About **Michael Parkin**

Michael Parkin received his training as an economist at the Universities of Leicester and Essex in England. Currently in the Department of Economics at the University of Western Ontario, Canada, Professor Parkin has held faculty appointments at Brown University, the University of Manchester, the University of Essex, and Bond University. He has served on the editorial boards of the *American Economic Review* and the *Journal of Monetary Economics* and as managing editor of the *Canadian Journal of Economics*. Professor Parkin's research on macroeconomics, monetary economics, and international economics has resulted in over 160 publications in journals and edited volumes, including the *American Economic Review*, the *Journal of Political Economy*, the *Review of Economic Studies*, the *Journal of Monetary Economics*, and the *Journal of Money, Credit and Banking*. It became most visible to the public with his work on inflation that discredited the use of wage and price controls. Michael Parkin also spearheaded the movement toward European monetary union. Professor Parkin is an experienced and dedicated teacher of introductory economics.

Preface

To change the way students see the world—this is my purpose in teaching economics, and it has remained my goal in preparing the third edition of this text. There is no greater satisfaction for a teacher than to share the joy of students who have begun to understand the powerful lessons of the economic approach. But these lessons are hard to learn. Every day in my classroom, I relive the challenges of gaining the insights that we call the economist's way of thinking and recall my own early struggles to master this discipline. In preparing this edition, I have been privileged to draw on the experiences not only of my own students but also of the many teachers and students who have used the two previous editions.

The principles of economics course is constantly evolving, and the past few years have seen some major shifts of emphasis, especially in macroeconomics. Today's principles course springs from today's issues—the slow-down in productivity growth, the information revolution, the emerging market economies of Central Europe and Asia, the expansion of global trade and investment. More and more, we recognize the value of teaching long-run fundamentals as a basis for understanding these issues and as a springboard to understanding short-run economic fluctuations. This book allows you to place an early emphasis on long-run fundamentals. And for the first time, it allows you to teach the theory of long-run economic growth, including "new" growth theory, using the familiar tools of supply and demand.

The Third Edition Approach

THIS EDITION HAS BEEN CRAFTED TO MEET three overriding goals:

- Focus on the core principles
- Use the core principles to explain the issues and problems of the 1990s
- Create a flexible teaching and learning tool.

Focus on Core Principles

The core principles of choice and opportunity cost, marginal analysis, substitution and incentives, and the power of the competitive process focus the micro chapters. The core tools of demand and supply are thoroughly explained and repeatedly used throughout both the micro and macro chapters. New ideas, such as dynamic comparative advantage, game theory and its applications, the modern theory of the firm, information, public choice, new growth theory, and real business cycle theory, also appear in this book. But they are described and explained by using the core principles—new ideas are explained by using familiar ideas and tools.

Explain the Issues and Problems of the 1990s

The core principles and tools are also used to help students understand the issues that confront them in today's world. Among the issues that are explored, some at length, are the environment, health care, widening income gaps, the productivity growth slowdown, restraining inflation, watching for the next recession, avoiding protectionism, and the consequences of the emerging economies of central Europe and Asia. These issues are studied repeatedly by using the same core principles.

Flexible Teaching and Learning Tool

One of the most exciting facts about economics is that its teachers hold strong views about what to teach and how to teach, yet they do not all hold the *same* view. This fact poses a special challenge to a textbook author, especially in the macro part of our subject. To be useful in a wide range of situations and to a diversity of teachers, a book must be flexible. This book can be used to teach all the traditional macro sequences, which place the main emphasis on short-term fluctuations in output, prices, and unemployment. It can support courses with a Keynesian emphasis or those with a monetarist emphasis. This book can also be used to teach a principles of macroeconomics course that places an early emphasis on long-term growth.

To signal this last possibility, the long-term growth chapter appears early in the book. But the order in which the chapters appear is only one of several orders in which they can be used. A table on p. xix shows some of the alternative possibilities.

Level and Viewpoint

The emphasis in this book on long-run fundamentals does not translate into "high level," nor does it translate into "bias." But this book does have a point of view. It is that economics is a serious, lively, and evolving science—a science that seeks to develop a body of theory that is powerful enough to explain the economic world around us and that pursues its task by building, testing, and rejecting economic models. In some areas the science has succeeded at its task, but in others it has some distance to go and controversy persists. Where matters are settled, I present what we know; where controversy persists, I present the alternative viewpoints. This positive approach to economics is, I believe, especially valuable for students as they prepare to function in a world in which simple ideologies have become irrelevant and in which familiar patterns in the economic landscape have shifted and blurred.

Always recalling my own early struggles with economics, I place the student at center stage and write for the student foremost. I am conscious that many students find economics hard. As a result, my goal has been to make the material as accessible as possible. I use a style that makes for an easy read and that doesn't intimidate. Each chapter opens with a clear list of learning objectives, a vignette that connects with the student's world and seeks to grab attention, and a statement of where we are heading. Once in the chapter, I don't reduce economics to a set of recipes to be memorized. Instead, I encourage students to try to understand each concept. To accomplish this goal, the book illustrates every principle with examples that have been selected both to hold the student's interest and to bring the subject to life. To encourage a sense of enthusiasm and confidence, when the book has explained a new principle, it puts it to work and uses it to illuminate a current real-world problem or issue.

Changes in the Third Edition

The structure of the microeconomics chapters remains consistent with the first two editions, but it reflects the central goals of the revision: to focus on core concepts, to explain current issues, and to be leaner and simpler. Chapter 1 is substantially new and sets the tone for the revision. It is organized around the themes of 'how economists think' and 'what economists do.' Chapter 3 uses lively new examples to illustrate the core concepts of scarcity, choice, and opportunity cost and gives a neat and accessible explanation of comparative advantage (and dynamic comparative advantage) and the gains from trade.

Chapter 4, the core demand and supply chapter, has a new opening section on money price, relative price, and opportunity cost and a new section that explains real-world price changes. Chapter 5 has a new illustration of the connection between elasticity and revenue and new international elasticity comparisons.

The revision of Chapter 8, an optional chapter on indifference curves, now has a section on labor-leisure and consumption-saving choices. Chapter 9 explains how agency relationships arise from incomplete information and how they lead to different types of business organizations. Chapter 10 has a simplified explanation of the connection between short-run and long-run cost and of the relationship between returns to scale and the shapes of the cost curves. Chapter 11 gets to the point of the competitive model more quickly and has a new explanation of competition and efficiency. Chapter 12 has a new expanded explanation and illustration of price discrimination between two groups with different demand elasticities. Chapter 13 has a more streamlined coverage of the game theory approach to oligopoly and a new section on contestable markets.

The chapters on markets and government reorganize and extend the comparable chapters of the second edition. Chapter 18 previews the entire range of government and public choice issues. The materi-

al on public goods in Chapters 19 and 20 of the second edition is brought together in this chapter. Chapter 19 (Chapter 18 in the second edition) discusses inequality and redistribution and includes a section on the interplay between health care and inequality and health-care reform. Chapter 20 (Chapter 21 in the second edition) includes new cases and examples, such as Microsoft and cable television. A new Chapter 21 explains externalities and illustrates these concepts with an extensive discussion of the economics of the environment, and the economics of knowledge—of education and research and development.

The structure of the macroeconomics chapters has been thoroughly rethought and reworked. Chapter 22 shows the entire macro landscape including its origins and rebirth in the Great Depression; the issues it explores of long-term growth, business cycles, unemployment, inflation, and international debts and deficits; the facts it seeks to explain, both current and historical, and in the United States and around the world; and the policy challenges it faces.

Chapter 23 has a streamlined treatment of the circular flow, new material on capital and investment, wealth and saving, and national saving and international borrowing. It also has an expanded evaluation of the meaning of real GDP. A new Chapter 24 describes the measurement of employment, unemployment, and real wage rates and explains labor market trends. Chapter 25 is also new. It explains investment, saving, and consumption decisions and the determination of the real interest rate. Chapters 24 and 25 are a foundation for studying both long-term growth and short-term fluctuations. Chapter 26 is a new chapter that makes growth theory accessible and relevant to the principles student. It describes the growth in the U.S. and world economies, explains growth accounting, and describes the sources of the productivity growth slowdown of the 1970s. The chapter also describes the growth of Asian economies and reviews policies for faster growth.

Chapter 27 draws on the best of the second edition's Chapter 24, but it now begins with long-run and short-run aggregate supply. In doing so, it sharpens the distinction between flexible and sticky price situations and paves the way for several chapters on short-run fluctuations. Chapter 28 draws heavily on material from Chapters 25 and 26 in the second edition and presents the Keynesian aggregate expenditure model and multiplier. The treatment of the multiplier has been carefully revised and simplified.

Chapter 29 is completely new. It describes the federal budget process and studies the effects of fiscal policy and proposals for deficit reduction. Chapters 30 and 31 cover money, the banking system, and monetary policy. The coverage is similar to the second edition, but it has been streamlined and is more accessible.

Chapter 32 has a simpler and clearer explanation of the modern theory of inflation and the connections between inflation and unemployment and inflation and interest rates. Chapter 33 is substantially new. It incorporates the material on the Great Depression found in the second edition but also includes an explanation of Keynesian, monetarist, rational expectations, and real business cycle theories. Chapter 34 is another big picture chapter, similar in intent to the second edition's Chapter 33, but clearer and more accessible. It shows how fiscal and monetary policy have been used to achieve both short-term and long-term objectives.

The book ends with chapters that focus on the global economy. Chapter 35 has an expanded description of U.S. trade, a description of GATT, and a new section that uses core principles to evaluate and debunk the arguments for protection. Chapter 36 provides one of the clearest treatments of exchange rate determination currently available. Finally, Chapter 37 combines discussions of growth and development and economic systems in transition into one chapter. The coverage of current problems in Eastern and Central Europe and Asia focuses on the core principles of incentives and efficiency.

Features that Enhance the Learning Process

THIS THIRD EDITION, LIKE ITS PREDECESSORS, IS packed with special features designed to enhance the learning process.

The Art Program: Showing the Economic Action

The first and second editions of this book set new standards with their highly successful and innovative art programs. My goal has always been to show clearly "where the economic action is." The figures and diagrams in this book continue to generate enormously positive feedback, confirming my view that graphical analysis is the most important tool for teaching and learning economics. But it is a tool that gives many students much difficulty. Because many students find graphs hard to work with, the art has been designed both to be visually attractive and engaging and to communicate economic principles unambiguously and clearly. In the third edition the crystal clear style of the data-based art that reveals the data and trends has been retained. In addition, diagrams that illustrate economic processes now consistently distinguish among key economic players (firms, households, governments, and markets).

We observe a consistent protocol in style, notation, and use of color, which includes:

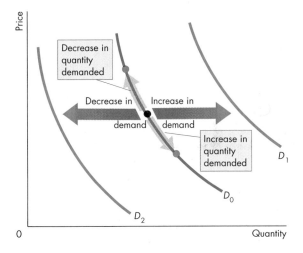

- Highlighting shifted curves, points of equilibrium, and the most important features in red
- Using arrows in conjunction with color to lend directional movement to what are usually static presentations
- Pairing graphs with data tables from which the curves have been plotted
- Using color consistently to underscore the content and referring to such use of color in the text and captions
- Labeling key pieces of information in graphs with boxed notes
- Rendering each piece electronically so that precision is achieved

The entire art program has been developed with the study and review needs of the student in mind. It has the following features:

- Marking the most important figures and tables with a red icon and listing them at the end of the chapter under "key figures and tables"
- Using complete, informative captions that encapsulate major points in the graph so that students can preview or review the chapter by skimming through the art

Interviews: Leading Economists Lend a Hand

Substantive interviews with famous economists were another popular feature in the first and second editions. I am continuing the tradition and have included all new interviews—seven in total—each with an economist who has contributed significantly to advancing thinking and practice in our discipline. One of the interviews is with a recent Nobel Laureate: Douglass North. The interviews encourage students to participate in the conversations as the economists discuss their areas of specialization, their unique contributions to economics, and their general insights that are relevant to beginning students.

An interview opens each of the book's seven parts, and each interview has been carefully edited to be self-contained. Because each interview discusses topics that are introduced formally in the subsequent chapters, students can use it as a preview to some of the terminology and theory they are about to encounter. A more careful reading afterward will give students a fuller appreciation of the discussion. Finally, the whole series of interviews can be approached as an informal symposium on the subject matter of economics as it is practiced today.

Reading Between the Lines: News Articles for Critical Thinking

Another feature of the previous editions that has been consistently well received is "Reading Between the Lines." A major goal of the principles course that "Reading Between the Lines" is designed to pursue is to help students build critical thinking skills and use economic principles to interpret daily news events (and their coverage in the media). I have updated all of the news articles in this edition and have selected

topics that appeal to students, such as the baseball strike of 1994–1995, the value of a college degree, the value of college grades not being too soft, the antitrust suit against Microsoft, and entrepreneurship in Russia. Each "Reading Between the Lines" spread contains three passes at a story. It begins with a facsimile (usually abbreviated) of an actual newspaper or magazine article. These news stories come from major newspapers and magazines, including the *Economist, New York Times, Wall Street Journal, Chicago Tribune, Detroit Free Press, Los Angeles Times*, and *Fortune*. The second pass presents a digest of the article's essential points. Finally, the third pass provides an economic analysis of the article. In order not to disrupt the flow of the material, these features are placed at the end of each chapter, before the chapter summary.

Economics in History: Path-breaking Ideas

The "Economics in History" feature helps students trace the evolution of path-breaking economic ideas and recognize the universality of their application, not only to the past but also to the present. For example, Adam Smith's powerful ideas about the division of labor apply to the creation of a computer chip as well as to the pin factory of the eighteenth century. In order not to disrupt the flow of the material, these features are located between chapters.

Learning Aids: Pedagogy that Leads to Active Learning

The careful pedagogical plan has been refined to ensure that this book complements and reinforces classroom learning. Each chapter contains the following pedagogical elements:

Objectives   Each chapter opens with a list of objectives that enable students to set their goals as they begin the chapter.

Chapter Openers   Intriguing puzzles, paradoxes, or metaphors frame the important questions that are unraveled and resolved as the chapter progresses.

Highlighted In-Text Reviews   Succinct summaries for review are interspersed throughout the chapter. In this edition these in-text reviews have a list format that is designed to give the student a more easily digested statement of the key points.

Key Terms   Highlighted within the text, these concepts form the first part of a three-tiered review of economic vocabulary. These terms are repeated with page references at the chapter ends and compiled in the end-of-book glossary.

Key Figures and Tables   The most important figures and tables are identified with the red icon and listed at chapter end.

End-of-Chapter Study Material   In the third edition we worked hard to create truly effective end-of-chapter review questions and problems and have added many new ones. As a new feature, we have included a substantial number of diagram problems. In addition, each chapter has a multipart problem based on the "Reading Between the Lines" feature. Many of the problems can be worked by using the *Economics in Action* software package; these problems are identified by an icon (◆). Each chapter ends with a summary organized around its major headings, a list of key terms with page references, a list of key figures and tables with page references, review questions, and problems.

Flexibility: Navigating the Principles Course

One semester or quarter is a short amount of time to accomplish the goals of the principles course and a powerful example of the fundamental economic problem: Our wants exceed our resources and we must make choices. To facilitate these choices, a text must be flexible and contain much optional material. A table at the end of this preface explains which chapters form the core, which are extensions or applications, and the prerequisites for each chapter.

There is much variety in how we approach macroeconomics at the principles level. Therefore a text must be flexible enough to support a number of different teaching styles and course organizations. An additional table at the end of this preface illustrates how the chapters can be organized to support several different courses.

The Teaching and Learning Package

ADDISON-WESLEY'S EDITORS, THE SUPPLEMENTS authors, and I have worked closely together to ensure that our integrated text and supplements package provides students and teachers with a seamless learning and teaching experience. The authors of the components are outstanding economists and teachers who have brought their own human capital (and that of their students) to the job of ensuring that the supplements are of the highest quality and value. The package contains three broad components:

- Tools to enhance learning
- Tools to enhance teaching
- Tools for the electronic classroom

Tools to Enhance Learning

Study Guide   Available in microeconomics and macroeconomics split versions, the all-new third edition study guide was prepared by Mark Rush of the University of Florida. Carefully coordinated with the main textbook, each chapter of the study guide contains:

- Key concepts
- Helpful hints
- True/false questions that may not be true or false and that ask students to explain their answers
- Multiple-choice questions
- Short-answer problems
- Common questions or misconceptions that the student is asked to explain as if he or she were the teacher

At the end of each part, students get to test their cumulative understanding in a number of ways. A "Reading Between the Lines" exercise asks them to apply what they've learned by analyzing a news article and answering short-answer questions. Each multiple-choice test simulates a midterm test by presenting a selection of questions similar to those in the test bank for the chapters in each part of the book.

Several elements of the study guide are geared to building critical thinking: True/False/Uncertain questions, multiple-choice answers that include explanations of why the answer is correct, "You're the Teacher" sections, and "Reading Between the Lines" exercises. Other elements are geared to making studying economics a bit easier: The key concepts are a study aid; the helpful hints focus on ways to better understand the principles or to avoid common pitfalls; the multiple-choice questions are plentiful and include explanations of why an answer is correct; the part tests allow students to simulate an exam.

The study guide includes an essay, "Should the Study of Economics Be Part of Your Future?," written by Robert Whaples of Wake Forest University. This essay describes the value of studying economics for both majors and non-majors. It includes information on career options for those with an economics degree, what the study of economics entails, what graduate school is like, and references for further reading.

Economics in Action Interactive Software   The second edition supplements package included truly interactive software to support student mastery of economic principles. Students across the country have used this path-breaking and widely acclaimed computer learning tool to increase their success in the principles course. With the third edition they will have fun working the tutorials and testing themselves ahead of their midterm exams. And they'll find the real-world data both illuminating and useful for projects. New releases of the software have the following features:

- Step-by-step, graph-based tutorials that actively engage students in exploring economic concepts
- A graphing tool that allows students to graph real-world economic data
- A self-testing facility that simulates a multiple-choice-test setting and gathers results
- A problem-solving tool that allows students to solve homework problems from the text

Tools to Enhance Teaching

Test Bank   Revised test items were prepared by David Denslow of the University of Florida and Robert Rossana of Wayne State University to thoroughly reflect the content and terminology of the third edition. The file includes over 5,000 multiple-choice questions, about one third of which are new to this edition. All questions have been reviewed

carefully for accuracy by Robert Horn and Ehsan Ahmed of James Madison University. Each chapter includes a section of questions that are taken directly from the study guide and *Economics in Action* software and a section of questions that parallel those in the study guide and *Economics in Action* software.

Computerized Test Bank   Testing software is available for DOS, Windows, and Macintosh. It includes all questions in the printed test bank. This software gives instructors the ability to add questions, edit questions, scramble question order and answer options, export to a word processor, and more.

Instructor's Manual   A revised instructor's manual has been prepared by Mark Rush of the University of Florida. The instructor's manual is designed to integrate the teaching and learning package, serving as a guide to all supplements. Each chapter includes a chapter outline, changes in the third edition, teaching suggestions, the big picture (how the chapter relates to what has come before and what comes later), cross-references to the acetates, software units, additional discussion questions, answers to the review questions, and answers to the problems.

An introductory section written by Byron Brown of Michigan State University and Dennis Hoffman of Arizona State University presents technology ideas for professors who are just getting started with electronic teaching tools. This section talks about teaching in a multimedia classroom, how to use electronic tools in the lecture, and how to integrate *Economics in Action* into the course.

Acetates and Overlays   Key figures from the text are rendered in full color on the acetates. Several figures include overlays that make it easy to walk through the figure as you lecture. The acetates are enlarged and simplified to be more legible in large classrooms. They are available to qualified adopters of the textbook (contact your Addison-Wesley sales representative).

Tools for the Electronic Classroom

Electronic Lecture Support   A complete lecture framework in Microsoft PowerPoint is available for Macintosh and Windows. Prepared by Tony Lima of California State University–Hayward, this lecture support system is organized by chapter and includes key figures from the text in addition to speaking notes. Some of the PowerPoint slides simulate the overlays in the full-color acetates.

MacNeil/Lehrer Business Reports   Once again, an Addison-Wesley exclusive offers adopters videos that have been carefully selected to illustrate the core principles through topical yet timeless news stories. The package includes video selections for microeconomic, macroeconomic, and international topics. The videos are free to adopters.

Economics in Action Software   Instructors can use *Economics in Action* interactive software in the classroom. Its full-screen display makes it possible to use as "electronic transparencies" to do live graph manipulation. Instructors can also have students use the real-world data in *Economics in Action* to complete various course projects. Additionally, *Economics in Action* is a helpful review tool for instructors to use with their students or assign to their students to help reinforce economic principles before tests or exams.

The Parkin Internet Exchange   A new element of the Parkin package is on-line support that includes mailing list discussion groups, access to information through ftp, and a World Wide Web home page. Teachers who are using the third edition texts (and others) can share teaching tips; concerns about the principles course; ideas for using the book, supplements, and *Economics in Action* interactive software; and other topics of mutual interest through a mailing list. To subscribe to the Parkin mailing list, send an e-mail message to `majordomo@aw.com`. The body of the message should say only "subscribe ParkinPr." Discussion threads from the mailing list, new "Reading Between the Lines" analyses, interviews, issues of the *Economic Times,* data sets for *Economics in Action* interactive software, and more will be available through ftp and the Parkin home page on aw.com.

An Internet discussion group is also available for students using the third edition. Students can chat with other students about the course, the book, projects, economics, and other relevant topics on their own majordomo mailing list. To subscribe to the student mailing list, send an e-mail message to `majordomo@aw.com`. The body of the message should say only "subscribe ParkinSt."

Whether you are a teacher or a student, you can reach all of these Internet services and more at `http://www.aw.com/he` on the World Wide Web. The Parkin home page includes access to the mailing lists and materials for ftp; a demo of

Economics in Action interactive software; and links to economic resources and other discussion groups on the Internet and Web.

Finally, if you have questions, comments, or suggestions for improvement, you can submit them via e-mail to Addison Wesley's economics editors at `ParkinEd@aw.com` or to me at `parkin@vaxr.sscl.uwo.ca.`

Acknowledgments

THE ENDEAVOR OF CREATING A PRINCIPLES TEXT involves the creative collaboration and contribution of many people. Although the extent of my debts cannot be fully acknowledged, it is nevertheless a joy to record my gratitude to the many people who have helped, some without realizing just how helpful they were.

I thank those of my current and former colleagues at the University of Western Ontario who have taught me a great deal that can be found in these pages: Jim Davies, Jeremy Greenwood, Ig Horstmann, Peter Howit, Greg Huffman, David Laidler, Phil Reny, Chris Robinson, John Whalley, and Ron Wonnacott. I also thank Doug McTaggart of Bond University and Christopher Findlay of the University of Adelaide, co-authors of the Australian edition. Their suggestions arising from their adaptation of the first two editions have been extremely helpful in preparing this edition.

It is a special pleasure to acknowledge my debt and express my thanks to the several thousand students whom I have been privileged to teach. The instant feedback that comes from the look of puzzlement or enlightenment has taught me, more than anything else, how to teach economics.

Producing a text such as this is a team effort, and the members of the Addison-Wesley "Parkin Team" are full co-producers of this book. I have been fortunate to work with a sequence of extraordinary editors. On the first two editions, from which this edition has grown, Barbara Rifkind played a crucial role, and I want to thank her for the legacy that is still visible in this edition. This edition has been inspired by a truly outstanding editor, Denise Clinton. The new approach to macro could not have been brought to fruition without her clear-headed vision and tough empirical approach. I am enormously impressed by and grateful to her. Marilyn Freedman has been my senior development editor for two editions now, and I thank her again for her personal and professional commitment. I thank Yvonne Linton, who did the preliminary market research in the summer of 1993 from which this revision began. I also thank Susan D. Howard, who assisted Marilyn, did much of the photo research, and helped me in a hundred small but important ways. And I thank Larry Rungren and the Bedford Free Public Library for the research assistance they provided to Marilyn and me. Loren Hilgenhurst Stevens has been my senior production editor for two editions, and I renew my thanks to her for directing the design and production effort. I also thank Nancy Fenton, who doubled with Loren and took the production reins when Loren took maternity leave. I thank two outstanding marketing managers, Craig Bleyer, who played a crucial role in helping to shape this revision and ensure that it sensitively reflects market needs, and Mark Childs, who launched the book in the market. Cindy Johnson has once more played a pivotal role in managing all the supplements. Her skill and commitment have ensured that the book and the supplements form a truly integrated and effective teaching and learning package that meets the highest standards. I thank Lena Buonanno, who played a key role in coordinating a long sequence of conference calls that were a crucial part of my search for the right way to restructure and redefine introductory macroeconomics. Lena also took care of the interviews and helped the interviewees and me make our conversations accessible to our student readers. Barbara Willette has again been copyeditor, and I thank her for continuing to coax yet better English from my keyboard. Karen Lehman has designed all three editions of this book, and with each edition she has raised the design to new heights. I thank her for her continued inspiration, which has inspired me. I also thank Mark Dalton, a vice president in the higher education group, and Michael Payne, an executive editor, for their deep support of this project and for ensuring that it is directed by the most talented editors in the business.

I thank the supplements authors: Mark Rush, David Denslow, Robert Rossana, Tony Lima, Robert Whaples, Byron Brown, and Dennis Hoffman. Mark has played a crucial role in the creation of this edition and has been a constant source of good advice and good humor. He helped me digest the reviews and distill the consensus, and he acted as an accuracy reviewer and supplier of news articles for and reviewer of the "Reading Between the Lines" features. Kathleen Possai also helped my search for good stories for "Reading Between the Lines," and she reviewed the supplements, including *Economics in Action*. Robert Whaples was another extraordinary reviewer who went well beyond the call of duty or the scope of the checkbook in his manuscript, accuracy, and study guide reviews; his participation in a lengthy macro conference call; and his writing of an essay for the study guide. I am deeply grateful to Carol Dole and Malcolm Robinson for their accuracy reviews of page proof. Byron Brown and Dennis Hoffman have written excellent essays for the instructor's manual, and J. Peery Cover provided outstanding advice on how to make the instructor's manual even more helpful. Others who helped me shape my ideas for the new macro sequence are Andy Dane (who also wrote the video guide), David Hakes, John Edgren, Tony O'Brien, Joseph Daniels, Robert Gillette, Robert Rossana, Fred Jungman, Michael Carter, Art Welch, Jerry Babb, Richard Gosselin, Robert Parks, Paul Schmitt, Gary Shelley, John Graham, Janet Mitchell, James Eden, and Lee Weissert.

I thank Richard Parkin, who has provided outstanding support in creating the electronic art manuscript and final art files and has contributed many ideas that have improved the figures in this book.

Like the previous editions, this one owes an enormous debt to Robin Bade. I dedicate this book to her and again thank her for her work. She has read every word that I have written, commented in detail on every draft, created many of the end-of-chapter review questions and problems, inspired me when I have been flagging, and managed the entire project from its initial conception through its three editions and through seven editions published in other countries. I could not have written this book without the unselfish help she has given me. My thanks to her are unbounded.

The empirical test of this book's value continues to be made in the classroom. I would appreciate hearing from instructors and students about how I can continue to improve it in future editions.

Michael Parkin
Department of Economics
University of Western Ontario
London, Ontario, N6A 5C2

REVIEWERS

Tajudeen Adenekan, Bronx Community College; **Milton Alderfer**, Miami-Dade Community College; **William Aldridge**, Shelton State Community College; **Stuart Allen**, University of North Carolina–Greensboro; **Alan Anderson**, Fordham University; **Jeff Ankrom**, Wittenberg University; **Fatma Antar**, Manchester Community Technical College; **Kofi Apraku**, University of North Carolina–Asheville; **Moshen Bahmani-Oskooee**, University of Wisconsin–Milwaukee; **Donald Balch**, University of South Carolina; **Mehmet Balcilar**, Wayne State University; **A. Paul Ballantyne**, University of Colorado; **Valerie Bencivenga**, Cornell University; **Ben Bernanke**, Princeton University; **Margot Biery**, Tarrant County Community College South; **John Bittorowitz**, Ball State University; **Sunne Brandmeyer**, University of South Florida; **Baird Brock**, Central Missouri State University; **Jeffrey Buser**, Columbus State Community College; **Tania Carbiener**, Southern Methodist University; **Kevin Carey**, University of Miami; **Michael Carter**, University of Massachusetts–Lowell; **Adhip Chaudhuri**, Georgetown University; **Gopal Chengalath**, Texas Tech University; **Daniel Christiansen**, Albion College; **John J. Clark**, Community College of Allegheny County–Allegheny Campus; **Meredith Clement**, Dartmouth College; **Michael B. Cohn**, U.S. Merchant Marine Academy; **Robert Collinge**, University of Texas–San Antonio; **Doug Conway**, Mesa Community College; **Larry Cook**, University of Toledo; **Bobby Corcoran**, Middle Tennesee State University; **James Peery Cover**, University of Alabama at Tuscaloosa; **Eleanor Craig**, University of Delaware; **Jim Craven**, Clark College; **David Culp**, Slippery Rock University; **Dan Dabney**, University of Texas–Austin; **Andrew Dane**, Angelo State University; **Joseph Daniels**, Marquette University; **David Denslow**, University of Florida; **Mark Dickie**, University of Georgia; **James Dietz**, California State University–Fullerton; **Carol Dole**, University of North Carolina–Charlotte; **Ronald Dorf**, Inver Hills Community College; **John Dorsey**, University of Maryland–College Park; **Amrik Singh Dua**, Mt. San Antonio College; **Thomas Duchesneau**, University of Maine–Orono; **Lucia Dunn**, Ohio State University; **Donald Dutkowsky**, Syracuse University; **John Edgren**, Eastern Michigan University; **David J.**

Eger, Alpena Community College; **Ibrahim Elsaify**, State University of New York–Albany; **M. Fazeli**, Hofstra University; **Philip Fincher**, Louisiana Tech University; **F. Firoozi**, University of Texas–San Antonio; **David Franck**, University of North Carolina–Charlotte; **Alwyn Fraser**, Atlantic Union College; **Eugene Gentzel**, Pensacola Junior College; **Robert Giller**, Virginia Polytechnic Institute and State University; **Robert Gillette**, University of Kentucky; **Maria Giuili**, Diablo College; **Richard Gosselin**, Houston Community College; **John Graham**, Rutgers University; **John Griffen**, Worcester Polytechnic Institute; **Robert Guell**, Indiana State University; **Jamie Haag**, University of Oregon; **Daniel Hagen**, Western Washington University; **David R. Hakes**, University of Northern Iowa; **Craig Hakkio**, Federal Reserve Bank–Kansas City; **Ann Hansen**, Westminster College; **Randall Haydon**, Wichita State University; **John Herrmann**, Rutgers University; **John M. Hill**, Delgado Community College; **Lewis Hill**, Texas Tech University; **Tom Hoerger**, Vanderbilt University; **Calvin Hoerneman**, Delta College; **Dennis Hoffman**, Arizona State University; **Jim H. Holcomb**, University of Texas–El Paso; **Harry Holzer**, Michigan State University; **Harold Hotelling, Jr.**, Lawrence Technical University; **Calvin Hoy**, County College of Morris; **Beth Ingram**, University of Iowa; **Michael Jacobs**, Lehman College; **Dennis Jansen**, Texas A&M University; **Frederick Jungman**, Northwestern Oklahoma State University; **Paul Junk**, University of Minnesota–Duluth; **Leo Kahane**, California State University–Hayward; **E. Kang**, St. Cloud State University; **Arthur Kartman**, San Diego State University; **Manfred Keil**, Northeastern University; **Rose Kilburn, M.S.**, Modesto Junior College; **Robert Kirk**, Indiana University–Purdue University at Indianapolis; **Norman Kleinberg**, City University of New York–Baruch College; **Robert Kleinhenz**, California State University–Fullerton; **Joseph Kreitzer**, University of St. Thomas; **David Lages**, Southwest Missouri State University; **Leonard Lardaro**, University of Rhode Island; **Kathryn Larson**, Elon College; **Luther D. Lawson**, University of North Carolina–Wilmington; **Elroy M. Leach**, Chicago State University; **Jay Levin**, Wayne State University; **Tony Lima**, California State University–Hayward; **William Lord**, University of Maryland–Baltimore County; **K. T. Magnusson**, Salt Lake City Community College; **Mark Maier**, Glendale Community College; **Beth Maloan**,

University of Tennessee–Martin; **Jean Mangan**, California State University–Sacramento; **Michael Marlow**, California Polytech; **Akbar Marvasti**, University of Houston–Downtown; **Wolfgang Mayer**, University of Cincinnati; **John McArthur**, Wofford College; **Amy McCormick**, College of William and Mary; **Gerald McDougall**, Wichita State University; **Richard McIntyre**, University of Rhode Island; **John McLeod**, Georgia Insititue of Technology; **Charles Meyer**, Iowa State University; **Peter Mieszkowski**, Rice University; **John Mijares**, University of North Carolina–Asheville; **Judith W. Mills**, Southern Connecticut State University; **Glen Mitchell**, Nassau Community College; **Jeannette C. Mitchell**, Rochester Institute of Technology; **Khan Mohabbat**, Northern Illinois University; **William Morgan**, University of Wyoming; **Joanne Moss**, San Francisco State University; **Edward Murphy**, Southwest Texas State University; **Kathryn Nantz**, Fairfield University; **William S. Neilson**, Texas A&M University; **Bart C. Nemmers**, University of Nebraska–Lincoln; **Anthony O'Brien**, Lehigh University; **Mary Olson**, Washington University; **Jim B. O'Niell**, University of Delaware; **Farley Ordovensky**, University of the Pacific; **Z. Edward O'Relley**, North Dakota State University; **Jan Palmer**, Ohio University; **Michael Palumbo**, University of Houston; **G. Hossein Parandvash**, Western Oregon State College; **Robert Parks**, Washington University; **David Pate**, St. John Fisher College; **Donald Pearson**, Eastern Michigan University; **Mary Anne Pettit**, Southern Illinois University–Edwardsville; **Kathy Phares**, University of Missouri–St. Louis; **William A. Phillips**, University of Southern Maine; **Dennis Placone**, Clemson University; **Charles Plot**, California Institute of Technology–Pasadena; **Kathleen Possai**, Wayne State University; **K. A. Quartey**, Talladega College; **Herman Quirmbach**, Iowa State University; **Vaman Rao**, Western Illinois University; **J. David Reed,** Bowling Green State University; **Robert H. Renshaw**, Northern Illinois University; **John Robertson**, Paducah Community College; **Malcolm Robinson**, University of North Carolina–Greensboro; **Thomas Romans**, State University of New York–Buffalo; **David R. Ross**, Bryn Mawr College; **Thomas Ross**, St. Louis University; **Robert J. Rossana**, Wayne State University; **Rochelle Ruffer**, Ithaca College; **Mark Rush**, University of Florida; **Gary Santoni**, Ball State University; **John Saussy**, Harrisburg Area Community College; **David Schlow**, Pennsylvania State University; **Paul Schmitt**, St. Clair County Community College; **Martin Sefton**, Indianapolis University; **Rod Shadbegian**, University of Massachusetts–Dartmouth; **Gerald Shilling**, Eastfield College; **Dorothy R. Siden**, Salem State College; **Scott Simkins**, University of North Carolina–Greensboro; **Chuck Skoro**, Boise State University; **Phil Smith**, DeKalb College; **William Doyle Smith**, University of Texas–El Paso; **Frank Steindl**, Oklahoma State University; **Jeffrey Stewart**, New York University; **Allan Stone**, Southwest Missouri State University; **Courtenay Stone**, Ball State University; **Mark Strazicich**, Ohio State University–Newark; **Robert Stuart**, Rutgers University; **Gilbert Suzawa**, University of Rhode Island; **David Swaine**, Andrews University; **Anthony Uremovic**, Joliet Junior College; **David Vaughn**, City University (Washington); **Francis Wambalaba**, Portland State University; **Rob Wassmer**, Wayne State University; **Paul A. Weinstein**, University of Maryland–College Park; **Lee Weissert**, St. Vincent College; **Robert Whaples**, Wake Forest University; **Mark Witte**, Northwestern University; **Willard E. Witte**, Indiana University; **Cheonsik Woo**, Clemson University; **Douglas Wooley**, Radford University; **John T. Young**, Riverside Community College; **Michael Youngblood**, Rock Valley College

Brief Contents

part 1 Introduction

Contents

Summary, Key Elements, Review Questions, and Problems appear at the end of each chapter.

Chapter 8

Possibilities, Preferences, and Choices 165

Chapter 9

Organizing Production 190

part 3 Markets for Factors of Production

Chapter 14

Pricing and Allocating Factors of Production 330

Chapter 20

Regulation and Antitrust Law 467

Chapter 21

Externalities, The Environment, and Knowledge 489

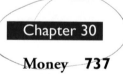

Chapter 30

Money   737

Money Makes the World Go Around   **738**

Chapter 31

The Federal Reserve and Monetary Policy   767

Temple of Secrets   **768**

Chapter 32

Inflation **795**

Chapter 33

The Business Cycle **824**

part 7 The Global Economy

part I

Introduction

Douglass North, who teaches economics and economic history at Washington University in St. Louis, was born in Cambridge, Massachusetts, in 1920. He was an undergraduate and graduate student at the University of California, Berkeley, where he earned his Ph.D. in 1952.

Professor North has pioneered the study of economic institutions such as stable government, the rule of law, and private property rights and the role these institutions play in fostering economic development and sustained

TALKING WITH **Douglass North**

income growth. He has used his ideas to explain why the United States and Western Europe have evolved from low-income agricultural societies 200 years ago into high-income complex societies today. In 1993, Professor North was awarded the Nobel Prize for Economic Science for this work. Michael Parkin talked with Professor North about his work and its relevance to today's—and tomorrow's—world.

Professor North, what attracted you to economics?

I grew up during the Great Depression of the 1930s. While I went to college in 1938, I was a concerned young man, and I became a Marxist because a Marxist had answers, or at least avowed to have answers, to the economic concerns that were so prevalent during the Depression. If the market economy of capitalism was replaced by the planned economy of socialism, the Depression and other economic ills could, we then believed, be cured.

As a student at the University of California at Berkeley, I looked for courses that were directed to researching and understanding why some countries are rich and others are poor. Economic history seemed to me to be most related to this area.

When I graduated from college I was going to be a lawyer. However, World War II broke out, and I spent four years in the Merchant Marines. During those four years, I just took a whole slew of books and read and read. You don't have much else to do when you're going around the world at ten miles an hour. I decided that I wanted to save the world—like any good Marxist wanted to—and I decided that the way to save it was to understand what made economies work badly or work well. And I've been pursuing that utopian goal ever since.

How did you abandon your Marxist beginning? Was there a sudden revelation or was it a gradual process?
Converting from Marxism was a very slow process. My first teaching job was at the University of Washington in Seattle in 1950. I used to play chess every day with my colleague, Donald Gordon. He was a good economist, and over three years of playing chess every day and talking economics, I gradually evolved away from Marxism and became a mainstream economist.

What are the key economic principles that guide your work—the principles and perspectives the economist brings to a study of long-term historical processes?
There are two. The first is the importance of transactions costs—the costs that people incur in order to do business with each other.

Economics attempts to understand how societies cope with the problem of scarcity—with the fact that people's wants always outstrip their limited resources. Traditionally, economists have focused on how resources are allocated at a moment of time—what determines today's allocation of spending between high schools and hospitals, computers and cars. Economic history deals with how societies evolve over time and tries to discover why some societies become wealthy while others remain poor. I became convinced that the economic way of reasoning underlying the economic principles is the right way to understand how societies evolve over time. But this conviction led me on a long trail.

Back in the days when I was learning economics, economic theories were based on the *assumption* that people could specialize and exchange their products in markets that function efficiently. They

ignored transaction costs—the costs that people incur when they do business with each other and the costs that governments and firms incur to make markets work. So the first problem was to think about how exchange takes place in the face of large transactions costs.

And the second principle?
The second principle is that transactions costs depend crucially on the way that human beings structure the economic order—on their institutions. And this fact gave me my second problem, to think about how institutions evolve to make markets work better over time.

When an economist talks about economic institutions, what exactly is he or she talking about? What are these institutions?
Institutions are rules of the society that structure the interaction among people. Institutions are made up of formal rules, like constitutions and statute law, and common rules and regulations. But they're also more than that. They are the informal ways by which people deal with each other every day, which you could think of as norms of behavior.

Institutions are the framework within which all of human interaction—political, social, and economic—takes place. And so, understanding how those work, why they work well in some circumstances, and why they work badly in others is the key, really, to the wealth of nations. Some examples of economic institutions include antitrust laws, patent laws, and bankruptcy laws.

The institutions that have evolved in the United States have brought economic development and prosperity while those that evolved in the former Soviet Union and that

to some degree still prevail in Russia and other Eastern European countries have brought stagnation and poverty. Can economists explain the radically different institutional evolution of the United States and Eastern Europe?
This question is at the very heart of what economic history should be about and in part is about. How did a country's economy get to where it is today? Why did countries, such as the former Soviet Union, evolve differently? A lot of my research, including my work in U.S. economic history, attempts to research and understand the incremental process of institutional change.

In order to have efficient markets, a country needs to structure a set of rules and regulations to provide incentives for people to do productive and creative things.

The United States first inherited a set of institutions—among them common law and property rights—from Great Britain. These institutions made Britain the leading nation in the world by the end of the eighteenth century. The United States took Britain's institutions over, modified them, and elaborated on them. The result has been two and a half centuries of economic growth. Much of the rest of the world, and Russia in particular, evolved institutions that didn't work very well.

In the evolution of Britain and the United States, the governments evolved a set of rules that provided a lot of freedom and latitude for people to make contracts and agreements among themselves. These rules produced economic efficiency on an unparalleled scale and led to sustained economic growth, which is the foundation of successful economies.

Third World countries and Eastern Europe chose different economic paths. Communism, for example, was an institution that did not provide sustained economic growth.

The goal of research in economic development and economic history is to understand exactly what it was that led to this very differential process of change between countries like the United States, Britain, and Russia.

Are there lessons in the economic histories of the United States and Western Europe from which Eastern Europe can learn?
How to make countries change is a very complicated process. Countries need to develop efficient markets. Increases in productivity underlie a country's economic growth. In order to achieve productivity increases, investment is required in a number of areas including human capital, physical capital, technological knowledge, and research and development.

What is unique to every country is how to get from one kind of an economy to another. The first step is to start from where people are. The degree to which you can change at any moment of time is a function of the perceptions and knowledge and ideas that people

have at a moment of time, as well as the existing institutions.

The economic growth of a country depends on its institutions. People can specialize, develop their human skills, and create profitable businesses only if they live under a framework of laws and property rights and have a

system of courts that enforce those property rights. Ultimately, and this is the most difficult of all things, you've got to have political stability which will perpetuate institutions conducive to economic development and income growth.

How do you explain the economic success of China and economic failure of Russia?
China had political authoritarianism at the top, and those authorities have either deliberately or accidentally loosened control in the provinces. The result has made for a very lucrative combination of local communist party officials teaming up with entrepreneurs, who got their capital and sometimes their training from the governments of Hong Kong and Taiwan, being let loose to pursue business ventures. And that's a unique situation. This certainly doesn't appear likely to happen in the former Soviet Union.

I think the biggest economic lessons are from Asia, the very successful countries of South Korea, Taiwan, and so on. They're interesting because they've shown that sometimes a proper dose of government can accelerate the process of creating efficient markets. Clearly, it teaches an impor-

The biggest economic lessons are from Asia, the very successful countries of South Korea, Taiwan, and so on.

tant lesson: In order to have efficient markets, a country needs to structure a set of rules and regulations to provide incentives for people to do productive and creative things and to produce better-quality goods at lower cost. And that takes a market with a set of rules that provides incentives for people to do that. It doesn't happen automatically. What Asia has shown us is that sometimes governments can in fact hasten the evolution of efficient markets.

Can you identify some of the key stages in which the U.S. government played a critical role in nurturing development of the rule of law, property rights, and the market economy?
The United States inherited economic and political rules from Great Britain. These rules provided the basis for efficient property rights and for the transfer of land, which was the biggest asset during the colonial period. Not only did

the United States create an efficient economic market, but it also created effective political markets. The Constitution of the United States was established, 11 years after that country's independence from Britain, to address growing trade and economic developments. It established a set of very efficient economic rules for the operation of the country. The Senate and House of Representatives were established and given power to, among other things, collect taxes, regulate commerce with other nations, regulate the value of money, and establish rules of bankruptcy.

How would you characterize the changes that are taking place in today's global and national economy?

I look at economic revolutions as changes in knowledge that fundamentally changed the whole economic social organization of societies. The origin and development of agriculture were the first economic revolution. This economic revolution probably occurred in the eighth millennium B.C. Agriculture completely altered the pace of economic and all other kinds of human change. Human beings settled down into villages and towns. This eventually led to the growth of exchange and to the whole basis for civilization. Agriculture enormously increased productivity potential and the potential for human progress.

The next real fundamental economic change was the application of science to technology. I would say there's never been a time in human history in which there's been as dramatic a setting of change as we're seeing in the world we live in today. I think it's extraordinary. It's a very exciting world to live in, particularly for an economic historian. I have argued that something happened in the

nineteenth century, which I call the Second Economic Revolution: there was a systematic wedding of science to technology that led to the development of the disciplines of physics, chemistry, genetics, and biology. This revolution has completely changed the way in which all of modern economic activity takes place and the way that human beings live and interact.

The personal and social implications of that revolution are enormous. As a result of this revolution, we live packed together in huge cities, many of which are plagued by crime on a scale that frightens us, and we depend for

our economic well-being on millions of people we do not know. Many people have benefited from the advances in technology and enjoy unimagined high living standards, while many others have been left behind and are not sharing in the prosperity that the second economic revolution has created. So, combined with the prosperity of this economic revolution, we've created a set of social, political, and

economic problems that we haven't figured out how to solve. And they may overwhelm us down the road.

What is your advice to a student who is just setting out to become an economist? How should the student approach his or her work? What are the things to study?

You should find excitement and challenge in the things you do and pursue them. At a university, this means that you ought to bug your professors. You should be continually trying to get a lot out of them. I think most university students don't get out of school what they

I think the most important thing in the world is to have a creative, stimulating, exciting life.... Find out what things excite you, and pursue them all your life.

could. Both in and out of class, you should ask questions and pursue the answers to those questions. I think that's terribly important.

I think the most important thing in the world is to have a creative, stimulating, exciting life. Everybody can do that in their own way, depending on their own curiosities, interests, and talents. Find out what things excite you, and pursue them all your life.

Chapter

1

What Is Economics?

**After studying
this chapter,
you will be
able to:**

■ Identify the kinds of questions that
economics seeks to answer

■ Explain why all economic questions arise
from scarcity

■ Explain why scarcity forces people to
make choices and face costs

■ Explain how economists think and
describe what they do

■ Describe the functions and the
components of the economy

Twenty years ago, almost no one watched a movie at home. But what was once a luxury enjoyed by only the wealthiest Americans is today an event enjoyed by millions. Why? Because advances in video and communications technologies have slashed the cost of home movies. The technologies that are transforming our homes are revolutionizing our farms, mines, factories, and assembly lines. Video cameras guide robots that pick fruit, mine coal, make steel, and assemble cars. As a result, millions of traditional jobs have disappeared, and millions of new jobs have been created. These facts raise the first set of economic questions:

Economic Questions

How does technological change affect the goods people consume and the jobs they do both here in the United States and around the world?

Movie stars, pop singers, news anchors, outstanding sports men and women, lawyers, doctors, and the chief executive officers of big companies earn large incomes. Gas pump attendants, supermarket checkout clerks, and day-care workers earn just a few dollars an hour. On the average, men earn more than women and whites earn more than minorities. These facts raise a second set of economic questions:

What determines people's incomes? Why are women paid less than men, even when they do jobs that seem similar? And why are minorities persistently paid less than other workers?

Over the years, the scope of government has expanded. When the founding fathers established the United States, the main business of government was to provide law and order. Today, governments provide social insurance and education, as well as national defense. They also regulate food and drug production, nuclear energy, and agriculture. Also, over the years, we've become more aware of our fragile environment. Chemicals called CFCs (chlorofluorocarbons), used in a wide variety of products from coolants in refrigerators and air conditioners to plastic phones and cleaning solvents for computer circuits, are believed to damage the atmosphere's protective ozone layer. Burning fossil fuels—coal and oil—adds carbon dioxide and other gases to the atmosphere, which prevents infrared radiation from escaping and might result in what has been called the "greenhouse effect." These facts raise a third set of economic questions:

What is the most effective role for government in economic life? Can government help us to protect our environment and be as effective as private enterprise at producing goods and services?

Since the late 1970s, China has been undergoing a dramatic economic transformation. Incomes in that country have grown at more than 10 percent a year—doubling every 7 years. In some cities—such as Shanghai—incomes have grown by more then 20 percent in some years. And China is not alone. Rapid income growth has occurred in Hong Kong, India, Indonesia, Malaysia, Singapore, South Korea, Taiwan, and Thailand. Incomes continue to grow in the rich countries of the world—the United States and Canada, Japan, Western Europe, and Australia and New Zealand—but the pace of expansion in these countries has slowed in comparison with the 1960s. In stark contrast to the growth miracles, Russian incomes shrank by an alarming 12 percent in 1993. Incomes also shrank in the Czech Republic and Hungary. These facts raise a fourth set of economic questions:

Why do incomes grow at an incredibly rapid rate in some countries, grow at a slower rate in other countries, and even fall in a few countries?

During the Great Depression—the early 1930s—unemployment afflicted almost one fifth of the work force in the industrial world. The Great Depression was a period of extreme hardship. But high unemployment is not unusual. For the past several years, unemployment has been near or above 10 percent in Canada, Britain, France, and Italy. And in the United States, when the average unemployment rate is 7 percent—as it was in 1993—the unemployment rate among young people (16- to 19-year-olds) is 20 percent, and among young African-Americans it is 40 percent. These facts raise a fifth set of economic questions:

What causes unemployment and why are some countries and groups more severely affected than others? Why are there so few good jobs for young Americans, especially for young African-Americans and Hispanic-Americans?

In 1993, the cost of living in Brazil rose by 2,500 percent. This meant that on the Copacabana beach, a pineapple that cost 15 cruzeiros on January 1 cost 390 cruzeiros by the end of the year. In that same year, prices in Russia rose by almost 1,000 percent. In contrast, prices in the United States increased by only 3 percent. But in the late 1970s, prices in the United States were rising by more than 10 percent a year. These facts raise a sixth set of economic questions:

Why do prices rise and why do some countries sometimes experience rapid price increases while others have stable prices?

In the 1960s, almost all the cars and trucks on the highways of the United States were made by Ford, General Motors, and Chrysler. In 1993, more than one fifth of the cars were imported. And cars are not exceptional. We now import most of our television sets, clothing, and computers. Governments impose taxes (called tariffs) on imports and also restrict the quantities of some goods that may be imported. They also enter into agreements with other governments, such as the North American Free Trade Agreement (NAFTA) between the United States, Canada, and Mexico. These facts raise a seventh set of economic questions:

What determines the amount of trade between nations and how do international trade agreements affect jobs and prosperity in the United States and other countries?

◆ These seven questions give you a sense of what economics is about. But they don't tell you what economics *is*. They don't tell you how to identify an *economic* question and distinguish it from a non-economic question. Nor do they tell you how economists think about economic questions and seek answers to them. How do economists identify *economic* questions? And how do they think about economic issues?

How Economists Think

ECONOMISTS, AS INDIVIDUALS, ARE LIKE everyone else. They have their own private objectives and agendas and have opinions about all sorts of economic and non-economic issues. You have perhaps already thought that the seven economic questions are very political. They are. They have an enormous influence on the quality of human life, and they generate fierce argument and debate.

Economists, as professionals, try to stand clear of the emotion and to approach their work with the detachment, rigor, and objectivity of a scientist. The first step in this process is to identify the fundamental problem from which all economic questions stem. That fundamental problem—*the* economic problem—is the fact that we have limited resources but unlimited wants.

Scarcity

When wants exceed the resources available to satisfy them, there is **scarcity.** Scarcity is everywhere. People want good health and long life, material comfort, security, physical and mental recreation, and knowledge. None of these wants is completely satisfied for everyone, and everyone has some unsatisfied wants. While many Americans have all the material comfort they want, many others do not. No one feels entirely satisfied with her or his state of health and expected length of life. No one feels entirely secure, even in this post–Cold War era, and no one has enough time for sport, travel, vacations, movies, theater, reading, and other leisure pursuits.

Scarcity is not *poverty*. The poor and the rich alike face scarcity. Everyone faces scarcity. A child wants a 75¢ can of soft drink and a 50¢ pack of gum but has only $1.00 in her pocket. She experiences scarcity. A student wants to go to a party on Saturday night but also wants to spend that same night catching up on late assignments. He experiences scarcity. Even parrots face scarcity—there just aren't enough crackers to go around.

Choice and Opportunity Cost

Faced with scarcity, people must make choices. When we cannot have everything we want, we choose

Not only do I want a cracker—we all want a cracker!

Drawing by Modell; ©1985 The New Yorker Magazine, Inc.

among the available alternatives. **Economics** is the study of the *choices* people make to cope with *scarcity*. Because scarcity forces choice, economics is sometimes called the *science of choice*—the science that explains the choices that people make and predicts how choices change as circumstances change.

Choosing more of one thing means having less of something else. Expressed another way, in making choices, we face costs. Whatever we choose to do, we could have chosen to do something else instead. There is no such thing as a free lunch. This popular phrase is not just a clever throwaway line. It expresses in a vivid way the central idea of economics—that every choice involves a cost.

Economists use the term *opportunity cost* to emphasize that making choices in the face of scarcity implies a cost. The **opportunity cost** of any action is the best alternative forgone. The best action that you choose *not* to do—the forgone alternative—is the cost of the action that you choose to do.

Opportunity cost is the *best* alternative forgone. It is not *all* the *possible* alternatives forgone. An example will make this clear. Your economics lecture is at 8:30 on a Monday morning. You contemplate two alternatives to attending the lecture: staying in bed for an hour or jogging for an hour. You can't stay in bed *and* jog for that same hour. The opportunity cost of attending the lecture is not the cost of an hour in bed *and* the cost of jogging for an hour. If these are the only alternatives you contemplate, then you have to decide which one you would do if you did not go to the lecture. The opportunity cost of attending a lecture for a jogger is a forgone hour of exercise; the opportunity cost of attending a lecture for a late sleeper is a forgone hour in bed.

Money Cost Versus Real Cost   We often express cost in terms of money. But this is just a convenient unit and is not a measure of opportunity cost. For example, the $40 spent on a book is not available for spending on four $10 CDs or on one $40 concert ticket. To calculate the opportunity cost of the book, we need to know the *best* alternative forgone. If CDs are the *best* alternative, the opportunity cost of the book is four CDs. If concert tickets are the *best* alternative, the opportunity cost of the book is one concert ticket.

It is especially vital to look behind the money costs when the amount that money will buy has changed. For example, a book that costs $40 today cost $25 in 1985. You can't conclude from this fact that the opportunity cost of a book has increased. To calculate the change in the opportunity cost of a book, you need to know the money cost of the best alternative forgone in 1985 and today. If CDs are the best alternative, and if in 1985 a CD cost $25 and today it cost $10, the opportunity cost of a book has indeed increased—from one CD in 1985 to four CDs today. Why? Because book prices have increased and CD prices have decreased. But if concert tickets are the best alternative to books, and if in 1985 a concert ticket cost $12.50 and today it cost $40, the opportunity cost of a book has fallen from two tickets in 1985 to one ticket today. Why? Because concert ticket prices have increased faster than book prices.

The key points are that it is fine to express opportunity cost in money units as long as you remember that this is just a convenient measure and that you can't compare opportunity costs between different times when the value of money has changed.

Time Cost   The opportunity cost of a good or service includes the value of the time spent obtaining it. If it takes an hour to visit your dentist, the value of that hour must be added to the amount you paid your dentist. We can convert time into a money cost by using a person's hourly wage rate. If you spend an hour visiting your dentist, the opportunity cost of that visit (expressed in units of money) is the amount that you paid to your dentist plus the value of the time lost by not doing something else. Again, it's important to keep reminding yourself that the opportunity cost is not the money itself but the goods and services that you would have bought with the money.

External Cost   Not all of the opportunity costs that you incur are the result of your own choices. Sometimes others make choices that impose opportunity costs on you. And your own choices can impose opportunity costs on others. For example, when you enjoy a cold drink from your refrigerator, part of its opportunity cost, borne by others, is the increased carbon dioxide in the atmosphere resulting from burning coal to generate the electricity that powers your refrigerator.

Marginal Analysis

Marginal analysis is a fundamental idea that permeates economics. The core of the idea is that people make choices in small steps—or *at the margin*. They decide whether to do a little bit more or a little bit less of an activity. To make such a decision, they compare the cost of a little bit more of the activity with its benefit. For example, to decide when to stop reading this book, you compare the cost of sticking with it for another five minutes with the benefit you expect (hope) it will bring. When you get to the point at which the cost of another five minutes reading exceeds the benefit, you quit.

The cost of a small increase in an activity is called **marginal cost**[1]. For example, suppose your personal computer has 2 megabytes of memory, and you are thinking about increasing its memory to 3 megabytes. The marginal cost of increasing your computer's memory is the cost of the *additional* megabyte of memory you are thinking about installing.

The benefit that arises from a small increase in an activity is called **marginal benefit**. For example, marginal benefit is the benefit you will get from 1 additional megabyte of memory in your computer, not the benefit you'll get from all 3 megabytes that you will have if you add 1 more megabyte. The reason is that you already have the benefit from 2 megabytes, so you don't count the benefit of these 2 megabytes as resulting from the decision you are now making.

To make your decision about computer memory, you compare the marginal cost of 1 megabyte with its

---

[1]The term *marginal cost* has a narrower technical definition: the cost of increasing output by one unit. This technical use of the term is just a special case of its more general meaning used here.

marginal benefit. If the marginal benefit exceeds the marginal cost, you buy the extra memory. If the marginal cost exceeds the marginal benefit, you stick with what you've got.

By evaluating marginal costs and marginal benefits, people are able to use their scarce resources in the way that makes them as well off as possible.

Substitution and Incentives

When opportunity costs change, people change their actions. A central principle of economics—the **principle of substitution**—is that when the opportunity cost of an activity increases, people substitute other activities which have lower opportunity costs in its place. Every activity has a *substitute*. Skiing is a substitute for skating; surfing is a substitute for skin diving; drinking Coke is a substitute for drinking Pepsi; studying economics is a substitute for taking dance training. A substitute might be similar to the original—Pepsi and Coke—or quite different—economics and dance.

If the opportunity cost of Coke increases, some people will substitute Pepsi for Coke; if the opportunity cost of studying economics increases (by a really large amount), some people will substitute dance for economics. The closer the substitutes, the greater is the degree of switching that takes place when the opportunity cost changes.

Substituting away from more costly activities toward less costly ones is responding to incentives. An **incentive** is an inducement to take a particular action. The inducement may be a reward—a carrot—or a penalty—a stick. Changes in opportunity costs—in marginal costs—and changes in marginal benefits change the incentives that people face and lead to changes in their actions.

Whenever some unusual event disrupts the normal state of affairs, the economist always asks: How will opportunity costs change and what substitutions will arise from the changed incentives? For example, a frost kills Florida's orange crop and sends the price of orange juice through the roof. This increase in price, with all other prices remaining unchanged, increases the opportunity cost of drinking orange juice and gives people an incentive to substitute other fruit juices in its place. Or a bumper broccoli crop sends the price of broccoli tumbling. This decrease in price, with all other prices remaining unchanged, decreases the opportunity cost of eating broccoli and gives people an incentive to substitute broccoli for cauliflower and other vegetables.

Competition and Second Round Effects

Scarcity leads to *competition*. Each individual competes with other individuals for goods and services. This competition takes many forms. For example, producers compete with each other for market share and seek the highest profit available. People compete with each other for jobs and seek the highest wages available (for a given amount of work effort). Shoppers compete with each other for bargains and seek the lowest prices available. And students compete with each other for concert tickets, parking spaces, and places in heavily demanded courses.

Because of competition, the ultimate effects of an economic disturbance (the second round effects) are different from the initial effects (the first round effects). And the second round effects usually dominate the first round effects. For example, the first round effect of a Florida frost is an increase in the price of orange juice and a substitution of other fruit juices (say apple juice) for orange juice. The second round effects are the consequences of the increased competition for scarce apples. Juice drinkers compete with apple eaters for the available apples, and the price of apples increases. People now search for yet other substitutes—guava juice perhaps. As these second round effects play out, a long chain of substitutions and price changes take place, all triggered by a simple frost in Florida.

Economists try to predict second round effects by considering all the main substitutions that are likely as people compete with each other for the available resources. Trying to predict the number of vacant parking spaces in New York City is a good example of the importance of the effects of competition and of the distinction between first round and second round effects. The first round effect of a shopper going home is a vacant parking space. But the first round effect is short-lived. Competition for parking spaces results in vacant spaces being filled almost immediately. So, taking account of competition and second round effects, you predict that there are rarely any vacant spaces!

"And now a traffic update: A parking space has just become available on Sixty-fifth Street between Second and Third. Hold it! A bulletin has just been handed to me. That space has been taken."

Drawing by H. Martin; ©1987 The New Yorker Magazine, Inc.

R E V I E W

The economic way of thinking is based on five core ideas:

■ All economic problems arise from scarcity, and scarcity forces people to make choices and evaluate opportunity cost.

■ Opportunity cost is the *best* alternative forgone, not the money cost, and includes time cost and external cost.

■ Decisions are made by comparing *marginal benefit* and *marginal cost.*

■ When the opportunity cost of an activity increases, the incentive to substitute an alternative activity increases.

■ Competition creates ripples along the chain of substitution—second round effects—that dominate the first round effects.

You've examined the types of questions that economists try to answer. You've also seen something of the way economists think and have learned the five core ideas that guide that thinking. Your next task is to move beyond ideas to action and to study the things that economists do.

What Economists Do

ECONOMISTS WORK ON A WIDE ARRAY OF problems, just a small sample of which are covered by the questions at the start of this chapter. Economic questions can be divided into two big groups: microeconomic questions and macroeconomic questions.

Microeconomics and Macroeconomics

Microeconomics is the study of the decisions of people and businesses and the interaction of those decisions in markets. The goal of microeconomics is to explain the prices and quantities of individual goods and services. Microeconomics also studies the effects of government regulation and taxes on the prices and quantities of individual goods and services. For example, microeconomics studies the forces that determine the prices of cars and the quantities of cars produced and sold. It also studies the effects of regulations and taxes on the prices and quantities of cars.

Macroeconomics is the study of the national economy and the global economy and the way that economic aggregates grow and fluctuate. The goal of macroeconomics is to explain *average* prices and the *total* employment, income, and production. Macroeconomics also studies the effects of government actions—taxes, spending, and the deficit—on total jobs and incomes. For example, macroeconomics studies the forces that determine the average cost of living in the United States, the total value of the nation's production, and the effects of the federal budget on these variables.

Although microeconomics and macroeconomics have their own separate focuses, they use a common set of tools and ideas. Some problems have a microeconomic and a macroeconomic dimension. An example is the invention of video games and the growth of the market in multimedia products. Microeconomics explains the effects of this invention on the prices of games, the quantity of games produced, and the number of people employed making games. Macroeconomics explains the effects of this invention on total spending and jobs in the economy as a whole.

Economists not only work on a wide range of questions but also approach their work in a variety of ways. The different approaches can be summarized under two broad heads:

- Economic science
- Economic policy

Economic science is the attempt to *understand* the economic world, and economic policy is the attempt to *improve* it. Another way of putting the distinctions is this: Science makes *predictions,* while policy offers *prescriptions.* Policy and science overlap in many ways, and policy cannot get very far without science—it is not possible to make something work better without first understanding it. Let's take a closer look at these two approaches that economists take to their work.

Economic Science

Economics is a social science (along with political science, psychology, and sociology), and a major task of economists is to discover how the economic world works. In pursuit of this goal, economists (like all scientists) distinguish between two types of statements:

- What *is*
- What *ought* to be

Statements about what *is* are called *positive* statements. They say what is currently believed about the way the world operates. A positive statement might be right or wrong. And a positive statement can be tested by checking it against the facts. Statements about what *ought* to be are called *normative* statements. These statements depend on values and cannot be tested.

To see the distinction between positive and normative statements, consider the controversy over global warming. Some scientists believe that centuries of the burning of coal and oil are increasing the carbon dioxide content of the earth's atmosphere and leading to higher temperatures that eventually will have devastating consequences for life on this planet. "Our planet is warming because of an increased carbon dioxide buildup in the atmosphere" is a positive statement. It can (in principle and with sufficient data) be tested. "We ought to cut back on our use of carbon-based fuels such as coal and oil" is a normative statement. You may agree with or disagree with this statement, but you can't test it. It is based on values. Health care reform

provides an economic example of the distinction. "Universal health care will cut the amount of work time lost to illness" is a positive statement. "Every American should have equal access to health care" is a normative statement.

It is the task of economic science to discover and catalog positive statements that are consistent with what we observe in the world and that enable us to understand how the economic world works. This task is a large one that can be broken into three steps:

- Observation and measurement
- Model building
- Testing models

Observation and Measurement   Economists keep track of the amounts and locations of natural and human resources, of people's wages and work hours, of the prices and quantities of the different goods and services produced, of interest rates and the amounts borrowed and lent, of taxes and government spending, and of the quantities of goods and services bought from and sold to other countries. This list gives a flavor of the array of things that economists can observe and measure.

Model Building   The second step toward understanding the economic world is to build economic models. An **economic model** is a description of some aspect of the economic world that includes only those features of the world that are needed for the purpose at hand. What a model includes and what it leaves out result from *assumptions* about what is essential and what are inessential details.

You can see how ignoring details is useful— even essential—to our understanding by thinking about a model that you use every time you need a book from your school library. That model is the library catalog and floor plan. It is a model that guides you to the locations of the books. The catalog doesn't tell you whether the book you want is red or blue, and the floor plan doesn't tell you where the telephone cables run. These details don't affect your search for a book.

An economic model tells us how a number of variables are determined by a number of other variables. For example, a model of the economic effects of the 1994 Los Angeles earthquake might tell us the effects of the earthquake and the government's relief efforts on the number of houses and apartments, rents and prices, jobs, and commuting times.

Testing Models   A model's predictions may correspond to or be in conflict with the facts. By comparing the model's predictions with the facts, we are able to test a model and develop an economic theory. An **economic theory** is a generalization that summarizes what we think we understand about the economic choices that people make and the performance of industries and entire economies. It is a bridge between an economic model and the real economy.

A theory is created by a process of building and testing models. For example, you have a theory that if you follow the library floor plan (a model), you will get to the second floor stacks (reality). When you follow the floor plan, you are testing your theory. Suppose the floor plan doesn't show that the second floor stacks can be reached only by taking the north elevator. When you take the south elevator and hit a dead-end, you have tested your theory. This particular theory must be rejected. But you can develop a new theory based on a model that does include the essential assumption about the solid wall between the south elevator and the second floor stacks.

Figure 1.1 illustrates the process of developing theories by building and testing models. We begin by building a model. The model's implications are used to generate predictions about the world. These predictions and their test form the basis of a theory. When the predictions of a theory are in conflict with the facts, either the theory is discarded in favor of a superior alternative or we return to the model-building stage, modifying our assumptions and creating a new model.

While Fig. 1.1 shows the logical structure of the search for new knowledge, it does not describe the actual processes that are followed. In practice, scientific discovery is a human activity marked by stabs in the dark, blind alleys, flashes of insight, and, occasionally, revolutionary new views. Also, some models are discarded even when they fit the facts, and others are clung to even when they fail. Albert Einstein, the great physicist, put it well when he said,

> Creating a new theory is not like destroying an old barn and erecting a skyscraper in its place. It is rather like climbing a mountain, gaining new and wider views, discovering new connections between our starting point and its rich environment. But the point from which we started still exists and can be seen, although it appears smaller and forms a tiny part of our broad view gained by the mastery of the obstacles on our adventurous way up.[2]

---

[2]These words are attributed to Einstein in a letter by Oliver Sacks to *The Listener*, 88 (2279), November 30, 1972, 756.

FIGURE   1.1

How Economic Theories Are Developed

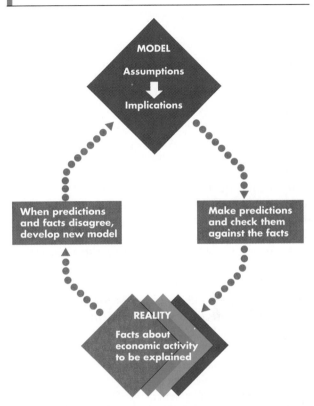

Economists develop economic theories by building and testing economic models. An economic model is based on *assumptions* about what is essential and what can be ignored and the *implications* of those assumptions. The implications of a model form the basis of *predictions* about the world. Economists test these predictions by checking them against the facts. If the predictions are in conflict with the facts, the model-building process begins again with new assumptions. Only when the predictions agree with the facts has a useful theory been developed.

Economics is a young science and a long way from having achieved its goal of explaining and understanding economic activity. Its birth can be dated fairly precisely to 1776 and the publication of Adam Smith's *The Wealth of Nations* (see *Economics in History,* pp. 64–65). In the closing years of the twentieth century, economics has managed to discover a sizable number of useful generalizations. In many areas, however, we are still going around the circle—changing assumptions, performing new logical deductions, generating new predictions, and getting wrong answers yet again. The gradual accumulation of correct answers gives most practitioners some faith that their methods will, eventually, provide usable answers to the big economic questions.

But progress in economics comes slowly, and economists must be careful how they proceed. Let's look at some of the obstacles to progress in economics.

Unscrambling Cause and Effect   It is difficult in economics to isolate forces and identify what is a cause and what is the effect. The logical tool that all scientists use for identifying cause and effect is *ceteris paribus*. ***Ceteris paribus*** is a Latin term that means "other things being equal" or "if all other relevant things remain the same." All successful attempts to understand the world use this device. By changing one factor at a time and holding all the other relevant factors constant, we isolate the factor of interest and are able to investigate its effects in the clearest possible way.

Economic models (like the models in all other sciences) enable the influence of one factor at a time to be isolated in the imaginary world of the model. Indeed, one of the strengths of model building is that model building enables us to imagine what would happen if only one factor changed. But *ceteris paribus* can be a problem in economics when we try to test a model.

In the laboratory sciences, such as chemistry and physics, experiments are performed that actually hold all the relevant factors constant except for the one under investigation. In the non-experimental sciences such as economics (and astronomy), we usually observe the outcomes of the *simultaneous* operation of several—perhaps many—factors. As a result, it is hard to sort out the effects of each individual factor and to compare the effects with what a model predicts. To cope with this problem, economists take three complementary approaches.

First, they look for pairs of events in which other things were equal (or similar). An example might be to study the effects of unemployment insurance on the unemployment rate by comparing the United States with Canada on the presumption that the people in the two economies are sufficiently similar. Second, economists have developed statistical tools—called *econometrics*—that unscramble the separate factors that simultaneously influence economic behavior. Third, economists are beginning to design experiments that are undertaken in economic

laboratories. This relatively new and exciting approach puts real subjects (usually students) in a decision-making situation and varies their incentives in some way to discover how they respond to one factor at a time.

Economists work hard to avoid *fallacies*—errors of reasoning that lead to a wrong conclusion. But two fallacies are common, and you need to be on your guard to avoid them. They are the

- Fallacy of composition
- *Post hoc* fallacy

Fallacy of Composition   The fallacy of composition is the (false) statement that what is true of the parts is true of the whole or that what is true of the whole is true of the parts. For one tuna fishing firm (a part), using bigger nets and boats enables more tuna to be caught. But if all the tuna fishing firms (the whole) use bigger nets and boats, overfishing will eventually result and everyone will catch fewer tuna.

The fallacy of composition arises mainly in macroeconomics, and it stems from the fact that the parts interact with each other to produce an outcome for the whole that might differ from the intent of the parts. For example, a firm lays off some workers to cut costs and improve its profits. If all firms take similar actions, incomes fall and so does spending. The firm sells less, and its profits don't improve.

Post Hoc Fallacy   Another Latin phrase—*post hoc ergo propter hoc*—means "after this, therefore because of this." The *post hoc* fallacy is the error of reasoning from timing to cause and effect. You see a flash of lightning and some seconds later hear a clap of thunder. But the lightning did not *cause* the thunder. The flash and the clap were the *simultaneous* effect of—were *caused* by—an electrical disturbance in the atmosphere.

Unraveling cause and effect is extremely difficult in economics. And just looking at the timing of events often doesn't help. For example, the stock market booms, and some months later the economy expands—jobs and incomes grow. Did the stock market boom cause the economy to expand? Possibly, but perhaps businesses started to plan the expansion of production because a new technology that lowered costs had become available. As knowledge of the plans spread, the stock market reacted to *anticipate* the economic expansion. To disentangle cause and effect, economists use economic models and data and, to the extent that they can, perform experiments.

We've now looked at the way in which economists try to understand the world—economic science. Let's now study economic policy to see how economists try to contribute to improving economic performance.

Economic Policy

Economic policy is the attempt to devise government actions and to design institutions that might improve economic performance. Economists play two distinct roles in the formulation of economic policy.

First, they try to predict the consequence of alternative policies. For example, economists who work on health care reform try to predict the cost, benefits, and effectiveness of alternative ways of financing and organizing the health care industry. Economists who work on environmental issues attempt to predict the cost and quality of urban air resulting from changes in auto emission standards. And economists who study financial markets try to predict the effects of interest rate changes on the stock market and employment.

Second, economists evaluate alternative policies on the scale of better to worse. To do this, economists must state the policy *objectives*. Provided that there is clarity and openness about the policy objectives, this type of policy analysis can be as objective and scientific as the development of economic theories. And over the years, by responding to the societies of which they are a part and interpreting sentiments expressed in the political arena, economists have developed criteria for judging social and political outcomes on the better-to-worse scale. Four objectives of policy have emerged:

- Efficiency
- Equity
- Growth
- Stability

Efficiency When **economic efficiency** has been achieved, production costs are as low as possible and consumers are as satisfied as possible with the combination of goods and services that is being produced. Three distinct conditions produce economic efficiency: efficient production, efficient consumption, and efficient exchange.

Efficient production is achieved when each firm produces its output at the least possible cost. Cost includes costs borne by the firm and costs borne by others—*external* costs. Efficient consumption is achieved when everyone buys the goods and services that make them as well off as possible by their own evaluations. And efficient exchange is achieved when everyone specializes to earn a living by doing the job that gives him or her the maximum possible economic benefit. When economic efficiency is achieved, it is not possible to make one person better off without at the same time making someone else worse off.

Equity **Equity** is economic justice or fairness. An efficient economy is not necessarily an equitable or just one. Economic efficiency could bring very large incomes to a few people and very low incomes to the vast majority. Such a situation would be regarded as inequitable by the majority but possibly not by everyone. Economists have succeeded in arriving at a widely accepted definition of efficiency, but attaining the same degree of consensus on a definition of equity or economic justice is elusive. Equity remains a matter on which reasonable people disagree.

Growth **Economic growth** is the increase in incomes and production per person. It results from the ongoing advance of technology, the accumulation of ever larger quantities of productive equipment and ever rising standards of education. Poor societies are transformed into rich ones by economic growth. But economic growth has a cost. It often uses up exhaustible natural resources. And it sometimes destroys natural vegetation and damages the environment. But these are not inevitable drawbacks of economic growth, and countries can, if they choose to do so, devote resources to enriching and protecting the environment.

Economic growth can be encouraged or discouraged by the policies that governments adopt. For example, tax incentives for research and development might stimulate growth, while tax penalties that encourage resource conservation might retard it. In reaching policy conclusions, economists must take a view about the desirable growth rate and the effects of the policies being considered on growth.

Stability **Economic stability** is the absence of wide fluctuations in the economic growth rate, the level of employment, and average prices. Almost the whole of macroeconomics has developed to understand these problems, and many macroeconomists specialize in designing policies to tame an unstable economy.

Agreement and Disagreement

Economists have a reputation for being a divided lot. Perhaps you've heard the joke: "If you laid all the economists in the world end to end, they still wouldn't reach agreement." There is a hint of truth in the joke, but only a hint. The fact is that there is a remarkable degree of consensus among economists on a wide range of issues. Table 1.1 gives a flavor of this consensus.

Some disagreements are about what is possible—*positive* matters—and some are about what is desirable—*normative* matters. Disagreements on positive issues arise when the available evidence is insufficient for a clear conclusion to be reached, and disagreements on normative issues arise from differences in values or priorities. It is hardly surprising that economists have such disagreements, since they are just a reflection of similar disagreements in the larger society of which economists are members.

You now know the types of questions that economists try to answer and that all economic questions and economic activity arise from scarcity. You know something about the way economists think and about the work they do. In the chapters that follow, you are going to study economic activity and discover how the U.S. economy and the global economy work. But before we do that, we need to stand back and take an overview of our economy.

TABLE 1.1

Agreement and Disagreement Among Economists

	Percentage of economists who	
Positive propositions	**Agree**	**Disagree**
Rent ceilings cut the availability of housing	93	7
A tax cut can help to achieve full employment	90	9
A minimum wage increases unemployment of young workers	79	21
Big firms in the United States are likely to collude	71	28
Lower unemployment brings higher inflation in the short run	59	39
Lower marginal income tax rates increase work effort	55	44
The U.S. trade deficit arises because our firms can't compete	48	52
A lower capital gains tax would promote economic growth	49	50
Normative propositions		
The distribution of income in the United States should be more equal	73	27
Antitrust laws should be enforced more vigorously to curtail monopoly power	72	28
The level of government spending should be reduced	55	45
Positive propositions about economic efficiency		
Tariffs and import quotas usually reduce economic well-being	93	7
A large federal budget deficit has an adverse effect on the economy	84	16
Cash payments benefit welfare recipients more than transfers-in-kind of equal value	84	15
Pollution taxes are more efficient than pollution limits	78	21
Economic evidence suggests that there are too many resources in American agriculture	73	21

Source: Richard M. Alston, J. R. Kearl, and Michael B. Vaughan, "Is there a Consensus Among Economists," *American Economic Review,* 82, (May 1992), pp. 203–209.

The Economy: An Overview

THE ECONOMY IS A MECHANISM THAT ALLOCATES scarce resources among alternative uses. This mechanism achieves five things:

- What
- How
- When
- Where
- Who

1. *What* goods and services will be produced and in *what* quantities? Will more cable companies offer pay-per-view service, or will more movie theaters be built? Will young professionals vacation in Europe or live in large houses? Will more high-performance sports cars or more trucks and station wagons be made?

2. *How* will the various goods and services be produced? Will a supermarket operate with three checkout lines and clerks using laser scanners or six checkout lines and clerks keying in prices by hand? Will workers weld station wagons by hand, or will robots do the job? Will farmers keep track of their livestock feeding schedules and inventories by using paper and pencil records or personal computers? Will credit card companies use computers or clerks to read charge slips?

3. *When* will the various goods and services be produced? Will a supermarket operate 24 hours a day, 7 days a week, or just 12 hours a day, 6 days a week? Will a car factory close for the summer and lay off its workers? Will there be a surge of house building in the spring, bringing higher wages and longer hours for construction workers? Will crude oil be used now or saved for later?

4. *Where* will the various goods and services be produced? Will American Express process its charge slips and accounts in New York, or will it hire less costly labor in Barbados and transfer its records by satellite? Will Honda make its cars in Japan and then ship them to the United States, or will it open a factory in Ohio and export cars from the United States to Japan? Will Boeing build airplanes in Seattle, or will it close its oper-

ations there and open a new assembly plant in Beijing?

5. *Who* will consume the various goods and services? The distribution of economic benefits depends on the distribution of income. People with high incomes are able to consume more goods and services than people with low incomes. Who gets to consume what thus depends on income. Will the ski instructor consume more than the lawyer's secretary? Will the people of Hong Kong consume more than the people of Ethiopia?

To understand how an economy works, we must identify its components and see how they interact with each other. Figure 1.2 shows a picture of an economy. This picture illustrates a *closed economy*—an economy that has no links to other economies. We can gain a lot of insight by studying a closed-economy model. In reality, the only closed economy is the economy of the entire world—the global economy. During the 1980s, the global economy became a highly integrated mechanism for allocating scarce resources and deciding *what, how, when, and where* the various goods and services will be produced and *who* will consume them.

The economy shown in Fig. 1.2 contains two types of components:

- Decision makers
- Markets

Decision Makers

Decision makers are the economic actors. They make the choices. Figure 1.2 identifies three types of decision makers:

1. Households
2. Firms
3. Governments

A *household* is any group of people living together as a decision-making unit. Every individual in the economy belongs to a household. Some households consist of a single person; others consist either of families or of groups of unrelated individuals, such as two or three students sharing an apartment. Each household has unlimited wants and limited resources.

FIGURE   I.2
A Picture of an Economy

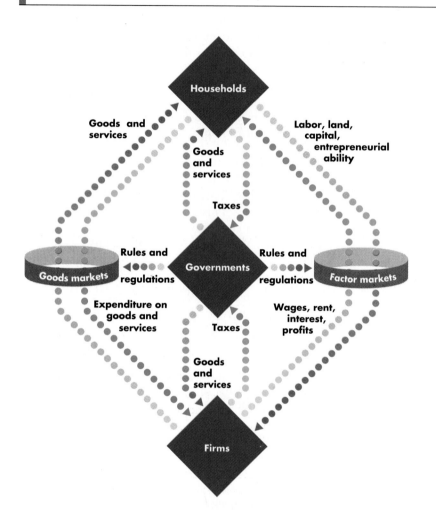

Households, firms, and governments make economic decisions. Households decide how much of their labor, land, capital, and entrepreneurial ability to sell or rent (the red flows) in exchange for wages, rent, interest, and profits (the green flows). They also decide how much of their income to spend on the various types of goods and services available. Firms decide how much labor, land, and capital to hire and how much of the various types of goods and services to produce. Governments decide which goods and services they will provide and the taxes that households and firms will pay.

These decisions by households, firms, and governments are coordinated in markets—the goods market and factor markets—that are regulated by rules that governments establish and enforce. In these markets, prices constantly adjust to keep buying and selling plans consistent.

A *firm* is an organization that uses resources to produce goods and services. All producers are called firms, no matter how big they are or what they produce. Car makers, farmers, banks, and insurance companies are all firms.

A *government* is a many-layered organization that sets laws and rules, operates a law-enforcement mechanism (courts and police forces), taxes households and firms, and provides public goods and services such as national defense, public health, transportation, and education. By changing laws and rules, taxes and spending, governments try to influence the choices that households and firms make.

Markets

In ordinary speech, the word *market* means a place where people buy and sell goods such as fish, meat, fruits, and vegetables. In economics, *market* has a more general meaning. A **market** is any arrangement that enables buyers and sellers to get information and to do business with each other. An example is the market in which oil is bought and sold—the world oil market. The world oil market is not a place. It is the network of oil producers, oil users, wholesalers, and brokers who buy and sell. In the world oil market, decision makers do not meet physically. They make deals throughout the world by telephone, fax, and direct computer link.

Figure 1.2 identifies two types of markets: goods markets and factor markets. *Goods markets* are those in which goods and services are bought and sold. *Factor markets* are those in which factors of production are bought and sold.

Factors of production are the economy's productive resources. They are classified under four headings:

1. Labor
2. Land
3. Capital
4. Entrepreneurial ability

Labor is the time and effort that people devote to producing goods and services. It is rewarded with wages. **Land** is all the natural resources used to produce goods and services. The return to land is rent. **Capital** is all the equipment, buildings, tools, and other manufactured goods used to produce other goods and services. The return to capital is interest. **Entrepreneurial ability** is a special type of human resource that organizes the other three factors of production, makes business decisions, innovates, and bears business risk. Entrepreneurship is rewarded with profit.

Households and firms make decisions that result in the transactions in the goods markets and factor markets shown in Fig. 1.2. Households decide how much of their labor, land, and capital to sell or rent in factor markets. They receive incomes in the form of wages, rent, interest, and profit. Households also decide how to spend their incomes on goods and services produced by firms.

Firms decide the quantities of factors of production to hire, how to use them to produce goods and services, what goods and services to produce, and in what quantities. They sell their output in goods markets.

The flows resulting from these decisions by households and firms are shown in Fig. 1.2. The red flows are the factors of production that go from households to firms and the goods and services that go from firms to households. The green flows in the opposite direction are the payments made in exchange for these items.

A public choice process determines the rules and regulations imposed by governments, the taxes governments raise, and the goods and services they provide. These public choices by governments are also shown in Fig. 1.2.

Coordinating Decisions

Perhaps the most striking thing about the choices made by households, firms, and governments is that they surely must come into conflict with each other. For example, households choose how much work to do and what type of work to specialize in, but firms choose the type and quantity of labor to employ in the production of various goods and services. In other words, households choose the types and quantities of labor to sell, and firms choose the types and quantities of labor to buy. Similarly, in markets for goods and services, households choose the types and quantities of goods and services to buy, while firms choose the types and quantities to sell.

How is it possible for the millions of individual decisions made by households, firms, and governments to be consistent with each other? What makes households want to sell the same types and quantities of labor that firms want to buy? What happens if the number of people wanting to work as airline pilots exceeds the number of pilots that airlines want to hire? How do firms know what to produce so that households will buy their output? What happens if firms want to sell more hamburgers than households want to buy?

Markets Coordinate Decisions   Markets coordinate individual decisions through price adjustments. To see how, think about the market for hamburgers in your local area. Suppose that at the current price, the quantity of hamburgers being offered for sale is less than the quantity that people would like to buy. Some people who want to buy hamburgers are not able to do so. To make the choices of buyers and sellers compatible, buyers must scale down their appetites and more hamburgers must be offered for sale. An increase in the price of hamburgers produces this outcome. Because there is a shortage of hamburgers, their price rises. The higher price encourages producers to offer more hamburgers for sale. The higher price also curbs the appetite for hamburgers and changes some lunch plans. Fewer people buy hamburgers, and more buy hot dogs (or some other alternative to hamburgers). More hamburgers (and more hot dogs) are offered for sale.

Now imagine the opposite situation. At the current price, more hamburgers are available than people want to buy. In this case, to make the choices of buyers and sellers compatible, more hamburgers must be bought and fewer must be offered for sale. A fall in the price of hamburgers achieves this outcome. Because there is a surplus of hamburgers, the price falls. And the lower price discourages the production of hamburgers and encourages consumption. Decisions to produce and sell and to buy and consume are continuously adjusted and kept in balance with each other by price adjustments.

Sometimes prices get stuck or fixed. For example, the government might impose a rent ceiling or a minimum wage that prevents the price adjustments that would make the plans of buyers and sellers consistent. Other mechanisms then begin to operate. One possibility is that customers wait in line and get served on a first-come-first-served basis. Another is that inventories operate as a temporary safety valve. If the price is fixed too low, firms sell more than they would like and their inventories shrink. If the price is fixed too high, firms sell less than they would like and their inventories pile up. Waiting lines and inventory changes are only a temporary solution to inconsistent buying and selling plans. Eventually, a price adjustment is needed.

We've seen how decisions coordinated in markets determine *what* gets produced—in the example, how many hamburgers are produced. Decisions coordinated in markets also determine *how* goods and services are produced. For example, hamburger producers can use gas, electric power, or charcoal to cook their hamburgers. Which fuel is used depends in part on the flavor that the producer wants to achieve. It also depends on the cost of the different fuels. If a fuel becomes very expensive, as did oil in the 1970s, less of it is used and more of other fuels are used. By substituting one fuel for another as the costs of the different fuels change, the market solves the question of how to produce.

Market-coordinated decisions also determine *when* goods and services are produced. If consumer spending on fast food falls temporarily and prices drop below the level that covers the wage bill and other expenses, hamburger and hot dog producers close down and lay off their workers. If consumer spending rises and fast food prices rise, firms respond by producing more hamburgers and hot dogs.

The market-coordinated decisions also determine *where* goods and services are produced. If the cost of making beef patties in the United States rises above the cost of making beef patties in Mexico, McDonald's and other fast food firms switch their production of patties to the low-cost source.

Finally, market-coordinated decisions determine *who* consumes the goods and services produced. Those skills, talents, and resources that are rare but highly valued command a high price, and their owners receive a large share of the economy's output. Those skills, talents, and resources that are common and less highly valued command a low price, and their owners receive a small share of the economy's output.

Alternative Coordination Mechanisms   The market is one of two alternative coordination mechanisms. The other is a command mechanism. A *command mechanism* is a method of determining *what*, *how*, *when*, and *where* goods and services are produced and *who* consumes them, using a hierarchical organization structure in which people carry out the instructions given to them. The best example of a hierarchical organization structure is the military. Commanders make decisions requiring actions that are passed down a chain of command. Soldiers and marines on the front line take the actions they are ordered to take.

An economy that relies on a command mechanism is called a *command economy*. Examples of command economies in today's world are becoming rare, and only North Korea falls squarely into this category. But the economies of Cuba and China have significant command sectors. Before they embarked on programs of reform in the late 1980s, the Soviet Union and other countries of Eastern Europe also had command economies.

An economy that uses a market coordinating mechanism is called a *market economy*. But most real-world economies use both markets and commands to coordinate economic activity. An economy that relies on both markets and command mechanisms is called a *mixed economy*.

The U.S. economy relies extensively on the market as a mechanism for coordinating the decisions of individual households and firms. But the U.S. economy also uses command mechanisms. The economy of the armed forces is a command economy. Command mechanisms are also employed in other government organizations and within large firms. There is also a command element in our legal system. By enacting laws and establishing regulations and agencies to monitor the market economy, governments influence the economic decisions of households and firms and change our economic course.

Thus the United States depends mainly on the market mechanism but also partly on a command mechanism, so the U.S. economy is a mixed economy.

International Linkages

We've looked at a closed economy—one that has no links with any other economy—and noted that the only closed economy is the entire world. A national economy like the U.S. economy is an *open economy.* It has economic links with other economies.

Figure 1.3 illustrates the economic links between the U.S. economy and the rest of the world. Firms in the open U.S. economy sell some of their production to the rest of the world. These sales are U.S. exports of goods and services. Also, firms, households, and governments in the United States buy goods and services from firms in other countries. These purchases are U.S. imports of goods and services. These export and import transactions take place in world goods markets and are illustrated in the figure.

The total values of exports and imports are not necessarily equal to each other. When U.S. exports exceed U.S. imports, we have a surplus. When U.S. imports exceed U.S. exports, we have a deficit. A country with a surplus lends to the rest of the world, and a country with a deficit borrows from the rest of the world. These international lending and borrowing transactions take place in the world financial markets and are illustrated in Fig. 1.3.

The volume of international transactions is large. In 1994, U.S. businesses sold more than 10 percent of their production to other countries and U.S. imports exceeded 11 percent of total spending. Total world exports and imports exceeded $8 trillion in 1994, which is larger than the total value of all the goods and services produced in the United States.

FIGURE 1.3
The Global Economy

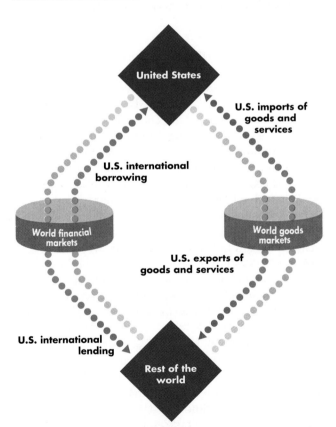

The U.S. economy buys and sells goods and services in world goods markets. What it buys are U.S. imports, and what it sells are U.S. exports. Also, U.S. firms set up business in other countries, and foreign firms set up business in the United States. The U.S. economy also borrows from and lends to the rest of the world. These transactions take place in the world's financial markets.

R E V I E W

■ An economy is a mechanism that determines what goods and services are produced; how, when, and where they are produced; and who consumes them.

■ Choices made by households, firms, and governments are coordinated through markets for goods and services and factors of production.

■ Choices are sometimes coordinated by command mechanisms.

◆ In the next chapter, we will study some of the tools that economists use to describe economic performance and to build economic models. Then, in Chapter 3, we will build an economic model and use that model to sharpen our understanding of opportunity cost and to study the way in which people make choices about what to produce.

SUMMARY

How Economists Think

Economists see all economic questions as arising from scarcity—from the fact that wants exceed resources. Economists study the ways people cope with scarcity. Scarcity forces people to make choices and face opportunity costs. The opportunity cost of any action is the best alternative action that could have been undertaken in its place.

Two fundamental ideas permeate economics: *the margin* and *substitution*. People make decisions at the margin. They evaluate actions in incremental steps. All actions have substitutes. The higher the opportunity cost of an action, the greater is the incentive for people to seek a substitute—an alternative—action. Scarcity forces people to compete for scarce resources. (pp. 8–11)

What Economists Do

Economists work on microeconomics—the study of the decisions of individual households and firms—and macroeconomics—the study of the economy as a whole and the way it fluctuates and expands over time. They attempt to *understand* the economic world and to *improve* economic performance by studying economic policy.

In their attempt to understand the economic world, economists distinguish between *positive* statements—statements about what is—and *normative* statements—statements about what ought to be. Like other scientists, they try to develop theories that enable them to make sense of the world. They pursue this task by building and testing economic models—abstract, logical constructions that contain assumptions about what is essential and what can be ignored and the implications of those assumptions. The main obstacles to progress in economics are the fact that we observe the outcomes of the *simultaneous* operation of several—perhaps many—factors and that it is difficult to disentangle cause and effect. To cope with these problems, economists use the *ceteris paribus* ("other things remaining the same") assumption and develop statistical and experimental methods for isolating the factors of interest. Economists are careful to avoid the fallacy of composition (the false statement "what is true of the parts is true of the whole or what is true of the whole is true of the parts") and the *post hoc* fallacy (the false statement "after this, therefore because of this").

In conducting economic policy analysis, economists often try to evaluate alternative policies on a better-to-worse scale. To do this, they must choose policy *objectives*. Four objectives of policy are efficiency, equity, growth, and stability. Of these, equity (or economic justice) is the most elusive and difficult to define.

Economists have disagreements, but they agree on a surprisingly wide range of questions. (pp. 11–16)

The Economy: An Overview

People have unlimited wants but limited resources or factors of production—of labor, land, capital, and entrepreneurial ability. The economy is a mechanism that allocates scarce resources among competing uses, determining *what*, *how*, *when*, and *where* goods and services are produced and *who* will consume them.

The economy's two key components are decision makers and markets. Economic decision makers are households, firms, and governments. Households decide how much of their labor, land, and capital to sell or rent and how much of the various goods and services to buy. Firms decide what factors of production to hire and which goods and services to produce. Governments decide what goods and services to provide to households and firms and how much to raise in taxes.

The decisions of households, firms, and governments are coordinated through markets in which prices adjust to keep buying plans and selling plans consistent. Alternatively, coordination can be achieved by a command mechanism. The U.S. economy relies mainly on markets, but there is a command element in the actions taken by governments and large firms that also influences the allocation of resources. The U.S. economy is a mixed economy.

National economies are interlinked in the global economy. Countries exchange large quantities of goods and services—exports and imports—and undertake international borrowing and lending. (pp. 17–21)

K E Y   E L E M E N T S

Key Figure

Key Terms

R E V I E W   Q U E S T I O N S

1. What is economics?
2. Give some examples, different from those in the chapter, of the questions that economics tries to answer.
3. What is scarcity and how is it different from poverty?
4. Why does scarcity force people to make choices?
5. Why does scarcity force people to face costs?
6. What is *opportunity cost*?
7. Why does the money we spend on something not tell us its opportunity cost?
8. Why is the time taken to do something part of its opportunity cost?
9. What is *marginal* cost and why is it the relevant cost for making a decision?
10. What is an external cost?
11. What is the *principle of substitution*?
12. What is an *incentive* and how do people respond to incentives?
13. Why does scarcity imply competition?
14. Why does competition lead to second round effects that determine the consequences of an economic disturbance?
15. Distinguish between microeconomics and macroeconomics.
16. Distinguish between positive and normative statements and list three examples of each type of statement.
17. What is an economic model?
18. What does *ceteris paribus* mean?
19. What is the fallacy of composition? Give an example.
20. What is the *post hoc* fallacy? Give an example.
21. Explain the difference between economic theory and economic policy.
22. What are the four main goals of economic policy?
23. Name the main economic decision makers.
24. List the economic decisions made by households, firms, and governments.
25. What is a market?
26. What is a command mechanism?
27. How does the market determine what, how, when, and where things will be produced and who will consume them?

P R O B L E M S

1. You plan to go to school this summer. If you do, you won't be able to take your usual job that pays $6,000 for the summer and you won't be able to live at home for free. The cost of your tuition will be $2,000, textbooks $200, and living expenses $1,400. What is the opportunity cost of going to summer school?

2. On Valentine's Day, Bernie and Catherine exchanged gifts: Bernie sent Catherine red roses and Catherine bought Bernie a box of chocolates. Each spent $15. They also spent $50 on dinner and split the cost evenly. Did either Bernie or Catherine incur any opportunity costs? If so, what were they? Explain your answer.

3. Nancy asks Beth to be her maid of honor at her wedding. Beth accepts. Which of the following are part of Beth's opportunity cost of being Nancy's maid of honor? Explain why they are or are not.
   a. The $200 she spent on a new outfit for the occasion
   b. The $50 she spent on a party for Nancy's friends
   c. The money she spent on a haircut a week before the wedding
   d. The weekend visit she missed for her grandmother's 75th birthday—the same weekend as the wedding
   e. The $10 she spent on lunch on the way to the wedding

4. The local mall has free parking, but the mall is always very busy and it usually takes 30 minutes to find a parking space. Today when you found a vacant spot, Harry also wanted it. Is parking really free at this mall? If not, what did it cost you to park today? When you parked your car today, did you impose any costs on Harry? Explain your answers.

5. Which of the following statements are positive and which are normative?

   a. A cut in wages will reduce the number of people who are willing to work.
   b. High interest rates prohibit many young people from buying their first home.
   c. No family ought to pay more than 25 percent of its income in taxes.
   d. The government should reduce the number of minority members in the military and increase the number of whites.
   e. The government ought to supply a medical insurance scheme for everyone free of charge.
   f. The government ought to behave in such a way as to ensure that resources are used efficiently.

6. You have been hired by Soundtrend, a company that makes and markets tapes, records, and compact discs (CDs). Your employer is going to start selling these products in a new region that has a population of 10 million people. A survey has indicated that 50 percent of people buy only popular music, 10 percent buy only classical music, and no one buys both types of music. Another survey suggests that the average income of a pop music fan is $10,000 a year and that of a classical fan is $50,000 a year. On the basis of a third survey, it appears that, on the average, people with low incomes spend one quarter of 1 percent of their income on tapes, records, and CDs, while people with high incomes spend 2 percent of their income on these products.

   Build a model to enable Soundtrend to predict how much will be spent on pop music and classical music in this region in one year. In doing so:

   a. List your assumptions.
   b. Work out the implications of your assumptions.
   c. Highlight the potential sources of errors in your predictions.

Making and Using Graphs

- Make and interpret a scatter diagram, a time-series graph, and a cross-section graph

- Distinguish between linear and nonlinear relationships and between relationships that have a maximum and a minimum

- Define and calculate the slope of a line

- Graph relationships among more than two variables

Benjamin Disraeli, British prime minister in the late nineteenth century, is reputed to have said that there are three kinds of lies: lies, damned lies, and statistics. One of the most powerful ways of conveying statistical information is in the form of a graph. And like statistics, graphs can lie. But the right graph does not lie. It reveals a relationship that would otherwise be obscure.

Three Kinds of Lies

◆ Graphs are a modern invention. They first appeared in the late eighteenth century, long after the discovery of logarithms and calculus. But today, in the age of the personal computer and video display, graphs have become as important as words and numbers. How do economists use graphs? What types of graphs do they use? What do graphs reveal and what can they hide? ◆ The seven big questions that you studied in Chapter 1—the questions that economics tries to answer—are difficult ones. They involve relationships among a large number of variables. Virtually nothing in economics has a single cause. Instead, a large number of variables interact with each other. It is often said that in economics, everything depends on everything else. Changes in the quantity of ice cream consumed are caused by changes in the price of cream, the temperature, and many other factors. How can we make and interpret graphs of relationships among several variables?

In this chapter, you are going to look at the kinds of graphs that are used in economics. You are going to learn how to make them and read them. You are also going to learn how to calculate the strength of the effect of one variable on another. There are no graphs or techniques used in this book that are more complicated than those explained and described in this chapter. If you are already familiar with graphs, you may want to skip (or skim) this chapter. Whether you study this chapter thoroughly or give it a quick pass, you can use it as a handy reference and return to it whenever you feel that you need extra help understanding the graphs that you encounter in your study of economics.

Graphing Data

GRAPHS REPRESENT A QUANTITY AS A DISTANCE on a line. Figure 2.1 gives two examples. Part (a) shows temperature, measured in degrees Fahrenheit, as the distance on a scale. Movements from left to right show increases in temperature. Movements from right to left show decreases in temperature. The point marked 0 represents zero degrees Fahrenheit. To the right of 0, the temperatures are positive. To the left of 0, the temperatures are negative (as indicated by the minus sign in front of the numbers).

Figure 2.1(b) provides another example. This time altitude, or height, is measured in thousands of feet above sea level. The point marked zero represents sea level. Points to the right of 0 represent feet above sea level. Points to the left of 0 (indicated by a minus sign) represent feet below sea level. There are no rigid rules about the scale for a graph. The scale is determined by the range of the variable being graphed and the space available for the graph.

Each graph in Fig. 2.1 shows just a single variable. Marking a point on either of the two scales indicates a particular temperature or a particular height. Thus point *a* represents 32°F, the freezing point of water. Point *b* represents 20,320 feet, the height of Mount McKinley, the highest mountain in North America.

Graphing a single variable does not usually reveal much. Graphs become powerful when they show how two variables are related to each other.

Two-Variable Graphs

To construct a two-variable graph, we set two scales perpendicular to each other. Figure 2.2 shows how this looks for temperature and height. Temperature is shown as it was before, but height is now shown by movements up and down a vertical scale.

The two scale lines in Fig. 2.2 are called *axes*. The vertical line is called the *y-axis,* and the horizontal line is called the *x-axis*. The letters *x* and *y* appear

---

FIGURE 2.2

Graphing Two Variables

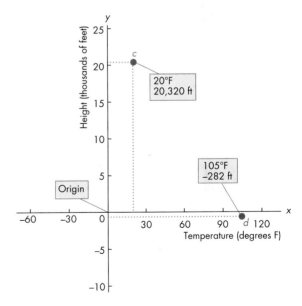

The relationship between two variables is graphed by drawing two axes perpendicular to each other. Height is measured here on the y-axis, and temperature on the x-axis. Point c represents the top of Mt. McKinley, 20,320 feet above sea level (measured on the y-axis) with a temperature of 20°F (measured on the x-axis). Point d represents Death Valley, 282 feet below sea level with a temperature of 105°F.

FIGURE 2.1

Graphing a Single Variable

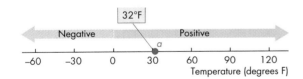

(a) Temperature

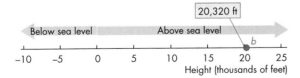

(b) Height

All graphs have a scale that measures a quantity as a distance. The two scales here measure temperature and height. Numbers to the right of zero are positive. Numbers to the left of zero are negative.

on the axes of Fig. 2.2. Each axis has a zero point shared by the two axes. The zero point, common to both axes, is called the *origin*.

To show something in a two-variable graph, we need two pieces of information. For example, Mount McKinley is 20,320 feet high, and on a particular day, the temperature at its peak is 20°F. We show this information in Fig. 2.2 by marking the height of the mountain on the *y*-axis at 20,320 feet and the temperature on the *x*-axis at 20°F. We can identify the values of the two variables that appear on the axes by marking point *c*.

Two lines, called *coordinates*, can be drawn from point *c*. The line running from *c* to the horizontal axis is the *y*-coordinate, because its length is the same as the value marked off on the *y*-axis. Similarly, the line running from *c* to the vertical axis is the *x*-coordinate, because its length is the same as the value marked off on the *x*-axis.

Figure 2.2 also illustrates that at Death Valley in the Mojave Desert, the lowest point in the United States at 282 feet *below* sea level, the temperature is 105°F. This information is shown by point *d*.

Economists use graphs similar to the one in Fig. 2.2 to reveal and describe the relationships among economic variables. The main types of graphs used in economics are:

■ Scatter diagrams
■ Time-series graphs
■ Cross-section graphs

Let's look at each of these types of graphs.

Scatter Diagrams

A **scatter diagram** plots the value of one economic variable against the value of another variable. Such a graph is used to reveal whether a relationship exists between two economic variables. It is also used to describe a relationship.

The Relationship Between Consumption and Income
Figure 2.3 shows a scatter diagram of the relationship between consumption and income. The *x*-axis measures average income, and the *y*-axis measures average consumption. Each point shows consumption per person (on the average) and income per person in the United States in a given year between 1984 and 1994. The points for all eleven

years are "scattered" within the graph. Each point is labeled with a two-digit number that shows us its year. For example, the point marked 89 shows us that in 1989, consumption per person was $13,000 and income per person was $14,000.

This graph shows us that a relationship exists between average income and average consumption. The dots form a pattern that shows us that when income increases, consumption also increases.

Breaks in the Axes Each axis in Fig. 2.3 has a break in it, as shown by the small gaps. The breaks indicate that there are jumps from the origin, 0, to the first values recorded. The breaks are used because

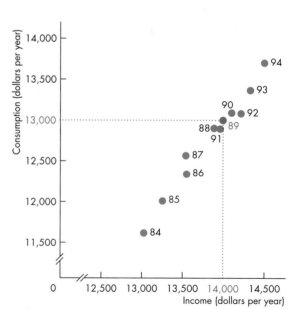

FIGURE 2.3

A Scatter Diagram

A scatter diagram shows the relationship between two variables. This scatter diagram shows the relationship between average consumption and average income during the years 1984 to 1994. Each point shows the values of the two variables in a specific year, and the year is identified by the two-digit number. For example, in 1989, average consumption was $13,000 and average income was $14,000. The pattern formed by the points shows that as income increases, so does consumption.

in the period covered by the graph, consumption was never less than $11,500 and income was never less than $12,500. With no breaks in the axes of this graph, there would be a lot of empty space, all the points would be crowded into the top right corner, and we would not be able to see whether a relationship existed between these two variables. By breaking the axes, we are able to bring the relationship into view. In effect, we use a zoom lens to bring the relationship into the center of the graph and magnify it so that it fills the graph.

The ranges of the variables plotted on the axes of a graph are an important feature of a graph, and it is a good idea to get into the habit of always looking closely at the values and the labels on the axes before you start to interpret a graph.

Other Relationships   Figure 2.4 shows two other scatter diagrams. Part (a) shows the relationship

between the percentage of households owning a VCR and the average price of a VCR. The pattern formed by the points shows us that as the price of a VCR falls, a larger percentage of households own one.

Part (b) looks at inflation and unemployment in the United States. The pattern formed by the points in this graph does not reveal a clear relationship between the two variables. The graph shows us, by its lack of a distinct pattern, that there is no simple relationship between inflation and unemployment.

Correlation and Causation   A scatter diagram that shows a clear relationship between two variables, such as Fig. 2.3 or Fig. 2.4(a), tells us that the two variables have a high correlation. When a high correlation is present, we can predict the value of one variable from the value of the other variable. But correlation does not imply causation. Sometimes a high correlation is just a coincidence, but sometimes it

---

FIGURE   2.4
More Scatter Diagrams

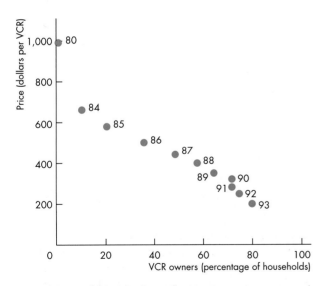

(a) VCR ownership and price

Part (a) is a scatter diagram that plots the price of a VCR against VCR ownership for 1980 and each year from 1984 to 1993. This graph shows that as the price of a VCR has fallen, the percentage of households owning one has increased.

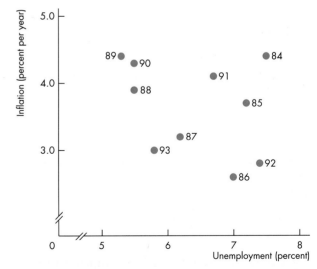

(b) Unemployment and Inflation

Part (b) is a scatter diagram that plots the inflation rate against the unemployment rate. This graph shows that inflation and unemployment are not closely related.

does arise from a causal relationship. It is likely, for example, that high income causes high consumption (Fig. 2.3) or that a falling price of VCRs causes their more widespread ownership.

A scatter diagram enables us to see the relationship between two economic variables. But it does not give us a clear picture of how those variables evolve over time. To see the evolution of economic variables, we use a time-series graph.

Time-Series Graphs

A **time-series graph** measures time (for example, months or years) on the *x*-axis and the variable or variables in which we are interested on the *y*-axis. Figure 2.5 shows a time-series graph. Time is measured in years on the *x*-axis. The variable that we are

interested in—the price of coffee—is measured on the *y*-axis. This time-series graph conveys an enormous amount of information quickly and easily:

1. It shows us the *level* of the price of coffee—when it is *high* and *low*. When the line is a long way from the *x*-axis, the price is high. When the line is close to the *x*-axis, the price is low.

2. It shows us how the price *changes*—whether it *rises* or *falls*. When the line slopes upward, as in 1976, the price is rising. When the line slopes downward, as in 1980, the price is falling.

3. It shows us the *speed* with which the price is changing—whether it is rising or falling *quickly* or *slowly*. If the line is very steep, then the price is rising or falling quickly. If the line is not steep, the price is rising or falling slowly. For example, the price rose very quickly in 1976 and 1977. The price went up again in 1982 but slowly. Similarly, when the price was falling in 1978, it fell quickly, but during the mid-1960s, it fell more slowly.

A time-series graph also reveals whether there is a trend. A **trend** is a general tendency for a variable to rise or fall. You can see that the price of coffee had a general tendency to fall from the mid-1970s to the early 1990s. That is, although there were ups and downs in the price, there was a general tendency for it to fall.

A time-series graph also lets us compare different periods quickly. Figure 2.5 shows that the 1960s were different from the 1970s. The price of coffee fluctuated more violently in the 1970s than it did in the 1960s. This graph conveys a wealth of information, and it does so in much less space than we have used to describe only some of its features.

Comparing Two Time-Series Sometimes we want to use a time-series graph to compare two different variables. For example, suppose you want to know whether the balance of the government's budget fluctuates with the unemployment rate. You can examine the government's budget balance and the unemployment rate by drawing a graph of each of them on the same time scale. But we can measure the government's budget balance either as a surplus or as a deficit. Figure 2.6(a) plots the budget surplus. The scale of the unemployment rate is on the left side of the figure, and the scale of the government's budget surplus is on the right. The orange line shows unemployment, and the blue line shows the government's

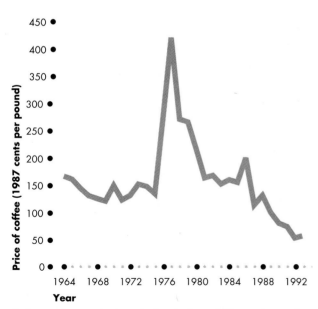

A time-series graph plots the level of a variable on the *y*-axis against time (day, week, month, or year) on the *x*-axis. This graph shows the price of coffee (in 1987 cents per pound) each year from 1964 to 1994. It shows us when the price of coffee was *high* and when it was *low*, when the price *increased* and when it *decreased* and when it changed *quickly* and when it changed *slowly*.

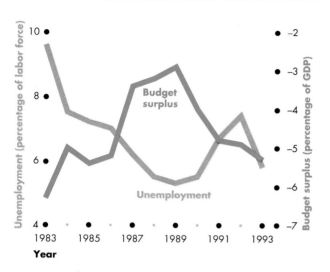

FIGURE 2.6
Time-Series Relationships

(a) Unemployment and budget surplus

(b) Unemployment and budget deficit

These two graphs show the unemployment rate and the balance of the government's budget. The unemployment line is identical in the two parts. Part (a) shows the budget surplus—taxes *minus* spending—on the right scale. It is hard to see a relationship between the budget surplus and unemployment. Part (b) shows the budget as a deficit—spending *minus* taxes. It inverts the scale of part (a). With the scale for the budget balance inverted, the graph reveals a tendency for unemployment and the budget deficit to move together.

budget surplus. You will probably agree that it is pretty hard work figuring out from Fig. 2.6(a) just what the relationship is between the unemployment rate and the government's budget.

In Fig. 2.6(b) the scale for the government's budget balance is measured as a deficit. That is, we flip the right-side scale over. You can now see more clearly the relationship between these two variables.

Cross-Section Graphs

A **cross-section graph** shows the values of an economic variable for different groups in a population at a point in time. Figure 2.7 is an example of a cross-section graph. It shows average income per person across the ten largest metropolitan areas in the United States in 1990. This graph uses bars rather than dots and lines, and the length of each bar indicates average income per person. Figure 2.7 enables you to compare the average incomes per person in these ten cities. And you can do so much more quickly and clearly than by looking at a list of numbers.

FIGURE 2.7
A Cross-Section Graph

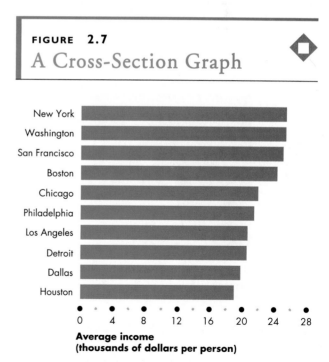

A cross-section graph shows the level of a variable across the members of a population. This graph shows the average income per person in each of the ten largest cities in the United States.

Misleading Graphs

All types of graphs—time-series graphs, scatter diagrams, and cross-section graphs—can mislead. A cross-section graph gives a good example. Figure 2.8 dramatizes a point of view rather than revealing the facts. A quick glance at this graph gives the impression that the average income per person in Chicago is about one half the average income per person in New York. But a closer look reveals that the scale on the axis has been stretched, and incomes between zero and $18,000 have been chopped off the graph. If, when you look at a graph, you make it a habit to look first at the numbers on the axes, you will not be misled, even if the intention of the graph is to mislead you. You can often see misleading graphs in the media. Keep your eyes open for such graphs in the newspapers and magazines you read and learn how to avoid being misled by them.

FIGURE   2.8

A Misleading Graph

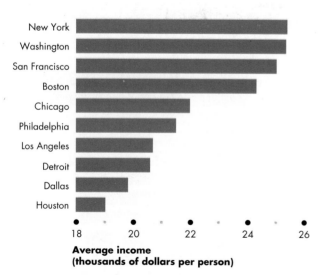

A graph can mislead when it distorts the scale on one of its axes. Here, the scale measuring average income per person has been stretched by chopping off the incomes between zero and $18,000. The result is that the comparison of incomes across cities is distorted. Incomes in the lower-income cities are made to look much smaller than they are in comparison with the higher-income cities.

Now that we have seen how we can use graphs in economics to show economic data and relationships between variables, let us examine how economists use graphs in a more abstract way in economic models.

Graphs Used in Economic Models

THE GRAPHS USED IN ECONOMICS ARE NOT always designed to show data. Another use of graphs is to show the relationships among the variables in an economic model. Although you will encounter many different kinds of graphs in economics, there are some patterns. Once you have learned to recognize them, they will instantly convey to you the meaning of a graph. There are graphs that show each of the following:

- Variables that go up and down together
- Variables that move in opposite directions
- Variables that have a maximum or a minimum
- Variables that are unrelated

Let's look at these four cases.

Variables That Go Up and Down Together

Figure 2.9 shows graphs of the relationships between two variables that move up and down together. A relationship between two variables that move in the same direction is called a **positive relationship** or a **direct relationship**. Such a relationship is shown by a line that slopes upward. The figure shows three types of relationships, one shown by a straight line and two by curved lines. A relationship shown by a straight line is called a **linear relationship**. But all the lines in these three graphs are called curves. Any line on a graph—no matter whether it is straight or curved—is called a *curve*.

Figure 2.9(a) shows a linear relationship between the number of miles traveled in 5 hours and speed. For example, point *a* shows us that we will travel 200 miles in 5 hours if our speed is 40 miles an hour. If we double our speed to 80 miles an hour, we will travel 400 miles in 5 hours.

Part (b) shows the relationship between distance sprinted and recovery time (the time it takes the heart

---

FIGURE 2.9

Positive (Direct) Relationships

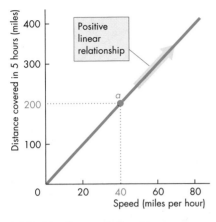

(a) Positive linear relationship

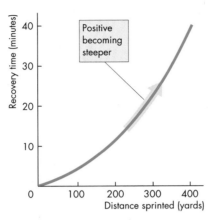

(b) Positive becoming steeper

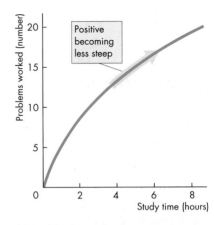

(c) Positive becoming less steep

Each part of this figure shows a positive (direct) relationship between two variables. That is, as the value of the variable measured on the *x*-axis increases, so does the value of the variable measured on the *y*-axis. Part (a) shows a linear relationship—as the two variables increase together we move along a straight line. Part (b) shows a positive relationship such that as the two variables increase together we move along a curve that becomes steeper. Part (c) shows a positive relationship such that as the two variables increase together we move along a curve that becomes flatter.

---

rate to return to normal). This relationship is an upward-sloping one shown by a curved line that starts out fairly flat but then becomes steeper as we move along the curve away from the origin.

Part (c) shows the relationship between the number of problems worked by a student and the amount of study time. This relationship is shown by an upward-sloping curved line that starts out fairly steep and becomes flatter as we move away from the origin.

Variables That Move in Opposite Directions

Figure 2.10 shows relationships between things that move in opposite directions. A relationship between variables that move in opposite directions is called a **negative relationship** or an **inverse relationship.**

Part (a) shows the relationship between the number of hours available for playing squash and the number of hours for playing tennis. One extra hour spent playing tennis means one hour less playing squash and vice versa. This relationship is negative and linear.

Part (b) shows the relationship between the cost per mile traveled and the length of a journey. The longer the journey, the lower is the cost per mile. But as the journey length increases, the cost per mile decreases, and the fall in the cost is smaller, the longer the journey. This feature of the relationship is shown by the fact that the curve slopes downward, starting out steep at a short journey length and then becoming flatter as the journey length increases.

Part (c) shows the relationship between the amount of leisure time and the number of problems worked by a student. Increasing leisure time produces an increasingly large reduction in the number of problems worked. This relationship is a negative one that starts out with a gentle slope at a small number of leisure hours and becomes steeper as the number of leisure hours increases.

FIGURE 2.10

Negative (Inverse) Relationships

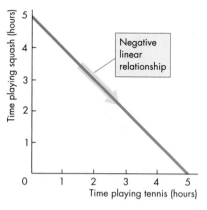

(a) Negative linear relationship

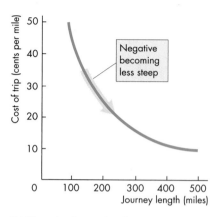

(b) Negative becoming less steep

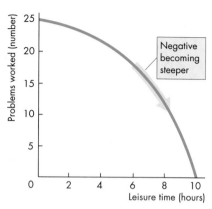

(c) Negative becoming steeper

Each part of this figure shows a negative (inverse) relationship between two variables. Part (a) shows a linear relationship—as one variable increases and the other variable decreases we travel along a straight line. Part (b) shows a negative relationship such that as the journey length increases the curve becomes flatter. Part (c) shows a negative relationship such that as the leisure time increases the curve becomes steeper.

Variables That Have a Maximum and a Minimum

Many relationships in economic models have a maximum or a minimum. For example, firms try to make the maximum possible profit and to produce at the lowest possible cost. Figure 2.11 shows relationships that have a maximum or a minimum.

Part (a) shows the relationship between rainfall and wheat yield. When there is no rainfall, wheat will not grow, so the yield is zero. As the rainfall increases up to 10 days a month, the wheat yield also increases. With 10 rainy days each month, the wheat yield reaches its maximum at 40 bushels an acre (point *a*). Rain in excess of 10 days a month starts to lower the yield of wheat. If every day is rainy, the wheat suffers from a lack of sunshine and the yield falls back to zero. This relationship is one that starts out sloping upward, reaches a maximum, and then slopes downward.

Part (b) shows the reverse case—a relationship that begins sloping downward, falls to a minimum, and then slopes upward. An example of such a relationship is the gasoline cost per mile as the speed of travel varies. At low speeds, the car is creeping along in a traffic snarl-up. The number of miles per gallon is low, so the gasoline cost per mile is high. At very high speeds, the car is traveling faster than its most efficient speed, and again the number of miles per gallon is low and the gasoline cost per mile is high. At a speed of 55 miles an hour, the gasoline cost per mile traveled is at its minimum (point *b*). This relationship is one that starts out sloping downward, reaches a minimum, and slopes upward.

Variables That Are Unrelated

There are many situations in which one variable is unrelated to another. No matter what happens to the value of one variable, the other variable remains constant. Sometimes we want to show the independence between two variables in a graph. Figure 2.12 shows two ways of achieving this. In Fig. 2.12(a), your grade in economics is shown on the *y*-axis against the price of bananas on the *x*-axis. Your grade (75 percent in this example) is unrelated to the price of bananas. The relationship between these two variables is shown by a horizontal straight line. This line neither slopes upward nor downward. In part (b), the output of French wine is shown on the *x*-axis and the num-

FIGURE 2.11
Maximum and Minimum Points

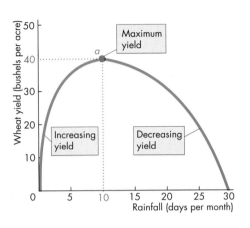

(a) Relationship with a maximum

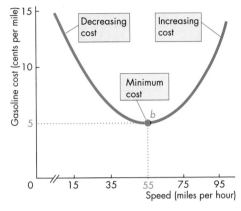

(b) Relationship with a minimum

Part (a) shows a relationship that has a maximum point, *a*. The curve slopes upward as it rises to its maximum point, is flat at its maximum, and then slopes downward. Part (b) shows a relationship with a minimum point, *b*. The curve slopes downward as it falls to its minimum, is flat at its minimum, and then slopes upward.

ber of rainy days a month in California is shown on the *y*-axis. Again, the output of French wine (3 billion gallons a year in this example) is unrelated to the number of rainy days in California. The relationship between these two variables is shown by a vertical straight line.

Figures 2.9 through 2.12 show ten different shapes of graphs that we will encounter in economic models. In describing these graphs, we have talked about the slopes of curves. The concept of slope is an intuitive one. But it is also a precise technical concept. Let's look more closely at the concept of slope.

FIGURE 2.12
Variables That Are Unrelated

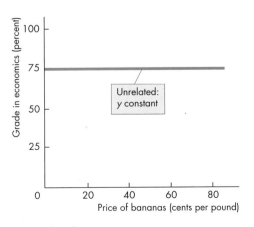

(a) Unrelated: *y* constant

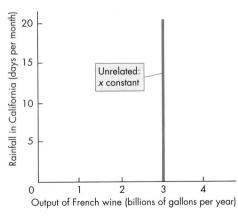

(b) Unrelated: *x* constant

This figure shows how we can graph two variables that are unrelated to each other. In part (a), a student's grade in economics is plotted at 75 percent regardless of the price of bananas on the *x*-axis. The curve is horizontal. In part (b), the output of the vineyards of France does not vary with the rainfall in California. The curve is vertical.

The Slope of a Relationship

WE CAN MEASURE THE INFLUENCE OF ONE variable on another by the slope of the relationship. The **slope** of a relationship is the change in the value of the variable measured on the y-axis divided by the change in the value of the variable measured on the x-axis. We use the Greek letter Δ (*delta*) to represent "change in." Thus Δy means the change in the value of the variable measured on the y-axis, and Δx means the change in the value of the variable measured on the x-axis. Therefore the slope of the relationship is

$$\Delta y \,/\, \Delta x.$$

If a large change in the variable measured on the y-axis (Δy) is associated with a small change in the variable measured on the x-axis (Δx), the slope is large and the curve is steep. If a small change in the variable measured on the y-axis (Δy) is associated with a large change in the variable measured on the x-axis (Δx), the slope is small and the curve is flat.

We can make the idea of slope sharper by doing some calculations.

The Slope of a Straight Line

The slope of a straight line is the same regardless of where on the line you calculate it. Thus the slope of a straight line is constant. Let's calculate the slopes of the lines in Fig. 2.13. In part (a), when x increases

---

FIGURE 2.13
The Slope of a Straight Line

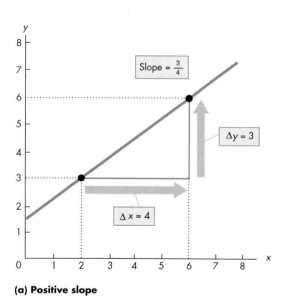

(a) Positive slope

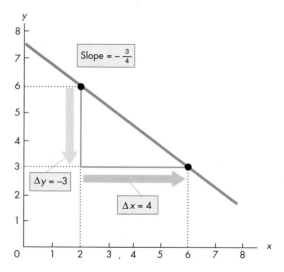

(b) Negative slope

To calculate the slope of a straight line, we divide the change in the value of the variable measured on the y-axis (Δy) by the change in the value of the variable measured on the x-axis (Δx), as we move along the curve.

Part (a) shows the calculation of a positive slope. When x increases from 2 to 6, Δx equals 4. That change in x brings

about an increase in y from 3 to 6, so Δy equals 3. The slope ($\Delta y/\Delta x$) equals 3/4.

Part (b) shows the calculation of a negative slope. When x increases from 2 to 6, Δx equals 4. That increase in x brings about a decrease in y from 6 to 3, so Δy equals −3. The slope ($\Delta y/\Delta x$) equals −3/4.

from 2 to 6, y increases from 3 to 6. The change in x is +4—that is, Δx is 4. The change in y is +3—that is, Δy is 3. The slope of that line is

$$\frac{\Delta y}{\Delta x} = \frac{3}{4}.$$

In part (b), when x increases from 2 to 6, y decreases from 6 to 3. The change in y is *minus* 3—that is, Δy is –3. The change in x is *plus* 4—that is, Δx is 4. The slope of the curve is

$$\frac{\Delta y}{\Delta x} = \frac{-3}{4}.$$

Notice that the two slopes have the same magnitude (3/4), but the slope of the line in part (a) is positive (+3/+4 = 3/4), while that in part (b) is negative

(–3/+4 = –3/4). The slope of a positive relationship is positive; the slope of a negative relationship is negative.

The Slope of a Curved Line

The slope of a curved line is trickier. The slope of a curved line is not constant. Its slope depends on where on the line we calculate it. There are two ways to calculate the slope of a curved line: you can calculate the slope at a point or you can calculate the slope across an arc of the line. Let's look at the two alternatives.

Slope at a Point   To calculate the slope at a point on a curve, you need to construct a straight line that has the same slope as the curve at the point in question. Figure 2.14 shows how this is done. Suppose

---

FIGURE 2.14

The Slope of a Curve

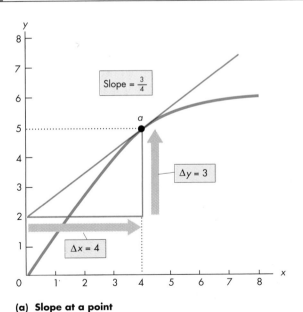

(a) Slope at a point

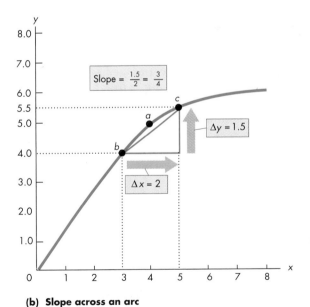

(b) Slope across an arc

To calculate the slope of the curve at point *a*, draw the red line that just touches the curve at *a*—the tangent. The slope of this straight line is calculated by dividing the change in *y* by the change in *x* along the line. When *x* increases from 0 to 4, Δx equals 4. That change in *x* is associated with an increase in *y* from 2 to 5, so Δy equals 3. The slope of the red line is 3/4. So the slope of the curve at point *a* is 3/4.

To calculate the average slope of the curve along the arc *bc*, draw a straight line from *b* to *c* in part (b). The slope of the line *bc* is calculated by dividing the change in *y* by the change in *x*. In moving from *b* to *c*, Δx equals 2, and Δy equals 1.5. The slope of the line *bc* is 1.5 divided by 2, or 3/4. So the slope of the curve across the arc *bc* is 3/4.

you want to calculate the slope of the curve at point *a*. Place a ruler on the graph so that it touches point *a* and no other point on the curve, then draw a straight line along the edge of the ruler. The straight red line in part (a) is this line, and it is the tangent to the curve at point *a*. If the ruler touches the curve only at point *a*, then the slope of the curve at point *a* must be the same as the slope of the edge of the ruler. If the curve and the ruler do not have the same slope, the line along the edge of the ruler will cut the curve instead of just touching it.

Having found a straight line with the same slope as the curve at point *a*, you can calculate the slope of the curve at point *a* by calculating the slope of the straight line. Along the straight line, as *x* increases from 0 to 4 ($\Delta x = 4$) *y* increases from 2 to 5 ($\Delta y = 3$). Therefore the slope of the line is

$$\frac{\Delta y}{\Delta x} = \frac{3}{4}.$$

Thus the slope of the curve at point *a* is 3/4.

Slope across an Arc   Calculating a slope across an arc is similar to calculating an average slope. An arc of a curve is a piece of a curve. In Fig. 2.14(b), we are looking at the same curve as in part (a), but instead of calculating the slope at point *a*, we calculate the slope across the arc from *b* to *c*. Moving along the arc from *b* to *c*, *x* increases from 3 to 5 and *y* increases from 4 to 5.5. The change in *x* is 2 ($\Delta x = 2$), and the change in *y* is 1.5 ($\Delta y = 1.5$). Therefore the slope of the line is

$$\frac{\Delta y}{\Delta x} = \frac{1.5}{2} = \frac{3}{4}.$$

Thus the slope of the curve across the arc *bc* is 3/4.

This calculation gives us the slope of the curve between points b and c. The actual slope calculated is the slope of the straight line from b to c. This slope approximates the average slope of the curve along the arc bc. In this particular example, the slope across the arc bc is identical to the slope of the curve at point a, in both part (a) and part (b). But the calculation of the slope of a curve does not always work out so neatly. You might have some fun constructing counter-examples.

Graphing Relationships Among More Than Two Variables

WE HAVE SEEN THAT WE CAN GRAPH A SINGLE variable as a point on a straight line and we can graph the relationship between two variables as a point formed by the *x*- and *y*-coordinates in a two-dimensional graph. You may be thinking that although a two-dimensional graph is informative, most of the things in which you are likely to be interested involve relationships among many variables, not just two. For example, the amount of ice cream consumed depends on the price of ice cream and the temperature. If ice cream is expensive and the temperature is low, people eat much less ice cream than when ice cream is inexpensive and the temperature is high. For any given price of ice cream, the quantity consumed varies with the temperature, and for any given temperature, the quantity of ice cream consumed varies with its price.

Figure 2.15 shows a relationship among three variables. The table shows the number of gallons of ice cream consumed each day at various temperatures and ice cream prices. How can we graph these numbers?

To graph a relationship that involves more than two variables, we consider what happens if all but two of the variables are held constant. When we hold other things constant, we are using the *ceteris paribus* assumption that is described in Chapter 1, p. 14. An example is shown in Fig. 2.15(a). There, you can see what happens to the quantity of ice cream consumed when the price of ice cream varies while the temperature is held constant. The line labeled 70°F shows the relationship between ice cream consumption and the price of ice cream when the temperature stays at 70°F. The numbers used to plot that line are those in the third column of the table in Fig. 2.15. For example, when the temperature is 70°F, 10 gallons are consumed when the price is 60¢ a scoop and 18 gallons are consumed when the price is 30¢. The curve labeled 90°F shows the consumption of ice cream when the price varies and the temperature is 90°F.

We can also show the relationship between ice cream consumption and temperature while holding the price of ice cream constant, as shown in Fig. 2.15(b). The curve labeled 60¢ shows how the consumption of ice cream varies with the temperature when ice cream costs 60¢, and a second curve shows the relationship when ice cream costs 15¢. For example, at 60¢ a scoop, 10 gallons are consumed when the temperature is 70°F and 20 gallons when the temperature is 90°F.

Figure 2.15(c) shows the combinations of temperature and price that result in a constant consumption of ice cream. One curve shows the combination that results in 10 gallons a day being consumed, and the other shows the combination that results in 7 gallons a day being consumed. A high price and a high temperature lead to the same consumption as a lower price and a lower temperature. For example, 10 gallons of ice cream are consumed at 90°F and 90¢ per scoop, at 70°F and 60¢ per scoop and at 50°F and 45¢ per scoop.

◆ With what you have learned about graphs, you can move forward with your study of economics. There are no graphs in this book that are more complicated than those that have been explained here.

FIGURE 2.15

Graphing a Relationship among Three Variables

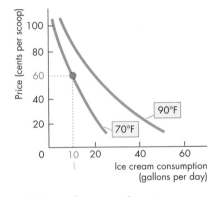

(a) Price and consumption at a given temperature

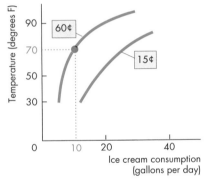

(b) Temperature and consumption at a given price

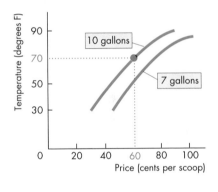

(c) Temperature and price at a given consumption

Price (cents per scoop)	Ice Cream Consumption (gallons per day)			
	30°F	**50°F**	**70°F**	**90°F**
15	12	18	25	50
30	10	12	18	37
45	7	10	13	27
60	5	7	10	20
75	3	5	7	14
90	2	3	5	10
105	1	2	3	6

The quantity of ice cream consumed depends on its price and the temperature. The table gives some hypothetical numbers that tell us how many gallons of ice cream are consumed each day at different prices and different temperatures. For example, if the price is 60¢ per scoop and the temperature is 70°F, 10 gallons of ice cream are consumed. This set of values is highlighted in the table and each part of the figure. To graph a relationship among three variables, the value of one variable is held constant.

Part (a) shows the relationship between price and consumption when temperature is held constant. One curve holds temperature at 90°F and the other at 70°F. Part (b) shows the relationship between temperature and consumption when price is held constant. One curve holds the price at 60¢ and the other at 15¢. Part (c) shows the relationship between temperature and price when consumption is held constant. One curve holds consumption at 10 gallons and the other at 7 gallons.

S U M M A R Y

Graphing Data

Three types of graphs used to show economic data are scatter diagrams, time-series graphs, and cross-section graphs. Each graph reveals the nature of the relationship between variables. But a graph can be misleading if its scale is distorted. (pp. 27–32)

Graphs Used in Economic Models

Five types of graphs used to show relationships among variables in economic models are: positive (an upward-sloping curve), negative (a downward-sloping curve), unrelated (a horizontal or vertical curve), positive and then negative (a maximum), and negative and then positive (a minimum). (pp. 32–35)

The Slope of a Relationship

The slope of a relationship is calculated as the change in the value of the variable measured on the y-axis divided by the change in the value of the variable measured on the x-axis—$\Delta y/\Delta x$. A straight line has a constant slope, but a curved line has a varying slope. To calculate the slope of a curved line, we calculate the slope at a point or across an arc. (pp. 36–38)

Graphing Relationships Among More Than Two Variables

To graph a relationship among more than two variables, we hold constant the values of all the variables except two. We then plot the value of one of the variables against the value of another. (pp. 38–39)

K E Y   E L E M E N T S

Key Figures

Key Terms

R E V I E W   Q U E S T I O N S

1. What are the three types of graphs used to show economic data?

2. Give an example of a scatter diagram.

3. Give an example of a time-series graph.

4. Give an example of a cross-section graph.

5. List three things that a time-series graph shows quickly and easily.

6. What do we mean by trend?

7. How can a graph mislead?

8. Draw some graphs to show the relationships between two variables:
   a.   That move in the same direction
   b.   That move in opposite directions

c. That have a maximum
d. That have a minimum

9. Which of the relationships in question 8 is a positive relationship and which a negative relationship?

10. What is the definition of the slope of a curve?

11. What are the two ways of calculating the slope of a curved line?

12. How do we graph relationships among more than two variables?

P R O B L E M S

◆ 1. The inflation rate in the United States and the interest rate on U.S. treasury bills between 1974 and 1994 were as follows:

Year	Inflation rate (percent per year)	Interest rate (percent per year)
1974	11.0	7.9
1975	9.1	5.8
1976	5.8	5.0
1977	6.5	5.3
1978	7.6	7.2
1979	11.3	10.0
1980	13.5	11.5
1981	10.3	14.0
1982	6.2	10.7
1983	3.2	8.6
1984	4.3	9.6
1985	3.6	7.5
1986	1.9	6.0
1987	3.6	5.8
1988	4.1	6.7
1989	4.8	8.1
1990	5.4	7.5
1991	4.2	5.4
1992	3.0	3.4
1993	3.0	3.0
1994	2.9	4.3

Draw a time-series graph of these data and use your graph to answer the following questions:

a. In which year was inflation highest?
b. In which year was inflation lowest?
c. In which years did inflation increase?
d. In which years did inflation decrease?
e. In which year did inflation increase most?
f. In which year did inflation decrease most?
g. What have been the main trends in inflation?
h. Draw a scatter diagram showing the relationship between inflation and the interest rate.
i. Does a relationship exist between inflation and the interest rate? If so, what kind of a relationship?

◆ 2. Use the following information to draw a graph showing the relationship between two variables x and y.

x	0	1	2	3	4	5	6	7	8
y	0	1	4	9	16	25	36	49	64

a. Is the relationship between x and y positive or negative?
b. Does the slope of the relationship rise or fall as the value of x rises?

◆ 3. Using the data in problem 2,
a. Calculate the slope of the relationship between x and y when x equals 4.
b. Calculate the slope of the arc when x rises from 3 to 4.
c. Calculate the slope of the arc when x rises from 4 to 5.
d. Calculate the slope of the arc when x rises from 3 to 5.
e. What do you notice that is interesting about your answers to (b), (c), and (d) compared with your answer to (a)?

Production, Growth, and Trade

After studying this chapter, you will be able to:

- Define the production possibility frontier

- Define production efficiency

- Calculate opportunity cost

- Explain how economic growth expands production possibilities but does not provide free gifts

- Explain comparative advantage

- Explain why people specialize and how they gain from trade

We live in a style that surprises our grandparents and would have astonished our great grandparents. Most of us live in more spacious homes than they did. We eat more, grow taller, and are even born larger than they were. Video games, cellular phones, gene splices, personal computers, and microwave ovens did not exist even twenty years ago. But today it is hard to imagine life without them.

Making the Most of It

Economic growth has made us richer than our grandparents. But it has not liberated us from scarcity. Why not? Why, despite our immense wealth, must we still make choices and face costs? Why are there no "free lunches"? ◆ We see an incredible amount of specialization and trade in the world. Each one of us specializes in a particular job—as a lawyer, a car maker, a home maker. We have become so specialized that one farm worker can feed 100 people. Less than one sixth of the U.S. work force is employed in manufacturing. More than half of the work force is employed in wholesale and retail trade, banking and finance, government, and other services. Why do we specialize? How do we benefit from specialization and trade? ◆ Over many centuries, institutions and social arrangements have evolved that we take for granted. One of them is markets. Another is property rights and a political and legal system that protects them. Yet another is money. Why have these arrangements evolved? And how do they extend our ability to specialize and increase production?

◆ These are the questions that we tackle in this chapter. We begin by studying the limits to production and the concept of production efficiency. We next learn how to measure opportunity cost. We also discover how we can increase production by specializing and trading with each other.

The Production Possibility Frontier

PRODUCTION IS THE CONVERSION OF LABOR, land, capital, and entrepreneurial ability into goods and services. We defined the factors of production in Chapter 1, but let's briefly recall what they are.

Labor is the time and effort that people devote to producing goods and services. It includes the physical and mental activities of the many thousands of people who make cars and cola, gum and glue, wallpaper and watering cans. *Land* is the gifts of nature that are used to produce goods and services. It includes the air, the water, and the land surface as well as the minerals that lie beneath the surface of the earth. *Capital* is the goods that have been produced and can now themselves be used in the production of other goods and services. Examples include the interstate highway system, the fine buildings of great cities, dams and power projects, airports and jumbo jets, car production lines, shirt factories, and cookie shops.

A special kind of capital is called human capital. **Human capital** is the skill and knowledge of people, which arise from their education and on-the-job training. You are getting human capital right now as you work on your economics course and other subjects. And your human capital will continue to grow when you get a full-time job and become better at it. Human capital improves the *quality* of labor.

Labor, land, and capital are organized by a fourth factor of production, *entrepreneurial ability*. Entrepreneurs come up with new ideas about what, how, when, and where to produce, make the key business decisions, and bear the risks that arise from their decisions.

Goods and services are all the valuable things that people produce. Goods are tangible—cars, spoons, VCRs, and bread. Services are intangible—haircuts, amusement park rides, and telephone calls. There are two types of goods: capital goods and consumption goods. *Capital goods* are goods that are used to produce other goods. Examples of capital goods are buildings, computers, auto-assembly lines, and telephones. *Consumption goods* are goods that are bought by households. Some are *durable* consumption goods such as shoes and shirts, and some are *nondurable* goods such as dill pickles and toothpaste. *Consumption* is the process of using goods and services.

The quantities of goods and services that can be produced are limited by the available resources and by technology. That limit is described by the production possibility frontier. The **production possibility frontier** (*PPF*) marks the boundary between those combinations of goods and services that can be produced and those that cannot.

To study the production possibility frontier, we consider just two goods at a time. They could be any two goods. In focusing on two goods, we hold the quantities produced of all the other goods constant—we use the *ceteris paribus* assumption. By this device, we look at a *model* of the economy—a model in which everything remains the same except the production of the two goods that we are (currently) interested in.

Let's begin by looking at the production possibility frontier for a single firm—one that produces denim jeans.

A Firm's Production Possibility Frontier

Mark's Jeans, Inc. employs 50 workers (labor). It has a small site (land), and it has a building that contains cutting and sewing machines (capital). Mark is the entrepreneur, and he uses these given amounts of labor, land, and capital to produce two types of jeans, baggy and Western cut. Mark's resources can produce a maximum of 5,000 jeans a week, in any combination of baggy and Western cut.

Figure 3.1 illustrates Mark's production possibilities. With his fixed quantities of labor, land, and capital, the maximum quantity of jeans he can produce is 5,000 a week. If he uses all his resources to produce baggys, he can produce no Western cuts. This combination of jeans, 5,000 baggys and no Western cuts, is one of Mark's *production possibilities*—shown in the table as possibility *a*. But there are other possibilities, and some of these are also shown in the table. For example, a second possibility is *b*. In this case, Mark uses one fifth of his resources to produce Western cuts and the rest to produce baggys. He produces 4,000 Western cuts and 1,000 baggys a week—and he continues to produce a total of 5,000 jeans a week. The pattern continues to possibility *f*, in which Mark devotes all his resources to producing Western cuts. In this case, he produces 5,000 Western cuts a week and no baggys.

FIGURE 3.1
Production Possibility Frontier for Jeans

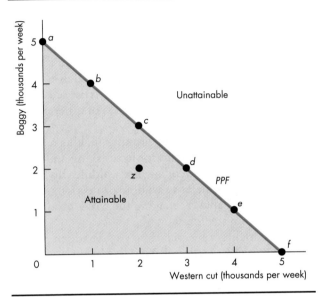

The table lists six points on Mark's production possibility frontier for Western cuts and baggys. Row *a* tells us that if he produces no Western cuts, the maximum quantity of baggys that he can produce is 5,000 a week. The rows of the table are graphed as points *a, b, c, d, e,* and *f* in the figure. The line passing through these points is Mark's *production possibility frontier* (PPF). It separates what Mark can attain from what he cannot attain. Mark can produce at any point inside the orange area or on the frontier. Points outside the frontier are unattainable. Points *inside* the frontier such as point *z* are *inefficient* because resources are being wasted or misallocated. At such points, it is possible for Mark to use his resources to produce more of either or both kinds of jeans.

Possibility	Western cuts (thousands per week)		Baggys (thousands per week)
a	0	and	5
b	1	and	4
c	2	and	3
d	3	and	2
e	4	and	1
f	5	and	0

The numbers in the table are plotted in the graph shown in Fig. 3.1. Thousands of Western cuts are measured on the horizontal axis, and thousands of baggys on the vertical axis. Points *a, b, c, d, e,* and *f* represent the numbers in the corresponding row of the table.

Mark does not have to produce jeans in batches of 1,000, as in the table. He could produce 1 Western cut and 4,999 baggys a week or any other combination that totals 5,000. All the other feasible allocations of Mark's resources enable him to produce the combinations of baggys and Western cuts described by the line that joins points *a, b, c, d, e,* and *f.* This line shows Mark's production possibility frontier for baggys and Western cuts, given his fixed resources. He can produce at any point on the frontier or at any point inside it, within the orange area. These are his attainable points. Points outside the frontier are unattainable. To produce at points beyond the frontier, Mark would need more resources. But more resources are not available to him—he can't attain points outside the frontier.

Production Efficiency

Production efficiency is achieved when it is not possible to produce more of one good without producing less of some other good. Production efficiency occurs only at points *on* the production possibility frontier. Possible production points *inside* the frontier, such as point *z,* are *inefficient.* They are points at which resources are being either wasted or misallocated. Resources are wasted when they are idle but could be working. For example, Mark might not run all his sewing machines all of the time. Resources are *misallocated* when they are assigned to inappropriate tasks. For example, Mark might assign a skilled cutter to sewing and a skilled sewer to cutting. This would be like assigning a pitcher to batting and a batter to pitching. Each works hard, but the team does not perform as well as it could. The allocation is inefficient.

If Mark is producing inefficiently at a point such as *z,* he can use his resources more efficiently and produce more jeans of either or both types. Mark will strive to avoid waste and try to produce at a point on the production possibility frontier—he will try to produce efficiently.

Although Mark will try to be efficient, he must choose among the many efficient points along his *PPF.* And in choosing among the efficient points, he faces opportunity costs. Let's explore Mark's opportunity costs.

A Firm's Opportunity Cost of Production

The *opportunity cost* of an action is the best alternative forgone. Of all the things you choose not to do—the alternatives forgone—the best one is the opportunity cost of the action you choose. The concept of opportunity cost can be made precise by using the production possibility frontier. Along the frontier, Mark is producing only two goods, so it is easy to work out the best alternative forgone. Given Mark's current resources and technology, he can produce more Western cuts only if he produces fewer baggys. Thus the opportunity cost of producing an additional Western cut is the quantity of baggys forgone. Similarly, the opportunity cost of producing an additional baggy is the quantity of Western cuts forgone. For example, at point *c* in Fig. 3.1, Mark produces fewer Western cuts and more baggys than at point *d*. If he chooses point *d* over point *c*, the additional 1,000 Western cuts *cost* 1,000 baggys. One Western cut costs one baggy—and one baggy costs one Western cut.

In this example, the opportunity costs of producing more of either type of jeans are the same. They are also constant, regardless of how many of each type is produced. That is, at any point on the *PPF*, one Western cut costs one baggy. These opportunity costs are constant because the resources used to produce jeans are equally productive regardless of the type of jeans produced.

Opportunity Costs Are Inescapable

The lesson we've learned by studying a model of a denim jeans factory is a fundamental one: We face trade-offs. A **trade-off** is a constraint that entails giving up one thing to get something else. For Mark, the trade-off is between baggys and Western cuts, and his *PPF* defines the terms of the trade-off. Your own budget is another example of a trade-off. With your fixed financial resources, you must make a trade-off between going to the movies and buying magazines.

Trade-offs arise in every imaginable real-world situation. At any given point in time, the world has a fixed amount of labor, land, capital, and entrepreneurial ability. By using the available technologies, these resources can be employed to produce goods and services. But there is a limit to what goods and

services can be produced. This limit defines a boundary between what is attainable and what is not attainable. This boundary is the real-world economy's production possibility frontier, and it defines the trade-offs that we must make. On the frontier, producing more of any one good or service requires producing less of some other goods or services.

For example, a presidential candidate who promises better welfare and better education is making a trade-off. By devoting more resources to these activities, less resources are available for defense or for private consumption. The opportunity cost of better welfare and educational services is less of other goods and services.

An environmental lobby group is making a trade-off when it campaigns for less logging and greater conservation of endangered wildlife. By devoting more resources to wildlife protection, less resources are avilable for making the paper products that come from the forests.

On a smaller scale each time you decide to rent a video, you make a trade-off. You decide not to use part of your limited income to buy soda, or popcorn, or some other good. The opportunity cost of renting one more video is having less of something else.

R E V I E W

- The production possibility frontier (*PPF*) is the boundary between attainable and unattainable levels of production.
- Points on the *PPF* and inside it are attainable, and points outside the *PPF* are unattainable.
- Points *on* the *PPF* are *efficient*, and points inside it are *inefficient*.
- Choosing among efficient points on the *PPF* involves a *trade-off* and an *opportunity cost*.
- The opportunity cost of producing an additional unit of one good is the decrease in the number of units of another good that can be produced.

Along the production possibility curve for jeans, Mark's opportunity costs are constant. But constant opportunity costs are unusual. Generally, the opportunity cost of producing a good increases as the quantity of that good produced increases. Let's look at this more general case.

Increasing Opportunity Cost

ALMOST ALL THE AVAILABLE LABOR, LAND, AND capital is *relatively* more productive in some activities than in others. Some people are creative and good at making entertaining movies, while others are well-coordinated and good at performing challenging physical tasks. Some land is good for farming, while other land is good for shopping malls. Most capital (tools, machines, and buildings) is custom-designed to do a small range of jobs—cutting and sewing machines, automobile assembly lines, or schools.

When each worker, each plot of land, and each piece of capital is allocated to the task in which it is relatively most productive, the economy is at a point on its production possibility frontier. But there are many points on the frontier. And as the economy moves along its *PPF* and produces more of one good or service and less of some others, factors of production must be assigned to tasks for which they are an increasingly poor match. Let's consider a contemporary example of the age-old *trade-off* between military expenditure and private consumption (sometimes called the guns and butter trade-off). Our guns will be missiles, and our butter will be video games.

Missiles Versus Video Games

The economy's production possibility frontier for missiles and video games shows the limits to the production of these two goods, given the total resources available to produce them. Figure 3.2 shows this production possibility frontier.

Suppose that in a year, 4,000 games and 2,000 missiles are produced—point *e* in Fig. 3.2 and possibility *e* in the table. The figure shows other production possibilities. For example, in a tense international situation, we might stop producing games and put all the creative people who devise them and all the programmers, assembly line workers, computers, buildings, and other resources used to produce games into the defense industry to produce missiles. This case is shown as point *a* in the figure and possibility *a* in the table. The quantity of missiles produced increases to 4,000 a year, and games

FIGURE 3.2

Production Possibility Frontier for Missiles and Video Games

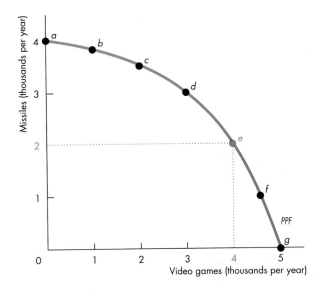

Possibility	Games (thousands of games)		Missiles (thousands of missiles)
a	0.0	and	4.0
b	1.0	and	3.8
c	2.0	and	3.5
d	3.0	and	3.0
e	4.0	and	2.0
f	4.6	and	1.0
g	5.0	and	0.0

The production possibility frontier for missiles and video games, *PPF*, is bowed outward because resources are not equally productive in all activities. Production is at point e—4,000 games and 2,000 missiles a year. If the economy moves from e to f, a small increase in the quantity of games produced is achieved at the cost of a large decrease in the quantity of missiles produced. If the economy moves back from f to e a large increase in the quantity of missiles is achieved at the cost of a small decrease in the quantity of games produced.

production dries up. Alternatively, in a calm international situation, we might close down the missile program and switch the resources into producing games. This case is 5,000 games are produced—possibility *g*.

The Bowed-Out Frontier

Pay attention to the shape of the production possibility frontier in Fig. 3.2. When a large quantity of missiles and a small quantity of games are produced—between points *a* and *d*—the frontier has a gentle slope. When a large quantity of games and a small quantity of missiles are produced—between points *e* and *f*—the frontier is steep. The whole frontier bows outward.

These features of the production possibility frontier are a reflection of the fact that not all resources are equally productive in all activities. Game inventors and programmers can work on missiles, so if they switch from making games to building missiles—moving along the frontier from *e* toward *a*—the production of missiles increases. But these people are not as good at building missiles as the original defense industry workers. So for a small increase in the quantity of missiles produced, the production of games falls a lot.

Similarly, defense workers can produce games, but they are not as good at that activity as the people who are currently making games. So when defense workers switch to producing games, the quantity of games produced increases by only a small amount, and the quantity of missiles produced falls a lot.

Measuring Opportunity Cost

We can measure the opportunity cost of missiles and of games by using the production possibility frontier in Fig. 3.2. To do so, we calculate how many missiles must be given up to get more games and how many games must be given up to get more missiles.

If all the available resources are used to produce missiles, 4,000 missiles and no games are produced. If now we decide to produce 1,000 games, how many missiles do we have to give up? You can work out the answer in Fig. 3.2. To produce 1,000 games, we move from *a* to *b*, and the quantity of missiles decreases by 200 to 3,800 a year. So the opportunity cost of the first 1,000 games is 200 missiles. If we

decide to produce another 1,000 games, how many missiles must we give up? This time, we move from *b* to *c*, and the quantity of missiles decreases by 300.

Figure 3.3(a) illustrates these opportunity costs. The first two rows of table (a) set out the opportunity costs that we have just calculated. The table also lists the opportunity costs of producing an additional 1,000 games by moving along the production possibility frontier from *c* to *d*, from *d* to *e*, and from *e* to *g*. To be sure that you understand how to calculate the opportunity cost, you might want to work out another example on your own. Calculate the opportunity cost of moving from *e* to *g*.

We've just worked out the opportunity cost of missiles. We can use the same idea to calculate the opportunity cost of games. If all the resources are used to produce games, we produce 5,000 a year and have no missiles. If we decide to produce 1,000 missiles, how many games must we give up? Again, you can work out the answer by using the information in Fig. 3.2. To build 1,000 missiles, we move from *g* to *f*, and the quantity of games decreases by 400 to 4,600 a year. So the opportunity cost of the first 1,000 missiles is 400 games. If we decide to build another 1,000 missiles a year, how many games must we give up? This time, we move from *f* to *e*, and the quantity of games decreases by 600.

Figure 3.3(b) shows these opportunity costs. The first two rows of table (b) show the opportunity costs that we have just calculated. The table also lists the opportunity costs of producing an additional 1,000 missiles by moving along the production possibility frontier from *e* to *d* and from *d* to *a*. You might want to work out another example on your own to be sure that you understand what is going on. Calculate the opportunity cost of moving from *d* to *a*.

Opportunity Cost Is a Ratio

The opportunity cost of producing one additional unit of a good is a ratio. It is the decrease in the quantity produced of one good divided by the increase in the quantity produced of another good as we move along the production possibility frontier. For example, in Fig. 3.3, the opportunity cost of one of the first 1,000 missiles is the decrease in the quantity of games, 400, divided by the increase in the quantity of missiles, 1,000. That is, the opportunity cost of 1 missile is 0.4 game.

FIGURE 3.3

Increasing Opportunity Cost

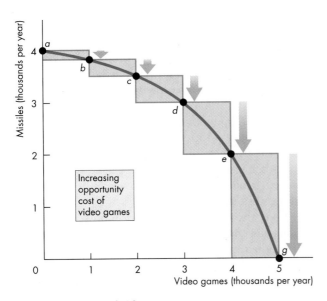

(a) Opportunity cost of video games

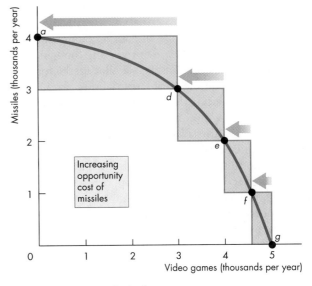

(b) Opportunity cost of missiles

(a) As the production of games increases:

First 1,000 games cost 200 missiles

Second 1,000 games cost 300 missiles

Third 1,000 games cost 500 missiles

Fourth 1,000 games cost 1,000 missiles

Fifth 1,000 games cost 2,000 missiles

(b) As the production of missiles increases:

First 1,000 missiles cost 400 games

Second 1,000 missiles cost 600 games

Third 1,000 missiles cost 1,000 games

Fourth 1,000 missiles cost 3,000 games

The tables record the opportunity costs of games and missiles, and the graphs illustrate the opportunity costs by the bars and arrows.

In part (a), the opportunity cost of games increases

from 200 missiles for the first 1,000 games to 2,000 missiles for the fifth 1,000 games. In part (b), the opportunity cost of missiles increases from 400 games for the first 1,000 missiles to 3,000 games for the fourth 1,000 missiles.

Because opportunity cost is a ratio, the opportunity cost of producing good X (the quantity of units of good Y forgone) is always equal to the inverse of the opportunity cost of producing good Y (the number of units of good X forgone). Let's check this proposition by returning to Fig. 3.3. To increase the production of games from 4,600 to 5,000 a year, an increase of

400, the quantity of missiles must decrease from 1,000 to zero. The opportunity cost of the extra 400 games is 1,000 missiles, or 2.5 missiles forgone per game. Similarly, an extra 1,000 missiles costs 400 games, so the opportunity cost of 1 missile is 0.4 game, and the opportunity cost of 1 game is 2.5 missiles (1/0.4 = 2.5).

Increasing Opportunity Costs Are Everywhere

Increasing opportunity cost and the bowed-out production possibility frontier are two different ways of expressing the same idea: Resources are not equally productive in all activities. Just about every activity that you can think of is one with an *increasing* opportunity cost. Two examples are producing food and producing health care services. We allocate the most skillful farmers and the most fertile land to producing food. And we allocate the best doctors and less fertile land to producing health care services. If we shift fertile land and tractors away from farming and ask farmers to become hospital porters, the production of food drops drastically and the increase in the production of health care services is small. The opportunity cost of a unit of health care services rises. Similarly, if we shift our resources away from health care toward farming, we must use more doctors and nurses as farmers and more hospitals as hydroponic tomato factories. The decrease in the production of health care services is large, but the increase in food production is small. The opportunity cost of producing a unit of food rises.

This example is extreme and unlikely, but these same considerations apply to any pair of goods that you can imagine: housing and diamonds, wheelchairs and golf carts, pet food and breakfast cereals. Given our limited resources, producing more of one thing always means producing less of something else, and because resources are not equally productive in all activities, the more of anything that we produce, the higher is its opportunity cost.

R E V I E W

- The *PPF* is bowed outward and the opportunity cost of producing a good increases as more of it is produced.
- The bowed-out frontier and increasing opportunity cost arise because resources are not equally productive in all activities and the resources most suitable for any given activity are used first.

We've seen how the production possibility frontier shows the limits to production. And we've seen how we can use the production possibility frontier to measure opportunity cost. Our next task is to study the forces that make our production possibilities grow.

Economic Growth

THE PRODUCTION POSSIBILITY FRONTIER THAT defines the boundary between what is attainable and what is unattainable is not static. It is constantly changing. Sometimes the production possibility frontier shifts *inward,* reducing our production possibilities. For example, when an earthquake hit Los Angeles in 1994, the freeway system was damaged and so could not handle as many cars as before the earthquake. Productivity decreased, and the production possibility frontier shifted inward. At other times, the frontier shifts outward. For example, as the quake-damaged freeways of Los Angeles were restored, production possibilities expanded and the frontier shifted outward.

Over the years, our production possibilities have undergone enormous expansion. The expansion of our production possibilities is called **economic growth**. As a consequence of economic growth, we can now produce much more than we could a hundred years ago and quite a bit more than even ten years ago. By 2000, if the same pace of growth continues, our production possibilities will be even greater. By pushing out the frontier, can we avoid the constraints imposed on us by our limited resources? Can we avoid opportunity costs? Is the economist's quip about there being no free lunches wrong?

The Cost of Shifting the Frontier

We are going to discover that although we can and do shift the production possibility frontier outward over time, we cannot have economic growth without incurring costs. The faster we push the *PPF* outward, the more we will have in the future but the less we can consume at the present time. Let's investigate the costs of growth by examining why economies grow and how the choice between the future and the present is made.

The two key factors that influence economic growth are technological progress and capital accumulation. **Technological progress** is the development of new and better ways of producing goods and services and the development of new goods. **Capital accumulation** is the growth of capital resources. As a consequence of technological progress and capital accumulation, we have an enormous quantity of cars and airplanes that enable us to produce more transportation than when we had only horses and carriages; we have satellites that make transcontinental communications possible on a scale that is much larger than that produced by the earlier cable technology. But to develop new technologies and accumulate capital, we must bear an opportunity cost. That opportunity cost is the decrease in the quantity of consumption goods and services because resources are switched from producing goods and services and used in research and development and to make new machines and other forms of capital. To understand these opportunity costs, let's return to Mark's denim jeans factory.

Technological Change and Capital Accumulation

Given its resources, Mark's factory can produce 5,000 jeans a week. But Mark and his workers do not have to produce jeans. They can do other activities instead. For example, they can spend some of their time installing new cutting and sewing machines.

Suppose that Mark spends part of his working time keeping abreast of the latest developments in jeans-making technology. One day, he learns of a recent *technological change* that he can use in his factory. To implement his idea, he must get some of his workers to stop making jeans and to work on installing some computer-controlled cutting and sewing machines that use the new technology— *capital accumulation.*

But Mark's workers are not all equally productive in all activities. Some workers are relatively more productive at making jeans, and others are relatively more productive at installing machines.

In assigning workers to tasks, Mark strives to be efficient. So the workers he assigns to installing machines are those who are relatively more productive in that activity. But the more workers he assigns to installing machines, the less suitable they are for that task, and the more suitable they are for making jeans. So to increase the number of machines installed, jeans production falls by an increasing amount. Mark's *PPF* for jeans and machines is bowed outward like that for video games and missiles.

Mark's production possibilities for jeans and machines are shown in Fig. 3.4. His production

FIGURE 3.4
Economic Growth in a Jeans Factory

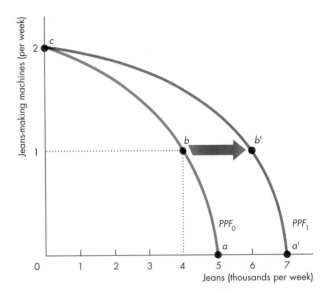

If Mark devotes all his resources to producing jeans, he installs no new machines and produces 5,000 jeans a week (point *a*). If he devotes sufficient resources to installing 1 new machine, his jeans production falls to 4,000 a week (point *b*). But when the new machine is in place, Mark can increase his production to a point on the red *PPF*. For example, if he returns to using all his resources to produce jeans, he can produce at point *a'* (7,000 a week). If he continues to devote resources to installing 1 additional machine, he can produce at point *b'* (6,000 jeans a week). So by installing machines, Mark can shift his *PPF* outward. But he cannot avoid opportunity cost. To shift the frontier outward and increase his *future* production possibilities, Mark must decrease his *current* production of jeans.

possibility frontier initially is the blue curve *abc*. If Mark devotes no resources to installing machines, he produces at point *a*. If he devotes one fifth of his resources to installing machines, he produces 4,000 jeans and installs 1 machine at point *b*. If he produces no jeans, he installs 2 machines at point *c*.

If Mark produces at point *a* in Fig. 3.4, his future production possibilities remain stuck on the blue production possibility frontier. But if he moves to point *b* in Fig. 3.4 and installs 1 machine, he increases his future production possibilities. An increase in the number of machines enables Mark to produce more jeans. As a consequence, Mark's production possibility frontier rotates outward as shown by the arrow. Mark's production possibilities expand and he experiences economic growth.

The amount by which Mark's production possibilities expand depends on how much of his resources he devotes to technological change and capital accumulation. If he devotes no resources to this activity, the frontier remains at *abc*—the original blue curve. If he cuts the current production of jeans and installs one machine (point *b*), then his frontier moves out in the future to the position shown by the red curve in Fig. 3.4. The less resources he devotes to current production of jeans and the more resources he devotes to installing machines, the greater is the expansion of his production possibilities.

But economic growth is not free for Mark. To make it happen, he devotes more resources to installing new machines and less to producing jeans. There is no free lunch. Also, economic growth is no magic formula for abolishing scarcity. On the new production possibility frontier, Mark continues to face opportunity costs.

The ideas about economic growth that we have explored in the setting of a denim jeans factory also apply to individual households and to nations. Let's see why.

The Economic Growth of Households

To expand its production possibilities, a family must forgo current consumption and devote resources to accumulating captial. It can accumulate claims to the income from real capital or it can accumulate human capital. For example, by forgoing current consumption and undertaking full-time schooling, members of a household can increase their earning potential and increase their future consumption. *Reading Between the Lines* on pp. 60–61 explores the opportunity cost and the benefits of human capital choices.

The Economic Growth of Nations

If as a nation we devote all our resources to producing food, clothing, housing, vacations, and other consumer goods and none to research, development, and the accumulation of capital, we will have no more capital and no better technologies in the future than we have at present. Our production possibilities in the future will be the same as today. To expand our production possibilities in the future, we must produce fewer consumption goods today. The resources that we free up today enable us to accumulate capital and to develop better technologies for producing consumption goods in the future. The decrease in the output of consumption goods today is the opportunity cost of economic growth and the attainment of more consumption goods in the future.

The experiences of the United States and some East Asian economies, such as Hong Kong's, provide a striking example of the effects of our choices on the rate of economic growth. In 1960, the production possibilities per person in the United States were more than four times those in Hong Kong (see Fig. 3.5). The United States devotes one fifth of its resources to accumulating capital and the other four fifths to consumption. In 1960, the United States was at point *a* in Fig. 3.5(a). But Hong Kong devotes more than one third of its resources to accumulating capital and less than two thirds to consumption. In 1960, Hong Kong was at point *a* in Fig. 3.5(b). Since 1960, both countries have experienced economic growth, but growth in Hong Kong has been much more rapid than in the United States. Because Hong Kong devotes a bigger fraction of its resources to accumulating capital, its production possibilities expand more quickly.

If Hong Kong's production possibilities per person continue to grow as quickly as they have done during the past few decades, Hong Kong will catch up with and possibly even overtake the United States in the near future. If Hong Kong continues to devote such a large proportion of its resources to accumulating capital (at point *b* on its 1995 production possibility frontier), it will most likely continue to grow more rapidly than the United States and its frontier will move out beyond our own. If Hong Kong increases its consumption and decreases its capital accumulation (moving to point *c* on its 1995 production possibility frontier), then its rate of economic growth will slow down to that of our own.

Hong Kong has been the fastest-growing East Asian economy, but others such as Singapore, Taiwan, South Korea, and recently China have performed similarly to Hong Kong, and they too are gaining on the United States.

FIGURE **3.5**

Economic Growth in the United States and Hong Kong

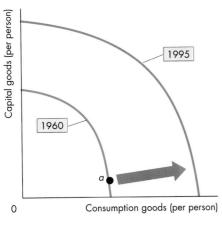

(a) United States

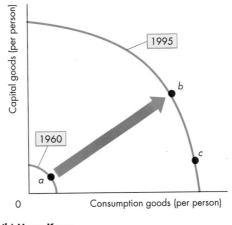

(b) Hong Kong

In 1960, the production possibilities per person in the United States, part (a), were much larger than those in Hong Kong, part (b). But Hong Kong devotes more of its resources to accumulating capital than does the United States so its production possibility frontier has shifted out more quickly than has that of the United States. In 1995, the two production possibilities per person were similar.

REVIEW

■ Economic growth results from technological change and capital accumulation.

■ The opportunity cost of faster economic growth is a decrease in current consumption.

■ By decreasing current consumption, we can devote more resources to developing new technologies and accumulating capital and can speed up the rate of economic growth.

Gains from Trade

PEOPLE CAN PRODUCE FOR THEMSELVES ALL THE goods that they consume, or they can concentrate on producing one good (or perhaps a few goods) and then trade with others—exchange some of their own products for the products of others. Concentrating on the production of only one good or a few goods is called *specialization*. We are going to discover how people gain by specializing in the production of the good in which they have a *comparative advantage* and trading with each other.

Comparative Advantage

A person has a **comparative advantage** in an activity if that person can perform the activity at a lower opportunity cost than anyone else. Differences in opportunity costs arise from differences in individual abilities and from differences in the characteristics of other resources.

No one excels at everything. One person is an outstanding pitcher but a poor catcher; another person is a brilliant lawyer but a poor teacher. In almost all human endeavors, what one person does easily, someone else finds difficult. The same applies to land and capital. One plot of land is fertile but has no mineral deposits: another plot of land has outstanding views but is infertile. One machine has great precision but is difficult to operate; another machine is fast but often breaks down.

Although no one excels at everything, some people excel and can outperform others in many activities. But such a person does not have a *comparative* advantage in every activity. For example, John Grisham is a better lawyer than most people. But he is an even better writer of fast-paced thrillers. His *comparative* advantage is writing.

Differences in individual abilities and differences in the quality of other resources mean that there are differences in individual opportunity costs of producing various goods. Such differences give rise to comparative advantage. Let's take a closer look at the idea of comparative advantage by returning again to Mark's denim jeans factory.

We've seen that Mark can produce jeans or install machines. But he can also modify his machines and produce other goods. Suppose that one of these goods is denim skirts. Figure 3.6(a) shows Mark's production possibility frontier for jeans and skirts. As we already know from Fig. 3.1, if Mark uses all his resources to make jeans, he can produce 5,000 a week. The *PPF* in Fig. 3.6(a) tells us that if he uses all his resources to make skirts, he can produce 10,000 skirts a week. But to produce skirts, Mark must decrease his production of jeans. And for each 1,000 skirts produced, he must decrease his production of jeans by 500. Mark's opportunity cost of producing 1 skirt is 0.5 jeans.

Similarly, if Mark wants to increase his production of jeans, he must decrease his production of skirts. And for each 1,000 jeans produced, he must decrease his production of skirts by 2,000. So Mark's opportunity cost of producing 1 pair of jeans is 2 skirts.

Another factory, operated by Marjorie, can also produce skirts and jeans. But Marjorie's factory has machines that are custom made for skirt production, so they are more suitable for producing skirts than jeans. Also, Marjorie's work force is more accustomed to making skirts.

This difference between the two factories means that Marjorie's production possibility frontier— shown in Fig. 3.6(b)—is different from Mark's. If Marjorie uses all her resources to make skirts, she can produce 25,000 a week. If she uses all her resources to make jeans, she can produce 2,000 a week. To produce jeans, Marjorie must decrease her production of skirts. For each 1,000 additional jeans produced, she must decrease her production of skirts by 12,500. Marjorie's opportunity cost of producing 1 pair of jeans is 12.5 skirts.

Similarly, if Marjorie wants to increase her production of skirts, she must decrease her production of jeans. For each 1,000 additional skirts produced, she must decrease her production of jeans by 80. So Marjorie's opportunity cost of producing 1 skirt is 0.08 jeans.

Mark and Marjorie can be *diversified* and produce both jeans and skirts. Suppose, for example, that Mark and Marjorie each produces the same quantities of jeans and skirts—1,400 jeans and 7,100 skirts. That is, each produces at point *a* on their production possibility frontiers. Their total production is 2,800 jeans and 14,200 skirts.

In which of the two goods does Marjorie have a comparative advantage? Recall that comparative advantage is a situation in which one person's opportunity cost of producing a good is less than another person's opportunity cost of producing that same good. Marjorie has a comparative advantage in producing skirts.

You can see her comparative advantage by looking at the production possibility frontiers for Marjorie and Mark in Fig. 3.6. Marjorie's production possibility frontier is steeper than Mark's. To produce one more skirt, Marjorie gives up fewer jeans than Mark. Hence Marjorie's opportunity cost of a skirt is less than Mark's. This means that Marjorie has a comparative advantage in producing skirts.

Mark's comparative advantage is in producing jeans. His production possibility frontier is flatter than Marjorie's. This means that Mark gives up fewer skirts to produce one more pair of jeans than Marjorie does. Mark's opportunity cost of producing jeans is less than Marjorie's, so Mark has a comparative advantage in jeans production.

Achieving the Gains from Trade

If Mark, who has a comparative advantage in jeans production, puts all his resources into that activity, he can produce 5,000 jeans a week—point *b* on his *PPF*. If Marjorie, who has a comparative advantage in skirt production, puts all her resources into that activity, she can produce 25,000 skirts a week—point *b* on her *PPF*. By specializing, Mark and Marjorie together can produce 5,000 jeans and 25,000 skirts a week.

To achieve the gains from specialization, Mark and Marjorie must trade with each other. Suppose they agree to the following deal: Each week, Marjorie

FIGURE 3.6
The Gains from Specialization and Trade

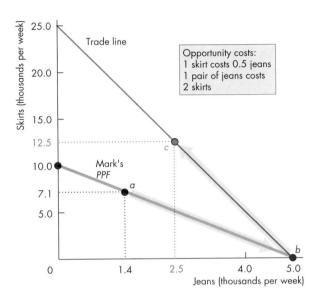

(a) Mark's factory

Mark (part a) and Marjorie (part b) each produces at point *a* on their respective *PPF*. For Mark, the opportunity cost of 1 pair of jeans is 2 skirts and the opportunity cost of 1 skirt is 0.5 jeans. For Marjorie the opportunity cost of 1 pair of jeans is 12.5 skirts—higher than Mark's—and the opportunity cost of 1 skirt is 0.08 jeans—lower than Mark's. Marjorie has a comparative advantage in skirts, and Mark has a comparative advantage in jeans.

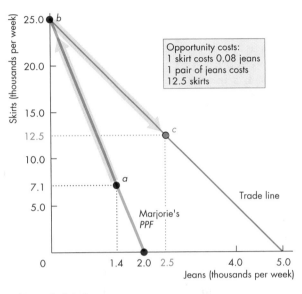

(b) Marjorie's factory

If Marjorie specializes in skirts and Mark specializes in jeans, each produces at point *b* on her or his respective *PPF*. They then exchange skirts for jeans along the red "Trade line." Marjorie buys jeans from Mark for less than her opportunity cost of producing them, and Mark buys skirts from Marjorie for less than his opportunity cost of producing them. Each goes to point *c*—a point *outside* his or her *PPF*—where each has 2,500 jeans and 12,500 skirts per week.

produces 25,000 skirts, Mark produces 5,000 jeans, and Marjorie supplies Mark with 12,500 skirts in exchange for 2,500 jeans. With this deal in place, Mark and Marjorie move along the red "Trade line" to point *c*. At this point, each has 12,500 skirts and 2,500 jeans—an additional 1,100 jeans and an additional 5,400 skirts. These are the gains from specialization and trade, and both parties to the trade share the gains.

Marjorie, who can produce jeans at an opportunity cost of 12.5 skirts per pair can buy jeans from Mark for a price of 5 skirts per pair. Mark, who can produce skirts at an opportunity cost of 0.5 jeans per skirt can buy skirts from Marjorie at a price of 0.2

jeans per skirt. Marjorie gets her jeans more cheaply, and Mark gets his skirts more cheaply. By specialization and trade, Mark and Marjorie get quantities of skirts and jeans that are *outside* their individual production possibility frontiers.

Absolute Advantage

We've seen that Mark has a comparative advantage in producing jeans and Marjorie has a comparative advantage in producing skirts. We've also seen that Mark can produce a larger quantity of jeans than Marjorie and Marjorie can produce a larger quantity of skirts than Mark. Neither Mark nor Marjorie can produce more of *both* goods than the other.

If by using the same quantities of inputs, one person can produce more of *both* goods than someone else can, that person is said to have an **absolute advantage** in the production of both goods. In our example, neither Mark nor Marjorie has an absolute advantage.

It is tempting to suppose that when a person (or country) has an absolute advantage, it is not possible to benefit from specialization and exchange. But this line of reasoning is wrong. To see why, let's look again at the case of Mark and Marjorie. Suppose that Marjorie invents and patents a production process that makes her *four* times as productive as she was before. With her new technology, Marjorie can produce 100,000 skirts a week (4 times the original 25,000) if she puts all her resources into that activity. Alternatively, she can produce 8,000 jeans (4 times the original 2,000) if she puts all her resources into that activity. Notice that Marjorie now has an absolute advantage in producing both goods.

We have already worked out that the gains from specialization arise when each person specializes in producing the good in which he or she has a *comparative* advantage. Recall that a person has a comparative advantage in producing a particular good if that person can produce the good at a *lower opportunity cost* than anyone else. Mark's opportunity costs remain exactly the same as they were before. What has happened to Marjorie's opportunity costs now that she has become four times as productive?

You can work out Marjorie's opportunity costs by doing exactly the same calculation that you've done before. And you can see that her opportunity costs have not changed. Marjorie can produce four times as much of *both* goods as before. But to increase the production of jeans by 1,000 along her new production possibility frontier, she must decrease her production of skirts by 12,500, so her opportunity cost of 1 pair of jeans is still 12.5 skirts. And to increase her production of skirts by 1,000, she must decrease her production of jeans by 80, so her opportunity cost of 1 skirt is 0.08 jeans.

When Marjorie becomes four times as productive as before, each unit of her resources produces more output, but her opportunity costs remain the same. To produce one more pair of jeans costs the same in terms of the quantity of skirts forgone as it did previously. Since neither Marjorie's nor Mark's opportunity costs

have changed, Marjorie continues to have a comparative advantage in producing skirts, and Mark continues to have a comparative advantage in producing jeans. Mark can buy skirts from Marjorie at a lower price than his own opportunity cost of producing them. And Marjorie can buy jeans from Mark for a lower price than her opportunity cost of producing them. So they can both continue to gain by specialization and trade.

The key point to recognize is that it is *not* possible for *anyone,* even someone who has an absolute advantage, to have a comparative advantage in everything. So gains for specialization and trade are always available.

Dynamic Comparative Advantage

Comparative advantage is not a static concept. At any given point in time, the resources available and the technologies in use determine the comparative advantages that individuals and nations have. But as technological change and capital accumulation shift the production possibility frontiers outward, so comparative advantages change. Also, people get better at doing what they do repeatedly. Just by repeatedly producing a particular good or service, people can become more productive in that activity, a phenomenon called **learning-by-doing**. Learning-by-doing is the basis of *dynamic* comparative advantage. **Dynamic comparative advantage** is a comparative advantage that a person (or country) possesses as a result of having specialized in a particular activity and, as a result of learning-by-doing, having become the producer with the lowest opportunity cost.

Dynamic comparative advantage applies to individuals, firms, and countries. Some people have a steep learning curve—they initially do not seem to be very different from anyone else, but through practice and hard work they become outstanding in some activity. Boeing, the world's largest maker of wide-bodied jet aircraft has pursued dynamic comparative advantage. As Boeing's labor force and management have gained experience in building wide-bodied aircraft, they have successively lowered costs and strengthened their comparative advantage.

Singapore, South Korea, Hong Kong, and Taiwan are examples of countries that have pursued dynamic comparative advantage vigorously. They have developed industries in which initially they might not have had a comparative advantage and, through learning-by-doing, have become low opportunity cost producers of high-technology products. An example is the decision to develop a genetic engineering industry in Singapore. Singapore probably did not have a comparative advantage in genetic engineering initially. But it might develop one as its scientists and production workers become more skilled in this activity.

R E V I E W

- Production increases if people specialize in the activity in which they have a comparative advantage.
- A person has a comparative advantage in producing a good if that person's opportunity cost of producing the good is lower than everyone else's.
- Differences in opportunity cost are the source of gains from specialization and trade.
- If, by using the same quantities of inputs, a person can produce more of all goods than someone else, then that person has an absolute advantage.
- Even people who have an absolute advantage gain by specializing in the activities in which they have a comparative advantage and trading.
- Dynamic comparative advantage can result from learning-by-doing.

The Evolution of Trading Arrangements

INDIVIDUALS AND COUNTRIES HAVE GAINED BY specializing in the production of those goods and services in which they have a comparative advantage and trading—see *Economics in History*, pp. 64–65. But to reap the gains from trade from billions of people specializing in millions of different activities, trade must be organized. And to organize trade, social arrangements have evolved. The most important of these arrangements are:

- Markets
- Property rights
- Money

Markets

We defined a *market* in Chapter 1 as any arrangement that enables buyers and sellers to get information and to do business with each other. Markets might be physical locations, such as a wholesale meat or fish market. Or they might be electronic links, such as the world oil market.

But all markets share a common feature. They link the producers and the consumers of goods and services together. Sometimes those links are direct—as in the market for haircuts—and sometimes they are indirect and involve many layers of producers of services and traders—as in the market for milk.

Markets work by pooling an enormous amount of information about the plans of buyers and sellers and summarizing this information in just one number, a price. The price moves in response to the decisions of buyers and sellers. It rises when there is a shortage and falls when there is a relative abundance. The price is a signal to buyers and sellers. Each potential buyer or seller knows her or his own opportunity cost of producing a good or service. By comparing this opportunity cost with the market price, each person can decide whether to become a buyer or a seller. Someone who can produce a good (or service) at an opportunity cost that is less than the market price can gain from producing and selling that good (or service). Someone who can produce a good at an opportunity cost that is greater than the market price can gain by buying the good rather than producing it.

Markets are one of the social arrangements that enable people to specialize and gain from the increased production that results from specialization. But markets would not work very smoothly without property rights and money.

Property Rights

Property rights are social arrangements that govern the ownership, use, and disposal of factors of production and goods and services. *Real property* includes land and buildings—the things we call property in ordinary speech—and durable goods such as plant and equipment. *Financial property* includes stocks and bonds and money in the bank. *Intellectual property* is the intangible product of creative effort. This type of property includes books, music, computer programs, and inventions of all kinds and is protected by copyrights and patents.

With no property rights, or with weakly enforced property rights, the incentive to specialize and produce the goods in which each person has a comparative advantage is weakened, and some of the potential gains from specialization and trade are lost. If people can take possession of whatever they have the ability to obtain for themselves—steal—then a good deal of time, energy, and resources must be devoted not to production, but to protecting possessions.

Establishing property rights is one of the greatest challenges facing Russia and other Eastern European nations as they seek to develop market economies. In countries where property rights are well established, such as the United States, upholding intellectual property rights is proving to be a challenge in the face of modern technologies that make it relatively easy to copy audio and video material, computer programs, and books.

Money

Markets and property rights enable people to specialize and trade their output. But *how* do they trade? There are two possible ways:

1. Barter
2. Monetary exchange

Barter   **Barter** is the direct exchange of one good or service for another. This method of trading severely limits the amount of exchange that takes place. Imagine that you have oranges, but you want to get apples. You look for someone with apples who wants oranges. Economists call this a *double coincidence of wants*—when person A wants to sell exactly what person B wants to buy and person B wants to sell exactly what person A wants to buy. As the term implies, such occurrences are coincidences and do not arise frequently. Another way of trading by barter is to undertake a sequence of exchanges. Failing to find someone with apples who wants oranges, you might trade oranges for plums, plums for pomegranates, pomegranates for pineapples, and then eventually pineapples for apples.

Although it is a cumbersome way of doing business, quite a large amount of barter takes place. For example, before the recent changes in Eastern Europe, hairdressers in Warsaw, Poland, obtained their barbershop equipment from England in exchange for hair clippings that they supplied to London wigmakers. Today, Australian meat processors swap cans of meat for Russian salmon, crabmeat, and scallops, and Australian wool growers swap wool for Russian electrical motors.

Although barter does occur, it is inefficient. Fortunately, a better alternative has evolved.

Monetary Exchange   *Monetary exchange* is a system of trading in which a commodity or token that we call *money* serves as the means of payment and the medium of exchange. Money lowers the cost of making a transaction and makes millions of transactions possible that otherwise would not be worth undertaking. Imagine the chain of barter transactions you'd have to go through every day to get your coffee, Coke, textbooks, professor's time, video, and all the other goods and services you consume. In a monetary exchange system, you exchange your time and effort for money and use that money to buy the goods and services you consume, cutting out the incredible hassle you would face each day in a world of barter.

Metals such as gold, silver, and copper have long served as money. Most commonly, they serve as money by being stamped as coins. Primitive societies have traditionally used commodities such as seashells as money. During the Civil War and for several years afterward, people used postage stamps as money. Prisoners of war in German camps in World War II used cigarettes as money. Using cigarettes as a medium of exchange should not be confused with barter. When cigarettes play the role of money, smokers and nonsmokers buy and sell goods by using cigarettes as a means of payment.

In modern societies, governments provide paper money. The banking system also provides money in the form of checking accounts. Checking accounts can be used for settling debts simply by writing an instruction—writing a check—to the bank requesting that funds be transferred to another checking account. Electronic links between bank accounts, which are now becoming more widespread, enable direct transfers between different accounts without any checks being written.

◆ You have now begun to see how economists go about the job of trying to answer economic questions. The fact of scarcity and the associated concept of opportunity cost allow us to understand why people specialize, why they trade with each other, and why they have developed social arrangements such as markets, property rights, and money. One simple fact, scarcity, and its direct implications, choice and opportunity cost, explain so much!

SUMMARY

The Production Possibility Frontier

Production, which is the conversion of factors of production into goods and services, is limited by the resources available and by technology. The production possibility frontier is the boundary between production levels that are attainable and those that are not attainable when all the available resources are being used to their limit. Production can take place at any point on or inside the production possibility frontier, but it is not possible to produce outside the frontier. Points on the production possibility frontier are efficient, and points inside the frontier are inefficient. Along the production possibility frontier, the opportunity cost of producing more of one good is the amount of the other good that must be given up. Opportunity cost is inescapable and confronts people with *trade-offs*. (pp. 44–46)

Increasing Opportunity Cost

Opportunity cost is measured as the increase in the quantity of one good divided by the decrease in the quantity of the other good as we move along the production possibility frontier. As the quantity produced of a good increases, so does the opportunity cost of producing it. Equivalently, the production possibility frontier is bowed outward. The production possibility frontier is bowed outward and the opportunity cost increases because resources are not equally productive in all activities and the most suitable resources for a given activity are used first in that activity. That is, factors of production are allocated efficiently by being assigned to the tasks for which they are the best available match. As the economy moves along its *PPF*, producing more of one good and less of another, factors of production are assigned to tasks for which they are an increasingly poor match and so the opportunity cost increases. (pp. 47–50)

Economic Growth

The production possibility frontier changes over time, partly because of natural forces, for example, earthquakes, and partly because of the choices that we make about what to produce and consume, how much research and development to undertake, and how much capital to accumulate. If we use some of today's resources for research and development and to produce capital goods, we can produce more goods and services in the future—the economy grows. But growth cannot take place without incurring costs. The opportunity cost of economic growth (of more goods and services in the future) is consuming fewer goods and services in the present. (pp. 50–53)

Gains from Trade

A person has a comparative advantage in producing a good if that person can produce the good at a lower opportunity cost than everyone else. Production can be increased if people specialize in the activity at which they have a comparative advantage. Each person produces the good for which her or his opportunity cost is less than everyone else's, and goods produced at the lowest possible opportunity cost are exchanged—traded.

When a person is more productive than another person—is able to produce more output from the same quantities of inputs—that person has an absolute advantage. But having an absolute advantage does not mean there are no gains from specialization and trade. Even if someone is more productive than other people in all activities, as long as the other person has a lower opportunity cost of some good, then gains from specialization and trade are available.

Comparative advantage changes over time, and dynamic comparative advantage arises from learning-by-doing. (pp. 53–57)

The Evolution of Trading Arrangements

Exchange in the real world involves the specialization of billions of people in millions of different activities. To make it worthwhile for each individual to specialize and to enable societies to reap the gains from trade, social arrangements have evolved. The most important of these are markets, property rights, and money. These arrangements enable people to specialize, exchanging factors of production and goods and services for money and money for factors of production and goods and services. As a result, they reap the gains from specialization and trade. (pp. 57–58)

Opportunity Cost: Cost and Benefit of a Degree

THE CHICAGO TRIBUNE, JULY 22, 1994

Study Finds College Costly, But Worth It

BY MICHAEL ARNDT

WASHINGTON—Burdened by the hefty cost of college—and the trendline showing ever-higher expenses in the years ahead—many people are questioning whether a degree is worth it.

It is.

A college degree can mean at least $600,000 in additional earnings over a typical 43.5-year career, while an advanced degree can lift lifetime income by as much as $2.2 million, the Census Bureau projects in a report Friday. The report is the first to make such lifetime projections. ...

The American Council on Education forecasts that a student at a public university will spend $9,876 in the coming school year on tuition fees, room, board, and supplies. ...

At private universities, costs are ... an average of $23,704.

Borrowing to pay the entire bill for four years of school at a private university could leave a student owing almost $100,000 plus interest.

While these expenses could strain the budgets of even affluent families, researchers say the potential payoffs justify the outlays. ...

According to the Census Bureau report, high school graduates earned an average of $18,737 in 1992. The average college graduate, by comparison, earned $32,629, while people with advanced degrees had an average income of $48,653.

Over time, these differentials equal huge sums of money. Citing 1992 income figures, the Census Bureau projects that an average high school graduate will make $821,000 over a lifetime of work, while a college graduate will earn $1.4 million, or $600,000 more.

Incomes continue rising with education, the report finds. People with master's degrees will earn an average of $1.8 million over their careers. Meanwhile, those with doctorates will earn $2.1 million, and people with professional degrees, such as medical doctors and lawyers will make $3 million.

At the other end of the socioeconomic spectrum, people without high school diplomas will earn an average of $609,000 over their lifetimes.

Essence of THE STORY

■ In 1994-95, average tuition fees, room, board, and supplies for a year of study at a public university were $9,876 and those at a private university were $23,704.

■ According to data reported by the Census Bureau, the potential payoffs justify the outlays on education.

■ In 1992, average earnings were $18,737 for high school graduates, $32,629 for college graduates, and $48,653 for people with advanced degrees.

■ The Census Bureau projects average lifetime earnings to be $609,000 for people without high school diplomas, $821,000 for high school graduates, $1.4 million for college graduates, $1.8 million for people with master's degrees, $2.1 million for people with doctorates, and $3 million for people such as medical doctors and lawyers with professional degrees.

Economic

A N A L Y S I S

■ The opportunity cost of school is forgone consumption, which equals the amount spent on school plus forgone earnings.

■ For a high school graduate, the opportunity cost of a four-year college degree is $114,000. This amount is $9,876 annual expenses plus $18,737 (the annual income of a high school graduate) in annual forgone earnings, multiplied by 4.

■ The payoff from a degree is an increase in lifetime income from the $821,000 of a high school graduate to the $1.4 million of a college graduate.

■ Figure I shows this opportunity cost and payoff. By selecting point *a* on the blue *PPF*, the student decreases consumption from $821,000 to $707,000—an opportunity cost of $114,000.

■ The red *PPF* shows the expanded possibilities with a college degree—a lifetime consumption possibility of $1,286,000 ($1.4 million earnings minus $114,000 cost).

■ For a college graduate, the opportunity cost of a four-year professional degree is $225,000. This amount is the sum the annual expenses of $23,704 and the annual forgone earnings of $32,629, multiplied by 4.

■ The payoff from a professional degree is an increase in lifetime income from the $1,286,000 for a college graduate to $3 million.

■ Figure 2 shows this opportunity cost and payoff. By selecting point *b* on the blue *PPF*, the student forgoes $225,000 of consumption—from $1,286,000 to $1,061,000—which is the opportunity cost of the professional degree.

■ The red *PPF* shows the expanded possibilities with a professional degree—a lifetime consumption possibility of $2,775,000 ($3 million earnings minus $225,000 cost).

■ The greater the resources devoted to education, the greater are the future consumption possibilities. The future benefits of education exceed the costs by a significant amount.

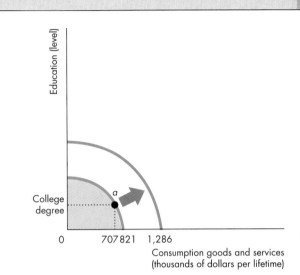

Figure 1 High School Graduates' Choices

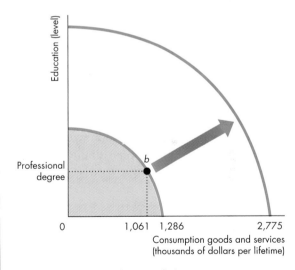

Figure 2 College Graduates' Choices

K E Y   E L E M E N T S

Key Figures

Key Terms

R E V I E W   Q U E S T I O N S

1. How does the production possibility frontier
   illustrate scarcity?
2. How does the production possibility frontier
   illustrate production efficiency?
3. How does the production possibility frontier
   illustrate opportunity cost?
4. Why does the production possibility frontier
   bow outward for most goods?
5. Why does opportunity cost generally increase as
   the quantity produced of a good increases?
6. What shifts the production possibility frontier
   outward and what shifts it inward?

7. Explain how our choices influence the pace of
   economic growth.
8. What is the opportunity cost of economic
   growth?
9. Why do people specialize and trade?
10. What are the gains from specialization and
    trade? How do they arise?
11. What is the difference between comparative
    advantage and absolute advantage?
12. Why do social arrangements such as markets,
    property rights, and money become necessary?

P R O B L E M S

1. Suppose that Leisureland produces only two
   goods—food and sunscreen. The table gives its
   production possibilities.
   a. Draw a graph of Leisureland's production
       possibility frontier.
   b. What are the opportunity costs of produc-
       ing food and sunscreen in Leisureland? List
       them at each output given in the table.
   c. Why are the opportunity costs the same at
       each output level?

Food (pounds per month)		Sunscreen (gallons per month)
300	and	0
200	and	50
100	and	100
0	and	150

2. Busyland produces only food and sunscreen,
   and its production possibilities are:

Food (pounds per month)		Sunscreen (gallons per month)
150	and	0
100	and	100
50	and	200
0	and	300

  a. Draw a graph of Busyland's production possibility frontier.

  b. What are the opportunity costs of producing food and sunscreen in Busyland? List them at each output given in the table.

◆ 3. Suppose that in problems 1 and 2, Leisureland and Busyland do not specialize and trade with each other. Leisureland produces and consumes 50 pounds of food and 125 gallons of sunscreen per month. Busyland produces and consumes 150 pounds of food per month and no sunscreen. Now the countries begin to trade with each other.

  a. What good does Leisureland export and what good does it import?

  b. What good does Busyland export and what good does it import?

  c. What is the maximum quantity of food and sunscreen that the two countries can produce if each country specializes in the activity at which it has a comparative advantage?

◆ 4. Suppose that Busyland becomes three times as productive as in problem 2.

  a. Show, on a graph, the effect of the increased productivity on Busyland's production possibility frontier.

  b. Has Busyland's opportunity costs of producing food and sunscreen changed? Explain.

  c. Does Busyland now have an absolute advantage in producing both goods?

  d. Can Busyland gain from specialization and trade with Leisureland now that it is three times as productive? If so, what will it produce?

  e. What are the total gains from trade? On what do these gains depend?

◆ 5. Andy and Bob work at Mario's Pizza Palace. In an eight-hour day, Andy can make 240 pizzas or 100 ice cream sundaes, and Bob can make 80 pizzas or 80 ice cream sundaes. Who does Mario assign to make the ice cream sundaes? Who makes the pizzas? Explain your answer.

6. Wendell enjoys playing tennis but the more time he spends on tennis, the lower is his grade in economics. The figure shows the trade-off he faces.

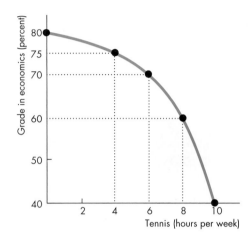

Calculate the opportunity cost of two hours of tennis if Wendell increases the time he plays tennis from:

  a. 4 to 6 hours a week.

  b. 6 to 8 hours a week.

7. By using the figure in problem 6, describe the relationship between the time Wendell spends playing tennis and the opportunity cost of an hour of tennis.

8. After you have studied the *Reading Between the Lines* on pp. 60–61:

  a. Draw a figure to show the relationship between the opportunity cost of education and the amount of education undertaken.

  b. Describe the relationship in (a).

  c. Draw a figure to show the relationship between the payoff from education and the amount of education undertaken.

  d. Describe the relationship in (c).

  e. Explain why the news article says that the "potential payoffs justify the outlays on education." Do you agree?

> "*It is not from the benevolence of the butcher, the brewer, or the baker that we expect our dinner, but from their regard to their own interest.*"
>
> ADAM SMITH, *THE WEALTH OF NATIONS*

Understanding the Sources of Economic Wealth

THE ISSUES AND IDEAS

Why do some nations become wealthy and others remain poor? Adam Smith was one of the first to try to answer this question. At the time that Smith was pondering this question, between 1760 and 1830, an "industrial revolution" was taking place. During these years, new technologies were invented and applied to the manufacture of cotton and wool, iron, transportation, and agriculture.

Smith wanted to understand the sources of economic wealth, and he brought his acute powers of observation and abstraction to bear on this question. His answer:

- The division of labor
- Free domestic and international markets

Smith identified the division of labor as the source of "the greatest improvement in the productive powers of labor." The division of labor became even more productive when it was applied to creating new technologies. Scientists and engineers, trained in extremely narrow fields, became specialists at inventing. Their powerful skills accelerated the advance of technology, so that by the 1820s, machines could make consumer goods faster and more accurately than any craftsman could. And by the 1850s, machines could make other machines that labor alone could never have made.

But, said Smith, the fruits of the division of labor are limited by the extent of the market. To make the market as large as possible, there must be no impediments to free trade both within a country and among countries. Smith argued that when each person makes the best possible economic choice, that choice leads as if by "an invisible hand" to the best outcome for society as a whole.

THEN...

ADAM SMITH speculated that one person, working hard, using the hand tools available in the 1770s, might possibly make 20 pins a day. Yet, he observed, by using those same hand tools but breaking the process into a number of individually small operations in which people specialize—by the division of labor—ten people could make a staggering 48,000 pins a day. One draws out the wire, another straightens it, a third cuts it, a fourth points it, a fifth grinds it. Three specialists make the head, and a fourth attaches it. Finally, the pin is polished and packaged. But a large market is needed to support the division of labor: one factory employing ten workers would need to sell more than 15 million pins a year.

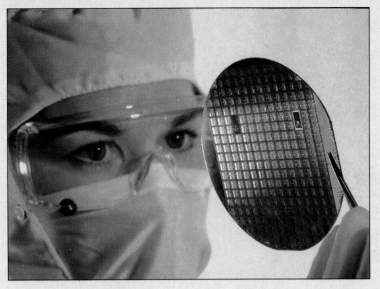

MEMORY CHIPS give your computer its instant recall ability, logic chips provide its number-crunching power, and custom chips make your camera idiot-proof. The computer chip is an extraordinary example of the productivity of the division of labor. Designers lay out a chip's intricate circuits. Printers and cameras transfer an image of the design to glass plates that work like stencils. Workers prepare silicon wafers on which the circuits will be printed. Some slice the wafers, others polish them, others bake them, and yet others coat them with a light-sensitive chemical. Machines transfer a copy of the circuit onto the wafer. Chemicals then etch the design onto the wafer. A further series of processes deposit atoms that act as transistors and aluminum that connects the transistors. Finally, a diamond saw or laser separates the hundreds of chips on the wafer. Every stage in the process of creating a computer chip, from its conception to its final separation from the wafer, uses other computer chips. And like the pin of the 1770s, the computer chip of the 1990s needs a large market—a global market—to support the huge quantities in which chips are produced.

THE ECONOMIST: ADAM SMITH

Adam Smith was a giant of a scholar who made extraordinary contributions in ethics and jurisprudence as well as economics. Born in 1723 in Kirkcaldy, a small fishing town near Edinburgh, Scotland, he was the only child of the town's customs officer (who died before Adam was born).

His first academic appointment, at age 28, was as Professor of Logic at the University of Glasgow. He subsequently became tutor to a wealthy Scottish duke, whom he accompanied on a two-year grand European tour, following which he received a pension of £300 a year—ten times the average income at that time.

With the financial security of his pension, Smith devoted ten years to writing *An Inquiry into the Nature and Causes of **The Wealth of Nations***. This book, published in 1776, established economics as a science. Many people had written on economic issues before Adam Smith, but it was he who made economics a science. Smith's account was so broad and authoritative that no subsequent writer on economics could advance ideas without tracing their connections with those of Smith's ideas.

4

Demand and Supply

After studying
this chapter,
you will be
able to:

- Distinguish between a money price and a
  relative real price

- Explain the main influences on demand

- Explain the main influences on supply

- Explain how prices are determined by
  demand and supply

- Explain how quantities bought and sold
  are determined

- Explain why some prices fall, some rise,
  and some fluctuate

- Make predictions about price changes
  using the demand and supply model

Slide, Rocket, and Roller Coaster

Slide, rocket, and roller coaster—Disneyland rides? No. Commonly used descriptions of the behavior of prices. ◆ CD players have taken a price slide. In 1983, when they first became available, their price tag was around $800—$1,100 in today's money. Now you can buy one for less than $200, and during the time that CD players have been with us, the quantity bought has increased steadily. Why has there been a slide in the price of CD players? And why hasn't the increase in the quantity bought kept their price high? ◆ The price of health care is an example of a rocket. Ever higher prices have not deterred people from buying health-care services—on the contrary, the amount of services bought have increased steadily every year. Why have people continued to seek ever larger amounts of health-care services when its price has rocketed? ◆ The prices of bananas, corn, coffee, wheat, and other agricultural commodities are examples of roller coasters. Why does the price of bananas roller-coaster even when people's tastes for them hardly change at all? ◆ Although prices may slide, rocket, and roll, many of the things we buy have remarkably steady prices. The price of the audiocassette tapes that we play in a Walkman is an example. But despite its steady price, the number of tapes bought has increased each year. Why do firms sell more tapes even though they're not able to get higher prices for them, and why do people buy more tapes even though their price is no lower than it was a decade ago?

◆ We will discover the answers to these and similar questions by studying the theory of demand and supply. The central aim of this theory is to explain prices and quantities. But first, we're going to take a closer look at the concept of price. Just what do we mean by price?

Opportunity Cost and Price

ECONOMIC ACTIONS ARISE FROM SCARCITY—WANTS exceed the resources available to satisfy them. Faced with *scarcity,* people must make choices. And in making choices, they are confronted with *opportunity costs.* Choices are influenced by opportunity costs. If the opportunity cost of a good or service increases, people look for less costly substitutes—the *principle of substitution*—and decrease their purchases of the more costly item.

We are going to build on these fundamental ideas and principles and study both the way people respond to *prices* and the forces that determine prices. But before we do that, we need to understand the relationship between opportunity cost and price.

The *opportunity cost* of an action is the best alternative forgone. When you buy a cup of coffee, you forgo something. If the best thing forgone is some gum, then the opportunity cost of buying a cup of coffee is a *quantity* of gum forgone. To calculate this quantity, we need to know the prices of the two goods.

The *price* of an object is the number of dollars that must be given up in exchange for it. Economists refer to this everyday idea of price as the *money price.* If the money price of coffee is $1 a cup and the money price of gum is 50¢ a pack, then the opportunity cost of one cup of coffee is two packs of gum. To calculate this opportunity cost, we divide the price of a cup of coffee by the price of a pack of gum and find the *ratio* of one price to the other. The ratio of one price to another is called a **relative price**, and a *relative price is an opportunity cost.* It is the price of good *X* divided by the price of good *Y,* and it tells us how many units of good *Y* must be given up to get one more unit of good *X.*

There are trillions of relative prices—coffee to gum, coffee to Coke, coffee to everything else, gum to Coke, gum to everything else, Coke to everything else—and we need a convenient way of expressing relative prices. The normal way of expressing a relative price is in terms of a "basket" of all goods and services rather than in terms of one particular good or service. That is, we divide the money price of a good by the money price of a "basket" of all goods (called a *price index*). The resulting relative price tells us the opportunity cost of an item in terms of how much of the "basket" of all goods must be given up to buy it.

Figure 4.1 gives an example of the distinction between a money price and a relative price. The green curve shows the money price of wheat and tells us that the money price has fluctuated but has tended to rise. The red curve shows the relative price of wheat measured in 1994 dollars. This curve tells us about the opportunity cost of wheat. It shows what the price would have been each year if prices *on the average* had been the same as they were in 1994. The relative price of wheat peaked in 1974 and has tended to fall since that year.

The theory of demand and supply that we are about to study determines *relative prices,* and the word "price" means *relative* price. When we predict

FIGURE 4.1

The Price of Wheat

The money price of wheat—the number of dollars that must be given up for a bushel of wheat—has fluctuated between $1.50 and $4.80. But the *relative* price or *opportunity cost* of wheat, expressed in 1994 dollars, has fluctuated between $4.00 and $15.00 and has tended to decrease. This fact is obscured by the behavior of the money price of wheat.

Source: International Financial Statistics Yearbook, International Monetary Fund, Washington, DC, 1994.

that a price will fall, we do not mean that its *money* price will fall—although it might. We mean that its *relative* price will fall. That is, its price will fall *relative* to the average price of other goods and services.

Let's now begin our study of demand and supply, starting with demand.

Demand

IF YOU DEMAND SOMETHING, THEN YOU'VE MADE A plan to buy it. Demands are different from wants. *Wants* are the unlimited desires or wishes that people have for goods and services. How many times have you thought that you would like something "if only you could afford it" or "if it weren't so expensive"? Scarcity guarantees that many—perhaps most—of our wants will never be satisfied. Demand reflects a decision about which wants to satisfy.

The **quantity demanded** of a good or service is the amount that consumers plan to buy during a given time period at a particular price. The quantity demanded is not necessarily the same amount as the quantity actually bought. Sometimes the quantity demanded is greater than the amount of goods available, so the quantity bought is less than the quantity demanded.

The quantity demanded is measured as an amount per unit of time. For example, suppose a person consumes one cup of coffee a day. The quantity of coffee demanded by that person can be expressed as 1 cup per day or 7 cups per week or 365 cups per year. Without a time dimension, we cannot tell whether a particular quantity demanded is large or small.

What Determines Buying Plans?

The amount of any particular good or service that consumers plan to buy depends on many factors. The main ones are:

■ The price of the good
■ The prices of related goods
■ Income
■ Expected future prices
■ Population
■ Preferences

Let's first focus on the relationship between the quantity demanded and the price of a good. To study this relationship, we hold constant all other influences on consumers' planned purchases. We can then ask: How does the quantity demanded of the good vary as its price varies?

The Law of Demand

The law of demand states:

Other things remaining the same, the higher the price of a good, the smaller is the quantity demanded.

Why does a higher price reduce the quantity demanded? There are two reasons,[1]

1. Substitution effect
2. Income effect

Substitution Effect   When the price of a good rises, other things remaining the same, its price rises relative to the prices of all other goods. Equivalently, its opportunity cost increases. Although each good is unique, it has substitutes—other goods that serve almost as well. As the opportunity cost of a good increases, people buy less of that good and more of its substitutes.

Income Effect   When the price of a good rises, other things remaining the same, the price rises relative to people's incomes. Faced with a higher price and an unchanged income, the quantities demanded of at least some goods and services must be decreased. Normally, the good whose price has increased will be one of the goods bought in a smaller quantity.

To see the substitution effect and the income effect at work, think about blank audiocassette tapes, which we'll refer to as "tapes." Many different goods provide a service similar to that provided by a tape, for example, a compact disc, a prerecorded tape, a radio or television broadcast, and a live concert. Tapes sell for about $3 each.

---

[1]We can derive the law of demand from a *marginal analysis* of consumers' choices. One way to study these choices is based on the idea of *diminishing marginal utility* (the more of a good you consume, the less benefit you derive from one extra unit), which is explained in Chapter 7. Another way is based on a model of the substitution effect and income effect, which is explained in Chapter 8.

If the price of a tape doubles to $6 while the prices of all the other goods remain constant, the quantity of tapes demanded decreases. People substitute compact discs and prerecorded tapes for blank tapes and, faced with a tighter budget, buy fewer tapes as well as less of other goods and services.

If the price of a tape falls to $1 while the prices of all the other goods remain constant, the quantity of tapes demanded increases. People now substitute blank tapes for compact discs and prerecorded tapes and, with a budget that has some slack from the lower price of tapes, buy more tapes as well as more of other goods and services.

Demand Schedule and Demand Curve

The table in Fig. 4.2 sets out the demand schedule for tapes. A *demand schedule* lists the quantities demanded at each different price when all the other influences on consumers' planned purchases—such as the prices of related goods, income, expected future prices, population, and preferences—remain the same. For example, if the price of a tape is $1, the quantity demanded is 9 million tapes a week. If the price of a tape is $5, the quantity demanded is 2 million tapes a week. The other rows of the table show the quantities demanded at prices of $2, $3, and $4.

Figure 4.2 shows the demand curve for tapes. A **demand curve** shows the relationship between the quantity demanded of a good and its price, all other influences on consumers' planned purchases remaining the same. It is a graph of a demand schedule. By convention, the quantity demanded is measured on the horizontal axis, and the price is measured on the vertical axis. The points on the demand curve labeled *a* through *e* represent the rows of the demand schedule. For example, point *a* on the graph represents a quantity demanded of 9 million tapes a week at a price of $1 a tape.

Willingness and Ability to Pay   Another way of looking at the demand curve is as a willingness-and-ability-to-pay curve. It tells us the highest price that someone is willing and able to pay for the last unit bought. If a large quantity is bought, that price is low; if a small quantity is bought, that price is high. In Fig. 4.2, if 9 million tapes are bought each week, the highest price that someone is willing to pay for the 9 millionth tape is $1. But if only 2 million tapes are bought each week, someone is willing to pay $5 for the last tape bought.

FIGURE   4.2

The Demand Curve

	Price (dollars per tape)	Quantity (millions of tapes per week)
a	1	9
b	2	6
c	3	4
d	4	3
e	5	2

The table shows a demand schedule listing the quantity of tapes demanded at each price if all other influences on buyers' plans remain the same. At a price of $1 a tape, 9 million tapes a week are demanded; at a price of $3 a tape, 4 million tapes a week are demanded. The demand curve shows the relationship between quantity demanded and price, everything else remaining the same. The demand curve slopes downward: As price decreases, the quantity demanded increases.

The demand curve can be read in two ways. For a given price, it tells us the quantity that people plan to buy. For example, at a price of $3 a tape, the quantity demanded is 4 million tapes a week. For a given quantity, the demand curve tells us the maximum price that consumers are willing and able to pay for the last tape bought. For example, the maximum price that consumers will pay for the 6 millionth tape is $2.

A Change in Demand

The term **demand** refers to the entire relationship between the quantity demanded and the price of a good, other things remaining the same. The demand for tapes is described by both the demand schedule and the demand curve in Fig. 4.2. To construct a demand schedule and a demand curve, we hold constant all the other influences on consumers' buying plans. What are the effects of each of those other influences?

1. Prices of Related Goods The quantity of tapes that consumers plan to buy depends in part on the prices of related goods and services that fall into two categories: substitutes and complements.

A **substitute** is a good that can be used in place of another good. For example, a bus ride substitutes for a train ride; a hamburger substitutes for a hot dog; a pear substitutes for an apple. As we have noted, tapes have many substitutes—prerecorded tapes, compact discs, radio and television broadcasts, and live concerts. If the price of one of these substitutes increases, people economize on its use and buy more tapes. For example, if the price of a compact disc rises, more tapes are bought and there is more taping of other people's discs—the demand for tapes increases.

A **complement** is a good that is used in conjunction with another good. Some examples of complements are hamburgers and french fries, party snacks and drinks, spaghetti and meat sauce, running shoes and jogging pants. Tapes also have complements: Walkmans, tape recorders, and stereo tape decks. If the price of one of these complements increases, people buy fewer tapes. For example, if the price of a Walkman rises, fewer Walkmans are bought and, as a consequence, fewer tapes are bought—the demand for tapes decreases.

2. Income Another influence on demand is consumer income. Other things remaining the same, when income increases, consumers buy more of most goods, and when income decreases, they buy less of most goods. Although an increase in income leads to an increase in the demand for *most* goods, it does not lead to an increase in the demand for *all* goods. **Normal goods** are those for which demand increases as income increases. **Inferior goods** are those for which demand decreases as income increases. An example of an inferior good is public transportation. The biggest users of public transportation are people with low incomes. As incomes increase, the demand for public transportation declines as more expensive, but more convenient, private transportation is substituted for it.

3. Expected Future Prices If the price of a good is expected to rise in the future and if the good can be stored, the opportunity cost of obtaining the good for future use is lower now than it will be when the price has increased. So people retime their purchase—they substitute over time. They buy more of the good before its price is expected to rise (and less after), so the current demand for the good increases.

For example, suppose that Florida is hit by a severe frost that damages the season's orange crop. You expect the price of orange juice to soar. So, anticipating the higher price, you fill your freezer with enough frozen juice to get you through the next six months. Your current demand for frozen orange juice has increased (and your future demand has decreased).

Similarly, if the price of a good is expected to fall in the future, the opportunity cost of buying the good in the present is high relative to what it is expected to be in the future. So again, people retime their purchases. They buy less of the good before its price is expected to fall (and more after), so the current demand for the good decreases.

Computer prices are constantly falling, and this fact poses a dilemma. Will you buy a new computer now, in time for the start of the school year, or will you wait until the price has fallen some more? Because people expect computer prices to keep falling, the current demand for computers is less (the future demand is greater) than it otherwise would be.

4. Population Demand also depends on the size and the age structure of the population. Other things remaining the same, the larger the population, the greater is the demand for all goods and services, and the smaller the population, the smaller is the demand for all goods and services.

For example, the demand for car parking space or movies or tapes or just about anything you can imagine, is much greater in New York City (population 8.5 million) than it is in Boise City, Idaho (population 320,000).

Also, other things remaining the same, the larger the proportion of the population in a given age group, the greater is the demand for the types of goods and services used by that age group.

For example, in 1995, there were about 3.3 million 19 year olds in the United States compared with almost 4 million in 1990. As a result, the demand for college places decreased during the 1990s. During these same years, the number of people living in the United States aged 85 years and over increased from 3 million in 1990 to 3.7 million. As a result, the demand for nursing home services increased.

5. Preferences   Demand depends on preferences. *Preferences* are an individual's attitudes toward goods and services. For example, a rock music fanatic has a much greater taste for tapes than does a tone-deaf workaholic. As a consequence, even if they have the same incomes, their demands for tapes will be very different.

Table 4.1 summarizes the influences on demand and the direction of those influences.

Movement Along Versus a Shift of the Demand Curve

Changes in the factors that influence buyers' plans cause either a movement along the demand curve or a shift of the demand curve.

TABLE 4.1

The Demand for Tapes

THE LAW OF DEMAND

The quantity of tapes demanded

Decreases if:	*Increases if:*
■ The price of a tape rises	■ The price of a tape falls

CHANGES IN DEMAND

The demand for tapes

Decreases if:	*Increases if:*
■ The price of a substitute falls	■ The price of a substitute rises
■ The price of a complement rises	■ The price of a complement falls
■ Income falls*	■ Income rises*
■ The price of a tape is expected to fall in the future	■ The price of a tape is expected to rise in the future
■ The population decreases	■ The population increases

*A tape is a normal good.

Movement Along the Demand Curve   If the price of a good changes but everything else remains the same, there is a movement along the demand curve. For example, if the price of a tape changes from $3 to $5, the result is a movement along the demand curve, from point *c* to point *e* in Fig. 4.2. The negative slope of the demand curve reveals that a decrease in the price of a good or service increases the quantity demanded—the law of demand.

A Shift of the Demand Curve   If the price of a good remains constant but some other influence on buyers' plans changes, there is a change in demand for that good. We illustrate a change in demand as a shift of the demand curve. For example, a fall in the price of the Walkman—a complement of tapes—increases the demand for tapes. We illustrate this increase in demand for tapes with a new demand schedule and a new demand curve. If the price of the Walkman falls, consumers buy more tapes regardless of whether the price of a tape is high or low. That is what a shift of the demand curve shows. It shows that more tapes are bought at each and every price.

Figure 4.3 illustrates such a shift. The table sets out the original demand schedule when the price of a Walkman is $200 and the new demand schedule when the price of a Walkman is $50. These numbers record the change in demand. The graph in Fig. 4.3 illustrates the corresponding shift of the demand curve. When the price of the Walkman falls, the demand curve for tapes shifts rightward.

A Change in Quantity Demanded Versus a Change in Demand   A point on the demand curve shows the quantity demanded at a given price. A movement along the demand curve shows a **change in the quantity demanded**. The entire demand curve shows demand, and a shift of the demand curve shows a **change in demand**.

Figure 4.4 illustrates and summarizes these distinctions. If the price of a good falls when everything else remains the same, the quantity demanded of that good increases, and there is a movement down the demand curve D_0. If the price rises when everything else remains the same, the quantity demanded decreases, and there is a movement up the demand curve D_0.

When any other influence on buyers' planned purchases changes, the demand curve shifts, and there is a *change* (an increase or a decrease) *in demand*. A rise in income (for a normal good), in population, in the price of a substitute, or in the

FIGURE 4.3
An Increase in Demand

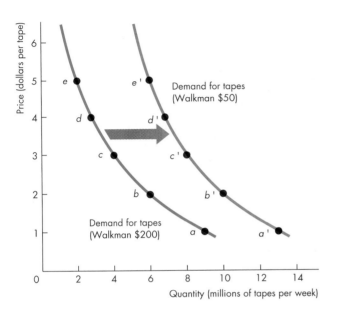

FIGURE 4.4
A Change in the Quantity Demanded Versus a Change in Demand

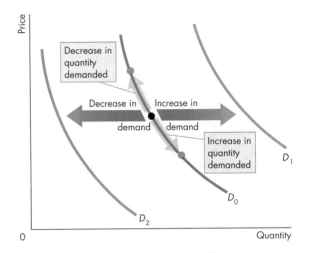

When the price of the good changes, there is a movement along the demand curve and *a change in the quantity demanded* of the good. For example, if the demand curve is D_0, a rise in the price of the good produces a decrease in the quantity demanded and a fall in the price of the good produces an increase in the quantity demanded. The blue arrows on demand curve D_0 represent these movements along the demand curve.

If some other influence on buying plans changes that increases the quantity people plan to buy, the demand curve shifts rightward (from D_0 to D_1) and *demand increases*. If some other influence on buying plans changes that reduces the quantity people plan to buy, the demand curve shifts leftward (from D_0 to D_2) and *demand decreases*.

Original demand schedule (Walkman $200)		New demand schedule (Walkman $50)		
Price (dollars per tape)	**Quantity** (millions of tapes per week)		**Price** (dollars per tape)	**Quantity** (millions of tapes per week)
a	1	9	*a'* 1	13
b	2	6	*b'* 2	10
c	3	4	*c'* 3	8
d	4	3	*d'* 4	7
e	5	2	*e'* 5	6

A change in any influence on buyers' plans other than the price of the good itself results in a new demand schedule and a shift of the demand curve. A change in the price of a Walkman changes the demand for tapes. At a price of $3 a tape (row *c* of the table), 4 million tapes a week are demanded when the Walkman costs $200 and 8 million tapes a week are demanded when the Walkman costs only $50. A *fall* in the price of a Walkman *increases* the demand for tapes because the Walkman is a complement of tapes. When demand *increases,* the demand curve shifts *rightward,* as shown by the shift arrow and the resulting red curve.

expected future price of the good or a fall in the price of a complement shifts the demand curve rightward (to the red demand curve D_1). This represents an *increase in demand.* A fall in income (for a normal good), in population, in the price of a substitute, or in the expected future price of the good or a rise in the price of a complement shifts the demand curve leftward (to the red demand curve D_2). This represents a *decrease in demand.* (For an inferior good, the effects of changes in income are in the direction opposite to those described above.)

■ The *quantity demanded* is the amount of a good that consumers plan to buy during a given period of time at a particular price. Other things remaining the same, the quantity demanded increases as price decreases.

■ *Demand* is the relationship between quantity demanded and price, other things remaining the same.

■ When the price of the good changes and all other influences on buying plans remain the same, there is a *change in the quantity demanded* and a *movement along the demand curve*.

■ When any influence on buying plans other than the price of the good changes, there is a *change in demand* and a *shift of the demand curve*.

Supply

WHEN SOMEONE HAS A SUPPLY OF A GOOD OR service, they have a definite plan to sell it. The amount of a good or service that producers plan to sell during a given time period at a particular price is called the **quantity supplied.** The quantity supplied is the maximum amount that producers are willing to sell at a given price and in given conditions. The quantity supplied is not necessarily the same as the quantity actually sold. If consumers do not want to buy the quantity producers plan to sell, their sales plans will be frustrated. Like the quantity demanded, the quantity supplied is expressed as an amount per unit of time.

What Determines Selling Plans?

The amount that producers plan to sell of any particular good or service depends on many factors. The main ones are

- The price of the good
- The prices of factors of production
- The prices of other goods produced
- Expected future prices
- The number of suppliers
- Technology

Let's first look at the relationship between the price of a good and the quantity supplied. To study this relationship, we hold constant all the other influences on the quantity supplied. We ask: How does the quantity supplied of a good vary as its price varies?

The Law of Supply

The law of supply states:

Other things remaining the same, the higher the price of a good, the greater is the quantity supplied.

Why does a higher price lead to a greater quantity supplied? It is because of increasing opportunity cost. The opportunity cost of supplying an additional unit of the good increases as the quantity produced increases. So the higher the price of a good, the more willing are producers to incur the higher opportunity cost of an increase in production.

Supply Schedule and Supply Curve

The table in Fig. 4.5 sets out the supply schedule for tapes. A *supply schedule* lists the quantities supplied at each different price when all other influences on the amount producers plan to sell remain the same. For example, if the price of a tape is $1, no tapes are supplied. If the price of a tape is $4, 5 million tapes are supplied each week.

Figure 4.5 illustrates the supply curve for tapes. A **supply curve** shows the relationship between the quantity supplied and the price of a good, everything else remaining the same. It is a graph of a supply schedule. The points on the supply curve labeled *a* through *e* represent the rows of the supply schedule. For example, point *d* represents a quantity supplied of 5 million tapes a week at a price of $4 a tape.

Minimum Supply Price Just as the demand curve has two interpretations, so too does the supply curve. It shows the quantity that producers plan to sell at each possible price. It also shows the minimum price at which the last unit will be supplied. For producers to be willing to supply the 3 millionth tape each week, the price must be at least $2 a tape. For producers to be willing to supply the 5 millionth tape each week, they must get at least $4 a tape.

A Change in Supply

The term **supply** refers to the entire relationship between the quantity supplied of a good and its price, other things remaining the same. The supply of tapes

FIGURE 4.5

The Supply Curve

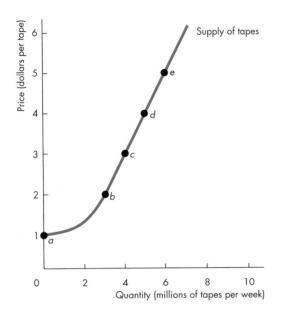

	Price	Quantity
	(dollars per tape)	(millions of tapes per week)
a	1	0
b	2	3
c	3	4
d	4	5
e	5	6

The table shows the supply schedule of tapes. For example, at $2 a tape, 3 million tapes a week are supplied; at $5 a tape, 6 million tapes a week are supplied. The supply curve shows the relationship between the quantity supplied and price, everything else remaining the same. The supply curve usually slopes upward: As the price of a good increases, so does the quantity supplied.

A supply curve can be read in two ways. For a given price, it tells us the quantity that producers plan to sell. For example, at a price of $3 a tape, producers plan to sell 4 million tapes a week. The supply curve also tells us the minimum price at which a given quantity will be offered for sale. For example, the minimum price that will bring forth a quantity supplied of 4 million tapes a week is $3 a tape.

is described by both the supply schedule and the supply curve in Fig. 4.5. To construct a supply schedule and a supply curve, we hold constant all the other influences on suppliers' plans. Let's now consider these other influences.

1. Prices of Factors of Production The prices of the factors of production used to produce a good influence its supply. For example, an increase in the prices of the labor and the capital equipment used to produce tapes increases the cost of producing tapes, so the supply of tapes decreases.

2. Prices of Other Goods Produced The supply of a good can be influenced by the prices of other goods. For example, if an automobile assembly line can produce either sports cars or sedans, the quantity of sedans produced will depend on the price of sports cars, and the quantity of sports cars produced will depend on the price of sedans. These two goods are *substitutes in production*. An increase in the price of a substitute in production lowers the supply of the good. Goods can also be complements in production. *Complements in production* arise when two things are, of necessity, produced together. For example, cattle produce beef and cowhide. An increase in the price of any one of these byproducts of cattle increases the supply of the other.

Blank tapes and prerecorded tapes are substitutes in production. An increase in the price of prerecorded tapes encourages producers to use their equipment to produce more prerecorded tapes, and so the supply of blank tapes decreases.

3. Expected Future Prices If the price of a good is expected to rise in the future, and if the good can be stored, the return from selling the good in the future is higher than it is in the present. So producers substitute over time. They offer a smaller quantity of the good for sale before its price is expected to rise (and a greater quantity later), so the current supply decreases. Similarly, if the price of a good is expected to fall in the future, the return from selling it in the present is high relative to what is expected. So again, producers substitute over time. They offer to sell more of the good before its price is expected to fall (and less later), so the current supply increases.

4. The Number of Suppliers Other things remaining the same, the larger the number of producers supplying a good, the larger is the supply of the good.

5. Technology   New technologies that enable producers to use less of each factor of production or cheaper factors of production lower the cost of production and increase supply. For example, the development of a new technology for tape production by Sony and Minnesota Mining and Manufacturing (3M) has lowered the cost of producing tapes and increased their supply. Over the long term, changes in technology are the most important influence on supply.

Table 4.2 summarizes the influences on supply and the directions of those influences.

Movement Along Versus a Shift of the Supply Curve

Changes in the factors that influence producers' planned sales cause either a movement along the supply curve or a shift of the supply curve.

Movement Along the Supply Curve   If the price of a good changes but everything else influencing suppliers' planned sales remains constant, there is a movement along the supply curve. For example, if the price of a tape increases from $3 to $5, there will be a movement along the supply curve from point *c* (4 million tapes a week) to point *e* (6 million tapes a week) in Fig. 4.5. The positive slope of the supply curve reveals that an increase in the price of a good or service increases the quantity demanded of it—the law of supply.

A Shift of the Supply Curve   If the price of a good remains the same but another influence on suppliers' planned sales changes, supply changes and there is a shift of the supply curve. For example, as we have already noted, technological advances lower the cost of producing tapes and increase their supply. As a result, the supply schedule changes. The table in Fig. 4.6 provides some hypothetical numbers that illustrate such a change. The table contains two supply schedules: one based on the original technology and one based on new technology. With the new technology, more tapes are supplied at each price. The graph in Fig. 4.6 illustrates the resulting shift of the supply curve. When tape-producing technology improves, the supply curve of tapes shifts rightward, as shown by the shift arrow and the red supply curve.

A Change in Quantity Supplied Versus a Change in Supply   A point on the supply curve shows the quantity supplied at a given price. A movement along

---

TABLE 4.2
The Supply of Tapes

THE LAW OF SUPPLY

The quantity of tapes supplied

Decreases if:	*Increases if:*
■ The price of a tape falls	■ The price of a tape rises

CHANGES IN SUPPLY

The supply of tapes

Decreases if:	*Increases if:*
■ The price of a factor of production used to produce tapes increases	■ The price of a factor of production used to produce tapes decreases
■ The price of a substitute in production rises	■ The price of a substitute in production falls
■ The price of a complement in production falls	■ The price of a complement in production rises
■ The price of a tape is expected to rise in the future	■ The price of a tape is expected to fall in the future
■ The number of firms supplying tapes decreases	■ The number of firms supplying tapes increases
	■ More efficient technologies for producing tapes are discovered

---

the supply curve shows a **change in the quantity supplied**. The entire supply curve shows supply. A shift of the supply curve shows a **change in supply**.

Figure 4.7 illustrates and summarizes these distinctions. If the price of a good falls and everything else remains the same, the quantity supplied of that good decreases and there is a movement down the supply curve S_0. If the price of a good rises and everything else remains the same, the quantity supplied increases, and there is a movement up the supply curve S_0. When any other influence on selling plans changes, the supply curve shifts and there is a *change in supply*. If the supply curve is S_0 and, say, a technological change reduces the amounts of the factors of production needed to produce the good, then supply increases and the supply curve shifts to the red supply curve S_1. If production costs rise, supply decreases and the supply curve shifts to the red supply curve S_2.

FIGURE 4.6
An Increase in Supply

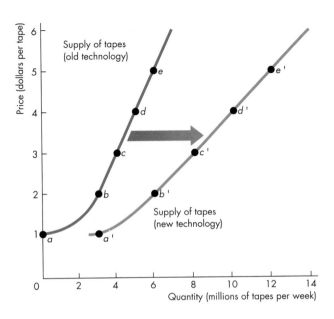

Original supply schedule Old technology			New supply schedule New technology		
	Price (dollars per tape)	**Quantity** (millions of tapes per week)		**Price** (dollars per tape)	**Quantity** (millions of tapes per week)
a	1	0	a'	1	3
b	2	3	b'	2	6
c	3	4	c'	3	8
d	4	5	d'	4	10
e	5	6	e'	5	12

A change in any influence on sellers other than the price of the good itself results in a new supply schedule and a shift of the supply curve. For example, if Sony and 3M invent a new, cost-saving technology for producing tapes, the supply of tapes changes.

At a price of $3 a tape, 4 million tapes a week are supplied when the producers use the old technology (row *c* of the table) and 8 million tapes a week are supplied with the new technology. An advance in technology *increases* the supply of tapes, and the supply curve shifts *rightward*, as shown by the shift arrow and the resulting red curve.

FIGURE 4.7
A Change in the Quantity Supplied Versus a Change in Supply

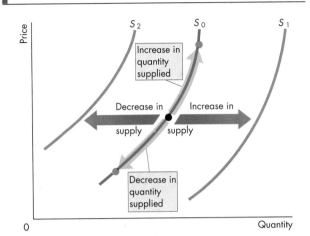

If the supply curve is S_0, a rise in the price *increases the quantity supplied*, and a fall in the price *decreases the quantity supplied*. The blue arrows on curve S_0 show these movements along the supply curve. If some other influence on supply changes that increases the quantity that producers plan to sell, the supply curve shifts rightward (from S_0 to S_1) and there is an *increase in supply*. If some other influence on supply changes that decreases the quantity the producers plan to sell, the supply curve shifts leftward (from S_0 to S_2) and there is a *decrease in supply*.

R E V I E W

- The *quantity supplied* is the amount of a good that producers plan to sell during a given period at a given price. Other things remaining the same, the quantity supplied increases as price increases.
- *Supply* is the relationship between quantity supplied and price, other things remaining the same.
- When the price of the good changes, other things remaining the same, there is a *change in the quantity supplied* and a *movement along the supply curve*.
- Changes in other influences on selling plans *change supply* and *shift the supply curve*.

Let's now bring demand and supply together and see how prices and quantities are determined.

Price Determination

WE HAVE SEEN THAT WHEN THE PRICE OF A good rises, the quantity demanded decreases and the quantity supplied increases. We are now going to see how adjustments in price coordinate the choices of buyers and sellers.

Price as a Regulator

The price of a good regulates the quantities demanded and supplied. If the price is too high, the quantity supplied exceeds the quantity demanded. If the price is too low, the quantity demanded exceeds the quantity supplied. There is one price, and only one price, at which the quantity demanded equals the quantity supplied. Let's work out what that price is.

The table in Fig. 4.8 shows the demand schedule (from Fig. 4.2) and the supply schedule (from Fig. 4.5). If the price of a tape is $1, the quantity demanded is 9 million tapes a week, but no tapes are supplied. The quantity demanded exceeds the quantity supplied by 9 million tapes a week. In other words, at a price of $1 a tape, there is a shortage of 9 million tapes a week. This shortage is shown in the final column of the table. At a price of $2 a tape, there is still a shortage, but only of 3 million tapes a week. If the price of a tape is $5, the quantity supplied exceeds the quantity demanded. The quantity supplied is 6 million tapes a week, but the quantity demanded is only 2 million. There is a surplus of 4 million tapes a week. The one price at which there is neither a shortage nor a surplus is $3 a tape. At that price, the quantity demanded is equal to the quantity supplied—4 million tapes a week.

Figure 4.8 shows the market for tapes. The demand curve (of Fig. 4.2) and the supply curve (of Fig. 4.5) intersect when the price is $3 a tape. At that price, the quantity demanded and supplied is 4 million tapes a week. At each price *above* $3 a tape, the quantity supplied exceeds the quantity demanded. There is a surplus of tapes. For example, at $4 a tape the surplus is 2 million tapes a week, as shown by the blue arrow in the figure. At each price *below* $3 a tape, the quantity demanded exceeds the quantity supplied. There is a shortage of tapes. For example, at $2 a tape, the shortage is 3 million tapes a week, as shown by the red arrow in the figure.

FIGURE 4.8

Equilibrium

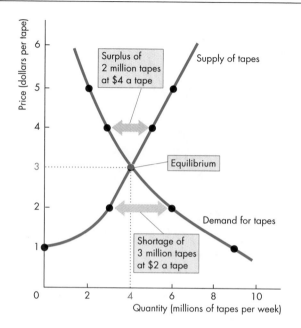

Price (dollars per tape)	Quantity demanded	Quantity supplied	Shortage (–) or surplus (+)
	(millions of tapes per week)		
1	9	0	–9
2	6	3	–3
3	4	4	0
4	3	5	+2
5	2	6	+4

The table lists the quantities demanded and quantities supplied as well as the shortage or surplus of tapes at each price. If the price is $2 a tape, 6 million tapes a week are demanded and 3 million are supplied. There is a shortage of 3 million tapes a week, and the price rises. If the price is $4 a tape, 3 million tapes a week are demanded and 5 million are supplied. There is a surplus of 2 million tapes a week, and the price falls. If the price is $3 a tape, 4 million tapes a week are demanded and 4 million are supplied. There is neither a shortage nor a surplus. Neither buyers nor sellers have any incentive to change the price. The price at which the quantity demanded equals the quantity supplied is the equilibrium price.

Equilibrium

An *equilibrium* is a situation in which opposing forces balance each other. Equilibrium in a market occurs when the price is such that the opposing forces of the plans of buyers and sellers balance each other. The **equilibrium price** is the price at which the quantity demanded equals the quantity supplied. The **equilibrium quantity** is the quantity bought and sold at the equilibrium price.

To see why equilibrium occurs where the quantity demanded equals the quantity supplied, we need to see how buyers and sellers behave if there is a shortage or a surplus.

A Shortage Forces the Price Up   Suppose the price of a tape is $2. Consumers plan to buy 6 million tapes a week, and producers plan to sell 3 million tapes a week. Consumers can't force producers to sell, so the quantity actually offered for sale is 3 million tapes a week. In this situation, powerful forces operate to increase the price and move it toward the equilibrium price. Some people, unable to find the tapes they planned to buy, offer to pay more. And some producers, noticing lines of unsatisfied consumers, move their prices up. As buyers try to outbid one another, and as producers push their prices up, the price rises toward its equilibrium. The rising price reduces the shortage because it decreases the quantity demanded and increases the quantity supplied. When the price has increased to the point at which there is no longer a shortage, the forces moving the price stop operating, and the price comes to rest at its equilibrium.

A Surplus Forces the Price Down   Suppose the price of a tape is $4. Producers plan to sell 5 million tapes a week, and consumers plan to buy 3 million tapes a week. Producers cannot force consumers to buy, so the quantity that is actually bought is 3 million tapes a week. In this situation, powerful forces operate to lower the price and move it toward the equilibrium price while eliminating the surplus. Some producers, unable to sell the quantities of tapes they planned to sell, cut their prices. In addition, some producers scale back production. And some buyers, noticing shelves of unsold tapes, offer to buy for a lower price. As producers try to undercut one another, and as buyers make lower price offers, the price falls toward its equilibrium. The falling price reduces the surplus because it increases the quantity demanded and decreases the quantity supplied. When the price has decreased to the point at which there is no longer a surplus, the forces moving the price stop operating, and the price comes to rest at its equilibrium.

The Best Deal Available for Buyers and Sellers
Both situations we have just examined result in price changes. In the first case, the price starts out at $2 and is bid upward. In the second case, the price starts out at $4 and producers undercut each other. In both cases, prices change until they hit the price of $3 a tape. At that price, the quantity demanded and the quantity supplied are equal, and neither buyers nor sellers can do business at a better price. Consumers pay the highest price they are willing to pay for the last unit bought, and producers receive the lowest price at which they are willing to supply the last unit sold.

When people freely make bids and offers and when buyers seek the lowest price and sellers seek the highest price, the price at which trade takes place is the equilibrium price—the quantity demanded equals the quantity supplied.

R E V I E W

- The *equilibrium price* is the price at which buyers' and sellers' plans match each other—the price at which the quantity demanded equals the quantity supplied.
- At prices below the equilibrium, there is a shortage and the price rises.
- At prices above the equilibrium, there is a surplus and the price falls.
- Only at the equilibrium price are there no forces acting on the price to make it change.

The theory of demand and supply that you have just studied is now a central part of economics. But that was not always so. Only 100 years ago, the best economists of the day were quite confused about matters that today students in introductory courses can get right—see *Economics in History* on pp. 94–95.

You'll discover in the rest of this chapter that the theory of demand and supply helps us to understand and make predictions about changes in prices—including the price slides, rockets, and roller coasters described in the chapter opener.

Predicting Changes in Price and Quantity

THE THEORY WE HAVE JUST STUDIED PROVIDES us with a powerful way of analyzing influences on prices and the quantities bought and sold. According to the theory, a change in price stems from either a change in demand or a change in supply or a change in both. Let's look first at the effects of a change in demand.

A Change in Demand

What happens to the price and quantity of tapes if the demand for tapes increases? We can answer this question with a specific example. If the price of a Walkman falls from $200 to $50, the demand for tapes increases, as is shown in the table in Fig. 4.9. (Recall that tapes and Walkmans are complements and that when the price of a complement falls, the demand for the good increases.) The original demand schedule and the new one are set out in the first three columns of the table. The table also shows the supply schedule for tapes.

The original equilibrium price is $3 a tape. At that price, 4 million tapes a week are demanded and supplied. When demand increases, the price that makes the quantity demanded equal the quantity supplied is $5 a tape. At this price, 6 million tapes are bought and sold each week. When demand increases, both the price and the quantity increase.

Figure 4.9 shows these changes. The figure shows the original demand for and supply of tapes. The original equilibrium price is $3 a tape, and the quantity is 4 million tapes a week. When demand increases, the demand curve shifts rightward. The equilibrium price rises to $5 a tape, and the quantity supplied increases to 6 million tapes a week, as highlighted in the figure. There is an increase in the quantity supplied but *no change in supply*. That is, the supply curve does not shift.

The exercise that we've just conducted can easily be reversed. If we start at a price of $5 a tape, with 6 million tapes a week being bought and sold, we can then work out what happens if demand decreases to its original level. You can see that the decrease in demand lowers the equilibrium price to $3 a tape and decreases the equilibrium quantity to 4 million tapes

FIGURE 4.9

The Effects of a Change in Demand

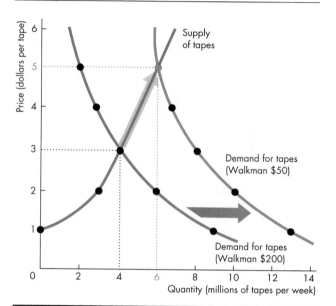

Price (dollars per tape)	Quantity demanded (millions of tapes per week)		Quantity supplied (millions of tapes per week)
	Walkman $200	Walkman $50	
1	9	13	0
2	6	10	3
3	4	8	4
4	3	7	5
5	2	6	6

With the price of a Walkman at $200, the demand for tapes is the blue curve. The equilibrium price is $3 a tape and the equilibrium quantity is 4 million tapes a week. When the price of a Walkman falls from $200 to $50, the demand for tapes increases and the demand curve shifts rightward to become the red curve. At $3 a tape, there is now a shortage of 4 million tapes a week.

The price of a tape rises to a new equilibrium of $5 a tape. As the price rises to $5, the quantity supplied increases—shown by the blue arrow on the supply curve—to the new equilibrium quantity of 6 million tapes a week. Following an increase in demand, the quantity supplied increases but supply does not change—the supply curve does not shift.

a week. Such a decrease in demand might arise from a decrease in the price of compact discs or of CD players. (CDs and CD players are substitutes for tapes.)

We can now make our first two predictions, other things remaining the same:

■ When demand increases, both the price and the quantity increase.
■ When demand decreases, both the price and the quantity decrease.

A Change in Supply

Suppose that Sony and 3M introduce a new cost-saving technology in their tape production plants. The new technology increases the supply of tapes. The new supply schedule (the same one that was shown in Fig. 4.6) is presented in the table in Fig. 4.10. What are the new equilibrium price and quantity? The answer is highlighted in the table: The price falls to $2 a tape, and the quantity increases to 6 million a week. You can see why by looking at the quantities demanded and supplied at the old price of $3 a tape. The quantity supplied at that price is 8 million tapes a week, and there is a surplus of tapes. The price falls. Only when the price is $2 a tape does the quantity supplied equal the quantity demanded.

Figure 4.10 illustrates the effect of an increase in supply. It shows the demand curve for tapes and the original and new supply curves. The initial equilibrium price is $3 a tape, and the original quantity is 4 million tapes a week. When the supply increases, the supply curve shifts rightward. The equilibrium price falls to $2 a tape, and the quantity demanded increases to 6 million tapes a week, highlighted in the figure. There is an increase in the quantity demanded but *no change in demand*. That is, the demand curve does not shift.

The exercise that we've just conducted can be reversed. If we start out at a price of $2 a tape with 6 million tapes a week being bought and sold, we can work out what happens if supply decreases to its original level. The decrease in supply shifts the supply curve leftward. The equilibrium price rises to $3 a tape, and the equilibrium quantity decreases to 4 million tapes a week. Such a decrease in supply might arise from an increase in the cost of labor or raw materials.

FIGURE 4.10
The Effects of a Change in Supply

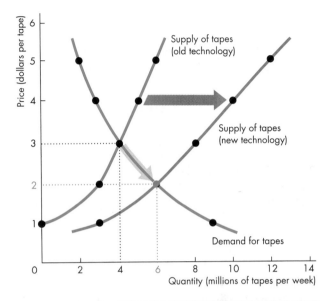

Price	Quantity demanded	Quantity supplied (millions of tapes per week)	
(dollars per tape)	(millions of tapes per week)	(old technology)	(new technology)
1	9	0	3
2	6	3	6
3	4	4	8
4	3	5	10
5	2	6	12

With the old technology, the supply of tapes is shown by the blue supply curve. The equilibrium price is $3 a tape, and the equilibrium quantity is 4 million tapes a week. When the new technology is adopted, the supply of tapes increases and the supply curve shifts rightward to become the red curve.

At $3 a tape, there is now a surplus of 4 million tapes a week. The price of a tape falls to a new equilibrium of $2 a tape. As the price falls to $2, the quantity demanded increases—shown by the blue arrow on the demand curve—to the new equilibrium quantity of 6 million tapes a week. Following an increase in supply, the quantity demanded increases but demand does not change—the demand curve does not shift.

We can now make two more predictions, other things remaining the same:

■ When supply increases, the quantity increases and the price falls.
■ When supply decreases, the quantity decreases and the price rises.

Reading Between the Lines on pp. 86–89 explores two further examples of changes in demand and supply—in the markets for pagers and for coffee.

A Change in Both Demand and Supply

In the above exercises, either demand or supply changed, but only one at a time. In each of these cases, we can predict the direction of change of the price and the quantity. But if demand and supply change together, we cannot always say what will happen to both the price and the quantity. We'll look at two cases in which both demand and supply change. First, we'll see what happens when they both change in the same direction—both demand and supply increase (or decrease) together. Then we'll look at the case in which they move in opposite directions—demand decreases and supply increases or demand increases and supply decreases.

Demand and Supply Change in the Same Direction   We've seen that an increase in the demand for tapes increases the price of tapes and increases the quantity bought and sold. And we've seen that an increase in the supply of tapes lowers the price of tapes and increases the quantity bought and sold. Let's now examine what happens when both of these changes happen to occur together.

The table in Fig. 4.11 brings together the numbers that describe the original quantities demanded and supplied and the new quantities demanded and supplied after the fall in the price of the Walkman and the improved tape production technology. These same numbers are illustrated in the graph. The original (blue) demand and supply curves intersect at a price of $3 a tape and a quantity of 4 million tapes a week. The new (red) supply and demand curves also intersect at a price of $3 a tape but at a quantity of 8 million tapes a week.

An increase in either demand or supply increases the quantity. Therefore when both demand and supply increase, so does quantity.

FIGURE 4.11

The Effects of an Increase in Both Demand and Supply

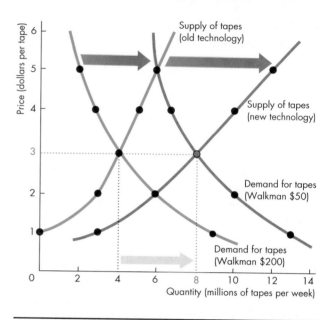

	Original quantities (millions of tapes per week)		New quantities (millions of tapes per week)	
Price (dollars per tape)	**Quantity demanded** (Walkman $200)	**Quantity supplied** (old technology)	**Quantity demanded** (Walkman $50)	**Quantity supplied** (new technology)
1	9	0	13	3
2	6	3	10	6
3	4	4	8	8
4	3	5	7	10
5	2	6	6	12

When a Walkman costs $200 and the old technology is used to produce tapes, the price of a tape is $3 and the quantity is 4 million tapes a week. A fall in the price of a Walkman increases the demand for tapes, and improved technology increases the supply of tapes. The new supply curve intersects the new demand curve at $3 a tape, the same price as before, but the quantity increases to 8 million tapes a week. These increases in demand and supply increase the quantity but leave the price unchanged.

An increase in demand increases the price, and an increase in supply lowers the price, so we can't say for sure which way the price will change when demand and supply increase together. In this example, the increases in demand and supply are such that the rise in price brought about by an increase in demand is offset by the fall in price brought about by an increase in supply—so the price does not change. But notice that if demand had increased slightly more than shown in the figure, the price would have risen. If supply had increased by slightly more than shown in the figure, the price would have fallen.

We can now make two more predictions:

■ When *both* demand and supply increase, the quantity increases and the price increases, decreases, or remains constant.

■ When *both* demand and supply decrease, the quantity decreases and the price increases, decreases, or remains constant.

Demand and Supply Change in Opposite Directions   Let's now see what happens when demand and supply change together but move in *opposite* directions. We'll look yet again at the market for tapes, but this time supply increases and demand decreases. An improved production technology increases the supply of tapes as before. But now the price of CD players falls. A CD player is a *substitute* for tapes. With less costly CD players, more people buy them and switch from buying tapes to buying discs, and the demand for tapes decreases.

The table in Fig. 4.12 describes the original and new demand and supply schedules, and these schedules are shown as the original (blue) and new (red) demand and supply curves in the graph. The original demand and supply curves intersect at a price of $5 a tape and a quantity of 6 million tapes a week. The new supply and demand curves intersect at a price of $2 a tape and at the original quantity of 6 million tapes a week.

A decrease in demand or an increase in supply lowers the price. Therefore when a decrease in demand and an increase in supply occur together, the price falls.

A decrease in demand decreases the quantity, and an increase in supply increases the quantity, so we can't say for sure which way the quantity will change when demand decreases and supply increases at the same time. In this example, the decrease in demand and the increase in supply are such that the increase

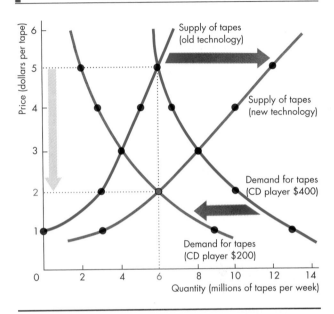

FIGURE 4.12

The Effects of a Decrease in Demand and an Increase in Supply

Price (dollars per tape)	Original quantities (millions of tapes per week)		New quantities (millions of tapes per week)	
	Quantity demanded (CD player $400)	Quantity supplied (old technology)	Quantity demanded (CD player $200)	Quantity supplied (new technology)
1	13	0	9	3
2	10	3	6	6
3	8	4	4	8
4	7	5	3	10
5	6	6	2	12

When a CD player costs $400 and the old technology is used to produce tapes, the price of a tape is $5 and the quantity is 6 million tapes a week. A fall in the price of a CD player decreases the demand for tapes, and improved technology increases the supply of tapes. The new supply curve intersects the new demand curve at $2, a lower price, but in this case the quantity remains constant at 6 million tapes a week. This decrease in demand and increase in supply lowers the price but leaves the quantity unchanged.

in quantity brought about by an increase in supply is offset by the decrease in quantity brought about by a decrease in demand—so the quantity does not change. But notice that if demand had decreased slightly more than shown in the figure, the quantity would have decreased. And if supply had increased by slightly more than shown in the figure, the quantity would have increased.

We can now make two more predictions:

- When demand decreases and supply increases, the price falls and the quantity increases, decreases, or remains constant.
- When demand increases and supply decreases, the price rises and the quantity increases, decreases, or remains constant.

CD Players, Health Care, and Bananas

Earlier in this chapter, we looked at some facts about prices and quantities of CD players, health care, and bananas. Let's use the theory of demand and supply that we have just studied to explain the movements in the prices and quantities of those goods.

A Price Slide: CD Players   Figure 4.13(a) shows the market for CD players. In 1983, when CD players were first manufactured, very few producers made them, and the supply was small. The supply curve was S_0. In 1983, there weren't many titles on CDs and the demand for CD players was small. The demand curve was D_0. The quantities supplied and demanded in 1983 were equal at Q_0, and the price was $1,100 (1994 dollars). As the technology for making CD players improved and as more and more factories began to produce CD players, the supply increased by a large amount, and the supply curve shifted rightward from S_0 to S_1. At the same time, increases in incomes, a decrease in the price of CDs, and an increase in the number of titles on CDs increased the demand for CD players. But the increase in demand was much smaller than the increase in supply. The demand curve shifted rightward from D_0 to D_1. With the new demand curve D_1 and the new supply curve S_1, the equilibrium price fell to $170, and the quantity increased to Q_1. The large increase in supply combined with a smaller increase in demand resulted in an increase in the quantity of CD players and a dramatic fall in the price. Figure 4.13(a) shows the CD player price slide.

A Price Rocket: Health Care   Figure 4.13(b) shows the market for health-care services. In 1980, the supply curve for health-care services was S_0. Advances in medical technology have greatly increased the range and complexity of conditions that can be treated and have increased the supply of health-care services. But large increases in doctors' compensation and costs have escalated the cost of providing health care and have decreased supply. The net change in supply resulting from these two opposing forces has been an increase. The supply curve has shifted rightward from S_0 to S_1. At the same time that supply increased by a relatively modest amount, the demand for health care increased enormously. Some of the increase resulted from higher incomes, some from an aging population, and some from a demand for newly available treatments. The combination of these influences on demand resulted in the demand curve shifting from D_0 to D_1. The combined effect of a large increase in demand and a small increase in supply was an increase in the quantity from Q_0 to Q_1 and an increase in price from 100 (an index number) in 1980 to 160 in 1994. Figure 4.13(b) shows the health-care price rocket.

A Price Roller Coaster: Bananas   Figure 4.13(c) shows the market for bananas. The demand for bananas—curve D—does not change much over the years. But the supply of bananas, which depends mainly on the weather, fluctuates between S_0 and S_1. With good growing conditions, the supply curve is S_1. With bad growing conditions, supply decreases and the supply curve is S_0. As a consequence of fluctuations in supply, the quantity fluctuates between Q_0 and Q_1. The price of bananas fluctuates between 32 cents per pound (1994 cents), the maximum price, and 23 cents per pound, the minimum price. Figure 4.13(c) shows the bananas price roller coaster.

◆   By using the theory of demand and supply, you can explain past fluctuations in prices and quantities and also make predictions about future fluctuations. But you will want to do more than predict whether prices are going to rise or fall. In your study of microeconomics, you will learn to predict *by how much* they will change. In your study of macroeconomics, you will learn to explain fluctuations in the economy as a whole. In fact, the theory of demand and supply can help answer almost every economic question.

FIGURE 4.13
Price Slide, Rocket, and Roller Coaster

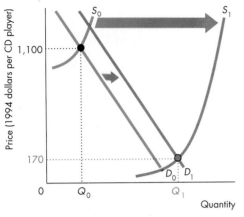

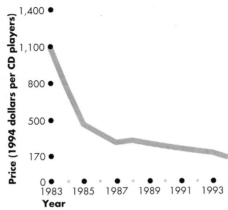

(a) Price slide: CD players

A large increase in the supply of CD players, from S_0 to S_1 combined with a small increase in demand, from D_0 to D_1, resulted in an increase in the quantity of CD players bought and sold from Q_0 to Q_1. The average price of CD players fell from $1,100 in 1982 to $170 in 1994—a price slide.

Source: U.S Bureau of the Census, *Statistical Abstract of the United States: 1994* (114th edition.) Washington, DC, 1994.

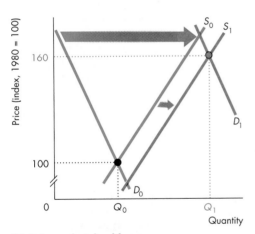

(b) Price rocket: health care

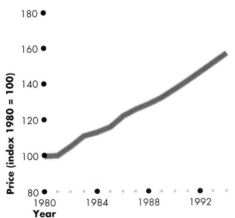

A large increase in demand for health care, from D_0 to D_1, combined with a small increase in the supply, has resulted in an increase in the quantity of health care, from Q_0 to Q_1 and a rise in the price of health care from 100 in 1980 to 160 in 1994—a price rocket.

Source: Economic Report of the President, 1994.

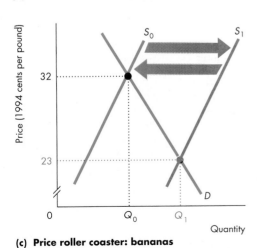

(c) Price roller coaster: bananas

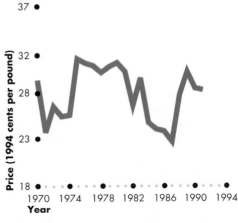

The demand for bananas remains constant at D. But supply fluctuates between S_0 and S_1. As a result, the price of bananas has fluctuated between 23 cents per pound and 32 cents per pound—a price roller coaster.

Source: International Financial Statistics Yearbook, International Monetary Fund, Washington, D.C., 1993.

Demand and Supply: Price of Pagers

THE BOSTON GLOBE, MAY 6, 1994

At Your Beep and Call

BY MICHAEL PUTZEL

WASHINGTON—Don't look now, but somebody's trying to get your attention.

Spurred by better, cheaper technology and a price war that has brought the cost down to consumer levels, all sorts of people are using beepers these days.

The Bugaboo Creek Family Steak House in Seekonk, Mass., is among a growing number of busy restaurants that hand pagers to customers when they arrive and then beep them when their tables are ready.

Kid Klubhouse, a day-care center in Tigard, Ore., loans a pager to each parent who drops a child off in the morning and beeps the parent for advice if there's a problem with the child during the day.

And get this one: A dairy farmer in Japan calls his cows in at milking time every evening by dialing the number for his lead bovine, who has a vibrating pager strapped to her neck and knows to head for the barn when she feels the tickle. I don't have the farmer's name, but people in the industry swear this is a true story.

Motorola, which makes 85 percent of the pagers sold or leased in this country, says there are 18 million pagers in service in the United States, and the company estimates that figure will more than double within three years.

The manufacturer has recently introduced two new lines aimed at the nonbusiness user, which is where the action is in this growth industry. Pagers—the preferred term since many of them don't "beep" anymore—now come in hot colors like "Bimini Blue" and "Totally Teal." And there is an increasing array of features, from musical signaling to automatic relaying of news bulletins. ...

On the horizon is a Seiko watch that goes on sale later this year with a built-in pager that has limited text messages and reports sports and winning lottery numbers. Two-way pagers that will let you reply to a beeped message are in development, to be announced soon.

With the purchase price of cellular phones falling even faster than pagers, it might seem reasonable to expect wireless telephones to replace beepers. But an analyst who specializes in watching developments in wireless technology said there is no indication that is going to happen in the foreseeable future, and studies show continued growth of pager sales at about 25 percent a year. ...

Reprinted by permission.

Economic

A N A L Y S I S

■ Figure 1 shows the market for pagers. The demand curve is *D* and initially, the supply curve is S_0. The price of a pager is $300, and 1 million pagers a year are bought.

■ The lower the price of a pager, other things remaining the same, the more uses people find for pagers—calling diners to the table at a restaurant, alerting parents to problems at a day-care center, even calling cows for milking.

■ As technology has advanced and as new firms have entered the pager market, supply has increased and the supply curve in Fig. 1 has shifted rightward to S_1.

■ If this were the only change in the market for pagers, the price of a pager would have fallen to $200 in this example, and there would have been an increase in the quantity of pagers demanded—shown by a movement along the demand curve—to 7 million a year.

■ But another change has influenced the market for pagers. Technological advances have increased the supply and decreased the prices of all forms of wireless communication, including the cellular telephone, which is a *substitute* for a pager.

■ The fall in the price of a cellular telephone (a substitute for a pager) has decreased the demand for pagers. The leftward shift of the demand curve from D_0 to D_1 in Fig. 2 illustrates this decrease in demand.

■ The decrease in the demand for pagers has lowered the price even farther, to $100 in this example, and brought a decrease in the quantity supplied—shown by the movement along the supply curve in Fig. 2.

■ Because the supply of pagers has increased and the demand for pagers has decreased, the price of a pager has fallen.

■ But because the increase in the quantity demanded in Fig. 1 is larger than the decrease in the quantity supplied in Fig. 2, the quantity of pagers bought has increased.

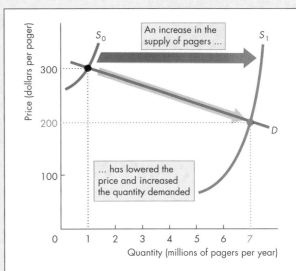

Figure 1

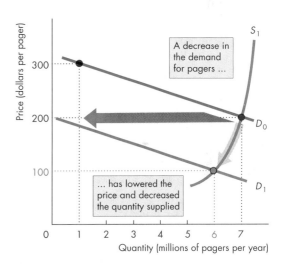

Figure 2

Demand and Supply: Price of Coffee

USA TODAY, AUGUST 4, 1994

Coffee Is a Force We Can't Resist

BY ELLEN BEUBORNE AND
MICHELINE MAYNARD

If you haven't had that first cup of coffee yet, better gulp it before reading on.

The price of coffee soared 150% this summer, and there's nothing you can do about it—short of switching to cola or tea.

Debra Craig, a cashier at Ralph's supermarket in Long Beach, Calif., says shelf prices for java jumped three times in three weeks. But that hasn't slowed coffee sales.

"Sometimes, I think coffee is like gasoline. You need it for fuel," she says. When the price of avocados hit $1.69 a piece, shoppers howled. But when some coffee brands shot up 40 cents a pound last month, customers pretended not to notice.

Craig hasn't even needed to flash the memo her manager wrote, blaming hikes on back-to-back frosts in Brazil. "You may grumble, but there's no way you'll take it off the (conveyor) belt and put it back on the shelf," Craig says. ...

We grumble, but we keep on buying. Coffee is a force we can't resist.

How did it happen?

Half of us won't start the day without a cup. In a year, we consume an average 10 to 15 pounds per person; in world-leading Finland, 37.5 pounds is the norm. ...

Coffee is a cultural mainstay. It's the national drink, as tea is to England. Coffee break, coffee klatch, coffee table, coffee house are all proper nouns here. Blame Boston as the root of all things coffee: The USA's first coffeehouse, the London Coffee House, opened there in 1689, predating the Salem witch trials and the Boston Tea Party. Revolutionaries Daniel Webster, Paul Revere and John Adams later hung out at the Green Dragon coffee house there. And the first public reading of the Declaration of Independence was held at still another Beantown coffeehouse, The Bunch of Grapes. ...

© Copyright 1994, USA Today. Reprinted with permission.

Essence of THE STORY

■ Fifty percent of Americans begin the day with coffee, and average consumption is 10 to 15 pounds per person per year.

■ The price of coffee increased by 150 percent in the summer of 1994.

■ The price increase was blamed on back-to-back frosts in Brazil.

■ People grumbled but kept on buying coffee. The higher price did not decrease coffee sales.

■ When the price of avocados increased to $1.69 each, shoppers howled.

Economic

A N A L Y S I S

■ Figure 1 shows the market for coffee. The demand curve for coffee, *D* reflects the fact that people regard other beverages (such as tea and cola) as poor substitutes for coffee. Even a large price rise brings a small decrease in the quantity demanded.

■ With normal coffee production in Brazil, the supply curve is S_0, the (wholesale) price is $1.00 per pound, and the quantity of coffee bought and sold is Q_0.

■ Back-to-back frosts in Brazil (a major supplier) decreases the supply of coffee, and the supply curve shifts leftward to S_1.

■ At a price of $1.00 a pound, the quantity of coffee supplied falls to Q_2 and creates a shortage of coffee, which brings a price rise of $1.50—an increase of 150 percent—to $2.50.

■ As the price rises, the quantity of coffee demanded decreases—a movement along the demand curve for coffee.

■ Also, as the price rises, the quantity of coffee sup-

plied increases—a movement along the new supply curve for coffee. (This increase in the quantity supplied comes from other regions and possibly from roasters' inventories).

■ Figure 2 shows the market for avocados, also mentioned in the news story.

■ The demand curve for avocados reflects the fact that people can easily find close substitutes for them. So a relatively small price increase brings a large decrease in the quantity demanded.

■ A poor avocado crop decreases the supply of avocados from S_0 to S_1.

■ At the original price of 99 cents per avocado, the quantity supplied falls to Q_2 and creates a shortage of avocados.

■ The price rises to $1.69. The rise in price brings a huge decrease in the quantity demanded and only a small increase in the quantity supplied. The quantity decreases to Q_1.

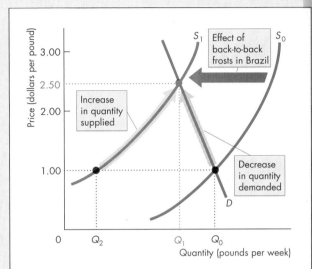

Figure 1 Coffee

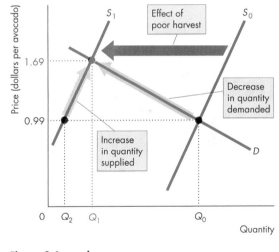

Figure 2 Avocados

SUMMARY

Opportunity Cost and Price

Opportunity cost is measured by a relative price —the money price of one good or service divided by the money price of another good or service. A convenient way to express opportunity cost and relative price is in terms of a "basket" of all other goods and services—the price of one good divided by the price (index) of a basket of all goods. The theory of demand and supply explains how relative prices are determined. (pp. 68–69)

Demand

The quantity demanded of a good or service is the amount that consumers plan to buy during a given time period at a particular price. The quantity that consumers plan to buy of any good depends on:

- The price of the good
- The prices of related goods—substitutes and complements
- Income
- Expected future prices
- Population
- Preferences

Other things remaining the same, the higher the price of a good, the smaller is the quantity demanded of that good. The relationship between the quantity demanded and price, all other influences on buying plans remaining the same, is illustrated by the demand schedule or demand curve. A change in the price of a good produces a movement along the demand curve for that good. Such a movement is called a change in the quantity demanded.

Changes in all other influences on buying plans change demand. When demand changes, there is a new demand schedule and the demand curve shifts. When demand increases, the demand curve shifts rightward; when demand decreases, the demand curve shifts leftward. (pp. 69–74)

Supply

The quantity supplied of a good or service is the amount that producers plan to sell during a given time period at a particular price. The quantity that producers plan to sell of any good or service depends on:

- The price of the good
- The prices of factors of production
- The prices of other goods produced
- Expected future prices
- The number of suppliers
- Technology

Other things remaining the same, the higher the price of a good, the larger is the quantity supplied of that good. The relationship between the quantity supplied and price, all other influences on selling plans remaining the same, is illustrated by the supply schedule or supply curve. A change in the price of a good produces a movement along the supply curve for that good. Such a movement is called a change in the quantity supplied.

Changes in all other influences on selling plans change supply. When supply changes, there is a new supply schedule and the supply curve shifts. When supply increases, the supply curve shifts rightward; when supply decreases, the supply curve shifts leftward. (pp. 74–77)

Price Determination

Price regulates the quantities supplied and demanded. The higher the price, the greater is the quantity supplied and the smaller is the quantity demanded. There is one price at which the quantity demanded equals the quantity supplied. That price is the equilibrium price. At higher prices, there is a surplus—an excess of the quantity supplied over the quantity demanded—and the price falls. At lower prices, there is a shortage—an excess of the quantity demanded over the quantity supplied—and the price rises. (pp. 78–79)

Predicting Changes in Price and Quantity

Changes in demand and supply lead to changes in price and in the quantity bought and sold. An increase in demand leads to a rise in price and to an increase in quantity. A decrease in demand leads to a fall in price and to a decrease in quantity. An increase in supply leads to an increase in quantity and to a fall in price. A decrease in supply leads to a decrease in quantity and a rise in price.

Simultaneous increases in demand and supply increase the quantity bought and sold, but the price can rise, fall, or remain constant. If the increase in demand is larger than the increase in supply, the price rises. If the increase in demand is smaller than the increase in supply, the price falls. If demand and supply increase by the same amounts, the price does not change. Simultaneous opposing changes in demand and supply such as an increase in supply and a decrease in demand decrease the price, but the quantity can increase, decrease, or remain constant. If the decrease in demand is larger than the increase in supply, the quantity decreases. If the decrease in demand is smaller than the increase in supply, the quantity increases. If the decrease in demand equals the increase in supply, the quantity does not change. (pp. 80–85)

K E Y   E L E M E N T S

Key Figures and Tables

Key Terms

R E V I E W   Q U E S T I O N S

1. Distinguish between a money price and a relative price. Which is an opportunity cost and why?
2. Define the quantity demanded of a good or service.
3. Define the quantity supplied of a good or service.
4. List the main factors that influence the amount that consumers plan to buy and say whether an increase in the factor increases or decreases consumers' planned purchases.
5. List the main factors that influence the quantity that producers plan to sell and say whether an increase in that factor increases or decreases firms' planned sales.
6. State the law of demand and the law of supply.
7. If a fixed amount of a good is available, what does the demand curve tell us about the price that consumers are willing to pay for that fixed quantity?
8. If consumers are willing to buy only a certain fixed quantity, what does the supply curve tell us about the price at which firms will supply that quantity?
9. Distinguish between:
   a. A change in demand and a change in the quantity demanded

b. A change in supply and a change in the quantity supplied

10. Why is the price at which the quantity demanded equals the quantity supplied the equilibrium price?

11. What is the effect on the price of a tape and the quantity of tapes sold if:
a. The price of CDs increases?

b. The price of a Walkman increases?
c. The supply of CD players increases?
d. Consumers' incomes increase and firms producing tapes switch to new cost-saving technology?
e. The prices of the factors of production used to make tapes increase?

P R O B L E M S

1. Suppose that one of the following events occurs:
a. The price of gasoline rises.
b. The price of gasoline falls.
c. All speed limits on highways are abolished.
d. A new fuel-efficient engine that runs on cheap alcohol is invented.
e. The population doubles.
f. Robotic production plants lower the cost of producing cars.
g. A law banning car imports from Japan is passed.
h. The rates for auto insurance double.
i. The minimum age for drivers is increased to 19 years.
j. A massive and high-grade oil supply is discovered in Mexico.
k. The environmental lobby succeeds in closing down all nuclear power stations.
l. The price of cars rises.
m. The price of cars falls.
n. The summer temperature is 10 degrees lower than normal.

State which of the above events will produce the following effects. Note that each event might have more than one effect.
(i) A movement along the demand curve for gasoline.
(ii) A shift of the demand curve for gasoline rightward.
(iii) A shift of the demand curve for gasoline leftward.
(iv) A movement along the supply curve of gasoline.
(v) A shift of the supply curve of gasoline rightward.

(vi) A shift of the supply curve of gasoline leftward.
(vii) A movement along the demand curve for cars.
(viii) A movement along the supply curve of cars.
(ix) A shift of the demand curve for cars rightward.
(x) A shift of the demand curve for cars leftward.
(xi) A shift of the supply curve of cars rightward.
(xii) A shift of the supply curve of cars leftward.
(xiii) An increase in the price of gasoline.
(xiv) A decrease in the equilibrium quantity of oil.

◆2. The demand and supply schedules for gum are as follows:

Price	Quantity demanded	Quantity supplied
(cents per pack)	(millions of packs a week)	
10	200	0
20	180	30
30	160	60
40	140	90
50	120	120
60	100	140
70	80	160
80	60	180
90	40	200

a. What is the equilibrium price of gum?
b. What is the equilibrium quantity of gum? Suppose that a huge fire destroys one half

of the gum-producing factories. The supply of gum decreases to one half of the amount shown in the above supply schedule.

   c. What is the new equilibrium price of gum?
   d. What is the new equilibrium quantity of gum?
   e. Has there been a shift in or a movement along the supply curve of gum?
   f. Has there been a shift in or a movement along the demand curve for gum?
   g. As the gum factories destroyed by fire are rebuilt and gradually resume gum production, what will happen to:
       (i)   The price of gum?
       (ii) The quantity of gum bought?
       (iii) The demand for gum?
       (iv) The supply curve of gum?

◆ 3. Suppose the demand and supply schedules for gum are those in problem 2. An increase in the teenage population increases the demand for gum by 40 million packs per week.
   a. Write out the new demand schedule for gum.
   b. What is the new equilibrium quantity of gum?
   c. What is the new equilibrium price of gum?
   d. Has there been a shift in or a movement along the demand curve for gum?
   e. Has there been a shift in or a movement along the supply curve of gum?

◆ 4. Suppose the demand and supply schedules for gum are those in problem 2. An increase in the teenage population increases the demand for gum by 40 million packs per week, and simultaneously the fire described in problem 2 occurs, wiping out one half of the gum-producing factories.
   a. Draw a graph of the original and new demand and supply curves.

   b. What is the new equilibrium quantity of gum?
   c. What is the new equilibrium price of gum?

5. Fill in the following table by inserting in each column an up arrow ↑ for increase, a down arrow ↓ for decrease and a question mark ? for indeterminate (can increase or decrease depending on the size of the change in demand and supply). Hint: To fill in this table, draw a separate demand and supply diagram for each case.

	Increase in demand	No change in demand	Decrease in demand
Increase in supply	P Q	P Q	P Q
No change in supply	P Q	P — Q —	P Q
Decrease in supply	P Q	P Q	P Q

6. Study the story about the market for pagers (*Reading Between the Lines,* pp. 86–87), and then:

   a. Describe the changes in the price of a pager and to the quantity sold.
   b. By drawing a demand-supply diagram, explain the changes in the price and quantity of pagers.
   c. Say which of the following occurred: a change in demand, a change in supply, a change in the quantity demanded, a change in the quantity supplied.

7. Study the story about the market for coffee (*Reading Between the Lines,* pp. 88–89) and then:

   a. Describe what happened when back-to-back frosts occurred in Brazil.
   b. Explain why the quantity of coffee demanded decreased and why the quantity of coffee supplied increased.

"...if any accident should move the scale of production from its equilibrium position, there will be instantly brought into play forces tending to push it back; just as, if a stone hanging by a string is displaced from its equilibrium position, the force of gravity will at once tend to bring it back ...;"

ALFRED MARSHALL, *PRINCIPLES OF ECONOMICS*

Discovering the Laws of Demand and Supply

THE ISSUES AND IDEAS

How are prices determined? Antoine-Augustin Cournot was the first to answer this question by using demand and supply, in the 1830s. But it was the development and expansion of the railroads during the 1850s that gave the newly emerging theory its first practical applications. Railroads in the 1850s were as close to the cutting edge of technology as airlines are today. And just as in the airline industry today, competition among the railroads was fierce.

In England, Dionysius Lardner used demand and supply to show railroad companies how they could increase their profits by cutting rates on long-distance business on which competition was fiercest, and by raising them on short-haul business on which they had less to fear from other transportation suppliers.

The principles that were first worked out by Lardner in the 1850s are used by economists today to calculate the freight rates and passenger fares that will give airlines the largest possible profit. And the rates that result have a lot in common with the railroad rates of the nineteenth century. The airlines have local routes that feed like the spokes of a wheel into a hub on which there is little competition and on which they charge high fares (per mile), and they have long-distance routes between hubs on which they compete fiercely with other airlines and on which fares per mile are lowest.

In France, Jules Dupuit worked out how to use demand theory to calculate the value of railroad bridges. His work was the forerunner of what is today called *cost-benefit analysis*. Working with the very same principles invented by Dupuit, economists today calculate the costs and benefits of highways and airports, of dams and power stations.

THEN...

DUPUIT used the law of demand to determine whether a bridge or canal would be valued enough by its users to justify the cost of building it. Lardner first worked out the relationship between the cost of production and supply and used demand and supply theory to explain the costs, prices, and profits of railroad operations. He also used the theory to discover ways of increasing revenue by raising rates on short-haul business and lowering them on long-distance freight.

TODAY, using the same principles devised by Dupuit, economists calculate whether the benefits of expanding airports and air traffic control facilities are sufficient to cover their costs, and airline companies use the principles developed by Lardner to set their prices and to decide when to offer "seat sales." Like the railroads before them, the airlines charge a high price per mile on short flights, for which they face little competition and a low price per mile on long flights, for which competition is fierce.

Antoine-Augustin Cournot

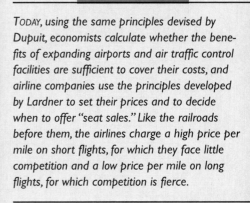

THE ECONOMISTS: ANTOINE AUGUSTIN COURNOT AND ALFRED MARSHALL

Antoine-Augustin Cournot (1801–1877), professor of mathematics at the University of Lyon, France, drew the first demand curve in the 1830s. The first practical application of demand theory, by Jules Dupuit (1804–1866), a French engineer/economist, was the calculation of the benefits from building a bridge—and, given that a bridge had been built, of the correct toll to charge for its use.

The laws of demand and supply and the connection between the costs of production and supply were first worked out by Dionysius Lardner (1793–1859), an Irish professor of philosophy at the University of London. Known satirically among scientists of the day as "Dionysius Diddler," Lardner worked on an amazing range of problems from astronomy to

Alfred Marshall

railway engineering to economics. A colorful character, he would have been a regular guest of David Letterman if late-night talk shows had been around in the 1850s. Lardner visited the École des Ponts et Chaussées (the School of Bridges and Roads) in Paris and must have learned a great deal from Dupuit, who was doing his major work on economics at the time.

Many others had a hand in refining the theory of demand and supply, but the first thorough and complete statement of the theory as we know it today was that of Alfred Marshall (1842–1924), professor of political economy at the University of Cambridge who, in 1890, published a monumental treatise—Principles in Economics—a work that became the textbook on economics for almost half a century. Marshall was an outstanding mathematician, but he kept mathematics and even diagrams in the background. His own supply and demand diagram (reproduced here at its original size) appears only in a footnote.

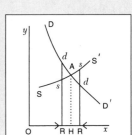

Chapter 5

Elasticity

After studying this chapter, you will be able to:

- Define and calculate the price elasticity of demand

- Explain what determines the elasticity of demand

- Use elasticity to determine whether a price change will increase or decrease total revenue

- Define and calculate other elasticities of demand

- Define and calculate the elasticity of supply

OPEC's Dilemma

You are the chief economic strategist for OPEC (the Organization of Petroleum Exporting Countries), and you want to increase OPEC's revenue. But you have a dilemma. You know that to increase the price of oil, you must restrict its supply. You also know that to sell more oil, you must lower its price. What will you recommend: restrict supply or lower the price? Which action will increase OPEC's revenue? ◆ As OPEC's economic strategist, you need to know a lot about the demand for oil. For example, as the world economy grows, how will that growth translate into an increase in demand for oil? What about substitutes for oil? Will we discover inexpensive methods to convert coal and tar sands into usable fuel? Will nuclear energy become safe and cheap enough to compete with oil? ◆ OPEC is not the only organization with a dilemma. A bumper grape crop is good news for wine consumers. It lowers the price of wine. But is it good news for grape growers? Do they get more revenue? Or does the lower price more than wipe out their gains from larger quantities sold? ◆ The government also faces a dilemma. Looking for greater tax revenue to balance its budget, it decides to increase the tax rates on tobacco and alcohol. Do the higher tax rates bring in more tax revenue? Or do people switch to substitutes for tobacco and alcohol on such a large scale that the higher tax rate brings in less tax revenue?

◻ In this chapter, you will learn how to tackle questions such as the ones just posed. You will learn how we can measure in a precise way the responsiveness of the quantities bought and sold to changes in prices and other influences on buyers or sellers.

Elasticity of Demand

LET'S BEGIN BY LOOKING A BIT MORE CLOSELY AT your task as OPEC's economic strategist. You are trying to decide whether to advise a cut in production that decreases supply and shifts the supply curve leftward. To make this decision, you need to know how the quantity of oil demanded responds to a change in price. You also need some way to measure that response.

The Responsiveness of the Quantity Demanded to Price

To understand the importance of the responsiveness of the quantity of oil demanded to a change in its price, let's compare two possible scenarios in the oil industry, shown in Fig. 5.1. In the two parts of the figure, the supply curves are identical but the demand curves differ.

The supply curve S_0 in each part of the figure shows the initial supply. In both cases, it intersects the demand curve at a price of $10 a barrel and a quantity of 40 million barrels a day. Suppose that you contemplate a decrease in supply that shifts the supply curve from S_0 to S_1. In part (a), the new supply curve S_1 intersects the demand curve D_a at a price of $30 a barrel and a quantity of 23 million barrels a day. In part (b), with demand curve D_b, the same supply curve shift increases the price to $15 a barrel and decreases the quantity to 15 million barrels a day. You can see that in part (a), the price increases by more and the quantity decreases by less than it does in part (b). What happens to the total revenue of the oil producers in these two cases?

The **total revenue** from the sale of a good equals the price of the good multiplied by the quantity sold. This amount is equal to the buyers' expenditures on the good. An increase in price has two opposing effects on total revenue. It increases the revenue on each unit sold (blue area). But an increase in price also leads to a decrease in the quantity sold, which decreases revenue (red area). Either of these two opposing effects could be larger. In case (a), the first effect is larger (blue area exceeds red area), so total revenue increases. In case (b), the second effect is larger (red area exceeds blue area), so total revenue decreases.

FIGURE 5.1

Demand, Supply, and Total Revenue

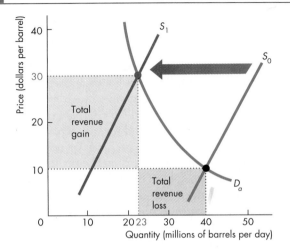

(a) More total revenue

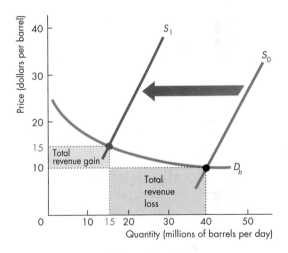

(b) Less total revenue

If supply is cut from S_0 to S_1, the price rises and the quantity decreases. In part (a), total revenue—the quantity multiplied by price—increases from $400 million to $690 million a day. The increase in total revenue from a higher price (blue area) exceeds the decrease in total revenue from smaller sales (red area). In part (b), total revenue decreases from $400 million to $225 million a day. The increase in total revenue from a higher price (blue area) is less than the decrease in total revenue from smaller sales (red area). These two different responses of total revenue arise from different responses of the quantity demanded to a change in price.

Slope Depends on Units of Measurement

The difference between these two cases is the responsiveness of the quantity demanded to a change in price. Demand curve D_a is steeper than demand curve D_b. But we can't compare two demand curves simply by their slopes, because the slope of a demand curve depends on the units in which we measure the price and quantity. Also, we often need to compare the demand curves for different goods and services. For example, when deciding by how much to change tax rates, the government needs to compare the demand for oil and the demand for tobacco. Which is more responsive to price? Which can be taxed at an even higher rate without decreasing the tax revenue? Comparing the slope of the demand curve for oil with the slope of the demand curve for tobacco has no meaning because oil is measured in gallons and tobacco in pounds—completely unrelated units.

To overcome these problems, we need a measure of responsiveness that is independent of the units of measurement of prices and quantities. Elasticity is such a measure.

Elasticity: A Units-Free Measure

The **price elasticity of demand** is a units-free measure of the responsiveness of the quantity demanded of a good to a change in its price, other things remaining the same. It is calculated by using the formula

$$\text{Price elasticity of demand} = \frac{\text{Percentage change in quantity demanded}}{\text{Percentage change in price}}.$$

Elasticity is a units-free measure because the percentage change in a variable is independent of the units in which the variable is measured. For example if we measure a price in dollars, an increase from $1.00 to $1.50 is a $0.50 increase. If we measure a price in cents, an increase from 100¢ to 150¢ is a 50¢ increase. The first increase is 0.5 of a unit and the second increase is 50 units, but they are both 50 percent increases.

Minus Sign and Elasticity When the price of a good *increases* along a demand curve, the quantity demanded *decreases*. Because a *positive* price change results in a *negative* change in the quantity demanded, the price elasticity of demand is a negative number. But it is the magnitude, or *absolute value*, of the price elasticity of demand that tells us how responsive—how elastic—demand is. To compare elasticities, we use the magnitude of the price elasticity of demand and ignore the minus sign.

Calculating Elasticity

To calculate the elasticity of demand, we need to know the quantities demanded at different prices, all the other influences on consumers' buying plans remaining the same. Let's assume that we have the relevant data on prices and quantities demanded of oil and calculate the elasticity of demand for oil.

Figure 5.2 zooms in on the demand curve for oil and shows how the quantity demanded responds to a small change in price. Initially the price is $9.50 a barrel and 41 million barrels a day are sold—the original point in the figure. Then the price increases to $10.50 a barrel and the quantity demanded decreases to 39 million barrels a day—the new point in the figure. When the price increases by $1 a barrel, the quantity demanded decreases by 2 million barrels a day.

To calculate the elasticity of demand, we express the changes in price and quantity demanded as percentages of the *average price* and the *average quantity*. By using the average price and average quantity, we calculate the elasticity at a point on the demand curve midway between the original point and the new point. The original price is $9.50 and the new price is $10.50, so the average price is $10. The $1 price increase is 10 percent of the average price. That is,

$$\Delta P / P_{ave} = 10\%.$$

The original quantity demanded is 41 million barrels and the new quantity demanded is 39 million barrels, so the average quantity demanded is 40 million barrels. The 2 million barrel decrease in the quantity demanded is 5 percent of the average quantity. That is,

$$\Delta Q / Q_{ave} = 5\%.$$

So the price elasticity of demand, which is the percentage change in the quantity demanded (5 percent) divided by the percentage change in price (10 percent) is 0.5. That is:

$$\text{Price elasticity of demand} = \frac{\%\Delta Q}{\%\Delta P}$$

$$= \frac{5\%}{10\%} = 0.5.$$

FIGURE 5.2

Calculating the Elasticity of Demand

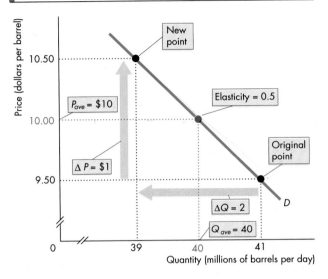

The elasticity of demand is calculated by using the formula*

$$\text{Price elasticity of demand} = \frac{\text{Percentage change in quantity demanded}}{\text{Percentage change in price}}$$

$$= \frac{\%\Delta Q}{\%\Delta P}$$

$$= \frac{\dfrac{\Delta Q}{Q_{ave}}}{\dfrac{\Delta P}{P_{ave}}}$$

$$= \frac{\dfrac{2}{40}}{\dfrac{1}{10}} = 0.5.$$

This calculation measures the elasticity at an average price of $10 a barrel and an average quantity of 40 million barrels.

*In the formula, the Greek letter delta (Δ) stands for "change in" and %Δ stands for "percentage change in."

Average Price and Quantity We use the *average* price and *average* quantity to avoid having two values for the elasticity of demand, depending on whether the price increases or decreases. A price increase of $1 is 10.5 percent of $9.50, and 2 million barrels is 4.9 percent of 41 million barrels. If we use these numbers to calculate the elasticity, we get 0.47. A price decrease of $1 is 9.5 percent of $10.50, and 2 million barrels is 5.1 percent of 39 million barrels. If we use

these numbers to calculate the elasticity, we get 0.54. By using the average price and average quantity demanded, the elasticity is 0.5 regardless of whether the price increases or decreases.

Percentages and Proportions Elasticity is the ratio of the *percentage* change in the quantity demanded to the percentage change in the price. It is also, equivalently, the proportionate change in the quantity demanded divided by the proportionate change in the price. The proportionate change in price is $\Delta P/P_{ave}$, and the proportionate change in quantity demanded is $\Delta Q/Q_{ave}$. The percentage changes are the proportionate changes multiplied by 100. So when we divide one percentage change by another, the 100s cancel and the result is the same as we get by using the proportionate changes.

Inelastic and Elastic Demand

Figure 5.3 shows three demand curves that cover the entire range of possible elasticities of demand. In Fig. 5.3(a), the quantity demanded is constant regardless of the price. If the quantity demanded remains constant when the price changes, then the elasticity of demand is zero and demand is said to be **perfectly inelastic.** One good that has a very low elasticity of demand (perhaps zero over some price range) is insulin. Insulin is of such importance to some diabetics that they will buy the quantity that keeps them healthy at almost any price. And even at low prices, they have no reason to buy more than the quantity that keeps them healthy.

If the percentage change in the quantity demanded is less than the percentage change in price, then the magnitude of the elasticity of demand is between zero and 1, and demand is said to be **inelastic.** The demand curve in Fig. 5.3(a) illustrates an inelastic demand.

If the percentage change in the quantity demanded exceeds the percentage change in price, then the magnitude of the elasticity is greater than 1, and demand is said to be **elastic**. The dividing line between inelastic and elastic demand is the case in which the percentage change in the quantity demanded equals the percentage change in price. In this case, the elasticity of demand is 1, and demand is said to be **unit elastic**. The demand illustrated in Fig. 5.3(b) is an example of unit elastic demand.

If the quantity demanded is infinitely responsive to a price change, then the magnitude of the elasticity

FIGURE 5.3

Inelastic and Elastic Demand

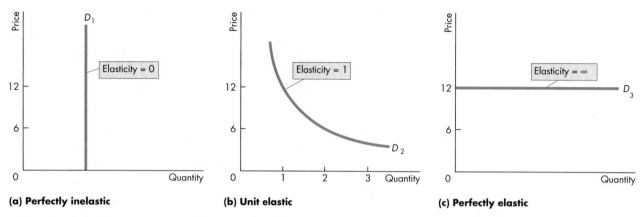

(a) Perfectly inelastic   **(b) Unit elastic**   **(c) Perfectly elastic**

Each demand illustrated here has a constant elasticity. The demand curve in part (a) is for a good that has a zero elasticity of demand. The demand curve in part (b) is for a good with a unit elasticity of demand. And the demand curve in part (c) is for a good with an infinite elasticity of demand.

---

of demand is infinity, and demand is said to be **perfectly elastic.** The demand curve in Fig. 5.3(c) is an example of perfectly elastic demand. An example of a good that has a very high elasticity of demand (almost infinite) is marker pens from the campus bookstore and from the convenience store next door. If the two stores offer pens for the same price, some people buy from one and some from the other. But if the bookstore increases the price of pens, even by a small amount, while the shop next door maintains the lower price, the quantity of pens demanded from the bookstore will fall to zero. Marker pens from the two stores are perfect substitutes for each other.

Elasticity Along a Straight-Line Demand Curve

Elasticity is not the same as slope, but the two are related. To understand how they are related, let's look at elasticity along a straight-line demand curve—a demand curve that has a constant slope.

Figure 5.4 illustrates the calculation of elasticity along a straight-line demand curve. Let's calculate the elasticity of demand at an average price of $40 a barrel and an average quantity of 4 million barrels a day. To do so, imagine that the price rises from $30 a barrel to

$50 a barrel. The change in the price (ΔP) is $20, and the average price (P_{ave}) is $40 (average of $30 and $50), which means that the proportionate change in price is

$$\frac{\Delta P}{P_{ave}} = \frac{20}{40}.$$

At a price of $30 a barrel, the quantity demanded is 8 million barrels a day. At a price of $50 a barrel, the quantity demanded is zero. So the change in the quantity demanded (ΔQ) is 8 million barrels a day, and the average quantity (Q_{ave}) is 4 million barrels a day (the average of 8 million and zero), so the proportionate change in the quantity demanded is

$$\frac{\Delta Q}{Q_{ave}} = \frac{8}{4}.$$

Dividing the proportionate change in the quantity demanded by the proportionate change in the price gives

$$\frac{\Delta Q/Q_{ave}}{\Delta P/P_{ave}} = \frac{8/4}{20/40} = 4.$$

By using this same method, we can calculate the elasticity of demand at any price and quantity along the demand curve. Because the demand curve is a

FIGURE 5.4

Elasticity Along a Straight-Line Demand Curve

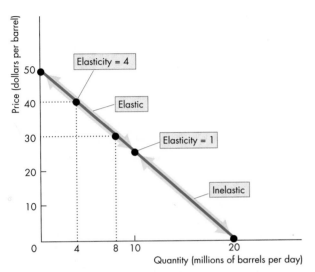

On a straight-line demand curve, elasticity decreases as the price falls and the quantity demanded increases. Demand is unit elastic at the midpoint of the demand curve (elasticity is 1). Above the midpoint, demand is elastic, and below the midpoint, demand is inelastic.

straight line, a $20 price change brings an 8 million barrel quantity change at every average price. So in the elasticity formula, $\Delta Q = 8$ and $\Delta P = 20$ regardless of average quantity and average price. But the lower the average price, the greater is the average quantity demanded. So the lower the average price, the less elastic is demand.

Check this proposition by calculating the elasticity of demand at the midpoint of the demand curve, where the price is $25 a barrel and the quantity demanded is 10 million barrels a day. The proportionate change in price is $20/$25 = 0.8, and the proportionate change in the quantity demanded is 8/10 = 0.8, so the elasticity of demand is 1. On *all* straight-line demand curves, the price elasticity is 1 at the midpoint. Above the midpoint, demand is elastic, and below the midpoint, demand is inelastic. Demand is perfectly elastic (elasticity is infinity) where the quantity demanded is zero and perfectly inelastic (elasticity is zero) where the price is zero.

The Factors that Influence the Elasticity of Demand

Actual values of elasticities of demand have been estimated from the average spending patterns of consumers, and some examples for the United States are set out in Table 5.1. You can see that these real-world elasticities of demand range from 1.52 for metals, the most elastic in the table, to 0.12 for food, the least elastic in the table. What makes the demand for some goods elastic and the demand for others inelastic? Elasticity depends on three main factors:

- The closeness of substitutes
- The proportion of income spent on the good
- The time elapsed since a price change

Closeness of Substitutes The closer the substitutes for a good or service, the more elastic is the demand for it. For example, oil has substitutes but none that are very close (imagine a steam-driven, coal-fueled car or a nuclear-powered jetliner). As a result, the demand for oil is inelastic. In contrast, metals have good substitutes such as plastics, so the demand for metals is elastic.

In everyday language we call some goods, such as food and housing, *necessities* and other goods, such as exotic vacations, *luxuries*. Necessities are goods that have poor substitutes and that are crucial for our well-being, so generally, they have inelastic demands. Luxuries are goods that usually have many substitutes and so have elastic demands.

The degree of substitutability between two goods also depends on how narrowly (or broadly) we define them. For example, even though oil does not have a close substitute, different types of oil are close substitutes for each other. Saudi Arabian Light, a particular type of oil, is a close substitute for Alaskan North Slope, another particular type of oil. If you happen to be the economic advisor to Saudi Arabia (as well as the OPEC economic strategist!), you will not contemplate a unilateral price increase. Even though Saudi Arabian Light has some unique characteristics, other oils can easily substitute for it, and most buyers will be very sensitive to its price relative to the prices of other types of oil. So the demand for Saudi Arabian Light is highly elastic.

This example, which distinguishes between oil in general and different types of oil, applies to many other goods and services. The elasticity of demand for meat in general is low, but the elasticity of demand

TABLE 5.1

Some Real-World Price Elasticities of Demand

Good or Service	Elasticity
Elastic Demand	
Metals	1.52
Electrical engineering products	1.39
Mechanical engineering products	1.30
Furniture	1.26
Motor vehicles	1.14
Instrument engineering products	1.10
Professional services	1.09
Transportation services	1.03
Inelastic Demand	
Gas, electricity, and water	0.92
Oil	0.91
Chemicals	0.89
Beverages (all types)	0.78
Clothing	0.64
Tobacco	0.61
Banking and insurance services	0.56
Housing services	0.55
Agricultural and fish products	0.42
Books, magazines, and newspapers	0.34
Food	0.12

Sources: Ahsan Mansur and John Whalley, "Numerical Specification of Applied General Equilibrium Models: Estimation, Calibration, and Data," *in Applied General Equilibrium Analysis,* eds. Herbert E. Scarf and John B. Shoven (New York: Cambridge University Press, 1984), 109, and Henri Theil, Ching-Fan Chung, and James L. Seale, Jr., *Advances in Econometrics, Supplement 1, 1989, International Evidence on Consumption Patterns* (Greenwich, Conn: JAI Press Inc., 1989). Reprinted with permission.

for beef, lamb, or chicken is high. The elasticity of demand for personal computers is low, but the elasticity of demand for a Compaq, Dell, or IBM is high.

Proportion of Income Spent on the Good

Other things remaining the same, the higher the proportion of income spent on a good, the more elastic is the demand for it. If only a small fraction of income is spent on a good, then a change in its price

has little impact on the consumer's overall budget. In contrast, even a small rise in the price of a good that commands a large part of a consumer's budget induces the consumer to make a radical reappraisal of expenditures.

To appreciate the importance of the proportion of income spent on a good, consider your own elasticity of demand for textbooks and chewing gum. If the price of textbooks doubles (increases 100 percent), there will be a big decrease in the quantity of textbooks bought. There will be an increase in sharing and in illegal photocopying. If the price of chewing gum doubles, also a 100 percent increase, there will be almost no change in the quantity of gum demanded. Why the difference? Textbooks take a large proportion of your budget, while gum takes only a tiny portion. You don't like either price increase, but you hardly notice the effects of the increased price of gum, while the increased price of textbooks puts your budget under severe strain.

Figure 5.5 shows the proportion of income spent on food and the price elasticity of demand for food in 20 countries. This figure confirms the general tendency we have just described. The larger the proportion of income spent on food, the more price elastic is the demand for food. For example, in Tanzania, a poor African nation where average incomes are 3.3 percent of incomes in the United States and where 62 percent of income is spent on food, the price elasticity of demand for food is 0.77. In contrast, in the United States, where 12 percent of income is spent on food, the elasticity of demand for food is 0.12. These numbers confirm that in a country that spends a large proportion of income on food, an increase in the price of food forces people to make a bigger adjustment to the quantity of food bought than in a country in which a small proportion of income is spent on food.

Time Elapsed Since Price Change The greater the time elapsed since a price change, the more elastic is demand. When a price changes, consumers often continue to buy similar quantities of a good for a while. But given enough time, they find acceptable and less costly substitutes. As this process of substitution occurs, the quantity purchased of an item that has become more expensive gradually declines.

To describe the effect of time on demand we distinguish between two time-frames:

1. Short-run demand
2. Long-run demand

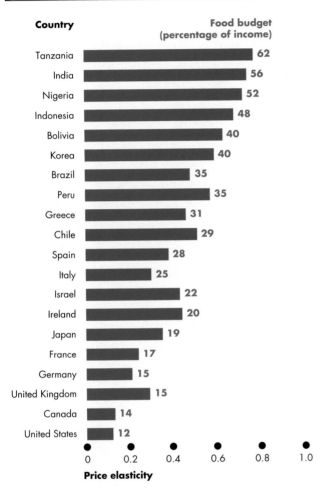

FIGURE 5.5
Price Elasticities in 20 Countries

As income increases and the proportion of income spent on food decreases, the demand for food becomes less elastic.

Source: Henri Theil, Ching-Fan Chung, and James L. Seale, Jr., *Advances in Econometrics, Supplement 1, 1989, International Evidence on Consumption Patterns* (Greenwich, Conn: JAI Press Inc., 1989).

Short-run demand describes the response of buyers to a change in the price of a good *before* sufficient time has elapsed for all the possible substitutions to be made. Long-run demand describes the response of buyers to a change in price *after* sufficient time has elapsed for all the possible substitutions to be made.

An example of a long-lasting price increase was the fourfold rise in the price of oil that occurred during

1973 and 1974. The higher price of oil led to sharp increases in the costs of home heating and gasoline. Initially, consumers maintained consumption at more or less their original levels. Then, gradually, buyers responded to higher oil and gasoline prices by using their existing capital—furnaces and gas guzzlers—in a way that economized on the more expensive fuel. But there were severe limits in the extent to which people felt it worthwhile to cut back on their consumption of the now much more costly fuel. Thermostats could be turned down, but that imposed costs—costs of discomfort. Drivers could lower their average speed and economize on gasoline. But that also imposed costs—costs of increases in travel time and forgone trips. So the short-run buyer response in the face of this sharp price increase was a relatively small decrease in the consumption of oil. Demand was inelastic.

But with a longer time to respond to the higher price of oil, many more options become available. And as these additional options are used, the quantity of oil demanded decreased further—demand became more elastic. People bought more energy-efficient capital. As yet more time elapsed, technological advances made even more economies on fuel possible. Furnaces and electric power generators became more fuel-efficient. Cars became smaller, on the average, and car and airplane engines became more fuel-efficient.

The short-run and long-run demand curves for oil in 1974 looked like those in Fig. 5.1. Look back at that figure and refresh your memory about the demand curves in parts (a) and (b). The short-run demand curve is D_a, and the long-run demand curve is D_b. The price of oil in 1974 was $10 a barrel, and 40 million barrels a day were bought and sold. At that price and quantity, long-run demand, D_b, is much more elastic than short-run demand, D_a.

REVIEW

- Elasticity of demand measures the responsiveness of the quantity demanded of a good or service to a change in its price.
- The elasticity of demand is the percentage change in the quantity demanded of a good divided by the percentage change in its price.
- The elasticity of demand for a good is determined by the closeness of substitutes for it, the proportion of income spent on it, and the time lapse since its price changed.

Elasticity, Total Revenue, and Expenditure

This chapter began with a dilemma. How can a producer of oil (or anything else) increase total revenue: by decreasing production to increase price, or by lowering price to sell a larger quantity? We can now answer this question.

The change in a producer's total revenue depends on the extent to which the quantity sold changes as the price changes—the elasticity of demand. If demand is elastic, a 1 percent price cut increases the quantity sold by more than 1 percent and total revenue increases. If demand is unit elastic, a 1 percent price cut increases the quantity sold by 1 percent and so total revenue does not change. And if demand is inelastic, a 1 percent price cut increases the quantity sold by less than 1 percent and total revenue decreases.

Total Revenue Test We can use this relationship between elasticity and total revenue to estimate elasticity using a total revenue test. The **total revenue test** is a method of estimating the price elasticity of demand by observing the change in total revenue that results from a price change (with all other influences on the quantity sold remaining unchanged). If a price cut increases total revenue, demand is elastic; if a price cut decreases total revenue, demand is inelastic; and if a price cut leaves total revenue unchanged, demand is unit elastic.

Figure 5.6 shows the connection between the elasticity of demand and total revenue. Part (a) shows the same demand curve that you studied in Fig. 5.4. Over the price range from $50 to $25, demand is elastic. Over the price range from $25 to zero, demand is inelastic. At a price of $25, demand is unit elastic.

Figure 5.6(b) shows total revenue. At a price of $50, the quantity sold is zero, so total revenue is also zero. At a price of zero, the quantity demanded is 20 million barrels a day, but at zero price, total revenue is again zero. A price cut in the elastic range brings an increase in total revenue—the percentage increase in the quantity demanded is greater than the percentage decrease in price. And a price cut in the inelastic range brings a decrease in total revenue—the percentage increase in the quantity demanded is less than the percentage decrease in price. At the point of unit elasticity, total revenue is at a maximum. A small price change on either side of $25 keeps total revenue constant. The loss in total revenue from a lower price is offset by a gain in total revenue from a greater quantity sold.

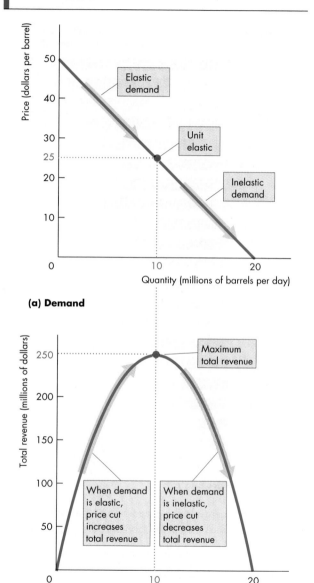

FIGURE 5.6

Elasticity and Total Revenue

(a) Demand

(b) Total revenue

When demand is elastic, in the price range from $50 to $25, a decrease in price (part a) brings an increase in total revenue (part b). When demand is inelastic, in the price range from $25 to zero, a decrease in price (part a) brings a decrease in total revenue (part b). When demand is unit elastic, at a price of $25 (part a), total revenue is at a maximum (part b).

We have seen that long-run demand is more elastic than short-run demand. It is possible, therefore, that a price cut will decrease total revenue in the short run but increase total revenue in the long run. This outcome occurs if short-run demand is inelastic but long-run demand is elastic.

So far, we've studied the most widely used elasticity—the *price* elasticity of demand. But there are some other useful elasticity of demand concepts. Let's look at them.

More Elasticities of Demand

BUYING PLANS ARE INFLUENCED BY MANY factors other than price. Among these other factors are the prices of other goods and incomes. We can calculate an elasticity of demand for each of these other factors as well as for price. Let's examine some of these additional elasticities.

Cross Elasticity of Demand

The quantity of any good that consumers plan to buy depends on the prices of its substitutes and complements. We measure these influences by using the concept of the cross elasticity of demand. The **cross elasticity of demand** is a measure of the responsiveness of the demand for a good to a change in the price of a substitute or complement, other things remaining the same. It is calculated by using the formula

$$\text{Cross elasticity of demand} = \frac{\text{Percentage change in quantity demanded}}{\text{Percentage change in the price of a substitute or complement}}.$$

The cross elasticity of demand is positive for a substitute and negative for a complement. Figure 5.7 makes it clear why. When the price of coal—a substitute for oil—rises, the demand for oil increases and the demand curve for oil shifts rightward from D_0 to D_1. Because an increase in the price of coal brings an increase in the demand for oil, the cross elasticity of demand for oil with respect to the price of coal is positive. When the price of a car—a complement of oil—rises, the demand for oil decreases and the demand curve for oil shifts leftward from D_0 to D_2.

FIGURE 5.7
Cross Elasticity of Demand

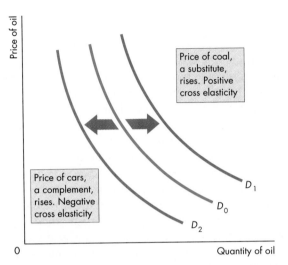

When the price of coal increases, the demand for oil, a *substitute* for coal, increases and the demand curve for oil shifts rightward from D_0 to D_1. The cross elasticity of the demand for oil with respect to the price of coal is *positive*. When the price of a car increases, the demand for oil, a *complement* of cars, decreases and the demand curve for oil shifts leftward from D_0 to D_2. The cross elasticity of the demand for oil with respect to the price of a car is *negative*.

Because an increase in the price of a car brings a decrease in the demand for oil, the cross elasticity of demand for oil with respect to the price of a car is negative.

Income Elasticity of Demand

As income grows, how does the demand for a particular good change? The answer depends on the income elasticity of demand for the good. The **income elasticity of demand** is a measure of the responsiveness of demand to a change in income, other things remaining the same. It is calculated by using the formula

$$\text{Income elasticity of demand} = \frac{\text{Percentage change in quantity demanded}}{\text{Percentage change in income}}.$$

Income elasticities of demand can be positive or negative and fall into three interesting ranges:

1. Greater than 1 (*normal* good, income elastic)
2. Between zero and 1 (*normal* good, income inelastic)
3. Less than zero (*inferior* good)

Figure 5.8 illustrates these three cases. Part (a) shows an income elasticity of demand that is greater than 1. As income increases, the quantity demanded increases, but the quantity demanded increases faster than income. Examples of goods in this category are ocean cruises, custom clothing, international travel, jewelry, and works of arts.

Part (b) shows an income elasticity of demand that is between zero and 1. In this case, the quantity demanded increases as income increases, but income increases faster than the quantity demanded. Examples of goods in this category are food, clothing, furniture, newspapers, and magazines.

Part (c) shows an income elasticity of demand that eventually becomes negative. In this case, the quantity demanded increases as income increases until it reaches a maximum at income *m*. Beyond that point, as income continues to increase, the quantity demanded declines. The elasticity of demand is positive but less than 1 up to income *m*. Beyond income *m*, the income elasticity of demand is negative. Examples of goods in this category are small motorcycles, potatoes, and rice. Low-income consumers buy most of these goods. At low income levels, the demand for such goods increases as income increases. But as income increases above point *m*, consumers replace these goods with superior alternatives. For example, a small car replaces the motorcycle; fruit, vegetables, and meat begin to appear in a diet that was heavy in rice or potatoes.

Real-World Income Elasticities of Demand

Table 5.2 shows estimates of some income elasticities of demand in the United States. Necessities such as food and clothing are income inelastic, while luxuries such as airline and foreign travel are income elastic.

FIGURE 5.8
Income Elasticity of Demand

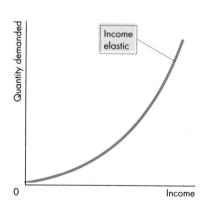

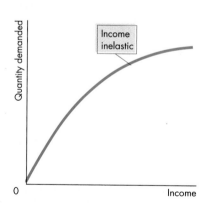

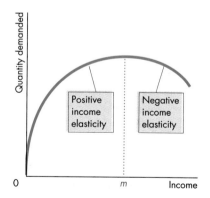

(a) Elasticity greater than 1

(b) Elasticity between zero and 1

(c) Elasticity less than 1 and becomes negative

Income elasticity of demand has three ranges of values. In part (a), income elasticity of demand is greater than 1. In this case, as income increases, the quantity demanded increases but by a bigger percentage than the increase in income. In part (b), income elasticity of demand is between zero and 1. In this case, as income increases, the quantity demanded increases but by a smaller percentage than the increase in income. In part (c), the income elasticity of demand is positive at low incomes but becomes negative as income increases above level *m*. Maximum consumption of this good occurs at the income *m*.

TABLE 5.2

Some Real-World Income Elasticities of Demand

Good or Service	Elasticity
Elastic Demand	
Airline travel	5.82
Movies	3.41
Foreign travel	3.08
Housing services	2.45
Electricity	1.94
Restaurant meals	1.61
Local buses and trains	1.38
Gasoline and oil	1.36
Haircutting	1.36
Cars	1.07
Unit Elastic Demand	
Dentists' services	1.00
Inelastic Demand	
Shoes and other footwear	0.94
Tobacco	0.86
Shoe repairs	0.72
Alcoholic beverages	0.62
Furniture	0.53
Clothing	0.51
Newspapers and magazines	0.38
Telephone	0.32
Food	0.14

Sources: H.S. Houthakker and Lester D. Taylor, *Consumer Demand in the United States* (Cambridge, Mass.: Harvard University Press, 1970), and Henri Theil, Ching-Fan Chung, and James L. Seale, Jr., *Advances in Econometrics, Supplement 1, 1989, International Evidence on Consumption Patterns* (Greenwich, Conn: JAI Press Inc., 1989). Reprinted with permission.

FIGURE 5.9

Income Elasticities in 20 Countries

As income increases, the income elasticity of demand for food decreases. For low-income consumers, a larger percentage of any increase in income is spent on food than for high-income consumers.

Source: Henri Theil, Ching-Fan Chung, and James L. Seale, Jr., *Advances in Econometrics, Supplement 1, 1989, International Evidence on Consumption Patterns* (Greenwich, Conn: JAI Press Inc., 1989).

What is a necessity and what is a luxury depend on the level of income. For people with a low income, food and clothing can be luxuries. So the *level* of income has a big effect on income elasticities of demand. Figure 5.9 shows this effect on the income elasticity of demand for food in 20 countries. In countries with low incomes, such as Tanzania and India, the income elasticity of demand for food is high while in countries with high incomes, such as the United States, it is low. A 10 percent increase in income leads to an increase in the demand for food of 7.5 percent in India and only 1.5 percent in the United States. These numbers confirm that necessities have a lower income elasticity of demand than luxuries.

Elasticity of Supply

IN 1994, THE U.S. AUTO INDUSTRY EXPANDED and increased its demand for steel. There was a *change in demand* for steel. Both car producers and steel producers were very interested in the likely changes in the price of steel that this increase in demand would bring—see *Reading Between the Lines* on pp. 112–113. A change in demand shifts the demand curve and leads to a *movement along the supply curve*. To predict the changes in price and quantity, we need to know how responsive the quantity supplied is to the price of a good. That is, we need to know the elasticity of supply.

The **elasticity of supply** measures the responsiveness of the quantity supplied of a good to a change in its price. It is calculated by using the formula

$$\text{Elasticity of supply} = \frac{\text{Percentage change in quantity supplied}}{\text{Percentage change in price}}.$$

There are two extreme cases of the elasticity of supply. If the quantity supplied is fixed regardless of the price, the supply curve is vertical and the elasticity of supply is zero. Supply is perfectly inelastic. If there is a price at which suppliers are willing to sell any quantity demanded, the supply curve is horizontal and the elasticity of supply is infinite. Supply is perfectly elastic. Table 5.3 on page 114 gives a compact glossary of all the demand and supply elasticities that you've studied.

The magnitude of the elasticity of supply depends on:

- Factor substitution possibilities
- Time frame for the supply decision

Factor Substitution Possibilities

Some goods and services are produced by using unique or rare factors of production. These items have a low, and perhaps zero, elasticity of supply. Other goods and services are produced by using factors of production that are more common and that can be allocated to a wide variety of alternative tasks. Such items have a high elasticity of supply.

A Van Gogh painting has been produced by a unique type of labor—Van Gogh's. No other factor of production can be substituted for this labor. And there is just one of each painting, so its supply curve is vertical and its elasticity of supply is zero. At the other extreme, wheat can be grown on land that is almost equally good for growing corn. So it is just as easy to grow wheat as corn, and the opportunity cost of wheat in terms of forgone corn is almost constant. As a result, the supply curve of wheat is almost horizontal and its elasticity of supply is very large. Similarly, when a good is produced in many different countries (for example, sugar and beef), the supply of the good is a highly elastic supply.

The supply of most goods and services lies between the two extremes. The quantity produced can be increased but only by incurring higher cost. If a higher price is offered, the quantity supplied increases. Such goods and services have an elasticity of supply between zero and infinity.

Elasticity of Supply and the Time Frame for Supply Decisions

To study the influence of the length of time elapsed since a price change, we distinguish three time frames of supply:

- Momentary supply
- Short-run supply
- Long-run supply

Momentary Supply When the price of a good rises or falls, the *momentary supply curve* shows the response of the quantity supplied immediately following a price change.

Some goods, such as fruits and vegetables, have a perfectly inelastic momentary supply—a vertical supply curve. The quantities supplied depend on crop-planting decisions made earlier. In the case of oranges, for example, planting decisions have to be made many years in advance of the crop being available.

Other goods, such as long-distance phone calls, have an elastic momentary supply. When many people simultaneously make a call, there is a big surge in the demand for telephone cable, computer switching, and satellite time, and the quantity bought increases (up to the physical limits of the telephone system) but the price remains constant. Long-distance carriers monitor fluctuations in demand and re-route calls to ensure that the quantity supplied equals the quantity demanded without raising the price.

Long-Run Supply The *long-run supply* curve shows the response of the quantity supplied to a change in price after all the technologically possible ways of adjusting supply have been exploited. In the case of oranges, the long run is the time it takes new plantings to grow to full maturity—about 15 years. In some cases, the long-run adjustment occurs only after a completely new production plant has been built and workers have been trained to operate it—typically a process that might take several years.

Short-Run Supply The *short-run supply curve* shows how the quantity supplied responds to a price change when only *some* of the technologically possible adjustments to production have been made. The first adjustment that is usually made is in the amount of labor employed. To increase output in the short run, firms work their labor force overtime and perhaps hire additional workers. To decrease their output in the short run, firms lay off workers or reduce their hours of work. With the passage of time, firms can make additional adjustments, perhaps training additional workers or buying additional tools and other equipment. The short-run response to a price change, unlike the momentary and long-run responses, is not a unique response but a sequence of adjustments.

Three Supply Curves Figure 5.10 shows three supply curves that correspond to the three time frames. They are the supply curves in the world market for oranges in a given week in which the price is $2 a pound and the quantity of oranges grown is 3 million pounds. Each supply curve passes through that point. Momentary supply is perfectly inelastic, as shown by the blue curve *MS*. As time passes, the quantity supplied becomes more responsive to price and is shown by the short-run supply curve, *SS*. As yet more time passes, the supply curve becomes the red long-run curve *LS*, the most elastic of the three supplies.

The momentary supply curve is vertical because, on a given day, no matter what the price of oranges, producers cannot change their output. They have picked, packed, and shipped their crop to market, and the quantity available for that day is fixed. The short-run supply curve slopes upward because producers can take actions quite quickly to change the quantity supplied in response to a price change. They can, for example, stop picking and leave oranges to rot on the tree if the price falls by a large amount. Or

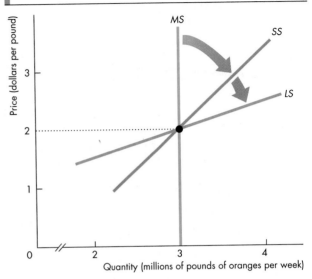

FIGURE 5.10

Supply: Momentary, Short-Run, and Long-Run

The momentary supply curve, *MS*, shows how quantity supplied responds to a price change the moment that it occurs. The blue momentary supply curve shown here is perfectly inelastic. The purple short-run supply curve, *SS*, shows how the quantity supplied responds to a price change after some adjustments to production have been made. The red long-run supply curve, *LS*, shows how the quantity supplied responds to a price change when all the technologically possible adjustments to the production process have been made.

they can use more fertilizers and improved irrigation and increase the yields of their existing trees if the price rises. In the long run, they can plant more trees and increase the quantity supplied even more in response to a given price rise.

◆ You have now studied the theory of demand and supply, and you have learned how to measure the responsiveness of the quantity demanded to changes in prices and income. You have also learned how to measure the responsiveness of the quantity supplied to a change in the price. All the elasticities that you've met in this chapter are summarized in Table 5.3. In the next chapter, we are going to use what we have learned to study some real-world markets—markets in action.

Elasticity: Cars and Steel

THE DETROIT FREE PRESS, JUNE 11, 1994

Demand for Autos May Raise Steel Prices

BY SUE ZEIDLER, REUTERS

PITTSBURGH—Steelmakers—enjoying their strongest business prospects in 15 years—are likely to win price increases in negotiations with the nation's automakers that could boost 1995 earnings, industry experts say.

"Last year's round of talks with the automakers locked in 1994 shipments at prices only marginally above 1993 levels," said Mike Gambardella of J.P. Morgan. "Price increases this year could be in the 3–5 percent range, which should provide a strong boost to earnings," he said.

The auto industry is the biggest consumer of steel in the United States, taking a 17 percent chunk of all steel produced.

With car sales on a sharp rebound, demand for steel is booming. This year Detroit is expected to buy 15.5 million tons of steel, up a sharp 17.5 percent from last year's 13.2 million tons.

It takes about one ton of steel to build a car, but Detroit is using even more because of a booming demand for light trucks and sport-utility vehicles, which use about 1.5 tons of steel each.

"Certainly, the market conditions augur well for sellers," USX Chief Executive Officer Charles Correy said.

Carmakers, likely to earn a combined $14 billion this year, are also likely to hang tough in negotiations to keep costs under control.

General Motors Corp. is the biggest buyer of steel in the nation, followed by Ford Motor Co. and Chrysler Corp. Chrysler has recently started talks on supply contracts for the 1995 model year, because its current steel supply contracts expire July 31.

Analysts said there were rumors that opening bids by the steel suppliers had price increases as high as 10 to 20 percent. But industry sources said the rumors were untrue. ...

Reprinted with permission of Reuters.

Essence of THE STORY

■ Increases in car sales brought increased earnings for car makers in 1994.

■ The auto industry takes 17 percent of total U.S. steel production and is the nation's biggest consumer of steel. (A car takes 1 ton of steel, and a truck takes 1.5 tons.)

■ The increase in car sales increased the demand for steel.

■ In 1994, the auto industry was expected to buy 15.5 million tons of steel, up 17.5 percent from 13.2 million tons in 1993.

■ Steel prices were predicted to increase during 1994 by an amount in the 3–5 percent range.

■ Rumors that the steel suppliers were seeking a price increase in the 10–20 percent range were said to be untrue.

Economic

A N A L Y S I S

■ The rise in the price of steel in 1994 depends on the magnitude of the increase in the demand for steel and on the *elasticity of supply* of steel.

■ The auto industry takes 17 percent of total U.S. steel production and the quantity of steel bought by the auto industry in 1993 was 13.2 million tons.

■ These two bits of information imply that U.S. steel production in 1993 was 78 million tons—13.2 million tons is 17 percent of 78 million tons.

■ The auto industry was expected to buy 15.5 million tons of steel in 1994, up 17.5 percent in 1993.

■ Let's assume the increase in sales of steel to the rest of the economy is 3 percent, the average growth rate of the economy in 1994.

■ The story implies an increase in the quantity of steel supplied in 1994 of 4 million tons to 82 million tons.

■ If the 1994 price rise is 4 percent (the middle of the 3–5 percent range), then the supply curve for steel must be S_A in Fig. 1.

■ You can calculate the elasticity of supply midway between the 1993 and 1994 points. The percentage change in the quantity supplied $\Delta Q/Q_{ave}$ is 4/80, and the percentage change in price $\Delta P/P_{ave}$ is 4/102.

■ The elasticity of supply is

$$\frac{\dfrac{\Delta Q}{Q_{ave}}}{\dfrac{\Delta P}{P_{ave}}} = \frac{\dfrac{4}{80}}{\dfrac{4}{102}} = 1.275.$$

Supply is elastic.

■ If the 1994 price rise is 15 percent (the middle of the 10-20 percent range), then the supply curve for steel must be S_B in Fig. 2. In this case, the elasticity is

$$\frac{\dfrac{\Delta Q}{Q_{ave}}}{\dfrac{\Delta P}{P_{ave}}} = \frac{\dfrac{4}{80}}{\dfrac{15}{107.5}} = 0.36.$$

Supply is inelastic.

■ The elasticity of supply of steel is unlikely to be as low as 0.36. Steel can be imported and U.S. steel producers have plenty of spare capacity. So a price increase of 4 percent looks more likely than the rumored increase of 10–20 percent.

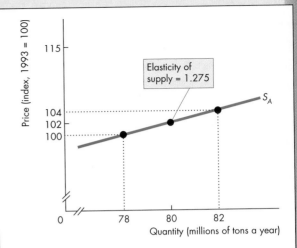

Figure 1

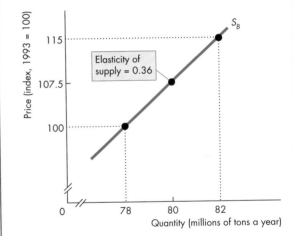

Figure 2

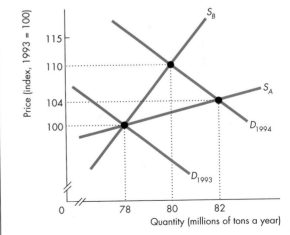

Figure 3

TABLE 5.3

A Compact Glossary of Elasticities

PRICE ELASTICITIES OF DEMAND

A relationship is described as	When its magnitude is	Which means that
Perfectly elastic or infinitely elastic	Infinity	The smallest possible increase in price causes an infinitely large decrease in the quantity demanded*
Elastic	Less than infinity but greater than I	The percentage decrease in the quantity demanded exceeds the percentage increase in price
Unit elastic	I	The percentage decrease in the quantity demanded equals the percentage increase in price
Inelastic	Greater than zero but less than I	The percentage decrease in the quantity demanded is less than the percentage increase in price
Perfectly inelastic or completely inelastic	Zero	The quantity demanded is the same at all prices

CROSS ELASTICITIES OF DEMAND

A relationship is described as	When its value is	Which means that
Perfect substitutes	Infinity	The smallest possible increase in the price of one good causes an infinitely large increase in the quantity demanded of the other good
Substitutes	Positive, less than infinity	If the price of one good increases, the quantity demanded of the other good also increases
Independent	Zero	The quantity demanded of one good remains constant, regardless of the price of the other good
Complements	Less than zero	The quantity demanded of one good decreases when the price of the other good increases

INCOME ELASTICITIES OF DEMAND

A relationship is described as	When its value is	Which means that
Income elastic (normal good)	Greater than I	The percentage increase in the quantity demanded is greater than the percentage increase in income
Income inelastic (normal good)	Less than I but greater than zero	The percentage increase in the quantity demanded is less than the percentage increase in income
Negative income elastic (inferior good)	Less than zero	When income increases, quantity demanded decreases

ELASTICITIES OF SUPPLY

A relationship is described as	When its magnitude is	Which means that
Perfectly elastic	Infinity	The smallest possible increase in price causes an infinitely large increase in the quantity supplied
Elastic	Less than infinity but greater than I	The percentage increase in the quantity supplied exceeds the percentage increase in the price.
Inelastic	Greater than zero but less than I	The percentage increase in the quantity supplied is less than the percentage increase in the price.
Perfectly inelastic	Zero	The quantity supplied is the same at all prices.

*In each description, the directions of change may be reversed. For example, in this case: The smallest possible *decrease* in price causes an infinitely large *increase* in the quantity demanded.

S U M M A R Y

Elasticity of Demand

Elasticity of demand is a measure of the responsiveness of the quantity demanded of a good to a change in its price. It enables us to calculate the effect of a change in supply on price, quantity bought, and total revenue. Elasticity of demand is calculated as the percentage change in the quantity demanded divided by the percentage change in price.

The larger the magnitude of the elasticity of demand, the greater is the responsiveness of the quantity demanded to a given change in price. When the percentage change in the quantity demanded is smaller than the percentage change in price, demand is inelastic. When the percentage change in the quantity demanded equals the percentage change in price, demand is unit elastic. And when the percentage change in the quantity demanded is larger than the percentage change in price, demand is elastic. Along a straight-line demand curve, demand is elastic at prices above the midpoint, unit elastic at the midpoint, and inelastic at prices below the midpoint.

Elasticity depends on how easily one good serves as a substitute for another, the proportion of income spent on the good, and the length of time that has elapsed since the price change. We use two time frames to analyze demand: short run and long run. Short-run demand describes the initial response of buyers to a price change. Long-run demand describes the response of buyers to a price change after all possible adjustments have been made. Short-run demand is usually less elastic than long-run demand.

If demand is elastic, a decrease in price leads to an increase in total revenue. If demand is unit elastic, a decrease in price leaves total revenue unchanged. And if demand is inelastic, a decrease in price leads to a decrease in total revenue. (pp. 99–107)

More Elasticities of Demand

Cross elasticity of demand measures the responsiveness of demand for one good to a change in the price of another good (a substitute or a complement). Cross elasticity of demand is calculated as the percentage change in the quantity demanded of one good divided by the percentage change in the price of another good. The cross elasticity of demand with respect to the price of a substitute is positive. The cross elasticity of demand with respect to the price of a complement is negative.

Income elasticity of demand measures the responsiveness of demand to a change in income. Income elasticity of demand is calculated as the percentage change in the quantity demanded divided by the percentage change in income. The larger the income elasticity of demand, the greater is the responsiveness of demand to a given change in income. When income elasticity is between zero and 1, demand is income inelastic. In this case, as income increases, demand increases but the percentage of income spent on the good decreases. When income elasticity is greater than 1, demand is income elastic. In this case, as income increases, demand increases and the percentage of income spent on the good also increases. When income elasticity is less than zero, demand is negative income elastic. In this case, as income increases, demand decreases. For normal goods, the income elasticity of demand is positive. For inferior goods, the income elasticity of demand is negative. In this case, as income increases, demand decreases. (pp. 107–109)

Elasticity of Supply

Elasticity of supply measures the responsiveness of the quantity supplied of a good to a change in its price. Elasticity of supply is calculated as the percentage change in the quantity supplied of a good divided by the percentage change in its price. Supply elasticities are usually positive and range between zero (vertical supply curve) and infinity (horizontal supply curve).

Supply decisions have three time frames: momentary, long run, and short run. Momentary supply refers to the response of suppliers to a price change at the instant that the price changes. Long-run supply refers to the response of suppliers to a price change when all the technologically feasible adjustments in production have been made. Short-run supply refers to the response of suppliers to a price change after some adjustments in production have been made. For many goods, momentary supply is perfectly inelastic. Supply becomes more elastic as suppliers have more time to respond to price changes. (pp. 110–111)

K E Y   E L E M E N T S

Key Figures and Table

Key Terms

R E V I E W   Q U E S T I O N S

1. Define the price elasticity of demand.

2. Why is elasticity a more useful measure of responsiveness than slope?

3. Draw a graph, or describe the shape of a demand curve, that represents a good that has an elasticity of demand equal to:
   a. Infinity.
   b. Zero.
   c. Unity.

4. Which item in each of the following pairs has the larger elasticity of demand:
   a. *People* magazine or magazines
   b. Vacations or vacations in Florida
   c. Broccoli or vegetables

5. What three factors determine the size of the elasticity of demand?

6. What do we mean by short-run demand and long-run demand?

7. Explain why the short-run demand curve is usually less elastic than the long-run demand curve.

8. What is the connection between elasticity and total revenue? If the elasticity of demand for dental work is 1, by how much does a 10 percent increase in the price of dental work change total revenue?

9. Define the cross elasticity of demand. Is the cross elasticity of demand positive or negative?

10. Define the income elasticity of demand.

11. Give an example of a good whose income elasticity of demand is:
    a. Greater than 1.
    b. Positive but less than 1.
    c. Less than zero.

12. State the sign (positive or negative) of the following elasticities:
    a. The cross elasticity of demand for ice cream with respect to the price of frozen yogurt
    b. The cross elasticity of demand for corn ready to be popped with respect to the price of popcorn machines
    c. The income elasticity of demand for Caribbean cruises
    d. The income elasticity of demand for toothpaste
    e. The elasticity of supply of Irish salmon

13. Define the elasticity of supply. Is the elasticity of supply positive or negative?

14. Give an example of a good whose elasticity of supply is:
    a. Zero.
    b. Greater than zero but less than infinity.
    c. Infinity.

15. What do we mean by momentary, short-run, and long-run supply?

16. Why is momentary supply perfectly inelastic for many goods?

17. Why is long-run supply more elastic than short-run supply?

P R O B L E M S

◆ 1. The demand schedule for videotape rentals is:

Price (dollars per videotape)	Quantity demanded (number per day)
0	150
1	125
2	100
3	75
4	50
5	25
6	0

a. At what price is the elasticity of demand equal to:
   (i)   1.
   (ii) Infinity.
   (iii) Zero.
b. At what price is total revenue maximized?
c. Calculate the elasticity of demand for a rise in rental price from $4 to $5.

◆ 2. Assume that the demand for videotape rentals in problem 1 increases by 10 percent at each price.

a. Draw the old and new demand curves.
b. Calculate the elasticity of demand for a rise in the rental price from $4 to $5. Compare your answer with that of problem 1(c).

◆ 3. You have been hired as an economic consultant by OPEC and given the following schedule showing the world demand for oil:

Price (dollars per barrel)	Quantity demanded (millions of barrels per day)
10	60
20	50
30	40
40	30
50	20

Your advice is needed on the following questions:
a. If the price rises from $20 to $30 a barrel, will the total revenue from oil sales increase or decrease?
b. What will happen to total revenue if the supply of oil is decreased further and the price rises to $40 a barrel?
c. What is the price that will achieve the highest total revenue?

d. What quantity of oil will be sold at the price that answers problem 3(c)?
e. What are the values of the price elasticity of demand for price changes of $10 a barrel at average prices of $15 and $45 a barrel?
f. What is the elasticity of demand at the price that maximizes total revenue?
g. Over what price range is the demand of oil inelastic?

◆ 4. The following table gives some data on the demand for long-distance telephone calls:

Price (cents per minute)	Quantity demanded (millions of minutes per day)	
	Short-Run	Long-Run
10	700	1,000
20	500	500
30	300	0

At a price of 20¢ a minute:
a. Calculate the elasticity of short-run demand.
b. Calculate the elasticity of long-run demand.
c. Is the demand for calls more elastic in the short run or the long run?

5. In problem 4, does total expenditure on calls increase or decrease as the price of a call decreases from 20¢ a minute to 10¢ a minute?

◆ 6. The following table gives some data on the supply of long-distance phone calls:

Price (cents per minute)	Quantity supplied (millions of minutes per day)	
	Short-Run	Long-Run
10	300	0
20	500	500
30	700	10,000

At 20¢ a minute, calculate the elasticity of:
a. Short-run supply.
b. Long-run supply.

7. In problem 6, which supply is more elastic and why? Compare the elasticities of supply when the price of a call is 15¢ a minute and when it is 25¢ a minute.

Markets in Action

After studying
this chapter,
you will be
able to:

- Explain the short-run and long-run effects of a change in supply on price and on the quantity bought and sold

- Explain the short-run and long-run effects of a change in demand on price and on the quantity bought and sold

- Explain the effects of price controls

- Explain how sales taxes affect prices

- Explain how making a good or service illegal affects its price and the quantity consumed

- Explain why farm prices and revenues fluctuate

- Explain how inventories and speculation limit price fluctuations

In 1906, San Francisco suffered a devastating earthquake that destroyed more than half the city's homes but killed very few people. How did the San Francisco housing market cope with this enormous shock? What happened to rents and to the quantity of housing services available? Did rents have to be controlled to keep housing affordable? ◆ Almost every day, new machines are invented that save labor and increase productivity. How do labor markets cope with the consequences of technological change? Does a falling demand for labor drive wages lower and lower? Is it necessary to have minimum wage laws to prevent wages from falling? ◆ Almost everything we buy is taxed. How do taxes affect the prices and quantities of the things we buy? Do prices increase by the full amount of the tax so that we, the buyers, pay? Or does the seller bear part of the tax? ◆ Trading in items such as drugs, automatic firearms, and enriched uranium is prohibited. How does the prohibition of trade affect the actual amounts of prohibited goods consumed? And how does it affect the prices paid by those who trade illegally? ◆ In 1988, grain yields were extremely low as crops were devastated by drought. But in 1991, yields were high. How do farm prices and revenues react to such output fluctuations? How do the actions of speculators and official agencies influence farm revenues?

◻ In this chapter, we use the theory of demand and supply (of Chapter 4) and the concept of elasticity (of Chapter 5) to answer questions such as those just posed. We're going to begin by studying how a market responds to a severe supply shock.

Turbulent Times

Housing Markets and Rent Ceilings

To SEE HOW AN UNREGULATED MARKET COPES with a supply shock, let's transport ourselves to San Francisco in April 1906, as the city is suffering from a massive earthquake and fire. You can sense the enormity of San Francisco's problems by reading some headlines from the *New York Times* on the first days of the crisis. On April 19, 1906:

Over 500 Dead, $200,000,000 Lost in San Francisco Earthquake
Nearly Half the City Is in Ruins and 50,000 Are Homeless

On April 20, 1906:

Army of Homeless Fleeing from Devastated City
200,000 Without Shelter and Facing Famine

And on April 21, 1906:

San Francisco's New Peril; Gale Drives Fire Ferryward
Fighting Famine and Disease Among the 200,000 Refugees
San Francisco Multitudes Camped Out Shelterless and in Want

The commander of federal troops in charge of the emergency described the magnitude of the problem:

> Not a hotel of note or importance was left standing. The great apartment houses had vanished . . . two hundred-and-twenty-five thousand people were . . . homeless.[1]

Almost overnight, more than half the people in a city of 400,000 had lost their homes. Temporary shelters and camps alleviated some of the problem, but it was also necessary to utilize the apartment buildings and houses left standing. As a consequence, they had to accommodate 40 percent more people than they had before the earthquake.

The *San Francisco Chronicle* was not published for more than a month after the earthquake. When the newspaper reappeared on May 24, 1906, the city's housing shortage—what would seem to be a major news item that would still be of grave importance—

was not mentioned. Milton Friedman and George Stigler describe the situation:

> *There is not a single mention of a housing shortage!* The classified advertisements listed sixty-four offers of flats and houses for rent, and nineteen of houses for sale, against five advertisements of flats or houses wanted. Then and thereafter a considerable number of all types of accommodation except hotel rooms were offered for rent.[2]

How did San Francisco cope with such a devastating reduction in the supply of housing?

The Market Response to a Decrease in Supply

Figure 6.1 shows the market for housing in San Francisco. The demand curve for housing is *D*. There are two supply curves: the short-run supply curve, which is labeled *SS*, and the long-run supply curve, which is labeled *LS*. The short-run supply curve shows how the quantity of housing supplied varies as the price (rent) varies while the number of houses and apartment buildings remains constant. This supply response arises from a variation in the intensity with which existing buildings are used. The quantity of housing supplied increases if families decide to rent out rooms that they previously used themselves, and the quantity supplied decreases if families decide to use rooms that they previously rented out to others.

The long-run supply curve shows how the quantity supplied varies after enough time has elapsed for new apartment buildings and houses to be erected or existing buildings to be destroyed. The long-run supply curve is shown as being perfectly elastic. We do not actually know that the long-run supply curve is perfectly elastic, but it is a reasonable assumption. It implies that the cost of building an apartment is pretty much the same regardless of whether there are 50,000 or 150,000 apartments in existence.

The equilibrium price (rent) and quantity are determined at the point of intersection of the *short-run* supply curve and the demand curve. Before the earthquake, the equilibrium rent is $16 a month and the quantity is 100,000 units of housing.[3] In addition (for simplicity), the housing market is assumed

---

[1] Reported in Milton Friedman and George J. Stigler, "Roofs or Ceilings? The Current Housing Problem," in *Popular Essays on Current Problems*, vol. 1, no. 2 (New York: Foundation for Economic Education, 1946), 3–159.

[2] *Ibid.*, 3.

[3] These numbers are close to the actual monthly rent and quantity of housing in San Francisco in 1906. (Average monthly incomes were about $46 in 1906.)

FIGURE **6.1**

The San Francisco Housing Market in 1906

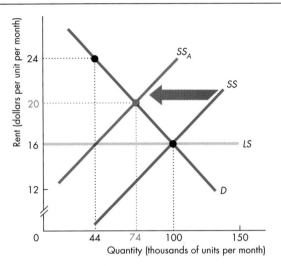

(a) After earthquake

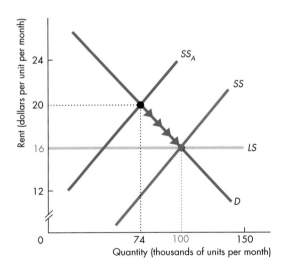

(b) Long-run adjustment

Part (a) shows that before the earthquake 100,000 housing units were rented at $16 a month. After the earthquake, the short-run supply curve shifts from SS to SS_A. The rent rises to $20 a month, and the quantity of housing decreases to 74,000 units.

With rents at $20 a month, there is profit in building new apartments and houses. As the building program proceeds, the short-run supply curve shifts rightward (part b). Rents gradually fall to $16 a month, and the quantity of housing increases gradually to 100,000 units—as shown by the arrowed line.

to be on its long-run supply curve, *LS*. Let's now look at the situation immediately after the earthquake.

Figure 6.1(a) reflects the new situation. The destruction of buildings decreases the supply of housing and shifts the short-run supply curve *SS* leftward to *SS_A*. If people use the remaining housing units with the same intensity as before the earthquake and if the rent remains at $16 a month, only 44,000 units of housing are available. But rents do not remain at $16 a month. With only 44,000 units of housing available, the maximum rent that someone is willing to pay for the last available apartment is $24 a month. So to get an apartment, prospective tenants offer to pay a higher rent than $16. As people try to outbid each other for the available apartments, rents rise. In Fig. 6.1(a), the rent rises to $20 a month. As the rent rises, people economize on their use of space and make spare rooms, attics, and basements available to others. The quantity of housing supplied increases to 74,000 units.

The response that we've just seen takes place in the short run. What happens in the long run?

Long-Run Adjustments

With sufficient time for new apartments and houses to be constructed, supply will increase. The long-run supply curve tells us that in the long run, housing will be supplied at a rent of $16 a month. Because the rent of $20 a month exceeds the long-run supply price of housing, there will be a rush to build new apartments and houses. As time passes, more apartments and houses are built, and the short-run supply curve gradually shifts rightward.

Figure 6.1(b) illustrates the long-run adjustment. As more housing is built, the short-run supply curve shifts rightward and intersects the demand curve at lower rents and larger quantities. The market equilibrium follows the arrows down the demand curve. The process ends when there is no further profit in building new housing units. Such a situation occurs at the original rent of $16 a month and the original quantity of 100,000 units of housing.

The analysis of the short-run and long-run response of a housing market that we've just studied applies to a wide range of other markets. And it applies regardless of whether the initial shock is to supply (as it is here) or demand. *Reading Between the Lines* on pp. 136–137 looks at another example, the market for mohair, that experienced both supply and demand shocks in 1994.

A Regulated Housing Market

We've just seen how a housing market responds to a decrease in supply. And we've seen that a key part of the adjustment process is a rise in rents. Suppose the government passes a law to stop rents from rising. Such a law is called a price ceiling. A **price ceiling** is a regulation that makes it illegal to charge a price higher than a specified level. When a price ceiling is applied to rents in housing markets, it is called a **rent ceiling**. How does a rent ceiling affect the way the housing market works?

The effect of a price (rent) ceiling depends on whether it is imposed at a level that is above or below the equilibrium price (rent). A price ceiling set above the equilibrium price has no effect. The reason is that the price ceiling does not constrain the market forces. The force of the law and the market forces are not in conflict. But a price ceiling below the equilibrium price has powerful effects on a market. The reason is that it attempts to prevent the price from regulating the quantities demanded and supplied. The force of the law and the market forces are in conflict, and one (or both) of these forces must yield to some degree. Let's study the effects of a price ceiling set below the equilibrium price by returning to San Francisco.

What would have happened in San Francisco if a rent ceiling of $16 a month—the rent before the earthquake—had been imposed? This question and some answers are illustrated in Fig. 6.2. At a rent of $16 a month, the quantity of housing supplied is 44,000 units and the quantity demanded is 100,000 units. So there is a shortage of 56,000 units of housing.

When the quantity demanded exceeds the quantity supplied, what determines the quantity actually bought and sold? The answer is the smaller quantity—the quantity supplied. Suppliers cannot be forced to offer housing for rent, and at a monthly rent of $16, they are willing to offer only 44,000 units.

So the immediate effect of a rent ceiling of $16 a month is that only 44,000 units of housing are available and a demand for a further 56,000 units is unsatisfied. But the story does not end here. Somehow, the 44,000 units of available housing must be allocated among the people demanding 100,000 units. How is this allocation achieved?

In an unregulated market, the shortage would drive the rent up, as shown in Fig. 6.1(a), and the price mechanism would regulate the quantities demanded and supplied and allocate the scarce housing resources. As long as one person was willing to pay a higher price than another person's minimum

FIGURE 6.2
A Rent Ceiling

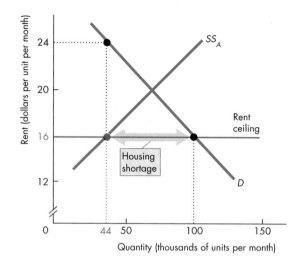

If there had been a rent ceiling of $16 a month, then the quantity of housing supplied after the earthquake would have been stuck at 44,000 units. People would willingly have paid $24 a month for the 44,000th unit. Because the last unit of housing available is worth more than the regulated rent, frustrated buyers will spend time searching for housing, and frustrated buyers and sellers will make deals in a black market.

supply price, the price would rise and the quantity of housing available would increase. When a rent ceiling tries to block this market mechanism by making rent increases illegal, two developments occur. They are:

■ Search activity
■ Black markets

Search Activity

When the quantity demanded exceeds the quantity supplied, many suppliers have nothing to sell and many demanders have nothing to buy. So unsatisfied demanders devote time and other resources searching for a supplier. The time spent looking for someone with whom to do business is called **search activity**. Even in markets in which prices adjust freely to keep the quantities demanded and supplied equal, search activity takes place. But when price is regulated, search activity increases.

Search activity is costly. It uses time and other resources, such as telephones, cars, and gasoline that could have been used in other productive ways. Frustrated would-be renters scan the newspapers, not for housing ads but for death notices! Any information about newly available housing is useful. And they race to be first on the scene when news of a possible supplier breaks. The *total cost* of housing is equal to the rent—the regulated price—plus the cost of the time and other resources spent searching—an unregulated price. So rent ceilings increase the opportunity cost of housing. They might control the rent portion of the cost of housing, but they do not control the total cost. And the total cost may well be *higher* than the unregulated market price.

Black Markets

A **black market** is an illegal trading arrangement in which buyers and sellers do business at a price higher than the legally imposed price ceiling. There are many examples of markets, in addition to housing markets, that are regulated in some way and in which economic forces result in black market trading. Most states, for example, ban ticket scalping, but this method of allocating scarce tickets for big games and rock concerts is common.

In regulated housing markets, a black market usually takes the form of a buyer and a seller colluding to avoid the rent ceiling. They have a written agreement that uses the regulated rent but have an unwritten side-deal that changes the actual rent. The level of the black market rent depends mainly on how tightly the government polices its rent ceiling regulations, the chances of being caught violating them, and the scale of the penalties imposed for violations.

At one extreme, the chance of being caught violating a rent ceiling is small. In this case, the black market will function similarly to an unregulated market, and the black market rent and quantity traded will be close to the unregulated equilibrium. At the other extreme, where policing is highly effective and where large penalties are imposed on violators, the rent ceiling will restrict the quantity traded. In the San Francisco example, with strict enforcement of the rent ceiling, the quantity of housing available is restricted to 44,000 units. A small number of people will offer housing for sale at $24 a month—the highest price that a buyer is willing to pay—and the government will detect and punish some of these black market traders.

Rent Ceilings in Practice

There are many modern examples of rent ceilings, but the best is New York City, where rent ceilings have been used since World War II (when they were introduced as a temporary measure). One consequence of New York's rent ceilings is that families that have lived in the city for a long time—including some rich and famous ones—enjoy incredibly low rents, while newcomers to the city pay high rents for hard-to-find apartments. At the same time, landlords in Harlem and the Bronx abandon unprofitable housing units, leaving entire city blocks occupied only by rats and drug dealers.

When rent ceilings are in force, frustrated renters and landlords constantly seek ways of increasing rents that do not violate the letter of the law but defeat its purpose. One common way is for a new tenant to pay a high price for worthless fittings—$2,000 for threadbare drapes. Another is for the tenant to pay for new locks and keys—a device called "key money."

But to the extent that the law does prevent the rent from adjusting to bring the quantity demanded into equality with the quantity supplied, factors other than rent must allocate the scarce housing. One of these factors is discrimination on the basis of race, ethnicity, or sex.

The effects of rent ceilings in New York and in other cities such as London and Paris have led Assar Lindbeck, chairman of the economic science Nobel Prize committee to suggest that rent ceilings are the most effective means yet for destroying cities, even more effective than the hydrogen bomb.

R E V I E W

- A decrease in the supply of housing increases equilibrium rents.
- In the short run, higher rents result in a decrease in the quantity of housing demanded and an increase in the quantity supplied as existing houses and apartments are used more intensively.
- In the long run, higher rents stimulate building. The supply of housing increases, and rents fall.
- Rent ceilings limit the ability of the housing market to respond to change and can result in a permanent housing shortage.

We next look at the effects of a price floor—a minimum price. To do so, we'll study the labor market.

The Labor Market and Minimum Wages

FOR MOST OF US, THE LABOR MARKET IS THE most important market in which we participate. It is the market that influences the jobs we get and the wages we earn. Firms decide how much labor to demand, and households decide how much labor to supply. The wage rate balances the quantity demanded and the quantity supplied and determines the level of employment. But the labor market is constantly being bombarded by shocks, and wages and employment prospects are constantly changing. The most pervasive source of these shocks is the advance of technology.

Labor-saving technology is constantly being invented. As a result, the demand for certain types of labor, usually the least skilled types, is constantly decreasing. How does the labor market cope with this continuous decrease in the demand for low-skilled labor? Doesn't it mean that the wages of the low-skilled workers are constantly falling? Let's find out.

Figure 6.3 shows the market for low-skilled labor. Other things remaining the same, the lower the wage rate, the greater is the quantity of labor demanded by firms. The demand curve for labor, *D* in part (a), shows this relationship between the wage rate and the quantity of labor demanded. Other things remaining the same, the higher the wage rate, the greater is the quantity of labor supplied by households. But the longer the period of adjustment, the greater is the elasticity of supply of labor. Thus there are two supply curves: a short-run supply curve *SS* and a long-run supply curve *LS*.

The short-run supply curve shows how the number of hours of labor supplied by a given number of workers changes as the wage rate changes. To get workers to work more hours, firms must offer higher wages, so the short-run supply curve slopes upward.

The long-run supply curve shows the relationship between the quantity of labor supplied and the wage rate after enough time has passed for people to acquire new skills and find new types of jobs. The number of people in the low-skilled labor market depends on the wage rate in this market compared with other opportunities. If the wage rate is high enough, people will enter this market. If the wage rate is too low, people will leave it. Some will seek training to enter the higher-skilled labor markets, and others will leave the labor force and work at home or retire.

FIGURE 6.3

A Market for Low-skilled Labor

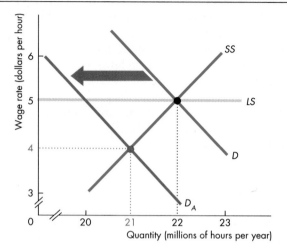

(a) After invention

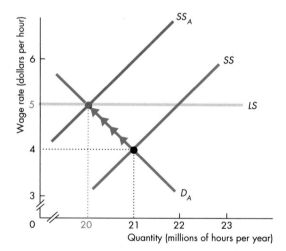

(b) Long-run adjustment

Part (a) shows the immediate effect of a labor-saving invention on the market for low-skilled labor. Initially, the wage rate is $5 an hour and 22 million hours of labor a year are employed. A labor-saving invention shifts the demand curve from *D* to D_A. The wage rate falls to $4 an hour, and employment decreases to 21 million hours a year. With the lower wage, some workers leave this market, and the short-run supply curve starts to shift gradually to SS_A (part b). The wage rate gradually increases, and the employment level decreases. In the long run, the wage rate returns to $5 an hour, and employment falls to 20 million hours a year.

Because people can freely enter and leave the low-skilled labor market, the long-run supply curve is elastic. In Fig. 6.3, for simplicity, the long-run supply curve is assumed to be perfectly elastic (horizontal). The low-skilled labor market is in equilibrium at a wage rate of $5 an hour, and 22 million hours of labor are employed.

What happens if a labor-saving invention decreases the demand for low-skilled labor? Figure 6.3(a) shows the short-run effects of such a change. The demand curve before the new technology is introduced is D. After the introduction of the new technology, the demand curve shifts leftward, to D_A. The wage rate falls to $4 an hour, and the quantity of labor employed decreases to 21 million hours. This short-run effect on wages and employment is not the end of the story.

People who are now earning only $4 an hour look around for other opportunities. They see many other jobs (in markets for other types of skills) that pay wages above $4 an hour. One by one, workers decide to go back to school or they take jobs that pay less but offer on-the-job training. As a result, the short-run supply curve begins to shift leftward.

Figure 6.3(b) shows the long-run adjustment. As the short-run supply curve shifts leftward, it intersects the demand curve D_A at higher wage rates and lower levels of employment. In the long run, the short-run supply curve shifts all the way to SS_A. At this point, the wage has returned to $5 an hour, and employment has decreased to 20 million hours a year.

Sometimes, the adjustment process that we've just described takes place quickly. At other times, it is a long, drawn-out affair. If the adjustment process is long and drawn out, wages remain low for a long period. In such a situation, the government is tempted to intervene in the labor market by legislating a minimum wage to protect the lowest-paid workers.

The Minimum Wage

A **minimum wage law** is a regulation that makes hiring labor below a specified wage illegal. If the minimum wage is set *below* the equilibrium wage, it has no effect. The law and the market forces are not in conflict. But if a minimum wage is set *above* the equilibrium wage, the minimum wage is in conflict with the market forces and does have some effects on the labor market. Let's study these effects by returning to the market for low-skilled labor.

Suppose that when the wage falls to $4 an hour (in Fig. 6.3a), the government imposes a minimum wage of $5 an hour. What are the effects of this law? Figure 6.4 shows the minimum wage as the horizontal red line labeled "Minimum wage." At this minimum wage, 20 million hours of labor are demanded (point *a*) and 22 million hours of labor are supplied (point *b*) so 2 million hours of available labor go unemployed.

What are the workers doing with their unemployed hours? They are searching for work. With only 20 million hours of labor employed, there are many people willing to supply their labor for wage rates much lower than the minimum wage. In fact, the 20 millionth hour of labor will be supplied for as

FIGURE 6.4

Minimum Wage and Unemployment

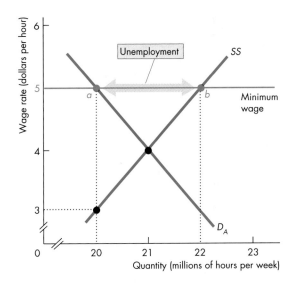

The demand curve for labor is D_A, and the supply curve is SS. In an unregulated market, the wage rate is $4 an hour, and 21 million hours of labor a year are employed. If a minimum wage of $5 an hour is imposed, only 20 million hours are hired but 22 million hours are available. Unemployment—*ab*—of 2 million hours a year is created. With only 20 million hours being demanded, some workers will willingly supply that 20 millionth hour for $3. These frustrated unemployed workers will spend time and other resources looking for a job.

little as $3. How do we know that there are people willing to work for as little as $3 an hour?

Look again at Fig. 6.4. As you can see, when only 20 million hours of work are available, the lowest wage at which workers are willing to supply that 20 millionth hour—read off from the supply curve—is $3 an hour. Someone who manages to find a job will earn $5 an hour—$2 an hour more than the lowest wage rate at which someone is willing to work. Therefore it pays the unemployed to spend time and effort looking for work. Even though only 20 million hours of labor actually get employed, each person spends time and effort searching for one of the scarce jobs.

The Minimum Wage in Reality

The Fair Labor Standards Act makes it illegal to hire a worker for less than $4.25 an hour. Economists do not agree on the effects of the minimum wage or on how much unemployment it causes. But they do agree that minimum wages bite hardest on the low-skilled workers. Because there is a preponderance of low-skilled workers among the young—they have had less opportunity to obtain work experience and acquire skills—we would expect the minimum wage to cause more unemployment among young workers than among older workers. That is exactly what happens. The unemployment rate for teenagers is more than twice the average. Although many factors other than the minimum wage influence unemployment among young people, it is almost certainly the case that part of the higher unemployment among the young arises from the impact of minimum wage laws.

R E V I E W

■ A decrease in the demand for low-skilled labor lowers the equilibrium wage.

■ In the short run, lower wages result in a decrease in the quantity of low-skilled labor supplied and bring forth an increase in the quantity demanded.

■ In the long run, lower wages encourage some people to leave the labor force and others to train and obtain more skill. The supply of low-skilled labor decreases, and wages rise.

■ Minimum wage regulations limit the ability of the labor market to respond to change and result in persistent unemployment.

Next we study the effects of taxes.

Taxes

LAST YEAR THE FEDERAL, STATE, AND LOCAL governments raised more than $500 billion—an average of $2,000 per person—by taxing the goods and services that we buy. These taxes include the state sales tax and special taxes on gasoline, alcoholic beverages, and tobacco. When you buy a good or service that is taxed you pay the amount on the price tag *plus* an additional amount, the *tax*. What are the effects of taxes on the prices and quantities of goods bought and sold? Do the prices of the goods and services you buy increase by the full amount of the tax? Because the sales tax is added to the price of a good or service, isn't it obvious that you, the consumer, pay the entire tax? Isn't the price higher than it otherwise would be by an amount equal to the tax? It can be, but usually it isn't. And it is even possible that you actually pay none of the tax, forcing the seller to pay it for you. Let's see how we can make sense of these apparently absurd statements.

Who Pays the Sales Tax?

To study the effect of the sales tax, we need to start by looking at a market in which there is no such tax. We'll then introduce a sales tax and see the changes it brings.

Figure 6.5 shows the market for CD players. The demand curve is *D*, and the supply curve is *S*. The equilibrium price of a CD player is $100, and the quantity is 5,000 players a week.

Suppose the federal government puts a $10 sales tax on CD players. What are the effects of this tax on the price and quantity of CD players? To answer this question, we need to work out what happens to demand and supply in the market for CD players.

When a good is taxed, it has two prices: a price that excludes the tax and a price that includes it. Consumers respond only to the price that includes the tax. Producers respond only to the price they receive—the price that excludes the tax. The tax is like a wedge between these two prices.

Let's think of the price on the vertical axis of Fig. 6.5 as the price paid by the consumer that *includes* the tax. When a tax is imposed, there is no change in demand—the demand curve does not shift. Regardless of whether the price includes some tax or not, it is the total price including the tax that influences the quantity demanded.

FIGURE 6.5

The Sales Tax

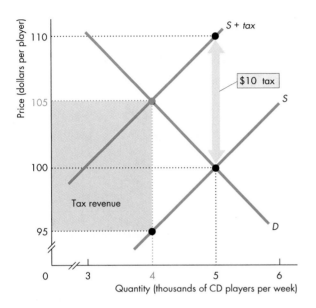

The demand curve for CD players is D, and the supply curve is S. With no sales tax, the price is $100 a player and 5,000 players a week are bought and sold. Then a sales tax of $10 a player is imposed. The price on the vertical axis is the price *including* the tax. The demand curve does not change, but the supply decreases and the supply curve shifts leftward. The curve S + tax shows the terms on which sellers will make CD players available. The vertical distance between the supply curve S and the new supply curve S + tax equals the tax—$10 a player.

The new equilibrium is at a price of $105 with 4,000 CD players a week bought and sold. The sales tax increases the price by less than the tax, decreases the price received by the supplier, and decreases the quantity bought and sold. It brings in revenue to the government equal to the blue area.

But the supply curve *does* shift. When a sales tax is imposed on a good, it is offered for sale at a higher price than in a no-tax situation. Supply of the good decreases, and the supply curve shifts leftward to S + tax. To determine the position of this new supply curve, we add the tax to the minimum price that suppliers are willing to accept for each quantity sold. For example, with no tax, suppliers are willing to sell 4,000 players a week for $95 a player. So with a $10 tax, they will supply 4,000 players a week for $105—a price that includes the tax. Similarly, with

no tax, suppliers are willing to sell 5,000 players a week at a price of $100, so they will supply this quantity for $110 including the tax. The new supply curve S + tax lies to the left of the original curve—supply has decreased—and the vertical distance between the original supply curve S and the new supply curve S + tax equals the tax. The curve S + tax describes the terms on which the good can be bought.

A new equilibrium is determined where the new supply curve intersects the demand curve—at a price of $105 and a quantity of 4,000 CD players a week. The $10 sales tax has increased the price paid by the consumer by only $5 ($105 versus $100), which is less than the $10 tax. And it has decreased the price received by the supplier by $5 ($95 versus $100). The $10 tax paid is made up of the higher price to the buyer and the lower price to the seller.

The tax brings in tax revenue to the government equal to the tax per item multiplied by the items sold. The blue area in Fig. 6.5 illustrates the tax revenue. The $10 tax on CD players brings in a tax revenue of $40,000 a week.

In this example, the buyer and the seller split the tax equally; the buyer pays $5 a player and so does the seller. This equal sharing of the tax is a special case and does not usually occur. But some split of the tax between the buyer and seller is usual. Cases in which either the buyer or the seller pays the entire tax can, however, occur. Let's look at these.

Tax Division and Elasticity of Demand

The division of the burden of a tax between buyers and sellers depends in part, on the elasticity of demand. Again, there are two extreme cases:

- Perfectly inelastic demand—buyer pays.
- Perfectly elastic demand—seller pays.

Perfectly Inelastic Demand   Figure 6.6(a) shows the market for insulin, a vital daily medication of diabetics. The quantity demanded is 100,000 doses a day, regardless of the price. That is, a diabetic would sacrifice all other goods and services rather than not consume the insulin dose that provides good health and survival. The demand for insulin reflects this fact and is perfectly inelastic, as shown by the vertical curve D. The supply curve of insulin is S. With no tax, the price is $2 a dose, and the 100,000 doses a day that keep the population of diabetics healthy are bought.

FIGURE 6.6

Sales Tax and the Elasticity of Demand

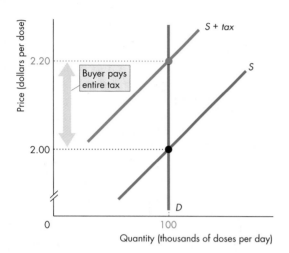

(a) Inelastic demand

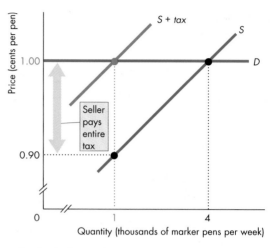

(b) Elastic demand

Part (a) shows the market for insulin. The demand for insulin is perfectly inelastic. With no tax, the price is $2 a dose and 100,000 doses a day are bought. A sales tax of 20¢ a dose increases the price at which sellers are willing to make insulin available and shifts the supply curve to S + tax. The price rises to $2.20 a dose, but the quantity bought does not change. Buyers pay the entire tax.

Part (b) shows the market for pink marker pens. The demand for pink marker pens is perfectly elastic. With no tax the price of a pink marker pen is $1 and 4,000 a week are bought. A sales tax of 10¢ a pink pen shifts the supply curve to S + tax. The price remains at $1 a pen, and the quantity of pink markers sold decreases to 1,000 a week. Suppliers pay the entire tax.

If insulin is taxed at 20¢ a dose, we must add the tax to the minimum price at which the drug companies are willing to sell insulin to determine the terms on which it will be available to consumers. The result is a new supply curve S + tax. The price rises to $2.20 a dose, but the quantity does not change. The buyer pays the entire sales tax of 20¢ a dose.

Perfectly Elastic Demand   Figure 6.6(b) shows the market for pink marker pens. Aside from a few pink freaks, no one cares whether they use a pink, blue, yellow, or green marker pen. If pink markers are less expensive than the others, everyone will use pink. If pink markers are more expensive than the others, no one will use them. The demand for pink marker pens is perfectly elastic at the price of other colored marker pens—$1 a pen in Fig. 6.6(b). The demand curve for pink markers is the horizontal curve D. The supply curve is S. With no tax, the price of a pink marker is $1, and 4,000 a week are bought at that price.

If a sales tax of 10¢ a pen is levied on pink marker pens, we must add the tax to the minimum price at which suppliers are willing to sell them to determine the terms on which pink marker pens will be available to consumers. The new supply curve is S + tax. The price remains at $1 a pen, and the quantity decreases to 1,000 a week. The 10¢ sales tax has left the price paid by the consumer unchanged but has decreased the amount received by the supplier by the full amount of the sales tax—10¢ a pen. As a result, sellers decrease the quantity offered for sale.

We've seen that when demand is perfectly inelastic, the buyer pays the entire tax, and when demand is perfectly elastic, the supplier pays it. In the usual case, in which demand is neither perfectly inelastic nor perfectly elastic, the tax is split between the buyer and the seller. But the division depends on the elasticity of demand. The more inelastic the demand, the larger is the portion of the tax paid by the buyer.

FIGURE 6.7

Sales Tax and the Elasticity of Supply

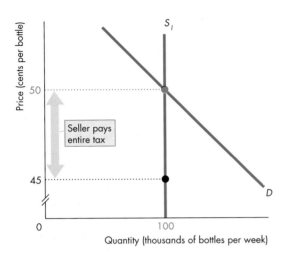

(a) Inelastic supply

(b) Elastic supply

Part (a) shows the market for water from a mineral spring. Supply is perfectly inelastic. With no tax the price is 50¢ a bottle. The sales tax of 5¢ decreases the price received by sellers, but the price remains at 50¢ a bottle, and the number of bottles bought remains the same. Suppliers pay the entire tax.

Part (b) shows the market for sand. Supply is perfectly elastic. With no tax the price is 10¢ a pound and 5,000 pounds a week are bought. The sales tax of 1¢ a pound increases the minimum price at which sellers are willing to supply to 11¢ a pound. The supply curve shifts to S_E + *tax*. The price increases to 11¢ a pound. Buyers pay the entire tax.

Tax Division and Elasticity of Supply

The division of the burden of a tax between buyers and sellers also depends, in part, on the elasticity of supply. There are two extreme cases:

- Perfectly inelastic supply—seller pays.
- Perfectly elastic supply—buyer pays.

Perfectly Inelastic Supply   Figure 6.7(a) shows the market for water from a mineral spring that flows at a constant rate that can't be controlled. The quantity supplied is 100,000 bottles a week, regardless of the price. The supply is perfectly inelastic, and the supply curve is S_I. The demand curve for the water from this spring is D. With no tax, the price is 50¢ a bottle, and the 100,000 bottles that flow from the spring are bought at that price.

Suppose this spring water is taxed at 5¢ a bottle. Even if the price received by the spring owners fell by

the full amount of the tax, they would still produce the same quantity—100,000 bottles a week. Consumers, on the other hand, are willing to buy the 100,000 bottles available each week only if the price is 50¢ a bottle. So the price remains at 50¢ a bottle, and the suppliers pay the entire tax. The sales tax of 5¢ a bottle reduces the price received by suppliers to 45¢ a bottle.

Perfectly Elastic Supply   Figure 6.7(b) shows the market for sand from which computer-chip makers extract silicon. A virtually unlimited quantity of this sand is available, and its owners are willing to supply any quantity at a price of 10¢ a pound. The supply is perfectly elastic, and the supply curve is S_E. The demand curve for sand is D. With no tax, the price is 10¢ a pound, and 5,000 pounds a week are bought.

If this sand is taxed at 1¢ a pound, we must add the tax to the minimum price at which the suppliers are willing to sell the sand to determine the terms on which this sand will be available to computer-chip makers. Because with no tax the suppliers of sand are willing to supply any quantity at 10¢ a pound, with the 1¢ tax they are willing to supply any quantity at 11¢ a pound along the curve $S_E + tax$. A new equilibrium is determined where the new supply curve intersects the demand curve—at a price of 11¢ a pound and a quantity of 3,000 pounds a week. The sales tax has increased the price paid by consumers by the full amount of the tax—1¢ a pound—and has decreased the quantity sold.

We've seen that when supply is perfectly inelastic, the seller pays the entire tax, and when supply is perfectly elastic, the buyer pays it. In the usual case, in which supply is neither perfectly inelastic nor perfectly elastic, the tax is split between the seller and the buyer. But the division depends on the elasticity of supply. The more elastic the supply, the larger is the portion of the tax paid by the buyer.

Sales Taxes in Practice

We've looked at the range of possible effects of a sales tax by studying the extreme cases. In practice supply and demand are rarely perfectly elastic or perfectly inelastic. They lie somewhere in between, like in the first example we studied. But some items tend toward one of the extremes. For example, a heavily taxed item such as alcohol, tobacco, or gasoline has a low elasticity of demand. Consequently the buyer pays most of the tax. Also, because demand is inelastic, the quantity bought does not decrease much and the government collects a large tax revenue.

It is unusual to tax an item heavily if its demand is elastic. But in 1991, the Federal government was scraping around for every dollar it could find to decrease its deficit. It came up with a plan to put a 10 percent "luxury tax" on pleasure boats, private airplanes, high-priced cars, furs, and jewelry, which it estimated would bring in $300 million a year. But the government did not reckon on the elasticity of demand for these items to be as large as it turned out to be. The quantities of pleasure boats and other luxury items bought decreased by up to 90 percent and the amount of tax revenue collected by the government in 1991 was only $30 million, one tenth the amount it expected. The luxury tax was quickly abandoned.

This short-lived experiment with a luxury tax explains why the items that are taxed are those that have inelastic demands and why buyers pay most of the taxes.

REVIEW

■ The effect of a sales tax depends on the elasticities of supply and demand.

■ For a given supply, the less elastic the demand, the larger is the price increase, the smaller is the quantity decrease and the larger is the portion of the tax paid by the buyer.

■ For a given demand, the more elastic the supply, the larger is the price increase, the larger is the quantity decrease and the larger is the portion of the tax paid by the buyer.

Taxes are just one method used to change prices and quantities. Another is to prohibit trade in a good.

Markets for Prohibited Goods

THE MARKETS FOR MANY GOODS AND SERVICES are regulated, and buying and selling some goods is prohibited—the goods and services are illegal. The best known examples of such goods are drugs, such as marijuana, cocaine, and heroin.

Despite the fact that these drugs are illegal, trade in them is a multibillion dollar business. This trade can be understood by using the same economic models and principles that explain trade in legal goods.

As you study the market for drugs, remember that economics tries to answer questions about how the economic world works. It neither condones or condemns the activities it seeks to explain. As a well-informed citizen, you may have an opinion about drugs and about public policy toward them. What you learn about the economics of markets for illegal goods is one input into developing your opinion. But it is not a substitute for your moral judgments and does not help you to develop those judgments. What follows is a value free analysis of how markets for prohibited goods work and not an argument about how they ought to be regulated and controlled.

To study the market for prohibited goods, we're first going to examine the prices and quantities that would prevail if these goods were not prohibited. Next, we'll see how prohibition works. Then we'll see how a tax might be used to limit the consumption of these goods.

A Free Market for Drugs

Figure 6.8 shows a market for drugs. The demand curve, *D,* shows that, other things remaining the same, the lower the price of drugs, the larger is the quantity of drugs demanded. The supply curve, *S,* shows that, other things remaining the same, the lower the price of drugs, the smaller is the quantity supplied. If drugs were not prohibited, the quantity bought and sold would be Q_c and the price would be P_c.

Prohibition on Drugs

When a good is prohibited, the cost of trading in the good increases. By how much the cost increases and on whom the cost falls depend on the penalties for violating the law and the effectiveness with which the law is enforced. The larger the penalties for violation and the more effective the policing, the higher are the costs. Penalties may be imposed on sellers, buyers, or both.

Penalties on Sellers   Drug dealers in the United States face large penalties if their activities are detected. For example, a marijuana dealer could pay a $200,000 fine and serve a 15-year prison term. A heroin dealer could pay a $500,000 fine and serve a 20-year prison term. These penalties are part of the cost of supplying illegal drugs, and they bring a decrease in supply—a leftward shift in the supply curve. To determine the new supply curve, we add the cost of breaking the law to the minimum price that drug dealers are willing to accept. In Fig. 6.8, the cost of breaking the law by selling drugs (*CBL*) is added to the minimum price that dealers will accept, and the supply curve shifts leftward to *S + CBL*. If penalties are imposed only on sellers, the market moves from point *c* to point *a*. The price increases, and the quantity bought decreases.

Penalties on Buyers   In the United States, it is illegal to *possess* drugs such as marijuana, cocaine, and heroin. For example, possession of marijuana can bring a prison term of 1 year and possession of heroin can bring a prison term of 2 years. Penalties fall on buyers, and the cost of breaking the law must be subtracted from the value of the good to determine the maximum price buyers are willing to pay. Demand decreases, and the demand curve shifts leftward. In Fig. 6.8, the demand curve shifts to *D – CBL*. If penalties are imposed only on buyers, the market

FIGURE **6.8**

The Market for a Prohibited Good

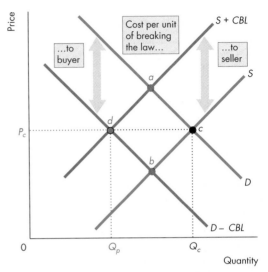

The demand curve for drugs is *D*, and the supply curve is *S*. With no prohibition on drugs, the quantity consumed is Q_c at a price of P_c—point *c*. If selling drugs is illegal, the cost of breaking the law by selling drugs (*CBL*) is added to the other costs and supply decreases to *S + CBL*. The price rises, and the quantity consumed decreases—point *a*. If buying drugs is illegal, the cost of breaking the law is subtracted from the maximum price that buyers are willing to pay, and demand decreases to *D – CBL*. The price falls, and the quantity consumed decreases—point *b*. If both buying and selling are illegal, both the supply and demand curves shift, the quantity consumed decreases even more, but (in this example) the price remains at its unregulated level—point *d*.

moves from point *c* to point *b*. The price and the quantity bought decrease.

Penalties on Both Sellers and Buyers   If penalties are imposed on sellers *and* buyers, both supply and demand decrease, and both the supply curve and the demand curve shift. In Fig. 6.8 the costs of breaking the law are the same for both buyers and sellers, so both curves shift leftward by the same amounts. The market moves to point *d*. The price remains at the competitive market price, but the quantity bought decreases to Q_p.

The larger the penalty and the greater the degree of law enforcement, the larger is the decrease in demand and/or supply and the greater is the shift of the demand and/or supply curve. If the penalties are heavier on sellers, the price will rise above P_c, and if the penalties are heavier on buyers, the price will fall below P_c. In the United States, the penalties on sellers are much larger than those on buyers. As a result, the decrease in supply is much larger than the decrease in demand. The quantity of drugs traded decreases and the price increases compared with an unregulated market.

With high enough penalties and effective law enforcement, it is possible to decrease demand and/or supply to the point at which the quantity bought is zero. But in reality, such an outcome is unusual. It does not happen in the case of illegal drugs. The key reason is the high cost of law enforcement and insufficient resources for the police to achieve effective enforcement. Because of this situation, some people suggest that drugs (and other illegal goods) should be legalized and sold openly but also be taxed at a high rate in the same way that legal drugs such as alcohol are taxed. How would such an arrangement work?

Legalizing and Taxing Drugs

Figure 6.9 shows what happens if drugs are legalized and taxed. With no tax, the quantity of drugs is Q_c and the price is P_c. Now suppose that drugs are taxed at a rate chosen to make the quantity bought the same as with a prohibition. The tax added to the supply price shifts the supply curve to $S + tax$. Equilibrium occurs at a quantity of Q_P. The price paid by consumers increases to P_b, and the price received by suppliers decreases to P_s. The government collects a tax revenue equal to the blue area in the figure.

Illegal Trading to Evade the Tax   It is likely that an extremely high tax rate would be needed to cut drug consumption to the level prevailing with a prohibition. It is also likely that many drug dealers and consumers would try to cover up their activities to evade the tax. If they did act in this way, they would face the cost of breaking the law—the tax law. If the penalty for tax law violation is as severe and as effectively policed as drug-dealing laws, the analysis we've already conducted applies also to this case. The quantity of drugs consumed would depend on the penalties for law breaking and on the way in which

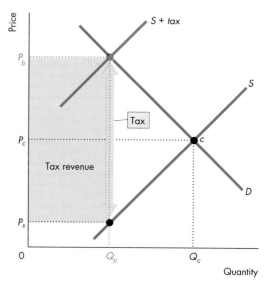

FIGURE 6.9

Legalizing and Taxing Drugs

Drugs are legalized but taxed at a high rate. The tax added to the supply price shifts the supply curve from S to $S + tax$. The quantity bought decreases to Q_p, the price paid by consumers increases to P_b, and the price received by suppliers decreases to P_s. The government collects a tax revenue equal to the blue shaded area.

the penalties are assigned to buyers and sellers. Tax revenue would fall short of the blue area in Fig. 6.9.

Some Pros and Cons of Taxes Versus Prohibition
So which works more effectively, prohibition or taxing? The comparison we've just made suggests that the two methods can be made to be equivalent if the taxes and penalties are set at the appropriate levels. But there are some other differences.

In favor of taxes and against prohibition is the fact that the tax revenue can be used to make law enforcement more effective. It can also be used to run a more effective education campaign against drugs. In favor of prohibition and against taxes is the fact that a prohibition sends a signal that may influence preferences, decreasing the demand for drugs. Also, some people intensely dislike the idea of the government profiting from trade in harmful substances.

■ Penalizing sellers of an illegal good increases the cost of selling the good and decreases the supply of it.

■ Penalizing buyers of an illegal good decreases the willingness to pay for the good and decreases the demand for it.

■ Penalizing either buyers or sellers decreases the quantity of an illegal good.

■ The price of an illegal good increases if penalties on sellers are higher than those on buyers, and the price decreases if penalties on buyers are higher than those on sellers.

■ Taxing a good at a sufficiently high rate can achieve the same consumption level as prohibition.

Stabilizing Farm Revenue

WHEN FLOODS COVERED VAST TRACTS OF THE Midwest in the summer of 1993, many farmers saw their crops wiped out. Farm output fluctuates a great deal because of fluctuations in the weather. How do changes in farm output affect farm prices and farm revenues? And how might farm revenues be stabilized? The answers to these questions depend on how the markets for agricultural products are organized. We'll begin by looking at an unregulated agricultural market.

An Unregulated Agricultural Market

Figure 6.10 illustrates the market for wheat. In both parts, the demand curve for wheat is *D*. Once farmers have harvested their crop, they have no control over the quantity supplied, and supply is inelastic along a *momentary supply curve*. In normal climate conditions, the momentary supply curve is MS_0 (in both parts of the figure).

The price is determined at the point of intersection of the momentary supply curve and the demand curve. In normal conditions, the price is $2 a bushel. The quantity of wheat produced is 20 billion bushels, and farm revenue is $40 billion. Suppose the opportunity cost to farmers of producing wheat is also $40 billion. Then in normal conditions, farmers just cover their opportunity cost.

FIGURE 6.10
Harvests, Farm Prices, and Farm Revenue

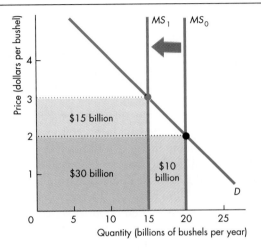

(a) Poor harvest: revenue increases

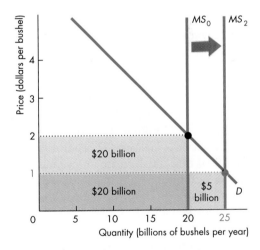

(b) Bumper harvest: revenue decreases

The demand curve for wheat is *D*. In normal times, the supply curve is MS_0, and 20 million bushels are sold for $2 a bushel. In part (a), a poor harvest decreases supply to MS_1. The price rises to $3 a bushel, and farm revenue increases to $45 billion—the $15 billion increase from the higher price (light blue area) exceeds the $10 billion decrease from the smaller quantity (red area). In part (b), a bumper harvest increases supply to MS_2. The price falls to $1 a bushel, and farm revenue decreases to $25 billion—the $20 billion decrease from the lower price (light blue area) exceeds the $5 billion increase from the increase in the quantity sold (red area).

Poor Harvest Suppose there is a bad growing season, resulting in a poor harvest. What happens to the price of wheat and the revenue of farmers? These questions are answered in Fig. 6.10(a). Supply decreases, and the momentary supply curve shifts leftward to MS_1, where 15 billion bushels of wheat are produced. With a decrease in supply, the price increases to $3 a bushel.

What happens to total farm revenue? It *increases* to $45 billion. A decrease in supply has brought an increase in price and an increase in farm revenue. The reason is that the demand for wheat is *inelastic*. The percentage decrease in the quantity demanded is less than the percentage increase in price. You can verify this fact by noticing in Fig. 6.10(a) that the increase in revenue from the higher price ($15 billion light blue area) exceeds the decrease in revenue from the smaller quantity ($10 billion red area). Farmers are now making a profit in excess of their opportunity cost.

Although total farm revenue increases when there is a poor harvest, some farmers, whose entire crop is wiped out, suffer a fall in revenue. Others, whose crop is unaffected, make an enormous gain.

Bumper Harvest Figure 6.10(b) shows what happens in the opposite situation, when there is a bumper harvest. Now supply increases to 25 billion bushels, and the momentary supply curve shifts rightward to MS_2. With the increased quantity supplied, the price falls to $1 a bushel. Farm revenues also decline—to $25 billion. They do so because the demand for wheat is inelastic. To see this fact, notice in Fig. 6.10(b) that the decrease in revenue from the lower price ($20 billion light blue area) exceeds the increase in revenue from the increase in the quantity sold ($5 billion red area).

Elasticity of Demand In the example we've just worked through, demand is inelastic. If demand is elastic, the price fluctuations go in the same directions as those we've worked out, but revenues fluctuate in the opposite directions. Bumper harvests increase revenue, and poor harvests decrease it. But the demand for most agricultural products is inelastic, and the case we've studied is the relevant one.

Because farm prices fluctuate, institutions have evolved to stabilize them. There are two types of institutions:

■ Speculative markets in inventories
■ Farm price stabilization policy

Speculative Markets in Inventories

Many goods, including a wide variety of agricultural products, can be stored. These inventories provide a cushion between production and consumption. If production decreases, goods can be sold from inventory; if production increases, goods can be put into inventory.

In a market that has inventories, we must distinguish production from supply. The quantity produced is not the same as the quantity supplied. The quantity supplied exceeds the quantity produced when goods are sold from inventory. And the quantity supplied is less than the quantity produced when goods are put into inventory. Supply therefore depends on the behavior of inventory holders.

The Behavior of Inventory Holders Inventory holders speculate. They hope to buy at a low price and sell at a high price. That is, they hope to buy goods and put them into inventory when the price is low and sell them from inventory when the price is high. They make a profit or incur a loss equal to their selling price minus their buying price and minus the cost of storage.[4]

But how do inventory holders know when to buy and when to sell? How do they know whether the price is high or low? To decide whether a price is high or low, inventory holders forecast future prices. If the current price is above its expected future level, they sell goods from inventory. If the current price is below its expected future level, they buy goods to put into inventory. This behavior by inventory holders makes the supply perfectly elastic at the future price expected by inventory holders.

Let's work out what happens to price and quantity in a market in which inventories are held when production fluctuates. Let's look again at the wheat market.

Fluctuations in Production In Fig. 6.11 the demand curve for wheat is D. Inventory holders expect the future price to be $2 a bushel. The supply curve is S—supply is perfectly elastic at the price expected by inventory holders. Production fluctuates between Q_1 and Q_2.

---

[4] We will suppose that the cost of storage is so small that we can ignore it. This assumption, though not essential, enables us to see more sharply the effects of inventory holders' decisions on prices.

FIGURE 6.11

How Inventories Limit Price Changes

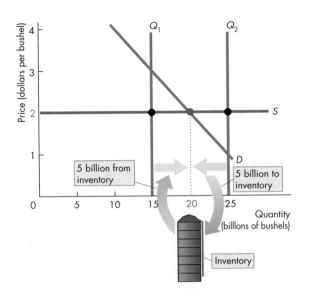

Inventory holders supply wheat from inventory if the price rises above $2 a bushel and take wheat into inventory if the price falls below $2 a bushel, making supply (S) perfectly elastic. When production decreases to Q_1, 5 billion bushels are supplied from inventory; when production increases to Q_2, 5 billion bushels are added to inventory. The price remains at $2 a bushel.

When production fluctuates and there are no inventories, the price and the quantity fluctuate. We saw this result in Fig. 6.10. But if there are inventories, the price does not fluctuate. When production is low, at Q_1 or 15 billion bushels, inventory holders sell 5 billion bushels from inventory, and the quantity bought by consumers is 20 billion bushels. The price remains at $2 a bushel. When production is high, at Q_2 or 25 billion bushels, inventory holders buy 5 billion bushels, and consumers continue to buy 20 billion bushels. Again, the price remains at $2 a bushel. Inventories reduce price fluctuations. In Fig. 6.11, the price fluctuations are entirely eliminated. When there are costs of carrying inventories and when inventories become almost depleted, some price fluctuations do occur, but these fluctuations are smaller than those occurring in a market without inventories.

Farm Revenue Even if inventory speculation succeeds in stabilizing prices, it does not stabilize farm revenue. With the price stabilized, farm revenue fluctuates as production fluctuates. But now bumper harvests bring larger revenues than poor harvests. The reason is that now farmers, in effect, face a perfectly elastic demand for their output.

Farm Price Stabilization Policy

Most governments intervene in agricultural markets. The most extensive such intervention occurs in the European Union. But it also occurs in the United States, where intervention is designed to stabilize the prices of many agricultural products, such as grains, milk, eggs, tobacco, rice, peanuts, and cotton.

Government intervention in agriculture is extremely costly to taxpayers. It usually takes the form of price floors set above the equilibrium price—similar to the minimum wage that we studied earlier—and above the production cost of efficient farms. The result is persistent surpluses, which a government agency must mop up. The price stabilization agency buys more than it sells and ends up with large inventory. Such has been the outcome in Europe, where they have mountains of butter and lakes of wine! The cost of buying and storing the inventory falls on taxpayers, and the main gainers are the large, efficient farms.

R E V I E W

- The demand for most farm products is inelastic.
- With no inventories, a poor harvest (a decrease in supply) increases price and increases farm revenue, and a bumper harvest (an increase in supply) decreases price and decreases farm revenue.
- Inventory holders speculate by trying to buy at a low price and sell at a high price. Successful speculation reduces price fluctuations.
- Farm price stabilization policies also limit price fluctuations but usually create surpluses.

◆ We've now completed our study of demand and supply and its applications. You've seen how this model enables us to predict prices movements and also how it enables us to understand a wide variety of real-world events.

The Market for Mohair

THE HOUSTON CHRONICLE, JUNE 16, 1994

Young Designers Discover Magic of Mohair— and Texas Profits

BY LINDA GILLAN GRIFFIN

ROCK SPRINGS, Texas—Most European and New York fashion designers have never been to the rocky, arid wilds of West Texas, but their latest creations are spreading smiles across the faces of Angora goat growers here.

Mohair fashions, from sweaters to suits to ball gowns, are included in many French, Italian and U.S. designers' fall and winter collections. The trend couldn't have come at a better time for the goat ranchers.

Mohair, the hair of Angora goats, is not to be confused with wool, the shorn hair of sheep, or with angora, the hair of Angora rabbits, which is often used in sweaters and warm, fluffy fabrics. Mohair is lighter than wool, takes dye better and can be woven into fabrics as fine as cashmere.

Texas is the mohair capital of the United States, which provides 45 percent of the world's supply, and Rock Springs is at its heart. Angora goat ranching had fallen on hard times, however. Beset with stiff foreign competition, ranchers had long enjoyed a federal subsidy, but last fall Congress did not reapprove that subsidy.

Ranchers began cutting anticipated losses by selling off older goats to Mexico, where they were more likely to be eaten than raised for their mohair.

But now an increase in mohair demand, coupled with the possibility of a short supply, is driving prices up dramatically— more than 100 percent in less than three months. Since April, prices in Texas have gone from 90 cents to $1.94 per pound for adult mohair. And political turmoil in South Africa, which barely leads the United States as the No. 1 producer of mohair (each produces approximately 45 percent of the world's supply), has threatened to further reduce supply.

"We've got no idea where the U.S. price will go," said Duery Menzies, executive director of the Mohair Council of America, headquartered in San Angelo, Texas.

It's impossible to determine how much of the price increase is due to the mohair fashions expected to hit store racks in August and how much is due to goat politics. ... If spring collections include mohair fashions prices could skyrocket. ...

Reprinted with permission of The Houston Chronicle.

Essence of THE STORY

■ Fashion houses around the world increased the amount of mohair used in their fall and winter (1994) designs.

■ The United States (mainly West Texas) and South Africa each provides 45 percent of the world's supply of mohair to a highly competitive world market.

■ Congress ended the federal subsidy to U.S. goat ranchers in the fall of 1993.

■ Goat ranchers reacted to the end of the subsidy by selling older goats to Mexico, which probably used them for meat.

■ Political turmoil in South Africa threatened to reduce supply further.

■ Between April and July 1994, the price of mohair increased by more than 100 percent—from 90 cents to $1.94 per pound.

■ It is impossible to say where the price will go— it could skyrocket.

Economic

A N A L Y S I S

■ Figure 1 shows the market for mohair before any of the changes reported in the news article. The demand curve is D_0, and the supply curve is S_0. The price of mohair is 90¢ a pound, and Q_0 pounds of mohair a year are bought and sold.

■ Figure 2 shows the effects of two events in the market for mohair. New fashion trends increased demand, and the demand curve shifted rightward to D_1. The end of a federal subsidy decreased supply as ranchers sold goats, and the supply curve shifted leftward to S_1.

■ The increase in demand and the decrease in supply increased the price to $1.94 a pound and increased the quantity of mohair bought and sold to Q_1.

■ Figure 3 shows the long-run response of the market for mohair. With a price of $1.94 a pound, ranchers in Texas and in South Africa and other parts of the world increase their herd sizes, and the supply of mohair gradually increases—the supply curve shifts rightward to S_2.

■ In Fig. 3, the long-run supply curve, LS, is perfectly elastic at the initial price of 90¢ a pound (an assumption).

■ It is impossible to predict how high the price of mohair will be *in the short run*, but in the long run, there is not much doubt that the price will fall as suppliers respond to the currently high price.

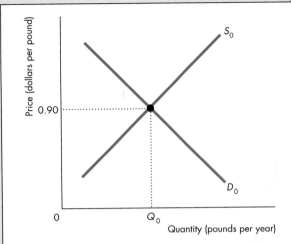

Figure 1

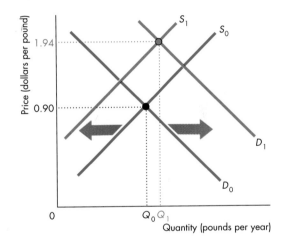

Figure 2

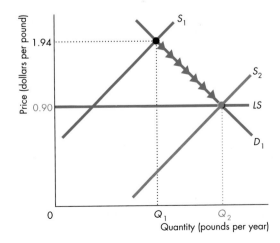

Figure 3

S U M M A R Y

Housing Markets and Rent Ceilings

A decrease in the supply of housing decreases short-run supply and increases equilibrium rents. Higher rents increase the quantity of housing supplied in the short run and stimulate building activity, which increases supply in the long run. Rents decrease, and the quantity of housing increases.

If a rent ceiling prevents rents from increasing, there is no inducement to increase the quantity supplied in the short run or the long run. As a result, the quantity of housing is less than what it would be in an unregulated market. People spend time searching for housing, and the cost of housing, including the value of the time spent searching, might exceed the cost in an unregulated market. (pp. 120–123)

The Labor Market and Minimum Wages

A decrease in the demand for low-skilled labor lowers the wage and reduces employment. The lower wage encourages people with low skill to acquire more skill. As they do so, the short-run supply of low-skilled labor decreases. The wage rises gradually to its original level, and employment decreases.

If the government imposes a minimum wage above the equilibrium wage, a decrease in the demand for labor will result in an increase in unemployment and an increase in the amount of time spent searching for a job. Minimum wages bite hardest on people having the fewest skills, and such workers tend to be young people. (pp. 124–126)

Taxes

When a good or service is taxed, usually the price increases and the quantity bought decreases but the price increases by less than the tax. The tax is paid partly by the buyer and partly by the seller. The portion of the tax paid by the buyer and by the seller depends on the elasticity of demand and the elasticity of supply. The less elastic the demand and the more elastic the supply, the greater is the price increase, the smaller is the quantity decrease, and the larger is the portion of the tax paid by the buyer. But if demand is perfectly elastic or supply is perfectly inelastic, the seller pays the entire tax. And if demand is perfectly inelastic or supply is perfectly elastic, the buyer pays the entire tax. (pp. 126–130)

Markets for Prohibited Goods

Penalties on sellers of an illegal good increase the cost of selling the good and decrease its supply. Penalties on buyers decrease their willingness to pay and decrease the demand for the good. The higher the penalties and the more effective the law enforcement, the smaller is the quantity bought. The price is higher or lower than the unregulated price, depending on whether penalties on sellers or buyers are higher. Effective law enforcement and high enough penalties will decrease demand and supply to the point at which the good disappears.

A tax set at a sufficiently high rate will also decrease the quantity of drug consumption, but there will be a tendency for the tax to be evaded. If the penalty for tax law violation is as severe and as effectively policed as drug-dealing laws, the quantity of drugs consumed will remain at the prohibition level, but the tax revenue will be lower than it would be without the tax evasion. Tax revenue from a drug tax could be used to make law enforcement more effective and to pay for a campaign against drugs. But prohibiting drugs sends a signal that may influence preferences, decreasing the demand for drugs. (pp. 130–133)

Stabilizing Farm Revenue

Farm revenues fluctuate because crop yields vary as climatic conditions fluctuate. The demand for most farm products is inelastic, so a decrease in supply increases the price and increases farm revenue, while an increase in supply decreases price and decreases farm revenues. Inventory holders and official agencies act to stabilize farm prices and revenues.

Inventory holders buy at a low price and sell at a high price. As a result, supply is perfectly elastic at the future price expected by inventory holders. When production is low, inventory holders sell from inventory, preventing the price from rising. When production is high, inventory holders buy, preventing the price from falling. Farm price stabilization policies set price floors above the equilibrium price that create persistent surpluses. (pp. 133–135)

K E Y   E L E M E N T S

R E V I E W   Q U E S T I O N S

1. Describe what happens to the rent and to the quantity of housing available if an earthquake suddenly and unexpectedly reduces the supply of housing. Trace the evolution of the rent and the quantity of housing rented over time.

2. What is a rent ceiling? In the situation described in question 1, how will things be different if a rent ceiling is imposed?

3. Describe what happens to the price and quantity in a market in which there is an increase in supply. Trace the evolution of the price and quantity in the market over time.

4. Describe the effects of an increase in the demand for a good on its price and the quantity bought and sold of it. Trace the evolution of the price and quantity in the market over time.

5. Describe what happens to the wage rate and quantity of labor employed when there is a decrease in demand for labor. Trace the evolution of the wage rate and employment over time.

6. What is a price floor? In the situation described in question 5, how are things different if a minimum wage is introduced?

7. Why does a minimum wage create unemployment?

8. When a government regulation prevents a price from changing, what forces come into operation to achieve an equilibrium?

9. How does the imposition of the sales tax on a good influence the supply of and demand for that good? How does it influence the price of the good and the quantity bought?

10. When a sales tax is imposed on a good or service with a perfectly elastic demand, who pays the tax?

11. When a sales tax is imposed on a good or service with a perfectly elastic supply, who pays the tax?

12. How does a prohibition of the sale of a good affect the demand for and supply of the good? How does it affect the price of the good and the quantity bought?

13. How does a prohibition of the consumption of a good affect the demand for and supply of the good? How does it affect the price of the good and the quantity bought?

14. Explain the alternative ways in which the consumption of harmful drugs can be controlled. What are the arguments for and against each method?

15. Why do farm revenues fluctuate?

16. Do farm revenues increase or decrease when there is a bumper crop and there are no inventories? Why?

17. Explain why speculation can stabilize the price of a storable commodity but does not stabilize the revenues of the producers of such a commodity.

18. How can farm prices be stabilized? Is such stabilization profitable?

P R O B L E M S

◆ 1. The demand for and supply of rental housing in your town are as follows:

Rent (dollars per month)	Quantity demanded (units of housing)	Quantity supplied
100	20,000	0
150	15,000	5,000
200	10,000	10,000
250	5,000	15,000
300	2,500	20,000
350	1,500	25,000

   a. What is the equilibrium rent?
   b. What is the equilibrium quantity of rented housing?

◆ 2. Now suppose that a rent ceiling of $150 a month is imposed in the housing market described in problem 1.
   a. What is the quantity of housing rented?
   b. What is the shortage of housing?
   c. What is the maximum price that demanders will be willing to pay for the last unit available?

◆ 3. The demand for and supply of teenage labor are as follows:

Wage rate (dollars per month)	Quantity demanded (hours per month)	Quantity supplied
2	3,000	1,000
3	2,500	1,500
4	2,000	2,000
5	1,500	2,500
6	1,000	3,000

   a. What is the equilibrium wage rate?
   b. What is the level of employment?
   c. What is the level of unemployment?
   d. If the government imposes a minimum wage of $3 an hour for teenagers, how many hours do teenagers work?
   e. If the government imposes a minimum wage of $5 an hour for teenagers, what are the employment and unemployment levels?
   f. If there is a minimum wage of $5 an hour and demand increases by 500 hours, what is the level of unemployment?

◆ 4. The following table illustrates three supply curves for train travel:

Price (cents per passenger mile)	Quantity supplied (billions of passenger miles)		
	Momentary	Short-run	Long-run
10	500	300	100
20	500	350	200
30	500	400	300
40	500	450	400
50	500	500	500
60	500	550	600
70	500	600	700
80	500	650	800
90	500	700	900
100	500	750	1,000

   a. If the price is 50 cents a passenger mile, what is the quantity supplied in:
     (i) The long run?
     (ii) The short run?
   b. Suppose that the price is initially 50 cents but that it then rises to 70 cents. What will be the quantity supplied:
     (i) Immediately following the price rise?
     (ii) In the short run?
     (iii) In the long run?

◆ 5. Suppose that the supply of train travel is the same as in problem 4. The following table gives two demand schedules—original and new:

Price (cents per passenger mile)	Quantity demanded (billions of passenger miles)	
	Original	New
10	10,000	10,300
20	5,000	5,300
30	2,000	2,300
40	1,000	1,300
50	500	800
60	400	700
70	300	600
80	200	500
90	100	400
100	0	300

a. What are the original equilibrium price and quantity?
b. After the increase in demand has occurred, what are:
    (i)   The momentary equilibrium price and quantity?
    (ii) The short-run equilibrium price and quantity?
    (iii) The long-run equilibrium price and quantity?

◆ 6. The short-run and long-run demand for train travel is as follows:

Price	Quantity demanded (billions of passenger miles)	
(cents per passenger mile)	Short-run	Long-run
20	650	5,000
30	600	2,000
40	550	1,000
50	500	500
60	450	400
70	400	300
80	350	200
90	300	100
100	250	0

The supply of train travel is the same as in problem 4.
a. What are the long-run equilibrium price and quantity of train travel?
b. Serious floods destroy one fifth of the trains and train tracks. Supply falls by 100 billion passenger miles. What happens to the price and the quantity of train travel in:
    (i)   The short run?
    (ii) The long run?

◆ 7. The following are the demand and supply schedules for chocolate brownies.

Price	Quantity demanded	Quantity supplied
(cents per brownie)	(millions per day)	
50	5	3
60	4	4
70	3	5
80	2	6
90	1	7

a. If there is no tax on brownies, what is their price and how many are produced and consumed?
b. If a tax of 20¢ a brownie is introduced, what happens to the price of a brownie and the number produced and consumed?
c. How much tax does the government collect and who pays it?

◆ 8. Calculate the elasticity of demand in Fig. 6.10 when the price of wheat is $3 a bushel. Does its magnitude imply that farm revenues fluctuate in the same direction as price fluctuations or in the opposite direction?

◆ 9. On Turtle Island, the government is considering ways of stabilizing farm prices and farm revenues. Currently, the egg market is competitive, and the demand for and supply of eggs are as follows:

Price	Quantity demanded	Quantity supplied
(dollars per month)	(dozens per week)	
1.20	3,000	500
1.30	2,750	1,500
1.40	2,500	2,500
1.50	2,250	3,500
1.60	2,000	4,500

a. Calculate the competitive equilibrium price and the quantity bought and sold.
b. The government introduces a floor price of $1.50 a dozen. Calculate the market price, the quantity of eggs bought and sold, and farm revenues. Calculate the surplus of eggs.
c. Calculate the amount the government must spend on eggs to maintain the floor price.

10. Study the *Reading Between the Lines* on pp. 136–137 on the market for mohair.
a. How much of the price increase is due to mohair fashion and how much is due to good politics? Explain your answer.
b. What would be the effects of political turmoil in South Africa on the market for mohair? Draw a figure to illustrate your answer.
c. If mohair suddenly becomes unfashionable, what will happen to its price?

part 2 Markets for Goods and Services

Ernst Berndt, who teaches at the Sloan School of Management at MIT, was born in Crespo, Entre Rios, Argentina, in 1946 and immigrated to the United States in 1949. He was an undergraduate at Valparaiso University and a graduate student at the University of Wisconsin–Madison, where he earned his Ph.D. in 1972. Professor Berndt became world-renowned for his econometric work on the demand for energy during the mid-1970s, when OPEC was increasing the world oil price. However, he has worked on a wide range of issues in applied microeconomics, including productivity measurement, the effects of deregulation of certain industries, and the pricing of pharmaceutical products. Professor Berndt is the author of *The Practice of Econometrics, Classic and Contemporary* (Addison-Wesley, 1991) and of dozens of articles on applied econometrics. Michael Parkin talked with Professor Berndt about his work and the challenges faced by microeconomists today.

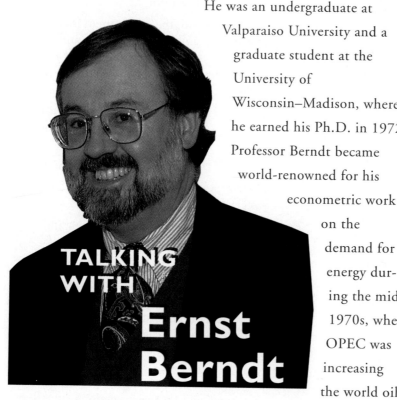

TALKING WITH Ernst Berndt

Professor Berndt, how did you get into economics?
I'm a bit embarrassed to begin this interview by answering that question. When I was a first-year undergraduate student, I found myself choosing between a 7:30 A.M. engineering class and an 8:30 A.M. economics principles class. I chose the 8:30 class. Luckily, my economics professor, Paul Heyne, was an absolutely superb lecturer who communicated the essential principles with great enthusiasm and clarity. He inspired me, and I've been hooked on economics ever since.

What are the core principles of economics that you find yourself repeatedly turning to in your research and teaching?
There are two principles that I keep encountering. First, as consumers, our wants for goods and services are essentially unlimited, and since resources are limited, we need a mechanism to ration the use of resources. The price system, where prices are determined in markets, is such a mechanism. Second, to understand markets, it is critical to distinguish between what people pay on the average for the items they buy—the average price—and what they pay for an additional unit of a good—the marginal price.

Can you give a practical example that illustrates these principles?

The Internet, an electronic super-highway that links computers in universities, research institutions, governments, and businesses, nicely illustrates these principles. As a member of the Internet, you can receive and send data electronically to anyone on the network worldwide. But there is a data overload—unlimited wants confronting limited resources—and a debate is raging on how to handle it.

One reason for the explosion in demand for access to the Internet is that most Internet users enjoy free access at the margin. That is, institutions and individuals typically pay a flat or monthly fee, but then have unlimited use of the electronic network at a zero price. So, while the average price is positive, the marginal price is zero. Traditional network engineers advocate reducing congestion on the Internet by building more capacity. Economists, however, are arguing that it makes more sense to charge users so-called congestion fees at times of peak system demand.

> *... the most important characteristic of a successful econometrician is an attitude of critical evaluation. ...when reading this textbook, I hope readers ask themselves... "How could I test this theory with real-world data?"*

Perfect competition and monopoly are the first two market structures that a student of economics encounters. Yet these market types are rare in reality. Why are they worth studying?

In real-world markets, we seldom see either perfect competition or pure monopoly. But understanding these two extreme market structures gives us enormous insight into real-world markets. Take, for example, the patent system that awards limited monopoly status to the successful innovator, such as a pharmaceutical company that discovers, develops, tests, and markets a new drug. Although the drug company has temporary monopoly patent protection for the new product, it still faces competition from other chemical entities that can serve as substitutes in medical treatments.

While the up-front costs, or premanufacturing costs, of basic drug research and development are very large, the marginal cost of producing a drug tablet are usually very small. Hence, to maximize profits, we can expect the price set by the monopolist to be where marginal revenue equals marginal cost and where the latter is approximately zero. At the price set, demand is close to being unit elastic (see Chapter 5, p. 101). However, once patent protection expires, generic drug manufacturers can enter, and then the market structure can be expected to approach that of a perfectly competitive market, where price falls so that the price equals marginal costs ($P = MC$).

Not surprisingly, a generic drug often sells for less than half the price of the equivalent patented drug. Understanding monopoly and perfect competition helps us to comprehend forthcoming changes in the pharmaceutical market, for in the next five years a very large number of drugs once considered breakthrough drugs will face loss of patent protection.

> *As a member of the Internet, you can receive and send data electronically to anyone on the network worldwide. But there is a data overload—unlimited wants confronting limited resources.*

You're an econometrician. What exactly is econometrics? How does it differ from economics? Can a beginning student do econometrics, or is it a subject only for advanced students?

Econometrics is a blend of economics, statistics and applied mathematics, and data analysis. The econometrician's goal is to give empirical content to economic theory. To pursue this goal, econometricians gather and then employ data in an effort to assess the validity of economic theory. They also look for empirical evidence suggesting changes in an economic theory. They do this by comparing the predictions of alternative theories with real-world events.

Because econometrics integrates economics, statistics, and mathematics, it is typically studied by more advanced undergraduate students.

Can you explain the most important discovery you have made as an economist?

In the 1970s, energy prices suddenly increased as the OPEC cartel gained market strength. Many energy analysts said that higher energy prices would prove near-fatal to the world's growing economies, for energy demand and economic growth are inextricably linked. These analysts believed that it was impossible to conserve energy inputs and that, as a result, the ratio of energy inputs to production output would not be reduced. Implicitly, these people were saying that the price elasticity of demand for energy was zero and that price-induced energy conservation was not possible. However, in research I completed with a colleague, David Wood, we found that in the United States, the price elasticity of industrial demand for energy was about a half, not zero.

...drugs once considered breakthrough drugs will face loss of patent protection.

Moreover, we found that while energy was a complementary input with capital, it is substitutable with labor. Today, we know that not only is the demand for energy price-responsive, but so too is the supply of energy. Not surprisingly, OPEC has not been able to sustain the high energy prices of the 1970s because demand growth has slowed and many new energy supplies have been discovered and developed.

What can an undergraduate do to prepare for a career in economics and econometrics?

Because econometrics is a blend of various disciplines, it requires a good background in several sets of courses. I strongly believe, however, that the most important characteristic of a successful econometrician is an attitude of critical evaluation. For example, when reading this textbook, I hope readers ask themselves questions such as "How could I test this theory with real-world data?" or "What type of data would suggest that this theory might be wrong?" The right time to develop these skills of critical evaluation is now, in this principles course, for those skills are absolutely essential in becoming a successful applied econometrician.

OPEC has not been able to sustain the high energy prices of the 1970s because demand growth has slowed and many new energy supplies have been discovered and developed.

Utility and Demand

After studying this chapter, you will be able to:

- Explain the connection between individual demand and market demand

- Define total utility and marginal utility

- Explain the marginal utility theory of consumer choice

- Use marginal utility theory to predict the effects of changing prices

- Use marginal utility theory to predict the effects of changing income

- Define and calculate consumer surplus

- Explain the paradox of value

We need water to live. We don't need diamonds for much besides decoration. If the benefits of water far outweigh the benefits of diamonds, why, then, does water cost practically nothing while diamonds are terribly expensive? ◆ When OPEC restricted its sale of oil in 1973, it created a dramatic rise in price, but people continued to use almost as much oil as they had before. Our demand for oil was price inelastic. But why? ◆ When the CD player was introduced in 1983, it cost more than $1,000, and consumers didn't buy very many. Since then, the price has decreased dramatically, and people are buying CD players in enormous quantities. Our demand for CD players is price elastic. What makes the demand for some things price elastic while the demand for others is price inelastic? ◆ Over the past 20 years, after the effects of inflation are removed, incomes in the United States have increased by 40 percent. Over that same period, expenditure on electricity has increased by more than 60 percent, while expenditure on transportation has increased by less than 20 percent. Thus the proportion of income spent on electricity has increased, and the proportion spent on transportation has decreased. Why, as incomes rise, does the proportion of income spent on some goods rise and that spent on others fall?

Water, Water, Everywhere

◻ In the preceding three chapters, we saw that demand has an important effect on the price of a good. But we did not analyze what exactly shapes a person's demand. This chapter examines household behavior and its influence on demand. It explains why demand is elastic for some goods and inelastic for others. It also explains why the prices of some things, such as diamonds and water, are so out of proportion to their total benefits.

Household Consumption Choices

A HOUSEHOLD'S CONSUMPTION CHOICES ARE determined by many factors, but we can summarize all of these factors under two concepts:

- Budget constraint
- Preferences

Budget Constraint

A household's consumption choices are constrained by its income and by the prices of the goods and services it buys. The household has a given amount of income to spend and cannot influence the prices of the goods and services it buys.

The limits to a household's consumption choices are described by its *budget line*. Let's consider Lisa's household. Lisa has an income of $30 a month to spend. She buys two goods—movies and soda. Movies cost $6 each; soda costs $3 a six-pack. If Lisa spends all her income, she will reach the limits to her consumption of movies and soda.

Figure 7.1 illustrates Lisa's possible consumption levels of movies and soda. Rows *a* through *f* in the table show six possible ways of allocating $30 to these two goods. For example, Lisa can see 2 movies for $12 and buy 6 six-packs for $18 (row *c*). The same possibilities are presented by rows *a* through *f* in the figures. The line passing through these points is Lisa's budget line.

Lisa's budget line is a constraint on her choices. It marks the boundary between what is affordable and what is unaffordable. She can afford all the points on the line and inside it. She cannot afford points outside the line. The constraint on her consumption depends on prices and on her income, and the constraint changes when prices and her income change.

Preferences

How does Lisa divide her $30 between these two goods? The answer depends on her likes and dislikes—her *preferences*. Economists use the concept of utility to describe preferences. The benefit or satisfaction that a person gets from the consumption of a good or service is called **utility**. But what exactly is utility and in what units can we measure it? Utility is an abstract concept, and its units are arbitrary.

FIGURE 7.1

Consumption Possibilities

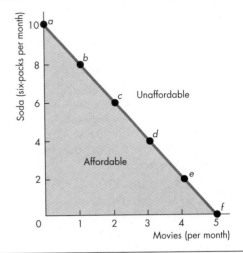

Possibility	Movies		Soda	
	Quantity	Expenditure (dollars)	Six-packs	Expenditure (dollars)
a	0	0	10	30
b	1	6	8	24
c	2	12	6	18
d	3	18	4	12
e	4	24	2	6
f	5	30	0	0

Rows *a* through *f* in the table show six possible ways that Lisa can allocate $30 to movies and soda. For example, Lisa can buy 2 movies and 6 six-packs (row *c*). The combination in each row costs $30. These possibilities are points *a* through *f* in the figure. The line through those points is a boundary between what Lisa can afford and what she cannot afford. Her choices must lie along the line *af* or inside the orange area.

Temperature—An Analogy Temperature is an abstract concept, and the units of temperature are arbitrary. You know when you feel hot, and you know when you feel cold. But you can't *observe* temperature. You can observe water turning to steam if it is hot enough or turning to ice if it is cold enough. You can construct an instrument, called a thermometer, that can help you to predict when such changes will occur. The scale on the thermometer is what we call temperature. But the units in which we measure temperature are arbitrary. For example, we can accurately predict that when a Celsius thermometer shows a temperature of 0, water will turn to ice. But the units of measurement do not matter because this same event also occurs when a Fahrenheit thermometer shows a temperature of 32.

The concept of utility helps us make predictions about consumption choices in much the same way that the concept of temperature helps us make predictions about physical phenomena. Admittedly marginal utility theory is not as precise as the theory that enables us to predict when water will turn to ice or steam.

Let's now see how we can use the concept of utility to describe preferences.

Total Utility

Total utility is the total benefit or satisfaction that a person gets from the consumption of goods and services. Total utility depends on the person's level of consumption—more consumption generally gives more total utility. Table 7.1 shows Lisa's total utility from movies and soda. If she sees no movies, she gets no utility from movies. If she sees 1 movie in a month, she gets 50 units of utility. As the number of movies she sees in a month increases, her total utility increases; if she sees 10 movies a month, she gets 250 units of total utility. The other part of the table shows Lisa's total utility from soda. If she drinks no soda, she gets no utility from soda. As the amount of soda she drinks increases, her total utility increases.

Marginal Utility

Marginal utility is the change in total utility resulting from a one-unit increase in the quantity of a good consumed. The table in Fig. 7.2 shows the calculation of Lisa's marginal utility of movies. When the number of movies she sees increases from 4 to 5 movies a month, her total utility from movies increases from 150 units to 175 units. Thus for Lisa, the marginal utility of seeing a fifth movie each month is 25 units. Notice that marginal utility appears midway between the quantities of movies. It does so because it is the *change* in consumption from 4 to 5 movies that produces the *marginal* utility of 25 units. The table displays calculations of marginal utility for each number of movies seen.

TABLE 7.1

Lisa's Total Utility from Movies and Soda

Movies		Soda	
Quantity per month	Total utility	Six-packs per month	Total utility
0	0	0	0
1	50	1	75
2	88	2	117
3	121	3	153
4	150	4	181
5	175	5	206
6	196	6	225
7	214	7	243
8	229	8	260
9	241	9	276
10	250	10	291
11	256	11	305
12	259	12	318
13	261	13	330
14	262	14	341

Figure 7.2(a) illustrates the total utility that Lisa gets from movies. The more movies Lisa sees in a month, the more total utility she gets. Part (b) illustrates her marginal utility. This graph tells us that as Lisa sees more movies, the marginal utility that she gets from watching movies decreases. For example, her marginal utility decreases from 50 units for the first movie to 38 units from the second and 33 units from the third. We call this decrease in marginal utility as the quantity of the good consumed increases the principle of **diminishing marginal utility**.

Marginal utility is positive but diminishes as the consumption of a good increases. Why does marginal utility have these two features? In Lisa's case, she likes movies, and the more she sees the better. That's why marginal utility is positive. The benefit that Lisa gets from the last movie seen is its marginal utility. To see why marginal utility diminishes, think about the following two situations: In one, you've just been

FIGURE 7.2
Total Utility and Marginal Utility

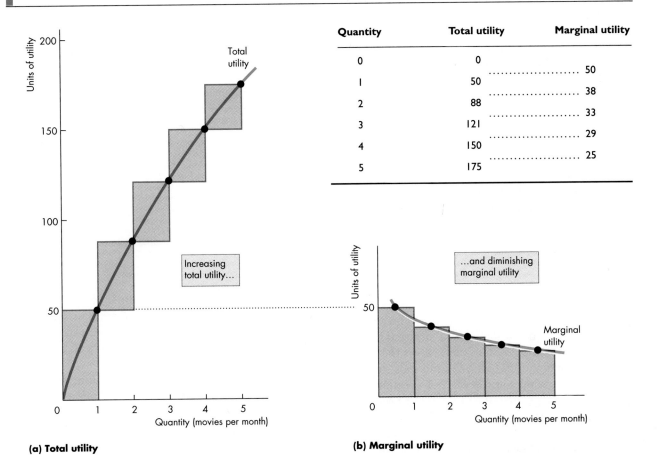

Quantity	Total utility	Marginal utility
0	0	
		50
1	50	
		38
2	88	
		33
3	121	
		29
4	150	
		25
5	175	

(a) Total utility

(b) Marginal utility

The table shows that as Lisa sees more movies her total utility from movies increases. The table also shows her marginal utility—the change in total utility resulting from the last movie seen. Marginal utility declines as consumption increases. The figure graphs Lisa's total utility and marginal utility from

movies. Part (a) shows her total utility. It also shows as a bar the extra total utility she gains from each additional movie—her marginal utility. Part (b) shows how Lisa's marginal utility from movies diminishes by placing the bars shown in part (a) side by side as a series of declining steps.

studying for 29 evenings. An opportunity arises to see a movie. The utility you get from that movie is the marginal utility from seeing one movie in a month. In the second situation, you've been on a movie binge. For the past 29 nights, you have not even seen an assignment. You are up to your eyeballs in movies. You are happy enough to go to a movie on yet one more night. But the thrill that you get out of that thirtieth movie in 30 days is not very large. It is the marginal utility of the thirtieth movie in a month.

R E V I E W

■ Consumption possibilities are limited by the consumer's income and the price of goods.

■ Consumers' preferences can be described by using the concept of utility, and marginal utility theory assumes that the greater the quantity of a good consumed, the larger is total utility, and as the quantity of a good consumed increases, the marginal utility from that good decreases.

Maximizing Utility

A HOUSEHOLD'S INCOME AND THE PRICES THAT it faces limit the utility that it can obtain. The key assumption of marginal utility theory is that, taking into consideration the income available for spending and the prices they face, households consume the quantities of goods and services that maximize total utility. The assumption of utility maximization is a way of expressing the fundamental economic problem. People's wants exceed the resources available to satisfy those wants, so they must make hard choices. In making choices, they try to get the maximum attainable benefit—they try to maximize total utility.

Let's see how Lisa allocates $30 a month between movies and soda to maximize her total utility. We'll continue to assume that movies cost $6 each and soda costs $3 a six-pack.

The Utility-Maximizing Choice

The most direct way of calculating how Lisa spends her income as to maximize her total utility is by making a table like Table 7.2. This table shows the same affordable combinations of movies and soda that you can find on her budget line in Fig. 7.1. The table records three things: first, the number of movies seen and the total utility derived from them (the left side of the table); second, the number of six-packs consumed and the total utility derived from them (the right side of the table); and third, the total utility derived from both movies and soda (the center column).

The first row of Table 7.2 records the situation if Lisa watches no movies and buys 10 six-packs. In this case, she gets no utility from movies and 291 units of total utility from soda. Her total utility from movies and soda (the center column) is 291 units. The rest of the table is constructed in the same way.

The consumption of movies and soda that maximizes Lisa's total utility is highlighted in the table. When Lisa consumes 2 movies and 6 six-packs of soda, she gets 313 units of total utility. This is the best Lisa can do, given that she has only $30 to spend and given the prices of movies and six-packs. If she buys 8 six-packs of soda, she can see only 1 movie and gets 310 units of total utility, 3 less than the maximum attainable. If she sees 3 movies and drinks only 4 six-packs, she gets 302 units of total utility, 11 less than the maximum attainable.

TABLE 7.2

Lisa's Utility-Maximizing Combinations

Movies		Total utility from movies and soda	Soda	
Quantity per month	Total utility		Total utility	Six-packs per month
0	0	291	291	10
1	50	310	260	8
2	88	313	225	6
3	121	302	181	4
4	150	267	117	2
5	175	175	0	0

We've just described a consumer equilibrium. A **consumer equilibrium** is a situation in which a consumer has allocated his or her income in the way that, given the prices of goods and services, maximizes his or her total utility.

In finding Lisa's consumer equilibrium, we measured her *total* utility from the consumption of movies and soda. There is a better way of determining a consumer equilibrium, which does not involve measuring total utility at all. Let's look at this alternative.

Equalizing Marginal Utility per Dollar Spent

Another way to find out the allocation that maximizes a consumer's total utility is to make the marginal utility per dollar spent on each good equal for all goods. The **marginal utility per dollar spent** is the marginal utility obtained from the last unit of a good consumed divided by the price of the good. For example, Lisa's marginal utility from seeing the first movie is 50 units of utility. The price of a movie is $6, which means that the marginal utility per dollar spent on movies is 50 units divided by $6, or 8.33 units of utility per dollar.

Total utility is maximized when all the consumer's income is spent and when the marginal utility per dollar spent is equal for all goods.

Lisa maximizes total utility when she spends all her income and consumes movies and soda such that

$$\frac{\text{Marginal utility from movies}}{\text{Price of a movie}} = \frac{\text{Marginal utility from soda}}{\text{Price of soda}}.$$

Call the marginal utility from movies MU_m, the marginal utility from soda MU_s, the price of a movie P_m, and the price of soda P_s. Then Lisa's utility is maximized when she spends all her income and when

$$\frac{MU_m}{P_m} = \frac{MU_s}{P_s}.$$

Let's use this formula to find Lisa's utility-maximizing allocation of her income.

Table 7.3 sets out Lisa's marginal utilities (which are calculated from Table 7.1) and her marginal utility per dollar spent on each good. For example, in row b, Lisa's marginal utility from movies is 50 units, and since movies cost $6 each, her marginal utility per dollar spent on movies is 8.33 units per dollar (50 units divided by $6). Each row exhausts Lisa's income of $30. You can see that Lisa's marginal utility per dollar spent on each good, like marginal utility itself, decreases as more of the good is consumed.

Total utility is maximized when the marginal utility per dollar spent on movies is equal to the marginal utility per dollar spent on soda—possibility c—when Lisa consumes 2 movies and 6 six-packs.

Figure 7.3 shows why the rule "equalize marginal utility per dollar spent on all goods" works. Suppose that instead of consuming 2 movies and 6 six-packs (possibility c), Lisa consumes 1 movie and 8 six-packs (possibility b). She then gets 8.33 units of utility from the last dollar spent on movies and 5.67 units from the last dollar spent on soda. Lisa can increase her total utility by buying less soda and seeing more movies. If she spends a dollar less on soda and a dollar more on movies, her total utility from soda decreases by 5.67 units and her total utility from movies increases by 8.33 units. Lisa's total utility increases by 2.66 units.

FIGURE 7.3

Equalizing Marginal Utilities per Dollar Spent

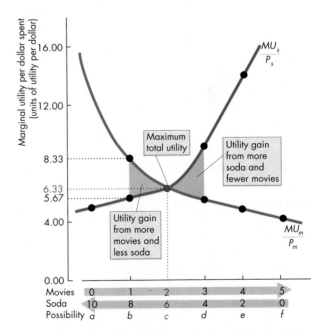

If Lisa consumes 1 movie and 8 six-packs (possibility b), she gets 8.33 units of utility from the last dollar spent on movies and 5.67 units of utility from the last dollar spent on soda. She can get more total utility by seeing one more movie. If she consumes 4 six-packs and 3 movies (possibility d), she gets 5.50 units of utility from the last dollar spent on movies and 9.33 units of utility from the last dollar spent on soda. She can get more total utility by seeing one fewer movie. When Lisa's marginal utility per dollar spent on both goods is equal, her total utility is maximized.

TABLE 7.3

Equalizing Marginal Utilities per Dollar Spent

	Movies ($6 each)			Soda ($3 per six-pack)		
	Quantity	Marginal utility	Marginal utility per dollar spent	Six-pack	Marginal utility	Marginal utility per dollar spent
a	0	0		10	15	5.00
b	1	50	8.33	8	17	5.67
c	2	38	6.33	6	19	6.33
d	3	33	5.50	4	28	9.33
e	4	29	4.83	2	42	14.00
f	5	25	4.17	0	0	

Or suppose that Lisa consumes 3 movies and 4 six-packs (possibility *d*). In this situation, her marginal utility from the last dollar spent on movies is less than her marginal utility from the last dollar spent on soda. Lisa can now increase her total utility by spending less on movies and more on soda.

The Power of Marginal Analysis   The method we've just used to maximize Lisa's utility is an example of the power of *marginal analysis*. By comparing the marginal gain from having more of one good with the marginal loss from having less of another good, Lisa is able to ensure that she gets the maximum attainable utility.

In the example, Lisa consumes at the point at which the marginal utility per dollar spent on movies and soda are equal. Because we buy goods and services in indivisible lumps, the numbers don't always work out so precisely. But the basic approach always works. The rule to follow is very simple: If the marginal utility per dollar spent on movies exceeds the marginal utility per dollar spent on soda, buy more movies and less soda; if the marginal utility per dollar spent on soda exceeds the marginal utility per dollar spent on movies, buy more soda and fewer movies.

More generally, if the marginal gain from an action exceeds the marginal loss, take the action. You will meet this principle time and again in your study of economics. And you will find yourself using it every time you make your own economic choices.

Units of Utility   In calculating the utility-maximizing allocation of income in Table 7.3 and Fig. 7.3, we have not used the concept of total utility at all. All the calculations have been performed by using marginal utility and price. By making the marginal utility per dollar spent equal for both goods, we know that Lisa has maximized her total utility.

This way of viewing maximum utility is important; it means that the units in which utility is measured do not matter. We could double or halve all the numbers measuring utility, or multiply them by any other positive number, or square them, or take their square roots. None of these transformations of the units used to measure utility makes any difference to the outcome. It is in this respect that utility is analogous to temperature. Our prediction about the freezing of water does not depend on the temperature scale; our prediction about maximizing total utility does not depend on the units of utility.

R E V I E W

- A consumer chooses the quantities of goods and services that maximize total utility.
- The consumer does so by spending all the available income and by making the marginal utility per dollar spent on each good equal.
- When marginal utilities per dollar spent are equal for all goods, a consumer cannot reallocate spending to get more total utility.

Predictions of Marginal Utility Theory

LET'S NOW USE MARGINAL UTILITY THEORY TO make some predictions. What happens to Lisa's consumption of movies and soda when their prices change and when her income changes?

A Fall in the Price of Movies

To determine the effect of a change in price on consumption requires three steps. First, determine the combinations of movies and soda that just exhaust the income at the new prices. Second, calculate the new marginal utilities per dollar spent. Third, determine the combinations that make the marginal utilities per dollar spent on movies and soda equal.

Table 7.4 shows the combinations of movies and soda that exactly exhausts Lisa's $30 of income when movies cost $3 each and soda costs $3 a six-pack. Her preferences do not change when prices change, so her marginal utility schedule remains the same as that in Table 7.3. But now we divide her marginal utility from movies by $3, the new price of a movie, to get the marginal utility per dollar spent on movies.

To find how Lisa responds to the fall in the price of a movie compare her new utility-maximizing allocation (Table 7.4) with her original allocation (Table 7.3). She watches more movies (up from 2 to 5 a month) and drinks less soda (down from 6 to 5 six-packs a month). That is, Lisa substitutes movies for soda. Figure 7.4 illustrates these effects. In part (a), a fall in the price of a movie produces a movement along Lisa's demand curve for movies, and in part (b), it shifts her demand curve for soda.

TABLE 7.4
How a Change in Price of Movies Affects Lisa's Choices

Movies ($3 each)		Soda ($3 per six-pack)	
Quantity	Marginal utility per dollar spent	Six-packs	Marginal utility per dollar spent
0		10	5.00
1	16.67	9	5.33
2	12.67	8	5.67
3	11.00	7	6.00
4	9.67	6	6.33
5	8.33	5	8.33
6	7.00	4	9.33
7	6.00	3	12.00
8	5.00	2	14.00
9	4.00	1	25.00
10	3.00	0	

FIGURE 7.4
A Fall in the Price of Movies

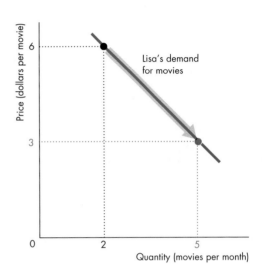

(a) Movies

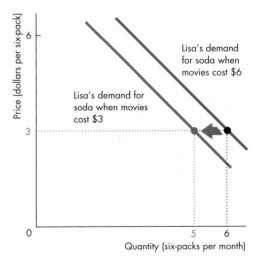

(b) Soda

When the price of a movie falls and the price of soda remains constant, the quantity of movies demanded by Lisa increases, and in part (a), Lisa moves along her demand curve for movies. Also, Lisa's demand for soda decreases, and in part (b), her demand curve for soda shifts leftward.

A Rise in the Price of Soda

Table 7.5 shows the combinations of movies and soda that exactly exhaust Lisa's $30 of income when movies cost $3 each and soda costs $6 a six-pack. Now we divide her marginal utility from soda by $6, the new price of a six-pack, to get the marginal utility per dollar spent on soda.

The effect of the rise in the price of soda on Lisa's consumption is seen by comparing her new utility-maximizing allocation (Table 7.5) with her previous allocation (Table 7.4). Lisa responds to a rise in the price of soda by drinking less soda (down from 5 to 2 six-packs a month) and watching more movies (up from 5 to 6 a month). That is, Lisa substitutes movies for soda when the price of soda rises. Figure 7.5 illustrates these effects. In part (a), a rise in the price of soda produces a movement along Lisa's demand curve for soda, and in part (b), it shifts her demand curve for movies.

TABLE 7.5

How a Change in Price of Soda Affects Lisa's Choices

Movies ($3 each)		Soda ($6 per six-pack)	
Quantity	Marginal utility per dollar spent	Six-packs	Marginal utility per dollar spent
0		5	4.17
2	12.67	4	4.67
4	9.67	3	6.00
6	7.00	2	7.00
8	5.00	1	12.50
10	3.00	0	

Marginal utility theory predicts these two results:

- When the price of a good rises, the quantity demanded of that good decreases
- If the price of one good rises, the demand for another good that can serve as a substitute increases.

Does this sound familiar? It should. These predictions of marginal utility theory correspond to the assumptions that we made about demand in Chapter 4. There we *assumed* that the demand curve for a good sloped downward, and we *assumed* that a rise in the price of a substitute increased demand.

We have now seen that marginal utility theory predicts how the quantities of goods and services that people demand respond to price changes. The theory helps us to understand both the shape and the position of the demand curve and how the demand curve for one good shifts when the price of another good changes. Marginal utility theory also helps us to understand one further thing about demand—how it changes when income changes. Let's study the effects of a change in income on consumption.

FIGURE 7.5

A Rise in the Price of Soda

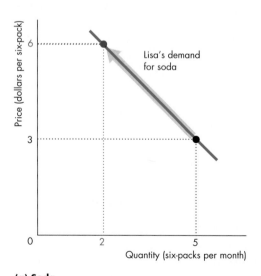

(a) Soda

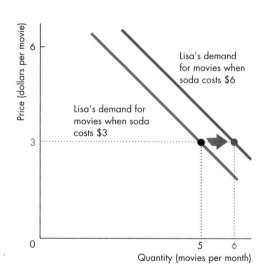

(b) Movies

When the price of soda rises and the price of movies remains constant, the quantity of soda demanded by Lisa decreases, and in part (a), Lisa moves along her demand curve for soda.

Also, Lisa's demand for movies increases, and in part (b), her demand curve for movies shifts rightward.

A Rise in Income

Let's suppose that Lisa's income increases to $42 a month and that movies cost $3 each and a six-pack costs $3. We saw in Table 7.4 that with these prices and with an income of $30 a month, Lisa consumes 5 movies and 5 six-packs a month. We want to compare this consumption of movies and soda with Lisa's consumption at an income of $42. The calculations for the comparison are shown in Table 7.6. With $42, Lisa can buy 14 movies a month and no soda or 14 six-packs a month and no movies or any combination of the two goods as shown in the rows of the table. We calculate the marginal utility per dollar spent in exactly the same way as we did before and find the quantities at which the marginal utilities per dollar spent on movies and on soda are equal. With an income of $42, the marginal utility per dollar spent on each good is equal when Lisa watches 7 movies and drinks 7 six-packs of soda a month.

By comparing this situation with that in Table 7.4, we see that with an additional $12 a month, Lisa consumes 2 more six-packs and 2 more movies. This response arises from Lisa's preferences, as described by her marginal utilities. Different preferences produce different quantitative responses. A higher income always brings a larger consumption of a *normal* good and a smaller consumption of an *inferior* good. For Lisa, soda and movies are normal goods. When her income increases, Lisa buys more of both goods.

You have now completed your study of the marginal utility theory of a household's consumption decisions and Table 7.7 summarizes the key assumptions, implications, and predictions of the theory.

TABLE 7.6

Lisa's Choices with an Income of $42 a Month

Movies ($3 each)		Soda ($3 per six-pack)	
Quantity	Marginal utility per dollar spent	Six-packs	Marginal utility per dollar spent
0		14	3.67
1	16.67	13	4.00
2	12.67	12	4.33
3	11.00	11	4.67
4	9.67	10	5.00
5	**8.33**	9	5.33
6	7.00	8	5.67
7	6.00	7	6.00
8	5.00	6	6.33
9	4.00	**5**	**8.33**
10	3.00	4	9.33
11	2.00	3	12.00
12	1.00	2	14.00
13	0.67	1	25.00
14	0.33	0	

TABLE 7.7

Marginal Utility Theory

Assumptions

- A consumer derives utility from the goods consumed.
- Each additional unit of consumption yields additional total utility; marginal utility is positive.
- As the quantity of a good consumed increases, marginal utility decreases.
- A consumer's aim is to maximize total utility.

Implication

Total utility is maximized when all the available income is spent and when the marginal utility per dollar spent is equal for all goods.

Predictions

- Other things remaining the same, the higher the price of a good, the smaller is the quantity bought (the law of demand).
- The higher the price of a good, the greater is the consumption of substitutes for that good.
- The higher the consumer's income, the greater is the quantity demanded of normal goods.

Individual Demand and Market Demand

One purpose of marginal utility theory is to explain how an individual household spends its income and an individual household's demand. But the main purpose of the theory is to explain market demand. Let's look at the connection between the individual demand and market demand.

The relationship between the total quantity demanded of a good and its price is called **market demand**. And the relationship between the quantity demanded of a good by a single individual and its price is called *individual demand.*

Figure 7.6 illustrates the relationship between individual demand and market demand. In this example, Lisa and Chuck are the only people. The market demand is the total demand of Lisa and Chuck. At $3 a movie, Lisa demands 5 movies a month and Chuck demands 2, so the total quantity demanded by the market is 7 movies a month. Lisa's demand curve for movies in part (a) and Chuck's in part (b) sum *horizontally* to give the market demand curve in part (c).

The market demand curve is the horizontal sum of the individual demand curves and is formed by adding the quantities demanded by each individual at each price.

Because marginal utility theory predicts that individual demand curves slope downward, it also predicts that market demand curves slope downward.

FIGURE 7.6

Individual and Market Demand Curves

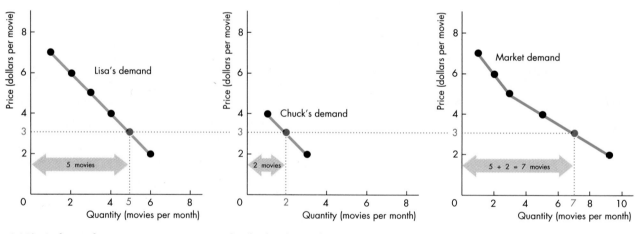

(a) Lisa's demand   **(b) Chuck's demand**   **(c) Market demand**

Price	Quantity of movies demanded		
(dollars per movie)	Lisa	Chuck	Market
7	1	0	1
6	2	0	2
5	3	0	3
4	4	1	5
3	5	2	7
2	6	3	9

The table and diagram illustrate how the quantity of movies demanded varies as the price of a movie varies. In the table, the market demand is the sum of the individual demands. For example, at a price of $3, Lisa demands 5 movies and Chuck demands 2 movies, so the total quantity demanded in the market is 7 movies. In the diagram, the market demand curve is the horizontal sum of the individual demand curves. Thus when the price is $3, the market demand curve shows that the quantity demanded is 7 movies, the sum of the quantities demanded by Lisa and Chuck.

Marginal Utility and the Real World

Marginal utility theory can be used to answer a wide range of questions about the real world. The theory is used in *Reading Between the Lines* on pp. 160–161 to interpret some recent trends in consumer choices in Japan. The theory also sheds light on why the demand for CD players is price elastic while the demand for oil is price inelastic and why the demand for electricity is income elastic while the demand for transportation is income inelastic. Elasticities are determined by preferences. The feature of our preferences that determines elasticity is the step size with which marginal utility declines—the steepness of the marginal utility steps in Fig. 7.2(b).

If marginal utility declines in big steps, a small change in the quantity bought brings a big change in the marginal utility per dollar spent. So it takes a big change in price or income to bring a small change in the quantity demanded—demand is inelastic. Conversely, if marginal utility diminishes slowly, even a large change in the quantity bought brings a small change in the marginal utility per dollar spent. So it takes only a small price change to bring a large quantity change—demand is elastic.

But marginal utility theory can do much more than explain households' *consumption* choices. It can be used to explain *all* the choices made by households. One of these choices, the allocation of time between work in the home, office, or factory and leisure, is the theme of *Economics in History* on pp. 188–189.

REVIEW

- When the price of a good falls and the prices of other goods and a consumer's income remain the same, the consumer increases consumption of the good whose price has fallen and decreases demand for other goods.
- These changes result in a movement along the demand curve for the good whose price has changed and shifts in the demand curves for other goods whose prices have remained constant.
- When a consumer's income increases, the consumer can afford to buy more of all goods, and the quantity bought increases for all *normal* goods.

Criticisms of Marginal Utility Theory

MARGINAL UTILITY THEORY HELPS US TO understand the choices people make and to predict how those choices change in response to price and income changes. But there are some criticisms of this theory. Let's look at them.

Utility Can't Be Observed

Agreed—we can't observe utility. But we do not need to observe it to use it. We can and do observe the quantities of goods and services that people consume, the prices of those goods and services, and people's incomes. Our goal is to understand the consumption choices that people make and to predict the effects of changes in prices and incomes on these choices. To make such predictions, we *assume* that people derive utility from their consumption, that more consumption yields more utility, that marginal utility diminishes, and that people attempt to maximize total utility. From these assumptions, we make predictions about the directions of change in consumption when prices and incomes change. As we've already seen, the actual numbers that we use to express utility do not matter. Consumers maximize total utility by making the marginal utility per dollar spent on each good equal. As long as we use the same scale to express utility for all goods, we'll get the same answer regardless of the units on our scale. In this regard, utility is similar to temperature—water freezes when it's cold enough, and that occurs independently of the temperature scale used.

"People Aren't That Smart"

Some critics maintain that marginal utility theory must be wrong because it assumes that people are supercomputers—or at least rocket scientists. It implies, such critics say, that people look at the marginal utility of every good at every different quantity they might consume, divide those numbers by the prices of the goods, and then find the quantities at which the marginal utility per dollar spent is the same for each good.

This criticism of marginal utility theory confuses the actions of people in the real world with those of people in a model economy. A model economy is no more an actual economy than a model railway is an actual railway. The people in the model economy perform the calculations that we have just described. People in the real world simply decide which is the best deal available. In doing so, they implicitly do the calculations that economists do explicitly. We observe people's consumption choices, not their mental gymnastics. Marginal utility theory says that the consumption patterns we observe in the real world are similar to those implied by a model economy in which people do compute the quantities of goods that maximize total utility. We test how closely the model economy resembles reality by checking the predictions of the model against observed consumption choices.

Marginal utility theory also has some broader implications that provide an interesting way of testing its usefulness. Let's examine two of these.

Implications of Marginal Utility Theory

WE ALL LOVE BARGAINS—PAYING LESS FOR something than its usual price. One implication of marginal utility theory is that we almost *always* get a bargain when we buy something. That is, we place a higher total value on the things we buy than the amount that it costs us. Let's see why.

Consumer Surplus and the Gains from Trade

People can gain by specializing in the production of the things in which they have a comparative advantage and then trading with each other. These gains are explored in Chapter 3, pp. 42–65. Marginal utility theory gives us a way of measuring the value to consumers of the gains from trade.

When Lisa buys movies and soda, she exchanges her income for them. Does Lisa profit from this exchange? Are the dollars she has to give up worth more or less than the movies and soda are worth to her? As we are about to discover, the principle of diminishing marginal utility guarantees that Lisa, and everyone else, gets more value from the things she buys than the amount of money she gives up in exchange.

Calculating Consumer Surplus

The **value** a consumer places on a good is the maximum amount that the person would be willing to pay for it. The amount actually paid for a good is its price. **Consumer surplus** is the difference between the value of a good and its price. When people can buy any chosen quantity of a good at a given price, diminishing marginal utility guarantees that a consumer always makes some consumer surplus. To understand why, let's look again at Lisa's choices.

Figure 7.7(a) shows Lisa's demand curve for movies when she has $30 a month to spend. If Lisa were able to watch only 1 movie a month, she would be willing to pay $7 to see it. She would be willing to pay $6 to see a second movie, $5 to see a third, and so on.

Luckily for Lisa, she has to pay only $3 for each movie she sees—the market price of a movie. Although she values the first movie she sees in a month at $7, she pays only $3, which is $4 less than she would be willing to pay. The second movie she sees in a month is worth $6 to her. The difference between the value she places on the movie and what she has to pay is $3. The third movie she sees in a month is worth $5 to her, which is $2 more than she has to pay for it, and the fourth movie is worth $4, which is $1 more than she has to pay for it. Figure 7.7(a) highlights the difference between the value she places on the first, second, third, and fourth movies and the price she pays ($3). These differences are a gain to Lisa. The total amount that Lisa is willing to pay for the 5 movies is $25 (the sum of $7, $6, $5, $4, and $3). She actually pays $15 (5 movies multiplied by $3). The extra value she receives is $10. This amount is Lisa's consumer surplus. From watching 5 movies a month, she gets $10 worth of value in excess of what she has to spend to see them.

Suppose there are a million consumers similar, but not quite identical, to Lisa. Some are willing to pay $8 for the first movie. At $7.99, yet more movies are demanded. And as the price falls a penny at a time, the quantity of movies demanded increases. For the market as a whole, the consumer surplus is the entire area under the demand curve and above the market price line as shown in Fig. 7.7(b). In this case the consumer surplus can be calculated as the area of the triangle. That area equals the base (5 million movies) multiplied by the height ($5 a movie—$8 minus $3) divided by 2, that is, $12.5 million.

Let's now look at another implication of marginal utility theory.

FIGURE 7.7
Consumer Surplus

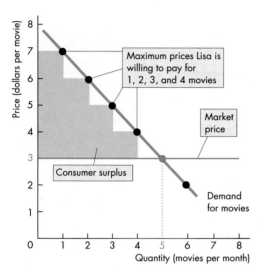

(a) Lisa

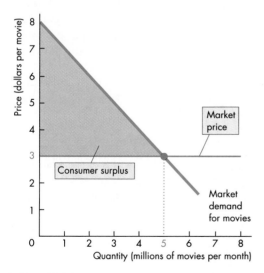

(b) Market

In part (a), Lisa is willing to pay $7 for the first movie, $6 for the second, $5 for the third, $4 for the fourth, and $3 for the fifth. She pays $3 for each movie and has a consumer surplus on the first four movies equal to $10 ($4 + $3 + $2 + $1). In part (b), the entire market has a consumer surplus shown by the green triangle. Its value is $12.5 million (the area of the triangle is equal to its base—5 million movies a month—multiplied by its height—$5 a movie—divided by 2).

The Paradox of Value

For centuries, philosophers have been puzzled by a paradox that we raised at the start of this chapter. Water, which is essential to life itself, costs little, but diamonds, which are useless compared to water, are expensive. Why? Adam Smith tried to solve this paradox. But not until the theory of marginal utility had been developed could anyone give a satisfactory answer.

You can solve this puzzle by distinguishing between *total* utility and *marginal* utility. The total utility that we get from water is enormous. But remember, the more we consume of something, the smaller is its marginal utility. We use so much water that the marginal utility—the benefit we get from one more glass of water—diminishes to a tiny value. Diamonds, on the other hand, have a small total utility relative to water, but because we buy few diamonds, they have a high marginal utility.

When a household has maximized its total utility, it has allocated its budgets in the way that makes the marginal utility per dollar spent equal for all goods. That is, the marginal utility from a good divided by the price of the good is equal for all goods. This equality of marginal utilities per dollar spent holds true for diamonds and water: Diamonds have a high price and a high marginal utility. Water has a low price and a low marginal utility. When the high marginal utility of diamonds is divided by the high price of diamonds, the result is a number that equals the low marginal utility of water divided by the low price of water. The marginal utility per dollar spent is the same for diamonds as for water.

◆ We've now completed our study of marginal utility theory of consumption. We've used that theory to examine how Lisa allocates her income between the two goods that she consumes—movies and soda. We've also seen how the theory can be used to resolve the paradox of value. Furthermore, we've seen how the theory can be used to explain our real-world consumption choices.

In the next chapter, we're going to study an alternative theory of household behavior. To help you see the connection between the marginal utility theory of this chapter and the more modern theory of consumer behavior of the next chapter, we'll continue with the same example. We'll meet Lisa again and discover another way of understanding how she gets the most out of her $30 a month.

Utility Theory: Camping in Japan

THE BOSTON GLOBE, MAY 15, 1994

Japan's Happy Campers

BY CHARLES A. RADIN

KITAKARUIZAWA, Japan—Sales of Coleman camping gear are soaring. So are those of camping vehicles. And the first Kampground of America, the Holiday Inn of campsites, has just opened.

The Japanese, it seems, are discovering the pleasures of sleeping under the stars.

"The increase has been very rapid in the past five years," says Akio Shindo, a campground manager.

It is not exactly a predictable development. The highly urbanized Japanese typically have enjoyed their nature in tamed, often enclosed, settings. This is, after all, the land of indoor beaches and ski slopes.

And while it would be too much to say the woods are teeming with them, the ranks of Japanese auto-campers—who drive to rural campsites and commune with nature in tents or recreational vehicles—are swelling. US companies, which with some justification see themselves as world champions of this sort of recreation, are rushing to cash in.

Kampgrounds in America, Inc. attributes the rise in camping's popularity to the expanded leisure time available to Japanese families, the economic recession (which presumably increases the appeal of lower-cost vacations) and a heightened ecological awareness among the Japanese. Others cite media attention on camping, increased emphasis in Japan on parent-child relations, and the proliferation of camping facilities. ...

The number of Japanese going camping at least once a year has more than tripled since 1984 to 13.5 million. There are now more than 37,000 "camping cars"—defined by the Japan Auto Camp Association as specially rigged vehicles with sleeping accommodations—up from about 1,500 in 1979, when the association started keeping count.

The trend seems certain to continue. A 1993 survey by the government-affiliated Leisure Development Center placed camping third on the list of new activities in which Japanese vacationers would most like to participate in the future. While Japanese still go camping in far fewer numbers than Canadians, Australians and Americans—the leading camping nations—Japan has passed Germany's participation rate and is fast closing in on the United Kingdom, according to the camping association. ...

Reprinted by permission.

- The leading camping nations are Canada, Australia, and the United States.

- Japan is a highly urbanized country, and the Japanese have a reputation for indoor leisure pursuits.

- Since 1980, the demand for camping and camping equipment in Japan has increased and especially so during the past five years.

- The number of Japanese going camping has more than tripled since 1984 to 13.5 million, and the number of camping vehicles has increased from 1,500 in 1979 to more than 37,000.

- The trend is expected to continue.

- Possible reasons for camping becoming popular in Japan are an increase in leisure time, economic recession, a heightened ecological awareness, media attention to camping, increased emphasis on parent-child relations, and a proliferation of camping facilities.

Economic

A N A L Y S I S

■ If Japanese households allocate their incomes between camping and other goods and services to maximize total utility, they make the marginal utility per dollar spent the same for all goods. That is:

$$\frac{\text{Marginal utility of camping}}{\text{Price of camping}} =$$

$$\frac{\text{Marginal utility of other goods}}{\text{Price of other goods}}.$$

■ Two possible income effects could have caused an increase in camping in Japan. They are:

1. Camping is an inferior good (suggested in the news story) and incomes have fallen
2. Camping is a normal good and incomes have increased

■ As Japanese income per person increased during the 1980s, so did the quantity of camping (indicated by camping vehicles or campers), as shown in the figure. Because camping and incomes both increased, camping is a normal good.

■ Camping is even a luxury good—the percentage increase in the quantity of camping exceeds the percentage increase in income, so its income elasticity of demand is greater than one.

■ After 1990, income growth stopped but camping continued to increase. The increase in camping after 1990 could have resulted from:

1. A fall in the price of camping
2. A change in preferences

■ The price of camping has fallen. This price includes the time and effort needed to find and get to a campsite. The proliferation of campsites and of information about them has lowered the price of camping in Japan. So Japanese families have maximized utility by substituting lower price camping for other activities.

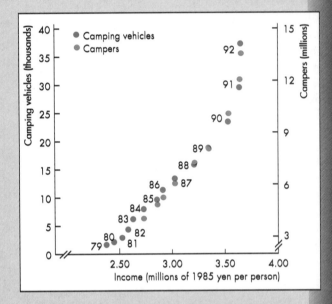

■ The heightened ecological awareness might have changed preferences. If it has done so, the marginal utility from camping has increased relative to the marginal utility from other goods. But the increase in camping can be explained by changes in prices and incomes.

■ As incomes in Japan continue to increase again during the mid-1990s, the demand for camping will continue to increase, as predicted in the news article.

S U M M A R Y

Household Consumption Choices

A household's consumption choices are determined by the constraints it faces and by its preferences. A household's consumption possibilities are constrained by its income and by the prices of the goods it wants to buy. Some combinations of goods are affordable and some are unaffordable. A household's preferences are described by using the concept of utility. The household derives utility from the goods consumed, and the household's total utility increases as consumption of the good increases. The change in total utility resulting from a one-unit increase in the consumption of a good is called marginal utility. Marginal utility declines as consumption increases. This assumption is the basis of the marginal utility theory. Marginal utility theory assumes that people buy the combination that is affordable and that maximizes total utility. (pp. 147–149)

Maximizing Utility

The consumer's goal is to maximize total utility, given the income available to be spent and the prices of the goods and services bought. Total utility is maximized when all the available income is spent and when the marginal utility per dollar spent on each good is equal. If the marginal utility per dollar spent on one good exceeded that on antoher, then it would be possible to increase total utility by reallocating dollars. By spending less on the good with the low marginal utility per dollar spent and more on the good with the high marginal utility per dollar spent, total utility would increase (pp. 150–152)

Predictions of Marginal Utility Theory

Marginal utility theory predicts how prices and income affect the amounts of each good consumed. First, it predicts the law of demand. That is, other things remaining the same, the higher the price of a good, the smaller is the quantity demanded of that good. Second, it predicts that, other things remaining the same, the higher the consumer's income, the greater is the consumption of all normal goods.

The marginal utility theory implies that the demand curve of an individual household slopes downward. The relationship between the price of a good and the quantity demanded by an individual household is called individual demand. Market demand is the sum of all individual demands, and the market demand curve is found by summing horizontally all the individual demand curves. Because individual demand curves slope downward, so do market demand curves. (pp. 152–157)

Criticisms of Marginal Utility Theory

Some people criticize marginal utility theory because utility cannot be observed. But utility does not need to be observed to be used. Marginal utility theory predicts that the ratio of marginal utility to price is equal for all goods. Any arbitrary units can be used to represent utility.

Another criticism is that consumers can't be as smart as the theory implies. In fact, the theory makes no predictions about the thought processes of consumers. It makes predictions only about their actions and assumes that people spend their income in what seems to them to be the best possible way. (pp. 157–158)

Implications of Marginal Utility Theory

Marginal utility theory implies that when we buy goods and services, we usually get more value for our expenditure than the money we spend. We benefit from consumer surplus, which is equal to the difference between the maximum amount that we are willing to pay for a good and the price that we actually pay.

Marginal utility theory resolves the paradox of value. When we talk loosely about value, we are thinking of *total* utility. But price is related to *marginal* utility. A good such as water, which we consume in large amounts, has a high total utility but a low marginal utility, while a good such as diamonds, which we consume in small amounts, has a low total utility and a high marginal utility. (pp. 158–159)

K E Y E L E M E N T S

Key Figures and Table

Key Terms

R E V I E W Q U E S T I O N S

1. What is a household's budget constraint?

2. What determines a household's consumption possibilities?

3. What do we mean by utility?

4. Distinguish between total utility and marginal utility.

5. How does the marginal utility from a good change as:
   a. The household increases the amount of the good it consumes
   b. The household decreases the amount of the good it consumes

6. Susan is a consumer. When is Susan's total utility maximized?
   a. When she has spent all her income
   b. When she has spent all her income, and marginal utility is equal for all goods
   c. When she has spent all her income, and the marginal utility per dollar spent is equal for all goods

   Explain your answers.

7. What does the term "marginal utility per dollar spent" mean?

8. Explain what happens to the marginal utility per dollar spent on a good as:
   a. More dollars are spent on the good
   b. Fewer dollars are spent on the good

9. What does marginal utility theory predict about the effect of a change in price on the quantity of a good consumed?

10. What does marginal utility theory predict about the effect of a change in the price of one good on the consumption of another good?

11. What does marginal utility theory predict about the effect of a change in income on consumption of a good?

12. What is the relationship between individual demand and market demand?

13. How do we construct a market demand curve from individual demand curves?

14. How would you answer someone who says that marginal utility theory is useless because utility cannot be observed?

15. How would you respond to someone who tells you that marginal utility theory is useless because people are not smart enough to compute a consumer equilibrium in which the marginal utility per dollar spent is equal for all goods?

16. What is the value a consumer places on a good?

17. What is consumer surplus? How is consumer surplus calculated?

18. What is the paradox of value? How does marginal utility theory resolve it?

P R O B L E M S

◆ 1. Calculate Lisa's marginal utility from soda from the numbers given in Table 7.1. Draw two graphs, one of her total utility and the other of her marginal utility from soda. Make your graphs look similar to those in Fig. 7.3.

◆ 2. Max enjoys windsurfing and snorkeling. He obtains the following utility from each of these sports:

Half-hours per month	Utility from windsurfing	Utility from snorkeling
1	60	20
2	110	38
3	150	53
4	180	64
5	200	70
6	206	75
7	211	79
8	215	82
9	218	84

a. Draw graphs showing Max's utility from windsurfing and from snorkeling.

b. Compare the two utility graphs. Can you say anything about Max's preferences?

c. Draw graphs showing Max's marginal utility from windsurfing and from snorkeling.

d. Compare the two marginal utility graphs. Can you say anything about Max's preferences?

◆ 3. Max has $35 to spend. Equipment for windsurfing rents for $10 a half-hour, while snorkeling equipment rents for $5 a half-hour. By using this information, together with that given in problem 2, how long will Max choose to windsurf and to snorkel?

◆ 4. Max's sister gives him $20 to spend on his leisure pursuits, so he now has $55 to spend. How long will Max now windsurf and snorkel?

5. If Max has only $55 to spend and the rent on windsurfing equipment decreases to $5 a half-hour, how will Max now spend his time windsurfing and snorkeling?

6. Does Max's demand curve for windsurfing slope downward or upward?

7. Max takes a Club Med holiday, the cost of which includes unlimited sports activities. There is no extra charge for any equipment. Max decides to spend a total of three hours each day on windsurfing and snorkeling. How does Max allocate his three hours between windsurfing and snorkeling?

◆ 8. Shirley's and Dan's demand schedules are:

Price (cents per carton)	Quantity demanded (cartons per week)	
	By Shirley	By Dan
10	12	6
30	9	5
50	6	4
70	3	3
90	1	2

If Shirley and Dan are the only two individuals, show that the market demand curve is the horizontal sum of Shirley's and Dan's demand curves.

◆ 9. Sara's demand for windsurfing is given by:

Price (dollars per half-hour)	Time windsurfing (half-hours per month)
12.50	8
15.00	6
17.50	4
20.00	2

a. If windsurfing costs $17.50 a half-hour, what is Sara's consumer surplus?

b. If windsurfing costs $12.50 a half-hour, what is Sara's consumer surplus?

10. Study *Reading Between the Lines* on pp. 160–161 on camping in Japan and then:

a. Explain why the increase in camping is consistent with marginal utility theory

b. Predict the effect on the quantity of camping of a tax on camper vehicles

c. Predict the effect on the quantity of camping of a large increase in income per person.

Possibilities, Preferences, and Choices

After studying
this chapter,
you will be
able to:

- Calculate and graph a household's budget
  line

- Work out how the budget line changes
  when prices or income changes

- Make a map of preferences by using
  indifference curves

- Explain the choices that households make

- Predict the effects of price and income
  changes on consumption choices

Like the continents floating on the earth's mantle, our spending patterns change steadily over time. On such subterranean movements, business empires rise and fall. Goods such as home videos and microwave popcorn now appear on our shopping lists, while 78 rpm phonograph records and horse-drawn carriages have disappeared. Miniskirts appear, disappear, and reappear in cycles of fashion. ◆ But the glittering surface of our consumption obscures deeper and slower changes in how we spend. In the last few years, we've seen a proliferation of gourmet food shops and designer clothing boutiques. Yet we spend a smaller percentage of our income today on food and clothing than we did in 1950. At the same time, the percentage of our income spent on fuel, housing, and medical care has grown steadily. Why does consumer spending change over the years? How do people react to changes in income and changes in the prices of the things they buy? ◆ Similar subterranean movements govern the way we spend our time. For example, the average workweek has fallen steadily from 70 hours a week in the nineteenth century to 35 hours a week today. Although the average workweek is now much shorter than it once was, far more people now have jobs. This change has been especially dramatic for women, who are much more likely to work outside the home than they were in previous generations. Why has the average workweek declined? And why do more women work? ◻ We're going to study a model of choice that predicts the effects of changes in prices and incomes on what people buy, how much work they do, and how much they borrow and lend.

Subterranean Movements

Consumption Possibilities

CONSUMPTION CHOICES ARE LIMITED BY INCOME and by prices. A household has a given amount of income to spend and cannot influence the prices of the goods and services it buys. It takes prices as given. The limits to a household's consumption choices are described by its **budget line**.

To make the concept of the household's budget line clear, we'll consider a concrete example—the household of Lisa.[1] Lisa has an income of $30 a month to spend. She buys two goods—movies and soda. Movies cost $6 each; soda costs $3 for a six-pack. If Lisa spends all of her income, she will reach the limits to her consumption of movies and soda.

In Fig. 8.1, each row of the table shows an affordable way for Lisa to consume movies and soda. Row *a* says that she can buy 10 six-packs of soda and see no movies. You can see that this combination of movies and soda exhausts her monthly income of $30. Row *f* says that Lisa can watch 5 movies and drink no soda—another combination that exhausts the $30 available. Each of the other rows in the table also exhausts Lisa's income. (Check that each of the other rows costs exactly $30.) The numbers in the table define Lisa's consumption possibilities. We can graph Lisa's consumption possibilities as points *a* through *f* in Fig. 8.1.

Divisible and Indivisible Goods Some goods—called divisible goods—can be bought in any quantity desired. Examples are gasoline and electricity. We can best understand the model of household choice we're about to study if we suppose that all goods and services are divisible. For example, Lisa can consume a half a movie a month *on the average* by seeing one movie every two months. When we think of goods as being divisible, the consumption possibilities are not just the points *a* through *f* shown in Fig. 8.1, but those points plus all the intermediate points that form the line running from *a* to *f*. Such a line is a budget line.

Lisa's budget line is a constraint on her choices. It marks the boundary between what is affordable and

---

[1]If you have read the preceding chapter on marginal utility theory, you have already met Lisa. This tale of her thirst for soda and zeal for movies will sound familiar to you—up to a point. But in this chapter, we're going to use a different method for representing preferences—one that does not require us to resort to the idea of utility.

FIGURE 8.1

The Budget Line

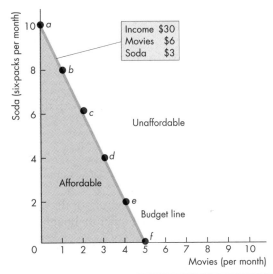

Income	$30
Movies	$6
Soda	$3

Consumption possibility	Movies (per month)	Soda (six-packs per month)
a	0	10
b	1	8
c	2	6
d	3	4
e	4	2
f	5	0

Lisa's budget line shows the boundary between what she can and cannot afford. The rows of the table list Lisa's affordable combinations of movies and soda when her income is $30, the price of soda is $3 a six-pack, and the price of a movie is $6. For example, row *a* tells us that Lisa exhausts her $30 income when she buys 10 six-packs and sees no movies. The figure graphs Lisa's budget line. Points *a* through *f* on the graph represent the rows of the table. For divisible goods, the budget line is the continuous line *af*. To calculate the equation for Lisa's budget line, start with expenditure equal to income:

$$\$3Q_s + \$6Q_m = \$30.$$

Divide by $3 to obtain

$$Q_s + 2Q_m = 10.$$

Subtract $2Q_m$ from both sides to obtain

$$Q_s = 10 - 2Q_m.$$

what is unaffordable. She can afford any point on the line and inside it. She cannot afford any point outside the line. The constraint on her consumption depends on prices and her income, and the constraint changes when prices or her income changes. Let's see how by studying an equation that describes her consumption possibilities.

The Budget Equation

We can describe the budget line by using a *budget equation*. The budget equation starts with the fact that

$$\text{Expenditure} = \text{Income}.$$

In Lisa's case, expenditure and income equal $30 a week.

Expenditure is equal to the sum of the price of each good multiplied by the quantity bought. For Lisa,

$$\text{Expenditure} = \text{Price of soda} \times \text{Quantity of soda}$$
$$+ \text{Price of movie} \times \text{Quantity of movies}.$$

Call the price of soda P_s, the quantity of soda Q_s, the price of a movie P_m, the quantity of movies Q_m, and income y. Using these symbols, Lisa's budget equation is

$$P_s Q_s + P_m Q_m = y.$$

Or, using the prices Lisa faces, $3 for a six-pack and $6 for a movie, and Lisa's income, $30, we get

$$\$3 Q_s + \$6 Q_m = \$30.$$

Lisa can choose any quantities of soda (Q_s) and movies (Q_m) that satisfy this equation. But notice that the quantity of movies she sees influences the quantity of soda she consumes. To find the relationship between these quantities, let's rearrange the equation. Divide both sides of the equation by the price of soda (P_s) to get

$$Q_s + \frac{P_m}{P_s} \times Q_m = \frac{y}{P_s}.$$

Now subtract the term $P_m/P_s \times Q_m$ from both sides of this equation to give

$$Q_s = \frac{y}{P_s} - \frac{P_m}{P_s} \times Q_m.$$

For Lisa, income (y) is $30, the price of a movie (P_m) is $6, and the price of a six-pack (P_s) is $3. So Lisa must choose the quantities of movies and soda to satisfy the equation

$$Q_s = \frac{\$30}{\$3} - \frac{\$6}{\$3} \times Q_m ,$$

or

$$Q_s = 10 - 2 Q_m .$$

This equation tells us how Lisa's consumption of soda (Q_s) varies as her consumption of movies (Q_m) varies. To interpret the equation, go back to the budget line of Fig. 8.1 and check that the equation you've just derived delivers that budget line. Begin by setting Q_m equal to zero. In this case, the budget equation tells us that Q_s, the quantity of soda, is y/P_s, which is $30/$3, or 10 six-packs. This combination of Q_m and Q_s is the same as that shown in row *a* of the table in Fig. 8.1. Setting Q_m equal to 5 makes Q_s equal to zero (row *f* of the table). Check that you can derive the other rows.

The budget equation contains two variables chosen by the household (Q_m and Q_s) and two variables (y/P_s and P_m/P_s) that the household takes as given. Let's look more closely at these variables.

Real Income A household's **real income** is the maximum quantity of a good that the household can afford to buy. In the budget equation, real income is y/P_s. This quantity is the maximum number of six-packs that Lisa can buy and is Lisa's real income in terms of soda. It is equal to her money income divided by the price of soda. Lisa's income is $30 and the price of soda is $3 a six-pack, so her real income in terms of soda is 10 six-packs. In Fig. 8.1, real income is the point at which the budget line intersects the y-axis.

Relative Price A **relative price** is the price of one good divided by the price of another good. In Lisa's budget equation, the variable P_m/P_s is the relative price of a movie in terms of soda. For Lisa, P_m is $6 a movie and P_s is $3 a six-pack, so P_m/P_s is equal to 2 six-packs per movie. That is, to see one more movie, Lisa must give up 2 six-packs.

You've just calculated Lisa's opportunity cost of a movie. Recall that the opportunity cost of an action is the best alternative forgone. For Lisa to see 1 more movie a month, she must forgo 2 six-packs. You've also calculated Lisa's opportunity cost of soda. For Lisa to consume 2 more six-packs a month, she must give up seeing 1 movie. So her opportunity cost of 2 six-packs is 1 movie.

The relative price of a movie in terms of soda is the magnitude of the slope of Lisa's budget line. To calculate the slope of the budget line, recall the formula for slope (Chapter 2): Slope equals the change in the variable measured on the *y*-axis divided by the change in the variable measured on the *x*-axis as we move along the line. In Lisa's case (Fig. 8.1), the variable measured on the *y*-axis is the quantity of soda, and the variable measured on the *x*-axis is the quantity of movies. Along Lisa's budget line, as soda decreases from 10 to 0 six-packs, movies increase from 0 to 5. Therefore the magnitude of the slope of the budget line is 10 six-packs divided by 5 movies, or 2 six-packs per movie. The magnitude of this slope is exactly the same as the relative price we've just calculated. It is also the opportunity cost of a movie.

A Change in Prices   When prices change, so does the budget line. The lower the price of the good measured on the horizontal axis, other things remaining the same, the flatter is the budget line. For example, if the price of a movie falls from $6 to $3, real income in terms of soda does not change but the relative price of a movie falls. The budget line rotates outward and becomes flatter as shown in Fig. 8.2(a). The higher the price of the good measured on the horizontal axis, other things remaining the same, the steeper is the budget line. For example, if the price of a movie rises from $6 to $12, the relative price of a movie increases. The budget line rotates inward and becomes steeper as shown in Fig. 8.2(a).

A Change in Income   A change in *money income* changes real income but does not change relative prices. The budget line shifts, but its slope does not change. The bigger a household's money income, the bigger is real income and the farther to the right is the budget line. The smaller a household's money income, the smaller is real income and the farther to the left is the budget line. Figure 8.2(b) shows the effect of a change in money income on Lisa's budget line. The initial budget line is the same one that we began with in Fig. 8.1 when Lisa's income is $30. The new budget line shows how much Lisa can consume if her income falls to $15 a month. The new budget line is parallel to the old one but closer to the origin. The two budget lines are parallel—have the same slope—because the relative price is the same in both cases. The new budget line is closer to the origin than the initial one because Lisa's real income has decreased.

Changes in Prices and Income

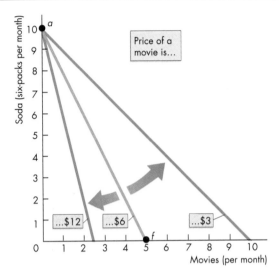

(a) A change in price

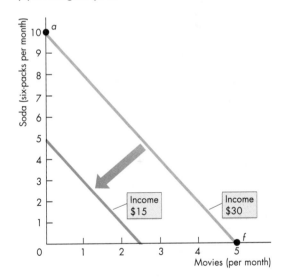

(b) A change in income

In part (a), the price of a movie changes. A fall in the price from $6 to $3 rotates the budget line outward and makes it flatter. A rise in the price from $6 to $12 rotates the budget line inward and makes it steeper.

In part (b), income falls from $30 to $15 while the prices of movies and soda remain constant. The budget line shifts leftward, but its slope does not change.

R E V I E W

- The budget line describes the limits to a household's consumption, which depends on its income and the prices of the goods that it buys.
- The position of the budget line depends on real income, and its slope depends on the relative price.
- A change in the price of one good changes the relative price and changes the slope of the budget line. If the price of the good measured on the horizontal axis rises, the budget line becomes steeper.
- A change in money income changes real income and shifts the budget line, but its slope does not change. A decrease in income shifts the budget line inward.

We've studied the limits to what a household can consume. Let's now see how we can describe the household's preferences.

Preferences and Indifference Curves

PREFERENCES ARE A PERSON'S LIKES AND DISLIKES. A key assumption about preferences is that they do not depend on prices or income. The things you like and dislike do not depend on what you can afford. When a price changes, or when your income changes, you make a new choice, but the preferences that guide that choice don't change. We are going to discover a very neat idea—that of drawing a map of a person's preferences.

A preference map is based on the intuitively appealing assumption that people can sort all the possible combinations of goods they might consume into three groups: preferred, not preferred, and indifferent. To make this idea more concrete, let's ask Lisa to tell us how she ranks various combinations of movies and soda. Figure 8.3 illustrates part of her answer.

Lisa tells us that she currently consumes 2 movies and 6 six-packs a month at point *c* in Fig. 8.3. She then lists all the combinations of movies and soda that she regards as equally acceptable to her as her current consumption. When we plot the combinations of movies and soda that Lisa tells us she likes just as much as the combination at point *c*, we get the green

FIGURE 8.3

Mapping Preferences

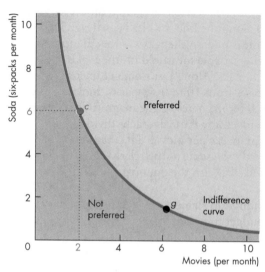

If Lisa drinks 6 six-packs of soda and sees 2 movies a month, she consumes at point *c*. Lisa can compare all other possible combinations of soda and movies to point *c* and rank them on the scale preferred to point *c*, not preferred to point *c*, or indifferent. The boundary between points that she prefers to point *c* and those that she does not prefer to point *c* is an indifference curve. Lisa is indifferent between points such as *g* and *c* on the indifference curve. She prefers any point above the indifference curve (yellow area) to any point on it, and she prefers any point on the indifference curve to any point below it (gray area).

curve in Fig. 8.3. This curve is the key element in a map of preferences and is called an indifference curve.

An **indifference curve** is a line that shows combinations of goods among which a consumer is *indifferent*. The indifference curve in Fig. 8.3 tells us that Lisa is just as happy to consume 2 movies and 6 six-packs a month at point *c* as to consume the combination of movies and soda at point *g* or at any other point along the curve.

Lisa goes on to tell us that starting from any combination of movies and soda, she prefers to have more movies and no less soda or more soda and no fewer movies. We can interpret Lisa as saying that the indifference curve defines the boundary between combinations of goods that she prefers to those on the indifference curve and combinations that she does not prefer. Lisa prefers any combination in the yellow area above the indifference curve to any combination on the indifference curve. And she prefers any combination on the indifference curve to any combination in the gray area below the indifference curve.

The indifference curve shown in Fig. 8.3 is just one of a whole family of such curves. This indifference curve appears again in Fig. 8.4. It is labeled I_1 and passes through points c and g. Two other indifference curves are I_0 and I_2. Lisa prefers any point on indifference curve I_2 to any point on indifference curve I_1, and she prefers any point on I_1 to any point on I_0. We refer to I_2 as being a higher indifference curve than I_1 and I_1 as being higher than I_0.

Indifference curves never intersect. To see why, consider indifference curves I_1 and I_2 in Fig. 8.4. We know that Lisa prefers point j to point c. We also

know that Lisa prefers any point on indifference curve I_2 to any point on indifference curve I_1. If these indifference curves did intersect, Lisa would be indifferent between the combination of goods at the intersection point and combinations c and j. But we know that Lisa prefers j to c, so there cannot be an intersection point. Hence the indifference curves never intersect.

A preference map consists of a series of indifference curves. The indifference curves shown in Fig. 8.4 are only a part of Lisa's preference map. Her entire map consists of an infinite number of indifference curves; each one slopes downward, and none of them intersects. They resemble the contour lines on a map that measure the height of a mountain. An indifference curve joins points representing combinations of goods among which a consumer is indifferent in much the same way that contour lines on a map join points of equal height above sea level. By looking at the shape of the contour lines on a map, we can draw conclusions about the terrain. In the same way, by looking at the shape of a person's indifference curves, we can draw conclusions about preferences. But interpreting a preference map requires a bit of work. It also requires some way of describing the shape of the indifference curves. In the next two sections, we'll learn how to "read" a preference map.

Marginal Rate of Substitution

The **marginal rate of substitution** (MRS) is the rate at which a person will give up good y (the good measured on the y-axis) to get more of good x (the good measured on the x-axis) and at the same time remain indifferent (remain on the same indifference curve). The marginal rate of substitution is measured from the slope of an indifference curve. If the indifference curve is steep, the marginal rate of substitution is high. The person is willing to give up a large quantity of good y in exchange for a small quantity of good x while remaining indifferent. If the indifference curve is flat, the marginal rate of substitution is low. The person is willing to give up only a small amount of good y in exchange for a large amount of good x to remain indifferent.

Figure 8.5 shows you how to calculate the marginal rate of substitution. The curve labeled I_1 is one of Lisa's indifference curves. Suppose that Lisa drinks 6 six-packs and watches 2 movies at point c in the figure. Her marginal rate of substitution is calculated by measuring the magnitude of the slope of the indifference

FIGURE 8.4
A Preference Map

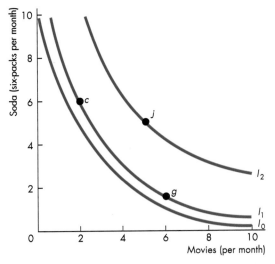

A preference map consists of an infinite number of indifference curves. Here, we show just three—I_0, I_1, and I_2—that are part of Lisa's preference map. Each indifference curve shows points among which Lisa is indifferent. For example, she is indifferent between point c and point g on indifference curve I_1. But she prefers any point on a higher indifference curve to any point on a lower indifference curve. For example, Lisa prefers point j to point c or g, so she prefers any point on indifference curve I_2 to any point on indifference curve I_1.

curve at point *c*. To measure this magnitude, place a straight line against, or tangent to, the indifference curve at point *c*. The slope of that line is the change in the quantity of soda divided by the change in the quantity of movies as we move along the line. As soda consumption decreases by 10 six-packs, movie consumption increases by 5. So at point *c* Lisa is willing to give up soda for movies at the rate of 2 six-packs per movie. Her marginal rate of substitution is 2.

Now, suppose that Lisa consumes 6 movies and 1 1/2 six-packs at point *g* in Fig. 8.5. What is her marginal rate of substitution at this point? The answer is found by calculating the magnitude of the slope of the indifference curve at point *g*. That slope is the same as the slope of the tangent to the differ-

ence curve at point *g*. Here, as soda consumption decreases by 4.5 six-packs, movie consumption increases by 9. So at point *g* Lisa is willing to give up soda for movies at the rate of 1/2 six-pack per movie. Her marginal rate of substitution is 1/2.

Notice that if Lisa drinks a lot of soda and does not see many movies, her marginal rate of substitution is large. If she watches a lot of movies and does not drink much soda, her marginal rate of substitution is small. This feature of the marginal rate of substitution is the central assumption of the theory of consumer behavior and is referred to as the diminishing marginal rate of substitution. The assumption of **diminishing marginal rate of substitution** is a general tendency for the marginal rate of substitution to diminish as the consumer moves along an indifference curve, increasing consumption of the good measured on the *x*-axis and decreasing consumption of the good measured on the *y*-axis.

Your Own Diminishing Marginal Rate of Substitution You may be able to appreciate why we assume the principle of a diminishing marginal rate of substitution by thinking about your own preferences for movies and soda. Suppose you consume 10 six-packs of soda a week and see no movies. How many six-packs are you willing to give up in exchange for seeing one movie a week? Your answer to this question is your marginal rate of substitution between soda and movies when you consume no movies. For example, if you are willing to give up 4 six-packs to see 1 movie, your marginal rate of substitution between soda and movies is 4. Now suppose that you consume 6 six-packs and see 1 movie a week. How many six-packs are you now willing to give up to see one additional movie a week? Your answer to this question is your marginal rate of substitution between soda and movies when you see 1 movie a week. If your answer is a smaller number than when you see no movies, your preferences display a diminishing marginal rate of substitution between soda and movies. The greater the number of movies you see, the smaller is the quantity of soda you are willing to give up to see one additional movie.

The shape of the indifference curves incorporates the principle of the diminishing marginal rate of substitution because the curves are bowed toward the origin. The tightness of the bend of an indifference curve tells us how willing a person is to substitute one good for another while remaining indifferent. Let's look at some examples that will clarify this point.

FIGURE 8.5

The Marginal Rate of Substitution

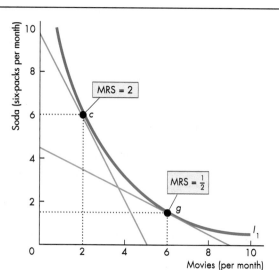

The magnitude of the slope of an indifference curve is called the marginal rate of substitution (MRS). The marginal rate of substitution tells us how much of one good a person is willing to give up to gain more of another good while remaining indifferent—that is, staying on the same indifference curve. The red line at point *c* tells us that Lisa is willing to give up 10 six-packs to see 5 movies. Her marginal rate of substitution at point *c* is 10 divided by 5, which equals 2. The red line at point *g* tells us that Lisa is willing to give up 4.5 six-packs to see 9 movies. Her marginal rate of substitution at point *g* is 4.5 divided by 9, which equals 1/2.

Degree of Substitutability

Most of us would not regard movies and soda as being close substitutes for each other. We probably have some fairly clear ideas about how many movies we want to see each month and how many cans of soda we want to drink. Nevertheless, to some degree, we are willing to substitute between these two goods. No matter how big a soda freak you are, there is surely some increase in the number of movies you can see that will compensate you for being deprived of a can of soda. Similarly, no matter how addicted you are to the movies, surely some number of cans of soda will compensate you for being deprived of seeing one movie. A person's indifference curves for movies and soda might look something like those shown in Fig. 8.6(a).

Close Substitutes Some goods substitute so easily for each other that most of us do not even notice which we are consuming. A good example concerns different brands of personal computers. Dell, Compaq, and Toshiba are all clones of the IBM PC, but most of us can't tell the difference between the clones and the IBM. The same holds true for marker pens. Most of us don't care whether we use a marker pen from the campus bookstore or the local supermarket. When two goods are perfect substitutes for each other, their indifference curves are straight lines that slope downward, as Fig. 8.6(b) illustrates. The marginal rate of substitution is constant.

Complements Some goods cannot substitute for each other at all. Instead they are complements. The complements in Fig. 8.6(c) are left and right running shoes. Indifference curves of perfect complements are L-shaped. One left running shoe and one right running shoe are as good as one left shoe and two right ones. Having two of each is preferred to having one of each, but having two of one and one of the other is no better than having one of each.

The extreme cases of perfect substitutes and perfect complements shown here don't often happen in reality. They do, however, illustrate that the shape of the indifference curve shows the degree of substitutability

---

FIGURE 8.6

The Degree of Substitutability

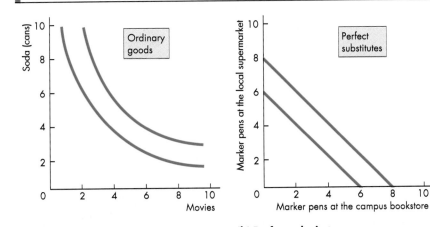

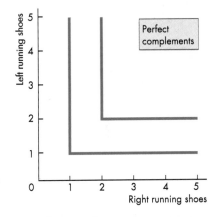

(a) Ordinary goods

(b) Perfect substitutes

(c) Perfect complements

The shape of the indifference curves reveals the degree of substitutability between two goods. Part (a) shows the indifference curves for two ordinary goods: movies and soda. To consume less soda and remain indifferent, one must see more movies. The number of movies that compensates for a reduction in soda increases as less soda is consumed. Part (b) shows the indifference curves for two perfect substitutes. For the consumer to remain indifferent, one fewer marker pen from the local supermarket must be replaced by one extra marker pen from the campus bookstore. Part (c) shows two perfect complements—goods that cannot be substituted for each other at all. Having two left running shoes with one right running shoe is no better than having one of each. But having two of each is preferred to having one of each.

"With the pork I'd recommend an Alsatian white or a Coke."

Drawing by Weber; © 1988 The New Yorker Magazine, Inc.

between two goods. The more perfectly substitutable the two goods, the more nearly are their indifference curves straight lines and the less quickly does the marginal rate of substitution fall. Poor substitutes for each other have tightly curved indifference curves, approaching the shape of those shown in Fig. 8.6(c).

As you can see in the cartoon, according to the waiter's preferences, Coke and Alsatian white wine are perfect substitutes and are each complements with pork. We hope the customers agree with him.

REVIEW

■ A person's preferences can be represented by a preference map that consists of a series of indifference curves.

■ For most goods, indifference curves slope downward, bow toward the origin. They never intersect.

■ The magnitude of the slope of an indifference curve is called the marginal rate of substitution.

■ The marginal rate of substitution diminishes as a person consumes less of the good measured on the y-axis and more of the good measured on the x-axis.

The two components of the model of household choice are now in place: the budget line and the preference map. We will now use these components to work out the household's choice.

The Household's Consumption Choice

WE ARE NOW GOING TO BRING LISA'S BUDGET line and indifference curves together and discover her best affordable choice of movies and soda. What are the quantities of movies and soda that Lisa *chooses* to buy? In Fig. 8.7, you can see her budget line from Fig. 8.1 and her indifference curves from Fig. 8.4. First focus on point h on indifference curve I_0. Point h is on Lisa's budget line, so we know that she can afford it. But does she *choose* this combination of movies and soda over all the other affordable combinations? No, she does not. To see why not, consider point c, where she consumes 2 movies and 6 six-packs. Point c is also on Lisa's budget line, so we know she can afford to consume at this point. But point c is on indifference curve I_1, a higher indiffer-

---

FIGURE 8.7
The Best Affordable Point

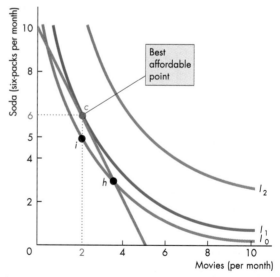

Lisa's best affordable point is c. At that point, she is on her budget line and also on the highest attainable indifference curve. At a point such as h, Lisa is willing to give up more movies in exchange for soda than she has to. She can move to point i, which is just as good as point h and have some unspent income. She can spend that income and move to c, a point that she prefers to point i.

ence curve than I_0. Therefore we know that Lisa prefers point c to point h.

Is there any affordable point that Lisa prefers to point c? There is not. All Lisa's other affordable consumption points—all the other points on or below her budget line—lie on indifference curves that are below I_1. Indifference curve I_1 is the highest indifference curve on which Lisa can afford to consume.

Let's look more closely at Lisa's best affordable choice.

Properties of the Best Affordable Point

The best affordable point—point c in this example—has two properties. It is:

■ On the budget line
■ On the highest attainable indifference curve

On the Budget Line The best affordable point is *on* the budget line. If Lisa chooses a point inside the budget line, there will be an affordable point on the budget line at which she can consume more of both goods. Lisa prefers that point to the one inside the budget line. The best affordable point cannot be outside the budget line because Lisa cannot afford such a point.

On the Highest Attainable Indifference Curve
The chosen point is on the highest attainable indifference curve. At this point, the indifference curve has the same slope as the budget line. Stated another way, the marginal rate of substitution between the two goods (the magnitude of the slope of the indifference curve) equals their relative price (the magnitude of the slope of the budget line).

To see why this condition describes the best affordable point, consider point h in Fig. 8.7, which Lisa regards as inferior to point c. At point h, Lisa's marginal rate of substitution is less than the relative price—indifference curve I_0 is flatter than Lisa's budget line. As Lisa gives up movies for soda and moves up indifference curve I_0, she moves inside her budget line and has some income left over. She can move to point i, for example, where she consumes 2 movies and 5 six-packs and has $3 to spare. She is indifferent between the combination of goods at point i and the combination at point h. But she prefers point c to point i, since at c, she has more soda than at i and sees the same number of movies.

By moving along her budget line from point h toward point c, Lisa passes through a number of indifference curves (not shown in the figure) located between indifference curves I_0 and I_1. All of these indifference curves are higher than I_0, and therefore any point on them is preferred to point h. Once Lisa gets to point c, she has reached the highest attainable indifference curve. If she keeps moving along the budget line, she will start to encounter indifference curves that are lower than I_1.

R E V I E W

■ Affordable combinations of goods lie on or inside the consumer's budget line.
■ The consumer's preferences are described by indifference curves.
■ The consumer's best affordable allocation of income occurs when all income is spent (on the budget line) and when the marginal rate of substitution (the magnitude of the slope of the indifference curve) equals the relative price (the magnitude of the slope of the budget line).

We will now use this model of household choice to make some predictions about changes in consumption patterns when income and prices change.

Predicting Consumer Behavior

LET'S START BY LOOKING AT THE EFFECT OF A change in price. By studying the effect of a change in price on a consumer's choice, other things held constant, we can derive a consumer's demand curve.

A Change in Price

The effect of a change in price on the quantity of a good consumed is called the **price effect**. We will use Fig. 8.8(a) to work out the price effect of a fall in the price of a movie. We start with movies costing $6 each, soda costing $3 a six-pack, and Lisa's income at $30 a month. In this situation, she consumes at point c, where her budget line is tangent to her highest attainable indifference curve, I_1. She consumes 6 six-packs and 2 movies a month.

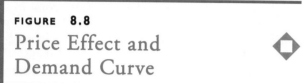

FIGURE 8.8

Price Effect and Demand Curve

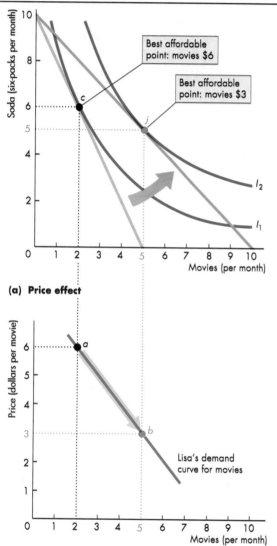

(a) Price effect

(b) Demand curve

Initially, Lisa consumes at point c (part a). If the price of a movie falls from $6 to $3, she consumes at point j. The increase in movies from 2 to 5 per month and the decrease in soda from 6 to 5 six-packs is the price effect.

Part (b) shows Lisa's demand curve for movies. When the price of a movie is $6, she sees 2 movies a month, at point a. When the price of a movie falls to $3, she sees 5 movies a month, at point b. Lisa's demand curve traces out her best affordable quantity of movies as the price of a movie varies.

Now suppose that the price of a movie falls to $3. We've already seen how a change in price (in Fig. 8.2a) affects the budget line. With a lower price of a movie, the budget line rotates outward and becomes flatter. The new budget line is the dark orange one in Fig. 8.8(a). Lisa's best affordable point is j, where she consumes 5 movies and 5 six-packs of soda. As you can see, Lisa drinks less soda and watches more movies now that movies cost less. She reduces her soda consumption from 6 to 5 six-packs and increases the number of movies she sees from 2 to 5 a month. Lisa substitutes movies for soda when the price of a movie falls and the price of soda and her income remain constant.

The Demand Curve

A demand curve shows the relationship between the quantity demanded of a good and its price, when all other influences on buying plans are constant. In Chapter 4, we asserted that the demand curve slopes downward and that it shifts when the consumer's income changes or when the price of another good changes. We can now derive a demand curve from a consumer's budget line and indifference curves. By doing so, we can see that the law of demand and the downward-sloping demand curve are consequences of the consumer's choosing his or her best affordable combination of goods.

Let's derive Lisa's demand curve for movies. We do so by lowering the price of a movie and finding her best affordable point at different prices. We just did this for two movie prices in Fig. 8.8(a). Figure 8.8(b) highlights these two prices and two points that lie on Lisa's demand curve for movies. When the price of a movie is $6, Lisa sees 2 movies a month at point a. When the price falls to $3, she increases the number of movies she sees to 5 a month at point b. The entire demand curve is made up of these two points plus all the other points that tell us Lisa's best affordable consumption of movies at each movie price—more than $6, between $6 and $3, and less than $3—given the price of soda and Lisa's income. As you can see, Lisa's demand curve for movies slopes downward—the lower the price of a movie, the more movies she watches each month. This is the law of demand.

Next, let's examine how Lisa adjusts her consumption when her income changes.

A Change in Income

The effect of a change in income on consumption is called the **income effect**. Let's work out the income effect by examining how consumption changes when income changes and prices remain constant. Figure 8.9(a) shows the income effect when Lisa's income falls. With an income of $30 and with a movie costing $3 and soda $3 a six-pack, she consumes at point j—5 movies and 5 six-packs. If her income falls to $21, she consumes at point ℓ—consuming 4 movies and 3 six-packs. Thus when Lisa's income falls, she consumes less of both goods. For Lisa, movies and soda are normal goods.

The Demand Curve and the Income Effect   A change in income leads to a shift in the demand curve, as shown in Fig. 8.9(b). With an income of $30, Lisa's demand curve is D_0, the same as in Fig. 8.8. But when her income falls to $21, she plans to see fewer movies at each price, so her demand curve shifts leftward to D_1.

Substitution Effect and Income Effect

We've now worked out the effects of a change in the price of a movie and the effects of a change in Lisa's income on her consumption of movies and soda. We've discovered that when her income increases, she increases her consumption of both goods. Movies and soda are *normal goods*. When the price of a movie falls, Lisa increases her consumption of movies and decreases her consumption of soda. A fall in the price of a normal good leads to an increase in the consumption of that good. To see why this change occurs, we separate the price effect into two parts. One part is called the substitution effect; the other part is called the income effect.

 Figure 8.10 illustrates the price effect and its separation into a substitution effect and an income effect. Part (a) shows the price effect that you worked out in Fig. 8.8. Let's see how that price effect comes about, first by isolating the substitution effect.

Substitution Effect   The **substitution effect** is the effect of a change in price on the quantities consumed when the consumer (hypothetically) remains

FIGURE   **8.9**

Income Effect and change in Demand

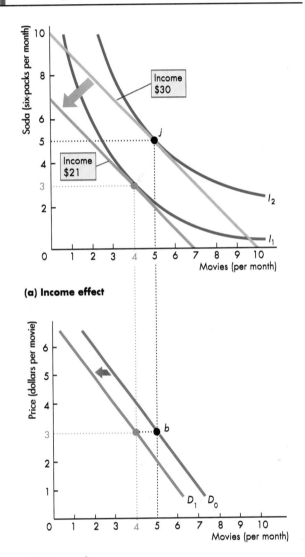

(a) Income effect

(b) Demand curve

A change in income shifts the budget line and changes the best affordable point and changes consumption. In part (a), when Lisa's income decreases from $30 to $21, she consumes less of both movies and soda. In part (b), Lisa's demand curve for movies when her income is $30 is D_0. When Lisa's income decreases to $21, her demand curve for movies shifts leftward to D_1. Lisa's demand for movies decreases because she now sees fewer movies at each price.

FIGURE 8.10

Price Effect, Substitution Effect, and Income Effect

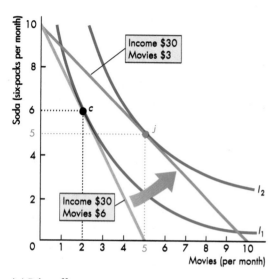

(a) Price effect

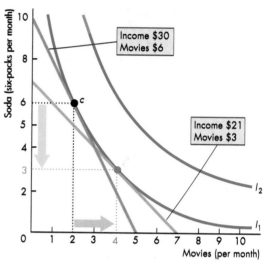

(b) Substitution effect

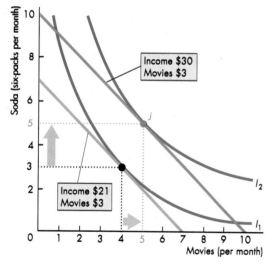

(c) Income effect

The price effect can be separated into a substitution effect and an income effect. Part (a) shows the price effect and it is the same as Fig. 8.8(a).

To calculate the substitution effect (part b), when the price of a movie falls, imagine that Lisa's income decreases so that her best affordable point remains on her original indifference curve I_1. The substitution effect of the price change is the move from c to ℓ.

To calculate the income effect (part c), reverse Lisa's imaginary income cut while holding prices constant at their new level. The increase in income shifts the budget line outward, and the quantities of movies and soda consumed increase. The income effect of the price change is the move from ℓ to j.

indifferent between the original and the new combinations of goods consumed. To work out Lisa's substitution effect, we have to imagine that when the price of a movie falls, Lisa's income also decreases by an amount that is just enough to leave her on the same indifference curve as before.

Figure 8.10(b) illustrates the substitution effect. When the price of a movie falls from $6 to $3, let's suppose (hypothetically) that Lisa's income decreases to $21. What's special about $21? It is the income that is just enough, at the new price of a movie, to keep Lisa's best affordable point on the same indifference curve as her original consumption point c. Lisa's budget line in this situation is the light orange line shown in Fig. 8.10(b). With the new price of a movie and the new smaller income, Lisa's best affordable point is ℓ on indifference curve I_1. The move from c to ℓ isolates the substitution effect of the price change. The substitution effect of the fall in the price of a movie is an increase in the consumption of movies from 2 to 4 and a decrease in the consumption of soda. The direction of the substitution effect never varies: When the relative price of a good falls, the consumer substitutes more of that good for the other good.

Income Effect   To calculate the substitution effect, we gave Lisa a $9 pay cut. Now let's give Lisa her $9 back. The $9 increase in income shifts Lisa's budget line outward, as shown in Fig. 8.10(c). The slope of the budget line does not change because both prices remain constant. This change in Lisa's budget line is similar to the one illustrated in Fig. 8.9, where we study the effect of income on consumption. As Lisa's budget line shifts outward, her consumption possibilities expand, and her best affordable point becomes j on indifference curve I_2. The move from ℓ to j isolates the income effect of the price change. In this example, as Lisa's income increases, she increases her consumption of both movies and soda. For Lisa, movies and soda are normal goods.

Price Effect   Figure 8.10 shows how the price effect in part (a) is broken into two effects: the substitution effect in part (b) and the income effect in part (c). In part (b), Lisa is indifferent between the two situations. Her income falls at the same time that the price of a movie falls, and she substitutes movies for soda. The substitution effect always works in the same direction—the consumer slides along an indifference curve to buy more of the good whose relative price has fallen and less of the good whose relative price has risen. In part (c), prices are constant at their new level and Lisa's income returns to its original level. The direction of the income effect depends on whether the good is normal or inferior. By definition, normal goods are ones whose consumption increases as income increases. For Lisa, movies and soda are normal goods because the income effect increases their consumption. Both the income effect and the substitution effect increase Lisa's consumption of movies.

The arrows in parts (b) and (c) of Fig. 8.10 show the substitution and income effects of a price change. The move from point c to point ℓ in part (b)

is the substitution effect, and the move from point ℓ to point j in part (c) is the income effect. For movies, the income effect reinforces the substitution effect with the result that Lisa increases her consumption of movies. For soda, the substitution effect and the income effect work in opposite directions with the result that Lisa decreases her consumption of soda.

The example that we have just studied is that of a change in the price of a normal good. The effect of a change in the price of an inferior good is different. Recall that an inferior good is one whose consumption decreases as income increases. For an inferior good, the income effect is negative. Thus for an inferior good, a lower price does not always lead to an increase in the quantity demanded. The lower price has a substitution effect that increases the quantity demanded. But the lower price also has a negative income effect that reduces the demand for the inferior good. Thus the income effect offsets the substitution effect to some degree.

Back to the Facts

We started this chapter by observing how consumer spending has changed over the years. We can use the indifference curve model to explain those changes. Spending patterns are interpreted as being the best choices households can make, given their preferences and incomes and given the prices of the goods they consume. Changes in prices and incomes lead to changes in the best affordable choice and change consumption patterns.

Sometimes, prices change because taxes change (which we studied in Chapter 6, pp. 126–130). *Reading Between the Lines* on pp. 180–181 shows you how when taxes changed the price of boating, consumers changed their spending patterns and made new best affordable choices.

Models based on the same ideas that you've studied here are used to explain the actual changes that occur and to measure the response of consumption to changes in prices and in income—the price elasticity and income elasticity of demand. You met some measures of these elasticities in Chapter 5. Most of those elasticities were measured by using the model that we've studied here (but models that have more than two goods).

The model of household choice can do much more than explain consumption choices. It can be used to explain a wide range of other household choices. Let's look at some of these.

Indifference Curves: Increased Boating Costs

THE DETROIT FREE PRESS, JULY 6, 1994

Boaters Feel Torpedoed by Taxes, Fees

By Mike Magner

WASHINGTON—As they hit the waters this summer, the nation's 11 million recreational boaters are in danger of being swamped by their old Uncle Sam.

Higher taxes on diesel fuel, a huge increase in the licensing fee for marine radios and a threatened cut in federal grants for safety programs are all weighing down boaters. That hits hard in Michigan, which leads the nation in the number of registered boats—877,581 in 1992, the last year for which figures were available.

"Once again it appears the boating public is being targeted as rich 'fat cats' and being squeezed for money," said Patricia Kearns, a Maryland boater and technical adviser to the American Boat and Yacht Council.

Added federal tax burdens on boaters this year come in the wake of two aborted attempts by Congress to lighten boaters' wallets.

A user fee to help fund U.S. Coast Guard services was imposed in 1990 but replaced in 1992 after an outcry from boating groups. A 10-percent luxury tax on new boats was repealed last year after scuttling sales for two years.

But to replace the luxury tax, Congress boosted the diesel fuel tax by 20 percent, from 20.1 cents to 24.4 cents a gallon, beginning Jan. 1. It also told the Federal Communications Commission to raise the fee for a 10-year marine radio license from $35 to $115. The fees will take effect July 18.

"It's like being in a boat on a swell. You go up and down," said Michael Sciulla, vice president of the Boat Owners Association of the United States, the nation's largest boating group, with 500,000 members.

Sciulla said many members of Congress seem to think all boaters are wealthy yacht owners. "That doesn't hold water. The average boater's income is $35,000, and the average boat size is 16 feet." ...

Reprinted by permission.

Essence of THE STORY

■ The United States has 11 million recreational boaters, 877,581 of whom are in Michigan (1992 figures).

■ The average boater has an income of $35,000 a year and owns a 16-foot boat (according to the Boat Owners Association).

■ The cost of boating increased in 1994 because of higher taxes on diesel fuel—up by 20 percent from 20.1 cents to 24.4 cents a gallon—and an increase in the license fee for marine radios—up from $35 to $115 for a ten-year license.

■ Two taxes on boaters—a user fee to help fund U.S. Coast Guard services, imposed in 1990, and a 10 percent luxury tax on new boats—were repealed.

■ The luxury tax caused new boat sales to plummet.

Economic

A N A L Y S I S

■ Figure 1 shows indifference curves for used boats and new boats. A used boat is a close substitute for a new boat so the indifference curves do not bow much—the marginal rate of substitution does not diminish very quickly (see Fig. 8.6).

■ Figure 1 also shows the budget line for boats. With no luxury tax on new boats, the budget line is the line labeled *a*. The number of new boats bought in a year is N_0, and the number of used boats bought is U_0.

■ A luxury tax on new boats increases the relative price of a new boat, and the budget line rotates inward to *b*. Because new boats and used boats are close substitutes, the quantity of new boats bought decreases sharply to N_1 and the number of used boats bought increases to U_1. The tax has a large effect on the number of new boats bought.

■ Figure 2 illustrates boaters' preferences between boating and other recreational activities. Boating and other activities are poor substitutes so the marginal rate of substitution diminishes quickly—the indifference curves are tightly bowed.

■ The slope of the budget line depends on the relative price of boating in terms of other recreational activities. Three events in the news story increased the relative price of boating: Coast Guard fees, the diesel tax, and the radio license fee.

■ The increase in the relative price of boating rotates the budget line inward from *a* to *b* and has an income effect and a substitution effect that decrease the quantity of boating from B_0 to B_1 and decrease the quantity of other recreational activities from A_0 to A_1.

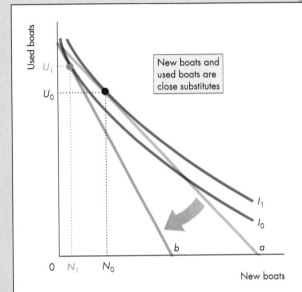

New boats and used boats are close substitutes

Figure 1

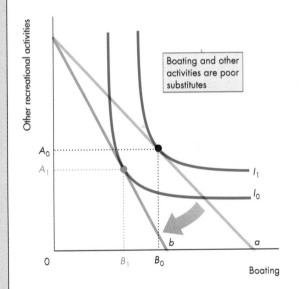

Boating and other activities are poor substitutes

Figure 2

Other Household Choices

HOUSEHOLDS MAKE MANY CHOICES OTHER THAN those about how to spend their income on the various goods and services available. We can use the model of consumer choice to understand many other household choices. Some of these are discussed in *Economics in History* on pp. 188–189. Here we'll study two key choices:

- How much labor to supply
- How much to save

Labor Supply

Every week, we allocate our 168 hours between working—called *labor*—and all other activities—called *leisure.* How do we decide how to allocate our time between labor and leisure? We can answer this question by using the theory of household choice.

The more hours we spend on *leisure,* the smaller is our income. The relationship between leisure and income is described by an *income-time budget line.* Figure 8.11 shows Lisa's income-time budget line. If Lisa devotes the entire week to leisure—168 hours— she has no income and is at point *z.* By supplying labor in exchange for a wage, she can convert hours into income along the income-time budget line. The slope of that line is determined by the hourly wage rate. If the wage rate is $5 an hour, Lisa faces the lowest budget line. If she worked for 68 hours a week, she would make an income of $340 a week. If the wage rate is $10 an hour, she faces the middle budget line. And if the wage rate is $15 an hour, she faces the highest budget line. Lisa buys leisure by not supplying labor and by forgoing income. The opportunity cost of an hour of leisure is the hourly wage rate forgone.

Lisa must choose a point on a time budget line. That is, she must choose how many hours of labor to supply. We can study this choice by looking at Lisa's indifference curves. Income and leisure are goods, just like movies and soda, and Lisa has indifference curves for income and leisure.

Figure 8.12(a) shows Lisa's indifference curves for income and leisure. The magnitude of the slope of an indifference curve tells us Lisa's marginal rate of substitution—the rate at which she is willing to give up income to get one more hour of leisure while remaining indifferent.

FIGURE 8.11

The Income-Time Budget Line

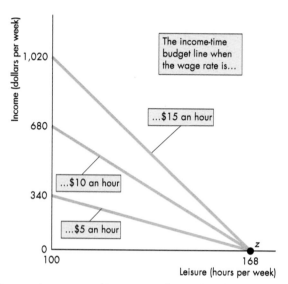

The income-time budget line when the wage rate is...

...$15 an hour

...$10 an hour

...$5 an hour

Time can be converted into income by working for a wage. If no work is done, the household has 168 hours of leisure per week and no income, at point z. The higher the wage rate, the steeper is the income-time budget line.

Lisa chooses her best attainable point. This choice of income and time allocation is just like her choice of movies and soda. She gets onto the highest possible indifference curve by making her marginal rate of substitution between income and leisure equal to her wage rate. Lisa's choice depends on the wage rate she can earn. At a wage rate of $5 an hour, Lisa chooses point *a* and works 20 hours a week (168 minus 148) for an income of $100 a week. At a wage rate of $10 an hour, she chooses point *b* and works 35 hours a week (168 minus 133) for an income of $350 a week. And at a wage rate of $15 an hour, she chooses point *c* and works 30 hours a week (168 minus 138) for an income of $450 a week.

Figure 8.12(b) shows Lisa's choices of hours to work at different wage rates in the form of her labor supply curve. This curve shows that as the wage rate increases from $5 an hour to $10 an hour, Lisa increases the quantity of labor supplied from 20 hours a week to 35 hours a week. But when the wage rate increases to $15 an hour, she decreases her quantity of labor supplied to 30 hours a week.

FIGURE 8.12

The Supply of Labor

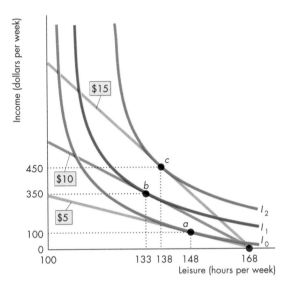

(a) Time allocation decision

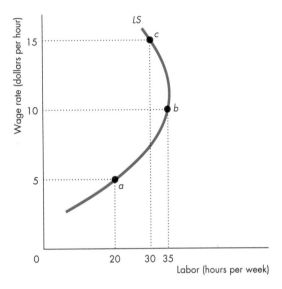

(b) Labor supply curve

In part (a), at a wage rate of $5 an hour, Lisa takes 148 hours of leisure and works 20 hours a week at point *a*. If the wage rate increases from $5 to $10, she decreases her leisure to 133 hours and increases her work to 35 hours a week at point *b*. But if the wage rate increases from $10 to $15, Lisa *increases* her leisure to 138 hours and *decreases* her work to 30 hours a week at point *c*.

Part (b) shows Lisa's labor supply curve—the change in Lisa's hours of work as the wage rate changes. Lisa's labor supply curve slopes upward between points *a* and *b* and then bends back between points *b* and *c*. The reason is that leisure is a normal good, and at a high enough wage rate, the positive income effect of a higher wage rate outweighs the negative substitution effect.

Lisa's supply of labor is similar to that described for the economy as a whole at the beginning of this chapter. As wage rates have increased, work hours have decreased. At first, this pattern seems puzzling. We've seen that the hourly wage rate is the opportunity cost of leisure. So a higher wage rate means a higher opportunity cost of leisure. This fact on its own leads to a decrease in leisure and an increase in work hours. But instead, we've cut our work hours. Why? Because our incomes have increased. As the wage rate increases, incomes increase, so people demand more of all normal goods. Leisure is a normal good, so as incomes increase, people demand more leisure.

The higher wage rate has both a *substitution effect* and an *income effect*. The higher wage rate increases the opportunity cost of leisure and so leads to a substitution effect away from leisure. And the higher

wage rate increases income and so leads to an income effect toward more leisure.

This theory of household choice can explain the facts about work patterns described at the beginning of this chapter. First, it can explain why the average workweek has fallen steadily from 70 hours in the nineteenth century to 35 hours today. The reason is that as wage rates have increased, although people have substituted work for leisure, they have also decided to use their higher incomes in part to consume more leisure. Second, the theory can explain why more women now have jobs in the labor market. The reason is that increases in their wage rates and improvements in their job opportunities have lead to a substitution effect away from working at home and toward working in the labor market.

Let's now see how the theory of household choice explains saving decision.

Saving

Each year, we allocate our income between consumption and saving. By saving, we decrease our *current* consumption and increase our *future* consumption. The choice of how much to consume and how much to save can also be understood by using the same model of household choice that explains the allocation of income to movies and soda.

The more we spend on *current* consumption, the less we can spend on *future* consumption. The relationship between current consumption and future consumption is described by a *lifetime budget line*. Figure 8.13 shows two possible lifetime budget lines for Lisa. Lisa earns $20,000 a year in her working years, and she can consume her entire income each year, and save nothing for her retirement at point *z*. The slope of the lifetime budget line depends on the interest rate. Other things remaining the same, the higher the interest rate, the steeper is the lifetime budget line. This means that the higher the interest rate, the larger is the amount of future consumption that can be done with a given amount of saving. Along the light orange budget line, the interest rate is 50 percent compounded to Lisa's retirement. (An annual interest rate of 1.6 percent compounds 50 percent of 25 years.) Along this lifetime budget line, if Lisa decreases her consumption while she is working by $1 (if she saves $1), she can spend an additional $1.50 after she retires. Along the dark orange line, the interest rate is 100 percent compounded to Lisa's retirement. (An annual interest rate of 3 percent compounds to 100 percent over 25 years). Along the budget line, if Lisa decreases her consumption in her working years by $1, she can spend an additional $2 after she retires.

Lisa must choose a point on her lifetime budget line. If she spends her entire income each year while she is working, she has nothing to spend when she retires and is at point *z* in Fig. 8.13. By decreasing current consumption, Lisa can increase future consumption along the lifetime budget line. For example, along the light orange lifetime budget line, by saving $8,000, Lisa moves to point *a*, at which she consumes $12,000 a year while she is working and also $12,000 a year after she retires. Lisa has smoothed out her consumption over her life.

The choice that Lisa makes depends on her preferences. And her preferences are represented by indifference curves for current consumption and future consumption. These indifference curves are similar to

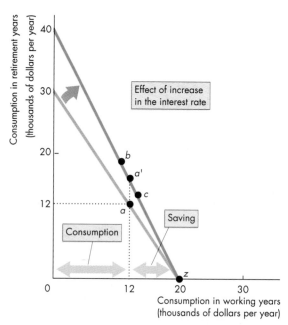

FIGURE 8.13

The Saving Decision

During her working years, Lisa earns $20,000 a year. If she consumes all her income, her consumption when she retires is zero, point *z*. By saving, Lisa can make her retirement consumption equal to her working years consumption at point *a*. An increase in the interest rate increases Lisa's current and future consumption possibilities. The substitution effect of the higher interest rate induces an increase in saving, but the income effect of the higher interest rate induces a decrease in saving. Depending on her preferences, Lisa might move to point *a'* (no change in saving), *b* (an increase in saving), or *c* (a decrease in saving).

those for any pair of goods—movies and soda or leisure and income.

Lisa chooses the amount of consumption and saving by making the marginal rate of substitution between current and future consumption equal to the interest rate. Suppose that when the interest rate is 50 percent, Lisa chooses point *a* in Fig. 8.13. She has a current income of $20,000 a year, consumes $12,000 a year, and saves $8,000 a year. What happens to Lisa's consumption and saving if the interest rate rises? A rise in the interest rate rotates the budget line outward as shown in the figure. With a higher interest rate, the opportunity cost of current consumption increases. So Lisa substitutes future consumption for current consumption. But the higher interest rate expands Lisa's consumption possibilities in both the current and future periods. This increase in her consumption possibilities creates an *income effect* that leads to an increase in both current and future consumption.

The outcome for current consumption and saving is ambiguous. If the income effect is smaller than the substitution effect, Lisa moves to *b* in Fig. 8.13. Here, current consumption decreases, saving increases, and future consumption increases. If the income effect is larger than the substitution effect, Lisa moves to *c*. Here, current consumption increases, saving decreases, and future consumption increases. If the income effect offsets the substitution effect, Lisa moves to *a'*. Here, current consumption and saving remain constant, and future consumption increases.

If Lisa is an average consumer, she will move from *a* to *b* when the interest rate rises. That is, the substitution effect will outweigh the income effect. The effect of the interest rate on saving appears to be small.

◆ We have now completed our study of household choices. We've seen how we can derive a demand curve from a model of household choice. And we've seen that the demand curve obeys the law of demand: Other things remaining the same, when the price of a good falls, the quantity demanded of that good increases. We've also seen how the model of household choice can be applied to a wide range of other choices, including the supply of labor and saving.

In the chapters that follow, we're going to study the choices made by firms. We'll see how, in the pursuit of profit, firms make choices governing the supply of goods and services and the demand for factors of production (inputs). After completing these chapters, we'll then bring the analysis of households and firms together and study their interactions in markets for goods and services and factors of production.

S U M M A R Y

Consumption Possibilities

The budget line shows the limits to a household's consumption given its income and the prices of goods. The budget line is the boundary between what the household can and cannot afford.

The point at which the budget line intersects the *y*-axis is the household's real income in terms of the good measured on that axis. The magnitude of the slope of the budget line is the relative price of the good measured on the *x*-axis in terms of the good measured on the *y*-axis.

A change in price changes the slope of the budget line. The lower the price of the good measured on the *x*-axis, the flatter is the budget line. A change in income shifts the budget line (rightward for an increase and leftward for a decrease) but does not change its slope. (pp. 167–170)

Preferences and Indifference Curves

A consumer's preferences can be represented by indifference curves. An indifference curve joins all the combinations of goods among which the consumer is indifferent. A consumer prefers any point above an indifference curve to any point on it and any point on an indifference curve to any point below it. Indifference curves bow toward the origin.

The magnitude of the slope of an indifference curve is called the marginal rate of substitution. A key assumption is that the marginal rate of substitution diminishes as consumption of the good measured on the *y*-axis decreases and consumption of the good measured on the *x*-axis increases. (pp. 170–174)

The Household's Consumption Choice

A household consumes at its best affordable point. Such a point is on the budget line and on the highest attainable indifference curve. At that point, the indifference curve and the budget line have the same slope—the marginal rate of substitution equals the relative price. (pp. 174–175)

Predicting Consumer Behavior

The change in the quantity bought that results from a change in the price of a good is called the price effect. Other things remaining the same, when the price of a good falls, a household buys more of that good. The change in the quantity bought that results from a change in income is called the income effect. Other things remaining the same, when income increases, a household buys more of all (normal) goods.

The price effect can be divided into a substitution effect and an income effect. The substitution effect is calculated as the change in consumption resulting from the change in price accompanied by a (hypothetical) change in income that leaves the consumer indifferent between the original situation and the new situation. The substitution effect of a price change always results in an increase in consumption of the good whose relative price has decreased. The income

effect of a price change is the effect of (hypothetically) restoring the consumer's original income but keeping the price of the good constant at its new level. For a normal good, the income effect reinforces the substitution effect. For an inferior good, the income effect offsets the substitution effect. (pp. 175–179)

Other Household Choices

The indifference curve model of household choice enables us to understand how a household allocates its time between leisure and work and its lifetime resources between current consumption and future consumption. (pp. 182–185)

KEY ELEMENTS

Key Figures

Key Terms

REVIEW QUESTIONS

1. What determines the limits to a household's consumption choices?
2. What is the budget line?
3. What determines the intercept of the budget line on the *y*-axis?
4. What determines the slope of the budget line?
5. What do all the points on an indifference curve have in common?
6. What is the marginal rate of substitution?
7. What two conditions are satisfied when a consumer makes the best affordable consumption choice?
8. What is the effect of a change in income on consumption?
9. What is the effect of a change in price on consumption?
10. What is the price effect?
11. Define and distinguish between the income effect and the substitution effect of a price change.
12. What is the opportunity cost of leisure?
13. Why might the labor supply curve bend backward?
14. What is the opportunity cost of current consumption?

P R O B L E M S

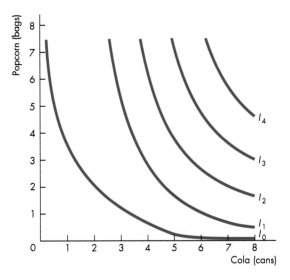

1. Sara has an income of $12 a week. Popcorn costs $3 a bag, and cola costs $3 a can.
   a. What is Sara's real income in terms of cola?
   b. What is her real income in terms of popcorn?
   c. What is the relative price of cola in terms of popcorn?
   d. What is the opportunity cost of a can of cola?
   e. Calculate the equation for Sara's budget line (placing bags of popcorn on the left side).
   f. Draw a graph of Sara's budget line with cola on the x-axis.
   g. In part (f), what is the slope of Sara's budget line? What is it equal to?

2. Sara's income and the prices she faces are the same as in problem 1. Her preferences are shown by her indifference curves in the figure.
   a. What are the quantities of popcorn and cola that Sara buys?
   b. What is Sara's marginal rate of substitution of popcorn for cola at the point at which she consumes?

3. Now suppose that in the situation described in problem 1, the price of cola falls to $1.50 per can and the price of popcorn and Sara's income remain constant.
   a. Find the new quantities of cola and popcorn that Sara buys.
   b. Find two points on Sara's demand curve for cola.
   c. Find the substitution effect of the price change.
   d. Find the income effect of the price change.
   e. Is cola a normal good or an inferior good for Sara?
   f. Is popcorn a normal good or an inferior good for Sara?

4. Jerry buys cookies that cost $1 each and comic books that cost $2 each. Each month, Jerry buys 20 cookies and 10 comic books. He spends all of his income. Next month, the price of cookies will fall to 50¢, but the price of a comic book will rise to $3.
   a. Will Jerry be able to buy 20 cookies and 10 comic books next month?
   b. Will he want to?

   c. If he changes his consumption, which good will he buy more of and which will he buy less of?
   d. Which situation does Jerry prefer: cookies at $1 and comic books at $2 or cookies at 50¢ and comic books at $3?
   e. When the prices change next month, will there be an income effect and a substitution effect at work or just one of them? If there is only one effect at work, which one will it be?

5. Now suppose that in the situation described in problem 4, the prices of cookies and comic books next month remain at $1 and $2, respectively. Jerry gets a pay raise of $10 a month. He now buys 16 comic books and 18 cookies. For Jerry, are cookies and comic books normal goods or inferior goods?

6. Study *Reading Between the Lines* on p. 180–181, and then explain what happens to the quantities of new boats and used boats bought if:
   a. the maintenance cost of used boats increases. Distinguish carefully between income effects and substitution effects.
   b. a technological advance in boat building decreases the price and increases the quality of new boats. Again, distinguish carefully between income effects and substitution effects. Do the indifference curves move? Why or why not?

> *"Economy is the art of making the most of life."*
>
> GEORGE BERNARD SHAW, *MAN AND SUPERMAN*

Understanding Human Behavior

THE ISSUES AND IDEAS

The economic analysis of human behavior in the family, the workplace, the markets for goods and services, the markets for labor services, and financial markets is based on the idea that our behavior can be understood as a response to scarcity. Everything we do can be understood as a choice that maximizes total utility subject to the constraints imposed by our limited resources and technology. If people's preferences are stable in the face of changing constraints, then we have a chance of predicting how they will respond to an evolving environment.

The incredible change that has occurred over the past 100 years in the way women allocate their time can be explained as the consequence of changing constraints. Technological advances have equipped the nation's factories with machines that have increased the productivity of both women and men, thereby raising the wages they can earn. The increasingly technological world has increased the return to education for both women and men and has led to a large increase in the number of high school and college graduates of both sexes. And, equipped with a wide array of gadgets and machines that cut the time of household jobs, an increasing proportion of women have joined the labor force.

This economic view may not be correct, but it is a powerful one. And if it is correct, the changing attitudes toward women are a consequence, not a cause, of their economic advancement.

THEN...

ECONOMISTS EXPLAIN people's actions as the consequence of choices that maximize total utility subject to constraints. In the 1890s, fewer than 20 percent of women chose market employment, and most of those who did had low-paying and unattractive jobs. The other 80 percent of women chose non-market work in the home. What were the constraints that led to these choices?

BY 1995, MORE than 60 percent of women were in the labor force, and although many had low-paying jobs, more and more women were found in the professions and in executive positions. What brought about this dramatic change compared with 100 years earlier? Was it a change in preferences or a change in the constraints that women face?

William Stanley Jevons

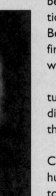

THE ECONOMISTS: BENTHAM, JEVONS, AND BECKER

Many economists have contributed to our understanding of human behavior, but three stand out from the rest. They are Jeremy Bentham (1748–1832), William Stanley Jevons (1835–1882), and Gary Becker (1930–   ).

Bentham, who lived in London (and whose embalmed body is preserved to this day in a glass cabinet in the University of London), was the first to use the concept of utility to explain and prescribe human choices. The distinction between explanation and prescription was not a sharp one in Bentham's day. He was one of the first to propose pensions for the retired, guaranteed employment, minimum wages, and social benefits such as free education and free medical care.

Jeremy Bentham

Jevon's main claim to fame in his own day was his proposal—wrong as it turned out—that economic fluctuations are caused by sunspots. He was a co-discoverer of the concept of marginal utility, and it was he who developed the theory explained in this chapter.

Gary Becker teaches both economics and sociology at the University of Chicago. He has used the ideas of Bentham and Jevons to explain a wide range of human choices, including the choices made by women about how many children to bear and how much and what type of work to do.

Organizing Production

After studying
this chapter,
you will be
able to:

■ Explain what a firm is and describe the
economic problems that *all* firms face

■ Define and explain the principal-agent
problem

■ Describe and distinguish between
different forms of business organization

■ Explain how firms raise the funds to
finance their operations

■ Calculate a firm's opportunity cost and
economic profit

■ Explain why firms coordinate some
economic activities and markets
coordinate others

On a July day in 1977, a tiny new firm was born that grew into a giant—Apple Computer. But that day was not unusual. Every day, a new successful firm is born. Apple began its life when two Stanford University students produced the world's first commercially successful personal computer in a backyard garage. From that modest start, Apple has grown into a giant. ◆ Apple is one of some 20 million firms that operate in the United States today. They range from multinational giants, such as Apple and Sony, to small family restaurants and corner stores. Three quarters of all firms are operated by their owners, as Apple once was. But corporations (like Apple today) account for 85 percent of all business sales. What are the different forms a firm can take? Why do some remain small while others become giants? Why are most firms owner-operated? ◆ Firms spend billions of dollars on buildings and production lines and on developing and marketing new products. How does a firm get the funds needed to pay for all these activities? What do investors expect in return when they put funds into a firm? And how do we measure a firm's economic health? ◆ Most of the components of an IBM personal computer are made by other firms. Another firm, Microsoft, created the operating system for the PC. Microsoft has now outgrown IBM, and its products such as DOS and Windows have become household names. Why doesn't IBM make its own computer components? Why didn't it create its own operating system? Why did it leave these activities to other firms? How do firms decide what to make themselves and what to buy in the marketplace from other firms?

◇ In this chapter, we are going to learn about firms and the choices they make to cope with scarcity. We begin by studying the economic problems and choices that all firms face.

An Apple a Day

The Firm and Its Economic Problem

THERE ARE 20 MILLION FIRMS IN THE UNITED States, and they differ enormously in size and in the scope of what they do. What do they have in common? What is the distinguishing characteristic of a firm? What are the different ways in which firms are organized? Why are there different forms of organization? These are the questions we'll tackle first.

What is a Firm?

A **firm** is an institution that hires factors of production and that organizes those factors to produce and sell goods and services. Firms exist because of scarcity. They help us to cope with the fundamental economic problem of scarcity and they enable us to use our scarce resources efficiently. But each firm faces its own economic problem. That is, each firm must strive to get the most it can out of the scarce resources it controls. To do so, a firm must decide on the following:

■ Which goods and services to produce and in what quantities

■ Which of its inputs to produce itself and which to buy from other firms

■ Which techniques of production to use

■ Which factors of production to employ and in what quantities

■ How to organize its management structure

■ How to compensate its factors of production and suppliers

For the majority of firms, these decisions are made so that the firm makes the maximum possible profit. And for every firm, whether it is motivated by profit or some other goal, these decisions are made so that the firm produces its output at the lowest possible cost.

In the rest of this chapter and in Chapters 10 through 13, we are going to study the actions a firm must take to be efficient. And we are going to see how we can predict a firm's behavior by working out its efficient response to a change in its circumstances. But we are going to begin by looking a bit more closely at the fundamental problem the firm faces.

The fundamental problem for a firm is *organization*—the firm organizes the production of goods and services by combining and coordinating the factors of production it hires. Firms organize production by using a mixture of two systems:

■ Command systems

■ Incentive systems

Command Systems

A command system is a method of coordinating the factors of production that a firm hires that is based on a managerial hierarchy. A chief executive is at the top of the managerial ladder and directs the senior managers. The senior managers direct the middle managers, who in turn direct operations managers. This lowest level of management controls the workers who produce the goods and services. Commands pass downward through the managerial hierarchy and information passes upward. Managers spend most of their time collecting and processing information about the performance of the people under their control and making decisions about commands to issue and how best to get those commands implemented.

The number of layers of management depends on the complexity of the business and on the technology available for managing information. In the smallest and simplest organizations, perhaps one or two layers of managers are all that are needed. But in large organizations that undertake complex tasks, several layers of management are found. The computer and information revolution of the 1980s and 1990s has decreased the number of layers needed and has brought a big shake-out of middle managers.

Despite the enormous efforts they make to be well-informed, managers always have incomplete information about what is happening in the divisions of the firm under their control. It is for this reason that firms use incentive systems as well as command systems to organize production.

Incentive Systems

Incentive systems are market-like mechanisms that firms create inside their organizations. Such systems operate at all levels, from the chief executive down to the factory floor and the sales force. And they arise because a firm's owners and managers cannot know everything that is relevant to the efficient operation of their business. What did John Sculley (a former president of Apple Computer) contribute to the success and subsequent problems faced by Apple? What role did Lee Iaccoca play in the fortunes of Chrysler? These questions cannot be answered with certainty even long after the event. Yet Apple and Chrysler must put chief executive officers (CEOs) like these in charge of operations and give them *incentives* to succeed, even when the contribution they make cannot be measured directly.

At the bottom of the management ladder, some workers are more diligent than others and it is often difficult for managers to know who is working and who is shirking. Did sales fall last month because the sales force slacked off or because of some other unknown factor? Again, firms must devise incentives to ensure that the sales force works effectively.

Because of incomplete information, firms do not simply demand factors of production and pay for them as if they were buying toothpaste at the drugstore. Instead, they enter into contracts and devise compensation packages that strengthen incentives and raise productivity. These contracts and compensation packages are called agency relationships and they are an attempt to solve what is called the principal-agent problem.

The Principal-Agent Problem

The **principal-agent problem** is to devise compensation rules that induce an *agent* to act in the best interest of a *principal*. For example, the relationship between the stockholders of the Bank of America and the bank's managers is an agency relationship. The stockholders (the principals) must induce the managers (agents) to act in the stockholders' best interest. Another example of an agency relationship is that between Microsoft Corporation (a principal) and its programmers working on a new version of Windows (agents). Microsoft must induce the programmers to work in the best interest of the firm.

Coping with the Principal-Agent Problem

Agents, whether they are managers or workers, pursue their own goals and often impose costs on a principal. For example, the goal of a stockholder of the Bank of America (a principal) is to maximize the bank's profit.

But the bank's profit depends on the actions of its managers (agents) who have their own goals. Perhaps a manager takes a customer to a ball game on the pretense that she is building customer loyalty, when in fact she is simply taking on-the-job leisure. This same manager is also a principal and her tellers are agents. The manager wants the tellers to work hard and attract new customers so she can meet her operating targets. But the tellers enjoy conversations with each other and keep customers waiting in line. Nonetheless, the bank constantly strives to find ways of improving performance and increasing profits.

The principal-agent problem cannot be solved just by giving orders and having workers obey them. In most firms, it isn't possible for the shareholders to monitor the managers or even for the managers to monitor the workers. To achieve their goal, the firm's owners (principals) must induce its managers (agents) to pursue the maximum possible profit. And the managers (principals) must induce the workers (agents) to work efficiently. Each principal attempts to do this by creating incentives that induce each agent to work in the interests of the principal. The three main ways of coping with the principal-agent problem are:

■ Ownership

■ Incentive pay

■ Long-term contracts

Ownership By assigning a manager or worker ownership (or part-ownership) of a business, it is sometimes possible to induce a job performance that increases a firm's profits. Part-ownership schemes for senior managers are quite common, but they are less common for workers. When United Airlines was running into problems a few years ago, it adopted this solution and made all its employees owners of the company.

Incentive pay Incentive pay schemes—pay related to performance—are very common. They are based on a wide variety of performance criteria. For example, managers often share in a firm's profits for meeting profit targets, and workers get bonuses for meeting production or sales targets.

Long-term contracts Long-term contracts are a way of coping with the principal-agent problem because they tie the long-term fortunes of managers and workers (agents) to the success of the principal(s)— the owner(s) of the firm.

The principal-agent problem has been tackled with a variety of innovative management structures and the arrangements. You can study a leading example—that of Motorola—in *Reading Between the Lines* on pp. 208-209.

A further fundamental problem that all firms must cope with is uncertainty about the future.

Uncertainty about the Future

Firms' decisions are based on their expectations of the consequences of their actions. But expectations often turn out to be wrong. The main problem is that almost every firm must commit to a project and spend huge amounts on it *before* it knows whether it will be able to sell its output in sufficient quantities and at a sufficiently high price to cover its outlays. For example, 30 years ago, French and British airplane makers spent several years and millions of dollars building a supersonic transatlantic passenger plane—the Concorde. They expected to be able to sell enough of these technologically sophisticated airplanes to recover their cost. But it turns out that too few people value the Concorde's extra speed for it to generate sales revenues equal to its cost. On a smaller scale, millions of people try their luck at opening coffee shops and other small businesses. They spend several thousand dollars setting up a business before they know how much revenue their business will earn. And many of them turn out to be too optimistic. The revenue falls short of the cost and the business fails.

The facts of incomplete information and uncertainty about the future give rise to different forms of business organization. Let's look at these different forms.

The Forms of Business Organization

The three main forms of business organization are:

- Proprietorship
- Partnership
- Corporation

Which form a firm takes influences its management structure, how it compensates factors of production, how much tax its owners pay, and who receives its profits and is liable for its debts if it goes out of business.

Proprietorship   A *proprietorship* is a firm with a single owner—a proprietor—who has unlimited liability. *Unlimited liability* is the legal responsibility for all the debts of a firm up to an amount equal to the entire wealth of the owner. If a proprietorship cannot pay its debts, the personal property of the owner can be claimed by those to whom the firm owes money. Corner stores, computer programmers, and artists are all examples of proprietorships.

The proprietor makes the management decisions and is the firm's sole residual claimant. A firm's *residual claimant* is the person who receives the firm's profits and is responsible for its losses. The profits of a proprietorship are part of the income of the proprietor. They are added to the proprietor's other income and taxed as personal income.

Partnership   A *partnership* is a firm with two or more owners who have unlimited liability. Partners must agree on an appropriate management structure and on how to divide the firm's profits among themselves. As in a proprietorship, the profits of a partnership are taxed as the personal income of the owners. But each partner is legally liable for all the debts of the partnership (limited only by the wealth of an individual partner). Liability for the full debts of the partnership is called *joint unlimited liability*. Most law firms are partnerships.

Corporation   A *corporation* is a firm owned by one or more limited liability stockholders. *Limited liability* means that the owners have legal liability only for the value of their initial investment. This limitation of liability means that if the corporation becomes bankrupt, the owners of the corporation, unlike the owners of a proprietorship or partnership, cannot be forced to use their personal wealth to pay the corporation's debts.

The stock of a corporation is divided into shares. A *share* is a fraction of the stock of a corporation. Shares in many corporations are bought and sold on stock markets such as the New York Stock Exchange.

Some corporations, no bigger than a proprietorship, have just one effective owner and are managed in the same way as a proprietorship. Large corporations have elaborate management structures headed by a CEO and senior vice-presidents responsible for such areas as production, finance, marketing, and research. These senior executives are in turn served by a series of specialists. Each layer in the management structure knows enough about what happens in the layer below it to exercise control, but the entire management consists of specialists who concentrate on a narrow aspect of the corporation's activities.

The corporation receives its financial resources from its owners—the stockholders—and by borrowing. Corporations sometimes borrow from banks, but they can also borrow directly from households by issuing bonds—loans on which they pay a fixed number of dollars of interest.

If a corporation makes a profit, the residual claimants to that profit are the stockholders, who receive dividends. If a corporation incurs a loss on such a scale that it becomes bankrupt, the residual loss is absorbed by the banks and other corporations to whom the troubled corporation is in debt. The stockholders themselves, by virtue of their limited liability, are responsible for the debt of the corporation only up to the value of their initial investment.

The profits of a corporation are taxed independently of the incomes of its stockholders, so corporate profits are, in effect, taxed twice. After the corporation has paid tax on its profits, the stockholders themselves pay taxes on the income they receive as dividends on stocks. The stockholders also pay tax on capital gains when they sell a stock. A **capital gain** is the income received by selling a stock (or a bond) for a higher price than the price paid for it. Corporate stocks generate capital gains when a corporation retains some of its profit and reinvests it in profitable activities instead of paying dividends. So even retained earnings are effectively taxed twice because the capital gains they generate are taxed.

The Pros and Cons of the Different Types of Firms

Because each of the three main types of firms exists, each type obviously has advantages in particular situations. Each type also has its disadvantages, a fact that explains why it has not driven out the other two. These pros and cons of each type of firm are summarized in Table 9.1.

TABLE 9.1

The Pros and Cons of Different Types of Firms

Type of firm	Pros	Cons
Proprietorship	■ Easy to set up ■ Simple decision making ■ Profits taxed only once as owner's income	■ Bad decisions not checked by need for consensus ■ Owner's entire wealth at risk ■ Firm dies with owner ■ Capital is expensive ■ Labor is expensive
Partnership	■ Easy to set up ■ Diversified decision making ■ Can survive withdrawal of partner ■ Profits taxed only once as owners' incomes	■ Achieving consensus may be slow and expensive ■ Owners' entire wealth at risk ■ Withdrawal of partner may create capital shortage ■ Capital is expensive
Corporation	■ Owners have limited liability ■ Large-scale, low-cost capital available ■ Professional management not restricted by ability of owners ■ Perpetual life ■ Long-term labor contracts cut labor costs	■ Complex management structure can make decisions slow and expensive ■ Profits taxed twice as company profit and as stockholders' income

FIGURE 9.1

Relative Importance of the Three Main Types of Firms

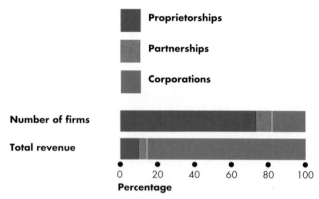

Proprietorships

Partnerships

Corporations

Number of firms

Total revenue

0   20   40   60   80   100
Percentage

(a) Number of firms and total revenue

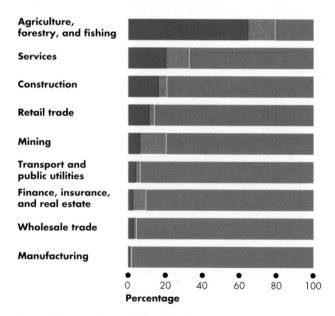

Agriculture, forestry, and fishing

Services

Construction

Retail trade

Mining

Transport and public utilities

Finance, insurance, and real estate

Wholesale trade

Manufacturing

0   20   40   60   80   100
Percentage

(b) Total revenue in various industries

Three quarters of all firms are proprietorships, almost one fifth are corporations, and only a twentieth are partnerships. Corporations account for 86 percent of business revenue (part a). But proprietorships and partnerships account for a significant percentage of business revenue in some industries (part b).

Source: U.S. Bureau of the Census, *Statistical Abstract of the United States: 1994,* 114th ed. (Washington, D.C.: 1994): 539 and 665.

The Relative Importance of Different Types of Firms

Figure 9.1(a) shows the relative importance of the three main types of firms in the U.S. economy. The figure also shows that the revenue of corporations is much larger than that of the other types of firms. Although only 18 percent of all firms are corporations, they generate 86 percent of revenue.

Figure 9.1(b) shows the percentage of total revenue accounted for by the different types of firms in various industries. Proprietorships account for a large percentage of revenue in agriculture, forestry, and fishing and in the service sector. They also account for a large percentage in construction and retail trades. Partnerships are more prominent in agriculture, forestry, and fishing; services; mining; and finance, insurance, and real estate than in other sectors of the economy. Corporations are important in all sectors and in manufacturing have the field almost to themselves.

Why do corporations dominate the business scene? Why do the other forms of business survive? And why are proprietorships and partnerships more prominent in some sectors? The answer to these questions lies in the pros and cons of the different forms of business organization that are summarized in Table 9.1 above. Corporations dominate because most businesses use a large amount of capital. Proprietorships and partnerships operate where flexibility in decision making is critical.

R E V I E W

- A firm is any institution that hires factors of production and organizes the production and sale of goods and services.
- Firms strive to be efficient and most firms aim to maximize profit, but they face uncertainty and have incomplete information. To cope with these problems, firms enter into relationships—principal-agent relationships—with owners, managers, workers, and other firms and devise efficient legal structures and compensation schemes.
- Each main type of firm—proprietorship, partnership, and corporation—has its advantages and disadvantages, and each type plays a role in every sector of the economy.

Business Finance

EVERY YEAR, FIRMS RAISE BILLIONS OF DOLLARS to enable them to buy capital equipment and to finance their inventory holdings. For example, an airline may raise hundreds of millions of dollars to buy a bigger fleet of jets. A steel manufacturer may raise hundreds of millions of dollars to build a new plant. A software producer may raise millions of dollars to pay programmers to develop a new computer game. Let's see how firms raise funds.

How Firms Raise Funds

All firms get some of their funds from their owners. The owner's stake in a business is called **equity**. Firms also borrow some of the funds they need from banks. Proprietorships and partnerships raise additional funds by borrowing from friends. The more permanent structure of corporations gives them two ways of raising large amounts of money that are not generally available to households and unincorporated businesses. They are

- Selling stock
- Selling bonds

Selling Stock

One major way in which a corporation can raise funds is by selling stock. Funds raised in this way are the corporation's *equity* because the stockholders of a corporation are its owners. They have bought shares of the corporation's stock.

Corporations sell shares of their stock, and these shares are regularly traded on stock exchanges. A *stock exchange* is an organized market for trading in stock. The biggest stock exchanges in the United States are the New York Stock Exchange (NYSE), the National Association of Securities Dealers Automated Quotations (NASDAQ), and the American Stock Exchange (ASE). Other major stock exchanges are in Boston, Philadelphia, Chicago, and San Francisco.

Figure 9.2 shows an example of a firm raising funds by selling stock. In February 1994, Reebok International Ltd. sold 3 million shares of stock for $33.125 a share thereby raising $99,375,000. A firm that raises funds by selling stock is not obligated to

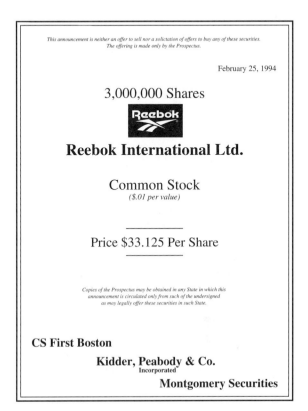

This announcement is neither an offer to sell nor a solicitation of offers to buy any of these securities. The offering is made only by the Prospectus.

February 25, 1994

3,000,000 Shares

Reebok International Ltd.

Common Stock
(*$.01 per value*)

Price $33.125 Per Share

Copies of the Prospectus may be obtained in any State in which this announcement is circulated only from such of the undersigned as may legally offer these securities in such State.

CS First Boston

Kidder, Peabody & Co.
Incorporated

Montgomery Securities

A share of the stock in a company entitles its holder to receive a dividend (if the directors vote to pay one). Reebok sold 3,000,000 shares of stock at $33.125 a share, thereby raising $99,375,000 of additional funds.

make dividend payments to its stockholders. But stockholders expect a dividend or a capital gain—otherwise no one will buy the shares.

Selling Bonds

A **bond** is a legally enforceable debt obligation to pay specified amounts of money at specified future dates. Usually, a bond specifies that a certain amount of money called the *redemption value* of the bond will be paid at a certain future date, called the *maturity date*. In addition, another amount will be paid each year between the date of sale of the bond and the maturity date. The amount of money paid each year is called the *coupon payment*.

Figure 9.3 gives an example of bond financing. On July 12, 1994, Kinpo Electronics Inc., a company based in Taiwan that plans to take on Apple Computers, Motorola, and Texas Instruments in a bid for the world market in personal digital assistants,

---

FIGURE 9.3

Selling Bonds

This announcement appears as a notice of record only.

Kinpo Electronics, Inc.

US $44,000,000

3 per cent. Bonds due 2001

Issue Price: 100 per cent.

Jardine Fleming

Indosuez Capital	China Development Corporation
J. Henry Schroder Wagg & Co. Limited	Swiss Bank Corporation
Capital Securities Hong Kong Limited	Nomura International
Droedner Bank	Morgan Stanley & Co.

Nikko Europe Plc

Finanical Advisor to the Company in the ROC
China Development Corporation

July 1994

A bond is an obligation to make coupon payments and a redemption payment. Kinpo, a producer of computer components and personal digital assistants, sold bonds to raise $44 million in 1994. The company promised to pay $3 per $100 borrowed each year as a coupon payment and to redeem the bonds in 2001.

---

raised $44 million by selling bonds. On that day, Kinpo committed itself to making a coupon payment of $1.32 million (the equivalent of an interest rate of 3 percent a year) on July 12 each year through 2001 and to repaying the $44 million on July 12, 2001. So the total amount that Kinpo committed to pay is $53.24 million, the $44 million borrowed plus $1.32 million a year for seven years.

When a firm makes a financing decision, it tries to minimize its cost of funds. If the cost of raising funds is lower by selling bonds than from any other source, the firm will choose this method of financing. But how does it decide how much to borrow? To answer this question, we need to understand a key principle of business and personal finance.

Discounting and Present Value

When a firm raises funds, it receives money in the current period and takes on an obligation to make a series of payments in *future* periods. For example, Kinpo received $44 million in 1994 and took on an obligation to pay out $53.24 million through 2001. But also when a firm raises funds, it does so because it plans to use them to generate a future net inflow of cash from its business operations. For example, Kinpo borrowed $44 million because it planned to use it to manufacture and sell computer components and products that would bring in some future revenue.

To decide whether to borrow and how much to borrow, a firm must somehow compare money today with money in the future. If you are given a choice between a dollar today and a dollar a year from today, you will choose a dollar today. A dollar today is worth more to you than a dollar in the future because you can invest today's dollar to earn interest. The same is true for a firm. To compare an amount of money in the future with an amount of money in the present, we calculate the present value of the future amount of money. The **present value** of a future amount of money is the amount that, if invested today, will grow to be as large as that future amount when the interest that it will earn is taken into account. Let's express this idea with an equation:

Future amount = Present value + Interest income.

The interest income is equal to the present value multiplied by the interest rate, r, so

Future amount = Present value + ($r \times$ Present value)

or

$$\text{Future amount} = \text{Present value} \times (1 + r).$$

If you have $100 today and the interest rate is 10 percent a year ($r = 0.1$), one year from today you will have $110—the original $100 plus $10 interest. Check that the above formula delivers that answer: $100 × 1.1=$110.

The formula that we have just used calculates a future amount one year from today from the present value and an interest rate. To calculate the present value, we just work backward. Instead of multiplying the present value by $(1 + r)$, we divide the future amount by $(1 + r)$. That is,

$$\text{Present value} = \frac{\text{Future amount}}{(1 + r)}.$$

You can use this formula to calculate present value. Calculating present value is called discounting. **Discounting** is the conversion of a future amount of money to its present value. Let's check that we can use the present value formula by calculating the present value of $110 one year from now when the interest rate is 10 percent a year. You'll be able to guess that the answer is $100 because we just calculated that $100 invested today at 10 percent a year becomes $110 in one year. Thus it follows immediately that the present value of $110 in one year's time is $100. But let's use the formula. Putting the numbers into the above formula, we have

$$\text{Present value} = \frac{\$110}{(1 + 0.1)}$$

$$= \frac{\$110}{(1.1)}$$

Calculating the present value of an amount of money one year from now is the easiest case. But we can also calculate the present value of an amount any number of years in the future. As an example, let's see how we calculate the present value of an amount of money that will be available two years from now.

Suppose that you invest $100 today for two years at an interest rate of 10 percent a year. The money will earn $10 in the first year, which means that by the end of the first year, you will have $110. If the interest of $10 is invested, then the interest earned in the second year will be a further $10 on the original $100 plus $1 on the $10 interest. Thus the total interest earned in the second year will be $11. The total interest earned overall will be $21 ($10 in the first year and $11 in the second year). After two years, you will have $121. From the definition of present value, you can see that the present value of $121 two years hence is $100. That is, $100 is the present amount that, if invested at 10 percent interest, will grow to $121 two years from now.

To calculate the present value of an amount of money two years in the future, we use the formula

$$\text{Present value} = \frac{\begin{array}{c}\text{Amount of money}\\ \text{two years in future}\end{array}}{(1 + r)^2}.$$

Let's check that the formula works by calculating the present value of $121 two years in the future when the interest rate is 10 percent a year. Putting these numbers into the formula gives

$$\text{Present value} = \frac{\$121}{(1 + 0.1)^2}$$

$$= \frac{\$121}{(1.1)^2}$$

$$= \frac{\$121}{1.21}$$

$$= \$100.$$

We can calculate the present value of an amount of money any number of years in the future by using a formula based on the two that we've already used. The general formula is

$$\text{Present value} = \frac{\begin{array}{c}\text{Amount of money}\\ n \text{ years in future}\end{array}}{(1 + r)^n}.$$

For example, if the interest rate is 10 percent a year, $100 to be received 10 years from now has a present value of $38.55. That is, if $38.55 is invested today at an interest rate of 10 percent, it will accumulate to $100 in 10 years. (You might check that calculation on your pocket calculator.)

Present Value and Marginal Analysis

Firms use the concept of present value to make their financing decisions. But they use it together with another fundamental principle, marginal analysis. In making any decision, only the additional benefit—*marginal benefit*—and additional cost—*marginal cost*—resulting from that decision are relevant. By evaluating the marginal benefit and marginal cost of borrowing, a firm is able to maximize its profit. Marginal benefit minus marginal cost is net benefit, and the present value of net benefit is called *net* present value.

The firm decides how much to borrow by calculating the net present value of borrowing one additional dollar—the marginal dollar borrowed. If the net present value of the marginal dollar borrowed is positive, then the firm increases its profit by increasing the amount it borrows. If the net present value of the marginal dollar borrowed is negative, then the firm increases its profit by *decreasing* its borrowing. When the present value of the marginal dollar borrowed is zero, then the firm is maximizing its profit.

REVIEW

- Firms finance their purchases of capital equipment by selling bonds—promises of a fixed income independent of the firm's profit—and selling stock—opportunities to share in the firm's profit.
- Firms borrow if doing so increases the net present value of their cash flow.

We've seen how firms pursue maximum profits by establishing appropriate types of business organizations and by raising funds in the most profitable way. But how do firms measure their performance? How do they calculate their costs and profits? These are the questions we now study.

Opportunity Cost and Economic Profit

A FIRM'S OPPORTUNITY COST OF PRODUCING A good is the best alternative action that the firm forgoes to produce it. Equivalently, it is the firm's best alternative use for the factors of production it employs to produce a good. Opportunity cost is a real alternative forgone. But so that we can compare the opportunity cost of one action with that of another action, we often express opportunity cost in units of money. Even though we express opportunity cost in money units, it is the real alternative forgone

and not the money value of that alternative.

A firm's opportunity cost of production has two components:

1. Explicit costs
2. Implicit costs

Explicit costs are paid directly in money—*money costs*. Implicit costs (measured in units of money) are opportunities forgone but not paid for directly in money. It is easy to measure explicit costs but harder to measure implicit costs.

A firm incurs explicit costs when it pays for a factor of production at the same time as it uses it. The money cost is the amount paid for the factor of production, but this same amount could have been spent on something else, so it is also the opportunity cost (expressed in dollars) of using this factor of production. For example, if a pizza restaurant hires a waiter, the wages paid are both the money cost and the opportunity cost of hiring the waiter—the firm pays the waiter at the same time as it uses the services of the waiter. Labor is the factor of production whose money cost typically equals its opportunity cost.

A firm incurs implicit costs when it uses the following factors of production:

- Capital
- Inventories
- Owner's resources

Cost of Capital

The cost of using capital equipment is an implicit cost because a firm usually buys its equipment—lays out some money—and then uses the equipment over a future period. For example, GM buys an assembly line, pays for it this year, and uses it for several years. What is the opportunity cost of using capital equipment bought several years earlier? This opportunity cost has two components:

- Depreciation
- Interest

Depreciation **Economic depreciation** is the change in the market price of a piece of capital over a given period. It is calculated as the market price of the capital at the beginning of the period minus its market price at the end of the period. For example, suppose that United Airlines has a Boeing 747 jumbo jet that it could have sold on December 31, 1994, for $5 million. Suppose also that it could sell the same airplane on December 31, 1995, for $4 million. The $1 million fall in the market value is the economic depreciation of the airplane during 1995. It is part of the opportunity cost of using the airplane during 1995.

Economic depreciation occurs for a variety of reasons. The most common is that an older piece of equipment has a shorter future life. Also, it is often more costly to maintain in good working order. But economic depreciation also occurs because a piece of equipment has become obsolete. It still works fine and might do so for many years, but there is something new that works even better. For example, suppose Kinko bought some new copiers on January 1, 1995, that it expected to operate for three years. Then, during 1995, a faster copier became available, and the market price of the slower copiers fell by 90 percent. This 90 percent fall in price is the opportunity cost of using the copiers in 1995. Even though the copiers are new and still work fine, their economic depreciation—and opportunity cost—during 1995 is large.

Interest The funds used to buy capital (buildings, plant, and equipment) could have been used for some other purpose. And in their next best alternative use, they would have yielded a return—an interest income. This forgone interest is part of the opportunity cost of using the capital. It is an opportunity cost regardless of whether a firm borrows the funds it uses to buy its capital. To see why, think about two cases: The firm borrows or uses its previous earnings.

If a firm borrows the money, then it makes an explicit interest payment, so the interest is an explicit cost. If the firm uses its own funds, then the opportunity cost is the amount that could have been earned by allocating those funds to their best alternative use. Suppose the best alternative is for the firm to put the money in a bank deposit. The interest forgone is part of the opportunity cost of using the capital.

Implicit Rental Rate To measure the opportunity cost of using capital (buildings, plant, and equipment), we calculate the sum of economic depreciation and interest costs. This opportunity cost is the income that the firm forgoes by using the assets itself and not renting them to another firm instead. The firm actually rents the assets to itself. When a firm rents assets to itself, it pays an **implicit rental rate** for their use.

People commonly rent houses, apartments, cars, telephones, and videotapes. And firms commonly rent photocopiers, earth-moving equipment, satellite launching services, and so on. If a piece of equipment is rented, a dollar payment called an *explicit* rental rate is made. If a piece of equipment is bought and used by its owner rather than rented to someone else, an *implicit* rental rate is paid. The owner-user of a piece of equipment could have rented the equipment to someone else instead. The income forgone is the opportunity cost of using the equipment. That opportunity cost is the *implicit* rental rate.

Market forces bring about an equality of the explicit rental rate and implicit rental rate. If renting had a lower opportunity cost than buying, everyone would want to rent and no one would want to buy. So some renters would not be able to find anyone to rent from, and the (explicit) rental rate would rise. If renting had a higher opportunity cost than buying, everyone would want to buy and no one would want to rent. So owners would not be able to find anyone to rent to, and the (explicit) rental rate would fall. Only when the opportunity cost of renting and buying are equal—when the explicit rental rate and the implicit rental rate are equal—is there no incentive to switch between buying and renting.

Sunk Cost The *past economic depreciation* of the firm's capital (buildings, plant, and equipment) is **sunk cost**. When the capital was purchased, an opportunity was forgone. But that past forgone opportunity is a bygone. The opportunity cannot be retrieved. Sunk cost is not an *opportunity cost*. In the Kinko copier example, Kinko incurred a high opportunity cost during 1995 when the market price of its slow copiers fell. But as Kinko looks forward to 1996, the fall in the value of its copiers in 1995 is a sunk cost. The opportunity cost of using the copiers during 1996 does *not* include that fall in value.

Accounting Measures Accountants measure depreciation, but they do not usually measure *economic depreciation*. Instead, they assess this fall in the value of a piece of capital by applying a conventional depreciation rate to the original purchase price. The conventions used are based on Internal Revenue Service rules and on standards established by the Federal Accounting Standards Board (FASB). For buildings, a conventional depreciation period is 20 years. Thus if a firm buys a new office building for

$100,000, its accounts show one twentieth of that amount, $5,000, as a cost of production each year. At the end of the first year, the firm's accounts record the value of the building as $95,000 (the original cost minus the $5,000 depreciation). Different depreciation rates are used for different types of capital. For example, for cars and computers, the conventional depreciation period is 3 years.

These accounting measures of depreciation do not measure economic depreciation and are not a correct measure of the depreciation component of the opportunity cost of using capital.

Cost of Inventories

Inventories are stocks of raw materials, semifinished goods, and finished goods held by firms. The opportunity cost of using an item from inventory is its current market price. Firms hold inventories to make the production process efficient. So when an item is taken out of inventory, it must be replaced by a new item. The cost of that new item is the opportunity cost of using the item taken from inventory. Another line of reasoning leads to the same conclusion. An alternative to *using* an item from inventory is to sell it for its current market price. So the opportunity forgone is the current market price.

To measure the cost of using inventories, accountants frequently use a money cost method called FIFO, which stands for "First In, First Out." This method of calculating the cost of an item taken from inventory assumes that the first item placed into the inventory is the first one out. An alternative accounting measure is called LIFO, which stands for "Last In, First Out." This money cost of an item taken from inventory is the cost of the last one placed into the inventory. Some firms have small inventories or inventories that turn over very quickly. In such cases, the money cost of using an item from inventory and its opportunity cost are the same. When a production process requires inventories to be held for a long time, the two costs might differ. If prices are constant over long periods of time, FIFO and LIFO measure opportunity cost. But if prices are changing, FIFO is not a measure of opportunity cost, although LIFO is a good approximation to it if the price most recently paid is similar to the price paid to replace the used item.

Cost of Owner's Resources

The owner of a firm often puts a great deal of time and effort into organizing the firm. But the owner could have worked at some other activity and earned a wage. The opportunity cost of the owner's time spent working for the firm is the wage income forgone by not working in the best alternative job.

In addition to supplying labor to the firm, its owner also supplies *entrepreneurial ability*—the factor of production that organizes the business, makes business decisions, innovates, and bears the risk of running the business. These activities would not be undertaken without the expectation of a return. The expected return for supplying entrepreneurial ability is called **normal profit**. Normal profit is part of a firm's opportunity cost, because it is the cost of a forgone alternative. The forgone alternative is running another firm.

Usually, the owner of a firm withdraws cash from the business to meet living expenses. Accountants regard such withdrawals of cash as part of the owner's profit from the business rather than as part of the opportunity cost of the owner's time and entrepreneurial ability. But to the extent that they compensate for wages forgone and risk, they are part of the firm's opportunity cost.

Economic Profit

What is the bottom line—the profit or loss of the firm? A firm's **economic profit** is equal to its total revenue minus its opportunity cost. Its opportunity cost is the explicit and implicit costs of the best alternative actions forgone, including *normal profit*.

Economic profit is not the same as what accountants call profit. For the accountant, a firm's profit is equal to its total revenue minus its money cost and its conventional depreciation.

Opportunity Cost and Economic Profit: An Example

To help you get a clearer picture of the concepts of a firm's opportunity cost and economic profit, we'll look at a concrete example. And we'll contrast the economist's concepts of opportunity cost and economic profit with the accounting measures of cost and profit.

Rocky owns a shop that sells bikes. His revenue, cost, and profit appear in Table 9.2. The accountant's calculations of Rocky's cost are on the left side, and the economist's calculations of Rocky's opportunity cost are on the right.

Rocky sold $300,000 worth of bikes during the year. This amount appears as his total revenue in both the accountant's and the economist's statement. The wholesale cost of bikes was $150,000, he bought $20,000 worth of utilities and other services, and he paid out $50,000 in wages to his mechanic and sales clerk. Rocky also paid $12,000 in interest to the bank. All of the items just mentioned appear in both the accountant's and the economist's statement. The remaining items differ between the two statements; some notes at the foot of the table explain the differences.

The accountant's depreciation calculation is based on conventional life assumptions for Rocky's capital. The economist calculates the cost of Rocky's time, funds invested in the firm, and risk-bearing and also calculates economic depreciation. The accountant says that Rocky's costs are $254,000 and his profit is $46,000. In contrast, the economist says that Rocky's year in business had an opportunity cost of $299,500 and yielded an economic profit of $500.

The accountant's calculation of Rocky's profit does not tell Rocky his economic profit because it omits some components of opportunity cost and measures others incorrectly. The economist's measure of economic profit tells Rocky how his business is doing compared with what he can normally expect. Any positive economic profit is good news for Rocky because his normal profit—the normal return to his entrepreneurial ability—is part of the opportunity cost of running his business.

TABLE 9.2

Rocky's Mountain Bikes' Revenue, Cost, and Profit Statement

The accountant		**The economist**	
Item	**Amount**	**Item**	**Amount**
Total revenue	$300,000	Total revenue	$300,000
Costs:		Costs:	
Wholesale cost of bikes	150,000	Wholesale cost of bikes	150,000
Utilities and other services	20,000	Utilities and other services	20,000
Wages	50,000	Wages	50,000
Depreciation	22,000	Fall in market value of assets[a]	10,000
		Rocky's wages (implicit)[b]	40,000
Bank interest	12,000	Bank interest	12,000
		Interest on Rocky's money invested	
		in firm (implicit)[c]	11,500
		Normal profit (implicit)[d]	6,000
Total cost	$254,000	Opportunity cost	$299,500
Profit	$46,000	Economic profit	$500

[a]The fall in the market value of the assets of the firm gives the opportunity cost of not selling them one year ago. That is part of the opportunity cost of using them for the year.
[b]Rocky could have worked elsewhere for $40 an hour, but he worked 1000 hours on the firm's business, which means that the opportunity cost of his time is $40,000.

[c]Rocky has invested $115,000 in the firm. If the current interest rate is 10% a year, the opportunity cost of those funds is $11,500.
[d]Rocky could avoid the risk of running his own business, and he would be unwilling to take on the risk for a return of less than $6,000. This is his *normal profit.* (The magnitude of normal profit is assumed.)

R E V I E W

- A firm's economic profit is equal to its total revenue minus its opportunity cost of production.
- Opportunity cost differs from money cost. Money cost measures cost as the money spent to hire inputs. Opportunity cost measures cost as the value of the best alternative forgone.
- The main differences between money cost and opportunity cost arise from the cost of capital and inventories and the cost of the resources supplied directly by the owner. But opportunity cost also includes normal profit—the expected return for bearing risk.

We are interested in measuring the opportunity cost of production, not for its own sake but so that we can compare the efficiency of alternative methods of production. What do we mean by efficiency?

Economic Efficiency

HOW DOES A FIRM CHOOSE AMONG ALTERNATIVE methods of production? What is the most efficient way of producing? There are two concepts of efficiency: technological efficiency and economic efficiency. **Technological efficiency** occurs when it is not possible to increase output without increasing inputs. **Economic efficiency** occurs when the cost of producing a given output is as low as possible.

Technological efficiency is an engineering matter. Given what is technologically feasible, something can or cannot be done. Economic efficiency depends on the prices of the factors of production. Something that is technologically efficient may not be economically efficient. But something that is economically efficient is always technologically efficient. Let's study technological efficiency and economic efficiency by looking at an example.

Suppose that there are four methods of making TV sets:

a. *Robot production.* One person monitors the entire computer-driven process.

b. *Production line.* Workers specialize in a small part of the job as the emerging TV set passes them on an production line.

c. *Human production.* Workers specialize in a small part of the job but walk from bench to bench to perform their tasks.

d. *Hand-tool production.* A single worker uses a few hand tools to make a TV set.

Table 9.3 sets out the amount of labor and capital required to make 10 TV sets a day by each of these four methods. Are all of these alternative methods technologically efficient? By inspecting the numbers in the figure, you will be able to see that method c is not technologically efficient. It requires 100 workers and 10 units of capital to produce 10 TV sets. Those same 10 TV sets can be produced by method b with 10 workers and the same 10 units of capital. Therefore method c is not technologically efficient.

Are any of the other methods not technologically efficient? The answer is no: Each of the other three methods is technologically efficient. Method a uses less labor and more capital than method b, and method d uses more labor and less capital than method b.

What about economic efficiency? Are all three methods economically efficient? To answer that question, we need to know the labor and capital costs. Let's suppose that labor costs $75 per person-day and that capital costs $250 per machine-day. Recall that economic efficiency occurs with the least expensive production process. Table 9.4 calculates the costs of using the four different methods of production. As you can see, the least expensive method of producing a TV set is b. Method a uses less labor but more capital. It costs much more to make a TV set by using method a than by using method b. Method d, the

---

TABLE 9.3

Four Ways of Making 10 TV Sets a Day

		Quantities of inputs	
	Method	Labor	Capital
a	Robot production	1	1,000
b	Production line	10	10
c	Human production	100	10
d	Hand-tool production	1,000	1

TABLE 9.4

The Costs of Four Ways of Making 10 TV Sets a Day

Method	Labor cost ($75 per day)		Capital cost ($250 per day)		Total cost	Cost per TV set
a	$75	+	$250,000	=	$250,075	$25,007.50
b	750	+	2,500	=	3,250	325.00
c	7,500	+	2,500	=	10,000	1,000.00
d	75,000	+	250	=	75,250	7,525.00

other technologically efficient method, uses much more labor and hardly any capital. Like method *a*, it costs far more to make a TV set by using method *d* than by using method *b*.

Method *c* is technologically inefficient. It uses the same amount of capital as method *b* but 10 times as much labor. It is interesting to notice that although method *c* is technologically inefficient, it costs less to produce a TV set by using method *c* than it does by using methods *a* and *d*. But method *b* dominates method *c*. Because method *c* is not technologically efficient, there is always a method available that has a lower cost. That is, a method that is technologically inefficient is never economically efficient.

Although *b* is the economically efficient method in this example, method *a* or *d* could be economically efficient in other circumstances. Let's see when.

First, suppose that labor costs $150 a person-day and capital costs only $1 a machine-day. Table 9.5 now shows the costs of making a TV set. In this case, method *a* is economically efficient. Capital is now sufficiently cheap relative to labor that the method

that uses the most capital is the economically efficient method.

Now suppose that labor costs only $1 a day while capital costs $1,000 a day. Table 9.6 shows the costs in this case. As you can see, method *d*, which uses a lot of labor and little capital, is now the least expensive method of producing a TV set. Method *d* is now the economically efficient method.

A firm that does not use the economically efficient method of production makes a smaller profit. Natural selection favors firms that choose the economically efficient method of production and goes against firms that do not. In extreme cases, an inefficient firm might go bankrupt or be taken over by another firm that can see the possibilities for lower cost and greater profit. Efficient firms will be stronger and better able to survive temporary adversity than will inefficient ones.

Our final topic in this chapter goes back to the economic fundamentals from which we began. It examines the reasons why firms coordinate the production of some goods and services and why markets coordinate some others.

TABLE 9.5

The Costs of Three Ways of Making 10 TV Sets: High Labor Costs

Method	Labor cost ($150 per day)		Capital cost ($1 per day)		Total cost	Cost per TV set
a	$150	+	$1,000	=	$1,150	$115.00
b	1,500	+	10	=	1,510	151.00
d	150,000	+	1	=	150,001	15,000.10

TABLE   9.6

The Costs of Three Ways of Making 10 TV Sets: High Capital Costs

Method	Labor cost ($1 per day)		Capital cost ($1000 per day)		Total cost	Cost per TV set
a	$1	+	$1,000,000	=	$1,000,001	$100,000.10
b	10	+	10,000	=	10,010	1,001.00
d	1,000	+	1,000	=	2,000	200.00

Firms and Markets

AT THE BEGINNING OF THIS CHAPTER, WE defined a firm as an institution that hires factors of production and organizes them to produce and sell goods and services. To organize production, firms coordinate the economic decisions and activities of many individuals. But firms are not the only coordinators of economic decisions. As we learned in Chapter 4, markets also coordinate decisions. By adjusting prices, markets make the decisions of buyers and sellers consistent—make the quantities demanded equal to the quantities supplied for different goods and services.

An example of market coordination is the production of a rock concert. A promoter hires a stadium, some stage equipment, audio and video recording engineers and technicians, some rock groups, a superstar, a publicity agent, and a ticket agent—all market transactions—and sells tickets to thousands of rock fans, audio rights to a recording company, and video and broadcasting rights to a television network—another set of market transactions. If rock concerts were produced like corn flakes, the firm producing them would own all the capital used (stadiums, stage, sound and video equipment) and would employ all the labor needed (singers, engineers, sales persons, and so on).

What determines whether a firm or markets coordinate a particular set of activities? The answer is cost. Taking account of the opportunity cost of time as well as the costs of the other inputs, people use the method that costs least. In other words, they use the economically efficient method.

Firms coordinate economic activity when they can perform a task more efficiently than markets. In such a situation, it is profitable to set up a firm. If markets can perform a task more efficiently than a firm, people will use markets, and any attempt to set up a firm to replace such market coordination will be doomed to failure.

Why Firms?

There are three key reasons why, in many instances, firms are more efficient than markets as coordinators of economic activity. Firms achieve

- Lower transactions costs
- Economies of scale
- Economies of team production

Transactions Costs   The idea that firms exist because there are activities in which they are more efficient than markets was first suggested by University of Chicago economist and Nobel Laureate Ronald Coase. Coase focused on the firm's ability to reduce or eliminate transactions costs. **Transactions costs** are the costs arising from finding someone with whom to do business, of reaching an agreement about the price and other aspects of the exchange, and of ensuring that the terms of the agreement are fulfilled. *Market* transactions require buyers and sellers to get together and to negotiate the terms and conditions of their trading. Sometimes, lawyers have to be hired to draw up contracts. A broken contract leads to still more expenses. A *firm* can lower such transactions costs by reducing the number of individual transactions undertaken.

Consider, for example, two ways of getting your creaking car fixed.

Firm coordination: You take the car to the garage. Parts and tools as well as the mechanic's time are coordinated by the garage owner, and your car gets fixed. You pay one bill for the entire job.

Market coordination: You hire a mechanic who diagnoses the problems and makes a list of the parts and tools needed to fix them. You buy the parts from the local wrecker's yard and rent the tools from ABC Rentals. You hire the mechanic again to fix the problems. You return the tools and pay your bills—wages to the mechanic, rental to ABC, and the cost of the parts used to the wrecker.

What determines the method that you use? The answer is cost. Taking account of the opportunity cost of your own time as well as the costs of the other inputs that you would have to buy, you will use the method that costs least. In other words, you will use the economically efficient method.

The first method requires that you undertake only one transaction with one firm. It's true that the firm has to undertake several transactions—hiring the labor and buying the parts and tools required to do the job. But the firm doesn't have to undertake those transactions simply to fix your car. One set of such transactions enables the firm to fix hundreds of cars. Thus there is an enormous reduction in the number of individual transactions that take place if people get their cars fixed at the garage rather than going through an elaborate sequence of market transactions.

Economies of Scale   When the cost of producing a unit of a good falls as its output rate increases, **economies of scale** exist. Many industries experience economies of scale; automobile manufacturing is an example. One firm can produce 4 million cars a year at a lower cost per car than 200 firms each producing 20,000 cars a year. Economies of scale arise from specialization and the division of labor that can be reaped more effectively by firm coordination rather than market coordination.

Team Production   A production process in which the individuals in a group specialize in mutually supportive tasks is *team production*. Sport provides the best example of team activity. Some team members specialize in pitching and some in batting, some in

defense and some in offense. The production of goods and services offers many examples of team activity. For example, production lines in automobile and TV manufacturing plants work most efficiently when individual activity is organized in teams, each specializing in a small task. You can also think of an entire firm as being a team. The team has buyers of raw material and other inputs, production workers, and salespeople. There are even specialists within these various groups. Each individual member of the team specializes, but the value of the output of the team and the profit that it earns depend on the coordinated activities of all the team's members. The idea that firms arise as a consequence of the economies of team production was first suggested by Armen Alchian and Harold Demsetz of the University of California at Los Angeles.

Because firms can economize on transactions costs, reap economies of scale, and organize efficient team production, it is firms rather than markets that coordinate most of our economic activity. But there are limits to the economic efficiency of firms. If a firm becomes too big or too diversified in the things that it seeks to do, the cost of management and monitoring per unit of output begins to rise, and at some point, the market becomes more efficient at coordinating the use of resources. IBM is an example of a firm that became too big to be efficient. In an attempt to restore efficient operations, IBM split up its large organization into a number of "Baby Blues," each of which specializes in a segment of the computer market.

Sometimes firms enter into long-term relationships with each other that effectively cut out ordinary market transactions and make it difficult to see where one firm ends and another begins. For example, GM has long-term relationships with suppliers of windows, tires, and other parts. Wal-Mart has long-term relationships with suppliers of the goods it sells in its stores. Such relationships make transactions costs lower than they would be if GM or Wal-Mart went shopping on the open market each time it wanted new supplies.

◆ In the next chapter, we are going to study more choices of firms. We will study their production decisions, how they minimize costs, and how they choose the amounts of labor and capital to employ. Then, in Chapters 11 through 13, we discover how firms behave in a variety of different market situations to maximize their profits.

A Firm in Action

FORTUNE, APRIL 18, 1994

Keeping Motorola on a Roll

by Ronald Henkoff

MENTION MOTOROLA, ...and the accolades fairly gush: titan of TQM, epitome of empowerment, tribune of training, icon of innovation, prince of profits.

At issue now is whether Motorola can keep getting better as it keeps getting bigger, whether this huge, decentralized, multinational corporation with headquarters in Schaumburg, Illinois, can avoid falling victim to the bureaucracy, complacency, and hubris that have afflicted so many other large American businesses.

Motorola's sales jumped 27.5% to a record $17 billion last year, propelling the company to the No. 23 spot on the FORTUNE 500. Earnings surged 127% to $1 billion, and analysts expect another knockout year in 1994. ...

Sales of cellular phones—the company's flagship product—are booming, up 43% in the U.S. last year, according to Herschel Shosteck Associates, a Silver Spring, Maryland, telecommunications research firm. Motorola, which commands a 45% share of the worldwide market, continues to attract new customers as it makes phones smaller, lighter, cheaper, and easier to use.

Increasingly multinational, Motorola—which generated 56% of its revenues overseas last year—is spreading the wonders of wireless communication to Asia, Eastern Europe, and Latin America. Countries with archaic state-run phone systems have seized on wireless networks as a relatively inexpensive means of quickstepping into the future.

With $6 billion in semiconductor sales last year, Motorola has become the world's No. 3 producer of chips, behind Intel and NEC, says Dataquest, a San Jose market research firm. ...

This company strives to measure every task performed by every one of its 120,000 employees, and calculates that it saved $1.5 billion by reducing defects and simplifying processes last year. ...

As part of its quality drive, Motorola has invested new meaning in the phrase "team spirit." At the cellular equipment plant in Arlington Heights, Illinois, self-directed teams hire and fire their co-workers, help select their supervisors, and schedule their own work (in consultation with other teams). Last year, the factory's 1,003 workers also mustered into no fewer than 168 special teams dedicated to improving quality [and] cutting costs. ...

Essence of THE STORY

■ Motorola is the world's leading producer of cellular phones (a 45 percent share) and the third largest producer of computer chips (behind Intel and NEC).

■ In 1993, Motorola's sales increased by 27.5 percent to $17 billion (earning the company the rank of 23 in the FORTUNE 500), its earnings increased by 127 percent to $1 billion, and it generated 56 percent of its revenues overseas.

■ The company has 120,000 employees organized in self-directed teams that hire and fire their co-workers, help select their supervisors, and (in consultation with other teams) schedule their own work.

■ Motorola's challenge is to keep getting better as it keeps getting bigger and to avoid falling victim to the inflexibilities that afflict many large American businesses.

Economic

A N A L Y S I S

■ Figure I shows the growth of Motorola's sales since 1984.

■ Part of Motorola's success arises from the diversity of its products (cellular telephones, computer chips, and many other electronic items), the diversity of its markets (the entire world), and the world boom in wireless communications technology.

■ For countries such as China and those of Eastern Europe that have either limited or dilapidated telecommunications systems, the cost of installing the latest generation of wireless technology is lower than the cost of installing the traditional cable technology. This cost advantage for wireless communications brings a rapid growth in the demand for products in which Motorola specializes.

■ Motorola operates in markets for new products, and its profitability depends on its ability to develop and market ever better products at competitive prices.

■ Innovative management and organization are a key to Motorola's success.

■ Figure 2 shows two management structures. Part (a) is a traditional management *hierarchy*. Managers control subordinates and are responsible to superiors. For some activities, such a management structure is usually inflexible and inefficient.

■ Part (b) is a flexible, market-like management structure similar to that of Motorola. The company uses a wide array of principal-agent relationships and creates self-managed teams. For example, one team might work on developing a new computer chip, another on a project to sell pagers to Russia, and yet another on producing and selling cellular phones to China.

■ Motorola's teams are profit centers—like small firms within a firm—each one of which is accountable for its own economic success. Motorola uses incentive systems that confront its employees with market-like signals and monitors all its employees closely.

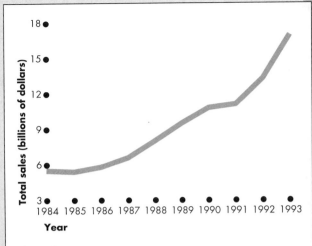

Figure 1

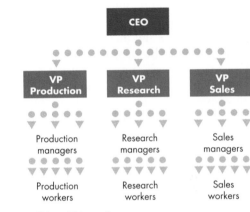

(a) Traditional hierarchy

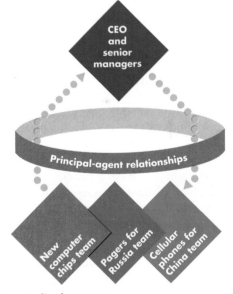

(b) Decentralized structure

Figure 2

S U M M A R Y

The Firm and Its Economic Problem

Firms hire and organize factors of production to produce and sell goods and services. Firms strive to be efficient—to produce output at the lowest possible cost and to maximize profit. Uncertainty and incomplete information place limits on what a firm can attain. To operate efficiently, a firm's owners (principals) must induce its managers (agents) to pursue the maximum possible profit. And the managers (principals) must induce the workers and other firms (agents) to work efficiently. But incentive schemes are imperfect, and firms constantly strive to find ways of improving performance and increasing profits.

The main forms of business organization are proprietorships, partnerships, and corporations. Proprietorships are easy to set up, and they face lower taxes than corporations, but they are riskier and face higher costs of capital and labor. Partnerships can draw on diversified expertise, but they can also involve decision conflicts. Corporations have limited liability, so they can obtain large-scale capital at a relatively low cost. They can hire professional management, but complex management structures can slow down decisions. Corporation profits are taxed twice: as company profit and as stockholder income. Proprietorships are the most common form of business organization, but corporations account for most of the economy's production. (pp. 192–196)

Business Finance

Firms get funds from their owners and from the sale of stock and bonds. A firm gets its funds from the source that costs least. When a firm raises funds, it receives money in the current period and takes on an obligation to make a series of payments in future periods. The firm compares money received today with money paid out in the future by calculating the present value of the future payments by using the formula

$$\text{Present value} = \frac{\substack{\text{Amount of money} \\ n \text{ years in future}}}{(1 + r)^n}.$$

A firm decides how much to borrow by calculating the net present value of borrowing one additional dollar—the marginal dollar borrowed. It increases its borrowing up to the point at which the present value of the marginal dollar borrowed is zero. At this amount of borrowing, the firm is maximizing its profit. (pp. 197–200)

Opportunity Cost and Economic Profit

Economic profit is calculated as total revenue minus opportunity cost. The *opportunity cost* of producing a good is the best alternative action that was forgone to produce it. It has two components: explicit costs and implicit costs. Explicit costs are paid directly in money—*money costs*. Implicit costs (measured in units of money) are opportunities forgone but not paid for directly in money. A firm's implicit costs arise from its use of capital, inventories, and resources provided by its owner.

The opportunity cost of capital is made up of economic depreciation—the change in the market price of a capital asset over a period—plus the interest on the funds used to buy capital. Interest is an opportunity cost even if the funds used are not borrowed. Interest is forgone on an alternative investment. The opportunity cost of using capital is the sum of economic depreciation and interest and is an *implicit rental rate*. Past economic depreciation of a capital asset is not a current opportunity cost. It is a *sunk cost*—a bygone. The opportunity cost of using an item from inventory is its current replacement cost. The opportunity cost of the resources supplied by a firm's owner is the income forgone by not working in the best alternative job and normal profit for supplying entrepreneurial ability. (pp. 200–204)

Economic Efficiency

There are two concepts of efficiency: technological efficiency and economic efficiency. A method of production is technologically efficient when it is not possible to increase output without using more inputs. A method of production is economically efficient when the cost of producing a given output is as low as possible. Economic efficiency requires technological efficiency. Economic efficiency also takes into account the relative prices of inputs. Economically efficient firms have a better chance of surviving than do inefficient ones. (pp. 204–206)

Firms and Markets

Firms coordinate economic activities when they can perform a task more efficiently—at lower cost—than markets. Firms can economize on transactions costs and achieve the benefits of economies of scale and of team production. (pp. 206–207)

K E Y   E L E M E N T S

Key Figure and Tables

Figure 9.1   Relative Importance of the Three Main Types of Firms, 196

Table 9.1   The Pros and Cons of Different Types of Firms, 195

Table 9.2   Rocky's Mountain Bikes' Revenue, Cost, and Profit Statement, 203

Table 9.3   Four Ways of Making 10 TV Sets a Day, 204

Key Terms

Bond, 197
Capital gain, 195

Discounting, 199
Economic depreciation, 200
Economic efficiency, 204
Economic profit, 202
Economies of scale, 207
Equity, 197
Firm, 192
Implicit rental rate, 201
Normal profit, 202
Present value, 198
Principal-agent problem, 193
Sunk cost, 201
Technological efficiency, 204
Transactions costs, 206

R E V I E W   Q U E S T I O N S

1. What is a firm and what is the fundamental economic problem that all firms face?
2. What factors make it difficult for a firm to get the most out of its resources?
3. What is a principal-agent relationship and why does it arise?
4. In what ways can a principal cope with the principal-agent problem?
5. What are the main forms of business organizations and the advantages and disadvantages of each?
6. What is the most common type of business and which type produces most of the economy's output?
7. What are the main ways in which firms can raise funds?
8. Describe and contrast a bond and a stock.
9. What do we mean by net present value?
10. What determines the value of a bond?
11. Explain how a firm uses marginal analysis when it makes a financing decision.
12. Distinguish between money cost and opportunity cost. What are the main items of opportunity cost that don't get counted as part of money cost?
13. Distinguish between implicit costs and explicit costs.
14. Distinguish between profit as defined by accountants, normal profit, and economic profit.
15. Distinguish between technological efficiency and economic efficiency.
16. Why do firms, rather than markets, coordinate such a large amount of economic activity?

P R O B L E M S

1. Soap Bubbles, Inc. has a bank loan of $1 million on which it is paying an interest rate of 10 percent a year. The firm's financial advisor suggests paying off the loan by selling bonds. To sell bonds valued at $1 million, Soap Bubbles, Inc. must offer the following deal: One year from today, pay the bond holders $9 for each $100 of bonds; two years from today, redeem the bonds for $114 per $100 of bonds.
   a. Does it pay Soap Bubbles to sell the bonds to repay the bank loan?
   b. What is the present value of the profit or loss that would result from repaying the bank loan and selling the bonds?

2. One year ago, Jack and Jill set up a vinegar bottling firm (called JJVB). In that year:

   a. Jack and Jill put $50,000 of their own money into the firm.
   b. They bought equipment for $30,000 and an inventory of bottles and vinegar for $15,000.
   c. They hired one employee to help them for an annual wage of $20,000.
   d. JJVB's sales for the year were $100,000.
   e. Jack gave up his previous job, at which he earned $30,000, and spent all his time working for JJVB.
   f. Jill kept her old job, which paid $30 an hour, but gave up 10 hours of leisure each week (for 50 weeks) to work for JJVB.
   g. The cash expenses of JJVB were $10,000 for the year.
   h. The inventory at the end of the year was worth $20,000.
   i. The market value of the equipment at the end of the year was $28,000.

   j. JJVB's accountant depreciated the equipment over 5 years.

      (i) Construct JJVB's profit and loss account as recorded by its accountant.
      (ii) Construct JJVB's profit and loss account based on opportunity cost rather than money cost concepts.
      (iii) What is JJVB's economic profit?

3. There are three methods that you can use to do your income tax return: a personal computer, a pocket calculator, or a pencil and paper. With a PC, you complete the task in an hour; with a pocket calculator, it takes 12 hours; and with a pencil and paper, it takes two days. The PC and its software cost $1,000, the pocket calculator costs $10, and the pencil and paper cost $1.

   a. Which, if any, of the above methods is technologically efficient?
   b. Suppose that your wage is $5 an hour. Which of the above methods is economically efficient?
   c. Suppose that your wage is $50 an hour. Which of the above methods is economically efficient?
   d. Suppose that your wage is $500 an hour. Which of the above methods is economically efficient?

4. Study *Reading Between the Lines* on pp. 208–209 and explain:

   a. The main principal-agent problem that Motorola faces.
   b. The key ways in which Motorola has tried to cope with its principal-agent problem.

Output and Costs

After studying this chapter, you will be able to:

- Explain what limits the profit a firm can make

- Explain the relationship between a firm's output and its costs

- Derive a firm's short-run cost curves

- Explain how cost changes when a firm's plant size changes

- Derive a firm's long-run average cost curve

Size does not guarantee survival in business. Of the 100 largest companies in the United States in 1917, only 22 still remained in that league in 1994. But remaining small does not guarantee survival either. Every year, millions of small businesses close down. Call a random selection of restaurants and fashion boutiques from *last* year's yellow pages and see how many have vanished. What does a firm have to do to be one of the survivors? ◆ Firms

Survival of the Fittest

differ in lots of ways—from Mom-and-Pop's convenience store to multinational giants producing hi-tech goods. But regardless of their size or what they produce, all firms must decide how much to produce and how to produce it. How do firms make these decisions? ◆ Most car makers in the United States can produce far more cars than they can sell. Why do car makers have expensive equipment lying around that isn't fully used? Many electric utilities in the United States don't have enough production equipment on hand to meet demand on the coldest and hottest days and have to buy power from other producers. Why don't such firms have a bigger production plant so that they can supply the market themselves?

◇ We are going to answer these questions in this chapter. To do so, we are going to study the economic decisions of a small, imaginary firm—Swanky, Inc., a producer of knitted sweaters. The firm is owned and operated by Sidney. By studying Swanky's economic problems and the way Sidney solves them, we will be able to get a clear view of the problems that face all firms—small ones like Swanky as well as the giants.

The Firm's Objective and Constraints

To understand and predict the behavior of firms, we need to know what they are trying to achieve—what their objectives are and the constraints they face. We'll begin by looking at what firms are trying to achieve.

The Objective: Profit Maximization

Individual firms and the entrepreneurs that run them have many different objectives. And if you asked a group of entrepreneurs what their objectives were, you'd get lots of different answers. Some would talk about making a quality product, others about business growth, others about market share, and others about work force job satisfaction. All of these objectives might be pursued, but they are not the fundamental objective. They are means to a deeper objective, which is achieving the largest possible profit—*profit maximization*.

The firm that we will study has this single objective of profit maximization. A firm that seeks to maximize profit is one that tries to use its scarce resources efficiently. And a firm that maximizes profit has the best chance of surviving in a competitive environment and of avoiding being taken over by another firm.

Two types of constraints limit the profit a firm can make. They are:

- Market constraints
- Technology constraints

Market Constraints

A firm's market constraints are the conditions under which it can buy its inputs and sell its output. On the output side, people have a limited demand for each good or service and will buy additional quantities only at lower prices. On the input side, people have a limited supply of the factors of production that they own and will supply additional quantities only at higher prices.

We'll study these market constraints on firms in Chapters 11 through 16. Swanky, the firm that we'll study in this chapter, is small and cannot influence the prices at which it sells its output or buys its inputs. For such a firm, the market constraints are a set of given prices.

Technology Constraints

A firm's technology constraints are the limits to the quantity of output that can be produced by using given quantities of inputs—factors of production. To maximize profit, a firm chooses a *technologically efficient* method of production. It does not use more inputs than necessary to produce a given output. Equivalently, it does not waste resources. But a firm must also choose the *economically efficient* technique—the technique that produces a given output at the lowest possible cost. (See Chapter 9, pp. 204–205.)

The possibilities that are open to a firm depend on the length of the planning period over which it is making its decisions. A firm that plans to change its output rate tomorrow has fewer options than one that plans to change its output rate six months from now. In studying the way a firm's technology constrains its actions, we distinguish between two planning horizons: the short run and the long run.

The Short Run and the Long Run

The **short run** is a period of time in which the quantity of at least one input is fixed and the quantities of the other inputs can be varied. The **long run** is a period of time in which the quantities of all inputs can be varied. Inputs whose quantity can be varied in the short run are called *variable inputs*. Inputs whose quantity cannot be varied in the short run are called *fixed inputs*.

There is no specific time that can be marked on the calendar to separate the short run from the long run. In some cases—for example, a Laundromat or a copying service—the short run is a month or two. New premises can be rented and new machines installed quickly. In other cases—for example, an electric power company or a railroad company—the short run is several years. Bigger power generators and additional track and rolling stock take a few years to build.

In the short run, Swanky has a fixed amount of capital—knitting machines—so to vary its output in the short run, it must vary the quantity of labor employed. For Swanky, the knitting equipment is the fixed input and labor is the variable input. In the long run, Swanky can vary the quantity of both inputs—knitting machines and labor employed.

Let's look more closely at the short-run technology constraint.

Short-Run Technology Constraint

To increase output in the short run, a firm must increase the quantity of a variable input. The effect of change in the quantity of a variable input can be described using three related concepts:

- Total product
- Marginal product
- Average product

Total Product

The total output produced with a given quantity of a fixed input is called **total product**. The *total product curve* shows the maximum output attainable with a given amount of capital as the amount of labor employed is varied. Equivalently, the relationship between total product and the amount of labor employed can be described by a schedule that lists the amounts of labor required with the given amount of capital to produce given amounts of output.

Figure 10.1 shows Swanky's total product schedule and curve. When employment is zero, no sweaters are knitted. As employment increases, so does the number of sweaters knitted. Swanky's total product curve, *TP*, is based on the schedule in the figure. Points *a* through *f* on the curve correspond to the same rows in the table.

The total product curve is similar to the *production possibility frontier* (explained in Chapter 3). It separates the attainable output levels from those that are unattainable. All the points that lie above the curve are unattainable. Points that lie below the curve, in the orange area, are attainable. But they are inefficient—they use more labor than is necessary to produce a given output. Only the points *on* the total product curve are technologically efficient.

Marginal Product

The **marginal product** of an input is the increase in total product divided by the increase in the quantity of the input employed, when the quantity of all other inputs is constant. For example, the marginal product of labor is the increase in total product divid-

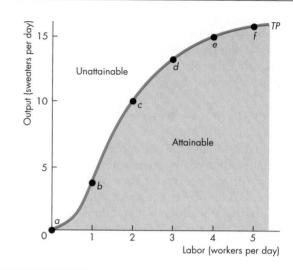

FIGURE 10.1

Total Product

	Labor (workers per day)	Output (sweaters per day)
a	0	0
b	1	4
c	2	10
d	3	13
e	4	15
f	5	16

The table shows how many sweaters Swanky can produce when it uses 1 knitting machine and different amounts of labor. For example, using 1 knitting machine, 2 workers can produce 10 sweaters a day (row c). The total product curve, *TP*, is based on these data. Points *a* through *f* on the curve correspond to the rows of the table. The total product curve separates the attainable output from the unattainable.

ed by the increase in the quantity of labor employed, when the quantity of capital is constant. Equivalently, it is the change in total product resulting from a one-unit increase in the quantity of labor employed.

Table 10.1 shows the calculation of Swanky's marginal product of labor. For example, when the quantity of labor increases from 2 to 3 workers, total product increases from 10 to 13 sweaters. The change in total product—3 sweaters—is the marginal product of going from 2 to 3 workers.

Figure 10.2 illustrates Swanky's marginal product of labor. Part (a) reproduces the total product curve that you met in Fig. 10.1. Part (b) shows the marginal product curve, *MP*. In part (a), the orange bars illustrate the marginal product of labor. The height of each bar measures marginal product. Marginal product is also measured by the slope of the total product curve. Recall that the slope of a curve is the change in the value of the variable measured on the *y*-axis—output—divided by the change in the variable measured on the *x*-axis—labor input—as we move along the curve. A one-unit increase in labor input, from 2 to 3 workers, increases output from 10 to 13 sweaters, so the slope from point *c* to point *d* is 3, the same as the marginal product that we've just calculated.

TABLE 10.1

Calculating Marginal Product and Average Product

	Labor (workers per day)	Output (sweaters per day)	Marginal product (sweaters per worker)	Average product (sweaters per worker)
a	0	0		
			 4	
b	1	4		4.00
			 6	
c	2	10		5.00
			 3	
d	3	13		4.33
			 2	
e	4	15		3.75
			 1	
f	5	16		3.20

Marginal product of an input is the change in total product resulting from a one-unit increase in an input. For example, when labor increases from 2 to 3 workers a day (row *c* to row *d*), total product increases from 10 to 13 sweaters. The marginal product of going from 2 to 3 workers is 3 sweaters.

Average product of an input is total product divided by the quantity of an input employed. For example, 3 workers produce 13 sweaters a day, so the average product of 3 workers is 4.33 sweaters per worker.

FIGURE 10.2

Marginal Product

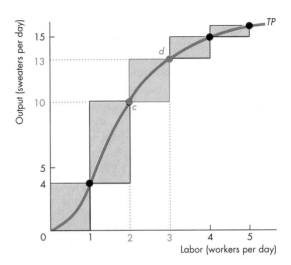

(a) Total product

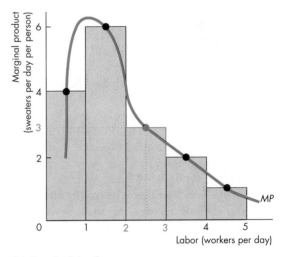

(b) Marginal product

Marginal product is illustrated by the orange bars. For example, when labor increases from 2 to 3, marginal product is the orange bar whose height is 3 sweaters. (Marginal product is shown midway between the labor inputs to emphasize that it is the result of *changing* inputs.) The steeper the slope of the total product curve (*TP*) in part (a), the larger is marginal product (*MP*) in part (b). Marginal product increases to a maximum (when 1 worker is employed in this example) and then declines—diminishing marginal product.

We've calculated the marginal product of labor for a series of unit increases in the amount of labor. But labor is divisible into smaller units than one person. It is divisible into hours and even minutes. By varying the amount of labor in the smallest imaginable units, we can draw the marginal product curve shown in Fig. 10.2(b). The *height* of this curve measures the *slope* of the total product curve at a point. Part (a) shows that an increase in employment from 2 to 3 workers increases output from 10 to 13 sweaters (an increase of 3). The increase in output of 3 sweaters appears on the vertical axis of part (b) as the marginal product of going from 2 to 3 workers. We plot that marginal product at the midpoint between 2 and 3 workers. Notice that marginal product shown in Fig. 10.2(b) reaches a peak at 1 unit of labor, and at that point, marginal product is more than 6. The peak occurs at 1 unit of labor because the total product curve is steepest at 1 unit of labor.

Average Product

The **average product** of an input is equal to total product divided by the quantity of the input employed. Average product tells us how productive, on the average, a factor of production is. Table 10.1 shows Swanky's average product of labor. For example, 3 workers can knit 13 sweaters a day, so the average product of labor is 13 divided by 3, which is 4.33 sweaters per worker.

Figure 10.3 illustrates Swanky's average product of labor, *AP*, and shows the relationship between average product and marginal product. Points *b* through *f* on the average product curve correspond to those same rows in Table 10.1. Average product increases from 1 to 2 workers (its maximum value at point *c*) but then decreases as yet more workers are employed. Notice also that average product is largest when average product and marginal product are equal. That is, the marginal product curve cuts the average product curve at the point of maximum average product. For employment levels at which marginal product exceeds average product, average product is increasing. For employment levels at which marginal product is less than average product, average product is decreasing.

The relationships between the average and marginal product curves that you've just seen are a general feature of the relationship between the average and marginal values of any variable. Let's look at a familiar example.

FIGURE 10.3
Average Product

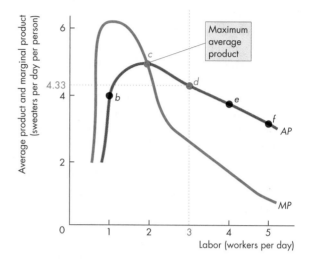

The figure shows the average product of labor and the connection between the average product and marginal product. With 1 worker per day, marginal product exceeds average product, so average product is increasing. With 2 workers per day, marginal product equals average product, so average product is at its maximum. With more than 2 workers per day, marginal product is less than average product, so average product is decreasing.

Marginal Grade and Grade Point Average

Figure 10.4 shows the performance over five semesters of Sidney, a part-time student who takes one course per semester. First, he takes calculus and his grade is a 2. This grade is his marginal grade. It is also his grade point average (GPA). In the next semester, Sidney takes French and gets a 3. French is Sidney's marginal course and his marginal grade is 3. His GPA rises to 2.5. Because his marginal grade exceeds his average grade, it pulls his average up. In the third semester, Sidney takes economics and gets a 4—his new marginal grade. Because his marginal grade exceeds his GPA, it again pulls his average up. His GPA is now 3, the average of 2, 3, and 4. The fourth semester, he takes history and gets a 3. Because his marginal grade is equal to his average, his GPA does not change. In the fifth semester, Sidney takes

English and gets a 2. Because his marginal grade, a 2, is below his GPA of 3, his GPA falls.

This everyday relationship between marginal and average values agrees with that between marginal and average product. Sidney's GPA increases when his marginal grade exceeds his GPA. His GPA falls when his marginal grade is below his GPA. And his GPA is constant when his marginal grade equals his GPA.

The Shapes of the Product Curves

Now let's get back to studying production. The total, marginal, and average product curves are different for different firms and different types of goods. Ford Motor Company's product curves are different from those of Jim's Burger Stand, which in turn are different from those of Sidney's sweater factory. But the shapes of the product curves are similar, because almost every production process has two features:

- Increasing marginal returns initially
- Diminishing marginal returns eventually

Increasing Marginal Returns **Increasing marginal returns** occur when the marginal product of an additional worker exceeds the marginal product of the previous worker. If Sidney employs just one worker at Swanky, that person has to learn all the aspects of sweater production: running the knitting machines, fixing breakdowns, packaging and mailing sweaters, buying and checking the type and color of the wool. All these tasks must be done by that one person. If Sidney hires a second person, the two workers can specialize in different parts of the production process. As a result, two workers produce more than twice as much as one. The marginal product of the second worker is greater than the marginal product of the first worker. Marginal returns are increasing.

Diminishing Marginal Returns *Increasing* marginal returns do not always occur, but all production processes eventually reach a point of *diminishing* marginal returns. **Diminishing marginal returns** occur when the marginal product of an additional worker is less than the marginal product of the previous worker. If Sidney hires a third worker, output increases but not by as much as it did when he added the second worker. In this case, after two workers are hired, all gains from specialization and the division of labor have been exhausted. By hiring a third worker, the factory produces more sweaters, but the equipment is being operated closer to its limits. There are

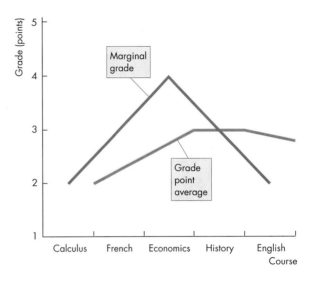

FIGURE 10.4

Marginal Grade and Grade Point Average

Sidney's first course is calculus, for which he gets a 2. His marginal grade is 2, and his GPA is 2. He then gets a 3 for French, which pulls his GPA up to 2.5. Next he gets a 4 for economics, which pulls his GPA up again to 3. For his next course, history, he gets a 3, which maintains his GPA. Then he gets a 2 for English. This marginal grade is below his GPA, and it pulls his average down.

even times when the third worker has nothing to do because the plant is running without the need for further attention. Adding yet more and more workers continues to increase output but by successively smaller amounts. Marginal returns are diminishing. This phenomenon is such a pervasive one that it is called a "law"—"the law of diminishing returns." The **law of diminishing returns** states that

As a firm uses more of a variable input, with a given quantity of fixed inputs, the marginal product of the variable input eventually diminishes.

Because marginal product eventually diminishes, so does average product. Recall that average product decreases when marginal product is less than average product. If marginal product is diminishing, it must eventually become less than average product, and when it does so, average product begins to decline.

■ When marginal product exceeds average product, average product increases; when marginal product is less than average product, average product decreases; and when marginal product and average product are equal, average product is at its maximum.

■ Initially, as the labor input increases, marginal product and average product might increase.

■ But as the labor input increases further, marginal product eventually declines—the law of diminishing returns.

Why does Swanky care about total product, marginal product, and average product and whether marginal product and average product are increasing or decreasing? Swanky cares because the product curves influence its costs and the way costs change with the quantity of sweaters produced.

Short-Run Cost

TO PRODUCE MORE OUTPUT IN THE SHORT RUN, a firm must employ more labor. But if the firm employs more labor, its costs increase. Thus to produce more output, a firm must increase its costs. Let's study Swanky's costs to see how a firm's costs change with the level of production.

Swanky is a small firm, and we'll assume that it cannot influence the prices it pays for its inputs. Given the prices of its inputs, Swanky's lowest attainable cost of production for each output level is determined by its technology constraint. Let's see how.

Total Cost

A firm's **total cost** is the sum of the costs of all the inputs it uses in production. It includes the cost of renting land, buildings, and equipment; the wages paid to the firm's work force; and normal profit. Total cost is divided into two categories: fixed cost and variable cost.

A **fixed cost** is the cost of a fixed input. Because the quantity of a fixed input does not change as output changes, a fixed cost is a cost that is inde-

pendent of the output level. For example, GM can change its output of cars without changing the amount it spends on advertising. The cost of advertising is a fixed cost.

A **variable cost** is a cost of a variable input. Because to change its output, a firm must change the quantity of variable inputs, a variable cost is a cost that varies with the output level. For example, to produce more cars, GM must run its assembly lines for longer hours and hire more labor. The cost of this labor is a variable cost.

Total fixed cost is the total cost of the fixed inputs. **Total variable cost** is the total cost of the variable inputs. We call total cost TC, total fixed cost TFC, and total variable cost TVC. The total cost of production is the sum of total fixed cost and total variable cost. That is,

$$TC = TFC + TVC.$$

Table 10.2 shows Swanky's total cost and its division into total fixed cost and total variable cost. Swanky has one knitting machine; this is its fixed input. To produce more sweaters, Sidney must hire more labor; the first two columns show how many sweaters can be produced at each level of employment. This is Swanky's technology constraint.

Swanky rents its knitting machine for $25 a day. This amount is its total fixed cost. It hires workers at a wage rate of $25 a day, and its total variable cost is equal to the total wage bill. For example, if Swanky employs 3 workers, its total variable cost is (3 × $25), which equals $75. Total cost is the sum of total fixed cost and total variable cost. For example, when Swanky employs 3 workers, its total cost is $100—total fixed cost of $25 plus total variable cost of $75.

Marginal Cost

A firm's **marginal cost** is the increase in its total cost divided by the increase in its output. Equivalently, it is the change in total cost that results from a unit increase in output. For example, when output increases from 10 to 13 sweaters, total cost increases from $75 to $100. The change in output is 3 sweaters, and the change in total cost is $25. The marginal cost of one of those 3 sweaters is ($25 ÷ 3), which equals $8.33.

Notice that when Swanky hires a second worker, marginal cost decreases, but when a third, a fourth,

TABLE 10.2

Calculating a Firm's Costs

Labor (workers per day)	Output (sweaters per day)	Total fixed cost (TFC)	Total variable cost (TVC)	Total cost (TC)	Marginal cost (MC)	Average fixed cost (AFC)	Average variable cost (AVC)	Total cost (ATC)
		(dollars per day)				(dollars per sweater)		
0	0	25	0	25		—	—	—
					6.25			
1	4	25	25	50		6.25	6.25	12.50
					4.17			
2	10	25	50	75		2.50	5.00	7.50
					8.33			
3	13	25	75	100		1.92	5.77	7.69
					12.50			
4	15	25	100	125		1.67	6.67	8.33
					25.00			
5	16	25	125	150		1.56	7.81	9.38

and a fifth worker are employed, marginal cost successively increases. Marginal cost eventually increases because each additional worker produces a successively smaller addition to output—*the law of diminishing returns.* The law of diminishing returns means that each additional worker produces a successively smaller addition to output. So to get an additional unit of output, ever more workers are required. Because more workers are required to produce one additional unit of output, the cost of the additional output—marginal cost—must eventually increase.

Average Cost

Average cost is the cost per unit of output. There are three average costs:

1. Average fixed cost
2. Average variable cost
3. Average total cost

Average fixed cost (*AFC*) is total fixed cost per unit of output. **Average variable cost** (*AVC*) is total variable cost per unit of output. **Average total cost** (*ATC*) is total cost per unit output. The average cost concepts are calculated from the total cost concepts as follows:

$$TC = TFC + TVC.$$

Divide each total cost term by the quantity produced, *Q*, to give

$$\frac{TC}{Q} = \frac{TFC}{Q} + \frac{TVC}{Q}$$

or,

$$ATC = AFC + AVC.$$

Average total cost equals average fixed cost plus average variable cost. Table 10.2 shows the calculation of average total cost. For example, when output is 10 sweaters, average fixed cost is ($25 ÷ 10), which equals $2.50, average variable cost is ($50 ÷ 10), which equals $5.00, and average total cost is ($75 ÷ 10), which equals $7.50. Equivalently, average total cost is equal to average fixed cost ($2.50) plus average variable cost ($5.00).

Short-Run Cost Curves

Figure 10.5(a) illustrates Swanky's short-run costs as the total cost curves. Total fixed cost is a constant $25. It appears in the figure as the horizontal green curve *TFC*. Total variable cost and total cost both increase with output. They are graphed as the purple total variable cost curve (*TVC*) and the blue total cost curve (*TC*). The vertical distance between those two curves is equal to total fixed cost—as shown by the

FIGURE 10.5
Short-Run Costs

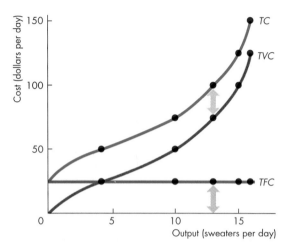

(a) Total costs

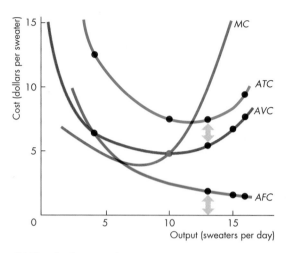

(b) Marginal cost and average costs

The short-run costs calculated in Table 10.2 are illustrated in the graphs. Part (a) shows the total cost curves. Total cost (*TC*) increases as output increases. Total fixed cost (*TFC*) is constant—it graphs as a horizontal line—and total variable cost (*TVC*) increases in a similar way to total cost. The vertical distance between the total cost curve and the total variable cost curve is total fixed cost, as illustrated by the two arrows.

Part (b) shows the average and marginal cost curves. Average fixed cost (*AFC*) decreases as output increases. The average total cost curve (*ATC*) and average variable cost curve (*AVC*) are U-shaped. The vertical distance between these two curves is equal to average fixed cost, as illustrated by the two arrows. The marginal cost curve (*MC*) is also U-shaped. It intersects the average variable cost curve and the average total cost curve at their minimum points.

two arrows. Because total fixed cost is a constant $25, the distance between the purple total variable cost curve and the blue total cost curve is a constant $25. Use your ruler to check that the distance is a constant $25.

Figure 10.5(b) shows the average cost curves. The green average fixed cost curve (*AFC*) slopes downward. As output increases, the same constant fixed cost is spread over a larger output. When Swanky produces 4 sweaters, average fixed cost is $6.25; when total product increases to 16 sweaters, average fixed cost decreases to $1.56.

The blue average total cost curve (*ATC*) and the purple average variable cost curve (*AVC*) are U-shaped. The vertical distance between the average total cost and average variable cost curves is equal to average fixed cost—as indicated by the two arrows. That distance shrinks as output increases because average fixed cost declines with increasing output.

Figure 10.5(b) also illustrates the marginal cost curve. It is the red curve *MC*. This curve is also U-shaped. The marginal cost curve intersects the average variable cost curve and the average total cost curve at their minimum points. That is, when marginal cost is less than average cost, average cost is decreasing, and when marginal cost exceeds average cost, average cost is increasing. This relationship holds for both the *ATC* curve and the *AVC* curve and is just another example of the relationship you saw in Figure 10.4 for Sidney's course grades.

Why the Average Total Cost Curve Is U-Shaped

Average total cost, *ATC*, is the sum of average fixed cost, *AFC*, and average variable cost, *AVC*. So the shape of the *ATC* curve combines the shapes of the

AFC and *AVC* curves. The U-shape of the average total cost curve arises from the influence of two opposing forces:

■ Spreading fixed cost over a larger output
■ Eventually diminishing returns

When output increases, the firm spreads its fixed costs over a larger output and its average fixed cost decreases—its average fixed cost curve slopes downward.

When output increases, diminishing returns eventually set in. That is, to produce an additional unit of output, ever larger amounts of labor are required. So average variable cost eventually increases, and the firm's *AVC* curve eventually slopes upward.

The shape of the average total cost curve combines these two effects. Initially, as output increases, both average fixed cost and average variable cost decrease, so average total cost decreases and the *ATC* curve slopes downward. But as output increases further and diminishing returns set in, average variable cost begins to increase. Eventually, average variable cost increases more quickly than average fixed cost decreases, so average total cost increases and the *ATC* curve slopes upward. At the output level at which declining average fixed cost offsets increasing average variable cost, average total cost is constant and at its minimum.

Cost Curves and Product Curves

A firm's cost curves are determined by its technology and its product curves. Figure 10.6 shows the links between the product curves and the cost curves. The upper part of the figure shows the average product curve and the marginal product curve—like those in Fig. 10.3(b). The lower part of the figure shows the average variable cost curve and the marginal cost curve—like those in Fig. 10.5(b).

Notice that over the output range in which marginal product and average product are rising, marginal cost and average variable cost are falling. Then, at the point of maximum marginal product, marginal cost is a minimum. At output levels above this point, marginal product diminishes and marginal cost increases. But there is an intermediate range of output over which average product is still rising and average variable cost is falling. Then an output is reached at which average product is a maximum and average variable cost is a minimum. At outputs above this level, average product diminishes and average variable cost increases.

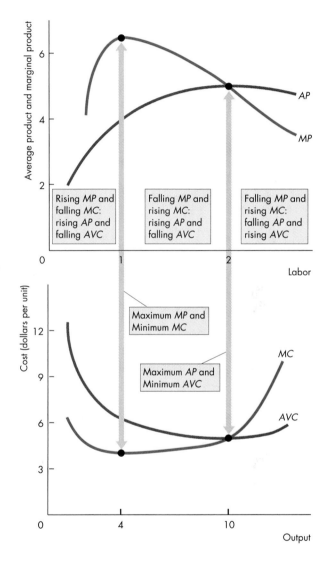

FIGURE 10.6

Product Curves and Cost Curves

A firm's cost curves are linked to its product curves. Over the range of rising marginal product, marginal cost is falling. When marginal product is a maximum, marginal cost is a minimum. Over the range of rising average product, average *variable* cost is falling. When average product is a maximum, average variable cost is a minimum. Over the range of diminishing marginal product, marginal cost is rising. And over the range of diminishing average product, average *variable* cost is rising.

TABLE 10.3
A Compact Glossary of Costs

Term	Symbol	Definition	Equation
Fixed cost		Cost that is independent of the output level; cost of a fixed input	
Variable cost		Cost that varies with the output level; cost of a variable input	
Total fixed cost	TFC	Cost of the fixed inputs	
Total variable cost	TVC	Cost of the variable inputs	
Total cost	TC	Cost of all inputs	$TC = TFC + TVC$
Output (total product)	TP	Output produced	
Marginal cost	MC	Change in total cost resulting from a one-unit increase in total product	$MC = \Delta TC \div \Delta TP$
Average fixed cost	AFC	Total fixed cost per unit of output	$AFC = TFC \div TP$
Average variable cost	AVC	Total variable cost per unit of output	$AVC = TVC \div TP$
Average total cost	ATC	Total cost per unit of output	$ATC = AFC + AVC$

Shifts in the Cost Curves

The position of a firm's short-run cost curves depend on technology, described by its product curves, and by the prices it pays for its factors of production. If technology changes or if factor prices change, the firm's costs change and its cost curves shift.

A technological change that increases productivity shifts the product curves upward and shifts the cost curves downward. For example, advances in robotic production techniques have increased productivity in the automobile industry. As a result, the product curves of Chrysler, Ford, and GM have shifted upward, and their cost curves have shifted downward. But the relationships between their product curves and cost curves have not changed. The curves are still linked in the way shown in Fig. 10.6.

An increase in factor prices increases costs and shifts the cost curves. But the way the curves shift depends on which factor prices change. A change in rent or some other component of *fixed* cost shifts the fixed cost curves (*TFC* and *AFC*) upward and shifts the total cost curve (*TC*) upward but leaves the variable cost curves (*AVC* and *TVC*) and the marginal cost curve (*MC*) unchanged. A change in wages or some other component of *variable* cost shifts the variable curves (*TVC* and *AVC*) upward and shifts the

total cost curve (*TC*) and the marginal cost curve (*MC*) upward but leaves the fixed cost curves (*AFC* and *TFC*) unchanged. *Reading Between the Lines* on pp. 230–231 shows how the cost curves of Digital Equipment Corporation were affected by its decision to expand the production of disk drives in Malaysia instead of Colorado.

You've now completed your study of short-run costs. All the concepts that you met are summarized in a compact glossary in Table 10.3.

R E V I E W

■ A firm's short-run cost curves show the relationships between short-run cost and output.

■ Marginal cost eventually increases because of *diminishing returns*—each additional worker produces a successively smaller addition to output.

■ Average fixed cost decreases because as output increases, fixed costs are spread over a larger output.

■ The average total cost curve is U-shaped because as output increases it combines the influences of falling average fixed cost and eventually diminishing returns.

Plant Size and Cost

WE HAVE STUDIED HOW THE COST OF production varies for a given sweater plant when different quantities of labor are used. We are now going to see how the cost of production varies when both plant size and the quantity of labor are varied. That is, we are going to study a firm's long-run costs. **Long-run cost** is the cost of production when a firm uses the economically efficient quantity of labor and plant size.

The behavior of long-run cost depends on the firm's production function. A **production function** is the relationship between the maximum output attainable and the quantities of *all* inputs used.

The Production Function

Figure 10.7 shows Swanky's production function. The table lists the total product for four different plant sizes and five different quantities of labor. The numbers for Plant 1 are for the sweater factory whose short-run product and cost curves we've just studied. The other three plants have 2, 3, and 4 machines. If Sidney doubles the plant size to 2 knitting machines, the various amounts of labor can produce the outputs shown in the second column of the table. The other two columns show the outputs of yet larger plants.

The numbers in the table are graphed as the four total product curves in Fig. 10.7. Each total product curve has the same basic shape, but the larger the number of knitting machines, the larger is the number of sweaters knitted each day by a given number of workers.

Diminishing Returns

Diminishing returns occur in all four plants as the labor input increases. You can check that fact by doing calculations for the larger plants similar to those you've already done for a plant with one machine. Regardless of the plant size, as the labor input increases, its marginal product (eventually) decreases.

Diminishing Marginal Product of Capital Just as we can calculate the marginal product of labor for each plant size, we can also calculate the marginal product of capital for each quantity of labor. The *marginal product of capital* is the change in total product divided by the change in capital employed when

FIGURE 10.7
The Production Function

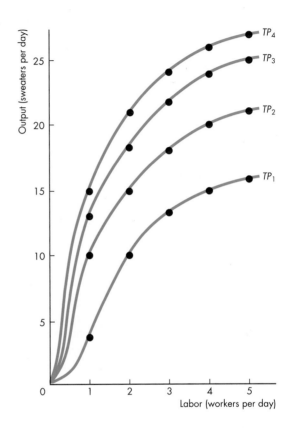

Labor	Output (sweaters per day)			
(workers per day)	Plant 1	Plant 2	Plant 3	Plant 4
1	4	10	13	15
2	10	15	18	21
3	13	18	22	24
4	15	20	24	26
5	16	21	25	27
Knitting machines (number)	1	2	3	4

The table shows the total product data for four plant sizes. These numbers are graphed as the total product curves TP_1, TP_2, TP_3, and TP_4. The bigger the plant, the larger is the total product for any given amount of labor employed. But each total product curve displays diminishing marginal product.

the amount of labor employed is constant. Equivalently, it is the change in output resulting from a one-unit increase in the quantity of capital employed. For example, if Swanky has 3 workers and increases the number of machines from 1 to 2, output increases from 13 to 18 sweaters a day. The marginal product of capital is 5 sweaters per day. The marginal product of capital diminishes, just like the marginal product of labor. For example, if with 3 workers, Swanky increases the number of machines from 2 to 3, output increases from 18 to 22 sweaters per day. The marginal product of the third machine is 4 sweaters per day, down from 5 sweaters per day for the second machine.

The law of diminishing returns tells us what happens to output when a firm changes one input, either labor or capital, and holds the other input constant. But what happens to a firm's output if it changes *both* labor and capital?

Returns to Scale

A change in scale occurs when there is an equal percentage change in the use of all the firm's inputs. For example, if Swanky has been employing one worker and has one knitting machine and then doubles its use of both inputs (to use two workers and two knitting machines), the scale of the firm will double. **Returns to scale** are the increases in output that result from increasing all inputs by the same percentage. There are three possible cases:

■ Constant returns to scale
■ Increasing returns to scale
■ Decreasing returns to scale

Constant Returns to Scale   **Constant returns to scale** occur when the percentage increase in a firm's output is equal to the percentage increase in its inputs. If constant returns to scale are present and a firm doubles all its inputs, its output exactly doubles. Constant returns to scale occur if an increase in output is achieved by replicating the original production process. For example, General Motors can double its production of Cavaliers by doubling its production facility for those cars. It can build an identical production line and hire an identical number of workers. With the two identical production lines, GM produces exactly twice as many cars.

Increasing Returns to Scale   **Increasing returns to scale** occur when the percentage

increase in output exceeds the percentage increase in inputs. If increasing returns to scale are present and a firm doubles all its inputs, its output more than doubles. Increasing returns to scale occur in production processes in which increased output enables a firm to increase the division of labor and to use more specialized labor and capital. For example, if GM produces only 100 cars a week, each worker and each machine must be capable of performing many different tasks. But if it produces 10,000 cars a week, each worker and each piece of equipment can be highly specialized. Workers specialize in a small number of tasks at which they become highly proficient. General Motors might use 100 times more capital and labor, but the number of cars produced increases more than a hundredfold. General Motors experiences increasing returns to scale.

Decreasing Returns to Scale   **Decreasing returns to scale** occur when the percentage increase in output is less than the percentage increase in inputs. If decreasing returns to scale are present and a firm doubles all its inputs, its output less than doubles. Decreasing returns to scale occur in all production processes at some output rate, but perhaps at a very large one. The most common source of decreasing returns to scale is the increasingly complex management and organizational structure required to control a large firm. The larger the organization, the greater is the number of layers in the management pyramid and the greater are the costs of monitoring and maintaining control of the production and marketing process.

Returns to Scale at Swanky   Swanky's production possibilities, set out in Fig. 10.7, display both increasing returns to scale and decreasing returns to scale. If Sidney has 1 knitting machine and employs 1 worker, his factory will produce 4 sweaters a day. If he doubles the firm's inputs to 2 knitting machines and 2 workers, the factory's output increases almost fourfold to 15 sweaters a day. If he increases the firm's inputs by another 50 percent to 3 knitting machines and 3 workers, output increases to 22 sweaters a day—an increase of less than 50 percent. Doubling Swanky's scale from 1 to 2 units of each input gives rise to increasing returns to scale, but the further increase from 2 to 3 units of each input gives rise to decreasing returns to scale.

Whether a firm experiences increasing, constant, or decreasing returns to scale affects its long-run costs. Let's see how.

Short-Run Cost and Long-Run Cost

The cost curves in Fig. 10.5 apply to a plant with one knitting machine. There is a set of short-run cost curves like those shown in Fig. 10.5 for each different plant size. Let's look at the short-run costs for the four plants set out in Fig. 10.7 and see how the plant size affects the cost curves.

We've already studied the costs of a plant with 1 knitting machine. We'll call the average total cost curve for that plant ATC_1 in Fig. 10.8. The average total cost curve for larger plants (with 2, 3, and 4 knitting machines, respectively) are also shown in Fig. 10.8 as ATC_2 (for 2 machines), ATC_3 (for 3 machines), and ATC_4 (for 4 machines). The average total cost curve for each plant size has the same basic U-shape. And because larger plants produce larger outputs with the same amount of labor, the ATC curves for successively larger plants lie farther to the right. Which of these cost curves Swanky operates on depends on its plant size. For example, if Swanky has 1 machine, then its average total cost curve is ATC_1 and it costs $7.69 per sweater to knit 13 sweaters a day. But Swanky can produce 13 sweaters a day with any of these four plant sizes. If it uses 2 machines, the average total cost curve is ATC_2 and the average total cost of a sweater is $6.80. And if it uses 4 machines, the average total cost curve is ATC_4 and the average total cost of a sweater is $9.50. If Swanky wants to produce 13 sweaters a day, the economically efficient plant size is 2 machines—the plant size with the lowest average total cost of production.

FIGURE 10.8

Short-Run Costs

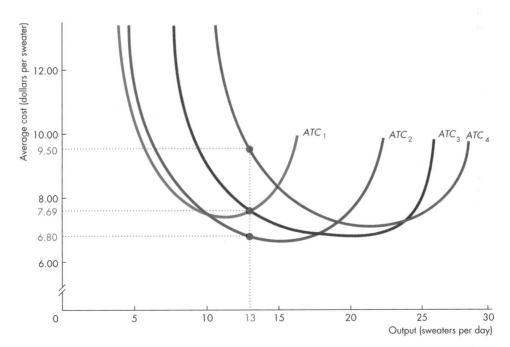

The figure shows short-run average total cost curves for four different plants. Swanky can produce 13 sweaters a day with 1 knitting machine on ATC_1 or with 3 knitting machines on ATC_3 for an average cost of $7.69 per sweater. It can produce the same number of sweaters by using 2 knitting machines on ATC_2 for $6.80 per sweater or with 4 machines on ATC_4 for $9.50 per sweater. If Swanky produces 13 sweaters a day, the least-cost method of production—the long-run method—is with 2 machines on ATC_2.

The Long-Run Average Cost Curve

The *long-run average cost curve* traces the relationship between the lowest attainable average total cost and output when both capital and labor inputs can be varied. This curve is illustrated in Fig. 10.9 as *LRAC*.

The long-run average cost curve is derived directly from the short-run average total cost curves that we have just reviewed in Fig. 10.8. As you can see, ATC_1 has the lowest average total cost for all output rates up to 10 sweaters a day. ATC_2 has the lowest average total cost for output rates between 10 and 18 sweaters a day. ATC_3 has the lowest average total cost for output rates between 18 and 24 sweaters a day.

And ATC_4 has the lowest average total cost for output rates in excess of 24 sweaters a day.

The segment of each of the four average total cost curves for which that plant has the lowest average total cost is highlighted in dark blue in Fig. 10.9. The scallop-shaped curve made up of these four segments is the long-run average cost curve.

Swanky will be on its long-run average cost curve if it does the following: To produce up to 10 sweaters a day, it uses 1 machine; to produce between 10 and 18 sweaters a day, it uses 2 machines; to produce between 18 and 24 sweaters, it uses 3 machines; and, finally, to produce more than 24 sweaters, it uses 4 machines. Within these ranges, Swanky varies its output by varying only the amount of labor employed.

FIGURE 10.9

Long-Run Average Cost Curve

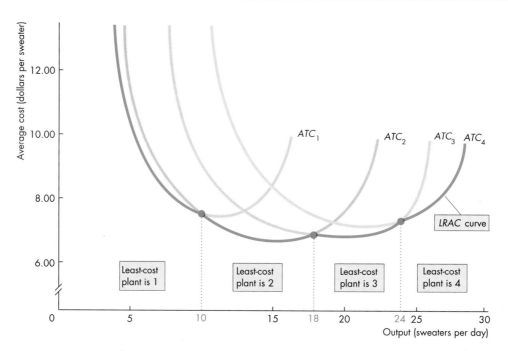

In the long run, Swanky can vary both capital and labor inputs. The long-run average cost curve traces the lowest attainable average total cost of production. Swanky produces on its long-run average cost curve, if it uses 1 machine to produce up to 10 sweaters a day, 2 machines to produce between 10 and 18 sweaters a day, 3 machines to produce between 18 and 24 sweaters a day, and 4 machines to produce more than 24 sweaters a day. Within these ranges, Swanky varies its output by varying its labor input.

Economies and Diseconomies of Scale

Economies of scale are present when, as output increases, long-run average cost decreases. When economies of scale are present, the *LRAC* curve slopes downward. Swanky experiences economies of scale for outputs up to 15 sweaters a day. **Diseconomies of scale** are present when, as output increases, long-run average cost increases. When diseconomies of scale are present, the LRAC curve slopes downward. At ouptuts greater than 15 sweaters a day, Swanky experiences diseconomies of scale.

In general, plant size can be changed in small increments so that there is an infinite number of plant sizes and an infinite number of short-run average total cost curves, one for each plant size.

Figure 10.10 illustrates this general case. With an infinite number of plant sizes, the long-run average cost curve is smooth, not scalloped like Swanky's. For outputs up to Q_1, there are economies of scale. For outputs that exceed Q_2, there are diseconomies of scale. For outputs between Q_1 and Q_2, there are neither economies of scale nor diseconomies of scale.

Each plant produces a single output at a lower cost than any other plant can produce it. For example, the quantity Q_0 can be produced at least cost by the plant with the short-run average cost curve $SRAC_0$. This least cost is ATC_0.

The first time the long-run average cost curve appeared in print, it was drawn incorrectly. Take a look at *Economics in History* (pp. 242–243) to see why. You will understand the connection between the short-run and long-run average cost curves more thoroughly after you have studied that material.

You've now studied the principles of long-run cost. Let's use what you've learned to answer some questions about real businesses.

Producing Cars and Generating Electric Power

At the beginning of this chapter, we noted that most car makers can produce more cars than they can sell. We posed the question: Why do car makers have expensive equipment lying around that isn't fully used? You can see the answer in Fig. 10.10. Car producers experience economies of scale. Given the output that they can sell, the minimum cost of production occurs on a short-run average total cost curve that looks like $SRAC_a$.

We also noted that many electric utilities don't have enough production equipment to meet demand on the coldest and hottest days and have to buy pow-

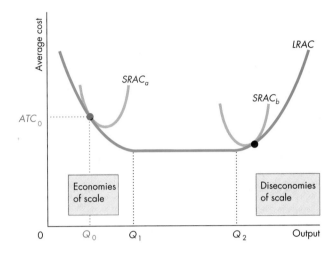

FIGURE 10.10

Economies of Scale

If capital can be varied in small units, the number of plant sizes is infinitely large, and there is an infinitely large number of short-run average total cost curves. Each short-run average total cost curve touches the long-run average cost curve at a single point. For example, the short-run average total cost curve ($SRAC_a$) touches the long-run average cost curve ($LRAC$) at the output rate Q_0 and average total cost ATC_0. For outputs up to Q_1, there are economies of scale; for outputs between Q_1 and Q_2, there are constant costs; and for outputs greater than Q_2, there are diseconomies of scale.

er from other producers. You can now see why this happens and why they don't build a bigger plant. Power producers experience diseconomies of scale. Given the output that they can sell on a normal day, they have short-run average total cost curves like $SRAC_b$. If they had larger plants, their average total costs of producing their normal output would increase.

We've now studied how a firm's costs vary as it changes its inputs and its output. We've seen that diminishing marginal product gives rise to increasing marginal and average costs. We've also seen how the long-run cost curve takes its shape from economies and diseconomies of scale.

Our next task is to study the interactions of firms and households in markets for goods and services and see how prices, outputs, and profits are determined.

Cost Curves in Action

THE BOSTON GLOBE, JULY 3, 1994

Digital Surges in Malaysia

BY MITCHELL ZUCKOFF AND AARON ZITNER

PENANG, Malaysia—On a single day in May the two faces of Digital Equipment Corp. were on display on opposite sides of the globe.

On one side, at company headquarters in Maynard, Mass., chief executive Robert B. Palmer was solemnly announcing that Digital may cut as many as 20,000 jobs in a dramatic bid to return to profitability.

At virtually the same hour in Malaysia, a buoyant Larry Larson was celebrating a milestone in the construction of Digital's newest plant, a $25 million disk drive manufacturing center that within a year could employ 3,000 workers.

"The growth of this business has been phenomenal, so we're doing everything we can to keep up," said Larson, Digital's Asia-Pacific program manager....

Its newest outpost is on this lush resort island at the northern end of the Straits of Malacca, where many of the biggest names in the electronics industry have found a home amid palm trees and the fading mansions of a bygone colonial era.

Digital's Penang plant official-ly began operations four weeks ago, just seven months after the

ground-breaking. It is expected to produce 1 million drives a year, most of which Digital sells to Compaq Computer Corp., Dell Computer Corp. and other compa-nies for use in high-end personal computers, workstations and servers....

Wages at the electronics firms are higher than the average pay of most Malaysian workers, although lower than US workers doing the same jobs. Larson declined to reveal the wage Digital will pay its new workers. "There's a basic range here that everybody operates in," he said. "We'll be in that range."

According to Dataquest, aver-age hourly pay for assembly and test laborers in Malaysia is $1.41, considerably below Singapore's $4.30, but considerably above China's 47 cents....

There were an assortment of reasons to build in Asia. ... First, demand for disk drives was begin-ning to outstrip capacity at Digital's other manufacturing plant, in Colorado Springs, Colo. ... Another reason was Penang itself.

"There is a tremendous cal-iber and availability of technical personnel in Penang, combined with excellent infrastructure and low labor cost," Larson said.

Reprinted by permission.

Essence of THE STORY

■ Digital Equipment Corp. is expanding its business in Asia. It has opened a $25 million disk drive manufacturing cen-ter that will employ 3,000 workers and produce a million disk drives a year.

■ Wages of electronics workers in Malaysia are $1.41 an hour. This wage is much lower than that in the United States and also lower than the $4.30 in Singapore. In China, the wage is even lower, at 47 cents an hour.

■ The demand for disk drives was beginning to outstrip capacity at Digital's other manufactur-ing plant in Colorado Springs.

■ Digital decided to expand in Penang, Malaysia, because of the high caliber and availability of technical personnel there as well as good infrastructure and low labor costs.

Economic

A N A L Y S I S

■ Figure 1 shows the average fixed cost curve, AFC_{US}, and average total cost curve, ATC_{US}, of producing disk drives at Digital's plant in Colorado Springs.

■ Average total cost is at a minimum when the plant produces 0.5 million disk drives a year (an assumed number) and the cost per drive is C_{US}.

■ To increase production in Colorado Springs, Digital would incur ever higher costs as it moved up its ATC_{US} curve.

■ Digital can be more efficient by producing disk drives in Malaysia. Figure 2 shows why.

■ The fixed cost of producing disk drives in Malaysia is probably greater than in Colorado because a new plant must be built ($25 million) and new space must be purchased or rented. The average fixed cost curve in Malaysia shifts upward from that in Colorado to AFC_M.

■ But the labor cost, which is part of *variable cost*, is lower in Malaysia than in Colorado. So the average variable cost in Malaysia is below that in Colorado.

■ The decrease in average variable cost exceeds the increase in average fixed costs, so the average total cost curve in Malaysia shifts downward from that in Colorado to ATC_M.

■ By expanding in Malaysia rather than in Colorado, Digital can produce disk drives at a lower price and be competitive.

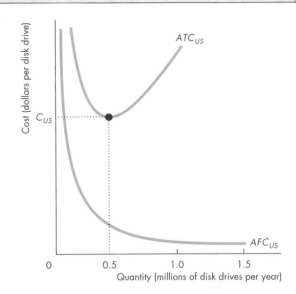

Figure 1 Colorado plant

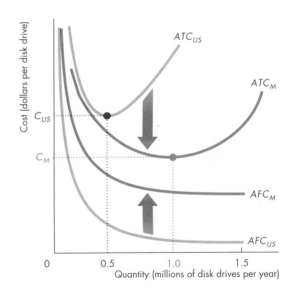

Figure 2 Malaysia plant

The Firm's Objective and Constraints

Firms aim to maximize profit. To do so, they try to use their scarce resources efficiently. Profit is constrained by the market and by technology. The market constrains profit because people have limited demands for each good or service and a limited supply of each factor of production. Technology constrains profit because the maximum quantity that can be produced depends on the quantities of inputs employed. To maximize profit, a firm chooses a technologically efficient method of production. The actions a firm can take depend on its planning horizon. In the short run, the quantity of at least one input—usually capital—is fixed, and the quantities of the other inputs—usually labor—can be varied. In the long run, the quantities of all inputs can be varied. (p. 215)

Short-Run Technology Constraint

A firm's short-run technology constraint determines how much additional output can be produced by a given increase in its variable input. It is described by a total product curve. The total product curve separates attainable output levels from unattainable output levels.

The slope of the total product curve is the marginal product of labor. Initially, marginal product increases as the quantity of labor increases. But eventually, marginal product diminishes—the law of diminishing returns. Average product also increases initially and eventually diminishes. Average product increases when marginal product exceeds average product. Average product decreases when marginal product is less than average product. And average product is at a maximum and constant when marginal product equals average product. (pp. 216–220)

Short-Run Cost

Total cost is the sum of total fixed cost and total variable cost. As output increases, total cost increases because total variable cost increases. A firm's average costs and marginal cost depend on how much a firm produces. Average fixed cost decreases as output increases. Average variable cost, average total cost, and marginal cost are U-shaped. At small output levels, they decline as output increases. They pass through a minimum point, which occurs at a different output for each cost, and then eventually increase as output increases. When marginal cost is less than average cost, average cost is decreasing. When marginal cost equals average cost, average cost is at its minimum. When marginal cost exceeds average cost, average cost is increasing.

Average variable cost is linked to average product. At the output level at which average product is at a maximum, average variable cost is at a minimum. Over the output range in which average product is increasing, average variable cost is decreasing, and over the output range in which average product is decreasing, average variable cost is increasing.

Marginal cost is linked to marginal product. At the output level at which marginal product is at a maximum, marginal cost is at a minimum. The output range over which marginal product is increasing, marginal cost is decreasing, and the output range over which marginal product is decreasing, marginal cost is increasing. (pp. 220–224)

Plant Size and Cost

Long-run cost is the cost of production when all inputs—labor and capital—have been adjusted to their economically efficient levels. The behavior of long-run cost depends on the firm's production function, the relation of output to inputs. As a firm uses more labor while holding capital constant, it eventually experiences diminishing returns. When it uses more capital while holding labor constant, it also eventually experiences diminishing returns. When the firm increases all its inputs in equal proportions, it experiences returns to scale. Returns to scale can be constant, increasing, or decreasing.

There is a set of short-run cost curves for each different plant size. There is one least-cost plant for each output. The larger the output, the larger is the plant that will minimize average total cost.

The long-run average cost curve traces out the lowest attainable average total cost at each output when both capital and labor inputs can be varied. With economies of scale, the long-run average cost curve slopes downward. With diseconomies of scale, the long-run average cost curve slopes upward.

There is no distinction between fixed cost and variable cost in the long run. Since all inputs are variable, all costs are also variable. (pp. 225–229)

KEY ELEMENTS

Key Figures and Tables

Key Terms

REVIEW QUESTIONS

1. Why do firms try to maximize profit?
2. What are the constraints on a firm's ability to maximize profit?
3. Distinguish between the short run and the long run.
4. What does a firm's total product curve show?
5. What does a firm's marginal product curve show?
6. What does a firm's average product curve show?
7. Explain the relationships between a firm's total product curve and its marginal product curve.
8. Explain the relationship between a firm's average product curve and its marginal product curve.
9. What is the law of diminishing returns? What does this law imply about the shapes of the total, marginal, and average product curves?
10. Why does a firm's marginal product at first increase and eventually diminish?
11. Define total cost, total fixed cost, and total variable cost. What is the relationship among the three concepts of total cost?
12. Explain how the three total cost measures change as total product increases.
13. Define marginal cost. Why does marginal cost eventually increase as total product increases?
14. Define average total cost, average variable cost, and average fixed cost. What is the relationship among the three average cost concepts?
15. Explain how the three average cost measures change as total product increases.
16. What is the relationship between average variable cost and marginal cost and between average total cost and marginal cost?
17. Explain the relationship between the average product curve and average variable cost curve and between the marginal product curve and the marginal cost curve.
18. What is the relationship between the long-run average cost curve and the short-run average total cost curves?
19. What effects do economies of scale and diseconomies of scale have on the shape of the long-run average cost curve?

P R O B L E M S

◆ 1. The total product schedule of Rubber Duckies, Inc., a firm that makes rubber boats, is described by the following:

Labor (workers per week)	Output (rubber boats per week)
1	1
2	3
3	6
4	10
5	15
6	21
7	26
8	30
9	33
10	35

a. Draw the total product curve.
b. Calculate the average product of labor and draw the average product curve.
c. Calculate the marginal product of labor and draw the marginal product curve.
d. What is the relationship between average product and marginal product when Rubber Duckies produces fewer than 30 boats a week? Why?
e. What is the relationship between average and marginal product when Rubber Duckies produces more than 30 boats a week? Why?

◆ 2. Suppose that the price of labor is $400 a week, the total fixed cost is $1,000 a week, and the total product schedule is the same as in problem 1.
a. Calculate total cost, total variable cost, and total fixed cost for each level of output.
b. Draw the total cost, total variable cost, and total fixed cost curves.
c. Calculate average total cost, average fixed cost, average variable cost, and marginal cost at each level of output.
d. Draw the following cost curves: average total cost, average variable cost, average fixed cost, and marginal cost.

◆ 3. Suppose that total fixed cost increases to $1,100 a week. What will now happen to the firm's short-run cost curves in problem 2?

◆ 4. Suppose that total fixed cost remains at $1,000 a week but that the price of labor increases to $450 a week. Using these new costs, rework problem 2.

5. Rubber Duckies, Inc., can buy an additional factory. If it does so and operates two factories, its total product schedule is:

Labor (workers per week)	Output (rubber boats per week)
1	2
2	6
3	12
4	20
5	30
6	42
7	52
8	60
9	66
10	70

The total fixed cost of operating its current factory is $1,000 a week and the total fixed cost of operating the additional factory is also $1,000 a week. The wage rate is $400 a week.
a. Calculate the total cost for each of the outputs given for the new factory.
b. Calculate Rubber Duckies' average total cost of each output given.
c. Draw Rubber Duckies' long-run average cost curve.
d. Over what output range would it be efficient for Rubber Duckies to operate one factory?
e. Over what output range would it be efficient for Rubber Duckies to operate two factories?

6. Study *Reading Between the Lines* on pp. 230–231 and then explain why
a. Digital has opened a factory in Malaysia.
b. Digital's average variable cost is higher in the United States than in Malaysia.
c. Digital's average fixed cost is probably lower in the United States than in Malaysia.

Producing at Least Cost

This appendix describes a set of useful tools for studying a firm's long-run production and costs. The tools are *isoquants* and *isocost lines*.

Isoquants

FIGURE A10.1 SHOWS SWANKY'S PRODUCTION function. The figure highlights that Swanky can use three different combinations of labor and capital to produce 15 sweaters a day and two different combinations to produce 10 and 21 sweaters a day. These combinations, and many others not shown in the figure, can be illustrated by using an isoquant map.

An Isoquant Map

An **isoquant** is a curve that shows the different combinations of labor and capital required to pro-

duce a given quantity of output. The word *isoquant* means "equal quantity"—*iso* meaning equal and *quant* meaning quantity. There is an isoquant for each output level. A series of isoquants is called an **isoquant map**. Figure A10.2 shows an isoquant map with three isoquants: one for 10 sweaters, one for 15 sweaters, and one for 21 sweaters. Each isoquant shown is based on the production function in Fig. A10.1.

Although all goods and services can be produced by using a variety of alternative methods of production or techniques, the ease with which capital and labor can be substituted for each other varies from industry to industry. The shape of the production function reflects the ease with which inputs can be substituted for each other. Therefore the production function can be used to calculate the degree of substitutability between inputs. Such a calculation involves a new concept—the marginal rate of substitution of labor for capital.

FIGURE A10.1
Swanky's Production Function

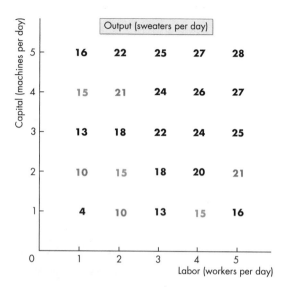

The figure shows how many sweaters can be produced per day by various combinations of labor and capital inputs. For example, by using 1 worker and 2 machines, Swanky can produce 10 sweaters a day; and by using 4 workers and 2 knitting machines, Swanky can produce 20 sweaters.

FIGURE A10.2
An Isoquant Map

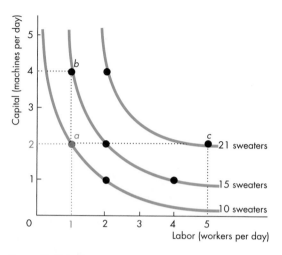

The figure illustrates an isoquant map, but one that shows only 3 isoquants—those for 10, 15, and 21 sweaters a day. These curves correspond to the production function shown in Fig. A10.1. If Swanky uses 2 machines and 1 worker (point *a*), it produces 10 sweaters. If it uses 4 machines and 1 worker (point *b*), it produces 15 sweaters. And if it uses 2 machines and 5 workers (point *c*), it produces 21 sweaters.

Marginal Rate of Substitution

The **marginal rate of substitution of labor for capital** is the decrease in capital needed per unit increase in labor so that output remains constant. The marginal rate of substitution is the magnitude of the slope of the isoquant. Figure A10.3 illustrates this relationship. The figure shows the isoquant for 13 sweaters a day. Pick any point on this isoquant and imagine increasing labor by the smallest conceivable amount and decreasing capital by the amount necessary to keep output constant at 13 sweaters. As we increase the labor input and decrease the capital input so as to keep output constant at 13 sweaters a day, we travel down along the isoquant.

The marginal rate of substitution of labor for capital at point *a* is the magnitude of the slope of the straight red line that is tangent to the isoquant at point *a*. The slope of the isoquant at point *a* equals the slope of the red line. To calculate that slope, let's

move along the red line from 5 knitting machines and no workers to 2.5 workers and no knitting machines. Capital decreases by 5 knitting machines, and labor increases by 2.5 workers. The magnitude of the slope is 5 divided by 2.5, which equals 2. Thus when Swanky uses technique *a* to produce 13 sweaters a day, the marginal rate of substitution of labor for capital is 2.

The marginal rate of substitution of labor for capital at point *b* is the magnitude of the slope of the straight red line that is tangent to the isoquant at point *b*. Along this red line, if capital decreases by 2.5 knitting machines, labor increases by 5 workers. The magnitude of the slope is 2.5 knitting machines divided by 5, which equals 1/2. Thus when Swanky uses technique *b* to produce 13 sweaters a day, the marginal rate of substitution of labor for capital is 1/2.

The marginal rates of substitution we've just calculated obey the **law of diminishing marginal rate of substitution**, which states that

FIGURE **A10.3**

FIGURE **A10.3**
The Marginal Rate of Substitution

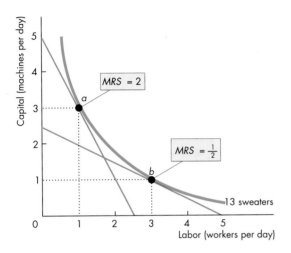

The marginal rate of substitution is measured by the magnitude of the slope of the isoquant. To calculate the marginal rate of substitution at point *a*, use the red line that is tangential to the isoquant at point *a*. Calculate the slope of that line to find the slope of the isoquant at point *a*. The magnitude of the slope at point *a* is 2. Thus at a point *a*, the marginal rate of substitution of labor for capital is 2. The marginal rate of substitution at point *b* is found from the slope of the red line tangential to the isoquant at that point. That slope is 1/2. Thus the marginal rate of substitution of labor for capital at point *b* is 1/2.

The marginal rate of substitution of labor for capital diminishes as the amount of labor increases and the amount of capital decreases.

You can now see that the law of diminishing marginal rate of substitution determines the shape of the isoquant. When the capital input is large and the labor input is small, the isoquant is steep and the marginal rate of substitution of labor for capital is large. As the capital input decreases and the labor input increases, the isoquant becomes flatter and the marginal rate of substitution of labor for capital diminishes. Only curves that are bowed toward the origin have this feature; hence isoquants are always bowed toward the origin.

Isoquants are very nice, but what do we do with them? The answer is that we use them to work out a

FIGURE **A10.4**
Swanky's Input Possibilities

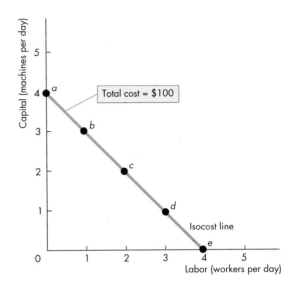

For a given total cost, Swanky's input possibilities depend on input prices. If labor and capital cost $25 a day each, for a total cost of $100 Swanky can employ the combinations of capital and labor shown by the points *a* through *e*. The line passing through these points is an isocost line. It shows all possible combinations of capital and labor that Swanky can hire for a total cost of $100 when capital and labor cost $25 a day each.

firm's least-cost technique of production. But to do so, we need to illustrate the firm's costs in the same sort of figure that contains the isoquants.

Isocost Lines

A FIRM'S COSTS CAN BE ILLUSTRATED BY ISOCOST lines. An **isocost line** shows all the combinations of capital and labor that can be bought for a given total cost. For example, suppose Swanky is going to spend $100 a day producing sweaters. Knitting-machine operators can be hired for $25 a day, and knitting machines can be rented for $25 a day. The points *a*, *b*, *c*, *d*, and *e* in Fig. A10.4 show five possible combinations of labor and capital that Swanky can employ for $100. For example, point *b* shows that Swanky can use 3 machines (costing $75) and 1 worker (costing

$25). If Swanky can employ workers and machines for fractions of a day, then any combination along the line *ae* will cost Swanky $100 a day. This line is Swanky's isocost line for a total cost of $100.

The Isocost Equation

The isocost line can be described by an equation. We'll work out the isocost equation by using symbols that apply to any firm and with numbers that describe Swanky's situation.

The variables that affect the firm's total cost (TC) are the prices of the inputs—the price of labor (P_L) and the price of capital (P_K)—and the quantities of the inputs employed—the quantity of labor (L) and the quantity of capital (K). In Swanky's case, we're going to look at the amount of labor and capital that can be employed when each input costs $25 a day and the total cost is $100. The cost of the labor employed ($P_L L$) plus the cost of the capital employed ($P_K K$) is the firm's total cost (TC). That is,

$$P_L L + P_K K = TC$$

and in Swanky's case,

$$25L + 25K = 100.$$

To calculate the isocost equation, divide the firm's total cost by the price of capital and then subtract $(P_L/P_K)L$ from both sides of the resulting equation. The isocost equation is

$$K = TC/P_K - (P_L/P_K)L$$

It tells us how the firm can vary its capital input as it varies its labor input, holding total cost constant. Swanky's isocost equation is

$$K = 4 - L.$$

This equation corresponds to the isocost line in Fig. A10.4.

The Effect of Input Prices

Along the isocost line that we have just calculated, capital and labor cost $25 a day each. Therefore, to decrease its capital input by 1 unit and keep its total cost at $100 a day, the firm must increase the labor input by 1 unit. The magnitude of the slope of the isocost line shown in Fig. A10.4 is 1. The slope tells us that 1 unit of labor costs 1 unit of capital.

If factor prices change, the slope of the isocost line changes. If the wage rate rises to $50 a day and the rental rate of a machine remains at $25 a day, then 1 worker costs 2 machines and the isocost line becomes steeper—line *B* in Fig. A10.5. If the wage rate remains at $25 a day and the rental rate of a machine rises to $50 a day, then 1 machine costs 2 workers and the isocost line becomes less steep—line *C* in Fig. A10.5.

The higher the relative price of labor, the steeper is the isocost line. The magnitude of the slope of the isocost line measures the relative price of labor in terms of capital—that is, the price of labor divided by the price of capital. As the price of either capital or labor changes, so too does the relative price of labor and the slope of the isocost line.

FIGURE **A10.5**

Input Prices and the Isocost Line

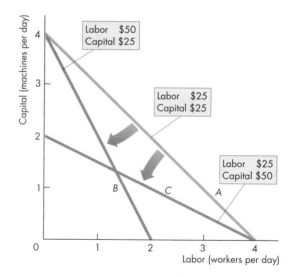

The slope of the isocost line depends on the relative input prices. Three cases are shown (each for a total cost of $100). If the prices of labor and capital are $25 a day each, the isocost line is line A. If the price of labor rises to $50 but the price of capital remains $25, the isocost line becomes steeper and is line B. If the price of capital rises to $50 and the price of labor remains constant at $25, the isocost line becomes flatter and is line C.

The Isocost Map

An **isocost map** shows a series of isocost lines, each for a different total cost when the price of each input is constant. With a larger total cost, larger quantities of all the inputs can be employed. Figure A10.6 illustrates an isocost map. In that figure, the middle isocost line is the one in Fig. A10.4. It is the isocost line for a total cost of $100 when capital and labor cost $25 a day each. The other two isocost lines in Fig. A10.6 are for a total cost of $125 and $75, when the input prices are constant at $25 each.

The Least-Cost Technique

The **least-cost technique** is the combination of inputs that minimizes total cost of producing a given output. Let's suppose that Swanky wants to produce 15 sweaters a day. What is the least-cost way of doing this?

The answer can be seen in Fig. A10.7. The isoquant for 15 sweaters is shown, and the three points on that isoquant (marked *a*, *b*, and *c*) illustrate the three techniques of producing 15 sweaters that are shown in Fig. A10.1. The figure also contains two isocost lines—each drawn for a price of capital and a price of labor of $25. One isocost line is for a total cost of $125, and the other is for a total cost of $100.

First, consider point *a*. Swanky can produce 15 sweaters at point *a* by using 1 worker and 4 machines. The total cost when Swanky uses this technique of production is $125. Point *c*, which uses 4 workers and 1 machine, is another technique by

---

FIGURE **A10.7**

The Least-Cost Technique of Production

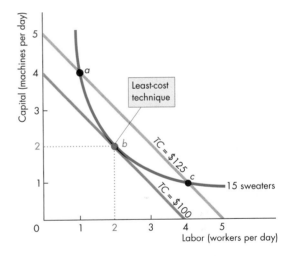

The least-cost technique of producing 15 sweaters is 2 machines and 2 workers (point *b*) and the total cost is $100. An output of 15 sweaters can be produced by using 4 machines and 1 worker (point *a*) or 1 machine and 4 workers (point *c*). But with either of these techniques, the total cost is greater, at $125. At *b*, the isoquant for 15 sweaters is tangential to the isocost line for $100. The isocost line and the isoquant have the same slope. If the isoquant intersects the isocost line—for example, at *a* and *c*—the least-cost technique has not been found. With the least-cost technique, the marginal rate of substitution (slope of isoquant) equals the relative price of the inputs (slope of isocost line).

FIGURE **A10.6**

An Isocost Map

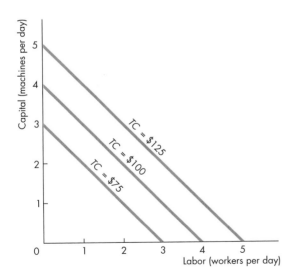

This isocost map shows three isocost lines, one for a total cost of $75, one for $100, and one for $125. For each isocost line, the prices of capital and labor are $25 a day each. The slope of each isocost line is equal to the price of labor divided by the price of capital—a constant. The larger the total cost, the farther is the isocost line from the origin.

which the firm can produce 15 sweaters for a cost of $125.

Next look at point *b*. At this point, Swanky uses 2 machines and 2 workers to produce 15 sweaters at a total cost of $100. Point *b* is the *least-cost technique* or the *economically efficient technique* for producing 15 sweaters when knitting machines and workers cost $25 a day each.

Notice that although there is only one way in which Swanky can produce 15 sweaters for $100, there are several ways of producing 15 sweaters for more than $100. Techniques shown by points *a* and *c* are two examples. All the points between *a* and *b* and all the points between *b* and *c* are also ways of producing 15 sweaters for a cost that exceeds $100 but is less than $125. That is, there are isocost lines between those shown, for total costs between $100 and $125. Those isocost lines cut the isoquant for 15 sweaters at the points between *a* and *b* and between *b* and *c*. Swanky can also produce 15 sweaters for a cost that exceeds $125. That is, the firm can change its technique of production by moving along the isoquant to a point above point *a* or to a point to the right of point *c*. All of these ways of producing 15 sweaters are economically inefficient.

You can see that Swanky cannot produce 15 sweaters for less than $100 by imagining the isocost line for $99. That isocost line will not touch the isoquant for 15 sweaters. That is, the firm cannot produce 15 sweaters for $99. At $25 for a unit of each input, $99 will not buy the inputs required to produce 15 sweaters.

Marginal Rate of Substitution Equals Relative Input Price

At the least-cost technique point *b*, the slope of the isoquant is equal to the slope of the isocost line. Equivalently, when a firm is using the least-cost technique of production, the marginal rate of substitution between the inputs equals their relative price. Recall that the marginal rate of substitution is the magnitude of the slope of an isoquant. Relative input prices are measured by the magnitude of the slope of the isocost line. We've just seen that producing at least cost means producing at a point where the isocost line is tangential to the isoquant. Because the two curves are tangential, their slopes are equal. Hence the marginal rate of substitution (the magnitude of the slope of isoquant) equals the relative input price (the magnitude of the slope of isocost line).

Marginal Product and Marginal Cost in the Long Run

WHEN LONG-RUN COST IS MINIMIZED, THE MARginal cost of increasing output by using one more unit of capital is equal to the marginal cost of increasing output by using one more unit of labor. To see why, we're first going to learn about the relationship between the marginal rate of substitution and marginal product.

Marginal Rate of Substitution and Marginal Products

The marginal rate of substitution and the marginal products are linked together in a formula:

The marginal rate of substitution of labor for capital equals the marginal product of labor divided by the marginal product of capital.

The change in output resulting from a change in inputs is determined by the marginal products of the inputs. That is,

$$\text{Change in output} = (MP_L \times \Delta L) + (MP_K \times \Delta K).$$

That is, the change in output equals the marginal product of labor, MP_L multiplied by the change in labor, ΔL, plus the marginal product of capital, MP_K, multiplied by the change in the capital, ΔK.

Suppose that Swanky wants to change its inputs but remain on an isoquant—that is, it wants to change its inputs of labor and capital but produce the same number of sweaters. To remain on an isoquant, the change in output must be zero. We can make the change of output zero in the above equation; doing so yields the equation

$$MP_L \times \Delta L = -MP_K \times \Delta K.$$

Divide both sides of this equation by the increase in labor (ΔL) and also divide both sides by the marginal product of capital (MP_K) to give

$$MP_L / MP_K = -\Delta K / \Delta L$$

This equation tells us that, when Swanky remains on an isoquant, the decrease in its capital input (ΔK) divided by the increase in its labor input (ΔL) is equal to the marginal product of labor (MP_L)

divided by the marginal product of capital (MP_K). The decrease in capital divided by the increase in labor when we remain on a given isoquant is the marginal rate of substitution of labor for capital. What we have discovered, then, is that the marginal rate of substitution of labor for capital equals the ratio of the marginal product of labor to the marginal product of capital.

Marginal Cost

When the least-cost technique is employed, the slope of the isoquant and the isocost line are the same. That is,

$$MP_L / MP_K = P_L / P_K$$

Rearrange the above equation in the following way. First, multiply both sides by the marginal product of capital and then divide both sides by the price of labor. We then get

$$MP_L / P_L = MP_K / P_K$$

This equation says that the marginal product of labor per dollar spent on labor is equal to the marginal product of capital per dollar spent on capital. In other words, the extra output from the last dollar spent on labor equals the extra output from the last dollar spent on capital. This makes sense. If the extra output from the last dollar spent on labor exceeds the extra output from the last dollar spent on capital, it will pay the firm to use less capital and use more labor. By doing so, it can produce the same output at a lower total cost. Conversely, if the extra output from the last dollar spent on capital exceeds the extra output from the last dollar spent on labor, the firm can lower its cost of producing a given output by

using less labor and more capital. A firm achieves the least-cost technique of production only when the extra output from the last dollar spent on all the inputs is the same.

Marginal cost with fixed capital and variable labor equals marginal cost with fixed labor and variable capital. To see this proposition, simply flip the last equation over and write it as

$$P_L / MP_L = P_K / MP_K .$$

Expressed in words, this equation says that the price of labor divided by its marginal product must equal the price of capital divided by its marginal product. But what is the price of an input divided by its marginal product? The price of labor divided by the marginal product of labor is marginal cost when the capital input is held constant. To see why this is so, first recall the definition of marginal cost: *Marginal cost* is the change in total cost resulting from a unit increase in output. If output increases because one more unit of labor is employed, total cost increases by the cost of the extra labor, and output increases by the marginal product of the labor. So marginal cost is the price of labor divided by the marginal product of labor. For example, if labor costs $25 a day and the marginal product of labor is 2 sweaters, then the marginal cost of a sweater is $12.50 ($25 divided by 2).

The price of capital divided by the marginal product of capital has a similar interpretation. The price of capital divided by the marginal product of capital is marginal cost when the labor input is constant. As you can see from the above equation, with the least-cost technique of production, marginal cost is the same regardless of whether the capital input is constant and more labor is used or the labor input is constant and more capital is used.

> *"Outside the firm, price movements direct production, which is co-ordinated through a series of exchange transactions on the market. Within a firm, these market transactions are eliminated ..."*
>
> RONALD H. COASE *"THE NATURE OF THE FIRM"*

Understanding Firms and Costs

THE ISSUES AND IDEAS

Why do firms exist? They exist, said Ronald Coase, because they enable us to avoid costs arising from market transactions. Without firms, each individual would need to find the best way of selling her or his own resources in a wide range of markets. The time cost of these activities would be extremely large. With firms, each person sells her or his resources to just one firm—the one offering the highest price—and managers direct the resources hired by the firm to their highest value uses.

How do firms' costs change as output changes? Jacob Viner answered this question by drawing a firm's short-run and long-run cost curves. But he didn't get it right, and his mistake can reinforce your understanding of the short-run average cost curve ($SRAC$) and the long-run average cost curve ($LRAC$).

Viner asked his assistant to draw a long-run average cost curve that satisfied two conditions:

- Not rise above any $SRAC$ curve at any point
- Pass through the minimum point of each $SRAC$ curve

Each $SRAC$ curve in Fig. 1 is never below the $LRAC$ and thus satisfies Viner's first condition. But the $LRAC$ curves do not satisfy the second condition—that it pass through the minimum points of each $SRAC$. Viner's wrong version is shown in Fig. 2. Viner's curve does pass through the minimum points of the $SRAC$ curves but it rises above $SRAC$. The curve in Fig. 1 is a long-run average cost curve, and Viner's curve in Fig. 2 is not.

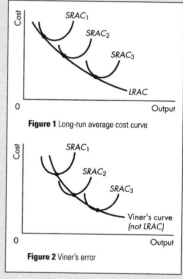

Figure 1 Long-run average cost curve

Figure 2 Viner's error

MANY GOODS cost more to market than to produce. By finding ways to economize on marketing costs, a new firm can find a niche in which to set out on the road to becoming a major player. Dell Computers is such a firm. It buys computers and parts at the lowest possible prices and sells straight to the consumer by direct mail. Dell has cut transaction costs and established itself as a significant player in the global computer market.

Ronald Coase

THE ECONOMISTS: JACOB VINER AND RONALD COASE

The development of our understanding of the working of firms started in the 1930s, and many economists contributed to our advancing knowledge. Two important contributors were Ronald Coase (1910–) and Jacob Viner (1892–1970).

Coase was born in England but has spent most of his life in the United States, which he first visited as a 20-year-old on a traveling scholarship during the depths of the Great Depression. It was on that visit, and before he had completed his bachelor's degree, that he wrote the paper "The Nature of the Firm" which the Swedish Academy of Sciences cited 60 years later as a main contribution to economics when it awarded him the Nobel Prize for Economic Science.

Viner was born in Montreal, Canada, the son of a poor immigrant family from Eastern Europe. He was educated at McGill University and Harvard and taught at the University of Chicago and Princeton. Viner's main contribution was to explain the nature of a firm's costs, and it was he who first described the firm's cost curves that are explained in this chapter.

Jacob Viner

Competition

**After studying
this chapter
you will be
able to:**

- Define perfect competition

- Explain how price and output are
  determined in a competitive industry

- Explain why firms sometimes shut down
  temporarily and lay off workers

- Explain why firms enter and leave an
  industry

- Predict the effects of a change in demand
  and of a technological advance

- Explain why perfect competition is
  efficient

Hot Rivalry in Ice Cream

Ice cream is big business. In the United States in 1994, more than a billion pounds were bought—an average of sixteen pounds per person—at a cost of more than $10 billion. Competition in the ice cream industry is fierce. National names such as Baskin-Robbins and Häagen-Dazs compete with Ben and Jerry's, Bart's, Annabel's, and hundreds of private label store brands for a place in a crowded market. New firms enter and try their luck while other firms are squeezed out of the business. How does competition affect prices and profits? What causes some firms to enter an industry and others to leave it? What are the effects on profits and prices of new firms entering and old firms leaving an industry? ◆ In 1994, on the average, eight million people were unemployed. Of these, more than a million were unemployed because they had been laid off by firms seeking to trim their costs and avoid bankruptcy. Ice cream producers, computer makers, and firms in almost every sector of the economy laid off workers in 1994, even though the economy was expanding and the total number of jobs was growing. Why do firms lay off workers? When will a firm temporarily shut down, laying off its workers? ◆ Over the past few years, there has been a dramatic fall in the prices of personal computers. For example, a slow computer cost almost $4,000 a few years ago, and a fast one costs only $2,000 today. What goes on in an industry when the price of its output decreases sharply? What happens to the profits of the firms producing such goods?

◈ Ice cream, computers, and most other goods are produced by more than one firm, and these firms compete with each other for sales. To study competitive markets, we are going to build a model of a market in which competition is as fierce and extreme as possible—more extreme than in the examples we've just considered. We call this situation "perfect competition."

Perfect Competition

PERFECT COMPETITION IS AN EXTREME FORM OF competition. **Perfect competition** arises when:

- There are many firms, each selling an identical product.
- There are many buyers.
- There are no restrictions on entry into the industry.
- Firms in the industry have no advantage over potential new entrants.
- Firms and buyers are completely informed about the prices of the products of each firm in the industry.

An industry can have a large number of firms only if the demand for its product is large relative to the output level at which average total cost is a minimum. For example, the worldwide demand for corn, rice, and other basic grains is many thousands of times larger than the output that can be produced by a single farm at minimum average cost.

The conditions that define perfect competition imply that no firm can influence the price at which it sells its output. Firms in perfect competition are said to be price takers. A **price taker** is a firm that cannot influence the price of a good or service.

The key reason why a perfectly competitive firm is a price taker is that it produces a tiny fraction of the total output of a particular good and buyers are well-informed about the prices of other firms.

Imagine that you are a wheat farmer in Kansas. You have a thousand acres under cultivation—which sounds like a lot. But then you go on a drive, first heading west. The flat lands turn into rolling hills as you head toward the Rocky Mountains, but everywhere you look, you see thousands and thousands of acres of wheat. The sun goes down in the west behind millions of acres of golden plants. The next morning, it rises in the east above the same scene. Driving to Colorado, Oklahoma, Texas, and back up to Nebraska and the Dakotas reveals similar vistas. You also find unbroken stretches of wheat in Canada, Argentina, Australia, and Ukraine. Your thousand acres is a drop in the ocean.

Nothing makes your wheat any better than any other farmer's, and all the buyers of wheat know the price at which they can do business. If everybody else sells their wheat for $3 a bushel, and you want $3.10,

why would people buy from you? They can simply go to the next farmer, and the one after that, and the next and buy all they need for $3. You are a price taker. A price-taker faces a perfectly elastic demand curve.

The market demand for wheat is not perfectly elastic. The market demand curve is downward-sloping, and its elasticity depends on the substitutability of wheat for other grains such as barley, rye, corn, and rice. However, the demand for wheat from farm *A* is perfectly elastic because wheat from farm *A* is a *perfect substitute* for wheat from farm *B*.

Perfect competition does not occur frequently in the real world. But competition in many industries is so fierce that the model of perfect competition we're about to study is of enormous help in predicting the behavior of the firms in these industries. Ice cream making and retailing, farming, fishing, wood pulping and paper milling, the manufacture of paper cups and plastic shopping bags, grocery retailing, photo finishing, lawn service, plumbing, painting, dry cleaning, and the provision of laundry services are all examples of industries that are highly competitive.

Profit and Revenue

The goal of a firm is to maximize profit, which is the sum of normal profit and economic profit. **Normal profit** is the return that a firm's owner could obtain in the best alternative business. So it is a forgone alternative or *opportunity cost* and part of the firm's total cost. **Economic profit** is equal to total revenue minus total cost.

Total revenue is the value of a firm's sales. It equals the price of the firm's output multiplied by the number of units of output sold (price × quantity). **Average revenue** is total revenue divided by the total quantity sold—revenue per unit sold. Because total revenue equals price multiplied by quantity sold, average revenue (total revenue divided by quantity sold) equals price. **Marginal revenue** is the change in total revenue divided by the change in quantity sold. That is, marginal revenue is the change in total revenue resulting from a one-unit increase in the quantity sold. In perfect competition, the price is constant when the quantity sold changes. So the change in total revenue resulting from a one-unit increase in the quantity sold equals price. Therefore, in perfect competition, marginal revenue equals price.

Figure 11.1 sets out an example of these revenue concepts for Swanky, Inc. The table shows three different quantities of sweaters sold. For a price taker, as the quantity sold varies, the price stays constant—in this example at $25 a sweater. Total revenue is equal to price multiplied by quantity sold. For example, if Swanky sells 8 sweaters, total revenue is 8 times $25, which equals $200. Average revenue is total revenue divided by quantity. Again, if Swanky sells 8 sweaters, average revenue is total revenue ($200) divided by quantity (8), which equals $25 a sweater. Marginal revenue is the change in total revenue resulting from a one-unit change in quantity. For example, when the quantity sold increases from 7 to 8, total revenue increases from $175 to $200, so marginal revenue is $25 a sweater. (Notice that in the table, marginal revenue appears *between* the lines for the quantities sold to remind you that marginal revenue results from the *change* in the quantity sold.)

Suppose that Swanky is one of a thousand similar small producers of sweaters. Figure 11.1(a) shows the demand and supply curves for the entire sweater

industry. Demand curve *D* intersects supply curve *S* at a price of $25 a sweater and a quantity of 7,000 sweaters. Figure 11.1(b) shows Swanky's demand curve. Because the firm is a price taker, its demand curve is perfectly elastic—the horizontal line at $25. The figure also illustrates Swanky's average and marginal revenues. Because average revenue and marginal revenue equal price, the firm's demand curve is also its average revenue curve (*AR*) and its marginal revenue curve (*MR*). That is, the firm's demand curve tells us the revenue per sweater sold and the change in total revenue that results from selling one more sweater. Swanky's total revenue curve, *TR* (part c), shows the total revenue for each quantity sold. For example, when Swanky sells 7 sweaters, total revenue is $175 (point *a*). Because each additional sweater sold brings in a constant amount—$25—the total revenue curve is an upward-sloping straight line.

FIGURE 11.1

Demand, Price, and Revenue in Perfect Competition

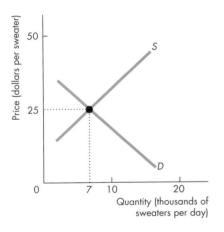

(a) Sweater industry

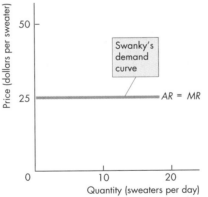

(b) Swanky's demand, average revenue, and marginal revenue

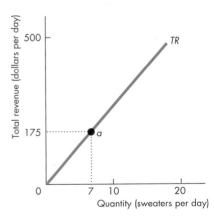

(c) Swanky's total revenue

Quantity sold (Q) (sweaters per day)	Price (P) (dollars per sweater)	Total revenue (TR = P × Q) (dollars)	Average revenue (AR = TR/Q) (dollars per sweater)	Marginal revenue (MR = ΔTR/ΔQ) (dollars per sweater)
7	25	175	25	
				25
8	25	200	25	
				25
9	25	225	25	

The industry demand and supply curves determines the market price. In part (a), the price is $25 a sweater and 7,000 sweaters are bought and sold. Swanky faces a perfectly elastic demand curve at the market price of $25 a sweater, part (b). The table calculates Swanky's total revenue, average revenue, and marginal revenue. Part (b) shows that Swanky's demand curve is also its average revenue curve (*AR*) and marginal revenue curve (*MR*). Part (c) shows Swanky's total revenue curve (*TR*). Point *a* corresponds to the first row of the table.

The Firm's Decisions in Perfect Competition

Firms in a perfectly competitive industry face a given market price and have the revenue curves that you've studied. These revenue curves summarize the market constraint faced by a perfectly competitive firm.

Firms also have a technology constraint, which is described by the product curves (total product, average product, and marginal product) that you studied in Chapter 10. The technology available to the firm determines its costs, which are described by the cost curves (total cost, average cost, and marginal cost) that you also studied in Chapter 10.

The task of the competitive firm is to make the maximum profit possible, given the constraints it faces. To achieve this objective, a firm must make four key decisions: two in the short run and two in the long run.

Short-Run Decisions

The short run is a time frame in which each firm has a given plant and the number of firms in the industry is fixed. But many things can change in the short run and the firm must react to these changes. For example, the price for which the firm can sell its output might have a seasonal fluctuation or it might fluctuate with general business fluctuations.

The firm must react to such short-run price fluctuations and decide:

1. Whether to produce or to shut down
2. If the decision is to produce, what quantity to produce

Long-Run Decisions

The long run is a time frame in which each firm can change the size of its plant and decide whether to leave the industry. Other firms can decide to enter the industry. So in the long run, both the plant size of each firm and the number of firms in the industry can change. Also in the long run, the constraints facing firms can change. For example, the demand for the good can permanently fall. Or technological advance can change the industry's costs.

The firm must react to such long-run changes and decide:

1. Whether to increase or decrease its plant size
2. Whether to stay in the industry or leave it

The Firm and the Industry in the Short Run and the Long Run

To study a competitive industry, we begin by looking at an individual firm's short-run decisions. We then see how the short-run decisions of all firms in a competitive industry combine to determine the industry price, output, and economic profit. Then we turn to the long run and study the effects of long-run decisions on the industry price, output, and economic profit. All the decisions we study are driven by the single objective: to maximize profit.

Profit-Maximizing Output

A perfectly competitive firm maximizes profit by choosing its output level. One way of finding the profit-maximizing output is to study a firm's total revenue and total cost curves and to find the output level at which total revenue exceeds total cost by the largest amount. Figure 11.2 shows how to do this for Swanky, Inc. The table lists Swanky's revenue and total cost at different outputs, and part (a) of the figure shows Swanky's total revenue and total cost curves. These curves are graphs of the numbers shown in the first three columns of the table. The total revenue curve (*TR*) is the same as that in Fig. 11.1(c). The total cost curve (*TC*) is similar to the one that you met in Chapter 10. As output increases, so does total cost.

Economic profit equals total revenue minus total cost. The fourth column of the table in Fig. 11.2 shows Swanky's economic profit, and part (b) of the figure illustrates these numbers as Swanky's profit curve. This curve shows that Swanky makes an economic profit at outputs between 4 and 12 sweaters a day. At outputs less than 4 sweaters a day, Swanky incurs an economic loss. It also incurs an economic loss if output exceeds 12 sweaters a day. At outputs of 4 sweaters and 12 sweaters a day, total cost equals total revenue and Swanky's economic profit is zero. An output at which total cost equals total revenue is called a *break-even point*. The firm's economic profit is zero but because normal profit is part of total cost, a firm makes normal profit at a break-even point. That is, at the break-even point, the owner of the firm makes profit equal to the best alternative return forgone.

Notice the relationship between the total revenue, total cost, and profit curves. Economic profit is measured by the vertical distance between the total

FIGURE   11.2

Total Revenue, Total Cost, and Economic Profit

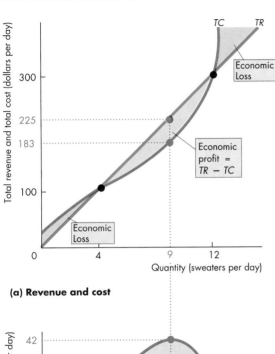

(a) Revenue and cost

(b) Economic profit and loss

Quantity (Q) (sweaters per day)	Total revenue (TR) (dollars)	Total cost (TC) (dollars)	Economic profit (TR – TC) (dollars)
0	0	22	–22
1	25	45	–20
2	50	66	–16
3	75	85	–10
4	100	100	0
5	125	114	11
6	150	126	24
7	175	141	34
8	200	160	40
9	225	183	42
10	250	210	40
11	275	245	30
12	300	300	0
13	325	360	–35

The table lists Swanky's total revenue, total cost, and economic profit. Part (a) graphs the total revenue and total cost curves. Economic profit, in part (a), is the height of the blue area between the total cost and total revenue curves. Swanky makes maximum economic profit, $42 a day ($225 – $183), when it produces 9 sweaters—the output at which the vertical distance between the total revenue and total cost curves is at its largest. At outputs of 4 sweaters a day and 12 sweaters a day, Swanky makes zero economic profit—these are break-even points. At outputs less than 4 and greater than 12 sweaters a day, Swanky incurs an economic loss. Part (b) of the figure shows Swanky's profit curve. The profit curve is at its highest when profit is at a maximum and cuts the horizontal axis at the break-even points.

revenue and total cost curves. When the total revenue curve in part (a) is above the total cost curve, between 4 and 12 sweaters, the firm is making an economic profit, and the profit curve in part (b) is above the horizontal axis. At the break-even point, where the total cost and total revenue curves intersect, the profit curve intersects the horizontal axis. The profit curve is at its highest when the distance between *TR* and *TC* is greatest. In this example, profit maximization occurs at an output of 9 sweaters a day. At this output, Swanky's economic profit is $42 a day.

Marginal Analysis

Another way of finding the profit-maximizing output is to use *marginal analysis*. To use marginal analysis, a firm compares its marginal revenue, *MR,* with its marginal cost, *MC.* As output increases, marginal revenue is constant and marginal cost eventually increases. If marginal revenue exceeds marginal cost (if *MR > MC*), then the extra revenue from selling one more unit exceeds the extra cost incurred to produce it, so profit increases if output increases. If marginal revenue is less than marginal cost (if *MR < MC*), then the extra revenue from selling one more unit is less than the extra cost incurred to produce it, so profit increases if output *decreases*. If marginal revenue equals marginal cost (if *MR = MC*), profit is maximized. The rule *MR = MC* is a prime example of marginal analysis. Let's check that this rule works to find the profit-maximizing output by returning to Swanky's sweater factory.

Look at Fig. 11.3. The table records Swanky's marginal revenue and marginal cost. Focus on the highlighted rows of the table. If Swanky increases output from 8 sweaters to 9 sweaters, marginal revenue is $25 and marginal cost is $23. Because marginal revenue exceeds marginal cost, economic profit increases. The last column of the table shows that profit increases from $40 to $42, an increase of $2. This profit from the ninth sweater is shown as the blue area in the figure.

If Swanky increases output from 9 sweaters to 10 sweaters, marginal revenue is still $25, but marginal cost is $27. Because marginal revenue is less than marginal cost, economic profit decreases. The last column of the table shows that profit decreases from $42 to $40. This loss from the tenth sweater is shown as the red area in the figure.

Swanky maximizes profit by producing 9 sweaters a day, the quantity at which marginal revenue equals marginal cost.

Economic Profit in the Short Run

In the short run, when a firm has set its marginal cost equal to its marginal revenue and maximized profit, it might make an economic profit, break even (making normal profit), or incur an economic loss. To determine which of these three possible outcomes occurs, we need to compare the firm's total revenue and total cost. Alternatively, we can compare price with average total cost. If price exceeds average total

FIGURE 11.3
Profit-Maximizing Output

Quantity (Q) (sweaters per day)	Total revenue (TR) (dollars)	Marginal revenue (MR) (dollars per sweater)	Total cost (TC) (dollars)	Marginal cost (MC) (dollars per sweater)	Economic profit (TR – TC) (dollars)
7	175		141		34
		25		19	
8	200		160		40
		25		23	
9	225		183		42
		25		27	
10	250		210		40
		25		35	
11	275		245		30

Another way of finding the profit-maximizing output is to determine the output at which marginal revenue equals marginal cost. The table shows that if output increases from 8 to 9 sweaters, marginal cost is $23, which is less than the marginal revenue of $25. If output increases from 9 to 10 sweaters, marginal cost is $27, which exceeds the marginal revenue of $25. The figure shows that marginal cost and marginal revenue are equal when Swanky produces 9 sweaters a day. If marginal revenue exceeds marginal cost, an increase in output increases economic profit. If marginal revenue is less than marginal cost, an increase in output decreases economic profit. If marginal revenue equals marginal cost, economic profit is maximized.

cost, a firm makes an economic profit. If price equals average total cost, a firm breaks even—makes normal profit. If price is less than average total cost, a firm incurs an economic loss. But the economic loss incurred is its minimum possible loss. Profit maximization implies loss minimization. Let's look more closely at these three possible outcomes for a firm.

Three Possible Profit Outcomes Figure 11.4 shows the three possible profit outcomes in the short run. In part (a), price exceeds average total cost (*ATC*), and Swanky makes an economic profit. Price and marginal revenue (*MR*) are $25 a sweater, and the profit-maximizing output is 9 sweaters a day. Swanky's total revenue is $225 a day (9 × $25). Average total cost is $20.33 a sweater, and total cost is $183 a day (9 × $20.33). Swanky's economic profit is $42 a day, total revenue of $225 minus total cost of $183. Economic profit also equals economic profit per sweater, which is $4.67 ($25.00 – $20.33), multiplied by the number of sweaters ($4.67 × 9 = $42). The blue rectangle shows this economic profit. The height of that rectangle is profit per sweater, $4.67, and the length is the quantity of sweaters produced,

9 a day, so the area of the rectangle measures Swanky's economic profit of $42 a day.

In part (b), price equals average total cost and Swanky breaks even—makes normal profit and zero economic profit. Price and marginal revenue are $20 a sweater, and the profit-maximizing output is 8 sweaters a day. At this output, average total cost is at its minimum.

In part (c), price is less than average total cost and Swanky incurs an economic loss. Price and marginal revenue are $17 a sweater, and the profit-maximizing (loss-minimizing) output is 7 sweaters a day. Swanky's total revenue is $119 a day (7 × $17). Average total cost is $20.14 a sweater, and total cost is $141 a day (7 × $20.14). Swanky's economic loss is $22 a day, total revenue of $119 minus total cost of $141. Economic loss also equals economic loss per sweater, which is $3.14 ($20.14 – $17.00), multiplied by the number of sweaters ($3.14 × 7 = $22). The red rectangle shows this economic loss. The height of that rectangle is economic loss per sweater, $3.14, and the length is the quantity of sweaters produced, 7 a day, so the area of the rectangle measures Swanky's economic loss of $22 a day.

FIGURE 11.4

Three Possible Profit Outcomes in the Short Run

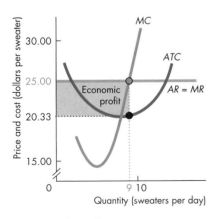

(a) Economic profit

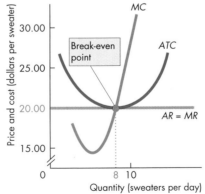

(b) Normal profit

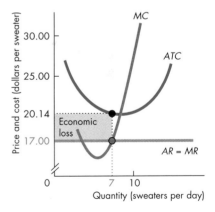

(c) Economic loss

In the short run, firms might make an economic profit, break even (making a normal profit), or incur an economic loss. If the market price exceeds the average total cost of producing the profit-maximizing output, the firm makes an economic profit (the blue rectangle in part a). If price equals minimum average total cost, the firm breaks even and makes a normal profit (part b). If the price is below minimum average total cost, the firm incurs an economic loss (the red rectangle in part c).

The Firm's Short-Run Supply Curve

A perfectly competitive firm's short-run supply curve shows how the firm's profit-maximizing output varies as the market price varies, other things remaining the same. Figure 11.5 shows how to derive Swanky's supply curve. Part (a) shows Swanky's marginal cost and average variable cost curves, and part (b) shows its supply curve. There is a direct link between the marginal cost and average variable cost curves and the supply curve. Let's see what that link is.

Temporary Plant Shutdown   In the short run, a firm cannot avoid incurring its fixed costs but it can avoid variable costs. If a firm produces no output, it incurs a loss equal to its total fixed cost. This loss is the largest that a firm will incur. If the price falls below average variable cost, the firm's profit-maximizing action is to shut down temporarily, lay off its workers, and produce nothing. A firm's **shutdown point** is the output and price at which the firm just covers its total variable cost. At the shutdown point, the firm incurs a loss equal to its total fixed cost. If a firm did produce at a price below its average variable cost, the firm's loss would exceed its total fixed cost. Such a firm would not maximize its profit (minimize its loss). Figure 11.5(a) shows the shutdown point. When the price is $17, the marginal revenue curve is MR_0 and the firm produces 7 sweaters a day at the shutdown point s. At a price below $17, the firm shuts down.

The Short-Run Supply Curve   If the price is above minimum average variable cost, Swanky maximizes profit by producing the output at which marginal cost equals price. We can determine the quantity produced at each price from the marginal cost curve. At a price of $25, the marginal revenue curve is MR_1, and Swanky maximizes profit by producing 9 sweaters. At a price of $31, the marginal revenue curve is MR_2 and Swanky produces 10 sweaters.

Swanky's short-run supply curve, shown in Fig. 11.5(b), has two separate parts: First, at prices that exceed minimum average variable cost, the supply curve is the same as the marginal cost curve above the shutdown point (s). Second, at prices below minimum average variable cost, Swanky shuts down and produces nothing. Its supply curve runs along the vertical axis. At a price of $17, Swanky is indifferent between shutting down and producing 7 sweaters a day. Either way, it incurs a loss of $25 a day.

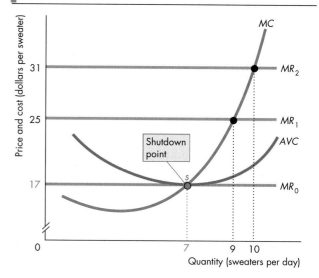

FIGURE 11.5
Swanky's Supply Curve

(a) Marginal cost and average variable cost

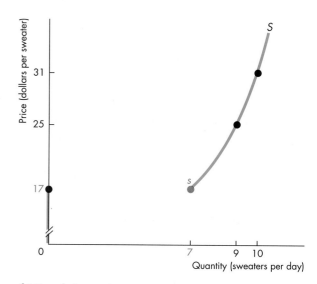

(b) Swanky's supply curve

Part (a) shows Swanky's profit-maximizing output at various market prices. At $25 a sweater, Swanky produces 9 sweaters. At $17 a sweater, Swanky produces 7 sweaters. At any price below $17 a sweater, Swanky produces nothing. Swanky's shutdown point is s. Part (b) shows Swanky's supply curve—the number of sweaters Swanky will produce at each price. It is made up of its marginal cost curve (part a) at all points above its average variable cost curve and the vertical axis at all prices below minimum average variable cost.

Short-Run Industry Supply Curve

The **short-run industry supply curve** shows how the quantity supplied by the industry varies as the market price varies when the plant size of each firm and the number of firms in the industry remain the same. The quantity supplied by the industry at a given price is the sum of the quantities supplied by all firms in the industry at that price. To construct the industry supply curve, we sum horizontally the supply curves of the individual firms.

Suppose that the competitive sweater industry consists of 1,000 firms exactly like Swanky. Figure 11.6 illustrates the industry supply curve. Each of the 1,000 firms in the industry has a supply schedule like Swanky's. The table lists the quantities supplied by a firm and by the industry at each price. At a price below $17, every firm in the industry will shut down; the industry will supply nothing. At $17, each firm is indifferent between shutting down and producing 7 sweaters. Because each firm is indifferent, some firms will produce sweaters and others will shut down. The quantity supplied by the industry can be anything between 0 (all firms shut down) and 7,000 (all firms produce 7 sweaters a day each). Thus at $17, the industry supply curve is horizontal. As the price rises above $17, each firm increases its quantity supplied, and the quantity supplied by the industry increases by 1,000 times that of each firm.

The supply schedules set out in the table form the basis of the industry supply curve in Fig. 11.6. At each price, the quantity supplied by the industry is 1,000 times the quantity supplied by a single firm. At a price of $17 a sweater, a firm supplies either nothing or 7 sweaters a day, so the industry supplies any quantity between zero and 7,000 sweaters. Over that range the industry supply curve is perfectly elastic.

FIGURE 11.6

Industry Supply Curve

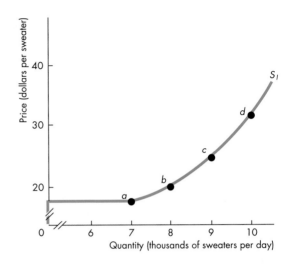

	Price (dollars) per sweater)	Quantity supplied by Swanky, Inc. (sweaters per day)	Quantity supplied by industry (sweaters per day)
a	17	0 or 7	0 to 7,000
b	20	8	8,000
c	25	9	9,000
d	31	10	10,000

The industry supply schedule is the sum of the supply schedules of all individual firms. An industry that consists of 1,000 identical firms has a supply schedule similar to that of the individual firm, but the quantity supplied by the industry is 1,000 times as large as that of the individual firm (see table). The industry supply curve is S_I. Points a, b, c, and d correspond to the rows of the table. At the shutdown price of $17, each firm produces either 0 or 7 sweaters per day. The industry supply curve is perfectly elastic at the shutdown price.

REVIEW

- In perfect competition, a firm is a price taker and its marginal revenue equals the market price.
- If price exceeds average variable cost, a firm maximizes profit by producing the output at which marginal cost equals marginal revenue (equals price). The lowest price at which a firm produces is equal to its minimum average variable cost.
- In the short run, a firm can make an economic profit, break even (make zero economic profit and earn normal profit), or incur an economic loss.

The maximum economic loss that a firm incurs is equal to its total fixed cost.

So far, we have studied a single firm in isolation. We have seen that the firm's profit-maximizing actions depend on the market price, which the firm takes as given. But how is the market price determined? Let's find out.

Output, Price, and Profit in the Short Run

To DETERMINE THE MARKET PRICE AND THE quantity bought and sold in a perfectly competitive market, we need to study the market as a whole. That is, we need to study how market demand and market supply interact. We begin this process by studying a perfectly competitive market in the short run.

Short-Run Equilibrium

The industry demand and supply determines market price and industry output. Figure 11.7(a) shows three different possible short-run equilibrium positions. The supply curve S is the same as S_I in Fig. 11.6. If the demand curve is D_1, the equilibrium price is $25 and industry output is 9,000 sweaters a day. If the demand curve is D_2, the price is $20 and industry output is 8,000 sweaters a day. If the demand curve is D_3, the price is $17 and industry output is 7,000 sweaters a day.

Figure 11.7(b) shows the situation facing each individual firm. With demand curve D_1, the price is $25 a sweater, so each firm produces 9 sweaters a day and makes an economic profit (the blue rectangle); if the demand curve is D_2, the price is $20 a sweater, so each firm produces 8 sweaters a day and makes a zero economic profit (normal profit); and if the demand curve is D_3, the price is $17 a sweater, so each firm produces 7 sweaters a day and incurs an economic loss (the red rectangle).

If the demand curve shifts farther leftward than D_3, the price remains constant at $17 because the industry supply curve is horizontal at that price. Some firms continue to produce 7 sweaters a day, and others shut down. Firms are indifferent between these two activities, and, whichever they choose, they incur an economic loss equal to total fixed cost. The number of firms continuing to produce is just enough to satisfy the market demand at a price of $17.

FIGURE 11.7

Short-Run Equilibrium

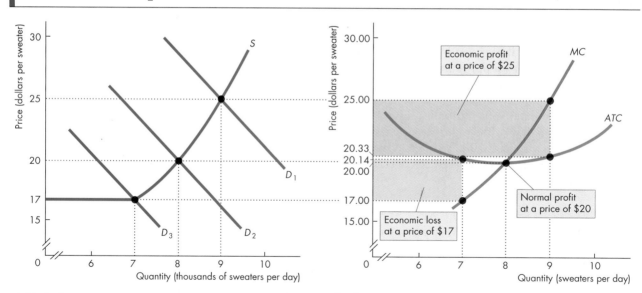

(a) Industry

(b) Firm

In part (a), the competitive sweater industry's supply curve is S. If demand is D_1, the price is $25 and the industry produces 9,000 sweaters. If demand is D_2, the price is $20 and industry output is 8,000 sweaters. If demand is D_3, the price is $17 and industry output is 7,000 sweaters. In part (b), when the price is $25, an individual firm makes an economic profit; when price is $20, it breaks even (makes normal profit); and when the price is $17, it incurs an economic loss.

In the short run, the number of firms and the plant size of each firm are fixed. In the long run, these features of an industry can change. Also, there are forces at work that will disturb some of the short-run situations we've just examined. Let's now look at the forces that operate in the long run.

Output, Price, and Profit in the Long Run

IN SHORT-RUN EQUILIBRIUM, A FIRM MIGHT MAKE an economic profit, incur an economic loss, or break even (make normal profit). Although each of these three situations is a short-run equilibrium, only one of them is a long-run equilibrium. To see why, we need to examine the forces at work in a competitive industry in the long run.

In the long run, an industry adjusts in two ways: The number of firms in the industry changes, and firms change the scale of their plants. Let's study the effects of these two forces in a competitive industry.

The number of firms in an industry changes as a result of entry and exit. *Entry* is the act of setting up a new firm in an industry. *Exit* is the act of a firm leaving an industry. Entry and exit are triggered by economic profit and economic loss, and entry and exit change economic profit and loss. Let's first see how economic profit and loss trigger entry and exit.

Economic Profit and Economic Loss as Signals

An industry in which firms are making an economic profit attracts new entrants; an industry in which firms are incurring an economic loss induces exits; and an industry in which firms are making normal profit (zero economic profit) induces neither entry nor exit. Thus economic profit and economic loss are the signals to which firms respond in making entry and exit decisions.

Temporary economic profits and temporary economic losses that are random, like the winnings and losings at a casino, do not trigger entry or exit. But the prospect of persistent economic profit or loss does.

Entry and exit influence market price, the quantity produced, and economic profit. The immediate effect of entry and exit is to shift the industry supply curve. If more firms enter an industry, the industry supply curve shifts rightward: Supply increases. If firms exit an industry, the industry supply curve shifts leftward: Supply falls. Let's see what happens when new firms enter an industry.

The Effects of Entry

Figure 11.8 shows the effects of entry. Suppose that the demand curve for sweaters is D and the industry supply curve is S_A, so sweaters sell for $23, and 7,000 sweaters are being produced. Firms in the industry are making an economic profit. These economic profits are a signal for firms to enter the industry. As new firms enter, the industry supply curve shifts rightward to S_0. With the greater supply and

FIGURE 11.8

Entry and Exit

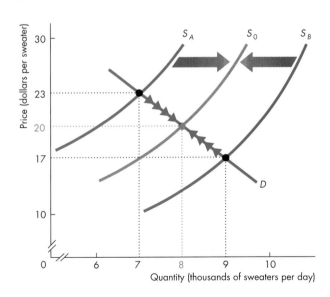

When new firms enter the sweater industry, the industry supply curve shifts rightward, from S_A to S_0. The equilibrium price falls from $23 to $20, and the quantity produced increases from 7,000 to 8,000 sweaters. When firms exit the sweater industry, the industry supply curve shifts leftward, from S_B to S_0. The equilibrium price rises from $17 to $20, and the quantity produced decreases from 9,000 to 8,000 sweaters.

unchanged demand, the market price falls from $23 to $20 a sweater and the quantity produced increases from 7,000 to 8,000 sweaters a day.

As the price falls, Swanky, like each other firm in the industry, moves down along its supply curve and decreases output. That is, for each existing firm in the industry, the profit-maximizing output decreases. Because the price falls and each firm sells less, economic profit decreases. When the price falls to $20, economic profit disappears and each firm makes a normal profit.

You have just discovered a key proposition:

As new firms enter an industry, the price falls and the economic profit of each existing firm decreases.

A good example of this process has occurred in the last few years in the personal computer industry. When IBM introduced its first personal computer in the early 1980s, there was little competition and the price of PCs gave IBM a big profit. But very quickly, new firms such as Compaq, NEC, Dell, and a host of others entered the industry with machines that were technologically identical to IBM's. In fact, they were so similar that they came to be called "clones." The massive wave of entry into the personal computer industry shifted the supply curve rightward and lowered the price and the economic profit for all firms.

Let's now see what happens when firms leave an industry.

The Effects of Exit

Figure 11.8 also shows the effects of exit. Suppose that the demand curve is D and the supply curve is S_B, so the market price is $17 and 9,000 sweaters are being produced. Firms in the industry are incurring an economic loss. These economic losses are a signal for some firms to exit the industry. As firms exit, the supply curve shifts leftward to S_0. With the decrease in supply, industry output decreases from 9,000 to 8,000 sweaters and the price rises from $17 to $20.

As the price rises, Swanky, like each other firm in the industry, moves up along its supply curve and increases output. That is, for each existing firm in the industry, the profit-maximizing output increases. Because the price rises and each firm sells more, economic loss decreases. When the price rises to $20, economic loss disappears and each firm makes a normal profit.

You have just discovered a second key proposition:

As firms leave an industry, the price rises and the economic loss of each remaining firm decreases.

An example of a firm leaving an industry is International Harvester, a manufacturer of farm equipment. For decades, people associated the name "International Harvester" with tractors, combines, and other farm machines. But International Harvester wasn't the only maker of farm equipment. The industry became intensely competitive, and the firm began losing money. Now the company has a new name, Navistar International, and it doesn't make tractors any more. After years of losses and shrinking revenues, it got out of the farm business in 1985 and started to make trucks.

International Harvester exited because it was incurring an economic loss. Its exit decreased supply and made it possible for the remaining firms in the industry to break even.

Long-Run Equilibrium

Long-run equilibrium occurs in a competitive industry when firms are earning normal profit and economic profit is zero. If the firms in a competitive industry make an economic profit, new firms enter the industry and the industry supply curve shifts rightward. As a result, the market price falls and so does the firm's economic profit. Firms continue to enter and economic profit continues to decrease as long as firms in the industry are earning positive economic profits. Only when the economic profit has been eliminated and normal profit is being made do firms stop entering.

If the firms in a competitive industry incur an economic loss, some of the firms exit the industry and the industry supply curve shifts leftward. As a result, the market price rises and the economic loss of each firm remaining in the industry shrinks. Firms continue to leave and economic loss continues to shrink as long as firms in the industry are incurring economic losses. Only when the economic loss has been eliminated and normal profit is being made do firms stop exiting.

So in long-run equilibrium in a competitive industry, firms neither enter nor exit the industry. Each firm in the industry earns normal profits.

Let's now examine the second way in which the competitive industry adjusts in the long run—by firms in the industry changing their plant size.

Changes in Plant Size

A firm changes its plant size if, by doing so, its economic profit increases. Figure 11.9 shows a situation in which Swanky can increase its profit by increasing its plant size. With its current plant, Swanky's marginal cost curve is MC_0, and its short-run average total cost curve is $SRAC_0$. The market price is $25 a sweater, so Swanky's marginal revenue curve is MR_0, and Swanky maximizes profit by producing 6 sweaters a day.

Swanky's long-run average cost curve is $LRAC$. By increasing its plant size—installing more knitting machines—Swanky can move along its long-run average cost curve. As Swanky increases its plant size, its short-run marginal cost curve shifts rightward.

FIGURE 11.9
Plant Size and Long-Run Equilibrium

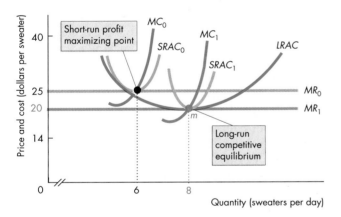

Initially, Swanky's plant has marginal cost curve MC_0 and short-run average total cost curve $SRAC_0$. The market price is $25 a sweater, and Swanky's marginal revenue is MR_0. The short-run profit-maximizing quantity is 6 sweaters a day. Swanky can increase its profit by increasing its plant size. If all firms in the sweater industry increase their plant sizes, the short-run industry supply increases and the market price falls. In long-run equilibrium, a firm operates with the plant size that minimizes its average cost. Here, Swanky operates the plant with short-run marginal cost MC_1 and short-run average cost $SRAC_1$. Swanky is also on its long-run average cost curve $LRAC$ and produces at point m. Its output is 8 sweaters a day, and its average total cost equals the price of a sweater—$20.

Recall that a firm's short-run supply curve is linked to its marginal cost curve. As Swanky's marginal cost curve shifts rightward, so does its supply curve. If Swanky and the other firms in the industry increase their plants, the short-run industry supply curve shifts rightward and the market price falls. The fall in the market price limits the extent to which Swanky can profit from increasing its plant size.

Figure 11.9 also shows Swanky in a long-run competitive equilibrium. This situation arises when the market price has fallen to $20 a sweater. Marginal revenue is MR_1, and Swanky maximizes profit by producing 8 sweaters a day. In this situation, Swanky cannot increase its profit by changing its plant size. It is producing at minimum long-run average cost (point m on $LRAC$).

Because Swanky is producing at minimum long-run average cost, it has no incentive to change its plant size. Either a bigger plant or a smaller plant has a higher long-run average cost. If Fig. 11.9 describes the situation of all firms in the sweater industry, the industry is in long-run equilibrium. No firm has an incentive to change its plant size. Also, because each firm is making zero economic profit (normal profit), no firm has an incentive to enter the industry or to leave it.

R E V I E W

Long-run equilibrium in a competitive industry is described by three conditions:

- Firms maximize short-run profit by producing the quantity that makes marginal cost equal to marginal revenue and price.
- Economic profits are zero, so no firm has an incentive to enter or to leave the industry.
- Long-run average cost is at a minimum, so no firm has an incentive to change its plant size.

We've seen how economic loss triggers exit, which eventually eliminates the loss, and we've seen how economic profit triggers entry, which eventually eliminates the profit. In the long run, normal profit is earned. But a competitive industry is rarely in a long-run equilibrium. It is restlessly evolving toward such an equilibrium and the constraints that firms in the industry face are constantly changing. The two most persistent sources of change are in tastes and technology. Let's see how a competitive industry reacts to such changes.

Changing Tastes and Advancing Technology

INCREASED AWARENESS OF THE HEALTH HAZARD of smoking has caused a decrease in the demand for tobacco and cigarettes. The development of inexpensive car and air transportation has caused a huge decrease in the demand for long-distance trains and buses. Solid-state electronics have caused a large decrease in the demand for TV and radio repair. The development of good-quality inexpensive clothing has decreased the demand for sewing machines. What happens in a competitive industry when there is a permanent decrease in the demand for its products?

The development of the microwave oven has produced an enormous increase in demand for paper, glass, and plastic cooking utensils and for plastic wrap. The demand for almost all products is steadily increasing as a result of increasing population and increasing incomes. What happens in a competitive industry when the demand for its product increases?

Advances in technology are constantly lowering the costs of production. New biotechnologies have dramatically lowered the costs of producing many food and pharmaceutical products. New electronic technologies have lowered the cost of producing just about every good and service. What happens in a competitive industry when technological change lowers its production costs?

Let's use the theory of perfect competition to answer these questions.

A Permanent Change in Demand

Figure 11.10(a) shows a competitive industry that initially is in long-run equilibrium. The demand curve is D_0, the supply curve is S_0, the market price is P_0, and industry output is Q_0. Figure 11.10(b) shows a single firm in this initial long-run equilibrium. The firm produces q_0 and makes a normal profit and zero economic profit.

Now suppose that demand decreases and the demand curve shifts leftward to D_1, as shown in part (a). The price falls to P_1, and the quantity supplied by the industry decreases from Q_0 to Q_1 as the industry slides down its short-run supply curve S_0. Part (b) shows the situation facing a firm. Price is now below the firm's minimum average total cost, so the firm incurs an economic loss. But to keep its loss to a

minimum, the firm adjusts its output to keep marginal cost equal to price. At a price of P_1, each firm produces an output of q_1.

The industry is now in short-run equilibrium but not long-run equilibrium. It is in short-run equilibrium because each firm is maximizing profit. But it is not in long-run equilibrium because each firm is incurring an economic loss—its average total cost exceeds the price.

The economic loss is a signal for some firms to leave the industry. As they do so, short-run industry supply decreases and the supply curve shifts leftward. As industry supply decreases, the price rises. At each higher price, a firm's profit-maximizing output is greater, so the firms remaining in the industry increase their output as the price rises. Each firm slides up its marginal cost or supply curve (part b). That is, as firms exit the industry, industry output decreases but the output of the firms that remain in the industry increases. Eventually, enough firms leave the industry for the industry supply curve to have shifted to S_1 (part a). At this time, the price has returned to its original level, P_0. At this price, the firms remaining in the industry produce q_0, the same quantity that they produced before the decrease in demand. Because firms are now making normal profits and zero economic profit, no firm wants to enter or exit the industry. The industry supply curve remains at S_1, and industry output is Q_2. The industry is again in long-run equilibrium.

The difference between the initial long-run equilibrium and the final long-run equilibrium is the number of firms in the industry. A permanent decrease in demand has decreased the number of firms. Each remaining firm produces the same output in the new long-run equilibrium as it did initially and earns a normal profit. In the process of moving from the initial equilibrium to the new one, firms that remain in the industry incur economic losses.

The market for mainframe computers is one that has experienced a decrease in demand in recent years. As personal computers have become faster and cheaper, more and more data processing has been done on people's desktops rather than in big computer laboratories. The effects of this decrease in demand have been similar to those we have just studied. You can learn more about the market for mainframe computers by studying *Reading Between the Lines* on pp. 264–265.

We've just worked out how a competitive industry responds to a permanent *decrease* in demand. A permanent increase in demand triggers a similar

FIGURE   11.10

A Decrease in Demand

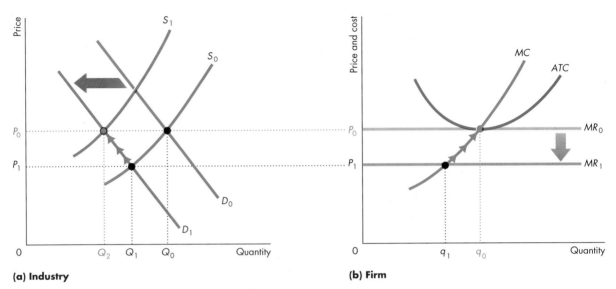

(a) Industry

(b) Firm

An industry starts out in long-run competitive equilibrium. Part (a) shows the industry demand curve D_0, the industry supply curve S_0, the equilibrium quantity Q_0, and the market price P_0. Each firm sells its output at price P_0, so its marginal revenue curve is MR_0 in part (b). Each firm produces q_0 and makes a normal profit. Demand decreases permanently from D_0 to D_1 (part a). The equilibrium price falls to P_1, each firm decreases its output to q_1 (part b), and industry output decreases to Q_1 (part a).

In this new situation, firms incur economic losses and some firms leave the industry. As they do so, the industry supply curve gradually shifts leftward, from S_0 to S_1. This shift gradually raises the market price from P_1 back to P_0. While the price is below P_0, firms incur economic losses and some firms leave the industry. Once the price has returned to P_0, each firm makes a normal profit. Firms have no further incentive to leave the industry. Each firm produces q_0, and industry output is Q_2.

response, except in the opposite direction. The increase in demand brings a higher price, economic profit, and entry. Entry increases industry supply and eventually lowers the price to its original level.

We've now studied about the effects of a permanent change in taste that brings a permanent change in demand for a good. To study these effects, we began and ended in a long-run equilibrium and examined the process that takes a market from one equilibrium to another. It is this process, not the equilibrium points, that describes the real world.

One feature of the predictions that we have just generated seems odd: In the long run, regardless of whether demand increases or decreases, the price returns to its original level. Is this outcome inevitable? In fact, it is not. It is possible for the long-run equilibrium price to remain the same, rise, or fall.

External Economies and Diseconomies

The change in the long-run equilibrium price depends on external economies and external diseconomies. **External economies** are factors beyond the control of an individual firm that lower its costs as the *industry* output increases. **External diseconomies** are factors outside the control of a firm that raise the firm's costs as industry output increases. With no external economies or external diseconomies, a firm's costs remain constant as the industry output changes.

Figure 11.11 illustrates these three cases and introduces a new supply concept: the long-run industry supply curve. A **long-run industry supply curve** shows how the quantity supplied by an industry varies as the market price varies after all the possible adjustments have been made, including changes in plant size and the number of firms in the industry.

Part (a) shows the case we have just studied—no external economies or diseconomies. The long-run industry supply curve (LS_A) is perfectly elastic. In this case, a permanent increase in demand from D_0 to D_1 has no effect on the price in the long run. The increase in demand brings a temporary increase in price to P_S and a short-run quantity increase from Q_0 to Q_S. Entry increases short-run supply from S_0 to S_1, which lowers the price to its original level, P_0, and increases the quantity to Q_1.

Part (b) shows the case of external diseconomies. The long-run supply industry curve (LS_B) slopes upward. A permanent increase in demand from D_0 to D_1 increases the price in both the short run and the long run. As in the previous case, the increase in demand brings a temporary increase in price to P_S and a short-run quantity increase from Q_0 to Q_S. Entry increases short-run supply from S_0 to S_1, which lowers the price to P_2 and increases the quantity to Q_2.

One source of external diseconomies is conges-

tion. The airline industry provides a good example. With bigger airline industry output, there is more congestion of airports and airspace, which results in longer delays and extra waiting time for passengers and airplanes. These external diseconomies mean that as the output of air transportation services increases (in the absence of technological advances), average cost increases. As a result, the long-run supply curve is upward sloping. So a permanent increase in demand brings an increase in quantity and a rise in the price. Technological advances decrease costs and *shift* the long-run supply curve downward. So even an industry that experiences external diseconomies might have falling prices over the long run.

Part (c) shows the case of external economies. In this case, the long-run industry supply curve (LS_C) slopes downward. A permanent increase in demand from D_0 to D_1 increases the price in the short run and lowers it in the long run. Again, the increase in demand brings a temporary increase in price to P_S, and a short-run quantity increase from Q_0 to Q_S. Entry increases short-run supply from S_0 to S_3, which lowers the price to P_3 and increases the quantity to Q_3.

FIGURE 11.11

Long-Run Changes in Price and Quantity

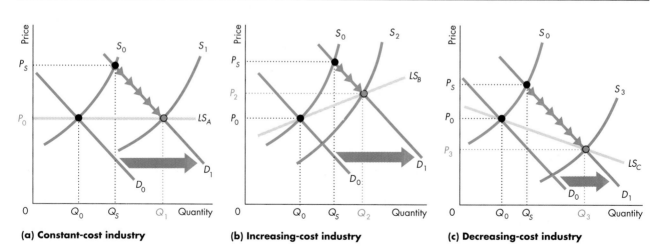

(a) Constant-cost industry

(b) Increasing-cost industry

(c) Decreasing-cost industry

Three possible changes in price and quantity occur in the long run. When demand increases from D_0 to D_1, entry occurs and the industry supply curve shifts from S_0 to S_1. In part (a), the long-run supply curve, LS_A, is horizontal. The quantity increases from Q_0 to Q_1 and the price remains constant at P_0. In part (b),

the long-run supply curve is LS_B; the price rises to P_2, and the quantity increases to Q_2. This case occurs in industries with external diseconomies. In part (c), the long-run supply curve is LS_C; the price falls to P_3, and the quantity increases to Q_3. This case occurs in an industry with external economies.

One of the best examples of external economies is the growth of specialist support services for an industry as it expands. As farm output increased in the nineteenth and early twentieth centuries, the services available to farmers expanded and average farm costs fell. For example, new firms specialized in the development and marketing of farm machinery and fertilizers. As a result, average farm costs decreased. Farms enjoyed the benefits of external economies. As a consequence, as the demand for farm products increased, the output increased but the price fell.

Over the long term, the prices of many goods and services have fallen, not because of external economies but because of technological change. Let's now study this influence on a competitive market.

Technological Change

Industries are constantly discovering lower-cost techniques of production. Most cost-saving production techniques cannot be implemented, however, without investing in new plant and equipment. As a consequence, it takes time for a technological advance to spread through an industry. Some firms whose plants are on the verge of being replaced will be quick to adopt the new technology, while other firms whose plants have recently been replaced will continue to operate with an old technology until they can no longer cover their average variable cost. Once average variable cost cannot be covered, a firm will scrap even a relatively new plant (embodying an old technology) in favor of a plant with a new technology.

New technology allows firms to produce at a lower cost. As a result, as firms adopt a new technology, their cost curves shift downward. With lower costs, firms are willing to supply a given quantity at a lower price, or, equivalently, they are willing to supply a larger quantity at a given price. In other words, industry supply increases, and the industry supply curve shifts rightward. With a given demand, the quantity produced increases and the price falls.

Two forces are at work in an industry undergoing technological change. Firms that adopt the new technology make an economic profit. So there is entry by new-technology firms. Firms that stick with the old technology incur economic losses. They either exit the industry or switch to the new technology.

As old-technology firms disappear and new-technology firms enter, the price falls and the quantity produced increases. Eventually, the industry arrives at a long-run equilibrium in which all the firms use the new technology, and make a zero economic profit (a normal profit). Because in the long run competition eliminates economic profit, technological change brings only temporary gains to producers. But the lower prices and better products that technological advances bring are permanent gains for consumers.

The process that we've just described is one in which some firms experience economic profits and others experience economic losses. It is a period of dynamic change for an industry. Some firms do well, and others do badly. Often, the process has a geographical dimension—the expanding new technology firms bring prosperity to what was once the boondocks and traditional industrial regions decline. Sometimes, the new-technology firms are in a foreign country, while the old-technology firms are in the domestic economy. The information revolution of the 1990s has produced many examples of changes like these. Commercial banking, traditionally concentrated in New York, San Francisco, and other large cities now flourishes in Charlotte, North Carolina, which has become the nation's number three commercial banking city. Television shows and movies, traditionally made in Los Angeles and New York, are now made in large numbers in Orlando. Technological advances are not confined to the information and entertainment industry. Even milk production is undergoing a major technological change.

R E V I E W

- A decrease in demand in a competitive industry brings a fall in price, economic loss, and exit. Exit decreases industry supply, which brings a rise in price. In the long run, enough firms exit for those remaining to make a normal profit.

- An increase in demand in a competitive industry brings a rise in price, economic profit, and entry. Entry increases industry supply, which brings a fall in price. In the long run, enough firms enter for the economic profit to decrease to zero and leave firms making a normal profit.

- A new technology lowers costs, increases industry supply, and lowers price. New-technology firms make an economic profit and enter. Old-technology firms incur an economic loss and exit. In the long run, all remaining firms adopt the new technology and make normal profit.

Competition and Efficiency

IS PERFECT COMPETITION EFFICIENT? TO ANSWER this question, we need to describe the conditions that prevail when efficiency has been achieved.

Allocative Efficiency

Allocative efficiency occurs when no resources are wasted. If someone can be made better off without making someone else worse off, resources are being wasted and efficiency has not been achieved. To achieve allocative efficiency, three conditions must be satisfied. They are:

1. Producer efficiency
2. Consumer efficiency
3. Exchange efficiency

Producer efficiency occurs when firms cannot decrease the cost of producing a given output by changing the factors of production used. Two separate conditions must be met to achieve producer efficiency. The first is *technological efficiency,* which is achieved when a firm is producing the maximum possible output from its factors of production. The second is *economic efficiency*, which is achieved when a firm is using the combination of inputs that minimizes the cost of producing a given output.

A firm achieves producer efficiency if it operates at a point on its marginal cost curve, or equivalently, on its supply curve. An industry achieves producer efficiency if it produces at a point on the industry supply curve. If all firms in all industries minimize cost, the economy is at a point on its *production possibility frontier* (See Chapter 3, pp. 44–46).

Consumer efficiency occurs when consumers cannot make themselves better off—cannot increase utility—by reallocating their budget. Consumer efficiency is achieved at all points along a demand curve.

Exchange efficiency occurs when the price at which a transaction takes place equals marginal social cost and also equals marginal social benefit. **Marginal social cost** is the cost of producing one additional unit of output, including external costs. **Marginal social benefit** is the dollar value of the benefit from one additional unit of consumption, including any external benefits. **External costs** are costs not borne by the producer but borne by other members of society, such as the costs of pollution.

External benefits are benefits accruing to people other than the buyer of a good, such as the pleasure we get from well-designed buildings and beautiful works of art in public galleries. As long as *someone* buys these things, *everyone* can enjoy them.

Figure 11.12 illustrates allocative efficiency. The marginal social benefit curve is *MSB*, and the marginal social cost curve is *MSC*. Imagine that output is restricted to Q_0. Marginal social cost is C_0 and marginal social benefit is B_0. Producers are willing to supply more of the good for a price lower than B_0. Consumers are willing to buy more of the good for a price higher than C_0. Everyone would like to trade more. But once output has increased to Q^*, the benefit to the consumer of the last unit equals its cost of production. To make more of the good available to one person would impose a cost on some other person greater than the benefit received. Allocative efficiency occurs at a quantity Q^* and price P^*. In this situation, no one can be made better off without someone else being made worse off—no resources are being wasted.

Efficiency of Perfect Competition

Perfect competition delivers allocative efficiency if there are no external costs and benefits. In such a case, all the benefits accrue to the buyers of a good and the costs are borne by its producer. In that case, the marginal social benefit curve is the same as the industry demand curve and the marginal social cost curve is the industry supply curve. With perfect competition, price and quantity are determined at the point of intersection of the demand and supply curves. Hence, in Fig. 11.12, a perfectly competitive market produces an output Q^* at a price P^* and allocative efficiency is achieved.

Adam Smith believed each participant in a competitive market is "led by an invisible hand to promote an end [efficiency] which was no part of his intention." You can see the invisible hand at work in the cartoon. When there is no demand for ice cream but there is a demand for shade, the ice cream vendor temporarily exits the ice cream market and enters the sunshade market. A transaction occurs that makes two people better off.

There are two main obstacles to allocative efficiency:

1. External costs and external benefits
2. Monopoly

FIGURE 11.12
Allocative Efficiency

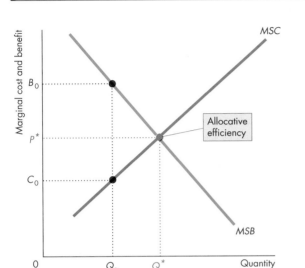

Allocative efficiency requires *producer efficiency,* which occurs when firms are on their supply curves; *consumer efficiency,* which occurs when consumers are on their demand curves; and *exchange efficiency,* which occurs when price equals marginal social cost (*MSC*) and also equals marginal social benefit (*MSB*). Allocative efficiency occurs at output Q^*. If output is Q_0, marginal social cost, C_0, is less than marginal social benefit, B_0. The benefit from one additional unit of output exceeds its cost. A perfectly competitive market is allocative efficient if there are no external costs and external benefits.

External Costs and External Benefits   Such goods as national defense, the enforcement of law and order, the provision of clean drinking water, and the disposal of sewage and garbage are examples of goods and services with enormous external benefits. Left to competitive markets, too small a quantity of them would be produced. The production of steel and chemicals can generate air and water pollution and perfect competition might produce too large a quantity of these goods. Government institutions and policies (in Chapters 19 and 21) arise, in part, because of external costs and benefits.

Monopoly   Monopoly (in Chapter 12) restricts output to below its competitive level to raise price and increase profit. Government policies (in Chapter 20) arise to limit such use of monopoly power.

Drawing by M. Twohy; © 1985 The New Yorker Magazine, Inc.

◆ We have now completed our study of perfect competition. Although many markets approximate the model of perfect competition, many do not. Our next task, in Chapters 12 and 13, is to study markets that depart from perfect competition. When we have completed this study, we'll have a toolkit of alternative models of markets that will enable us to study all the possible situations that arise in the real world. We begin, in the next chapter, by going to the opposite extreme of perfect competition—pure monopoly. Then, in Chapter 13, we'll study the markets between perfect competition and pure monopoly—monopolistic competition and oligopoly (competition among a few producers).

Competition: The Market for Mainframe Computers

THE CHICAGO TRIBUNE, MAY 9, 1994

A Bit of Stability Seen Returning to Mainframe Market

BLOOMBERG BUSINESS NEWS

SUNNYVALE, Calif.—Prices for mainframe computers, those dinosaurs, finally seem to have steadied.

The big names in the $19 billion global mainframe market were profitable or approaching the break-even point in the first quarter after three years of collapsing prices.

"We were quite pleased with our first quarter because we ran ahead of expectations," said Edward Thompson, chief financial officer of Amdahl Corp., which competes in mainframes against International Business Machines Corp., Fujitsu Ltd. and Hitachi Ltd. "Pricing was a little more stable than expected."

Amdahl's ... revenue of $378.8 million fell less than 1 percent from the same period last year. Over the last four quarters, Amdahl revenue has dipped more than 30 percent.

The mainframe-maker has lost more than $587 million since 1991, its last profitable year. It has axed almost half its 10,000 employees and undergone a wrenching change as its bread-and-butter IBM-compatible mainframes fell out of favor when computer customers turned to cheaper personal computers and workstations. ...

In the last five years sales of mainframes, which run the computer operations of banks, phone companies and airlines, fell to about 2,775 machines from 4,700, International Data Corp. estimates. Dollar revenue from mainframes fell about 40 percent from $30 billion in 1988.

Since 1990 prices for top-of-the-line IBM Enterprise System 9000s, Amdahl 5995Ms or Hitachi GX 8824s have been halved. Last year IBM scrapped list prices for its mainframes, which used to run as high as $25 million.

"Prices just can't go down any more," says David Carlson, a pricing expert with Spectrum Economics in Palo Alto, Calif. "What was going on is that you had sufficiently high profits for mainframes and there was a relative lack of competition, so that you could charge prices way above the cost of production."

But shipments of more than 150 million PCs and tens of thousands of workstations at competitive prices shifted computer processing from the traditional data center to the desktop.

Now mainframes may be coming back. Corporate computer users need ever-more-powerful file servers to run their networks of PCs. What server could have more power than a mainframe? ...

Reprinted by permission.

Economic

A N A L Y S I S

■ The mainframe computer market has a small number of producers, but it is highly competitive. The industry is fairly easy to enter, and some firms, such as Amdahl, account for a small proportion of total sales. (The data in the news story imply that Amdahl has a 7 percent market share.)

■ We can interpret Amdahl and other small producers as being price takers.

■ Part (a) of the figure shows the mainframe market. The supply curve is S. In 1988, the demand curve was D_{88}. The market price was P_{88}, and the quantity of mainframes sold was Q_{88}.

■ Because of competition from low-cost PCs and workstations, the demand for mainframes decreased. By 1993, the demand curve was D_{93}. The market price fell to P_{93}, and the quantity sold decreased to Q_{93}.

■ Part (b) of the figure shows the situation facing a single (small) producer such as Amdahl. The firm's marginal cost curve is MC, and its average total cost curve is ATC.

■ Assuming that Amdahl is a price taker, its marginal revenue curve is horizontal at the market price.

■ In 1988, Amdahl's marginal revenue curve was MR_{88}. Amdahl's profit-maximizing quantity was q_{88}. At this quantity, Amdahl's marginal cost equals marginal revenue (price).

■ Amdahl made an economic profit, shown by the blue rectangle in part (b).

■ By 1993, the market price had fallen to P_{93}, and Amdahl's marginal revenue curve had shifted to MR_{93}. Amdahl's profit-maximizing quantity fell to q_{93}.

■ In 1993, Amdahl incurred an economic loss, shown by the red rectangle in part (b).

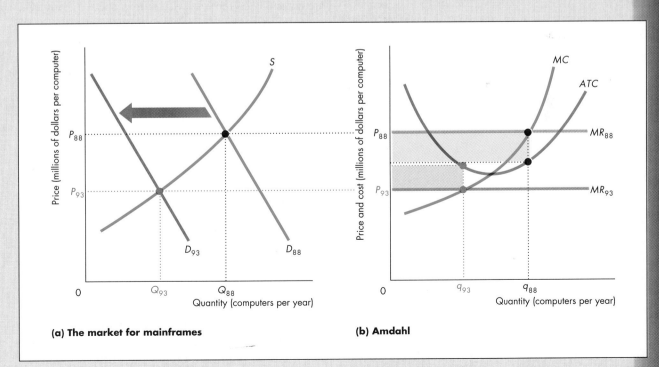

(a) The market for mainframes

(b) Amdahl

S U M M A R Y

Perfect Competition

A perfectly competitive firm is a price taker. It chooses how much to produce, whether to temporarily shut down, its scale, and whether to permanently leave an industry. The firm's choices are motivated by its desire to maximize profit.

If price is greater than average total cost, the firm makes an economic profit. If price equals average total cost, the firm breaks even—makes a normal profit. If price is below average total cost, the firm incurs an economic loss. If price is below minimum average variable cost, the firm maximizes profit by temporarily shutting down. When price equals minimum average variable cost, the firm incurs an economic loss equal to its total fixed costs whether it produces the profit-maximizing output or shuts down.

The firm's supply curve is the upward-sloping part of its marginal cost curve above minimum average variable cost and the vertical axis at all prices below its minimum average variable cost. (pp. 246–253)

Output, Price, and Profit in the Short Run

The short-run industry supply curve shows how the total quantity supplied in the short run by all the firms in an industry varies as the market price varies.

Equality of the quantity supplied and the quantity demanded determines the market price. Each firm takes the market price as given and chooses the output that maximizes profit. In short-run equilibrium, each firm can make an economic profit, incur an economic loss, or break even. (pp. 254–255)

Output, Price, and Profit in the Long Run

If the firms in an industry make economic profits, new firms enter the industry and existing firms might increase their plant size. If the firms in an industry incur economic losses, some firms will leave the industry and the remaining firms might decrease their plant size. Entry and exit and changes in plant size change the short-run industry supply. As firms enter, the short-run industry supply increases. As firms exit, the short-run industry supply decreases.

Entry decreases the economic profit of existing firms, and exit decreases the economic loss of remaining firms. In long-run equilibrium, economic profit is zero and firms make normal profit. No firm will enter or leave the industry, and no firm will increase or decrease its plant size.

Long-run equilibrium occurs when each firm produces the output that maximizes profit (marginal revenue equals marginal cost); economic profit is zero (normal profit is earned), so there is no entry or exit; and each firm produces at the point of minimum long-run average cost, so it has no incentive to change its plant size. (pp. 255–257)

Changing Tastes and Advancing Technology

In a perfectly competitive market, a permanent decrease in demand leads to a smaller industry output and a smaller number of firms in the industry. A permanent increase in demand leads to an increase in industry output and an increase in the number of firms in the industry. If there are no external economies or diseconomies, the market price remains constant in the long run as demand changes. If there are external economies, price falls in the long run as demand increases. If there are external diseconomies, price increases in the long run as demand increases.

New technology increases the industry supply, and in the long run the market price falls and the quantity sold increases. Firms that are slow to change to the new technology will incur economic losses and eventually will go out of business. Firms that are quick to adopt the new technology will make economic profits initially, but in the long run they will make zero economic profit. (pp. 258–261)

Competition and Efficiency

Allocative efficiency occurs when no one can be made better off without making someone else worse off. Three conditions for allocative efficiency—producer efficiency, consumer efficiency, and exchange efficiency—occur in perfect competition when there are no external costs and external benefits.

The two main obstacles to the achievement of allocative efficiency are the existence of external costs and external benefits and monopoly. (pp. 262–263)

KEY ELEMENTS

REVIEW QUESTIONS

1. What are the main features of a perfectly competitive industry?

2. Why can't a perfectly competitive firm influence the industry price?

3. List the four key decisions that a firm in a perfectly competitive industry has to make to maximize profit.

4. Why is marginal revenue equal to price in a perfectly competitive industry?

5. When will a perfectly competitive firm temporarily stop producing?

6. In a perfectly competitive industry, what is the connection between the firm's supply curve and its marginal cost curve?

7. In a perfectly competitive industry, what is the relationship between a firm's supply curve and the short-run industry supply curve?

8. When will firms enter an industry and when will they leave it?

9. What happens to the short-run industry supply curve when firms enter a competitive industry?

10. What is the effect of entry on the market price and quantity produced?

11. What is the effect of entry on economic profit?

12. Trace the effects of a permanent increase in demand on price, quantity sold, number of firms, and economic profit.

13. Trace the effects of a permanent decrease in demand on price, quantity sold, number of firms, and economic profit.

14. What are external economies and external diseconomies?

15. Under what circumstances will a perfectly competitive industry have
    a. A perfectly elastic long-run supply curve
    b. An upward-sloping long-run supply curve
    c. A downward-sloping long-run supply curve

16. What is allocative efficiency and under what circumstances does it arise?

17. What are external costs and external benefits?

18. What is economic efficiency?

19. What is consumer efficiency?

20. What are marginal social cost and marginal social benefit?

21. Under what conditions is perfect competition not allocatively efficient?

P R O B L E M S

1. Quick Copy is one of the many copy shops near the campus. The figure shows Quick Copy's cost curves.
   a. If the market price of copying one page is 10 cents, what is Quick Copy's profit-maximizing output?
   b. Calculate Quick Copy's profit.

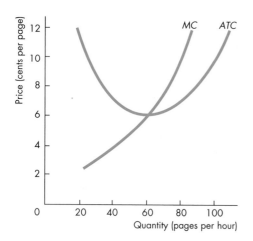

◆ 2. Pat's Pizza Kitchen is a price taker. It has the following hourly costs:

Output (pizzas per hour)	Total cost (dollars per hour)
0	10
1	21
2	30
3	41
4	54
5	69
6	86

   a. If pizzas sell for $14, what is Pat's profit-maximizing output per hour? How much economic profit does Pat make?
   b. What is Pat's shutdown point?
   c. Derive Pat's supply curve.
   d. What range of prices will cause Pat to leave the pizza industry?
   e. What range of prices will cause other firms with costs identical to Pat's to enter the industry?
   f. What is the long-run equilibrium price of pizzas?

◆ 3. The market demand schedule for cassettes is as follows:

Price (dollars per cassettes)	Quantity demanded (cassettes per week)
3.65	500,000
4.40	475,000
5.20	450,000
6.00	425,000
6.80	400,000
7.60	375,000
8.40	350,000
9.20	325,000
10.00	300,000
10.80	275,000
11.60	250,000
12.40	225,000
13.20	200,000
14.00	175,000
14.80	150,000

The market is perfectly competitive, and each firm has the following cost structure:

Output (cassettes per week)	Marginal cost	Average variable cost (dollars per cassette)	Average total cost
150	6.00	8.80	15.47
200	6.40	7.80	12.80
250	7.00	7.00	11.00
300	7.65	7.10	10.43
350	8.40	7.20	10.06
400	10.00	7.50	10.00
450	12.40	8.00	10.22
500	12.70	9.00	11.00

There are 1,000 firms in the industry.
   a. What is the market price?
   b. What is the industry's output?
   c. What is the output of each firm?
   d. What is the economic profit of each firm?
   e. What is the shutdown point?

f. What is the long-run equilibrium price?

g. What is the number of firms in the long run?

◆ 4. The same demand conditions as those in problem 3 prevail, and there are still 1,000 firms in the industry, but fixed costs increase by $980.

a. What is the short-run profit-maximizing output for each firm?

b. Do firms enter or exit the industry in the long run?

c. What is the new long-run equilibrium price?

d. What is the new long-run equilibrium number of firms in the industry?

◆ 5. The same cost conditions as those in problem 3 prevail, and there are 1,000 firms in the industry, but a fall in the price of compact discs decreases the demand for cassettes, and the demand schedule becomes as follows:

Price (dollars per cassette)	Quantity demanded (cassettes per week)
2.95	500,000
3.54	475,000
4.13	450,000
4.71	425,000
5.30	400,000
5.89	375,000
6.48	350,000
7.06	325,000
7.65	300,000
8.24	275,000
8.83	250,000
9.41	225,000
10.00	200,000
10.59	175,000
11.18	150,000

a. What is the short-run profit-maximizing output for each firm?

b. Do firms enter or exit the industry in the long run?

c. What is the new long-run equilibrium price?

d. What is the new long-run equilibrium number of firms in the industry?

6. Why have the prices of pocket calculators and VCRs fallen?

7. What has been the effect of an increase in world population on the wheat market and the individual wheat farmer?

8. How has the diaper service industry been affected by the decrease in the U.S. birth rate and the development of disposable diapers?

9. The graph illustrates the copy market. There are no external costs and benefits from making copies.

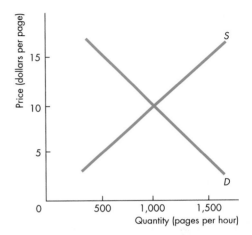

a. What is the allocatively efficient number of copies per hour?

b. If the industry produced 500 copies an hour, are the copy shops economically efficient?

c. If the copy price were 15 cents a page and students made 500 copies an hour, is this outcome consumer efficient?

d. If the copy industry created external costs of 1 cent a page, would the allocatively efficient output be larger or smaller than that when the industry created no external costs?

10. After you have studied *Reading Between the Lines* on pp. 264–265, answer the following questions.

a. What have been the main influences on the demand for mainframe computers over the past five years?

b. What have been the main influences on the costs of producers of mainframe computers over the past five years?

c. How have the influences on demand and costs affected price, quantity, profit, and entry and exit in the mainframe computer industry?

Chapter

12

Monopoly

After studying this chapter, you will be able to:

- Define monopoly and explain the conditions under which it arises

- Distinguish between legal monopoly and natural monopoly

- Explain how a monopoly determines its price and output

- Define price discrimination and explain why it leads to a bigger profit

- Compare the performance of a competitive industry and a monopoly

- Define rent seeking and explain why it arises

- Explain the gains from monopoly

You have been reading a lot in this book about firms that want to maximize profit. But perhaps you've been looking around at some of the places where you do business and wondering whether they are really so intent on profit. After all, don't you get a student's discount when you get a haircut? Don't museums and movie theaters give discounts to students, too? And what about the airline that

The Profits of Generosity

gives a discount for buying a ticket in advance? Are your barber and movie theater owner, as well as the museum and airline operators, simply generous folks to whom the model of profit-maximizing firms does not apply? Aren't they simply throwing profit away by cutting ticket prices and offering discounts? ◆ When you buy electric power, you don't shop around. You buy from your electric power utility, which is your only available supplier. If you live in New York City and want cable TV service, you only have one option: buy from Manhattan Cable. These are examples of a single producer of a good or service controlling its supply. Such firms are obviously not like firms in perfectly competitive industries. They don't face a market-determined price. They can choose their own price. How do such firms behave? How do they choose the quantity to produce and the price at which to sell it? How does their behavior compare with firms in perfectly competitive industries? Do such firms charge prices that are too high and that damage the interests of consumers? Do such firms bring any benefits?

◇ In this chapter we study markets in which an individual firm can influence the quantity of goods supplied and exert an influence on price. We also compare the performance of a firm in such markets with that of a competitive market and examine whether monopoly is as efficient as competition.

How Monopoly Arises

THE SUPPLIERS OF LOCAL PHONE SERVICES, GAS, electricity, and water are monopolies. A **monopoly** is an industry that produces a good or service for which no close substitute exists and in which there is one supplier that is protected from competition by a barrier preventing the entry of new firms. The suppliers of local phone services, gas, electricity, and water are local monopolies—monopolies restricted to a given location. Microsoft Corp., the software developer that created Windows, the operating system used by PCs, is an example of a global monopoly.

No Close Substitutes

The first key feature of a monopoly is that the good or service produced has no close substitute. If a good does have a close substitute, even though only one firm produces it, that firm effectively faces competition from the producers of substitutes.

Water supplied by a local public utility is an example of a good that does not have close substitutes. While it does have a close substitute for drinking—bottled mineral water—it has no effective substitutes for showering or washing a car.

Innovation and technological change create new products. Some of these are substitutes for existing products and so weaken existing monopolies. For example, since the arrival of national couriers such as FedEx and UPS and the development of the fax machine, the first-class letter monopoly of the U.S. Postal Service has been weakened. Similarly, the arrival of satellite dishes has weakened the monopoly of local cable television companies. Advances in telecommunication technology have ended the telephone monopoly. Competition among long-distance carriers came first, and later, cellular telephones began to undermine the monopoly in local calls.

Other new products have poor substitutes and so create new monopolies. An example is Microsoft's monopoly in Windows. Similarly, research in the pharmaceutical industry is constantly creating new monopolies in drugs.

Barriers to Entry

The second key feature of a monopoly is the existence of barriers preventing the entry of new firms. **Barriers to entry** are legal or natural impediments protecting a firm from competition from potential new entrants.

Legal Barriers to Entry   Legal barriers to entry create legal monopoly. A **legal monopoly** is a market in which competition and entry are restricted by the granting of a public franchise, license, patent or copyright, or in which a firm has acquired ownership of a significant portion of a key resource.

The first type of legal barrier to entry is a public franchise. A *public franchise* is an exclusive right granted to a firm to supply a good or service. An example of a public franchise is the U.S. postal service, which has the exclusive right to carry first-class mail. Another common public franchise occurs on freeways and turnpikes where particular firms are given exclusive rights to sell gasoline and food.

A second legal barrier is a government license. A *government license* controls entry into particular occupations, professions, and industries. Government licensing in the professions is the most common example of this type of barrier to entry. For example, a license is required to practice medicine, law, dentistry, schoolteaching, architecture, and a variety of other professional services. Licensing does not create monopoly, but it does restrict competition.

A *patent* is an exclusive right granted to the inventor of a product or service. A *copyright* is an exclusive right granted to the author or composer of a literary, musical, dramatic, or artistic work. Patents and copyrights are valid for a limited time period that varies from country to country. In the United States, a patent is valid for 20 years. Patents protect inventors by creating a property right and thereby encourage invention by preventing others from copying an invention until sufficient time has elapsed for the inventor to have reaped some benefits. They also stimulate *innovation*—the use of new inventions—by encouraging inventors to publicize their discoveries and offer them for use under license. *Reading Between the Lines* on p. 290–291 describes some of the consequences of a firm being granted a legal monopoly on a particular type of soybean seed.

In some industries, the government does not grant a legal monopoly, but a single firm acquires ownership of a significant proportion of a key resource. A past example of this type of monopoly is Alcoa, an aluminum producer that controlled a large proportion of the sources of supply of aluminum during the 1930s. A modern example is DeBeers, a South African firm that controls more than 80 percent of the world's supply of natural diamonds.

Natural Barriers to Entry   Natural barriers to entry give rise to natural monopoly. **Natural monopoly** occurs when one firm can supply the entire market at a lower price than two or more firms can. This situation arises when demand limits sales to a quantity at which economies of scale exist. Figure 12.1 shows such a situation. Here, the demand curve for electric power is D and the average total cost curve is ATC. Because average total cost decreases as output increases, economies of scale prevail over the entire length of the ATC curve. One firm can produce 4 million kilowatt-hours at 5 cents a kilowatt-hour. At this price, the quantity demanded is 4 million kilowatt-hours. So if the price was 5 cents, one firm could supply the entire market. If two firms shared the market, it would cost each of them 10 cents a kilowatt-hour to produce a total of 4 million

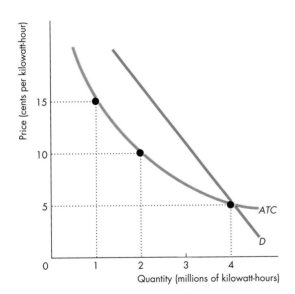

FIGURE 12.1

Natural Monopoly

The demand curve for electric power is D and the average total cost curve is ATC. Economies of scale exist over the entire ATC curve. One firm can produce a total output of 4 million kilowatt-hours at a cost of 5 cents a kilowatt-hour. This same total output costs 10 cents a kilowatt-hour with two firms and 15 cents a kilowatt-hour with four firms. So one firm can meet the market demand at a lower cost than two or more firms can, and the market is a natural monopoly.

kilowatt-hours. If four firms shared the market, it would cost each of them 15 cents a kilowatt-hour to produce a total of 4 million kilowatt-hours. So, in conditions like those shown in Fig. 12.1, one firm can supply the entire market at a lower cost than two or more firms can. Electric power utilities are an example of natural monopoly. Another example is natural gas distribution.

Most monopolies in the real world, whether legal or natural, are regulated in some way by government or by government agencies. We will study such regulation in Chapter 20. Here we will study unregulated monopoly for two reasons. First, we can better understand why governments regulate monopolies and the effects of regulation if we also know how an unregulated monopoly behaves. Second, even in industries with more than one producer, firms often have a degree of monopoly power arising from locational advantages or from differences in product quality protected by patents. The theory of monopoly sheds light on the behavior of such firms and industries.

We begin by studying the behavior of a single-price monopoly. A *single-price monopoly* is a monopoly that charges the same price for each and every unit of its output. How does a single-price monopoly determine the quantity to produce and the price to charge for its output?

Single-Price Monopoly

THE STARTING POINT FOR UNDERSTANDING HOW a single-price monopoly chooses its price and output is to work out the relationship between the demand for the good produced by the monopoly and the monopoly's revenue.

Demand and Revenue

Because in a monopoly there is only one firm, the demand curve facing that firm is the industry demand curve. Let's look at an example: Bobbie's Barbershop, the sole supplier of haircuts in Cairo, Nebraska. The demand schedule that Bobbie faces is set out in Table 12.1. At a price of $20, Bobbie sells no haircuts. The lower the price, the more haircuts per hour Bobbie is able to sell. For example, at a price of $12, consumers demand 4 haircuts per hour (row *e*), and at a price of $4, they demand 8 haircuts per hour (row *i*).

TABLE 12.1

Single-Price Monopoly's Revenue

Price (P) (dollars per haircut)	Quantity demanded (Q) (haircuts per hour)	Total revenue (TR = P × Q) (dollars)	Marginal revenue (MR = ΔTR/ΔQ) (dollars per haircut)
a	20	0	0	
				18
b	18	1	18	
				14
c	16	2	32	
				10
d	14	3	42	
				6
e	12	4	48	
				2
f	10	5	50	
				−2
g	8	6	48	
				−6
h	6	7	42	
				−10
i	4	8	32	
				−14
j	2	9	18	
				−18
k	0	10	0	

The table shows Bobbie's demand schedule—the number of haircuts demanded per hour at each price. Total revenue (*TR*) is price multiplied by quantity sold. For example, row *c* shows that when the price is $16 a haircut, 2 haircuts are sold and total revenue is $32. Marginal revenue (*MR*) is the change in total revenue resulting from a one-unit increase in the quantity sold. For example, when the price falls from $16 to $14 a haircut, the quantity sold increases from 2 to 3 haircuts and total revenue increases by $10. Marginal revenue is $10. Total revenue rises through row *f*, in which 5 haircuts are sold for $10, and it falls thereafter. Over the output range in which total revenue increases, marginal revenue is positive; over the output range in which total revenue decreases, marginal revenue is negative.

Total revenue (*TR*) is the price (*P*) multiplied by the quantity sold (*Q*). For example, in row *d*, Bobbie sells 3 haircuts at $14 each, so total revenue is $42. *Marginal revenue* (*MR*) is the change in total revenue (Δ*TR*) resulting from a one-unit increase in the quantity sold. For example, if the price falls from $18 (row

b) to $16 (row *c*), the quantity sold increases from 1 to 2 haircuts. Total revenue rises from $18 to $32, so the change in total revenue is $14. Because the quantity sold increases by 1 haircut, marginal revenue equals the change in total revenue and is $14. Marginal revenue is placed between the two rows to emphasize that marginal revenue relates to the *change* in the quantity sold.

Figure 12.2 shows Bobbie's demand curve (*D*). Each row of Table 12.1 corresponds to a point on the demand curve. For example, row *d* in the table and

FIGURE 12.2

Demand and Marginal Revenue for a Single-Price Monopoly

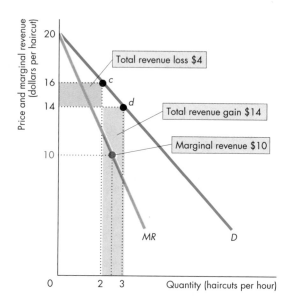

The monopoly demand curve (*D*) is based on the numbers in Table 12.1. At a price of $16 a haircut, Bobbie sells 2 haircuts an hour. If she lowers the price to $14, she sells 3 haircuts an hour. The sale of the third haircut brings a revenue gain of $14 (the price charged for the third haircut). But there is a revenue loss of $4 ($2 per haircut) on the 2 haircuts that she could have sold for $16 each. The marginal revenue (extra total revenue) from the third haircut is the difference between the revenue gain and the revenue loss—$10. The marginal revenue curve (*MR*) shows the marginal revenue at each level of sales. Marginal revenue is lower than price.

point *d* on the demand curve tell us that at a price of $14, Bobbie sells 3 haircuts. The figure also shows Bobbie's marginal revenue curve (*MR*). Notice that the marginal revenue curve lies below the demand curve. That is, at each level of output, marginal revenue is less than price. Why is marginal revenue less than price? It is because when the price is lowered to sell one more unit, there are two opposing effects on total revenue. The lower price results in a revenue loss, and the increased quantity sold results in a revenue gain. For example, at a price of $16, Bobbie sells 2 haircuts (point *c*). If she reduces the price to $14, she sells 3 haircuts and has a revenue gain of $14 on the third haircut. But she charges the same price for all haircuts, so she receives only $14 on the first two as well—$2 less than before. As a result, she loses $4 of revenue on the first 2 haircuts. She must deduct this amount from the revenue gain of $14. Marginal revenue—the difference between the revenue gain and the revenue loss—is $10.

Figure 12.3 shows Bobbie's demand curve (*D*), marginal revenue curve (*MR*), and total revenue curve (*TR*) and illustrates the connections between them. Again, each row in Table 12.1 corresponds to a point on the curves. For example, row *d* in the table and point *d* on the graphs tell us that when 3 haircuts are sold for $14 each (part a), total revenue is $42 (part b). Notice that as the quantity sold increases, total revenue rises to a peak of $50 (point *f*) and then declines. To understand the behavior of total revenue, notice what happens to marginal revenue as the quantity sold increases. Over the range 0 to 5 haircuts, marginal revenue is positive. When more than 5 haircuts are sold, marginal revenue becomes negative. The output range over which marginal revenue is positive is the same as that over which total revenue increases. The output range over which marginal revenue is negative is the same as that over which total revenue declines. The output at which marginal revenue is 0 is the same as that at which total revenue is at a maximum.

Revenue and Elasticity

The elasticity of demand is the absolute value of the percentage change in the quantity demanded divided by the percentage change in price. The demand for a good can be:

1. Elastic
2. Inelastic
3. Unit elastic

Demand is *elastic* if a 1 percent decrease in price results in a greater than 1 percent increase in the quantity demanded. When demand is elastic, the elasticity of demand is greater than 1. Demand is *inelastic* if a 1 percent decrease in price results in a less than 1 percent increase in the quantity demanded. When demand is inelastic, the elasticity of demand is less than 1. Demand is *unit elastic* if a 1 percent decrease in price results in a 1 percent increase in the quantity demanded. When demand is unit elastic, the elasticity of demand is 1.

The elasticity of demand influences the change in total revenue resulting from a change in price. A fall in the price increases the quantity demanded along the firm's demand curve. But what happens to total revenue? If demand is elastic, total revenue increases—the increase in revenue from the increase in quantity sold outweighs the decrease in revenue from the lower price. If demand is inelastic, total revenue decreases—the increase in revenue from the increase in quantity sold is outweighed by the decrease in revenue from the lower price. If demand is unit elastic, total revenue does not change—the increase in revenue from the increase in quantity sold offsets the decrease in revenue from the lower price. (Chapter 5, pp. 106–107, explains the relationship between total revenue and elasticity more fully.)

Figure 12.3 illustrates the relationship between marginal revenue, total revenue, and elasticity. As the price of a haircut gradually falls from $20 to $10, the quantity of haircuts demanded increases from 0 to 5 an hour. Over this output range, marginal revenue is positive (part a) and total revenue increases (part b). The demand for haircuts is elastic. As the price falls from $10 to $0 a haircut, the quantity of haircuts demanded increases from 5 to 10 an hour. Over this output range, marginal revenue is negative (part a) and total revenue decreases (part b). The demand for haircuts is inelastic. When the price is $10 a haircut, marginal revenue is zero and total revenue is a maximum. The demand for haircuts is unit elastic.

Monopoly Demand Always Elastic The relationship that you have just discovered implies that a profit-maximizing monopoly never produces an output in the inelastic range of its demand curve. If it did so, marginal revenue would be negative—each additional unit sold would lower total revenue. In such a situation, if the firm charges a higher price and produces a smaller quantity its profit increases because its total revenue rises and its total cost falls. But what price and quantity does a profit-maximizing monopoly choose?

FIGURE 12.3

A Single-Price Monopoly's Revenue Curves

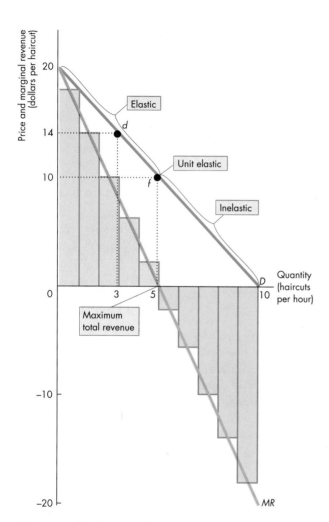

(a) Demand and marginal revenue curves

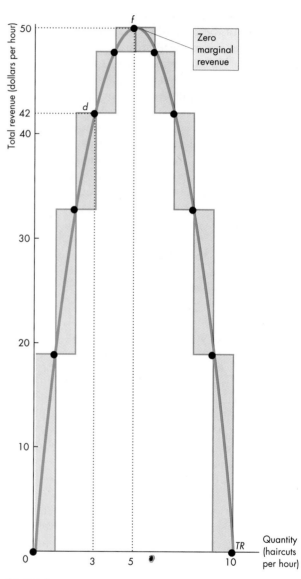

(b) Total revenue curve

Bobbie's demand curve (*D*) and marginal revenue curve (*MR*), shown in part (a), and total revenue curve (*TR*), shown in part (b), are based on the numbers in Table 12.1. For example, at a price of $14, Bobbie sells 3 haircuts an hour (point *d* in part a) for a total revenue of $42 (point *d* in part b). Over the range 0 to 5 haircuts an hour, total revenue is increasing and marginal revenue is positive, as shown by the blue bars. Over the range

5 to 10 haircuts an hour, total revenue declines—marginal revenue is negative, as shown by the red bars. Over the range of output for which marginal revenue is positive, demand is elastic. At the level of output at which marginal revenue is zero, demand is unit elastic. Over the range of output for which marginal revenue is negative, demand is inelastic.

Price and Output Decision

To determine the output level and price that maximize a monopoly's profit, we need to study the behavior of both revenue and costs as output varies. A monopoly faces the same types of technology and cost constraints as a competitive firm. But it faces a different market constraint. The competitive firm is a price taker, whereas the monopoly's production decision influences the price it receives. Let's see how.

Bobbie's revenue, which we studied in Table 12.1, is shown again in Table 12.2. The table also contains information on Bobbie's costs and economic profit. Total cost (TC) rises as output increases, and so does total revenue (TR). Economic profit equals total revenue minus total cost. As you can see in the table, the maximum profit ($12) occurs when Bobbie sells 3 haircuts for $14 each. If she sells 2 haircuts for $16 each or 4 haircuts for $12 each, her economic profit will be only $8.

You can see why 3 haircuts is Bobbie's profit-maximizing output by looking at the marginal revenue and marginal cost columns. When Bobbie increases output from 2 to 3 haircuts, her marginal revenue is $10 and her marginal cost is $6. Profit increases by the difference—$4 an hour. If Bobbie increases output yet further, from 3 to 4 haircuts, her

marginal revenue is $6 and her marginal cost is $10. In this case, marginal cost exceeds marginal revenue by $4, so profit decreases by $4 an hour. When marginal revenue exceeds marginal cost, profit increases if output increases. When marginal cost exceeds marginal revenue, profit increases if output decreases. When marginal cost and marginal revenue are equal, profit is maximized.

The information set out in Table 12.2 is shown graphically in Fig. 12.4. Part (a) shows Bobbie's total revenue curve (TR) and total cost curve (TC). Economic profit is the vertical distance between TR and TC. Bobbie maximizes her profit at 3 haircuts an hour—economic profit is $42 minus $30, or $12.

A monopoly, like a competitive firm, maximizes profit by producing the output at which marginal cost equals marginal revenue. Figure 12.4(b) shows Bobbie's demand curve (D) and marginal revenue curve (MR) along with her marginal cost curve (MC) and average total cost curve (ATC). Bobbie maximizes her profit by doing 3 haircuts an hour. But what price does she charge for a haircut? To set the price, the monopolist uses the demand curve and finds the highest price at which it can sell the profit-maximizing output. In Bobbie's case, the highest price at which she can sell 3 haircuts an hour is $14.

TABLE 12.2

A Monopoly's Output and Price Decision

Price (P) (dollars per haircut)	Quantity demanded (Q) (haircuts per hour)	Total revenue (TR = P × Q) (dollars)	Marginal revenue (MR =ΔTR/ΔQ) (dollars per haircut)	Total cost (TC) (dollars)	Marginal cost (MC = ΔTC/ΔQ) (dollars per haircut)	Profit (TR − TC) (dollars)
20	0	0		20		−20
			18		1	
18	1	18		21		−3
			14		3	
16	2	32		24		+8
			10		6	
14	3	42		30		+12
			6		10	
12	4	48		40		+8
			2		15	
10	5	50		55		−5

This table gives the information needed to find the profit-maximizing output and price. Total revenue (TR) equals price multiplied by the quantity sold. Profit equals total revenue minus total cost (TC). Profit is maximized when the price is $14 and 3 haircuts are sold. Total revenue is $42, total cost is $30, and economic profit is $12 ($42 − $30).

A Monopoly's Output and Price

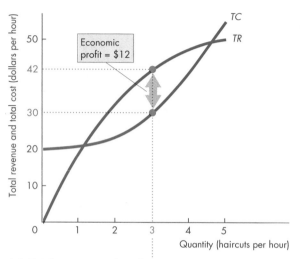

(a) Total revenue and total cost curves

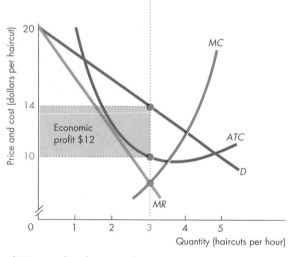

(b) Demand and marginal revenue and cost curves

This figure graphs the numbers in Table 12.2. In part (a) economic profit is the vertical distance total revenue (*TR*) minus total cost (*TC*), and it is maximized at 3 haircuts an hour. In part (b) economic profit is maximized when marginal cost (*MC*) equals marginal revenue (*MR*). The price is determined by the demand curve (*D*) and is $14. Economic profit, the blue rectangle, is $12—the profit per haircut ($4) multiplied by 3 haircuts.

All firms maximize profit by producing the output at which marginal revenue equals marginal cost. For a competitive firm, price equals marginal revenue, so price also equals marginal cost. For a monopoly, price exceeds marginal revenue, so price also exceeds marginal cost.

A monopoly charges a price that exceeds marginal cost, but does it always make an economic profit? In Bobbie's case, when she produces 3 haircuts an hour, her average total cost is $10 (read from the *ATC* curve) and her price is $14 (read from the *D* curve). Her profit per haircut is $4 ($14 minus $10). Bobbie's economic profit is shown by the blue rectangle, which equals the profit per haircut ($4) multiplied by the number of haircuts (3), for a total of $12.

Bobbie makes a positive economic profit. But suppose that the owner of the shop that Bobbie rents increases Bobbie's rent. If Bobbie pays an additional $12 an hour, her fixed cost increases by $12 an hour. Her marginal cost and marginal revenue don't change, so her profit-maximizing output remains at 3 haircuts an hour. Her profit decreases by $12 an hour to zero. If Bobbie pays more than an additional $12 an hour for her shop rent, she incurs an economic loss. If this situation were permanent, Bobbie would go out of business. But entrepreneurs are a hardy lot, and Bobbie might find another shop where the rent is less.

If firms in a perfectly competitive industry are making a positive economic profit, new firms enter. That does not happen in a monopolistic industry. Barriers to entry prevent new firms from entering. So in a monopolistic industry, a firm can make a positive economic profit and continue to do so indefinitely. Sometimes that profit is large, as in the international diamond business.

REVIEW

- A monopoly maximizes profit by producing an output at which marginal cost equals marginal revenue.
- At the profit-maximizing output, the monopoly charges the price that consumers are willing to pay, which is determined by the demand curve.
- Because in a monopoly, price exceeds marginal revenue, price also exceeds marginal cost.
- A monopoly can make a positive economic profit even in the long run because of barriers to entry.

Price Discrimination

MOVIE THEATERS OFTEN CHARGE STUDENTS AND senior citizens a lower price than other adults to see a movie. Movie theaters practice price discrimination. **Price discrimination** is the practice of charging some customers a lower price than others for an identical good or of charging an individual customer a lower price on a large purchase than on a small one, even though the cost of servicing all customers is the same. Another example is the common practice of barbers and hairdressers giving discounts to senior citizens and students. Price discrimination can be practiced in varying degrees. *Perfect price discrimination* occurs when a firm charges a different price for each unit sold and charges each consumer the maximum price that he or she is willing to pay for the unit. Though firms in the real world do not practice perfect price discrimination, it shows the limit to which price discrimination can be taken.

Not all price *differences* imply price *discrimination*. In many situations, goods that are similar but not identical have different costs and sell for different prices *because* they have different costs. For example, the marginal cost of producing electricity depends on the time of day. If an electric power company charges a higher price for consumption between 7:00 and 9:00 in the morning and between 4:00 and 7:00 in the evening than it does at other times of the day, this practice is not called price discrimination. Price discrimination charges varying prices to consumers, not because of differences in the cost of producing the good but because of differences in consumer's elasticities of demand for the good.

At first sight, it appears that price discrimination contradicts the assumption of profit maximization. Why would a movie operator allow children to see movies at half price? Why would a hairdresser or barber charge students and senior citizens less? Aren't these producers losing profit by being nice?

Deeper investigation shows that far from losing profit, price discriminators actually make a bigger profit than they would otherwise. Thus a monopoly has an incentive to try to find ways of discriminating among groups of consumers and charging each group the highest possible price. Some people may pay less with price discrimination, but others pay more. How do firms make more profit when they practice price discrimination?

Price Discrimination and Consumer Surplus

Demand curves slope down because the value that an individual places on a good falls as the quantity consumed of that good increases. When all the units consumed can be bought for a single price, consumers benefit. The benefit is the value the consumers get from each unit of the good minus the price actually paid for it. We call this benefit *consumer surplus*. (If you need to refresh your understanding of consumer surplus, flip back to Chapter 7, page 158.) Price discrimination can be seen as an attempt by a monopoly to capture the consumer surplus (or as much of the surplus as possible) for itself.

Discriminating among Units of a Good

One form of price discrimination charges each single buyer a different price on each unit of a good bought. An example of this type of discrimination is a discount for bulk buying. The larger the order, the larger is the discount—and the lower is the price. This type of price discrimination works because each individual's demand curve slopes downward. Note that some discounts for bulk arise from lower costs of production for greater bulk. In these cases, such discounts are not price discrimination.

To extract every dollar of consumer surplus from every buyer, the monopolist would have to offer each individual customer a separate price schedule based on that customer's own demand curve. Clearly, such price discrimination cannot be carried out in practice because a firm does not have enough information about each consumer's demand curve.

Discriminating among Individuals

Even when it is not possible to charge each individual a different price for each unit bought, it might still be possible to discriminate among individuals. This possibility arises from the fact that some people place a higher value on consuming one more unit of a good than do other individuals. By charging such an individual a higher price, the producer can obtain some of the consumer surplus that would otherwise accrue to their customers.

Discriminating between Groups

Price discrimination often takes the form of discriminating between different groups of consumers on the basis of age, employment status, or some other easily distinguished characteristic. This type of price discrimination works only if each group has a different price elasticity of demand for the product. But this situation is a common one. For example, the elasticity of demand for haircuts is lower for businesspeople than for students, and the elasticity of demand for air travel is lower for business travelers than for vacation travelers. Let's see how an airline exploits the differences in demand by business and vacation travelers and increases its profit by price discriminating.

Global Air has a monopoly on an exotic route. Figure 12.5(a) shows the demand curve (D) and the marginal revenue curve (MR) for travel on this route. It also shows Global Air's marginal cost curve (MC). Marginal cost is constant, and fixed cost is zero. Global Air is a single-price monopoly and maximizes its profit by producing the output at which marginal revenue equals marginal cost. This output is 10,000 trips a year. The price at which Global can sell 10,000 trips is $1,500 per trip. Global Air's total revenue is $15 million a year. Its total cost is $10 million

a year, so its economic profit is $5 million a year, as shown by the blue rectangle in part (a).

Global is struck by the fact that most of its customers are business travelers. Global knows that its exotic route is ideal for vacationers, but it also knows that to attract more of these travelers, it must offer a lower fare than $1,500. At the same time, Global knows that if it cuts the fare, it will lose revenue on its business travelers. So Global decides to price discriminate between the two groups.

Global's first step is to determine the demand curve of business travelers and the demand curve of vacation travelers. The market demand curve (in Fig. 12.5a) is the horizontal sum of the demand curves for these two types of traveler (see Chapter 7, pp. 156–157). Global determines that the demand curve for business travel is D_B in Fig. 12.5(b) and the demand curve for vacation travel is D_V in Fig. 12.5(c). At the single fare of $1,500, the 10,000 trips that Global sells is made up of 6,000 to business travelers and 4,000 to vacation travelers. At $1,500 a trip, business travelers buy more trips than vacation travelers—there are 6,000 business trips and 4,000 vacation trips—but at this price, the demand for business travel is much less elastic than vacation travel. As the price decreases below $1,500, the demand for busi-

---

FIGURE 12.5

A Single Price of Air Travel

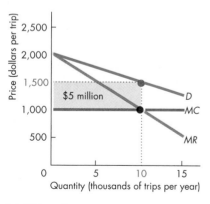

(a) All travelers

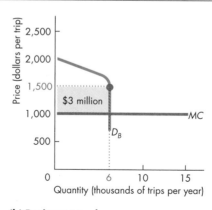

(b) Business travelers

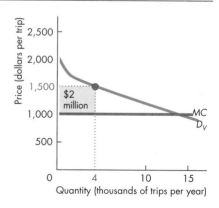

(c) Vacation travelers

Part (a) shows the demand curve (D), marginal revenue curve (MR), and marginal cost curve (MC), for a route on which Global Airlines has a monopoly. As a single-price monopoly, Global maximizes profit by selling 10,000 trips a year at $1,500 a trip. Its profit is $5 million, which is shown by the

blue rectangle in part (a). The demand curve in part (a) is the horizontal sum of the demand curves for business travel (D_B) in part (b) and for vacation travel (D_V) in part (c). Global sells 6,000 trips to business travelers for a profit of $3 million and 4,000 trips to vacation travelers for a profit of $2 million.

ness travel becomes perfectly inelastic while the demand for vacation travel is more elastic.

Profiting by Price Discriminating

Global uses the profit-maximization rule: produce the quantity at which marginal revenue equals marginal cost and set the price at the level the consumer is willing to pay. But now that Global has separated its market into two parts, it has two marginal revenue curves. Global's marginal revenue curve for business travel is MR_B in Fig 12.6(a) and its marginal revenue curve for vacation travel is MR_V in Fig. 12.6(b).

In Fig. 12.6(a), marginal revenue from business travel equals marginal of $1,000 at 5,000 trips a year. The price that business travelers are willing to pay for this quantity of trips is $1,700 a trip, up $200 on the current price. In Fig. 12.6(b), marginal revenue from vacation travel equals marginal cost of $1,000 at 7,000 trips a year. The price that vacation travelers are willing to pay for this quantity of trips is $1,500 a trip, *down* $150 on the current price.

If Global can charge its business travelers a fare of $1,700 and its vacation travelers a fare of $1,350, it can increase its sales from 10,000 to 13,000 trips a year and can increase its economic profit from $5 million a year to $5.95 million. On business travelers, it can make $3.5 million a year, which is $700 per trip on 5,000 trips. This economic profit is shown by the blue rectangle in Fig. 12.6(a). On vacation travelers, Global can make $2.45 million a year, which is $350 per trip on 7,000 trips. The blue rectangle in Fig. 12.6(b) illustrates this economic profit.

How can Global get its business travelers to pay $1,700? If it offers fares to vacation travelers for $1,350, won't business travelers claim to be vacationers? Not with the deal that Global comes up with.

Global has noticed that its business travelers never make reservations more than three weeks in advance. It conducts a survey, which reveals that these travelers never know more than a month in advance when they will need to travel. Its survey also reveals that vacation travelers always know at least a month in advance of their travel plans. So Global

---

FIGURE 12.6

Price Discrimination

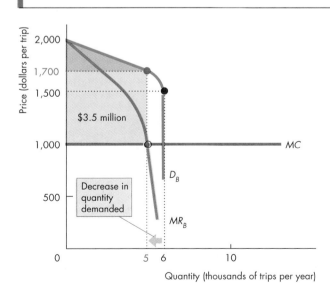

(a) Business travelers

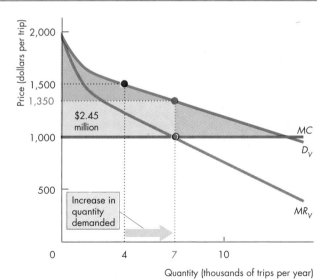

(b) Vacation travelers

The marginal revenue curve for business travel is (MR_B) in part (a) and for vacation travel is (MR_V) in part (b). Global maximizes profit by making marginal revenue equal to marginal cost for each type of travel. By increasing the business fare to $1,700 and by cutting the vacation fare to $1,350, Global increases its

economic profit. It now sells 5,000 business trips for a profit of $3.5 million (the blue rectangle in part a) and 7,000 vacation trips for a profit of $2.45 million (the blue rectangle in part b), so its total profit increases from $5 million with no price discrimination to $5.95 million with discrimination.

offers a deal to all travelers: a basic fare of $1,700, but if a traveler buys a non-refundable ticket one month in advance of the date of travel, the fare is discounted by $350 to $1,350. By price discriminating between business and vacation travelers, Global increases the quantity of trips sold from 10,000 to 13,000 and increases its profit by $0.95 million a year.

More Perfect Price Discrimination

Global can do even better. Some of the business travelers are willing to pay more than $1,700 a trip. They make a consumer surplus, as shown by the green triangle in Fig. 12.6(a). Also, most of the vacation travelers who are paying $1,350 a trip are willing to pay more. They make a consumer surplus, as shown by the green triangle in Fig. 12.6(b). Further, some potential vacation travelers are not willing to pay $1,350 but are willing to pay at least $1,000. With a price of $1,000 a trip, these potential vacation travelers would make a consumer surplus equal to the orange triangle in Fig. 12.6(b).

Global gets creative. It comes up with a host of special deals. For higher prices, it offers priority reservations and frills to the business travelers. (These deals don't change Global's marginal cost.) It refines the list of restrictions on its discount fares and creates many different fare categories, the lowest of which has lots of restrictions but is $1,000 a trip.

The quantity of seats sold increases until Global is selling 20,000 trips a year, 6,000 to business travelers at various prices between $1,500 and almost $2,000 and 14,000 to vacationers at prices ranging between $1,000 and $1,700 a trip. Global is now almost a perfect price discriminator.

Figure 12.7 shows that if Global is able to perfectly price discriminate, it captures the entire consumer surplus.

Price Discrimination in Practice

You can now see why price discrimination is profitable. Global's special offer—"Normal fare: $1,700, 30-day advance purchase special: $1,350"—is no

---

Perfect Price Discrimination

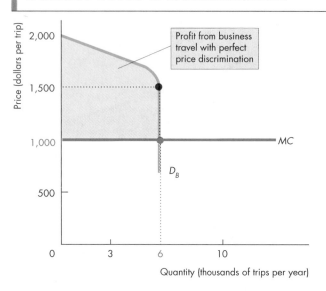

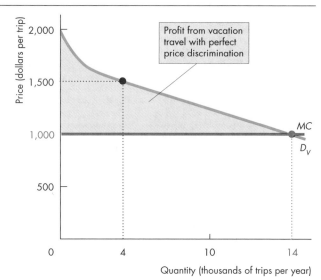

(a) Business travelers

By offering a wide array of special fares, restrictions, and deals, Global tries to perfectly price discriminate. If it succeeds, it sells 6,000 trips to buiness travelers and 14,000 trips to vaca-

(b) Vacation travelers

tion travelers and it captures the entire consumer surplus. Its economic profit increases to the magnitude shown by the blue areas under the two demand curves.

generous gesture. It is profit-maximizing behavior. The model of price discrimination that you have just studied explains a wide variety of familiar pricing practices, even by firms that are not pure monopolies.

For example, real airlines, not just the imaginary Global, offer lower fares for advance-purchase tickets than for last-minute travel. Last-minute travelers usually have a lower elasticity of demand than vacation travelers who can plan ahead. Retail stores of all kinds hold seasonal "sales" when they reduce their prices, often by substantial amounts. These "sales" are a form of price discrimination. Each season, the newest fashions carry a high price tag, but retailers do not expect to sell all their stock at such high prices. At the end of the season, they sell off what is left at a discount. Thus such stores discriminate between buyers who have an inelastic demand (for example, those who want to be instantly fashionable) and buyers who have a more elastic demand (for example, those who pay less attention to up-to-the-minute fashion and more attention to price).

Limits to Price Discrimination

If price discrimination is profitable, why don't more firms do it? What limits price discrimination?

Profitable price discrimination can take place only under certain conditions. First, it is possible to price discriminate only if the good cannot be resold. If a good can be resold, then customers who get the good for the low price can resell it to someone who is willing to pay a higher price. Price discrimination breaks down. It is for this reason that price discrimination

Would it bother you to hear how little I paid for this flight?

From William Hamilton, "Voodoo Economics," ©1992 by The Chronicle Publishing Company, p.3. Reprinted with permission of Chronicle Books.

usually occurs in markets for services rather than in markets for storable goods. One major exception, price discrimination in the sale of fashion clothes, works because at the end of the season when the clothes go on sale, the fashion plates are looking for next season's fashions. People buying on sale have no one to whom they can resell the clothes at a higher price.

Second, a price-discriminating monopoly must be able to identify groups with different elasticities of demand. The characteristics used for discrimination must also be within the law. These requirements usually limit price discrimination to cases based on age, employment status, or the timing of the purchase.

Despite these limitations, there are some ingenious criteria used for discriminating. For example, American Airlines discriminates between four different passenger groups on many of its international flights. The economy class alternatives between New York and London in the summer of 1995 were:

- $1,284—no restrictions
- $759—7-day advance purchase
- $688—14-day advance purchase, mid-week only
- $618—30-day advance purchase, mid-week only

These different prices discriminate between different groups of customers with different elasticities of demand. The $1,284 fare is probably paid by last-minute business travelers who have a lower elasticity of demand, and the $616 fare is probably paid by vacationers who have a higher elasticity of demand.

R E V I E W

- Price discrimination can increase a monopoly's profit.
- By charging the highest price for each unit of the good that each person is willing to pay, a monopoly perfectly price discriminates and captures all of the consumer surplus.
- Most price discrimination takes the form of discriminating among different groups of customers with different elasticities of demand.
- People with a lower elasticity of demand pay a higher price, and people with a higher elasticity of demand pay a lower price.
- A price-discriminating monopoly produces a larger output than a single-price monopoly.

Comparing Monopoly and Competition

WE HAVE NOW STUDIED A VARIETY OF WAYS IN which firms and households interact in markets for goods and services. In Chapter 11, we saw how perfectly competitive firms behave and discovered the price and output at which they operate. In this chapter, we have studied the price and output of a single-price monopoly and a monopoly that price discriminates. How do the quantities produced, prices, and profits of these different types of firms compare with each other?

To answer this question, let's imagine an industry made up of a large number of identical competitive firms. We will work out what the price charged and quantity produced will be in that industry. Then we will imagine that a single firm buys out all the individual firms and creates a monopoly. We will then work out the price charged and quantity produced by the monopoly, first when it charges a single price and second when it price discriminates.

Price and Output

We will conduct the analysis by using Fig. 12.8. The industry demand curve is D, and the industry supply curve is S. In perfect competition, the market equilibrium occurs where the supply curve and the demand curve intersect.

In Perfect Competition The quantity produced by the industry is Q_C, and the price is P_C. Each firm takes the price P_C and maximizes its profit by producing the output at which its own marginal cost equals the price. Because each firm is a small part of the total industry, there is no incentive for any firm to try to manipulate the price by varying its output.

With Single-Priced Monopoly Now suppose that this industry is taken over by a single firm. No changes in production techniques occur, so the new combined firm has costs identical to those of the original separate firms. The new single firm recognizes that by varying output, it can influence price. It also recognizes that its marginal revenue curve is MR. To maximize profit, the firm chooses an output at which marginal revenue equals marginal cost.

FIGURE 12.8

Monopoly and Competition Compared

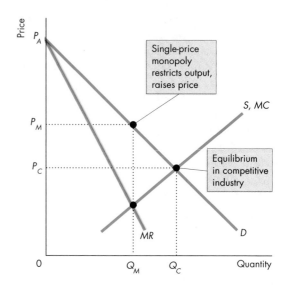

A competitive industry has a demand curve D and a supply curve S. Equilibrium occurs where the quantity demanded equals the quantity supplied at quantity Q_C and price P_C. If all the firms in the industry are taken over by a single producer that sells the profit-maximizing output for a single price, marginal revenue is MR and the competitive industry supply curve, S, becomes the monopoly's marginal cost curve, MC. The monopoly produces the output at which marginal revenue equals marginal cost. A single-price monopoly produces Q_M and sells that output for the price P_M. A perfectly price-discriminating monopoly produces Q_C and charges a different price for each unit sold. The prices charged range from P_A to P_C.

Monopoly restricts output and raises the price. But the more perfectly a monopoly can price discriminate, the closer its output gets to the competitive output.

But what is the monopoly's marginal cost curve? To answer this question, you need to recall the relationship between the marginal cost curve and the supply curve of a competitive firm. The supply curve of an individual competitive firm is its marginal cost curve above minimum average variable cost. The industry supply curve is the industry's marginal cost curve. (The supply curve has also been labeled MC to remind you of this fact.) Therefore, when the industry is taken over by a single firm, that firm's marginal cost curve is the same as what used to be the competitive industry's supply curve.

We have seen that a competitive industry always operates at the point of intersection of its supply and demand curves. In Fig. 12.8, the price is P_C and the industry produces the quantity Q_C. In contrast, the single-price monopoly maximizes profit by restricting output to Q_M, where marginal revenue equals marginal cost. Because the marginal revenue curve is below the demand curve, output Q_M will always be smaller than output Q_C. The monopoly charges the price for which output Q_M can be sold, and that price, which is determined by the demand curve, is P_M. We have just established a key proposition:

Compared to a perfectly competitive industry, a single-price monopoly restricts its output and charges a higher price.

With Perfect Price Discrimination   If a monopoly can perfectly price discriminate, it will charge a different price on each unit sold and increase output to Q_C. The highest price charged is P_A, and the lowest price charged is P_C, the price in a competitive market. The price P_A is the highest that is charged because at yet higher prices, nothing can be sold. The price P_C is the lowest charged because when a monopoly perfectly price discriminates, its demand curve is also its marginal revenue curve and at prices below P_C, marginal cost exceeds marginal revenue. We have just established a second key proposition:

The more perfectly the monopoly can price discriminate, the closer its output gets to the competitive output.

We've seen how the output and price of a monopoly compare with those in a competitive industry. Let's now compare the efficiency of the two types of market.

Allocative Efficiency

Whether monopoly is less efficient than competition depends on how successfully the monopoly can price discriminate. A single-price monopoly is inefficient and a perfect-price discriminating monopoly is efficient. Let's look at these two cases.

Inefficiency of a Single-Price Monopoly   Figure 12.9 compares perfect competition and a single-price monopoly. Under perfect competition (part a), consumers pay P_C for each unit bought. The maximum price that consumers are willing to pay for each unit is shown by the demand curve (D). This price measures the value of the good to the consumer. The value of a good minus its price is **consumer surplus**. (See Chapter 7, pp. 158–159, for a more detailed explanation of consumer surplus.)

In Fig. 12.9(a), consumer surplus is shown by the green triangle. A single-price monopoly (part b) restricts output to Q_M and sells that output for P_M. Consumer surplus decreases to the smaller green triangle. Consumers lose partly by having to pay more for the good and partly by getting less of it. But is the consumers' loss equal to the monopoly's gain? Is there simply a redistribution of the gains from trade? A closer look at Fig. 12.9(b) will convince you that there is a reduction in the gains from trade. Some of the loss in consumer surplus accrues to the monopoly—the monopoly gets the difference between the higher price (P_M) and P_C on the quantity sold (Q_M). So the monopoly takes the part of the consumer surplus shown by the blue rectangle. This portion of the loss of consumer surplus is not a loss to society. It is a redistribution from consumers to the monopoly.

What, though, has become of the rest of the consumer surplus? The answer is that because output has been restricted, it is lost. But more than that has been lost. The total loss resulting from the smaller monopoly output (Q_M) is the gray triangle in Fig. 12.9(b). The part of the gray triangle above P_C is the loss of consumer surplus, and the part of the triangle below P_C is a loss of producer surplus. **Producer surplus** is the difference between a producer's revenue and the opportunity cost of production. It is calculated as the sum of the differences between price and the marginal cost of producing each unit of output. Under competition, the producer sells the output between Q_M and Q_C for a price of P_C. The marginal cost of producing each extra unit of output through that range is shown by the marginal cost (supply) curve. Thus the vertical distance between the marginal cost curve and price represents a producer surplus. Part of the producer surplus is lost when a monopoly restricts output to less than its competitive level.

The gray triangle, which measures the total loss of both consumer and producer surplus, is called the deadweight loss. **Deadweight loss** measures allocative inefficiency as the reduction in consumer and

FIGURE 12.9

Allocative Inefficiency of Monopoly

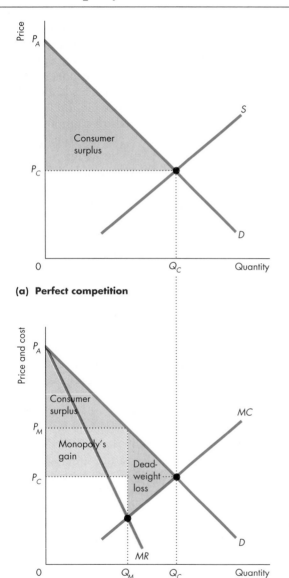

(a) Perfect competition

(b) Monopoly

In perfect competition (part a), the quantity Q_C is sold at the price P_C. Consumer surplus is shown by the green triangle. In long-run equilibrium, firms' economic profits are zero and consumer surplus is maximized. A single-price monopoly (part b) restricts output to Q_M and increases the price to P_M. Consumer surplus is the smaller green triangle. The monopoly takes the blue rectangle and creates a deadweight loss (the gray triangle).

producer surplus resulting from a restriction of output below its efficient level. The reduced output and higher price result in the monopoly's capturing some of the consumer surplus. It also results in the elimination of the producer surplus and the consumer surplus on the output that a competitive industry would have produced but that the monopoly does not.

Usually a monopoly produces an output well below that at which average total cost is a minimum. It has far more capacity than it uses. But even if a monopoly produces the quantity at which average total cost is a minimum, which it might, the consumer does not have the opportunity of buying the good at that price. The price paid by the consumer always exceeds marginal cost.

Efficiency of Perfect Price Discrimination The deadweight loss if the monopoly practices perfect price discrimination is zero. A perfect price discriminator produces the same output as the competitive industry would. The price of the last item sold is P_C, the same as its marginal cost. Consumer surplus is zero but deadweight loss is also zero. So perfect price discrimination achieves allocative efficiency. But what about the distribution of the gains from trade?

Redistribution

Under perfect competition, the consumer surplus is the green triangle in Fig. 12.9(a). Because of free entry, the long-run equilibrium economic profit of each perfectly competitive firm is zero. We've just seen that the creation of monopoly reduces consumer surplus. Further, in the case of a single-price monopoly, a deadweight loss arises. But what happens to the distribution of surpluses between producers and consumers? The answer is that the monopoly always wins. In the case of a single-price monopoly (Fig. 12.9b), the monopoly gains the blue rectangle at the expense of the consumer, but it loses part of its producer surplus—its share of the deadweight loss. This loss reduces its gain. But there is always a net gain for the monopoly and a net loss for the consumer. We also know that because there is a deadweight loss, the consumer loses more than the monopoly gains.

In the case of a perfect price-discriminating monopoly, there is no deadweight loss but there is an even larger redistribution of the gains from trade away from consumers to the monopoly. In this case, the monopoly captures the entire consumer surplus, the green triangle in Fig. 12.9(a).

It is because it creates a deadweight loss that monopoly is inefficient. It imposes a cost on society. This cost might be avoided by the breakup of a monopoly, and a considerable amount of law and regulation, which is described and explained in Chapter 20, is directed at this problem.

R E V I E W

■ The creation of a monopoly results in a redistribution of economic gains away from consumers and to the monopoly producer.

■ If a monopoly can perfectly price discriminate, it produces the same output as a competitive industry and achieves allocative efficiency but it captures the entire consumer surplus.

■ If a monopoly cannot perfectly price discriminate, it restricts output below what a competitive industry would produce and creates a deadweight loss. The monopoly is allocatively inefficient—the consumers' loss exceeds the monopoly's gain.

Rent Seeking

The activity of searching out a monopoly from which an economic profit can be made is called **rent seeking**. The term "rent seeking" is used because "rent" (or "economic rent") is a general term that includes consumer surplus, producer surplus, and economic profit. We've seen that a monopoly makes its economic profit by diverting part of the consumer surplus to itself. Thus the pursuit of an economic profit by a monopolist is rent seeking. It is the attempt to capture some consumer surplus.

Rent seeking is a profitable activity and one that is widely pursued. It is profitable because a monopoly can make an economic profit in the long run. A firm in a competitive industry can make an economic profit only in the short run because freedom of entry brings new firms and results in economic profit being competed away. In a monopoly, barriers to entry prevent this process. Because a monopoly can make an economic profit in the long run, there is an incentive to acquire a monopoly—to rent seek.

What do rent seekers do? One form of rent seeking is the searching out of existing monopoly rights that can be bought for a lower price than the monopoly's economic profit—that is, seeking to acquire existing monopoly rights. An example of this type of rent-seeking activity is the purchase of taxicab licenses. In most cities, taxicabs are regulated. The city restricts both the fares and the number of taxis that can operate. Operating a taxi results in economic profit or rent. A person who wants to operate a taxi must buy a license from someone who already has one.

But buying an existing monopoly does not ensure an economic profit. The reason is that there is freedom of entry into the activity of rent seeking. Rent seeking is like perfect competition. If an economic profit is available, a new entrant will try to get some of it. Competition among rent seekers pushes up the price that must be paid for a monopoly right to the point at which only a normal profit can be made by operating the monopoly. The economic profit—the rent—goes to the person who created the monopoly in the first place. For example, competition for the right to operate a taxi in New York City leads to a price of more than $100,000, which is sufficiently high to eliminate long-run economic profit for the taxi operator. But the person who acquired the right in the first place collects the economic rent. This type of rent seeking transfers wealth from the buyer to the seller of the monopoly.

Although a great deal of rent-seeking activity involves searching out existing monopoly rights that can be profitably bought, much of it is devoted to the creation of monopoly. This type of rent-seeking activity takes the form of lobbying and seeking to influence the political process. Such influence is sometimes sought by making campaign contributions in exchange for legislative support or by indirectly seeking to influence political outcomes through publicity in the media or more direct contacts with politicians and bureaucrats. An example of a monopoly right created in this way is the government-imposed restrictions on the quantities of textiles that may be imported into the United States. Another is a regulation that limits the number of oranges that may be sold in the United States. These are regulations that restrict output and increase price.

This type of rent seeking is a costly activity that uses up scarce resources. In aggregate, firms spend billions of dollars lobbying Congress, state legislators, and local officials in the pursuit of licenses and laws that create barriers to entry and establish a monopoly right. Everyone has an incentive to rent seek, and because there are no barriers to entry into the rent-seeking activity, there is a great deal of competition for new monopoly rights.

What determines the value of the resources that a person will use to obtain a monopoly right? The answer is the monopoly's economic profit. If the value of resources spent trying to establish a monopoly exceeds the monopoly's economic profit, the net result is an economic loss. But as long as the value of the resources used to create a monopoly falls short of the monopoly's economic profit, there is an economic profit to be earned. With no barrier to entry into rent seeking, the value of the resources used up in rent seeking equals the monopoly's economic profit.

Because of rent seeking, monopoly imposes a social cost that exceeds the deadweight loss. That social cost equals the deadweight loss plus the value of resources used in rent seeking—the monopoly's entire economic profit because that is the value of the resources that it pays to use in rent seeking. Thus the social cost of monopoly is the deadweight loss plus the monopoly's economic profit.

Gains from Monopoly

So far, compared to perfect competition, monopoly has come out in a pretty bad light. If monopoly is so bad, why do we put up with it? Why don't we have laws that crack down on monopoly so hard that it never rears its head? We do indeed have laws that limit monopoly power (see Chapter 20). We also have laws that regulate those monopolies that exist. But monopoly is not all bad. Let's look at its potential advantages and some of the reasons for its existence.

The main reasons why monopoly might have some advantages are:

- Economies of scale and economies of scope
- Incentive to innovate

Economies of Scale and Scope   A firm experiences *economies of scale* when an increase in its production of a good or service brings a decrease in the average total cost of producing it—see Chapter 10, pp. 225–229. **Economies of scope** arise when an increase in the *range of goods produced* brings a decrease in average total cost. Economies of scope occur when highly specialized (and usually expensive) technical inputs can be shared by different goods. For example, McDonald's can produce both hamburgers and french fries at an average total cost that is lower than what it would cost two separate firms to produce the two goods because at McDonald's hamburg-

ers and french fries share the use of specialized food storage and preparation facilities. Firms producing a wide range of products can hire specialist computer programmers, designers, and marketing experts whose skills can be used across the product range, thereby spreading their costs and lowering the average total cost of production of each of the goods.

Large-scale firms that have control over supply and can influence price—and that therefore behave like the monopoly firm that we've been studying in this chapter—can reap these economies of scale and scope. Small, competitive firms cannot. As a consequence, there are situations in which the comparison of monopoly and competition that we made earlier in this chapter is not a valid one. Recall that we imagined the takeover of a large number of competitive firms by a monopoly firm. But we also assumed that the monopoly would use exactly the same technology as the small firms and have the same costs. But if one large firm can reap economies of scale and scope, its marginal cost curve will lie below the supply curve of a competitive industry made up of thousands of small firms. It is possible for such economies of scale and scope to be so large as to result in a larger output and lower price under monopoly than a competitive industry would achieve.

Figure 12.10 illustrates such a situation. Here, the demand curve (D) is the same regardless of whether the industry is a competitive one or a monopoly. With a competitive industry, the supply curve is S, the quantity produced is Q_C, and the price is P_C. The marginal revenue curve for a monopoly is MR. With a monopoly that can exploit economies of scale and scope, the marginal cost curve is MC_M. The monopoly maximizes profit by producing the output (Q_M) at which marginal revenue equals marginal cost. The price that maximizes profit is P_M. By exploiting a superior technology that is not available to each small firm, the monopoly is able to achieve a larger output and lower price than the competitive industry.

There are many examples of industries in which economies of scale are so significant that they lead to an outcome similar to that shown in Fig. 12.10. Public utilities such as gas, electric power, water, local telephone service, and garbage collection are all such cases. There are also many examples in which a combination of economies of scale and economies of scope arise. Some examples are the brewing of beer, the manufacture of refrigerators and other household appliances, the manufacture of pharmaceuticals, and the refining of petroleum.

When Economies of Scale and Scope Make Monopoly More Efficient

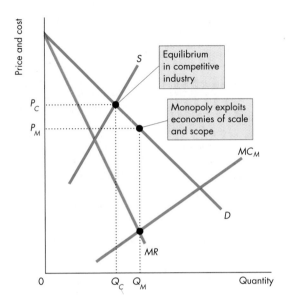

In some industries, economies of scale and economies of scope result in the monopoly's marginal cost curve (MC_M) lying below the competitive industry supply curve (S). In such a case, it is possible that the single-price monopoly output (Q_M) exceeds the competitive output (Q_C) and that the monopoly price (P_M) is below the competitive price (P_C).

Incentives to Innovate

Innovation is the first-time application of new knowledge in the production process. Innovation may take the form of developing a new product or a lower-cost way of making an existing product. Controversy has raged over whether large firms with monopoly power or small competitive firms lacking such monopoly power are the most innovative. It is clear that some temporary monopoly power arises from innovation. A firm that develops a new product or process and patents it obtains an exclusive right to that product or process for the term of the patent.

But does the granting of a monopoly, even a temporary one, to an innovator increase the pace of innovation? One line of reasoning suggests that it

does. With no protection, an innovator is not able to enjoy the profits from innovation for very long. Thus the incentive to innovate is weakened. A contrary argument is that monopolies can afford to be lazy while competitive firms cannot. Competitive firms must strive to innovate and cut costs even though they know that they cannot hang on to the benefits of their innovation for long. But that knowledge spurs them on to greater and faster innovation.

A matter such as this one cannot be resolved by listing arguments and counterarguments. It requires a careful empirical investigation. Many such investigations have been conducted, but the evidence is mixed. It shows that large firms do more research and development than do small firms. It also shows that large firms are significantly more prominent at the development end of the research and development process. But measuring research and development is measuring the volume of inputs into the process of innovation. What matters is not input but output. Two measures of the output of research and development are the number of patents and the rate of productivity growth. On these measures, there is no clear evidence that big is best. But there is a clear pattern in the process of diffusion of technological knowledge. After innovation, a new process or product spreads gradually through the industry, with large firms jumping on the bandwagon more quickly than the remaining small firms. Thus large firms speed the process of diffusion of technological advances.

In determining public policy toward monopoly (Chapter 20), laws and regulations are designed that balance the gains from monopoly (economies of scale and scope and innovation) against the deadweight loss and redistribution it generates.

◆ We've now studied two market structures: perfect competition and monopoly. We've discovered the conditions under which perfect competition achieves allocative efficiency and compared the efficiency of competition with that of monopoly.

Although there are examples of markets in the U.S. economy that are highly competitive or highly monopolistic, most markets lie somewhere between these two extremes. In the next chapter, we're going to study this middle ground between monopoly and competition. We're going to discover that many of the lessons that we learned from these two extreme models are still relevant and useful in understanding behavior in real-world markets.

Monopoly in Action: Soybean Seed

Seed Sales Sow Controversy

BY TIMOTHY J. MCNULTY

SPENCER, Iowa—The way Becky Winterboer figures it, if she hadn't spilled that bag of seed corn on her gravel driveway years ago, she wouldn't be worrying now about how the U.S. Supreme Court is going to rule.

The young farm wife and her husband, Denny, ... were not about to let the 50 pounds of seed go to waste, So ... [they] ... bought a $5 hand-held filter to strain the bits of gravel and dirt out of the corn.

One idea led to another; Winterboer ... discovered a much larger machine, a marvelous solid-oak contraption more than 60 years old ... [that] ... could strain whole bushels of soybean seeds.

With such a machine, Winterboer thought, he would clean not only his own soybeans but also help other farmers sift their soybean harvests to extract ... seeds. And that is exactly what happened.

...

"Heck," the meticulous Winterboer said one day after becoming disgusted at cleaning raccoon droppings and chicken feathers from another farmer's crop. ... "Why not just sell them my own seeds?"

And that is what landed the Winterboers in big, big trouble.

Asgrow Seed Co. ... suspected the Winterboers were creating a serious business out of selling bags of soybean seed .... To prove that, they hired an agent to buy several bags of soybean seed from them surreptitiously, and then Asgrow sued the couple for violating a federal statute, the Plant Variety Protection Act. ... The plant variety act gives seed companies a patent-like protection for 17 years after developing new strains of soybean, wheat and cotton seeds ....

But Congress included a farmers' exemption, in the act, allowing a bonafide farmer the right to save his soybean crop to use later or to sell as seed. The law, however, does not spell out how much or how little the farmer can reserve. ...

[Asgrow] alleges that the Winterboers planted 265 acres in soybeans and sold almost their entire harvest, more than 10,000 bushels, as seed. At the time, Asgrow charged $16 for a bushel of new soybean seed, while the Winterboers sold their second-generation seed at $8.70 a bushel. ...

After a two-day trial at the federal court in Sioux City, Iowa, the judge ruled in Asgrow's favor. ...

Denny Winterboer says Asgrow initially demanded $160,000. Faced with such financial pain, even ruin, the couple decided to appeal. ...

... the farm family rebounded last year when a three-judge panel unanimously overturned the lower court ruling. ...

... the case [is now] before the Supreme Court ...

Essence of THE STORY

■ The Plant Variety Protection Act gives seed companies a patent-like protection for 17 years after developing new strains of soybean, wheat, and cotton seeds.

■ The act allows farmers such as the Winterboers to sell their own seed, but it does not say how much seed a farmer may sell.

■ Asgrow Seed Co. alleged that the Winterboers sold more than 10,000 bushels as seed and sued the Winterboers for violating the Plant Variety Protection Act.

■ Asgrow's price was $16 a bushel (for new seed); the Winterboers' price was $8.70 a bushel (for second-generation seed).

■ A federal court ruled in Asgrow's favor, but the Winterboers appealed and won the appeal. The case is now before the Supreme Court.

Economic

A N A L Y S I S

■ The Plant Variety Protection Act granted a monopoly to Asgrow to produce and sell soybean seeds.

■ Figure 1 shows that Asgrow's maximizes profit by producing Q_m bushels of soybean seeds, which it sells for $16 a bushel. It makes an economic profit shown by the blue rectangle.

■ Figure 2 shows that the Winterboers can produce seed at marginal cost MC_F and that as a small producer they are a price taker. Second generation seed sells for $8.70 a bushel.

■ To maximize profit, the Winterboers produce 10,000 bushels a year.

■ It is rational for Asgrow to try to preserve its monopoly and to use resources up to its total economic profit to do so.

■ One competitor like the Winterboers is not a problem but dozens of competitors will force the price of seed down and erode Asgrow's economic profit.

■ Asgrow estimated the 10,000 bushels sold by the Winterboers cost it $160,000—10,000 × $16.

■ This amount exceeds the cost imposed on Asgrow by the Winterboers because Asgrow has some variable costs. The variable cost of 10,000 bushels must be subtracted from the $160,000 of lost revenue to calculate the damage done to Asgrow.

■ Seed companies such as Asgrow are protected so they can conduct research and develop new seeds that ultimately will increase farm efficiency—increase farm output by more than the resulting increase in the cost of seeds.

■ But to the extent that research and the development of new seeds is done in publicly funded universities and agricultural research institutions, the case for protecting seed companies is weakened.

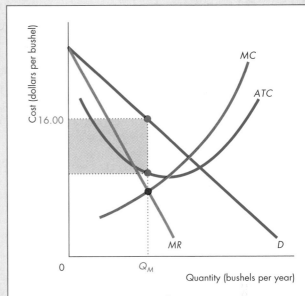

Figure 1 Asgrow's "monopoly"

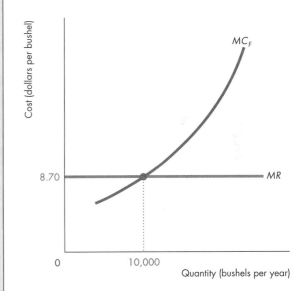

Figure 2 The Winterboers

S U M M A R Y

How Monopoly Arises

A monopoly is an industry that produces a good or service for which no close substitute exists and in which there is one supplier. Monopoly arises because barriers to entry prevent competition. Barriers to the entry of new firms may be legal or natural. Legal barriers take the form of public franchise, government license, patent, copyright, or a single firm has significant control of a resource. Natural barriers exist when economies of scale are so large that a single firm can supply an entire market at a lower average total cost than can several firms. (pp. 272–273)

Single-Price Monopoly

A single-price monopoly is a firm that charges the same price for each unit of output. The monopoly's demand curve is the market demand curve for the good. For a single-price monopoly, marginal revenue is less than price. Total revenue rises at first, but above some output level, it begins to decline. When total revenue is rising, marginal revenue is positive. When total revenue is falling, marginal revenue is negative. When total revenue is a maximum, marginal revenue is zero. When marginal revenue is positive (total revenue is rising), the elasticity of demand is greater than 1. The elasticity of demand equals 1 when marginal revenue is zero.

A monopoly's technology and costs behave in a way similar to those of any other type of firm. The monopoly maximizes profit by producing the output that makes marginal revenue equal to marginal cost and by charging the maximum price that consumers are willing to pay for that output. The price charged always exceeds marginal cost. (pp. 273–278)

Price Discrimination

Price discrimination is the practice of charging some consumers a lower price than others for an identical item or charging an individual customer a lower price on a large purchase than on a small one. Price discrimination is an attempt by the monopoly to convert consumer surplus into economic profit. Perfect price discrimination extracts all the consumer surplus. Such a monopoly charges a different price for each unit sold and obtains the maximum price that each consumer is willing to pay for each unit bought. With perfect price discrimination, the monopoly's demand curve is also its marginal revenue curve and the monopoly produces the same output as would a perfectly competitive industry.

A monopoly can discriminate between different groups of customers on the basis of age, employment status, or other easily distinguishable characteristics. Such price discrimination increases the monopoly's profit if each group has a different price elasticity of demand for the product. To maximize profit with price discrimination, the monopoly produces an output such that marginal cost equals marginal revenue but then charges each group the maximum price that it is willing to pay. These prices will be different.

Price discrimination can be practiced only when it is impossible for a buyer to resell the good and when consumers with different elasticities can be identified. (pp. 279–283)

Comparing Monopoly and Competition

A single-price monopoly charges a higher price and produces a smaller quantity than a perfectly competitive industry. A perfectly price discriminating monopoly produces the competitve quantity and sells the last unit for the competitive price.

A single-price monopoly captures consumer surplus by restricting output and creates a deadweight loss. The more a monopoly price discriminates, the smaller is the deadweight loss, the smaller is consumer surplus, and the larger is the monopoly's economic profit.

Monopoly imposes costs that equal its deadweight loss plus the cost of the resources devoted to rent-seeking—searching out profitable monopoly opportunities. At most, the resources used in rent seeking are equal in value to the economic profit that the monopoly might attain. So the maximum cost of monopoly equals deadweight loss plus its economic profit.

In industries with large economies of scale and scope, a monopoly's output can be higher and its price lower than a competitive industry could achieve. Monopoly might be more innovative than competition. (pp. 284–289)

KEY ELEMENTS

Key Figures and Table

Key Terms

REVIEW QUESTIONS

1. What is a monopoly? What are some examples of monopoly in your state?
2. How does monopoly arise?
3. What are barriers to entry? Give some examples of the various barriers to entry.
4. Distinguish between a legal monopoly and a natural monopoly. Give examples of each type.
5. Explain why a monopoly has to lower its price to be able to sell a larger quantity.
6. Explain why a monopoly's marginal revenue decreases as it sells a larger quantity.
7. Explain why marginal revenue is always less than the price for a single-price monopoly.
8. Why does a monopoly's total revenue initially increase as output increases but eventually decrease as output continues to increase?
9. Does a single-price monopoly operate on the inelastic part of its demand curve? Explain why it does or does not.
10. Explain how a single-price monopoly chooses its output and price.
11. Compare the price charged by a monopoly and its marginal revenue at its profit-maximizing output.
12. Does a monopoly always make a positive economic profit in the short run? Explain why or why not.
13. Does a monopoly make zero economic profit in the long run? Explain why or why not.
14. Can any monopoly price discriminate? If yes, why? If no, why not?
15. Explain why a single-price monopoly produces a smaller output than an equivalent competitive industry.
16. Is a single-price monopoly as efficient as competition?
17. What are consumer surplus and producer surplus?
18. What is deadweight loss?
19. Show graphically the deadweight loss under perfect price discrimination.
20. As far as allocative efficiency is concerned, is a single-price monopoly better or worse than perfect price discrimination? Why?
21. Monopoly redistributes consumer surplus. Explain why the consumer loses more under perfect price discrimination than under single-price monopoly.
22. Explain why people engage in rent-seeking activities.
23. When taking account of the cost of rent seeking, what is the social cost of monopoly?
24. What are economies of scale and economies of scope? What effects, if any, do they have on the allocative efficiency of monopoly?

P R O B L E M S

1. The figure illustrates the situation facing the publisher of the only newspaper containing local news in an isolated community. Use the figure to answer the following questions.

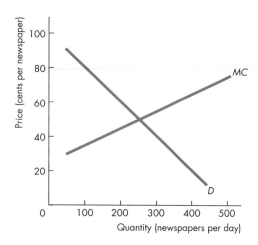

a. What quantity of newspapers will maximize the publisher's profit?
b. What price will the publisher charge for a daily newspaper?
c. What is the publisher's daily total revenue?
d. At the price charged for a newspaper, is the demand for newspapers elastic or inelastic? Why?

2. Refer to problem 1.
a. What is the allocatively efficient quantity of newspapers to print each day? Explain your answer.
b. Calculate the consumer surplus of the readers of the newspaper.
c. Calculate the deadweight loss created by the newspaper publisher.

3. Refer to the newspaper industry in problem 1. If this industry were allocatively efficient,
a. How many newspapers would be printed?
b. What would be the price of a newspaper?
c. What would be the consumer surplus of the readers of newspapers?
d. What would be the deadweight loss?

♦ 4. Minnie's Mineral Springs, a single-price monopoly, faces the following demand schedule for bottled mineral water:

Price (dollars per bottle)	Quantity demanded (bottles)
10	0
8	1
6	2
4	3
2	4
0	5

a. Calculate Minnie's total revenue schedule.
b. Calculate its marginal revenue schedule.
c. At what price is the elasticity of demand equal to 1?

♦ 5. Minnie's in problem 4 has the following total cost:

Quantity produced (bottles)	Total cost (dollars)
0	1
1	3
2	7
3	13
4	21
5	31

Calculate the profit-maximizing levels of
a. Output
b. Price
c. Marginal cost
d. Marginal revenue
e. Economic profit
f. Is Minnie's allocatively efficient? Explain your answer.

♦ 6. Suppose that Minnie's can perfectly price discriminate. Calculate its profit-maximizing
a. Output
b. Total revenue
c. Economic profit
d. Is Minnie's allocatively efficient? Explain your answer.

◆7. What is the maximum price that someone would be willing to pay Minnie's for a license to operate its mineral spring?

8. Two demand schedules for round-trip flights between New York and Mexico City are set out below. The schedule for weekday travelers is for those making round-trips on weekdays and returning within the same week. The schedule for weekend travelers is for those who stay through the weekend. (The former tend to be business travelers, and the latter tend to be vacation and pleasure travelers.)

Weekday travelers		Weekend travelers	
Price (dollars per round-trip)	**Quantity demanded** (thousands of round-trips)	**Price** (dollars per round-trip)	**Quantity demanded** (thousands) of round-trips)
1500	0		
1250	5		
1000	10		
750	15	750	0
500	15	500	5
250	15	250	10
0	15	0	15

The marginal cost of a round-trip is $500. If a single-price monopoly airline controls the New York-Mexico City route, use a graph to find out the following:
  a. What price is charged?
  b. How many passengers travel?
  c. What is the consumer surplus for weekday travelers?
  d. What is the consumer surplus for weekend travelers?
  e. Is the market allocatively efficient? Explain your answer.

9. If the airline in problem 8 discriminates between round-trips within a week and round-trips through the weekend,
  a. What is the price for the round-trip within the week?
  b. What is the price of the airline ticket with a weekend stay?
  c. What is the consumer surplus for weekday travelers?

  d. What is the consumer surplus for weekend travelers?
  e. Is the market allocatively efficient? Explain your answer.

10. If the airline in problem 8 could practice perfect price discrimination:
  a. Calculate the travelers' consumer surplus.
  b. Calculate the deadweight loss created by the airline.

◆11. Barbara runs a truck stop on the prairies, miles from anywhere. She has a monopoly and faces the following demand schedule for meals:

Price (dollars per meal)	**Quantity demanded** (meals per week)
5.00	0
4.50	20
4.00	40
3.50	60
3.00	80
2.50	100
2.00	120
1.50	140
1.00	160

Barbara's marginal cost and average total cost are a constant $2 per meal.
  a. If Barbara charges all customers the same price for a meal, what price is it?
  b. What is the consumer surplus of all the customers who buy a meal from Barbara?
  c. What is the producer surplus?
  d. What is the deadweight loss?

12. Study *Reading Between the Lines* on pp. 290–291 and then answer the following questions.
  a. Why has Asgrow been granted a monopoly in the production of soybean seed?
  b. Is Asgrow allocatively efficient? Explain why or why not.
  c. In Fig. 1 on p. 291, shade in the consumer surplus of the buyers of seed.
  d. In Fig. 1 on p. 291, shade in the deadweight loss created by Asgrow.
  e. Are any gains from trade redistributed from the buyers of soybean seed to Asgrow?

Monopolistic Competition and Oligopoly

After studying this chapter, you will be able to:

- Define monopolistic competition and oligopoly

- Explain how price and output are determined in a monopolistically competitive industry

- Explain why the price might be sticky in an oligopoly industry

- Explain how price and output are determined when an industry has one dominant firm and several small firms

- Use game theory to make predictions about price wars and competition among small numbers of firms

Every week, we receive a newspaper stuffed with supermarket fliers describing this week's "specials," providing coupons and other enticements, all designed to grab our attention and persuade us that A&P, Kroger, Safeway, Alpha Beta, Winn Dixie, Stop & Shop, Shop 'n' Save, and H.E.B.'s have the best deals in town. One claims the lowest price, another the best brands, yet another the best value for money even if its prices are not the lowest.

Fliers and War Games

How do firms locked in fierce competition with other firms set their prices, pick their products, and choose the quantities to produce? How are the profits of such firms affected by the actions of other firms? ◆ Until recently, only one firm made the chips that drive IBM and compatible PCs: Intel Corporation. During 1994, the prices of powerful personal computers based on Intel's fast 486 and Pentium chips collapsed. The reason: Intel suddenly faced competition from new chip producers such as Advanced Micro Devices Inc. and Cyrix Corp. The price of Intel's Pentium processor, set at more than $1,000 when it was launched in 1993, fell to less than $350 by spring 1995, and the price of a Pentium-based computer fell to less than $2,000. How did competition among a small number of chip makers bring such a rapid fall in the price of chips and computers?

◆ The theories of monopoly and perfect competition do not predict the kind of behavior that we've just described. There are no fliers and coupons, best brands, or price wars in perfect competition because each firm produces an identical product and is a price taker. And there are none in monopoly because each monopoly firm has the entire market to itself. To understand coupons, fliers, and price wars, we need the richer models explained in this chapter.

Varieties of Market Structure

WE HAVE STUDIED TWO TYPES OF MARKET
structure—perfect competition and monopoly. In
perfect competition, a large number of firms produce
identical goods and there are no barriers to the entry
of new firms into the industry. In this situation, each
firm is a price taker, and in the long run, there is no
economic profit. The opposite extreme, monopoly, is
an industry in which there is one firm. That firm is
protected by barriers preventing the entry of new
firms. The firm sets its price to maximize profit and
might enjoy economic profit even in the long run.

Many real-world industries are not well described
by the models of perfect competition and monopoly.
They lie somewhere between these two cases. Two
other market models have been developed to study
the industries that lie between perfect competition
and monopoly. They are:

1. Monopolistic competition
2. Oligopoly

Monopolistic competition is a market structure in which a large number of firms compete with
each other by making similar but slightly different
products. Making a product slightly different from
the product of a competing firm is called **product
differentiation**. Because of product differentiation,
a monopolistically competitive firm has an element
of monopoly power. The firm is the sole producer of
the particular version of the good in question. For
example, in the market for microwave popcorn, only
Nabisco makes Planters Premium Select. Only
General Mills makes Pop Secret. And only American
Popcorn makes Jolly Time. Each of these firms has a
monopoly on a particular brand of microwave popcorn. Differentiated products are not necessarily different in an objective sense. For example, the different brands of aspirin are chemically identical and
differ only in their packaging. What matters is that
consumers perceive the products to be differentiated.

Oligopoly is a market structure in which a
small number of producers compete with each other.
There are hundreds of examples of oligopolistic
industries. Computer software, airplane manufacture,
and international air transportation are but a few. In
some oligopolistic industries, each firm produces an
almost identical product, while in others, products
are differentiated. For example, oil and gasoline are
essentially the same whether they are made by Texaco
or Exxon. But Chrysler's Cirrus is a differentiated
product from Chevrolet's Lumina and Ford's Taurus.

Many factors must be taken into account to
determine which market structure describes a particular real-world market. But one of these factors is the
extent to which the market is dominated by a small
number of firms. To measure this feature of markets,
economists have developed indexes called measures of
concentration. Let's look at these measures.

Measures of Concentration

To tell how close to the competitive or monopolistic
extreme an industry comes or where in between these
extremes it lies, economists have developed two measures of industrial concentration. They are:

1. The four-firm concentration ratio
2. The Herfindahl-Hirschman Index

The Four-Firm Concentration Ratio   The **four-
firm concentration ratio** is the percentage of the
value of sales accounted for by the four largest firms
in an industry. The range of the concentration ratio is
from almost zero for perfect competition to 100 percent for monopoly. This ratio is the main measure
used to assess market structure.

Table 13.1 sets out two hypothetical concentration ratio calculations, one for tires and one for printing. In this example, there are 14 firms in the tire
industry. The biggest four have 80 percent of the sales
of the industry, so the four-firm concentration ratio
for that industry is 80 percent. In the printing industry, with 1,004 firms, the top four firms account for
only 0.5 percent of total industry sales. In that case,
the four-firm concentration ratio is 0.5 percent.

The idea behind calculating four-firm concentration ratios is to get information about the degree of
competitiveness of a market: A low concentration
ratio indicates a high degree of competition, and a
high concentration ratio indicates an absence of competition. In the extreme case of monopoly, the concentration ratio is 100 percent—the largest (and
only) firm makes the entire industry sales. The four-
firm concentration ratio is also regarded as a useful
indicator of the likelihood of collusion among firms
in an oligopoly. If the ratio exceeds 60 percent, it is
likely that firms will collude and behave like a
monopoly. If the ratio is less than 40 percent, it is
likely that the firms will compete effectively.

TABLE 13.1

Concentration Ratio Calculations

Tiremakers		Printers	
Firm	**Sales** (millions of dollars)	**Firm**	**Sales** (millions of dollars)
Top, Inc.	200	Fran's	2.5
ABC, Inc.	250	Ned's	2.0
Big, Inc.	150	Tom's	1.8
XYZ, Inc.	100	Jill's	1.7
Top 4 sales	700	Top 4 sales	8.0
Other 10 firms' sales	175	Other 1,000 firms' sales	1,592.0
Industry sales	**875**	Industry sales	**1,600.0**

Four-firm concentration ratios:

Tiremakers: $\dfrac{700}{875} \times 100 = 80\%$ Printers: $\dfrac{8}{1,600} \times 100 = 0.5\%$

The Herfindahl-Hirschman Index   The **Herfindahl-Hirschman Index**—also called the HHI—is calculated as the square of market share (percentage) of each firm summed over the largest 50 firms (or summed over all the firms if there are fewer than 50) in a market. For example, suppose there are four firms in a market. The market shares of the firms are 50 percent, 25 percent, 15 percent, and 10 percent. The Herfindahl-Hirschman Index is calculated as

$$HHI = 50^2 + 25^2 + 15^2 + 10^2 = 3,450.$$

If each of the largest 50 firms has a market share of 0.1 percent, the HHI is $0.1^2 \times 50 = 0.5$. Such a market is perfectly competitive. If a market has only one firm that has a 100 percent market share, the HHI is $100^2 = 10,000$. Such a market is a monopoly.

The HHI is used as an indicator of monopoly power. It became a popular measure during the 1980s, when the Justice Department used it to classify markets. If the HHI is less than 1,800, a market is regarded as being competitive. (An HHI less than 1,000 is highly competitive, and one between 1,000 and 1,800 is moderately competitive.) But if the HHI exceeds 1,800, a market is regarded as being highly concentrated. The Justice Department scrutinizes any mergers of firms in markets in which the HHI exceeds 1,800.

Although the HHI has an official status, most users of the two measures find the concentration ratio more intuitive than the HHI and point out that the formula for the HHI is not derived from any theory or observations and is arbitrary.

Table 13.2 summarizes the characteristics of perfect competition, monopolistic competition, oligopoly, and monopoly and their concentration ratios.

Limitations of Concentration Measures

Although concentration ratios and HHIs are useful, they have some limitations and must be supplemented by other information to determine a market's structure. There are three key problems:

■ The geographical scope of the market

■ Barriers to entry and firm turnover

■ The correspondence between a market and an industry

Geographical Scope of Market   Concentration ratio data are based on a national view of the market. Many goods are sold in a national market, but some are sold in a regional market and some in a

TABLE 13.2

Market Structure

Characteristics	Perfect competition	Monopolistic competition	Oligopoly	Monopoly
Number of firms in industry	Many	Many	Few	One
Product	Identical	Differentiated	Either identical or differentiated	No close substitutes
Barriers to entry	None	None	Scale and scope economies	Scale and scope economies or legal barriers
Firm's control over price	None	Some	Considerable	Considerable or regulated
Concentration ratio	0	Low	High	100
HHI	Less than 1,000	1,000 to 1,800	More than 1,800	10,000
Examples	Wheat, corn	Food, clothing	Automobiles, cereals	Local phone service, electric and gas utilities

global one. The newspaper industry is a good example of one for which the local market is more relevant than the national market. Thus although the concentration ratio for newspapers is not high, there is a high degree of concentration in the newspaper industry in most cities. The automobile industry is an example of one for which there is a global market. Thus although the biggest four U.S. car producers account for 92 percent of all cars sold by U.S. producers, they account for a smaller percentage of the total U.S. car market (including imports) and a smaller percentage of the global market for cars.

Barriers to Entry and Turnover Measures of concentration do not tell us how severe are the barriers to entry in an industry. Some industries are highly concentrated but have virtually free entry and experience an enormous amount of turnover of firms. An example is the market in local restaurants. Many small towns have few restaurants. But there are no restrictions on entering the restaurant industry, and indeed firms do enter and exit with great regularity.

Even if there is not much entry and exit, an industry might be competitive because of the potential for entry—because the few firms in the market face potential competition from many firms that can easily enter the market.

Market and Industry The classifications used to calculate concentration ratios allocate every firm in the U.S. economy to a particular industry. But markets for particular goods do not usually correspond to industries.

The main problem is that markets are usually much narrower than industries. For example, the pharmaceutical industry, which has a low concentration ratio, operates in many separate markets for individual products (drugs and treatments), each one of which has almost no substitute. So this industry, which looks competitive, operates in many somewhat monopolistic markets.

Another problem arises from the fact that firms make many products. For example, Westinghouse makes electrical equipment and, among other things, gas-fired incinerators and plywood. So this one firm operates in at least three separate markets. But Westinghouse is classified by the Department of Commerce as being in the electrical goods and equipment industry.

A further problem arises from the fact that firms switch from market to market depending on the profit opportunities that exist. Many firms have built their initial organization on one product but then diversified into a wide variety of others. For example, Motorola, which today produces a wide variety of wireless communications products, has diversified from being a TV and computer chip maker. Motorola produces no TVs today. Publishers of newspapers, magazines, and textbooks are today rapidly diversifying into multimedia products.

Despite their limitations, combined with information about the geographical scope of the market, barriers to entry, and the extent to which large, multiproduct firms straddle a variety of markets, concentration ratios provide a basis for determining the degree of competition in an industry.

Concentration Measures for the U.S. Economy

Figure 13.1 shows a selection of concentration ratios and HHIs for the United States calculated by the Department of Commerce. Motor vehicles, light bulbs, refrigerators, chewing gum, and breakfast cereals are highly concentrated oligopolies. Industries from macaroni and spaghetti to commercial printing are highly competitive. Chocolate products and cookies and crackers are moderately concentrated.

FIGURE 13.1

Some Concentration Measures in the United States

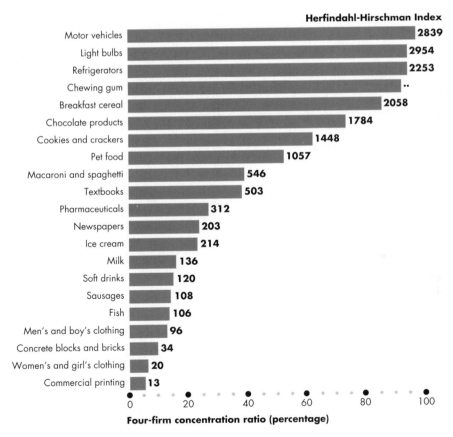

Measured by the four-firm concentration ratio and the Herfindahl-Hirschman Index, the industries producing motor vehicles, light bulbs, and refrigerators are highly concentrated, while the industries producing commercial printing, women's dresses, and concrete blocks and bricks are highly competitive. The industries producing pet foods and textbooks have an intermediate degree of concentration.

Source: U.S. Department of Commerce, *Concentration Ratios in Manufacturing,* MC82-S-7, Washington D.C., 1986.

Market Structures in the U.S. Economy

Figure 13.2 shows the market structure of the U.S. economy and the trends in market structure between 1939 and 1980. (Comparable data for the 1980s and 1990s are not available.) Over this period, the U.S. economy became increasingly competitive.

In 1980, three quarters of the value of goods and services bought and sold in the United States was traded in markets that are essentially competitive—markets that have almost perfect competition or monopolistic competition. Monopoly and the dominance of a single firm, which are found mainly in public utilities and public transportation, accounted for about 5 percent of sales. Oligopoly, which is found mainly in manufacturing, accounted for about 18 percent of sales.

FIGURE 13.2

The Market Structure of the U.S. Economy

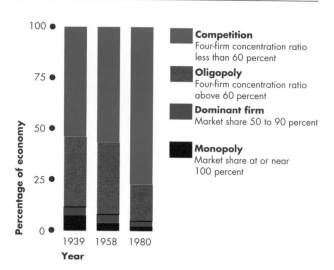

The market structure of three quarters of the U.S. economy is effectively competitive (perfect competition or monopolistic competition), one fifth is oligopoly, and the rest is monopoly. The economy became more competitive between 1939 and 1980.

Source: William G. Shepherd, "Causes of Increased Competition in the U.S. Economy, 1939-1980," *Review of Economics and Statistics,* November 1982, pp. 613–626.

Monopolistic Competition

MONOPOLISTIC COMPETITION ARISES IN AN industry in which:

- A large number of firms compete.
- Each firm produces a differentiated product, which is a close but not a perfect substitute for the products of the other firms.
- Firms are free to enter and exit.

Makers of running shoes, pizza producers, auto-service stations, family restaurants, and realtors are all examples of firms that operate in monopolistic competition. In monopolistic competition, as in perfect competition, the industry consists of a large number of firms and each firm supplies a small part of the total industry output. Because each firm is small, no one firm can effectively influence what other firms do. If one firm changes its price, this action has no effect on the actions of the other firms.

Unlike perfect competition and like monopoly, a firm in monopolistic competition faces a downward-sloping demand curve. The reason is that the firm's product is differentiated from the products of its competitors. Some people will pay more for one variety of the product, so when its price rises, the quantity demanded falls but it does not (necessarily) fall to zero. For example, Adidas, Asics, Diadora, Etonic, Fila, New Balance, Nike, Puma, and Reebok all make differentiated running shoes. Other things remaining the same, if the price of Adidas running shoes rises and the prices of the other shoes remain constant, Adidas sells fewer shoes and the other producers sell more. But Adidas shoes don't disappear unless the price rises by a large amount. Because a firm in monopolistic competition faces a downward-sloping demand curve, it maximizes profit by choosing both its price and its output.

Like competition and unlike monopoly, in monopolistic competition there is free entry and free exit. As a consequence, a firm in monopolistic competition cannot make an economic profit in the long run. When economic profit is being made, new firms enter the industry. This entry lowers prices and eventually eliminates economic profit. When economic losses are incurred, some firms leave the industry. This exit increases prices and profits and eventually eliminates the economic loss. In long-run equilibrium, firms neither enter nor leave the industry and the firms in the industry make zero economic profit.

Price and Output in Monopolistic Competition

Figure 13.3 shows how price and output are determined by a firm in a monopolistically competitive industry. Part (a) deals with the short run, and part (b) deals with the long run. Let's concentrate initially on the short run. The demand curve D shows the demand for the firm's own variety of the product. For example, it is the demand for Bayer aspirin rather than for painkillers in general or for McDonald's hamburgers rather than for hamburgers in general. The curve labeled MR is the marginal revenue curve associated with the demand curve. The figure also shows the firm's average total cost (ATC) and marginal cost (MC). The firm maximizes profit in the short run by producing output Q_S, where marginal revenue equals marginal cost, and charging the price P_S. The

firm's average total cost is C_S, and the firm makes a short-run economic profit, as measured by the blue rectangle.

So far, the monopolistically competitive firm looks just like a monopoly. It produces the quantity at which marginal revenue equals marginal cost and then charges the price that buyers are willing to pay for that quantity, determined by the demand curve. The key difference between monopoly and monopolistic competition lies in what happens next.

There is no restriction on entry in monopolistic competition, so economic profit attracts new entrants. As new firms enter the industry, the firm's demand curve and marginal revenue curve start to shift leftward. At each point in time, the firm maximizes its short-run profit by producing the quantity at which marginal revenue equals marginal cost and by charging the price that buyers are willing to pay

---

FIGURE 13.3

Monopolistic Competition

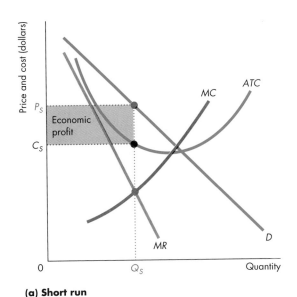

(a) Short run

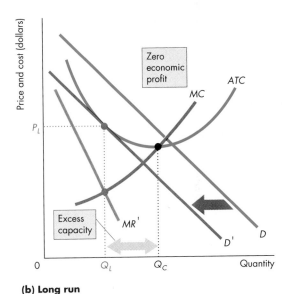

(b) Long run

Profit is maximized where marginal revenue equals marginal cost. Part (a) shows the short-run outcome. Profit is maximized by producing quantity Q_S and selling it for price P_S. Average total cost is C_S, and the firm makes an economic profit (the blue rectangle). Economic profit encourages new entrants in the long run.

Part (b) shows the long-run outcome. The entry of new

firms decreases each firm's demand, and shift the demand curve and marginal revenue curve leftward. When the demand curve has shifted to D', the marginal revenue curve is MR' and the firm is in long-run equilibrium. The output that maximizes profit is Q_L, the price is P_L, and economic profit is zero. Because each firm produces less output than its capacity Q_C, it has excess capacity.

for this quantity. But as the demand curve shifts leftward, the profit-maximizing quantity and price fall.

Figure 13.3(b) shows the long-run equilibrium. The firm produces Q_L and sells it at a price of P_L. In this situation, the firm is making zero economic profit. There is no incentive for firms to enter or exit.

Excess Capacity A firm's *capacity* output is the output produced when average total cost is a minimum—the output at the bottom of the U-shaped *ATC* curve (Q_C in Fig. 13.3b). In monopolistic competition, in the long run, firms always have *excess capacity*. In Fig. 13.3(b), the firm produces Q_L and has excess capacity of $Q_C - Q_L$. That is, firms produce less output than that which minimizes average total cost. As a consequence, the consumer pays a price that exceeds minimum average total cost. This result arises from the fact that the firm faces a downward-sloping demand curve. The demand curve slopes down because of product differentiation—because one firm's product is not a perfect substitute for another firm's product. Thus it is product differentiation that produces excess capacity.

You can see the excess capacity in monopolistic competition all around you. Family restaurants (except for the truly outstanding ones) almost always have a few empty tables. You can always get a pizza delivered in less than 30 minutes. It is rare that every pump at a gas station is in use with customers waiting in line. There is always an abundance of realtors ready to help find or sell a home.

Efficiency of Monopolistic Competition

When we studied a perfectly competitive industry, we discovered that in some circumstances, such an industry achieves allocative efficiency. A key feature of allocative efficiency is that price equals marginal cost. Recall that price measures the value placed on the last unit bought by the consumer and marginal cost measures the firm's opportunity cost of producing the last unit. We also discovered that monopoly is allocatively inefficient because it restricts output below the level at which price equals marginal cost. As we have just discovered, monopolistic competition shares this feature with monopoly. Even though there is zero economic profit in long-run equilibrium, the monopolistically competitive industry produces an output at which price equals average total cost but exceeds marginal cost.

Because in monopolistic competition, price exceeds marginal cost, this market structure, like monopoly, is allocatively inefficient. The marginal cost of producing one more unit of output is less than the marginal benefit to the consumer, determined by the price the consumer is willing to pay. But the inefficiency of monopolistic competition arises from product differentiation—from product variety. Variety is valued by consumers, but it is achievable only if firms make differentiated products. So the loss in allocative efficiency that occurs in monopolistic competition must be weighed against the gain of greater product variety.

Product Innovation

Another source of gain from monopolistically competitive industries is product innovation. Monopolistically competitive firms are constantly seeking out new products that will provide them with a competitive edge, even if only temporarily. A firm that manages to introduce a new and differentiated variety will temporarily face a steeper demand curve than before and will be able to temporarily increase its price. It will make an economic profit. New firms that make close substitutes for the new product will enter and compete away the economic profit arising from this initial advantage.

Selling Costs

A large and increasing proportion of the prices we pay goes to cover the cost of selling the good, not the cost of making it. When you visit a major shopping mall, you see store designs, indoor gardens, and waterfalls that might be movie sets. The cost of these items are just a part of selling costs. Others are the costs of glossy catalogs and brochures, magazine and television advertising, and the salaries, airfares, and hotel bills of salespeople. All these costs are incurred because monopolistically competitive firms strive to differentiate their products from those of other firms. Some product differentiation is achieved by designing and introducing products that are actually different from those of the other firms in the industry. But firms also attempt to differentiate the consumer's perception of the product. Marketing and advertising are the principal means whereby firms seek to achieve this end. But selling costs increase a monopolistically competitive firm's costs above those of a competitive firm or a monopoly that does not incur such selling costs.

To the extent that selling costs provide consumers with services that are valued and with information about the precise nature of the differentiation of products, they serve a valuable purpose to the consumer and enable a better product choice to be made. But the opportunity cost of the additional services and information must be weighed against the gain to the consumer.

The bottom line on the question of allocative efficiency of monopolistic competition is ambiguous. In some cases, the gains from extra product variety unquestionably offset the selling and marketing costs and the extra cost arising from excess capacity. The tremendous varieties of books and magazines, clothing, food, and drinks are examples of such gains. It is less easy to see the gains from being able to buy brand-name drugs that have a chemical composition identical to that of a generic alternative. But some people do willingly pay more for the brand-name alternative.

R E V I E W

■ In monopolistic competition, a large number of firms compete with each other, but because each firm produces a differentiated product, it faces a downward-sloping demand curve.

■ In the short run, firms can make economic profit.

■ Economic profit stimulates entry. In the long run, firms make zero economic profit—normal profit.

■ In long-run equilibrium, price equals average total cost but exceeds marginal cost, and the quantity produced is less than that which minimizes average total cost.

■ The cost of monopolistic competition is excess capacity and high advertising expenditure; the gain is a wide product variety and valuable information to the consumer.

You've seen that monopolistic competition is a blend of monopoly and competition. As in monopoly, each firm faces a downward-sloping demand curve and sets its price. But as in perfect competition economic profit triggers entry, so in long-run equilibrium, economic profits are completed away and firms make normal profit.

Oligopoly, which we now study, is fundamentally different from the other market types because each firm must take account of its actions on other firms.

Oligopoly

IN OLIGOPOLY, A SMALL NUMBER OF PRODUCERS compete with each other. The quantity sold by any one producer depends on that producer's price *and* on the other producers' prices and quantities sold. Each firm must take into account the effects of its own actions on the actions of other firms.

To see the interplay between prices and sales, suppose you run one of the three gas stations in a small town. If you lower your price and your two competitors don't lower theirs, your sales increase, but the sales of the other two firms decrease. In such a situation, the other firms will, most likely, lower their prices too. If they do cut their prices, your sales and profits will take a tumble. So before deciding to cut your price, you try to predict how the other firms will react and you attempt to calculate the effects of those reactions on your own profit.

A variety of models have been developed to explain the determination of price and quantity in oligopoly markets, and no one theory has been found that can explain all the different types of behavior that we observe in such markets. The models fall into two broad groups: traditional models and game theory models. We'll look at examples of both types, starting with two traditional models.

The Kinked Demand Curve Model

The kinked demand curve model is a model of oligopoly based on assumptions about the beliefs of each firm concerning the reactions of another firm (or firms) to its own actions. These beliefs are:

1. If I increase my price, I will be on my own—others will not follow me.

2. If I decrease my price, so will everyone else.

Figure 13.4 shows a demand curve (*D*) that reflects these beliefs. The demand curve has a kink occurring at the current price, which is *P*. At prices above *P*, the demand curve is relatively elastic. It reflects the belief that if the firm raises its price above *P*, its price will be higher than the price set by the other firms. So the quantity demanded will fall by a relatively large amount. At prices below *P*, the demand curve is less elastic. It reflects the belief that if the firm lowers its price, the other firms will lower their prices too. So the quantity demanded will increase by a relatively small amount.

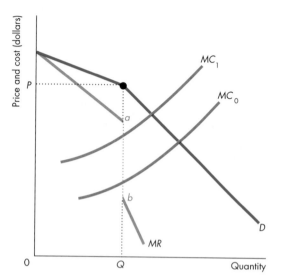

FIGURE 13.4

The Kinked Demand Curve Model

The price in an oligopoly market is *P*. Each firm believes it faces the demand curve *D*. At prices above *P*, demand is relatively elastic because the firm believes that its price increases will not be matched by other firms. At prices below *P*, demand is less elastic because the firm believes that its price cuts will be matched. Because the demand curve is kinked, the marginal revenue curve, *MR*, has a break *ab*. Profit is maximized by producing *Q*. The marginal cost curve passes through the break in the marginal revenue curve. Marginal cost changes inside the range *ab* leave the price and quantity unchanged.

The kink in demand curve *D* creates a break in the marginal revenue curve (*MR*). To maximize profit, the firm produces the quantity that makes marginal cost and marginal revenue equal. But that output, *Q*, is where the marginal cost curve passes through the discontinuity in the marginal revenue curve—the gap *ab*. If marginal cost fluctuates between *a* and *b*, as shown in the figure by the marginal cost curves *MC₀* and *MC₁*, the firm will change neither its price nor its quantity of output. Only if marginal cost fluctuates outside the range *ab* will the firm change its price and quantity produced.

Thus the kinked demand curve model predicts that price and quantity will be insensitive to small cost changes but will respond if cost changes are large enough. That is, the price will be sticky.

But there are two problems with the kinked demand curve model:

- It does not tell us how the price, *P*, is determined.
- It does not tell us what happens if firms discover that their belief about the demand curve is incorrect.

Suppose, for example, that marginal cost increases by enough to cause the firm to increase its price and that all firms experience the same increase in marginal cost, so they all increase their prices together. Each firm bases its action on the belief that other firms will not match its price increase, but that belief is incorrect. The firm's beliefs are inconsistent with reality, and the demand and marginal revenue curves that summarize those beliefs (such as those in Fig. 13.4) are not the correct ones for the purpose of calculating the new profit-maximizing price and output. A firm that bases its actions on beliefs that are wrong does not maximize profit and might well end up incurring an economic loss, leading to its eventual exit from the industry.

The kinked demand curve model is an attempt to understand price and output determination in an oligopoly in which the firms are of similar size. Another traditional model deals with the case in which firms differ in size and one firm dominates the industry.

Dominant Firm Oligopoly

A dominant firm oligopoly arises when one firm—the dominant firm—has a substantial cost advantage over the other firms and produces a large part of the industry output. The dominant firm sets the market price and the other firms are price takers. An example of a dominant firm oligopoly is a large gasoline retailer or a big video rental company that dominates its market in a particular city.

To see how a dominant firm oligopoly works, suppose that 11 firms operate gas stations in a city. Big-G is the dominant firm. It sells 50 percent of the city's gas. The other firms are small, and each sells 5 percent of the city's gas.

Figure 13.5 shows the market for gas in this city. In part (a), the demand curve *D* tells us how the total quantity of gas demanded in the city is influenced by its price. The supply curve *S₁₀* is the supply curve of the 10 small suppliers. These firms are price takers.

Part (b) shows the situation facing Big-G, the dominant firm. Big-G's marginal cost curve is *MC*. The demand curve for gasoline facing Big-G is *XD*.

This curve is found by working out the amount of excess demand arising from the rest of the market. It graphs the difference between the quantity demanded and the quantity supplied in the rest of the market at each price. Thus, for example, at a price of $1 a gallon, the distance *ab* in part (a) measures the excess quantity demand in the rest of the market. That same distance *ab* at the price of $1 a gallon in part (b) provides us with one point, point *b*, on Big-G's demand curve, *XD*.

If Big-G sold gasoline in a perfectly competitive city gas market, it would be willing to supply it at the prices indicated by its marginal cost curve. The city market would operate at the point of intersection of Big-G's marginal cost curve and its demand curve. But Big-G can do better for itself than that. Because it controls 50 percent of the city's gas market, it can restrict its sales, decreasing the amount of gas available and increasing its price.

To maximize its profit, Big-G operates like a monopoly. Big G's demand curve is the excess demand curve *XD*. To operate like a monopoly, Big-G must calculate its marginal revenue and find its marginal revenue curve. The curve is *MR* in Fig. 13.5(b). This curve tells us the extra revenue Big-G gets from selling one more gallon of gas. To maximize profit, Big-G sells the quantity that makes its marginal revenue equal to its marginal cost. Thus it sells 10,000 gallons of gas for $1 a gallon. With this price and quantity of sales, Big-G makes the biggest possible profit. The 10 small firms are price takers, so they take the price of $1 a gallon and behave competitively. The quantity of gas demanded in the entire city at $1 a gallon is 20,000 gallons, as shown in part (a). Of this amount, 10,000 gallons are sold by Big-G and 10,000 gallons are sold by the 10 small firms that sell 1,000 gallons each.

FIGURE 13.5

A Dominant Firm Oligopoly

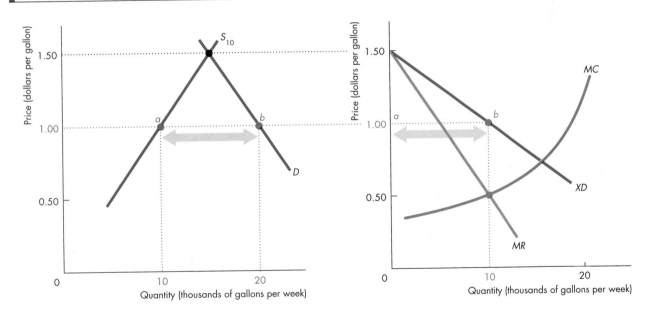

(a) Ten small firms and market demand

(b) Big-G's price and output decision

The demand curve for gas in a city is *D* in part (a). There are 10 small competitive firms that together have a supply curve of S_{10}. In addition, there is 1 large firm, Big-G, shown in part (b). Big-G faces the demand curve *XD*, determined as market demand *D* minus the supply of the other 10 firms S_{10}—the demand that is not satisfied by the small firms. Big-G's margin-

al revenue is *MR*, and marginal cost is *MC*. Big-G sets its output to maximize profit by equating marginal cost, *MC*, and marginal revenue, *MR*. This output is 10,000 gallons per week. The price at which Big-G can sell this quantity is $1 a gallon. The other 10 firms take this price, and each firm sells 1,000 gallons per week.

REVIEW

- If a firm believes that a price cut will be matched by other firms but a price rise will not, the firm faces a demand curve with a kink at the current price and quantity and a marginal revenue curve with a break in it.
- If a firm faces a kinked demand curve, its price will be sticky.
- If one firm dominates a market because its costs are lower than the other firms' costs, the dominant firm acts like a monopoly and sets its profit-maximizing price.
- When the dominant firm sets the price, the other firms take this price and act like competitive firms.

The dominant firm model of oligopoly works for markets in which there is a producer that has a cost advantage over all the other firms. But the model doesn't explain why the dominant firm has a cost advantage or what happens if some of the smaller firms acquire the same technology and costs as the dominant firm. Also it does not predict prices and quantities in markets in which firms are of similar size. The kinked demand curve model attempts to deal with this alternative case. But, as we've seen, that model has some weaknesses.

The weaknesses of traditional theories of oligopoly and a widespread dissatisfaction with them is one of the main forces leading to the development of new oligopoly models based on game theory.

Game Theory

THE TOOL THAT ECONOMISTS USE TO ANALYZE *strategic behavior*—behavior that takes into account the expected behavior of others and the mutual recognition of interdependence—is called **game theory**. Game theory was invented by John von Neumann in 1937 and extended by von Neumann and Oskar Morgenstern in 1944. Today, it is a major research field in economics.

Game theory seeks to understand oligopoly as well as political and social rivalries by using a method of analysis specifically designed to understand games of all types, including the familiar games of everyday life. We will begin our study of game theory, and its application to the behavior of firms, by considering those familiar games.

Familiar Games: What They Have in Common

What is a game? At first thought, the question seems silly. After all, there are many different games. There are ball games and parlor games, games of chance and games of skill. What do games of such diversity and variety have in common? In answering this question, we will focus on those features of games that are relevant for game theory and for analyzing oligopoly as a game. All games have three things in common:

- Rules
- Strategies
- Payoffs

Let's see how these common features of games apply to a game called "the prisoners' dilemma." This game, it turns out, captures some of the essential features of oligopoly, and it gives a good illustration of how game theory works and how it leads to predictions about the behavior of the players.

The Prisoners' Dilemma

Art and Bob have been caught red-handed, stealing a car. Facing airtight cases, they will receive a sentence of two years each for their crime. During his interviews with the two prisoners, the district attorney begins to suspect that he has stumbled on the two people who were responsible for a multimillion-dollar bank robbery some months earlier. But this is just a suspicion. The district attorney has no evidence on which he can convict them of the greater crime unless he can get them to confess. The district attorney decides to make the prisoners play a game with the following rules.

Rules Each prisoner (player) is placed in a separate room, and there is no communication between them. Each is told that he is suspected of having carried out the bank robbery and that:

If both he and his accomplice confess to the larger crime, each will receive a sentence of 3 years.

If he alone confesses and his accomplice does not, he will receive an even shorter sentence of 1 year while his accomplice will receive a 10-year sentence.

Strategies In game theory, as in ordinary games, **strategies** are all the possible actions of each player. The strategies in the prisoners' dilemma game are very simple. Each prisoner (player) can do only one of two things:

- Confess to the bank robbery.
- Deny having committed the bank robbery.

Payoffs   Because there are two players, each with two strategies, there are four possible outcomes:

1. Neither player confesses.
2. Both players confess.
3. Art confesses but Bob does not.
4. Bob confesses but Art does not.

Each prisoner can work out exactly what will happen to him—his *payoff*—in each of these four situations. We can tabulate the four possible payoffs for each of the prisoners in what is called a payoff matrix for the game. A **payoff matrix** is a table that shows the payoffs for every possible action by each player for every possible action by each other player.

Table 13.3 shows a payoff matrix for Art and Bob. The squares show the payoffs for each prisoner—the red triangle in each square shows Art's and the blue triangle shows Bob's. If both prisoners confess (top left), each gets a prison term of 3 years. If Bob confesses but Art denies (top right), Art gets a 10-year sentence and Bob gets a 1-year sentence. If Art confesses and Bob denies (bottom left), Art gets a 1-year sentence and Bob gets a 10-year sentence. Finally, if both of them deny (bottom right), neither can be convicted of the bank robbery charge but both are sentenced for the car theft—a 2-year sentence.

Equilibrium   The equilibrium of a game occurs when player *A* takes the best possible action given the action of player *B* and player *B* takes the best possible action given the action of player *A*. In the case of the prisoners' dilemma, the equilibrium occurs when Art makes his best choice given Bob's choice and when Bob makes his best choice given Art's choice. Let's find the equilibrium of the prisoners' dilemma game.

Look at the situation from Art's point of view. Art realizes that his outcome depends on the action Bob takes. If Bob confesses, it pays Art to confess also, for in that case, he will be sentenced to 3 years rather than 10 years. But if Bob does not confess, it still pays Art to confess for in that case he will receive 1 year rather than 2 years. Art reasons that, regardless of Bob's action, his own best action is to confess.

The problem from Bob's point of view is identical to Art's. Bob knows that if Art confesses, he will receive 10 years if he does not confess and 3 years if

TABLE 13.3
Prisoners' Dilemma Payoff Matrix

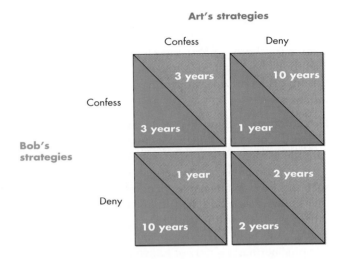

Each square shows the payoffs for the two players, Art and Bob, for each possible pair of actions. In each square, the red triangle shows Art's payoff and the blue triangle shows Bob's. For example, if both confess, the payoffs are in the top left square. The equilibrium of the game is for both players to confess and each gets a 3-year sentence.

he does. Therefore if Art confesses, it pays Bob to confess. Similarly, if Art does not confess, Bob will receive 2 years for not confessing and 1 year if he confesses. Again, it pays Bob to confess. Bob's best action, regardless of Art's action, is to confess.

Nash Equilibrium   The equilibrium concept that we have used—player *A* takes the best possible action given the action of player *B* and player *B* takes the best possible action given the action of player *A*—is called a **Nash equilibrium**; it is so named because it was first proposed by John Nash of Princeton University, who received the Nobel Prize for Economic Science in 1994.

Each prisoner sees that, regardless of what the other prisoner does, his own best action is to confess. Because each player's best action is to confess, each will confess, each will get a 3-year prison term, and the district attorney will have solved the bank robbery. This is the equilibrium of the game.

The prisoners' dilemma is a game that has a special kind of Nash equilibrium called a dominant strategy equilibrium. A *dominant strategy* is a strategy that is the same regardless of the action taken by the other player. In other words, each player has a unique best action regardless of what the other player does. A **dominant strategy equilibrium** occurs when there is a dominant strategy for each player. In the prisoners' dilemma, no matter what Bob does, Art's best strategy is to confess; and no matter what Art does, Bob's best strategy is to confess. Thus the equilibrium of the prisoners' dilemma is that each player confesses.

The Dilemma   Now that you have found the solution to the prisoners' dilemma, you can better appreciate the nature of the dilemma. The dilemma arises for each prisoner as he contemplates the consequences of confessing and not confessing. Each prisoner knows that if both he and his accomplice remain silent about the bank robbery, they will be sentenced to only 2 years for stealing the car. But neither prisoner has any way of knowing that his accomplice will remain silent and refuse to confess. Each knows that if the other confesses and he denies, the other will receive only a 1-year sentence while he himself will receive a 10-year sentence. Each poses the following questions: Should I deny and rely on my accomplice to deny so that we will both get only 2 years? Or should I confess in the hope of getting just 1 year (provided that my accomplice denies) but knowing that if my accomplice does confess, we will both get 3 years in prison? The dilemma is resolved by finding the equilibrium of the game.

A Bad Outcome   For the prisoners, the equilibrium of the game, with each confessing, is not the best outcome. If neither of them confesses, each will get only 2 years for the lesser crime. Isn't there some way in which this better outcome can be achieved? It seems that there is not, because the players cannot communicate with each other. Each player can put himself in the other player's place, and so each player can figure out that there is a dominant strategy for each of them. The prisoners are indeed in a dilemma. Each knows that he can serve 2 years only if he can trust the other not to confess. But each prisoner also knows that it is not in the best interest of the other not to confess. Thus each prisoner knows that he has to confess, thereby delivering a bad outcome for both.

Let's now see how we can use the ideas we've just developed to understand price fixing, price wars, and the behavior of firms in oligopoly.

Oligopoly Game

To UNDERSTAND HOW AN OLIGOPOLY GAME works, it is revealing to study a special case of oligopoly called duopoly. **Duopoly** is a market structure in which there are two producers of a commodity competing with each other. There are few cases of duopoly on a national and international scale but many cases of local duopolies. For example, in some communities, there are two suppliers of milk, two local newspapers, two taxi companies, two car rental firms, or two college bookstores. But the main reason for studying duopoly is not its "realism." It is the fact that it captures all the essential features of oligopoly and yet is more manageable to analyze and understand.

To study a duopoly game, we're going to build a model of a duopoly industry.[1] Suppose that only two firms, Trick and Gear, make a particular kind of electric switchgear. Our goal is to make predictions about the prices charged and the outputs produced by each of the two firms. We are going to pursue that goal by constructing a duopoly game that the two firms will play. To set out the game, we need to specify the strategies of the players and the payoff matrix.

We will suppose that the two firms enter into a collusive agreement. A **collusive agreement** is an agreement between two (or more) producers to restrict output in order to raise prices and profits. Such an agreement is illegal in the United States and is undertaken in secret. A group of firms that has entered into a collusive agreement to restrict output and increase prices and profits is called a **cartel**. The strategies that firms in a cartel can pursue are to:

- Comply
- Cheat

Complying simply means sticking to the agreement. Cheating means breaking the agreement in a manner designed to benefit the cheating firm.

Because each firm has two strategies, there are four possible combinations of actions for the two firms:

- Both firms comply.
- Both firms cheat.
- Trick complies and Gear cheats.
- Gear complies and Trick cheats.

---

[1]The model is inspired by a real-world case known as "the incredible electrical conspiracy." But don't lose sight of the fact that what follows is a *model*. It is not a description of a real historical episode.

We need to work out the payoffs to each firm from each of these four possible sets of actions. To do that, we need to explore the costs and demand conditions in the industry.

Cost and Demand Conditions

The cost of producing switchgears is the same for both Trick and Gear. The average total cost curve (*ATC*) and the marginal cost curve (*MC*) for each firm are shown in Fig. 13.6(a). The market demand curve for switchgears (*D*) is shown in Fig. 13.6(b). Each firm produces an identical switchgear product, so one firm's switchgear is a perfect substitute for the other's. The market price of each firm's product, therefore, is identical. The quantity demanded depends on that price—the higher the price, the smaller is the quantity demanded.

Notice that in this industry, there is room for only two firms. For each firm, the *minimum efficient scale* of production is 3,000 switchgears a week. When the price equals the average total cost of production at the minimum efficient scale, total industry demand is 6,000 switchgears a week. There is no room for three firms in this industry. If there were three firms, at least one of them would incur an economic loss and exit. Thus the number of firms that an industry can sustain depends on the relationship between cost and the industry's demand conditions.

In the model industry that we're studying here, the particular cost and demand conditions assumed are designed to generate an industry in which two firms can survive in the long run. In real-world oligopoly and duopoly, barriers to entry may arise from economies of scale of the type featured in our model industry but there are other possible barriers as well (as discussed in Chapter 12, pp. 272–273).

FIGURE 13.6
Costs and Demand

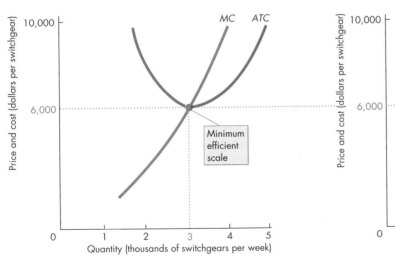

(a) Individual firm

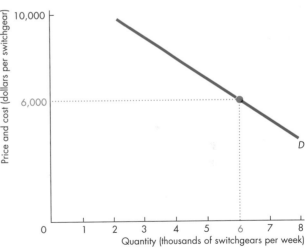

(b) Industry

Part (a) shows the costs facing Trick and Gear, two duopolies that make switchgears. Each firm faces identical costs. The average total cost curve for each firm is *ATC*, and the marginal cost curve is *MC*. For each firm, the minimum efficient scale of production is 3,000 switchgears per week and the average total cost of producing that output is $6,000 a unit. Each firm makes zero economic profit (that is, normal profit).

Part (b) shows the industry demand curve. At a price of $6,000, the quantity demanded is 6,000 switchgears per week. With only two firms in the industry, each firm will make normal profit. But with more than two firms in the industry, they will incur economic losses. Sooner or later one firm will exit the industry. There is room for only two firms in this industry.

Colluding to Maximize Profits

Let's begin by working out the payoffs to the two firms if they collude to make the maximum industry profit by acting like a monopoly. The calculations that the two firms will perform are exactly the same calculations that a monopoly performs. (You studied these calculations in Chapter 12, pp. 273–278.) The only additional thing that the duopolists have to do is to agree on how much of the total output each of them will produce.

The price and quantity that maximize industry profit for the duopolists are shown in Fig. 13.7. Part (a) shows the situation for each firm, and part (b) shows the situation for the industry as a whole. The curve labeled MR is the industry marginal revenue curve. The curve labeled MC_I is the industry marginal cost curve if each firm produces the same level of output. That curve is constructed by adding together the outputs of the two firms at each level of marginal cost. That is, at each level of marginal cost, industry output is twice as much as the output of each individual firm. Thus the curve MC_I in part (b) is twice as far to the right as the curve MC in part (a).

To maximize industry profit, the duopolists agree to restrict output to the rate that makes the industry marginal cost and marginal revenue equal. That output rate, as shown in part (b), is 4,000 switchgears a week. The highest price for which the 4,000 switchgears can be sold is $9,000 each. Let's suppose that Trick and Gear agree to split the market equally so that each firm produces 2,000 switchgears a week. The average total cost (ATC) of producing 2,000 switchgears a week is $8,000, so the profit per unit is $1,000 and economic profit is $2 million (2,000 switchgears × $1,000 per unit). The economic profit

---

Colluding to Make Monopoly Profits

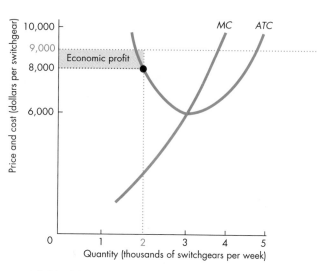

(a) Individual firm

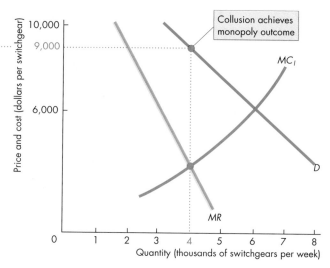

(b) Industry

If Trick and Gear come to a collusive agreement, together they can act as a monopoly and maximize profit. To maximize profit, the firms first calculate the industry marginal cost curve, MC_I (part b), which is the horizontal sum of the two firms' marginal cost curves, MC (part a). Next they calculate the industry marginal revenue, MR. They then choose the output rate that makes marginal revenue equal to marginal cost (4,000 switchgears per week). They agree to sell that output

for a price of $9,000, the price at which 4,000 switchgears are demanded.

Each firm has the same costs, so each produces half the total output—2,000 switchgears per week. Average total cost is $8,000 per unit, so each firm makes an economic profit of $2 million (blue rectangle)—2,000 switchgears multiplied by $1,000 profit per unit.

of each firm is represented by the blue rectangle in Fig. 13.7(a).

We have just described one possible outcome for the duopoly game: The two firms collude to produce the monopoly profit-maximizing output and divide that output equally between themselves. From the industry point of view, this solution is identical to a monopoly. A duopoly that operates in this way is indistinguishable from a monopoly. The economic profit that is made by a monopoly is the maximum total profit that can be made by colluding duopolists.

Cheating on a Collusive Agreement

There are two possible cheating situations: one in which one firm cheats and one in which both firms cheat.

One Firm Cheats What is the effect of one firm cheating on a collusive agreement? How much extra profit does the cheating firm make? What happens to the profit of the firm that sticks to the agreement in the face of cheating by the other firm? Let's work out the answers to these questions.

There are many different ways for a firm to cheat. We will work out just one possibility. Suppose that Trick convinces Gear that there has been a fall in industry demand and that it cannot sell its share of the output at the agreed price. It tells Gear that it plans to cut its price in order to sell the agreed 2,000 switchgears each week. Because the two firms produce a virtually identical product, Gear has no alternative but to match Trick's price cut.

In fact, there has been no fall in demand, and the lower price has been calculated by Trick to be exactly the price needed to sell the additional output that it plans to produce. Gear, though lowering its price in line with that of Trick, restricts its output to the previously agreed level.

Figure 13.8 illustrates the consequences of Trick cheating in this way. Part (a) shows what happens to Gear (the complier); part (b) shows what happens to Trick (the cheat); and part (c) shows what is happening in the industry as a whole.

FIGURE 13.8

Cheating on a Collusive Agreement

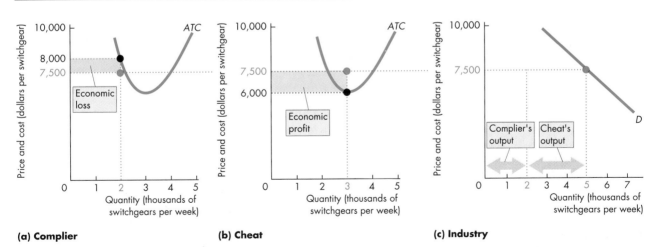

(a) Complier   **(b) Cheat**   **(c) Industry**

One firm, shown in part (a), complies with the agreement and produces 2,000 switchgears. The other firm, shown in part (b), cheats on the agreement and increases its output to 3,000 switchgears. Given the market demand curve, shown in part (c), and with a total production of 5,000 switchgears a week, the market price falls to $7,500.

At this price, the complier in part (a) incurs an economic loss of $1 million ($500 × 2,000 units) shown by the red rectangle. In part (b), the cheat makes an economic profit of $4.5 million ($1,500 × 3,000 units), shown as the blue rectangle.

Suppose that Trick decides to increase its output from 2,000 to 3,000 switchgears a week—the output at which average total cost is minimized. It recognizes that if Gear sticks to the agreement to produce only 2,000 switchgears a week, total output will be 5,000 a week, and given demand in part (c), the price will have to be cut to $7,500 a unit.

Gear continues to produce 2,000 switchgears a week at a cost of $8,000 a unit and incurs a loss of $500 a unit or $1 million a week. This economic loss is represented by the red rectangle in part (a). Trick produces 3,000 switchgears a week at an average total cost of $6,000 each. With a price of $7,500, Trick makes a profit of $1,500 a unit and therefore an economic profit of $4.5 million. This economic profit is the blue rectangle in part (b).

We have now described a second possible outcome for the duopoly game—one of the firms cheats on the collusive agreement. In this case, the industry output is larger than the monopoly output and the industry price is lower than the monopoly price. The total economic profit made by the industry is also smaller than the monopoly's economic profit. Trick (the cheat) makes an economic profit of $4.5 million, and Gear (the complier) incurs an economic loss of $1 million. The industry makes an economic profit of $3.5 million. Thus the industry profit is $0.5 million less than the economic profit a monopoly would make. But the profit is distributed unevenly. Trick makes a bigger economic profit than it would under the collusive agreement, while Gear incurs an economic loss.

We have just worked out what happens if Trick cheats and Gear complies with the collusive agreement. A similar outcome would arise if Gear cheated and Trick complied with the agreement. The industry profit and price would be the same, but in this case Gear (the cheat) would make an economic profit of $4.5 million and Trick (the complier) would incur an economic loss of $1 million.

There is yet another possible outcome: Both firms cheat on the agreement.

Both Firms Cheat   Suppose that instead of just one firm cheating on the collusive agreement, both firms cheat. In particular, suppose that each firm behaves in exactly the same way as the cheating firm that we have just analyzed. Each tells the other that it is unable to sell its output at the going price and that it plans to cut its price. But because both firms cheat, each will propose a successively lower price. As long

as price exceeds marginal cost, each firm has an incentive to increase its production—to cheat. Only when price equals marginal cost is there no further incentive to cheat. This situation arises when the price has reached $6,000. At this price, marginal cost equals price. Also, price equals minimum average total cost. At a price of less than $6,000, each firm incurs an economic loss. At a price of $6,000, each firm covers all its costs and makes zero economic profit (makes normal profit). Also, at a price of $6,000, each firm wants to produce 3,000 switchgears a week, so the industry output is 6,000 switchgears a week. Given the demand conditions, 6,000 switchgears can be sold at a price of $6,000 each.

Figure 13.9 illustrates the situation just described. Each firm, shown in part (a), produces 3,000 switchgears a week, and at this output level average total cost is a minimum ($6,000 per unit). The market as a whole, shown in part (b), operates at the point at which the demand curve (D) intersects the industry marginal cost curve. This marginal cost curve is constructed as the horizontal sum of the marginal cost curves of the two firms. Each firm has lowered its price and increased its output to try to gain an advantage over the other firm. Each has pushed this process as far as it can without incurring an economic loss.

We have now described a third possible outcome of this duopoly game: Both firms cheat. If both firms cheat on the collusive agreement, the output of each firm is 3,000 switchgears a week and the price is $6,000. Each firm makes zero economic profit.

The Payoff Matrix

Now that we have described the strategies and payoffs in the duopoly game, let's summarize the strategies and the payoffs in the form of the game's payoff matrix and then calculate the equilibrium.

Table 13.4 sets out the payoff matrix for this game. It is constructed in exactly the same way as the payoff matrix for the prisoners' dilemma in Table 13.3. The squares show the payoffs for the two firms—Gear and Trick. In this case, the payoffs are profits. (In the case of the prisoners' dilemma, the payoffs were losses.)

The table shows that if both firms cheat (top left), they achieve the perfectly competitive outcome—each firm makes zero economic profit. If both firms comply (bottom right), the industry makes the monopoly profit and each firm earns an

FIGURE 13.9

Both Firms Cheat

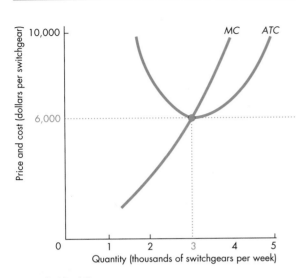

(a) Individual firm

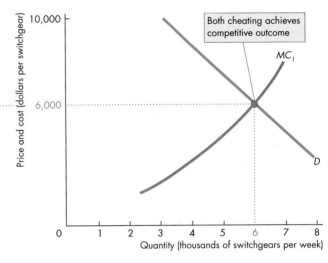

(b) Industry

If both firms cheat by increasing their output and lowering the price, the collusive agreement completely breaks down. The limit to the breakdown of the agreement is the competitive equilibrium. Neither firm will want to cut the price below $6,000 (minimum average total cost), for to do so will result in losses. Part (a) shows the situation facing each firm. At a price of $6,000, the firm's profit-maximizing output is 3,000 switchgears per week. At that output rate, price equals mar-

ginal cost, and it also equals average total cost. Economic profit is zero. Part (b) describes the situation in the industry as a whole. The industry marginal cost curve (MC_I)—the horizontal sum of the individual firms' marginal cost curves (MC)—intersects the demand curve at 6,000 switchgears per week and at a price of $6,000. This output and price are the ones that would prevail in a competitive industry.

economic profit of $2 million. The top right and bottom left squares show what happens if one firm cheats while the other complies. The firm that cheats collects an economic profit of $4.5 million, and the one that complies incurs a loss of $1 million.

This duopoly game is, in fact, the same as the prisoners' dilemma that we examined earlier in this chapter; it is a duopolists' dilemma.

The Duopolists' Dilemma

You can see why the duopolists have a dilemma by thinking about the situation that each faces. Under a collusive agreement, the colluding firms restrict output to make their joint marginal revenue equal to their joint marginal cost. They set the highest price for which the quantity produced can be sold—a price that is higher than marginal cost. In such a situation,

each firm recognizes that if it cheats on the agreement and raises its output, even though the price will fall below that agreed to, more will be added to its revenue than to its cost, so its profit will increase. Because each firm recognizes this fact, there is a temptation for each firm to cheat. The dilemma is just like that of the prisoners. If each firm could rely on the other one not to cheat, their joint profit would be maximized. But because it is in the individual best interest of each firm to cheat, each firm is led to that action. Let's confirm that this is the outcome of the duopolists' dilemma by finding its equilibrium.

Equilibrium of the Duopolists' Dilemma

To find the equilibrium, let's look at things from Gear's point of view. Gear reasons as follows: Suppose

TABLE 13.4

Duopoly Payoff Matrix

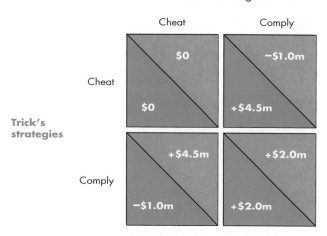

Each square shows the payoffs from a pair of actions. For example, if both firms comply with the collusive agreement, the payoffs are recorded in the bottom right square. The red triangle shows Gear's payoff, and the blue triangle shows Trick's. The equilibrium is a Nash equilibrium in which both firms cheat.

that Trick cheats. If we comply with the agreement, we incur an economic loss of $1 million. If we also cheat, we make zero economic profit. Zero economic profit is better than a $1 million loss, so it will pay us to cheat. But suppose Trick complies with the agreement. If we cheat, we will make an economic profit of $4.5 million, and if we comply, we will make an economic profit of $2 million. A $4.5 million profit is better than a $2 million profit, so it again pays us to cheat. Thus regardless of whether Trick cheats or complies, it pays us to cheat. Gear's dominant strategy is to cheat.

Trick comes to the same conclusion as Gear. Therefore both firms will cheat. The equilibrium of the duopoly game is that both firms cheat on the agreement. Although there are only two firms in the industry, the price and quantity are the same as in a competitive industry. Each firm makes zero economic profit.

Although we have done this analysis for only two firms, it would not make any difference (other than to increase the amount of arithmetic) if we were to play the game with three, four, or more firms. In other

words, though we have analyzed duopoly, the game theory approach can also be used to analyze oligopoly. The analysis of oligopoly is much harder, but the essential ideas that we have learned also apply to oligopoly.

Repeated Games

The first game that we studied, the prisoners' dilemma, was played just once. The prisoners did not have an opportunity to observe the outcome of the game and then play it again. The duopolist game just described was also played only once. In contrast, most real-world duopolists do get opportunities to play repeatedly against each other. This fact suggests that real-world duopolists might find some way of learning to cooperate so that their efforts to collude are more effective.

If a game is played repeatedly, one player always has the opportunity to penalize the other player for previous "bad" behavior. If Trick refuses to cooperate this week, then Gear can refuse to cooperate next week (and vice versa). If Gear cheats this week, perhaps Trick will cheat next week. Before Gear cheats this week, shouldn't it take account of the possibility of Trick cheating next week?

What is the equilibrium of this more complicated prisoners' dilemma game when it is repeated indefinitely? Actually, there is more than one possibility. One is the Nash equilibrium that we have just analyzed. Both players cheat and each makes zero economic profit forever. In such a situation, it will never pay one of the players to start complying unilaterally; to do so would result in a loss for that player and a profit for the other. The price and quantity will remain at the competitive levels forever.

But another equilibrium is possible—one in which the players make and share the monopoly profit. How might this equilibrium come about? Why wouldn't it always pay each firm to try to get away with cheating? The key to answering this question is the fact that when a prisoners' dilemma game is played repeatedly, the players have an increased array of strategies. Each player can punish the other player for previous actions.

There are two extremes of punishment. The smallest penalty that one player can impose on the other is what is called "tit for tat." A *tit-for-tat strategy* is one in which a player cooperates in the current period if the other player cooperated in the previous period but cheats in the current period if the other player cheated in the previous period. The most severe form of punishment that one player can impose on the other arises in what is called a trigger strategy. A *trigger strategy* is one in which a player cooperates if the other player cooperates but plays the Nash equilibrium strategy forever thereafter if the other player cheats. Because a tit-for-tat strategy and a trigger strategy are the extremes of punishment—the most mild and most severe—there are evidently other intermediate degrees of punishment. For example, if one player cheats on the agreement, the other player could punish by refusing to cooperate for a certain number of periods. In the duopoly game between Gear and Trick, a tit-for-tat strategy keeps both players cooperating and earning monopoly profits. Let's see why.

If both firms stick to the collusive agreement in period 1, each makes an economic profit of $2 million. Suppose that Trick contemplates cheating in period 2. The cheating produces a quick $4.5 million economic profit and inflicts a $1 million economic loss on Gear. Adding up the profits over two periods of play, Trick comes out ahead by cheating ($6.5 million compared with $4 million if it did not cheat). The next period, Gear punishes Trick with its tit-for-tat response and cheats. If Trick reverts to cooperating, to induce Gear to cooperate in period 4, Gear now makes an economic profit of $4.5 million and Trick incurs an economic loss of $1 million. Adding up the profits over four periods of play, Trick would have made more profit by cooperating. In that case, its economic profit would have been $8 million compared with $7.5 million from cheating and generating Gear's tit-for-tat response.

What is true for Trick is also true for Gear. Because each firm makes a larger profit by sticking with the collusive agreement, both firms do so and the monopoly price, quantity, and profit prevail in the industry. This equilibrium is called a **cooperative equilibrium**—an equilibrium resulting from each player's rational response to the credible threat of the other player to inflict heavy damage if the agreement is broken. But for this strategy to work, the threat must be credible; that is, each player must recognize that it is in the interest of the other player to respond with a "tit for tat." The tit-for-tat strategy is credible because if one player cheats, it clearly does not pay the other player to continue complying. So the threat of cheating in the next period is credible and sufficient to support the monopoly equilibrium outcome.

In reality, whether a cartel works like a one-play game or a repeated game depends primarily on the number of players and the ease of detecting and punishing cheating. The larger the number of players, the harder it is to maintain a cartel. The market for cellular telephone calls is restricted by regulation to two players, and as you can see in *Reading Between the Lines* on pp. 322–323, the high price of cellular telephone calls can be understood as the outcome of a repeated game between two players. The larger the number of players, the harder it is to achieve a monopoly outcome.

R E V I E W

- A collusive agreement to restrict output and raise price creates a game like the prisoners' dilemma.
- Because price exceeds marginal cost, each firm can increase its profit at the expense of the other firm by cheating on the agreement and increasing production.
- If the game is played once, the agreement breaks down because the equilibrium strategy for each firm is to cheat.
- If the game is played repeatedly, punishment strategies such as tit-for-tat can be used that enable the agreement to persist.

Games and Price Wars

The theory of price and output determination under duopoly can help us understand real-world behavior and, in particular, price wars. Some price wars can be interpreted as the implementation of a tit-for-tat strategy. We've seen that with a tit-for-tat strategy in place, firms have an incentive to stick to the monopoly price. But fluctuations in demand lead to fluctuations in the monopoly price, and sometimes, when the price changes, it might seem to one of the firms that the price has fallen because the other has cheated. In this case, a price war will break out. The price war will end only when each firm has satisfied itself that the other is ready to cooperate again. There will be cycles of price wars and the restoration of collusive agreements. Fluctuations in the world price of oil can be interpreted in this way.

Some price wars arise from the entry of a small number of firms into an industry that had been a monopoly. Although the industry has a small number of firms, the firms are in a prisoners' dilemma, and they cannot impose effective penalties for price cutting. The behavior of prices and outputs in the computer chip industry during 1994 and 1995 can be explained in this way. Until 1994, the market for CPU chips for IBM compatible computers was dominated by one firm, Intel Corporation, which was able to make maximum economic profit by producing the quantity of chips at which marginal cost equaled marginal revenue. The price of Intel's chips was set to ensure that the quantity demanded equaled the quantity produced. Then in 1994 and 1995, with the entry of a small number of new firms, the industry became an oligopoly. If the firms had maintained Intel's price and shared the market, together they could have made economic profits equal to Intel's profit. But the firms were in a prisoners' dilemma. So prices tumbled to competitive levels.

The Incredible Electrical Conspiracy

Price-fixing arrangements such as those we've just studied are illegal in the United States. This means that any conspiracies by firms to fix prices have to be undertaken in secrecy. As a result, we get to know about such agreements only after they have been cracked by the Justice Department.

One famous price-fixing arrangement, involving almost 30 firms, has been called "the incredible electrical conspiracy."[2] For most of the 1950s, 30 producers of electrical equipment, including such giants as General Electric and Westinghouse, fixed prices "on items ranging from $2 insulators to huge turbine generators costing several million dollars."[3]

Although the electrical equipment pricing conspiracy operated throughout the entire decade of the 1950s, the individual firms conspiring often changed. In particular, General Electric sometimes participated in the price-fixing agreement and sometimes dropped out, undercutting the agreed price and dragging down the industry price and profit in much the way that the model that we've studied predicts.

Preserving Secrecy Because collusion is illegal, one special problem that colluding firms face is hiding the fact of their collusion and preserving secrecy. "The incredible electrical conspiracy" provides a fascinating view of one way in which this problem has been solved. The particular device used in this conspiracy was called the "phases of the moon" pricing formula.

> [These pricing formulas were listed on] sheets of paper, each containing a half dozen columns of figures. . . . One group of columns established the bidding order of the seven switchgear manufacturers—a different company, each with its own code number, phasing into the priority position every two weeks (hence "phases of the moon"). A second group of columns, keyed into the company code numbers, established how much each company was to knock off the agreed-upon book price. For example, if it were No 1's (G.E.'s) turn to be low bidder at a certain number of dollars off book, then all Westinghouse (No 2), or Allis-Chalmers (No 3) had to do was look for their code number in the second group of columns to find how many dollars they were to bid *above* No 1. These bids would then be fuzzed up by having a little added to them or taken away by companies 2, 3, etc. Thus, there was not even a hint that the winning bid had been collusively arrived at.[4]

Before stumbling on the "phases of the moon" papers, the Justice Department was having a very hard time proving conspiracy, but, with the formula in hand, it was able to put the conspiracy under the spotlight and end it.

Other Strategic Variables

We have focused here on firms that play a simple game and consider only two possible strategies—complying and cheating—concerning two variables—price and quantity produced. But the approach that we have used can be extended to deal with a much wider range of choices facing firms. For example, a firm has to decide whether to mount an expensive advertising campaign; whether to modify its product; how reliable to make its product (the more reliable a product, usually, the more expensive it is to produce); whether to price discriminate and, if so, among which groups of customers and to what

[2]Richard A. Smith, "The Incredible Electrical Conspiracy," Part I and Part II, *Fortune* (April 1961): 132 and (May 1961): 161.
[3]James V. Koch, *Industrial Organization and Prices*, 2nd ed. (Englewood Cliffs, N.J.: Prentice-Hall, 1980): 423.

[4]Richard A. Smith, "The Incredible Electrical Conspiracy," Part II, *Fortune* (May 1961): 210. ©1961 Time Inc. All rights reserved.

degree; whether to undertake a large research and development (R&D) effort aimed at lowering production costs, or whether to enter or leave an industry. All of these choices can be analyzed by using game theory. The basic method that you have studied can be applied to these problems by working out the payoff for each of the alternative strategies and then finding the equilibrium of the game.

We'll look at two examples. The first is an R&D game and the second is an entry-deterrence game—a game in which a firm tries to prevent other firms from entering an industry.

An R&D Game

Disposable diapers were first marketed in 1966. The two market leaders from the start of this industry have been Procter & Gamble (makers of Pampers) and Kimberly-Clark (makers of Huggies). Procter & Gamble has about 60 to 70 percent of the total market, and Kimberly-Clark has about 25 percent. When the disposable diaper was first introduced in 1966, it had to be cost-effective in competition with reusable, laundered diapers. A costly research and development effort resulted in the development of machines that could make disposable diapers at a low enough cost to achieve that initial competitive edge. But as the industry has matured, a large number of firms have tried to get into the business and take market share away from the two industry leaders, and the industry leaders themselves have battled each other to maintain or increase their own market share.

The disposable diaper industry is one in which technological advances that result in small decreases in the average total cost of production can provide an individual firm with an enormous competitive advantage. The current machines can produce disposable diapers at a rate of 3,000 an hour—a rate that represents a tenfold increase on the output rate of just a decade ago. The firm that develops and uses the least-cost technology gains a competitive edge, undercutting the rest of the market, increasing its market share, and increasing its profit. But the research and development effort that has to be undertaken to achieve even small cost reductions is itself very costly. This cost of research and development has to be deducted from the profit resulting from the increased market share that lower costs achieve. If no firm does R&D, every firm can be better off, but if one firm initiates the R&D activity, all must.

Each firm is in a research and development dilemma situation that is similar to the game played by Art and Bob. Although the two firms play an ongoing game against each other, it has more in common with the one-shot game than a repeated game. The reason is that research and development is a long-term process. Effort is repeated, but payoffs occur only infrequently and uncertainly.

Table 13.5 illustrates the dilemma (with hypothetical numbers) for the R&D game that Kimberly-Clark and Procter & Gamble are playing. Each firm has two strategies: to spend $25 million a year on R&D or to spend nothing on R&D. If neither firm spends on R&D, they make a joint profit of $100 million: $30 million for Kimberly-Clark and $70

TABLE 13.5

Pampers Versus Huggies: An R&D Game

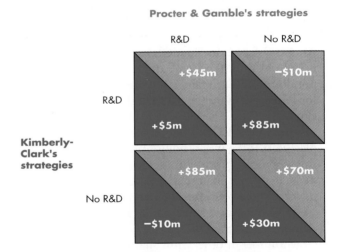

Procter & Gamble's strategies

If both firms undertake R&D, their payoffs are those shown in the top left square. If neither firm undertakes R&D, their payoffs are in the bottom right square. When one firm undertakes R&D and the other one does not, their payoffs are in the top right and bottom left squares. The red triangle shows Procter & Gamble's payoff, and the blue triangle shows Kimberly-Clark's. The dominant strategy equilibrium for this game is for both firms to undertake R&D. The structure of this game is the same as that of the prisoners' dilemma.

million for Procter & Gamble (bottom right square of the payoff matrix). If each firm conducts R&D, market shares are maintained but each firm's profit is lower, by the amount spent on R&D (top left square of the payoff matrix). If Kimberly-Clark pays for R&D but Procter & Gamble does not, Kimberly-Clark gains a large part of Procter & Gamble's market. Kimberly-Clark profits, and Procter & Gamble loses (top right square of the payoff matrix). Finally, if Procter & Gamble invests in R&D and Kimberly-Clark does not, Procter & Gamble gains market share from Kimberly-Clark, increasing its profit while Kimberly-Clark incurs a loss (bottom left square).

Confronted with the payoff matrix in Table 13.5, the two firms calculate their best strategies. Kimberly-Clark reasons as follows: If Procter & Gamble does not undertake R&D, we make $85 million if we do and $30 million if we do not; therefore it pays to conduct R&D. If Procter & Gamble conducts R&D, we lose $10 million if we don't and make $5 million if we do. Again, R&D pays off. Thus conducting R&D is a dominant strategy for Kimberly-Clark. Doing it pays, regardless of Procter & Gamble's decision.

Procter & Gamble reasons similarly: If Kimberly-Clark does not undertake R&D, we make $70 million if we follow suit and $85 million if we conduct R&D. It therefore pays to conduct R&D. If Kimberly-Clark does undertake R&D, we make $45 million by doing the same and lose $10 million by not doing R&D. Again, it pays to conduct R&D. So for Procter & Gamble, R&D is also a dominant strategy.

Because R&D is a dominant strategy for both players, it is the Nash equilibrium. The outcome of this game is that both firms conduct R&D. They make less profit than they would if they could collude to achieve the cooperative outcome of no R&D.

The real-world situation has more players than Kimberly-Clark and Procter & Gamble. There are a large number of other firms sharing a small portion of the market, all of them ready to eat into the market share of Procter & Gamble and Kimberly-Clark. So the R&D effort by these two firms not only serves the purpose of maintaining shares in their own battle, but also helps to keep barriers to entry high enough to preserve their joint market share.

Let's now study an entry-deterrence game in which a firm tries to prevent other firms from entering an industry. Such a game is played in a type of market called a contestable market.

Contestable Markets

A **contestable market** is a market in which one firm (or a small number of firms) operates but in which both entry and exit are free so that the firm (or firms) in the market faces perfect competition from *potential* entrants. Examples of contestable markets are routes served by airlines and by barge companies that operate on the major waterways. These markets are contestable because even though only one or a few firms actually operate on a particular air route or river, other firms could enter those markets if an opportunity for economic profit arose and could exit those markets if the opportunity for economic profit disappeared. The potential entrance prevents the firm (or few firms) from making an economic profit.

If the HHI is used to determine the degree of competition, a contestable market appears to be uncompetitive. But a contestable market behaves as if it were perfectly competitive. You can see why by thinking about a game that we'll call an entry-deterrence game.

Entry-deterrence game   In the entry-deterrence game we'll study, there are two players. One player is Agile Air, the only firm operating on a particular route. The other player is Wanabe Inc., a potential entrant making a normal profit in its current business. The strategies for Agile Air are to set its price at the monopoly profit-maximizing level or at the competitive (zero economic profit) level. The strategies for Wanabe are to enter and set a price just below that of Agile or to not enter.

Table 13.6 shows the payoffs for the two firms. If Wanabe does not enter, Agile earns a normal profit by setting a competitive price or earns maximum monopoly profit (a positive economic profit) by setting the monopoly price. If Wanabe does enter and undercuts Agile's price, Agile incurs an economic loss regardless of whether it sets its price at the competitive or monopoly level. The reason is that Wanabe takes the market with the lower price, so Agile incurs a cost but has zero revenue. If Agile sets a competitive price, Wanabe earns a normal profit if it does not enter or incurs an economic loss if it enters and undercuts Agile by setting a price that is less than average total cost. If Agile sets the monopoly price, Wanabe earns a positive economic profit by entering or a normal profit by not entering.

The Nash equilibrium for this game is a competitive price at which Agile Air earns a normal profit and Wanabe does not enter. If Agile raised the price to the

TABLE 13.6

Agile Versus Wanabe: An Entry-Deterrence Game

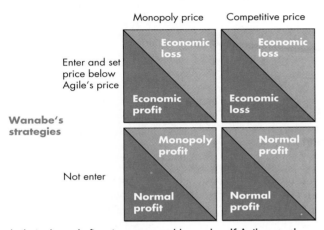

Agile's strategies

Agile is the only firm in a contestable market. If Agile sets the monopoly price, Wanabe earns an economic profit by entering and undercutting Agile's price or a normal profit by not entering. So if Agile sets the price at the monopoly level, Wanabe will enter. If Agile sets the competitive price, Wanabe earns a normal profit if it does not enter or incurs an economic loss if it enters. So if Agile sets the price at the competitive level, Wanabe will not enter. With entry, Agile incurs an economic loss regardless of the price its sets. The Nash equilibrium of this game is for Agile to set the competitive price, for Wanabe to not enter, and for both firms to make normal profit.

monopoly level, Wanabe would enter and by undercutting Agile's price would take all the business, leaving Agile with an economic loss equal to total cost. Agile avoids this outcome by sticking with the competitive price and deterring Wanabe from entering.

Limit Pricing **Limit pricing** is the practice of charging a price below the monopoly profit-maximizing price and producing a quantity greater than that at which marginal revenue equals marginal cost in order to deter entry. The game that we've just studied is an example of limit pricing but the practice is more general. For example, a firm can use limit pricing to try to convince potential entrants that its own costs are so low that new entrants will incur an economic loss if they enter the industry. To see how this works, let's go back to Agile and Wanabe.

Wanabe knows the current market price but does not know Agile's costs and profit. It can infer those costs though. Suppose Wanabe believes that marginal revenue is 50 percent of price. If the price is $100, then Wanabe estimates that marginal revenue is $50. Wanabe might assume that Agile is maximizing profit by setting marginal revenue equal to marginal cost. Given this assumption, Wanabe estimates Agile's marginal cost to be $50. If Wanabe's marginal cost is greater than $50, it can't compete with Agile, so it will drop the idea of entering this industry. But if its marginal cost is less than $50, it might not only be able to enter the industry but also to drive Agile out.

Recognizing that Wanabe (and other potential entrants) reason in this way, Agile might decide to use limit pricing to send a false but possibly believable signal to them. It might cut its price to (say) $80 to make Wanabe believe that its marginal cost is only $40 (50 percent of $80). The lower Wanabe believes Agile's marginal cost to be, the less likely is Wanabe to enter. The strategic use of limit pricing makes it possible, in some situations, for a firm (or group of firms) to maintain a monopoly or collusive oligopoly and limit entry.

◆ We have now studied the four main market structures—perfect competition, monopolistic competition, oligopoly, and monopoly—and have discovered how prices and outputs, revenue, cost, and economic profit are determined. We have used these models to make predictions about behavior and to assess the efficiency of alternative market structures.

A key element in our analysis of the markets for goods and services is the behavior of costs. Costs are determined partly by technology and partly by the prices of factors of production. We have treated those factor prices as given. We are now going to see how factor prices are themselves determined. Factor prices interact with the goods market that we have just studied in two ways. First, they determine the firm's production costs. Second, they determine household incomes and therefore influence the demand for goods and services. Factor prices also affect the distribution of income.

Firms decide *how* to produce; the interactions of households and firms in the markets for goods and services decide *what* will be produced. But the factor prices determined in the markets for factors of production determine *for whom* the various goods and services are produced.

Duopoly in Action: Cellular Phones

Wall Street Journal, May 5, 1994

Cellular-Phone Rates Spark Static from Users

BY GAUTAM NAIK

... The cellular industry has grown at explosive rates since its launch a decade ago. In 1993 alone, the number of customers surged 45% to 16 million, while revenue zoomed 40% to $10.9 billion. Despite this growth, it isn't a whole lot cheaper to make a cellular call today than it was 10 years ago. While long-distance charges have fallen roughly 40% in the past decade, by one measure even the *lowest* average cellular rates around the country have come down only 9% in eight years.

One major reason is the lack of competition. The Federal Communications Commission in 1981 decreed that each cellular market should be restricted to just two cellular carriers, and typically the entrenched local phone company is one of them. And unlike regular phone service, cellular doesn't have to answer to regulators.

The FCC holds out the hope of more competition. It has set plans to auction licenses for "personal communications services," which would introduce up to seven new rivals in each market. But the auctions aren't until the fall, and any new services are two years away. For now, cellular providers argue that their rates aren't all that high and that high-volume customers can get substantial discounts. ...

Even carriers admit they will be forced to lower per-minute rates when competitors arrive. Some users ask: If they can lower prices then, why not now? Barry Goodstadt of Electronic Data Systems Corp. offers one answer: "Cellular firms clearly have room to lower prices. But they know they have competition coming. So you get your margins while you can."

Per-minute costs hardly vary among the two carriers in many major cities. In New York, Nynex charges up to 59 cents per minute during peak hours whether the call is incoming or outgoing; rival Cellular One of Paramus, N.J.,... charges 65 cents. In Los Angeles, the two cellular carriers charge 45 cents and 41 cents a minute.

- The cellular phone industry has grown rapidly. In 1993, customers increased 45% and revenue increased 40%.

- The Federal Communications Commission (FCC) restricts each cellular market to two carriers, but the FCC does not regulate the firms.

- The two carriers in many major cities have similar rates: 65¢ and 59¢ per minute in New York and 45¢ and 41¢ per minute in Los Angeles.

- In the past decade, long-distance rates have fallen 40 percent, while cellular rates have fallen 9 percent in eight years.

- In fall 1994, FCC will auction up to seven new licenses in each market.

- The new competition will force rates to fall. One observer says cellular firms could cut rates now but are getting their economic profit while they can.

Economic

A N A L Y S I S

■ Figure I shows a profitable cellular company. The firm's demand curve is *D*, its marginal revenue curve is *MR*, its marginal cost curve is *MC*, and its average total cost curve is *ATC*—all based on hypothetical numbers.

■ The firm maximizes profit by producing the quantity (millions of minutes of calls per year) at which marginal revenue equals marginal cost. This quantity is 100 million minutes a year, and the price is 60¢ a minute. The firm makes an economic profit of $40 million.

■ Figure 2 shows the situation after the FCC's auctions and after sufficient time has elapsed for entry. If consumers regard the services of each firm as being identical, each firm will be a price taker and will face a horizontal marginal revenue curve. Price will fall to 20¢, and economic profit will fall to zero. Each firm will earn normal profits.

■ Even before new competitors arrive, each of the two firms in the market faces a temptation to cut price. Table I shows the payoff matrix for the prisoners' dilemma game they might play.

■ By holding the price high, each firm makes $40 million (bottom right square) and is in the situation shown in Fig. 1. If one firm cuts its price and the other does not, the price cutter gains and the other firm loses (top right and bottom left squares). If both firms cut the price, each makes a normal profit (top left square) and is in the situation shown in Fig. 2.

■ Because the two firms are playing a repeated game, they can maintain a high price if each believes the other will play a tit-for-tat strategy (see pp. 316–317).

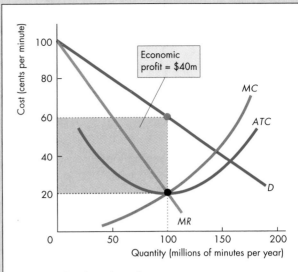

Figure 1 Firm in a duopoly

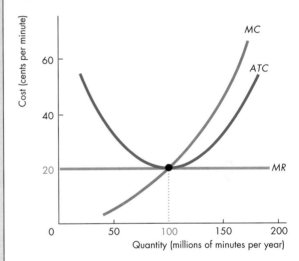

Figure 2 Firm in perfect competition

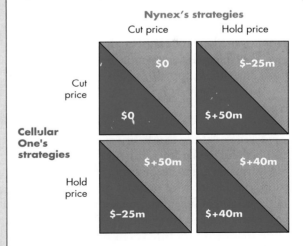

Table 1 Payoff matrix

S U M M A R Y

Varieties of Market Structure

Two market structures lie between monopoly and perfect competition: monopolistic competition and oligopoly. Monopolistic competition occurs when a large number of firms compete with each other by making slightly different products. Oligopoly is a situation in which a small number of producers compete with each other. A market with a small number of firms can be competitive if low barriers to entry bring competition from potential entrants.

The four-firm concentration ratio and the Herfindahl-Hirschman Index measure the degree of competitiveness in a market and are indicators of monopoly power. In the United States, most industries are effectively competitive, but some significant oligopoly and monopoly elements exist. (pp. 298–302)

Monopolistic Competition

Under monopolistic competition, each firm produces a differentiated product and so faces a downward-sloping demand curve. The firm has to choose its price and its output level. Because there is free entry, in long-run equilibrium, zero economic profit is earned. When profit is maximized, marginal cost equals marginal revenue, and average total cost equals price in the long run. But average total cost is not at its minimum. That is, in monopolistic competition, firms operate with excess capacity. Monopolistic competition is inefficient because marginal cost is less than price. But the inefficiency must be weighed against product variety. (pp. 302–305)

Oligopoly

In oligopoly, the quantity that a firm sells depends on the firm's price and on the other firms' prices and quantities sold. Firms take into account the effects of their own actions on the behavior of other firms and the effects of the actions of other firms on their own profits.

The kinked demand curve model is based on the assumption that each firm believes its price cuts will be matched by its rivals but its price increases will not be matched. If these beliefs are correct, each firm faces a kinked demand curve for its product, the kink occurring at the current price, and has a break in its marginal revenue curve. To maximize profit, the firm produces the quantity that makes marginal cost and marginal revenue equal, an output level such that the marginal cost curve passes through the break in the marginal revenue curve. Fluctuations in marginal cost inside the range of the break in marginal revenue have no effects on either price or output.

The dominant firm model of oligopoly assumes that an industry consists of one large firm and a large number of small firms. The large firm acts like a monopoly and sets a profit-maximizing price. The small firms take this price as given and act like perfectly competitive firms. (pp. 305–308)

Game Theory

Game theory is a method of analyzing strategic behavior that focuses on three aspects of a game: rules, strategies, and payoffs. Given their payoffs, the players choose strategies, and the combined strategies lead to an outcome—the equilibrium of the game. In a classic game called the prisoners' dilemma, two prisoners, each acting in his own best interest, confess to a crime. (pp. 308–310)

Oligopoly Game

An oligopoly game with two firms—a duopoly game—can be constructed in which the firms consider colluding to achieve a monopoly profit. The firms may in fact collude, or one may cheat on the collusive agreement to make a bigger profit at the expense of the other firm. Such a game is a prisoners' dilemma. If the game is played only once, the equilibrium is for both firms to cheat. The industry output and price are the same as in perfect competition.

If a game is repeated indefinitely, there is an opportunity for one player to punish another player for previous "bad" behavior. In such a situation, a tit-for-tat strategy can produce an equilibrium in which both firms stick to the agreement and the price and output are the same as in a monopoly.

Firms in oligopolistic industries have to make a large range of decisions: whether to enter or leave an industry; how much to spend selling the product; whether to modify its product; whether to undertake research and development. All these choices result in payoffs for the firm and the other firms in the industry and can be studied by using game theory. (pp. 310–321)

K E Y   E L E M E N T S

Key Figures and Tables

Key Terms

R E V I E W   Q U E S T I O N S

1. What are the main varieties of market structure? What are the main characteristics of each of those market structures?

2. Explain how a firm can differentiate its product.

3. What is a four-firm concentration ratio? If the four-firm concentration ratio is 90 percent, what does that mean?

4. What is the Herfindahl-Hirschman Index and what does a large value of that index indicate?

5. Give some examples of U.S. industries that have a high concentration ratio and of U.S. industries that have a low concentration ratio.

6. What is the value of the four-firm concentration ratio for each market structure?

7. What is the value of the Herfindahl-Hirschman Index for each market structure?

8. How do monopolistic competition and perfect competition differ?

9. Is monopolistic competition efficient? Explain your answer.

10. Why might the demand curve facing an oligopoly be kinked, and what happens to a firm's marginal revenue curve if its demand curve is kinked?

11. In what circumstances might the dominant firm model of oligopoly be relevant?

12. List the key features that all games have in common.

13. What is the prisoners' dilemma?

14. What is a Nash Equilibrium?

15. What is a dominant strategy equilibrium?

16. How do duopoly and oligopoly differ?

17. What is the essential feature of both duopoly and oligopoly?

18. What are the features of duopoly that make it reasonable to treat duopoly as a game between two firms?

19. What is meant by a repeated game?

20. Explain what a tit-for-tat strategy is.

21. What is a price war? What is the effect of a price war on the profit of the firms in the industry and on the profitability of the industry itself?

22. What is a contestable market? Will the Herfindahl-Hirschman Index reveal such a market? How does a contestable market operate.

23. What is limit pricing? How might a firm try to use limit pricing to increase its economic profit?

P R O B L E M S

1. The figure shows the situation facing Lite and Kool Inc., a producer of running shoes.

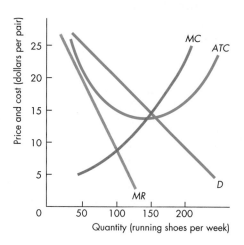

a. What quantity does Lite and Kool produce?
b. What price does it charge?
c. How much profit does Lite and Kool make?

2. A monopolistically competitive industry is in long-run equilibrium as illustrated in Fig. 13.3(b). Demand for the industry's product increases, increasing the demand for each firm's output. Using diagrams similar to those in Fig. 13.3, analyze the short-run and long-run effects on price, output, and economic profit of this increase in demand.

3. Another monopolistically competitive industry is in long-run equilibrium, as illustrated in Fig. 13.3(b), when it experiences a large increase in wages. Using diagrams similar to those in Fig. 13.3, analyze the short-run and long-run effects on price, output, and economic profit of this increase in wages.

4. A firm with a kinked demand curve experiences an increase in its variable cost. Explain the effects on the firm's price, output, and economic profit/loss.

5. An industry with one very large firm and 100 very small firms experiences an increase in the demand for its product. Use the dominant firm model to explain the effects on

a. The price, output, and economic profit of the large firm

b. The price, output, and economic profit of a typical small firm

6. Describe the game known as the prisoners' dilemma. In describing the game:

a. Make up a story that motivates the game.
b. Work out a payoff matrix.
c. Describe how the equilibrium of the game is arrived at.

7. Consider the following game. There are two players, and each is asked a question. They can answer the question honestly, or they can lie. If both answer honestly, each receives a payoff of $100. If one answers honestly and the other lies, the liar gains at the expense of the honest player. In that event, the liar receives a payoff of $500 and the honest player gets nothing. If both lie, then each receives a payoff of $50.

a. Describe this game in terms of its players, strategies, and payoffs.
b. Construct the payoff matrix.
c. What is the equilibrium for this game?

8. Two firms, Soapy and Suddies Inc., are the only producers of soap powder. They collude and agree to share the market equally. If neither cheats on the agreement, each makes $1 million economic profit. If either firm cheats, the cheater increases its economic profit to $1.5 million while the firm that abides by the agreement incurs an economic loss of $0.5 million. Neither firm has any way of policing the other's actions.

a. Describe the best strategy for each firm in a game that is played once.
b. What is the economic profit for each firm if both cheat?
c. Construct the payoff matrix of a game that is played just once.
d. What is the equilibrium if the game is played once?
e. If this duopolist game can be played many times, describe some of the strategies that each firm may adopt.

9. Use the oligopoly game to explain why producers of pet foods spend so much on advertising.

10. Study *Reading Between the Lines* on pp. 322–323 and then explain what will happen to the rates charged by cellular phone companies once the new licenses are auctioned.

James J. Heckman teaches economics and econometrics at the Department of Economics, University of Chicago and also is associated with the National Opinion Research Center (NORC) at the University of Chicago. He was born in Chicago, Illinois, in 1944 and was an undergraduate at Colorado College and graduate student at Princeton University, where he earned his Ph.D. in 1971. Professor Heckman is widely respected for studying practical issues that affect our lives such as employment, welfare, education, and wages. He studies these issues by using very large amounts of microeconomic data that keep track of people's choices over long periods of time about where to live, what kind of work to do, and what they spend and save. Michael Parkin talked with Professor Heckman about his work and about the problems that economists face when they use quantitative methods to analyze people's economic behavior.

TALKING WITH James Heckman

Professor Heckman, what did you study at Colorado College?
The benefit of attending a liberal arts college such as Colorado College was that I could study a variety of disciplines. I was initially attracted to physics. But I realized that it was easier to do math than physics, so I majored in mathematics and took some physics courses that interested me as well as courses in anthropology, history, and philosophy.

I took a few courses in economics as well, some of which were excellent. They were readings courses that covered classical economists such as David Ricardo and Adam Smith. During my study of economics, I developed a sense that I could affect things in the world.

Can you describe the kinds of data that are available to economists? Can undergraduates get easy access to the large data bases that you use? How?
We are in an age in which a lot of good data are available. There are some very powerful computer programs that people can use to access data. For example, 30 years ago, the U.S. Bureau of the Census would store census records on large reels of tape. Technology was primitive. This made access to information time consuming and difficult. Today, however, the Bureau of the Census uses easily available formats that allow for easy and quick

access to information. A student can gain access to the individual records of the census much more easily today than 30 years ago.

Computers allow us to access large longitudinal data sets. A longitudinal data set is a record of the activities of individuals over many years. It contains information about people's schooling, jobs, job turnover, wage rates, income, assets, family circumstances, and more. Such data enable us to discover how responsive people are to changes in the incentives they face.

One such survey, the Michigan Panel Survey of Income Dynamics, has followed the economic activities of the same people for more than 25 years. This survey tells researchers on a month-by-month basis, and in some cases on a week-by-week basis, about births, deaths, marriages, changes in income, and many other variables. So longitudinal data really allow you to track those individuals over time in a consistent, uniform way.

How do people get selected to participate in the surveys that generate economic data?
Initially, the selection is random. For example, the initial Panel Survey of Income Dynamics was a random sample of the population in 1966 and 1967. A companion subsample was also designed to keep track of the profile of low-income population of the United States. But the random sample drawn in the late 1960s is not an accurate reflection of the U.S. population in 1994. The main reason is the massive amount of in-migration from abroad.

There are some other accuracy issues to consider with surveys. Accuracy is diminished because there are segments of the population that are not well represented. The homeless, for example, are much less likely to get into these

surveys than others. Many researchers and scholars are therefore worried about the quality of the data.

Is it easy to replicate work that people have done using large data sets?
People have a lot of difficulty replicating the work of other empirical scholars, and this is a serious issue. The problem is analogous to that of replicating the

results of experiments in the laboratory sciences. The really excellent empirical scholars provide very clear instruction on how to reproduce their data. If a person is clear enough about how the data were selected and what statistics were calculated, somebody can duplicate that study. Unfortunately, such clarity is rare.

Have we uncovered any stable patterns and relationships about the choices that people make—choices about family size, schooling, work hours?
The environment changes, technologies change, and the notion of capturing or understanding all of the forces giving rise to change is unrealistic. But there are some interesting findings.

One is that economic incentives are an important factor in

Nobody can be a good economist who is only an economist. You have to read broadly. . . . It is also important to recognize diversity in human behavior and the ability of the human mind to respond to situations in creative ways.

most decision-making processes. For example, incentives affect peoples' choices about entering and exiting the work force, or migrating to a region, or moving from one location to another.

Another finding is that male and female labor supplies respond very similarly to wages. You would not have thought so 20 years ago.

As more women have worked, their labor supply responses to wages has come to resemble that of men.

Can we use the data from surveys to study the effects of government policies? For example, can we learn about the effects of welfare payments on joblessness?
There is a scarcity of economic knowledge on the consequences of many government policies and programs. Many well-intentioned people do not understand the negative incentives built into certain kinds of social programs such as welfare. The biggest empirical problem in this area is the precise measurement of incentives confronting potential participants in welfare programs. I think once we accurately measure the incentives facing people, we'll understand much better how to alleviate the incentive problems.

I think a major contribution of economists is to understand that people respond to incentives. A major contribution of microeconomists is to demonstrate that the better you measure the incentive, the stronger generally is the measured response to the incentive.

Can we use the kind of studies that you do to figure out how to make government policies work?
Economists rarely design government programs. That is usually the work of politicians and bureaucrats. However, economists reduce the ignorance about the way the world actually works. Economics is most effective in combating bad policies. Economics—labor economics, in particular— has been very effective in demonstrating that certain policies have been either harmful or wasteful. For example, a major finding is that one of the reasons for high European unemployment is high benefit levels paid to the unemployed. Such studies about incentives have helped central bankers, politicians, and the

public realize that welfare payments could actually account for high levels of unemployment. Once economists research and understand a phenomenon like this, it is possible to suggest some kind of policy change.

Is there any evidence at all, in all the studies that you are aware of, that the labor supply curve eventually bends backwards—that at some high wage rate, the quantity of labor supplied decreases if the wage rate increases?
I have seen some evidence from less developed countries that would suggest a backward-bending labor supply curve. In the United States, both men and women seem to have upward-sloping labor supply curves—the quantity of labor supplied increases as the wage rate increases, other things remaining the same. This is certainly the case for participation in the workplace. But the response of hours worked to the wage rate tends to be weak once people work the first hour. The backward-bending labor supply curve has gotten more support in textbooks than it has in reality.

If an undergraduate wants to become an economist and do the kind of work that you do, what should he or she begin by studying? What are the essential courses in the undergraduate program?
If you are interested in empirical work, I think you have to keep an open mind. I think economic theory and basic economic intuitions are really essential to organize data. I feel that a background in mathematics and some quantitative skills is essential. These skills are probably more easily acquired in structured settings—but the fact of the matter is that nobody can be a good economist who is only an economist. You have to read broadly. For example, courses in literature, history, and philosophy are important. I found philosophy to be

incredibly helpful. Rigorous philosophy involves clarifying and defining terms as precisely as you can, and I think economics requires the very same skills and abilities. In conducting careful empirical research, it is important to be precise in your definitions of ideas and at the same time to be open-minded about alternative explanations for the data. It is also important to recognize diversity in human behavior and the ability of the human mind to respond to situations in creative ways.

I would also suggest that you read very widely and find the best professors. When I went to college, I studied with some first-rate minds. I found that some of the most informative minds that I have encountered are people who were

The environment changes, technologies change and the notion of capturing and understanding all the forces giving rise to change is unrealistic.

never famous in a very public way but who had very high standards and a sense of intellectual and personal integrity that was hard not to seize on and be inspired by.

I say go work with the best people, the most interesting people, the ones who challenge you the most.

Pricing and Allocating Factors of Production

After studying this chapter, you will be able to:

- Explain how firms choose the quantities of labor, capital, and land to demand

- Explain how households choose the quantities of labor, capital, land, and entrepreneurship to supply

- Explain how wages, interest, rent, and normal profit are determined in competitive factor markets

- Explain the concept of economic rent and distinguish between economic rent and transfer earnings

Many Happy Returns

It may not be your birthday, and even if it is, chances are you are spending most of it working. But at the end of the week or month (or, if you're devoting all your time to college, when you graduate), you will receive the *returns* from your labor. Those returns vary a lot. Pedro Lopez, who spends his chilly winter days in a small container suspended from the top of Chicago's John Hancock Tower cleaning windows, makes a happy return of $12 an hour. Dan Rather, who puts on a 30-minute news show each weekday evening makes a very happy return of $3.6 million a year. Students working at what have been called "McJobs"—serving fast food or laboring in the fields of southern California—earn just a few dollars an hour. Why aren't *all* jobs well-paid? ◆ Most of us have little trouble spending our pay. But most of us do manage to save some of what we earn. What determines the amount of saving that people do and the returns they make on that saving? How do the returns on saving influence the allocation of savings across the many industries and activities that use our capital resources? ◆ Some people receive income from supplying land, but the amount earned varies enormously with the land's location and quality. For example, an acre of farmland in Iowa rents for about $1,000 a year, while a block on Chicago's "Magnificent Mile" rents for several million dollars a year. What determines the rent that people are willing to pay for different blocks of land? Why are rents so enormously high in big cities and so relatively low in the great farming regions of the nation? ◈ In this chapter we study the markets for factors of production—labor, capital, land, and entrepreneurship—and learn how their prices and people's incomes are determined.

Factor Prices and Incomes

GOODS AND SERVICES ARE PRODUCED BY USING the four factors of production—*labor, capital, land,* and *entrepreneurship*. (These factors of production are defined in Chapter 1, p. 19.) The owners of factors of production supply factor *services* and firms demand factor *services*. These factor services are *flows*—quantities *per unit of time*. Firms hire the *services* of factors of production and in return for the use of their factor services, factor owners receive incomes. These incomes are determined by the prices of the factor services—called *factor prices*. The factor prices are the *wage* rate for labor, the *interest* rate for capital, the *rental* rate for land, and the rate of *normal profit* for entrepreneurship.

In addition to the four factor incomes, a residual income, *economic profit* (or *economic loss*) is paid to (or borne by) firms' owners. A firm's owners might be the suppliers of any of the four factors of production. For a small firm, the owner is usually the entrepreneur. For a large corporation, the owners are the stockholders. In some cases, for example United Airlines, a large part of the stock is owned by the firm's employees.

Factor Prices and Opportunity Costs

Factor prices, which generate incomes for the owners of factors of production, are *opportunity costs* for the firms that employ the factors. The wage rate is the opportunity cost of labor, the interest rate is the opportunity cost of capital, the land rental rate is the opportunity cost of land, and normal profit is the opportunity cost of entrepreneurship. This idea of factor prices as opportunity costs helps you to better understand the nature of the prices of the services of capital and land.

Why is the interest rate the factor price for capital? Why isn't the capital factor price the price of a piece of machinery—the price of a knitting machine for Swanky's sweater factory, the price of a computer for a tax consultant, or the price of an automobile assembly line for GM?

The answer is that these prices are not opportunity costs of *using* capital. They are prices at which capital can be bought *and sold*—the prices at which a piece of capital can change hands. But they are not the prices that must be paid for the use of capital. The opportunity cost of *using* capital is the best alter-native forgone. This alternative is using the funds tied up in the capital to earn some interest. So the interest rate paid on the funds tied up in the capital is the opportunity cost of using capital. These funds may be borrowed, in which case there is an explicit payment of interest to the lender. Or the funds may be owned by the firm, in which case there is an *implicit* interest cost—the interest that could have been earned by using those funds in some other way. Land is similar to capital. The opportunity cost of using land is its rental rate, not its purchase price.

An Overview of a Competitive Factor Market

We're going to learn how a competitive market for the services of a factor of production determines the price, the quantity used, and the income of the factor. But markets exist for only three of the factors of production—labor, capital, and land. The fourth factor, entrepreneurship, is special. It is demanded and supplied by each individual entrepreneur, who constantly seeks out economic profit opportunities. Entrepreneurs flow into industries that yield an economic profit, out of industries that incur an economic loss, and remain in industries that yield a normal profit. Entrepreneurs organize firms that create a demand for the other three factors of production. Let's look at a factor market.

We can study a factor market and the forces that determine the price and quantity in that market by using the model of demand and supply. The quantity of a factor of production demanded depends on the factor's price. That is, the quantity of labor demanded depends on the wage rate, the quantity of capital demanded depends on the interest rate, and the quantity of land demanded depends on the rental rate. The law of demand applies to factors of production just as it does to goods and services. The lower the price of a factor of production, other things remaining the same, the greater is the quantity demanded of the factor of production. Figure 14.1 shows the demand curve for a factor of production as the curve labeled *D*.

The quantity supplied of a factor of production also depends on its price. With a possible exception that we'll identify later in this chapter, the law of supply applies to factors of production. The higher the price of a factor of production, other things remaining the same, the greater is the quantity supplied of

FIGURE 14.1

Demand and Supply in a Factor Market

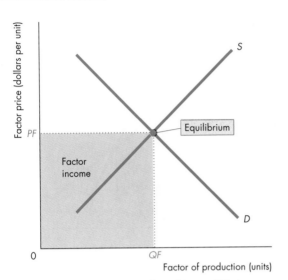

The demand curve for a factor of production (*D*) slopes downward, and the supply curve (*S*) slopes upward. Where the demand and supply curves intersect, the factor price (*PF*) and the quantity of a factor used (*QF*) are determined. The factor income is the product of the factor price and the quantity of the factor, as represented by the blue rectangle.

the factor. Figure 14.1 shows the supply curve of a factor of production as the curve labeled *S*.

The point of intersection of the factor demand and factor supply curves determines the equilibrium factor price. Figure 14.1 shows such an equilibrium: *PF* is the factor price, and *QF* is the quantity of the factor used.

The income earned by a factor of production is its price multiplied by the quantity used. In Fig. 14.1, the price is measured by the distance from the origin to *PF*, and the quantity used is measured by the distance from the origin to *QF*. The factor income is the product of these two distances and equals the blue rectangle in the figure.

All influences on the quantity of a factor that a firm plans to employ other than its price result in a shift in the factor demand curve. We'll study what those influences are in the next section. For now, let's simply work out the effects of a change in the demand for a factor of production on the price of a factor, the quantity used of it, and the factor income.

An increase in demand for a factor of production, as illustrated in Fig. 14.2(a), shifts the demand curve rightward, leading to an increase in its price and an increase in the quantity of the factor used. Thus when the demand curve shifts from D_0 to D_1, the price increases from PF_0 to PF_1 and the quantity used increases from QF_0 to QF_1. An increase in the demand for a factor of production increases that factor's income. The dark blue area in Fig. 14.2(a) illustrates the increase in income.

When the demand for a factor of production decreases, its demand curve shifts leftward. Figure 14.2(b) illustrates the effects of a decrease in demand. The demand curve shifts leftward from D_0 to D_2, the price decreases from PF_0 to PF_2, and the quantity used decreases from QF_0 to QF_2. When the demand for a factor of production decreases, the income of that factor also decreases. The light blue area in Fig. 14.2(b) illustrates the decrease in income.

The extent to which a change in the demand for a factor of production changes the factor price and the quantity used depends on the elasticity of supply. If the supply curve is very flat (supply is elastic), the change in the quantity used is large and the change in price is small. If the supply curve is very steep (supply is inelastic), the change in the price is large and the change in the quantity used is small.

A change in the supply of a factor of production changes the price and quantity used of the factor as well as its income. An increase in supply results in a decrease in the factor price and an increase in the quantity used. A decrease in supply results in an increase in the factor price and a decrease in the quantity used. But whether a change in supply increases or decreases the factor's income depends on the elasticity of demand for the factor.

Suppose that the quantity used of the factor illustrated in Fig. 14.3 decreases from 3 units to 2 units. Initially, the price is $10 a unit. If the demand for the factor is shown by the curve D_0, the decrease in supply results in an increase in the price of the factor but a decrease in the factor's income. You can see that income decreases by multiplying the factor price by the quantity used. Initially, when the quantity is 3 units and the price is $10, the factor's income is $30 ($20 light blue area plus $10 red area). When the quantity decreases to 2 units and the price increases to $14, income decreases by the $10 (red area) but increases by the $8 (dark blue area) for a net decrease of $2 to $28. Over the range of the price change that we've just considered, the demand for the factor is elastic.

FIGURE 14.2

Changes in Demand

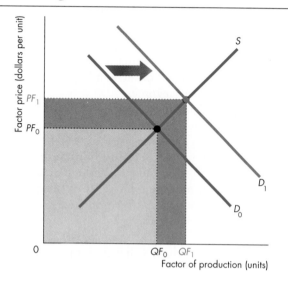

(a) An increase in demand

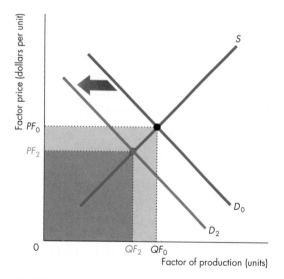

(b) A decrease in demand

An increase in the demand for a factor of production (part a) shifts its demand curve rightward—from D_0 to D_1. The quantity used increases from QF_0 to QF_1, and the price increases from PF_0 to PF_1. The factor income increases, and that income increase is shown by the dark blue area. A decrease in the demand for a factor of production (part b), from D_0 to D_2, results in a decrease in the quantity used, from QF_0 to QF_2, and a decrease in the factor price, from PF_0 to PF_2. The decrease in demand results in a decrease in the factor income. That decrease in income is illustrated by the light blue area.

FIGURE 14.3

Factor Income and Demand Elasticity

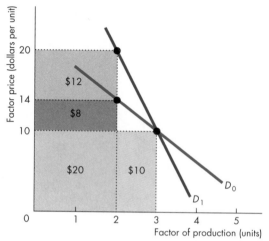

A decrease in the quantity used of a factor of production might result in a decrease or an increase in the factor's income. If the demand curve is D_0 (an elastic demand over the relevant range), a decrease in the quantity from 3 to 2 results in a decrease in the factor income from $30 to $28. If the demand curve is D_1 (an inelastic demand over the relevant range), a decrease in the quantity from 3 to 2 results in an increase in the factor's income from $30 to $40.

Conversely, suppose that the demand for the factor is shown by the curve D_1. In this case, when the quantity decreases to 2 units, the price increases to $20 a unit. Income increases to $40. The smaller quantity lowers income by $10 (red area), but the higher factor price increases income by $20 (dark blue plus green areas). Over the range of the price change that we've just considered, the demand for the factor is inelastic.

We've just seen how demand and supply in a factor market determine the price, quantity used, and income of a factor of production. We're going to spend the rest of this chapter exploring more closely the influences on the demand for and supply of factors of production. We're also going to study the influences on the elasticities of supply of and demand for factors. These elasticities are important because of their effects on factor prices and the incomes earned. Let's begin by studying the demand for factors of production.

Demand for Factors

THE DEMAND FOR A FACTOR OF PRODUCTION IS A
derived demand. A **derived demand** is a demand
for an item not for its own sake but to use it in the
production of goods and services. A firm's derived
demand for factors depends on the constraints the
firm faces—its technology constraint and its market
constraint. It also depends on the firm's objective. We
will study the behavior of firms whose objective is to
maximize profit.

Profit Maximization

In the short run, a firm's factors of production fall
into two categories: variable and fixed. In most
industries, the variable factor is labor and the fixed
factors are capital (i.e., plant, machinery, and buildings) and land. A firm makes short-run changes in
output by changing the quantity of labor it employs.
It makes long-run changes in output by changing the
quantities of labor, capital, and land it employs.

A profit-maximizing firm produces the output at
which marginal cost equals marginal revenue. This
principle holds true whether the firm is in a perfectly
competitive industry, in monopolistic competition, in
oligopoly, or a monopoly. If one more unit of output
adds less to total cost than it adds to total revenue, the
firm can increase its profit by producing more.

We can also state the condition for maximum
profit in terms of the marginal cost of a factor of production and the marginal revenue that the factor generates. Let's look at these two concepts.

Marginal Cost of a Factor   The marginal cost of a
factor of production is the addition to a firm's total
cost that results from employing one more unit of a
factor. For a firm that buys its factors of production
in competitive factor markets, the marginal cost of a
factor is the price of the factor. That is, in a competitive factor market, each firm is such a small user of
the factor that it has no influence on the price it must
pay for each unit employed. The firm simply has to
pay the going factor price—market wage rate for
labor, interest rate for capital, and rent for land.

Marginal Revenue Product   To maximize profit, a
firm must compare the marginal cost of a factor with
the marginal revenue that the factor generates, which
is called marginal revenue product. **Marginal revenue product** is the change in total revenue resulting from employing one more unit of a factor of production while the quantity of all other factors
remains constant.

The concept of *marginal revenue product* sounds
a bit like the concept of *marginal revenue* that you
have met before. These concepts are indeed related,
but there is a crucial distinction between the two.
Marginal revenue product is the extra revenue generated as a result of employing one extra unit of a factor; marginal revenue is the extra revenue generated
as a result of selling one additional unit of output.

Quantity of Factor Demanded   To maximize
profit, a firm hires the quantity of a factor of production that makes the marginal revenue product of the
factor equal to its price. If the marginal revenue product of a factor exceeds its price, the firm can increase
its profit by increasing the quantity of the factor
employed. If the marginal revenue product of a factor
is less than its price, the firm can increase its profit by
decreasing the quantity of the factor employed. But if
the marginal revenue product of a factor is equal to
its price, the firm can only decrease its profit by
changing the quantity of the factor employed. At this
point, the firm is maximizing profit.

As the price of a factor varies, the quantity
demanded of it also varies. The lower the price of a
factor, the larger is the quantity demanded of that
factor. Let's illustrate this proposition by working
through an example—that of labor.

The Firm's Demand for Labor

A *total product schedule* describes a firm's short-run
technology constraint. The first two columns of Table
14.1 set out the total product schedule for a car wash
operated by Max's Wash 'n' Wax. (This total product
schedule is similar to the one we studied in Chapter
10, Fig. 10.1.) The numbers tell us how the maximum number of car washes each hour varies as the
amount of labor employed varies. The third column
of Table 14.1 shows the *marginal product of labor*—
the change in output resulting from a one-unit
increase in the quantity of labor employed.

Max's market constraint is the demand curve for
his product. If, in the goods market, a firm is a
monopoly or is engaged in monopolistic competition
or oligopoly, the demand curve for its product is
downward-sloping. If a firm is perfectly competitive,
the demand curve for its product is perfectly elastic—
the firm is a price taker. Assume that the car wash

market is perfectly competitive. Max can sell as many washes as he chooses at a constant price of $4 a wash. Given this information, we can calculate Max's total revenue (fourth column) by multiplying the number of cars washed per hour by $4. For example, if 9 cars are washed each hour (row *c*), total revenue is $36.

The fifth column shows the calculation of marginal revenue product of labor—the change in total revenue per unit increase in labor. For example, if Max hires a second worker (row *c*), total revenue increases from $20 to $36, so marginal revenue product of labor is $16.

There is an alternative way of calculating the marginal revenue product of labor. The marginal product of labor tells us how many washes an additional worker produces. Marginal revenue tells us the change in total revenue from selling one more wash. So an additional worker changes total revenue by an amount that equals marginal product multiplied by marginal revenue. That is, marginal revenue product equals marginal product multiplied by marginal revenue. For a perfectly competitive firm, marginal revenue equals price, so marginal revenue product equals marginal product multiplied by price.

To see that this method works, let's use the numbers in Table 14.1. Multiply the marginal product of

hiring a second worker—4 car washes an hour—by marginal revenue—$4 a wash—and notice that the answer is $16, the same as we have already calculated.

Notice that as the quantity of labor increases, the marginal revenue product of labor falls. When Max hires the first worker, the marginal revenue product of labor is $20. If Max hires a second worker, the marginal revenue product of labor is $16. Marginal revenue product of labor continues to decline as Max hires more workers.

Marginal revenue product diminishes as Max hires more workers because of the principle of diminishing returns that we first studied in Chapter 10. With each additional worker hired, the marginal product of labor falls and so brings in a smaller marginal revenue product. Because Max's Wash 'n' Wax is a perfectly competitive firm, the price of each additional car wash is the same and brings in the same marginal revenue.

If Max had a monopoly in car washing, he would have to lower his price to sell more washes. In this case, the marginal revenue product of labor diminishes even more quickly than in perfectly competitive conditions. For a monopoly, marginal revenue product diminishes because of diminishing marginal product of labor and also because of diminishing marginal revenue.

TABLE 14.1

Marginal Revenue Product at Max's Wash 'n' Wax

	Quantity of labor (L) (workers)	Output (Q) (car washes per hour)	Marginal product ($MP = \Delta Q/\Delta L$) (washes per worker)	Total revenue ($TR = P \times Q$) (dollars)	Marginal revenue product ($MRP = \Delta TR/\Delta L$) (dollars per worker)
a	0	0		0	
			5		20
b	1	5		20	
			4		16
c	2	9		36	
			3		12
d	3	12		48	
			2		8
e	4	14		56	
			1		4
f	5	15		60	

The marginal revenue product of labor is the change in total revenue that results from a one-unit increase in labor. Max operates in a perfectly competitive car wash market and can sell any quantity of washes at $4 a wash. To calculate marginal revenue product, first work out total revenue. If Max hires 1 worker (row *b*), output is 5 washes an hour and total revenue is $20. If he hires 2 workers (row *c*), output is 9 washes an hour and total revenue is $36. By hiring the second worker, total revenue rises by $16—the marginal revenue product of labor is $16.

The Labor Demand Curve

Figure 14.4 shows how the labor demand curve is derived from the marginal revenue product curve. The *marginal revenue product curve* graphs the marginal revenue product of a factor at each quantity of the factor hired. Figure 14.4(a) illustrates the marginal revenue product curve for workers employed by Max. The horizontal axis measures the number of workers that Max hires, and the vertical axis measures the marginal revenue product of labor. The blue bars show the marginal revenue product of labor as Max employs more workers. These bars correspond to the numbers in Table 14.1. The curve labeled *MRP* is Max's marginal revenue product curve.

The firm's demand for labor curve is its marginal revenue product curve. You can see Max's demand for labor curve (*D*) in Fig. 14.4(b). The horizontal axis measures the number of workers hired—the same as in part (a). The vertical axis measures the wage rate in dollars per hour. The demand for labor curve is exactly the same as the firm's marginal revenue product curve. For example, when Max employs 3 workers an hour, his marginal revenue product is $10 an hour, as

in Fig. 14.4(a); and at a wage rate of $10 an hour, Max hires 3 workers an hour, as in Fig. 14.4(b).

Why is the demand for labor curve identical to the marginal revenue product curve? Because the firm hires the profit-maximizing quantity of labor. If the cost of hiring one more worker—the wage rate—is less than the additional revenue that the worker brings in—the marginal revenue product of labor—then the firm can increase its profit by employing one more worker. Conversely, if the cost of hiring one more worker is greater than the additional revenue that the worker brings in—the wage rate exceeds the marginal revenue product—then the firm can increase its profit by employing one fewer worker. But if the cost of hiring one more worker is equal to the additional revenue that the worker brings in—the wage rate equals the marginal revenue product—then the firm cannot increase its profit by changing the number of workers it employs. The firm is making the maximum possible profit. Thus the quantity of labor demanded by the firm is such that the wage rate equals the marginal revenue product of labor.

Table 14.2 is a compact glossary of the factor market terms that you've just learned.

FIGURE 14.4

The Demand for Labor at Max's Wash 'n' Wax

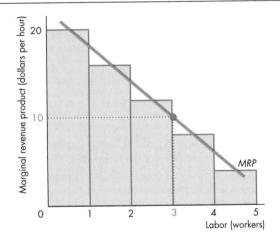

(a) Marginal revenue product

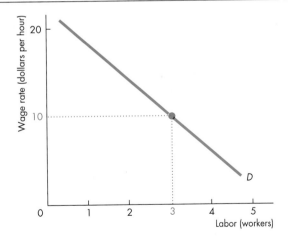

(b) Demand for labor

Max's Wash 'n' Wax operates in a perfectly competitive car wash market and can sell any quantity of washes at $4 a wash. The blue bars in part (a) represent the firm's marginal revenue product of labor. They are based on the numbers in Table 14.1. The orange line is the firm's marginal revenue product of

labor curve. Part (b) shows Max's demand for labor curve. This curve is identical to Max's marginal revenue product curve. Max demands the quantity of labor that makes the wage rate, which is the marginal cost of labor, equal to the marginal revenue product of labor.

TABLE 14.2

A Compact Glossary of Factor Market Terms

Factors of production	Labor, capital, land, and entrepreneurship
Factor prices	Wage—price of labor; interest—price of capital; rent—price of land; normal profit—price of entrepreneurship
Marginal product	The additional output produced by employing one additional unit of a factor; for example, the marginal product of labor is the additional output produced by employing one more person
Marginal revenue	The change in total revenue resulting from selling one additional unit of output
Marginal revenue product	The change in total revenue resulting from hiring one additional unit of a factor of production; for example, the marginal revenue product of labor is the additional total revenue resulting from selling the output produced by employing one more person

TABLE 14.3

Two Conditions for Maximum Profit

SYMBOLS

Marginal product	**MP**
Marginal revenue	**MR**
Marginal cost	**MC**
Marginal revenue product	**MRP**
Factor price	**PF**

TWO CONDITIONS FOR MAXIMUM PROFIT

1.   **MR = MC**   2.   **MRP = PF**

EQUIVALENCE OF CONDITIONS

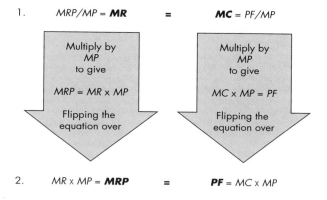

The two conditions for maximum profit are marginal revenue (*MR*) equals marginal cost (*MC*) and marginal revenue product (*MRP*) equals the price of the factor (*PF*). These two conditions are equivalent because marginal revenue product (*MRP*) equals marginal revenue (*MR*) multiplied by marginal product (*MP*) and the factor price (*PF*) equals marginal cost (*MC*) multiplied by marginal product (*MP*).

Two Conditions for Profit Maximization

When we studied firms' output decisions, we discovered that a condition for maximum profit is that marginal revenue equals marginal cost. We've now discovered another condition for maximum profit: Marginal revenue product of a factor equals the factor's price. These two conditions are equivalent to each other, as Table 14.3 shows. When a firm produces the quantity of output that maximizes profit, marginal revenue equals marginal cost and the firm's technology and market constraints imply that the firm is employing the amount of labor that makes the marginal revenue product of labor equal to the wage rate.

We have just derived the law of demand as it applies to the labor market. And we've discovered that the same principles that apply to the demand for goods and services apply here as well. The demand

for labor curve slopes downward. Other things remaining the same, the lower the wage rate (the price of labor), the greater is the quantity of labor demanded. Let's now study the influences that change in the demand for labor and shift in the demand for labor curve.

Changes in the Demand for Labor

The position of a firm's demand for labor curve depends on three factors:

1. The price of the firm's output
2. The prices of other factors of production
3. Technology

The higher the price of a firm's output, the greater is the quantity of labor demanded by the firm, other things remaining the same. The price of output affects the demand for labor through its influence on marginal revenue product. A higher price for the firm's output increases marginal revenue, which, in turn, increases the marginal revenue product of labor. A change in the price of a firm's output leads to a shift in the firm's demand for labor curve. If the price of the firm's output increases, the demand for labor increases.

The other two influences on the demand for labor have their main effects not in the short run but in the long run. The *short-run demand for labor* is the relationship between the wage rate and the quantity of labor demanded when the quantities of the other factors are fixed and labor is the only variable factor. The *long-run demand for labor* is the relationship between the wage rate and the quantity of labor demanded when all factors can be varied. A change in the relative price of factors of production—such as the relative price of labor and capital—leads to a substitution away from the factor whose relative price has increased and toward the factor whose relative price has decreased. Thus if the price of using capital decreases relative to that of using labor, the firm substitutes capital for labor, increasing the quantity of capital demanded and decreasing its demand for labor.

Finally, a new technology that influences the marginal product of labor also affects the demand for labor. For example, the development of electronic telephones with memories and a host of clever features decreased the marginal product of telephone operators and so decreased the demand for telephone operators. This same new technology increased the marginal product of telephone engineers and so increased the demand for telephone engineers. Again, these effects are felt in the long run when the firm adjusts all its factors and incorporates new technologies into its production process. Table 14.4 summarizes the influences on a firm's demand for labor.

We saw in Fig. 14.2 the effects of a change in the demand for a factor. We can now say why the demand for labor curve shifts. For example, an increase in the price of the firm's output, an increase in the price of

TABLE 14.4

A Firm's Demand for Labor

THE LAW OF DEMAND

The quantity of labor demanded by a firm

Decreases if:	*Increases if:*
■ The wage rate increases	■ The wage rate decreases

CHANGES IN DEMAND

A firm's demand for labor

Decreases if:	*Increases if:*
■ The firm's output price decreases	■ The firm's output price increases
■ The prices of other factors decrease	■ The prices of other factors increase
■ A new technology decreases the marginal product of labor	■ A new technology increases the marginal product of labor

capital, or a new technology that increases the marginal product of labor shifts the demand for labor curve from D_0 to D_1 in Fig. 14.2(a). A decrease in the price of the firm's output, a decrease in the price of capital, or a new technology that lowers the marginal product of labor shifts the demand curve for labor from D_0 to D_2 in Fig. 14.2(b).

Market Demand

So far, we've studied only the demand for labor by an individual firm. Let's now look at the market demand. The market demand for a factor of production is the total demand for that factor by all firms. Thus the concept of the market demand for labor curve is exactly like the concept of the market demand curve for a good or service. The market demand curve for a good or service is obtained by adding together the quantities demanded of that good by all households at each price. The market demand curve for labor is obtained by adding together the quantities of labor demanded by all firms at each wage rate.

Elasticity of Demand for Labor

The elasticity of demand for labor measures the responsiveness of the quantity of labor demanded to the wage rate. We calculate this elasticity in the same way that we calculate a price elasticity: The elasticity of demand for labor equals the magnitude of the percentage change in the quantity of labor demanded divided by the percentage change in the wage rate.

The demand for labor is less elastic in the short-run, when only labor can be varied, than in the long run, when labor and other factors can be varied. The elasticity of demand for labor depends on:

- The labor intensity of the production process
- How rapidly the marginal product of labor diminishes
- The elasticity of demand for the product
- The substitutability of capital for labor

Labor Intensity   A labor-intensive production process is one that uses a lot of labor and little capital—a process that has a high ratio of labor to capital. Home building is an example. The larger the labor-capital ratio, the more elastic is the demand for labor, other things remaining the same. Let's see why.

If wages are 90 percent of total cost, a 10 percent increase in the wage rate increases total cost by 9 percent. Firms will be extremely sensitive to such a large change in total cost. If the wage rate increases, firms will decrease the quantity of labor demanded by a large amount. But if wages are 10 percent of total cost, a 10 percent increase in the wage rate increases total cost by 1 percent. Firms will be less sensitive to this increase in cost. If the wage rate increases in this case, firms will decrease the quantity of labor demanded by a small amount.

How Rapidly Marginal Product Diminishes   The more rapidly the marginal product of labor diminishes, the less elastic is the demand for labor, other things remaining the same. In some activities, marginal product diminishes quickly. For example, the marginal product of one bus driver is high, but the marginal product of a second driver on the same bus is close to zero. In other activities, marginal product diminishes slowly. For example, hiring a second window cleaner on a team almost doubles the amount of glass that can be cleaned in an hour—the marginal product of the second window cleaner is almost the same as the first.

The Elasticity of Demand for the Product   The greater the elasticity of demand for the good, the larger is the elasticity of demand for the factors of production used to produce it. To see why, think about what happens when the wage rate increases. An increase in the wage rate increases marginal cost and decreases the supply of the good. The decrease in the supply of the good increases the price of the good and decreases the quantity demanded of the good and the quantities of the factors used to produce it. The greater the elasticity of demand for the good, the larger is the decrease in the quantity demanded of the good and so the larger is the decrease in the quantities of the factors of production used to produce it.

The Substitutability of Capital for Labor   The substitutability of capital for labor influences the long-run elasticity of demand for labor but not the short-run elasticity. In the short run, capital is fixed. In the long run, capital can be varied, and the more easily capital can be substituted for labor in production, the more elastic is the long-run demand for labor. For example, it is fairly easy to substitute robots for assembly line workers in car factories and automatic picking machines for labor in vineyards and orchards. At the other extreme, it is difficult (though not impossible) to substitute computers for newspaper reporters, bank loan officers, and teachers. The more readily capital can be substituted for labor, the more elastic is the firm's demand for labor in the long run.

R E V I E W

- A firm chooses the quantity of labor to employ so that its profit is maximized.
- Profit is maximized when the marginal revenue product of labor equals the wage rate.
- The marginal revenue product of labor curve is the firm's demand for labor curve. The lower the wage rate, the greater is the quantity of labor demanded.
- The short-run elasticity of demand for labor depends on the labor intensity of production, how rapidly marginal product diminishes, and the elasticity of demand for the product.
- The long-run elasticity of demand for labor depends on these same three conditions and on how easily capital can be substituted for labor.

Supply of Factors

THE SUPPLY OF FACTORS IS DETERMINED BY THE decisions of households. Households allocate the factors of production that they own to their most rewarding uses. The quantity supplied of any factor of production depends on its price. Usually, the higher the price of a factor of production, the larger is the quantity supplied. There is a possible exception to this general law of supply concerning the supply of labor. It arises from the fact that people have preferences about how they use their time.

Let's examine the household's factor supply decisions, beginning with the supply of labor.

Supply of Labor

A household chooses the number of hours per week of labor to supply as part of its time allocation decision. Time is allocated between two broad activities:

1. Market activity
2. Nonmarket activity

Market activity is the same thing as supplying labor. **Nonmarket activity** consists of everything else: leisure, nonmarket production activities including education and training, shopping, cooking, and other activities in the home. The household obtains a return from market activity in the form of a wage. Nonmarket activities generate a return in the form of goods and services produced in the home, a higher future income, or leisure, which is valued for its own sake and which is classified as a good.

In deciding how to allocate its time between market activity and nonmarket activity, a household weighs the returns that it can get from the different activities. We are interested in the effects of the wage rate on the household's allocation of its time and on how much labor it supplies.

Wages and Quantity of Labor Supplied To induce a household to supply labor, it must be offered a high enough wage rate. Households value nonmarket activities either because the time is used in some productive activity or because of the value they attach to leisure. For it to be worthwhile to supply labor, a household has to be offered a wage rate that is at least equal to the value it places on the last hour it spends in nonmarket activities. This wage rate—the lowest one for which a household will supply labor to the market—is called its **reservation wage**. At wage rates below the reservation wage, the household supplies no labor. Once the wage rate reaches the reservation wage, the household begins to supply labor. As the wage rate rises above the reservation wage, the household varies the quantity of labor that it supplies. But a higher wage rate has two offsetting effects on the quantity of labor supplied: a *substitution effect* and an *income effect*.

Substitution Effect Other things remaining the same, the higher the wage rate, the more time people allocate to market activity and the less they allocate to nonmarket activities. Suppose, for example, that the market price of laundry services is $10 an hour. If the wage rate available to a household is less than $10 an hour, the household will provide its own laundry services—a nonmarket activity. If the household's wage rate rises above $10 an hour, it will be worthwhile for the household to allocate more hours to market activity and use part of its income to buy laundry services. The higher wage rate induces a switch of time from nonmarket activities to market activities.

Income Effect The higher the household's wage rate, the higher is its income. A higher income, other things remaining the same, induces an increase in demand for most goods. Leisure, a component of nonmarket activity, is one of those goods. Because an increase in income creates an increase in the demand for leisure, it also creates a decrease in the amount of time allocated to market activities and therefore to a fall in the quantity of labor supplied.

Backward-Bending Household Supply of Labor Curve The substitution effect and the income effect operate in opposite directions. The higher the wage rate, the greater is the quantity of labor supplied via the substitution effect but the smaller is the quantity of labor supplied via the income effect. At low wage rates, the substitution effect is larger than the income effect. As the wage rate rises, the household supplies more labor. But as the wage rate continues to rise, there comes a point at which the substitution effect and the income effect just offset each other. At that point, a change in the wage rate has no effect on the quantity of labor supplied. If the wage rate continues to rise, the income effect begins to dominate the substitution effect and the quantity of labor supplied declines. The household's supply of labor curve does not slope upward throughout its entire length but begins to bend back on itself. It is called a *backward-bending supply curve*.

Figure 14.5(a) shows three individual household labor supply curves. Each household has a different reservation wage and each household's labor supply curve is backward-bending.

Market Supply   The quantity of labor supplied to the entire market is the total quantity supplied by all households. The market supply of labor curve is the sum of the supply curves of all the individual households. Figure 14.5(b) shows the market supply curve (S_M) derived from the supply curves of the three households (S_A, S_B, S_C) in Fig. 14.5(a). At wage rates of less than $1 an hour, the three households do only nonmarket activities such as laundry and cooking, and they do not supply any market labor. The household most eager to supply market labor has a reservation wage of $1 an hour. As the wage rate rises from $1 to $4 an hour, household A increases the quantity of labor that it supplies to the market. The reservation wage of household B is $4 an hour, so as the wage rate rises above $4 an hour, the quantity of labor supplied in the market is the sum of the labor supplied by households A and B. When the wage rate reaches $7

an hour, household C begins to supply some labor to the market. At wage rates above $7 an hour, the quantity supplied in the market is equal to the sum of the quantities supplied by the three households.

Notice that the market supply curve S_M, like the individual household supply curves, eventually bends backward. But the market supply curve has a long upward-sloping section. The reason is that the reservation wage rates of individual households are not equal and at higher wage rates, additional households reach their reservation wage and so begin to supply labor.

Supply to Individual Firms   We've studied the labor supply decisions of individual households and seen how those decisions add up to the market supply. But how is the supply of labor to each individual firm determined? The answer to this question depends on the degree of competitiveness in the labor market. In a perfectly competitive labor market (that we study here), each firm faces a perfectly elastic supply of labor. That is, the firm can hire any quantity of labor at the market wage rate. This situation arises because the individual firm is such a small part of the total labor market that it has no influence on the wage rate.

FIGURE 14.5

The Supply of Labor

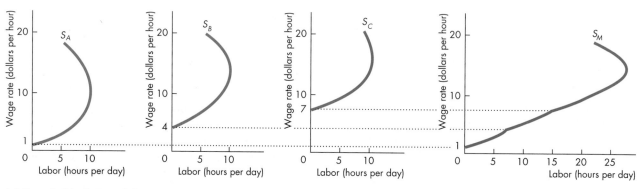

(a) Households A, B, and C

Part (a) shows the labor supply curves of three households (S_A, S_B, and S_C). Each household has a reservation wage below which it will supply no labor. As the wage rises, the quantity of labor supplied increases to a maximum. If the wage continues to rise, the quantity of labor supplied begins to decrease. Each

(b) Market

household's supply curve eventually bends backward. Part (b) shows how, by adding the quantities of labor supplied by the households at each wage rate, we derive the market supply curve of labor (S_M). The market supply curve has a long upward-sloping region before it bends backward.

- The labor supply curve is backward bending.
- The market supply of labor curve is the sum of the supply curves of individual households and is upward-sloping.
- In a perfectly competitive labor market, each firm faces a perfectly elastic supply curve.

Supply of Capital

The supply of capital is more indirect than the supply of labor. It is determined by households' saving decisions. If households supplied capital in the same direct way that they supply labor, then all the buildings, machines, and other equipment would be owned by households and rented to firms. In fact, most capital is owned by firms, who in effect rent it to themselves. Households supply the funds, called *financial capital*, that firms use to buy capital. Households lend some of these funds to firms by buying their stocks and bonds and by making deposits in banks, which the banks lend to firms. Households also lend funds to firms in the form of retained earnings—profits that have not been paid out to the firm's owners, their stockholders.

The total amount of capital that firms can acquire and use depends on the total quantity of financial capital. This quantity is a *stock*—a quantity at a point in time. The stock of financial capital depends on the amounts that households have saved in previous years. Saving is a *flow*—a quantity per year—that adds to the stock of financial capital.

The most important factors determining a household's saving are:

- Current income and expected future income
- The interest rate

Current Income and Expected Future Income

A household with a current income that is low compared with its expected future income saves little and might even have negative saving. A household with a current income that is high compared with its expected future income saves a great deal in the present to be able to consume more in the future. The stage in the household's life cycle is the main factor influencing whether current income is high or low compared with expected future income. Young households typi-

cally have a low current income compared with their expected future income, while older working households have a high current income relative to their expected future income. The consequence of this pattern in income over the life cycle is that young people have negative saving and older working people have positive saving. Thus the young incur debts (such as consumer credit) to acquire durable goods and to consume more than their income, while older working people save and accumulate assets (often in the form of pension and life insurance arrangements) to provide for their retirement years.

The Interest Rate The interest rate is the opportunity cost of consuming in the current year rather than in the following year. If the interest rate is 10 percent a year, $100 consumed in the current year costs $110 of consumption in the following year. So by consuming $100 in the current year rather than in the following year, consumption falls by $10 or 10 percent of current consumption. Equivalently, $100 saved (not consumed) in the current year brings the possibility of increasing consumption by $110 in the following year—a net increase in consumption of $10 or 10 percent.

Other things remaining the same, the higher the interest rate, the greater is the amount of saving and the greater is the quantity of capital supplied. With a high interest rate, people have a strong incentive to cut consumption and increase their saving in order to take advantage of the high returns available. With a low interest rate, people have only a weak incentive to cut their consumption and save.

The Supply Curve of Capital

The quantity of capital supplied in the market is the sum of the quantities supplied by all the individual households. The market supply curve of capital shows how the quantity of capital supplied varies as the interest rate varies. In the short run, the supply of capital is inelastic and might even be perfectly inelastic. The vertical supply curve SS in Fig. 14.6 illustrates such a case. The reason is that households find it difficult to change their consumption plans quickly in response to changes in the interest rate. But given sufficient time to make the necessary substitutions, they do respond to a change in the interest rate. As a result, the long-run supply of capital is much more elastic. The supply curve LS in Fig. 14.6 illustrates such a case.

FIGURE 14.6

Short-Run and Long-Run Supply of Capital

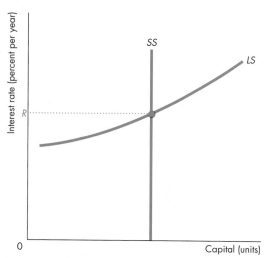

The long-run supply of capital (LS) is highly elastic. In the long run, if the interest rate is above R, households increase their saving and the quantity of capital supplied increases. Also, in the long run, if the interest rate is below R, households decrease their saving and the quantity of capital supplied decreases. The short-run supply of capital (SS) is inelastic (perfectly inelastic in the figure). In the short run, there is a fixed amount of capital and this quantity cannot be varied, no matter what the interest rate.

Supply to Individual Firms   In the short run, a firm can vary its labor but not its capital. Thus in the short run, the firm faces a fixed supply of capital. It has a specific set of capital assets. For example, an auto producer has a production assembly line; a laundromat operator has a number of washing machines and dryers; the campus print shop has a number of photocopying and other printing machines. These pieces of capital cannot be quickly disposed of or added to.

In the long run, a firm can vary all its factors—capital as well as labor. A firm operating in a competitive capital market can obtain any amount of capital it chooses at the going market interest rate. Thus it faces a perfectly elastic supply of capital.

Let's complete our analysis of the supply of factors of production by examining the supply of land.

Supply of Land

Land is the quantity of natural resources, and its aggregate quantity supplied cannot be changed by any individual decisions. Individual households can vary the amount of land they own, but whatever land is acquired by one household is sold by another, so the aggregate quantity of land supplied of any particular type and in any particular location is fixed, regardless of the decisions of any individual household. This fact means that the supply of each particular piece of land is perfectly inelastic. Figure 14.7 illustrates such a supply. Regardless of the rent available, the quantity of land supplied on Chicago's "Magnificent Mile" is a fixed number of square feet.

Expensive land can be, and is, used more intensively than inexpensive land. For example, high-rise buildings enable land to be used more intensively. However, to use land more intensively, it has to be combined with another factor of production—capital. Increasing the amount of capital per block of land does not change the supply of land itself. But it does enable land to become more productive. Rising land prices strengthen the incentive to find ways of

FIGURE 14.7

The Supply of Land

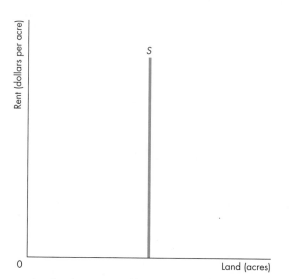

The supply of a given piece of land is perfectly inelastic. No matter what the rent, no more land than the quantity that exists can be supplied.

increasing its productivity. These issues are explored more fully in *Economics in History* on pp. 354–355.

Although the supply of each type of land is fixed and its supply is perfectly inelastic, each individual firm, operating in competitive land markets, faces an elastic supply of land. For example, Fifth Avenue in New York City has a fixed amount of land, but Doubleday, the bookstore, could rent some space from Saks, the department store. Each firm can rent the quantity of land that it demands at the going rent, as determined in the marketplace. Thus provided that land markets are highly competitive, firms are price takers in these markets, just as they are in the markets for other factors of production.

R E V I E W

■ The supply of capital is determined by households' saving decisions.

■ Other things remaining the same, the higher the interest rate, the greater is the amount of capital supplied. The supply of capital to individual firms is inelastic in the short run but perfectly elastic in the long run.

■ The supply of land is fixed—is perfectly inelastic. But the supply of land to individual firms is elastic.

We've now seen how demand and supply in factor markets determine incomes, and we've probed more deeply into the influences on the demand for and supply of factors of production. Let's now use what we've learned to see why some factors of production earn high incomes and others earn low ones. Let's also learn about economic rent and transfer earnings.

Incomes, Economic Rent, and Transfer Earnings

WE SAW AT THE BEGINNING OF THIS CHAPTER— in Figs. 14.1. 14.2, and 14.3—that the price of a factor of production and the quantity of it used are determined by the interaction of demand and supply. We've seen that demand is determined by marginal productivity and supply is determined by the resources available and by households' choices about their use. The interaction of demand and supply in factor markets determines who receives a large income and who receives a small income.

Large and Small Incomes

Why does a national news anchor earn a large income? It is because such a person has a very high marginal revenue product—reflected in the demand for her or his services—and the supply of people with the combination of talents needed for this kind of job is small—reflected in the supply. Equilibrium occurs at a high wage rate and a small quantity employed.

Why do McJobs pay low wages? It is because they have a low marginal revenue product—reflected in the demand—and many households are able and willing to supply their labor for these jobs. Equilibrium occurs at a low wage rate and a large quantity employed.

If the demand for news anchors increases, their incomes increase by a large amount and the number of news anchors barely changes. If the demand for workers in McJobs increases, the number of people doing these jobs increases by a large amount and the wage rate barely changes.

The demand for that block of land is determined by its marginal revenue product. The marginal revenue product in turn depends on the uses to which the land can be put. In a central business district such as Manhattan, the marginal revenue product is high because a large number of people are concentrated in that area, making it a prime place for conducting business.

The rent charged for a piece of land depends entirely on its marginal revenue product—the demand for it. If demand increases, the rent rises. If demand decreases, the rent falls. The quantity of land supplied remains constant.

Is coffee expensive in New York City because land rents are high, or are land rents high because people in New York City are willing to pay a high price for coffee? If you asked McDonald's financial director this question, the answer you would get is that McDonald's charges a high price for coffee at its 57th Street restaurant because of the high rent it pays for the land. But this answer is not deep enough. The rent is high because McDonald's marginal revenue product of that land is high. That is, the rent of a New York City block is determined by the demand for it, and that the demand, in turn, is determined by its marginal revenue product. Land has a high marginal revenue product because someone is willing to pay a high price to the use the land.

You can get a further insight into factor incomes by learning about the distinction between economic rent and transfer earnings.

Economic Rent and Transfer Earnings

The total income of a factor of production is made up of its economic rent and its transfer earnings. **Economic rent** is the income received by the owner of a factor over and above the amount required to induce that owner to offer the factor for use. Any factor of production can receive an economic rent. The income required to induce the supply of a factor of production is called **transfer earnings**. Transfer earnings are the opportunity cost of using a factor of production—the value of the factor in its next best use.

Figure 14.8 illustrates the concepts of economic rent and transfer earnings. The figure shows the market for a factor of production. It could be *any* factor of production—labor, capital, or land. The demand curve for the factor of production is D, and its supply curve is S. The factor price is PF, and the quantity of the factor used is QF. The income of the factor is the sum of the yellow and green areas. The yellow area below the supply curve measures transfer earnings, and the green area above the supply curve but below the factor price measures economic rent.

To see why the area below the supply curve measures transfer earnings, recall that a supply curve can be interpreted in two different ways. One interpretation is that a supply curve indicates the quantity supplied at a given price. But the alternative interpretation of a supply curve is that it shows the minimum price at which a given quantity is willingly supplied. If suppliers receive only the minimum amount required to induce them to supply each unit of the factor of production, they will be paid a different price for each unit. The prices will trace the supply curve, and the income received is entirely transfer earnings—the yellow area in Fig. 14.8.

The concept of economic rent is similar to the concept of consumer surplus that you met in Chapter 7 (pp. 158–159). Recall that consumer surplus is the difference between the maximum price the household would be willing to pay, as indicated by the demand curve, and the price the household pays for a good. In a parallel sense, economic rent is the difference between the factor price a household actually receives and the minimum factor price at which it would be willing to supply a given amount of a factor of production.

Economic rent is not the same thing as *rent*. Rent is the price paid for the services of land. Economic rent is a component of the income received by any factor of production.

The portion of the income of a factor of production that consists of economic rent depends on the elasticity of the supply of the factor of production. When the supply of a factor of production is perfectly inelastic, its entire income is economic rent. Most of Garth Brook's and Pearl Jam's income is economic rent. Also, a large part of the income of a major league baseball player is economic rent (see *Reading Between the Lines*, pp. 348–349). When the supply of a factor of production is perfectly elastic, none of its income is economic rent. Most of the income of a baby sitter is transfer earnings. In general, when the supply curve is neither perfectly elastic nor perfectly inelastic (like that illustrated in Fig. 14.8), some part of the factor income is economic rent and the other part is transfer earnings.

Figure 14.9 illustrates the three possibilities. Part (a) of the figure shows the market for a particular parcel of land in New York City. The quantity of land is fixed in size at L acres. Therefore the supply curve of the land is vertical—perfectly inelastic. No matter

---

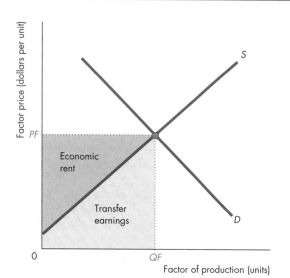

FIGURE 14.8

Economic Rent and Transfer Earnings

The total factor income is made up of its economic rent and its transfer earnings. Transfer earnings are measured by the yellow area under the supply curve, and economic rent is measured by the green area above the supply curve and below the factor price.

FIGURE 14.9
Economic Rent and Supply Elasticity

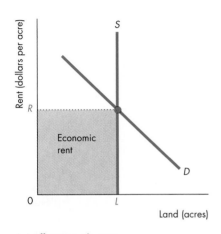

(a) All economic rent

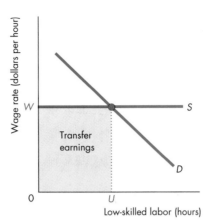

(b) All transfer earnings

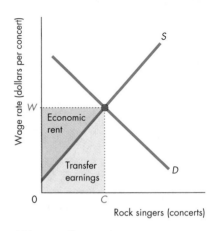

(c) Intermediate case

When the supply of a factor of production is perfectly inelastic (the supply curve is vertical), as in part (a), the entire factor income is economic rent. When the supply of the factor of production is perfectly elastic, as in part (b), the factor's entire income is transfer earnings. When a factor supply curve slopes upward, as in part (c), part of the factor income is economic rent and part is transfer earnings. Land is the example shown in part (a); low-skilled labor in poor countries such as India and China in part (b); and rock singers in part (c).

what the rent on the land is, there is no way of increasing the quantity that can be supplied.

Suppose that the demand curve in Fig. 14.9(a) shows the marginal revenue product of this block of land. Then it commands a rent of *R*. The entire income accruing to the owner of the land is the green area in the figure. This income is *economic rent*.

Figure 14.9(b) shows the market for a factor of production that is in perfectly elastic supply. An example of such a market might be that for low-skilled labor in a poor country such as India or China. In those countries, large amounts of labor flock to the cities and are available for work at the going wage rate (in this case, *W*). Thus in these situations, the supply of labor is almost perfectly elastic. The entire income earned by this labor is transfer earnings. They receive no economic rent.

Figure 14.9(c) shows the market for rock singers. To induce rock singers to sing at a larger number of concerts, a higher income has to be offered—the supply curve of rock singers is upward-sloping. The demand curve—measuring the marginal revenue product of the rock singer—is labeled *D* in the figure. Equilibrium occurs where the rock singer

receives a wage of *W* and sings in *C* concerts. The green area above the rock singer's supply curve is economic rent, and the yellow area below the supply curve is the rock singer's transfer earnings. If the rock singer is not offered at least the amount of the transfer earnings, then the singer will withdraw from the rock concert market and perform alternative activities, such as recording CDs or teaching singing.

◆ We've now studied the markets for factors of production, and we've seen how the returns to these factors of production are determined. We've seen how the interaction of demand and supply determines factor prices and factor incomes. We've also seen how changes in demand and supply bring changes in factor prices and incomes. We've seen the crucial role played in determining the demand for a factor of production by the factor's marginal revenue product, and we've seen why some factors receive large incomes and others receive small incomes. Finally, we've distinguished between economic rent and transfer earnings.

In the next chapter, we're going to examine labor markets more closely and explain differences in wage rates among high- and low-skilled workers, males and females, and racial and ethnic minorities.

Economic Rent in Baseball

THE BOSTON GLOBE, SEPTEMBER 15, 1994

Baseball pulls plug on season

BY LARRY WHITESIDE

NEW YORK—Thirty-three days after the funeral, major league baseball has been declared dead for 1994. And obituaries for 1995 already are taking shape.

With the solemnity of a coroner, acting commissioner Bud Selig delivered the official word from Milwaukee, stating what had become obvious days ago: Because of a labor stalemate that triggered the players' strike of Aug. 12, the season will not continue, and there will be no postseason for the first time since 1904. The damages: the loss of 52 days and 669 games from the regular season, the elimination of the postseason and a threat to baseball's credibility and future.

Given that the major issues—revenue sharing and a salary cap demanded by owners and steadfastly resisted by players—are no closer to resolution than they were when the parting took place, prospects for next season are uncertain, perhaps downright bleak.

That was clearly the concern of all parties when Brewers owner Selig stepped to the podium at his County Stadium headquarters and sadly but firmly announced that by a vote of 26-2, owners decided to shut down the season. The end came not with a bang but with a fax. It was a fitting climax to a season that for more than a month has seen balls and strikes replaced by rhetoric. ...

"We're living in a different generation," said Selig. "And I know a lot of you don't understand that. But you're going to have to deal with it." ...

Baseball's decision to close its parks put an exclamation point on the game's eighth work stoppage since 1972. And it renders the entire season an aberration. For the first time in history, there were no league champions. ...

Reprinted by permission.

Economic

A N A L Y S I S

■ A Supreme Court ruling in 1922 exempted major league baseball from the antitrust laws that regulate the actions of monopolies and cartels.

■ The cartel of owners of major league clubs has the power to restrict the number and location of clubs, to control television rights, and to license baseball-related products.

■ But clubs compete for talented players, and players' wages have increased at an average annual rate of 12 percent since 1980 and 15 percent since 1990.

■ Figure 1 shows the market for players. The quantity of people of major-league quality is limited, and the figure assumes this quantity to be Q. The supply curve of major-league-quality players, S, is perfectly inelastic.

■ The demand for players depends on the demand by people to watch baseball and also on the owners' ability to collude to limit their demand.

■ In 1980, the demand for players was D_{80}. The average annual wage was $260,000 (in today's dollars). Players earned an economic rent shown by the dark green rectangle.

■ During the 1980s and 1990s, the demand to watch baseball both live and on television increased. Attendance at games increased steadily from 43 million in 1980 to more than 70 million in 1993.

■ This increase in the demand for baseball increased the demand for players, and the demand curve shifted rightward to D_{94}. The average annual wage increased to $1,200,000, and the players' economic rent increased by the amount shown by the pale green rectangle.

■ Figure 2 shows the situation facing a single club. The club must pay the going wage rate and so faces a perfectly elastic supply of players. In 1980, the club faced the supply curve S_{80}. The club's demand curve in 1980 was D_{80}, and the quantity of players hired was Q.

■ By 1994, the club's demand curve had shifted to D_{94}, and the wage rate confronting the club had increased to $1,200,000 a year, so the supply curve of players had shifted to S_{94}. The club continued to hire the same quantity of players, Q.

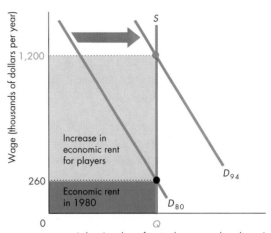

Figure 1 Market

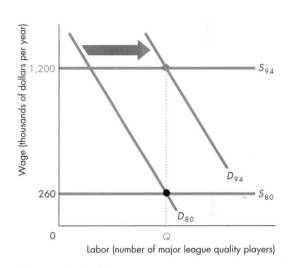

Figure 2 Single club

■ The owners want to limit the market demand for players and obtain a share of the economic rents earned by the players by imposing a salary cap. The players want the largest share of baseball revenues they can get and oppose the salary cap.

■ Unable to agree on how to share the economic rent from baseball, the players and owners destroyed it by canceling the balance of the season and postseason games.

SUMMARY

Factor Prices and Incomes

The factors of production—labor, capital, land, and entrepreneurship—earn a return—wages, interest, rent, and normal profit. Factor prices are opportunity costs and are determined by the demand for and supply of factors of production. Incomes are determined by the prices of factors of production and the quantities used.

An increase in the demand for a factor of production increases the factor's price and income; a decrease in the demand for a factor of production decreases its price and income.

An increase in supply increases the quantity used of a factor of production but decreases its price. A decrease in supply decreases the quantity used and increases the factor's price. Whether a change in supply leads to an increase or decrease in the income of a factor of production depends on the elasticity of demand for the factor. When demand is elastic, a decrease in supply leads to a decrease in the factor's income. When the demand for a factor is inelastic, a decrease in supply leads to an increase in the factor's income. (pp. 332–334)

Demand for Factors

A firm's demand for a factor stems from its attempt to maximize profit. The change in total revenue generated by hiring one more unit of a factor is called the marginal revenue product of the factor. A firm maximizes profit by hiring the quantity of a factor of production that makes the marginal revenue product of the factor equal to the factor's price. A firm's demand curve for a factor is exactly the same as that factor's marginal revenue product curve.

Firms can vary the amount of labor hired in both the short run and the long run but they can vary the amount of capital used only in the long run. The short-run elasticity of demand for labor depends on the labor intensity of the production process, on how rapidly the marginal product of labor diminishes, and on the elasticity of demand for the firm's product. The long-run elasticity of demand for labor depends on these three conditions and on the ease with which capital can be substituted for labor.

The market demand for labor is the sum of the demands by each individual firm. (pp. 335–340)

Supply of Factors

In choosing how much time to allocate to market activities, each household compares the wage rate that can be earned with the value of its time in other, nonmarket activities. At wage rates above the reservation wage, the quantity of labor supplied increases as long as the substitution effect of the higher wage rate is larger than the income effect. As the wage rate continues to rise, the income effect becomes larger than the substitution effect, and the quantity of labor supplied decreases.

The market supply curve of labor is the sum of the supply curves of all households. Like the household's labor supply curve, the market supply of labor curve eventually bends backward.

Households supply capital by saving, and firms use financial capital to buy physical capital. Saving and the quantity of capital supplied increase as the interest rate increases. The supply of capital to an individual firm is highly inelastic in the short run but highly elastic in the long run.

The supply of land is fixed and independent of its rent. But the supply of land to individual firms is elastic. (pp. 341–345)

Incomes, Economic Rent, and Transfer Earnings

In a competitive factor market, the intersection of the demand and supply curves determines the factor price and quantity used. High factor prices occur for factors of production that have a high marginal revenue product and a low supply. Low factor prices occur for factors of production with a low marginal revenue product and a high supply.

Economic rent is the income received by a factor owner over and above the amount needed to induce the owner to supply the factor of production for use. The rest of a factor's income is transfer earnings. Transfer earnings are opportunity costs but economic rent is not. When the supply of a factor is perfectly inelastic, its entire income is made up of economic rent. Factors that have a perfectly elastic supply receive only transfer earnings. In general, the supply curve of a factor is upward-sloping, and part of its income received is transfer earnings (below the supply curve) and part is economic rent (above the supply curve but below the factor price). (pp. 345–347)

KEY ELEMENTS

Key Terms

REVIEW QUESTIONS

1. Explain what happens to the price of a factor of production and its income if each of the following occurs:
   a. The demand for the factor increases.
   b. The supply of the factor increases.
   c. The demand for the factor decreases.
   d. The supply of the factor decreases.

2. Explain why the effect of a change in the supply of a factor on a factor's income depends on the elasticity of demand for the factor.

3. Define marginal revenue product and distinguish between marginal revenue product and marginal revenue.

4. Why does marginal revenue product of a factor decline as the quantity of the factor employed increases?

5. What is the relationship between the demand curve for a factor of production and its marginal revenue product curve? Why?

6. Show that the condition for maximum profit in the goods market—marginal cost equals marginal revenue—is equivalent to the condition for maximum profit in the factor market—marginal revenue product equals marginal cost of factor (equals factor price in a competitive factor market).

7. Review the main influences on the demand for a factor of production—the influences that shift the demand curve for a factor.

8. What determines the short-run and the long-run elasticity of demand for labor?

9. What determines the supply of labor?

10. Why might the supply of labor curve bend backward at a high enough wage rate?

11. Explain why national news anchors receive such large salaries.

12. Explain why fast-food servers are paid such a low wage rate.

13. What determines the supply of capital?

14. Explain why the supply of capital is more elastic in the long run than in the short run.

15. Explain why the price of a block of land is determined by its marginal revenue product.

16. Define economic rent and transfer earnings and distinguish between these two components of income.

17. Suppose that a factor of production is in perfectly inelastic supply. If the marginal revenue product of the factor decreases, what happens to the price, quantity used, income, transfer earnings, and economic rent of the factor?

PROBLEMS

1. The figure illustrates the market for blueberry pickers:

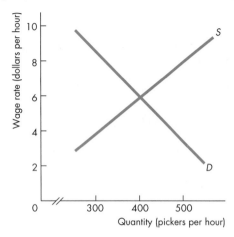

a. What is the wage rate paid to blueberry pickers?
b. How many blueberry pickers get hired?
c. What is the income received by blueberry pickers?
d. What is the marginal revenue product of blueberry pickers?
e. If the price of blueberries is $1 a carton, what is the marginal product of the last picker hired?

2. In problem 1, show on the figure the pickers'
a. Economic rent.
b. Transfer earnings.

3. In problem 1, if the demand for blueberry pickers increases by 100 a day,
a. What is the increase in the wage rate paid to the pickers?
b. How many additional pickers get hired?
c. What is the total income paid to pickers?
d. What now is the pickers' economic rent?
e. What now is the pickers' transfer earnings?

4. Wanda owns a fish shop. She employs students to sort and pack the fish. Students can pack the following amounts of fish in an hour:

Number of students	Quantity of fish (pounds)
1	20
2	50
3	90
4	120
5	145
6	165
7	180
8	190

a. Draw the marginal product curve of these students.
b. If Wanda can sell her fish for 50¢ a pound, draw the marginal revenue product curve.
c. Draw Wanda's demand for labor curve.
d. If all fish shops in Wanda's area pay their packers $7.50 an hour, how many students will Wanda employ?

5. The price of fish falls to 33.33¢ a pound, and fish packers' wages remain at $7.50 an hour.
a. What happens to Wanda's marginal product curve?
b. What happens to her marginal revenue product curve?
c. What happens to her demand for labor curve?
d. What happens to the number of students that she employs?

6. Fish packers' wages increase to $10 an hour, but the price of fish remains at 50¢ a pound.
a. What happens to the marginal revenue product curve?
b. What happens to Wanda's demand curve?
c. How many students does Wanda employ?

7. Using the information provided in problem 4, calculate Wanda's marginal revenue and marginal cost, marginal revenue product, and marginal cost of labor. Show that when Wanda is making maximum profit, marginal cost equals marginal revenue and marginal revenue product equals the marginal cost of labor.

8. You are given the following information about the labor market in an isolated town in the Amazon rainforest: Everyone works for logging companies, but there are many logging companies in the town. The market for logging workers is perfectly competitive. The town's labor supply is given as follows:

Wage rate (cruzeiros per hour)	Quantity of labor supplied (hours)
200	120
300	160
400	200
500	240
600	280
700	320
800	360

The market demand for labor from all the logging firms in the town is as follows:

Wage rate (cruzeiros per hour)	Quantity of labor demanded (hours)
200	400
300	360
400	320
500	280
600	240
700	200
800	160

a. What is the equilibrium wage rate, and how many hours of labor are employed?
b. What is total labor income?
c. How much of that labor income is economic rent and how much is transfer earnings? (You may find it easier to answer this question by drawing graphs of the demand and supply curves and then finding the economic rent and transfer earnings as areas on the graph in a manner similar to what was done in Fig. 14.8.)

9. Study *Reading Between the Lines* on pp. 348–349 and answer the following questions:
a. Why do the owners want a salary cap?
b. Why do the players not want a salary cap?
c. If owners had been successful in introducing a salary cap of say $1 million per player per year, how much economic rent would have been redistributed from players to owners in 1995?

> "*Men, like all animals, naturally multiply in proportion to the means of their subsistence.*"
>
> ADAM SMITH, *THE WEALTH OF NATIONS*

Running Out of Resources?

THE ISSUES AND IDEAS

Is there a limit to economic growth, or can we expand production and population without effective limit? One of the most influential answers to these questions was given by Thomas Malthus in 1798. He believed that population, unchecked, would grow at a geometric rate—1, 2, 4, 8, 16, ..., while the food supply would grow at an arithmetic rate—1, 2, 3, 4, 5, ... To prevent the population from outstripping the available food supply, there would be periodic wars, famines, and plagues. In Malthus's view, only a change in the moral code by which people live could prevent such periodic disasters.

As industrialization proceeded through the nineteenth century, Malthus's idea came to be applied to all natural resources, especially those that are exhaustible. A modern-day Malthusian, ecologist Paul Ehrlich, believes that we are sitting on a "population bomb" and that the government must limit both population growth and the resources that may be used each year.

In 1931, Harold Hotelling developed a theory of natural resources with different predications from those of Malthus. The Hotelling Principle is that the relative price of an exhaustible natural resource will steadily rise, bringing a decline in the quantity used and an increase in the use of substitute resources.

Julian Simon, a contemporary economist, has challenged both the Malthusian gloom and the Hotelling Principle. He believes that *people* are the "ultimate resource," and predicts that a rising population *lessens* the pressure on natural resources. A bigger population provides a larger number of resourceful people who can work out more efficient ways of using scarce resources. As these solutions are found, the prices of exhaustible resources actually fall. To demonstrate his point, in 1980, Simon bet Ehrlich that the prices of five metals—copper, chrome, nickel, tin, and tungsten—would fall during the 1980s. Simon won the bet!

THEN...

No MATTER *whether it is agricultural land, an exhaustible natural resource, or the space in the center of Chicago and no matter whether it is 1995 or, as shown here, 1892, there is a limit to what is available, and we persistently push against that limit. Economists see urban congestion as a consequence of the value of doing business in the city center relative to the cost. They see the price mechanism, bringing ever higher rents and prices of raw materials, as the means of allocating and rationing scarce natural resources. Malthusians, in contrast, explain congestion as the consequence of population pressure, and they see population control as the solution.*

HUNT.

IN TOKYO, the pressure on space is so great that in some residential neighborhoods, a parking space costs $1,700 a month. To economize on this expensive space—and to lower the cost of car ownership and hence boost car sales—Honda, Nissan, and Toyota, three of Japan's big car producers, have developed a parking machine that enables two cars to occupy the space of one. The most basic of these machines costs a mere $10,000—less than 6 months' parking fees.

Thomas Robert Malthus

THE ECONOMISTS: ROBERT MALTHUS AND HAROLD HOTELLING

Thomas Robert Malthus (1766–1834), an English parson and professor, was an extremely influential social scientist. In his best-selling *Essay on the Principle of Population*, published in 1798, he argued that population growth would outstrip food production. Modern-day Malthusians believe that his basic idea was right and that it applies to all natural resources.

The most profound work on the economics of natural resources is that of Harold Hotelling (1895–1973). Hotelling worked as a journalist, schoolteacher, and mathematical consultant before becoming an economics professor at Columbia University. He explained how the price mechanism allocates exhaustible resources, making them progressively more expensive. Their higher price encourages the development of new technologies, the discovery of new sources of supply, and the development of substitutes.

Harold Hotelling

Labor Markets

After studying
this chapter,
you will be
able to:

■ Explain why high-skilled workers earn
more, on the average, than low-skilled
workers

■ Explain why college graduates earn more,
on the average, than high school graduates

■ Explain why union workers earn higher
wages than nonunion workers

■ Explain why, on the average, men earn
more than women and whites earn more
than minorities

■ Predict the effects of a comparable-worth
program

As you well know, college is not just a party. Those exams and problem sets require a lot of time and effort. Are they worth the sweat that goes into them? What is the payoff? Is it sufficient to make up for the years of tuition, room and board, and lost wages? (You could, after all, be working for pay now instead of slogging through this economics course.) ◆ Many workers belong to labor

The Sweat of Our Brows

unions. Usually, union workers earn a higher wage than nonunion workers in comparable jobs. Why? How are unions able to get higher wages for their members than the wages that nonunion workers are paid? ◆ Among the most visible and persistent differences in earnings are those between men and women and between whites and minorities. White men, on the average, earn incomes that are one third higher than the incomes earned by black men and white women. Black men and white women earn more, in descending order, than Hispanic men, black women, and Hispanic women, who earn only 58 cents for each dollar earned by the average white man. Certainly, a lot of individuals defy the averages. But why do minorities and women so consistently earn less than white men? Is it because of discrimination and exploitation? Or is it because of economic factors? Or is it a combination of the two? ◆ Equal pay legislation has resulted in comparable-worth programs that try to ensure that jobs of equivalent value receive the same pay regardless of the pay set by the market. Can comparable-worth programs bring economic help to women and minorities?

◇ In this chapter, we answer questions such as these by continuing our study of labor markets. We begin by extending the competitive labor market model developed in Chapter 14 to analyze the effects of education and training on wages. We then study differences in union and nonunion wages and in pay among men, women, and minorities. Finally, we analyze the effects of comparable-worth laws.

Skill Differentials

EVERYONE IS SKILLED BUT THE VALUE THE MARKET places on different types of skills varies a great deal so that differences in skills lead to large differences in earnings. For example, a clerk in a law firm earns less than a tenth of the earnings of the attorney he assists. An operating room assistant earns less than a tenth of the earnings of the surgeon she works with. Differences in skills arise partly from differences in education and partly from differences in on-the-job training. Differences in earnings between workers with varying levels of education and training can be explained by using a model of competitive labor markets. In the real world, there are many different levels and varieties of education and training. To keep our analysis as clear as possible, we'll study a model economy in which there are just two different levels that result in two types of labor: high-skilled labor and low-skilled labor. We'll study the demand for and supply of these two types of labor and see why there is a difference in their wages and what determines that difference. Let's begin by looking at the demand for the two types of labor.

The Demand for High-Skilled and Low-Skilled Labor

High-skilled workers can perform a wide variety of tasks that low-skilled workers would perform badly or perhaps could not even perform at all. Imagine an untrained, inexperienced person performing surgery or piloting an airplane. High-skilled workers have a higher marginal revenue product than low-skilled workers. As we learned in Chapter 14, a firm's demand for labor curve is the same as the marginal revenue product of labor curve.

Figure 15.1(a) shows the demand curves for high-skilled and low-skilled labor. At any given level of employment, firms are willing to pay a higher wage rate to a high-skilled worker than to a low-skilled worker. The gap between the two wage rates measures the marginal revenue product of skill—for example, at an employment level of 2,000 hours, firms are willing to pay $12.50 for a high-skilled worker and only $5 for an low-skilled worker, a difference of $7.50 an hour. Thus the marginal revenue product of skill is $7.50 an hour.

The Supply of High-Skilled and Low-Skilled Labor

Skills are costly to acquire. Furthermore, a worker usually pays the cost of acquiring a skill before benefiting from a higher wage. For example, attending college usually leads to a higher income, but the higher income is not earned until after graduation. These facts imply that the acquisition of a skill is an investment. To emphasize the investment nature of acquiring a skill, we call that activity an investment in human capital. **Human capital** is the accumulated skill and knowledge of human beings.

The opportunity cost of acquiring a skill includes actual expenditures on such things as tuition and room and board and also costs in the form of lost or reduced earnings while the skill is being acquired. When a person goes to school full time, that cost is the total earnings forgone. However, some people acquire skills on the job. Such skill acquisition is called on-the-job training. Usually, a worker undergoing on-the-job training is paid a lower wage than one doing a comparable job but not undergoing training. In such a case, the cost of acquiring the skill is the difference between the wage paid to a person not being trained and that paid to a person being trained.

Supply Curves of High-Skilled and Low-Skilled Labor The position of the supply curve of high-skilled workers reflects the cost of acquiring the skill. Figure 15.1(b) shows two supply curves: one for high-skilled workers and the other for low-skilled workers. The supply curve for high-skilled workers is S_H, and that for low-skilled workers is S_L.

The high-skilled worker's supply curve lies above the low-skilled worker's supply curve. The vertical distance between the two supply curves is the compensation that high-skilled workers require for the cost of acquiring the skill. For example, suppose that the quantity of low-skilled labor supplied is 2,000 hours at a wage rate of $5 an hour. This wage rate compensates the low-skilled workers mainly for their time on the job. Consider next the supply of high-skilled workers. To induce 2,000 hours of high-skilled labor to be supplied, firms must pay a wage rate of $8.50 an hour. This wage rate for high-skilled labor is higher than that for low-skilled labor because high-skilled labor must be compensated not only for the time on the job but also for the time and other costs of acquiring the skill.

FIGURE 15.1
Skill Differentials

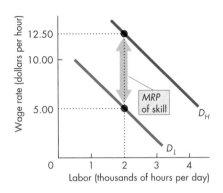

**(a) Demand for high-skilled
and low-skilled labor**

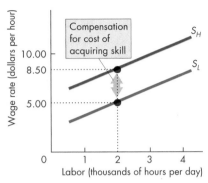

**(b) Supply of high-skilled
and low-skilled labor**

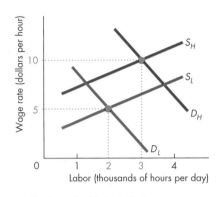

**(c) Markets for high-skilled
and low-skilled labor**

Part (a) illustrates the marginal revenue product of skill. Low-skilled workers have a marginal revenue product that gives rise to the demand curve marked D_L. High-skilled workers have a higher marginal revenue product than low-skilled workers. Therefore the demand curve for high-skilled workers, D_H, lies to the right of D_L. The vertical distance between these two curves is the marginal revenue product of the skill.

Part (b) shows the effects of the cost of acquiring skills on the supply curves of labor. The supply curve for low-skilled

workers is S_L. The supply curve for high-skilled workers is S_H. The vertical distance between these two curves is the required compensation for the cost of acquiring a skill.

Part (c) shows the equilibrium employment and the wage differential. Low-skilled workers earn a wage rate of $5 an hour and 2,000 hours of low-skilled labor are employed. High-skilled workers earn a wage rate of $10 and 3,000 hours of high-skilled labor are employed. The wage rate for high-skilled workers always exceeds that for low-skilled workers.

Wage Rates of High-Skilled and Low-Skilled Labor

To work out the wage rates of high-skilled and low-skilled labor, we have to bring together the effects of skill on the demand and supply of labor.

Figure 15.1(c) shows the demand curves and the supply curves for high-skilled and low-skilled labor. These curves are exactly the same as those plotted in parts (a) and (b). Equilibrium occurs in the market for low-skilled labor where the supply and demand curves for low-skilled labor intersect. The equilibrium wage rate is $5 an hour, and the quantity of low-skilled labor employed is 2,000 hours. Equilibrium in the market for high-skilled workers occurs where the supply and demand curves for high-skilled workers intersect. The equilibrium wage rate is $10 an hour, and the quantity of high-skilled labor employed is 3,000 hours.

As you can see in part (c), the equilibrium wage rate of high-skilled labor is higher than that of low-skilled labor. There are two reasons why this occurs: First, high-skilled labor has a higher marginal revenue product than low-skilled labor, so at a given wage rate, the quantity of high-skilled labor demanded exceeds that of low-skilled labor. Second, skills are costly to acquire, so at a given wage rate, the quantity of high-skilled labor supplied is less than that of low-skilled labor. The wage differential (in this case, $5 an hour) depends on both the marginal revenue product of the skill and the cost of acquiring it. The higher the marginal revenue product of the skill, the larger is the vertical distance between the demand curves. The more costly it is to acquire a skill, the larger is the vertical distance between the supply curves. The higher the marginal revenue product of the skill and the more costly it is to acquire, the larger is the wage differential between high-skilled and low-skilled workers.

Do Education and Training Pay?

There are large and persistent differences in earnings based on the degree of education and training. An indication of those differences can be seen in Fig. 15.2. This figure highlights two important sources of earnings differences. The first is the degree of education itself. The higher the level of education, other things remaining the same, the higher are a person's earnings. The second source of earnings differences apparent in Fig. 15.2 is age. Age is strongly correlated with experience and the degree of on-the-job training a person has had. Thus as a person gets older, up to middle age, earnings increase.

We can see from Fig. 15.2 that going through high school, college, and postgraduate education leads to higher incomes. But do they pay in the sense of yielding a higher income that compensates for the cost of education and for the delay in the start of earnings? For most people who go to college, college does indeed pay. Rates of return have been estimated to be in the range of 5 to 10 percent a year after allowing for inflation, which suggest that a college degree is a better investment than almost any other that a person can undertake.

Education is an important source of earnings differences. But there are others. One is the activities of labor unions. Let's see how unions affect wages and why, on the average, union wages exceed nonunion wages.

Union-Nonunion Wage Differentials

WAGE DIFFERENTIALS CAN ARISE FROM LABOR market monopolies. The main source of these monopolies is the labor union. A **labor union** is an organized group of workers whose purpose it is to increase wages and influence other job conditions for its members. The union seeks to restrict competition and, as a result, increases the price at which labor is traded.

There are two main types of union: craft unions and industrial unions. A **craft union** is a group of workers who have a similar range of skills but work for many different firms in many different industries and regions. Examples are the carpenters' union and the electrical workers union (IBEW). An **industrial union** is a group of workers who have a variety of skills and job types but work for the same firm or industry. The United Auto Workers (UAW) and the Steelworkers Union are examples of industrial unions.

Most unions are members of the AFL-CIO. The AFL-CIO was created in 1955 when two labor organizations combined: the American Federation of Labor (AFL), which was founded in 1886 to organize craft unions, and the Congress of Industrial Organizations (CIO), founded in 1938 to organize industrial unions. The AFL-CIO provides many services to member unions, such as training union organizers and acting as a national voice in the media and in the political arena.

Unions vary enormously in size. Craft unions are the smallest, and industrial unions are the biggest. Figure 15.3 shows the 12 largest unions in the United States—measured by number of members.

FIGURE 15.2

Education and Earnings

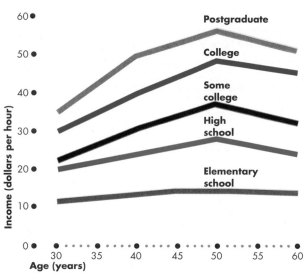

Earnings of male employees at various ages and with varying school levels are shown. Earnings increase with length of education and also with age but only up to the middle forties. Beyond that age, earnings decrease. These differences show the importance of experience and education in influencing skill differentials.

Source: U.S. Bureau of the Census, *Money Income in 1981 of Families and Persons in the United States, Current Population Reports,* Series P-60, No. 137 (1983), Table 48.

FIGURE 15.3

Unions with the Largest Membership

Each of the 12 largest labor unions in the United States, shown here, has more than 400,000 members.

Source: U.S. Bureau of the Census, *Statistical Abstract of the United States: 1994,* 114th edition, p. 438.

Union strength peaked in the 1950s, when 35 percent of the nonagricultural work force belonged to unions. That percentage has declined steadily since 1955 and is now only 12 percent. Changes in union membership, however, have been uneven. Some unions have declined dramatically, while others, especially those in the government sector such as the State, County, and Municipal Employees union, have increased in strength.

Union organization is based on a subdivision known as the local. The *local* is a subunit of a union that organizes the individual workers. In craft unions, the local is based on a geographical area; in industrial unions, the local is based on a plant or an individual firm.

There are three possible forms of organization for a local: an open shop, a closed shop, or a union shop. An *open shop* is an arrangement in which workers can be employed without joining the union—there is no union restriction on who can work in the "shop." A *closed shop* is an arrangement in which only union members can be employed by a firm. Closed shops have been illegal since the passage of the Taft-Hartley Act in 1947. A *union shop* is an arrangement in which a firm can hire nonunion workers, but in order for such workers to remain employed, they must join the union within a brief period specified by the union. Union shops are illegal in the 20 states that have passed right-to-work laws. A *right-to-work law* allows an individual to work at any firm without joining a union.

Unions negotiate with employers or their representatives in a process called **collective bargaining**. The main weapons available to the union and the employer in collective bargaining are the strike and the lockout. A *strike* is a group decision to refuse to work under prevailing conditions. A *lockout* is a firm's refusal to operate its plant and employ its workers. Each party uses the threat of a strike or a lockout to try to get an agreement in its own favor. Sometimes, when the two parties in the collective bargaining process cannot agree on the wage rate or other conditions of employment, they agree to submit their disagreement to binding arbitration. *Binding arbitration* is a process in which a third party—an arbitrator—determines wages and other employment conditions on behalf of the negotiating parties. A compact glossary on unions can be found in Table 15.1.

Though not labor unions in a legal sense, professional associations act, in many ways, like labor unions. A *professional association* is an organized group of professional workers such as lawyers, dentists, or physicians (an example of which is the American Medical Association—AMA). Professional associations control entry into the professions and license practitioners, ensuring the adherence to minimum standards of competence. But they also influence the compensation and other labor market conditions of their members.

Union's Objectives and Constraints

A union has three broad objectives that it strives to achieve for its members:

1. To increase compensation
2. To improve working conditions
3. To expand job opportunities

Each of these objectives contains a series of more detailed goals. For example, in seeking to increase members' compensation, a union operates on a variety of fronts: wage rates, fringe benefits, retirement pay, and such things as vacation allowances. In seeking to improve working conditions, a union is concerned with occupational health and safety as well as the environmental quality of the workplace. In seeking to expand job opportunities, a union tries to get greater job security for existing union members and to find ways of creating additional jobs for them.

A union's ability to pursue its objectives is restricted by two sets of constraints—one on the supply side and the other on the demand side of the labor market. On the supply side, the union's activities are limited by how well it can restrict nonunion workers from offering their labor in the same market. The larger the fraction of the work force controlled by the union, the more effective the union can be. For example, unions find it difficult to be effective in markets for low-skilled labor in southern California because of their inability to control the flow of nonunion, often illegal, labor from Mexico (see *Reading Between the Lines*, pp. 372–373). At the other extreme, unions in the construction industry can better pursue their goals because they can influence the number of people who can obtain skills as electricians, plasterers, and carpenters. The professional associations of dentists and physicians are best able to restrict the supply of dentists and physicians.

TABLE 15.1

A Compact Glossary on Unions

Labor union	An organized group of workers that attempts to increase wages and improve other conditions of employment for its members
AFL-CIO	A federation of unions formed in 1955 by a merger of the American Federation of Labor (AFL) and the Congress of Industrial Organization (CIO); provides services to member unions and acts as the voice in media and political arenas
Craft union	A union in which workers have a similar range of skills but work for many firms and in many different industries
Industrial union	A union in which workers have a variety of skills and job types but work in the same industry
Local	A subunit of a union that organizes individual workers. In craft unions, the local is geographical; in industrial unions, the local is based on a plant or a company
Open shop	A place of work that has no union restriction on who can work in the shop; here, the union bargains for its members but not for nonmembers
Closed shop	A place of work where only union members can be employed; illegal since 1947, when Congress passed the Labor-Management Relations Act (the Taft-Hartley Act)
Union shop	A place of work that may hire nonunion workers but only if they join the union within a specified period; illegal in 20 states where right-to-work legislation has been passed
Right-to-work law	A law that protects the right of an individual to work without joining a union
Collective bargaining	Negotiations between representatives of employers and unions on wages and other employment conditions
Strike	A group decision to refuse to work under prevailing conditions
Lockout	A firm's refusal to allow its labor force to work
Binding arbitration	Determination of wages and other employment conditions by a third party (an arbitrator) acceptable to both parties

These groups control the number of qualified workers by controlling either the examinations that new entrants must pass or entrance into professional degree programs.

On the demand side of the labor market, the constraint facing a union is the fact that it cannot force firms to hire more labor than the quantity that maximizes their profits. Anything that increases the wage rate or other employment costs decreases the quantity of labor demanded.

Let's see how a union operates in a competitive labor market.

Unions in a Competitive Labor Market

When a union operates in an otherwise competitive labor market, it seeks to increase wages and other compensation and to limit employment reductions by increasing demand for the labor of its members.

Figure 15.4 illustrates a labor market. The demand curve is D_C, and the supply curve is S_C. If the market is a competitive one with no union, the wage rate is $4 an hour and 100 hours of labor will be employed. Suppose that a union is formed to organize the workers in this market and that the union has sufficient control over the supply of labor to be able to artificially restrict that supply below its competitive level—to S_U. If that is all the union does, employment will fall to 85 hours of labor and the wage rate will rise to $5 an hour.

How Unions Try to Change the Demand for Labor

Unless unions can take actions that change the demand for the labor that it represents, it has to accept the fact that a higher wage rate can be obtained only at the price of lower employment. Recognizing the importance of the demand for labor, a union tries to make the demand for union labor inelastic and to increase the demand for it. If the union can make the demand for labor less elastic, it can increase the wage rate at a lower cost in terms of lost employment opportunities. And if it can increase the demand for labor, it might even be able to increase both the wage rate and the employment opportunities of its members. Some of the methods used by the unions to change the demand for the labor of its members are to:

FIGURE 15.4

A Union in a Competitive Labor Market

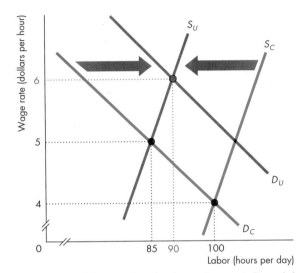

In a competitive labor market, the demand curve is D_C and the supply curve is S_C. Competitive equilibrium occurs at a wage rate of $4 an hour with 100 hours employed. By restricting employment below the competitive level, the union shifts the supply of labor to S_U. If the union can do no more than that, the wage rate will increase to $5 an hour, but employment will fall to 85 hours. If the union can increase the demand for labor (by increasing the demand for the good produced by union members or by raising the price of substitute labor) and shift the demand curve to D_U, then it can increase the wage rate still higher, to $6 an hour, and achieve employment of 90 hours.

- Increase the marginal product of union members
- Encourage import restrictions
- Support minimum wage laws
- Support immigration restrictions
- Increase demand for the good produced

Unions try to increase the marginal product of their members, which in turn increases the demand for their labor, by organizing and sponsoring training schemes, by encouraging apprenticeship and other on-the-job training activities, and by professional certification.

One of the best examples of import restrictions is the support by the United Auto Workers union (UAW) for import restrictions on foreign cars.

Unions support minimum wage laws to increase the cost of employing low-skilled labor. An increase in the wage rate of low-skilled labor leads to a decrease in the quantity demanded of low-skilled labor and to an increase in demand for high-skilled union labor, a substitute for low-skilled labor.

Restrictive immigration laws decrease the supply and increase the wage rate of low-skilled workers. As a result, the demand for high-skilled union labor increases.

Because the demand for labor is a derived demand, an increase in the demand for the good produced increases the demand for union labor. The best examples of attempts by unions in this activity are in the textile and auto industries. The garment workers' union urges us to buy union-made clothes, and the UAW asks us to buy only American cars made by union workers.

Figure 15.4 illustrates the effects of an increase in the demand for the labor of a union's members. If the union can also take steps that increase the demand for labor to D_U, it can achieve an even bigger increase in the wage rate with a smaller fall in employment. By maintaining the restricted labor supply at S_U, the union increases the wage rate to $6 an hour and achieves an employment level of 90 hours of labor.

Because a union restricts the supply of labor in the market in which it operates, its actions increase the supply of labor in nonunion markets. Workers who can't get union jobs must look elsewhere for work. This increase in supply in nonunion markets lowers the wage rate in those markets and further widens the union-nonunion differential. But low nonunion wages decrease the demand for union labor and limit the increase in wages that unions can achieve. For this reason, unions are strong supporters of minimum wage laws that keep nonunion wages high and limit the incentive to use nonunion labor.

Let's now turn our attention to the case in which employers have considerable influence in the labor market.

Monopsony

A **monopsony** is a market structure in which there is just a single buyer. With the growth of large-scale production over the last century, large manufacturing plants such as coal mines, steel and textile mills, and car manufacturers became the major employer of labor in some regions, and in some places a single firm employed almost all the labor. Such a firm has some monopsony power.

A monopsony can make a bigger profit than a group of firms that have to compete with each other for their labor. Figure 15.5 illustrates how a monopsony operates. The monopsony's marginal revenue product curve is *MRP*. This curve tells us the extra revenue the monopsony makes from selling the output produced by the last hour of labor hired. The curve labeled *S* is the supply curve of labor. This curve tells us how many hours are supplied at each wage rate. It also tells us the minimum wage that is acceptable at each level of labor supplied.

In deciding how much labor to hire, the monopsony recognizes that to hire more labor, it must pay a higher wage; equivalently, by hiring less labor, the monopsony can get away with paying a lower wage. The monopsony takes account of this fact when calculating its marginal cost of labor. The marginal cost of labor is shown by the curve *MCL*. The relationship between the marginal cost of labor curve and the supply curve is similar to the relationship between the marginal cost and average total cost curves that you studied in Chapter 10. The supply curve is like the average total cost of labor curve. For example, in Fig. 15.5, the

FIGURE 15.5

A Monopsony Labor Market

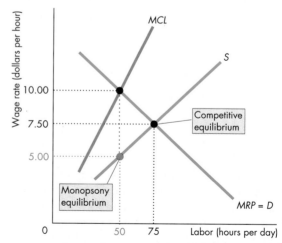

A monopsony is a market structure in which there is a single buyer. A monopsony in the labor market has marginal revenue product curve *MRP* and faces a labor curve *S*. The marginal cost of labor curve is *MCL*. Profit is maximized by making the marginal cost of labor equal to marginal revenue product. The monopsony hires 50 hours of labor and pays the lowest wage for which that labor will work, $5 an hour.

firm can hire 50 hours of labor at $5 an hour, so its average total cost is $5 an hour. The total cost of labor is $5 an hour multiplied by 50 hours, which equals $250 an hour. But suppose that the firm hires slightly less than 50 hours of labor, say 49 hours. The wage rate at which 49 hours of labor can be hired is just below $4.90 an hour. The firm's total labor cost is $240. Hiring the fiftieth hour of labor increases the total cost of labor from $240 to $250, which is $10. The curve *MCL* shows the $10 marginal cost of hiring the fiftieth hour of labor.

To calculate the profit-maximizing quantity of labor to hire, the firm sets the marginal cost of labor equal to the marginal revenue product of labor. That is, the firm wants the cost of the last worker hired to equal the extra total revenue brought in. In Fig. 15.5, this outcome occurs when the monopsony employs 50 hours of labor. What is the wage rate that the monopsony pays? To hire 50 hours of labor, the firm must pay $5 an hour, as shown by the supply of labor curve. The marginal revenue product of labor, however, is $10 an hour, which means that the firm makes an economic profit of $5 on the last hour of labor that it hires. Each worker is paid $5 an hour.

Compare this outcome with that in a competitive labor market. If the labor market shown in Fig. 15.5 were competitive, equilibrium would occur at the point of intersection of the demand curve and the supply curve. The wage rate would be $7.50 an hour and 75 hours of labor a day would be employed. So, compared with a competitive labor market, a monopsony decreases both the wage rate and the level of employment.

The ability of a monopsony to lower the wage rate and employment level and make an economic profit depends on the elasticity of labor supply. The more elastic the supply of labor, the less opportunity a monopsony has to cut wages and employment and make an economic profit.

Monopsony Tendencies   With today's low transportation costs, it is unlikely that many pure monopsonies remain. Workers can easily commute long distances to a job, and so for most people, there is not just one potential employer. But some firms do have a monopsony tendency. That is, while they are not pure monopsonies, they face an upward-sloping supply of labor curve and their marginal cost of labor exceeds the wage rate. Monopsony tendencies arise in isolated communities in which a single firm is the main employer. But in such situations, there is also, usually, a union. Let's see how unions and monopsonies interact.

Monopsony and Unions   When we studied monopoly in Chapter 12, we discovered that a single seller in a market is able to determine the price in that market. We have just studied monopsony—a market with a single buyer—and discovered that in such a market, the buyer is able to determine the price. Suppose that a union starts to operate in a monopsony labor market. A union is like a monopoly. It controls the supply of labor and acts like a single seller of labor. If the union (monopoly seller) faces a monopsony buyer, the situation is one of **bilateral monopoly**. In bilateral monopoly, the wage rate is determined by bargaining between the two sides. Let's study the bargaining process.

In Fig. 15.5, if the monopsony is free to determine the wage rate and the level of employment, it hires 50 hours of labor for a wage rate of $5 an hour. But suppose that a union represents the workers and can, if necessary, call a strike. Also suppose that the union agrees to maintain employment at 50 hours but seeks the highest wage rate the employer can be forced to pay. That wage rate is $10 an hour. That is, the wage rate equals the marginal revenue product of labor. It is unlikely that the union will get the wage rate up to $10 an hour. But it is also unlikely that the firm will keep the wage rate down to $5 an hour. The monopsony firm and the union will bargain over the wage rate, and the result will be an outcome between $10 an hour (the maximum that the union can achieve) and $5 an hour (the minimum that the firm can achieve).

The actual outcome of the bargaining depends on the costs that each party can inflict on the other as a result of a failure to agree on the wage rate. The firm can shut down the plant and lock out its workers, and the workers can shut down the plant by striking. Each party knows the other's strength and knows what it will lose if it does not agree to the other's demands. If the two parties are equally strong and they realize it, they will split the difference and agree to a wage rate of $7.50 an hour. If one party is stronger than the other—and both parties know that—the agreed wage will favor the stronger party. Usually, an agreement is reached without a strike or a lockout. The threat—knowledge that such an event can occur—is usually enough to bring the bargaining parties to an agreement. But when a strike or lockout does occur, it is often because one party has misjudged the costs each party can inflict on the other.

Monopsony has an interesting implication for the effects of minimum wage laws. Let's now study these effects.

Monopsony and the Minimum Wage

A minimum wage that exceeds the equilibrium wage in a competitive labor market decreases employment (see Chapter 6, pp. 124–126). A minimum wage in a monopsony labor market can *increase* both the wage rate and employment. Let's see how.

Suppose that the labor market is that shown in Fig. 15.6 and that the wage rate is $5 an hour with 50 hours of labor employed. The government now passes a minimum wage law that prohibits anyone from hiring labor for less than $7.50 an hour. Firms can hire labor for $7.50 an hour or more but not for less than that wage. The monopsony in Fig. 15.6 now faces a perfectly elastic supply of labor at $7.50 an hour up to 75 hours. Above 75 hours, a higher wage than $7.50 an hour must be paid to hire additional hours of labor. Because the wage rate is a fixed $7.50 an hour up to 75 hours, the marginal cost of labor is also constant at $7.50 up to 75 hours. Beyond 75 hours, the marginal cost of labor rises above $7.50 an hour. To maximize profit, the monopsony sets the marginal cost of labor equal to its marginal revenue product. That is, the monopsony hires 75 hours of labor at $7.50 an hour.

FIGURE 15.6
Minimum Wage in Monopsony

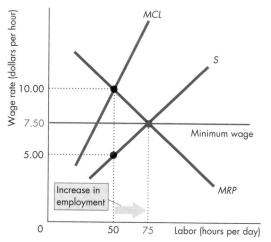

In a monopsony labor market, the wage rate is $5 an hour and 50 hours are hired. If a minimum wage law increases the wage rate to $7.50 an hour, employment increases to 75 hours.

The minimum wage law has made the supply of labor perfectly elastic and made the marginal cost of labor the same as the wage rate up to 75 hours. The law has not affected the supply of labor curve or the marginal cost of labor at employment levels above 75 hours. The minimum wage law has succeeded in raising the wage rate by $2.50 an hour and increasing the amount of labor employed by 25 hours.

The Scale of Union-Nonunion Wage Differentials

We have seen that unions can influence the wage rate by restricting the supply of labor and increasing the demand for labor. How much of a difference to wage rates do unions make in practice?

Union wage rates are, on the average, 30 percent higher than nonunion wage rates. In mining and financial services, union and nonunion wages are similar. In services, manufacturing, and transportation, the differential is between 11 and 19 percent. But in wholesale and retail trades, the differential is 28 percent, and in construction it is 65 percent.

These union-nonunion wage differentials do not give a true measure of the effects of unions, however. In some industries, union wages are higher than nonunion wages because union members do jobs that involve greater skill. Even without a union, those workers receive a higher wage. To calculate the effects of unions, we have to examine the wages of unionized and nonunionized workers who do nearly identical work. The evidence suggests that after allowing for skill differentials, the union-nonunion wage differential lies between 10 percent and 25 percent. For example, airline pilots who belong to the Air Line Pilots' Union earn about 25 percent more than nonunion pilots with the same level of skill.

REVIEW

- Differences in earnings based on skill or education level arise because high-skilled labor has a higher marginal revenue product than low-skilled labor and because skills are costly to acquire.
- Union workers have higher wage rates than nonunion workers because a union is able to control the supply of labor and, indirectly, influence the marginal revenue product of its members.

Wage Differentials Between Sexes and Races

THE OBJECTIVE OF THIS SECTION IS TO SHOW you how to use economic analysis to address a controversial and emotionally charged issue. Figure 15.7 gives a quick view of the earnings differences that exist between the sexes and the races and also shows how those differences have evolved since 1955. The wages of each race and sex group are expressed as a percentage of the wages of white men. In 1993, the most recent year for which we have data, these percentages ranged from 75 for white women and 73 for black men, to 59 for women of Hispanic origin.

Why do the differentials shown in Fig. 15.7 exist? Do they arise because there is discrimination against women and members of minority races, or is there some other explanation? These controversial questions

generate an enormous amount of passion. It is not my intention to make you angry, but that might happen as an unintended consequence of this discussion.

We are going to examine four possible explanations for these earnings differences:

■ Job types
■ Discrimination
■ Differences in human capital
■ Differences in degree of specialization

Job Types

Some of the difference in men's and women's wages arises from the fact that men and women do different jobs and, for the most part, men's jobs are better paid than women's jobs. But there are increasing numbers of women entering areas that were traditionally the preserve of men. This trend is particularly clear in professions such as architecture, medicine, economics, law, accounting, and pharmacology. The percentage of total enrollments in university courses in these subjects for women has increased from less than 20 percent in 1970 to approaching, and in some cases exceeding, 50 percent today. Women are also increasingly seen as bus drivers, police officers, and construction workers, all jobs traditionally done mainly by men.

But in many situations women and minorities earn less than white men, even when they do essentially the same job. One possible reason is that women and minorities are discriminated against. Let's see how discrimination might affect wage rates.

Discrimination

To see how discrimination can affect earnings, let's look at an example—the market for investment advisors. Suppose that there are two groups of investment advisors who are identical in their skills at picking good investments. One group consists of black females, and the other of white males. Figure 15.8(a) shows the supply curve of black females, S_{BF}, and Fig. 15.8(b) shows the supply curve of white males, S_{WM}. These supply curves are identical. The marginal revenue product of investment advisors, whether they are black female or white male, is also identical, as shown by the two curves labeled *MRP* in parts (a) and (b). (Their revenues are the fees their customers pay for investment advice.)

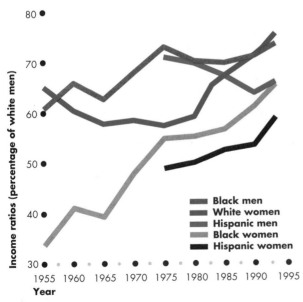

Year

■ Black men
■ White women
■ Hispanic men
■ Black women
■ Hispanic women

Wages of different race and sex groups are shown as percentages of white male wages. These differentials have persisted over many years but their magnitudes have changed.

Source: United States Bureau of the Census, *Statistical Abstract of the United States: 1994,* 114th edition, p. 429.

FIGURE 15.8
Discrimination

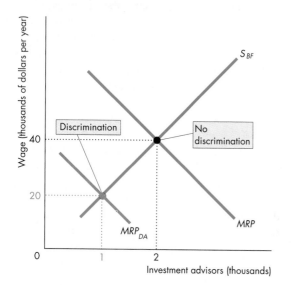

(a) Black females

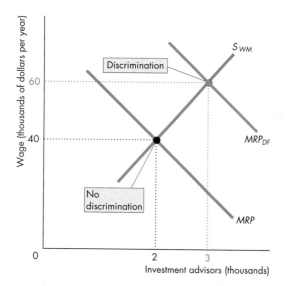

(b) White males

With no discrimination, the wage rate is $40,000 a year and 2,000 of each group are hired. With discrimination against blacks and women, the marginal revenue product curve in part (a) is MRP_{DA} and in part (b) MRP_{DF}. The wage rate for black women falls to $20,000 a year, and only 1,000 are employed. The wage rate for white men rises to $60,000 a year, and 3,000 are employed.

Suppose that everyone in this society is free of prejudice about race and sex. The market for black female investment advisors determines a wage rate of $40,000 a year, and there are 2,000 black female investment advisors. The white male investment advisor market also determines a wage rate of $40,000 a year, and there are 2,000 white male investment advisors.

In contrast, suppose that the customers of investment houses are prejudiced against women and against members of racial minorities. The two types of investment advisors are equally able, as before, but the degree of prejudice is so strong that the customers are not willing to pay as much for investment advice given by a black female as they will pay for advice from a white male. Because of the differences in the amounts that people are willing to pay, based purely on their prejudices, the marginal revenue products of the two groups are different. The ability of the two groups is the same, but the value that prejudiced consumers place on their outputs is not the same. Suppose that the marginal revenue product of the black females, when discriminated against, is the line labeled MRP_{DA}, where DA stands for "discriminated against." Suppose that the marginal revenue product for white males, the group discriminated in favor of, is MRP_{DF}, where DF stands for "discriminated in favor of." Given these marginal revenue product curves, the markets for the two groups of investment advisors will now determine very different wages and employment levels. Black females will earn $20,000 a year, and only 1,000 will work as investment advisors. White males will earn $60,000 a year, and 3,000 of them will work as investment advisors. Thus, purely on the basis of the prejudice of the demanders of investment advice, black women will earn one third the wages of white men, and three quarters of all investment advisors will be white men and only one quarter will be black women.

We've just examined a hypothetical example of how prejudice can produce differences in earnings. Economists disagree about whether prejudice actually causes wage differentials, and one line of reasoning suggests that it does not. In the example, the customers who buy from white men pay a higher service charge for investment advice than the customers who buy from black women. This price difference acts as an incentive to limit discrimination and encourages people who are prejudiced to buy from the people whom they are prejudiced against. This force could be so strong as to eliminate the effects of discrimination altogether. Suppose, as is true in manufacturing, that a firm's customers never meet its workers. If a manufacturing firm discriminated against women or minorities, it would not be able to compete with firms who hired these groups. So only those firms that do not discriminate are able to survive in a competitive industry. This line of reasoning suggests a test for discrimination. Customers who discriminate against women and minorities must pay a higher price for the services they buy from white males than the prices paid by those willing to buy from women and minorities. And firms that discriminate must make lower profit rates than those that do not.

But while you can recognize prejudice when you see it, you cannot easily measure it objectively. The model we've studied shows that sex and race differentials might come from prejudice. But without a way of directly measuring prejudice, we cannot test that model in a completely convincing way to see whether it is true.

We need to make another point as well. Our model of prejudice, like all economic models, is in an equilibrium, albeit an unhappy one. But simply because a model is in equilibrium does not mean that such a real situation is either desirable or inevitable. Economic theory makes predictions about the way things will be, not moral statements about the way things ought to be. Policies designed to bring equal wages and employment prospects to women and minorities can be devised. But to be successful, such policies must be based on careful economic analysis. Good intentions are not enough to bring about equality.

A further source of wage rate differences lies in differences in human capital. Let's now examine the effects of human capital on wage rates.

Human Capital Differences

Wages are compensation in part for time spent on the job and in part for the cost incurred in acquiring skill—human capital. The more human capital a person possesses, the more that person earns, other things being equal. It is impossible to measure human capital precisely, but there are some rough indicators, the three most useful of which are:

1. Years of schooling
2. Years of work experience
3. Number of job interruptions

In recent years, the median number of years in school for all races and both sexes are almost equal at

about 12 1/2 years. But this equality is recent. In 1960, whites, on the average, spent about 11 years in school, while blacks, on the average, had about 8 years of schooling. By 1970, that differential had been cut to 2 years, and today it has virtually disappeared.

Years of work experience and job interruptions are interrelated. For people of a given age and given amount of schooling, a person who has had fewer job interruptions has usually had more years of work experience. But interruptions to a career disrupt and reduce the effectiveness of job experience, slow down the accumulation of human capital, and even sometimes result in the depreciation of human capital through its lack of use. Historically and today, job interruptions are more serious for women than for men. Traditionally, women's careers have been interrupted for bearing and rearing children. This factor is a possible source of lower wages, on the average, for women. But just as education differences are virtually disappearing, so career interruptions for women are becoming less common. Maternity leave and day-care facilities are providing an increasing number of women with uninterrupted employment that makes their human capital accumulation more similar to that of men.

Thus it seems that human capital differences possibly can account for earnings differentials in the past and some of the differentials that still remain. The trends, however, suggest that wage differentials from this source will eventually disappear.

There is one final source of earnings differences that is likely to affect women's incomes adversely: the relative degree of specialization of women and men.

Degrees of Specialization

People undertake two kinds of production activities: They supply labor services to the market (market activities), and they undertake household production (nonmarket activities). *Household production* creates goods and services to be consumed within the household rather than to be supplied to the market. Such activities include cooking, cleaning, minor repair work, education, shopping, and various organizational services such as arranging vacations and leisure activities. Bearing and rearing children are other important nonmarket activities.

In Chapter 3, we discovered that people can gain from specializing in particular activities and trading their output with each other. Specialization and the gains from trade do not operate exclusively in the marketplace. They also operate within the household and among its members. It is not uncommon for each member of a household to specialize in a limited range of activities. For example, one does the shopping and cleaning while another does laundry and prepares meals. Specialization in bearing children is a biological necessity, although rearing them is not.

Consider, for example, a household that has two members—Bob and Sue. Bob and Sue have to choose how to allocate their time between nonmarket activities and market activity. One solution is for Bob to specialize in market activity and Sue to specialize in nonmarket activity. Another is for Sue to specialize in market activity and Bob in nonmarket activity. Or for one or both of them to be diversified in market and nonmarket activities.

The allocation chosen by Bob and Sue will depend on their preferences and on the market earning potential of each of them. The choice of an increasing number of households is for each person to be diversified between nonmarket and market activity. But most households still choose an allocation that has Bob almost fully specialized in market activity and Sue diversified in market and nonmarket activities. It seems likely that with this allocation, Bob will have higher earning potential in the marketplace than Sue. If Sue devotes time and effort to ensuring Bob's mental and physical well-being, the quality of Bob's market labor will be higher than if he were diversified. If the roles were reversed, Sue's would be able to supply market labor capable of earning more than Bob.

Economists have attempted to test whether the degree of specialization can account for earnings differentials between the sexes by examining the wages of men and women when, as far as possible, the degree of specialization is held constant. For example, if the degree of specialization is an important factor influencing a person's wage, then men and women of identical ages and educational backgrounds in identical occupations will be paid different wages depending on whether they are single, married to a spouse who specializes in household production, or married to a spouse who has paid employment. Single men and women who live alone, are equally specialized in household and market production, have the same amounts of human capital, and do similar jobs will be paid the same wage. To make nonmarket factors as similar as possible, economists have studied two groups: "never married" men and "never married" women. The available evidence suggests that, on the average, when they have the same amount of human capital—measured by years of schooling, work experience, and career interruptions—the wages of these two groups are not identical, but they are much closer than the difference between average wages for men and women. Women are paid, on the average, about 76 percent of the wage rates of men. When allowance is made for degree of specialization and human capital, this wage differential comes down to between 5 and 10 percent by some estimates. Some economists suspect that the remaining discrepancy stems from discrimination against women, although the difficulty of measuring such discrimination makes this hypothesis hard to test.

Because labor markets do not seem to treat everyone in the same way, governments intervene in these markets to modify the wages and employment levels that they determine. One potentially far-reaching intervention is comparable-worth laws. Let's see how these laws work.

Comparable-Worth Laws

CONGRESS PASSED THE EQUAL PAY ACT IN 1963 AND the Civil Rights Act in 1964. These acts require equal pay for equal work. They are attempts to remove the most blatant forms of discrimination between men and women and between whites and minorities. But many people believe that these acts do not go far enough. In their view, getting paid the *same* wage for doing the *same* job is just the first step that has to be taken. What's important is that jobs that are *comparable*—require the same levels of skills and responsibilities—receive the *same* wages, regardless of whether the jobs are done by men or women or by blacks or whites. Paying the same wage for different jobs that are judged to be comparable is called *comparable worth*.

Advocates of comparable-worth laws argue that wages should be determined by analyzing the characteristics of jobs and determining their worth on objective grounds. However, such a method of determining wage rates does not achieve the objectives sought by supporters of wage equality. Let's see why.

Figure 15.9 shows two markets: that for oil rig operators in part (a) and that for school teachers in part (b). The marginal revenue product curves (MRP_R and MRP_T) and the supply curves (S_R and S_T) are shown for each type of labor. Competitive equilibrium generates a wage rate W_R for oil rig operators and W_T for teachers.

Suppose that the knowledge and skills required in those two occupations—the mental and physical

FIGURE 15.9

The Problem with Comparable Worth

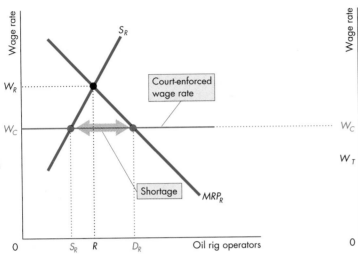

(a) Market for oil rig operators

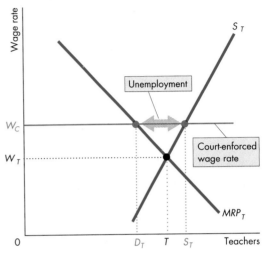

(b) Market for teachers

Part (a) shows the demand for and supply of oil rig operators, MRP_R and S_R, and part (b) shows the demand for and supply of school teachers, MRP_T and S_T. The competitive equilibrium wage rate for oil rig operators is W_R, and that for teachers is W_T. If an evaluation of the two jobs finds that they have comparable worth and rules that the wage rate W_C be paid to

both types of workers, such a wage creates a shortage of oil rig operators and a surplus of teachers. Oil producers search for labor-saving ways of producing oil (that are more expensive), and teachers search for other jobs (that are less desirable to them and probably are less well paid).

demands, the responsibilities, and the working conditions—result in a judgment that these two jobs are of comparable worth. The wage rate that is judged to apply to each of them is W_C, and the courts enforce this wage rate. What happens? First, there is a shortage of oil rig operators. Oil rig companies are able to hire only S_R workers at the wage rate W_C. They cut back their production or build more expensive labor-saving oil rigs. Also the number of teachers employed decreases. But this decrease occurs because school boards demand fewer teachers. At the higher wage W_C, school boards demand only D_T teachers. The quantity of teachers supplied is S_T, and the difference between S_T and D_T is the number of unemployed teachers looking for jobs. These teachers eventually accept nonteaching jobs (which they don't like as much as teaching jobs), quite likely at a lower rate of pay than that of teachers.

Thus legislated comparable wages for comparable work may have serious and costly unintended consequences.

REVIEW

■ Wage differences between the sexes and the races might arise from differences in the types of jobs done, discrimination, and differences in human capital.

■ Wage differences between the sexes might also arise from differences in the degree of specialization of women and men.

■ The equalization of human capital and of the degree of specialization will lead to smaller differentials and possibly will eliminate them.

■ Comparable-worth laws cannot, themselves, eliminate wage differences.

◆ In this chapter, we applied the factor markets model to understand a variety of phenomena in labor markets. In the next chapter, we apply this model to deal with markets for capital and for natural resources.

The Limits of Union Power

THE LOS ANGELES TIMES, MAY 10, 1994

Strikers Reap Harvest of Bitterness

BY MARK ARAX

STOCKTON—In the migrant labor camps of this Delta town, Diamond Walnut was a way out of the tomato and onion fields that trapped the lives of young single mothers like Toni Escobedo.

In good years, working as forklift drivers and plant supervisors—jobs traditionally not open to women—they brought home $32,000 in wages and had a health plan that was the envy of cannery workers in this depressed region where the Sacramento and San Joaquin rivers meet.

When the walnut processor and packer tottered on the edge of financial ruin a decade ago, there was no doubt what Escobedo and her fellow workers would do. They agreed to wage cuts as high as 35% to save the company they regarded as family.

Today, walking a weary picket line outside the giant plant where she worked for 23 years—a statistic in one of the nation's most bitter labor strikes—Escobedo still has trouble believing how fast it all went sour.

In 1991, as a flushed Diamond Walnut prepared to process and ship its biggest crop ever, she and 260 other full-time employees went on strike. The company, she said, had reneged on its promise to restore higher wages when the good times returned. ...

The company said it had no choice but to hire permanent replacements because of the timing of the strike. ...

To union workers and their supporters across the country, the fight at Diamond Walnut has become a touchstone in the debate over the right of employers to hire permanent replacement workers as a way to defang a strike and eventually bust a union. ...

[In the 1980s] ... to save the company, workers agreed to a new three-year contract that cut average hourly wages from $10.05 to $7.70. The company purchased new laser acoustical machines to speed up the process of culling the dark and light meat of the nut—automation that slashed the 600-member full-time work force in half.

Diamond Walnut quickly rebounded and has posted record sales in each of the past four years. Last year, the cooperative sold $204 million worth of walnuts—$58 million more than when the wage cuts went into effect. Grower proceeds nearly doubled to $11.2 million in the same period....

Reprinted by permission.

Essence of THE STORY

■ When Diamond Walnut, a walnut-processing cooperative, fell on hard times in the 1980s, its workers agreed to a wage cut from $10.05 to $7.70 an hour.

■ The company automated the culling process by purchasing laser acoustical machines and decreased its full-time work force from 600 to 300 people.

■ Times improved and each of the four years through 1993 saw record sales. In 1993, sales were $204 million—$58 million more than when wage cuts were agreed to.

■ In 1991, employees went on strike because, they claimed, the company had reneged on its promise to restore wages when conditions improved.

■ The company hired permanent replacements for the striking workers.

■ The dispute became a fight about the right of employers to hire permanent replacement workers when union workers strike.

Economic

A N A L Y S I S

■ Before hard times hit Diamond Walnut, its demand for full-time workers was D_0 in Fig. 1.

■ The competitive labor supply curve facing Diamond Walnut was S_C, but the union managed to influence the supply of full-time labor, so the firm faced the union supply curve S_U in Fig. 1.

■ Given the demand curve D_0 and the supply curve S_U, the average wage rate was $10.05 an hour and 600 full-time workers were employed.

■ The demand for labor is a derived demand and depends (among other factors) on the price of the good it is employed to produce—in this case, the price of walnuts.

■ A fall in the price of walnuts decreased the marginal revenue product of labor, which decreased the demand for labor and shifted the demand curve leftward to D_1 in Fig. 1.

■ Faced with this decrease in demand, the union agreed to a wage cut from $10.05 to $7.70. The supply curve changed from the union supply curve S_U to the competitive supply curve S_C.

■ With these changes in demand and supply, the level of employment remained constant at 600.

■ Diamond Walnut automated its operations, and this action decreased the demand for labor even further to D_2 in Fig. 2.

■ Because the supply of labor is perfectly elastic at $7.70 an hour (an assumption), this further decrease in the demand for labor decreased the quantity of labor hired but did not lower the wage rate below $7.70.

■ After Diamond Walnut automated, the price of walnuts and quantity of walnuts processed increased. So its demand for labor increased back toward D_1.

■ With an increase in the demand for labor, the union expected Diamond Walnut to restore the wage rate to its original level of $10.05. When the firm refused to do so, the union withdrew its labor by going on strike.

■ Diamond Walnut then hired nonunion replacement labor and operated on the competitive labor supply curve, S_C.

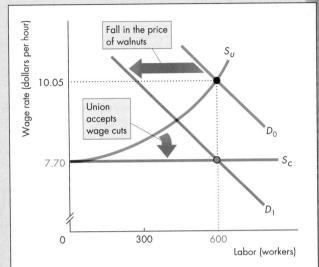

Figure 1 A fall in the price of walnuts

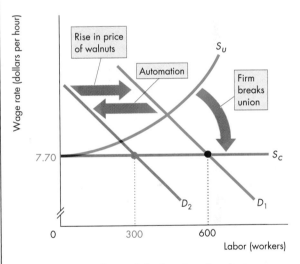

Figure 2 Automation and rise in price of walnuts

■ Only if the union can restrict the availability of nonunion labor can it get the wage rate to return to the level that prevailed before the new automated technology was introduced.

■ Even then, to get the wage rate back to its old level, the union must accept a decrease in employment.

S U M M A R Y

Skill Differentials

Skill differentials arise partly because high-skilled labor has a higher marginal revenue product than low-skilled labor and partly because skills are costly to acquire. Skills are costly to acquire because households have to invest in human capital to become skilled. Investment sometimes means direct payments such as tuition and other training fees and sometimes means working for a lower wage during on-the-job training. Because skills are costly to acquire, households supply high-skilled labor on terms that compensate them for both the time spent on the job and the costs of acquiring the skills. Thus the supply curve of high-skilled labor lies above the supply curve of low-skilled labor.

Wage rates of high-skilled and low-skilled labor are determined by demand and supply in the two labor markets. The equilibrium wage rate for high-skilled labor exceeds that for low-skilled labor. The difference in wages reflects the higher marginal product of skill and the cost to acquire skill. (pp. 358–360)

Union-Nonunion Wage Differentials

Labor unions influence wages by controlling the supply of labor. In competitive labor markets, unions obtain higher wages only at the expense of lower employment. Unions in competitive industries also influence the marginal revenue product of their members by supporting import restrictions, minimum wages, and immigration restrictions; by increasing demand for the good they produce; and by increasing the marginal productivity of their members.

In a monopsony—a market in which there is a single buyer—a union can increase the wage rate without sacrificing employment. Bilateral monopoly occurs when the union is a monopoly seller of labor, the firm is a monopsony buyer of labor, and the wage rate is determined by bargaining between the two parties. Also, in a monopsony, a minimum wage law can increase both the wage rate and the level of employment.

In practice, union workers earn an estimated 10 to 25 percent more than comparable nonunion workers. (pp. 360–366)

Wage Differentials Between Sexes and Races

Earnings differentials between men and women and between whites and minorities arise from differences in types of jobs, discrimination, differences in human capital, and differences in degree of specialization.

Well-paid jobs such as those in the legal, medical, and other professions, and in higher ranks of management are more likely to be held by white men than by women and minorities. Women and minorities are more likely to be discriminated against than white males, but discrimination is hard to measure objectively. Historically, white males have had more human capital than other groups, but human capital differences arising from schooling differences have been declining and have almost been eliminated.

Differentials based on work experience have kept women's pay below that for men because women's careers have traditionally been interrupted more frequently than those of men, resulting, on the average, in a smaller accumulation of human capital. This difference is smaller today than in the past. Differentials arising from different degrees of specialization are probably important and might persist. Men have traditionally been more specialized in market activity, on the average, than women. Women have traditionally undertaken both nonmarket (household production) activities and market activities. Attempts to test for the importance of the degree of specialization suggest that it is an important source of the difference between the earnings of men and women. (pp. 367–370)

Comparable-Worth Laws

Comparable-worth laws determine wages by using objective characteristics rather than what the market will pay to assess the value of different types of jobs. Determining wages through comparable worth will result in a decrease in the number of people employed in jobs on which the market places a lower value and shortages of workers that the market values more highly. Thus the attempt to achieve comparable wages for comparable work has costly, unintended consequences. (pp. 370–371)

KEY ELEMENTS

Key Figures and Table

Key Terms

REVIEW QUESTIONS

1. What is human capital? How is it acquired?
2. Explain why the demand curve for high-skilled labor lies to the right of the demand curve for low-skilled labor.
3. Explain why the supply curve for high-skilled labor lies to the left of the supply curve for low-skilled labor.
4. What is the influence of education and on-the-job-training on earnings?
5. Explain why skilled workers are paid more than low-skilled workers.
6. What is a labor union? What are the main types of labor unions?
7. What is collective bargaining? What are the main weapons available to a union and an employer?
8. How does a labor union try to influence wages?
9. What can a union do in a competitive labor market?
10. How might a union increase the demand for its members' labor?
11. Explain why the elasticity of supply of labor influences how much the union can raise the wage rate paid to union members.
12. What is monopsony? Where in the United States might a monopsony exist?
13. Explain why the supply of labor facing a monopsony is not the marginal cost of labor.
14. Explain why a monopsony maximizes its profit by paying labor a wage rate that is less than the marginal revenue product of labor.
15. Under what circumstances will the introduction of a minimum wage increase employment?
16. How big are the union-nonunion wage differentials in the United States today?
17. What are the four main reasons why sex and race differentials in earnings exist?
18. Why does discrimination against women influence the marginal revenue product of women?
19. What is the effect of discrimination in a particular profession on the basis of sex or race on:
    a. The wage rate paid to women and members of minorities?
    b. The number of women and members of minorities that get hired in that particular profession?
20. What are the wage differentials between women and men in the United States?
21. Is the wage differential between men and women all due to discrimination? Explain your answer.
22. What is a comparable-worth law?
23. How do comparable-worth laws work and what are their predicted effects?

PROBLEMS

1. The demand for and supply of low-skilled labor are given by the following schedule:

Hourly wage rate (dollars per hour)	Quantity supplied (hours per day)	Quantity demanded (hours per day)
2	2,000	8,000
3	3,000	7,000
4	4,000	6,000
5	5,000	5,000
6	6,000	4,000
7	7,000	3,000
8	8,000	2,000
9	9,000	1,000

 a. What is the wage rate of low-skilled labor?
 b. What is the quantity of low-skilled labor employed?

2. The workers in problem 1 can be trained—can obtain a skill—and their marginal productivity doubles. (The marginal product at each employment level is twice the marginal product of a low-skilled worker.) But the compensation for the cost of acquiring skill adds $2 an hour to the wage that must be offered to attract the high-skilled labor. What is:
 a. The wage rate of high-skilled labor?
 b. The quantity of high-skilled labor employed?

3. Suppose in problem 1 that high-skilled workers become unionized and the union restricts the amount of high-skilled labor to 5,000 hours. What is:
 a. The wage rate of high-skilled workers?
 b. The wage differential between low- and high-skilled workers?

4. If in problem 1, the government introduces a minimum wage rate of $6 an hour for low-skilled workers
 a. What is the wage rate paid to low-skilled workers?
 b. How many hours of low-skilled labor gets hired each day?

5. In an isolated part of the Amazon Basin a gold mining company faces the following labor market. The gold mine is a monopsony.
 a. What wage rate does the company pay?
 b. How many hours of labor does the gold mine hire?
 c. What is the marginal revenue product of the last hour of labor?
 d. How does the gold mine maximize its profit when it does not pay its workers their marginal revenue product?
 e. If the world price of gold increases, what happens to the wage rate paid and the number of workers hired?

6. If in problem 5 the government imposes a minimum wage rate of $1.50 a day,
 a. What wage rate does the gold mine pay?
 b. Does the gold mine increase or decrease the number of hours of labor it hires?

7. Study the *Reading Between the Lines* on pp. 372–373 and use the figure in the Economic Analysis to answer the following questions:
 a. If the union had not agreed to the wage cut when Diamond Walnut fell on hard times, how many workers would have been hired?
 b. If when Diamond Walnut had automated and the price of walnuts increased the wage rate had been $10.05, how many workers would have been hired?

Capital and Natural Resource Markets

After studying this chapter, you will be able to:

- Describe the structure of capital markets in the United States today

- Explain how the demand for and supply of capital are determined

- Explain how interest rates and stock prices are determined and why stock prices fluctuate

- Explain how the prices of natural resources are determined

- Explain how markets regulate the pace at which we use exhaustible resources such as oil

Panic filled the cavernous New York Stock Exchange on Monday, October 19, 1987. It had taken five years, from August 1982, for the average price of a common stock to climb 200 percent. But on that single day, stock prices fell an unheard-of 22 percent—knocking billions of dollars off the value of people's investments. The crash touched off other stock market plunges from Tokyo to London. Why does the stock market boom for several

Boom and Bust

years and then crash suddenly and spectacularly? ◆ The New York Stock Exchange, large as it is, is only a part of the capital market of the United States and the worldwide capital market. Every year, trillions of dollars flow through these markets. Savings flow through banks, insurance companies, and stock exchanges and end up financing the purchases of machinery, factory and office buildings, cars, and homes. How do the dollars people save and place on deposit in a bank enable Pepsi-Cola to open a new bottling plant? ◆ Many of our natural resources are exhaustible, and yet we are using them up at a rapid rate. Every year, we burn trillions of cubic feet of natural gas, billions of gallons of petroleum, and millions of tons of coal. We extract bauxite to make aluminum and iron ore to make steel. Aren't we one day going to run out of these and other natural resources? How are their prices determined? Do their prices rise to encourage conservation, or does the market need help to ensure that we do not pillage nature's exhaustible endowments?

◈ In this chapter, we study capital and natural resource markets. We'll find out what determines the amount of saving and investment and how interest rates and stock prices are determined. We'll also see how market forces encourage the conservation and discovery of exhaustible natural resources.

The Structure of Capital Markets

CAPITAL MARKETS ARE THE CHANNELS THROUGH which households' saving flows into firms. Firms use the financial resources they obtain in capital markets to buy capital goods. Capital goods—goods such as buildings, machines, airplanes, and computers—are bought and sold, and they are rented. The markets in which capital goods are bought, sold and rented are not capital markets. They are goods markets and factor rental markets. These markets coordinate the decisions of producers and buyers and of owners and renters of capital goods. In these markets, the forces of demand and supply, which you first met in Chapter 4, determine the prices and quantities of the various capital goods.

Capital markets coordinate the saving plans of households, which determine the supply of capital, and the investment plans of firms, which determine the demand for capital. The price of capital, which adjusts to make the quantity of capital supplied equal to the quantity demanded, is the interest rate.

The Flows of Funds

Figure 16.1 shows the main flows of saving through the capital markets. Households save part of their incomes and supply *financial capital*. Firms demand financial capital and use it to buy *physical capital*. Lying at the core of the financial markets are **financial intermediaries**, which are institutions that receive deposits, make loans, and facilitate transactions in markets for stocks, bonds, and loans. The best-known financial intermediaries are commercial banks and savings and loan associations, but others are money market funds, insurance companies, and retirement fund management companies. The green dotted lines in the figure illustrate the financial transactions. Households use their saving to buy stocks or bonds issued by firms and to make deposits with financial intermediaries. Financial intermediaries make loans to households and firms.

The three main types of capital markets are:

- Stock markets
- Bond markets
- Loan markets

FIGURE 16.1

Capital Market Flows

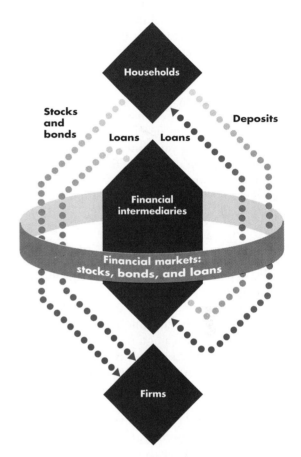

Households supply *financial* capital to firms, which use financial capital to buy *physical* capital. Households purchase stocks and bonds and make deposits in financial intermediaries. Financial intermediaries lend to both households and firms. The green dotted lines illustrate these financial transactions.

Stock Markets A **stock market** is a market in which the stocks of corporations are traded. The most famous stock market, the *New York Stock Exchange* (*NYSE*), located on Wall Street, New York City, handles more than 2,000 of the most actively traded stocks, many of which are those of household names such as General Motors, Boeing Aircraft, and Exxon. Another stock exchange in New York City, NASDAQ, handles stocks that are not quite as heavily traded as those on the NYSE. Stock exchanges in

Boston, Chicago, San Francisco, and other major cities handle the stocks of smaller regional companies. Outside the United States, London, Paris, Frankfurt, Tokyo, Toronto, and other large cities have long-established stock exchanges that specialize in trading the stocks of tens of thousands of foreign companies. In recent years, stock markets have begun to operate in Shanghai, Taipei, Bangkok, Seoul, and other centers in the emerging market economies of East Asia.

If you want to buy or sell a stock on a stock exchange, you must give an instruction to a *broker*, who in turn places a buy or sell order with a *specialist* who deals in the stock you want to trade. The specialist, who works on the *floor* of the stock exchange, continuously monitors demand and supply and tries to keep the price of the stock at the level at which the quantity demanded equals the quantity supplied.

Bond Markets A **bond market** is a market in which the bonds of corporations and governments are traded. The distinction between a stock and a bond, described in Chapter 9 (pp. 197–198), is that a stockholder receives a periodic dividend that depends on a firm's profit, while a bondholder receives a periodic fixed amount, called a coupon payment. Bond markets, like stock markets, are located in all the major financial centers. And bonds are issued in all the world's major currencies. For example, a business in Indonesia might borrow by issuing bonds denominated in Japanese yen or in United States dollars or in British pounds.

Also as in stock markets, if you want to buy or sell a bond, you must give an instruction to a broker who, working with specialist traders, maintains a balance between the quantities of bonds demanded and supplied.

Loan Markets A **loan market** is a market in which households, firms, and financial intermediaries make and receive loans. Financial intermediaries make loan markets function and are the major players in these markets. When you make a deposit in a bank, you make a loan to the bank and the bank uses the funds it receives from depositors to make loans to businesses and households. Loans to businesses are used to finance investment in capital equipment and inventories. Loans to households are used to finance the purchase of homes and consumer durable goods.

Let's begin to learn how capital markets work by studying the demand for capital.

The Demand for Capital

A FIRM'S DEMAND FOR *financial* CAPITAL STEMS from its demand for *physical* capital, and the amount that a firm plans to *borrow* in a given time period is determined by its planned *investment*.

Capital and Investment

Capital is a *stock*—the quantity of previously manufactured goods in existence at a given time that are used to produce other goods and services. **Gross investment** is a *flow*—the purchase of new capital goods during a given period. This amount is added to the capital stock. Capital is like the water in Lake Powell at a given point in time and gross investment is like the water flowing into the lake from the San Juan and Colorado Rivers during a given period. The inflow adds to the water in the lake. Depreciation is another flow. It is the amount of existing capital that wears out in a given period. Depreciation is like the water flowing out of Lake Powell into the Colorado River. This outflow decreases the water in the lake. The change in the capital stock during a given period is called **net investment** and equals gross investment minus depreciation. Similarly, the change in the amount of water in Lake Powell equals the inflow minus the outflow.

Investment Decisions

To decide how much to invest and borrow, a firm decides on the size of its capital stock. This decision is driven by its attempt to maximize profit.

As a firm increases the quantity of capital employed, other things remaining the same, the marginal revenue product of capital eventually diminishes. To maximize profit, a firm uses the rule: employ the quantity of capital that makes the marginal revenue product of capital equal to the price of using capital. The price of using capital is the interest rate. So a firm increases the quantity of capital employed until the additional revenue generated by using one extra unit of capital equals the interest rate.

The easiest way to see that the interest rate is the price of using capital is to think about capital that is actually rented. If a firm rents a computer from Computerland, it pays an annual rental rate. This rental rate gives Computerland a rate of return equal to the interest rate. If Computerland made a return less than the interest rate, it would sell some computers and buy some stocks and bonds that yield an interest rate higher than that on computers. If Computerland made a return greater than the interest rate, it would buy more computers and sell some stock or bonds that have an interest rate lower than that on computers.

But most capital is not rented. Firms *buy* buildings, plant, and equipment and operate them for several years. To decide how much capital equipment to buy, the firm compares the price to be paid here and now for the equipment with the returns—the future flow of marginal revenue product—that the equipment will generate over its life. The interest rate is still the price of using capital, even when it is bought rather than rented. The reason is that to decide how much capital to buy, the firm must convert a stream of *future* marginal revenue product into a *present value* so that it can be directly compared with the price of a new piece of capital equipment. Chapter 9 (pp. 198–200) explains the concept of present value.

The Net Present Value of a Computer   Let's see how a firm decides how much capital to buy by calculating the present value of a new computer. Table 16.1(a) summarizes the data. Tina runs Taxfile, Inc., a firm that sells advice to taxpayers. Tina is considering buying a new computer that costs $10,000. The computer has a life of two years, after which it will be worthless. If Tina buys the computer, she will pay $10,000 now and she expects to generate business that will bring in an additional $5,900 at the end of each of the next two years.

To calculate the present value, *PV*, of the marginal revenue product of a new computer, Tina uses the formula

$$PV = \frac{MRP_1}{(1+r)} + \frac{MRP_2}{(1+r)^2}.$$

Here, MRP_1 is the marginal revenue product received by Tina at the end of the first year. It is converted to a present value by dividing it by $(1 + r)$. The term MRP_2 is the marginal revenue product received at the end of the second year. It is converted to a present value by dividing it by $(1 + r)^2$.

Table 16.1(b) puts Tina's numbers into the present value formula and calculates the present value of the marginal revenue product of a computer. Tina

---

TABLE   16.1

Net Present Value of an Investment—Taxfile, Inc.

(a) Data

Price of computer	$10,000
Life of computer	2 years
Marginal revenue product	$5,900 at end of each year
Interest rate	4% a year

(b) Present value of the flow of marginal revenue product

$$PV = \frac{MRP_1}{1 + r} + \frac{MRP_2}{(1 + r)^2}$$

$$= \frac{\$5,900}{1.04} + \frac{\$5,900}{(1.04)^2}$$

$$= \$5,673 + \$5,455$$

$$= \$11,128$$

(c) Net present value of investment

$$NPV = PV \text{ of Marginal revenue product} - \text{Cost of computer}$$

$$= \$11,128 - \$10,000$$

$$= \$1,128$$

---

can borrow or lend at an interest rate of 4 percent a year. The present value (*PV*) of $5,900 one year in the future is $5,900 divided by 1.04 (4 percent as a proportion is 0.04). The present value of $5,900 two years in the future is $5,900 divided by $(1.04)^2$. Tina works out those two present values and then adds them to get the present value of the future flow of marginal revenue product, which is $11,128.

Tina's Decision to Buy   Tina decides whether to buy the computer by comparing the present value of its future flow of marginal revenue product with its purchase price. She makes this comparison by calculating the net present value (*NPV*) of the computer. **Net present value** is the present value of the future flow of marginal revenue product generated by the capital minus the cost of the capital. If net present value is positive, the firm buys additional capital. If the net present value is negative, the firm does not buy additional capital. Table 16.1(c) shows the calculation of Tina's net present value of a computer. The net present value is $1,128—greater than zero—so Tina buys the computer.

Tina can buy any number of computers that cost $10,000 and have a life of two years. But like all other factors of production, capital is subject to diminishing marginal returns. The greater the amount of capital employed, the smaller is its marginal revenue product. So if Tina buys a second computer or a third one, she gets successively smaller marginal revenue products from the additional machines.

Table 16.2(a) sets out Tina's marginal revenue products for one, two, and three computers. The marginal revenue product of one computer (the case just reviewed) is $5,900 a year. The marginal revenue product of a second computer is $5,600 a year, and the marginal revenue product of a third computer is $5,300 a year. Table 16.2(b) shows the calculations of the present values of the marginal revenue products of the first, second, and third computers.

You've seen that with an interest rate of 4 percent a year, the net present value of one computer is positive. At an interest rate of 4 percent a year, the present value of the marginal revenue product of a second computer is $10,562, which exceeds its price by $562. So Tina buys a second computer. But at an interest rate of 4 percent a year, the present value of the marginal revenue product of a third computer is $9,996, which is $4 less than the price of the computer. So Tina does not buy a third computer.

A Change in the Interest Rate We've seen that at an interest rate of 4 percent a year, Tina buys two computers but not three. Suppose that the interest rate is 8 percent a year. In this case, the present value of the first computer is $10,521 (see Table 16.2b), so Tina still buys one machine because it has a positive net present value. At an interest rate of 8 percent a year, the net present value of the second computer is $9,986, which is less than $10,000, the price of the computer. So, at an interest rate of 8 percent a year, Tina buys only one computer.

Suppose that the interest rate is even higher, at 12 percent a year. In this case, the present value of the marginal revenue product of one computer is $9,971 (see Table 16.2b). At this interest rate, Tina buys no computers.

TABLE 16.2
Taxfile's Investment Decision

(a) Data

Price of computer	$10,000
Life of computer	2 years
Marginal revenue product:	
Using 1 computer	$5,900 a year
Using 2 computers	$5,600 a year
Using 3 computers	$5,300 a year

(b) Present value of the flow of marginal revenue product

If $r = 0.04$ (4% a year):

Using 1 computer: $PV = \dfrac{\$5,900}{1.04} + \dfrac{\$5,900}{(1.04)^2} = \$11,128$

Using 2 computers: $PV = \dfrac{\$5,600}{1.04} + \dfrac{\$5,600}{(1.04)^2} = \$10,562$

Using 3 computers: $PV = \dfrac{\$5,300}{1.04} + \dfrac{\$5,300}{(1.04)^2} = \$9,996$

If $r = 0.08$ (8% a year):

Using 1 computer: $PV = \dfrac{\$5,900}{1.08} + \dfrac{\$5,900}{(1.08)^2} = \$10,521$

Using 2 computers: $PV = \dfrac{\$5,600}{1.08} + \dfrac{\$5,600}{(1.08)^2} = \$9,986$

If $r = 0.12$ (12% a year):

Using 1 computer: $PV = \dfrac{\$5,900}{1.12} + \dfrac{\$5,900}{(1.12)^2} = \$9,971$

These calculations trace Taxfile's demand schedule for capital, which shows the value of computers demanded by Taxfile at each interest rate. Other things remaining the same, as the interest rate rises, the quantity of capital demanded decreases. The higher the interest rate, the smaller is the quantity of *physical* capital demanded. But to finance the purchase of *physical* capital, firms demand *financial* capital. So the higher the interest rate, the smaller is the quantity of *financial* capital demanded.

Demand Curve for Capital

The quantity of capital demanded by a firm depends on the marginal revenue product of capital and the interest rate. A firm's demand curve for capital shows the relationship between the quantity of capital demanded and the interest rate, other things remaining the same. Figure 16.2 illustrates Taxfile's demand for computers (D_F). Points *a*, *b*, and *c* correspond to the example that we have just worked through. At an interest rate of 12 percent a year, Tina buys no computers—point *a*. At an interest rate of 8 percent, she buys 1 computer worth $10,000—point *b*. At an interest rate of 4 percent, she buys 2 computers worth $20,000—point *c*.

We've considered only one type of computer—one that costs $10,000. But Tina can buy different types of computers, the power of which can be expressed as a multiple or fraction of a $10,000 com-

puter. For example, there may be a $5,000 computer that has half the power of a $10,000 machine or a machine that costs $12,500 and has one and a quarter times the power of a $10,000 machine. If we consider all the different types of computers that Tina can buy, we generate not just the three points, *a*, *b*, and *c* but Taxfile's entire demand curve—the blue curve in Fig. 16.2.

The Market Demand for Capital

The market demand curve for capital is the horizontal sum of all the individual firm's demand curves. Figure 16.3 shows the market demand curve, which like the firm's demand curve slopes downward. When the interest rate rises, other things remaining the same, the quantity of capital demanded decreases along the demand curve. Figure 16.3 shows such a change by the movement along demand curve D_0.

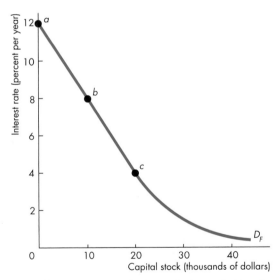

FIGURE 16.2

A Firm's Demand for Capital

The lower the interest rate, the larger is the capital stock demanded. At an interest rate of 12 percent a year, Taxfile demands no computers (point *a*). At 8 percent a year, the firm demands 1 computer worth $10,000 (point *b*). At 4 percent a year, the firm demands 2 computers worth $20,000 (point *c*). If Taxfile can buy computers of different types (fractions of a $10,000 computer), its demand for computers is shown by the demand curve passing through points *a*, *b*, and *c*.

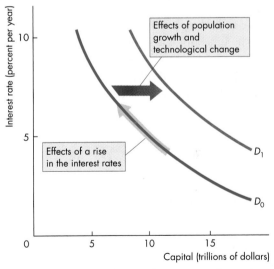

FIGURE 16.3

The Demand for Capital

Other things remaining the same, the quantity of capital demanded decreases as the interest rate rises and there is a movement along the demand curve for capital. Population growth steadily increases the demand for capital and shifts the demand curve steadily rightward. Advances in technology lead to fluctuations in the pace at which the demand curve shifts rightward.

Changes in the Demand for Capital The demand for capital changes when firms revise their expectations about the future marginal revenue product of capital. For example, Taxfile and other businesses might revise their expectations about marginal revenue product upward. If they do, the quantity of capital that has a positive present value increases at each interest rate. As a result, the demand of capital increases. The two main factors that change the marginal revenue product of capital and bring changes in the demand for capital are:

1. Population growth
2. Technological change

Population growth brings a steady increase in the demand for capital. Technological change brings fluctuations in the demand for capital. Technological change increases the demand for some types of capital and decreases the demand for other types. For example, the development of diesel engines for railroad transportation decreased the demand for steam engines and increased the demand for diesel engines. In this case, the railroad industry's overall demand for capital did not change much. In contrast, the development of desktop computers increased the demand for office computing equipment, decreased the demand for electric typewriters, and increased the overall demand for capital in the office. Figure 16.3 shows the increase in demand resulting from population growth and technological change by a shift in the demand curve from D_0 to D_1.

R E V I E W

- Firms' profit-maximization decisions determine the demand for capital—both *physical* and *financial*.

- The quantity of capital demanded depends on the marginal revenue product of capital and the interest rate.

- The higher the interest rate, the smaller is the present value of the future flow of marginal revenue product and the smaller is the quantity of capital demanded.

- The demand for capital increases as population grows and fluctuates as technology changes.

The Supply of Capital

THE QUANTITY OF CAPITAL SUPPLIED RESULTS from people's saving decisions. Saving is a *flow*, which equals income minus consumption. The current market value of a household's past saving, together with any inheritances it has received, is the household's **wealth**, which is a *stock*. Households hold their wealth as financial capital such as stocks, bonds, and bank deposits, and as physical capital such as houses, cars, and other consumer durable goods. The wealth that households hold as financial capital is used by firms to finance the purchase of physical capital. So for the economy, wealth equals the value of physical capital—the total value of the physical capital of both households and firms.

Portfolio Choices A household's decision about how to hold wealth is called a *portfolio choice*. In everyday language, we often refer to the purchase of stocks and bonds as investment. That everyday use of the word "investment" can cause confusion in economic analysis. It is to avoid this confusion that we use the term "portfolio choice" to refer to the choices that households make in allocating their wealth across the various assets available to them. *Investment* is the purchases of new physical capital.

The Saving Decision

The main factors that determine saving are:

- Income
- Expected future income
- Interest rate

Income Saving is the act of converting *current* income into *future* consumption. Usually, the higher a household's income, the more it plans to consume both in the present and in the future. But to increase *future* consumption, the household must save. So, other things remaining the same, the higher a household's income, the more it saves.

Expected Future Income Because a major reason for saving is to increase future consumption, the amount that a household saves depends not only on its current income but also on its *expected future income*. If a household's current income is high and its expected future income is low, it will have a high level of saving. But if its current income is low and its expected future income is high, it will have a low (perhaps even negative) level of saving.

Young people (especially students) usually have low current incomes compared with their expected future income. To smooth out their lifetime consumption, they consume more than they earn and incur debts. Such people have a negative amount of saving. In middle age, most people's incomes reach their peak. At this stage in life, saving is at its maximum. After retirement, people spend part of the wealth they have accumulated during their working lives.

Interest Rate   A dollar saved today grows into a dollar plus interest tomorrow. The higher the interest rate, the greater is the amount that a dollar saved today becomes in the future. Thus the higher the interest rate, the greater is the opportunity cost of current consumption. Interest rates have two influences on saving. They are:

1. Substitution effect
2. Income effect

1. *Substitution Effect.* Because a higher interest rate increases the future return from today's saving and increases the opportunity cost of current consumption, it stimulates saving. It encourages people to economize on current consumption and take advantage of the higher interest rate. That is, the substitution effect of interest rates on saving is positive. Other things remaining the same, the substitution effect of a higher interest rate is a greater quantity of saving.

2. *Income Effect.* A change in the interest rate changes a household's *future* income. Other things remaining the same, as a household's income increases so, too, does its consumption. But the effect of a change in the interest rate on a household's future income depends on whether the household is a net borrower or a net lender. For a net lender, an increase in interest rates increases future income, so it increases both current and future consumption and it decreases saving. The income effect opposes the substitution effect and saving might increase or decrease depending on the relative strengths of the two effects. For a net borrower, an increase in interest rates decreases future income and decreases both current and future consumption. So saving increases. In this case, the income effect of a higher interest rate reinforces the substitution effect.

For individual households that are net lenders, the effect of a change in the interest rate on saving is ambiguous, but for households that are net borrowers, and for the economy as a whole, there is no ambiguity: other things remaining the same, the higher the interest rate, the greater is the flow of saving in a given period and the greater is the stock of financial capital supplied.

Supply Curve of Capital

The quantity of capital supplied is the total value of accumulated saving—wealth. Figure 16.4 shows the supply curve of capital—the relationship between the quantity of capital supplied and the interest rate, other things remaining the same. An increase in the interest rate brings an increase in the quantity of capital supplied and a movement along the supply curve, as shown along the supply curve S_0. The supply curve is inelastic in the short run but probably quite elastic in the long run. The reason is that in any given year, the total amount of saving is small relative to the

FIGURE   16.4

The Supply of Capital

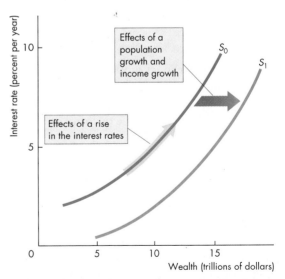

Other things remaining the same, the quantity of capital supplied increases as the interest rate rises and there is a movement along the supply curve for capital. An increase in population and rising incomes increase the supply of capital and shift the supply curve rightward.

stock of capital in existence. So even a large change in the saving rate brings only a small change in the quantity of capital supplied.

Changes in the Supply of Capital A change in any influence on saving, other than the interest rate, changes the amount of saving and shifts the supply curve of capital. The main influences on the supply of capital are income and its distribution and the size and age distribution of the population.

Other things remaining the same, an increase in income or an increase in the population brings an increase in the supply of capital. Also, other things remaining the same, the more unequally income is distributed, the higher is the saving rate. The reason is that low income and middle income families have low saving rates, while high income families have high saving rates. So the larger the proportion of total income earned by the highest income families, the greater is the amount of saving. Finally, and again other things remaining the same, the larger the proportion of middle-aged people, the higher is the saving rate. The reason is that middle-aged people do most of the saving as they build up a pension fund to provide an income in their retirement.

Any one of the factors that increases the supply of capital shifts the supply curve of capital rightward, as shown in Fig. 16.4, where the supply curve shifts from S_0 to S_1.

REVIEW

- The quantity of capital supplied is determined by saving decisions.
- Other things remaining the same, the higher the interest rate, the larger is the quantity of capital supplied.
- The supply of capital changes as a result of changes in income and its distribution and in the population and its age composition. Income growth and population growth bring a steady increase in the supply of capital.

We have studied the demand for and supply of capital. We now bring these two sides of the capital market together and study the determination of interest rates and asset prices. We'll then be able to answer some of the questions posed at the beginning of this chapter about the stock market and understand the forces that produce stock market booms and crashes.

Interest Rates and Stock Prices

SAVING PLANS AND INVESTMENT PLANS ARE coordinated through capital markets. Interest rates, stock prices, and bond prices adjust to make these plans compatible. We are now going to study the way in which these market forces work. We are also going to discover what determines the stock market value of a firm.

Two Sides of the Same Coin

Interest rates and stock (and bond) prices can be viewed as two sides of the same coin. We'll look first at interest rates, then at stock (and bond) prices, and finally at the connection between them. The interest rate on a stock is called a *stock yield* and is the dividend on the stock, expressed as a percentage of the price of the stock. The interest rate on a bond is called a *bond yield* and is the coupon payment of the bond, expressed as a percentage of the price of the bond. So to calculate a stock (or bond) yield, we divide the dividend on the stock (or the coupon payment of the bond) by its price. For example, if Taxfile, Inc. pays a dividend of $5 a share and if the price of a share is $50, then the stock yield is 10 percent ($5 divided by $50, expressed as a percent). If Taxfile's dividend is $5 and the stock price is $100, then the stock yield is 5 percent.

These calculations show that for a given dividend, the higher the price of a stock, the lower is its yield. This connection between the price of a stock and its yield or interest rate means that we can study the market forces in capital markets as simultaneously determining interest rates (yields) and stock and bond prices. We will first look at capital market equilibrium in terms of interest rate (or yield) determination and then in terms of the stock market value of a firm.

Equilibrium Interest Rate

Figure 16.5 shows the capital market. The horizontal axis measures the total quantity of capital. Notice that the axis is labeled "Capital stock and wealth." This label emphasizes the fact that the values of the capital stock and wealth are equivalent. The vertical axis measures the interest rate. The demand curve is D, and

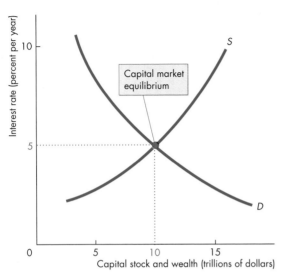

FIGURE 16.5

Capital Market Equilibrium ◆

Capital market equilibrium occurs when the interest rate is such that the quantity of capital demanded equals the quantity of capital supplied. The demand curve is D, and the supply curve is S. These curves intersect at an interest rate of 5 percent a year and a capital stock of $10 trillion.

the supply curve is S. Capital market equilibrium occurs where the quantity of capital supplied equals the quantity of capital demanded. In Fig. 16.5, this equilibrium is at an interest rate of 5 percent a year and $10 trillion of capital is supplied and demanded.

The market forces that bring about this equilibrium are the same as those that we studied in the markets for goods and services. If the interest rate exceeds 5 percent a year, the quantity of financial capital demanded is less than the quantity supplied. There is a surplus of funds in capital markets. In such a situation, as lenders compete to make loans, interest rates fall. The quantity of financial capital demanded increases as firms increase their borrowing and buy more capital goods. The interest rate continues to fall until lenders are able to lend all the funds they wish at that interest rate.

Conversely, if the interest rate is below 5 percent a year, the quantity of financial capital supplied is less than the quantity demanded. There is a shortage of funds in capital markets. Borrowers are unable to borrow all the funds they wish, so they offer a higher inter-

est rate. Interest rates increase until there are no unsatisfied borrowers. In either case, the interest rate converges on 5 percent a year, the equilibrium interest rate.

The institutions that specialize in trading in capital markets—banks, insurance companies, and specialized dealers—handle millions of dollars of business every day and maintain a nearly continuous equality between the quantity of capital demanded and the quantity supplied. These same competitive forces ensure that the interest rate is the same in all the capital markets, both across the nation and around the world.

The interest rate determined in Fig. 16.5 is the *average* interest rate. Interest rates on individual assets will be distributed around this average, based on the relative degree of riskiness of individual assets. An asset with a high degree of risk will earn an interest rate that exceeds the average, and a very safe asset will earn an interest rate that is below the average. The riskier asset earns a higher interest rate to compensate for the higher risk. For example, if the average interest rate is 5 percent a year as shown in Fig. 16.5, the interest rate on a bank deposit (a safer asset) might be 3 percent a year and that on the stock of a corporation (a riskier asset) might be 8 percent a year.

We've now seen how interest rates (yields) are determined. Let's look at the other side of the coin—stock (and bond) prices. To do so, we'll look at the stock market value of a firm.

Stock Market Value of a Firm

What determines the price of a firm's stock? The price of a firm's stock depends on the dividends the firm is expected to pay and on the interest rate. To see why, suppose that Pronto, a printing firm, is expected to pay a dividend of $10 a share in each future year and that the interest rate is 10 percent a year. The price of Pronto's stock will be $100 a share. At this price, Pronto's stock yields a return of 10 percent a year—the interest rate. If Pronto's stock could be bought for less than $100 a share, its expected yield would exceed 10 percent. In this case, people would buy Pronto's stock and its price would rise. If Pronto's stock costs more than $100 a share, its expected yield would be less than 10 percent a year. In this case, people would sell Pronto's stock and its price would fall. Only when Pronto's stock costs $100 a share and its yield is 10 percent—the same as the current interest rate—do people neither buy nor sell the stock. So only when its price is $100 does it remain constant. So if a firm is expected to pay a dividend of $10 a share and if the interest rate is 10 percent a year, the price of the firm's stock will be $100 a share. The stock market value of the firm equals the price of a share multiplied by the number of shares.

The price of a firm's stock increases if the expected dividend increases or if the interest rate falls. For example, if Pronto becomes more profitable and is expected to pay a dividend of $20 a share in each future year and the interest rate remains at 10 percent a year, the price of Pronto's stock will rise to $200 a share. And if Pronto is expected to pay a dividend of $10 a share each future year but the interest rate falls to 5 percent a year, the price of Pronto's stock will also rise to $200 a share.

Price-Earnings Ratio

A commonly used measure to describe the performance of a firm's stock is its price-earnings ratio. A *price-earnings ratio* is the current price of a share in a firm's stock divided by the most recent year's profit per share. In 1982, the average price-earnings ratio of the stocks that formed the Dow Jones Industrial Average was 8.1. By 1987, the price-earnings ratio had risen to 20.5, but that was a peak year. The ratio then declined, and in April 1995, it stood at 16.2.

What determines a price-earnings ratio? Why, in April 1995, was Bank of America's price-earnings ratio only 10 while Boeing's was 21? The higher a firm's *expected future* dividend, the higher is the *current* price of its stock. Expected future dividends depend on the firm's expected future profit. So the bigger the future profit is expected to be, the bigger is the future dividend people expected the firm to pay and the higher is the current price of its stock. Because the firm's price-earnings ratio is the ratio of its current price to its *current* profit, its price-earnings ratio depends on its expected future profit relative to its current profit. When expected future profit is high relative to current profit, the price-earnings ratio is high. Fluctuations in the price-earnings ratio arise from fluctuations in expected future profit relative to current profit.

Stock Market Volume and Prices

Sometimes stock prices rise or fall with little trading taking place. At other times, there is little change in stock prices but an enormous volume of trading. What determines the volume of stock traded?

We've seen that stock prices rise and fall because of changes in expected future dividends and changes in interest rates. Suppose expected future dividends increase and suppose the source of this expectation is so obvious that everyone can see it. Everyone agrees that a firm's profits are going to be higher in the future. In this situation, the price of the firm's stock rises but no one buys or sells shares. Shareholders are happy with the shares they already hold, and the price rises to make the expected yield (new expected dividend divided by new price) equal to the interest rate on other assets. If the price rises further so that the expected yield is less than the interest rate, people will sell the stock and buy other assets. Their actions will lower the price until the expected yield equals the interest rate.

Conversely, suppose that an event occurs that will change this firm's future profit, but it is difficult to forecast how it will change. Some people believe that dividends will increase, and others believe that they will decrease. Call the first group optimists and the second group pessimists. The optimists will buy this firm's stock, and the pessimists will sell it. The price will not necessarily change, but a large volume of shares will be traded. What increases the volume traded is the disagreement, not the event that triggered the change in expected profitability. A large volume of shares traded on the stock market implies a large amount of disagreement.

Large changes in stock prices with small volumes of shares traded imply a great deal of agreement that something fundamental has changed. Large volumes traded with hardly any price change means that the underlying changes are difficult to interpret: Some people predict that profitability will increase while others predict it will decrease.

Takeovers and Mergers

The theory of capital markets that you've now studied can be used to explain why takeovers and mergers occur. A **takeover** is the purchase of the stock of one firm by another firm. A takeover occurs when the stock market value of a firm is less than the present value of the expected future profits from operating the firm. For example, suppose that Taxfile, Inc. has a stock market value of $120,000. If the present value of its expected future profit is $150,000, someone will have an incentive to take over the firm. Takeover activity affects the stock market value of a firm, and often the threat of a takeover drives the stock market value to the point at which the takeover is no longer profitable.

But a takeover does occur if the profitability of the firm being taken over is expected to be larger after the takeover than it was before. One recent example that illustrates this possibility is the takeover of Paramount Pictures by Viacom Corp. Viacom is a large media company that owns, among other things, the Blockbuster retail video chain. It also owns companies that make video games. Viacom believed it could operate Paramount more profitably than Paramount could operate on its own. So Viacom was willing to offer a higher price for Paramount's stock than the current stock market value.

A **merger** is the combining of the assets of two firms to form a single, new firm. Mergers take place when two firms perceive that by combining their assets, they can increase their combined stock market values. For example, when the demand for high technology weapons systems decreased during the 1990s, Martin Marietta Corporation and Lockheed Corporation, two major defense contractors, merged and increased their profitability in the increasingly competitive global market for weapons systems.

R E V I E W

- An interest rate (or yield) is the dividend on a stock (or coupon payment on a bond) expressed as a percentage of the price of the stock (or bond).

- For a given dividend (or coupon payment), as the price of a stock (or bond) increases, its interest rate decreases.

- The average interest rate and stock (or bond) price makes the quantity of capital supplied equal to the quantity demanded.

- The market value of a firm's stock fluctuates because its expected dividend fluctuates. The price-earnings ratio fluctuates because current profit relative to expected future profit changes.

- Takeovers and mergers occur when the current stock market value of the firm is less than the present value of the expected future profits that another firm believes it can generate.

The lessons that we've just learned about capital markets have wider application than explaining fluctuations in the stock market. They also help us to understand how natural resource markets work. Let's now examine these important markets.

Natural Resource Markets

THE NONPRODUCED FACTORS OF PRODUCTION are **natural resources**. Natural resources fall into two categories: exhaustible and nonexhaustible. **Exhaustible natural resources** are natural resources that can be used only once and that cannot be replaced once they have been used. Examples of exhaustible natural resources are coal, natural gas, and oil—the so-called hydrocarbon fuels. **Nonexhaustible natural resources** are natural resources that can be used repeatedly without depleting what's available for future use. Examples of nonexhaustible natural resources are land, seas, rivers and lakes, rain, and sunshine. Plants and animals are also examples of nonexhaustible natural resources. By careful cultivation and husbandry, more of these natural resources can be produced to replace those used up in production and consumption activities.

Natural resources have two economic dimensions: a stock and a flow. Stocks are determined by nature and by the previous rate of use of resources and flows—rates of use—are determined by human choices. We first consider the stock dimension.

Supply and Demand in a Natural Resource Market

The stock of a natural resource supplied is the amount of the resource in existence. For example, the stock of oil supplied is the total volume of oil lying beneath the earth's surface. This amount is fixed independently of the price of the resource. Its supply is perfectly inelastic.

The actual stock supplied is not the same as the known (or proven) quantity. The known quantity of a natural resource is smaller than the actual quantity supplied, and the known quantity can increase even if the resource is being used up. The known quantity increases for two reasons. First, advances in technology enable ever less accessible resources to be discovered. Second, as the price of a natural resource rises, other things remaining the same, the incentive to widen the search for additional reserves is strengthened. Both of these factors operated to double the known reserves of oil between 1970 and 1995—see *Reading Between the Lines*, pp. 394–395. During this same period, the quantity of oil consumed exceeded the 1970 known reserves.

Demand for a Stock   The stock of a natural resource demanded is determined by the *expected* rate of return or expected interest rate from holding that stock of the natural resource. The reason is that firms buy stocks of natural resources as an alternative to buying stocks, bonds, or physical capital, and they do so in the expectation of making a return.

What determines the expected interest rate on the stock of a natural resource? The answer is the rate of economic profit available from extracting and selling the stock, plus the rate at which the price of the resource is expected to rise. If the market for the extracted resource is competitive, firms will make only a normal profit on their extraction activity, so the return from holding a natural resource comes from increases in the price of the resource. The faster the price of a natural resource increases, the higher is the return from owning that natural resource. Because firms don't know the future, they must forecast this interest rate and the forecasted or *expected* interest rate is equal to the *expected* percentage increase in the price of the resource.

Stock Equilibrium   Equilibrium occurs in the market for the stock of a natural resource when the price of the resource is *expected* to rise at a rate equal to the interest rate on similarly risky stocks and bonds. This proposition is called the **Hotelling Principle**.[1]

Why is the price of a natural resource expected to grow at a rate equal to the interest rate on similarly risky assets? It is to make the expected interest rate on the natural resource equal to the interest rate on other comparably risky stocks and bonds. Firms look for the highest returns they can find, holding risk constant. So if the expected interest rate on a stock of a natural resource exceeds that on stocks or bonds with similar risk, firms buy natural resources and sell stocks and bonds. Conversely, if the expected interest rate on a natural resource is less than that on stocks or bonds with similar risk, firms buy stocks and bonds and sell natural resources. Equilibrium occurs in the market for the stock of a natural resource when prices and expected future prices have adjusted to make the *expected* interest rate earned on the natural resource equal to the interest rate on similarly risky stocks and bonds.

[1]The Hotelling Principle, discovered by Harold Hotelling, first appeared in "Economics of Exhaustible Resources," *Journal of Political Economy* 39 (April 1931): 137–175.

Supply and demand in the market for the stock of a natural resource determine the interest rate from owning that stock, which means that they determine the future *expected rate of change* of the price. But what determines the *current price* of the resource? To determine the *current* price of a natural resource, we must consider not only the supply of and demand for the stock of the resource but also the demand for its use.

Price of a Natural Resource

To determine the price of a natural resource, we must consider the influences on the demand for the use of the natural resource. Then we will study the equilibrium that emerges from the interaction of the demand for the use of the resource—the demand for a *flow*—with the demand to own the natural resource—the demand for a *stock*.

Demand for the Use of a Natural Resource
Figure 16.6(a) shows the demand curve, *D*, for the flow of a natural resource for use in production. This demand curve is determined in a similar way to that for the services of any other factor of production. A firm in a perfectly competitive market maximizes profit by using the quantity of a natural resource that makes the marginal revenue product of the resource equal to its price. Marginal revenue product diminishes as the quantity of the resource used increases, so the lower the price of a resource, the greater is the quantity demanded for use in production.

For any resource, there is a price that is so high that no one uses the resource. The price at which no one uses a natural resource is called the **choke price**. It is the price at which the demand curve touches the price axis. In Fig. 16.6(a), the choke price is $144 a ton. Everything has substitutes, and at a high enough price—the choke price—only a substitute will be used. For example, we do not have to put soft drinks in aluminum cans; we can use plastic bottles instead. We do not have to power cars with gasoline; we can use alcohol, electricity, or natural gas instead. We do not have to generate electric power with coal, oil, or uranium; we can use solar or tidal energy instead. The natural resources that we *do* use are the least expensive resources available at the time they are used. They cost us less than the next best alternative would. For example, if the price of plastic is such as to make the price of plastic bottles more

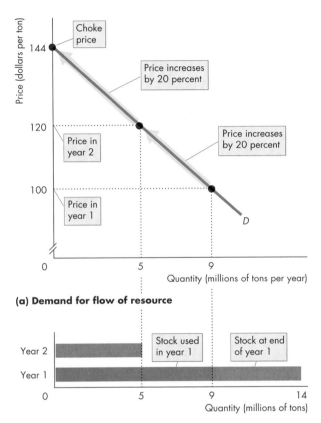

FIGURE 16.6

The Market for an Exhaustible Natural Resource

(a) Demand for flow of resource

(b) Stock available at start of each year

In part (a), at a price below $144 at ton—the *choke price*—the quantity demanded is positive and the lower the price, the larger is the quantity demanded. In part (b), the stock of the resource at the start of year 1 is 14 million tons. If the interest rate is 20 percent a year, the current price is $100 a ton. Starting from $100 a ton, the price rises by 20 percent a year to reach the choke price in two years. The demand curve (*D*) tells us that the quantity demanded (used) in the first year is 9 million tons and the quantity used in the second year is 5 million tons, so the stock of 14 million tons is exhausted after two years.

expensive than aluminum cans, soft drink producers will use aluminum cans. But as the price of aluminum increases, soft drink producers will substitute plastic bottles for aluminum cans.

Equilibrium Stock and Flow

The price of a natural resource and its rate of use depend on three things:

1. The interest rate
2. The demand for the flow of the resource
3. The stock of the resource

Figure 16.6 shows how these three factors combine to determine the price and rate of use of a natural resource. Let's start at the time the resource becomes depleted and work backwards. When the resource is depleted, the quantity supplied is zero, so the quantity demanded must also be zero. The price that makes the quantity demanded zero is the choke price. So at the end of the life of a resource, its price equals the choke price. In Fig. 16.6(a), the choke price is $144 a ton.

With a given stock of the resource, its price must be expected to rise at a rate equal to the interest rate. Given this fact, the price in the year before the resource is depleted must be less than the choke price by a percentage amount determined by the interest rate. In Fig. 16.6(a), the interest rate is 20 percent a year, so the price in the year before depletion is $120 a ton. A 20 percent price rise takes the price to the choke price of $144 a ton the following year. We now repeat this type of calculation. The price two years before depletion is yet lower and in the example is $100 a ton. A 20 percent increase takes the price to $120 a ton in the following year and to $144 a ton in two years.

We repeat this calculation for as many years as necessary until the accumulated amount of the resource used up, which is determined by the demand for the flow of the resource and the sequence of prices we've calculated, just exhausts the current stock of the resource. In Fig. 16.6, the stock is exhausted in only two years. (This short life lets you see the principles more clearly.) To see that the stock is depleted after two years, notice in part (b) of the figure that the stock at the start of year 1 is 14 million tons. In year 1, the price is $100 a ton and part (a) shows that the quantity used is 9 million tons. The blue bar in part (b) shows the stock used in year 1. In year 2, the price rises to $120 a ton and the quantity used is 5 million tons. The total quantity used, 9 million tons plus 5 million tons, exhausts the 14 million tons available at the start of year 1. The price of this natural resource starts at $100 a ton in year 1 and rises by 20 percent a year for two years until it reaches its choke price of $144 a ton, at which time the natural resource is depleted. That is, the current price of the natural resource and the rate at which it is used is determined by the interest rate, the demand for the flow of the resource and the current stock available.

The higher the interest rate, the lower is the current price of a natural resource. You can see this fact by recalling that the price must end up at the choke price. At a higher interest rate the price must rise more quickly and end up at the same price (as determined by the demand for the flow), so its current price must be lower. But a lower current price means that the resource will be used up at a faster rate.

The greater the marginal revenue product of the natural resource—the larger the demand for the flow of the natural resource—the higher is the current price of the resource. A greater marginal revenue product means that the demand curve for the resource lies farther to the right and that the choke price is higher. The higher current price decreases the quantity of the resource used to ensure that the current stock equals the quantities demanded over the remaining years of the life of the resource.

The larger the initial stock of the natural resource, the lower is the current price. The larger the known stock, the bigger is the quantity that must be used up before the choke price is reached. To induce an increase in the quantity used, the current price of the resource must be lower.

Expected Prices and Actual Prices

Equilibrium in the market for a natural resource determines the current price of the resource and the *expected* rate of change of its future price. But the actual price rarely follows its expected path. For example, *Reading Between the Lines* on pp. 394–395 shows (in Fig. 1) the path of the price of oil between 1970 and 1994. This price did not follow the path predicted by the Hotelling Principle. Also, the prices of metals have tended to fall, as Fig. 16.7 shows. This fact was the basis of a famous wager between a conservationist and an economist—see *Economics in History* on p. 354–355. Why do natural resource prices fluctuate and sometimes even fall rather than follow their expected path and increase over time?

The price of a natural resource depends on expectations about future events. In particular, it depends on expectations about the interest rate, the future demand for the use of the resource, and the

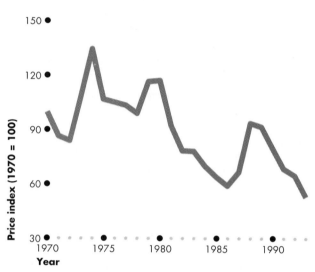

FIGURE 16.7

Falling Resource Prices

The prices of metals (here an average of the prices of aluminum, copper, iron ore, lead, manganese, nickel, silver, tin, and zinc) have tended to fall over time, not rise as predicted by the Hotelling Principle. The reason is that advances in technology have decreased the cost of extracting resources and greatly increased the exploitable known reserves.

Source: International Financial Statistics, International Monetary Fund, Washington, D.C. (various issues).

size of the known stock, which in turn depends on the technologies and costs of extracting it. Natural resource markets are constantly being bombarded by new information that leads to new expectations. For example, new information about the stock of a resource or the technologies available for its use or extraction can lead to sudden and perhaps quite large changes in the price of a natural resource.

All of these forces have been at work in many of the markets for exhaustible natural resources in recent years. The market for oil illustrates these effects very well. The discovery of new sources of supply and of new extraction technologies has resulted in previously unforeseen increases in the known stock of oil. The development of energy-efficient automobile and airplane engines has slowed the growth in the quantity of oil used for transportation to below what was expected in the early 1970s. The combination of these factors has led to a fall in the price of oil. And changes in interest rates—up and down—have brought fluctuations in the price of oil.

An additional force leading to price changes in natural resource markets in general and in the oil market in particular is the degree of competitiveness in the markets. The model market that we have been studying is a perfectly competitive one. But the real-world market for oil was until recently dominated by the OPEC cartel, an oligopoly similar to that analyzed in Chapter 13 (pp. 306–308). The declining power of the OPEC cartel contributed significantly to the decline in the price of oil during the 1980s.

Conservation and Doomsday

The theory of the price of a natural resource and its expected change over time has important implications for the popular debate about the use of natural resources. Many people fear that we are using the earth's exhaustible natural resources at such a rapid pace that we will eventually (and perhaps in the not very distant future) run out of sources of energy and other crucial raw materials. Such people urge a slowing down in the rate at which we use exhaustible natural resources so that the limited stocks available today will last longer.

This topic is an emotional one and generates passionate debate. It is also a matter that involves economic issues that can be understood by using the economic model of a depletable natural resource that you have just studied.

The economic analysis of an exhaustible natural resource market predicts that doomsday—the using up of the entire stock of a natural resource—will eventually arise if our use of natural resources is organized in competitive markets. The economic model also implies that a competitive market will provide an automatic conservation program arising from the steadily rising price. As the stock of a natural resource gets closer and closer to depletion, its price gets closer to the choke price—the price at which no one wants to use the resource any more. Each year, as the price rises, the quantity demanded of the flow declines.

But what if the resource gets completely used up? Don't we have a real problem then? We have the problem of scarcity but in no more acute a form than we had it before. Everything has substitutes. The resource that is no longer available was used because it was more efficient to use it than some alternative. For example, it is more efficient to generate electricity today by using coal and oil rather than solar power. It

is efficient to stop using an exhaustible resource only when a lower-cost alternative is available. This substitution might occur before the resource is depleted or at the same time as it becomes depleted. So the market economy handles the depleting stocks of natural resources by persistently forcing their prices up. Higher prices cause us to ration our use and eventually drive the quantity demanded of the flow to zero. This happens when the supply of the stock disappears.

But will a competitive market lead us to use our scarce exhaustible natural resources at an efficient rate? Perfectly competitive markets for goods and services achieve allocative efficiency if there are no external costs and benefits. (The allocative efficiency of a perfectly competitive market is explained in Chapter 11, pp. 262–263.) The same proposition applies to markets for natural resources. If there are no external costs or benefits arising from the use of a natural resource, then the rate of its use determined in a perfectly competitive exhaustible natural resource market is the efficient rate of use. But if external costs arise from the use of a natural resource, efficiency requires a slower rate of use of the resource than that in the competitive market. For example, if burning hydrocarbon fuels increases the carbon dioxide in the atmosphere and a warming of the earth's atmosphere results—the so-called greenhouse effect—the costs associated with this atmospheric change have to be added to the costs of using oil and coal as fuels. When these costs are taken into account, the allocatively efficient rate of use of these fuels is slower than that resulting from a perfectly competitive market. We examine ways in which government intervention can achieve allocative efficiency in such a situation in Chapter 20 (pp. 497–502).

◆ We have now studied the way in which factor markets allocate scarce productive resources—labor, capital, and land—and the determination of factor prices and factor incomes. The prices and quantities determined in factor markets in turn determine the distribution of income among individuals and families. And that income distribution determines *for whom* goods and services are produced. But that outcome is uncertain. People decide what type of work to do, how much to save, and what to do with their saving with no sure knowledge of the incomes they'll receive from their decisions. In the next chapter, we study uncertainty and its consequences in a more systematic way, and we discover some of the ways in which we cope with uncertainty.

Expanding the Sources of Oil

THE NEW YORK TIMES APRIL 24, 1994

2,860 Feet Under the Sea, a Record-Breaking Well

By AGIS SALPUKAS

GARDEN BANKS, Gulf of Mexico— During most of the hour-and-a-half helicopter ride out to Shell Oil's Auger offshore drilling platform, one can see rigs and platforms dotting the deep blue water below. Then, for 30 miles, there is nothing but water and sky. Finally the eye glimpses the four yellow hull towers of the 39,000-ton Auger platform and, gradually, the outlines of pipes, rigging, valves and living quarters rising 419 feet above the water.

Here, in pristine isolation, the Shell Oil Company nine days ago opened a well in water far deeper than humankind had ever ventured in search of petroleum wealth. Shell hopes the platform and its 14 wells will be producing 46,000 barrels of oil and 125 million cubic feet of natural gas a day by year's end.

If Shell's technology succeeds, the significance will run far deeper than the company's bottom line. The success of the Auger platform, 136 miles off the Louisiana shore, could open whole new regions of the Gulf of Mexico to offshore drilling, revitalizing the gulf oil industry and possibly giving the United States its largest oil-field since the development of Alaska's Prudhoe Bay in the 1960's.

But with oil selling for $17 a barrel or less these days, and with no previous experience in pumping oil from such underwater depths, Shell has no guarantee that it can make the $1.2 billion Auger platform pay off.

"The real question," said Phillip J. Carroll, Shell's president and chief executive, "is not whether the development can be done, but whether it can be done profitably."

Eight miles past the continental shelf, where the gulf's floor falls off sharply and beyond which offshore drilling has never before been attempted, the Auger platform floats tethered to an anchorage 2,860 feet—more than a half-mile—below. ...

Mr. Carroll said his company and others in the oil industry, through the use of seismic readings, have found evidence of petroleum in about 30 deep-water locations in the gulf. The combined reserves from those deposits alone have been estimated at between 3 and 4 billion barrels. "This is with only about 15 percent of the leased acreage having been explored," he said, venturing that deep-water fields in the gulf potentially hold 15 billion barrels—which would be even more than Prudhoe Bay. ...

Essence of THE STORY

■ In April 1994, the Shell Oil Company opened its Auger platform, a $1.2 billion, 39,000-ton offshore drilling platform, in water 2,860 feet deep, 136 miles off the Louisiana coast.

■ Shell planned to be producing 46,000 barrels of oil and 125 million cubic feet of natural gas a day by the end of 1994.

■ If it succeeds, the new technology could allow access to 15 billion barrels of oil reserves in the Gulf of Mexico, making the gulf a larger oil-field than Prudhoe Bay in Alaska.

■ In 1994, oil was selling for about $17 a barrel. At this price, and with no previous experience in pumping oil from such underwater depths, Shell was not sure it could make the Auger platform pay.

Economic

A N A L Y S I S

■ In Fig. 1, the green curve shows the path that the price of oil would have followed after 1970 according to the Hotelling Principle in the absence of any unanticipated changes in the demand for oil, the quantity and accessibility of oil reserves, and the degree of competition in the world market for oil. The price would have increased at the real interest rate, slightly more than 5 percent per year.

■ Figure 1 also shows the actual path of the price of oil since 1970 (the purple curve). To remove the effects of inflation, the actual price and the Hotelling price are shown in 1994 dollars (see Chapter 4, pp. 68–69).

■ The price of oil jumped in 1974 and 1979 because the world oil market became more monopolistic. These price increases occurred because the Organization of Petroleum Exporting Countries (OPEC) cartel limited production and decreased the world supply of oil.

■ The price of oil fell from 1981 through 1986 because at the high prices prevailing, new reserves were discovered and profitably accessed.

■ Also, advances in technology have led to the discovery of ever more oil reserves and have lowered the cost of extracting oil. The latest event in the ongoing process of change is the Auger offshore platform, which can access oil at ocean depths of half a mile.

■ Figure 2 shows how the cost of accessing oil reserves has changed. The quantity of world reserves of oil is shown on the x-axis, and the cost of accessing those reserves is shown on the y-axis.

■ In 1970, the marginal cost curve was MC_{70}. The curve becomes vertical at the quantity of proven reserves.

■ Technological advances have increased the quantity of proven reserves and have lowered the cost of extracting oil. The marginal cost curve has shifted rightward to MC_{94}.

■ If the price of oil is $17 a barrel, as it was in 1994, reserves up to the quantity Q_{94} can be profitably extracted. Shell Oil Company is not sure that the Auger can operate at a cost below $17 a barrel.

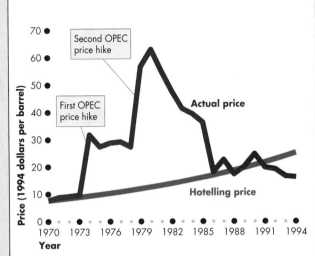

Figure 1

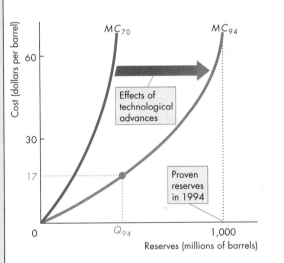

Figure 2

■ The $1.2 billion that Shell has spent building the Auger is sunk cost (not a pun—see Chapter 9, p. 201). Shell will operate the Auger as long as the *variable* cost of the oil it can pump does not exceed the price of oil.

■ But Shell and other oil companies such as Exxon and Conoco that also operate in the Gulf of Mexico will sink new wells in deep water only if they expect to cover the *total* cost (including normal profit) of the operation.

SUMMARY

The Structure of Capital Markets

Capital markets channel financial capital from households' saving to firms. Firms use the financial resources they obtain in capital markets to buy physical capital. Capital markets determine interest rates, which coordinate the saving plans of households and the investment plans of firms.

Financial intermediaries are key players in financial markets. They take deposits, make loans, and make markets for stocks, bonds, and loans work smoothly. The stocks of corporations are traded in stock markets such as the New York Stock Exchange. The bonds of corporations and governments are traded in bond markets. Loans are made in loan markets in which financial intermediaries play the main role. (pp. 379–380)

The Demand for Capital

Capital is a *stock*, and *investment* and *depreciation* are flows. Gross investment is the purchase of new capital during a given period that adds to the capital stock, and depreciation is the amount of existing capital that wears out in a given period.

The demand for capital is determined by firms' profit-maximization decisions. The quantity of capital demanded by a firm is such that the marginal revenue product of capital equals its factor cost—the interest rate. Other things remaining the same, the lower the interest rate, the greater is the present value of the future flow of marginal revenue product and the greater is the quantity of capital equipment a firm buys. The demand curve for capital is downward sloping.

The demand for capital changes when firms revise their expectations of the marginal revenue product of capital, the main influences on which are population growth and technological change. The demand curve for capital shifts steadily rightward as a result of population growth but technological change creates variability in the pace at which the demand for capital increases. (pp. 380–384)

The Supply of Capital

The quantity of capital supplied results from the saving decisions of households. Saving depends on current income and expected future income and on the extent to which households smooth their consumption over their lifetime. Saving also depends on the interest rate. Other things remaining the same, as interest rates rise, the quantity of capital supplied increases—the supply curve of capital is upward-sloping. Changes in the size and the age composition of the population and changes in income and its distribution change the supply of capital and shift the supply curve of capital over time. (pp. 384–386)

Interest Rates and Stock Prices

Interest rates and stock (or bond) prices can be viewed as two sides of the same coin. Interest rates and stock (or bond) prices adjust to achieve equality between the quantity of capital demanded and the quantity supplied. Interest rates on particular assets are distributed around the average rate according to the degree of riskiness of different types of assets. The price of a firm's stock may be high or low, relative to its current profit and is indicated by the price-earnings ratio. When people are in agreement about expected future dividends, there is little trading in a firm's stock, but when there is disagreement about the future, trading is heavy. If a firm's stock market value is low, relative to its earnings potential, the firm becomes a takeover target. (pp. 386–389)

Natural Resource Markets

Natural resources are the nonproduced factors of production. The price of a natural resource is determined by the interest rate, the marginal revenue product of the natural resource (which determines the demand for its flow), and the stock of the natural resource (which determines the supply). The price of a natural resource is such that its future price is expected to rise at a rate equal to the interest rate and to reach the choke price at the time at which the resource is exhausted. The actual price is constantly changing to take into account new information. Even though the future price is expected to increase, the actual price often decreases as a result of new information, leading to an increase in the estimate of the remaining stock or to a decrease in the demand for the flow of the resource. (pp. 389–393)

K E Y   E L E M E N T S

Key Figures

Key Terms

R E V I E W   Q U E S T I O N S

1. Briefly describe the structure of the capital markets.

2. Distinguish between financial capital and physical capital.

3. Give some examples of financial intermediaries and describe the role they play in capital markets.

4. Describe the main flows of funds in the capital markets.

5. Distinguish among the stock market, bond market, and loan market.

6. What is the net present value of an investment?

7. What are the main influences on the demand for capital?

8. Why does the quantity of capital demanded by a firm increase as the interest rate decreases?

9. What are the main factors that change the demand for capital and how do they change the demand curve for capital?

10. What are the influences of the interest rate on the amount of saving and the supply of capital?

11. How does the age structure of the population influence the supply of capital?

12. What is the relationship between the interest rate and the price of a stock or bond?

13. How is the interest rate determined?

14. How are stock prices and bond prices determined?

15. Distinguish between a takeover and a merger. Explain why takeovers and mergers occur.

16. What is an exhaustible resource? Give some examples.

17. Distinguish between the stock and the flow of an exhaustible natural resource.

18. Explain what determines the demand for and supply of a stock of an exhaustible natural resource.

19. Explain what determines the demand for a flow of an exhaustible natural resource.

20. Explain why the price of an exhaustible natural resource is expected to rise at a rate equal to the interest rate.

21. What determines the price of a natural resource?

22. Why do the prices of some natural resources fall over time?

P R O B L E M S

1. At the end of 1994, a firm had a production plant worth $1,000,000. The plant depreciated during 1995 by 10 percent. During the same year, the firm also bought new capital equipment for $250,000. What is the value of the firm's stock of capital at the end of 1995? What was the firm's gross investment during 1995? What was the firm's net investment during 1995?

2. After paying your taxes, you earn $20,000 per year for three years, and you spend $16,000 each year. How much do you save each year? If the interest rate is 5 percent a year, what happens to your wealth during this three-year period?

3. What are the different ways in which household saving can finance a firm's investment?

4. A firm is considering buying a new machine. It is estimated that the marginal revenue product of the machine will be $10,000 a year for five years. The machine will have no value at the end of five years. The interest rate is 10 percent a year.

   a. What is the maximum price that the firm will pay for the machine?
   b. If the machine costs $40,000, would the firm buy the machine at an interest rate of 10 percent? What is the highest interest rate at which the firm would buy the machine?

5. Suppose that exploration in China reveals a vast stock of natural gas that was previously undreamed of and that exceeds all the currently known stocks in China. What do you predict will happen to the world price of natural gas:

   a. At the moment the news of the discovery breaks?
   b. Over the following ten years?
   c. What will happen to the rate of use of natural gas?

6. If the government increases the tax on oil and makes it more costly for people to use oil, what do you predict will happen to:

   a. The price of oil at the moment the tax is imposed?
   b. The price of oil over the following ten years?
   c. The rate of use of oil?

7. You've been hired by Greenpeace to make the economic case for conserving the world's stock of copper. Set out your best case and anticipate the arguments that an economist opposing you would make.

8. Doomsday is close for zapton, an exhaustible natural resource, the remaining stock of which is 6 million tons. The marginal revenue product schedule for zapton is:

Quantity used (millions of tons)	Marginal revenue product (dollars per ton)
0	16.11
1	14.64
2	13.31
3	12.10
4	11.00
5	10.00

The interest rate is 10 percent a year.

   a. What is the choke price of zapton?
   b. What is the current price of zapton?
   c. If there is no change in the marginal revenue product schedule for zapton, after how many years is its stock exhausted?

9. In problem 8, a new use is discovered for zapton that increases its marginal revenue product. Does the:

   a. Choke price of zapton rise, fall, or remain unchanged?
   b. Current price of zapton rise, fall, or remain unchanged?
   c. Number of years to zapton's exhaustion increase, decrease, or remain unchanged?

10. Study the three graphs that show the prices of coal, iron ore, and lead (prices are in 1987 dollars to remove the effects of inflation).

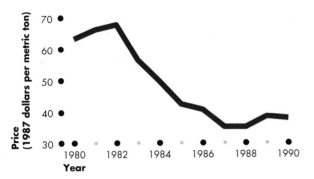

(a) Coal

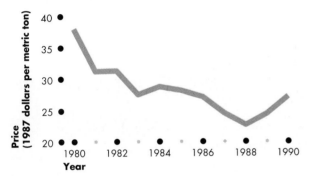

(b) Iron ore

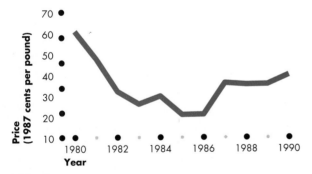

(c) Lead

How can you explain the trends in these prices using the theory of exhaustible resource markets that you've studied in this chapter?

11. Study *Reading Between the Lines* on pp. 394–395 and use the theory of the price of an exhaustible natural resource to predict the effects of advances in oil finding and extracting technology on:
    a. The price of oil
    b. The rate at which the price of oil is *expected* to change
    c. The choke price of oil

Uncertainty and Information

After studying
this chapter,
you will be
able to:

■ Explain how people make decisions when
they are uncertain about the consequences

■ Explain why people buy insurance and
how insurance companies make a profit

■ Explain why buyers search and sellers
advertise

■ Explain how markets cope with private
information

■ Explain how people use financial markets
to lower risk

Life is like a lottery. You work hard in school, but what will the payoff be? Will you get an interesting, high-paying job or a miserable, low-paying one? You set up a small summer business and work hard at it. But will you make enough income to keep you in school next year or will you get wiped out? How do people make a decision when they don't know its consequences? ◆ As you drive across an intersection on a green light, you see a car on

Lotteries and Lemons

your left that's still moving. Will it stop or will it run the red light? You buy insurance against such a risk, and insurance companies gain from your business. Why are we willing to buy insurance at prices that leave insurance companies with a gain? ◆ Buying a new car—or a used car—is fun, but it's also scary. You could get stuck with a lemon. And cars are not unique. Just about every complicated product you buy could be defective. How do car dealers and retailers induce us to buy what may turn out to be a lemon? ◆ People keep some of their wealth in the bank, some in mutual funds, some in bonds, and some in stocks. Some of these ways of holding wealth have a high return, and some have a low return. Why don't people put all their wealth in the place that has the highest return? Why does it pay to diversify?

◇ In this chapter, we answer questions such as these. In doing so, we will extend and enrich the more abstract models of markets that we studied in earlier chapters. We'll begin by explaining how people make decisions when they're uncertain about the consequences. We'll see how it pays to buy insurance, even if its price leaves the insurance company with a profit. We'll explain why we use scarce resources to generate and disseminate information. And we'll look at transactions in a wide variety of markets in which uncertainty and the cost of acquiring information play important roles.

Uncertainty and Risk

ALTHOUGH WE LIVE IN AN UNCERTAIN WORLD, we rarely ask what uncertainty is. Yet to explain how we make decisions and do business with each other in an uncertain world, we need to think more deeply about uncertainty. What exactly is uncertainty? We also live in a risky world. Is risk the same as uncertainty? Let's begin by defining uncertainty and risk and distinguishing between them.

Uncertainty is a situation in which more than one event may occur but we don't know which one. For example, when farmers plant their crops, they are uncertain about the weather during the growing season.

In ordinary speech, risk is the probability of incurring a loss (or some other misfortune). In economics, **risk** is a situation in which more than one outcome may occur and the *probability* of each possible outcome can be estimated. A *probability* is a number between zero and one that measures the chance of some possible event occurring. A zero probability means the event will not happen. A probability of one means the event will occur for sure—with certainty. A probability of 0.5 means that the event is just as likely to occur as not. An example is the probability of a tossed coin falling heads. In a large number of tosses, about half of them will be heads and the other half tails.

Sometimes, probabilities can be measured. For example, the probability that a tossed coin will come down heads is based on the fact that, in a large number of tosses, half are heads and half are tails; the probability that an automobile in Chicago in 1996 will be involved in an accident can be estimated by using police and insurance records of previous accidents; the probability that you will win a lottery can be estimated by dividing the number of tickets you have bought by the total number of tickets bought.

Some situations cannot be described by using probabilities based on past observed events. These situations may be unique events, such as the introduction of a new product. How much will sell and at what price? Because the product is new, there is no previous experience on which to base a probability. But the questions can be answered by looking at past experience with *similar* new products, supported by some judgments. Such judgments are called *subjective probabilities*.

Regardless of whether the probability of some event occurring is based on actual data or judg-ments—or even guesses—we can use probability to study the way in which people make decisions in the face of uncertainty. The first step in doing this is to describe how people assess the cost of risk.

Measuring the Cost of Risk

Some people are more willing to bear risk than others, but almost everyone prefers less risk to more, other things remaining the same. We measure people's attitudes toward risk by using their utility of wealth schedules and curves. The **utility of wealth** is the amount of utility a person attaches to a given amount of wealth. The greater a person's wealth, other things remaining the same, the higher is the person's total utility. Greater wealth brings higher total utility, but as wealth increases, each additional unit of wealth increases total utility by a smaller amount. That is, the *marginal utility of wealth diminishes*.

Figure 17.1 sets out Tania's utility of wealth schedule and curve. Each point *a* through *e* on Tania's utility of wealth curve corresponds to the row of the table identified by the same letter. You can see that as her wealth increases, so does her total utility of wealth. You can also see that her marginal utility of wealth diminishes. When wealth increases from $3,000 to $6,000, total utility increases by 20 units, but when wealth increases by a further $3,000 to $9,000, total utility increases by only 10 units.

We can use Tania's utility of wealth curve to measure her cost of risk. Let's see how Tonia evaluates two summer jobs that involve different amounts of risk.

One job, working as a painter, pays enough for her to save $5,000 by the end of the summer. There is no uncertainty about the income from this job and hence no risk. If Tania takes this job, by the end of the summer her wealth will be $5,000. The other job, working as a telemarketer selling subscriptions to a magazine, is risky. If she takes this job, her wealth at the end of the summer depends entirely on her success at selling. She might be a good salesperson or a poor one. A good salesperson makes $9,000 in a summer, and a poor one makes $3,000. Tania has never tried telemarketing, so she doesn't know how successful she'll be. She assumes she has an equal chance—a probability of 0.5—of making either $3,000 or $9,000. Which outcome does Tania prefer, $5,000 for sure from the painting job or a 50 percent chance of either $3,000 or $9,000 from the telemarketing job?

FIGURE 17.1
The Utility of Wealth

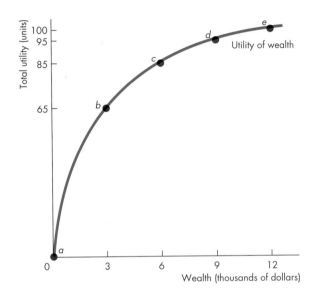

	Wealth (thousands of dollars)	Total utility (units)	Marginal utility (units)
a	0	0	
			65
b	3	65	
			20
c	6	85	
			10
d	9	95	
			5
e	12	100	

The table shows Tania's utility of wealth schedule, and the figure shows her utility of wealth curve. Utility increases as wealth increases, but the marginal utility of wealth diminishes.

FIGURE 17.2
Choice under Uncertainty

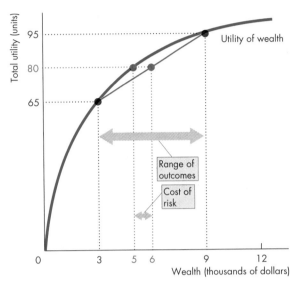

If Tania's wealth is $5,000 and she faces no risk, her utility is 80 units. If she faces an equal probability of having $9,000 with a utility of 95 or $3,000 with a utility of 65, her expected wealth is $6,000. But her expected utility is 80 units—the same as with $5,000 and no uncertainty. Tania is indifferent between these two alternatives. Tania's extra $1,000 of expected wealth is just enough to offset her extra risk.

When there is uncertainty, people do not know the *actual* utility they will get from taking a particular action. But it is possible to calculate the utility they *expect* to get. **Expected utility** is the average utility arising from all possible outcomes. So, to choose her summer job, Tania calculates the expected utility from each job. Figure 17.2 shows how she does this.

If Tania takes the painting job, she has $5,000 of wealth and 80 units of utility. There is no uncertain-

ty, so her expected utility equals her actual utility—80 units. But suppose she takes the telemarketing job. If she makes $9,000, her utility is 95 units, and if she makes $3,000, her utility is 65 units. Tania's *expected income* is the average of these two outcomes and is $6,000—($9,000 × 0.5) + ($3,000 × 0.5). This average is called a *weighted average*, the weights being the probabilities of each outcome (both 0.5 in this case). Tania's *expected utility* is the average of these two possible total utilities and is 80 units—(95 × 0.5) + (65 × 0.5).

Tania chooses the job that maximizes her expected utility. In this case, the two alternatives give the same expected utility—80 units—so she is indifferent between them. She is equally likely to take either job. The difference between Tania's expected wealth of $6,000 from the risky job and $5,000 from the no-risk job—$1,000—is just large enough to offset the additional risk that Tania faces.

The calculations that we've just done enable us to measure Tania's cost of risk. The cost of risk is the amount by which expected wealth must be increased to give the same expected utility as a no-risk situation. In Tania's case, the cost of the risk arising from an uncertain income of $3,000 or $9,000 is $1,000.

If the amount Tania can make from painting remains at $5,000 and the expected income from telemarketing also remains constant while its range of uncertainty increases, Tania will take the painting job. To see this conclusion, suppose that good telemarketers make $12,000 and poor ones make nothing. The average income from telemarketing is unchanged at $6,000, but the range of uncertainty has increased. The table in Fig. 17.1 shows that Tania gets 100 units of utility from a wealth of $12,000 and zero units of utility from a wealth of zero. Thus in this case, Tania's expected utility from telemarketing is 50 units—$(100 \times 0.5) + (0 \times 0.5)$. Because the expected utility from telemarketing is now less than that from painting, she chooses painting.

Risk Aversion and Risk Neutrality

There is an enormous difference between Bill Parcells, coach of the New England Patriots, who favors a cautious running game and Jim Kelly, quarterback of the Buffalo Bills, who favors a risky passing game. They have different attitudes toward risk. Bill is more *risk averse* than is Jim. Tania is also *risk averse*; other things remaining the same, she prefers less risk. The shape of the utility of wealth curve tells us about the attitude toward risk—about the person's degree of *risk aversion*. The more rapidly a person's marginal utility of wealth diminishes, the more risk-averse that person is. You can see this fact best by considering the case of *risk neutrality*. A risk-neutral person is one for whom risk is costless. Such a person cares only about *expected wealth* and does not mind how much uncertainty there is.

Figure 17.3 shows the utility of wealth curve of a risk-neutral person. It is a straight line and the marginal utility of wealth is constant. If this person has an expected wealth of $6,000, expected utility is 50 units regardless of the range of uncertainty around that average. An equal probability of having $3,000 or $9,000 gives the same expected utility as an equal probability of having $0 or $12,000, which is also the expected utility of a certain $6,000. Real people are risk averse, and their utility of wealth curves look

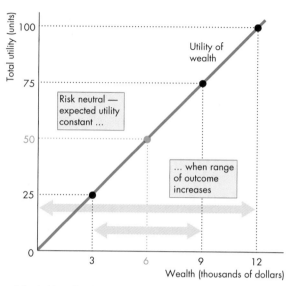

FIGURE 17.3
Risk Neutrality

People's dislike of risk implies a diminishing marginal utility of wealth. A (hypothetical) risk-neutral person has a linear utility of wealth curve and a constant marginal utility of wealth. For a risk-neutral person, expected utility does not depend on the range of uncertainty, and the cost of risk is zero.

like Tania's. But the case of risk neutrality illustrates the importance and the consequences of the shape of the utility of wealth curve for a person's degree of risk aversion.

REVIEW

- Faced with uncertain outcomes, people take the actions that maximize expected utility.
- The cost of risk can be measured as the amount by which expected wealth must be increased to give the same expected utility as in a no-risk situation.
- The cost of risk depends on the degree of *risk aversion*. The greater the degree of risk aversion, the greater is the cost of risk.
- For a *risk-neutral* person, risk is costless.

Most people are risk averse. Let's now see how insurance enables them to reduce the risk they face.

Insurance

ONE WAY OF REDUCING THE RISK WE FACE IS TO buy insurance. How does insurance reduce risk? Why do people buy insurance? And what determines the amount we spend on insurance? Before we answer these questions, let's look at the insurance industry in the United States today.

Insurance Industry in the United States

We spend close to 15 percent of our income, on the average, on private insurance. That's as much as we spend on housing and more than we spend on cars and food. In addition, we buy insurance through our taxes in the form of social security and unemployment insurance. When we buy private insurance, we enter into an agreement with an insurance company to pay an agreed price—called a *premium*—in exchange for benefits to be paid to us if some specified event occurs. The three main types of insurance we buy are:

- Life insurance
- Health insurance
- Property and casualty insurance

Life Insurance   Life insurance reduces the risk of financial loss in the event of death. More than 80 percent of households in the United States have life insurance, and the average amount of coverage is $110,000 per household. More than 2,400 companies supply life insurance, and the total premiums paid in a year are more than $400 billion. As you can see in Fig. 17.4, life insurance has been the greatest source of the insurance industry's business in recent years and has generated most of its profit.

Health Insurance   Health insurance reduces the risk of financial loss in the event of illness. It can provide funds to cover both lost earnings and the cost of medical care. This type of insurance is rapidly growing, but in recent years, it has not been highly profitable. Figure 17.4 illustrates its relative scale.

Property and Casualty Insurance   Property and casualty insurance reduces the risk of financial loss in the event of an accident involving damage to persons

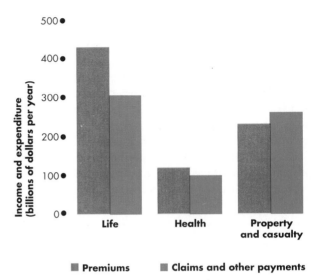

FIGURE 17.4

The Insurance Industry

Total expenditure on insurance is almost $800 billion a year. Most is spent on life insurance, and in recent years, this type of insurance has also been the most profitable.

Source: U.S. Bureau of the Census, *Statistical Abstract of the United States 1993* (114th edition), Washington, D.C., 1991, pp. 533–535.

or property. It includes auto insurance—its biggest component—workers' compensation, fire, earthquake, and professional malpractice insurance, and a host of smaller items. Figure 17.4 shows that we spend more on this type of insurance than on health insurance but not as much as on life insurance.

How Insurance Works

Insurance works by pooling risks. It is possible and profitable because people are risk averse. The probability of any one person having a serious auto accident is small, but the cost of an accident to the person involved is enormous. For a large population, the probability of one person having an accident is the proportion of the population that does have an accident. Because this probability can be estimated, the total cost of accidents can be predicted. An insurance company can pool the risks of a large population and share the costs. It does so by collecting premiums from everyone and paying out benefits to those who suffer a loss. If the insurance company does its calculations correctly, it collects at least as much in premiums as it pays out in benefits and operating costs.

To see why people buy insurance and why it is profitable, let's consider an example. Dan has the utility of wealth curve shown in Fig. 17.5. He owns a car worth $10,000, and that is his only wealth. If there is no risk of his having an accident, his utility will be 100 units. But there is a 10 percent chance (a probability of 0.1) that he will have an accident within a year. Suppose Dan does not buy insurance. If he does have an accident, his car is worthless, and with no insurance, he has no wealth and no utility. Because the probability of an accident is 0.1, the probability of *not* having an accident is 0.9. Dan's expected wealth, therefore, is $9,000 ($10,000 × 0.9

+ $0 × 0.1), and his expected utility is 90 units (100 × 0.9 + 0 × 0.1).

Given his utility of wealth curve, Dan has 90 units of utility if his wealth is $7,000 and he faces no uncertainty. That is, Dan's utility of a guaranteed wealth of $7,000 is the same as his utility of a 90 percent chance of having wealth of $10,000 and a 10 percent chance of having nothing. If the cost of an insurance policy that pays out in the event of an accident is less than $3,000 ($10,000 − $7,000), Dan will buy the policy. Thus Dan has a demand for auto insurance at premiums less than $3,000.

Suppose there are lots of people like Dan, each with a $10,000 car and each with a 10 percent chance of having an accident within the year. If an insurance company agrees to pay each person who has an accident $10,000, the company will pay out $10,000 to one tenth of the population, or an average of $1,000 per person. This amount is the insurance company's minimum premium for such insurance. It is less than the value of insurance to Dan because Dan is risk averse. He is willing to pay something to reduce the risk he faces.

Now suppose that the insurance company's operating expenses are a further $1,000 and that it offers insurance for $2,000. The company now covers all its costs—the amounts paid out to policyholders for their losses plus the company's operating expenses. Dan—and all the other people like him—will maximize their utility by buying this insurance.

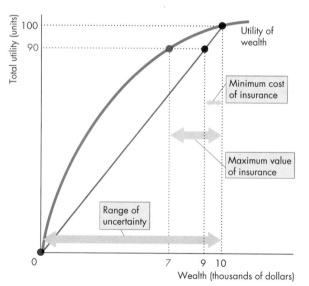

FIGURE 17.5

The Gains from Insurance

Dan has a car valued at $10,000 that gives him a utility of 100 units, but there is a 0.1 probability that he will have an accident, making his car worthless (wealth and utility equal to zero). With no insurance, his expected utility is 90 units and he is willing to pay up to $3,000 for insurance. An insurance company (with no operating expenses) can offer insurance to Dan and the rest of the community for $1,000. Hence there is a potential gain from insurance for both Dan and the insurance company.

R E V I E W

- Americans spend 15 percent of their income, on the average, on life, health, and property and casualty insurance.

- Insurance works by pooling risks. Every insured person pays in, but only those who suffer a loss are compensated.

- Insurance is worth buying and is profitable because people are risk averse and are willing to pay for lower risk.

Much of the uncertainty we face arises from ignorance. We just don't know all the things we could benefit from knowing. But knowledge or information is not free. We must make decisions about how much information to acquire. Let's now study the choices we make about obtaining information and see how incomplete information affects some of our transactions.

Information

WE SPEND A HUGE QUANTITY OF OUR SCARCE resources on economic information. **Economic information** includes data on the prices, quantities, and qualities of goods and services and factors of production.

In the models of perfect competition, monopoly, and monopolistic competition, information is free. Everyone has all the information he or she needs. Households are completely informed about the prices of the goods and services they buy and the factors of production they sell. Similarly, firms are completely informed.

In contrast, information is scarce in the real world. If it were not, we wouldn't need *The Wall Street Journal* and CNN. And we wouldn't need to shop around for bargains or spend time looking for a job. The opportunity cost of economic information—the cost of acquiring information on prices, quantities, and qualities of goods and services and factors of production—is called **information cost**.

The fact that many economic models ignore information costs does not make these models useless. They give us insights into the forces generating trends in prices and quantities over periods long enough for information limits not to be important. But to understand how markets work hour by hour and day by day, we must take information problems into account. Let's look at some of the consequences of information cost.

Searching for Price Information

When many firms sell the same good or service, there is a range of prices and buyers want to find the lowest price. But searching takes time and is costly. So buyers must balance the expected gain from further search against the cost of further search. To perform this balancing act, buyers use a decision rule called the *optimal-search rule*—or *optimal-stopping rule*. The optimal-search rule is:

- Search for a lower price until the expected marginal benefit of search equals the marginal cost of search.
- When the expected marginal benefit from additional search is less than or equal to the marginal cost, stop searching and buy.

To implement the optimal-search rule, each buyer chooses her or his own reservation price. The buyer's **reservation price** is the highest price that the buyer is willing to pay for a good. The buyer will continue to search for a lower price if the lowest price so far found exceeds the reservation price but will stop searching and buy if the lowest price found is less than or equal to the reservation price. At the buyer's reservation price, the expected marginal benefit of search equals the marginal cost of search.

Figure 17.6 illustrates the optimal-search rule. Suppose you've decided to buy a used Mazda Miata. Your marginal cost of search is $C per dealer visited and is shown by the horizontal orange line in the figure. This cost includes the value of your time, which is the amount that you could have earned by working instead of cruising around used car lots, and the amount spent on transportation and advice. Your

FIGURE 17.6

Optimal-Search Rule

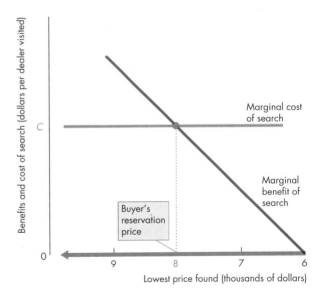

The marginal cost of search is constant at $C. As the lowest price found (measured from right to left on the horizontal axis) declines, the expected marginal utility of further search diminishes. The lowest price found at which the marginal cost equals the expected marginal benefit is the reservation price. The optimal-search rule is to search until the reservation price (or lower) is found and then buy at that lowest found price.

expected marginal benefit of visiting one more dealer depends on the lowest price that you've found. The lower the price you've already found, the lower is your expected marginal benefit of visiting one more dealer, as shown by the blue curve in the figure.

The price at which expected marginal benefit equals marginal cost is your reservation price—$8,000 in the figure. If you find a price equal to or below your reservation price, you stop searching and buy. If you find a price that exceeds your reservation price, you continue to search for a lower price. Individual shoppers differ in their marginal cost of search and so have different reservation prices. As a result, identical items can be found selling for a range of prices.

A Real Car Shopping Trip Real car shoppers are confronted with a much bigger problem than the one we've just studied. There are many more dimensions of the car they are looking for than its price. They could spend almost forever gathering information about the alternatives. But at some point in their search, they decide they've done enough looking and make a decision to buy. Your imaginary shopping trip to buy a used Mazda Miata rationalizes their decision. Real shoppers think, the benefits I expect from further search are insufficient to make it worth going on with the process. They don't do the calculations we've just done—at least, not explicitly—but their actions can be explained by those calculations. But buyers are not alone in creating information. Sellers do a lot of it too—in the form of advertising. Let's see what the effects of advertising are.

Advertising

Advertising constantly surrounds us—on television, radio, and billboards and in newspapers and magazines—and costs billions of dollars. How do firms decide how much to spend on advertising? Does advertising create information, or does it just persuade us to buy things we don't really want? What does it do to prices?

Advertising for Profit Maximization A firm's advertising decision is part of its overall profit-maximization strategy. Firms in perfect competition don't advertise because everyone has all the information there is. But firms selling differentiated products in monopolistic competition and firms locked in the struggle of survival in oligopoly advertise a lot.

The amount of advertising undertaken by firms in monopolistic competition is such that the marginal revenue product of advertising equals its marginal cost. The amount of advertising undertaken by firms in oligopoly is determined by the game they are playing. If that game is a *prisoners' dilemma*, they might spend amounts that lower their combined profits, but they can't avoid advertising without being wiped out by other firms in the industry.

Persuasion or Information Much advertising is designed to persuade us that the product being advertised is the best in its class. For example, the Pepsi advertisement tells us that Pepsi is really better than Coke. The Coca-Cola advertisement tells us that Coke is really better than Pepsi. But advertising also informs. It provides information about the quality and price of a good or service.

Does advertising mainly persuade or mainly inform? The answer varies for different goods and different types of markets. Goods whose quality can be assessed *before* they are bought are called *search goods*. Typically, the advertising of search goods mainly informs—gives information about price, quality, and location of suppliers. Examples of such goods are gasoline, basic foods, and household goods. Goods whose quality can be assessed only *after* they are bought are called *experience goods*. Typically, the advertising of experience goods mainly persuades—encourages the consumer to buy now and make a judgment later about quality, based on experience with the good. Examples of such goods are cigarettes, alcoholic beverages, and perfume.

Because most advertising involves experience goods, it is likely that advertising is more often persuasive rather than merely informative. But persuasive advertising doesn't necessarily harm the consumer. It might result in lower prices.

Advertising and Prices Advertising is costly, but does it increase the price of the good advertised? It might, but two lines of reasoning tell us that advertising can lower prices. The first is that if advertising is informative, it *increases* competition. By informing potential buyers about alternative sources of supply, advertising forces firms to keep their prices low. There is evidence of such effects, especially in retailing. The second is that if advertising enables firms to increase their output and reap economies of scale, it is possible that the price of the good will be lower with advertising than without it, provided that competition prevents monopoly pricing.

REVIEW

- Data on the prices, quantities, and qualities of goods and services and factors of production—economic information—is scarce, and people economize on its use.
- Buyers searching for price information stop when they find a price at or below their reservation price, the price that makes the expected marginal benefit of search equal the marginal cost of search.
- Sellers advertise to inform potential buyers of the good or to persuade them to buy it.
- Advertising can increase competition and may raise or lower the price of the advertised good.

Private Information

SO FAR WE HAVE LOOKED AT SITUATIONS IN which information is available to everyone and can be obtained with an expenditure of resources. But not all situations are like this. For example, someone might have private information. **Private information** is information that is available to one person but too costly for anyone else to obtain.

Private information affects many economic transactions. One is your knowledge about your driving. You know much more than your auto insurance company does about how carefully and defensively you drive. Another is your knowledge about your work effort. You know far more than your employer about how hard you work. Yet another is your knowledge about the quality of your car. You know whether it's a lemon. But the person to whom you are about to sell it does not and can't find out until after he or she has purchased it from you.

Private information creates two problems:

1. Moral hazard
2. Adverse selection

Moral hazard exists when one of the parties to an agreement has an incentive, *after the agreement is made*, to act in a manner that brings additional benefits to himself or herself at the expense of the other party. Moral hazard arises because it is too costly for the injured party to monitor the actions of the advantaged party. For example, Jackie hires Mitch as a salesperson and pays him a fixed wage regardless of his sales. Mitch faces a moral hazard. He has an incentive to put in the least possible effort, benefiting himself and lowering Jackie's profits. For this reason, salespeople are usually paid by a formula that makes their income higher the greater is the volume (or value) of their sales.

Adverse selection is the tendency for people to enter into agreements in which they can use their private information to their own advantage and to the disadvantage of the less informed party. For example, if Jackie offers salespeople a fixed wage, she will attract lazy salespeople. Hardworking salespeople will prefer *not* to work for Jackie because they can earn more by working for someone who pays by results. The fixed-wage contract adversely selects those with private information (knowledge about their work habits) who can use that knowledge to their own advantage and to the disadvantage of the other party.

A variety of devices have evolved that enable markets to function in the face of moral hazard and adverse selection. We've just seen one, the use of incentive payments for salespeople. Let's look at some more and also see how moral hazard and adverse selection influence three real-world markets:

- The market for used cars
- The market for loans
- The market for insurance

The Market for Used Cars

When a person buys a car, it might turn out to be a lemon. If the car is a lemon, it is worth less to the buyer and to everyone else than if it has no defects. Does the used car market have two prices reflecting these two values—a low price for lemons and a higher price for cars without defects? It does not. To see why, let's look at a used car market, first with no dealer warranties and second with warranties.

Used Cars without Warranties   To make the points as clearly as possible, we'll make some extreme assumptions. There are just two kinds of cars, lemons and those without defects. A lemon is worth $1,000 both to its current owner and to anyone who buys it. A car without defects is worth $5,000 to its current and potential future owners. Whether a car is a lemon is private information that is available only to the current owner. Buyers of used cars can't tell whether they are buying a lemon until *after* they have bought the car and learned as much about it as its current owner knows. There are no dealer warranties.

Because buyers can't tell the difference between a lemon and a good car, they are willing to pay only one price for a used car. What is that price? Are they willing to pay $5,000, the value of a good car? They are not, because there is at least some probability that they are buying a lemon worth only $1,000. If buyers are not willing to pay $5,000 for a used car, are the owners of good cars willing to sell? They are not, because a good car is worth $5,000 to them, so they hang onto their cars. Only the owners of lemons are willing to sell—as long as the price is $1,000 or higher. But, reason the buyers, if only the owners of lemons are selling, all the used cars available are lemons, so the maximum price worth paying is $1,000. Thus the market for used cars is a market for lemons, and the price is $1,000.

Moral hazard exists in the car market because sellers have an incentive to claim that lemons are good cars. But, given the assumptions in the above description of the car market, no one believes such claims. Adverse selection exists, resulting in only lemons actually being traded. The market for used cars is not working well. Good used cars just don't get bought and sold, but people want to be able to buy and sell good used cars. How can they do so? The answer is by introducing warranties into the market.

Used Cars with Warranties   Buyers of used cars can't tell a lemon from a good car, but car dealers sometimes can. For example, they might have regularly serviced the car. They know, therefore, whether they are buying a lemon or a good car and can offer $1,000 for lemons and $5,000 for good cars.[1] But how can they convince buyers that it is worth paying $5,000 for what might be a lemon? The answer is by giving a guarantee in the form of a warranty. The dealer *signals* which cars are good ones and which are lemons. A **signal** is an action taken outside a market that conveys information that can be used by that market. Students' grades are an example of a signal to the job market, and this familiar signal is explored in *Reading Between the Lines* on pp. 414–415. In the case of the used cars, dealers take actions in the market for car repairs that can be used by the market for cars. For each good car sold, the dealer gives a war-

ranty. The dealer agrees to pay the costs of repairing the car if it turns out to have a defect. Cars with a warranty are good; cars without a warranty are lemons.

Why do buyers believe the signal? It is because the cost of sending a false signal is high. A dealer who gives a warranty on a lemon ends up paying the high cost of repairs—and risks gaining a bad reputation. A dealer who gives a warranty only on good cars has no repair costs and a reputation that gets better and better. It pays to send an accurate signal. It is rational, therefore, for buyers to believe the signal. Warranties break the lemon problem and enable the used car market to function with two prices, one for lemons and one for good cars.

The Market for Loans

The market for bank loans is one in which private information plays a crucial role. Let's see how.

The quantity of loans demanded by borrowers depends on the interest rate. The lower the interest rate, the greater is the quantity of loans demanded—the demand curve for loans is downward-sloping. The supply of loans by banks and other lenders depends on the cost of lending. This cost has two parts. One is interest, and this interest cost is determined in the market for bank deposits—the market in which the banks borrow the funds that they lend. The other part of the cost of lending is the cost of bad loans—loans that are not repaid—called the default cost. The interest cost of a loan is the same for all borrowers. The default cost of a loan depends on the quality of the borrower.

Suppose that borrowers fall into two classes: low-risk and high-risk. Low-risk borrowers seldom default on their debts and then only for reasons beyond their control. For example, a firm might borrow to finance a project that fails and be unable to repay the bank. High-risk borrowers take high risks with the money they borrow and frequently default on their loans. For example, a firm might borrow to speculate in high-risk mineral prospecting that has a very small chance of paying off.

If banks could separate borrowers into the two risk categories, they would supply loans to low-risk borrowers at one interest rate and to high-risk borrowers at another, higher interest rate. But banks cannot separate their borrowers. They have no sure way of knowing whether they are lending to a low-risk or a high-risk borrower.

---

[1] In this example, to keep the numbers simple, we'll ignore dealers' profit margins and other costs of doing business and suppose that dealers buy cars for the same price as they sell them. The principles are the same with dealers' profit margins.

So the banks must charge a single interest rate to both low-risk and high-risk borrowers. If they offered loans to everyone at the low-risk interest rate, borrowers would face moral hazard and the banks would attract a lot of high-risk borrowers—adverse selection. Most borrowers would default, and the banks would incur economic losses. If the banks offered loans to everyone at the high-risk interest rate, most low-risk borrowers, with whom the banks would like to do profitable business, would be unwilling to borrow.

Faced with moral hazard and adverse selection, banks use *signals* to discriminate between borrowers, and they *ration* or limit loans to amounts below the amounts demanded. To restrict the amounts they are willing to lend to borrowers, banks use signals such as length of time in a job, ownership of a home, marital status, age, and business record.

Figure 17.7 shows how the market for loans works in the face of moral hazard and adverse selection. The demand for loans is D, and the supply is S. The supply curve is horizontal—perfectly elastic supply—because it is assumed that banks have access to a large quantity of funds that have a constant marginal cost of r. With no loan limits, the interest rate is r and the quantity of loans is Q. Because of moral hazard and adverse selection, the banks set loan limits based on signals and restrict the total loans to L. At the interest rate r, there is an excess demand for loans. A bank cannot increase its profit by making more loans because it can't identify the type of borrower taking the loans. Because the signals used mean that more high-risk borrowers are unsatisfied than low-risk borrowers, it is likely that additional loans will be biased toward high-risk (and high-cost) borrowers.

The Market for Insurance

People who buy insurance face a moral hazard problem, and insurance companies face an adverse selection problem. The moral hazard problem is that a person with insurance coverage for a loss has less incentive than an uninsured person to avoid such a loss. For example, a business with fire insurance has less incentive to take precautions against fire such as installing a fire alarm or sprinkler system than a business with no fire insurance. The adverse selection problem is that people who face greater risks are more likely to buy insurance. For example, a person with a family history of serious illness is more likely to buy health insurance than is a person with a family history of good health.

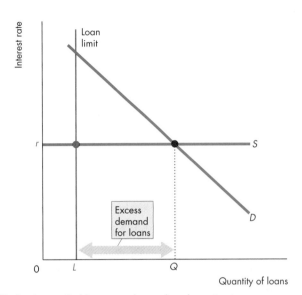

FIGURE 17.7

The Market for Loans

If a bank supplied loans on demand at the going interest rate r, the quantity of loans would be Q, but most of the loans would be taken by high-risk borrowers. Banks use signals to distinguish between low-risk and high-risk borrowers, and they ration loans. Banks have no incentive to increase interest rates and increase the quantity of loans because the additional loans would be to high-risk borrowers.

Insurance companies have an incentive to find ways around the moral hazard and adverse selection problems. By doing so, they can lower premiums and increase the amount of business they do. Real-world insurance markets have developed a variety of devices for overcoming or at least moderating these private information problems. Let's see how signals work in markets for insurance by looking at the example of auto insurance.

One of the clearest signals a person can give an auto insurance company is her or his driving record. Suppose that Dan is a good driver and rarely has an accident. If he can demonstrate to the insurance company that his driving record is impeccable over a long enough period, then the insurance company will recognize him as a good driver. Dan will work hard at establishing a reputation as a good driver because he will be able to get his insurance at a lower price.

If all drivers, good and bad alike, can establish good records, then simply having a good record will not convey any information. For the signal to be informative, it must be difficult for bad drivers to fake low risk by having a good record. The signals used in car insurance are the "no-claim" bonuses that drivers accumulate when they do not make an insurance claim.

Another device used by insurance companies is the deductible. A deductible is the amount of a loss that the insured person agrees to bear. For example, most auto insurance policies have the insured person paying the first few hundred dollars worth of damage. The premium varies with the deductible, and the decrease in the premium is more than proportionate to the increase in the deductible. By offering insurance with full coverage—no deductible—on terms that are attractive only to the highest-risk people and by offering coverage with a deductible on more favorable terms, insurance companies can do profitable business with everyone. High-risk people choose policies with low deductibles and high premiums, while low-risk people choose policies with high deductibles and low premiums.

REVIEW

- Private information creates moral hazard and adverse selection.
- In markets for cars, loans, and insurance, methods such as warranties, loan limits, and no-claim bonuses and deductibles have been devised to limit the problems caused by private information.

Managing Risk in Financial Markets

RISK IS A DOMINANT FEATURE OF MARKETS FOR stocks and bonds—indeed for any asset whose price fluctuates. One thing people do to cope with risky asset prices is diversify their asset holdings.

Diversification to Lower Risk

The idea that diversification lowers risk is very natural. It is just an application of not putting all one's eggs into the same basket. How exactly does diversifi-

cation reduce risk? The best way to answer this question is to consider an example.

Suppose there are two risky projects that you can undertake. Each involves investing $100,000. The two projects are independent of each other, but they both promise the same degree of risk and return.

On each project, you will either make $50,000 or lose $25,000, and the chance that either of these will happen is 50 percent. The expected return on each project is ($50,000 × 0.5) + (−$25,000 × 0.5), which is $12,500. But because the two projects are completely independent, the outcome of one project in no way influences the outcome of the other.

Undiversified Suppose you put all your eggs in one basket, investing the $100,000 in either Project 1 or Project 2. You will either make $50,000 or lose $25,000, and the probability of each of these outcomes is 50 percent. Your expected return is the average of these two outcomes—an expected return of $12,500. But in this case in which only one project is chosen, there is no chance that you will actually make a return of $12,500.

Diversified Suppose instead that you diversify by putting 50 percent of your money into Project 1 and 50 percent into Project 2. (Someone else is putting up the other money in these two projects.) Because the two projects are independent, you now have *four* possible returns:

1. Lose $12,500 on each project, and your return is −$25,000.
2. Make $25,000 on Project 1 and lose $12,500 on Project 2, and your return is $12,500.
3. Lose $12,500 on Project 1 and make $25,000 on Project 2, and your return is $12,500.
4. Make $25,000 on each project, and your return is $50,000.

Each of these four possible outcomes is equally probable—each has a 25 percent chance of occurring. You have lowered the chance that you will earn $50,000, but you have also lowered the chance that you will lose $25,000. And you have increased the chance that you will actually make your expected return of $12,500. By diversifying your portfolio of assets, you have reduced its riskiness while maintaining an expected return of $12,500.

If you are risk-averse—that is, if your utility of wealth curve looks like Tania's, which you studied earlier in this chapter—you'll prefer the diversified portfolio to the one that is not diversified. That is, your *expected utility* with a diversified set of assets is greater.

A common way to diversify is to buy stocks in different corporations. Let's look at the market in which these stocks are traded.

The Stock Market

The prices of the stocks are determined by demand and supply. But demand and supply in the stock market is dominated by one thing: the expected future price. If the price of a stock today is higher than the expected price tomorrow, people will sell the stock today. If the price of a stock today is less than its expected price tomorrow, people will buy the stock today. As a result of such trading, today's price equals tomorrow's expected price, and so today's price embodies all the relevant information that is available about the stock. A market in which the actual price embodies all currently available relevant information is called an **efficient market**.

In an efficient market, it is impossible to forecast changes in price. Why? If your forecast is that the price is going to rise tomorrow, you will buy now. Your action of buying today is an increase in demand today and increases *today's* price. It's true that your action—the action of a single trader—is not going to make much difference to a huge market like the New York Stock Exchange. But if traders in general expect a higher price tomorrow and they all act today on the basis of that expectation, then today's price will rise. It will keep on rising until it reaches the expected future price, because only at that price do traders see no profit in buying more stock today.

There is an apparent paradox about efficient markets. Markets are efficient because people try to make a profit. They seek a profit by buying at a low price and selling at a high price. But the very act of buying and selling to make a profit means that the market price moves to equal its expected future value. Having done that, no one, not even those who are seeking to profit, can *predictably* make a profit. Every profit opportunity seen by traders leads to an action that produces a price change that removes the profit opportunity for others. Even the probability of an intergalactic attack on New York City is taken into account in determining stock market prices—see the cartoon.

Thus an efficient market has two features:

"Drat! I suppose the market has already discounted this, too."

Drawing by Lorenz; © 1986 The New Yorker Magazine, Inc.

1. Its price equals the expected future price and embodies all the available information.
2. There are no forecastable profit opportunities available.

The key thing to understand about an efficient market such as the stock market is that if something can be anticipated, it will be, and the anticipation will affect the current price of a stock.

Volatility in Stock Prices   If the price of a stock is always equal to its expected future price, why is the stock market so volatile? The answer must be that expectations themselves are subject to fluctuation. Expectations depend on the information available. As new information becomes available, stock traders form new expectations about the future state of the economy and, in turn, new expectations of future stock prices. New information comes randomly, so prices change randomly.

◆ We've studied the way people cope with uncertainty and how markets work when there are important information problems. In the following chapters we're going to study some problems that the market economy has difficulty coping with and that give rise to government economic activity. We'll learn how government actions and programs modify the outcome of a pure market economy and influence the distribution of income and wealth.

Grades as Signals

THE CHICAGO TRIBUNE, MAY 4, 1994

Easy College A's Become Rampant

BY CAROL JOUZAITIS

PALO ALTO, Calif.—When Stanford University decided in 1970 to challenge its students, it didn't exactly make things tougher for them: It banished F's and made it easier for students to avoid low grades. ...

At Stanford today, an astonishing 91 percent of all letter grades are A's and B's, a substantial increase over 20 years ago.

"It's frankly preposterous" to argue that students are working that much harder than they did before, said biology department chairman Robert Simoni. Like most faculty members, he believes many of the high grades are undeserved.

Critics say widespread grade inflation in the nation's schools has made it difficult to distinguish between high performers and mediocre students. And students get a skewed view of their academic talents, which could affect their ability to compete in the real world. ...

Today's grades have little meaning. A's are handed out for a range of performance, from exceptional to ordinary. B's, once

an indicator of "good" work, now are considered a reward for "average" work. C's, once a common grade that meant "satisfactory," have come to be viewed as a "bad" grade ... And without F's, D's are akin to failure. ...

Academics refer to rampant grade inflation as the Lake Wobegon syndrome, the national desire to live in a place "where all students are above average," as in Garrison Keillor's mythical town.

Even the comic strip Doonesbury has taken up the issue, poking fun at law school applicants who beg for mercy when admissions officers insist their straight-A transcripts lack credibility.

Harvard magazine reported last year that 43 percent of all grades there were A's, twice as many as in the mid-1960s. The average Harvard undergraduate now carries a B-plus average.

The situation is similar, the magazine reported, at Princeton University, where A's account for 40 percent of grades. And at Brown University, there are no D's or F's as a matter of academic policy. ...

Essence of THE STORY

■ In 1970, Stanford University abolished F grades and by 1992–93, 91 percent of grades at Stanford were As and Bs, a substantial increase over the number 20 years ago. The situation is similar at many other universities, including Harvard, Princeton, and Brown.

■ Critics of grade inflation say that it makes it difficult to distinguish among students and students get a distorted view of their accomplishments, which could affect their ability to compete for jobs when they graduate.

■ Today, an A grade indicates a range of performance from exceptional to ordinary; a B indicates an "average" performance; a C has come to be viewed as a "bad" grade; and a D is regarded as failure.

Economic

A N A L Y S I S

Grades provide information about a student's academic performance that is used by students and other academic institutions to make decisions about graduate and professional school entry and by potential employers in the job market.

Employers value information about the likely performance of employees, and grades that are correlated with job performance act as *signals*.

Figure 1 shows the labor market for college graduates. The supply curve is *S*, and the *marginal revenue product curve* (see Chapter 14, p. 337) is *MRP*. The wage rate is *W*, and *Q* graduates are employed.

Suppose that graduates fall into two groups: Hs, who have high productivity and a marginal revenue product curve MRP_H, and Ls, who have low productivity and a marginal revenue product curve MRP_L.

With no information about individual performance, everyone is paid *W*. But the value of a high-productivity graduate is *H*, and the value of a low-productivity graduate is *L*.

Because the marginal revenue product of an H is greater than the wage rate, firms could increase profit by hiring more Hs. And because the marginal revenue product of an L is less than the wage rate, firms could increase profit by hiring fewer Ls.

Through grading performance on the job, firms might eventually distinguish the Hs and Ls. But if they could distinguish at the point of hiring, the market would be more efficient.

Figures 2 and 3 show what happens if the graduates are perfectly sorted in school. An H gets an A in school, and an L gets a B. The As (Fig. 2) get a wage rate of W_A, and the number employed increases to Q_A. The Bs (Fig. 3) get a wage rate of W_B, and the number employed decreases to Q_B.

In reality, college grades are not perfect signals. But colleges use grades to compete for students.

"Good" students gain by being identified as such. So other things remaining the same, the tougher its grading, the more "good" students a school attracts.

Schools balance the desire to get more students (soft grading) with the desire to get good students (tough grading).

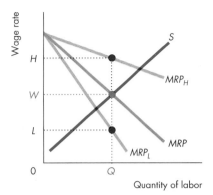

Figure 1 No grading

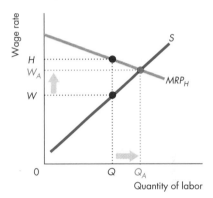

Figure 2 Perfect grading: As

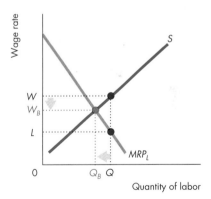

Figure 3 Perfect grading: Bs

SUMMARY

Uncertainty and Risk

Uncertainty is a situation in which more than one event may occur but we don't know which one. To describe uncertainty, we use the concepts of probability and risk. A probability is a number between zero and one that measures the chance of some possible event occurring. Risk is uncertainty with probabilities attached to each possible outcome. Sometimes the probabilities can be measured, and sometimes they cannot. When they cannot be measured, they are subjective probabilities.

A person's attitude toward risk, called the degree of risk aversion, is described by a utility of wealth schedule and curve. Greater wealth brings higher utility, but as wealth increases, the marginal utility of wealth diminishes. The cost of risk is the amount by which expected wealth must be increased to give the same expected utility as in a no-risk situation. Faced with uncertainty, people choose the action that maximizes expected utility. (pp. 402–404)

Insurance

We spend 15 percent of our income on insurance, one way in which we reduce the risk we face. The three main types of insurance are life, health, and property and casualty. Insurance works by pooling risks, and it pays people to insure because they are risk averse—they value risk reduction. By pooling risks, insurance companies can reduce the risks people face (from insured activities) at a low cost in terms of reduced expected wealth. The decrease in risk is valued more than the decrease in wealth. (pp. 405–406)

Information

Economic information includes data on the prices, quantities, and qualities of goods and services and factors of production. Buyers search for price information—looking for the least-cost source of supply. In doing so, they use the optimal-search rule of searching for a lower price until the expected marginal benefit of search equals the marginal cost of search. When the expected marginal benefit equals the mar-

ginal cost, the buyer stops searching and buys. There is a reservation price at which the expected marginal benefit of search equals the marginal cost of search. When a price equal to (or less than) the reservation price is found, the search ends and the item is bought.

Sellers advertise, sometimes to persuade and sometimes to inform. Advertising is part of a firm's profit-maximization strategy. The general presumption is that advertising increases prices. But advertising can also increase competition and enable economies of scale to be experienced, in which cases some prices might be lower because of advertising. (pp. 407–409)

Private Information

Private information is one person's knowledge that is too costly for anyone else to discover. Private information creates the problems of moral hazard—the use of private information to the advantage of the informed and the disadvantage of the uninformed—and adverse selection—the tendency for people to enter into agreements in which they can use their private information to their own advantage and to the disadvantage of the less informed party. Devices that enable markets to function in the face of moral hazard and adverse selection are incentive payments, guarantees such as warranties, rationing, and signals. (pp. 409–412)

Managing Risk in Financial Markets

Risk can be reduced by diversifying asset holdings, thereby combining the returns on projects that are independent of each other. A common way to diversify is to buy stocks in different corporations. Stock prices are determined by the expected future price of the stock. Expectations about future stock prices are based on all the information that is available and regarded as relevant. If the price is expected to rise, people buy and the actual price rises until it equals the expected price. If the price is expected to fall, people sell and the actual price falls until it equals the expected price. A market in which the price equals the expected price is an efficient market. (pp. 412–413)

KEY ELEMENTS

Key Figures

Key Terms

REVIEW QUESTIONS

1. Distinguish between uncertainty and risk.

2. How do we measure a person's attitude toward risk? How do these attitudes vary from one person to another?

3. What is a risk-neutral person and what does such a person's utility of wealth curve look like?

4. What is risk aversion and how could you tell which of two people are the more risk averse by looking at their utility of wealth curves?

5. Why do people buy insurance and why do insurance companies make a profit?

6. Why is information valuable?

7. What determines the amount of searching you do for a bargain?

8. Why do firms advertise?

9. Does advertising always increase prices? Why might it lower them?

10. What are moral hazard and adverse selection and how do they influence the way markets for loans and insurance work?

11. What is a lemon and how does the lemon problem arise?

12. Explain how the used car market works.

13. Why do firms give guarantees such as warranties?

14. Why do banks limit the amounts they are willing to lend?

15. How do deductibles make insurance more efficient and enable insurance companies to discriminate between high-risk and low-risk customers?

16. What is diversification?

17. What is the most common way of diversifying assets?

18. How does diversification lower risk?

19. How is stock price determined and what role does the expected future price play?

20. What is an efficient market? What types of markets are efficient?

P R O B L E M S

1. The figure shows Lee's utility of wealth curve.

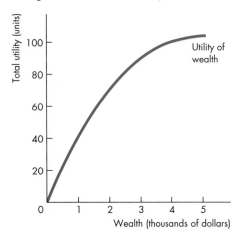

Lee is offered a job as a salesperson in which there is a fifty percent chance she will make $4,000 a month and a fifty percent chance she will make nothing.
   a. What is Lee's expected income from taking this job?
   b. What is Lee's expected utility from taking this job?
   c. How much (approximately) would another firm have to offer Lee with certainty to persuade her not to take the risky sales job?

2. The figure shows Colleen's utility of wealth curve.

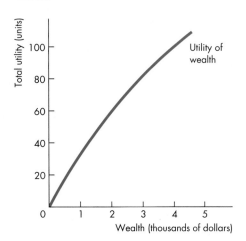

Colleen is offered the same kind of sales job as Lee in problem 1—a fifty percent chance of making $4,000 a month and a fifty percent chance of making nothing.

   a. What is Colleen's expected income from taking this job?
   b. What is Colleen's expected utility from taking this job?
   c. Explain who is more likely to be willing to take this risky job, Lee or Colleen.

3. Jimmy and Zenda have the following utility of wealth schedules:

Wealth	Jimmy's utility	Zenda's utility
0	0	0
100	200	512
200	300	640
300	350	672
400	375	678
500	387	681
600	393	683
700	396	684

Who is more risk averse, Jimmy or Zenda?

4. Suppose that Jimmy and Zenda in problem 3 have $400 each and that each sees a business project that involves committing the entire $400 to the project. They reckon that the project could return $600 (a profit of $200) with a probability of 0.85 or $200 (a loss of $200) with a probability of 0.15. Who goes for the project and who hangs onto the initial $400?

5. In problem 3, who is more likely to buy insurance, Jimmy or Zenda, and why?

6. A new wonder drug is discoverd by Merck that is expected to bring big profits. Describe in detail what happens in the stock market and how these actions influence the price of Merck's stock. Why would people diversify rather than put all their wealth into Merck's stock?

7. Study *Reading Between the Lines* on pp. 414–415 and then answer the following questions:
   a. Why do schools and colleges give students grades?
   b. Why might grade inflation cause problems for students, schools, and firms?
   c. What are the benefits of tough grading?
   d. Who gets the benefits and who bears the costs?

Glenn C. Loury teaches economics at Boston University. He was born in Chicago, Illinois, in 1948 and was an undergraduate at Northwestern University and a graduate student at MIT, where he earned his Ph.D. in 1976. Professor Loury is an economic theorist whose work covers a wide range of issues including game theory, exhaustible resources, oligopoly, externalities, poverty, and discrimination. Michael Parkin talked with Professor Loury about his work and about the problems of assessing the effects of government policies.

TALKING WITH Glenn Loury

Professor Loury, what attracted you to economics?

I was a math major in college during the late sixties and early seventies when there was a good deal of racial unrest in the United States and turmoil about the Vietnam War. While I enjoyed mathematics very much, I wanted to do work that had some relationship to the political and social issues that were so pressing. I happened to take an economics course and had a very good teacher, Jonathan Hughes, who got me excited about economics. I discovered that one could do quite a bit of formal analytical thinking while at the same time addressing oneself to questions of significance to society. It seemed to me economics was ideally suited to combine my aptitudes and interests in mathematics with my desire to be engaged in questions of social import.

You are a self-proclaimed conservative. Do your political views influence the issues you work on or the answers you get?

I think that's a subtle issue, and I suspect that for all of us, our political views at some level influence our work. The kind of question you find interesting to investigate is influenced by how you construe the world and what your basic values are. For example, the generation of economists before me, such as Robert Solow and James Tobin, were profoundly influenced by the Great Depression. Their interest in macroeconomics in part derived from a concern to understand the causes of the Depression. On the other hand, when you do an analysis, it is problematic if you simply won't see certain implications of the facts because they run contrary to your political beliefs.

Let's talk about one of our major social problems—poverty. Is it enough to give people equal opportunities, or must we redistribute income to deal with unequal outcomes? And if so, can private charity do the job or do we need government action—progressive taxes? Social Security? Welfare?
In American society, you walk along the streets in any big city and see people who are homeless. It seems to me on a purely ethical basis that that's not right. There are measures to address this problem. I would break these measures down into human capital strategies and redistribution strategies. The human capital strategies would involve investments in the capacities of disadvantaged persons to increase their market earnings: retraining displaced workers, ensuring that children get adequate nutrition and stimulation so that their cognitive development in the early years is at its maximum potential, investing in the primary and secondary educational institutions that youngsters in

poor communities attend, and training of welfare mothers so that they could be independent and self-supporting in the labor market. Redistribution strategies aim to provide a "safety net" of minimally adequate income to all families. Personally, I do not believe that income redistribution from the rich to the middle class should be a high priority in our society.

We've had some problems designing human capital programs that work effectively. Employment training programs in the United States for adult workers are, on the whole, relatively ineffective in enhancing lifetime earnings.

In my ideal world, there would be a negative income tax ... with a flat tax rate and a high enough grant that people would be able to afford at least a modest health insurance policy. ...

When one reads carefully the research about the effectiveness of Head Start, an early childhood investment program, one cannot avoid the conclusion that the record is quite mixed. The kinds of programs that have had the greatest effect at producing positive results have been very expensive enrichment programs in which there are visits of the Head Start officials to the family's home and in which the parents are

involved in the program along with the children. We need to keep trying to figure out how to do this better.

What is wrong with health care in the United States today, and what can we learn from economics about the most effective way of fixing its problems?
I don't believe that the only civilized system to the delivery of health care is one in which the government undertakes to ensure its provision to every individual. I do think there's a problem in the United States, but I don't think that the problem is that the

United States is the only advanced industrial country without a national health service. We have a very outstanding health care delivery system. The problem is that some people who need to have access to it do not have adequate access, and the access they do have is underwritten by the charity of the providing institutions, which then shifts the cost of the provision of that care to other payers. The people who require emergency services do not have the kind of ongoing maintenance health care, such as doctor's visits, that would prevent the onset of some more costly disease.

In my ideal world, there would be a negative income tax, which would guarantee every family a minimum annual income, with a flat tax rate and a high enough grant that people would be able to afford at least a modest health insurance policy along with the food that they need to eat, and the housing that they require, and so on. I would respect *their* choices about how elaborate their health insurance coverage should be.

What do you identify as the major externalities that need government action. What kind of action? Taxes/subsidies? Markets? Property rights?

The environment is the major policy area where externalities are important. When a business releases pollution into the environment, it imposes external costs on the community. In the air quality area, we think about the effects of various discharges into the atmosphere, which can lead to acid rain, among other things.

I think we should rely more on market devices to efficiently administer government's judgment about the extent to which pollution needs to be diminished. For example, the government doesn't have complete information about the cost of reducing pollution at all various sources. It can exploit the knowledge that individual producers have about their own costs by using a marketable permit scheme in which people can trade the rights to discharge pollution into the air. Such a pro-

Both law and education have limits on the extent to which they can shape people's preferences...

gram is included in the 1990 Clean Air Act. This act allows U.S. power plants to trade emission permits of sulfur dioxide emissions. These permits can be traded between plants at negotiated prices.

The larger question is the value that one places on the heritage of nature, which one cannot decide scientifically, but which is crucial for policy.

What are the main forms of discrimination that economic policy can correct and what is your assessment of the progress made in the United States in the past 20 years?

The 1954 United States Supreme Court case *Brown* v. *Board of Education of Topeka, Kansas* made various efforts to deal with discrimination. It outlawed the segregation of children in public schools based on race. Prior to this ruling, strict racial segregation existed in U.S public schools. The effects of the Supreme Court ruling over 40 years have been mixed, and the extent to which that effort has resulted in the substantive improvement of educational opportunity for black

youngsters in the United States has been relatively minor.

There have been some success stories, and certainly I think it was the right thing to do to outlaw legally separate school systems. However, the fact is that today in the large cities of the United States, where poor black youngsters are concentrated, they are still substantially in segregated school systems. Simply put, the white people have moved away. So long as people's underlying preferences were such that they wanted to avoid association, they could undo the efforts of the law by placing themselves outside of its jurisdiction, by withdrawing their children from the public schools and sending them to private schools, etc.

Both law and education have limits on the extent to which they can shape people's preferences, and there are easy and hard cases. As someone who respects individual freedom, I want to allow people a certain autonomy in their decisions about associations. One wouldn't want to intervene when a group of people who enjoy a certain kind of tradition choose to gather together. For example, there's no law that says churches have to be racially segregated, and yet many congregations of African-Americans are essentially homogeneously black by choice, and that suits everybody just fine.

Affirmative action is a very large policy area. Some use of the policy can be justified on the argument of the historical effects of past discrimination, but one needs to be exceedingly careful in its administration so that affirmative action encourages the development of more equal capacities to compete in the disadvantaged group instead of simply focusing on the end process of filling a certain number of positions in a particular job or school.

There are problems with relying purely on statistical measures of discrimination. The government or regulatory agency that relies on statistical measures might not have all the information relevant in any given case. A classic illustration of this is the concern about disparity in death penalty incidence between African-Americans and whites in the United States. The statistical disparity is not that African-Americans are disproportionately sentenced to death by juries relative to the number of times they're convicted of murder, but rather that the death sentence is disproportionately given in cases in which the victim is white relative to cases in which the victim is African-American. On that basis, some people have said that juries are acting as if they value white lives more than African-American lives. Others have said it may be that the factors which lead a jury to recommend a death penalty because the crime has been particularly egregious are relatively more frequent in the cases where the victim is white. Without further investigation and statistical summary, one cannot evaluate the hypotheses.

When an undergraduate who wants to become an economist seeks your advice on the choice of subjects, what do you say?
Outside of the economics courses that you're, of course, going to take, a student needs to study math. You must have some familiarity with linear algebra, statistics, and abstract reasoning. Beyond that, I would emphasize history. I think it's essential to understand something about how and why institutions evolve in a society. I would also encourage the student to learn something about politics. This may mean taking formal political science courses, or it may mean just reading and thinking about what's in the newspaper every day. The student should pay some attention to the ways in which decisions are made about collective questions in the society, both at the local and the national level.

Some use of [affirmative action] can be justified on the argument of historical effects of past discrimination, but one needs to be exceedingly careful in its administration …

Market Failure and Public Choice

After studying this chapter, you will be able to:

- Describe the structure and size of the government sector of the U.S. economy

- Explain how the economic role for government arises from market failure and inequity

- Distinguish between public goods and private goods and explain the free-rider problem

- Explain how the quantity of public goods is determined

- Explain why most of the government's revenue comes from income taxes and why some goods are taxed at a high rate

Government—the Solution or the Problem?

In 1993, the federal, state, and local governments in the United States employed 18.8 million people and spent $2.2 trillion. Independent government agencies employed yet another million people. Do we need this much government? Is government, as conservatives sometimes suggest, too big? Is government "the problem"? Or, despite its enormous size, is government too small to do all the things it must attend to? Is government, as liberals sometimes suggest, not contributing enough to economic life? ◆ Government touches many aspects of our lives. It is present at our birth, supporting the hospitals in which we are born and helping to train the doctors and nurses who deliver us. It is present throughout our education, supporting schools and colleges and helping to train our teachers. It is present throughout our working lives, taxing our incomes, regulating our work environment, and paying us benefits when we are unemployed. It is present throughout our retirement, paying us a small income and, when we die, taxing our bequests. And government provides services such as the enforcement of law and order and the provision of national defense. But the government does not make all our choices. We decide what work to do, how much to save, and what to spend our income on. Why does the government participate in some aspects of our lives but not others? ◆ Almost everyone, from the poor, single mother to the wealthy taxpayer, grumbles about government services. Why is the bureaucracy so unpopular? And what determines the scale on which public services are provided? ◆ In this chapter and the next three, we study the interactions of governments and markets. We begin by describing the government sector and explaining how, in the absence of a government, the market economy fails to achieve an efficient allocation of resources. We also explain how the scale of government is determined.

The Government Sector

THE GOVERNMENT SECTOR OF THE U.S. economy consists of more than 86,000 separate organizations, some tiny, like the Yuma, Arizona, School District, and some enormous, like the U.S. federal government. Total spending by the government sector equals 35 percent of total income in the United States, and 20 percent of the labor force is employed in the government sector.

There are three levels of government in the United States: federal, state, and local. The federal government has the largest expenditure—$1.5 trillion in 1993—but local government has the largest number of employees—close to 10 million. Each level of government is organized into branches and departments. The branches of government are the legislative, judicial, and executive, and the departments are the bureaucracies that run the day-to-day business of government. The largest federal government departments are Defense, Health and Human Services, and Treasury. Including military personnel, the Defense Department employs almost two thirds of federal government employees and spends almost one third of the federal budget. The Department of Health and Human Services, which administers welfare programs (including Social Security), spends more than one third of the federal budget. Even the Treasury Department spends close to one fifth of the federal budget (on debt interest and tax collection).

The Scale and Growth of Government

The scale of government has changed over the years, as Fig. 18.1(a) shows. In 1929, government expenditure was 10 percent of total expenditure. It jumped to 20 percent during the Great Depression years of the early 1930s, temporarily exploded during the years of World War II, and then increased steadily over three decades to reach 35 percent of total expenditure by 1993. Government employment has also grown, as Fig. 18.1(b) shows. But the government share of employment reached a peak in the mid-1970s and then began to decrease.

The growth of government expenditure and employment understates the growth of government influence on economic life. That influence stems not only from the government's share of expenditure and employment but also from the mushrooming of laws

FIGURE 18.1

The Size of Government

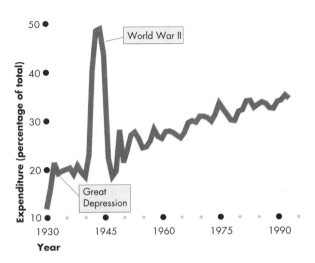

(a) Government expenditure

(b) Government employment

Government expenditure in the United States grew from 10 percent of the total expenditure in 1929 to 35 percent in 1993. Employment (excluding the military) grew from 10 percent of jobs in 1929 to 17 percent in 1993.

Source: The Economic Report of the President, 1988 and 1994.

and regulations that affect the economic actions of households and firms. We look at this aspect of government in Chapter 20, where we study regulation and antitrust.

Why does the government sector become an ever-larger part of the economy? And why has the government's share in employment begun to decline? We'll discover the answers to these and other questions about government later in this chapter and in the following three chapters. But first let's look at the economic role the government plays.

The Economic Theory of Government

WE ALL HAVE OPINIONS ON POLITICAL MATTERS, and some of those opinions are strongly held. As students of economics, our task is to understand, explain, and predict the economic choices that the government sector makes. Although we cannot suppress our political views, it is important, if we are to make progress in studying political behavior, to continually remind ourselves of the important distinction between positive and normative analysis. We first reviewed that distinction in Chapter 1 (p. 12). But because the distinction is so important for the economic study of political behavior, let's remind ourselves of what that distinction is.

Positive and Normative Analysis

An economic analysis of government choices may be either *positive* or *normative*. The positive analysis of government seeks to explain the reasons for and effects of government economic choices. A normative analysis seeks to evaluate the desirability of a government action and argues for or against some particular proposal. Positive analysis seeks to understand what *is*; normative analysis seeks to reach conclusions on what *ought* to be. The economic analysis used in both of these activities is similar. But the use to which the analysis is put differs.

Here we undertake a positive study of government action; that is, we seek to understand the reasons for and the effects of the actions that we see being undertaken by governments in the United States today. We do not seek to establish the desirability of any particular course of action or to argue for or against any particular policy.

Government economic activity arises, in part, because an unregulated market economy does not achieve an *efficient allocation of resources*, a situation called **market failure**. When market failure occurs, the market economy produces too many of some goods and services and too few of some others. In these cases, the marginal social cost of each good and service does not equal its marginal benefit. By reallocating resources, it is possible to make some people better off while making no one worse off. So some government activity is an attempt to modify the market outcome to moderate the effects of market failure.

Government economic activity also arises because an unregulated market economy does not achieve what most people regard as an *equitable distribution of income*. So some government activity is an attempt to modify the market outcome to redistribute income and wealth, sometimes from the rich to the poor, sometimes among the rich, and sometimes from the poor to the rich.

There are four broad problems that create market failure and inequity. They are:

- Public goods
- Economic inequality
- Monopoly
- Externalities

Public Goods

A **public good** is a good or service that can be consumed simultaneously by everyone and from which no one can be excluded. The first feature of a public good is called nonrivalry. A good is **nonrival** if for a given level of production, the consumption by one person does not decrease the consumption by another person. An example of nonrival consumption is watching a television show. The opposite of nonrival is rival. A good is **rival** if for a given level of production, the consumption by one person decreases the consumption by another person. An example of rival consumption is eating a hotdog.

The second feature of a public good is that it is nonexcludable. A good is **nonexcludable** if it is impossible, or extremely costly, to prevent someone from benefiting from a good. An example of a nonexcludable good is national defense. It would be difficult to exclude someone from being defended. The opposite of nonexcludable is excludable. A good is **excludable** if it is possible to prevent a person from enjoying the benefits of a good. An example of an excludable good is cable television. Cable companies can ensure that only those people who have paid the fee receive programs.

FIGURE 18.2
Public Goods and Private Goods

	Rival	Nonrival
Excludable	**Pure private goods** Food Car House	**Excludable and nonrival** Cable television Bridge Highway
Non-excludable	**Nonexcludable and rival** Fish in the ocean Air	**Pure public goods** Lighthouse National defense

A pure public good (bottom right) is one for which consumption is nonrival and from which it is impossible to exclude a consumer. Pure public goods pose a free-rider problem. A pure private good (top left) is one for which consumption is rival and from which consumers can be excluded. Some goods are nonexcludable but are rival (bottom left), and some goods are nonrival but are excludable (top right).

Source: Adapted from and inspired by E. S. Savas, *Privatizing the Public Sector*, Chatham House Publishers, Inc., Chatham, NJ., 1982, p. 34.

Figure 18.2 classifies goods according to these two criteria and gives some examples of goods in each category. Goods in the bottom right-hand corner are known as *pure* public goods. The classic example of a pure public good is a lighthouse. A modern example is national defense. One person's consumption of the security provided by our national defense system does not decrease the amount available for someone else—defense is nonrival. And the military cannot select those whom it will protect and those whom it will leave exposed to threats—defense is nonexcludable.

Many goods have a public element but are not pure public goods. An example is a highway. A highway is nonrival until it becomes congested. One more car on a highway with plenty of space does not reduce anyone else's consumption of transportation services. But once the highway becomes congested, one extra vehicle lowers the quality of the service available to everyone else—it becomes rival like a private good. Also, users can be excluded from a highway by toll-gates. Another example is fish in the ocean. Ocean fish

are rival because a fish taken by one person is not available for anyone else. Ocean fish are also nonexcludable because it is difficult (at least outside a country's territorial limits) to prevent anyone from taking them.

Public goods can create a free-rider problem. A **free rider** is a person who consumes a good without paying for it. Public goods create a *free-rider problem* because the quantity of the good that the person is able to consume is not influenced by the amount the person pays for the good. So no one has an incentive to pay for a public good. We'll see how government can help to cope with the free-rider problem later in this chapter. But first let's look at the other sources of government economic activity.

Economic Inequality

The market economy produces unequal incomes. It does so because many people own few resources or own resources that command a low price. Also, the market economy does not provide insurance against an unlucky draw in the income distribution sweepstakes. Economic inequality creates two types of problems. First, it creates a situation that many people regard as unfair. Second, it creates social and political unrest that can increase the crime rate and, in extreme cases, produce political insurrection and revolution.

To lessen the degree of inequality, governments redistribute income. They tax some people and pay benefits to others. But not all government redistribution goes from the rich to the poor. The creation of monopoly and government protection of cartels often redistributes income from the poor (and the middle) to the rich. We study inequality and the way governments try to lessen it in Chapter 19.

Monopoly

Rent seeking and *monopoly* prevent the allocation of resources from being efficient. Every business tries to maximize profit, and when monopoly power exists, it is usually possible to increase profit by restricting output and increasing price. Until fairly recently, for example, AT&T had a monopoly on long-distance telephone services, and the quantity of long-distance services was much smaller and the price much higher than they are today.

Although some monopolies arise from *legal barriers to entry*—barriers to entry created by governments—a major activity of government is to regulate monopoly and to enforce laws that prevent cartels and other restrictions on competition. We study these regulations and laws in Chapter 20.

Externalities

An **externality** is a cost or a benefit arising from an economic transaction that falls on people who do not participate in that transaction. For example, when a chemical factory (legally) dumps its waste into a river and kills the fish, it imposes an externality—in this case, an external cost—on the fisherman who lives downstream. External costs and benefits are not usually taken into account by the people whose actions create them. For example, the chemical factory does not take its effects on the fish into account when deciding whether to dump waste into the river. When a homeowner fills her garden with spring bulbs, she generates an external benefit for all the joggers and walkers who pass by. In deciding how much to spend on this lavish display, she takes into account only the benefits accruing to herself. We study externalities in Chapter 21.

Before we begin to study each of these problems from which government activity arises, let's look at the arena in which governments operate, the "political marketplace."

Public Choice and the Political Marketplace

GOVERNMENT IS A COMPLEX ORGANIZATION made up of millions of individuals, each with his or her *own* economic objectives. Government policy choices are the outcome of the choices made by these individuals. To analyze these choices, economists have developed a theory of the political marketplace that parallels theories of markets for goods and services—*public choice theory*.

In public choice theory, the actors in the political marketplace are:

- Voters
- Politicians
- Bureaucrats

The choices and interactions of these actors are illustrated in Fig. 18.3. Let's look at each in turn.

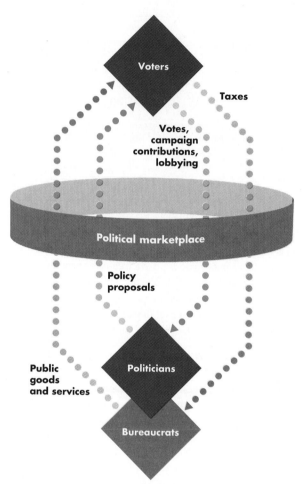

FIGURE 18.3
The Political Marketplace

Voters express their demands for policies by voting, making campaign contributions, and lobbying. Politicians propose policies to appeal to a majority of voters. Bureaucrats try to maximize the budgets of their bureaus. If voters are well-informed, the political equilibrium is efficient. If voters are rationally ignorant, the provision of public goods exceeds the efficient level.

Voters

Voters are the consumers of the political process. In markets for goods and services, people express their demands by their willingness to pay. In the political marketplace, they express their demands by voting, by making campaign contributions, and by lobbying.

Economic models of public choice assume that people support policies that they believe will make them better off and oppose policies that they believe will make them worse off. They neither oppose nor support—they are indifferent among—policies that they believe have no effect on them. Voters' *perceptions* rather than reality are what guide their choices.

Politicians

Politicians are the elected administrators and legislators in federal, state, and local government—from the chief executives (the president, state governor, or mayor) to members of the legislatures (state and federal senators and representatives and city councilors).

Economic models of public choice assume that the objective of a politician is to get elected and to remain in office. Votes to a politician are like dollars to a firm. To get enough votes, politicians form coalitions—political parties—that develop policy proposals, which they expect will appeal to a majority of voters.

Bureaucrats

Bureaucrats are the hired officials who work in government departments, again at the federal, state, and local levels, and who produce public goods and services. The most senior bureaucrats are hired by politicians. Junior bureaucrats are hired by senior ones.

Economic models of public choice assume that bureaucrats aim to maximize their own utility. To achieve this objective, they try to maximize the budget of the agency in which they work. The bigger the budget of the agency, the greater is the prestige of the agency chief and the larger is the opportunity for promotion for people farther down the bureaucratic ladder. Thus all the members of an agency have an interest in maximizing the agency's budget. To maximize their budgets, bureaucrats devise programs that they expect will appeal to politicians and help politicians to sell programs to voters.

Political Equilibrium

Voters, politicians, and bureaucrats make their economic choices to best further their own objectives. But each group is constrained in two ways: by the preferences of the other groups and by what is technologically feasible. The outcome of the choices of voters, politicians, and bureaucrats is the political

equilibrium. The **political equilibrium** is a situation in which the choices made by voters, politicians, and bureaucrats are all compatible and in which no group can improve its position by making a different choice.

Two types of political equilibrium are possible: efficient and inefficient. *Public interest* theory predicts that governments make choices that achieve efficiency. *Public choice* theory recognizes the possibility of inefficient outcomes—of *government failure* that parallels the possibility of market failure. We'll see to what extent public interest and public choice are better descriptions of reality.

Let's see how voters, politicians, and bureaucrats interact to determine the quantity of public goods.

Public Goods

WHY DOES THE GOVERNMENT PROVIDE GOODS and services—goods and services that can be consumed simultaneously by everyone and from which no one can be excluded—such as national defense, public health services, a legal system, and schools and highways? Why don't we leave the provision of these goods and services to private firms that sell their output in markets? Why don't we buy our national defense from North Pole Protection, Inc., a private firm that would compete for our dollars in the marketplace in the same way that McDonald's and Coca-Cola do? The answer to these questions lies in the free-rider problem.

The Free-Rider Problem

Suppose that for its effective national defense, a country must launch some communication and surveillance satellites. One satellite can do part of the job required. But the larger the number of satellites deployed, the greater is the degree of security.

Satellites are expensive, and to build them, resources are diverted from other productive activities. The larger the number of satellites installed, the greater is their marginal cost.

Our task is to work out the number of satellites to install to achieve allocative efficiency. We'll then examine whether private provision can achieve allocative efficiency, and we'll discover that it cannot—that there is a free-rider problem.

Cost-Benefit Analysis

The benefit provided by a satellite is based on the preferences and beliefs of the consumers of its services. The benefit is the *value* of the satellite's services. The *value* to an individual of a *private* good is the maximum amount that the person is willing to pay for one more unit of the good. And the individual's demand curve tells us this value. Similarly, the value to an individual of a *public* good is the maximum amount that the person is willing to pay for one more unit of the good.

To calculate the value a person places on one more unit of a public good, we use the concepts of total benefit and marginal benefit. *Total benefit* is the total dollar value that a person places on a given level of provision of a public good. The greater the quantity of a public good, the larger is a person's total benefit. **Marginal benefit** is the increase in total benefit that results from a one-unit increase in the quantity of a public good.

Figure 18.4 shows an example of the marginal benefit that arises from defense satellites for a society with just two members, Lisa and Max. Lisa's and Max's marginal benefits are graphed as MB_L and MB_M, respectively, in parts (a) and (b) of the figure. The marginal benefit from a public good is similar to the marginal utility from a private good—its magnitude diminishes as the quantity of the good increases. For Lisa, the marginal benefit of the first satellite is $80, and for the second it is $60. By the time 4 satellites are deployed, Lisa perceives no additional benefits. For Max, the marginal utility of the first satellite is $50, and for the second it is $40. By the time 4 satellites are deployed, Max perceives only $10 worth of marginal benefit.

Part (c) of the figure shows the economy's marginal benefit curve, MB (where the economy has only two people, Lisa and Max). An individual's marginal benefit curve for a public good is similar to the individual's demand curve for a private good. But the economy's marginal benefit curve for a public good is different from the market demand curve for a private good. To obtain the market demand curve for a private good, we add up the quantities demanded by each individual at each price. In other words, we sum the individual demand curves horizontally.[1] In contrast, to find the economy's marginal benefit curve of a public good, we add the marginal benefit of each

---

[1]The derivation of the market demand curve from the individual demand curves is explained in Fig. 7.1, p. 147.

FIGURE 18.4
Benefits of a Public Good

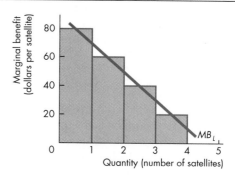

(a) Lisa's marginal benefit

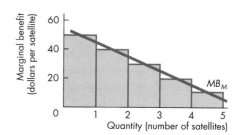

(b) Max's marginal benefit

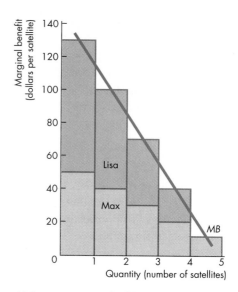

(c) Economy's marginal benefit

The marginal benefit to the economy at each quantity of the public good is the sum of the marginal benefits to each individual. The marginal benefit curves are MB_L for Lisa, MB_M for Max, and MB for the economy.

individual at each quantity of provision. That is, we sum the individual marginal benefit curves vertically. The resulting marginal benefit for the economy made up of Lisa and Max is the economy's marginal benefit curve graphed in part (c)—the curve *MB*.

In reality, an economy with two people would not buy any satellites—the total benefit falls far short

of the cost. But an economy with 250 million people might. To determine the efficient quantity, we need to take cost as well as benefit into account. The cost of a satellite is based on technology and the prices of the factors of production used to produce it. It is an opportunity cost and is derived in the same way as the cost of producing sweaters (explained in Chapter

---

FIGURE 18.5

The Efficient Quantity of a Public Good

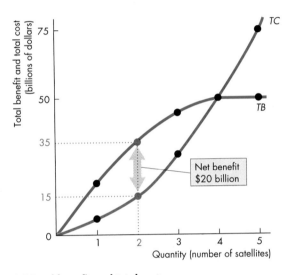

(a) Total benefit and total cost

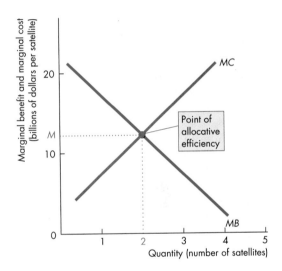

(b) Marginal benefit and marginal cost

Quantity (number of satellites)	Total benefit (billions of dollars)		Marginal benefit (billions of dollars per satellite)	Total cost (billions of dollars)		Marginal cost (billions of dollars per satellite)	Net benefit (billions of dollars)
0	0			0			0
			20			5	
1	20			5			15
			15			10	
2	35			15			20
			10			15	
3	45			30			15
			5			20	
4	50			50			0
			0			25	
5	50			75			−25

Total benefit and total cost are graphed in part (a) as the total benefit curve, *TB*, and the total cost curve, *TC*. Net benefit—the vertical distance between the two curves—is maximized when 2 satellites are installed.

Part (b) shows the marginal benefit curve, *MB*, and marginal cost curve, *MC*. When marginal cost equals marginal benefit, net benefit is maximized and allocative efficiency is achieved.

10). The efficient quantity is the one that maximizes *net benefit*—total benefit minus total cost.

Figure 18.5 illustrates the efficient quantity of satellites. The second and third columns of the table show the total and marginal benefits to an economy. The next two columns show the total and marginal cost of producing satellites. The final column shows net benefit. Total benefit, *TB,* and total cost, *TC,* are graphed in part (a) of the figure. Net benefit (total benefit minus total cost) is maximized when the vertical distance between the *TB* and *TC* curves is at its largest, a situation that occurs with 2 satellites. This is the efficient quantity.

The fundamental principles of marginal analysis that you have used to explain how consumers maximize utility and how firms maximize profit can also be used to calculate the efficient scale of provision of a public good. Figure 18.5(b) shows this alternative approach. The marginal benefit curve is *MB* and the marginal cost curve is *MC.* When marginal benefit exceeds marginal cost, net benefit increases if the quantity produced increases. When marginal cost exceeds marginal benefit, net benefit increases if the quantity produced decreases. Marginal benefit equals marginal cost with 2 satellites. So making marginal cost equal to marginal benefit maximizes net benefit and achieves allocative efficiency.

Private Provision

We have now worked out the quantity of satellites that maximizes net benefit. Would a private firm—North Pole Protection, Inc.—deliver that quantity? It would not. To do so, it would have to collect $15 billion to cover its costs—or $60 from each of the 250 million people in the economy. But no one would have an incentive to buy his or her "share" of the satellite system. Everyone would reason as follows: The number of satellites provided by North Pole Protection, Inc., is not affected by my $60. But my own private consumption is greater if I free-ride and do not pay my share of the cost of the satellite system. If I do not pay, I enjoy the same level of security and can buy more private goods. Therefore I will spend my $60 on other goods and free-ride on the public good. This is the free-rider problem.

If everyone reasons the same way, North Pole Protection has zero revenue and so provides no satellites. Because two satellites is the efficient level, private provision is inefficient.

Public Provision

Suppose there are two political parties, the Hawks and the Doves, that agree with each other on all issues except for satellites. The Hawks would like to provide 4 satellites at a cost of $50 billion, with benefits of $50 billion and a net benefit of zero, as shown in Fig. 18.6. The Doves would like to provide 1 satellite at a cost of $5 billion, a benefit of $20 billion, and a net benefit of $15 billion—see Fig. 18.6.

Before deciding on their policy proposals, the two political parties do a "what-if" analysis. Each party reasons as follows: If each party offers the satellite program it wants—Hawks 4 satellites and Doves 1 satellite—the voters will see that they will get a net

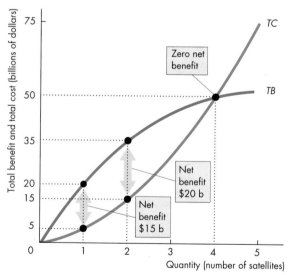

FIGURE 18.6

Provision of a Public Good in a Political System ◆

Net benefit is maximized if 2 satellites are installed, with a total benefit of $35 billion and a total cost of $15 billion. The Doves would like 1 satellite, and the Hawks would like 4. But each party recognizes that its only hope of being elected is to provide 2 satellites—the quantity that maximizes net benefit and so leaves no room for the other party to improve on. If voters are well-informed about the cost and benefit of a public good, competition between political parties for their votes achieves the efficient outcome.

benefit of $15 billion from the Doves and zero net benefit from the Hawks, and the Doves will win the election.

Contemplating this outcome, the Hawks realize that their party is too hawkish to get elected. They figure that they must offer net benefits in excess of $15 billion if they are to beat the Doves. So they scale back their proposal to 2 satellites. At this level of provision, total cost is $15 billion, total benefit is $35 billion, and net benefit is $20 billion. If the Doves stick with 1 satellite, the Hawks will win the election.

But contemplating this outcome, the Doves realize that the best they can do is to match the Hawks. They too propose to provide 2 satellites on exactly the same terms as the Hawks. If the two parties offer the same number of satellites, the voters are indifferent between the parties. They flip coins to decide their votes, and each party receives around 50 percent of the vote.

The result of the politicians' "what-if" analysis is that each party offers 2 satellites, so regardless of who wins the election, this is the quantity of satellites installed. And this quantity is efficient. It maximizes the perceived net benefit of the voters. Thus in this example, competition in the political marketplace results in the efficient provision of a public good. But for this outcome to occur, voters must be well-informed and evaluate the alternatives. We'll see below that they do not always have an incentive to do so.

In the example we've just studied, both parties propose identical policies. This tendency toward identical policies is called the principle of minimum differentiation.

The Principle of Minimum Differentiation The **principle of minimum differentiation** is the tendency for competitors to make themselves identical to appeal to the maximum number of clients or voters. You can see the principle of minimum differentiation in many familiar situations. Let's look at one.

Figure 18.7 shows a beach that is one mile long from *A* to *B*. Sunbathers lounge at equal intervals over the entire beach and buy their ice cream from the nearest vendor. Also, the farther they must walk, the fewer ice creams they buy. An ice cream vendor arrives at the beach and sets up a stand. Where will she locate? The answer is at position *C*—exactly halfway between *A* and *B*. By locating in this position, the farthest that anyone must walk to buy an ice

FIGURE **18.7**

The Principle of Minimum Differentiation

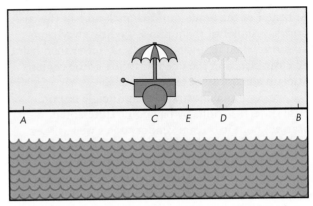

A beach stretches from *A* to *B*. Sunbathers are distributed at even intervals along the whole beach. An ice cream vendor sets up a stand at point *C*. The distance that people must walk for ice cream is the same no matter on which side of the ice cream stand they are located. If a second ice cream vendor sets up a stand, it will pay to place the stand exactly next to *C* in the middle of the beach. If the second stand is placed at *D*, only the customers on the beach between *E* and *B* will buy ice cream from *D*. Those between *A* and *E* will go to *C*. By moving as close to *C* as possible, the second ice cream vendor picks up half the ice cream customers.

cream is a mile (half a mile to the ice cream stand and half a mile back to the beach towel), so she gets the maximum possible number of customers.

Now suppose a second ice cream vendor arrives on the beach. Where will he place his ice cream stand? The answer is right next to the original one at point *C*. To understand why, imagine that the second vendor locates his stand at point *D*—halfway between *C* and *B*. How many customers will he attract and how many will go to the stand at *C*? The stand at *D* will pick up all the customers on the beach between *B* and *D*, because this stand is closer for them. It will also pick up all the customers between *D* and *E* (the point halfway between *C* and *D*), because they too will have a shorter trip for an ice cream by going to *D* than by going to *C*. All the people between *A* and *C* and all those between *C* and *E* will go to stand *C*. So the ice cream stand located at

C will pick up all the people on the beach between *A* and *E*, and the stand located at *D* will pick up all the people located between *E* and *B*.

Now suppose that the vendor with a stand at *D* moves to *C*. There are now two stands at *C*. Half the customers will go to the first vendor and the other half to the second vendor. Only by locating exactly in the center of the beach can each pick up half the customers. If either of them moves slightly away from the center, then that vendor picks up fewer than half the customers and the one remaining at the center picks up a majority of the customers.

This example illustrates the principle of minimum differentiation. By having no differentiation in location, both ice cream vendors do as well as they can and share the market evenly.

The principle of minimum differentiation has been used to explain a wide variety of choices: how supermarkets choose their locations, how the makers of automobiles and microwave popcorn design their products, and how political parties choose their platforms.

We have analyzed the behavior of politicians but not that of the bureaucrats who translate the choices of the politicians into programs. Let's now see how the economic choices of bureaucrats influence the political equilibrium.

The Role of Bureaucrats

We've seen, in Fig. 18.5 and Fig. 18.6, that 2 satellites at a cost of $15 billion maximizes net benefit and that competition between two political parties delivers this outcome. But will the Defense Department—the Pentagon—cooperate?

Suppose the objective of the Pentagon is to maximize the defense budget. To achieve its objective, the Pentagon will try to persuade the politicians that 2 satellites cost more than $15 billion. As Fig. 18.8 shows, if possible, the Pentagon would like to convince Congress that 2 satellites cost $35 billion—the entire benefit. And pressing its position even more strongly, the Pentagon will argue for more satellites. It will press for 4 satellites and a budget of $50 billion. In this situation, total benefit and total cost are equal and net benefit is zero.

The Pentagon wants to maximize its budget but won't the politicians prevent it from doing so to maximize votes? They will if voters are well-informed and know what is best for them. But voters might be

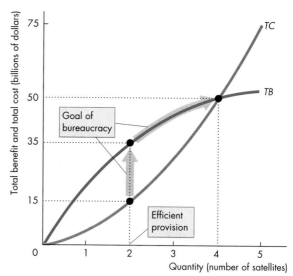

FIGURE 18.8
Bureaucratic Overprovision

The goal of a bureaucracy is to maximize its budget. A bureaucracy that maximizes its budget will seek to increase its budget so that its total cost equals total benefit and then to use its budget to expand output and expenditure. Here, the Pentagon tries to get $35 billion to provide 2 satellites. It would like to increase the quantity of satellites to 4 with a budget of $50 billion.

rationally ignorant. In this case, well-informed interest groups might enable the Pentagon to achieve its objective.

Voter Ignorance and Well-Informed Interest Groups   A principle of public choice theory is that it is rational for a voter to be ignorant about an issue unless that issue has a perceptible effect on the voter's income. **Rational ignorance** is the decision *not* to acquire information because the cost of doing so exceeds the expected benefit. For example, each voter knows that he or she can make virtually no difference to the defense policy of the U.S. government. Each voter also knows that it would take an enormous amount of time and effort to become even moderately well-informed about alternative defense technologies. So voters remain relatively uninformed about the technicalities of defense issues. (Though we are

using defense policy as an example, the same applies to all aspects of government economic activity.)

All voters are consumers of national defense. But not all voters are producers of national defense. Only a small number are in this latter category. Voters who own or work for firms that produce satellites have a direct personal interest in defense because it affects their incomes. These voters have an incentive to become well-informed about defense issues and to operate a political lobby aimed at furthering their own interests. In collaboration with the defense bureaucracy, these voters exert a larger influence than do the relatively uninformed voters who only consume this public good.

When the rationality of the uninformed voter and special interest groups are taken into account, the political equilibrium provides public goods in excess of the efficient quantity. So in the satellite example, 3 or 4 satellites might be installed rather than the efficient quantity, which is 2 satellites. An efficient outcome is predicted by public interest theory, and an inefficient overprovision is predicted by public choice theory.

Why Government Grows

We saw at the beginning of this chapter that government has grown over the years. Now that we know how the quantity of public goods is determined, we can explain part of the reason for the growth of government. Government grows, in part, because the demand for some public goods increases at a faster rate than the demand for private goods. There are two possible reasons for this growth:

- Voter preferences
- Inefficient overprovision

Voter Preferences The growth of government can be explained by voter preferences in the following way. As voters' incomes increase (as they usually do in most years), the demand for many public goods increases more quickly than income. (Technically, the *income elasticity of demand* for many public goods is greater than 1—see Chapter 5, pp. 107–108.) Many (and the most expensive) public goods are in this category. They include communication systems such as highways, airports, and air-traffic control systems; public health; education; and national defense. If politicians did not support increases in expenditures on these items, they would not get elected.

Inefficient Overprovision Inefficient overprovision might explain the *size* of government, but not its *growth rate*. It (possibly) explains why government is *larger* than its efficient scale, but it does not explain why governments use an increasing proportion of total resources. In fact, while government has accounted for a steadily rising proportion of total spending in the economy, government sector employment has shrunk relative to total employment since the mid-1970s (see Figure 18.1, p. 425). This change in employment is probably explained by the substitution of capital—such as computers—for labor.

Voters Strike Back

If government grows too large, relative to what voters are willing to accept, there might be a voter backlash against government programs and a large bureaucracy. The electoral success of Ronald Reagan during the 1980s and Republicans in the elections of 1994 might be interpreted as such a backlash.

Another way that voters—and politicians—can try to counter the tendency of bureaucrats to expand their budgets is to privatize the *production* of public goods. Government *provision* of a public good does not automatically imply that a government-operated bureau must *produce* the good. *Reading Between the Lines* on pp. 440–441 explores this distinction between public provision and public production further.

R E V I E W

- Private provision of a public good creates a free-rider problem and provides less than the efficient quantity of the good.

- Competition between politicians for votes can achieve an efficient quantity of a public good, provided that voters are well-informed.

- If consumers of a public good are less well-informed than producers of that good, bureaucrats supported by well-informed voters have a larger influence than uninformed voters and the quantity of public goods exceeds the efficient quantity.

We've now seen how voters, politicians, and bureaucrats interact to determine the quantity of a public good. But public goods must be paid for with taxes. How does the political marketplace determine the scale and variety of taxes that we pay?

Taxes

TAXES GENERATE THE FINANCIAL RESOURCES that governments use to provide voters with public goods and other benefits. For the federal government in 1994, 56 percent of total revenue came from income taxes and 38 percent from social insurance taxes. For state and local governments, 50 percent of total revenue came from sales taxes and 21 percent from income taxes. Why do income taxes provide such a large proportion of the government's revenue?

Income Taxes

Income taxes are a prominent source of government revenue because of the way they distribute the costs and benefits of government. The amounts that people pay in income tax and receive in benefits from government programs depend on their incomes. Other things being the same, the higher a person's income, the greater is the amount of income tax paid and the smaller is the amount of benefit received. So as a rule, high-income people tend to vote for a political party that proposes low benefits and a low income tax rate, while low-income people tend to vote for a political party that proposes high benefits and a high income tax rate. The politicians' task is to find the income tax rate and benefits program that attract the votes of a majority of voters.

A model of the attempt of politicians to balance the interests of the high-income voters and low-income voters is based on the median voter theorem.

The Median Voter Theorem The **median voter theorem** states that political parties will pursue policies that appeal most to the median voter. The median member of a population is the one in the middle—one half of the population lies on one side and one half on the other. Let's see how the median voter theorem applies to the questions of how large a benefits program and how large an income tax rate to impose.

Imagine a list of all the possible levels of benefits from government programs and the associated income tax rates needed to finance them. The list begins with the highest possible level of benefits and income tax rate and ends with no benefits and a zero income tax rate. We can identify each entry in the list by the income tax rate associated with it.

Next imagine arranging all the voters along a line running from A to D, as shown in Fig. 18.9. The voter who favors the highest income tax rate (and the highest benefit level) is at A. The voter who favors a zero tax rate (and no benefits) is at D. All the other voters are arranged along the line based on the tax rate (and benefits) that they favor most. The curve in the figure shows the tax rate favored most by each voter between A and D. The median voter in the example in Fig. 18.9 favors most a tax rate of 30 percent.

Suppose that two political parties propose similar but not quite identical income tax rates. The high-tax party proposes a tax rate of 61 percent and the low-tax party proposes a tax rate of 59 percent. Given this choice, all the voters between A and B prefer the higher tax rate and will vote for the high-tax party. All the voters between B and D prefer the lower tax and will vote for the low-tax party. The low-tax party will win the election.

Alternatively, suppose that the high-tax party proposes a tax rate of 11 percent and the low-tax party proposes a tax rate of 9 percent. The voters between A and C will vote for the high-tax party and those between C and D will vote for the low-tax party. This time, the high-tax party will win the election.

In either of the two situations we've just examined, the party that wins the election is the one closer to the position preferred by the median voter. So each party can improve its election performance by moving closer to the median than the other party. But each party has the same incentive, so each moves toward the median. Once the two parties are offering the tax rate favored most by the median voter, neither can increase its vote by changing its proposal. One party will get the votes between A and the median, and the other party will get the votes between the median and D.

All the voters except those at the median will be dissatisfied—for those between A and the median, the benefits and tax rate are too low, and for those between D and the median, the benefits and tax rate are too high. But no political party can propose programs other than those that can be financed with a 30 percent tax rate and expect to win the election. If the two parties propose identical programs and a 30 percent tax rate, the voters are indifferent and either don't vote or flip a coin to decide which party to vote for.

The median voter theorem implies the principle of minimum differentiation that we've already studied. Both political parties locate at the same point on the political spectrum. But this implication does not

FIGURE 18.9
Voting for Income Taxes

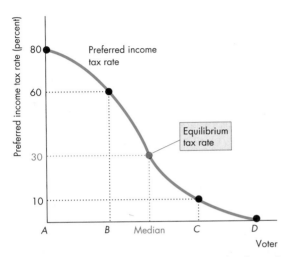

A political party can win an election by proposing policies that appeal to the median voter and to all voters on one side of the median. If the median voter favors a policy, that policy will be proposed. In the figure, voters have different preferences concerning the income tax rate (and benefit rate). They are ranked in descending order of their preferred tax. A's preferred tax rate is highest (80 percent) and D's is lowest (0 percent).

There are two political parties. If one proposes a 61 percent tax and the other a 59 percent tax, the low-tax party will win the election—voters between A and B will vote for the high-tax party, and those between B and D will vote for the low-tax party. If both parties propose low taxes—11 percent and 9 percent—the high-tax party will win. It will pick up the votes between A and C, leaving only the votes between C and D for the low-tax party. Each party has an incentive to move toward the tax rate preferred by the median voter. At that point, each party picks up half the votes and neither can improve its share.

mean that all political parties will be identical in all respects. One party might be ideologically aligned with the wealthy and another with the poor. The two parties will pursue similar policies but each will maintain a rhetoric designed to further the goals of their supporters. One party will talk about higher taxes and better programs and the other will talk about cutting taxes and programs, but neither will actually carry such policies to excess for fear of losing the support of the median voter.

Excise Taxes

An **excise tax** is a tax on the sale of a particular commodity. Let's study the effects of an excise tax by considering the tax on gasoline shown in Fig. 18.10. The demand curve for gasoline is D, and the supply curve is S. If there is no tax on gasoline, its price is 60¢ a gallon and 400 million gallons of gasoline a day are bought and sold.

Now suppose that a tax is imposed on gasoline at the rate of 60¢ a gallon. If producers are willing to supply 400 million gallons a day for 60¢ when there is no tax, then they are willing to supply that same quantity in the face of a 60¢ tax only if the price increases to $1.20 a gallon. That is, they want to get the 60¢ a gallon they received before plus the 60¢ that they now have to give the government in the form of a gasoline tax. As a result of the tax, the supply of gasoline decreases and the supply curve shifts leftward. The magnitude of the shift is such that the vertical distance between the original and the new supply curve is the amount of the tax. The new supply curve is the red curve, $S + tax$. The new supply curve intersects the demand curve at 300 million gallons a day and $1.10 a gallon. This situation is the new equilibrium after the imposition of the tax.

Why Tax Rates Vary

Why do we tax gasoline, alcohol, and tobacco at high rates and some goods not at all? One reason is that taxes create *deadweight losses*. (You first encountered the concept of deadweight loss when you studied monopoly in Chapter 12, pp. 285–286.) It is impossible to avoid deadweight losses from taxes, but by levying taxes at different rates on different commodities, the deadweight loss arising from raising a given amount of revenue can be minimized. Minimizing deadweight loss is consistent with maximizing the number of voters to whom the taxes will appeal.

Minimizing the Deadweight Loss of Taxes You can see that taxes create deadweight loss by looking again at Fig. 18.10. Without a tax, 400 million gallons of gasoline a day are consumed at a price of 60¢ a gallon. With a 60¢ tax, the price paid by the consumer rises to $1.10 a gallon and the quantity consumed declines to 300 million gallons a day. There is a loss of consumer surplus arising from this price increase and quantity decrease. The amount of consumer surplus lost is shown by the light gray triangle.

FIGURE 18.10

An Excise Tax

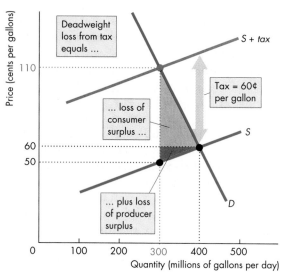

The demand curve for gasoline is D, and the supply curve is S. In the absence of any taxes, gasoline will sell for 60¢ a gallon and 400 million gallons a day will be bought and sold. When a tax of 60¢ a gallon is imposed, the supply curve shifts leftward to become the curve S + tax. The new equilibrium price is $1.10 a gallon, and 300 million gallons a day are bought and sold. The excise tax creates a deadweight loss represented by the gray triangle. The tax revenue collected is 60¢ a gallon on 300 million gallons, which is $180 million a day. The deadweight loss from the tax is $30 million a day. That is, to raise tax revenue of $180 million a day, a deadweight loss of $30 million a day is incurred.

On the 300 millionth gallon bought—the marginal unit bought—the consumer pays 110¢ compared with 60¢ in the absence of a tax. So 50¢ of consumer surplus is lost on this unit. On each successive unit up to the 400 millionth, there is a successively smaller loss of consumer surplus. The total amount of consumer surplus lost equals the area of the light gray triangle, which is $25 million dollars a day.[2]

There is also a loss of producer surplus. The amount of producer surplus lost is shown by the dark gray triangle. On the 300 millionth gallon sold—the marginal unit sold—the producer receives 50¢ compared with 60¢ in the absence of a tax. So 10¢ of producer surplus is lost on this unit. On each successive unit up to the 400 millionth, there is a successively smaller loss of producer surplus. The total amount of producer surplus lost equals the area of the dark gray triangle, which is $5 million dollars a day.[3]

The deadweight loss is the sum of the loss of consumer surplus and producer surplus, which is indicated by the two gray triangles in Fig. 18.10. The dollar value of that triangle is $30 million a day.

But how much revenue is raised by this tax? Because 300 million gallons of gasoline are sold each day and the tax is 60¢ a gallon, total revenue from the gasoline tax is $180 million a day (300 million gallons multiplied by 60¢ a gallon). Thus to raise tax revenue of $180 million dollars a day by using the gasoline tax, a deadweight loss of $30 million a day—one sixth of the tax revenue—is incurred.

One of the main influences on the deadweight loss arising from a tax is the elasticity of demand for the product. The demand for gasoline is fairly inelastic. As a consequence, when a tax is imposed, the quantity demanded falls by a smaller percentage than the percentage rise in price. In the example that we've just studied, the quantity demanded falls by 25 percent but the price increases by 83.33 percent.

To see the importance of the elasticity of demand, let's consider a different commodity—orange juice. So that we can make a quick and direct comparison, let's assume that the orange juice market is exactly as big as the market for gasoline. Figure 18.11 illustrates this market. The demand curve for orange juice is D, and the supply curve is S. Orange juice is not taxed, and so the price of orange juice is 60¢ a gallon—where the supply curve and the demand curve intersect—and the quantity of orange juice traded is 400 million gallons a day.

Now suppose that the government contemplates abolishing the gasoline tax and taxing orange juice instead. The demand for orange juice is more elastic than the demand for gasoline. It has many good sub-

---

[2]You can calculate the area of that triangle by using the formula (Base × height)/2. The base is 100 million gallons, the decrease in quantity. The height is the price increase—50¢. Multiplying 100 million gallons by 50¢ and dividing by 2 give $25 million a day.

[3]The base is 100 million gallons, the decrease in quantity. The height is the price decrease for the producer—10¢. Multiplying 100 million gallons by 10¢ and dividing by 2 give $5 million a day.

stitutes in the form of other fruit juices. The government wants to raise $180 million a day so that its total revenue is not affected by this tax change. The government's economists, armed with their statistical estimates of the demand and supply curves for orange juice that appear in Fig. 18.11, work out that a tax of 90¢ a gallon will do the job. With such a tax, the supply curve shifts leftward to become the curve labeled *S + tax*. This new supply curve intersects the demand curve at a price of $1.30 a gallon and at a

quantity of 200 million gallons a day. The price at which suppliers are willing to produce 200 million gallons a day is 40¢ a gallon. The government collects a tax of 90¢ a gallon on 200 million gallons a day, so it collects a total revenue of $180 million dollars a day—exactly the amount that it requires.

But what is the deadweight loss in this case? The answer can be seen by looking at the gray triangle in Fig. 18.11. The magnitude of that deadweight loss is $90 million.[4] Notice how much bigger the deadweight loss is from taxing orange juice than from taxing gasoline. In the case of orange juice, the deadweight loss is one half the revenue raised, while in the case of gasoline, it is only one sixth. What accounts for this difference? The supply curves are identical in each case, and the examples were also set up to ensure that the initial no-tax prices and quantities were identical. The difference between the two cases is the elasticity of demand: In the case of gasoline, the quantity demanded falls by only 25 percent when the price almost doubles. In the case of orange juice, the quantity demanded falls by 50 percent when the price only slightly more than doubles.

You can see why taxing orange juice is not on the political agenda of any of the major parties. Vote-seeking politicians seek out taxes that benefit the median voter. Other things being equal, this means that they try to minimize the deadweight loss of raising a given amount of revenue. Equivalently, they tax items with poor substitutes more heavily than items with close substitutes.

 We've seen that markets do not always achieve allocative efficiency—there is market failure. We've also seen how it is possible for public choices to overcome market failure in the provision of public goods. But we've also seen that bureaucrats can overprovide a public good. Finally, we've seen how public choices result in income taxes and high tax rates on items whose elasticity of demand is low. In the next three chapters, we are going to look more closely at the other sources of government economic actions—inequality, monopoly, and externalities—and the way public choices cope with them.

FIGURE 18.11
Why We Don't Tax Orange Juice

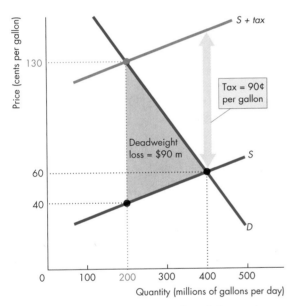

The demand curve for orange juice is *D*, and the supply curve is *S*. The equilibrium price is 60¢ a gallon, and 400 million gallons of juice a day are traded. To raise $180 million of tax revenue, a tax of 90¢ a gallon will have to be imposed. The introduction of this tax shifts the supply curve to *S + tax*. The price rises to $1.30 a gallon, and the quantity bought and sold falls to 200 million gallons a day. The deadweight loss is represented by the gray triangle and equals $90 million a day. The deadweight loss from taxing orange juice is much larger than that from taxing gasoline (Fig. 18.10) because the demand for orange juice is much more elastic than the demand for gasoline. Items that have a low elasticity of demand are taxed more heavily than items that have a high elasticity of demand.

---

[4]This deadweight loss is calculated in exactly the same way as our previous calculation of the deadweight loss from the gasoline tax. The loss of consumer surplus is 200 million gallons multiplied by 70¢, divided by 2, which equals $70 million a day. The loss of producer surplus is 200 million gallons multiplied by 20¢, divided by 2, which equals $20 million a day. The deadweight loss is the sum of the two losses, which equals $90 million a day.

Private Production of Public Goods

Wall Street Journal, June 22, 1993

Public Safety Poses Dangers to Taxpayers

BY TIM W. FERGUSON

Rural/Metro Corp. is a familiar name to those who've long championed the privatizing of public services. The Scottsdale, Ariz.-based company is the fire department for that town and 22 other spots in the Sun Belt. It provides paramedic service in even more places.

Now Rural/Metro is going public—that is, it's registered for an initial stock sale. Currently a $62 million annual operation, it wants to position itself for growth in a most sensitive area of contracting with the government.

The privatization of public safety—fire, rescue, police and jails—is not only touchy and tricky, it is increasingly timely. ...

In the total scheme of government, public safety is surprisingly small potatoes, maybe 4% of all federal, state and local expenditures. But the growth rate is ominous. ... Fire and paramedic spending has grown more than sixfold in 20 years—about the same as the growth rate for total state and local government. The police tab has risen by seven times, and "corrections," 15 times. ...

Corrections is understandably a hot turf for privatization right now. ... Private operation promises a cost reduction of 10% to 15% over standard public management, according to University of Florida Prof. Charles Taylor. He attributes that mainly to thinner top administrative ranks, less "red tape" in procurement and processing and lower pension costs. Wage levels will tend to be comparable, but employees at a company such as Corrections Corp. of America, the nation's largest private alternative, [keep labor costs under control] because they have a stake in the business [through] an Employee Stock Ownership Plan. ...

In nearly all situations to date, privatization in the public safety area has been a tentative, marginal response, a testing of the frontiers of what is politically acceptable ...

Essence of THE STORY

■ The privatization of public safety—fire, rescue, police, and jails—is politically sensitive but timely.

■ Public safety absorbs 4 percent of federal, state, and local expenditures. Fire and paramedic spending has grown more than sixfold in 20 years, police expenditure has increased sevenfold, and "corrections" spending has increased 15-fold.

■ According to University of Florida Professor Charles Taylor, privately operated correctional facilities cost 10 percent to 15 percent less to run than publicly managed ones.

■ The private sector has fewer top administrators, less "red tape," and lower pension costs.

■ Labor is also more efficient, and in some cases (for example, at Corrections Corp. of America), workers have a stake in the business.

Economic

A N A L Y S I S

■ Many public goods are produced privately. Examples are weapons systems for national defense, highways, legal services, and public health services.

■ Some correctional services, fire services, and policing services are also produced privately.

■ The figures compare the public and private production of a public good. In both figures, the total benefit of the public good is shown by TB, and the total cost is shown by TC. The efficient quantity is Q, which we'll assume the government decides to provide.

■ In Fig. 1, the good is produced by a public bureaucracy whose goal is to maximize its budget. B is the maximum budget that the voters will tolerate being spent to produce the quantity Q.

■ In Fig. 2, the government calls for bids from private firms to produce Q. The winning firm does the job for C, its opportunity cost (including normal profit).

■ The private firm has an incentive to cut costs by producing an inferior service, so it is monitored by a pubic bureaucracy whose goal is to maximize its own budget. B minus C is the maximum possible budget for the bureaucracy, given that C is already being spent to produce the good.

■ The case for private production is that a public monitoring bureau can't expand its budget by much and the total cost of private production is less than that of public production.

■ The case for public production is that it is more costly to monitor a private producer to ensure quality service than it is to produce the good publicly.

■ The issue is unresolved and is different for different goods and services. McDonnell Douglas, monitored by the Pentagon, produces aircraft at a lower cost than a government aircraft factory could. The U.S. Army produces national security services at a lower cost than (the fictitious) Private Army Corp. could.

■ American Express Corp. and Aetna Corp. could compete to administer Social Security. We don't know whether this arrangement would be efficient.

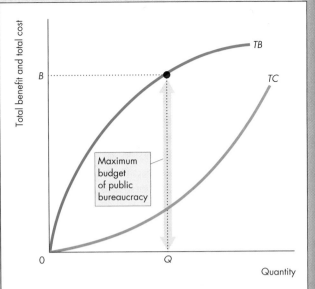

Figure 1 Public production

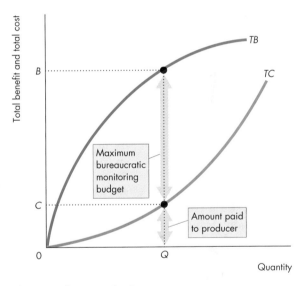

Figure 2 Private production

S U M M A R Y

The Government Sector

Total spending by the government sector equals 35 percent of total income in the United States, and 20 percent of the labor force is employed in the government sector. The biggest departments of government deal with the provision of defense and health and human services. The government share of the economy has grown over the years, increasing from 10 percent in 1929 to 35 percent in 1993. (pp. 425–426)

The Economic Theory of Government

Government economic actions arise in an attempt to cope with problems created by public goods, economic inequality, monopoly, and externalities. Public goods—goods and services that are nonrival (one person's consumption does not reduce the amount available for someone else) and nonexcludable (no one can be kept from sharing the consumption)—create a free-rider problem. Economic inequality, which arises because of an unequal distribution of the ownership of resources and an absence of private insurance against low income, results in an inequity problem. Monopoly, which can arise from natural or legal barriers to entry, and externalities, which arise because in many transactions parties who do not participate in the transaction are affected by its outcome, result in an inefficient allocation of resources. (pp. 426–428)

Public Choice and the Political Marketplace

To study government actions, we use public choice theory. Public choice theory is based on the idea that government operates in a political marketplace in which voters, politicians, and bureaucrats interact with each other. Voters are the consumers of the political process, and they express their demands through their votes, campaign contributions, and lobbying. Politicians propose policies, and their objective is to win elections. Bureaucrats implement policies, and their objective is to maximize their budgets. The outcome of the interaction of voters, politicians, and bureaucrats is a political equilibrium that might or might not be efficient. (pp. 428–429)

Public Goods

The efficient level of provision of a public good is the level at which total benefit minus total cost is at a maximum. Equivalently, it is the level at which marginal benefit equals marginal cost. The existence of public goods creates a free-rider problem—people have too little incentive to voluntarily pay for such goods. If public goods are provided privately, too small a quantity is provided.

A government can provide a public good and pay for it with tax revenue. People will vote for a political party that proposes to produce a public good on a scale at which total benefit exceeds total cost. Competition between political parties, each of which tries to appeal to the maximum number of voters, will lead both parties to propose the same policies—the principle of minimum differentiation.

Bureaucrats try to maximize their budgets, but they are constrained by what the voters will tolerate. If voters are well-informed, politicians will be elected who propose to provide the efficient quantity of a public good. But if voters are rationally ignorant, producer interests may result in voting to support taxes that provide public goods in quantities that exceed those that maximize net benefit. (pp. 429–435)

Taxes

Government revenue comes from income taxes, social insurance taxes, sales taxes, and excise taxes on gasoline, alcoholic beverages, and tobacco products, which are taxed at high rates.

Income tax rates are set to appeal to the median voter. Voters with high incomes pay for more benefits than they receive and prefer a lower tax rate. Voters with low incomes pay for fewer benefits than they receive and prefer a higher tax rate. The tax rate that wins elections is the one that appeals to the median voter. Even political parties that represent the interests of the rich and the poor propose taxes and benefits that appeal to the median voter. To do otherwise would lose the election.

The imposition of a tax on a good creates a deadweight loss, the size of which depends on the elasticity of demand. By taxing goods that have a low elasticity of demand, the deadweight loss of raising a given amount of tax revenue is minimized. (pp. 436–439)

K E Y E L E M E N T S

Key Figures

Figure 18.4   Benefits of a Public Good, 430
Figure 18.5   The Efficient Quantity of a Public Good, 431
Figure 18.6   Provision of a Public Good in a Political System, 432
Figure 18.7   The Principle of Minimum Differentiation, 433
Figure 18.8   Bureaucratic Overprovision, 434
Figure 18.9   Voting for Income Taxes, 437
Figure 18.10 An Excise Tax, 438
Figure 18.11 Why We Don't Tax Orange Juice, 439

Key Terms

Bureaucrats, 429
Excise tax, 437
Excludable, 426
Externality, 428
Free rider, 427
Marginal benefit, 430
Market failure, 426
Median voter theorem, 436
Nonexcludable, 426
Nonrival, 426
Political equilibrium, 429
Principle of minimum differentiation, 433
Public good, 426
Rational ignorance, 434
Rival, 426

R E V I E W Q U E S T I O N S

1. Describe the growth of the government sector of the U.S. economy over the past 60 years.
2. What is market failure and from what does it arise?
3. What is a public good? Give three examples.
4. What is the free-rider problem and how does government help to overcome it?
5. What is an externality?
6. Describe the three actors in the political marketplace.
7. Describe the economic functions of voters and explain how they make their economic choices.
8. Describe the economic functions of politicians and explain how they make their economic choices.
9. Describe the economic functions of bureaucrats and explain how they make their economic choices.
10. What is meant by political equilibrium?
11. What is the principle of minimum differentiation?
12. How does the principle of minimum differentiation explain political parties' policy platforms?
13. Explain why the quantity of a public good will likely exceed its efficient scale.
14. Why is it rational for voters to be ignorant?
15. What is the median voter theorem?
16. What features of political choices does the median voter theorem explain?

PROBLEMS

1. You are given the following information about a sewage disposal system that a city of 1 million people is considering installing:

Capacity (thousands of gallons a day)	Marginal private benefit to the average person (dollars)	Total cost (millions of dollars)
0		0
	100	
1		10
	80	
2		30
	60	
3		60
	40	
4		100
	20	
5		150

a. What is the capacity that achieves maximum net benefit?

b. How much will each person have to pay in taxes to pay for the efficient capacity level?

c. What is the political equilibrium if voters are well-informed?

d. What is the political equilibrium if voters are rationally ignorant and bureaucrats achieve the highest attainable budget?

2. Your local city council is contemplating upgrading its system for controlling traffic signals. The council believes that by installing computers, it can improve the speed of the traffic flow. The bigger the computer the council buys, the better job it can do. The mayor and the other elected officials who are working on the proposal want to determine the scale of the system that will win them the most votes. The city bureaucrats want to maximize the budget. Suppose that you are an economist who is observing this public choice. Your job is to calculate the quantity of this public good that achieves allocative efficiency.

a. What data would you need to reach your own conclusions?

b. What does the public choice theory predict will be the quantity chosen?

c. How could you, as an informed voter, attempt to influence the choice?

3. An economy with 9 groups of people, A through I, has net benefits from the following tax rates:

A	B	C	D	E	F	G	H	I
90	80	70	60	50	0	0	0	0

If two political parties compete for office what income tax rate would the parties propose?

4. In a competitive market for cookies:

Price (dollars per pound)	Quantity demanded (pounds per month)	Quantity supplied (pounds per month)
10	0	36
8	3	30
6	6	24
4	9	18
2	12	12
0	15	0

a. What are the equilibrium price and quantity bought and sold?

b. If cookies are taxed 10 percent:
   (i) What is the new price of cookies?
   (ii) What is the new quantity bought?
   (iii) What is the tax revenue?
   (iv) What is the deadweight loss?

5. Study *Reading Between the Lines* on pp. 440–441 and then answer the following:

a. What is the distinction between the public provision and public production of a public good? Give some examples, in addition to those in the news article, of public provision and private production as well as public provision and public production.

b. In what circumstances might voters support a political party that proposes to provide a public good by:
   (i) Buying it from a private producer rather than by producing it in a government bureau?
   (ii) Producing it in a government bureau rather than by buying it from a private producer?

Inequality, Redistribution, and Health Care

After studying this chapter, you will be able to:

- Describe the inequality in income and wealth in the United States

- Explain why wealth inequality is greater than income inequality

- Explain how economic inequality arises

- Explain the effects of taxes, social security, and welfare programs on economic inequality

- Explain the effects of health-care reform on economic inequality

Fifty-three stories above Manhattan is a penthouse with unobstructed views of Central Park, the Hudson River, and the city skyline. Its price? $4 million. "Now, you can be one of the enviable few to fly Around the World by Supersonic Concorde ... for just $32,000 per person," trumpets an advertisement in *The New Yorker*. Not quite within view of the $4 million penthouse, but not far from it, is Fort Washington Armory in

Riches and Rags

Upper Manhattan. What was opened as a temporary shelter in 1981 permanently houses close to 1,000 men who sleep in one football-field-sized room. These men live on the edge of despair and in fear of AIDS and other life-threatening diseases. ◆ Why are some people exceedingly rich while others are very poor and own almost nothing? Are the rich getting richer and the poor getting poorer? Does the information we have about the inequality of income and wealth in the United States paint an accurate picture or a misleading one? How do taxes, social security, welfare, and health-care programs influence economic inequality?

◇ In this chapter, we study economic inequality—its extent, its sources, and its potential remedies. We look at taxes and government programs that redistribute incomes and study their effects on economic inequality in the United States. We also study the different ways in which health care can be delivered and their effects on economic efficiency and equality. Let's begin by looking at some facts about economic inequality.

Economic Inequality in the United States

WE CAN STUDY INEQUALITY BY LOOKING AT either the distribution of income or the distribution of wealth. A family's income is the amount that it receives in a given period of time. A family's wealth is the value of the things it owns at a point in time. We can measure income inequality by looking at the percentage of total income received by a given percentage of families. And we can measure wealth inequality by looking at the percentage of total wealth owned by a given percentage of families.

In 1992, the average U.S. family income was $39,000. But there was considerable inequality around that average. The poorest 20 percent of families received less than 5 percent of total income. The next poorest 20 percent of families received less than 11 percent of total income. The richest 20 percent of families received almost 45 percent of total income.

The wealth distribution shows even greater inequality. Average family wealth in 1992 was $193,000. But the range was enormous. The poorest 90 percent of families owned about one third of total wealth. The next 9 percent owned another third of total wealth. And the wealthiest 1 percent of families owned the remaining one third of total wealth.

Lorenz Curves

Figure 19.1 shows the distributions of income and wealth. The table divides families into five groups, called *quintiles*, ranging from the lowest income (row *a*) to highest income (row *e*), and shows the percentages of income of each of these groups. For example, row *a* tells us that the lowest quintile of families receives 5 percent of total income. The table also shows the *cumulative* percentages of families and income. For example, row *b* tells us that the lowest two quintiles (lowest 40 percent) of families receive 16 percent of total income (5 percent for the lowest quintile and 11 percent for the next lowest). The data on cumulative income shares are illustrated by a Lorenz curve. A **Lorenz curve** graphs the cumulative percentage of income against the cumulative percentage of families.

If income were distributed equally to every family, the cumulative percentages of income received by the cumulative percentages of families would fall

FIGURE 19.1

Lorenz Curves for Income and Wealth

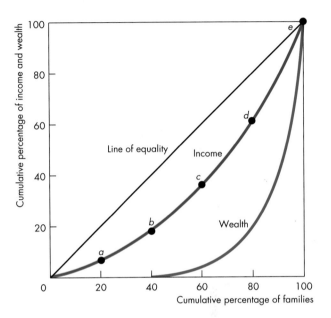

Families		Income		Wealth	
Percentage	Cumulative percentage	Per-centage	Cumulative percentage	Per-centage	Cumulative percentage
a Lowest 20	20	5	5	0	0
b Second 20	40	11	16	0	0
c Third 20	60	16	32	4	4
d Fourth 20	80	24	56	11	15
e Highest 20	100	44	100	85	100

The cumulative percentages of income and wealth are graphed against the cumulative percentage of families. If income and wealth were distributed equally, each 20 percent of families would have 20 percent of the income and wealth—the line of equality. Points *a* through *e* on the Lorenz curve for income correspond to the rows of the table. The Lorenz curves show that income and wealth are unequally distributed and wealth more unequally distributed than income.

Sources: Income: *Current Population Reports, Consumer Income,* Series P-60, Nos. 167 and 168 (Washington, D.C.: U.S. Department of Commerce, Bureau of the Census, 1990). Wealth: Robert D. Avery and Arthur B. Kennickell, "Measurement of Household Saving Obtained from First Differencing Wealth Estimates" (Washington, D.C.: Federal Reserve Board, February 1990).

along the straight line labeled "Line of equality." The actual distribution of income is shown by the Lorenz curve labeled "Income."

The figure also shows a Lorenz curve for wealth. This curve is based on the distribution described above, in which total wealth is divided approximately equally between the top 1 percent, the next 9 percent, and the bottom 90 percent of families.

The Lorenz curve shows the degree of inequality. The closer the Lorenz curve is to the line of equality, the more equal is the distribution. As you can see from the two Lorenz curves in Fig. 19.1, the Lorenz curve for wealth is much farther away from the line of equality than the Lorenz curve for income is, so the distribution of wealth is much more unequal than the distribution of income.

Inequality over Time

Figure 19.2 shows how the distribution of income has changed over the years. The first impression is that the distribution has been constant. But a closer look shows that from 1950 to about 1967, the distribution became more equal—the richest 20 percent received a slightly smaller share of total income, the poorest 20 percent received a slightly larger share, and the income shares of the three middle groups didn't change much. After 1967, the trends reversed and the distribution of income became less equal. The income shares of all three lower-income groups declined, and that of the two highest-income groups increased. The low-income groups suffer for a variety of reasons; one of them is increased international mobility and competition that is keeping down the wages of the low-skilled. The higher-income groups are gaining because rapid technological change has increased the value of and return to education.

Who Are the Rich and the Poor?

What are the characteristics of poor and rich families? The lowest-income household in the United States today is likely to be a black woman over 65 years of age who lives alone somewhere in the South and has fewer than eight years of elementary school education. The highest-income household in the United States today is likely to be a college-educated white married couple between 45 and 54 years of age living together with two children somewhere in the West.

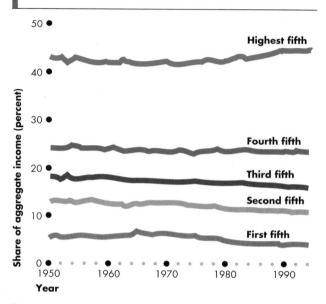

FIGURE 19.2

Trends in the Distribution of Income: 1950–1992

The distribution of income in the United States became more equal between 1950 and 1967 and less equal after 1967. The main changes were in the percentage of income earned by the highest fifth and the lowest fifth.

Source: Current Population Reports, Consumer Income, Series P-60, Nos. 162 (1993), 167, and 168 (1990) (Washington, D.C.: U.S. Department of Commerce, Bureau of the Census, 1993).

These snapshot profiles are the extremes in Fig. 19.3. That figure illustrates the importance of education, size of household, marital status, age of householder, race, and region of residence in influencing the size of a family's income. The range of variation associated with education is the largest. On the average, people who have not completed grade 9 earn $13,383 a year, while people with a bachelor's degree or more earn almost $54,000 a year. Four-person households have incomes that average more than $44,400 while one-person households have an average income of about $15,400. Single females, on the average, have incomes of $14,400 a year, while married couples earn an average joint income of $42,100 a year. The oldest and youngest households have lower incomes than middle-aged households. Black families have an average income of $18,700, while white families have an average income of more than $32,000. Finally, incomes are lowest in the South and highest in the

FIGURE **19.3**

The Distribution of Income by Selected Family Characteristics in 1994

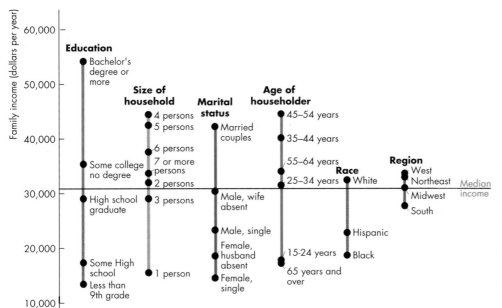

Education is the single biggest factor affecting family income distribution, but size of household, marital status, and age of householder are also important. Race and region of residence also play a role.

Source: *Statistical Abstract of the United States: 1994*, 114th edition (1991), p. 465.

West; those in the Northeast are fairly close to those in the West, and incomes in the Midwest lie midway between those in the West and those in the South.

Poverty

Families at the low end of the income distribution are so poor that they are considered to be living in poverty. **Poverty** is a state in which a family's income is too low to be able to buy the quantities of food, shelter, and clothing that are deemed necessary. Poverty is a relative concept. Millions of people living in Africa and Asia survive on incomes of less than $400 a year. In the United States, the poverty level is calculated each year by the Social Security Administration. In 1992, the poverty level for a four-person family was an income of $14,335. In that year, 37 million Americans were in families that had incomes below the poverty level. Many of these families benefited from Medicare and Medicaid, two government programs that benefit the poorest families and lift some of them above the poverty level.

The distribution of poverty by race is very unequal: 6.8 percent of white families, 20.9 percent of Hispanic origin families, and 25.4 percent of black families are below the poverty level. Poverty is also influenced by family status. More than 30 percent of families in which the householder is a female and no husband is present are below the poverty level, while fewer than 5 percent of other families are.

R E V I E W

- Income and wealth are distributed unequally, but wealth is distributed more unequally than income.
- From 1950 to 1967, the distribution of income became more equal, and after 1967 it became less equal.
- The main influences on a family's income, in decreasing order of importance, are education, household size, marital status, age of householder, race, and region of residence.

Comparing Like with Like

TO DETERMINE THE DEGREE OF INEQUALITY, WE compare one person's economic situation with another person's. But what is the correct measure of a person's economic situation? Is it income or is it wealth? And is it *annual* income, the measure we've used so far in this chapter, or income over a longer time period—for example, over a family's lifetime?

Wealth versus Income

Wealth is a stock of assets and income is the flow of earnings that results from the stock of wealth. Suppose that a person owns assets worth $1 million—has a wealth of $1 million. If the rate of return on assets is 5 percent a year, then this person receives an income of $50,000 a year from those assets. We can describe this person's economic condition by using either the wealth of $1 million or the income of $50,000. When the rate of return is 5 percent a year, $1 million of wealth equals $50,000 of income in perpetuity. Wealth and income are simply different ways of looking at the same thing.

But in Fig. 19.1, the distribution of wealth is much more unequal than the distribution of income. Why? It is because the wealth data measure tangible assets and exclude the value of human capital while the income data measure income from both tangible assets and human capital.

Table 19.1 illustrates the consequence of omitting human capital from the wealth data. Lee has twice the wealth and twice the income of Peter. But Lee's human capital is less than Peter's—$200,000 compared with $499,000. And Lee's income from human capital of $10,000 is less than Peter's income from human capital of $24,950. Lee's nonhuman capital is larger than Peter's—$800,000 compared with $1,000. And Lee's income from nonhuman capital of $40,000 is larger than Peter's income from nonhuman capital of $50.

The national wealth and income surveys record their incomes of $50,000 and $25,000 respectively, which indicates that Lee is twice as well off as Peter. And they record their tangible assets of $800,000 and $1,000 respectively, which indicates that Lee is 800 times as wealthy as Peter. Because the national survey of wealth excludes human capital, the income distribution is a more accurate measure of economic inequality than the wealth distribution.

TABLE 19.1				

Capital, Wealth, and Income

	Lee		Peter	
	Wealth	**Income**	**Wealth**	**Income**
Human capital	200,000	10,000	499,000	24,950
Nonhuman capital	800,000	40,000	1,000	50
Total	$1,000,000	$50,000	$500,000	$25,000

When wealth is measured to include the value of human capital as well as nonhuman capital, the distribution of income and the distribution of wealth display the same degree of inequality.

Annual or Lifetime Income and Wealth?

A typical family's income changes over time. It starts out low, grows to a peak when the family's workers reach retirement age, and then falls after retirement. Also, a typical family's wealth changes over time. Like income, it starts out low, grows to a peak at the point of retirement, and falls after retirement.

Suppose we look at three families that have identical lifetime incomes. One family is young, one is middle aged, and one is retired. The middle-aged family has the highest income and wealth, the retired family has the lowest, and the young family falls in the middle. The distributions of annual income and wealth in a given year are unequal but the distributions of lifetime income and wealth are equal. So some of the measured inequality arises from the fact that different families are at different stages in the life cycle and this overstates the degree of lifetime inequality.

REVIEW

■ The distribution of income is a more accurate indicator of the degree of inequality than the distribution of wealth because the wealth data exclude human capital.

■ The distribution of lifetime income is a more accurate indicator of the degree of inequality than the distribution of annual income because income varies over a family's life cycle.

Let's look at the sources of economic inequality.

Factor Prices, Endowments, and Choices

A FAMILY'S INCOME DEPENDS ON THE PRICES OF the factors of production supplied, the endowment of the factors the family owns, and the choices the family members make. To what extent do differences in income arise from differences in factor prices and from differences in the quantities of factors that people supply?

Labor Market and Wages

Wages are the biggest single source of income. To what extent do variations in wage rates account for the unequal distribution of income? Table 19.2 helps to answer this question. It sets out the average hourly earnings of private sector employees in seven industry groups in the United States in 1993. Average hourly earnings for all industries is $10.83. As a group, those working in construction earn $14.35, substantially more than the average. Those working in retail trade earn $7.29, substantially less than the average. Within each group, individual wage rates vary. For example, in the mining group, the highest-paid work is in coal mining ($17.25 an hour) and the lowest-paid work is in non-metallic minerals ($12.70 an hour). In the lowest-paid industry, retail trade, the highest-paid work is in automotive dealerships and service stations ($9.62 an hour), while the lowest-paid work is in eating and drinking places ($5.35 an hour).

The wage rate data in Table 19.2 tell us the highest-paid labor earns about 3.3 times as much as the lowest-paid labor. That is, makers of flat glass (glass for windows and mirrors), who earn $17.54 an hour, earn 3.3 times as much as those working in eating and drinking places, who earn $5.35 an hour.

One of the things that wage rate differences reflect is differences in skills or human capital. For example, the highest-paid workers in manufacturing are flat glass makers, while the lowest-paid workers make children's outerwear. The wage rate difference between these two categories probably reflects, to some degree, differences in training and skill. Similarly, transportation workers who operate highly sophisticated pipeline-transport networks have more skill than those who drive local trains or buses. Again, the wage rate difference reflects this difference in human capital.

TABLE 19.2
Average Hourly Earnings in 1993

Industry	Average hourly earnings (dollars)	
Mining		**14.60**
Coal mining	17.25	
Non-metallic minerals	12.70	
Manufacturing		**11.76**
Flat glass making	17.54	
Children's outerwear	6.39	
Construction		**14.35**
Transportation		**13.64**
Pipeline transport	16.93	
Local transit	9.99	
Retail trade		**7.29**
Automotive dealerships and service stations	9.62	
Eating and drinking places	5.35	
Finance, insurance, and real estate		**11.32**
Services		**10.81**
Computer and data processing	16.35	
Laundry and cleaning	7.28	
Average, all industries (private sector)		**10.83**

There is considerable inequality in average hourly earnings across different occupations. But the range of inequality is much lower than the inequality of income. For example, the highest-paid workers, coal miners, earn only 3.2 times the income of the lowest-paid workers, those who work in eating and drinking places.

Source: Statistical Abstract of the United States: 1994, 114th edition, pp. 422–425.

Differences in wage rates are one source of income inequality. Differences in endowments of factors of production are another.

Distribution of Endowments

There is a large amount of variety in a family's endowments of abilities. Physical and mental differences (some inherited, some learned) are such an obvious feature of human life that they hardly need mentioning. These differences across individuals have a normal, or bell-shaped, distribution—like the distribution of heights or weights.

The distribution of individual ability across individuals is a major source of inequality in income and wealth. But it is not the only source. If it were, the distributions of income and wealth would look like the bell-shaped curve that describes the distribution of heights. In fact, these distributions are skewed toward high incomes and look like the curve in Fig. 19.4. This figure shows income on the horizontal axis and the percentage of families receiving each income on the vertical axis. In 1992, the median household income—the income that separates households into two groups of equal size—was $30,786. The most common income—called the mode income—is less than the median income. The mean income—also called the average income—is greater than the median income and in 1992 was $39,020. A skewed distribution like the one shown in Fig. 19.4 is one in which many more people have incomes below the average than above it, a large number of people have low incomes, and a small number of people have high incomes. The distribution of (nonhuman) wealth has a similar shape to the distribution of income but is even more skewed.

The skewed shape of the distribution of income cannot be explained by the bell-shaped distribution of individual abilities. It results from the choices that people make.

Choices

While many poor families feel trapped and do not have many options open to them, a family's income and wealth depend partly on the choices that its members make. People choose how much of each of the factors of production that they own to supply. They also choose whether to baby-sit or look for a job in a bank, whether to put their savings in the bank or in stocks. We are going to discover that the choices people make exaggerate the differences among families. Their choices make the distribution of income more unequal than the distribution of abilities, and they make the distribution of income skewed.

FIGURE 19.4

The Distribution of Income

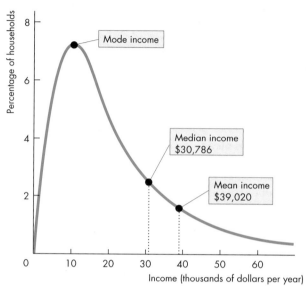

The distribution of income is unequal and is not symmetric around the mean income. There are many more people with incomes below the mean income than above it. Also, the distribution has a long, thin upper tail representing a small number of people earning very large incomes.

Wages and the Supply of Labor   Other things remaining the same, the quantity of labor that a person supplies usually increases as that person's wage rate increases. A person who has a low wage rate chooses to work fewer hours than a person who has a high wage rate. Compare two people, one whose wage rate is $10 an hour and another whose wage rate is $20 an hour. If each person works the same number of hours, one has an income that is twice as much as the others. But a higher wage rate can induce a greater number of hours of work. So if the person whose wage is $20 an hour chooses to work more hours, she earns an income that exceeds twice the income of the other person.

Thus because the quantity of labor supplied increases as the wage rate increases, the distribution of income is more unequal than the distribution of hourly wages. It is also skewed, like the distribution shown in Fig. 19.4. People whose wage rates are below the average tend to work fewer hours than the average, and their incomes bunch together below the average. People whose wage rates are above the average tend to work more hours than the average, and their incomes stretch out above the average.

Saving and Bequests   Another choice that results in unequal distributions in income and wealth is the decision to save and make bequests. A *bequest* is a gift from one generation to the next. The higher a family's income, the more that family tends to save and bequeath to later generations. By making a bequest, a family can spread consumption across the generations. One very common way in which people make bequests is to provide educational resources for the children and grandchildren.

Saving and bequests are not inevitably a source of increased inequality. If a family saves to redistribute an uneven income over the life cycle and enable consumption to be constant, the act of saving decreases the degree of inequality. If a lucky generation that has a high income saves a large amount and makes a bequest to a generation that is unlucky, this act of saving also decreases the degree of inequality. But there are two important features of bequests that do make intergenerational transfers of wealth a source of increased inequality:

- Debts cannot be bequeathed
- Mating is assortative

Debts Cannot Be Bequeathed   Although a person may die with debts that exceed assets—with negative wealth—debts cannot be forced onto other family members. Because a zero inheritance is the smallest inheritance that anyone can receive, bequests can only add to future generations' wealth and income potential.

The vast majority of people inherit nothing or a very small amount. A few people inherit enormous fortunes. As a result, bequests make the distribution of income and wealth not only more unequal than the distribution of ability and job skills but also more persistent. A family that is poor in one generation is more likely to be poor in the next. A family that is wealthy in one generation is likely to be wealthy in the next. But there is a tendency for income and wealth to converge, across generations, to the average. Although there can be long runs of good luck or bad luck, or good judgment or bad judgment, across the generations, such long runs are uncommon. But a feature of human behavior slows the convergence of wealth to the average and makes inequalities persist—assortative mating.

Assortative Mating   *Assortative mating* is the tendency for people to marry within their own socioeconomic class. In the vernacular, "like attracts like." Although there is a good deal of folklore that "opposites attract," perhaps such Cinderella tales appeal to us because they are so rare in reality. Marriage partners tend to have similar socioeconomic characteristics. Wealthy individuals seek wealthy partners. The consequence of assortative mating is that inherited wealth becomes more unequally distributed.

R E V I E W

- Income inequality arises from unequal wage rates, unequal endowments, and choices.
- Wage rates are unequal because of differences in skills or human capital.
- Endowments are unequal and have a bell-shaped distribution.
- The distribution of income is skewed because people with higher wage rates tend to work longer hours and so make a disproportionately larger income.
- The distribution of wealth is skewed because people with higher incomes save more, bequeath more to the next generation, and marry people with similar wealth.

We've now examined some of the reasons inequality exists. Next, we're going to see how the political marketplace modifies the outcome of the market economy and changes the distributions of income and wealth.

Income Redistribution

THE THREE MAIN WAYS THAT GOVERNMENTS IN the United States redistribute income are:

- Income taxes
- Income maintenance programs
- Provision of goods and services below opportunity cost

Income Taxes

The scale of redistribution of income achieved through income taxes depends on the form that the income taxes take. Income taxes may be progressive, regressive, or proportional. A **progressive income tax** is one that taxes income at a marginal rate that increases with the level of income. The term "marginal," applied to income tax rates, refers to the fraction of the last dollar earned that is paid in taxes. A **regressive income tax** is one that taxes income at a marginal rate that decreases with the level of income. A **proportional income tax** (also called a *flat-rate income tax*) is one that taxes income at a constant rate, regardless of the level of income.

The income tax rates that apply in the United States are composed of two parts: federal and state taxes. Some cities, such as New York City, also have an income tax. There is variety in the detailed tax arrangements in the individual states, but the tax system, at both the federal and state levels, is progressive. The poorest families pay no federal income tax, the middle-income families pay 15 percent of each additional dollar they earn, and successively richer families pay 28 percent and 31 percent of each additional dollar earned.

Income Maintenance Programs

Three main types of programs redistribute income by making direct payments (in cash, services, or vouchers) to people in the lower part of the income distribution. They are:

- Social security programs
- Unemployment compensation
- Welfare programs

Social Security The main social security program is OASDHI—Old Age, Survivors, Disability, and Health Insurance. Monthly cash payments to retired or disabled workers or their surviving spouses and children are paid for by compulsory payroll taxes on both employers and employees. In 1992, total social security expenditure was $286 billion, and 41 million people received an average monthly social security check of $689.

The other component of social security is Medicare, which provides hospital and health insurance for the elderly and disabled.

Unemployment Compensation To provide an income to unemployed workers, every state has established an unemployment compensation program. Under these programs, a tax is paid based on the income of each covered worker and a benefit is received by such a worker when he or she becomes unemployed. The details of the benefits vary from state to state. In 1992, more than 3 million people each week benefited from unemployment compensation programs and received a total of $25 billion.

Welfare Programs Four state-administered federal welfare programs provide income maintenance for families and individuals who do not qualify for social security or unemployment compensation. They are

1. Supplementary Security Income (SSI) program, designed to help the neediest elderly, disabled, and blind people
2. Aid to Families With Dependent Children (AFDC) program, designed to help families who have inadequate financial support
3. Food Stamp program, designed to help the poorest families obtain a basic diet
4. Medicaid, designed to cover the costs of medical care for families receiving help under the SSI and AFDC programs

Provision of Goods and Services below Cost

A great deal of redistribution takes place in the United States through the provision of goods and services by the government at prices far below the cost of production. The taxpayers who consume these goods and services receive a transfer in kind from the taxpayers who do not consume them. The two most important areas in which this form of redistribution takes place are education—both kindergarten through grade 12 and college and university—and health care.

In 1993, students enrolled in the University of California system paid annual tuition fees of around $3,000. The cost of one year's education at the University of California at Berkeley or San Diego in 1993 was more than $15,000. Thus families with a member enrolled in these institutions received a benefit from the government of more than $12,000 a year. Families with several college or university students received proportionately higher benefits.

Government provision of health-care services has grown to equal the scale of private provision. Programs such as Medicaid and Medicare bring high-quality and high-cost health care to millions of people who earn too little to buy such services themselves. As a result, these programs contribute a great deal to reducing inequality. Because the role of health care is so important, we study it more fully in the next major section of this chapter. But before doing so, we'll bring all the different methods of income redistribution together and look at the overall scale of redistribution they achieve. And we will examine some income redistribution reform proposals.

The Scale of Income Redistribution

A family's income in the absence of government redistribution is called *market income*. One way of measuring the scale of income redistribution is to calculate the percentage of market income paid in taxes and the percentage received in benefits at each income level. Making such a calculation in a way that takes into account the value of government-provided services is almost impossible. The only calculations that are available ignore this aspect of redistribution and focus on taxes and cash benefits.

The most recent year for which such a calculation has been done is 1980, and the results are shown in Fig. 19.5. This figure shows that the poorest 32 percent of the population received more benefits than they pay in taxes—they received net benefits. For example, people at the tenth percentile point (the point at which 10 percent are poorer and 90 percent are richer) received benefits equal to 50 percent of their market incomes, on the average (point *a* in the figure). In contrast, the richest 68 percent of the population paid more in taxes than they received in benefits—they paid net taxes. For example, the very richest people, on the average, paid 28 percent of their market incomes to the government in net taxes (point *c* in the figure). Those at the dividing line between these two groups broke even, paying as much in taxes as they received in benefits, on the average (point *b* in the figure).

Another measure of the scale of redistribution is provided by the sources of income of families at different points of the income distribution. The poorest 20 percent of families receive almost two thirds of their income in the form of payments from the government—called transfer income. The second 20 percent receives a third of its income in government transfers. In contrast, the richest 20 percent receive almost nothing from the government but receive a third of their income from capital—interest and dividends from financial assets. The proportion of income from capital for the other 80 percent of families is remarkably constant at about 8 percent.

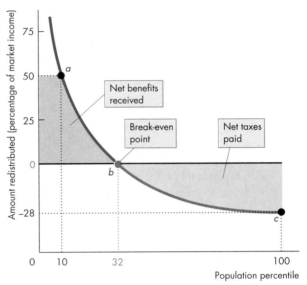

FIGURE 19.5

Income Redistribution in 1980

Taxes and income maintenance programs reduce the degree of inequality that the market generates. In 1980, the 32 percent of families with the lowest incomes received net benefits and the 68 percent of families with the highest market incomes paid net taxes. Families at the 10th percentile received 50 percent of their market income from income maintenance programs, those at the 32nd percentile broke even, and those with higher market incomes paid up to 28 percent of their incomes in taxes.

Source: Joseph A. Pechman, *Who Paid the Taxes, 1966–85?* (Washington, D.C.: The Brookings Institution, 1985), p. 54.

The Big Tradeoff

The redistribution of income creates what has been called the **big tradeoff**, a tradeoff between equity and efficiency. The big tradeoff arises because redistribution uses scarce resources and weakens incentives.

A dollar collected from a rich person does not translate into a dollar received by a poor person. Some of it gets used up in the process of redistribution. Tax-collecting agencies such as the Internal Revenue Service and welfare-administering agencies (as well as tax accountants and lawyers) use skilled labor, computers, and other scarce resources to do their work. The bigger the scale of redistribution, the greater is the opportunity cost of administering it.

Greater equality can be achieved only by taxing productive activities such as work and saving. Taxing people's income from their work and saving lowers the after-tax income they receive. This lower income makes them work and save less. Less work and less saving result in smaller output and less consumption not only for the rich who pay the taxes but also for the poor who receive the benefits. So the scale and methods of income redistribution involve striking a balance between greater equality and lower average consumption.

Some of the weakest incentives are those faced by families that benefit under programs such as Supplementary Security Income and Aid to Families With Dependent Children. When a person in one of these families gets a job, benefits are withdrawn and the family in effect pays a tax of 100 percent on its earnings. This marginal tax rate is higher than that paid by the wealthiest Americans, and it helps lock poor families in a welfare trap.

Reform Proposals

There are two broad ways in which the problem of the "big tradeoff" can be tackled. They are:

■ Piecemeal reforms
■ Radical reforms

Piecemeal Reforms   For practical reasons, most reforms that actually get implemented are piecemeal. They are a response to the most pressing problems of the day. The critical aspect of welfare that is receiving attention is the removal of disincentives to work and the encouragement of people on welfare to find jobs. This process began with the Family Support Act of 1988. Its Job Opportunities and Basic Skills (JOBS) program provides education and training; it provides incentives for young people to complete high school education; it provides benefits to two parent families to discourage family breakups; and it requires unpaid work—workfare—by one member of a two-parent welfare family.

In 1994, the Clinton administration's welfare reforms strengthened the incentives to work by expanding the Earned Income Tax Credit (EIC) scheme and extending Aid to Families With Dependent Children to low-income wage earners, see *Reading Between the Lines* on pp. 462–463. It is too early to assess the effects of these innovations.

Radical Reforms   A more radical reform proposal that is not on the current political agenda but is popular among economists is a negative income tax. A **negative income tax** gives every family a *guaranteed annual income* and decreases the family's benefit at a specified *benefit-loss rate* as its market income increases. For example, suppose the guaranteed annual income is $10,000 and the benefit-loss rate and the income tax rate are set at 25 percent. A family with no earnings receives the $10,000 guaranteed income. A family with earnings of $8,000 loses 25 percent of that amount—$2,000—and receives a total income of $16,000 ($8,000 earnings plus $10,000 guaranteed income minus $2,000 benefit loss). A family earning $40,000 receives an income of $40,000 ($40,000 earnings plus $10,000 guaranteed income minus $10,000 benefit loss). Such a family is at the break-even income level. Families with earnings exceeding $40,000 pay more in taxes than they receive in benefits.

Figure 19.6 illustrates a negative income tax and compares it with our current arrangements. In both parts of the figure, the horizontal axis measures *market income*—that is, income *before* taxes are paid and benefits are received—and the vertical axis measures income *after* taxes are paid and benefits are received. The 45° line shows the hypothetical case of "no redistribution."

Part (a) shows the current redistribution arrangements—the blue curve. Benefits of *G* are paid to those with no income. As incomes increase from zero to *A*, benefits are withdrawn, *lowering* income after redistribution below *G*. This arrangement creates a *welfare trap*—it does not pay a person to work if the income he or she can earn is less than *A*. The welfare trap is shown as the gray triangle in the figure. Over the income range *A* to *C*, each additional dollar of market income increases income after redistribution by a dollar. At incomes greater than *C*, income taxes are paid and at successively higher rates, so income after redistribution is smaller than market income.

Part (b) shows the negative income tax. The guaranteed annual income is *G,* and the break-even income is *B*. Families with market incomes below *B* receive a net benefit (blue area), and those with incomes above *B* pay taxes (red area). You can see why such a scheme is called a negative income tax. Every family receives a guaranteed minimum income, and every family pays a tax on its market income—losing benefits is like paying a tax—but families with market incomes below the break-even income receive more than they pay and so, in total, they pay a negative amount of tax.

FIGURE 19.6

Comparing Current Programs and a Negative Income Tax

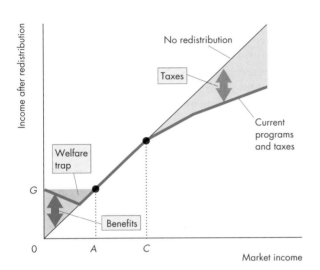

(a) Current redistribution arrangements

Part (a) shows the current redistribution arrangements—the blue curve. Benefits of *G* are paid to those with no income. As incomes increase from zero to *A*, benefits are withdrawn, *lowering* income after redistribution below *G* and creating a welfare trap—the gray triangle. As incomes increase from *A* to *C*, there is no redistribution. As incomes increase above *C*, income taxes are paid at successively higher rates.

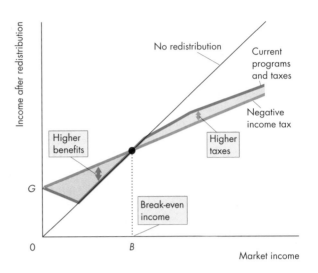

(b) A negative income tax

In part (b), a negative income tax gives a guaranteed annual income of *G* and decreases benefits at the same rate as the tax rate on incomes. The red line shows how market incomes translate into income after redistribution. Families with market incomes below *B*, the break-even income, receive net benefits. Those with market incomes above *B* pay net taxes.

A negative income tax removes the welfare trap and gives greater encouragement to low-income families to seek more employment, even at a low wage. It also overcomes many of the other problems arising from existing income maintenance programs.

So why don't we have a negative income tax scheme? The main reason is cost. The guaranteed annual income that puts a family of four on the official *poverty* income was $14,335 in 1992. With a benefit-loss rate equal to 20 percent—a rate similar to the income tax rate for most families—the break-even income is more than $65,000. This income is much higher than the average income, and the taxes on families with incomes above this level would increase substantially (as shown in Fig. 19.6b). Less generous negative income tax schemes are feasible, but most welfare experts believe that the more piecemeal approach to reform that is currently being pursued will yield a better outcome.

REVIEW

■ Governments redistribute income in the United States by using income taxes and income maintenance programs—social security, unemployment compensation, and welfare—and providing goods and services below cost.

■ The poorest 20 percent of families receive almost two thirds of their income from the government.

■ Existing programs discourage work and family life, create social tensions, and are costly to administer.

■ Welfare reform seeks to strengthen the incentive to find a job. A more radical reform proposal is a negative income tax.

Health and the cost of health care are major sources of inequality, and we now study the economics of health care and health-care reform.

Health-Care Reform

EXPENDITURE PER PERSON ON HEALTH CARE IS greater in the United States than any other country. Also, the percentage of total income spent on health care in the United States exceeds that of any other country. An American who has a good job and the comprehensive health insurance that goes with it enjoys a high degree of security and receives the highest quality health care. Let's look at the scale of spending on health care and at who does the spending.

Total spending on health care in the United States was 14 percent of total income in 1991 and, at its current trend, would reach 20 percent of total income by the year 2000. Almost 50 percent of the total health-care cost is met by the government, and this share has increased from 25 percent in 1965, as Fig. 19.7 shows. The government's share of the cost is made up of its expenditures on Medicare ($123 billion in 1991) and Medicaid ($101 billion in 1991) and the premiums it pays to private health-care insurance companies for government employees. The other 50 percent of the cost of health care is met by private health-care insurance (up from 25 percent of total payments in 1965 to 30 percent in 1991) and by direct payments by patients (*down* from 50 percent of total payments in 1965 to 20 percent in 1991).

Despite our large commitment of resources and our high quality of care, many people perceive health care in the United States to be in crisis. Why? There are two main problem areas:

1. Health care costs appear to be out of control.
2. Private health care insurance does not cover everyone.

Let's take a closer look at these problems.

Problem of Health-Care Costs

Health-care costs have increased more rapidly than consumer prices on the average, as Fig. 19.8 shows. Two separate factors create the gap between the rate of increase in health-care costs and average price increases—the health-care cost gap.

First, health care is a labor-intensive personal service with limited scope for labor-saving technological change. Health-care labor costs—wage rates of medical workers from surgeons to janitors—generally increase at a faster rate than do average prices, and because there is limited scope for labor-saving changes in health-care technology, these higher labor costs are reflected in higher costs for the final health-care product.

Second, the main effect of the technological change that does take place in health care is to improve the quality of the product. For example, the application of computer technology and advances in drugs have broadened the range of conditions that can be treated. But the cost of using new technologies to treat previously untreatable conditions steadily rises. Both sources of the health-care cost gap can be expected to persist.

Figure 19.9 shows the market for health care. Initially (say in 1980), the demand curve was D_0, the supply curve was S_0, the quantity was Q_0, and the price was P_0. Increasing incomes and advances in the

---

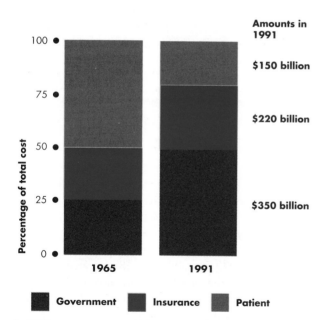

FIGURE 19.7

Who Pays for Health Care?

In 1991, government paid 50 percent of the total cost of health care, up from 25 percent in 1965. The direct payments by patients declined from 50 percent of the total in 1965 to 20 percent in 1991.

Source: Economic Report of the President, 1994.

The Rising Cost of Health Care

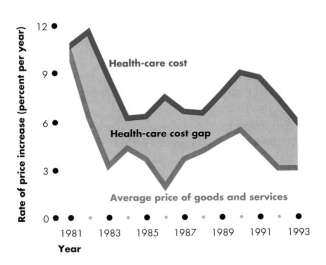

The cost of health care has increased much faster than the average price of other goods and services. The reasons are that health care is a labor-intensive industry—a personal service industry—so labor costs increase, and quality improvements have changed the nature of the product and increased its cost.

Source: Economic Report of the President, 1994.

The Market for Health Care

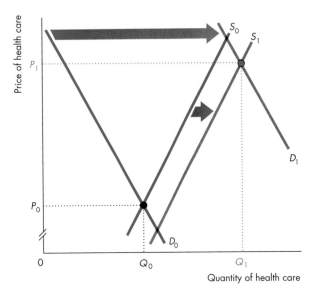

Initially (say in 1980), demand was D_0, supply was S_0, the quantity was Q_0, and the price was P_0. Increasing incomes and technological advances that expand the range of conditions that can be treated increase demand and shift the demand curve rightward to D_1. Advancing technology also increases supply, but increasing wages and more costly equipment and drugs counteract this increase in supply. The net result is that the supply curve shifts rightward to S_1. The quantity increases by a moderate amount, to Q_1, and the price increases steeply, to P_1.

medical conditions that can be treated increase the demand for health-care services, and the demand curve shifts rightward from D_0 to D_1. Technological advances in health care have increased supply of health-care services. But the increase in supply is smaller than the increase in demand because some factors have worked to decrease supply. One of these factors is the increasing wage rates of health-care workers; another is the increasing cost of ever more sophisticated health-care technologies. The net effect of the positive and negative influences on supply is a rightward shift in the supply curve to S_1. The quantity of health care has increased to Q_1—and the price has risen to P_1—a relatively large increase.

The forces at work that produce the changes shown in Fig. 19.9 do not appear to be temporary, and they may be expected to bring similar changes in the future.

Problems for Private Health-Care Insurance

In 1994, 51 percent of the health-care dollar was spent on 8 percent of the population. A further 32 percent was spent on 20 percent of the population. Health-care spending on the healthiest 72 percent of the population was 17 percent of total health-care cost.

Because the costs are high and the frequency of use is low, most people choose to finance their health care by insurance. But health-care insurance, like all types of insurance, faces two problems: *moral hazard* and *adverse selection*.[1] Moral hazard in health insur-

---

[1] These problems and other aspects of insurance are explained more fully in Chapter 17, pp. 409–412.

ance is the tendency for people who are covered by insurance to use more health services or to be less careful about avoiding health risks than they otherwise would. Adverse selection in health insurance is the tendency for people who know they have a greater chance than the average of falling ill to be the ones more likely to buy health insurance.

For example, a person might buy insurance only a few days before going on a ski trip to Colorado (adverse selection) and, covered by insurance, might then make a faster run down the ski slope, knowing that the cost of fixing a broken ankle will be borne, in part, by the insurance company (moral hazard). But the main adverse selection and moral hazard problems arise not from reckless young skiers, but from cautious physicians and patients who elect to perform tests and procedures that are demanded only because someone else is paying for them.

Insurance companies set their premium levels sufficiently high to cover claims arising from people who have been adversely selected and who face moral hazard. But to attract profitable business from low-risk customers, insurance companies give preference to the healthy and employed. They also limit the coverage of preexisting conditions and claims arising from major illness. The result is that many people are uninsured or are insured for minor problems but not for catastrophic illness.

Reform Proposals

Health-care reform is a major political issue. Almost always, when some feature of the economy is not working the way people want it to, some people reach the conclusion that the government must step in to deal with the problem and others reach the opposite conclusion and identify existing government intervention as the source of the problem. So it is with health care. We'll end our brief study of the economics of health care by examining a range of alternative proposals for improving the performance of the health-care sector.

A Bigger Role for Government?

The health-care plan proposed by President Clinton in 1993 (set out in the now-dead Health Care Security Act, 1993) is an example of an attack on the

problems facing health care that relies on a bigger role for government. The main features of the plan were:

1. Insurance companies would be required to offer a comprehensive package of health-care benefits to every citizen on equal terms and not reject any applicant.
2. People would be free to choose their doctor and their health plan.
3. Cost would be contained through increased competition and efficiency and by capping insurance premium increases.
4. Contributions to the cost of health care would be collected from everyone (with limited exceptions).

If insurance companies are required to provide universal coverage, their ability to select customers on the basis of health risk would be removed. The result would be better insurance for those who were previously excluded but higher insurance premiums for those who had qualified for insurance under the previous rules.

It is possible that some one-time cost savings might be achieved from more efficient administration of the insurance and health-care industries. For example, simplifying the administration of claims and reducing fraud—two measures featured in the plan—might decrease costs. But the scope for such cost cuts is limited. It was estimated (by President Clinton's economic advisors) that administration costs are 25 percent of hospital costs—about $70 billion in 1991—and that fraud accounts for 10 percent of total health-care costs—another $70 billion in 1991. Decreasing these components of health-care cost is likely to bring some benefit. But it cannot stop the process of rising prices.

If a premium cap—a spending ceiling—is imposed on insurance premiums, the total cost of health care might be limited. But spending ceilings create shortages. The quantity of health care demanded will exceed the quantity supplied. In this situation, some method other than the price mechanism will ration the scarce resources of health care.[2] One possible device is a queue—a waiting line for services. The evidence from Britain and Canada, two countries that ration health-care services by waiting lines, is that the people who are likely to wait longest and get the worst deal are those whom the current scheme serves least well.

---

[2] The effects of price ceilings are explained in Chapter 6, p. 122.

Make the Private Health-Care Market Work Better?   The federal government is already a major player in the health-care business. It pays for Medicaid and Medicare and tax laws encourage private employers to provide health-care insurance for their employees. Both of these government interventions create inefficiencies.

First, it is harder to contain cost increases and achieve the efficient operation of hospitals and other health-care delivery units when the bills are being paid by government funds rather than private funds. Removing the effects of inflation, the cost of Medicaid and Medicare has increased more than four-fold since 1970, while the cost of private health care has less than doubled.

Second, by providing tax incentives that encourage employers to buy medical insurance, the government has made the private part of health care less efficient. Although *employers* buy medical insurance, it is the *employees* who pay for it. The compensation package, which consists of dollars plus medical insurance, is determined by the forces of demand and supply. The amount that employers spend buying medical insurance is subtracted from the total compensation to determine the amount to be paid in dollars—the wage rate.

But the income tax laws interact with employer-provided medical insurance to create a big problem. Employees pay income tax on their wages, but not on the value of their medical insurance. So, suppose a firm and its workers are negotiating a new compensation package. Will wages rise by $100 per employee, or will medical insurance premiums rise by $100 per employee to improve the quality of medical insurance? (Improved medical insurance might take the form of a lower deductible or a wider coverage.)

If a firm's labor cost is going to increase by $100 per employee, the firm doesn't care whether it pays the $100 in higher wages or in improved health insurance. But the employees care. Because wages are taxed, an extra $100 in wages translates into around $60 in disposable income. So employees must compare the value of improved health insurance that costs $100 with an additional $60 of disposable income. If the value employees place on improved medical insurance that costs $100 exceeds $60, they will opt for the insurance rather than the higher wages. If employers were not permitted to shelter employees from income tax in this way, wages would be higher and people would decide for themselves how much medical insurance coverage to buy.

There would be a strengthened incentive to buy insurance at a lower cost with a larger deductible and smaller range of coverage. With a larger deductible, people would have a stronger incentive to economize on medical treatments and the moral hazard and adverse selection problems would be lessened.

But the fundamental problem is that rising health-care costs stem from forces that are going to persist. Advances in health-care technology can be expected to keep the demand for health care increasing briskly. And the increasing cost of applying new medical technologies and steadily rising wage rates for skilled health-care workers can be expected to keep supply growing more slowly than demand. The result: The price that balances the quantities demanded and supplied will continue to increase faster than the average rise in prices.

R E V I E W

- Health-care costs are high and rising and many people lack health-care insurance.
- Health-care costs increase more quickly than average prices because health care is a labor-intensive personal service and it experiences continuous improvements in product quality.
- Health-care insurance (like all types of insurance) faces *moral hazard* and *adverse selection* problems.
- Health-care reform plans call for either more government intervention—such as universal coverage, and a ceiling on insurance premiums—or less government intervention—such as an end to mandating employers to provide medical insurance.

◆   We've examined economic inequality in the United States, and we've seen that there is a large amount of inequality across families and individuals. Some of that inequality arises from comparing families at different stages in the life cycle. But even if we take a lifetime view, inequality remains. Some of that inequality arises from differences in wage rates. And economic choices accentuate those differences. We've seen that actions in the political marketplace redistribute income to alleviate the worst aspects of poverty.

Our next task is to look at the ways in which government actions modify the outcome of the market economy—the regulation of monopolies.

Reforming Welfare

THE LOS ANGELES TIMES, MAY 9, 1994

Welfare Reform Rhetoric Rings Hollow in the Delta

BY ELIZABETH SHOGREN

SHELBY, Miss.—Sitting in the tidy shack of a house she rents for $140 a month, Diane Walker is complaining about the severely slanted floor, the broken electrical fixtures and the water that rushes through the roof when it rains.

And in a still more hopeless tone, she laments her dismal prospects for bettering her family's lot.

"I've been looking for a job for about three years," said Walker, 32, adding that she has filled out applications at every factory and store in the area. "But you can't make somebody hire you."

Like many of the people living in the cheap houses, trailers and barrack-type apartments in her neighborhood, Walker supports herself and her three children with public-assistance checks and food stamps. Her sense of being trapped in the welfare system is common in the Mississippi Delta, a region where too few jobs and inadequate schools combine with other vestiges of a racist society to make poverty particularly intractable.

Federal officials designing welfare reform acknowledge that "ending welfare as we know it"—President Clinton's professed goal—may be impossible here and in other rural regions.

The Administration hopes to break the vicious cycle of welfare dependency by limiting Aid to Families With Dependent Children to a maximum of two years and by guaranteeing public service work for those who cannot get private sector jobs after two years on welfare. ...

But the "two years and out" formula may not make sense in chronically poor, remote areas where training, child care and jobs are in desperately short supply. ...

"That system will not work here," said Robert Gray, Shelby's mayor. "How can people go to work if there are no jobs?" ...

There are a lot of Shelbys in the United States. While the debate on welfare reform has centered on places such as South-Central Los Angeles, a quarter of the national poverty population in 1992—9.5 million people—lived in non-metropolitan areas. The poverty rate in rural areas was 17%, much higher than the national average of 11%. ...

Reprinted by permission.

Essence of THE STORY

■ The national average poverty rate (the percentage of people living below the official poverty level) is 11%. In rural areas, the rate is 17%, and in 1992, a quarter of the people living in poverty—9.5 million people—lived outside the metropolitan areas.

■ The poorest Americans are supported by public-assistance checks and food stamps.

■ The Clinton administration hopes to end long-term welfare dependency by limiting Aid to Families With Dependent Children (AFDC) to a maximum of two years and by guaranteeing public service work for people who cannot get private sector jobs.

■ Many people fear that in rural areas where the problem of poverty is deeply entrenched, there just aren't enough jobs for the reform to work.

Economic

A N A L Y S I S

■ In 1993, the Aid to Families With Dependent Children (AFDC) program paid some 5 million families a total of $23 billion—an average of $379 per family per month. Food stamps and other benefits are distributed under other programs.

■ Figure 1 shows a profile of AFDC recipients.

■ The Clinton administration's welfare reform plan has two components: carrots and sticks. The news story focuses on the main stick: the two-year limit for AFDC benefits.

■ The main carrots are expanded job training, help with job finding, child care, help with getting absent fathers to meet their child-care obligations, and a boost to the Earned Income Tax Credit (EIC) program, which is designed to make the welfare trap less severe.

■ A family in which at least one person has worked (full-time or part-time) during the year and that has at least one child and has no income outside the United States is eligible to receive an EIC based on the number of children and the family's income.

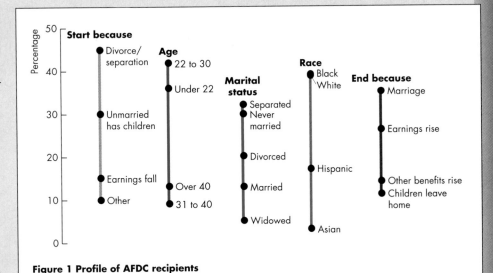

Figure 1 Profile of AFDC recipients

■ Figure 2 shows the effects of EIC for a married couple with two children in 1995. (The figure excludes the effects of other programs. EIC recipients are eligible for other benefits such as food stamps, Medicaid, and a housing subsidy.)

■ With a market income of less than $11,000, the family receives the maximum EIC, which is $3,370. As income increases above $11,000, the EIC decreases by 20 cents for each dollar earned. At an income of $27,000, the EIC is zero.

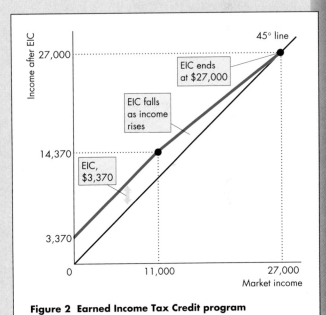

Figure 2 Earned Income Tax Credit program

■ The EIC is designed to encourage people to accept low-paying jobs rather than to rely entirely on welfare.

S U M M A R Y

Economic Inequality in the United States

The richest 1 percent of Americans own almost one third of the total wealth in the country. Income is distributed less unevenly than wealth. In the 1960s, inequality declined, and since 1967, it has increased. The poorest people in the United States are single black women with less than eight years of schooling who live in the South. The richest people live in the West and are college-educated, middle-aged, white families in which husband and wife live together. (pp. 447–449)

Comparing Like with Like

The measured distribution of wealth exaggerates the degree of inequality because it fails to take human capital into account. The distributions of annual income and wealth exaggerate the degree of lifetime inequality because they do not take into account the stage in the family's life cycle. (p. 450)

Factor Prices, Endowments, and Choices

Differences in income and wealth arise partly from differences in individual endowments and partly from differences in factor prices. Those differences get exaggerated by the economic choices that people make.

People who face a high hourly wage rate generally work longer than those who face a low wage rate. As a result, the distribution of income becomes more unequal than the distribution of wage rates. The distribution also becomes skewed. A large proportion of the population lies below the average and a small proportion lies above the average. Also, saving and bequests affect wealth across the generations. (pp. 451–453)

Income Redistribution

Governments in the United States today redistribute income through income taxes, income maintenance programs, and provision of goods and services below cost. Income taxes are progressive. The poorest families pay no federal income tax, middle-income families pay 15 percent of their taxable income, and the richest families pay 28 percent. Income maintenance programs are social security, unemployment compen-

sation, and welfare programs. Social security programs are OASDHI—Old Age, Survivors, Disability, and Health Insurance—and Medicare. Welfare programs provide income maintenance for families and individuals who do not qualify for social security or unemployment compensation.

Redistribution creates what has been called a "big tradeoff" between equity and efficiency. The big tradeoff arises because the process of redistribution uses resources and weakens incentives to work and save.

Income maintenance programs create a welfare trap that discourages work, so poverty is persistent. Reform of income maintenance programs seeks to lessen the severity of the welfare trap. A more radical reform known as negative income tax would encourage those on welfare to find work. (pp. 453–457)

Health-Care Reform

Total spending on health care in the United States was 14 percent of total income in 1991. Of this total, almost 50 percent is met by the government, 30 percent by private insurance payments, and 20 percent by direct payments by patients. The two main problem areas for health care are that its costs are high and rising and that many people lack health-care insurance.

Health-care costs have increased more rapidly than consumer prices on the average. Health care is a labor-intensive personal service and experiences continuous increases in demand because of improvements in product quality.

The problems facing health-care insurance arise from moral hazard—the tendency for people who are insured to take greater risks—and adverse selection—the tendency for people with the greatest chance of making an insurance claim to be the ones who buy insurance. Moral hazard increases premiums, and adverse selection limits coverage.

Some people suggest that health-care reform requires universal comprehensive health insurance and ceilings on insurance premiums (these were part of President Clinton's 1993 plan). Other people say that because the tax laws encourage employers to provide medical insurance to employees, incentives are weakened and the moral hazard and adverse selection problems are made more severe. The fundamental forces behind rising health-care costs are likely to persist. (pp. 458–461)

K E Y   E L E M E N T S

Key Figures

Key Terms

R E V I E W   Q U E S T I O N S

1. Which of the following describe the distributions of personal income and wealth in the United States today?
   a. The distributions of income and wealth are best represented by normal or bell-shaped curves.
   b. More than 50 percent of the population is wealthier than the average.
   c. More than 50 percent of the population is poorer than the average.

2. What is a Lorenz curve? How does a Lorenz curve illustrate inequality? Explain how the Lorenz curves for the distributions of income and wealth in the United States differ from each other.

3. Which is more unequally distributed, income or wealth? In answering this question, pay careful attention both to the way in which income and wealth are measured by official statistics and to the fundamental concepts of income and wealth.

4. How has the distribution of income in the United States changed over the past 20 years?

Which groups have received a larger share of total income and which have received a smaller share?

5. What is wrong with the way in which the official statistics measure the distribution of wealth?

6. Explain why the work/leisure choices made by individuals can result in a distribution of income that is more unequal than the distribution of ability. If ability is distributed normally (bell-shaped), will the resulting distribution of income also be bell-shaped?

7. Explain how the distribution of income and wealth is influenced by bequests and assortative mating.

8. What are the three main ways in which governments redistribute income in the United States?

9. What is a negative income tax and why don't we have one?

10. How did the 1993 Clinton health-care plan propose to tackle the problems of health care?

11. What was the main weakness in the 1993 Clinton health-care plan?

P R O B L E M S

1. Imagine an economy in which there are five people who are identical in all respects. Each lives for 70 years. For the first 14 of those years, they earn no income. For the next 35 years, they work and earn $30,000 a year from their work. For their remaining years, they are retired and have no income from labor. To make the arithmetic easy, let's suppose that the interest rate in this economy is zero; the individuals consume all their income during their lifetime and at a constant annual rate. What are the distributions of income and wealth in this economy if the individuals have the following ages:
   a. All are 45
   b. 25, 35, 45, 55, 65

   Is case (a) one of greater inequality than case (b)?

2. You are given the following information about income and wealth shares:

	Income shares (percent)	Wealth shares (percent)
Lowest 20%	5	0
Second 20%	11	1
Third 20%	17	3
Fourth 20%	24	11
Highest 20%	43	85

   Draw the Lorenz curves for income and wealth for this economy. Explain which of the two variables—income or wealth—is more unequally distributed.

3. An economy consists of 10 people, each of whom has the following labor supply schedule:

Wage rate (dollars per hour)	Hours worked per day
1	0
2	1
3	2
4	3
5	4

The people differ in ability and earn different wage rates. The distribution of *wage rates* is as follows:

Wage rate (dollars per hour)	Number of people
1	1
2	2
3	4
4	2
5	1

   a. Calculate the average wage rate.
   b. Calculate the ratio of the highest to the lowest wage rate.
   c. Calculate the average daily income.
   d. Calculate the ratio of the highest to the lowest daily income.
   e. Sketch the distribution of hourly wage rates.
   f. Sketch the distribution of daily incomes.
   g. What important lesson is illustrated by this problem?

4. After studying the *Reading Between the Lines* on pp. 462–463 answer the following questions:
   a. Describe the characteristics of the people most likely to be on welfare in the United States.
   b. What is the welfare trap?
   c. Explain why the Clinton administration's welfare reform plan will make the welfare trap less severe.
   d. Do you think that the Clinton administration's welfare reform plan will change the characteristics of the people most likely to be on welfare? How?

Chapter 2

Regulation and Antitrust Law

After studying
this chapter,
you will be
able to:

- Define regulation and antitrust law

- Distinguish between the public interest
  and capture theories of regulation

- Explain how regulation affects prices,
  outputs, profits, and the distribution of
  the gains from trade between consumers
  and producers

- Explain how antitrust law has been
  applied in a number of landmark cases

- Explain how antitrust law is used today

When you consume water, electric power, natural gas, cable TV, or local telephone service you buy from a regulated monopoly. Why are the industries that produce these goods and services regulated? How are they regulated? Do the regulations work in the public interest—the interest of all consumers and producers—or do they serve special interests—the interests of particular groups of

Public Interest or Special Interests?

consumers or producers? ◆ Cable TV has been on a regulatory roller coaster. It was initially regulated, but in 1984 it was deregulated. After deregulation, the profits of cable TV firms soared and in 1992, Congress acted to re-regulate the industry. Why was cable television deregulated and then re-regulated? ◆ In 1986, two mergers were proposed, one between PepsiCo and 7-Up and the other between Coca-Cola and Dr Pepper. But the government blocked these mergers with its antitrust laws. It used these same laws to break up the American Telephone and Telegraph Company (AT&T) and to create a number of regional telephone companies. This action brought competition into the market for long-distance telephone service by encouraging the entry of such firms as MCI and Sprint. What are the antitrust laws? How have they evolved over the years? How are they used today? Do they serve the public interest of consumers or the special interests of producers?

◻ This chapter studies government actions to influence markets for goods and services. It draws on your earlier study of how markets work and on your knowledge of consumer surplus and producer surplus. It shows how consumers and producers might redistribute those gains in the political marketplace, and it identifies who stands to gain and who stands to lose from various types of government intervention.

Market Intervention

THE GOVERNMENT INTERVENES IN MONOPOLISTIC and oligopolistic markets to influence prices, quantities produced, and the distribution of the gains from economic activity. It intervenes in two main ways:

■ Regulation
■ Antitrust law

Regulation

Regulation consists of rules administered by a government agency to influence economic activity by determining prices, product standards and types, and the conditions under which new firms may enter an industry. To implement its regulations, the government establishes agencies to oversee the regulations and ensure their enforcement. The first national regulatory agency to be set up in the United States was the Interstate Commerce Commission (ICC), established in 1887. Over the years since then, up to the late 1970s, regulation of the economy grew until, at its peak, almost a quarter of the nation's output was produced by regulated industries. Regulation applied to banking and financial services, telecommunications, gas and electric utilities, railroads, trucking, airlines and buses, many agricultural products, and even haircutting and braiding. Since the late 1970s, there has been a tendency to deregulate the U.S. economy.

Deregulation is the process of removing restrictions on prices, product standards and types, and entry conditions. In recent years, deregulation has occurred in domestic air transportation, telephone service, interstate trucking, and banking and financial services. Cable TV was deregulated in 1984 but re-regulated in 1992.

Antitrust Law

An **antitrust law** is a law that regulates and prohibits certain kinds of market behavior, such as monopoly and monopolistic practices. Antitrust law is enacted by Congress and enforced through the judicial system. Lawsuits under the antitrust laws may be initiated either by government agencies or by injured private parties.

The main thrust of antitrust law is the prohibition of monopoly practices of restricting output to achieve higher prices and profits. The first antitrust law—the Sherman Act—was passed in 1890. Successive acts and amendments have strengthened and refined the body of antitrust law. Antitrust law (like all law) depends as much on the decisions of the courts and of the Supreme Court as on the statutes passed by Congress. Over the 100 years since the passage of the Sherman Act, there have been some interesting changes in the court's interpretation of the law and in how vigorously the law has been enforced. We'll study these later in this chapter.

To understand why the government intervenes in the markets for goods and services and to work out the effects of its interventions, we need to identify the gains and losses that government actions can create. These gains and losses are the consumer surplus and producer surplus associated with different output levels and prices. Let's refresh our understanding of these concepts.

Surpluses and Their Distribution

Consumer surplus is the gain from trade accruing to consumers. It is calculated as the maximum price that consumers are willing to pay minus the price actually paid for each unit bought, summed over all the units bought (see Chapter 7, pp. 158–159). *Producer surplus* is the gain from trade accruing to producers. It is calculated as price minus marginal cost (opportunity cost) for each unit produced, summed over all the units produced (see Chapter 12, pp. 285–286). **Total surplus** is the sum of consumer surplus and producer surplus.

Figure 20.1 shows these surpluses. In Fig. 20.1(a) there is perfect competition. The market demand curve is D and the market supply curve is S. The price is P_C and the quantity is Q_C. Because the demand curve shows the maximum price that consumers are willing to pay for each unit bought, consumer surplus is the amount shown by the green triangle. Because the supply curve shows marginal cost, producer surplus is the amount shown by the blue triangle. Total surplus is the amount shown by the combined green and blue triangles.

In Fig. 20.1(b), the industry is a (single-price) monopoly. The supply curve for a perfectly competitive industry is the marginal cost curve for a monopoly.

FIGURE 20.1

Surpluses

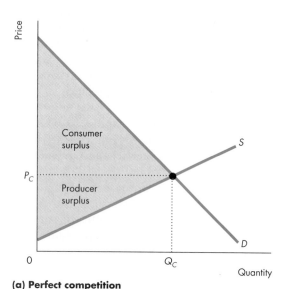

(a) Perfect competition

(b) Monopoly

With perfect competition (part a), consumer surplus is shown by the green triangle and producer surplus is shown by the blue triangle. Total surplus is the sum of these two triangles. With monopoly (part b), the firm restricts output and consumer surplus decreases, producer surplus increases, and a deadweight loss, which is shown by the gray triangle, arises. Total surplus is maximized under perfect competition.

The firm's marginal revenue curve is *MR*. To maximize profit, the firm restricts output to Q_M, the quantity at which marginal revenue equals marginal cost, and sells the quantity Q_M at the price P_M. Consumer surplus is shown by the smaller green triangle and producer surplus is shown by the blue area. Compared with perfect competition, consumer surplus is smaller and producer surplus is larger. Some of the consumer surplus becomes a producer surplus but some of it disappears. Also, some of the producer surplus is lost. The lost consumer surplus and producer surplus is *deadweight loss*, which is shown by the gray triangle (see Chapter 12, p. 286).

Total surplus is maximized when deadweight loss is zero. When output is restricted to increase the price and increase producer surplus, total surplus falls. Thus there is a tension between the special interest of producers and the public interest. This tension is the key to understanding the economic theory of regulation. Let's examine that theory.

Economic Theory of Regulation

THE ECONOMIC THEORY OF REGULATION IS part of the broader theory of public choice that is explained in Chapter 18. We're going to re-examine the main features of public choice theory but with an emphasis on the regulatory aspects of government behavior. We'll examine the demand for government actions, the supply of those actions, and the political equilibrium—the balancing of demands and supplies.

Demand for Regulation

The demand for regulation is expressed through political activity—voting, lobbying, and making campaign contributions. But engaging in political activity is costly and people demand political action only if the benefit that they individually receive from such action exceeds their individual costs in obtaining the action. The four main factors that affect the demand for regulation are:

1. Consumer surplus per buyer
2. Number of buyers
3. Producer surplus per firm
4. Number of firms

The larger the consumer surplus per buyer that results from regulation, the greater is the demand for regulation by buyers. Also, as the number of buyers increases, so does the demand for regulation. But numbers alone do not necessarily translate into an effective political force. The larger the number of buyers, the greater is the cost of organizing them, so the demand for regulation does not increase proportionately with the number of buyers.

The larger the producer surplus per firm that arises from a particular regulation, the larger is the demand for that regulation by firms. Also, as the number of firms that might benefit from some regulation increases, so does the demand for that regulation. But again, large numbers do not necessarily mean an effective political force. The larger the number of firms, the greater is the cost of organizing them.

For a given surplus, consumer or producer, the smaller the number of households or firms that share the surplus, the larger is the demand for the regulation that creates it.

Supply of Regulation

Regulation is supplied by politicians and bureaucrats. According to public choice theory, politicians choose policies that appeal to a majority of voters, thereby enabling themselves to achieve and maintain office. Bureaucrats support policies that maximize their budgets (see Chapter 18, pp. 428–429). Given these objectives of politicians and bureaucrats, the supply of regulation depends on the following three factors:

1. Consumer surplus per buyer
2. Producer surplus per firm
3. The number of people affected

The larger the consumer surplus per buyer or producer surplus per firm generated and the larger the number of people affected by a regulation, the greater is the tendency for politicians to supply that regulation. If regulation benefits a large number of people by enough for it to be noticed and if the recipients know the source of the benefits, that regulation appeals to politicians and is supplied. If regulation benefits a *small* number of people by a large amount per person, that regulation also appeals to politicians, provided that its costs are spread widely and are not easily identified. If regulation benefits a large number of people but by too small an amount per person to be noticed, that regulation does not appeal to politicians and is not supplied.

Political Equilibrium

In equilibrium, the regulation that exists is such that no interest group finds it worthwhile to use additional resources to press for changes and no group of politicians finds it worthwhile to offer different regulations. Being in a political equilibrium is not the same thing as everyone being in agreement. Lobby groups will devote resources to trying to change regulations that are already in place. Others will devote resources to maintaining the existing regulations. But no one will find it worthwhile to *increase* the resources they are devoting to such activities. Also, political parties might not agree with each other. Some support the existing regulations, and others propose different regulations. In equilibrium, no one wants to change the proposals that they are making.

What will a political equilibrium look like? The answer depends on whether the regulation serves the public interest or the interest of the producer. Let's look at these two possibilities.

Public Interest Theory The **public interest theory** is that regulations are supplied to satisfy the demand of consumers and producers to maximize total surplus—that is, to attain allocative efficiency. Public interest theory implies that the political process relentlessly seeks out deadweight loss and introduces regulations that eliminate it. For example, where monopoly practices exist, the political process will introduce price regulations to ensure that outputs increase and prices fall to their competitive levels.

Capture Theory The **capture theory** is that the regulations are supplied to satisfy the demand of producers to maximize producer surplus—that is, to maximize economic profit. The key idea of capture theory is that the cost of regulation is high and only those regulations that increase the surplus of small, easily identified groups and that have low organization costs are supplied by the political process. Such regulations are supplied even if they impose costs on others, provided that those costs are spread thinly and widely enough that they do not decrease votes.

The predictions of the capture theory are less clear-cut than the predictions of the public interest theory. According to the capture theory, regulations benefit cohesive interest groups by large and visible amounts and impose small costs on everyone else. But those costs are so small, in per-person terms, that no one finds it worthwhile to incur the cost of organizing an interest group to avoid them. To make these predictions concrete enough to be useful, the capture theory needs a model of the costs of political organization.

Whichever theory of regulation is correct, according to public choice theory, the political system delivers amounts and types of regulations that best further the electoral success of politicians. Because producer-oriented and consumer-oriented regulation are in conflict with each other, the political process can't satisfy both groups in any particular industry. Only one group can win. This makes the regulatory actions of government a bit like a unique product—for example, a painting by Rembrandt. There is only one original, and it will be sold to just one buyer. Normally, a unique commodity is sold through an auction; the highest bidder takes the prize. Equilibrium in the regulatory process can be thought of in much the same way: The suppliers of regulation will satisfy the demands of the higher bidder. If the producer demand offers a bigger return to the politicians, either directly through votes or indirectly through campaign contributions, then the producers' interests will be served. If the consumer demand translates into a larger number of votes, then the consumers' interests will be served by regulation.

R E V I E W

- The demand for regulation is expressed by consumers and producers who spend scarce resources voting, lobbying, and campaigning for regulations that best further their own interests.
- Regulation is supplied by politicians and bureaucrats. Politicians choose actions that appeal to a majority of voters, and bureaucrats choose actions that maximize their budgets.
- The regulation that exists is the political equilibrium that balances the opposing demand and supply forces. The political equilibrium either achieves efficiency—the public interest theory—or maximizes producer surplus—the capture theory.

We have now completed our study of the *theory* of regulation in the marketplace. Let's turn our attention to the regulations that exist in our economy today. Which theory of regulation best explains these real world regulations? Which regulations are in the public interest and which are in the interest of producers?

Regulation and Deregulation

THE PAST 20 YEARS HAVE SEEN DRAMATIC changes in the way in which the U.S. economy is regulated by government. We're going to examine some of these changes. To begin, we'll look at what is regulated and also at the scope of regulation. Then we'll turn to the regulatory process itself and examine how regulators control prices and other aspects of market behavior. Finally, we'll tackle the more difficult and controversial questions: Why do we regulate some things but not others? Who benefits from the regulations that we have—consumers or producers?

The Scope of Regulation

The first federal regulatory agency, the Interstate Commerce Commission (ICC), was set up in 1887 to control prices, routes, and the quality of service of interstate transportation companies—railroads, trucking lines, bus lines, water carriers, and, in more recent years, oil pipelines. Following the establishment of the ICC, the federal regulatory environment remained static until the years of the Great Depression. Then, in the 1930s, more agencies were established—the Federal Power Commission, the Federal Communications Commission, the Securities and Exchange Commission, the Federal Maritime Commission, the Federal Deposit Insurance Corporation, and, in 1938, the Civil Aeronautical Agency, which was replaced in 1940 by the Civil Aeronautics Board. There was a further lull until the establishment in the 1970s of the Postal Rate Commission, the Copyright Royalty Tribunal, and finally, the Federal Energy Regulatory Commission. In addition to these, there are many state and local regulatory commissions.

In the mid-1970s, almost one quarter of the economy was subject to some form of regulation. Heavily regulated industries—those subject both to price regulation and to regulation of entry of new firms—were electricity, natural gas, telephones, airlines, highway freight services, and railroads.

Regulation reached its peak in 1977. Since then, there has been a gradual deregulation process. Deregulation has had the most significant impact in the telecommunication, banking and finance, railroad, bus, trucking, and airline industries.

What exactly do regulatory agencies do? How do they regulate?

The Regulatory Process

Though regulatory agencies vary in size and scope and in the detailed aspects of economic life that they control, all agencies have features in common.

First, the bureaucrats who are the key decision makers in a regulatory agency are appointed by the administration or Congress in the case of federal agencies and by state and local governments. In addition, all agencies have a permanent bureaucracy made up of experts in the industry being regulated and often recruited from the regulated firms. Agencies have financial resources, voted by Congress or state or local legislatures, to cover the costs of their operations.

Second, each agency adopts a set of practices or operating rules for controlling prices and other aspects of economic performance. These rules and practices are based on well-defined physical and financial accounting procedures that are relatively easy to administer and to monitor.

In a regulated industry, individual firms are usually free to determine the technology that they will use in production. But they are not free to determine the prices at which they will sell their output, the quantities that they will sell, or the markets that they will serve. The regulatory agency grants certification to a company to serve a particular market and with a particular line of products, and it determines the level and structure of prices that will be charged. In some cases, the agency also determines the scale of output permitted.

To analyze the way in which regulation works, it is convenient to distinguish between the regulation of natural monopoly and the regulation of cartels. Let's begin with the regulation of natural monopoly.

Natural Monopoly

Natural monopoly was defined in Chapter 12 (p. 273) as an industry in which one firm can supply the entire market at a lower price than two or more firms can. As a consequence, a natural monopoly experiences economies of scale, no matter how large its output rate. Examples of natural monopolies include local distribution of cable television signals, electricity and gas, and urban rail services. It is much more

expensive to have two or more competing sets of wires, pipes, and train lines serving every neighborhood than it is to have a single set. (What is a natural monopoly changes over time as technology changes. With the introduction of fiber optic cables, both telephone companies and cable television companies can compete with each other in both markets, so what was once a natural monopoly is becoming a more competitive industry.)

Let's consider the example of cable TV, which is shown in Fig. 20.2. The demand curve for cable TV is *D*. The cable TV company's marginal cost curve is

FIGURE 20.2
Natural Monopoly: Marginal Cost Pricing

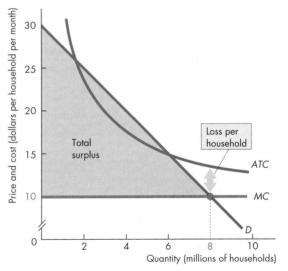

A natural monopoly is an industry in which average total cost is falling even when the entire market demand is satisfied. A cable TV operator faces the demand curve *D*. The firm's marginal cost is constant at $10 per household per month, as shown by the curve labeled *MC*. Fixed costs are large, and the average total cost curve, which includes average fixed cost, is shown as *ATC*. A marginal cost pricing rule that maximizes total surplus sets the price at $10 a month, with 8 million households being served. The resulting consumer surplus is shown as the green area. The firm incurs a loss on each household, indicated by the red arrow. To remain in business, the cable operator must either price discriminate or receive a subsidy.

MC. That marginal cost curve is (assumed to be) horizontal at $10 per household per month—that is, the cost of providing each additional household with a month of cable programming is $10. The cable company has a heavy investment in satellite receiving dishes, cables, and control equipment and so has high fixed costs. These fixed costs are part of the company's average total cost curve, shown as *ATC.* The average total cost curve slopes downward because as the number of households served increases, the fixed cost is spread over a larger number of households. (If you need to refresh your memory on how the average total cost curve is calculated, take a quick look back at Chapter 10, p. 221.)

Regulation in the Public Interest How will cable TV be regulated according to the public interest theory? In the public interest theory, regulation maximizes total surplus, which occurs if marginal cost equals price. As you can see in Fig. 20.2, that outcome occurs if the price is regulated at $10 per household per month and if 8 million households are served. Such a regulation is called a marginal cost pricing rule. A **marginal cost pricing rule** sets price equal to marginal cost. It maximizes total surplus in the regulated industry.

A natural monopoly that is regulated to set price equal to marginal cost incurs an economic loss. Because its average total cost curve is falling, marginal cost is below average total cost. Because price equals marginal cost, price is below average total cost. Average total cost minus price is the loss per unit produced. It's pretty obvious that a cable TV company that is required to use a marginal cost pricing rule will not stay in business for long. How can a company cover its costs and, at the same time, obey a marginal cost pricing rule?

One possibility is price discrimination. Some natural monopolies can fairly easily price discriminate. For example, local telephone companies can charge consumers a monthly fee for being connected to the telephone system and then charge a price equal to marginal cost for each local call. A cable TV operator can price discriminate by charging a one-time connection fee that covers its fixed cost and then charging a monthly fee equal to marginal cost.

But a natural monopoly cannot always price discriminate. When a natural monopoly cannot price discriminate, it can cover its total cost and follow a marginal cost pricing rule only if it receives a subsidy from the government. In such a case, the government

raises the revenue for the subsidy by taxing some other activity. But as we saw in Chapter 18, taxes themselves generate deadweight loss. Thus the deadweight loss resulting from additional taxes must be subtracted from the allocative efficiency gained by forcing the natural monopoly to adopt a marginal cost pricing rule.

It is possible that deadweight loss will be minimized by permitting the natural monopoly to charge a higher price than marginal cost rather than by taxing some other sector of the economy to subsidize the natural monopoly. Such a pricing arrangement is called an average cost pricing rule. An **average cost pricing rule** sets price equal to average total cost. Figure 20.3 shows the average cost pricing solution. The cable TV operator charges $15 a month and serves 6 million households. A deadweight loss arises, which is shown by the gray triangle in the figure.

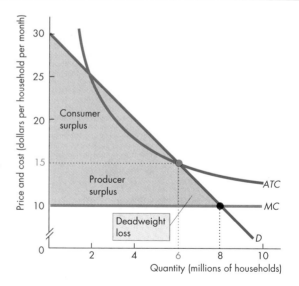

FIGURE 20.3

Natural Monopoly: Average Cost Pricing

Average cost pricing sets price equal to average total cost. The cable TV operator charges $15 a month and serves 6 million households. In this situation, the firm breaks even—average total cost equals price. Deadweight loss, shown by the gray triangle, is generated. Consumer surplus is reduced to the green area.

Capturing the Regulator   What does the capture theory predict about the regulation of this industry? According to the capture theory, regulation serves the interests of the producer, which means maximizing profit. To work out the price that achieves this goal, we need to look at the relationship between marginal revenue and marginal cost. A monopoly maximizes profit by producing the output at which marginal revenue equals marginal cost. The monopoly's marginal revenue curve in Fig. 20.4 is the curve *MR*. Marginal revenue equals marginal cost when output is 4 million households and the price is $20 a month. Thus a regulation that best serves the interest of the producer will set the price at this level.

But how can a producer go about obtaining regulation that results in this monopoly profit-maximizing outcome? To answer this question, we need to

look at the way in which agencies determine a regulated price. A key method used is called rate of return regulation.

Rate of Return Regulation   **Rate of return regulation** determines a regulated price by setting the price at a level that enables the regulated firm to earn a specified target percent return on its capital. The target rate of return is determined with reference to what is normal in competitive industries. This rate of return is part of the opportunity cost of the natural monopolist and is included in the firm's average total cost. By examining the firm's total cost, including the normal rate of return on capital, the regulator attempts to determine the price at which average total cost is covered. Thus rate of return regulation is equivalent to average cost pricing.

In Fig. 20.3, average cost pricing results in a regulated price of $15 a month with 6 million households being served. Thus rate of return regulation, based on a correct assessment of the producer's average total cost curve, results in a price that favors the consumer and does not enable the producer to maximize monopoly profit. The special interest group will have failed to capture the regulator, and the outcome will be closer to that predicted by the public interest theory of regulation.

But there is a feature of many real-world situations that the above analysis does not take into account: the ability of the monopoly firm to mislead the regulator about its true costs.

FIGURE   20.4

Natural Monopoly: Profit Maximization

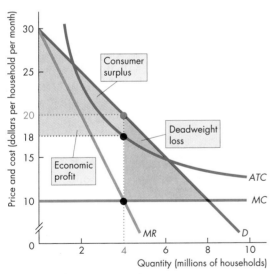

The cable TV operator would like to maximize profit. To do so, marginal revenue (MR) is made equal to marginal cost. At a price of $20 a month, 4 million households buy cable service. Consumer surplus is reduced to the green triangle. The deadweight loss increases to the gray triangle. The monopoly makes the profit shown by the blue rectangle. If the producer can capture the regulator, the outcome will be the situation shown here.

Inflating Costs   The managers of a firm might be able to inflate the firm's costs by spending part of the firm's revenue on inputs that are not strictly required for the production of the good. By this device, the firm's apparent costs exceed the true costs. On-the-job luxury in the form of sumptuous office suites, limousines, free baseball tickets (disguised as public relations expenses), company jets, lavish international travel, and entertainment are all ways in which managers can inflate costs.

If the cable TV operator manages to inflate its costs and persuade the regulator that its true average total cost curve is that shown as *ATC (inflated)* in Fig. 20.5, then the regulator, applying the normal rate of return principle, will regulate the price at $20 a month. In this example, the price and quantity will be the same as those under unregulated monopoly. It might be impossible for firms to inflate their costs by as much as the amount shown in the figure. But to the extent that costs can be inflated, the apparent average total cost curve lies somewhere between the true *ATC* curve and *ATC (inflated)*. The greater the ability of the firm to pad its costs in this way, the more closely its profit (measured in economic terms) approaches the maximum possible. The shareholders of this firm don't receive this economic profit because it gets used up in baseball tickets, luxury offices, and the other actions taken by the firm's managers to inflate the company's costs.

Incentive Regulation Schemes   Partly for the reasons we've just examined, rate of return regulation is increasingly being replaced by incentive regulation schemes. An **incentive regulation scheme** is a type of regulation that gives a firm an incentive to operate efficiently and keep costs under control. By 1990, 30 states had adopted incentive regulation schemes for telecommunications rather than traditional rate of return regulation. These new schemes take two main forms: price caps (adopted in California, New Jersey, Oregon, and Rhode Island) and earnings sharing plans (adopted in Colorado, Connecticut, Florida, Georgia, Kentucky, Tennessee, and Texas). Under a price cap regulation, the regulators set the maximum price that may be charged and hold that price cap for a number of years. If profits are considered too high, the price cap will be lowered. Under earnings sharing regulation, if profits rise above a certain level, they must be shared with the firm's customers. There is some evidence that under these types of regulations, local telephone companies are attempting to cut costs.

FIGURE 20.5
Natural Monopoly: Inflating Costs

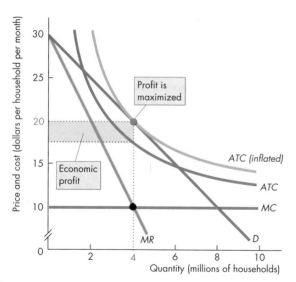

If the cable TV operator is able to inflate its costs to *ATC (inflated)* and persuade the regulator that these are genuine minimum costs of production, rate of return regulation results in a price of $20 a month—the profit-maximizing price. To the extent that the producer can inflate costs above average total cost, the price rises, output falls, and deadweight loss increases. The profit is captured by the managers, not the shareholders (owners) of the firm.

Public Interest or Capture?

It is not clear whether actual regulation produces prices and quantities that more closely correspond with the predictions of capture theory or with public interest theory. One thing is clear, however. Price regulation does not require natural monopolies to use the marginal cost pricing rule. If it did, most natural monopolies would make losses and receive hefty government subsidies to enable them to remain in business. But there are even exceptions to this conclusion. For example, many local telephone companies do appear to use marginal cost pricing for local telephone calls. They cover their total cost by charging a flat fee each month for being connected to their telephone system but then permitting each call to be made at its marginal cost—zero or something very close to it.

A test of whether natural monopoly regulation is in the public interest or the interest of the producer is to examine the rates of return earned by regulated natural monopolies. If those rates of return are significantly higher than those in the rest of the economy, then, to some degree, the regulator might have been captured by the producer. If the rates of return in the regulated monopoly industries are similar to those in the rest of the economy, then we cannot tell for sure whether the regulator has been captured or not, for we cannot know the extent to which costs have been inflated by the managers of the regulated firms.

Table 20.1 shows the rates of return in regulated natural monopolies as well as the economy's average rate of return. In the 1960s, rates of return in regulated natural monopolies were somewhat below the economy average; in the 1970s, those returns exceeded the economy average. Overall, the rates of return achieved by regulated natural monopolies were not very different from those in the rest of the economy. We can conclude from these data either that natural monopoly regulation does, to some degree, serve the public interest or that natural monopoly managers inflate their costs by amounts sufficiently large to disguise the fact that they have captured the regulator and that the public interest is not being served.

A final test of whether regulation of natural monopoly is in the public interest or the interest of producers is to study the changes in consumer surplus and producer surplus following deregulation. Microeconomists have researched this issue and their conclusions are summarized in Table 20.2. In the case of railroad deregulation, which occurred during the 1980s, both consumers and producers gained, and by large amounts. The gains from deregulation of telecommunications and cable television were smaller and accrued only to the consumer. These findings suggest that railroad regulation hurt everyone, while regulation of telecommunications and cable television hurt only the consumer.

We've now examined the regulation of natural monopoly. Let's next turn to regulation in oligopolistic industries—the regulation of cartels.

TABLE 20.1

Rates of Return in Regulated Monopolies

Industry	1962–69	1970–77
Electricity	3.2	6.1
Gas	3.3	8.2
Railroad	5.1	7.2
Average of above	3.9	7.2
Economy average	6.6	5.1

Source: Paul W. MacAvoy, *The Regulated Industries and the Economy* (New York: W.W. Norton, 1979), 49–60.

TABLE 20.2

Gains from Deregulating Natural Monopolies

Industry	Consumer surplus	Producer surplus	Total surplus
	(billions of 1990 dollars)		
Railroads	8.5	3.2	11.7
Telecommunications	1.2	0.0	1.2
Cable television	0.8	0.0	0.8
Total	10.5	3.2	13.7

Source: Clifford Winston, "Economic Deregulation: Days of Reckoning for Microeconomists," *Journal of Economic Literature,* XXXI, September 1993, pp. 1263–1289, and my calculations.

Cartel Regulation

A *cartel* is a collusive agreement among a number of firms that is designed to restrict output and achieve a higher profit for the cartel's members. Cartels are illegal in the United States and in most other countries. But international cartels can sometimes operate legally, such as the international cartel of oil producers known as OPEC (the Organization of Petroleum Exporting Countries).

Illegal cartels can arise in oligopolistic industries. An oligopoly is a market structure in which a small number of firms compete with each other. We studied oligopoly (and duopoly—two firms competing for a market) in Chapter 13. There we saw that if firms manage to collude and behave like a monopoly, they can set the same price and sell the same total quantity as a monopoly firm would. But we also discovered that in such a situation, each firm will be tempted to cheat, increasing its own output and profit at the expense of the other firms. The result of such cheating on the collusive agreement is the unraveling of the monopoly equilibrium and the emergence of a competitive outcome with zero economic profit for producers. Such an outcome benefits consumers at the expense of producers.

How is oligopoly regulated? Does regulation prevent monopoly practices or does it encourage those practices?

According to the public interest theory, oligopoly is regulated to ensure a competitive outcome.

Consider, for example, the market for trucking toma-toes from the San Joaquin Valley to Los Angeles, illustrated in Fig. 20.6. The market demand curve for trips is *D*. The industry marginal cost curve—and the competitive supply curve—is *MC*. Public interest regulation will regulate the price of a trip at $20, and there will be 300 trips a week.

How would this industry be regulated according to the capture theory? Regulation that is in the pro-ducer interest will maximize profit. To find the out-come in this case, we need to determine the price and quantity when marginal cost equals marginal rev-enue. The marginal revenue curve is *MR*. So marginal cost equals marginal revenue at 200 trips a week. The price of a trip is $30.

One way of achieving this outcome is to place an output limit on each firm in the industry. If there are 10 trucking companies, an output limit of 20 trips per company ensures that the total number of trips in a week is 200. Penalties can be imposed to ensure that no single producer exceeds its output limit.

All the firms in the industry would support this type of regulation because it helps to prevent cheating and to maintain a monopoly outcome. Each firm knows that without effectively enforced production quotas, every firm has an incentive to increase out-put. (For each firm, price exceeds marginal cost, so a greater output brings a larger profit.) So each firm wants a method of preventing output from rising above the industry profit-maximizing level, and the quotas enforced by regulation achieve this end. With this type of cartel regulation, the regulator enables a cartel to operate legally and in its own best interest.

What does cartel regulation do in practice? Although there is disagreement about the matter, the consensus view is that regulation tends to favor the producer. Trucking (when it was regulated by the Interstate Commerce Commission), taxicabs (regulat-ed by cities), and airlines (when they were regulated by the Civil Aeronautics Board) are specific examples in which profits of producers increased as a result of regulation. In some cases—and trucking is one of these—the work force, through unionization, also managed to take a large part of the producer surplus.

Some further evidence in support of the conclu-sion that regulation sometimes increases profit is pre-sented in Table 20.3. If regulation ensures a competi-tive outcome, rates of return in a regulated oligopoly

FIGURE 20.6
Collusive Oligopoly

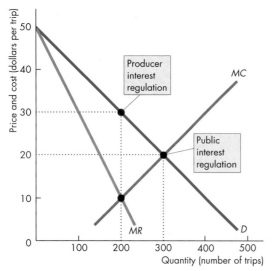

Ten trucking firms transport tomatoes from the San Joaquin Valley to Los Angeles. The demand curve is *D*, and the indus-try marginal cost curve is *MC*. Under competition, the *MC* curve is the industry supply curve. If the industry is competi-tive, the price of a trip will be $20 and 300 trips will be made each week. Producers will demand regulation that restricts entry and limits output to 200 trips a week where industry marginal revenue (*MR*) is equal to industry marginal cost (*MC*). This regulation raises the price to $30 a trip and results in each producer making maximum profit—as if it is a monopoly.

TABLE 20.3
Rates of Return in Regulated Oligopolies

Industry	Years	
	1962–69	1970–77
Airlines	12.8	3.0
Trucking	13.6	8.1
Economy average	6.6	5.1

Source: Paul W. MacAvoy, *The Regulated Industries and the Economy* (New York: W.W. Norton, 1978), 49–60.

will be no higher than those in the economy as a whole. As the numbers in Table 20.3 show, rates of return in airlines and trucking were close to twice the economy average rate of return in the 1960s. In the 1970s, the rate of return in trucking remained higher than the economy average (although by a smaller margin than had prevailed in the 1960s). Airline rates of return in the 1970s fell to below the economy average. The overall picture that emerges from examining data on rates of return is mixed. The regulation of oligopoly does not always result in higher profit, but there are many situations in which it does.

Further evidence on cartel and oligopoly regulation can be obtained from the performance of prices and profit following deregulation. If, following deregulation, prices and profit fall, then, to some degree, the regulation must have been serving the interest of the producer. In contrast, if, following deregulation, prices and profits remain constant or increase, then the regulation may be presumed to have been serving the public interest. Because there has been a substantial amount of deregulation in recent years, we may use this test of oligopoly regulation to see which of the two theories better fits the facts. The evidence is mixed, but in the cases of the airlines and trucking, the two main oligopolies to be deregulated, prices fell and there was a large increase in the volume of business. Table 20.4 summarizes the estimated effects of deregulation of airlines and trucking on consumer surplus, producer surplus, and total surplus. Most of the gains were in consumer surplus. In the case of the airlines, there was a gain in producer surplus as well. But in trucking, producer surplus decreased, which

suggests that regulation of this industry did benefit the producer.

Making Predictions

Most industries have a few producers and many consumers. In these cases, public choice theory predicts that regulation will protect producer interests because a small number of people stand to gain a large amount and so they will be fairly easy to organize as a cohesive lobby. Under such circumstances, politicians will be rewarded with campaign contributions rather than votes. But there are situations in which the consumer interest is sufficiently strong and well organized and thus able to prevail. There are also cases in which the balance switches from producer to consumer, as seen in the deregulation process that began in the late 1970s.

Deregulation raises some hard questions for economists seeking to understand and make predictions about regulation. Why were the transportation and telecommunication sectors deregulated? If producers gained from regulation and if the producer lobby was strong enough to achieve regulation, what happened in the 1970s to change the equilibrium to one in which the consumer interest prevailed? We do not have a complete answer to this question at the present time. But regulation had become so costly to consumers, and the potential benefits to them from deregulation so great, that the cost of organizing the consumer voice became a price worth paying.

One factor that increased the cost of regulation borne by consumers and brought deregulation in the transportation sector was the large increase in energy prices in the 1970s. These price hikes made route regulation by the ICC extremely costly and changed the balance in favor of consumers in the political equilibrium. Technological change was the main factor at work in the telecommunication sector. New satellite-based, computer-controlled long-distance technologies enabled smaller producers to offer low-cost services. These producers wanted a share of the business—and profit—of AT&T. Furthermore, as communication technology improved, the cost of communication fell and the cost of organizing larger groups of consumers also fell. If this line of reasoning is correct, we can expect to see more consumer-oriented regulation in the future. In practice, more consumer-oriented regulation often means deregulation—removing the regulations that are already in place to serve the interests of producer groups.

TABLE 20.4

Gains from Deregulating Oligopolies

Industry	Consumer surplus	Producer surplus	Total surplus
		(billions of 1990 dollars)	
Airlines	11.8	4.9	16.7
Trucking	15.4	−4.8	10.6
Total	27.2	0.1	27.3

Source: Clifford Winston, "Economic Deregulation: Days of Reckoning for Microeconomists," *Journal of Economic Literature,* XXXI, September 1993, pp. 1263–1289, and my calculations.

REVIEW

- Regulation of a natural monopoly in the public interest sets price equal to marginal cost or, to avoid a tax-financed subsidy, sets price equal to average total cost.
- In practice, natural monopolies face either rate of return regulation or incentive regulation schemes.
- With rate of return regulation, firms have an incentive to inflate costs and move as closely as possible to the profit-maximizing output. Incentive regulation—price caps and earnings sharing—encourages cost cutting.
- Cartel regulation that establishes output levels for each firm can help perpetuate a cartel and work against the public interest.

Let's now leave regulation and turn to the other main method of intervention in markets: antitrust law.

Antitrust Law

ANTITRUST LAW PROVIDES AN ALTERNATIVE WAY in which the government may influence the marketplace. As in the case of regulation, antitrust law can be formulated in the public interest, to maximize total surplus, or in private interests, to maximize the surpluses of particular special interest groups such as producers.

Landmark Antitrust Cases

The antitrust laws themselves are brief and easily summarized. The first antitrust law, the Sherman Act, was passed in 1890 in an atmosphere of outrage and disgust at the actions and practices of J.P. Morgan, John D. Rockefeller, and W.H. Vanderbilt—the so-called "robber barons." Ironically, the most lurid stories of the actions of these great American capitalists are not of their monopolization and exploitation of consumers but of their sharp practices against each other. Nevertheless, monopolies did emerge—for example, the spectacular control of the oil industry by John D. Rockefeller, Sr. The Sherman Act had little effect until the early part of this century, and in 1914, it was augmented by the Clayton Act and the

TABLE 20.5

Antitrust Laws

Name of law	Year passed	What the law prohibits
Sherman Act	1890	■ Combination, trust, or conspiracy to restrict interstate or international trade ■ Monopolization, or attempt to monopolize interstate or international trade
Clayton Act Robinson-Patman Amendment Cellar-Kefauver Amendment	1914 1936 1950	■ Price discrimination if the effect is to substantially lessen competition or create monopoly and if such discrimination is not justified by cost differences ■ Contracts that force other goods to be bought from same firm ■ Acquisition of competitors' shares or assets ■ Interlocking directorships among competing firms
Federal Trade Commission Act	1914	■ Unfair methods of competition and unfair or deceptive business practices

creation of the Federal Trade Commission, an agency charged with enforcing the antitrust laws. Table 20.5 gives a summary of the main antitrust laws.

The real force of any law arises from its interpretation. Interpretation of the antitrust laws has ebbed and flowed. At times, it has appeared to favor producers, and at other times, consumers. Let's see how.

Table 20.6 summarizes the landmark antitrust cases. The first cases were those of the American Tobacco Company and Standard Oil Company, decided in 1911. These two companies were found guilty of violations under the Sherman Act and ordered to divest themselves of large holdings in other companies. The breakup of John D. Rockefeller's Standard Oil Company resulted in the creation of the oil companies that today are household names, such as Amoco, Chevron, Exxon, and Sohio.

TABLE 20.6

Landmark Antitrust Cases

Case	Year	Verdict and consequence
American Tobacco Co. and *Standard Oil Co.*	1911	*Guilty*: Ordered to divest themselves of large holdings in other companies; "rule of reason" enunciated—only *unreasonable* combinations guilty under Sherman Act.
U.S. Steel Co.	1920	*Not guilty*: Although U.S. Steel had a very large market share (near monopoly), mere "size alone is not an offense"; application of the "rule of reason."
Socony-Vacuum Oil Co.	1940	*Guilty*: Combination was formed for purpose of price fixing; no consideration of "reasonableness" applied.
Alcoa	1945	*Guilty*: Too big—had too large a share of the market; end of "rule of reason."
General Electric, Westinghouse, and others	1961	*Guilty*: Price-fixing conspiracy; executives fined and jailed.
Brown Shoe	1962	*Guilty*: Ownership of Kinney, a retail chain, reduced competition; ordered to sell Kinney (Brown supplied 8 percent of Kinney's shoes, and Kinney sold 2 percent of nation's shoes).
Von's Grocery	1965	*Guilty*: Merger of two supermarkets in Los Angeles would restrain competition (the merged firm would have had 7 1/2 percent of the L.A. market).
IBM	1982	*Case dismissed* as being "without merit."
AT&T	1983	*Agreement* between AT&T and government that company would divest itself of all local telephone operating companies—80 percent of its assets.

In finding these companies to be in violation of the provisions of the Sherman Act, the Supreme Court enunciated the "rule of reason." The rule of reason states that monopoly arising from mergers and agreements among firms is not necessarily illegal. Only if there is an unreasonable restraint of trade does the arrangement violate the provisions of the Sherman Act. The rule of reason was widely regarded as removing the force of the Sherman Act itself. This view was reinforced in 1920 when U.S. Steel Company was acquitted of violations under the act even though it had a very large (more than 50 percent) share of the U.S. steel market. Applying the "rule of reason," the court declared that "size alone is not an offense."

Matters remained much as they were in 1920 until 1940, when the *Socony-Vacuum Oil Company* case resulted in the first chink in the armor of the "rule of reason." The court found Socony-Vacuum Oil Company guilty because a combination had been formed for the purpose of price fixing. The court ruled that no consideration of reasonableness should be applied to such a case. If the purpose of the agree-ment was price fixing, the automatic interpretation was to be that the agreement was unreasonable.

The "rule of reason" received its death blow in the *Alcoa* case, decided in 1945. Alcoa was judged to be in violation of the law because it was too big. It had too large a share of the aluminum market. A relatively tough interpretation of the law continued through the late 1960s. In 1961, General Electric, Westinghouse, and other electrical component manufacturers were found guilty of a price-fixing conspiracy. This case was the first one in which the executives (rather than the company itself) were fined and also jailed.

Tough antimerger decisions were taken in 1962 against Brown Shoe and in 1965 against Von's Grocery. In the first of these cases, Brown Shoe was required to divest itself of ownership of the Kinney shoe retail chain. This case is an example of the court ruling that a vertically integrated firm is capable of restraining competition. *Vertical integration* is the merger of two or more firms operating at different stages in a production process of a single good or service. For example, the merger of a firm that produces raw materials, a firm that converts those raw materials into a manufactured good, and a firm that retails the finished product creates a vertically integrated firm. The vertically integrated Brown Shoe and Kinney retail chain was ordered to be broken up even though Brown supplied only 8 percent of Kinney's shoes and Kinney sold only 2 percent of the nation's shoes.

Von's Grocery is an example of a horizontally integrated firm. *Horizontal integration* is a merger of two or more firms providing essentially the same product or service. In the *Von's Grocery* case, the court ruled that the combination of two supermarkets in Los Angeles would restrict competition even though the combined sales of the two firms would have been only 7 1/2 percent of total supermarket sales in the Los Angeles area.

Three Recent Antitrust Cases

Three recent antitrust cases have arisen in the high-technology computer and telecommunications industries.

The IBM Case   In the late 1960s, IBM was charged with anticompetitive practices. At that time, IBM faced little competition in the market for main-frame computers (the large computers used by banks, insurance companies, and universities and other research institutions). But it faced fierce competition from firms that produced peripherals such as tape drives and disk drives that were compatible with IBM's own peripherals. IBM reacted to this competition by cutting its prices on peripherals to the point at which its competitors could not cover their costs, while maintaining high prices on its computers. After 13 years of litigation, the IBM case was dismissed by the Department of Justice in 1982 as being "without merit." The entry of new firms during the 1970s had created a highly competitive market in both main-frame and microcomputers and substantially weakened the original case against IBM.

The AT&T Case   In 1974, AT&T was charged with violating the Sherman Act and accused of actions aimed at maintaining a monopoly in long-distance and local telephone communications. This case was resolved by an agreement between AT&T and the Department of Justice under which AT&T gave up its regional telephone business (which broke up into regional companies, known as "baby Bells") and competed in its long-distance business with new

carriers such as MCI and Sprint. But it was techno-logical changes in telecommunications as much as the law that made this outcome feasible.

The Microsoft Case   In 1993, the Department of Justice began to study the actions of Microsoft, the software company founded by Bill Gates that created DOS and Windows, the main operating systems for PCs. Microsoft's competitors claimed that the company monopolized the market for PC operating systems because of "per-processor" contracts. Under these contracts, computer makers paid Microsoft a royalty on every computer shipped, regardless of whether the computers had Microsoft software installed on them. This practice made it difficult for producers of other operating systems to compete with Microsoft. It has also been claimed that Microsoft frustrated (and continues to frustrate) competitors for its applications programs (such as word processors and spreadsheets) by giving other developers of applications an incomplete description of the code needed to work properly with Windows. The Justice Department and Microsoft reached an accord in 1994 but the case continues to be contro-versial and has been reopened. This antitrust case is examined further in *Reading Between the Lines* on pp. 484–485.

Current Mergers Rules

Today, the Department of Justice uses guidelines to determine which mergers it will examine and possibly block based on the Herfindahl-Hirschman index (HHI), which is explained in Chapter 13 (p. 299). A market in which the HHI is less than 1,000 is regard-ed as competitive. An index between 1,000 and 1,800 indicates a moderately concentrated market, and a merger in this market that would increase the index by 100 points is challenged by the Department of Justice. An index above 1,800 indicates a concen-trated market, and a merger in this market that would increase the index by 50 points is challenged. Figure 20.7(a) summarizes these guidelines.

The Department of Justice used these guidelines in analyzing two recently proposed mergers in the market for carbonated soft drinks. In 1986, PepsiCo announced its intention to buy 7-Up for $380 mil-lion. A month later, Coca-Cola said it would buy Dr Pepper for $470 million. Whether this market is con-centrated depends on how it is defined. The market

Department of Justice. Figure 20.7(b) shows how the HHI would have changed with the mergers. The PepsiCo and 7-Up merger would have increased the index by more than 300 points, the Coca-Cola and Dr Pepper merger would have increased it by more than 500 points, and both mergers together would have increased the index by almost 800 points. The Justice Department decided to define the market narrowly and, with increases of these magnitudes, blocked the mergers.

FIGURE 20.7
The HHI Merger Guidelines

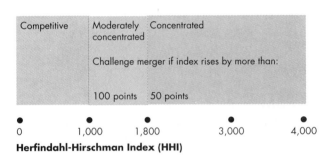

(a) The merger guidelines

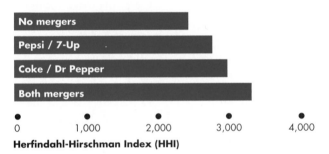

(b) Product mergers in soft drinks

The Justice Department scrutinizes proposed mergers if the HHI exceeds 1,000. Proposed mergers between producers of carbonated soft drinks were blocked in 1986 by application of these guidelines.

for all soft drinks, which includes *carbonated* drinks marketed by these four companies plus fruit juices and bottled water, has an HHI of 120, so it is highly competitive. But the market for *carbonated* soft drinks is highly concentrated. Coca-Cola has a 39 percent share, PepsiCo has 28 percent, Dr Pepper is next with 7 percent, then comes 7-Up with 6 percent. One other producer, RJR, has a 5 percent market share. So the five largest firms in this market have an 85 percent market share. If we assume that the other 15 percent of the market consists of 15 firms, each with a 1 percent market share, the Herfindahl-Hirschman index is

$$HHI = 39^2 + 28^2 + 7^2 + 6^2 + 5^2 + 15 = 2430.$$

With an HHI of this magnitude, a merger that increases the index by 50 points is examined by the

Public or Special Interest?

It is clear from the historical contexts in which antitrust law has evolved that its intent has been to protect and pursue the public interest and restrain the profit-seeking and anticompetitive actions of producers. But it is also clear from the above brief history of antitrust legislation and cases that from time to time the interest of the producer has had an influence on the way in which the law has been interpreted and applied. Nevertheless, the overall thrust of antitrust law appears to have been directed toward achieving allocative efficiency and therefore to serving the public interest.

There is a key difference between the ways in which antitrust law and regulation are administered. Regulation is administered by a bureaucracy. Antitrust law is interpreted and enforced by the legal process—the courts. Economists are now beginning to extend theories of public choice to include an economic analysis of the law and the way in which the courts interpret the law. It is interesting to speculate that the legal institutions that administer antitrust law are more sensitive to the public interest than the bureaucratic institutions that administer regulations.

◆ In this chapter, we've seen how the government intervenes in markets to affect prices, quantities, the gains from trade, and the division of those gains between consumers and producers when there is monopoly or oligopoly. We've seen that there is a conflict between the pursuit of the public interest—achieving allocative efficiency—and the pursuit of the special interests of producers—maximizing producer surplus or economic profit. The political and legal arenas are the places in which these conflicts are resolved. We've reviewed the two theories—public interest and capture—concerning the type and scope of government intervention.

Monopoly in PC Software?

FORTUNE, APRIL 18, 1994

Microsoft's Antitrust Blues

BY ALISON ROGERS

If Bill Gates were a chip, he'd be more powerful than a Pentium. Besides running Microsoft, the busy billionaire announced in late March a planned $9 billion outside partnership with cellular phone czar Craig McCaw to launch an 840-satellite communications network. And now Gates must turn his processing power toward a federal antitrust case that seems to be heating up.

Since last August the U.S. Department of Justice has been accumulating evidence of possible antitrust violations by Microsoft, and the case should spill out by summer. One charge: The company monopolizes the market for PC operating systems, the software that acts as your computer's central nervous system. Microsoft denies this, though the firm has a 77% market share with its DOS and Windows products.

Rivals such as Taligent, an alliance of Apple, IBM, and Hewlett-Packard, argue that Microsoft's licensing structure makes it a monopolist. Any computer retailer who wants to bundle Windows on one machine and get the best possible price has to buy a copy for *each* machine she offers. So why buy a rival operating system?

Justice may well wrangle Gates into signing a consent decree to abandon so-called per-processor licensing. But Microsoft's systems are so predominant that the company won't be hurt much by more competition.

Microsoft's other big market is applications software—spreadsheets, graphics, and the like. Here, Novell's planned acquisition of WordPerfect and of Borland's spreadsheet business, announced in late March, will create a battle of Goliath vs. Goliath. The new conglomerate is likely to press on with the charge that Microsoft has attempted to monopolize applications software.

When Microsoft writes applications, its developers have detailed maps of the underlying operating system. Microsoft also gives these maps to competitors, who charge that pieces of terrain are missing. Says Scott McNealy, CEO, of Sun Microsystems, a Microsoft competitor: "It's like trying to write a book without vowels." So while Microsoft's software runs seamlessly on Windows, theirs doesn't.

Though Microsoft maintains that it has done no wrong, Gates is not likely to bloody his company in a protracted litigation. Look for a last-minute settlement before a threatened San Francisco trial this summer.

Essence of THE STORY

■ In August 1993, the U.S. Department of Justice began accumulating evidence of possible antitrust violations by Microsoft Corp., the maker of the microcomputer operating systems DOS and Windows.

■ Microsoft Corp. has a 77 percent share of the market in PC operating systems for microcomputers and is a large producer of applications software.

■ Competitors claim that Microsoft's per-processor licensing scheme makes it a monopoly. To sell a computer and Windows bundle, a retailer must buy a copy of Windows for each machine sold.

■ Its competitors also claim that Microsoft has attempted to monopolize the market in applications software by denying other software developers full information about its operating systems.

■ Microsoft's founder, Bill Gates, is planning yet another venture, a $9 billion partnership in an 840-satellite communications network.

Economic

A N A L Y S I S

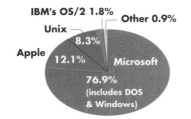

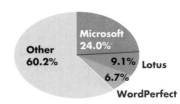

(a) Operating systems

(b) Applications software

Figure 1 Microsoft's market
Source: Fortune, April 18,1994, p.12.

■ To run the latest programs on a PC, you need a copy of DOS and a copy of Windows, both made by Microsoft. (A Mac needs the equivalent Apple operating system.)

■ In the market for microcomputer operating systems, Microsoft has a 77 percent share, Apple 12 percent, Unix 8 percent, IBM 2 percent, and others 1 percent (see Fig. 1a).

■ The Herfindahl-Hirschman Index for this market indicates a high degree of concentration.

■ Microsoft is also a significant producer of applications—word processing, spreadsheet, and graphing programs (see Fig. 1b).

■ The *fixed cost* of designing software is large, but the *marginal cost* of producing an additional copy is small, so a software producer faces a downward-sloping average total cost curve.

■ Figure 2 shows Microsoft's average total cost curve ATC and its marginal cost curve MC. The demand curve Microsoft faces is D.

■ If Microsoft acts as a single-price monopoly (Chapter 12, pp. 273–275), it maximizes profit by producing the quantity, Q_M, and by charging a price equal to P_M. Microsoft's economic profit is shown by the blue rectangle, consumer surplus by the green triangle, and deadweight loss by the gray triangle.

■ If the market were efficient, the number of copies of DOS and Windows sold would be Q_C.

■ According to the claims of its competitors, Microsoft acted like a monopoly by offering perprocessor licensing agreements: Computer retailers paid Microsoft a fee for each PC (processor) sold and Microsoft supplied copies of Windows for a lower price.

■ Microsoft agreed with the Department of Justice to end per-processor licensing in 1994.

■ But Microsoft remains free to price discriminate (Chapter 12, pp. 279–283) and its dominant market share continues to make it a tough firm to compete against.

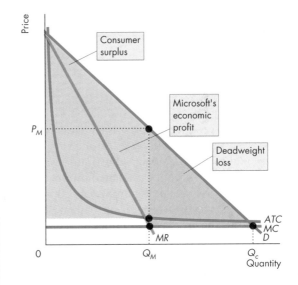

Figure 2 The market for DOS and Windows

■ Microsoft's alleged practice of withholding information about Windows from other producers of applications programs can be interpreted as an attempt to limit entry.

■ Bill Gates recognizes that economic profits don't last forever. His bid to establish a large satellite communications network appears to be a move to begin another potential monopoly by controlling the on-ramp to the information superhighway.

S U M M A R Y

Market Intervention

The government intervenes to regulate monopolistic and oligopolistic markets in two ways: regulation and antitrust law. In the United States, both of these methods are widely used. We seek to understand the reasons for and the effects of regulation.

Government action can influence consumer surplus, producer surplus, and total surplus. Consumer surplus is equal to the maximum price that consumers are willing to pay minus the price actually paid for each unit bought, summed over all units bought. Producer surplus is equal to the price minus the marginal cost (opportunity cost) for each unit produced, summed over all units produced. Total surplus is the sum of consumer surplus and producer surplus. Total surplus is maximized under competition. Under monopoly, producer surplus is increased, consumer surplus is decreased, and a deadweight loss is created. (pp. 469–470)

Economic Theory of Regulation

Consumers and producers express their demand for the regulation that influences their surpluses by voting, lobbying, and making campaign contributions. The larger the surplus that can be generated by a particular regulation and the smaller the number of people who are adversely affected, the larger is the demand for the regulation. But the greater the number of people, the greater is the cost of organizing them into an effective political lobby. Regulation is supplied by politicians, who pursue their own best interest. The larger the surplus per person generated and the larger the number of people affected by it, the larger is the supply of regulation. In equilibrium, the regulation that exists is such that no interest group finds it worthwhile to employ additional scarce resources to press for further changes. But the political equilibrium depends on whose interests are served by regulation. The public interest theory predicts that total surplus will be maximized; the capture theory predicts that producer surplus will be maximized. (pp. 470–472)

Regulation and Deregulation

Federal regulation began with the establishment of the Interstate Commerce Commission in 1887. A further expansion of regulation occurred in the 1930s. There was further steady growth of regulatory activity until the mid-1970s. Since 1978, the transportation, telecommunication, and financial sectors have been deregulated.

Regulation is conducted by regulatory agencies controlled by politically appointed bureaucrats and staffed by a permanent bureaucracy of experts. Regulated firms are required to comply with rules about price, product quality, and output levels. Two types of industries are regulated: natural monopolies and cartels. In both cases, regulation has enabled firms in the regulated industries to achieve profit levels that are equal to or greater than those attained on the average in the rest of the economy. Deregulation has brought gains for both consumers and producers, but the gains have been largest for consumers and in the case of trucking, producers lost from deregulation. (pp. 472–480)

Antitrust Law

Antitrust law is an alternative way in which the government can control monopoly and monopolistic practices. The first antitrust law, the Sherman Act, was passed in 1890, and the law was strengthened in 1914 when the Clayton Act was passed and the Federal Trade Commission was created.

The first landmark cases (against the American Tobacco Company and Standard Oil Company) established the "rule of reason," that monopoly arising from mergers is illegal only if there is an unreasonable restraint of trade; size alone is not illegal. The "rule of reason" was abandoned in a case against Alcoa in 1945 and a relatively tough interpretation of the law continued through the late 1960s.

Today, the Department of Justice uses guidelines to determine which mergers it will examine and possibly block based on the Herfindahl-Hirschman Index (HHI).

The intent of antitrust law is to protect and pursue the public interest and restrain the profit-seeking and anticompetitive actions of producers. This intent has been served most of the time. But sometimes the interest of the producer has influenced the way in which the law has been interpreted and applied. (pp. 480–483)

KEY ELEMENTS

Key Figures and Tables

Key Terms

REVIEW QUESTIONS

1. What are the two main ways in which the government can intervene in the marketplace?

2. What is consumer surplus? How is it calculated and how is it represented in a diagram?

3. What is producer surplus? How is it calculated and how is it represented in a diagram?

4. What is total surplus? How is it calculated and how is it represented in a diagram?

5. Why do consumers demand regulation? In what kinds of industries would their demands for regulation be greatest?

6. Why do producers demand regulation? In what kinds of industries would their demands for regulation be greatest?

7. Explain the public interest and capture theories of the supply of regulation. What does each theory imply about the behavior of politicians?

8. How is oligopoly regulated in the United States? In whose interest is it regulated?

9. What are the main antitrust laws in force in the United States today?

10. What is the "rule of reason"? When was this rule formulated? How has it been applied? When was it abandoned?

11. What are the landmark antitrust cases?

12. Describe the issues and outcome of the American Tobacco and Standard Oil cases?

13. What was the main difference between the American Tobacco and Standard Oil cases on the one hand and the U.S. Steel case on the other hand?

14. What was special about the Alcoa case?

15. Describe the case against IBM. How was the case settled?

16. Describe the case against AT&T. How was the case settled?

17. Describe the case against Microsoft.

18. How does the Department of Justice decide whether to challenge and possibly seek to block a merger?

19. What was the problem with mergers in the soft drink industry recently?

P R O B L E M S

1. Elixir Springs, Inc., is an unregulated natural monopoly that bottles Elixir, a unique health product with no substitutes. The total fixed cost incurred by Elixir Springs is $160,000, and its marginal cost is 10¢ a bottle. The demand for Elixir is as follows:

Price (cents per bottle)	Quantity demanded (thousands of bottles per year)
100	0
90	200
80	400
70	600
60	800
50	1,000
40	1,200
30	1,400
20	1,600
10	1,800
0	2,000

   a. What is the price of a bottle of water?
   b. How many bottles does Elixir Springs sell?
   c. Does Elixir Springs maximize total surplus or producer surplus?

2. The government regulates Elixir Springs in problem 1 by imposing a marginal cost pricing rule.
   a. What is the price of a bottle of Elixir?
   b. How many bottles does Elixir Springs sell?
   c. What is Elixir Springs producer surplus?
   d. What is the consumer surplus?
   e. Is the regulation in the public interest or in the private interest?

3. The government regulates Elixir Springs in problem 1 by imposing an average cost pricing rule.
   a. What is the price of a bottle of Elixir?
   b. How many bottles does Elixir Springs sell?
   c. What is Elixir Springs' producer surplus?
   d. What is the consumer surplus?
   e. Is the regulation in the public interest or in the private interest?

4. The value of the capital invested in Elixir Springs in problem 1 is $2 million. The government introduces a rate of return regulation requiring the firm to sell its water for a price that gives it a rate of return of 6 percent on its capital.
   a. What is the price of a bottle of Elixir?
   b. How many bottles does Elixir Springs sell?
   c. What is Elixir Springs' producer surplus?
   d. What is the consumer surplus?
   e. Is the regulation in the public interest or in the private interest?

5. Faced with the rate of return regulation of problem 4, Elixir Springs inflates its costs by paying a special bonus to its owner that it counts as a cost.
   a. Counting the bonus as part of the producer surplus, what is the size of the bonus that maximizes producer surplus and that makes the measured rate of return equal to 6 percent as required by the regulation?
   b. How many bottles does Elixir Springs sell?
   c. What is Elixir Springs' producer surplus?
   d. What is the consumer surplus?
   e. Is the regulation in the public interest or in the private interest?

6. After you have studied *Reading Between the Lines* on pp. 484–485, answer the following questions.
   a. Why do Microsoft's competitors claim that the firm is acting as a monopoly?
   b. If Microsoft and Unix proposed to merge their activities in the market for operating systems, what would the Department of Justice do and why?
   c. What would be the Department of Justice's attitude toward a merger between Apple and Unix?
   d. Describe Microsoft's "per-processor" agreements and explain their effects on economic efficiency and Microsoft's economic profit.

Externalities, the Environment, and Knowledge

After studying this chapter, you will be able to:

■ Explain how property rights can sometimes be used to overcome externalities

■ Explain how emission charges, marketable permits, and taxes can be used to achieve efficiency in the face of external costs

■ Explain how subsidies can be used to achieve efficiency in the face of external benefits

■ Explain how scholarships, below-cost tuition, and research grants make the quantity of education and invention more efficient

■ Explain how patents increase economic efficiency

We burn huge quantities of fossil fuels—coal, natural gas, and oil—that cause acid rain and possibly global warming. The persistent and large-scale use of chlorofluorocarbons (CFCs) may have caused irreparable damage to the earth's ozone layer, thereby exposing us to additional ultraviolet rays, which increases the incidence of skin cancer. We dump toxic waste into rivers, lakes, and oceans. These environmental issues are simultaneously everybody's problem and nobody's problem.

Greener and Smarter

What, if anything, can government do to protect our environment? How can government action help us to take account of the damage that we cause others every time we turn on our heating or air conditioning systems? ◆ Almost every day, we hear about a new discovery—in medicine, engineering, chemistry, physics, or even economics. The advance of knowledge seems boundless. And more and more people are learning more and more of what is already known. The stock of knowledge—what is known and how many people know it—is increasing, apparently without bound. We are getting smarter. But is our stock of knowledge advancing fast enough? Are we spending enough on research and development? Do we spend enough on education? Do enough people remain in school for long enough? And do we work hard enough at school? Would we be better off if we spent more on research and education?

◈ In this chapter we study the problems that arise because many of our actions affect other people, for ill or good, in ways that we do not usually take into account when we make our own economic choices. We study two big areas—the environment and the accumulation of knowledge—in which these problems are especially important. But first we study the general problem of externalities.

Externalities

A COST OR BENEFIT OF A PRODUCTION OR CONsumption activity that spills over to affect people other than those who decide the scale of the activity is called an **externality**. Externalities can be negative—external costs—or positive—external benefits. An *external cost* is the cost of producing a good or service that is not borne by its consumers but by other people. An *external benefit* is the benefit of consuming a good or service that does not accrue to its consumers but to other people. Let's consider some examples.

External Costs

When a chemical factory dumps toxic waste products into a river and kills the fish, it imposes an external cost on the members of the fishing club located downstream. Because these costs are not borne by the chemical factory, the chemical factory does not take these costs into account in deciding whether, and in what quantities, to dump waste into the river. When in the early 1980s a person in Los Angeles drove a car fueled by leaded gasoline, an external cost was imposed on everyone who tried to breathe the toxic air. Again, because most of these costs were not borne by the driver, they were not taken into account in deciding how often to drive.

Two particularly dramatic external costs have received a lot of attention in recent years. One arises from the use of chlorofluorocarbons (CFCs). These chemicals are used in a wide variety of products—from coolants in refrigerators and air conditioners to plastic phones to cleaning solvents for computer circuits. Although the precise chemistry of the process is not understood and is a subject of dispute, many atmospheric physicists believe that CFCs damage the atmosphere's protective ozone layer. Discoveries of depleted ozone over Antarctica in 1983 heightened fears of extended ozone depletion. The National Academy of Sciences has estimated that a 1 percent drop in ozone levels might cause a 2 percent rise in the incidence of skin cancer. Diminished ozone is also believed to be a possible cause of cataracts. But when you switch on the air conditioner on a steamy August evening, you do not count the cost of an increase in the incidence of skin cancer as part of the price that has to be paid for a comfortable night's sleep. You count only the cost that *you* incur.

The other external cost arises from burning fossil fuels that add carbon dioxide and other gases to the atmosphere that prevent infrared radiation from escaping. These gases are collectively known as "greenhouse gases" because they maintain the earth's temperature. An increase in the concentration of these gases might be responsible for an increase in the earth's average temperature—an increase that could continue into the next century and beyond. If the greenhouse scenario is correct (which is by no means certain), much of the Midwest will become a dust bowl and many eastern and Gulf Coast regions will disappear under an expanded Atlantic Ocean. But when you take a car trip and burn gasoline, a fossil fuel, you do not count as part of the cost the effects of a warmer planet. You compare your private benefit with your own cost.

Not all externalities are negative—they are not always external costs. Let's look at some activities that bring external benefits.

External Benefits

When a homeowner renovates her house and landscapes her yard, she generates an external benefit for her neighbors—their property values increase. In deciding how much to spend on this renovation and landscaping, she pays more attention to the pleasure she receives herself than to the increase in property values she creates for others.

The biggest external benefits are in our schools, colleges, and research laboratories. Well-educated people derive many benefits for themselves—such as higher incomes and the enjoyment of a wide range of artistic and cultural activities. But they also bring benefits to others through social interaction. People find more exciting partners and spouses, children get more imaginative parents, and we get to see more creative and entertaining movies and television shows. The list is almost endless. Despite all these external benefits, each one of us decides how much schooling to undertake by assessing our own costs and benefits, not those enjoyed by the wider community.

Health services also create external benefits. The pursuit of good health and personal hygiene reduces the risk that the people with whom we come into contact will be infected by transmitted diseases. Again, in making economic choices about the scale of resources to devote to health and hygiene, we mainly take account of the costs borne by ourselves and the benefits accruing to ourselves and not the greater benefit that our actions bring to others.

Market Failure and Public Choice

External costs and external benefits are a major source of *market failure*. The market economy tends to overproduce goods and services that have external costs and to underproduce goods and services that have external benefits. That is, externalities create inefficiency.

When market failure occurs, we must either live with the inefficiency it creates or try to achieve greater efficiency by making some *public choices* and using the instruments of government to intervene in the market economy. Governments can take several types of action to achieve a more efficient allocation of resources in the face of externalities to decrease production where there are external costs and increase it where there are external benefits. This chapter explains these actions. It begins this task by studying external costs that affect the environment.

Economics of the Environment

ENVIRONMENTAL PROBLEMS ARE NOT NEW, AND they are not restricted to rich industrial countries. Preindustrial towns and cities in Europe had severe sewage disposal problems that created cholera epidemics and plagues that killed tens of millions of people. Nor is the desire to find solutions to environmental problems new. The development in the fourteenth century of pure water supplies and of garbage and sewage disposal are examples of early contributions to improving the quality of the environment.

Popular discussions of the environment usually pay little attention to economics. They focus on physical aspects of the environment, not costs and benefits. A common assumption is that if people's actions cause *any* environmental degradation, those actions must cease. In contrast, an economic study of the environment emphasizes costs and benefits. An economist talks about the efficient amount of pollution or environmental damage. This emphasis on costs and benefits does not mean that economists, as citizens, do not share the same goals as others and value a healthy environment. Nor does it mean that economists have the right answers and everyone else has the wrong ones (or vice versa). Economics provides a set of tools and principles that clarify the issues. It does not provide an agreed list of solutions. The starting point for an economic analysis of the environment is the demand for a healthy environment.

The Demand for Environmental Quality

The demand for a clean and healthy environment has grown and is greater today than it has ever been. We express our demand for a better environment in a variety of ways. We join organizations that lobby governments for environmental regulations and policies. We vote for politicians who convince us that they have the environment polices that we want to see implemented. (All politicians at least pay lip service to the environment today.) And we buy "green" products and avoid hazardous products, even if we pay a bit more to do so. Figure 21.1 gives one indicator of

FIGURE 21.1

Membership of Environmental Groups

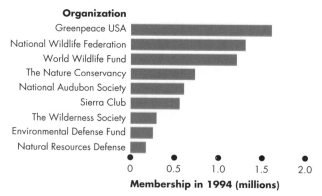

(a) Organizations

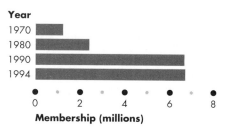

(b) Membership trend

In 1994, almost 7 million people were members of environmental groups. Membership doubled during the 1970s and almost tripled during the 1980s.

Sources: Outside, March 1994; Francis Cairncross, *Costing the Earth*, The Economist Books Ltd., p. 13.

the growth in the demand for a better environment: the growth in the number of people who pay subscriptions to environment organizations.

The demand for a better environment has grown for two reasons:

1. Increased incomes
2. Increased knowledge of the sources of environmental problems

As our incomes increase, we demand a larger range of goods and services, and one of these "goods" is a high-quality environment. We value clean air, unspoiled natural scenery, and wildlife, and we are willing to pay to protect these valuable resources.

As our knowledge of the effects of our actions on the environment grows, so we are able to take measures that improve the environment. For example, now that we know how sulfur dioxide causes acid rain and how clearing rain forests destroys natural

stores of carbon dioxide, we are able, in principle, to design measures that limit these problems.

Let's look at the range of environmental problems that have been identified and the actions that create those problems.

The Sources of Environmental Problems

Environmental problems arise from pollution of the air, water, and land, and these individual sources of pollution interact through the *ecosystem*.

Air Pollution   Figure 21.2(a) shows the five economic activities that create most of our air pollution. It also shows the relative contributions of each activity. More than two thirds of air pollution comes from road transportation and industrial processes. Only one sixth arises from electric power generation.

FIGURE   21.2

Air Pollution

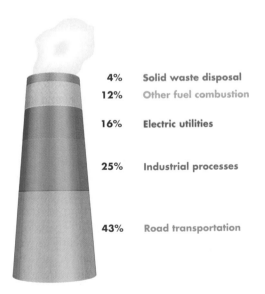

4%	Solid waste disposal
12%	Other fuel combustion
16%	Electric utilities
25%	Industrial processes
43%	Road transportation

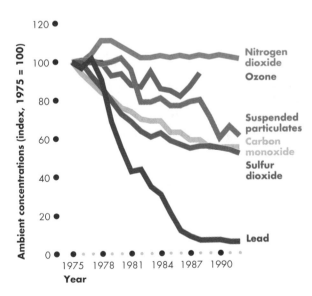

Part (a) shows that road transportation is the largest source of air pollution, followed by industrial processes and electric utilities. Part (b) shows that lead has almost been eliminated from our air and concentrations of carbon monoxide and sulfur dioxide and suspended particulates have decreased. But nitrogen dioxide and ozone have persisted at close to their 1975 levels.

Source: U.S. Environmental Protection Agency, *National Air Quality and Emissions Trends Report, 1994*, February 1994.

A common belief is that air pollution is getting worse. On many fronts, as we will see later in this chapter, *global* air pollution *is* getting worse. But air pollution in the United States is getting less severe for most substances. Figure 21.2(b) shows the trends in the concentrations of six air pollutants. While lead has been almost eliminated from our air and sulfur dioxide, carbon monoxide, and suspended particulates have been reduced substantially, levels of other pollutants have remained more stable.

While the facts about the sources and trends in air pollution are not in doubt, there is considerable disagreement in the scientific community about the *effects* of air pollution. The least controversial problem is *acid rain,* which is caused by sulfur dioxide and nitrogen oxide emissions from coal- and oil-fired generators of electric utilities. Acid rain begins with air pollution, and it leads to water pollution and damages vegetation.

More controversial are airborne substances (suspended particulates) such as lead from leaded gasoline. Some scientists believe that in sufficiently large concentrations, these substances (189 of which have currently been identified) cause cancer and other life-threatening conditions.

Even more controversial is *global warming,* which some scientists believe results from the carbon dioxide emissions of road transportation and electric utilities, methane created by cows and other livestock, nitrous oxide emissions of electric utilities and from fertilizers, and chlorofluorocarbons (CFCs) from refrigeration equipment and (in the past) aerosols. The earth's average temperature has increased over the past 100 years, but most of the increase occurred *before* 1940. Determining what causes changes in the earth's temperature and separating out the effect of carbon dioxide and other factors are proving to be very difficult.

Equally controversial is the problem of *ozone layer depletion.* There is no doubt that a hole in the ozone layer exists over Antarctica, and that the ozone layer protects us from cancer-causing ultraviolet rays from the sun. But how our industrial activity influences the ozone layer is simply not understood at this time.

One air pollution problem has almost been eliminated: lead from gasoline. In part, this happened because the cost of living without leaded gasoline, it turns out, is not high. But sulfur dioxide and the so-called greenhouse gases are a much tougher problem to tackle. Their alternatives are costly or have environmental problems of their own. The major sources of these pollutants are road vehicles and electric utilities. Road vehicles can be made "greener" in a variety of ways. One is with new fuels, and some alternatives being investigated are alcohol, natural gas, propane and butane, and hydrogen. Another way of making cars and trucks "greener" is to change the chemistry of gasoline. Refiners are working on reformulations of gasoline that cut tailpipe emissions. Similarly, electric power can be generated in cleaner ways by harnessing solar power, tidal power, or geothermal power. Technically possible, these methods are more costly than conventional carbon-fueled generators. Another alternative is nuclear power. This method is good for air pollution but bad for land and water pollution because there is no known safe method of disposing of spent nuclear fuel.

Water Pollution The largest sources of water pollution are the dumping of industrial waste and treated sewage in lakes and rivers and the runoff from fertilizers. A more dramatic source is the accidental spilling of crude oil into the oceans such as the *Exxon Valdez* spill in Alaska in 1989 and an even larger spill in the Russian Arctic in 1994. The most frightening is the dumping of nuclear waste into the ocean by the former Soviet Union.

There are two main alternatives to polluting the waterways and oceans. One is the chemical processing of waste to render it inert or biodegradable. The other, in wide use for nuclear waste, is to use land sites for storage in secure containers.

Land Pollution Land pollution arises from dumping toxic waste products. Ordinary household garbage does not pose a pollution problem unless dumped garbage seeps into the water supply. This possibility increases as less suitable landfill sites are used. It is estimated that 80 percent of existing landfills will be full by 2010. Some regions (New York, New Jersey, and other East Coast states) and some countries (Japan and the Netherlands) have run out of landfill space already. The alternatives to landfill are recycling and incineration. Recycling is an apparently attractive alternative, but it requires an investment in new technologies to be effective (see *Reading Between the Lines* on pp. 506–507). Incineration is a high-cost alternative to landfill, and it produces air pollution.

We've seen that the demand for a quality environment has grown, and we've described the range of environmental problems. Let's now look at the ways in which these problems can be handled. We'll begin by looking at property rights and how they relate to environmental externalities.

Property Rights and Environmental Externalities

Externalities arise because of an *absence* of property rights. **Property rights** are social arrangements that govern the ownership, use, and disposal of factors of production and goods and services. In modern societies a property right is a legally established title that is enforceable in the courts.

By thinking about the examples we've already reviewed, you can see that property rights are absent when externalities arise. No one owns the air, the rivers, and the oceans. So it is no one's private business to ensure that these resources are used in an efficient way. In fact, there is an incentive to use them more than if there were property rights.

Figure 21.3 illustrates how an environmental externality arises in the absence of property rights. A chemical factory (part a) upstream from a fishing club (part b) must decide how to dispose of its waste.

The *MB* curve in part (a) is the factory's marginal benefit curve. It tells us how much an additional ton of waste dumped into the river is worth to the factory. The value to the firm of dumping a marginal ton of waste in the river falls as the quantity increases. The *MB* curve is the firm's demand curve for the use of the river, which is a factor of production. The demand for a factor of production slopes downward because of the law of diminishing returns (see Chapter 14, pp. 335–340).

The *MSC* curve in part (b) is the marginal social cost curve. It tells us the cost imposed by the chemical factory on the fishing club by one additional ton of waste dumped into the river. The cost to the club of the firm dumping a marginal ton of waste in the river rises as the quantity increases.

If no one owns the river, the factory dumps the amount of waste that maximizes its total benefit. Because its marginal cost of waste disposal is zero, it dumps the quantity that makes its marginal benefit zero. The quantity dumped is 8 tons a week. The cost of this amount of waste, which is borne by the fishing club, is $200 a ton. The marginal social cost of the waste is $200 a ton and the marginal benefit is zero, so this outcome is inefficient. Stopping the dumping of waste is worth more to the fishing club than the benefit of dumping waste is worth to the factory.

Sometimes it is possible to correct an externality by establishing a property right where one does not currently exist. For example, suppose that the property right in the river was assigned to the chemical factory. Because the river is now the property of the factory,

FIGURE 21.3

An Externality

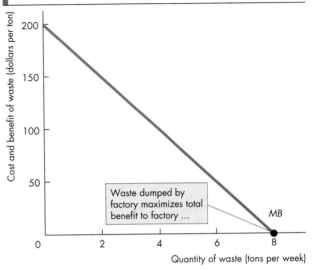

(a) Chemical factory

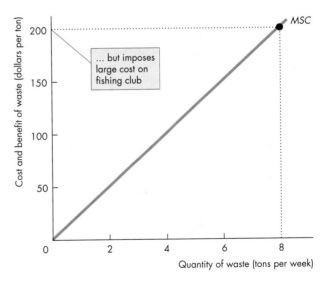

(b) Fishing club

A chemical factory's marginal benefit from dumping its waste into a river is MB (part a) and a fishing club's marginal cost of having waste dumped is MSC (part b). With no property rights, the factory maximizes total benefit by dumping 8 tons a week, the quantity at which the marginal benefit of dumping equals the marginal cost (zero). With this quantity of waste, the fishing club bears a marginal cost of $200 per ton. This outcome is inefficient because the marginal social cost exceeds the marginal benefit.

the fishing club must pay the factory for the right to fish in the river. But the price that the club is willing to pay depends on the number and quality of fish, which in turn depends on how much waste the factory dumps in the river. The greater the amount of pollution, the smaller is the amount the fishing club is willing to pay for the right to fish. Similarly, the smaller the amount of pollution, the greater is the amount the fishing club is willing to pay for the right to fish. The chemical factory is now confronted with the cost of its pollution decision. It might still decide to pollute, but if it does, it faces the opportunity cost of its actions—forgone revenue from the fishing club.

Suppose that the fishing club, not the chemical factory, owns the river. In this case the factory must pay a fee to the fishing club for the right to dump its waste. The more waste it dumps (equivalently, the more fish it kills), the more it must pay. Again, the factory faces an opportunity cost for the pollution it creates—the fee paid to the fishing club.

The Coase Theorem

We've considered two alternatives: assigning the property right to the polluter and to the victim of the pollution. Does it matter how property rights are assigned? At first thought, the assignment seems crucial. And until 1960, that is what everyone thought—including economists who had thought about the problem for longer than a few minutes. But in 1960, Ronald Coase had a remarkable insight, now known as the Coase theorem. The **Coase theorem** is the proposition that if property rights exist and transactions costs are low, private transactions are efficient. Equivalently, with property rights and low transactions costs, there are no externalities. All the costs and benefits are taken into account by the transacting parties. So it doesn't matter how the property rights are assigned.

Figure 21.4 illustrates the Coase theorem. It brings together the chemical factory's marginal benefit curve and the fishing club's marginal cost curve that you saw in Fig. 21.3. With property rights in place, the *MB* curve becomes the factory's demand curve for dumping waste. It tells us what the factory is willing to pay to dump. The *MSC* curve is the fishing club's supply curve of river use to the firm. It tells us what the club's members must be paid if they are to put up with inferior fishing and supply the firm with a permit to dump.

FIGURE 21.4

The Coase Theorem

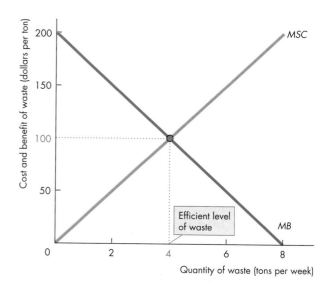

Pollution of a river imposes a marginal social cost, *MSC*, on the victim and provides a marginal benefit, *MB*, to the polluter. The efficient amount of pollution is the quantity that makes marginal benefit equal to marginal social cost—in this example, 4 tons per week. If the polluter owns the river, the victim will pay $400 a week ($100 a ton × 4 tons a week) to the polluter for the assurance that pollution will not exceed 4 tons a week. If the victim owns the river, the polluter will pay $400 for pollution rights to dump 4 tons a week.

The efficient level of waste is 4 tons a week. At this level, the club bears a cost of $100 for the last ton dumped into the river, and the factory gets a benefit of that amount. If waste disposal is restricted below 4 tons a week, an increase in waste disposal benefits the factory more than it costs the club. The factory can pay the club to put up with more waste disposal, and both the club and the factory can gain. If waste disposal exceeds 4 tons a week, an increase in waste disposal costs the club more than it benefits the factory. The club can now pay the factory to cut its waste disposal, and again, both the club and the factory can gain. Only when the level of waste disposal is 4 tons a week can neither party do any better. This is the efficient level of waste disposal.

The amount of waste disposal is the same regardless of who owns the river. If the factory owns it, the club pays $400 for fishing rights and for an agreement that waste disposal will not exceed 4 tons a week. If the club owns the river, the factory pays $400 for the right to dump 4 tons of waste a week. In both cases, the amount of waste disposal is the efficient amount.

Property rights work in this example because the transactions costs are low. The factory and the fishing club can easily sit down and negotiate the deal that produces the efficient outcome.

But in many situations, transactions costs are high and property rights cannot be enforced. Imagine, for example, the transactions costs if the 50 million people who live in the northeastern part of the United States and Canada tried to negotiate an agreement with the 20,000 factories that emit sulfur dioxide and cause acid rain! In a case such as this, governments resort to alternative methods of coping with externalities. They use:

1. Emission charges
2. Marketable permits
3. Taxes

Economics in History on pp. 508–509 reviews some examples of the use of these methods and how ideas about how to cope with externalities have changed. In the United States, the federal government has established an agency, the Environmental Protection Agency (EPA), to coordinate and administer the nation's environment policies. Let's look at the tools available to the EPA and see how they work.

Emission Charges

Emission charges are a method of using the market to achieve efficiency, even in the face of externalities. The government (or the regulatory agency established by the government) sets the emission charges, which are, in effect, a price per unit of pollution. The more pollution a firm creates, the more it pays in emission charges. This method of dealing with environmental externalities has been used only modestly in the United States, but it is common in Europe. For example, in France, Germany, and the Netherlands, water polluters pay a waste disposal charge.

To work out the emission charge that achieves efficiency, the regulator must determine the marginal social cost and marginal social benefit of pollution. **Marginal social cost** is the marginal cost incurred by the producer of a good—marginal private cost—

plus the marginal cost imposed on others—the external cost. **Marginal social benefit** is the marginal benefit received by the consumer of a good—marginal private benefit—plus the marginal benefit to others—the external benefit. To achieve efficiency, the price per unit of pollution must be set to make the marginal social cost of the pollution equal to its marginal social benefit.

Figure 21.5 illustrates an efficient emissions charge. The marginal benefit of pollution is *MB* and accrues to the polluters—there is no *external* benefit. The marginal social cost of pollution is *MSC* and is entirely an external cost. The efficient level of sulfur dioxide emissions is 10 million tons a year, which is achieved with an emission charge of $10 per ton. At this price, polluters do not find it worthwhile to buy the permission to pollute in excess of 10 million tons a year.

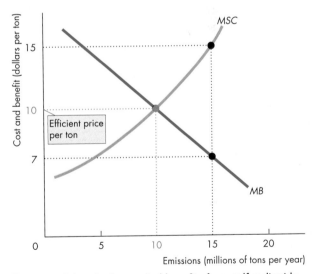

FIGURE 21.5
Emission Charges

Electric utilities obtain marginal benefits from sulfur dioxide emissions of *MB*, and everyone else bears a marginal social cost of *MSC*. The efficient level of pollution—10 million tons a year in this example—is achieved by imposing an emission charge on the utilities of $10 a ton. If the emission charge is set too low, at $7 a ton, the resulting amount of pollution is greater than the efficient amount—at 15 million tons a year in this example. In this case, the marginal social cost is $15 a ton, and it exceeds the marginal benefit of $7 a ton.

In practice, it is hard to determine the marginal benefit of pollution. And the people who are best informed about the marginal benefit, the polluters, have an incentive to mislead the regulators about the benefit. As a result, if a pollution charge is used, the most likely outcome is for the price to be set too low. For example, in Fig. 21.5, the price might be set at $7 per ton. At this price, polluters find it worthwhile to pay for 15 million tons a year. At this level of pollution, the marginal social cost is $15 a ton, and the amount of pollution exceeds the efficient level.

One way of overcoming excess pollution is to impose a quantitative limit. The most sophisticated way of doing this is with quantitative limits that firms can buy and sell—with marketable permits. Let's look at this alternative.

Marketable Permits

Instead of imposing emission charges on polluters, each potential polluter might be given a pollution limit. To achieve efficiency, marginal benefit and marginal cost must be assessed just as in the case of emission charges. Provided that these benefit-cost calculations are correct, the same efficient outcome can be achieved with quantitative limits as with charges. But in the case of quantitative limits, a cap must be set for each polluter. To set these caps at their efficient levels, the marginal benefit of *each* producer must be assessed. If firm *H* has a higher marginal benefit than firm *L*, an efficiency gain can be achieved by decreasing the cap of firm *L* and increasing that of firm *H*. It is virtually impossible to determine the marginal benefits of each firm, so in practice, quantitative restrictions cannot be allocated to each producer in an efficient way.

Marketable permits are a clever way of overcoming the need for the regulator to know every firm's marginal benefit schedule. Each firm can be allocated a permit to emit a certain amount of pollution, and firms may buy and sell such permits.

Figure 21.6 shows how such a system works and can achieve efficiency. Some firms have low marginal benefits from sulfur dioxide emissions, shown as MB_L in part (a). Others have a high marginal benefit,

FIGURE 21.6

Marketable Pollution Permits

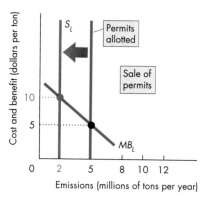

(a) Low-benefit firms

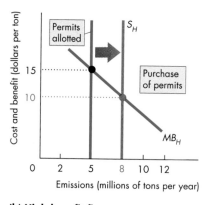

(b) High-benefit firms

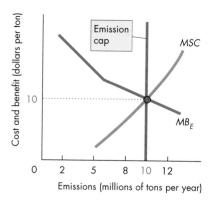

(c) Economy

Some firms obtain low marginal benefits from pollution, MB_L in part (a), and some obtain high marginal benefits, MB_H in part (b). Marginal benefit for the economy, MB_E in part (c), is the horizontal sum of the MB_L and MB_H curves. Marginal social cost is MSC in part (c). Permits for 10 million tons a year (the efficient level) are issued. Each type of firm gets 5 million tons a year. Initially, low-benefit firms value their permits at $5 a ton, and high-benefit firms value their permits at $15 a ton. High-benefit firms buy permits for 3 million tons of pollution from low-benefit firms for a market price of $10 a ton.

shown as MB_H in part (b). For the economy as a whole, the marginal benefit is MB_E in part (c). It is the horizontal sum of MB_L and MB_H. The marginal social cost of sulfur dioxide emissions is MSC, also shown in part (c). The efficient level of emissions is 10 million tons a year, the quantity at which marginal social cost equals marginal social benefit.

Suppose the EPA allocates permits for a total of 10 million tons of sulfur dioxide emissions a year. And suppose the permits are allocated equally to the two groups of firms—5 million tons each. The firms in part (a) value their last ton of pollution permitted at $5. The firms in part (b) value their last ton of pollution permitted at $15 a ton. With a market in permits, the firms in part (a) sell some of their permits to those in part (b). Both types of firm gain from the trade.

If the market in permits is competitive, the price at which firms trade permits is $10 per ton. At this price, low-benefit firms (part a) sell permits for 3 million tons of sulfur dioxide emissions to the high-benefit firms (part b). After these transactions, the low-benefit firms (part a) have S_L permits and the high-benefit firms (part b) have S_H permits, and the allocation is efficient.

The Market for Emissions in the United States

Markets for emission permits have operated in the United States since the Environmental Protection Agency first implemented air quality programs following the passage of the Clean Air Act in 1970.

Emissions trading has four elements: *netting, offsets, bubbles,* and *banking. Netting* is like trading inside a firm. A firm may create a new source of emissions by decreasing its emissions at another plant. *Offsets* are sufficiently large decreases in a firm's emissions in one area to gain it permission to create pollution in an already heavily polluted area. *Bubbles* enable a firm to sum all its emissions from a single plant and meet an aggregate limit for the plant. The name derives from the idea that there is an imaginary bubble placed over a plant and all the emissions leave through a single leakage point. *Banking* is saving current reductions in emissions for later use—putting permits in the bank.

Trading in lead pollution permits was very common during the 1980s, and this marketable permit program has been rated a success. It enabled lead to be virtually eliminated from the atmosphere of the United States (see Figure 21.1b). But this success might not easily translate to other situations because lead pollution has some special features. First, most lead pollution came from a single source, leaded gasoline. Second, lead in gasoline is easily monitored. Third, the objective of the program was clear: eliminate lead in gasoline.

The EPA is now considering using marketable permits to promote efficiency in the control of chlorofluorocarbons, the gases that are believed to damage the ozone layer.

Taxes and External Costs

Taxes can be used to provide incentives for producers or consumers to cut back on an activity that creates external costs. To see how taxes work, consider the market for transportation services. Figure 21.7 shows this market. The demand curve for transportation services, D, is also the marginal benefit curve, MB. This curve tells us how much consumers value each different quantity of transportation services. The curve MC measures the marginal *private* cost of producing transportation services—the costs directly incurred by the producers of these services.

The costs borne by the producers of transportation services are not the only costs. External costs arise from the airborne particulates and greenhouse gases caused by vehicle emissions. Further, one person's decision to use a highway imposes congestion costs on others. These costs also are external costs. When all the external marginal costs are added to the marginal cost faced by the producer, we obtain the marginal *social* cost of transportation services, shown by MSC in the figure.

If the transportation market is competitive and unregulated, road users will balance their own marginal cost, MC, against their own marginal benefit, MB, and travel Q_0 vehicle miles at a price (and cost) of P_0 per mile. At this scale of transportation services, the marginal social cost is SC_0. The marginal social cost minus the marginal private cost, $SC_0 - P_0$, is the marginal cost imposed on others—the marginal external cost.

Suppose the government taxes road transportation and that it sets the tax equal to the external marginal cost. By imposing such a tax, the government makes the suppliers of transportation services incur a marginal cost equal to the marginal social cost. That is, the marginal private cost plus the tax equals the marginal social cost. The market supply curve is now the same as the MSC curve. The price rises to P_1 a mile, and at this price, people travel Q_1 vehicle miles. The marginal cost of the resources used in producing

FIGURE 21.7
Taxes and Pollution

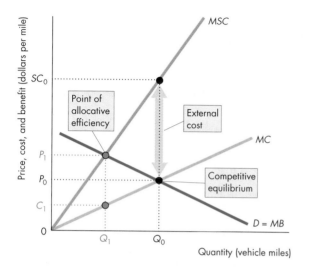

The demand curve for road transportation services is also the marginal benefit curve ($D = MB$). The marginal private cost curve is MC. If the market is competitive, output is Q_0 vehicle miles and the price is P_0 per vehicle mile. Marginal social cost is SC_0 per vehicle mile. Because of congestion and pollution, the marginal cost services exceeds the marginal private cost. Marginal social cost is shown by curve MSC. If the government imposes a tax so that producers of transportation services are confronted with the marginal social cost, the MSC curve becomes the relevant marginal cost curve for suppliers' decisions. The price increases to P_1 per vehicle mile, and the quantity decreases to Q_1 vehicle miles. Allocative efficiency is achieved.

Q_1 vehicle miles is C_1, and the marginal external cost is P_1 minus C_1. That marginal external cost is paid by the consumer through the tax.

The situation at the price P_1 and the quantity Q_1 is efficient. At a quantity greater than Q_1, marginal social cost exceeds marginal benefit, so net benefit increases by decreasing the quantity of transportation services. At a quantity less than Q_1, marginal benefit exceeds marginal social cost, so net benefit increases by increasing the quantity of transportation services.

A Carbon Fuel Tax?   A tax can be imposed on any activity that creates external costs. For example, we could tax *all* air-polluting activities. Because the car-

bon fuels that we use to power our vehicles and generate our electric power are a major source of pollution, why don't we have a broad-based tax on all activities that burn carbon fuel and set the tax rate high enough to give a large reduction in carbon emissions?

The question becomes even more pressing when we consider not only the current levels of greenhouse gases but also their projected future levels. In 1990, annual carbon emissions worldwide were a staggering 6 billion tons. By 2050, with current policies, that annual total is predicted to be 24 billion tons.

Uncertainty About Global Warming   Part of the reason we do not have a high, broad-based, carbon fuel tax is that the scientific evidence that carbon emissions produce global warming is not accepted by everyone. Climatologists are uncertain about how carbon emissions translate into atmospheric concentrations—about how the *flow* of emissions translates into a *stock* of pollution. The main uncertainty arises because carbon drains from the atmosphere into the oceans and vegetation at a rate that is not well understood. Climatologists are also uncertain about the connection between carbon concentration and temperature. And economists are uncertain about how a temperature increase translates into economic costs and benefits. Some economists believe that the costs and benefits are almost zero, while others believe that a temperature increase of 5.4 degrees Fahrenheit by 2090 will reduce the total output of goods and services by 20 percent.

Present Cost and Future Benefit   Another factor weighing against a large change in fuel use is that the costs would be borne now, while the benefits, if any, would accrue many years in the future. To compare future benefits with current costs, we must use an interest rate. If the interest rate is 1 percent a year, a dollar today becomes $2.70 in 100 years. If the interest rate is 5 percent a year, a dollar today becomes more than $131.50 in 100 years. So at an interest rate of 1 percent a year, it is worth spending $1 million in 1995 on pollution control to avoid $2.7 million in environmental damage in 2095. At an interest rate of 5 percent a year, it is worth spending $1 million today only if this expenditure avoids $131.5 million in environmental damage in 2095.

Because large uncertain future benefits are needed to justify small current costs, a general tax on carbon fuels is not a high priority on the political agenda.

International Factors A final factor against a large change in fuel use is the international pattern of the use of carbon fuels. Right now, carbon pollution comes in even doses from the industrial countries and the developing countries. But by 2050, three quarters of the carbon pollution will come from the developing countries (if the trends persist).

One reason for the high pollution rate in some developing countries (notably China, Russia, and other Eastern European countries) is that their governments *subsidize* the use of coal or oil. These subsidies lower producers' marginal costs and encourage the use of fuels. The result is that the quantity of carbon fuels consumed exceeds the efficient quantity—and by a large amount. It is estimated that by 2050, these subsidies will induce annual global carbon emissions of some 10 billion tons—about two fifths of total emissions. If the subsidies were removed, global emissions in 2050 would be 10 billion tons a year less.

A Global Warming Dilemma

With the high output rate of greenhouse gases in the developing world, the United States and the other industrial countries are faced with a global warming dilemma.[1] Decreasing pollution is costly and might bring benefits. But the benefits depend on all countries taking action to limit pollution. If one country acts alone, it bears the cost of limiting pollution and gets almost no benefits. So it is worthwhile taking steps to limit global pollution only if all nations act together.

Table 21.1 shows the global warming dilemma faced by the United States and the developing countries. The numbers are hypothetical. Each country (we'll call the developing countries a country) has two possible policies: to control carbon emissions or to pollute. If each country pollutes, it receives a zero net return (by assumption), shown in the top left square in the table. If each country controls carbon emissions, it bears the cost of using more expensive fuels and gets the benefit of less pollution. Its net return is $25 billion, as shown in the bottom right square of the table. If the United States controls carbon emissions but the developing countries do not, the United States alone bears the cost of using alter-

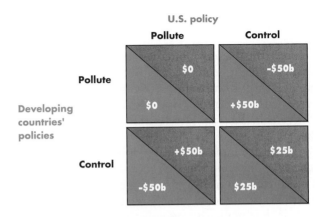

TABLE 21.1

A Global Warming Dilemma

If the United States and developing countries both pollute, their payoffs are those shown in the top left square. If both countries control pollution, their payoffs are shown in the bottom right square. When one country pollutes and the other one does not, their payoffs are shown in the top right and bottom left squares. The outcome of this game is for both countries to pollute. The structure of this game is the same as that of the prisoners' dilemma.

native fuels, and both the United States and the developing countries enjoy a lower level of pollution. In this example, the United States pays $50 billion more than it benefits and the developing countries benefit by $50 billion more than they pay, as shown in the top right corner of the table. Finally, if the developing countries control emissions and the United States does not, the developing countries bear the cost and the United States shares the gains, so the developing countries lose $50 billion and the United States gains this amount, as shown in the bottom left corner of the table.

Confronted with these possible payoffs, the United States and the developing countries decide their policies. The United States reasons as follows: If the developing countries do not control carbon emissions, we break even if we pollute and we lose $50 billion if we control our emissions. Conclusion: We are better off polluting. If the developing countries do control carbon emissions, we gain $50 billion if we pollute and $25 billion if we control emissions.

---

[1]This dilemma is like the "prisoners' dilemma" that is explained in Chapter 13 on pp. 308–310.

Again, we are better off polluting. The developing countries reach the same conclusion. So no one controls emissions, and pollution continues unabated.

Treaties and International Agreements

To break the dilemma, international agreements—treaties—might be negotiated. But such treaties must have incentives for countries to comply with their agreements. Otherwise, even with a treaty, the situation remains as we've just described and illustrated in Table 21.1.

One such international agreement is the *climate convention* that came into effect on March 21, 1994. This convention is an agreement among 60 countries to limit their output of greenhouse gases. But the convention does not have economic teeth. The poorer countries are merely asked to list their sources of greenhouse gases. The rich countries must show how, by 2000, they will return to their 1990 emissions levels.

To return to the 1990 emissions levels, the rich countries will need stiff increases in energy taxes, and such taxes will be costly. Energy taxes will induce a substitution toward more costly but cleaner alternative fuels. Without energy taxes, only a large technological advance in solar, wind, tidal, or nuclear power that makes these sources less costly than coal and oil can create the incentive needed to give up carbon fuels.

R E V I E W

- When externalities are present, the market allocation is not efficient.
- If an externality can be eliminated by assigning property rights, an efficient allocation can be achieved.
- If the government confronts firms with emission charges, imposes pollution limits, or imposes taxes equivalent to marginal external cost, it induces them to produce the efficient quantity of pollution, even in the face of externalities.
- When an externality goes beyond the scope of one country, effective international cooperation is necessary to achieve an efficient outcome.

Economics of Knowledge

KNOWLEDGE, THE THINGS PEOPLE KNOW AND understand, has a profound effect on the economy. The economics of knowledge is an attempt to understand that effect. It is also an attempt to understand the process of knowledge accumulation and the incentives people face to discover, to learn, and to pass on what they know to others. It is an economic analysis of the scientific and engineering processes that lead to the discovery and development of new technologies. And it is a study of the education process of teaching and learning.

You can think of knowledge as being both a consumer good and a factor of production. The demand for knowledge—the willingness to pay to acquire knowledge—depends on the marginal benefit it provides to its possessor. As a consumer good, knowledge provides utility, and this is one source of its marginal benefit. As a factor of production—part of the stock of capital—knowledge increases productivity, and this is another source of its marginal benefit.

Knowledge creates benefits not only for its possessor, but for others as well—external benefits. External benefits arise from education—passing on existing knowledge to others. When children learn the basics of reading, writing, and numbers in grade school, they are equipping themselves to be better neighbors for each other and better able to communicate and interact with each other. The process continues through high school and college. But when people make decisions about how much schooling to undertake, they undervalue the external benefits that it creates.

External benefits also arise from research and development activities that lead to the creation of new knowledge. Once someone has worked out how to do something, others can copy the basic idea. They do have to work to copy an idea, so they face an opportunity cost. But they do not usually have to pay the person who made the discovery to use it. When Isaac Newton worked out the formulas for calculating the rate of response of one variable to another—calculus—everyone was free to use his method. When a spreadsheet program called VisiCalc was invented, others were free to copy the basic idea. Lotus Corporation developed its 1-2-3 and later Microsoft created Excel, and both became highly successful, but they did not pay for the key idea first used in VisiCalc. When the first shopping mall was built and found to be a successful way of arranging retailing, everyone was free to copy the idea, and malls spread like mushrooms.

When people make decisions about the quantity of education to undertake or the amount of research and development to do, they balance the *private* marginal costs against the private marginal benefits. They undervalue the external benefits. As a result, if we were to leave education and research and development to unregulated market forces, we would get too little of these activities. To deliver them in efficient quantities, we make public choices through governments to modify the market outcome.

Three devices that governments can use to achieve an efficient allocation of resources in the presence of the external benefits from education and research and development are:

■ Subsidies
■ Below-cost provision
■ Patents and copyrights

Subsidies

A **subsidy** is a payment made by the government to producers that depends on the level of output. By subsidizing private activities, government can in principle encourage private decisions to be taken in the public interest. A government subsidy program might alternatively enable private producers to capture resources for themselves. Although subsidies cannot be guaranteed to work successfully, we'll study an example in which they do achieve their desired goal.

Figure 21.8 shows how subsidizing education can increase the amount of education undertaken and achieve allocative efficiency. Suppose that the marginal cost of producing a student-year of college education is a constant $20,000. We'll assume that all these costs are borne by the colleges and that there are no external costs. The marginal social cost is the same as the colleges' marginal cost and is shown by the curve *MC = MSC*. The maximum price that students (or parents) are willing to pay for an additional year of college determines the marginal private benefit curve and the demand curve for education. That curve is *MPB = D*. In this example, a competitive market in private college education results in 20 million students being enrolled in college with tuition at $20,000 a year.

Suppose that the external benefit—the benefit derived by people other than those who receive the education—results in marginal social benefits described by the curve *MSB*. Allocative efficiency occurs when marginal social cost equals marginal social benefit. In the example in Fig. 21.8, this equality occurs when 40 million students are enrolled in college. One way of getting 40 million students in college is to subsidize private colleges. In the example, a subsidy of $15,000 per student per year paid to the colleges does the job. With a subsidy of $15,000

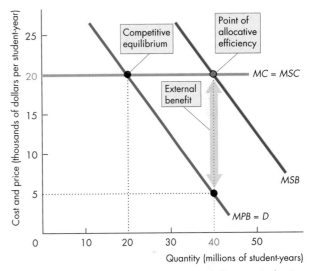

FIGURE 21.8

The Efficient Quantity of Education

The demand curve for education measures the marginal private benefit of education (*MPB = D*). The curve *MC* shows the marginal cost of education—in this example, $20,000 per student-year. If education is provided in a competitive market, tuition is $20,000 a year and 20 million students enroll. Education produces an external benefit, and adding the external benefit to the marginal private benefit gives marginal social benefit, *MSB*. Education has no external costs, so *MC* is also the marginal social cost of education, *MSC*. Allocative efficiency is achieved if the government provides education services to 40 million students a year, which is achieved by either subsidizing private colleges or providing education below cost in public colleges. In this example, students pay an annual tuition of $5,000 and the government pays a subsidy of $15,000.

and a marginal cost of $20,000, colleges earn an economic profit if the annual tuition exceeds $5,000. Competition among the colleges would drive the tuition down to $5,000, and at this price, 40 million students will enroll in college. So a subsidy can achieve an efficient outcome.

The lessons in this example can be applied to stimulating the rate of increase in the stock of knowledge—research and development. By subsidizing these activities, the government can move the allocation of resources toward a more efficient outcome. The mechanism that the government uses for this purpose is a research and development grant. In 1993, through agencies such as the National Science Foundation, the government made research and development grants of $51 billion. Of this total, $28 billion went to industry and $23 billion to universities and federally funded research and development centers.

Another way to achieve an efficient amount of education or research and development is through public provision below cost.

Below-Cost Provision

Instead of subsidizing private colleges, the government can establish it own colleges (public colleges) that provide schooling below cost. And instead of subsidizing research and development in industry and the universities, the government can establish its own research facilities and make discoveries available to others. Let's see how this approach works by returning to the example in Fig. 21.8.

By establishing public colleges with places for 40 million students, the government can supply the efficient quantity of college education. To ensure that this number of places is taken up, the public colleges would charge a tuition, in this example, of $5,000 a student per year. The government provides this tuition below its marginal cost of $20,000 a student per year. At this price, the number of people who choose to attend college makes the marginal social benefit of education equal to its marginal social cost.

We've now looked at two examples of how government action can help market participants take account of the external benefits deriving from education to achieve an outcome different from that of a private unregulated market. In reality, governments use both methods of encouraging an efficient quantity of education. They subsidize private colleges and universities, and they run their own institutions and

sell their services at below cost. But in education, the public sector is by far the larger. In research and development, subsidies to the private sector are far larger than the government direct provision.

Patents and Copyrights

Knowledge may well be the only factor of production that does not display *diminishing marginal productivity*. More knowledge (about the right things) makes people more productive. And there seems to be no tendency for the additional productivity from additional knowledge to diminish.

For example, in just 15 years, advances in knowledge about microprocessors have given us a sequence of processor chips that has made our personal computers increasingly powerful. Each advance in knowledge about how to design and manufacture a processor chip has brought apparently ever larger increments in performance and productivity. Similarly, each advance in knowledge about how to design and build an airplane has brought apparently ever larger increments in performance: Orville and Wilbur Wright's "Flyer 1" was a one-seat plane that could hop a farmer's field. The Lockheed Constellation was an airplane that could fly 120 passengers from New York to London, but with two refueling stops in Newfoundland and Ireland. The latest version of the Boeing 747 can carry 400 people nonstop from Los Angeles to Sydney or New York to Tokyo (flights of 7,500 miles that take 13 1/2 hours). These examples can be repeated again and again in fields as diverse as agriculture, biogenetics, communications, engineering, entertainment, medicine, and publishing.

A key reason why the stock of knowledge increases without diminishing returns is the sheer number of different techniques that can in principle be tried. Paul Romer explains this fact with an amazing example. Suppose, says Romer,

> that to make a finished good, 20 different parts have to be attached to a frame, one at a time. A worker could proceed in numerical order, attaching part one first, then part two....Or the worker could proceed in some other order, starting with part 10, then adding part seven....With 20 parts, a standard (but incredible) calculation shows that there are about 10^{18} different sequences one can use for assembling the final good. This number is larger than the total number of seconds that have elapsed since the big

bang created the universe, so we can be confident that in all activities, only a very small fraction of the possible sequences have ever been tried.[2]

Think about all the processes, all the products, and all the different bits and pieces that go into each, and you can see that we have only begun to scratch around the edges of what is possible.

Because knowledge is productive and creates external benefits, it is necessary to use public policies to ensure that those who develop new ideas face incentives that encourage an efficient level of effort. The main way of creating the right incentives is to provide the creators of knowledge with property rights in their discoveries—called **intellectual property rights**. The legal device for creating intellectual property rights is the patent or copyright. A **patent** or **copyright** is a government-sanctioned exclusive right granted to the inventor of a good, service, or productive process to produce, use, and sell the invention for a given number of years. A patent enables the developer of a new idea to prevent, for a limited number of years, others from benefiting freely from an invention. But to obtain the protection of the law, an inventor must make knowledge of the invention public.

Although patents encourage invention and innovation, they do so at an economic cost. While a patent is in place, its holder is a monopolist. And monopoly is another type of market failure. To maximize profit, a monopoly (patent holder) produces the quantity at which marginal cost equals marginal revenue. The monopoly sets the price above marginal cost and equal to the highest price at which the profit-maximizing quantity can be sold. In this situation, consumers value the good more highly (are willing to pay more for one more unit of it) than its marginal cost. So the quantity of the good available is less than the efficient quantity.

But without a patent, the effort to develop new goods, services, or processes is diminished and the flow of new inventions is slowed. So the efficient outcome is a compromise that balances the benefits of more inventions against the cost of temporary monopoly power in newly invented activities.

R E V I E W

- Knowledge is a consumer good and a factor of production that creates external benefits.
- External benefits arise both from education—passing on existing knowledge to others—and from research and development—creating new knowledge.
- Three devices used by governments to achieve an efficient stock of knowledge are subsidies, below-cost provision, and patents.
- Subsidies or below-cost provision can deliver an efficient amount of education.
- Knowledge does not seem to have diminishing returns, so incentives must exist to encourage the development of new ideas.
- Patents and copyrights can stimulate research, but they create a temporary monopoly, so the gain from more knowledge must be balanced against the loss from monopoly.

◆ We've now completed our study of *microeconomics*. We've learned how all economic problems arise from scarcity, that scarcity forces us to make choices, and that choice imposes cost—opportunity cost. Prices (*relative prices*) are opportunity costs and are determined by the interactions of buyers and sellers in markets. People choose what goods to buy and what factors of production to sell to maximize utility. Firms choose what goods to sell and what factors to buy to maximize profit. People and firms interact in markets, but the resulting equilibrium might be inefficient because of public goods, inequality, monopoly, and externalities. By providing public goods, redistributing income, curbing monopoly power, and coping with externalities, public choice modifies the market outcome.

The next part of this book studies *international economics*—the study of international trade and the problems of emerging market economies around the globe.

[2]From Paul Romer, "Ideas and Things," in *The Future Surveyed*, supplement to *The Economist*, 11 September, 1993, pp. 71–72. © 1993 The Economist Newspaper Group, Inc. Reprinted with permission. Further reproduction prohibited. The "standard calculation" that Romer refers to is the number of ways of selecting and arranging in order 20 objects from 20 objects—also called the number of permutations of 20 objects 20 at a time. This number is *factorial* 20, or 20! = $20 \times 19 \times 18 \times \ldots \times 2 \times 1 = 10^{18.4}$. A standard theory (challenged by observations made by the Hubbel space telescope in 1994) is that a big bang started the universe 15 billion years, or $10^{17.7}$ seconds, ago. Although $10^{18.4}$ and $10^{17.7}$ look similar, $10^{18.4}$ is *five* times as large as $10^{17.7}$, so if you started trying alternative sequences at the moment of the big bang and took only one second per trial, you would still have tried only one fifth of the possibilities. Amazing?

Efficient Markets in Recyclables

TIME, NOVEMBER 7, 1994

Treasure from Trash

BY BARBARA RUDOLPH

"Twenty-five soft-drink bottles can make a great sweater," says Rosie Rogers, who is neither a stand-up comic nor a fringe fashion designer. Rogers is a development engineer at Wellman, an American recycling firm—and she is totally serious. In an exhibit that opened last week at New York City's Fashion Institute for Technology, manufacturers showed off thermal underwear made from plastic bottles, gowns from garbage bags, and necklaces from telephone wires—born-again products that provided striking evidence of the upswing for recycling, or the business of giving trash a second life.

For years the industry has had a dirty secret: a fair amount of the so-called recycling activity was a sham. Amid the environmental fervor that followed Earth Day 1990, people in many countries began dutifully separating cans, bottles and newspapers from other trash and putting them in special collection containers. Some of this refuse—aluminum cans, for example—could easily be reused, but much of the material just piled up a recycling centers or was eventually dumped in landfills. Companies interested in the business had to figure out how to use the trash and develop the means to transform it into products consumers would buy. That required major investment in new technologies and factories. In the meantime, the glut of discarded paper and plastic drove down their value in the marketplace, and municipal-collection operations lost a great deal of money.

At last the picture is beginning to change. ... Plastics, typically the least desirable of recycled commodities, are ... in greater demand. One reason is this year's poor cotton harvest in China, which left textile manufacturers around the world scrambling for cotton substitutes. Old soft-drink bottles, it turns out, can be pulverized, treated with chemicals and reconstituted into synthetic fibers that look and feel like cotton....

Encouraged that uses can be found for more trash, towns and cities are setting up recycling operations at a rapid clip: in the U.S. the number of curbside pickup programs for reusable materials has grown from 600 in the late 1980s to more than 6,600....

A hopeful sign for the future can be found at the Chicago Board of Trade, one of the world's leading commodities markets. Next year it will begin trading a few recyclables, starting with certain types of plastic and glass. "This will be an international market for recyclable materials," says Michael Walsh, a senior economist at CBOT. With a place alongside gold, wheat and pork bellies, recyclables may become serious business indeed.

Reprinted by permission.

Essence of **THE STORY**

■ Until recently, not all of the paper and plastic waste separated from other trash was being recycled and the market prices of these items fell.

■ A big investment was needed to develop new technologies and factories to transform trash into products that consumers would buy.

■ New technology converts old soft-drink bottles into synthetic fibers that look and feel like cotton.

■ A poor cotton harvest in China in 1994 stimulated interest in cotton substitutes, so, with the new technology, plastic bottles are in greater demand.

■ Curbside pickup programs for reusable materials grew from 600 in the late 1980s to more than 6,600 in 1994.

■ In 1995, the Chicago Board of Trade will begin trading some types of recycled plastic and glass and create an international market in recyclable materials.

Economic

A N A L Y S I S

■ There are few externalities in the trash business, and a market mechanism operates with well-defined property rights that achieves an efficient allocation of trash.

■ When we sort our trash into various types of recyclables and other material, we do so at almost zero marginal cost to ourselves. (We might even benefit from lower garbage collection charges.)

■ Separated recyclables, collected by curbside (and other) programs, are sold to recyclers or dumped, depending on which method of disposal minimizes the collector's opportunity cost.

■ Figure I shows the market for used soft-drink bottles and the effect of recycling programs. Initially, demand was D_0, and supply was S_0. the equilibrium price was P_0, and the quantity was Q_0.

■ Trash separation programs increased the supply of bottles to S_1. With no change in demand, the price fell to zero. The quantity of bottles recycled increased to R, but many of the bottles collected were not sold to recyclers. They were dumped.

■ Recyclers had an incentive to find more ways of using old bottles. One way is to convert them into a cottonlike yarn.

■ A poor Chinese cotton harvest decreased the quantity available and increased the world price of cotton. With a high price of cotton, cotton users looked for lower-priced substitutes—the *principle of substitution* was at work.

■ The search for cotton substitutes and the low price of bottles gave recyclers the incentive to develop the technology and build the plants to turn bottles into cloth.

■ Figure 2 shows the effects of the new technology. The demand for bottles increased—the demand curve shifted rightward from D_0 to D_1. The price of bottles increased, and so did the quantity recycled.

■ With a higher price for bottles, the incentive to increase the number of curbside collection programs increased.

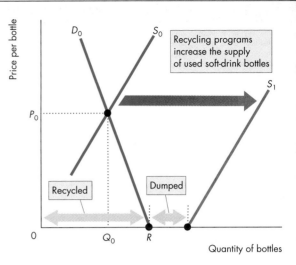

Figure 1 Market for used bottles

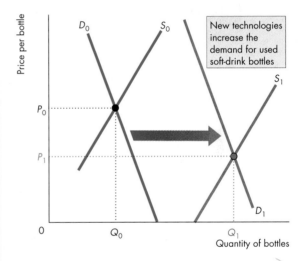

Figure 2 New technology

■ As business in recyclables grows, markets develop in which recyclables are traded. Like other traders, sellers of recyclables want to sell for the highest possible price and buyers want to buy for the lowest possible price. To achieve this outcome, the market in recyclables needs to be a global market. The Chicago Board of Trade is about to make such a market.

■ With global markets, the quantities of materials recycled make buyers' marginal benefits equal to sellers' marginal costs. These marginal benefits and marginal costs are marginal *social* benefits and costs because there are not externalities.

507

"The question to be decided is: is the value of fish lost greater or less than the value of the product which contamination of the stream makes possible."

RONALD H. COASE, *THE PROBLEM OF SOCIAL COST*

Understanding Externalities

THE ISSUES AND IDEAS

As knowledge accumulates, we are becoming more sensitive to environmental externalities. We are also developing more sensitive methods of dealing with them. But all the methods involve a public choice.

Urban smog forms when sunlight reacts with emissions from the tailpipes of automobiles and is both unpleasant and dangerous to breathe. Because of these external costs, emission standards are set by regulation and gasoline is taxed. Emission standards increase the cost of cars, and gasoline taxes increase the cost of the marginal mile traveled. The higher costs decrease the quantity demanded of road transportation and so decrease the amount of pollution created. Is the value of cleaner urban air worth the higher cost of transportation? The public choice of voters, regulators, and lawmakers answered this question.

Acid rain falls from clouds laden with the output of electric utility smokestacks. This external cost is being tackled with a market solution that to some extent replaces the values of lawmakers and bureaucrats with those of the people who bear the costs. This solution is marketable permits, the price and allocation of which is determined by the forces of demand and supply. Private choices determine the demand for pollution permits, but a public choice determines the supply.

As cars stream onto an urban freeway at morning rush hour, the highway clogs and becomes an expensive parking lot. Each rush hour traveler imposes external costs on all the others. Today, road users bear private congestion costs and do not face a share of the external congestion costs they create. But a market solution to this problem is now feasible. This solution would charge road users a toll that varies with time of day and degree of congestion. Confronted with the marginal social cost of his or her actions, each road user would make a choice, and the market for highway space would be efficient. Here a public choice to use a market solution leaves the final decision about the degree of congestion to private choices.

THEN...

CHESTER JACKSON, *a Lake Erie fisherman, recalls that when he began fishing on the lake, boats didn't carry drinking water. Fishermen drank from the lake. Speaking after World War II, Jackson observed, "Can't do that today. Those chemicals in there would kill you." Farmers used chemicals, such as the insecticide DDT, that got carried into the lake by runoff. Industrial waste and trash were also dumped into the lake in large quantities. As a result, Lake Erie became badly polluted during the 1940s and became incapable of sustaining a viable fish stock.*

TODAY, LAKE ERIE supports a fishing industry, just as it did in the 1930s. No longer treated as a garbage dump for chemicals, the lake is regenerating its ecosystem. Fertilizers and insecticides are now recognized as products that have potential externalities, and their external effects are assessed by the Environmental Protection Agency before new versions are put into widespread use. Dumping industrial waste into rivers and lakes is now subject to much more stringent regulations and penalties. Lake Erie's externalities problems have been solved by one of the methods available: government regulation.

James Buchanan

THE ECONOMISTS: THE PUBLIC INTEREST AND PUBLIC CHOICES

Externalities are solved by public choices. But for a time, economists lost sight of this fact. During the 1920s, Arthur Cecil Pigou (1877–1959) of Cambridge, England, pioneered a branch of economics designed to guide public choices—*welfare economics*. Pigou, who attended school with Winston Churchill and relaxed by climbing in the Swiss Alps with some of the best mountaineers of the day, devised rules that, if followed, would ensure that decisions about externalities were in the public interest. But the rules were not followed.

Arthur Cecil Pigou

Not until the 1950s did economists develop *public choice theory* and explain the choices that are actually made by politicians and bureaucrats. A leader in this field is 1986 Nobel laureate James Buchanan (1919–   ) of George Mason University. Working in the inspiring setting of his mountainside summer cottage near Blacksburg, Virginia, Buchanan has led us to appreciate that the solutions adopted to externalities depend not on the public interest, but on private interests—on private costs and benefits.

S U M M A R Y

Externalities

An externality is a cost or benefit of a production or consumption activity that spills over to affect people other than those who decide the scale of the activity. An external cost is the cost of producing a good or service that is not borne by its consumers but by other people. An external benefit is the benefit of consuming a good or service that does not accrue to its consumers but to other people.

The main external costs arise in connection with the environment and are the costs of air, land, and water pollution. The main external benefits are the benefits of education and scientific research.

External costs and external benefits are sources of market failure—they create inefficiency. There is a tendency for the market economy to overproduce goods and servcies that have external costs and to underproduce goods and services that have external benefits.

When market failure occurs, either we must put up with the inefficiency it creates or try to achieve greater efficiency by making public choices and using the instruments of government to intervene in the market economy. (pp. 491–492)

Economics of the Environment

Popular discussion of the environment frames the debate in terms of right and wrong. In contrast, economists emphasize costs and benefits and a need to find a way to balance the two.

The demand for environmental policies has grown because incomes have grown and awareness of the connection between actions and the environment has increased.

Air pollution arises from road transportation, electric utilities, and industrial processes. In the United States, the trends in most types of air pollution are downward. Water pollution arises from dumping industrial waste, treated sewage, and fertilizers into lakes and rivers and spilling oil and dumping waste into the oceans. Land pollution arises from dumping toxic waste products.

Externalities (environmental and others) arise when property rights are absent. Sometimes it is possible to overcome an externality by assigning a prop-erty right. The Coase theorem states that if property rights exist and transactions costs are low, private transactions are efficient—there are no externalities. In this case, the same efficient amount of pollution is achieved regardless of who has the property right, the polluter or the victim.

When property rights cannot be assigned, governments might overcome environmental externalities by using emission charges, marketable permits, or taxes. Marketable permits were used successfully to virtually eliminate lead from our air.

Global externalities, such as greenhouse gases and substances that deplete the earth's ozone layer, can be overcome only by international action. Each country acting alone has insufficient incentive to act in the interest of the world as a whole. But there is a great deal of scientific uncertainty and disagreement about the effects of greenhouse gases and ozone depletion and in the face of this uncertainty, international resolve to act is weak. Also, the world is locked in a type of "prisoners' dilemma" game, in which it is in every country's self-interest to let other countries carry the costs of environmental policies. (pp. 492–502)

Economics of Knowledge

Knowledge is both a consumer good and a factor of production that creates external benefits. External benefits from education—passing on existing knowledge to others—arise because the basic reading, writing, and number skills equip people to interact and communicate more effectively. External benefits from research and development—creating and applying new knowledge—arise because once someone has worked out how to do something, others can copy the basic idea.

To enable the efficient amount of education and innovation to take place, we make public choices through governments to modify the market outcome. Three devices are available to governments: subsidies, below-cost provision, and patents and copyrights.

Subsidies to private schools or the provision of public education below cost can achieve an efficient provision of education. Patents and copyrights create intellectual property rights and increase the incentive to innovate. But they do so by creating a temporary monopoly, the cost of which must be balanced against the benefit of more inventive activity. (pp. 502–505)

K E Y   E L E M E N T S

Key Figures

Key Terms

R E V I E W   Q U E S T I O N S

1. What are externalities? Give some examples of positive and negative externalities.
2. Why is an external cost a problem?
3. Why does the existence of external costs and external benefits lead to market failure?
4. How can external benefits pose an economic problem?
5. Describe how membership of environmental groups has changed since 1970.
6. Why has the demand for a better environment increased?
7. Describe the various types of pollution and identify their sources.
8. What are the main economic activities that cause air pollution?
9. What do property rights have to do with externalities?
10. State the Coase theorem. Under what conditions does the Coase theorem apply?
11. Explain why property rights assigned to either the polluter or the victim of pollution give an efficient amount of pollution if transactions costs are low.
12. What is an emission charge and how does it work?
13. What is a marketable pollution permit and how does it work?
14. How might a tax be used to overcome an external cost?
15. What are the pros and cons of a high, broad-based carbon tax and why don't we have such a tax?
16. Explain how the Environmental Protection Agency regulates the quality of air in the United States.
17. Which countries have high pollution rates?
18. Why do some countries have high pollution rates?
19. Is the efficient rate of pollution zero? Explain your answer.
20. What is the global warming dilemma?
21. What are the externalities problems posed by knowledge?
22. Why do we have free schooling?
23. What is a patent and how does it work?

P R O B L E M S

1. A trout farmer and a pesticide maker are located next to each other on the side of a lake. The pesticide maker can dispose of waste by dumping it into the lake or by trucking it to a safe land storage place. The marginal cost of trucking is a constant $100 a ton. The trout farmer's profit depends on how much waste the pesticide maker dumps into the lake and is as follows:

Quantity of waste (tons per week)	Trout farmer's profit (dollars per week)
0	1,000
1	950
2	875
3	775
4	650
5	500
6	325
7	125

   a. What is the efficient amount of waste to be dumped into the lake?
   b. If the trout farmer owns the lake, how much waste will be dumped and how much will the pesticide maker pay to the farmer for each ton dumped?
   c. If the pesticide maker owns the lake, how much waste will be dumped and how much will the farmer pay to the factory to rent space on the lake?

2. Using the information given in problem 1, suppose that no one owns the lake and that the government introduces a pollution tax.
   a. What is the tax per ton of waste dumped that will achieve an efficient outcome?
   b. Explain the connection between the answer to this problem and the answer to problem 1.

3. Using the information given in problem 1, suppose that no one owns the lake and that the government issues marketable pollution permits to both the farmer and the factory. Each may dump the same amount of waste in the lake, and the total that may be dumped is the efficient amount.

   a. What is the quantity that may be dumped into the lake?
   b. What is the market price of a permit? Who buys and who sells?
   c. What is the connection between the answer to this problem and the answers to problems 1 and 2?

4. The marginal cost of educating a student is $5,000 a year and is constant. The marginal private benefit schedule is as follows:

Quantity of education (student years)	Marginal private benefit (dollars per student-year)
0	10,000
1,000	5,000
2,000	3,000
3,000	2,000
4,000	1,500
5,000	1,250
6,000	1,100
7,000	1,000

   a. With no government involvement in education and if the schools are competitive, how many students are enrolled in school and what is the annual tuition?
   b. Suppose the external benefit from education is $4,000 per student year and is constant. If the government provides the efficient amount of education, how many school places does it offer and what is the annual tuition?

5. After you have studied *Reading Between the Lines* on pp. 506–507, answer the following questions:
   a. What are the costs of supplying used soft-drink bottles to be recycled?
   b. Who bears those costs?
   c. Are any of the costs external costs?
   d. What are the benefits of recycling soft-drink bottles?
   e. Who receives those benefits?
   f. Are any of the benefits external benefits?
   g. Why is the Chicago Board of Trade going to start trading recyclables?

part 5

Preliminaries and Long-Term Fundamentals

Christina Romer, who teaches economics and economic history at the University of California, Berkeley, was born in Alton, Illinois, in 1958. She was an undergraduate at the College of William and Mary and a graduate student at MIT, where she earned her Ph.D. in 1985. Professor Romer is best known for her meticulous work on the measurement of unemployment and production in the United States during the late nineteenth century and early twentieth century. She has also worked on a wide range of empirical macroeconomic questions such as the effects of the actions of the Federal Reserve on the business cycle. Michael Parkin talked with Professor Romer about her work and the relevance of macroeconomic history to the macroeconomic issues of the 1990s.

TALKING WITH Christina Romer

Professor Romer, how were you attracted to economics?

As a sophomore at William and Mary, I was all set to major in government and then go to law school. As part of the government major, however, I was required to take two semesters of economics. I found both the economic way of thinking and the issues that economics deals with fascinating. I especially liked the way that economics provides a framework for thinking logically about complex public policy issues such as government regulation of business, income maintenance programs, and international trade.

You brought a fresh approach and method to analyzing some old data on national income in the United States. What exactly did you do? What did you discover? And why is it important?

Most of our modern macroeconomic data, such as the unemployment rate and the index of industrial production (an index of the total output of the industrial sector), were first collected around World War II. Economists in the 1950s then pieced together bits of historical data to try to estimate what these same data series might have been in the late nineteenth and early twentieth centuries. I examined whether the methods used to construct these historical estimates may have introduced biases that distorted our view of the magnitude of the macroeconomic fluctuations that occurred before World War II. Since it was impossible to travel back in time and conduct the same surveys that we use today to measure unemployment or industrial production, I did just the reverse. I asked, what would the unemployment rate or the index of industrial production look like today if we inferred them from similar bits of data to those used in the pre–World War II era? I constructed time series of unemployment and the index of industrial production that were uniformly bad for the whole twentieth century. I found that the old methods tended to overstate the size of macroeconomic fluctuations. That is, unemployment and industrial production estimated using the historical methods fluctuate more than the modern survey data. For example, the estimates of the unemployment rate that I constructed using the old methods were much lower than the modern survey data in the boom of the 1960s and much higher in the recession of the mid-1970s. The same was true for industrial production using the old methods: It rose much faster than the modern index during booms and fell much more precipitously during recessions.

The finding that the historical estimates exaggerated the size of fluctuations in unemployment and industrial production is important because economists had made a great deal of the apparent decline in the size of business cycles over time. The series that combined constructed data before 1940 and survey data after 1940 showed

recessions becoming much milder over time. From this, many economists had concluded that monetary and fiscal policy had managed to ease, if not cure, the business cycle. I showed that much of this apparent stabilization was a figment of the data. If one uses data constructed the same way over the entire twentieth century, business cycles after the Great Depression of the 1930s are nearly as severe as those before 1929.

The most encouraging development [in macroeconomics] is the renewed emphasis on the importance of long-run growth.

could estimate the relationship between the two series of some period when both series existed.

Simon Kuznets, who was awarded the Nobel Prize in 1971 and who both pioneered the concept of GDP and constructed the historical time-series measures of GDP, understood that this was the most desirable method of adjusting the available historical data, and even attempted to implement it in the early 1950s. He couldn't

How crucial is the computer technology that we now take for granted to the kind of work that you do? Could people working in the 1950s have done what you have done, if they had thought of it?
For the data on gross domestic product (GDP), I tried to do more than show that the historical methods exaggerated the size of fluctuations. There were enough actual data for the period 1889–1929 that I tried to adjust the existing data to be more consistent with modern measures of GDP. In making those adjustments, computers were essential. Rather than just guessing how the data available related to the concept I needed to measure, I

do very many of these adjustments, however, because all of the empirical estimation had to be done by hand.

What was the catalyst that led you to reexamine old data that most people thought had nothing new to tell us?
I think that I saw something new in the old data simply because I was new to the field. Economic historians were well aware that the historical macroeconomic indicators were flawed, but to a young graduate student accustomed to modern data, the methods used to construct the historical series were truly shocking. My first encounter

with historical data came when I was working as a research assistant after my first year in graduate school. I was sent off to the basement of the library to gather historical price indexes. In the process, I was forced to read the long data appendixes in dusty old volumes. I still remember reading the entry describing how the price index for manufactured fuels and lighting products was constructed. It said that after 1890 the index included the prices of fuel oil, kerosene, gasoline, and many other products; before 1890 the index included only the prices of matches and candles. I immediately began to wonder if such changes in the way the data were constructed could have affected the many empirical conclusions that were derived from the historical indicators.

How do you see macroeconomics at the end of the twentieth century? What are its most pressing challenges? What are its most promising avenues of inquiry?
There are both encouraging and discouraging aspects to the state of macroeconomics at the end of the twentieth century. The most encouraging development is the renewed emphasis on the importance of long-run growth. For too long, macroeconomists have focused mainly on business cycles, forgetting that even small changes in long-term growth rates can have a much larger effect on standards of living than large recessions. The somewhat discouraging aspect of the state of macroeconomics is that current research emphasizes theory over empirical work.

While theoretical models of both growth and fluctuations are useful for clarifying our thinking,

most questions in macroeconomics are fundamentally empirical in nature. What is desperately needed are detailed quantitative and qualitative studies of the determinants of growth and the nature and importance of other macroeconomic relationships.

Is the current emphasis on long-run growth a fad? Where do you see the growth research program going? Does long-run growth now have a major place in the economics curriculum?
Economic research naturally proceeds in starts and stops. When someone discovers something new and interesting, other researchers start working in the area as well. We are currently in such a "research spurt" with long-run growth. Economists have learned a tremendous amount in recent years about why some countries are so much richer than others. If we run into theoretical roadblocks or diminishing returns, some of this research effort will be directed toward other topics and growth may stop being quite such a hot topic.

At the same time, however, I cannot imagine economists ever going back to teaching courses where long-run growth is relegated to a minor role. It is just too obvious that the fundamental determinant of living standards is not business cycles or Federal Reserve policy, but the average sustainable growth rate over long periods of time. Furthermore, the theoretical advances of the past decade have paved the way for much new empirical research. I predict that we will continue to discover important new facts about the growth process and that an emphasis on the long run will be the cornerstone of macroeconomics well into the 21st century.

I think that the effects of globalization on the U.S. macroeconomy are greatly overstated. The U.S. economy has always been substantially integrated with foreign markets...

How would you describe the divisions and debates in macroeconomics today?
The most significant division in macroeconomics today is largely a debate over technique rather than substance. Both new classical and new Keynesian macroeconomists believe that models of macroeconomic behavior need to include maximizing behavior on the part of consumers and producers, as well as assumptions about wage and price rigidity. But the techniques that the two camps advocate are quite different. New classical research uses models of artificial economies and then asks whether the behavior implied by the models bears any resemblance to actual macroeconomic behavior. New Keynesian research typically involves studying key macroeconomic relationships such as the effect of monetary policy on output and then estimating these relationships directly, often using large amounts of data generated by surveys or qualitative information about the state of policy.

What are the challenges created by the globalization of the economy?

Quite honestly, I think that the effects of globalization on the U.S. macroeconomy are greatly overstated. The U.S. economy has always been substantially integrated with foreign markets, and the expansion of that integration has not fundamentally altered the behavior of the economy or the effects of macroeconomic policy. For example, I recently conducted a study with my colleague and husband, David Romer, on the effect of greater integration of world financial markets on U.S. monetary policy. We found that even before the recent expansion of global ties, U.S. banks found quite innovative ways to maintain lending when the Federal Reserve tightened policy. They were only forced to reduce loans when the Federal Reserve supplemented reductions in the money supply with actions aimed at directly reducing credit, such as explicit credit controls or special reserve requirements. We showed that the recent increase in banks' ability to make loans during periods of tight money was not due to the globalization of financial markets, but simply to the fact that the Federal Reserve no longer supplements

Many policymakers are frighteningly unaware of the economic incentives and consequences of the policies they advocate. As a result, economists have a tremendous amount to contribute...

contractionary monetary policy with credit actions.

If you were an undergraduate again today, what would you study and why?

If I were an undergraduate again today, I would still study economics. After nearly ten years of working as an economist, I am more convinced than ever that economic analysis provides crucial insight into most of the important issues facing the country. Many policymakers are frighteningly unaware of the economic incentives and consequences of the policies they advocate. As a result, economists have a tremendous amount to contribute through participating in policy formation and through educating future generations of policymakers and voters.

Chapter 22

A First Look at Macroeconomics

After studying this chapter, you will be able to:

- Describe the origins of macroeconomics and the problems it deals with

- Describe the long-term trends and short-term fluctuations in economic growth, unemployment, inflation, and the balance of international payments

- Explain why economic growth, unemployment, inflation, and the balance of international payments are important

- Identify the macroeconomic policy challenges and describe the tools available for meeting them

During the past 100 years, the quantity of goods and services produced in the nation's farms, factories, shops, and offices has expanded more than twentyfold. In 1994, production expanded more quickly than the average and this rapid growth created a fear that the economy was overheating. How does an economy overheat? Why was rapid economic growth feared? Isn't more output always a good thing? ◆ One reason why overheating was feared was that by the end of

Overheating?

1994, unemployment was an unusually low 5 percent of the work force—about 7 million people. But how can the economy be overheating when 7 million people are unemployed? Why can't *everyone* who wants a job find one? ◆ Prices have increased slowly over the past few years. But with rapid production growth and falling unemployment, it was feared that inflation might break out again. That's what overheating means—an economy growing so quickly that inflation breaks out. What exactly is inflation, and why does it matter? ◆ A consequence of an overheated economy is that it sucks in goods and services from abroad on a large scale and brings a larger balance of international payments deficit. Why does it matter if we have a balance of international payments deficit? ◆ To prevent the economy from overheating and to prevent the opposite condition, an economic slowdown, the federal government and the nation's financial manager, the Federal Reserve Board, take policy actions. What kinds of actions do they take? How do those actions influence production, jobs, inflation, and the ability of Americans to compete in the global marketplace?

◻ These questions are the subject matter of macroeconomics—the branch of economics that seeks to understand economic growth, unemployment, inflation, and the balance of international payments and to design policies to improve macroeconomic performance. The macroeconomic events through which we are now living are tumultuous and exciting. With what you learn in these chapters, you will be able to understand these events, the policy challenges they bring, and the political debate they stir. ◆ Let's begin by looking at the origins of macroeconomics and the key issues it deals with.

Origins and Issues of Macroeconomics

ECONOMISTS BEGAN TO STUDY LONG-TERM ECO-nomic growth, inflation, and international payments as long ago as the 1750s, and this work was the beginning of macroeconomics. But modern macro-economics emerged much later, as a response to the **Great Depression**, a decade (1929–1939) of high unemployment and stagnant production throughout the world economy. In the depression's worst year, 1933, the production of U.S. farms, factories, shops, and offices was only 70 percent of its 1929 level, and 25 percent of the labor force was unemployed. These were years of human misery on a scale that is hard to imagine today. They were also years of extreme pes-simism about the ability of the market economy to work properly. Many people believed the Great Depression demonstrated that the economic system of private ownership and free markets was a failure. The perceived failure was so extreme that it raised the deeply disturbing question of whether liberal-democ-ratic political institutions could survive.

The science of economics had no solutions. The major alternative economic system of central plan-ning and the political system of socialism that went with it seemed increasingly attractive to many people. It was in this climate of economic depression and political and intellectual turmoil that modern macro-economics emerged with the publication in 1936 of John Maynard Keynes' *The General Theory of Employment, Interest, and Money* (see *Economics in History* on pp. 542–543).

Short-Term Versus Long-Term Goals

Keynes' theory was that depression and high unem-ployment result from insufficient private spending and that to cure these problems, the government must increase its spending. Keynes' focus was primar-ily on the *short term*. He wanted to cure an immedi-ate and serious problem almost regardless of what the *long-term* consequences of the cure might be. "In the long run," said Keynes, "we're all dead."

But Keynes believed that after his cure for depression had restored the economy to a normal condition, the long-term problems of inflation and economic growth would become the central ones. And he suspected that his cure for depression, increased government spending, might trigger infla-tion and also might lower the long-term growth rate of production. With a lower long-term growth rate, fewer jobs would be created. If this outcome did occur, a policy aimed at lowering unemployment in the short run might end up increasing it in the long run.

By the late 1960s and through the 1970s, these long-term concerns became a reality. Inflation increased, economic growth slowed down, and in some countries, unemployment became persistently high. The causes of these developments are complex. But they point to an inescapable conclusion: The long-term issues of inflation, slow growth, and persis-tent unemployment and the short-term issues of depression and economic fluctuations intertwine and are most usefully studied together. So although macroeconomics was reborn during the Great Depression, it has now returned to its older tradition. Today, macroeconomics is a subject that tries to understand the long-term issues of economic growth and inflation as well as short-term economic fluctua-tions and the unemployment these fluctuations bring.

The Road Ahead

There is no unique way to study macroeconomics. Because its rebirth was a product of depression, for many years the common practice was to pay most attention to short-term output fluctuations and unemployment, but to never completely lose sight of the long-term issues. When a serious inflation emerged during the 1970s, this topic returned to prominence. During the 1980s, when long-term growth had slowed in the United States and other rich industrial countries, economists redirected their energy toward that problem. In the 1990s, when information technologies continually shrink the globe, the international dimension of macroeconom-ics has become more prominent. The result of all these events is that modern macroeconomics is a broad subject that pays attention to all the issues we've just reviewed: long-term economic growth, unemploy-ment, inflation, and international economic activity.

Over the past 40 years, economists have devel-oped a clearer understanding of the forces that deter-mine macroeconomic performance and have devised policies that, while very imperfect, stand some chance of preventing the extremes of depression and inflation. Your main goal is to become familiar with the theories of macroeconomics and the policies they make possible. To set you on your path toward this goal, we're going to take a first look at the macroeconomic issues of economic growth, unemployment, inflation, and the balance of international payments and learn why they are problems that merit our attention.

Economic Growth

YOUR PARENTS ARE RICHER THAN YOUR GRANDparents were when they were young. But are you going to be richer than your parents? And are your children going to be richer than you? The answers depend on the rate of economic growth.

Economic growth is the expansion of the economy's capacity to produce goods and services. It is an expansion of the economy's production possibilities and can be pictured as an outward shift of the production possibility frontier (*PPF*)—see Chapter 3, pp. 50–53.

We measure economic growth by the increase in real gross domestic product. **Real gross domestic product** (also called **real GDP**) is the value of *aggregate* or *total* production—the output of all the nation's farms, factories, shops, and offices—measured in the prices of a single year. At the present time, real GDP in the United States is measured in the prices of 1987 (called 1987 dollars). We use the prices of a single year so that we can eliminate the influence of *inflation*—the increase in prices—and determine how much production has grown from one year to another. (The concept of real GDP is explained more fully in Chapter 23 on pp. 546–558.)

Real GDP is not a perfect measure of total production because it does not measure everything that is produced. For example, it does not include the things we produce for ourselves at home (preparing meals, doing laundry, house painting, gardening, and so on). Nor does it include things people produce but hide to avoid taxes—known as the underground economy.

Despite its shortcomings, real GDP is the broadest measure of total production available. Let's see what it tells us about economic growth in the United States.

Economic Growth in the United States

Figure 22.1 shows real GDP in the United States since 1960 and highlights two features of economic growth:

- The growth of potential GDP
- Fluctuations of real GDP around potential GDP

The Growth of Potential GDP When all the economy's labor, capital, land, and entrepreneurial ability are fully employed, real GDP is equal to **potential GDP**. The rate of long-term economic growth is measured by the growth rate of potential GDP and is shown by the steepness of the potential GDP line.

If you look closely at Fig. 22.1, you can see that the potential GDP line is steeper in the 1960s than in the 1970s and 1980s. During the 1960s, real GDP grew at an unusually rapid average rate of 4.1 percent a year. Growth slowed during the 1970s and early 1980s as a result of a **productivity growth slowdown**—a slowdown in the growth rate of output per person. Faster growth in potential GDP might have returned during the late 1980s and 1990s, but it is too soon to be sure about this possibility.

Why did the productivity growth slowdown occur? Was the United States alone in experiencing such an event? What are its consequences?

The "why" question is a big one and a hard one to answer fully. Many factors were at work but two were critical: energy price shocks and rapid inflation. The energy price shocks of 1973–1974 and 1989–1990 triggered the development of new energy-saving technologies and a high level of investment in energy efficient equipment. But these innovations and investments did not increase labor productivity. The rapid inflation of the 1970s brought increased uncertainty and made it hard for people to make wise long-term investment decisions. This brief explanation of the productivity growth slowdown is expanded on in Chapter 26 on pp. 632–633.

Was the United States alone in experiencing a productivity growth slowdown? No. We'll see examples from some other countries later in this chapter when we look at long-term growth around the world. And what are the consequences? We have much smaller incomes today than we would have had if productivity growth had not slowed. We'll expand on the consequences later in this chapter when we study the benefits and costs of economic growth.

FIGURE 22.1

Economic Growth in the United States: 1960–1994

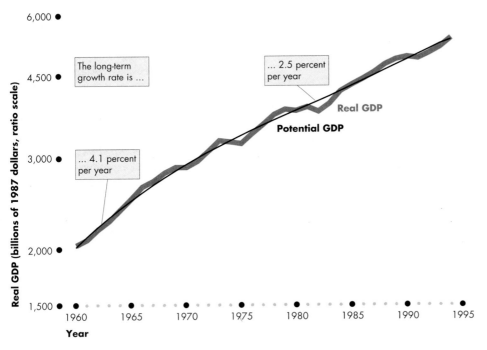

The long-term economic growth rate, measured by the growth of potential GDP, was 4.1 percent a year during the 1960s but slowed to 2.5 percent a year during the 1970s and 1980s. Real GDP fluctuates around potential GDP.

Source: U.S. Department of Commerce, *National Income and Product Accounts of the United States.*

Let's look at the second feature of economic growth, the fluctuations around trend.

Fluctuations Around Trend   Real GDP fluctuates around potential GDP in a business cycle. A **business cycle** is the periodic but irregular up-and-down movement in economic activity. It is measured by fluctuations in real GDP around potential GDP. When real GDP is less than potential GDP, some resources are underused. For example, some labor is unemployed and capital is underutilized. When real GDP is greater than potential GDP, some resources are being overused. For example, many people are working longer hours than they are willing to put up with in the long run and capital is being worked so intensively that there is no time to keep it in prime working order.

Business cycles are not regular, predictable, or repeating cycles like the phases of the moon. Their timing changes unpredictably. But cycles do have

some things in common. Every business cycle has two turning points:

1. Peak
2. Trough

and two phases:

1. Recession
2. Expansion

Figure 22.2 shows these features of the most recent business cycle in the United States. A *peak* is the upper turning point of a business cycle where an expansion ends and a recession begins. A peak occurred in the third quarter of 1990. A *trough* is the lower turning point of a business cycle where a recession ends and a recovery begins. A trough occurred in the second quarter of 1991.

A **recession** is a period during which real GDP decreases—the growth rate of real GDP is negative—

FIGURE 22.2

The Most Recent U.S. Business Cycle

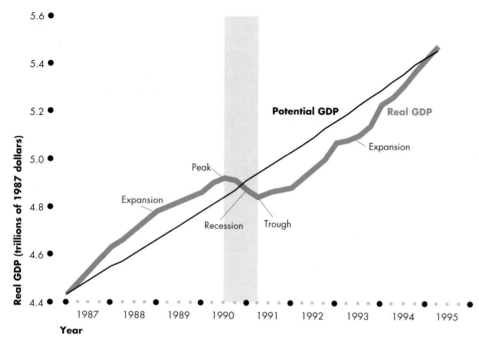

A business cycle has two turning points, a peak and a trough. In the most recent business cycle, the peak occurred in the third quarter of 1990 and the trough occurred in the second quarter of 1991. A business cycle has two phases: recession and expansion. The most recent recession ran from the peak in 1990 to the trough in 1991 when a new expansion began.

for at least two successive quarters. In Fig. 22.2, a recession followed the peak in the third quarter of 1990 and ended in the second quarter of 1991. This recession lasted for three quarters.

An **expansion** is a period during which real GDP increases. It begins at a trough and ends at a peak. In Fig. 22.2, an expansion ended at the 1990 peak and another expansion began at the 1991 trough. That expansion was still proceeding in the first quarter of 1995 when the graph ends.

The Recent Recession in Historical Perspective

The recession of 1990–1991 seemed pretty severe while we were passing through it, but compared with earlier recessions, it was relatively mild. You can see how mild it was by looking at Fig. 22.3, which shows a longer history of economic growth in the United States. The most precipitous decline in real GDP occurred during the Great Depression of the 1930s. A very large fall in real GDP also occurred in 1946 and 1947, immediately following World War II. In more recent times, severe decreases

in real GDP occurred during the mid-1970s—following oil price hikes by the Organization of Petroleum Exporting Countries (OPEC)—and during the early 1980s.

Each of these economic downturns was more severe than that in 1990–1991. But you can see that the Great Depression was much more severe than anything that followed it. This episode was so extreme that we don't call it a recession. We call it a depression. The term *depression* is used to describe an extremely severe decrease in production that brings extreme and prolonged hardship.

The fact that the last truly great depression occurred before governments started taking policy actions to stabilize the economy (and before the birth of macroeconomics) has led to speculation that perhaps macroeconomics has made a contribution to economic stability. We'll examine this speculation on a number of occasions in this book.

We've seen that real GDP in the United States has increased over the long term. But we've also seen that U.S. long-term growth slowed during the 1970s

FIGURE 22.3

Long-Term Economic Growth in the United States

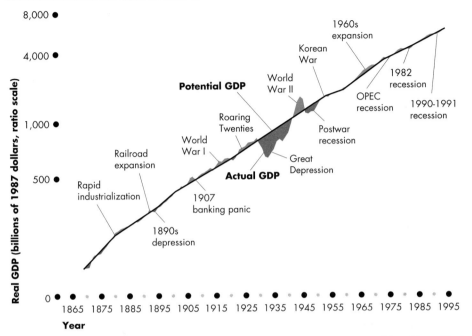

The thin black line shows potential GDP. Along this line, real GDP grew at an average rate of 3.3 percent a year between 1870 and 1994. The blue areas show when real GDP was above potential GDP, and the red areas show when it was below potential GDP. During some periods, such as World War II, real GDP expanded quickly. During other periods, such as the Great Depression and more recently in 1975 (following the OPEC oil price hike), 1982, and 1990–1991, real GDP declined.

Sources: 1869–1928, Christina D. Romer, "The Prewar Business Cycle Reconsidered: New Estimates of Gross National Product, 1869–1908," *Journal of Political Economy* 97, (1989) 1–37. 1929–1994, U.S. Department of Commerce, *National Income and Product Accounts of the United States.*

and 1980s. We've also seen that recessions have interrupted the broad upward sweep of real GDP. Is the U.S. experience typical? Do other countries share this experience? Let's see whether they do.

Economic Growth Around the World

A country might have a rapid growth rate of real GDP, but it might also have a rapid population growth rate. To compare growth rates over time and across countries, we use the growth rate of real GDP *per person*. Real GDP per person is real GDP divided by the population. For example, U.S. real GDP in 1993 was $5,133 billion, and the population of the United States was 258.2 million. So U.S. real GDP per person was $5,133 billion divided by 258.2 million, which equals $19,880.

Figure 22.4 shows real GDP per person between 1960 and 1990 for the world's three biggest economies: the United States, Japan, and Germany.

In these countries, three features of the paths of real GDP per person stand out:

- Similar productivity growth slowdowns
- Similar business cycles
- Different long-term trends in potential GDP

Similar Productivity Growth Slowdowns   The three countries shown in Fig. 22.4 have experienced similar productivity growth slowdowns. U.S. real GDP per person grew at a rate of 2.9 percent per year during the 1960s, but slowed to 1.5 percent a year during the 1970s and 1980s. In Germany, the growth of real GDP per person slowed from 3.5 percent a year during the 1960s to 2.0 percent a year during the 1970s and 1980s. In Japan, the slowdown was more spectacular, from 8.2 percent a year during the 1960s to 3.1 percent a year during the 1970s and 1980s.

The slowdown experienced by the United States, Japan, and Germany was also experienced by almost every country. The exceptions were the major oil producers.

FIGURE 22.4

Economic Growth in the Three Largest Economies

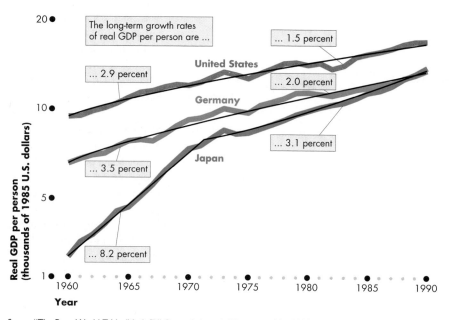

The long-term growth rates of real GDP per person are ...

... 1.5 percent

... 2.9 percent

United States

... 2.0 percent

Germany

... 3.1 percent

... 3.5 percent

Japan

... 8.2 percent

Real GDP per person (thousands of 1985 U.S. dollars)

Year

Economic growth in the three largest economies, the United States, Germany, and Japan, has followed a similar pattern. The growth rate in all three countries slowed during the 1970s, and each country has had similar business cycles. But Japan has grown fastest, and Germany too has grown faster than the United States.

Source: "The Penn World Table (Mark 5)," *Quarterly Journal of Economics*, May 1991, pp. 327–368. New computer disk supplement (Mark 5.5). The data use comparable international relative prices converted to 1985 U.S. dollars.

Similar Business Cycles   The three big economies have experienced similar business cycles. Each economy had an expansion running from the early or mid-1960s through 1973, a recession from 1973 to 1975, an expansion through 1979, another recession in the early 1980s, and a long expansion through the rest of the 1980s.

Like the common productivity growth slow-down, this common business cycle is also shared by most economies around the world.

Different Long-Term Trends in Potential GDP
Perhaps the most striking feature of Fig. 22.4 is the variation in the long-term growth rates of the three big economies. In 1960, real GDP per person was $9,800 in the United States, $6,600 in Germany, and $3,000 in Japan.[1] So in round numbers, in 1960, Germany produced twice as much per person as

Japan, and the United States produced three times as much per person than Japan.

But during the 1960s, Japan streaked upward like a rocket leaving Cape Canaveral. When U.S. long-term growth in real GDP per person was 2.9 percent a year, Germany achieved a rate of 3.5 percent a year, and real GDP per person in Japan grew at an astonishing 8.2 percent a year. These differences in the long-term growth trend survived the productivity growth slowdown. After the slowdown, even though Japan's growth rate more than halved, its growth of real GDP per person still exceeded the U.S. rate before the slowdown.

Because it has achieved such a high growth rate, Japan has narrowed the gap between its own production level and that of the United States. Japan has passed Germany.

Differences in growth rates like those shown in Fig. 22.4 can also be seen in the broader regions of the world. Figure 22.5 shows some average yearly growth rates of real GDP per person between 1973 and 1990. Among the industrial countries (shown by the red bars), Japan has grown the fastest and the coun-

---

[1] These dollars are based on prices in 1985 and have been calculated to make the most valid possible international comparison (see the source note on Fig. 22.4).

FIGURE 22.5

Long-Term Growth Rates Around the World: 1973–1990

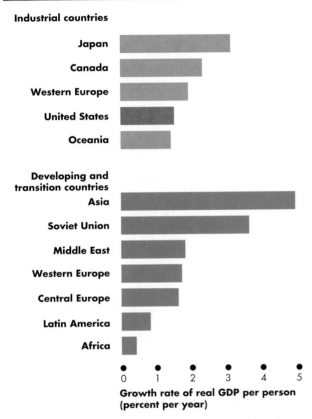

Industrial countries

Japan
Canada
Western Europe
United States
Oceania

Developing and transition countries

Asia
Soviet Union
Middle East
Western Europe
Central Europe
Latin America
Africa

0 1 2 3 4 5

**Growth rate of real GDP per person
(percent per year)**

After the productivity growth slowdown of the 1970s, the growth rate of real GDP per person has been lower in the United States than in some other industrial countries. The developing countries of Asia have had the most rapid growth rates and those of Latin America and Africa have had the slowest growth.

Source: "The Penn World Table (Mark 5)" *Quarterly Journal of Economics*, May 1991, pp. 327–368. New computer disk supplement (Mark 5.5). The data use comparable international relative prices converted to 1985 U.S. dollars.

times the U.S. growth rate. The slowest growth has been experienced by the developing countries in Africa and Latin America. With the exception of these regions, growth rates in the developing countries have exceeded that of the United States.

Benefits and Costs of Economic Growth

We've studied some facts about economic growth in the United States and around the world. But why is economic growth important? What are the benefits of economic growth? Does it matter if the long-term growth rate slows down as it did during the 1970s?

The main benefit of long-term economic growth is expanded consumption possibilities, including more health care for the poor and elderly, more cancer and AIDS research, more space research and exploration, better roads, and more and better housing. We can even have cleaner lakes, more trees, and cleaner air by devoting more resources to these environmental problems.

When the long-term growth rate slows, some of these benefits are lost, and the loss can be large. For example, if long-term economic growth had not slowed in the United States during the 1970s, GDP in 1994 would have been $8.7 trillion, or $33,000 per person. Instead, it was $6.7 trillion, or $26,000 per person. So if the long-term trend of the 1960s had persisted, as a nation we would have had $2 trillion more to spend. Each person (on the average) would have had $7,000 more. If the government had taken one third of this extra income, it could have provided more health care, education, day-care services, highways, space stations, and a super-collider with no decrease in its provision of other goods and services and its budget would be in a huge surplus. At the same time, you might have had almost another $5,000 a year to spend on whatever excited you.

Although economic growth brings enormous benefits, it also has costs that must be balanced against the benefits. The main cost of economic growth is the current consumption forgone. To sustain a high growth rate over a large number of years, resources must be devoted to advancing technology and accumulating capital rather than to producing goods and services for current consumption.

A second possible cost of faster long-term economic growth is more rapid depletion of exhaustible natural resources such as oil and natural gas. A third

tries of Oceania (Australia and New Zealand) have grown the slowest. The U.S. growth rate has been toward the low end of the range experienced by these countries. The developing countries and the countries in transition to a market economy have experienced a wide range of growth rates. The most rapid growth has occurred in Asia, where the average growth rate has been close to 5 percent a year—three

possible cost is environmental degradation such as increased pollution of the air, rivers, and oceans. But neither of these problems is inevitable. The technological advances that bring economic growth often help us to economize on natural resources and to achieve a cleaner environment. For example, more efficient internal combustion engines have decreased the amount of gasoline a car uses and cut tailpipe emissions.

A fourth possible cost of faster long-term economic growth is more frequent changes in what we produce, the job we do, and the place we live. Faster long-term growth means that the number of new businesses starting up increases and possibly existing businesses fail at a faster pace. With the birth and death of businesses, jobs are created and destroyed. Faster long-term growth increases the pace of job creation and possibly job destruction. In a fast-growing economy, people must be ready to accept changes in the jobs they do and the places in which they live and to bear the costs of these changes.

The choices that people make, both private choices and public choices made through government institutions, to balance the benefits and costs of economic growth determine the actual pace of economic growth. We'll study these choices and their consequences in Chapters 25 and 26.

REVIEW

- Economic growth is the expansion of production possibilities. The long-term trend in economic growth is measured by the growth rate of potential GDP.
- Long-term growth in the United States and other countries slowed during the 1970s and 1980s.
- Real GDP growth fluctuates in a business cycle. An *expansion* to a *peak* is followed by a *recession*, *trough*, and a new *expansion*.
- The main benefit of economic growth is expanded consumption possibilities. The main costs are less *current* consumption, possibly resource depletion and environmental pollution, and rapid changes in jobs and locations.

We've seen that real GDP grows and that it also fluctuates over the business cycle. Business cycles bring fluctuations in jobs and unemployment. Let's now examine this core macroeconomic problem.

Jobs and Unemployment

WHAT KIND OF LABOR MARKET WILL YOU ENTER when you graduate? Will there be plenty of good jobs to choose from, or will there be so much unemployment that you will be forced to take a low-paying job that doesn't use your education? The answer depends, to a large degree, on the total number of jobs available and on the unemployment rate.

Jobs

The U.S. economy is an incredible job-creating machine. In 1994, 123 million people had jobs. That number is 18 million more than in 1984 and 36 million more than in 1974. Every year, on the average, the U.S. economy creates an *additional* 1.8 million jobs.

When President Clinton took office, he set a goal of creating an additional 8 million jobs during his four-year term. In an average four-year period, the economy creates 7.2 million jobs, so President Clinton's goal was ambitious. But it was not an impossible goal because the pace of job creation and destruction fluctuates over the business cycle. More jobs are destroyed than created during a recession, so the number of jobs decreases. But more jobs are created than destroyed during an expansion, so the number of jobs increases. For example, during the recession of 1990–1991, the number of jobs fell by more than a million but through the expansion that followed, 2 million jobs a year were created each year. During the expansion of the 1980s, jobs were created at an even faster pace of 2.5 million jobs each year.

Unemployment

Although the U.S. economy is an incredible job-creating machine, not everyone who wants a job can find one. On any one day in a normal or average year, seven million people are unemployed, and during a recession or depression, unemployment rises above this level. For example, in the recession of 1991, almost nine million people were looking for jobs.

A person is defined as being **unemployed** if he or she does not have a job but is available for work, willing to work, and has made some effort to find work within the previous four weeks. The sum of the people who are unemployed and the people who are employed is called the **labor force**. The **unemployment rate** is the percentage of the people in the labor force who are unemployed. (The concepts of the labor force and unemployment are explained more fully in Chapter 24 on pp. 573–574.)

The unemployment rate is not a perfect measure of the underutilization of labor for two main reasons. First, it excludes discouraged workers. A **discouraged worker** is a person who does not have a job, is available for work, and willing to work but who has given up the effort to find work. Many people switch between the unemployment and discouraged worker categories in both directions every month. Second, the unemployment rate measures unemployed people rather than unemployed labor hours. It excludes those people who have a part-time job but who want a full-time job.

Despite these two limitations, the unemployment rate is the best available measure of underused labor resources. Let's look at some facts about unemployment.

Unemployment in the United States

Figure 22.6 shows the unemployment rate in the United States from 1929 through 1994. Two features stand out. First, during the Great Depression of the 1930s, the unemployment rate was extremely high. The highest unemployment rate on record—25 percent—occurred during this period, in 1933. This official rate probably overstates unemployment in 1933 because it counts as unemployed people who had make-work jobs created by governments. In the period since the Great Depression, the average unemployment rate has been close to 6 percent.

Second, although in recent years we have not experienced anything as devastating as the Great Depression, we have seen some high unemployment rates during recessions. The figure highlights three of them—the OPEC recession of the mid-1970s, the 1982 recession, and the 1990–1991 recession.

How does U.S. unemployment compare with unemployment in other countries?

FIGURE   22.6

Unemployment in the United States: 1929–1994

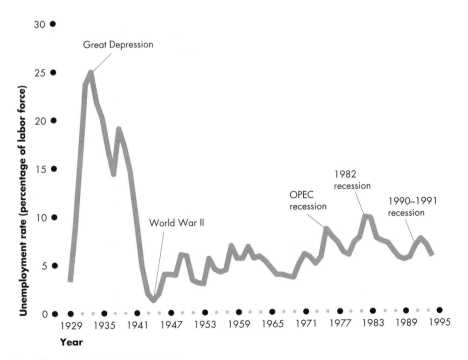

Unemployment is a persistent feature of economic life, but its rate varies. At its worst—during the Great Depression—25 percent of the labor force was unemployed. Even in recent recessions, the unemployment rate climbed toward 10 percent. Between the late 1960s and 1982, there was a general tendency for the unemployment rate to increase.

Source: Economic Report of the President, 1994.

Unemployment Around the World

Figure 22.7 shows the unemployment rate in Canada, Western Europe, and Japan, and compares those unemployment rates with that of the United States. Over the period shown in this figure, U.S. unemployment averaged 7 percent, much higher than Japanese unemployment, which averaged 2.5 percent, but lower than Canadian unemployment, which averaged 9.6 percent, and European unemployment, which averaged 8.1 percent.

U.S. unemployment fluctuates over the business cycle. It increases during a recession and decreases during an expansion. Like U.S. unemployment, Canadian and European unemployment also increases during recessions and decreases during expansions. The cycles in Canadian unemployment are similar to those in U.S. unemployment but the cycle in Europe is out of phase with the U.S. cycle. Also, European unemployment was on a rising trend through the 1980s. In contrast with the other countries, Japanese unemployment has remained remarkably stable.

We've looked at some facts about unemployment in the United States and in other countries. Let's now look at some of the consequences of unemployment that make it the serious problem that it is.

Why Unemployment Is a Problem

Unemployment is a serious economic, social, and personal problem. A prolonged spell of unemployment can permanently damage a person's job prospects. For example, Jody finishes law school at a time when the unemployment rate is high, and she just can't find a job in a law office. Desperately short of income, she becomes a taxi driver. After a year in this work, she discovers that she can't compete with the new crop of law graduates and is stuck with cab driving.

Many social problems become more severe in times of high unemployment. Among them are increases in theft, alcoholism, depression, suicide, and domestic violence. The main reason for the correlation between theft and unemployment is that some people, when they cannot earn an income from legal work, turn to illegal activities. As a result, the amount of theft increases. The other correlations arise from low incomes, increased uncertainty and fear, and increased personal frustration. These factors put family life under a strain and lead to an increase in child and spouse abuse. Also, many people who experience prolonged periods of unemployment lose their self-

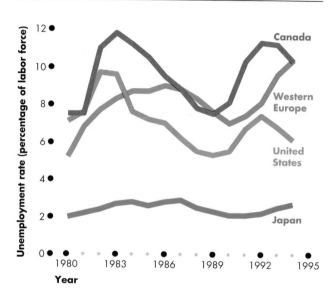

FIGURE 22.7

Unemployment in Industrial Economies

The unemployment rate in the United States has been lower than that in Canada and Western Europe but higher than that in Japan. The cycles in Canadian unemployment are similar to those in the United States. Western European unemployment has a cycle that is out of phase with the U.S. unemployment cycle. Unemployment in Japan is remarkably stable.

Source: Main Economic Indicators, OECD, Paris, 1995.

esteem. It is probably this aspect of unemployment that makes it so highly charged with political and social significance.

R E V I E W

■ On the average, the U.S. economy creates 1.8 million additional jobs a year.

■ The unemployment rate fluctuates, but unemployment never disappears.

■ Prolonged unemployment can permanently damage a person's job prospects, and a high unemployment rate brings increased social problems.

Let's now turn to the third major issue for macroeconomics: inflation.

Inflation

PRICES ON THE AVERAGE CAN BE RISING, FALLING, or stable. **Inflation** is a process of rising prices. We measure the *inflation rate* as the percentage change in the *average* level of prices or **price level**. A common measure of the price level is the *Consumer Price Index* (CPI). The CPI tells us how the average price of all the goods and services bought by a typical urban household changes from month to month. (The CPI is explained in Chapter 23, p. 556).

So that you can see in a concrete way how the inflation rate is measured, let's do a calculation. In December 1992, the CPI was 141.9, and in December 1993, it was 145.8, so the inflation rate during 1993 was

$$\text{Inflation} = \frac{145.8 - 141.9}{141.9} \times 100$$

$$= 2.7\%.$$

Inflation in the United States

Figure 22.8 shows the U.S. inflation rate from 1960 through 1994. You can see from this figure that during the early 1960s, the inflation rate was between 1 and 2 percent a year. Inflation began to increase in the late 1960s at the time of the Vietnam War. But the largest increases occurred in 1974 and 1980, years in which the actions of the Organization of Petroleum Exporting Countries (OPEC) resulted in exceptionally large increases in the price of oil. Inflation was brought under control in the early 1980s when Fed chairman Paul Volcker pushed interest rates up and people cut back on their spending. Since 1983, inflation has been relatively mild and during the 1990s, its rate has fallen yet further.

The inflation rate rises and falls over the years, but it rarely becomes negative. If the inflation rate is negative, the price *level* is falling. Since the 1930s, the price level has generally risen—the inflation rate has been positive. Thus even when the inflation rate is low, as it was in 1961 and 1986, the price level is rising.

FIGURE 22.8

Inflation in the United States: 1960–1994

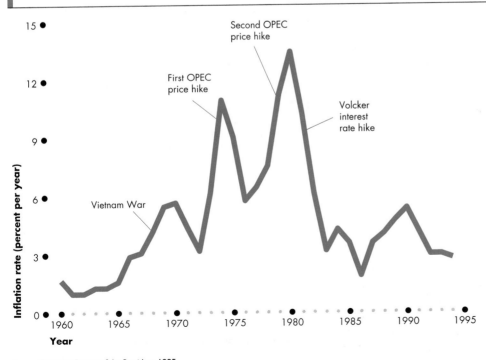

Inflation is a persistent feature of economic life in the United States. The inflation rate was low in the first half of the 1960s, but it increased during the Vietnam War years. It increased further with the OPEC oil price hikes but eventually declined in the early 1980s as a result of policy actions.

Source: *Economic Report of the President,* 1995.

Inflation Around the World

Figure 22.9 shows inflation around the world since 1970. It also shows the U.S. inflation rate in a broader perspective. Part (a) shows that the U.S. inflation rate has been similar to that of other industrial countries. You can also see that all the industrial countries shared the burst of double-digit inflation during the 1970s and the fall in inflation during the 1980s. Part (b) shows that the average inflation rate of industrial countries has been very low compared with that of the developing counties. Among the developing countries, the most extreme inflation has occurred in Latin America where, in 1990, the inflation rate almost hit 600 percent.

A period of inflation brings changes in two other key variables:

- Interest rates
- The foreign exchange rate

Inflation and Interest Rates

An **interest rate** is the amount received by a lender and paid by a borrower expressed as a percentage of the amount of the loan. For example, suppose you borrow $1,000 for one year and at the end of the year, you repay the $1,000 plus $60 of interest. In this case, you have paid an *interest rate* of 6 percent a year.

There are many interest rates in our economy. On a savings account at a bank, you receive the *savings deposit interest rate*. On a loan to buy a car, you pay the *consumer loan interest rate*. On the money the federal government borrows from banks, businesses, and people for up to one year, it pays the *treasury bill rate*. On the overnight loans that banks make to each other, they pay and receive the *federal funds rate*. On loans that banks make to big businesses, the banks earn the *prime rate*.

Although there are many interest rates, they all move up and down together. Usually, the higher the inflation rate, the higher are interest rates. You can see this relationship between inflation and interest rates in Fig. 22.10. This figure shows the prime rate alongside the inflation rate. As inflation increased during the 1960s and early 1970s, interest rates also increased, but not as quickly as inflation. The result, by 1974 and 1975, was that most interest rates were lower than the inflation rate. But as inflation increased in the late 1970s, interest rates rose and

FIGURE 22.9
Inflation Around the World

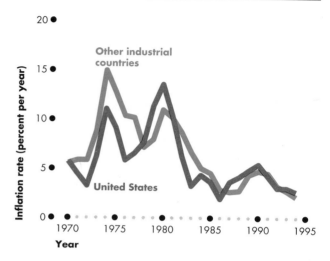

(a) The United States and other industrial countries

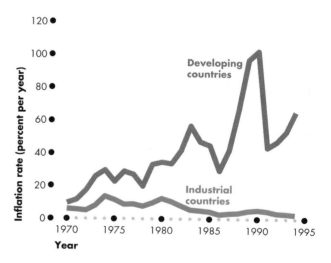

(b) Industrial countries and developing countries

Inflation in the United States is similar to that in the other industrial countries. Compared with the developing countries, inflation in the United States and the other industrial countries is low.

Source: International Monetary Fund, *International Financial Statistics Yearbook 1994,* Washington, D.C., 1994.

continued to rise into the early 1980s. When inflation decreased through the 1980s, interest rates also came down, but much more slowly than inflation.

FIGURE 22.10

Interest Rates and Inflation: 1960–1994

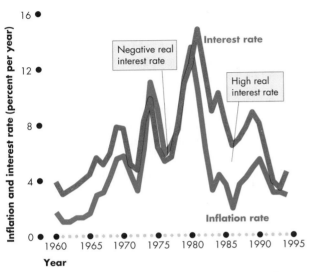

Interest rates and inflation generally fluctuate together. During the 1960s, they increased together, but inflation increased faster than interest rates and real interest rates fell. During the 1980s, when inflation decreased, interest rates did not fall as quickly and real interest rates increased. Real interest rates remained high until the 1990s.

Source: Economic Report of the President, 1995.

them for the fact that they will be repaid with money that buys less than the money they lend. And people who borrow are willing to pay such an interest rate. The interest rate calculated in terms of money is called the **nominal interest rate**. But when the value of money is falling, money itself is not a good measuring rod of value. So instead of calculating interest in terms of money, we calculate it in terms of the goods and services that the money will buy. The result is the **real interest rate**, which is the nominal interest rate minus the inflation rate.

Let's calculate a real interest rate. Suppose you borrow $1,000 for one year at a nominal interest rate of 6 percent a year. Suppose the inflation rate is 2 percent a year. At the end of the year, you pay $1,060 to repay the loan and pay the interest. But with 2 percent inflation, this $1,060 buys what about $1,040 would have bought at the beginning of the year. So the real interest paid is $40 and the real interest rate is only 4 percent a year (6 percent minus 2 percent).

You can see the real interest rate in Fig. 22.10. It is the vertical distance between the (nominal) interest rate and the inflation rate. During the 1960s, the real interest rate was positive but decreasing. It became negative in 1974 and 1975 and then positive again and quite high during the 1980s. During the 1990s, the real interest rate was lower but it remained positive.

Fluctuations in interest rates occur because of fluctuations in the inflation rate and in real interest rates. You will learn what determines real interest rates in Chapter 25 and what determines inflation and interest rates in Chapter 32.

Inflation and the Foreign Exchange Rate

All countries experience inflation. But inflation *rates* vary from one country to another. When inflation rates across countries differ over a prolonged period of time, the result is a change in the foreign exchange value of money. A *foreign exchange rate* is the rate at which one country's money (or currency) exchanges for another country's money. For example, in January 1995, one U.S. dollar exchanged for 100 Japanese yen. But in January 1970, you could get 360 yen for a dollar. The U.S. dollar has fallen in value against the Japanese yen. Part of the reason for this fall in the value of the U.S. dollar in terms of the Japanese yen is the fact that U.S. inflation has been higher than Japan's inflation.

The gap between interest rates and the inflation rate widened. In the 1990s, as inflation decreased, interest rates fell and the gap narrowed.

The Real Interest Rate When inflation is present, money is losing value. The *value of money* is the quantity of goods and services that can be bought with a given amount of money. When an economy experiences inflation, the value of money falls—you cannot buy as many groceries with $50 this year as you could last year. The rate at which the value of money falls is equal to the inflation rate. When the inflation rate is high, as it was in 1981, money loses its value at a rapid pace. When the inflation rate is low, as it was in 1993, the value of money falls slowly.

When money is losing value, people who have funds to lend are willing to do so only if they receive an interest rate that they expect will compensate

Why Inflation Is a Problem

Inflation is a problem because it makes the economy behave like a giant casino in which some people gain and some lose and no one can predict where the gains and losses will fall. Gains and losses occur because of unpredictable changes in the value of money. Money is used as a measuring rod of value in the transactions that we undertake. Borrowers and lenders, workers and employers all make contracts in terms of money. If the value of money varies unpredictably over time, then the amounts *really* paid and received—the quantity of goods that the money will buy—also fluctuate unpredictably. Measuring value with a measuring rod whose units vary is a bit like trying to measure a piece of cloth with an elastic ruler. The size of the cloth depends on how tightly the ruler is stretched.

In a rapid inflation, resources are diverted from productive activities to forecasting inflation. It becomes more profitable to forecast the inflation rate correctly than to invent a new product. Doctors, lawyers, accountants, farmers—just about everyone—can make themselves better off, not by practicing the profession for which they have been trained but by becoming amateur economists and inflation forecasters. From a social perspective, this diversion of talent resulting from inflation is like throwing our scarce resources onto the garbage heap. This waste of resources is a cost of inflation.

Inflation distorts taxes because it makes money incomes rise faster than *real* incomes. Money incomes, not real incomes, are taxed. This distortion does not affect wages because tax brackets change automatically with inflation. But it is a serious problem for income from capital. Inflation increases the money value of stocks, which are taxed as "capital gains." And inflation increases the nominal interest rate, which means that lenders, who receive their incomes in the form of interest end up paying a greater amount of income tax even though the higher nominal interest rate is only compensating them for the falling value of money.

The most serious type of inflation is called *hyper-inflation*—an inflation rate that exceeds 50 percent a month. Such high inflation rates are rare, but they occurred in Germany, Poland, and Hungary during the 1920s and in Hungary and China during the 1940s. At the height of these hyperinflations, workers were paid twice a day because money lost its value so quickly. As soon as they are paid, people rushed off to spend their wages before they lost too much value.

Prices were so high that a shopping cart of money was needed to buy just a handful of groceries. People who lingered too long in the coffee shop found that the price of their cup of coffee had increased between the time they placed their order and when the check was presented.

Hyperinflation is not just a historical curiosity. In 1994, the African nation of Zaire had a hyperinflation that peaked at a *monthly* inflation rate of 76 percent. Also in 1994, Brazil almost reached the hyperinflation stratosphere with a monthly inflation rate of 40 percent. A cup of coffee that cost 15 cruzeiros in 1980 would have cost 22 *billion* cruzeiros in 1994. With numbers this big, Brazil twice changed the name of its currency and twice lopped off three zeros to keep the magnitudes of monetary values manageable. Bank deposits in Brazil earn 30 percent a month interest—just about enough to keep up with inflation. With automatic teller machines on every street corner, people get cash at the moment they need it. When they take a taxi, they stop at an ATM at the end of the trip and get just enough cash for the fare. Hyperinflation and near hyperinflation like Brazil's bring economic chaos and severely disrupt normal economic life.

R E V I E W

- Inflation is a process of rising prices and a falling value of money.
- Fluctuations in the inflation rate bring fluctuations in interest rates.
- When U.S. inflation exceeds inflation in another country, the value of the dollar in terms of the money of the other country falls.
- Inflation is a serious problem because it brings unpredictable gains and losses to borrowers and lenders, workers and employers and because it distorts taxes and diverts resources from producing goods and services to predicting inflation.

We've now looked at economic growth and fluctuations, unemployment, and inflation. There is a fourth macroeconomic issue that generates a lot of excitement: the balance of international payments. What happens when a nation buys more from other countries that it sells to them? Does it face the problem that you and I would face if we spent more than we earned? Does it run out of money? Let's look at these questions.

International Payments

WHEN WE IMPORT GOODS AND SERVICES FROM the rest of the world, we make payments to foreigners. When we export goods and services to the rest of the world, we receive payments from foreigners. We keep track of the values of our imports and exports in our international current account.

The Current Account

The **current account** records the receipts from exports (the sale of goods and services to other countries), the payments for imports (the purchase of goods and services from other countries), the receipts of interest income from other countries, the payments of interest to other countries, and gifts and other transfers (such as international aid payments).

If our exports plus interest receipts from other countries exceed our imports plus interest payments to other countries plus gifts and other transfers, we have a current account surplus. If our imports plus interest payments to other countries plus gifts and other transfers exceed our exports plus interest received from other countries, we have a current account deficit.

The U.S. Current Account

Figure 22.11 shows the history of the U.S. current account since 1960. It shows that until the late 1970s, the United States usually had a current account surplus. When a deficit occurred, as it did in 1971 and 1972 and again in 1977 through 1979, it was small and short-lived. But after 1982, a persistent current account deficit emerged. And at times the deficit has been large. In 1985 and 1986, for example, it exceeded $150 billion each year.

The current account balance fluctuates with the business cycle. In a recession, imports fall and the deficit decreases (or the surplus increases). During an expansion, imports rise and the current account deficit increases. For example, during the recession of the mid-1970s the current account moved into a surplus, and during the expansion of the late 1970s it went into deficit. It returned briefly to surplus during the recession of 1981 and then plunged into a spectacular deficit during the long expansion of the

1980s. This deficit almost disappeared in the recession of 1990–1991 and then re-emerged in the 1990s expansion.

How can we have a persistent current account deficit? The answer is because we have a capital account surplus.

The Capital Account

The **capital account** records the receipts from foreign investments in the United States and U.S. investments in the rest of the world. When we have a current account deficit, we borrow from foreigners or we sell some U.S. assets to foreigners to pay for it. When we have a current account surplus, we loan our surplus to the rest of the world or we buy foreign assets.

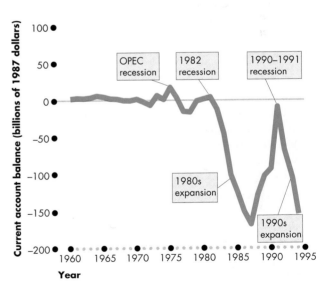

FIGURE 22.11

The U.S. Current Account Balance: 1960–1994

The U.S. current account records our exports and imports of goods and services. Up to the early 1980s, our current account was generally in surplus. During the expansion of the 1980s, a large deficit emerged. The deficit almost disappeared during the 1990–1991 recession, but it reappeared during the 1990s expansion.

Source: Economic Report of the President, 1995.

So a current account surplus is always matched by a capital account deficit and a current account deficit is always matched by a capital account surplus. We do not, as a nation, run out of cash to pay our bills. But is borrowing from the rest of the world a problem? It might be but it is not inevitably a problem.

Just like an individual can borrow to consume, so also can a nation. Borrowing to consume is usually not a good idea. It builds up a debt that grows as interest is added to the debt, and at some point the debt plus the interest must be paid off. But an individual or a nation can also borrow to invest in assets that earn interest. Borrowing to invest in assets that earn interest is potentially profitable. It creates an income stream that can pay off a debt and the interest on the debt. So long as the interest rate earned on the investment exceeds that on the debt, the deficit and the debt do not pose a problem.

You will learn more about the U.S. balance of international payments, why we have had a current account deficit for more than ten years, why the current account balance fluctuates with the business cycle, and whether we have been borrowing to consume or to invest in Chapters 25, 28, and 36.

R E V I E W

- The current account records the receipts from exports and the payments for imports.
- When imports exceed exports, we have a current account deficit.
- We have had a persistent current account deficit since 1982.
- The current account deficit is cyclical. It increases during an expansion and decreases during a recession.
- A current account deficit is matched by a capital account surplus.

We've now reviewed the problems that macroeconomics tries to understand—the problems of economic growth and fluctuations, jobs and unemployment, inflation, and international payments. The goal of macroeconomics is not only to understand these problems but also to devise policy actions that can improve macroeconomic performance. Let's close this chapter by looking at the macroeconomic policy challenges.

Macroeconomic Policy Challenges and Tools

FROM THE TIME OF ADAM SMITH'S *WEALTH OF Nations* and the founding of the United States in 1776 until the birth of modern macroeconomics in 1936, the general view among economists was that the proper role of government in economic life was to provide the legal framework in which people could freely pursue their own best interests. The macroeconomics of Keynes challenged this view and argued that government could (and should) take policy actions aimed at achieving and maintaining full employment.

In the United States, the policy goal of full employment became the declared objective of the government in 1946 with the passage of the Employment Act. This act, among other things, established a President's Council of Economic Advisers to advise the president and administration on macroeconomic policy. U.S. macroeconomic policy goals became more ambitious some 30 years later with the passage in 1978 of the Full Employment and Balanced Growth Act (known as the Humphrey-Hawkins Act).

Policy Challenges

Today, the widely agreed challenges for macroeconomic policy are to:

- Boost long-term growth
- Stabilize the business cycle
- Lower unemployment
- Keep inflation under control
- Lower the current account deficit

By boosting long-term growth, we can try to avoid the problems that have arisen over the past 20 years from the productivity growth slowdown of the mid-1970s. You've seen in this chapter how much that slowdown has cost us. By stabilizing the business cycle, we can try to smooth out the fluctuations in unemployment and in income growth. By lowering the unemployment rate, we can try to avoid some of the social problems that unemployment creates, and by keeping inflation under control, we can encourage people to focus on the activities at which they have a comparative advantage and not get diverted to becoming amateur inflation forecasters. Finally, by lowering our current account deficit, we borrow less from the rest of the world and cut our interest payments to other countries.

But these goals seem to be elusive. Do we have any hope of achieving them? Some economists are skeptical but most believe that we can at least move in the direction of achieving these goals. Let's look at the tools that can be used to pursue the macroeconomic policy challenges.

Policy Tools

Macroeconomic policy tools are divided into two broad categories:

- Fiscal policy
- Monetary policy

Fiscal Policy   **Fiscal policy** is the government's attempt to influence the economy by setting and changing taxes, government spending, and the government's deficit and debt. This range of policy actions is under the control of Congress and the administration. Fiscal policy can be used to try to change the total amount of spending or to change incentives so that investment and productivity increase. When the economy is in a recession, the government might cut taxes or increase its spending in an attempt to lower the unemployment rate. Conversely, when the economy is expanding and real GDP is above potential GDP, the government might increase taxes or cut its spending in an attempt to prevent the economy from overheating.

Each year throughout the 1980s and 1990s, the U.S. government has spent more than it has raised in taxes. When government spending exceeds tax revenues, the government has a **budget deficit**. At times, the government's budget deficit has been large.

The presence of a large deficit has created a new problem and a new objective for U.S. macroeconomic policy. The new problem is that with a large deficit, the total amount owed by the government increases every year. Since 1980, the total amount of U.S. federal government debt has increased more than fivefold. The new objective is to eliminate the federal government deficit. The existence of this new problem and objective has limited the scope for using fiscal policy to stabilize the business cycle.

Monetary Policy   **Monetary policy** consists of changes in interest rates and in the amount of money in the economy. This range of policy actions is under the control of the Federal Reserve (known more popularly as the Fed). When the economy is in recession, the Fed might lower interest rates and inject money into the economy in an attempt to lower the unemployment rate. And when the economy is expanding quickly, the Fed might increase interest rates in an attempt to prevent the economy from overheating. But whether the Fed is trying to stimulate an expansion or fight inflation, it must be cautious. If the Fed moves too vigorously, its actions to boost the economy might be the cause of overheating. And its actions to contain inflation might be the cause of recession.

By mid-1994, the Fed became concerned that the economy was overheating and heading toward a period of rising inflation (see *Reading Between the Lines* on pp. 536–537), and through the balance of that year, monetary policy was used to push interest rates up to discourage borrowing and spending and bring the growth of production back into line with the growth of potential GDP.

REVIEW

- The macroeconomic policy challenges are to boost long-term growth, stabilize the business cycle, lower unemployment, tame inflation, and prevent a large current account deficit.
- To meet these challenges, the federal government uses fiscal policy tools—taxes and government spending—and the Federal Reserve uses monetary policy tools—interest rates and the money supply.
- Since 1980, the government has had a large deficit. Eliminating this deficit is a new policy challenge.

◆ In your study of macroeconomics, you will find out what is currently known about the causes of long-term economic growth, business cycles, unemployment, inflation, and the international balance of payments and about the policy choices and challenges that Congress, the administration, and the Fed face. The next step in your pursuit of these goals is to learn more about macroeconomic measurement—about how we measure real GDP and the price level.

The Economy in 1994

THE ECONOMIST, DECEMBER 3, 1994

Mid-Western Thunder

Chicago—To hear the sound of three years of economic recovery in America's Mid-West, listen to the blast furnaces of USX Corporation's steelworks in Gary, Indiana. According to its owners, that hulking behemoth on the southern shore of Lake Michigan has made more steel than any other plant in the world—and right now its four casters and its hot- and cold-rolled sheet mills are cranking at maximum capacity. Demand for flat steel has never been higher. Just along the lake at Inland Steel, third-quarter earnings were up 80% over the third quarter of last year, and deliveries, at 1.28m tons, are the highest since 1981.

Most of that steel is being snapped up by the Mid-West's thundering manufacturers, ranging from cars to washing machines and machine tools, not to mention the host of other local industries whose business, as locals put it, is to "bend metal". And the market is getting tight. Imports of raw steel have shot up to make up for a domestic shortfall, and finished steel is on "allo-cation": If you are a customer who has not ordered before, you go to the end of the queue. Lead-times for deliveries have doubled this year, and prices, on average, have risen by 15%.

No one is complaining. What is good for steel is good for the rest of the Mid-Western economy. Unemployment in the region has been cruising along at almost one percentage point below the national average of 5.8%. In some areas it is down to 3%, and Madison, Wisconsin, with a non-seasonally-adjusted 1.9%, boasts the lowest rate in the nation. A recent national survey of hiring plans for the fourth quarter shows the Mid-West again leading the nation and things are looking strong into the first three months of 1995. Manufacturing leads the pace, but wholesale and retail trades are also more enthusiastic than they have been for 15 years; the boom is not confined to one sector. Mid-Western financial markets are flourishing, and even farmers have pulled a record year out of the hat. A bin-busting maize harvest is piled on the ground for lack of storage space. ...

Essence of THE STORY

■ In 1994, the economy of the Midwest was enjoying its third year of recovery.

■ Prominent in the recovery was the steel industry, which produced to capacity in 1994.

■ Steel boomed because makers of cars, washing machines, machine tools, and other "metal benders" also boomed.

■ Steel imports increased to fill the gap, but prices and delivery lags increased.

■ Unemployment in the Midwest was about one percentage point below the national average of 5.8 percent, and in Madison, Wisconsin, it was 1.9 percent.

■ Although manufacturing led the recovery, wholesale and retail trades, finance, and farming also performed well.

■ Prospects looked good for 1995.

Economic

A N A L Y S I S

■ During 1992–1995, the Midwest's economy and the U.S. economy were in a business cycle expansion phase. The expansion had four main features: production increased, unemployment decreased, prices began to rise more quickly, and imports increased.

■ The Midwest was in step with the rest of the economy, as the figures and the following analysis show.

■ Figure 1 shows real GDP surging toward potential GDP during 1994. Potential GDP is not known exactly, and the line in this figure is only one possible estimate.

■ Figure 2 shows that the unemployment rate fell steadily throughout the expansion phase to 6 percent in 1994(2) (the second quarter of 1994).

■ Figure 3 shows that inflation increased in 1994(2), bringing to an end its downward trend. This increase in inflation occurred at the same time that real GDP surged toward potential GDP.

■ Figure 4 shows that imports as a percentage of GDP increased throughout the expansion but especially quickly in 1994(2).

■ Taken together, these four figures point to the conclusion that in 1994(2), real GDP was close to potential GDP and that inflation might increase.

■ The policy makers at the Fed reached this conclusion and decided that they should try to slow the expansion to prevent excessive overheating and a serious upturn in the inflation rate in 1995.

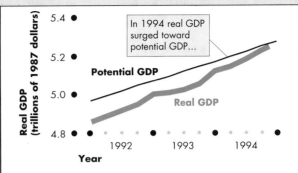

Figure 1 Real GDP

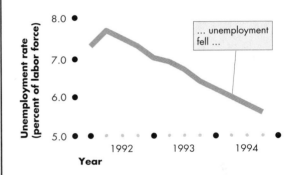

Figure 2 Unemployment

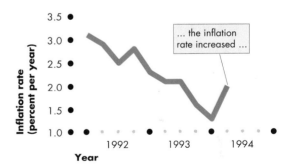

Figure 3 Inflation

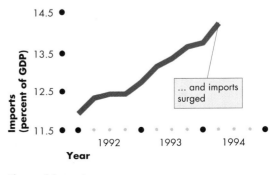

Figure 4 Imports

S U M M A R Y

Origins and Issues of Macroeconomics

Macroeconomics, which emerged during the mid-eighteenth century and was reborn during the Great Depression of the 1930s, studies economic growth and fluctuations, unemployment, inflation, and the balance of international payments. Its main purpose is to devise policies that will boost long-term economic growth, prevent the extremes of depression and inflation, and avoid large international payments deficits. (pp. 519–520)

Economic Growth

Economic growth is the expansion of the economy's capacity to produce goods and services, measured by the rate of increase in potential GDP. Real GDP fluctuates around potential GDP in a business cycle. Every business cycle has an expansion, peak, recession, trough, and new expansion.

To compare countries, we use the growth rate of real GDP per person—real GDP divided by the population. When we compare countries, we find similar productivity growth slowdowns and business cycles but different long-term trends in potential GDP.

The main benefit of long-term economic growth is expanded consumption possibilities, and the main costs are reduced current consumption, possible resource depletion and environmental pollution, and rapid and often costly changes in jobs. (pp. 520–526)

Jobs and Unemployment

The U.S. economy has created an *additional* 1.8 million jobs a year on the average. But on any day in an average year, 7 million people are unemployed.

Unemployment is a state in which people who do not have jobs are willing to work, are available for work, and have looked for work during the previous four weeks. Measured unemployment excludes discouraged workers and part-time workers who want to become full-time workers.

U.S. unemployment fluctuates over the business cycle. It rises during a recession and falls during an expansion. The U.S. unemployment rate is lower than the unemployment rate in Canada and Western Europe but higher than that in Japan.

Unemployment is a serious economic, social, and personal problem. It can permanently damage a person's job prospects. (pp. 526–528)

Inflation

Inflation is a process of rising prices. The inflation rate is measured by the percentage change in a price index such as the CPI. During the 1960s and 1970s, U.S. inflation was on an upward trend, but since 1980, it has been on a downward trend. U.S. inflation has been similar to that of the other industrial countries but mild compared to that of the developing countries.

Changes in the inflation rate lead to changes in interest rates and the foreign exchange rate.

Inflation is a problem because it lowers the value of money at an unpredictable rate and makes money less useful as a measuring rod of value. A rapid inflation diverts resources from productive activities to forecasting inflation. (pp. 529–532)

International Payments

Our receipts from exports (the sale of goods and services to foreigners), payments for imports (the purchase of goods and services from foreigners), international interest receipts and payments, and gifts and other transfers (such as international aid payments) are recorded in the current account. The United States has had a current account deficit since the early 1980s. The current account balance fluctuates with the business cycle; it decreases in a recession and increases in an expansion.

A current account deficit is financed by borrowing from abroad or by selling U.S. assets to foreigners. These transactions are recorded in the capital account. (pp. 533–534)

Macroeconomic Policy Challenges and Tools

The challenges for macroeconomic policy are to boost long-term growth, stabilize the business cycle, lower unemployment, tame inflation, and prevent a large current account deficit. The tools available for meeting these challenges are fiscal policy and monetary policy. (pp. 534–535)

K E Y   E L E M E N T S

Key Figures

Key Terms

R E V I E W   Q U E S T I O N S

1. What is economic growth and how is the long-term economic growth rate measured?

2. Is real GDP an ideal measure of total production? Explain why or why not.

3. Distinguish between real GDP and potential GDP.

4. Describe the productivity growth slowdown that occurred in the United States and other countries during the 1970s.

5. What is a business cycle? Describe its phases.

6. In what phase of the business cycle was the U.S. economy during 1975? 1980? 1985? 1994?

7. What are the benefits of long-term economic growth?

8. What are the costs of long-term economic growth?

9. What is unemployment?

10. What does the unemployment rate tell us about the amount of joblessness? Explain your answer.

11. Why is unemployment a serious problem?

12. What is inflation?

13. Explain the connection between inflation and interest rates and define the real interest rate.

14. Explain the connection between inflation and the foreign exchange rate.

15. Why is inflation a problem?

16. What are the main challenges and tools of macroeconomic policy?

P R O B L E M S

1. The figure shows real GDP per person in Barbados and Mexico during the 1980s.

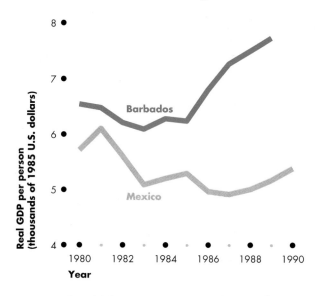

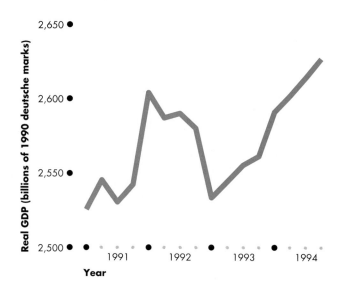

a. In which years was economic growth in Barbados positive?
b. In which years was economic growth in Barbados negative?
c. In which year was economic growth in Barbados fastest?
d. In which years was economic growth in Mexico positive?
e. In which years was economic growth in Mexico negative?
f. What is the most striking difference between real GDP per person in these two countries?
g. In which country is the average person becoming richer?

2. The figure shows real GDP in Germany from the first quarter of 1991 to the second quarter of 1994. Use the figure to answer the following questions:
a. How many recessions did Germany experience during this period?
b. In which quarters, if any, did Germany experience a business cycle peak?
c. In which quarters, if any, did Germany experience a business cycle trough?
d. In which quarters, if any, did Germany experience an expansion?

3. Obtain data on quarterly real GDP for the United States since the fourth quarter of 1994 and then update Fig. 22.2. You will find the data in the recent issues of the *Survey of Current Business,* which is published monthly by the U.S. Department of Commerce. (Find out if your school library has a subscription to STAT.*USA*, which gives you access to the latest data on the Internet.) Using what you have discovered, answer the following questions:
a. Is the U.S. economy now in a recession or an expansion?
b. If the economy is still in an expansion, how long has the expansion lasted?
c. During 1995, was the growth rate speeding up or slowing down?
d. Compare the expansion that ended in the 1990–1991 recession with the expansion that began in 1991. Which expansion is the longest, and during which expansion did real GDP grow most quickly?

4. Obtain data on unemployment in your home state. If your school library has the Bureau of the Census publication *Statistical Abstract of the United States* or the U.S. Department of Labor publication *Employment and Earnings*, you can get the data from there. You can also get the data on the Internet by accessing the Parkin Home Pages on the World Wide Web. The address is http://www.aw.com/he. Once there, go to Business & Economics, New Releases, Economics, Third Edition, and then Student Resources. The Student Resources Page will take you to a variety of helpful economics sites on the World Wide Web. You might, alternatively, call your local newspaper business desk for the information. Compare the behavior of unemployment in your home state with that in the United States as a whole. Why do you think your state might have a higher or a lower unemployment rate than the U.S. average?

◆ 5. Obtain data on inflation in the United States, Japan, Canada, and Germany since 1980. You will find these data in *International Financial Statistics* or the *Economic Report of the President* in your school library. Draw a graph of the data and answer the following questions. Which country has had:
   a. The highest inflation rate?
   b. The lowest inflation rate?
   c. The fastest rising inflation rate?
   d. The fastest falling inflation rate?

6. Study *Reading Between the Lines* on pp. 536–537 and then answer the following questions:
   a. In what phase of the business cycle was the U.S. economy during 1994 and how long had it been in that phase?
   b. When did the inflation rate begin to increase?
   c. When did the expansion begin?
   d. When did real GDP surge forward toward potential GDP?
   e. What happened to the unemployment rate during the expansion from 1992 to 1994?
   f. Why did imports increase sharply in 1994?
   g. Why did the Fed increase interest rates during 1994?

> "*The ideas of economists and political philosophers, both when they are right and when they are wrong, are more powerful than is commonly understood. Indeed the world is ruled by little else.*"

JOHN MAYNARD KEYNES (1883–1946), *THE GENERAL THEORY OF EMPLOYMENT, INTEREST AND MONEY*, CHAPTER 24, "CONCLUDING NOTES" (1936).

The Keynesian Revolution

THE ISSUES AND IDEAS

During the Industrial Revolution in England and on the European continent, new inventions destroyed jobs. Waves of new prosperity for the majority were accompanied by unemployment for a significant minority. In this climate, there was controversy as to whether the economy could expand indefinitely or whether it would reach a limit beyond which there would not be sufficient demand to buy the goods and services that could be produced.

Jean-Baptiste Say argued that in the long run, there can be no problem about supply outstripping demand. The production of goods and services, he claimed, creates incomes that are sufficient to buy those goods and services—supply creates its own demand. The idea that supply creates its own demand came to be known as *Say's Law*.

As the economies of the world became industrialized, they fluctuated in a business cycle—alternating recessions and expansions. But Say seemed to be correct. On the average, supply appeared to create its own demand.

But as the Great Depression of the 1930s became more severe and more prolonged, Say's Law looked less and less relevant. John Maynard Keynes revolutionized macroeconomic thinking by turning Say's Law on its head, arguing that real GDP does not depend on what can be produced—on supply. Instead, real GDP depends on what people are willing to buy—on demand, or as Keynes put it, on *effective demand*. It is possible, argued Keynes, for people to refuse to spend all of their incomes. If businesses also fail to spend on new capital, demand might be less than supply. In this case, resources might go unemployed and remain unemployed indefinitely.

THEN...

In 1766, James Hargreaves, an English weaver and carpenter, developed a simple hand-operated machine called the spinning jenny (pictured here). Using this machine, a person could spin 80 threads at once. Thousands of hand-wheel spinners, operators of machines that could spin only one thread at once, lost their jobs. They protested and tried to protect their jobs by wrecking spinning jennies. In the long run, the displaced hand-wheel spinners found work, often in factories that manufactured the machines that had destroyed their previous jobs. Since the earliest days of the Industrial Revolution to the present day, people have lost their jobs as new technologies have automated what human effort had previously been needed to accomplish.

ADVANCES IN computer technology have made it possible for us to dial our own telephone calls to any part of the world and get connected in a flash. A task that was once performed by telephone operators, who made connections along copper wires, is now performed faster and more reliably by computers, which make connections along fiber optic cables. Just as the Industrial Revolution transformed the textile industry, so today's Information Revolution is transforming the telecommunications industry. In the process, the mix of jobs is changing. There are fewer jobs for telephone operators but more jobs for telephone systems designers, builders, managers, and marketers. In the long run, as people spend the incomes they earn in their new and changing jobs, supply creates its own demand and just as Say predicted. But does supply create its own demand in the short run, when displaced workers are unemployed?

THE ECONOMISTS: JEAN-BAPTISTE SAY AND JOHN MAYNARD KEYNES

Jean-Baptiste Say

Say and Keynes would have had a lot to disagree about. Jean-Baptiste Say, born in Lyon, France, in 1767 (he was 9 years old when Adam Smith's *Wealth of Nations* was published), suffered the wrath of Napoleon for expressing the view that the government should not intervene in the economy. As a result, for several years he was forced to work as a journalist and then as a cotton manufacturer before resuming his career as an economics professor. In the early nineteenth century, Say was the most famous economist in both America and Europe. His book *Traité d' économie politique (A Treatise on Political Economy)*, published in 1803, became a best selling university economics textbook on both sides of the Atlantic.

John Maynard Keynes

John Maynard Keynes, born in England in 1883, was one of the truly great minds of the twentieth century. He wrote on probability as well as economics, represented the British government at the Versailles peace conference following World War I, was a master speculator in international financial markets (an activity that he conducted from bed every morning), and played a prominent role in establishing the International Monetary Fund and a new global financial system after World War II. He was a prominent member of the Bloomsbury Group, an astonishing circle of artists and writers that included E. M. Forster, Bertrand Russell, and Virginia Woolf. Keynes was a controversial and quick-witted figure. A critic once complained that Keynes was constantly shifting his position, to which Keynes retorted: "When I discover I am wrong, I change my mind. What do you do?"

Measuring GDP, Inflation, and Economic Growth

After studying this chapter, you will be able to:

- Distinguish between the *stocks* of capital and wealth and the *flows* of production, income, investment, and saving

- Describe the circular flow of income and expenditure, and explain why aggregate income, expenditure, and product are equal

- Explain how GDP is measured

- Explain how the Consumer Price Index (CPI) and the GDP deflator are measured

- Explain the shortcomings of changes in the CPI and the GDP deflator as measures of inflation

- Explain how *real* GDP is measured

- Explain the shortcomings of real GDP growth as a measure of improvements in economic well-being

When Motorola contemplates spending $1 billion developing a wireless communications system in China, it pays close attention to forecasts of China's real GDP through the next decade. When AT&T plans to expand its fiber optics network, it uses forecasts of long-term growth in the U.S. economy. The outcomes of many business decisions turn on the quality of forecasts of global and national macroeconomic conditions. ◆ Key inputs for

Economic
Barometers

making economic forecasts are the latest estimates of the gross domestic product, or GDP. The GDP data are a barometer of a nation's economy. Economists pore over the latest numbers looking at past trends and seeking patterns that might give a glimpse of the future. How do economic statisticians add up all the economic activity of the country to arrive at the number called GDP? What exactly *is* GDP? ◆ Most of the time, our economy grows and sometimes it shrinks. But to reveal the rate of growth (or shrinkage), we must remove the effects of inflation on GDP and assess how *real* GDP is changing. How do we remove the inflation component of GDP to reveal real GDP? ◆ From economists to homemakers, all types of people pay close attention to another economic barometer, the Consumer Price Index, or CPI. The Department of Labor publishes new figures each month, and analysts in newspapers and on TV quickly leap to conclusions about the causes of recent changes in prices and the prospects for future changes. How does the government determine the CPI? How well does it measure a consumer's living costs and the inflation rate? ◆ Some countries are rich while others are poor and only now are in the process of developing their industries and reaching their productive potential. How do we compare incomes in one country with incomes in another? How can we make international comparisons of GDP?

◈ In this chapter you are going to find out how economic statisticians measure real GDP and the price level. You are also going to learn how they use these measures to assess the economic growth rate and the inflation rate and to compare macroeconomic performance across countries.

Gross Domestic Product

WHAT EXACTLY IS GDP, HOW IS IT CALCULATED, what does it mean, and why do we care about it? You are going to discover the answers to these questions in this chapter. First, what *is* GDP? **Gross Domestic Product (GDP)** is the value of *aggregate* or *total* production of goods and services in a country during a given time period—usually a year. The GDP of the United States, which measures the value of aggregate production in the United States during a year, was $6,738 billion in 1994. How was this number calculated?

Two fundamental concepts form the foundation on which GDP measurements are made:

■ The distinction between stocks and flows

■ The equality of income, expenditure, and the value of production

Stocks and Flows

To keep track of our personal economic transactions and the economic transactions of a country, we distinguish between stocks and flows. A **stock** is a quantity that exists at a point in time. The water in a bathtub is a stock. So are the number of CDs that you own and the amount of money in your savings account. A **flow** is a quantity per unit of time. The water that is running from an open faucet into a bathtub is a flow. So are the number of CDs that you buy during a month and the amount of income that you earn during a month. GDP is another flow. It is the value of the goods and services produced in a country *during a given time period.*

Capital and Investment The key macroeconomic stock is capital. **Capital** is the plant, equipment, buildings, and inventories of raw materials and semi-finished goods that are used to produce other goods and services. The amount of capital in the economy is a crucial factor that influences GDP. Two macroeconomic *flows* change the *stock* of capital: investment and depreciation. **Investment** is the purchase of new plant, equipment, and buildings and the additions to inventories. Investment *increases* the stock of capital. **Depreciation** is the decrease in the stock of capital that results from wear and tear and the passage of time. Another name for depreciation is *capital consumption.* The total amount spent on adding to the stock of capital and on replacing depreciated

capital is called **gross investment**. The amount spent on adding to the stock of capital is called **net investment**. Net investment equals gross investment minus depreciation.

Figure 23.1 illustrates these concepts. On January 1, 1995, Mark's Jeans, Inc. had 3 sewing machines. This quantity was its initial capital. During 1995, Mark's scrapped an older machine. This quantity is its depreciation. After depreciation, Mark's stock of capital was down to 2 machines. But also during 1995, Mark's bought 2 new machines. This amount is its gross investment. By December 31, 1995, Mark's had 4 sewing machines so its capital had increased by 1 machine. This amount is Mark's net investment. Mark's net investment equals its gross investment (the purchase of 2 new machines) minus its depreciation (1 machine scrapped).

The example of Mark's Jeans factory can be applied to the economy as a whole. The nation's capital stock

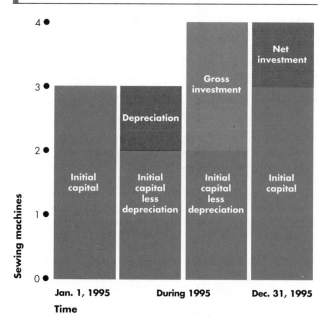

FIGURE 23.1

Capital and Investment

Mark's Jeans, Inc.'s capital stock at the end of 1995 equals its capital stock at the beginning of the year plus its net investment. Net investment is equal to gross investment less depreciation. Mark's gross investment is the 2 new sewing machines bought during the year, and its depreciation is the 1 sewing machine that Mark's scrapped during the year.

decreases because capital depreciates and increases because of gross investment. The change in the nation's capital stock from one year to the next equals its net investment.

Wealth and Saving   Another macroeconomic stock is **wealth**, which is the value of all the things that people own. What people *own*, a stock, is related to what they *earn*, a flow. People *earn* an *income*, which is the amount they receive during a given time period from supplying the services of factors of production. Income can be either consumed or saved. **Consumption expenditure** is the amount spent on consumption goods and services. **Saving** is the amount of income remaining after meeting consumption expenditures. Saving adds to wealth, and dissaving (negative saving) decreases wealth.

For example, suppose that at the end of the school year you have $250 in a savings account and some textbooks that are worth $300. That's all you own. Your wealth is $550. Suppose that you take a summer job and earn an income of $5,000. You are extremely careful and spend only $1,000 through the summer on consumption goods and services. At the end of the summer, when school starts again, you have $4,250 in your savings account. Your wealth is now $4,550. Your wealth has increased by $4,000, which equals your saving of $4,000. Your saving of $4,000 equals your income of $5,000 minus your consumption expenditure of $1,000.

National wealth and national saving work just like this personal example. The wealth of a nation at the start of a year equals its wealth at the start of the previous year plus its saving during the year. Its saving equals its income minus its consumption expenditure.

We'll make the idea of the nation's income and consumption expenditure more precise a bit later in this chapter. Before doing so, let's see what the stocks and flows that we've just learned about imply for the recurring theme of macroeconomics: short-term fluctuations in actual GDP and long-term growth in potential GDP.

The Short Term Meets the Long Term   You saw in Chapter 22 that potential GDP grows incessantly, year after year. You also saw that actual real GDP grows and fluctuates around potential GDP. Both the long-term growth in potential GDP *and* the short-term fluctuations in actual GDP are influenced by the stocks and flows that you've just studied. One of the reasons why potential GDP grows is

that the capital stock grows. One of the reasons that real GDP fluctuates is that investment fluctuates. So capital and investment as well as wealth and saving are part of the key to understanding the growth and fluctuations of GDP.

The flows of investment and saving together with the flows of income and consumption expenditure interact in a circular flow of income and expenditure. In this circular flow, income equals expenditure, which also equals the value of production. This amazing equality is the foundation on which a nation's economic accounts are built and from which its GDP is measured.

The Equality of Income, Expenditure, and the Value of Production

To see that for the economy as a whole income equals expenditure and also equals the value of production, we study the circular flow of income and expenditure.

Figure 23.2 illustrates the circular flow of income and expenditure. In the figure the economy consists of four sectors: households, firms, governments, and the rest of the world (the purple diamonds). It has three aggregate markets: factor markets, goods (and services) markets, and financial markets. Focus first on households and firms.

Households and Firms   Households sell and firms buy the services of labor, capital, land, and entrepreneurship in factor markets. For these factor services, firms pay income to households: wages for labor services, interest for the use of capital, rent for the use of land, and profits for entrepreneurship. Firms' retained earnings—profits that are not distributed to households—are also part of the household sector's income. (You can think of retained earnings as being income that households save and lend back to firms.) The *total income* received by all households in payment for the services of factors of production is *aggregate income*. Figure 23.2 shows aggregate income by the blue dots labeled Y.

Firms sell and households buy consumer goods and services—such as popcorn and soda, movies and chocolate bars, microwave ovens and inline skates, dental and dry cleaning services—in the markets for goods and services. The aggregate payment that households make for these goods and services is *consumption expenditure*. Figure 23.2 shows consumption expenditure by the red dots labeled C.

FIGURE 23.2
The Circular Flow of Income and Expenditure

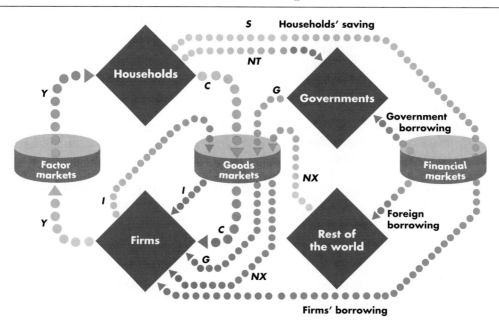

In the circular flow of income and expenditure, households receive incomes (*Y*) from firms (blue flow) and make consumption expenditures (*C*); firms make investment expenditures (*I*); governments purchase goods and services (*G*); the rest of the world purchases net exports (*NX*)—(red flows). Aggregate income (blue flow) equals aggregate expenditure (red flows).

Households' saving (*S*) and net taxes (*NT*) leak from the circular flow. Firms borrow to finance their investment expenditures, and governments and the rest of the world borrow to finance their deficits or lend their surpluses (green flows).

Firms buy and sell new capital equipment in the goods market. For example, IBM sells 1,000 PCs to General Motors, or Boeing sells an airplane to United Airlines. Some of what firms produce might not be sold at all and is added to inventory. For example, if GM produces 1,000 cars and sells 950 of them, the other 50 cars remain unsold and GM's inventory of cars increases by 50. When a firm adds unsold output to inventory, we can think of the firm as buying goods from itself. The purchase of new plant, equipment, and buildings and the additions to inventories are *investment*.

Figure 23.2 shows investment by the red dots labeled *I*. Notice that in the figure, investment flows from firms through the goods markets and back to firms. Some firms produce capital goods, and other firms buy them (and firms "buy" inventories from themselves).

Firms finance their investment by borrowing from households in financial markets. Households' saving flows into financial markets and firms' borrowing flows out of financial markets. Figure 23.2 shows these flows by the green dots labeled "Households' saving" or *S* and "Firms' borrowing." These flows are neither income nor expenditure. Income is a payment for the services of a factor of production, and expenditure is a payment for goods or services.

Governments   Governments buy goods and services, called **government purchases**, from firms. In Fig. 23.2 these government purchases are shown as the red flow *G*. Governments use taxes to pay for their purchases. Figure 23.2 shows taxes as net taxes by the green dots labeled *NT*. **Net taxes** are equal to taxes paid to governments minus transfer payments received from governments. *Transfer payments* are cash transfers from governments to households and firms such as social security benefits, unemployment compensation, and subsidies.[1]

When government purchases (G) exceed net taxes (NT), the government sector has a budget deficit, which it finances by borrowing in financial markets. This borrowing is shown by the green dots labeled "Government borrowing."

Rest of World Sector   Firms export goods and services to the rest of the world and import goods and services from the rest of the world. The value of exports minus the value of imports is called **net exports**. Figure 23.2 shows net exports by the red flow NX.

If value of exports exceeds the value of imports, net exports are positive and flow from the rest of the world to firms. But if the value of exports is less than the value of imports, net exports are negative and flow from firms to the rest of the world.

When net exports are positive, the rest of the world either borrows from the domestic economy or sells domestic assets that it has bought previously. These transactions take place in financial markets and they are shown by the green flow labeled "Foreign borrowing." When net exports are negative, the domestic economy either borrows from the rest of the world or sells foreign assets that it had previously acquired. Again, these transactions take place in financial markets. To illustrate this case in the figure, we would reverse the directions of the flows of net exports and foreign borrowing.

To help you keep track of the different types of flows that make up the circular flow of income and expenditure, they are color-coded. In Fig. 23.2, the red flows are expenditures on goods and services, the blue flow is income, and the green flows are financial transfers. The expenditure flows (red flows) are consumption expenditure, investment, government purchases, and net exports. The income flow (blue flow) is aggregate income. The financial transfers (green flows) are saving, net taxes, government borrowing, foreign borrowing, and firms' borrowing.

---

[1]The diagram does not show firms paying any (net) taxes. In reality, firms pay taxes and receive subsidies. You can think of net taxes paid by firms as being paid on behalf of the households that own the firms. For example, a tax on a firm's profit means that the households owning the firm receive less income. It is as if the households receive all the profit and then pay the tax on the profit. This way of looking at taxes makes Fig. 23.2 simpler but does not change any conclusions.

Gross Domestic Product   Gross domestic product is the value of *aggregate production* in a country during a year. Production can be valued in two ways:

1. By what buyers pay for it
2. By what it costs producers to make it

From the viewpoint of buyers, goods are worth the prices paid for them. From the viewpoint of producers, goods are worth what it costs to make them. It will be a real nuisance if these two values are different because we will then have two different measures of GDP. But if these two values are always equal, we will have a unique concept of GDP regardless of which one we use.

Fortunately, the two concepts of value do give the same answer. Let's see why.

Expenditure Equals Income   The total amount that buyers pay for the goods and services produced is *aggregate expenditure*. Let's focus on aggregate expenditure in Fig. 23.2. The expenditures on goods and services are shown by the red flows. Firms' revenues from the sale of goods and services equal consumption expenditure (C) plus investment (I) plus government purchases of goods and services (G) plus net exports (NX). The sum of these four flows is equal to aggregate expenditure on goods and services.

The total amount it costs producers to make goods and services is equal to the incomes paid for factor services. This amount is shown by the blue flow in Fig. 23.2.

The sum of the red flows equals the blue flow. The reason is that everything a firm receives from the sale of its output is paid out as incomes to the owners of the factors of production that it employs. That is,

$$Y = C + I + G + NX,$$

or aggregate income (Y) equals aggregate expenditure ($C + I + G + NX$).

The buyers of aggregate production pay an amount equal to aggregate expenditure, and the sellers of aggregate production pay an amount equal to aggregate income. Because aggregate expenditure equals aggregate income, these two methods of valuing aggregate production give the same answer. So aggregate production, GDP, equals aggregate expenditure or aggregate income.

The circular flow of income and expenditure is the foundation for measuring GDP. But it is also the foundation for understanding how the flows that we've just studied finance investment and translate into a growing capital stock.

How Investment Is Financed

Investment is financed by national saving and by borrowing from the rest of the world. **National saving** equals household saving plus government saving. Borrowing from the rest of the world equals the value of imports minus the value of exports (or the negative of net exports). Let's see how these sources of funds combine to finance investment.

National Saving   Look at the flows into and out of households in Fig. 23.2. Aggregate income (Y) flows in, and consumption expenditure (C), saving (S), and net taxes (NT) flow out. Everything received by households is either spent on consumption goods and services, saved, or paid in net taxes, so

$$Y = C + S + NT,$$

and household saving is

$$S = (Y - NT) - C.$$

Aggregate income minus net taxes ($Y - NT$) is called *disposable income*, so household saving equals disposable income minus consumption expenditure.

Government saving equals net taxes minus government purchases, ($NT - G$), which is the government budget surplus. If net taxes exceed government purchases, that is, if ($NT - G$) is positive, the government has a budget surplus and this surplus is added to household saving as an additional source of finance for investment. But if net taxes are less than government purchases, that is, if ($NT - G$) is negative, the government has a budget deficit and has to borrow funds. In this case, part of household saving is used to finance the government deficit.

National saving equals household saving plus government saving:

$$\text{National saving} = S + (NT - G).$$

But because household saving equals disposable income minus consumption expenditure,

$$\text{National saving} = (Y - NT) - C + (NT - G).$$

You can see that net taxes cancel in the above equation. Households pay them and governments receive them, so when we add household saving and government saving together, they wash out and we are left with

$$\text{National saving} = Y - C - G.$$

National saving equals aggregate income (GDP) minus consumption expenditure minus government purchases.

Borrowing From the Rest of the World   If foreigners spend more on U.S. goods and services than we spend on theirs, they must borrow from us to pay the difference. That is, if the value of U.S. exports (EX) exceeds the value of U.S. imports (IM), Americans must lend to the rest of the world an amount equal to $EX - IM$. In this situation, part of U.S. national saving flows to the rest of the world and is not available to finance investment.

Conversely, if we spend more on foreign goods and services than the rest of the world spends on ours, we must borrow from the rest of the world to pay the difference. That is, if the value of U.S. imports (IM) exceeds the value of U.S. exports (EX), Americans must borrow from the rest of the world an amount equal to $IM - EX$. In this case, part of the rest of the world's saving flows into the United States and becomes available to finance investment.

Investment Financing   The total funds available to finance investment equals national saving, $S + (NT - G)$, plus borrowing from the rest of the world, ($IM - EX$). This amount equals investment. That is,

$$I = S + (NT - G) + (IM - EX).$$

That is, investment (I) equals household saving (S) plus government saving ($NT - G$) plus borrowing from the rest of the world ($IM - EX$).

In 1994, investment in the United States was $1,033 billion. Saving was $1,068 billion. The government sector had a deficit of $133 billion, so government saving was −$133 billion. As a result, national saving was $935 billion. Net borrowing from the rest of the world, imports minus exports, was $98 billion. Adding this amount to national saving equals $1,033, the level of investment.

Injections and Leakages   You can think of the circular flow of income and expenditure as a system of tubes with liquid flowing through them. The flow of factor incomes equals the flow of expenditures. But some liquid leaks from the circular flow. The *leakages* from the circular flow are saving, net taxes, and imports. For the flows to not run dry, there must also be some injections into the circular flow. The *injections* are investment, government purchases of goods and services, and exports. You are going to see that injections always equal leakages.

Start with the investment financing equation that you've just seen:

$$I = S + (NT - G) + (IM - EX).$$

Add government purchases (*G*) and exports (*EX*) to both sides of this equation and you get

$$I + G + EX = S + NT + IM.$$

The left side is injections into the circular flow of income and expenditure, and the right side is leakages from the circular flow. So

$$\text{Injections} = \text{Leakages}.$$

REVIEW

- Production, income, expenditure, investment, and saving are flows—quantities per unit of time. Capital and wealth are stocks—quantities at a point in time. The flow of investment adds to the stock of capital, and the flow of saving adds to the stock of wealth.

- Aggregate expenditure (the sum of consumption expenditure, investment, government purchases, and net exports) equals aggregate income.

- Investment is financed by national saving plus borrowing from the rest of the world.

- Investment, government purchases, and exports are *injections* into the circular flow of income and expenditure, and saving, net taxes, and imports are *leakages* from the circular flow. Injections equal leakages.

Let's now see how economic statisticians at the Department of Commerce use the circular flow of income and expenditure to measure GDP.

Measuring U.S. GDP

TO MEASURE GDP, THE DEPARTMENT OF Commerce uses two approaches:

- Expenditure approach
- Factor incomes approach

The Expenditure Approach

The *expenditure approach* measures GDP by collecting data on consumption expenditure (*C*), investment (*I*), government purchases of goods and services (*G*), and net exports (*NX*). Table 23.1 illustrates this approach. The numbers refer to 1994 and are in billions of dollars. The name of the item used in the

---

TABLE 23.1

GDP: The Expenditure Approach

Item	Symbol	Amount in 1994 (billions of dollars)	Percentage of GDP
Personal consumption expenditures	C	4,628	68.7
Gross private domestic investment	I	1,033	15.3
Government purchases of goods and services	G	1,175	17.4
Net exports of goods and services	NX	−98	−1.4
Gross domestic product	Y	6,738	100.0

The expenditure approach measures GDP by adding together personal consumption expenditures (*C*), gross private domestic investment (*I*), government purchases of goods and services (*G*), and net exports (*NX*). In 1994, GDP measured by the expenditure approach was $6,738 billion. Two thirds of aggregate expenditure is on personal consumption goods and services.

Source: U.S. Department of Commerce, *Survey of Current Business* (March 1995), p. 7.

National Income and Product Accounts of the United States (published by the Department of Commerce) appears in the first column, and the symbol we have used in our GDP equations appears in the next column. To measure GDP using the expenditure approach, we add together personal consumption expenditures (*C*), gross private domestic investment (*I*), government purchases of goods and services (*G*), and net exports of goods and services (*NX*).

Personal consumption expenditures are the expenditures by households on goods and services produced in the United States. They include goods such as soda, CDs, books, and magazines as well as services such as insurance, banking, and legal advice. They do not include the purchase of new residential houses, which is counted as part of investment.

Gross private domestic investment is expenditure on capital equipment and buildings by firms and expenditure on new residential houses by households. It also includes the change in firms' inventories.

Government purchases of goods and services are the purchases of goods and services by all levels of government—from Washington to the local town hall. This item of expenditure includes the cost of providing national defense, law and order, street lighting, garbage collection, and so on. It does not include *transfer payments*. As we have seen, such payments do not represent purchases of goods and services but rather transfers of funds from government to households.

Net exports of goods and services are the value of exports minus the value of imports. When IBM sells a computer to Volkswagen, the German car producer, the value of that computer is part of U.S. exports. When your local Mazda dealer stocks up on RX7s, its expenditure is part of U.S. imports.

Table 23.1 shows the relative importance of the four items of aggregate expenditure. The largest component is personal consumption expenditures, and the smallest is net exports (negative in 1994).

Expenditures Not in GDP Aggregate expenditure, which equals GDP, does not include all the things that people and businesses buy. To distinguish total expenditure on GDP from other items of spending, we call the expenditure included in GDP *final expenditure*. Spending that is not part of final expenditure and not part of GDP include the purchase of:

■ Intermediate goods and services
■ Used goods
■ Financial assets

Intermediate goods and services are the goods and services that firms buy from each other and use as inputs in the goods and services that they eventually sell to final users. An example of an intermediate good is a computer chip that Dell Corp. buys from Intel Corp. A Dell computer is a final good, but an Intel chip is an intermediate good. To count the expenditure on intermediate goods and services as well as the expenditure on the final good involves counting the same thing twice—called *double counting*.

Some goods are sometimes intermediate goods and sometimes final goods. For example, the ice cream that you buy on a hot summer day is a final good, but the ice cream that a diner buys and uses to make sundaes is an intermediate good. Whether a good is intermediate or final depends on what it is used for, not on what it is.

Expenditure on *used* goods is not part of GDP because these goods were counted as part of GDP in the period in which they were produced and in which they were new goods. For example, a 1988 automobile was part of GDP in 1988. If the car is traded on the used car market in 1995, the amount paid for the car is not part of GDP in 1995.

Firms often sell *financial assets* such as bonds and stocks to finance purchases of newly produced capital goods. The expenditure on newly produced capital goods is part of GDP, but the expenditure on financial securities is not. GDP includes the amount spent on new capital, not the amount spent on pieces of paper.

Let's look at the second way of measuring GDP.

The Factor Incomes Approach

The *factor incomes approach* measures GDP by adding together all the incomes paid by firms to households for the services of the factors of production they hire—wages for labor, interest for capital, rent for land, and profits paid for entrepreneurship. Let's see how the factor incomes approach works.

The *National Income and Product Accounts* divide factor incomes into five categories:

1. Compensation of employees
2. Net interest
3. Rental income
4. Corporate profits
5. Proprietors' income

Compensation of employees is the total payments by firms for labor services. This item includes the net wages and salaries (called "take-home pay") that workers receive each week or month plus taxes withheld on earnings plus fringe benefits such as social security and pension fund contributions.

Net interest is the total interest payments received by households on loans made by them minus the interest payments made by households on their own borrowing. This item includes, on the plus side, payments of interest by firms to households on bonds and, on the minus side, households' interest payments on the outstanding balances on their credit cards.

Rental income is the payment for the use of land and other rented inputs. It includes payments for rented housing and imputed rent for owner-occupied housing. (Imputed rent is an estimate of what homeowners would pay to rent the housing they own and use themselves. By including this item in the national income accounts, we measure the total value of housing services, whether they are owned or rented.)

Corporate profits are the total profits made by corporations. Some of these profits are paid to households in the form of dividends, and some are retained by corporations as undistributed profits.

Proprietors' income is a mixture of the elements that we have just reviewed. The proprietor of an owner-operated business supplies labor, capital, and perhaps land and buildings to the business. It is difficult to split the income earned by an owner-operator into compensation for labor, payment for the use of capital, rent payments for the use of land or buildings, and profit, so the national income accounts lump all these separate incomes into a single category.

Table 23.2 shows these five factor incomes and their relative magnitudes. As you can see, wages and salaries (compensation of employees) make up by far the largest factor income.

The sum of these five components of factor incomes is called *net domestic income at factor cost*. It is not GDP. Two further adjustments are needed to get to GDP, one from factor cost to market price and another from net to gross.

Factor Cost to Market Price   When we add up all the final expenditures on goods and services, we arrive at a total called domestic product at *market price*. These expenditures are valued at the market prices that people pay for the various goods and services. Another way of valuing goods and services is at factor cost. *Factor cost* is the value of a good or service measured by adding together the costs of all the factors of production used to produce it. If the only economic transaction were between households and firms—if there were no government taxes or subsidies—the market price and factor cost values would be the same. But the presence of indirect taxes and subsidies makes these two methods of valuation differ.

An *indirect tax* is a tax paid by consumers when they buy goods and services. (In contrast, a *direct tax* is a tax on income.) State sales taxes and taxes on alcohol, gasoline, and tobacco products are indirect taxes. Because of indirect taxes, consumers pay more for some goods and services than producers receive. The market price is greater than the factor cost. For example, suppose there is a sales tax of 7 percent. If you buy a $1 chocolate bar, it costs you $1.07. The factor cost of the chocolate bar including profit is $1. The market price is $1.07 and the factor cost is $1.

A *subsidy* is a payment by the government to a producer. Payments made to grain growers and dairy

TABLE 23.2

GDP: The Factor Incomes Approach

Item	Amount in 1994 (billions of dollars)	Percentage of GDP
Compensation of employees	4,005	59.4
Rental income	28	0.4
Corporate profits	543	8.1
Net interest	420	6.2
Proprietors' income	474	7.0
Indirect taxes *less* Subsidies	553	8.2
Capital consumption (depreciation)	715	10.6
Gross domestic product	6,738	100.0

The sum of all factor incomes equals net domestic income. GDP equals net domestic income plus capital consumption (depreciation). In 1994, GDP measured by the factor incomes approach was $6,738 billion. The compensation of employees—labor income—was by far the largest part of total factor incomes.

Source: U.S. Department of Commerce, *Survey of Current Business* (March 1995), p. 9–10.

farmers are subsidies. Because of subsidies, consumers pay less for some goods and services than producers receive. The market price is less than the factor cost.

To use the factor incomes approach to measure GDP, we must add indirect taxes to total factor incomes and subtract subsidies. Making this adjustment brings us one step closer to GDP, but it does not quite get us there. We must make one further adjustment.

Net Domestic Product to Gross Domestic Product   If we total all the factor incomes and then add indirect taxes and subtract subsidies, we arrive at *net domestic product at market prices*. What do the words *gross* and *net* mean?

The word gross means *before* subtracting *depreciation*—the decrease in the value of the capital stock that results from wear and tear and the passage of time. Similarly, the word net means *after* subtracting depreciation.

A component of aggregate expenditure is *gross investment*—the purchase of new capital and the replacement of depreciated capital. So when we total all the expenditures, we arrive at a number that includes that amount of depreciation, a gross measure.

A component of aggregate factor incomes is the *net profit* of businesses—profit *after* subtracting the depreciation of capital. So when we total all the factor incomes, we arrive at a number that excludes depreciation, a net measure.

Table 23.2 summarizes these calculations and shows how the factor incomes approach leads to the same estimate of GDP as the expenditure approach.

Valuing the Output of Industries

The methods used to measure GDP can also be used to measure the contribution that an industry makes to GDP. But to measure the value of production of an individual industry, we must be careful to count only the value added by that industry. **Value added** is the value of a firm's production minus the value of the *intermediate goods* bought from other firms. Equivalently, it is the sum of the incomes (including profits) paid to the factors of production used by the firm to produce its output. Let's illustrate value added by looking at the production of a loaf of bread.

Figure 23.3 takes you through the brief life of a loaf of bread. It starts with the farmer, who grows the wheat. To do so, the farmer hires labor, capital equipment, and land. Wages are paid to farm workers, and interest and rent are paid. The farmer also earns a profit. The entire value of the wheat produced is the farmer's value added. The miller buys wheat from the farmer and turns it into flour. To do so, the miller hires labor and capital equipment. Wages are paid to mill workers, interest is paid on the capital, and the miller earns a profit. The miller has now added value to the wheat bought from the farmer. The baker buys flour from the miller. The price of the flour includes the value added by both the farmer and the miller. The baker adds more value by turning the flour into bread. Wages are paid to bakery workers, interest is paid on the capital used by the baker, and the baker earns a profit. The grocer buys the bread from the baker. The price paid by the grocer includes the value added by the farmer, the miller, and the baker. At this stage the value of the loaf is its *wholesale* value. The grocer adds further value by making the loaf available in a convenient

FIGURE 23.3

Value Added and Final Expenditure

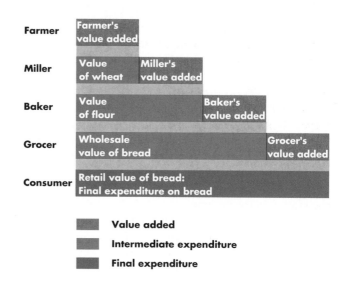

A consumer's expenditure on bread is equal to the sum of the value added at each stage in its production. Intermediate expenditure, for example the amount paid by the baker for the purchase of flour from the miller, equals the value added by the farmer and the miller. So to include intermediate expenditure and final expenditure double counts some value added.

place at a convenient time. The consumer buys the bread for a price—its *retail price*—that includes the value added by the farmer, the miller, the baker, and the grocer.

Final Goods and Intermediate Goods   To value output, we count only *value added* because the sum of the value added at each stage of production equals expenditure on the *final good*. By using value added, we avoid double counting. In the above example the only thing that has been produced and consumed is a loaf of bread—shown by the green bar in Fig. 23.3. The value added at each stage is shown by the red bars, and the sum of the red bars equals the green bar. The transactions involving intermediate goods, shown by the blue bars, are not part of value added and are not counted as part of the value of output or of GDP.

Aggregate Expenditure, Income, and GDP

You've seen that aggregate expenditure equals aggregate income. And you've seen that the Department of Commerce uses both aggregate expenditure and aggregate income to measure GDP. Why does it use two approaches when they are supposed to be the same? The answer is that although the two concepts of the value of aggregate production are identical, the actual measurements, which are based on samples of information, give slightly different answers. The expenditure approach uses data from surveys of retail stores, house building, and business investment, the accounts of the federal, state, and local government, customs records and many other sources. The factor incomes approach uses data supplied by the Internal Revenue Service. None of these sources gives a com-

plete coverage of all the items that make up aggregate expenditure and aggregate factor incomes. So by using the two approaches, the Department of Commerce can check one aggregate against the other. The small discrepancy between the approaches is used to adjust both approaches to make them equal.

Figure 23.4 shows this equality between the approaches to measuring GDP and summarizes the expenditure, income, and product concepts. It also shows the relative magnitudes of the components of aggregate expenditure and aggregate income.

REVIEW

- The *expenditure approach* to measuring GDP sums consumption expenditure, investment, government purchases, and net exports.
- The *factor incomes approach* to measuring GDP sums wages, interest, rent, and profits.
- To value the production of an industry, we calculate the value added of that industry.

So far, in our study of GDP and its measurement, we've been concerned with the dollar value of GDP and its components. But the dollar value of GDP can change either because prices change or because there is a change in the volume of goods and services produced—a change in *real* GDP. Let's now see how we measure the price level and distinguish between the dollar value and the real value of GDP.

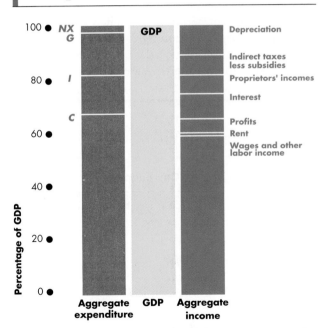

FIGURE 23.4

Aggregate Expenditure, Output, and Income

The red bar illustrates the components of aggregate expenditure as well as their relative magnitudes. Net exports, the smallest component, is shown here as a positive quantity, but in some years it is negative. The green bar illustrates the components of aggregate income and their relative magnitudes. The figure illustrates the equality between aggregate expenditure, aggregate income, and GDP (the yellow bar).

The Price Level and Inflation

THE PRICE LEVEL IS THE AVERAGE LEVEL OF PRICES measured by a *price index*. To construct a price index, we take a basket of goods and services and calculate its value in the current period and its value in a base period. The price index is the value of the basket in the current period expressed as a percentage of the value of the same basket in the base period.

The two main price indexes that are used to measure the price level in the United States today are:

- The Consumer Price Index
- The GDP deflator

The Consumer Price Index

The **Consumer Price Index (CPI)** measures the average level of prices of the goods and services that a typical urban American family consumes. The CPI is published every month by the Bureau of Labor Statistics in the U.S. Department of Labor. To construct the CPI, the Department of Labor first selects a base period. Currently, it is the three-year period 1982–1984. Then, during the base period, it surveys consumer spending patterns to determine the typical or average "basket" of goods and services that people buy in the base period. Around 400 different goods and services feature in the CPI.

Every month, the Department of Labor sends a team of observers to more than 50 urban centers in the United States to record the prices of the 400 items. When all the data are in, the CPI is calculated by valuing the basket of goods and services at the current month's prices. That value is expressed as a percentage of the value of the same basket in the base period.

To see more precisely how the CPI is calculated, let's work through a simplified example. Table 23.3 summarizes the calculations. Let's suppose that in the base period the typical consumer's basket contains 5 pounds of oranges, 6 haircuts, and 200 bus rides. The table shows the prices prevailing in the base period

and also the total expenditure. The typical consumer buys 200 bus rides at 70¢ each and so spends $140 on bus rides. Expenditure on oranges and haircuts is worked out in the same way. Total expenditure is the sum of expenditures on the three goods, which is $210.

To calculate the price index for the current period, we need only discover the prices of the goods in the basket in the current period. We do not need to know the quantities bought. Let's suppose that the prices are those set out in Table 23.3 under "Current period." We can now calculate the current period's value of the (base-period) basket of goods by using the current period's prices. For example, the current price of oranges is $1.20 per pound, so the current period's value of the base-period quantity (5 pounds) is 5 multiplied by $1.20, which is $6. The base-period quantities of haircuts and bus rides are valued at this period's prices in a similar way. The total value of the base-period basket in the current period is $231.

We can now calculate the CPI—the ratio of the current period's value of the basket to the base period's value, multiplied by 100. In this example the CPI for the current period is 110. The CPI for the base period is, by definition, 100. A CPI of 110 tells us that in the current period the price level is 10 percent higher than it was in the base period.

TABLE   23.3

The Consumer Price Index: A Simplified Calculation

Base-period basket	Base period		Current period	
	Price	**Expenditure**	**Price**	**Expenditure**
5 pounds of oranges	$ 0.80/pound	$ 4	$ 1.20/pound	$ 6
6 haircuts	$ 11.00 each	$ 66	$ 12.50 each	$ 75
200 bus rides	$ 0.70 each	$ 140	$ 0.75 each	$ 150
Total expenditure		$210		$231
CPI	$\dfrac{\$210.00}{\$210.00} \times 100 = 100$		$\dfrac{\$231.00}{\$210.00} \times 100 = 110$	

A fixed basket of goods—5 pounds of oranges, 6 haircuts, and 200 bus rides—is valued in the base period at $210. Prices change, and that same basket is valued at $231 in the current period. The CPI is equal to the current-period value of the basket divided by the base-period value of the basket, multiplied by 100. In the base period the CPI is 100, and in the current period the CPI is 110.

The GDP Deflator

The **GDP deflator** measures the average level of prices of all the goods and services that are included in GDP.

To calculate the GDP deflator, we use the formula

$$\text{GDP deflator} = \frac{\text{Nominal GDP}}{\text{Real GDP}} \times 100.$$

In this formula, **nominal GDP** is GDP valued in the current year's prices. It is the dollar value of GDP. And **real GDP** is GDP valued in the prices of a base year. Currently, the base year for the GDP deflator is 1987.

We are going to learn how to calculate the GDP deflator by studying an imaginary economy that produces just three final goods: a consumption good that households buy (oranges), a capital good that firms buy (computers), and a good that the government buys (red tape). Net exports are zero in this example. Table 23.4 summarizes the calculations of the GDP deflator in this economy.

To calculate nominal GDP we'll use the expenditure approach. The table shows that the economy's current output is 4,240 pounds of oranges, 5 computers, and 1,060 yards of red tape. To calculate nominal GDP, we work out the expenditure on each good in the current period and then total the three expenditures. Consumption expenditure (oranges) is $4,452, investment (computers) is $10,500, and government purchases (red tape) are $1,060, so nominal GDP is $16,012.

Now let's calculate real GDP, the real value of the economy's current output. To do so, we value the current-period output at the base-period prices. Because the base year is 1987, we refer to the units in which real GDP is measured as "1987 dollars." The table shows the prices for the base period. Real expenditure on oranges is 4,240 pounds of oranges valued at $1 per pound, which is $4,240. If we perform the same types of calculations for computers and red tape and add up the real expenditures, we arrive at a real GDP of $15,300.

Let's put the numbers we've found into the formula for the GDP deflator. Nominal GDP is $16,012, and real GDP is $15,300, so the GDP deflator is

$$\text{GDP deflator} = \frac{\$16,012}{\$15,300} \times 100 = 104.7.$$

TABLE 23.4

Nominal GDP, Real GDP, and the GDP Deflator: Simplified Calculations

Current-year output	Base-period values		Current-period values	
	Price	Expenditure	Price	Expenditure
4,240 pounds of oranges	$1/pound	$4,240	$1.05/pound	$4,452
5 computers	$2,000 each	$10,000	$2,100 each	$10,500
1,060 yards of red tape	$1/yard	$1,060	$1/yard	$1,060
	Real GDP	$15,300	**Nominal GDP**	$16,012

$$\text{GDP deflator} = \frac{\$16,012}{\$15,300} \times 100 = 104.7$$

An imaginary economy produces only oranges, computers, and red tape. In the current period, nominal GDP is $16,012. If the current-period quantities are valued at the base-period prices, we obtain a measure of real GDP, which is $15,300. The GDP deflator in the current period—which is calculated by dividing nominal GDP by real GDP in the current period and multiplying by 100—is 104.7.

When the current period is also the base period, nominal GDP equals real GDP, and the GDP deflator is 100. A GDP deflator of 104.7 tells us that the price level in the current period is 4.7 percent higher than it was in the base period.

You can think of nominal GDP as a balloon that is being blown up by growing production and rising prices. Figure 23.5 illustrates this idea. In part (a), real GDP is measured by the height of the red area and nominal GDP is measured by the height of the red area plus the green area. In part (b) the GDP deflator lets the inflation air out of the nominal GDP balloon—the contribution of rising prices—so that we can see what has happened to *real* GDP. The red balloon for 1987 shows real GDP in that year. The green balloon shows nominal GDP in 1994. The red balloon for 1994 shows real GDP for that year. To see real GDP in 1994, we use the GDP deflator to *deflate* nominal GDP.

What the Inflation Numbers Mean

A major purpose of the CPI and the GDP deflator is to measure inflation, and the measures are put to practical use. For example, the CPI is used to determine cost of living adjustments to Social Security payments and changes in tax brackets—the income ranges over which different income tax rates apply. How good a measure of inflation does the CPI or the GDP deflator give? Does a 2.7 percent increase in the CPI mean that the cost of living has increased by 2.7 percent? Does a 3 percent increase in the GDP deflator mean that the prices of the goods and services that make up real GDP have increased by 3 percent? Let's find out.

Measuring the inflation rate accurately is of crucial importance. It tells us how the value of money is changing, and it affects our assessment of changes in real GDP. A 1 percent upward bias in the estimated inflation rate translates into a 1 percent downward

---

FIGURE 23.5

The U.S. GDP Balloon

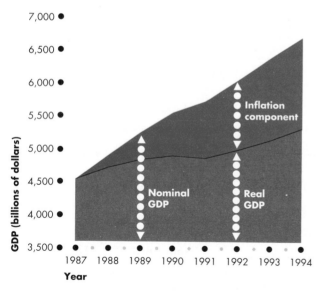

(a) Nominal GDP and real GDP

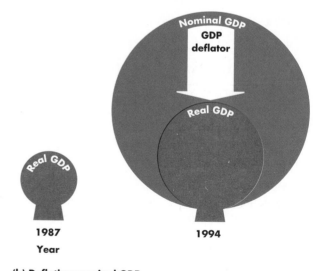

(b) Deflating nominal GDP

Part of the increase in GDP comes from inflation, and part comes from increased production—an increase in real GDP (part a). The GDP deflator lets the inflation air out of the GDP balloon (part b) so that we can see the extent to which production has grown.

Source: Economic Report of the President, 1995.

bias in the estimated growth rate of real GDP. A 1 percent a year bias sustained over ten years throws the estimate of real GDP off by more than 10 percent.

Despite the importance of getting the numbers right, the CPI and the GDP deflator give different views of the inflation rate, and neither index is a perfect measure. Figure 23.6 shows the difference in the two measures. The average inflation rate over the period shown is 4.9 percent a year for the CPI and 4.8 percent a year for the GDP deflator, and the CPI fluctuates more than the deflator.

Worse, *both* measures of inflation probably overstate the inflation rate. The main sources of bias are:

- New goods bias
- Quality change bias
- Substitution bias

New Goods Bias   New goods keep replacing old goods. For example, CDs have replaced LP records and PCs have replaced typewriters. If you want to compare the price level in 1995 with that in 1975, you somehow have to compare the price of a CD and a computer today with that of an LP and a typewriter in 1975. Because CDs and PCs are more expensive than LPs and typewriters, the arrival of these new goods puts an upward bias into the estimate of the price level.

Quality Change Bias   Most goods undergo constant quality improvement. Cars, computers, CD players, and even textbooks get better year after year. Improvements in quality often mean increases in price. But such price increases are not inflation. For example, suppose that a 1995 car is 5 percent better and costs 5 percent more than a 1994 car. Adjusted for the quality change, the price of the car has been constant. But in calculating the CPI, the price of the car will be counted as having increased by 5 percent.

Estimates have been made of the importance of quality change bias, especially for obvious changes such as those in cars and computers. Allowing for quality improvements changes the inflation picture by between 1 and 2 percentage points a year on the average, according to some economists. That is, correctly measured, the inflation rate might be as much as 2 percentage points a year less than the published numbers.

Substitution Bias   A change in the CPI measures the percentage change in the price of a *fixed* basket of goods and services. But changes in relative prices lead

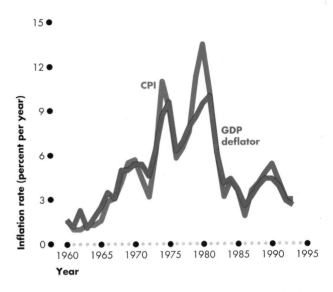

FIGURE 23.6

Two Measures of Inflation

The CPI and the GDP deflator have similar averages over the period shown here—4.9 percent a year for the CPI and 4.8 percent a year for the GDP deflator—but the CPI fluctuates more than the GDP deflator, and both measures probably overstate the inflation rate.

Source: Economic Report of the President, 1995.

consumers to seek less costly items. For example, by shopping more frequently at discount stores and less frequently at convenience stores, consumers can cut the prices they pay. By using discount fares on airplanes, they can cut the cost of travel. This kind of substitution of cheaper items for more costly items is not picked up by the CPI. Because consumers make such substitutions, a price index based on a fixed basket overstates the effects of a given price change on the inflation rate.

To reduce the bias problems, the Bureau of Labor Statistics revises the basket used for calculating the CPI about every 10 years. The current plan is to revise the CPI in 1998 by using a basket of goods and services based on spending patterns in 1993–1995. Yet despite periodic updating, the CPI is of limited value for making comparisons of the cost of living over long periods of time and even has shortcomings as a measure of year-to-year inflation rates.

■ The Consumer Price Index measures the average prices of a fixed basket of consumption goods and services bought by a typical urban family.

■ The GDP deflator measures the average prices of the goods and services that make up GDP.

■ The CPI and GDP deflator overstate the inflation rate by an estimated 1 to 2 percentage points a year.

You now know how inflation is calculated and what the inflation numbers mean. You also know that by letting the inflationary air out of the nominal GDP balloon, we can reveal real GDP. But what does real GDP really mean? Let's find out.

How Real GDP Is Used

ESTIMATES OF REAL GDP AND THE REAL GDP growth rate are used for many purposes. But the three main uses are to:

■ Make international comparisons of GDP

■ Assess changes in economic welfare over time

■ Determine the current phase of the business cycle

International Comparisons of GDP

To make international comparisons, the real GDP of one country must be converted into the same currency units as the real GDP of the other country. For example, in 1990 the real GDP of China was 1,769 billion yuan. In that year, $1 U.S. was worth 4.78 yuan. If we use this exchange rate to convert China's real GDP into U.S. dollars, we get a value of $370 billion. The population of China in 1990 was 1,139 million, so according to these estimates, real GDP per person in China in 1990 was $325. In comparison, U.S. real GDP in 1990 was $5,546 billion and the population of the United States was 250 million, so real GDP per person in the United States in 1990 was $22,200, some 68 times larger than real GDP per person in China.

This comparison of China and the United States makes China look extremely poor, and the official statistics published by the International Monetary Fund (IMF) and the World Bank give this impression. But data on China's real GDP in the Penn World Table (PWT) compiled by Robert Summers and Alan Heston, economists at the University of Pennsylvania, tell a remarkably different story. The difference arises from the prices used. The official statistics use Chinese prices converted to U.S. dollars at the market exchange rate. But these prices are misleading. Some goods that are expensive in the United States cost very little in China. If the prices of these items are converted into U.S. dollars, these items get a small weight in China's real GDP. If, instead, all the goods and services are valued at the prices prevailing in the United States, then a better comparison can be made. Such a comparison uses prices called *purchasing power parity prices*.

The result of this correction to the prices at which China's production is valued changes the picture by an incredible amount. Instead of real GDP per person in 1990 being $325, it was perhaps as much as $2,000—more than 6 times the official estimate. Figure 23.7 shows this amazing difference.

The World Bank and International Monetary Fund data tell us that China is a poor developing country. The Penn World Table data tell us that China has become a middle-income country. The Penn World Table data also tell us that China's real GDP exceeds Germany's, and China's economy is the third largest in the world after that in the United States and Japan.

Despite large differences in estimates of the *level* of China's real GDP, there is much less doubt about its growth rate. The economy of China is expanding at an extraordinary rate and it is for this reason that most businesses are paying a great deal of attention to the prospects of expanding their activities in China and the other Asian economies.

The alternative measures of China's real GDP are to some degree unreliable, and the truth is not known. But even if it were, there would still be problems in comparing the United States and China. These problems also affect comparisons in a single country over time. They arise because real GDP is an imperfect measure of economic welfare.

Economic Welfare

Economic welfare is a comprehensive measure of the general state of well-being. Improvements in economic welfare depend on the growth of real GDP.

FIGURE 23.7

Two Views of Real GDP in China

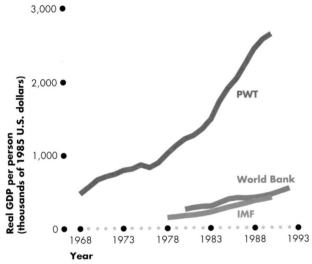

According to the official statistics of the International Monetary Fund (IMF) and the World Bank, China is a poor developing country. But according to an alternative view, Penn World Table (PWT), which is based on purchasing power prices, China has a real GDP more than 6 times the official view and has the world's third largest total production.

Sources: *International Financial Statistics Yearbook*, 1994, IMF, Washington, D.C., *World Development Report, 1994*, World Bank, Washington, D.C.; "The Penn World Table (Mark 5.5): An Expanded Set of International Comparisons, 1950–1988," *Quarterly Journal of Economics*, May 1991, pp. 327–368; new computer diskette, Mark 5.5, June 15, 1993; and the author's calculations.

But they also depend on many other factors that are not measured by GDP. Some of these factors are:

- Quality improvements
- Household production
- The underground economy
- Health and life expectancy
- Leisure time
- The environment
- Political freedom and social justice

Quality Improvements   The price indexes that we use to measure inflation give a downward-biased estimate of the growth rate of real GDP. When car prices rise because cars have gotten better (safer, faster, more fuel efficient, more comfortable), the CPI and the GDP deflator count the price increase as inflation. So what is really an increase in production is counted as an increase in price rather than an increase in real GDP. It is deflated away by the wrongly measured higher price level.

Household Production   An enormous amount of production takes place every day in our homes. Changing a light bulb, cutting the grass, washing the car, growing vegetables, and teaching a child to catch a ball are all examples of productive activities that do not involve market transactions and are not counted as part of GDP.

Household production has become much more capital intensive over the years. As a result, less labor is used in household production than in earlier periods. For example, a microwave meal that takes just a few minutes to prepare uses a great deal of capital and almost no labor. Because we use less labor and more capital in household production, it is not easy to work out whether household production has increased or decreased over time. But it is likely that market production counted in GDP has increasingly replaced household production. Two trends point in this direction. One is the trend in the number of people who hold jobs, which has increased from 60 percent in 1970 to 66 percent in 1994. The other is the trend in the purchase of traditionally home-produced goods and services in the market. For example, more and more families now eat in fast food restaurants—one of the fastest-growing industries in the United States—and use day-care services. This trend means that an increasing proportion of food preparation and child care that used to be part of household production are now measured as part of GDP.

The Underground Economy   The *underground economy* is the part of the economy that is purposely hidden from the view of the government in order to avoid taxes and regulations or because the goods and services being produced are illegal. Because underground economic activity is unreported, it is omitted from GDP.

The underground economy is easy to describe, even if it is hard to measure. It includes the production and distribution of drugs, production that uses illegal labor that is paid less than the minimum wage, and jobs done for cash to avoid paying income taxes. This last category might be quite large and includes tips earned by cab drivers, hairdressers, and hotel and restaurant workers. Estimates of the scale of the underground economy range between 6 and 20 percent of GDP ($400 billion to $1,300 billion) in the United States and much more in some countries.

Provided that the underground economy is a reasonably stable proportion of the total economy, its omission from GDP does not pose a problem. The growth rate of real GDP still gives a useful estimate of the long-term growth rate and of business cycle fluctuations. But sometimes, production shifts from the underground to the rest of the economy, and sometimes it shifts the other way. The underground economy expands relative to the rest of the economy if taxes become especially high or if regulations become especially restrictive. And the underground economy shrinks relative to the rest of the economy if the burdens of taxes and regulations are eased. During the 1980s, when tax rates were cut, there was an increase in the reporting of previously hidden income, and tax revenues increased. So some part (but probably a very small part) of the expansion of real GDP during the 1980s represented a shift from the underground economy rather than an increase in production.

Health and Life Expectancy   Good health and a long life—the hopes of everyone—do not show up in real GDP, at least not directly. A higher real GDP does enable us to spend more on medical research, health care, a good diet, and exercise equipment. And as real GDP has increased, our life expectancy has lengthened—from 70 years at the end of World War II to approaching 80 years today. Infant deaths and death in childbirth, two fearful scourges of the nineteenth century, have almost been eliminated.

But we face new health and life expectancy problems every year. AIDS and drug abuse are taking young lives at a rate that causes serious concern. When we take these negative influences into account, we see that real GDP growth overstates the improvements in economic welfare.

Leisure Time   Leisure time is an economic good that adds to our economic welfare. Other things being equal, the more leisure we have, the better off we are. Our time spent working is valued as part of GDP, but our leisure time is not. Yet from the point of view of economic welfare, that leisure time must be at least as valuable to us as the wage that we earn on the last hour worked. If it was not, we would

work instead of taking the leisure. Over the years, leisure time has steadily increased. The workweek has become shorter, more people take early retirement, and the number of vacation days has increased.

These improvements in economic well-being are not reflected in GDP.

The Environment   The environment is directly affected by economic activity. The burning of hydrocarbon fuels is the most visible activity that damages our environment. But it is not the only example. The depletion of exhaustible resources, the mass clearing of forests, and the pollution of lakes and rivers are other major environmental consequences of industrial production.

Resources that are used to protect the environment are valued as part of GDP. For example, the value of catalytic converters that help to protect the atmosphere from automobile emissions are part of GDP. But if we did not use such pieces of equipment and instead polluted the atmosphere, we would not count the deteriorating air that we were breathing as a negative part of GDP.

An industrial society possibly produces more atmospheric pollution than an agricultural society does. But such pollution does not always increase as we become wealthier. One of the things that wealthy people value is a clean environment, and they devote resources to protecting it. Compare the pollution that was discovered in East Germany in the late 1980s with pollution in the United States. East Germany, a relatively poor country, polluted its rivers, lakes, and atmosphere in a way that is unimaginable in the United States or in wealthy West Germany.

Political Freedom and Social Justice   Most people value political freedoms such as those provided by the U.S. Constitution. And they value social justice or fairness—equality of opportunity and of access to social security safety nets that protect people from the extremes of misfortune.

A country might have a very large real GDP per person but have limited political freedom and equity. For example, a small elite might enjoy political liberty and extreme wealth while the vast majority are effectively enslaved and live in abject poverty. Such an economy would generally be regarded as having less economic welfare than one that had the same amount of real GDP but in which political freedoms were enjoyed by everyone. Today, China has rapid real GDP growth but limited political freedoms, while Russia has a decreasing real GDP and an emerging democratic political system. Economists have no easy way to determine which of these countries is better off.

The Bottom Line   What is the bottom line? Do we get the wrong message about changes (or differences) in economic welfare by looking at changes (or differences) in real GDP? The influences omitted from real GDP are probably important and could be large. Developing countries have a larger underground economy and a larger amount of household production than do developed countries. So as an economy develops and grows, part of the apparent growth might reflect a switch from underground to regular production and from home production to market production. This measurement error overstates the rate of economic growth and the improvement in economic welfare.

Other influences on living standards include the amount of leisure time available, the quality of the environment, the security of jobs and homes, the safety of city streets, and so on. It is possible to construct broader measures that combine the many influences that contribute to human happiness. Real GDP will be one element in those broader measures, but it will by no means be the whole of them.

Phase of the Business Cycle

When the Fed decides to raise interest rates to slow an expansion that it believes is too strong, it looks at the latest estimates of real GDP and inflation. But don't the measures of inflation used to calculate real GDP overstate the inflation rate? They do, but not in a cyclical way. They are off by a similar amount every year. So while the possible mismeasurement of inflation might lead to wrong estimates of long-term real GDP growth, it probably does not cause a wrong assessment of the phase of the business cycle.

On the whole, the fluctuations in economic activity measured by real GDP probably tell a reasonably accurate story about the phase of the business cycle that the economy is in. When real GDP grows the economy is in a business cycle expansion and when real GDP shrinks (for two quarters), the economy is in a recession. Also, real GDP fluctuations are correlated with other indicators of the business cycle. For example, in a recession, jobs disappear and unemployment increases, inflation (eventually) subsides,

and imports decrease. Similarly, in an expansion, more jobs become available and unemployment falls, inflation (eventually) increases, and imports increase. By studying *Reading Between the Lines* on pp. 564–565, you can see how real GDP estimates during 1994 showed the economy to be in a strong business cycle expansion.

But real GDP fluctuations probably exaggerate or overstate the fluctuations in total production and economic welfare. The reason is that when business activity slows down in a recession, household production increases and so does leisure time. When business activity speeds up in an expansion, household production and leisure time decrease. Because household production and leisure time increase in a recession and decrease in an expansion, they are countercyclical. As a result, real GDP fluctuations tend to overstate the fluctuations in total production and in economic welfare. But the directions of change of real GDP, total production, (and economic welfare) are probably the same.

R E V I E W

- Real GDP is not an accurate measure of economic welfare because it undervalues quality improvements, omits some production, and ignores indicators of economic welfare such as health and life expectancy, leisure time, the environment, and political freedom.
- Real GDP probably understates the long-term growth rate and overstates business cycle fluctuations.

◆ In Chapter 22 we studied the macroeconomic performance of the United States in recent years—the growth and fluctuations in real GDP, unemployment, inflation, and the balance of international payments. We've now studied the methods used to measure some of these indicators of macroeconomic performance. We've seen how real GDP and the price level are measured, and we've seen what these measures mean.

In Chapter 24 we will learn about the labor market and the measurement of employment and unemployment. The chapters that follow build on this knowledge of the measurement and meaning of the indicators of macroeconomic performance and explain the choices and the interactions that determine the performance of the economy.

Diagnosing the Economy

Essence of **THE STORY**

THE CHICAGO TRIBUNE, JUNE 30, 1994

Strong 1st Quarter Surprises Economists

The economy grew at a surprisingly brisk annual rate of 3.4 percent in the first quarter as consumers spent freely despite severe winter weather, the Commerce Department said Wednesday in a revised report.

The final report on growth showed it up from previous estimates of 3 percent made a month ago and 2.6 percent originally. ...

Stronger consumer spending than first thought was the primary reason for revising first-quarter growth upward. But businesses also plowed more money into new plants and equipment.

"It doesn't fundamentally change my view that the strength of the economy is dissipating somewhat," said economist Christopher Probyn of DRI-McGraw Hill, a forecasting service in Lexington, Mass. However, he said the upward revision could signal a trend that influences the Federal Reserve to again raise interest rates.

The Fed already has boosted short-term rates four times this year. Members of its Open Market Committee will meet Tuesday and Wednesday to consider whether further hikes in interest rates are needed to support the stumbling dollar to ward off any possibility of inflation.

The only sector of the gross domestic product report that performed significantly more weakly than previously thought was trade, as exports were revised downward. Big deficits, especially in trade with Japan, have put the dollar under acute pressure. ...

GDP is widely expected to grow at a pace of around 4 percent in the current second quarter before leveling off in the second half for full-year growth of about 3 percent, the same as in 1993.

■ Real GDP grew at an annual rate of 3.4 percent in the first quarter of 1994.

■ This final estimate of growth in the first quarter of 1994 was up from an initial estimate of 2.6 percent and an interim estimate of 3 percent a month earlier.

■ Consumer spending and business investment were the main contributors to the revised growth estimate.

■ The only component of GDP that grew less quickly than previously thought was exports.

■ Economists expected the economy to grow at a rate of 4 percent a year in the second quarter of 1994 and then to slow to about 3 percent a year.

■ The Fed had increased interest rates four times in 1994, and it was believed that it might increase them again to help avoid an upturn in the inflation rate.

Economic

A N A L Y S I S

■ The Department of Commerce estimates each quarter's GDP three times. It makes an *initial* or *advanced estimate* one month after the quarter's end, an *interim* or *revised estimate* two months after a quarter's end, and a *final estimate* three months after a quarter's end.

■ These estimates are like a physician's diagnosis of a patient's state of health. The advanced estimate is like the physician's diagnosis based on the patient's temperature and blood pressure. The revised estimate is like the physician's diagnosis made after a more probing examination, and the final estimate is like the physician's diagnosis after studying the results of blood tests and X-rays.

■ Figure 1 shows how the diagnosis of the economic growth rate changed during 1994.

■ The long-term average growth rate of U.S. real GDP is 3 percent a year. If the economy is growing more quickly that 3 percent a year, it is moving toward potential GDP.

■ In the first quarter of 1994 the economy was actually growing faster than 3 percent a year,

according to the final estimate (the red bar), but the advanced estimate did not give that impression.

■ For the rest of 1994, real GDP grew faster than 3 percent a year and so the economy remained in the expansion phase of the business cycle.

■ Just as the physician monitors many features of a patient's health, the economist keeps track of many aspects of economic performance. A group of factors that are watched closely are combined into the Index of Leading Indicators—indicators that lead or precede the business cycle. These factors include work hours, unemployment insurance claims, factory orders, building permits issued, raw materials prices, stock prices, the money supply, and consumer expectations.

■ Figure 2 shows the percentage change in the Index of Leading Indicators alongside the growth rate of real GDP. You can see that, although the real GDP growth rate and the Index of Leading Indicators generally move up and down together, the index is not a perfect predictor of real GDP growth.

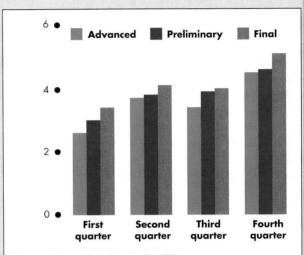

Figure 1 Growth Estimates in 1994

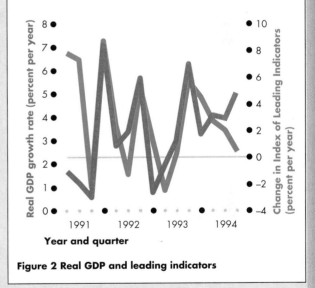

Figure 2 Real GDP and leading indicators

■ By monitoring the Index of Leading Indicators and its components along with real GDP growth, economists try to anticipate the future course of the economy.

■ Policy makers use these same indicators to decide the doses of economic medicine needed to maintain a sustainable rate of economic growth and avoid high rates of unemployment and inflation.

S U M M A R Y

Gross Domestic Product

Gross domestic product (GDP) is the value of aggregate production in a country during a given period (usually a year). The concept of GDP is based on the distinction between stocks and flows and the circular flow of expenditure and income.

Capital is the key macroeconomic stock, and investment is the flow that increases the stock of capital. Wealth is also a stock, and saving—income minus consumption expenditure—increases the stock of wealth.

The circular flow of income and expenditure arises from the expenditures of households, firms, governments, and the rest of the world and the payment of factor incomes by firms. Aggregate expenditure on goods and services equals aggregate income. The value of aggregate production—GDP—is equal to aggregate expenditure or aggregate income.

Injections into the circular flow—investment, government purchases, and exports—equal the leakages from the circular flow—saving, net taxes, and imports. Investment is financed by national saving plus borrowing from the rest of the world. (pp. 546–551)

Measuring U.S. GDP

Because aggregate expenditure, aggregate income, and the value of aggregate production are equal, national income accountants can measure GDP by using one of two approaches: the expenditure approach or the factor incomes approach.

The expenditure approach adds together consumption expenditure, investment, government purchases of goods and services, and net exports to arrive at an estimate of GDP. This approach includes only expenditure on new final goods and services. It does not include expenditure on intermediate goods and services, used goods, and financial services.

The factor incomes approach adds together the incomes paid to the factors of production—wages paid to labor, interest paid to capital, rent paid to

land, and profit paid to entrepreneurs. To use the factor incomes approach to estimate GDP, it is necessary to add indirect taxes less subsidies and depreciation.

To value the output of a firm or sector in the economy, we measure value added. The use of value added avoids double counting. (pp. 551–555)

The Price Level and Inflation

Two main indexes that measure the price level are the Consumer Price Index and the GDP deflator. The CPI measures the average price level of goods and services typically consumed by American families. It is measured as the ratio of the value of the typical (base-period) basket at current-period prices to its value at base-period prices, multiplied by 100. The GDP deflator measures the average price level of all goods and services that make up GDP. It is measured as the ratio of nominal GDP to real GDP, multiplied by 100. Real GDP is the current year's production valued at base-period prices.

Inflation is measured by the rate of change of the CPI or the GDP deflator. The CPI and the GDP deflator give an upward-biased measure of inflation because some goods disappear and new goods become available, the quality of goods and services change over time, and as relative prices change, consumers substitute less expensive items for more expensive items. (pp. 555–560)

How Real GDP Is Used

Real GDP is not a perfect measure of either aggregate production or economic welfare. It excludes quality improvements, household production, the underground economy, environmental damage, the contribution to economic welfare of health and life expectancy, leisure time, and political freedom and social justice. But the growth rate of real GDP gives a good indication of the phases of the business cycle. (pp. 560–563)

K E Y   E L E M E N T S

R E V I E W   Q U E S T I O N S

1. Distinguish between a stock and a flow.
2. What are the main macroeconomic stocks? What are the flows that change them?
3. List the components of aggregate expenditure.
4. What are the components of aggregate income?
5. Why does aggregate income equal aggregate expenditure?
6. Why does the value of output (or GDP) equal aggregate income?
7. Distinguish between government purchases of goods and services and transfer payments.
8. What are injections into the circular flow of income and expenditure? What are leakages?
9. Explain why injections into the circular flow of income and expenditure equal leakages from it.
10. How does the Department of Commerce measure GDP?
11. Explain the expenditure approach to measuring GDP.
12. Explain the factor incomes approach to measuring GDP.
13. What is the distinction between expenditure on final goods and expenditure on intermediate goods?
14. What is value added? How is it calculated?
15. What are the two main price indexes used to measure the price level?
16. How is the Consumer Price Index calculated?
17. How is the basket of goods and services used in constructing the CPI chosen? Is it the same basket in 1995 as it was in 1955? If not, how is it different?
18. Is the CPI a good measure to use to compare the cost of living today with that in the 1930s? If not, why not?
19. How is the GDP deflator calculated?
20. Is real GDP a good measure of economic welfare? If not, why not?
21. Is the growth of real GDP a good measure of the growth of real economic activity?
22. Compare the fluctuations of real GDP with the phases of the business cycle.

P R O B L E M S

1. The figure at the bottom of the page shows the flows of income and expenditure on Lotus Island during 1994. The amounts are thousands of dollars.

   Calculate Lotus Island's

   a. Aggregate expenditure.
   b. Aggregate income.
   c. GDP.
   d. Government budget deficit.
   e. Total value added.
   f. Household saving.
   g. Government saving.
   h. Foreign borrowing.
   i. National saving.

2. In problem 1, calculate the values of:

   a. Two leakages from the circular flow.
   b. Two injections into the circular flow.

3. In problem 1, calculate:

   a. Firms' borrowing.
   b. Government borrowing.
   c. Rest of the world's borrowing.

4. The following transactions took place in Ecoland last year:

Item	Billions of dollars
Wages paid to labor	800,000
Consumption expenditure	600,000
Taxes	250,000
Government transfer payments	50,000
Firms' profits	200,000
Investment	250,000
Government purchases	200,000
Exports	300,000
Saving	300,000
Imports	250,000

   a. Calculate Ecoland's GDP.
   b. Did you use the expenditure approach or the factor incomes approach to make this calculation?
   c. What extra information do you need to calculate net domestic product?

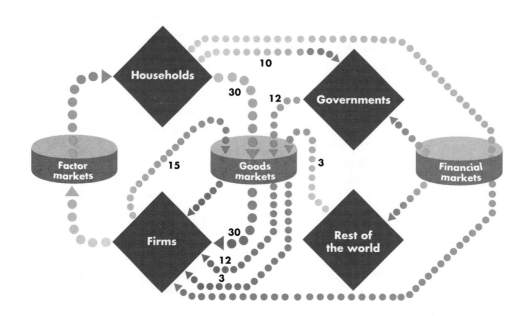

5. In problem 4,
   a. Calculate leakages from the circular flow of income and expenditure.
   b. Calculate injections into the circular flow of income and expenditure.
   c. Do injections equal leakages?

6. In problem 4, what is
   a. Household saving?
   b. Government saving?
   c. National saving?
   d. Borrowing from the rest of the world?

7. In problem 4, how is investment in Ecoland financed?

8. Cindy, the owner of The Great Cookie, spends $100 on eggs, $50 on flour, $45 on milk, $10 on utilities, and $60 on wages to produce 200 great cookies. Cindy sells her cookies for $1.50 each. Calculate the value added per cookie at The Great Cookie.

9. A typical family living on Sandy Island consumes only apple juice, bananas, and cloth. In the base year the typical family spent $40 on apple juice, $45 on bananas, and $25 on cloth. Prices in the base year were $4 a gallon for apple juice, $3 a pound for bananas, and $5 a yard for cloth. In the current year, apple juice costs $3 a gallon, bananas cost $4 a pound, and cloth costs $7 a yard. Calculate:

   a. The basket used in the CPI.
   b. The Consumer Price Index in the current year.
   c. The inflation rate between the base year and the current year.

10. An economy has the following real GDP and nominal GDP in 1993, 1994, and 1995:

Year	Real GDP	Nominal GDP
1993	$1,000 billion	$1,000 billion
1994	$1,050 billion	$1,200 billion
1995	$1,200 billion	$1,500 billion

   a. What was the GDP deflator in 1994?
   b. What was the GDP deflator in 1995?
   c. What is the inflation rate as measured by the GDP deflator between 1994 and 1995?
   d. What is the inflation rate as measured by the GDP deflator between 1993 and 1995?

11. Study *Reading Between the Lines* on pp. 564–565 and then answer the following questions:
   a. Which phase of the business cycle is the economy in if real GDP is growing at 4 percent a year?
   b. Which phase of the business cycle is the economy in if real GDP is growing at 1 percent a year?
   c. What problems might arise if real GDP grows at 4 percent a year for several quarters?
   d. What problems might arise if real GDP grows at 1 percent a year for several quarters?
   e. Why do policy makers look at indicators other than real GDP to diagnose the state of economic health?

Employment and Unemployment

After studying this chapter, you will be able to:

- Define the unemployment rate, the labor force participation rate, the employment-to-population ratio, and aggregate hours

- Describe the trends and fluctuations in the indicators of labor market performance

- Describe the sources of unemployment, its duration, and the groups that are most affected by it

- Explain the different types of unemployment

- Define the natural rate of unemployment and full employment

- Explain how employment and wage rates are determined by demand and supply in the labor market

Each month, we chart the course of the unemployment rate as a measure of U.S. economic health with the intensity with which a physician tracks a patient's temperature. How do we measure the unemployment rate? What does it tell us? Is it a reliable vital sign for the economy? ◆ June 1992 was a month in which unemployment peaked at almost 10 million. How can this large number of people be unemployed? How do people become unemployed? Do most of

Vital Signs

them get fired, or do most quit their jobs to look for better ones? How long do spells of unemployment last for most people? A week, two weeks, or several months? And how does the length of unemployment spells vary over the business cycle? ◆ You probably know that unemployment affects young people much more severely than older people. It also affects minorities much more severely than whites. Why isn't unemployment "shared" more equitably by all age and racial groups? ◆ Another feature of the labor market that we chart every month is the number of people working. This number fluctuates as the unemployment rate fluctuates, but it also trends upward. At the start of 1995, almost 125 million people in the United States had jobs. What does this vital sign tell us about the health of the U.S. economy? Does the number of jobs grow quickly enough to keep pace with increases in the population? ◆ Yet other signs of economic health are the hours people work and the wages they receive. Are work hours growing as quickly as the number of people with jobs? Are most of the new jobs full time or part time? Also, are most new jobs high-wage or low-wage jobs?

◗ These are the questions we study in this chapter. You will discover that a lot of ideas that people have about the U.S. labor market are just plain wrong. The economy has created millions of jobs and good jobs that pay higher and higher wages and benefits. But you'll also see some serious problems. Most people have seen a slowdown in their rate of wage increase, and many have seen their wages fall. So there have been big changes in the *distribution* of jobs and big changes in the spread between the highest and the lowest wages. We begin by looking at the key labor market indicators and the way they are measured.

Employment and Wages

REAL GDP DEPENDS ON THE QUANTITIES OF labor and capital employed, entrepreneurship, and the state of technology, which influences the productivity of the factors of production. In this chapter we study the forces that determine the quantity of labor employed, and we take an initial look at the productivity of labor. But we begin by learning how the state of the labor market is observed and measured.

Population Survey

Every month, the U.S. Census Bureau surveys 60,000 households and asks a series of questions about the age and job market status of its members. This survey is called the Current Population Survey. The Census Bureau uses the answers to estimate the size of the working-age population, the number of people employed, and the number unemployed.

Figure 24.1 shows the population categories used by the Census Bureau and the relationships among the categories. It divides the population into two groups, the working-age population and others who are too young to work or who live in institutions and are unable to work. The **working-age population** is the total number of people aged 16 years and over who are not in jail, hospital, or some other form of institutional care. The Census Bureau divides the working-age population into two groups: those in the labor force and those not in the labor force. It also divides the labor force into two groups: the employed and the unemployed. So the **labor force** is the sum of the employed and the unemployed.

To be counted as employed in the Current Population Survey, a person must have either a full-time job or a part-time job. To be counted as *un*employed, a person must be available for work and must be in one of three categories:

1. Without work, but has made specific efforts to find a job within the previous four weeks
2. Waiting to be called back to a job from which he or she has been laid off
3. Waiting to start a new job within 30 days

Anyone surveyed who satisfies one of these three criteria is counted as unemployed. People in the working-age population who are neither employed nor unemployed are classified as not in the labor force.

FIGURE 24.1
Population Labor Force Categories

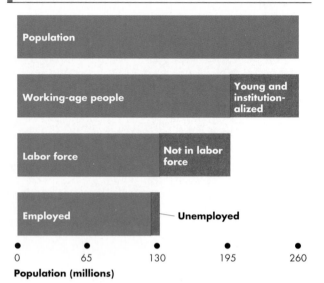

Population (millions)

The number of people employed plus the number unemployed make up the labor force. The labor force plus the people not in the labor force make up the working-age population. The working-age population plus young and institutionalized people make up the population.

Source: Economic Report of the President, 1995.

In 1994 the population of the United States was 260.7 million. There were 63.9 million people under 16 years of age or living in institutions. The working-age population was 196.8 million. Of this number, 65.8 million were not in the labor force. Most of these people were in school full time or had retired from work. The remaining 131 million people made up the U.S. labor force. Of these, 123 million were employed and 8 million were unemployed.

Three Labor Market Indicators

The Census Bureau calculates three indicators of the state of the labor market, which are shown in Fig. 24.2. They are:

- The unemployment rate
- The labor force participation rate
- The employment-to-population ratio

The Unemployment Rate   The amount of unemployment is an indicator of the extent to which people who want jobs can't find them. The **unemployment rate** is the percentage of the people in the labor force who are unemployed. That is,

$$\text{Unemployment rate} = \frac{\begin{array}{c}\text{Number of}\\\text{people unemployed}\end{array}}{\text{Labor force}} \times 100,$$

and

$$\text{Labor force} = \begin{array}{c}\text{Number of}\\\text{people employed}\end{array} + \begin{array}{c}\text{Number of}\\\text{people unemployed}\end{array}$$

In 1994 the number of people employed was 123 million and the number unemployed was 8 million. By using the above equations, you can verify that the labor force was 131 million (123 million plus 8 million) and the unemployment rate was 6.1 percent (8 million divided by 131 million, multiplied by 100).

Figure 24.2. shows the unemployment rate (orange line) and two other labor market indicators between 1960 and 1994. The average unemployment rate has been 6 percent, and it reached peak values during the OPEC recession and the recessions of 1982 and 1990–1991.

The Labor Force Participation Rate   The number of people who join the labor force is an indicator of the willingness of people of working age to take jobs. The **labor force participation rate** is the percentage of working-age population who are members of the labor force. That is,

$$\begin{array}{c}\text{Labor force}\\\text{participation rate}\end{array} = \frac{\text{Labor force}}{\text{Working-age population}} \times 100.$$

In 1994 the labor force was 131 million and the working-age population was 196.8 million. By using the above equation, you can calculate the labor force participation rate. It was 66.6 percent (131 million divided by 196.8 million, multiplied by 100).

The labor force participation rate (graphed in red and plotted on the left scale) has followed an upward trend and has increased from 59 percent during the early 1960s to 66 percent in the 1990s. It has also had some mild fluctuations. They result from unsuccessful job-seekers becoming discouraged

---

FIGURE   24.2

Employment, Unemployment, and the Labor Force: 1960–1994

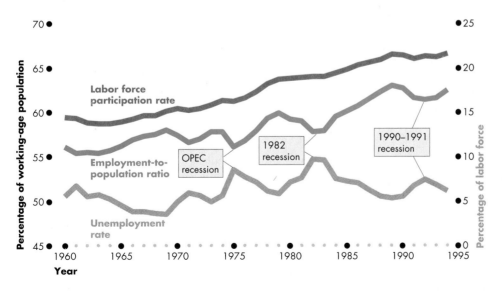

The unemployment rate increases in recessions and decreases in expansions. The labor force participation rate and the employment-to-population ratio have upward trends and fluctuate with the business cycle. The employment-to-population ratio fluctuates more than the labor force participation rate and reflects cyclical fluctuations in the unemployment rate. Fluctuations in the labor force participation rate arise mainly because of discouraged workers.

Source: Economic Report of the President, 1995.

workers. **Discouraged workers** are people who temporarily leave the labor force during a recession and who reenter the labor force during an expansion and become more active job seekers.

The Employment-to-Population Ratio   The number of people of working age who have jobs is an indicator of both the availability of jobs and the degree of match between people's skills and jobs. The **employment-to-population ratio** is the percentage of people of working age who have jobs. That is,

$$\text{Employment--to--population ratio} = \frac{\text{Number of people employed}}{\text{Working-age population}} \times 100.$$

In 1994, employment was 123 million and the working-age population was 196.8 million. By using the above equation, you can calculate the employment-to-population ratio. It was 62.5 percent (123 million divided by 196.8 million, multiplied by 100).

The employment-to-population ratio (graphed in blue and plotted against the left scale) has increased from 55 percent during the early 1960s to 62 percent the 1990s. The fact that the employment-to-population ratio has increased means that the U.S. economy has created jobs at a faster rate than the working-age population has grown. This labor market indicator also fluctuates, and its fluctuations coincide with but are opposite to those in the unemployment rate. It falls during a recession and increases during an expansion.

Why have the labor force participation rate and the employment-to-population ratio increased? The main reason is an increase in the number of women in the labor force. Figure 24.3 shows this increase. Between 1960 and 1994, the female labor force participation rate increased from 38 percent to 58 percent. Shorter work hours, higher productivity, and an increased emphasis on white-collar jobs have expanded the job opportunities and wages available to women. At the same time, technological advances have increased productivity in the home and freed women from some of their more traditional jobs outside the job market.

Figure 24.3 also shows another remarkable fact about the U.S. labor force: The labor force participation rate and the employment-to-population ratio for men have *decreased*. Between 1960 and 1994, the male labor force participation rate decreased from 83 percent to 75 percent. It has decreased because increasing numbers of men are remaining in school

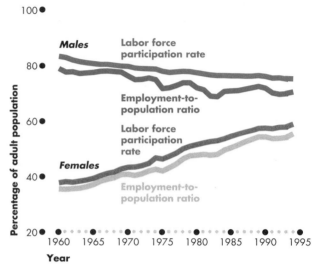

FIGURE   24.3

The Changing Face of the Labor Market

The upward trends in the labor force participation rate and the employment-to-population ratio are accounted for entirely by the increasing participation of women in the labor market. The male labor force participation rate and employment-to-population ratio have decreased.

Source: Economic Report of the President, 1995.

longer, some are retiring earlier, and some are specializing in the household jobs that previously were done almost exclusively by women.

Aggregate Hours

The three labor market indicators that we've just examined are useful signs of the health of the economy and directly measure what matters to most people: jobs. But they don't tell us the quantity of labor used to produce GDP and we cannot use them to calculate the productivity of labor. The productivity of labor is significant because it influences the wages people earn.

The reason why the number of people employed does not measure the quantity of labor employed is that jobs are not all the same. Some jobs are part time and involve just a few hours work a week. Others are full time, and some of these involve regular overtime work. For example, at two 7-11 stores the jobs might be different. One store might hire six students who work for three hours a day each. The other might hire two full-time workers who work nine hours a day each. The number of people employed in these two stores is eight, but the total hours worked by six of the eight is the same as the total hours worked by the other two. To determine the total amount of labor used to produce GDP, we measure labor in hours rather than in jobs. **Aggregate hours** are the total number of hours worked by all the people employed, both full time and part time, during a year.

Figure 24.4(a) shows aggregate hours in the U.S. economy from 1960 to 1994. Like the employment-to-population ratio, aggregate hours have an upward trend. But aggregate hours have not grown as quickly as have the number of people employed. Between 1960 and 1994 the number of people employed in the U.S. economy increased by 82 percent. During that same period, aggregate hours increased by only 62 percent. Why the difference? Because average hours per worker decreased.

Figure 24.4(b) shows average hours per worker. After hovering at almost 39 hours a week during the early 1960s, average hours per worker decreased to about 34 hours a week in the early 1990s. This shortening of the average workweek has arisen partly because of a decrease in the average hours worked by full-time workers but mainly because the number of part-time jobs has increased faster than the number of full-time jobs.

Fluctuations in aggregate hours and average hours per worker line up with the business cycle. Figure 24.4 highlights the past three recessions, during which aggregate hours decreased and average hours per worker decreased more quickly than trend.

Wage Rates

The **real wage rate** is the quantity of goods and services that an hour's work can buy. It is equal to the money wage rate (dollars per hour) divided by the price level. If we use the GDP deflator to measure the price level, the real wage rate is expressed in 1987 dollars because the GDP deflator is 100 in 1987. The real wage is a significant economic variable because it measures the reward for labor.

What has happened to the real wage rate in the United States? Figure 24.5 answers this question. It

FIGURE 24.4

Aggregate Hours: 1960–1994

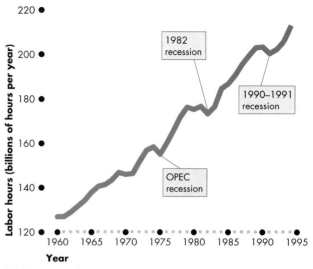

(a) Aggregate hours

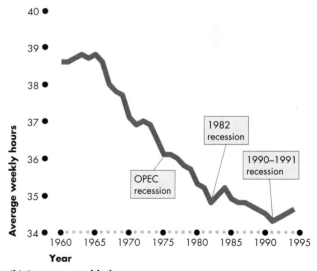

(b) Average weekly hours per person

Aggregate hours (part a) measure the total labor used to produce real GDP more accurately than does the number of people employed because an increasing proportion of jobs are part time. Between 1960 and 1994, aggregate hours increased by an average of 1.5 percent a year. Fluctuations in aggregate hours coincide with business cycle fluctuations. Aggregate hours have increased at a slower rate than the number of jobs because the average workweek has shortened (part b).

Source: Economic Report of the President, 1995, and the author's calculations.

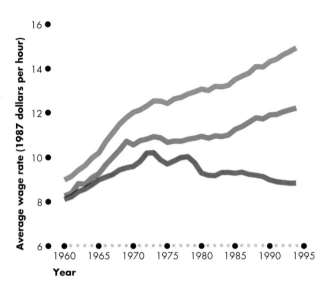

FIGURE 24.5

Real Wage Rates: 1960–1994

Total wages, salaries, and benefits divided by aggregate hours

Total wages and salaries divided by aggregate hours

Average hourly wage rate of private manufacturing nonsupervisory workers

The average hourly real wage rate of private manufacturing nonsupervisory workers peaked in 1973 and followed a downward path after that year. But broader measures of the average hourly real wage rate show an increase. All measures of average hourly real wage rates reflect a productivity growth slowdown of the 1970s.

Source: Economic Report of the President, 1995, and the author's calculations.

shows three measures of the average hourly real wage rate in the U.S. economy between 1960 and 1994.

The first measure of the real wage rate is the Department of Labor's calculation of the average hourly earnings of private manufacturing nonsupervisory workers. This measure of the hourly wage rate increased to a maximum of $10.20 in 1973 (in 1987 dollars) and then followed a twenty-year downward trend.

The second measure of the hourly real wage rate is based on the national income accounts. It is calculated by dividing total wages and salaries by aggregate hours. This measure of the average hourly wage rate is broader than the first and includes the incomes of

all types of labor, whether their rate of pay is calculated by the hour or not. It includes managers and supervisors and all types of workers. You can see that this measure did not follow a downward trend, but its growth rate slowed during the mid-1970s and remained low through the early 1980s. It then speeded up during the late 1980s and 1990s.

The decline in the average wage rate of manufacturing nonsupervisory workers and the slowdown in the growth rate of the broader measure of the average wage rate coincide with the *productivity growth slowdown* that you saw in Chapter 22. This productivity slowdown is the main reason for this behavior of average real wage rates.

There is another factor at work. An increasing proportion of labor compensation now takes the form of fringe benefits such as pension contributions and the payment by employers of health insurance premiums. To take this trend into account, Fig. 24.5 shows a third measure of the hourly real wage rate, which equals *total labor compensation*—wages, salaries, and benefits—divided by aggregate hours. This measure is the most comprehensive one available, and it shows that the average hourly wage rate has increased. But it also shows that no matter how we measure the hourly wage rate, the productivity growth slowdown also slowed real wage rate growth.

R E V I E W

- The labor force participation rate and the employment-to-population ratio have an upward trend; the unemployment rate and employment-to-population ratio fluctuate with the business cycle.
- The female labor force participation rate has increased, but the male labor force participation rate has decreased.
- Aggregate hours have not grown as quickly as the number of people employed because the average workweek has shortened.
- Average hourly real wage rates have grown, but their growth rate slowed with the productivity growth slowdown of the 1970s.

We've seen that employment grows and that employment and unemployment fluctuate with the business cycle. Let's now focus more sharply on unemployment.

Unemployment and Full Employment

How do people become unemployed, how long do they remain unemployed, and who is at greatest risk to become unemployed? Let's answer these questions by looking at the anatomy of unemployment.

The Anatomy of Unemployment

People become unemployed if they:

1. Lose their jobs
2. Leave their jobs
3. Enter or reenter the labor force

People end a spell of unemployment if they:

1. Are hired or recalled
2. Withdraw from the labor force

People who are laid off, either permanently or temporarily, from their jobs are called **job losers**. Some job losers become unemployed but some immediately withdraw from the labor force. People who voluntarily quit their jobs are called **job leavers**. Like job losers, some job leavers become unemployed and search for a better job while others withdraw from the labor force temporarily or permanently retire from work. People who enter or reenter the labor force are called **entrants** and **reentrants**. Entrants are mainly people who have just left school. Some entrants get a job right away and are never unemployed, but many spend time searching for their first job and during this period, they are unemployed. Reentrants are people who have previously withdrawn from the labor force. Most of these people are formerly discouraged workers. Figure 24.6 shows these labor market flows.

Let's see how much unemployment arises from the three different ways in which people can become unemployed.

The Sources of Unemployment Figure 24.7 shows unemployment by reason for becoming unemployed. Job losers are the biggest source of unemployment. Also, their number fluctuates a great deal. In

FIGURE 24.6

Labor Market Flows

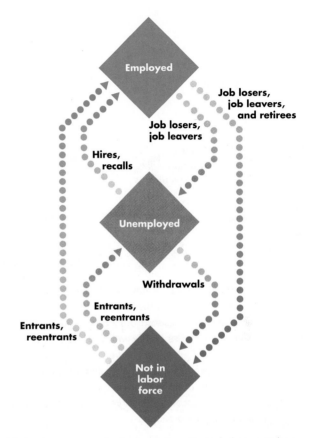

Unemployment results from employed people losing or leaving their jobs (job losers and job leavers) and from people entering the labor force (entrants and reentrants). Unemployment ends because people get hired or recalled or because they withdraw from the labor force.

the recession of 1990–1991, on any given day, more than 5 million of the 9.4 million people who were unemployed were job losers. In contrast, in the peak year of 1989, fewer than 3 million of the 6.5 million people who were unemployed were job losers.

Entrants and reentrants also are a large component of the unemployed and their number fluctuates mildly. On any given day, between 2.5 million and 3 million unemployed people are entrants and reentrants.

Job leavers are the smallest and most stable source of unemployment. On any given day, fewer than 1 million people are unemployed because they

FIGURE 24.7
Unemployment by Reasons

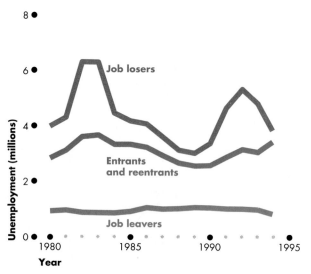

Everyone who is unemployed is either a job loser, a job leaver, or an entrant or reentrant into the labor force. Most of the unemployment that exists results from job loss. The number of job losers fluctuates more closely with the business cycle than do the numbers of job leavers and entrants and reentrants. Entrants and reentrants are the second most commonly unemployed people. Their number fluctuates with the business cycle because of discouraged workers. Job leavers are the least common unemployed people.

Source: Economic Report of the President, 1995.

FIGURE 24.8
Unemployment by Duration

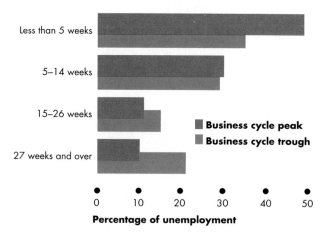

At the business cycle peak in 1989, when unemployment was at its lowest level, almost 50 percent of unemployment lasted for less than 5 weeks, 30 percent lasted for 5 to 14 weeks, and 20 percent lasted for 15 weeks or more. In the business cycle trough in 1992, when unemployment was at its highest level, only 34 percent of unemployment lasted for less than 5 weeks, 29 percent lasted for 5 to 14 weeks, and 37 percent lasted for 15 weeks or more.

Source: Economic Report of the President, 1995.

are job leavers. The number of job leavers is remarkably constant, although to the extent that it fluctuates, it does so in line with the business cycle: A slightly larger number of people leave their jobs in good times than in bad times.

The Duration of Unemployment Some people are unemployed for a week or two, and others are unemployed for periods of a year or more. The average duration of unemployment varies over the business cycle. Figure 24.8 compares some features of the duration of unemployment at the business cycle peak of 1989 when the unemployment rate was low and at the business cycle trough of 1992 when the unemployment rate was high. In 1989, when the unemployment rate hit a low of 5.3 percent, almost

50 percent of the unemployed were in that state for less than 5 weeks and fewer than 20 percent of the unemployed were jobless for longer than 15 weeks. In 1992, when unemployment reached a high of 7.4 percent, only 35 percent of the unemployed found a new job in less than 5 weeks and another 35 percent were unemployed for more than 15 weeks. At both low and high unemployment rates, about 30 percent of the unemployed are unemployed for between 5 weeks and 14 weeks.

The Demographics of Unemployment Figure 24.9 shows unemployment for different demographic groups. The figure shows that high unemployment rates occur among young workers and also among blacks. In the business cycle trough in 1992 the unemployment rate of black teenagers was almost 40 percent. Even at the business cycle peak in 1989 the percentage did not fall below 30 percent. The unemployment rates for white teenagers are less than half

FIGURE 24.9

Unemployment by
Demographic Group

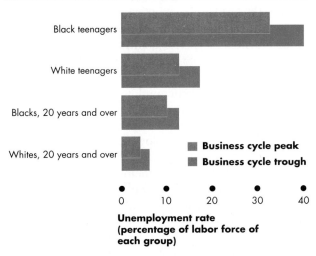

Black teenagers experience unemployment rates that average three times those of white teenagers, and teenage unemployment rates are much higher than those for people aged 20 years and over. Even in a business cycle trough, when unemployment is at its highest rate, only 6 percent of whites aged 20 years and over are unemployed.

Source: Economic Report of the President, 1995.

10,300,000 teenagers were in school. The ratio of teenage unemployment to the teenage population is less than 8 percent. That is, 20 percent of the teenage labor force or 8 percent of the teenage population is unemployed.

Types of Unemployment

Unemployment is classified into three types that are based on its causes. They are:

- Frictional
- Structural
- Cyclical

Frictional Unemployment Frictional unemployment is the unemployment that arises from normal labor turnover—from people entering and leaving the labor force and from the ongoing creation and destruction of jobs. Frictional unemployment is not usually regarded as a problem, but it is a permanent phenomenon.

The unending flow of people into and out of the labor force and the processes of job creation and job destruction create the need for people to search for jobs and for businesses to search for workers. Always there are businesses with unfilled jobs and people seeking jobs. Look in your local newspaper, and you will see that there are always some jobs being advertised. Businesses don't usually hire the first person who applies for a job, and unemployed people don't usually take the first job that comes their way. Instead, both firms and workers spend time searching out what they believe will be the best match available. By this process of search, people can match their own skills and interests with the available jobs and find a satisfying job and income. While these unemployed people are searching, they are frictionally unemployed.

The amount of frictional unemployment depends on the rate at which people enter and reenter the labor force and on the rate at which jobs are created and destroyed. During the 1960s the amount of frictional unemployment increased as a consequence of the post-war baby boom that began during the 1940s. By the 1960s the baby boom created a bulge in the number of people leaving school. As these people entered the labor force, the amount of frictional unemployment increased.

The amount of frictional unemployment is influenced by unemployment compensation. The greater the number of people covered by unemployment

those of black teenagers. The racial differences also exist for workers aged 20 years and over. The highest unemployment rates that whites 20 years and over experience are less than the lowest rates experienced by the other groups.

Why are teenage unemployment rates so high? There are three reasons. First, young people are still in the process of discovering what they are good at and trying different lines of work. So they leave their jobs more frequently than older workers. Second, firms sometimes hire teenagers on a short-term trial basis. So the rate of job loss is higher for teenagers than for other people. Third, most teenagers are not in the labor force but are in school. This fact means that the percentage of the teenage population that is unemployed is much lower than the percentage of the teenage labor force that is unemployed. In 1992, for example, 1,350,000 teenagers were unemployed and 5,400,00 were employed, and the teenage unemployment rate (all races) was 20 percent. But

insurance and the more generous the unemployment benefit, the longer is the average time taken in job search and the greater is the amount of frictional unemployment. In the United States, 93 percent of the labor force is covered by unemployment insurance, up from 83 percent in the 1970s and 69 percent in 1960. The average unemployment benefit has increased from 40 percent of average weekly wages in 1960 to 48 percent in 1995, but in 1960 the benefit was not taxed as it is today.

Structural Unemployment **Structural unemployment** is the unemployment that arises when changes in technology or international competition destroy jobs that use different skills or are located in different regions from the new jobs that are created. Structural unemployment usually lasts longer than frictional unemployment because it is often necessary to retrain and possibly relocate to find a job. For example, when a steel plant in Gary, Indiana, is automated, some jobs in that city are destroyed. Meanwhile, new jobs for security guards, life-insurance salespeople, and retail clerks are created in Chicago, Indianapolis, and other cities. The unemployed former steelworkers remain unemployed for several months until they move, retrain, and get one of these jobs. Structural unemployment is painful, especially for older workers for whom the best available option might be to retire early but with a lower income than they had expected.

At some times the amount of structural unemployment is modest. At other times it is large, and at such times, structural unemployment can become a serious long-term problem. It was especially large during the late 1970s and early 1980s when increases in the price of oil and an increasingly competitive international environment brought a decline in the number of jobs in traditional U.S. industries, such as auto and steelmaking, and an increase in the number of jobs in new industries, such as electronics and bioengineering, as well as in banking and insurance.

Cyclical Unemployment **Cyclical unemployment** is the fluctuating unemployment that coincides with the business cycle. Cyclical unemployment is a repeating short-term problem. The amount of cyclical unemployment increases during a recession and decreases during an expansion. An auto worker who is laid off because the economy is in a recession and who gets rehired some months later when the expansion begins has experienced cyclical unemployment.

Figure 24.10 illustrates cyclical unemployment in the United States between 1980 and 1994. Part (a) shows the fluctuations of real GDP around potential GDP. Part (b) shows fluctuations in the unemployment rate around a line labeled "Natural rate of unemployment." The **natural rate of unemployment** is the unemployment rate when there is no cyclical unemployment or, equivalently, when all the unemployment is frictional and structural. The divergence of the unemployment rate from the natural rate is cyclical unemployment.

In Fig. 24.10 the unemployment rate fluctuates around the natural rate of unemployment (part b) just as real GDP fluctuates around potential GDP (part a). When the unemployment rate equals the natural rate of unemployment, real GDP equals potential GDP. When the unemployment rate is less than the natural rate of unemployment, real GDP is greater than potential GDP. And when the unemployment rate is greater than the natural rate of unemployment, real GDP is less than potential GDP.

The unemployment rate fluctuates around the natural rate of unemployment. But it is possible that the natural rate itself depends on the path of the actual unemployment rate. So where the unemployment rate ends up depends on where it has been. Such a process is called **hysteresis**.

If hysteresis is present, then an increase in the unemployment rate brings an increase in the natural rate. A possible source of hysteresis is the fact that the human capital of unemployed workers depreciates and people who experience a long bout of unemployment usually find it difficult to get new jobs as good as the ones they have lost. An increase in the number of long-term unemployed people means an increase in the amount of human capital lost and possibly a permanent increase in the natural rate of unemployment. The hysteresis theory is controversial and has not yet been thoroughly tested.

Full Employment

There is always *some* unemployment—someone looking for a job or laid off and waiting to be recalled. So what do we mean by *full employment*? **Full employment** occurs when the unemployment rate equals the natural rate of unemployment. There can be quite a lot of unemployment at full employment, and the term "full employment" is an example of a technical economic term that does not correspond with everyday ideas. The term "natural rate of unemployment"

FIGURE **24.10**

Unemployment and Real GDP

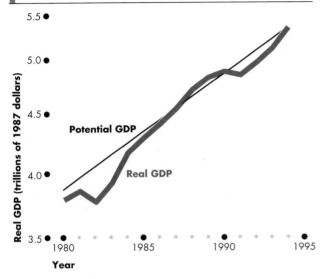

(a) Real GDP

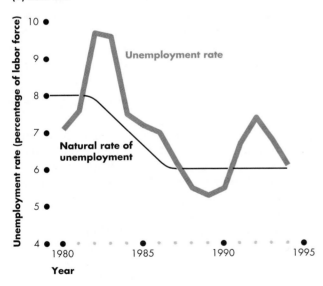

(b) Unemployment rate

As real GDP fluctuates around potential GDP (part a), the unemployment rate fluctuates around the natural rate of unemployment (part b). In the deep recession of 1982, unemployment reached almost 10 percent. In the milder recession of 1991–1992 the unemployment rate peaked at less than 8 percent. The natural rate of unemployment decreased during the 1980s.

Source: *Economic Report of the President*, 1995, and the author's assumptions.

is another example of a technical economic term that does not correspond with everyday language. For most people—especially for unemployed workers—there is nothing *natural* about unemployment. These terms remind us that frictions and structural changes are unavoidable features of the economy and that they create unemployment.

In Fig. 24.10(b) the natural rate of unemployment is 7 percent during the early 1980s and falls to 6 percent during the late 1980s, where it remains into the 1990s. This view of the natural rate of unemployment in the United States is an estimate that many economists would accept. But not every economist would accept this estimate.

There is not much controversy about the existence of a natural rate of unemployment. Nor is there much controversy that it fluctuates. The natural rate of unemployment arises from the existence of frictional and structural unemployment, and it fluctuates because the frictions and the amount of structural change fluctuate. But there is controversy about the magnitude of the natural rate of unemployment and the extent to which it fluctuates. Some economists believe that the natural rate of unemployment fluctuates frequently and that at times of rapid demographic and technological change, its rate can be high. Others think that it changes slowly.

R E V I E W

- The people who become unemployed are job losers, job leavers, and labor force entrants or reentrants.
- Unemployment can be *frictional* (normal labor market turnover), *structural* (a long-lasting decline in a region or industry), or *cyclical* (in line with the business cycle).
- When all the unemployment is frictional and structural (when there is no cyclical unemployment), the unemployment rate is equal to the *natural rate of unemployment.*
- When the unemployment rate is equal to the *natural rate of unemployment*, there is full employment.

We've *described* the trends and fluctuations in employment, wage rates, and unemployment and the anatomy of unemployment. It is now time to *explain* the trends and fluctuations. We begin by explaining the trends in employment and wage rates.

Explaining Employment and Wage Rates

WE CAN UNDERSTAND THE AMOUNT OF EMPLOYment and the wage rate by applying the model of demand and supply to the labor market.

Demand and Supply in the Labor Market

Figure 24.11 illustrates the labor market in 1994. The *x*-axis measures the quantity of labor employed as *aggregate hours*—billions of hours per year. The *y*-axis measures the real wage rate. The figure has two curves, a labor demand curve and a labor supply curve. In the labor market, firms demand labor and households supply labor.

The **labor demand curve** shows the quantity of labor that firms plan to hire at each possible real wage rate. The lower the real wage rate, the greater is the quantity of labor that firms plan to hire. That is, the labor demand curve slopes downward, just like the demand curves you studied in Chapter 4 (on p. 70.) The reason why the quantity of labor demanded depends on the *real* wage rate is that firms care only about the amount they pay for labor relative to the amount they get for their output. If money wages and prices change in the same proportion, the quantity of labor that firms plan to hire is unaffected.

The **labor supply curve** shows the quantity of labor that households plan to supply at each possible real wage rate. The higher the real wage rate, the greater is the quantity of labor that households plan to supply. That is, the labor supply curve slopes upward like the supply curves in Chapter 4 (on pp. 74–75). The reason why the quantity of labor supplied depends on the *real* wage rate is that households care only about the amount they are paid for their labor relative to the price they must pay for the things they buy. If money wages and prices change in the same proportion, the quantity of labor that households plan to supply is unaffected.

The reason why the quantity of labor demanded increases as the real wage rate decreases—why the labor demand curve slopes downward—is that firms strive to maximize profit. If the wage rate at which firms can hire labor falls relative to the price they can

FIGURE 24.11

The Labor Market

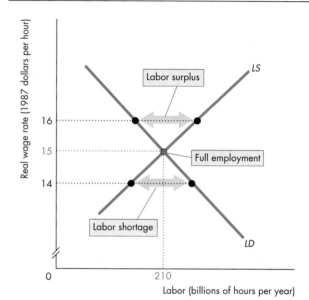

The labor demand curve, *LD*, shows the aggregate hours of labor that firms plan to hire at each real wage rate. The labor supply curve, *LS*, shows the aggregate hours that households plan to work at each real wage rate. In equilibrium the real wage rate is $15 an hour and 210 billion hours of labor are employed.

get for their output, the real wage rate decreases and they have an incentive to expand production and hire more labor. The reason why the quantity of labor supplied increases as the real wage rate increases—why the labor supply curve slopes upward—is that households strive to use their scarce time in the most efficient way. If the wage rate they are offered rises relative to the prices they must pay for goods and services, the real wage rate increases and they have a stronger incentive to work.

Labor demand and labor supply interact to determine the level of employment, unemployment, and real wage rate. In Fig. 24.11, at wage rates below $15 an hour, for example at $14 an hour, there is a labor shortage. People find jobs easily, but businesses are short of labor. But this situation doesn't last forever. Because there is a shortage of labor, the real wage rate rises toward the equilibrium wage rate of $15 an hour.

At wage rates above $15 an hour, for example at $16 an hour, there is a labor surplus. People have a hard time finding jobs, and businesses can easily hire all the labor they want. In this situation the real wage rate falls toward the equilibrium wage rate of $15 an hour.

At a wage rate of $15 an hour the quantity demanded equals the quantity supplied. There is neither a shortage nor a surplus of labor.

The Trends in Employment and Wage Rates

We can use the model of labor demand and labor supply to understand the long-term trends in aggregate hours and real wage rates. We saw in Fig. 24.4 that aggregate hours have increased steadily over the years. In 1960, aggregate hours were 125 billion, and in 1994 they were close to 210 billion. We also saw in Fig. 24.5 that the real wage rate has increased. The average real wage rate including benefits for the entire economy increased from $9 an hour in 1960 to $15 an hour in 1994.

Figure 24.12 shows how these changes came about. In 1960 the labor demand curve was LD_{60} and the labor supply curve was LS_{60}. The equilibrium real wage rate was $9 an hour, and 125 billion hours of labor were employed.

Throughout the period since 1960, labor has become more and more productive. The reason is that capital per worker has increased and technology has advanced. We will explore these reasons for this increased productivity in Chapter 26. But regardless of the reasons, the effect of an increase in labor productivity is an increase in the demand for labor. If an hour of labor can produce more output, firms are willing to pay a higher wage rate to hire that hour of labor. This increase in demand is shown by a rightward shift in the labor demand curve from LD_{60} to LD_{94}.

At the same time as labor became more productive and the demand for it increased, the population grew and so did the working-age population. With a larger working-age population, the supply of labor increased. This increase is shown by the rightward shift in the labor supply curve from LS_{60} to LS_{94}.

To predict the effects of an increase in *both* demand and supply, we need to know which had the larger increase. In this case, the increase in the demand for labor was larger than the increase in supply. As a result, both the quantity of labor employed and the average real wage rate increased.

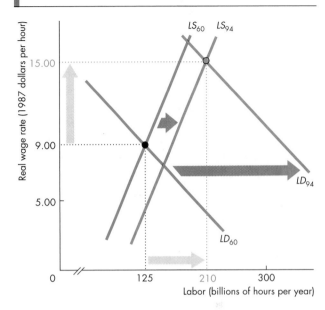

FIGURE 24.12

Explaining Labor Market Trends

In 1960 the labor demand curve was LD_{60}, and the labor supply curve was LS_{60}. The equilibrium real wage rate was $9 an hour, and 125 billion hours of labor were employed. Over the years, advances in technology increased the productivity of labor and increased the demand for labor. The demand curve shifted rightward to LD_{94}. At the same time an increase in the working-age population increased the supply of labor, and the labor supply curve shifted rightward to LS_{94}. But the labor supply curve shifted by less than the labor demand curve. Because both labor demand and labor supply increased, the quantity of labor employed increased. And because labor demand increased by more than labor supply, the real wage rate increased.

Changes in the Distribution of Jobs and Wage Rates

When we looked at the trends in wage rates, we saw that while total hourly compensation has grown, the average hourly wage rates of manufacturing non-supervisory workers has decreased. These changes have brought relative economic hardship to a large number of families. Why have these changes in wage rates occurred?

Figure 24.13 helps us to answer this question. It shows how structural change has increased some wages and employment opportunities and decreased others. The figure describes the U.S. labor market during the 1980s and early 1990s. Part (a) shows the labor market in manufacturing industries— those that produce goods—and part (b) shows the labor market in service industries. In each part, the *y*-axis measures the real wage rate and the *x*-axis measures the quantity of labor in terms of workers, not hours.

In 1980 the labor supply curve in manufacturing was LS_M and in services it was LS_{80}. The labor demand curve in each sector was LD_{80}. In manufacturing, the average real wage rate was $12.60 an hour and 20 million people had jobs. In services, the average real wage rate was $10.00 an hour and 18 million people had jobs.

During the 1980s and through 1993, technological change and international competition brought a decrease in the demand for labor in manufacturing. The demand curve shifted leftward to become LD_{93} in part (a). With no change (assumed) in supply, the real wage rate fell to $11.80 and the number of people with jobs in manufacturing decreased to 18 million. The 2 million people who lost their jobs had to search for a job in the service industries.

The same technological change and international competition that destroyed jobs in manufacturing created jobs in services. The demand for labor in services increased, and the labor demand curve shifted rightward. By 1993, the demand curve had become LD_{93} in part (b).

As people who had lost their jobs in manufacturing looked for jobs in services and as the growing population entered the labor market, the supply of labor in services increased. The labor supply curve shifted rightward. By 1993, the demand curve had become LS_{93} in part (b).

The increase in labor supply was smaller than the increase in labor demand. As a result the real wage rate increased to $10.80 and the number of people with jobs in services increased to 30 million.

The changes that we've just looked at break the labor market into just two parts. In reality, it has many parts and reallocations of labor take place among the many parts. Even while the total number of jobs in services was increasing, some service jobs were being destroyed. For example, jobs for directory assistance operators and television repair people virtually disappeared.

FIGURE 24.13

Labor Force Reallocation

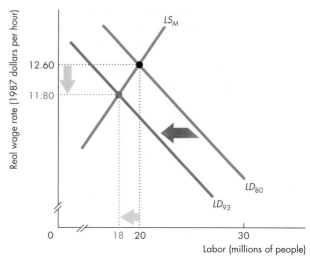

(a) Manufacturing

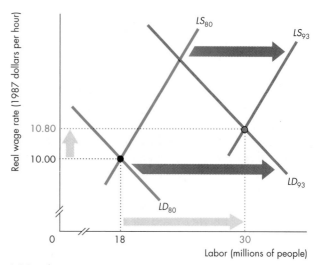

(a) Services

Between 1980 and 1993, the demand for labor in manufacturing decreased (part a) and the labor demand curve shifted leftward from LD_{80} to LD_{93}. In services, (part b) the demand for labor increased and the demand curve shifted rightward from LD_{80} to LD_{93}. In manufacturing, the supply of labor was constant (an assumption) at LS_M, but in services the supply of labor increased and the supply curve shifted rightward from LS_{80} to LS_{93}. In manufacturing, employment and the real wage rate decreased. In services, demand increased by more than supply, so both employment and the real wage rate increased.

REVIEW

- The *labor demand curve* shows the quantity of labor that firms plan to hire at each real wage rate. The labor demand curve slopes downward because a fall in the *real* wage rate gives firms a stronger incentive to increase production and hire more labor.
- The *labor supply curve* shows the quantity of labor that households plan to supply at each real wage rate. The labor supply curve slopes upward because a rise in the *real* wage rate gives households a stronger incentive to work.
- Labor demand and labor supply curves interact to determine the level of employment and the real wage rate.
- Both the real wage rate and employment have increased because labor demand and labor supply have increased but labor demand has increased by more than labor supply.

We've now studied the main trends in employment and wage rates, and we have seen how the demand and supply model can help us to understand those trends. Our next task is to explain unemployment.

Explaining Unemployment

WE'VE DESCRIBED HOW PEOPLE BECOME UNEMployed—they are job losers, job leavers, or labor force entrants and reentrants. And we have classified unemployment—it can be frictional, structural, and cyclical. But this description and classification do not *explain* unemployment. Why is there always some unemployment? Why does its rate fluctuate? Why are there trends in the unemployment rate? In particular, why was the unemployment rate lower during the 1960s than it is today?

If we want to design policies that can lower unemployment, we must answer these questions. We must understand the forces that generate unemployment and that cause its rate to change. Unemployment is ever present and its rate fluctuates for three reasons:

- Job search
- Job rationing
- Sticky wages

Job Search

Job search is the activity of people looking for acceptable vacant jobs. There might be as many jobs as there are people looking for jobs, but there are always some people who have not yet found suitable jobs. The reason is that the labor market is in a constant state of change. Jobs are destroyed and created as businesses fail and new businesses start up and as new technologies and new markets evolve. In the process, people lose jobs. Other people enter or reenter the labor market. Still other people leave their jobs to look for better ones, and others retire. This constant churning in the labor market means that there are always some people looking for jobs and these people are the unemployed. Job search takes place even when the quantity of labor demanded equals the quantity supplied. In this situation, some people have not yet found a job and some jobs have not yet been filled.

Job search explains frictional, structural, and cyclical unemployment. All three types of unemployment occur because job losers, job leavers, and labor force entrants and reentrants don't know about all the jobs available to them, so they must take time to *search* for an acceptable one. This search takes time, and the average amount of time varies. When there is a small amount of structural change and when the economy is close to a business cycle peak, search times are low and the unemployment rate is low. But when structural change is rapid and when the economy is in a recession, search times increase and the unemployment rate increases.

Although job search is cyclical, it also has slower changes that bring changes in the natural rate of unemployment. The main sources of these slower changes are:

- Demographic change
- Unemployment compensation
- Technological change

Demographic Change An increase in the proportion of the population that is of working age brings an increase in the entry rate into the labor force and an increase in the unemployment rate. This factor has been important in the U.S. labor market in recent years. The bulge in the birth rate that occurred in the late 1940s and early 1950s increased the proportion of new entrants into the labor force during the 1970s and brought an increase in the unemployment rate.

As the birth rate declined, the bulge moved into higher age groups and the proportion of new entrants declined during the 1980s. During this period the natural rate of unemployment decreased.

Unemployment Compensation The length of time that an unemployed person spends searching for a job depends, in part, on the opportunity cost of job search. With no income during a period of unemployment an unemployed person faces a high opportunity cost of job search. In this situation, search is likely to be short and an unattractive job is likely to be accepted as a better alternative to continuing a costly search process. With generous unemployment insurance benefits the opportunity cost of job search is low. In this situation, search is likely to be prolonged. An unemployed worker will hold out for the ideal job.

The opportunity cost of job search fell during the late 1960s and 1970s as unemployment benefits were extended to larger groups. As a result, the natural rate of unemployment increased during those years.

Technological Change Labor market flows and unemployment are influenced by the pace and direction of technological change. Sometimes, technological change brings a *structural slump*, a condition in which some industries die and some regions suffer while other industries are born and other regions flourish. When these events occur, labor turnover is high—the flows between employment and unemployment increase and the pool of those unemployed increases. The decline of industries in the "Rust Belt" and the rapid expansion of industries in the "Sun Belt" illustrate the effects of technological change and were a source of the increase in unemployment during the 1970s and early 1980s. The analysis of the changes in the reallocation of the U.S. labor force from manufacturing to services (Fig. 24.13) is also an example of the effects of technological change. While these changes were taking place, the natural rate of unemployment increased. *Reading Between the Lines* on pp. 588–589 also looks at some recent examples of the effects of technological change on employment in some of the nation's biggest companies.

Job search unemployment is present even when the quantity of labor demanded equals the quantity supplied. The other possible explanations of unemployment are based on the view that the quantity of labor demanded does not always equal the quantity supplied.

Job Rationing

Job rationing is the practice of paying employed people a wage that creates an excess supply of labor, a shortage of jobs, and increases the natural rate of unemployment. When there is job rationing, there are fewer available jobs than there are people looking for jobs. Three reasons why jobs might be rationed are:

- Efficiency wages
- Insider interest
- The minimum wage

Efficiency Wages Some firms can increase their labor productivity by paying wages above the competitive wage rate. The higher wage attracts a higher quality of labor, encourages greater work effort, and cuts down on the firm's labor turnover rate and recruiting costs. But the higher wage also adds to the firm's costs. So a firm offers a wage rate that balances productivity gains and additional costs. The wage rate that maximizes profit is called the **efficiency wage**.

The efficiency wage might be higher than the competitive equilibrium wage. If the wage were lower than the competitive wage, competition for labor would bid the wage up. With an efficiency wage above the competitive wage, some labor is unemployed and employed people have an incentive to perform well to avoid being fired.

Insider Interest Why don't firms cut their wage costs by offering jobs to unemployed workers for a lower wage rate than that paid to existing workers? One explanation, called **insider-outsider theory**, is that to be productive, new workers—outsiders—must receive on-the-job training from existing workers—insiders. If insiders train outsiders who are paid a lower wage, the insiders' bargaining position is weakened. So insiders will train outsiders only if everyone receives the same rate of pay.

When bargaining for a pay deal, unions represent the interests of insiders only, and so the agreed-on wage exceeds the competitive wage and there are always outsiders who are unable to find work. So the pursuit of rational self-interest by insiders is a further reason why the natural rate of unemployment is positive.

The Minimum Wage A minimum wage is legislated by the federal government at a level that is higher than what the market would determine. As a result, the quantity of labor supplied exceeds the quantity demanded. This source of unemployment explains why the unemployment rate of young people is persistently high.

Job rationing is a possible reason why the natural rate of unemployment is high. It is a source of persistent and possibly high frictional unemployment. The distinction between unemployment that arises from job search and that which arises from job rationing can be illustrated by musical chairs. If there are equal numbers of chairs (jobs) and players (people who want jobs), when the music stops and everyone searches for a chair, everyone finds one. If there are more players than chairs, when the music stops and everyone searches for a chair, some players can't find one. The chairs are rationed.

Job rationing is a source of long-term frictional unemployment. The final explanation of unemployment is one reason why unemployment is cyclical.

Sticky Wages

Wages do not change as often as prices do. So if the demand for labor decreases, the equilibrium real wage rate falls, but the actual real wage rate does not change immediately. Rather, it gradually falls toward its new equilibrium and it takes some time to get there. During this process of gradual wage adjustment, there is a surplus of labor and unemployment is temporarily high.

Figure 24.14 illustrates this type of unemployment. Initially, the demand for labor is LD_0 and the supply of labor is LS. The equilibrium level of employment is 210 billion hours and the real wage rate is $15 an hour. The demand for labor then decreases and the demand curve shifts leftward to LD_1. But the real wage rate is temporarily sticky at $15 an hour. At this real wage rate and in the new conditions, firms are willing to hire only 200 billion hours of labor. So there is a surplus of 10 billion hours and unemployment is created.

Eventually, as prices and wages change, the real wage rate falls to its equilibrium level. In this example, when the real wage rate has fallen to $14 an hour, the quantity of labor demanded equals the quantity supplied and the surplus of labor vanishes.

FIGURE 24.14

Sticky Wages and Unemployment

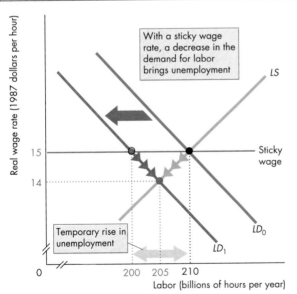

When the demand for labor is LD_0 and the supply of labor is LS, employment is 210 billion hours and the real wage rate is $15 an hour. The demand for labor decreases and the demand curve shifts leftward to LD_1 but the real wage rate is sticky at $15 an hour. Employment decreases to 200 billion hours and there is a surplus of 10 billion hours—10 billion hours of labor are unemployed. Eventually, the real wage rate falls to $14 an hour and employment increases to 205 billion hours.

R E V I E W

■ Unemployment is always present because of job search.

■ The natural rate of unemployment depends on the age distribution of the population, unemployment compensation, and technological change.

■ Some unemployment results from job rationing and sticky wages.

◆ You have now completed your study of labor markets. You have seen the trends and fluctuations in employment, unemployment, and wage rates, and you have seen how these trends and fluctuations are influenced by the forces of demand and supply and the shocks that change the pattern of jobs.

In the chapters that follow, you will return to some of the themes set out here. Chapter 25 continues to look at the long-term fundamentals. It explains how consumption, investment, and saving decisions are made, and it sets the scene for your study of economic growth in Chapter 26 and short-term fluctuations in Chapters 27 and 28.

Structural Change at Work

THE NEW YORK TIMES, MARCH 22, 1994

Job Losses Don't Let Up Even as Hard Times Ease

By LOUIS UCHITELLE

The economy is growing and American companies are prospering, but announcements of job cuts this year are more numerous than ever. While there are no good measures of how much "fat" still remains in corporate America, the pressures are such that cuts seem likely to continue....

This is an unusual moment. Although many American companies have become as efficient and modern as those in Japan and Germany, several forces have arisen that continue to push corporations to shed workers. Advances in technology are allowing companies to produce much more with fewer employees. With price increases hard to get, corporate America increasingly maintains profits by slicing labor costs. And job shedding has become fashionable—the mark of a good manager....

No End in Sight

"It is going to be a permanent condition, that companies are constantly reorganizing and reshaping themselves," said Audrey Freedman, a labor economist and consultant, referring to the job cutbacks that have become a regular event among prosperous as well as hard-pressed companies.

For a while last year, a dip in the number of announced job cutbacks raised hopes that the trend might be tapering off, that corporate America had finally eliminated most of its fat. But that turned out to be illusory.

In January, the announcements of staff cutbacks surged again, to 108,946,... according to Challenger, Gray & Christmas, Inc., a Chicago consulting firm that tallies job cuts. While there was a dip in February, the total of 143,564 for the first two months [of 1994] exceeded the record January-February levels of last year. ...

Cutting the Most

[Listed below are] American companies that since January 1, 1993, have announced the elimination of 10,000 or more jobs. ...Cuts may be stretched out over several years.

Company	Jobs to be eliminated
General Motors	69,650
Sears Roebuck	50,000
IBM	38,600
AT&T	33,625
Boeing	31,000
GTE	27,975
Nynex	22,000
Philip Morris	14,000
Procter & Gamble	13,000
Woolworth	13,000
Martin Marietta	12,060
Eastman Kodak	12,000
Xerox	11,200
McDonnell Douglas	10,968
Raytheon	10,624
Pacific Telesis	10,000

Essence of THE STORY

■ After a dip in 1993, and despite rapid economic growth, announcements of job cuts by U.S. companies reached a new high of 143,564 during January and February 1994.

■ Even though many U.S. companies are as efficient as those in Japan and Germany, advances in technology are allowing companies to shed more workers.

■ Job shedding has become the mark of a good manager.

■ A labor economist said that the constant reorganization and reshaping of companies is going to be a permanent condition.

Economic

A N A L Y S I S

■ Most of the job cuts reported in the news article and listed in the accompanying table will create *structural* unemployment.

■ Figure 1 shows the rate of job destruction in U.S. manufacturing industries during the 1980s. These data are compiled infrequently and are not yet available for the 1990s. But the 1980s data tell us a lot.

■ The rate of job destruction fluctuates with the business cycle. But on the average, about 1 percent of jobs get destroyed each month. And 1 percent of the labor force becomes unemployed.

■ Much of the job destruction arises because technological advances enable companies to produce more output with fewer workers. In fact, this process has been going on almost uninterrupted since the Industrial Revolution in the 1760s.

■ With a labor force of 122 million and a normal rate of job destruction, 1.2 million people would lose their jobs during January 1994.

■ The announced job cutbacks reported in this news article (and frequently reported in the media) are less than one tenth of total job losses. The reported job cuts are the losses in big companies that are shedding labor in large numbers.

■ Most job losses and most new jobs that are created are unreported because they happen in very small companies that often employ only one or two people.

■ Job cuts are serious for the people whom they affect. But they would be even more serious if jobs were not being created in even larger numbers.

■ Figure 1 also shows the rate of job creation and net change in the number of jobs in manufacturing. In most years, more jobs have been destroyed than created in the manufacturing industries. But (not shown in the figure) more jobs have been created in services than the number lost in manufacturing.

■ Technological change creates more jobs than it destroys. It increases the productivity of labor and leads to an increase in the demand for labor.

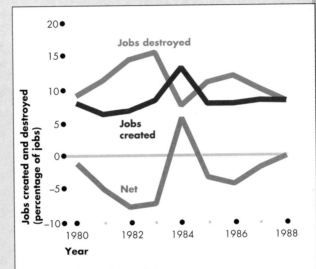

Figure 1 Job creation and destruction rates

Figure 2 Job creation and destruction and unemployment

Sources: Steven J. Davis, John C. Haltiwanger, and Scott Schuh, *Job Creation and Destruction*, U.S. Department of Commerce, Bureau of the Census, Center for Economic Studies, 1995 and *Economic Report of the President*, 1955.

■ Figure 2 shows the total amount of job creation and job destruction in manufacturing during the 1980s and the relationship between this number and the unemployment rate. It shows that the total amount of job creation and job destruction fluctuates in line with fluctuations in the unemployment rate.

SUMMARY

Employment and Wages

The population is divided into four labor market categories: employed, unemployed, not in the labor force, and young and institutionalized people. The labor force is the sum of the employed and the unemployed. The working-age population is the sum of the labor force and the people who are not in the labor force. The population is the sum of the working-age population and young and institutionalized people. These population categories are used to calculate the unemployment rate, the labor force anticipation rate, and the employment-to-population ratio.

The labor force participation rate and the employment-to-population ratio have an upward trend, and they fluctuate with the business cycle. The female labor force participation rate has increased; the male labor force participation rate has decreased.

Aggregate hours have an upward trend, and they fluctuate in line with the business cycle. But aggregate hours have not grown as quickly as the number of people employed because average hours per worker have decreased.

The average hourly real wage rate of private manufacturing nonsupervisory workers peaked in 1973 and then followed a downward trend. Broader measures of average hourly real wage rates do not decrease, but their growth rate slowed during the 1970s with the productivity growth slowdown. (pp. 572–576)

Unemployment and Full Employment

The unemployment rate rises because people lose their jobs (*job losers*), leave their jobs (*job leavers*), and enter and reenter the labor force (*entrants* and *reentrants*); the unemployment rate falls because people get hired or recalled or withdraw from the labor force.

The duration of unemployment fluctuates over the business cycle. But the business cycle has little influence on the demographic patterns in unemployment.

Unemployment can be *frictional* (normal labor market turnover), *structural* (a long-lasting decline in a region or industry), and *cyclical* (the business cycle).

When all the unemployment is frictional and structural, unemployment is at its natural rate, and there is *full employment*. The natural rate of unemployment fluctuates because of fluctuations in frictional and structural unemployment. (pp. 577–581)

Explaining Employment and Wage Rates

Employment and wage rates can be understood by applying the demand and supply model to the labor market.

The quantity of labor demanded increases if the *real* wage rate falls because the cost of labor falls relative to the price firms get for their output.

The quantity of labor supplied increases if the *real* wage rate increases because households face a stronger incentive to work. Labor demand and labor supply interact to determine the level of employment and the real wage rate.

The average real wage rate and total employment have increased over the years because both labor demand and labor supply have increased, but labor demand has increased by more than labor supply. Labor demand has increased because labor has become more productive, and labor supply has increased because the working-age population has grown.

Wage rates and job opportunities have expanded in some industries, mainly services, and have shrunk in other industries, mainly manufacturing. (pp. 582–585)

Explaining Unemployment

Unemployment arises from *job search, job rationing,* and *sticky wages*. The amount of job search unemployment fluctuates with the business cycle, but it also changes for other reasons, which bring changes in the natural rate of unemployment. These other reasons are demographic change, extension of coverage of unemployment insurance, and technological change. A high unemployment rate brings an increase in the natural rate of unemployment because the human capital of the long-term unemployed depreciates, and these people find it hard to get new jobs.

Job rationing, which can arise from efficiency wages, insider interest, and the minimum wage, can be a source of long-term frictional or structural unemployment. Sticky wages—the gradual adjustment of wage rates—can bring cyclical unemployment. (pp. 585–587)

K E Y   E L E M E N T S

Key Figures

Key Terms

R E V I E W   Q U E S T I O N S

1. What are the categories that the Census Bureau uses in its monthly survey to classify the population?

2. Define the unemployment rate, the labor force participation rate, and the employment-to-population ratio. What do these three indicators of labor market performance tell us?

3. Define aggregate hours. Why might aggregate hours be a more accurate measure of the total labor input than the number of people employed?

4. Name three measures of the average hourly real wage rate and describe how each one changed between 1970 and 1994.

5. How do people become unemployed? What is the most common way and what is the one that fluctuates most?

6. How does the duration of unemployment vary over the business cycle?

7. Which groups of the population experience the highest unemployment rates?

8. Distinguish between frictional, structural, and cyclical unemployment.

9. What is the natural rate of unemployment and what is full employment?

10. What is the relationship between the unemployment rate and real GDP over the business cycle?

11. Explain how demand and supply in the labor market determine the level of employment and the real wage rate.

12. What are the main changes in demand and supply in the labor market that have brought employment growth?

13. What are the main changes in demand and supply in the labor market that have brought a slowdown in the rate of increase in real wage rates and a fall in some real wage rates?

14. What are the three main explanations of unemployment?

P R O B L E M S

◆ 1. The Census Bureau measured the following numbers in December 1994: labor force 131.7 million, employment 124.6 million, working-age population 197.8 million. Calculate for that month the
   a. Unemployment rate.
   b. Labor force participation rate.
   c. Employment-to-population ratio

2. During 1994 the working-age population increased by 3.3 million, employment increased by 3.9 million, and the labor force increased by 2.8 million. What happened to the level of unemployment and what do you believe happened to the number of discouraged workers?

3. In January 1994 the unemployment rate was 6.7 percent. In December 1994 the unemployment rate was 5.4 percent. What do you predict happened in 1994 to the numbers of
   a. Job losers?
   b. Job leavers?
   c. Labor force entrants and reentrants?

◆ 4. The labor market in an economy is described by the figure. Initally, demand is LD_0 but then it decreases to LD_1.

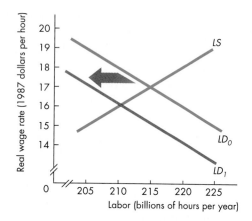

   a. What are the initial levels of employment hours and real wage rate?
   b. When the demand for labor decreases, what are the new levels of employment hours and real wage rate if wages are completely flexible?

   c. When the demand for labor decreases and if the real wage rate is sticky and does not change:
      (i)   What is the level of employment hours?
      (ii) What is the quantity of employment hours supplied?
      (iii) What is the number of hours that are unemployed?
      (iv) During the time that the real wage rate is stuck above its equilibrium level, is the unemployment rate greater than, less than, or equal to the natural rate of unemployment?

◆ 5. You are told the following facts about the economy of Big Time: All the people work in either fishing, Big Time's traditional economic activity, or video game production, Big Time's new found bonanza industry. The working-age population is growing by 1 million people a year and the number of jobs is growing by 1.2 million a year. But jobs in fishing are disappearing at a rate of 2 million a year and jobs are being created in video game production at a rate of 3.2 million a year. What do you predict is happening to wage rates, employment, and unemployment in Big Time both in total and in its two industries. Draw two labor market figures, one for the fishing industry and one for the video games industry, and show how the demand and supply curves are shifting and how wage rates and employment levels are changing.

6. Study *Reading Between the Lines* on pp. 588–589 and then answer the following questions:
   a. What is the number of jobs that disappear in a normal month?
   b. Roughly, what proportion of those jobs are in big, visible companies?
   c. What information would you need that is not supplied in the news article to determine whether the job losses reported will create frictional, structural, or cyclical unemployment?
   d. Which fluctuates most, the rate of job creation or the rate of job destruction?

Investment, Capital, and Interest

After studying this chapter, you will be able to:

- Describe the growth and fluctuations of investment and the capital stock

- Compare investment in the United States with that in other countries

- Describe the fluctuations in the real interest rate

- Explain how business investment decisions are made

- Explain how household saving and consumption decisions are made

- Explain how investment, saving, and consumption interact to determine the real interest rate

- Explain how net exports are determined and explain the role they play in influencing investment

Building the Global Village

When the World Soccer Cup final was played in Los Angeles in 1994, more than a billion soccer fans (one fifth of the world's population) watched the game live. This media event was made possible by an enormous investment in a global video network. An even larger investment in a vast network of computers, telecommunications equipment, and databases enables a grade school student in Alice Springs, Australia, to click her mouse button and surf the Internet or send an email message to her "pen-friend" in Akron, Ohio. How do businesses make the investment decisions that create the amazing tools that are building a global village? ◆ Each one of us decides how much income to save and how much to spend on consumption goods and services. Some of us spend everything we earn and can't wait for the next payday to come around. Others of us save large amounts of income. How do people make their saving and consumption decisions? ◆ Investment, saving, and consumption decisions combine to determine interest rates and the long-term growth of potential GDP. Fluctuations in investment create cycles in real GDP. How do investment, saving, and consumption decisions influence the interest rate you pay on your credit card balance and the interest rate you'll pay when you take a mortgage to buy a home? How do they influence the size of your pension when you retire?

◆ In this chapter, we study the decisions that determine the amount of capital in the economy and the return—the interest rate—that capital earns. The chapter parallels Chapter 24, which studies the decisions that determine the amount of labor in the economy and the return—the wage rate—that labor earns. When you have completed your study of these two topics, you will be able to combine them and learn about the forces that make potential GDP expand, which are explained in Chapter 26. We begin by looking at some facts about investment, capital, and interest rates in the United States and around the world.

Capital and Interest

THE TOTAL QUANTITY OF PLANT, EQUIPMENT, buildings, and inventories is the economy's **capital stock**. The purchase of new capital, called **gross investment**, increases the capital stock, and the wearing out and scrapping of existing capital, called **depreciation**, decreases the capital stock. The capital stock increases by the amount of **net investment,** which equals gross investment minus depreciation. (See Chapter 23, pp. 546–547.)

Figure 25.1 shows investment and capital in the United States from 1970 through 1994. In part (a), you can see that gross investment has grown and fluctuated. In the recession years (1975, 1982, and 1991), gross investment decreased, and in the expansion years, it grew quickly. Part of gross investment replaces worn-out capital. The green line labeled "Replacement investment" in Fig. 25.1(a) shows this amount. This component of investment has grown steadily, but it does not fluctuate much.

Figure 25.1(a) also shows net investment, the addition to the capital stock. Net investment fluctuates like gross investment. In the recession years, net investment fell to about $0.1 trillion ($100 billion). In business cycle peak years, it was close to $0.3 trillion ($300 billion) a year.

Figure 25.1(b) shows how the capital stock has changed over the years. It has grown every year and increased from around $8 trillion in 1970 to almost $14 trillion in 1994. The growth of the capital stock slowed during the recessions, but the growth rate has been steady.

The reason why the capital stock has grown every year is that net investment has been positive. The reason why the fluctuations in the growth rate of the capital stock are small is that net investment is small relative to the capital stock. When net investment falls to a low during a recession, the capital stock grows at about 1 percent a year. When net investment rises to a high during an expansion, the capital stock grows at about 3 percent a year. On the average, the capital stock has grown at a rate of 2 percent a year.

Figure 25.1 shows private investment and the privately owned capital stock. Private investment is business investment plus investment in new homes and additions to inventories. But some investment is public, and some of the capital stock is publicly owned. In the national income accounts, public investment is included in government purchases. Public investment

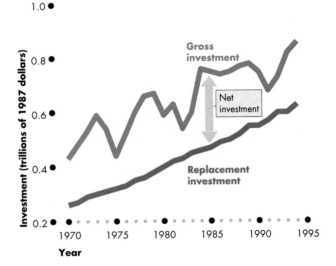

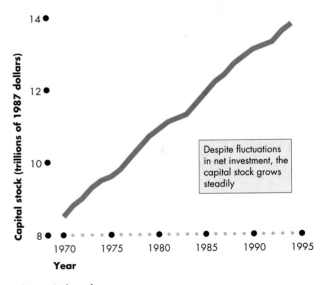

FIGURE **25.1**

Investment and the Capital Stock: 1970–1994

(a) Investment

(b) Capital stock

Net investment fluctuates between $0.1 trillion and $0.3 trillion a year and the capital stock has grown steadily to almost $14 trillion in 1994.

Source: U.S. Department of Commerce, *National Income and Product Accounts of the United States* and *The Capital Stock of the United States*.

is the part of government purchases that creates *social infrastructure capital.* The most basic element of social infrastructure capital is the body of laws and the legal institutions that enforce them. Without this social infrastructure our economy could not have developed. Other social infrastructure capital, for example, highways, dams and canals, schools, and state universities, enhances our productivity growth.

Investment Around the World

How does the amount of investment in the United States compare with that in other parts of the world? Figure 25.2 answers this question. Here investment includes business investment and government invest-

ment and so that we can make comparisons, we measure investment as a percentage of GDP.

Figure 25.2 shows that investment in the United States has fluctuated between about 16 percent and 22 percent of GDP. This investment rate is less than that in the other groups of countries shown in the figure—the industrial countries and the developing countries. The industrial countries are Canada, Japan, Australia, New Zealand, and 18 rich countries in Western Europe. The developing countries comprise the rest of the world. Investment in the industrial countries has fluctuated between about 21 percent and 26 percent of GDP and has been on a downward trend. Investment in the developing countries has fluctuated between about 23 percent and 28 percent of GDP. Investment in these countries has followed two distinct trends: an upward trend from 1970 through 1981 and a downward trend through the 1980s. Since 1975, the investment rate in the developing countries has exceeded that in the industrial countries.

Within the developing economies, those in Asia (such as Korea, Taiwan, and Malaysia) have the highest investment rates and those in Africa and Central and South America have the lowest investment rates. But most of these countries have higher investment rates than that of the United States.

Interest Rates

When we studied labor in Chapter 24, we discovered that over the years both the quantity of labor and the real wage rate per hour of labor have increased. We've seen that the capital stock has grown steadily over time. But what about the return on capital? Has the return to capital grown also? Let's find out.

The return on capital is the real interest rate. The **real interest rate** is equal to the interest rate on a loan minus the inflation rate—the rate at which prices are rising. For example, if the interest rate is 10 percent a year and the inflation rate is 4 percent a year, then the *real* interest rate is 6 percent a year.

Think about the following example. You borrow $1,000 to help finance a year in school. You plan to repay this loan after one year with the income from next summer's job. At the end of the year you pay out $1,100—the $1,000 borrowed plus $100 interest. If prices are rising by 4 percent a year, $1,040 is needed to buy the same goods and services that $1,000 bought a year earlier. So the people who loaned you

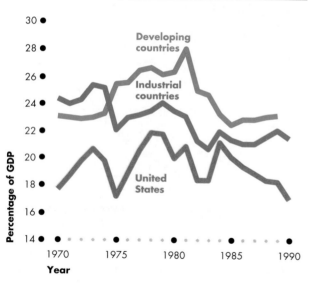

FIGURE 25.2

Investment in the United States and World: 1970–1990

Here investment includes business investment and government investment. Investment in the United States fluctuates between 16 percent and 22 percent of GDP. The United States has invested a smaller percentage of GDP than many other countries have. Since 1975, investment in the developing countries has been a larger percentage of GDP than it has been in the industrial countries.

Source: International Financial Statistics, Yearbook, 1994.

$1,000 need to receive $1,040 just to replace the purchasing power that they loaned. So only $60 of the interest is an addition to their purchasing power. This $60 is the *real* interest income, and the real interest rate is 6 percent a year—$60 as a percentage of the $1,000 loan.

Viewed from your perspective, the amount of summer work that earns $1,000 this year will earn $1,040 next. So when you borrow $1,000 this year, you know that you will get $40 from the higher wages (from inflation) and will only *really* pay $60 in interest, so the real interest rate that you face is 6 percent a year.

In the world economy, there are thousands of different interest rates. But real interest rates around the world move together. One real interest rate that fluctuates with many others is the real interest rate at which big U.S. corporations borrow. In 1995, this real interest rate was about 6 percent a year. The real interest rate at which homebuyers and risky businesses could borrow was higher, and the rate at which the U.S. government could borrow was lower. But all real interest rates tend to move up and down together.

In 1985, the real interest rate was at a peak level. In that year, big U.S. corporations could borrow at an interest rate of 11.5 percent a year and the inflation rate was only 3 percent a year, so the real interest rate was 8.5 percent a year. In contrast, in 1975, the real interest rate was *negative*. Big U.S. corporations could borrow at about 9 percent a year, and the inflation rate was about 10 percent a year, so the real interest rate was close to *minus* 1 percent a year.

Figure 25.3 shows the real interest rate facing big U.S. corporations from 1970 through 1994. Four periods are striking:

1. The 1970s—low (and negative in 1975)
2. Between 1980 and 1985—increased to exceed 8 percent
3. Between 1985 and 1989—decreased to about 5 percent
4. The 1990s—steady between 5 percent and 6 percent

The 1970s were years of economic turmoil that resulted from huge oil price hikes. The 1980s began with a deep recession but then saw the longest ever peacetime expansion. The 1990s also began with a recession and then had a rapid expansion. We'll learn in this chapter how these events influenced the real interest rate.

FIGURE 25.3

The Real Interest Rate

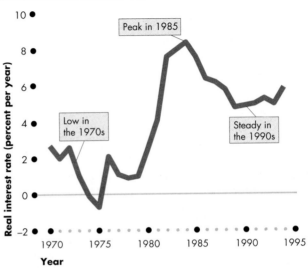

The real interest rate (here, the rate at which big U.S. corporations can borrow) was low during the 1970s and negative in 1975. It increased strongly between 1980 and 1985, and then it decreased through 1989. It has been relatively steady at between 5 percent and 6 percent a year during the 1990s.

Source: Economic Report of the President, 1995, and the author's calculations.

R E V I E W

- Net investment (gross investment minus depreciation) increases the capital stock.
- Net investment fluctuates but is usually positive, so the capital stock grows every year. Fluctuations in the growth rate of the capital stock are small because net investment is small relative to the capital stock.
- Government purchases include investment in social infrastructure capital.
- The U. S. investment rate (the percentage of GDP invested) is lower than the rate in many other countries, especially the developing countries.
- The return on capital is the real interest rate.

We've described investment. Let's now study the investment decisions that businesses make and what determines their demand for investment.

Investment Decisions

How does Chrysler decide how much to spend on a new car assembly plant? What determines AT&T's outlays on fiber optic communications systems? The main influences on business investment decisions are:

- The expected profit rate
- The real interest rate

The Expected Profit Rate

Other things remaining the same, the greater the expected profit rate from new capital, the greater is the amount of investment.

Imagine that Chrysler is trying to decide whether to build a new $100 million automobile assembly line that will produce cars for one year and then be scrapped. Chrysler expects a net revenue of $120 million from operating the plant. Net revenue is equal to total revenue from sales minus the cost of labor and materials. The firm's expected profit from this assembly line is $20 million, which equals $120 million (net revenue) minus $100 million (cost of the plant). The expected *profit rate* is 20 percent a year—($20 million ÷ $100 million) × 100.

Of the many influences on the expected profit rate, the two that stand out are:

1. The phase of the business cycle
2. Advances in technology

During a business cycle expansion, the expected profit rate increases, and during a recession, it decreases. The phase of the business cycle influences the expected profit rate because sales and the rate at which firms use their capital fluctuates over the business cycle. In an expansion, an increase in sales and an increase in the rate at which firms use their capital bring a higher profit rate. In a recession, a decrease in sales and a decrease in the rate at which firms use their capital bring a lower profit rate.

As technologies advance, profit expectations change. When a new technology first becomes available, firms expect to be on a learning curve and so expect a modest profit rate from the new technology. But as firms gain experience with a new technology, they expect costs to fall and the profit rate to increase.

The profit rate calculation does not include the firm's *opportunity cost* of the funds used to buy capital as a cost. Chrysler's profit rate that we've just done ignores the opportunity cost of the funds used to buy the assembly line. To decide whether to invest in a new assembly line, Chrysler compares the expected profit rate with the opportunity cost of the funds to be used. This opportunity cost is the real interest rate.

The Real Interest Rate

The funds used to finance investment might be borrowed, or they might be the financial resources of the firm's owners (the firm's retained earnings). But regardless of the source of the funds, the opportunity cost of the funds is the real interest rate. The real interest paid on borrowed funds is an obvious cost. The real interest rate is also the cost of using retained earnings because these funds could be loaned to another firm. The real interest income forgone is the opportunity cost of using retained earnings to finance an investment project. Other things remaining the same, the lower the real interest rate, the greater is the amount of investment.

In the Chrysler example, the expected profit rate is 20 percent a year. So it is profitable for Chrysler to invest as long as the real interest rate is less than 20 percent a year. That is, at real interest rates below 20 percent a year, Chrysler will build this assembly line, and at real interest rates in excess of 20 percent a year, it will not. Other projects will be profitable at higher real interest rates, and others will become unprofitable at lower real interest rates. Consequently, the higher the real interest rate, the smaller is the number of projects that are worth undertaking and the smaller is the amount of investment.

Investment Demand

Investment demand is the relationship between the level of planned investment and the real interest rate, all other influences on investment remaining the same. The *investment demand schedule* lists the planned investment at each real interest rate, all other influences on investment remaining the same, and the *investment demand curve* graphs this relationship.

Figure 25.4(a) shows an investment demand curve when the expected profit rate is average. Each point (*a* through *c*) corresponds to a row in the table. If the real interest rate is 6 percent a year, planned investment is

FIGURE 25.4

Investment Demand

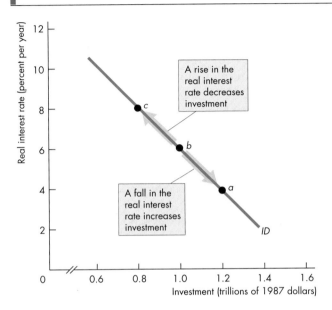

(a) The effect of a change in the real interest rate

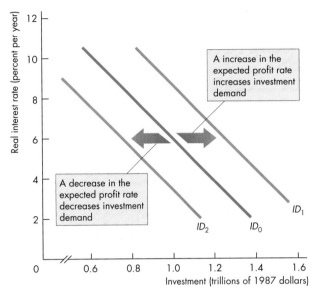

(b) The effect of a change in the expected profit rate

	Real interest rate (percent per year)	Investment (trillions of 1987 dollars)		
		Profit rate expectations		
		Low	**Average**	**High**
a	4	1.0	1.2	1.4
b	6	0.8	1.0	1.2
c	8	0.6	0.8	1.0

The table shows three investment demand schedules for low, average, and high profit expectations. Row *b* states that when the real interest rate is 6 percent a year, investment is $0.8 trillion a year with low profit expectations, $1.0 trillion with average expectations, and $1.2 trillion with high expectations. Part (a) shows the investment demand curve, *ID*, for average expectations. A change in the interest rate brings a movement along the investment demand curve. A change in profit expectations shifts the investment demand curve, shown in part (b). High expectations shift the curve rightward to ID_1 and low expectations shift it leftward to ID_2.

$1 trillion. A change in the real interest rate causes a movement along the investment demand curve. If the real interest rate rises to 8 percent a year, planned investment decreases to $0.8 trillion; there is a movement up the investment demand curve. If the real interest rate falls to 4 percent a year, planned investment increases to $1.2 trillion; there is a movement down the investment demand curve.

Figure 25.4(b) shows how the inevestment demand curve depends on the expected rate of profit. When firms expect an average profit rate, investment demand

is ID_0, the same as in part (a). But when the expected profit rate increases, investment demand increases and the investment demand curve shifts rightward to ID_1. When the expected profit rate decreases, investment demand decreases and the investment demand curve shifts leftward to ID_2. Fluctuations in the expected profit rate are the main source of fluctuations in investment demand.

We've studied the *theory* of investment demand. Let's now see how that theory helps us to understand the changes in investment in the United States.

Investment Demand in the United States

The theory of investment demand predicts that fluctuations in investment result from fluctuations in the real interest rate and in profit rate expectations. Figure 25.5 shows the relative importance of these two factors. The dots in the figure show the gross

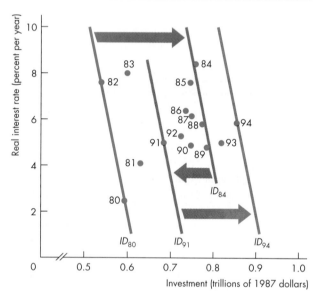

FIGURE   25.5

Investment Demand in the United States

The blue dots show the gross investment and the real interest rate in the United States for each year between 1980 and 1994. When the expected profit rate was low in the recession of the early 1980s, the investment demand curve was ID_{80}. As the expected profit rate increased during the 1980s, the investment demand curve shifted rightward. By 1984, it had shifted to ID_{84}. It remained close to ID_{84} through the late 1980s. When the expected profit rate decreased during the recession of 1991, the investment demand curve shifted leftward to ID_{91}. Then as the expected profit rate increased again in 1992 and 1993, the investment demand curve shifted rightward to ID_{94}. Swings in profit expectations are more important than changes in interest rates in creating fluctuations in gross investment.

Source: U.S. Department of Commerce, *National Income and Product Accounts of the United States,* and the author's assumptions.

investment and the real interest rate in the United States each year from 1980 to 1994. The figure also shows four U.S. investment demand curves—ID_{80}, ID_{84}, ID_{91}, and ID_{94}.

In the early 1980s, the investment demand curve was ID_{80}. The expected profit rate increased during the expansion in 1983 and 1984, and investment demand increased. This increase is shown by the rightward shift in the investment demand curve to ID_{84}. During the late 1980s, the investment demand curve remained close to ID_{84} but began to shift slightly leftward. Then, in 1990 and 1991, the expected profit rate decreased as the economy went into recession. Investment demand decreased, and the investment demand curve shifted leftward to ID_{91}. The expected profit rate increased again in the expansion of 1992–1994, and investment demand increased. The investment demand curve shifted rightward to ID_{94}.

You can see in Fig. 25.5 that investment fluctuates for two reasons: The real interest rate changes, which brings movements along an investment demand curve, and profit rate expectations change, which shift the investment demand curve. You can also see that changes in the expected profit rate (shifts of the investment demand curve) have created larger fluctuations in investment than have changes in the real interest rate (movements along the investment demand curve).

R E V I E W

- Investment depends on the expected profit rate and the real interest rate.
- Other things remaining the same, if the real interest rate falls, investment increases and there is a movement along the investment demand curve.
- When the expected profit rate increases, the investment demand curve shifts rightward; when the expected profit rate decreases, it shifts leftward.
- Changes in both the real interest rate and the expected profit rate play a role in creating fluctuations in investment in the United States but changes in the expected profit rate have the larger effect.

Next, we study the decisions that create the funds that finance investment: saving and consumption decisions.

Saving and Consumption Decisions

A NATION'S INVESTMENT IS FINANCED BY ITS national saving and by its borrowing from the rest of the world (see Chapter 23, pp. 550–551). National saving, which is the sum of private saving and government saving, is determined by decisions of households and by the government's fiscal policy. Here we'll focus on the major source of finance for investment: the saving decisions of households.

Households receive a *disposable income* (earned income—wages, dividends, interest, and profit—plus transfers from the government minus taxes), and they must decide how to allocate that income between saving and consumption expenditure. *Consumption expenditure* is the value of the consumption goods and services bought by households in a given time period and *saving* is defined as disposable income minus consumption expenditure. So the saving and consumption decision is a single decision. It is a decision about how to allocate disposable income between the two actions. Of the many factors that influence household saving and consumption expenditure decisions, the more important ones are:

- Real interest rate
- Disposable income
- Purchasing power of net assets
- Expected future income

Real Interest Rate

Other things remaining the same, the lower the real interest rate, the greater is the amount of consumption expenditure and the smaller is the amount of saving. So an increase in consumption this year means less saving this year, and the interest that could have been earned on that saving is forgone. Thus the opportunity cost of consumption is the real interest rate. This opportunity cost arises regardless of whether a person is a lender or a borrower. For a lender, increasing consumption this year means saving less this year and receiving less interest next year. For a borrower, increasing consumption this year means paying less off the loan this year and paying more interest next year.

The effect of the real interest rate on consumption expenditure is an example of the principle of substitution. If the opportunity cost of an action increases, people substitute other actions in its place. In this case, if the opportunity cost of current consumption increases, people cut current consumption and substitute future consumption for it.

For example, if the real interest rate on your student loan were 12 percent, you might cut your consumption expenditure (buy cheaper food, find lower-rent accommodations) and borrow a smaller amount. Similarly, with a 12 percent real interest rate, lenders try to cut back on current consumption to increase their lending and profit from the high real interest rate. But if the real interest rate on your student loan were 1 percent a year, you might increase your consumption and borrow a larger amount, while lenders might increase their current consumption and decrease their lending.

Disposable Income

The higher a household's disposable income, other things remaining the same, the greater is its consumption expenditure and the greater is its saving.

For example, a student works during the summer and earns a disposable income of $10,000. She spends the entire $10,000 on consumption during the year. When she graduates as an economics major, her disposable income jumps to $20,000 a year. She now spends $16,000 on consumption and saves $4,000. The increase in disposable income of $10,000 has brought an increase in consumption of $6,000 and an increase in saving of $4,000.

Purchasing Power of Net Assets

A household's assets are what it *owns*, and its debts are what it *owes*. A household's *net assets* are its assets minus its debts. The purchasing power of a household's net assets, the *real* value of its net assets, are the goods and services that its net assets can buy. The higher the purchasing power of a household's net assets, other things remaining the same, the greater is its consumption expenditure. That is, if two households have the same disposable income in the current year, the household with the larger net assets will spend a larger portion of current disposable income on consumption goods and services.

Look, for example, at the households of Patti and Tony. Both Patti and Tony are department store executives, and each earns a disposable income of $30,000 a year. In the past Patti saved and now has $15,000 in the bank and no debts. Tony has no money in the bank and owes $15,000 on his car loan. Patti spends most of her $30,000 each year, but Tony tries to keep his consumption at $25,000 so that he can pay off his car loan. (Paying off a loan is not consumption expenditure. When Tony bought his car, that was consumption expenditure. When his consumption is $25,000, he saves $5,000. Therefore what he pays off his loan is saving.)

The purchasing power of net assets is influenced by the price level. The higher the price level, other things remaining the same, the smaller is the purchasing power of net assets and the smaller is the amount of consumption expenditure. For example, if the price level rises by 10 percent, everything else remaining the same, Patti with $15,000 in a savings account experiences a $1,500 decrease in her purchasing power. Patti will probably cut her consumption and increase her saving. But the rise in the price level decreases the real value of Tony's debts, which is opposite to the effect on the real value of Patti's assets. As the purchasing power that Tony must give up to repay his debts decreases, he might increase his consumption expenditure. Most households have assets that exceed their debts, so an increase in the price level decreases consumption expenditure.

Expected Future Income

The higher a household's expected future income, other things remaining the same, the greater is its consumption expenditure. That is, if two households have the same disposable income in the current year, the household with the larger expected future income will spend a larger portion of current disposable income on consumption goods and services.

Look at Patti and Tony again. (Recall that both are department store executives and each earns a disposable income of $30,000 a year.) Patti has just been promoted and will receive a $10,000 pay raise next year. Tony has just been told that he will be fired at the end of the year. On receiving this news, Patti buys a new car—increases her consumption expenditure—and Tony cancels his winter vacation plans—decreases his consumption expenditure.

Although consumption expenditure and saving are influenced by several factors, we focus on two of them: the real interest rate and disposable income. The real interest rate, which is the opportunity cost of consumption, determines the long-run allocation

of disposable income between consumption expenditure and saving. Disposable income is the key short-run influence on consumption expenditure and saving. In the rest of this chapter, our focus is the long run and the real interest rate. In Chapters 27 and 28, we look at the short run and disposable income.

Consumption Demand and Saving Supply

If the real interest rate rises, other things remaining the same, consumption expenditure decreases and saving increases. The table in Fig. 25.6 shows an example of these relationships. It lists the levels of consumption expenditure and saving that occur at three levels of the real interest rate. The relationship between consumption expenditure and the real interest rate, other things remaining the same, is called **consumption demand,** and the relationship between saving and the real interest rate, other things remaining the same, is called **saving supply**.

Consumption Demand   Figure 25.6(a) shows the consumption demand curve for an economy. The x-axis measures consumption expenditure, and the y-axis measures the real interest rate. Along the consumption demand curve, the points labeled *a* through *c* correspond to the rows having the same letters in the table. For example, point *b* indicates a real interest rate of 6 percent a year and consumption expenditure of $3.6 trillion. If the real interest rate rises from 6 percent a year to 8 percent a year, consumption expenditure decreases from $3.6 trillion to $3.5 trillion and there is a movement along the consumption demand curve from *b* to *c*. If the real interest rate falls from 6 percent a year to 4 percent a year, consumption expenditure increases from $3.6 trillion to $3.7 trillion and there is a movement along the consumption demand curve from *b* to *a*.

Saving Supply   Figure 25.6(b) shows a saving supply curve for the same economy. The x-axis measures saving, and the y-axis measures the real interest rate. Again, the points marked *a* through *c* correspond to the rows of the table. For example, point *b* indicates that when the real interest rate is 6 percent a year, saving is $1.0 trillion. If the real interest rate rises from 6 percent a year to 8 percent a year, saving increases from $1 trillion to $1.1 trillion and there is a movement along the saving supply curve from *b*

FIGURE 25.6
Consumption Demand Curve and Saving Supply Curve

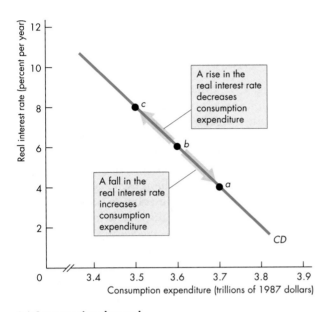

(a) Consumption demand

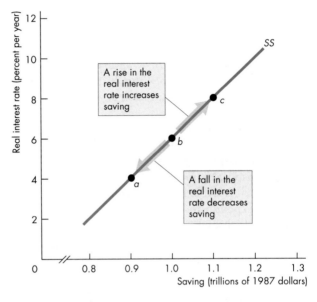

(b) Saving supply

The table shows consumption expenditure and saving at various levels of the real interest rate and for a disposable income of $4.6 trillion, all other influences on consumption and saving remaining the same. Part (a) of the figure shows the relationship between consumption expenditure and the real interest rate (the consumption demand curve). Part (b) shows the relationship between saving and the real interest rate (the saving supply curve). Points a through c on the consumption demand curve and saving supply curve correspond to the rows in the table. At each real interest rate, consumption expenditure plus saving equals disposable income. An increase in the real interest rate decreases consumption expenditure and increases saving. Their total remains unchanged.

	Real interest rate (percent per year)	Consumption expenditure	Saving	Disposable income
		(trillions of 1987 dollars)		
a	4	3.7	0.9	4.6
b	6	3.6	1.0	4.6
c	8	3.5	1.1	4.6

to *c*. If the real interest rate falls from 6 percent a year to 4 percent a year, saving decreases from $1 trillion to $0.9 trillion and there is a movement along the saving supply curve from *b* to *a*.

Along the consumption demand curve and saving supply curve, all the other influences on consumption and saving are constant. One of these influences, and one of the strongest influences, is dis-

posable income. Because disposable income is constant along the consumption demand and saving supply curves, consumption plus saving equals the constant level of disposable income. In the table in Fig. 25.6, disposable income is a constant $4.6 trillion. Because households can only consume or save their disposable income, consumption demand plus saving supply always equals disposable income.

Disposable Income, Consumption Expenditure, and Saving

You've seen how a change in the real interest rate brings changes in consumption expenditure and saving. And you've seen how these changes bring movements along the consumption demand curve and saving supply curve.

Changes in other influences on consumption expenditure and saving *change consumption demand* and also *change saving supply*: that is, these changes alter the quantity of consumption expenditure and saving at each interest rate. They are illustrated as shifts in the consumption demand curve and the saving supply curve. The most important of these other factors that change consumption demand and saving supply is disposable income.

When disposable income increases, both consumption expenditure and saving increase. The extent to which each increases is determined by the marginal propensity to consume and the marginal

propensity to save. The **marginal propensity to consume** (*MPC*) is the fraction of a *change* in disposable income that is consumed. It is calculated as the *change* in consumption expenditure (*C*) divided by the *change* in disposable income (*YD*) that brought it about; that is,

$$MPC = \frac{\text{Change in } C}{\text{Change in } YD}.$$

In Fig. 25.7, disposable income increases from $4.6 trillion to $4.9 trillion. This increase in disposable income increases consumption expenditure from $3.6 trillion to $3.8 trillion. The change in disposable income is $0.3 trillion, and the change in consumption expenditure is $0.2 trillion. The *MPC* is $0.2 trillion divided by $0.3 trillion, which equals 0.67.

The **marginal propensity to save** (*MPS*) is the fraction of a *change* in disposable income that is saved. It is calculated as the *change* in saving (*S*) divided by the *change* in disposable income (*YD*) that

FIGURE 25.7

An Increase in Disposable Income

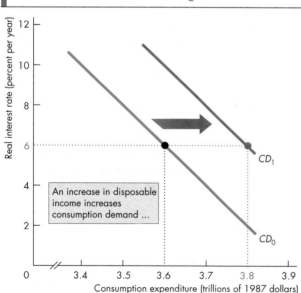

(a) Increase in consumption demand

An increase in disposable income increases both consumption demand and saving supply. The marginal propensity to consume, *MPC*, determines the increase in consumption demand, and the marginal propensity to save, *MPS*, determines the

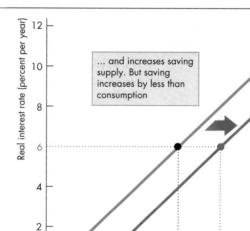

(b) Increase in saving supply

increase in saving supply, other things remaining the same. Here, the *MPC* is 0.67 and the *MPS* is 0.33. An increase in disposable income of $0.3 trillion increases consumption demand by $0.2 trillion and increases saving supply by $0.1 trillion.

brought it about; that is,

$$MPS = \frac{\text{Change in } S}{\text{Change in } YD}.$$

Again, in Fig. 25.7, when disposable income increases from $4.6 trillion to $4.9 trillion, saving increases from $1.0 trillion to $1.1 trillion. The change in disposable income is $0.3 trillion, and the change in saving is $0.1 trillion. The *MPS* is $0.1 trillion divided by $0.3 trillion, which equals 0.33.

Because an increase in disposable income increases both consumption expenditure and saving, it shifts both the consumption demand curve and the saving supply curve rightward. Figure 25.7 shows these shifts. But also, as in this example, because the marginal propensity to consume is generally greater than the marginal propensity to save, an increase in disposable income increases consumption expenditure by more than it increases saving.

Other Influences on Consumption Expenditure and Saving

The other influences on consumption expenditure and saving—the purchasing power of net assets and expected future income—change consumption expenditure and saving in opposite directions, other things remaining the same. That is, any change that increases consumption expenditure, with disposable income remaining constant, decreases saving. For example, an increase in the purchasing power of net assets increases consumption expenditure and decreases saving. Consumption demand increases by the same amount as saving supply decreases. The reason is that disposable income is constant and consumption plus saving sum to the constant amount of disposable income.

Figure 25.8 illustrates the effects of these changes on the consumption demand curve and the saving supply curve. An increase in the purchasing power of

---

FIGURE 25.8

Other Influences on Consumption Demand and Saving Supply

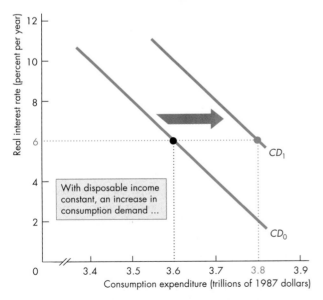

(a) Increase in consumption demand

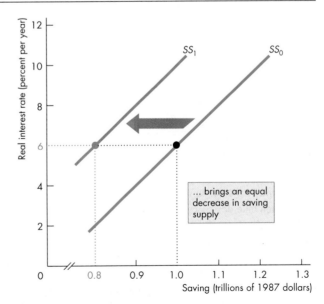

(b) Decrease in saving supply

With a given level of disposable income, an increase in the purchasing power of net assets or an increase in expected future income increases consumption demand and decreases saving supply. The consumption demand curve shifts rightward

from CD_0 to CD_1 (part a), and the saving supply curve shifts leftward from SS_0 to SS_1 in part (b). Because consumption expenditure plus saving always equal disposable income, the rightward shift of CD equals the leftward shift of SS.

net assets or an increase in expected future income increases consumption demand and decreases saving supply. The consumption demand curve shifts rightward as shown in Fig. 25.8(a) and the saving supply curve shifts leftward, as shown in Fig. 25.8(b). The two curves shift by the same amount but in opposite directions.

We've studied the *theory* of consumption demand and saving supply and identified the key influences on these decisions. Let's now see how that theory helps us to understand the changes in consumption expenditure and saving in the United States.

Consumption Demand and Saving Supply in the United States

All the influences on consumption and saving that we have isolated—the real interest rate, disposable income, the purchasing power of net assets, and expected future income—combine to determine fluctuations in consumption and saving in the United States. Let's first look at U.S. consumption.

Figure 25.9(a) shows the U.S. consumption demand curve. Each point identified by a blue dot represents consumption expenditure and the real

---

FIGURE **25.9**

Consumption Demand and Saving Supply in the United States

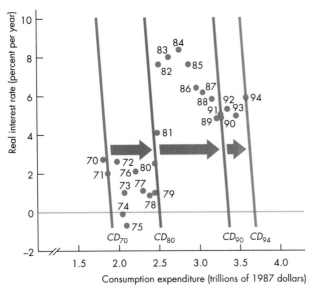

(a) Consumption demand

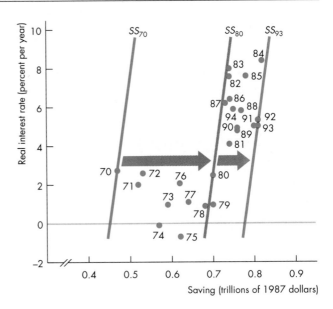

(b) Saving supply

Part (a) shows the consumption demand curve in the United States. Each blue dot represents consumption expenditure and the real interest rate for a particular year from 1970 through 1994. The blue curve CD_{70} is an estimate of the consumption demand curve for 1970. A large change in the real interest rate brings a small change in consumption expenditure. As disposable income increased, consumption demand increased and the consumption demand curve shifted rightward through CD_{80}, CD_{90}, and CD_{94}. Consumption demand increased by more during the 1980s than during the 1970s or the 1990s.

Part (b) shows the saving supply curve. Each blue dot represents saving and the real interest rate for a particular year from 1970 through 1994. The blue curve SS_{70} is an estimate of the saving supply curve for 1970. As disposable income increased, saving supply increased and the saving supply curve shifted rightward through SS_{80} and SS_{93}. Saving supply increased by much more during the 1970s than during the 1980s. In 1994, saving supply decreased despite a large increase in disposable income.

Source: U.S. Department of Commerce, *National Income and Product Accounts of the United States*, and the author's assumptions.

interest rate for a particular year. (The dots are for the years 1970–1994.) In 1970, the consumption demand curve was CD_{70}. This curve indicates that when the real interest rate rises, other things remaining the same, consumption expenditure decreases. But a large change in the real interest rate brings a small change in consumption expenditure.

Over time, the consumption demand curve has shifted rightward, mainly because disposable income has increased. During the 1970s, disposable income increased by $0.87 trillion and consumption expenditure increased by $0.64 trillion. The consumption demand curve shifted rightward to CD_{80}. During the 1980s, disposable income increased by $0.88 trillion and consumption expenditure increased by $0.82 trillion. So the consumption demand curve shifted rightward by a larger amount than in the 1970s to become CD_{90}. As disposable income increased during the 1990s, the consumption demand curve shifted farther rightward to CD_{94} in 1994.

Next, let's look at saving in the United States. Figure 25.9(b) shows the U.S. saving supply curve. Here, each point identified by a blue dot represents saving and the real interest rate for a particular year. In 1970, the saving supply curve was SS_{70}. The curve indicates that when the real interest rate rises, saving increases. But as in the case of consumption, a large change in the real interest rate brings a small change in saving.

Over time, the saving supply curve has shifted rightward and for the same reason that the consumption demand has shifted rightward—because disposable income has increased. But saving supply has not increased by as much as consumption demand. During the 1970s, when disposable income increased by $0.87 trillion, saving increased by $0.23 trillion and the saving supply curve shifted rightward to SS_{80}. During the 1980s, when disposable income increased by $0.88 trillion, saving increased by only $0.06 trillion. So the saving supply curve shifted rightward by a tiny amount (too small to show in Fig. 25.9b). As disposable income increased during the 1990s, saving supply increased again and the saving supply curve shifted rightward to SS_{93} . But in 1994, saving supply decreased, despite a large increase in disposable income.

The reason why saving supply has increased much less than consumption demand is that influences other than the interest rate and disposable income have tended to increase consumption expenditure and decrease saving. During the 1980s, these influ-

ences were the purchasing power of net assets and expected future incomes. With a booming stock market and increasing personal wealth, people were willing to consume more and save less. Expectations of continued rapid economic expansion, which increased expected future incomes, reinforced the effect of increasing personal wealth. The result was an increase in consumption expenditure that almost equaled the increase in disposable income.

You've now completed your review of the influences on consumption and saving in the United States between 1970 and 1994. *Reading Between the Lines* on pp. 616–617 takes a closer look at the effects of interest rates on consumption and saving during the 1990s recovery and expansion.

R E V I E W

- Consumption expenditure and saving decisions are influenced by the real interest rate, disposable income, the purchasing power of net assets, and expectations of future income.
- The consumption demand curve is the relationship between consumption expenditure and the real interest rate, other things remaining the same. The consumption demand curve slopes downward: The higher the real interest rate, the smaller is the amount of consumption expenditure, other things remaining the same.
- The saving supply curve is the relationship between saving and the real interest rate, other things remaining the same. The saving supply curve slopes upward: The higher the real interest rate, the greater is the level of saving, other things remaining the same.
- Between 1970 and 1994, the consumption demand curve in the United States shifted rightward as disposable income increased. The saving supply curve shifted rightward during the 1970s and between 1990 and 1993; but during the 1980s and in 1994, other influences on saving offset the influence of increased disposable income and saving stagnated.

We've now studied the decisions that determine investment, consumption expenditure, and saving and seen that both sets of decisions depend on the real interest rate. But how is the real interest rate determined?

Long-Run Equilibrium in the Global Economy

WE ARE NOW GOING TO SEE HOW INVESTMENT decisions together with consumption and saving decisions determine the real interest rate. To do so, we study the economy of the entire world. Why? Why don't we determine the real interest rate the way we determine the real wage rate by studying the national economy?

The reason is that there is a single world capital market. In contrast, each country has a national labor market. Immigration laws and nationality laws limit the free movement of labor in search of the highest available wage rate. So the supply of labor and the demand for labor in a national economy determine the national real wage rate. But the market in which the real interest rate is determined knows no such restrictions. Capital is free to roam the globe and seek the highest possible real rate of return. So the saving of one country is not necessarily used to finance the investment of that country.

Real interest rates are not identical in every country because some countries are riskier than others and have higher real interest rates. But rates move up and down together. For countries with equal risk, if the real interest rate in one country is higher than anywhere else, capital rushes into that country. The increase in the supply of capital lowers the real interest rate and brings it into line with that in other countries. If the return available in one country is lower than anywhere else, capital leaves that country. The decrease in the supply of capital raises the real interest rate and brings it into line with that in other countries. The world average real interest rate and changes in the real interest rate in each country are determined by global saving and global investment. So the real interest rate is determined by global saving and global investment.

Determining the Real Interest Rate: S = I

Figure 25.10 shows how the real interest rate is determined. The *ID* curve is the world investment demand curve. The *SS* curve is the world saving supply curve. The higher the real interest rate, the greater is the amount of saving and the smaller is the amount

FIGURE 25.10

The Saving Equals Investment Approach

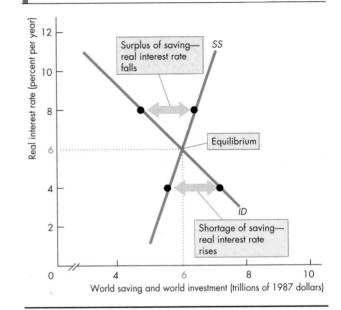

Real interest rate	Investment	Saving
(percent per year)	(trillions of 1987 dollars)	
a 4	7.2	5.6
b 6	6.0	6.0
c 8	4.8	6.4

The table sets out a world investment demand schedule and saving supply schedule and the figure shows the world investment demand curve, *ID*, and saving supply curve, *SS*. If the real interest rate is 4 percent a year, investment exceeds saving. There is a shortage of saving and the real interest rate rises. If the real interest rate is 8 percent a year, investment is less than saving. There is a surplus of saving and the real interest rate falls. When the real interest rate is 6 percent a year, investment equals saving. There is neither a shortage nor a surplus of saving and the real interest rate is at its equilibrium level.

of investment. In the figure, when the real interest rate exceeds 6 percent a year, saving exceeds investment. There is a surplus of saving. Borrowers have an easy time finding the loans they want, but lenders are unable to lend all the funds they have available. In this situation, the real interest rate falls. As it falls, planned investment increases and planned saving decreases. The interest rate continues to fall so long as there is a surplus of saving.

When the interest rate is less than 6 percent a year, saving is less than investment. There is a shortage of saving. Borrowers can't find the loans they want, but lenders are able to lend all the funds they have available. In this situation, the real interest rate rises. As it rises, there is a decrease in planned investment and an increase in planned saving. The interest rate continues to rise so long as there is a shortage of saving.

Regardless of whether there is a surplus or a shortage of saving, the real interest rate changes and is pulled toward an equilibrium level. In Fig. 25.10, this equilibrium is 6 percent a year. At this interest rate there is neither a surplus nor a shortage of saving. Investors can get the funds they demand and savers can lend all the funds they have available. The plans of savers and investors are consistent with each other.

Let's use this model of global saving and investment to explain changes in the real interest rate in the world economy.

Explaining Changes in the Real Interest Rate

In 1995, the real interest rate was unusually high. For the biggest and safest corporations, the real interest rate was about 6 percent a year and it was more than 6 percent a year for homebuyers and risky businesses. Ten years earlier in 1984, the real interest rate was even higher. In that year, it reached a peak level for big companies of 8.5 percent a year. In contrast, 20 years earlier in 1975, the real interest rate was *negative*. Big companies could borrow at about 9 percent a year and the inflation rate was about 10 percent a year. So the real interest rate was close to *minus 1* percent a year.

Figure 25.11 explains why these changes in the real interest rate occurred. Each dot represents world investment and world saving and the real interest rate for a particular year. Part (a) focuses on a short period from 1973 to 1975. In 1973, the saving supply curve was SS_{73} and the investment demand curve was ID_{73}. The real interest rate was 4 percent, and the amount of saving and investment in the world economy was $3.2 trillion.

In 1973, the price of a barrel of oil was $2.70. By 1975, this price was $10.70. Oil producers and exporters experienced a huge increase in income and their saving increased. The world saving supply curve shifted rightward to SS_{75}. Oil users and importers faced steep cost increases and a collapse of profits. With a low expected profit rate, investment demand decreased and the world investment demand curve shifted leftward to ID_{75}. So in 1975, world saving supply was high, world investment demand was low, and the real interest rate fell to −1 percent a year.

Figure 25.11(b) takes up the story at this point. Gradually, investment demand recovered and, except for severe recession in 1982, increased each year. By 1984, the investment demand curve had shifted rightward to ID_{84}. Through these same years, saving supply increased slowly. In fact, in 1984, the saving supply curve was the same as it had been in 1977. The reasons for this slow saving growth are complex. But one factor at work was the productivity growth slowdown of the 1970s. At first, the productivity growth slowdown was seen as temporary, so people still expected their future income to grow. With expected future income growth, consumption expenditure increased and saving decreased. The combination of a large increase in investment demand and a small increase in saving supply increased the real interest rate to 8.5 percent a year in 1984, and world investment and world saving increased to $4.2 trillion.

The rest of the 1980s saw a more rapid growth in the supply of saving relative to the increase in investment demand. A possible reason is that, by then, the productivity growth slowdown was perceived to be persisting and people expected the income growth rate to fall. As a result, consumption was cut and saving increased. By 1989, the investment demand curve had shifted rightward to ID_{89} and the saving supply curve had shifted to SS_{89}. As a result of these changes, the real interest rate fell to 5 percent a year.

You've now seen how saving and investment in the world economy determine the world real interest rate. There is another way of viewing the equilibrium interest rate. The equilibrium real interest rate also ensures that the quantity of world real GDP demanded equals the quantity of world real GDP supplied. This alternative view of the equilibrium real interest rate is interesting because it helps us to see more clearly how decisions in national economies are coordinated. Let's study the demand for world GDP and the way it is influenced by the real interest rate.

FIGURE 25.11

Explaining Changes in the Real Interest Rate

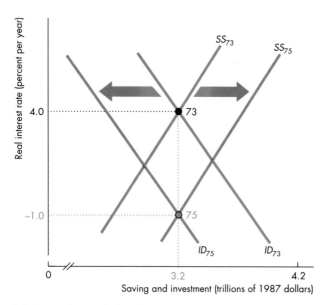

(a) Onset of growth slowdown

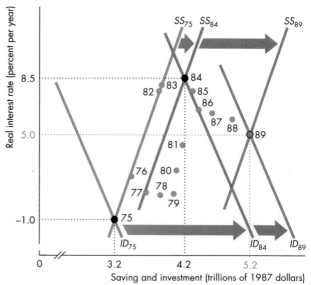

(b) 1975–1989

In 1973 (part a), world saving supply was SS_{73} and world investment demand was ID_{73}. The real interest rate was 4 percent a year. A large increase in the world price of oil increased world saving supply and decreased world investment demand. By 1975, world saving supply was SS_{75} and world investment demand was ID_{75}, and the real interest rate was negative. By 1984 (part b), a strong economic expansion was under way

and investment demand had increased to ID_{84}, but saving supply had not increased by much and was at SS_{84}. The real interest rate increased and reached a peak of 8.5 percent in 1984. During the rest of the 1980s, saving supply increased by more than investment demand, and by 1989, the saving supply curve was at SS_{89} and the investment demand curve was at ID_{89}. The real interest rate had fallen to 5 percent a year.

Sources: "The Penn World Table (Mark 5.5): An Expanded Set of International Comparisons, 1950–1988," *Quarterly Journal of Economics*, May 1991, pp. 327–368, New computer diskette, Mark 5.5, June 15, 1993, *International Financial Statistics, Yearbook*, 1994, *Economic Report of the President*, 1995, and the author's assumptions.

The Demand for Real GDP

The consumption demand curve tells us how consumption demand changes as the real interest rate changes, other things remaining the same, and the investment demand curve tells us how investment changes as the real interest rate changes other things remaining the same. Figure 25.12 shows these two demand curves for the world economy.

In part (a), world consumption expenditure is shown on the *x*-axis and the real interest rate on the *y*-axis. At point *b*, world consumption expenditure is $16 trillion at a real interest rate of 6 percent a year. Along this consumption demand curve, as real

interest rates rise, world consumption expenditure decreases. This consumption demand curve is related to the saving supply curve that you've already used in Fig. 25.10. At each real interest rate, consumption demand plus saving supply equals disposable income. In this example, disposable income is $22 trillion. At a real interest rate of 6 percent a year, world consumption expenditure is $16 trillion and world saving is $6 trillion.

Figure 25.12(b) shows the world investment demand curve. At point *b*, world investment is $6 trillion at an interest rate of 6 percent a year. Along this investment demand curve, as the real interest rate rises, world investment decreases.

Total demand for world real GDP equals consumption demand plus investment demand plus government demand. Figure 25.12(c) generates the demand curve for world GDP. First, it adds consumption demand and investment demand together to create the $C + I$ line. For example, when the real interest rate is 6 percent a year, $C + I$ is $22 trillion ($16 trillion of consumption expenditure and $6 trillion of investment). The rest of the $C + I$ line is constructed in a similar way.

Second, Fig. 25.12(c) adds government purchases to the $C + I$ line. We examine the influences on government purchases when we study fiscal policy in Chapter 29. Here, we will assume that whatever the factors that determine government purchases, they do not depend on the real interest rate. For this example, we assume that world government purchases are a constant $5 trillion. Adding this amount to the $C + I$ line at each real interest rate gives the $C + I + G$ line. This line tells us the quantity of real GDP demanded in the world economy as the real interest rate changes, all other influences on consumption expenditure, investment, and government purchases remaining the same.

FIGURE 25.12

Demand for Real GDP

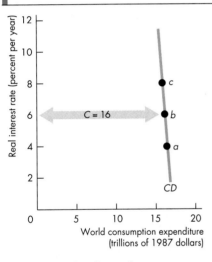

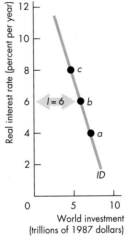

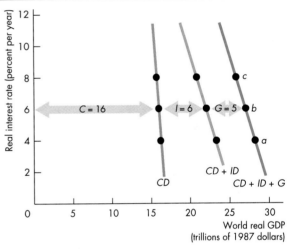

(a) Consumption demand (b) Investment demand (c) Demand for real GDP

	Real interest rate (percent per year)	Consumption expenditure (C)	Investment (I)	(C + I)	Government purchases (G)	(C + I + G)
		(trillions of 1987 dollars)				
a	4	16.4	7.2	23.6	5.0	28.6
b	6	16.0	6.0	22.0	5.0	27.0
c	8	15.6	4.8	20.4	5.0	25.6

The table shows global consumption, investment, government purchases, and total expenditure ($C + I + G$) at each of three real interest rates. By adding global consumption demand (part a) and global investment demand (part b), we get the $C + I$ line (part c). By adding global government purchases to this amount, we get the $C + I + G$ line, which shows how the demand for global real GDP changes as the real interest rate changes.

Determining the Real Interest Rate: $C + I + G = Y_{POT}$

The equilibrium real interest rate, which ensures that world saving equals world investment, also ensures that the quantity of world real GDP demanded equals the quantity of world real GDP supplied. You've just learned how to construct the $C + I + G$ line, which tells us the quantity of real GDP demanded in the global economy at each real interest rate. What determines the quantity of real GDP supplied in the global economy?

On the average, ignoring the ebb and flow of the business cycle, the quantity of real GDP supplied is potential GDP—Y_{POT}; that is, when there is full employment, the quantity of real GDP equals potential GDP.

Figure 25.13 shows the $C + I + G$ line. It also shows a vertical line labeled Y_{POT}, which is potential GDP for the global economy. Here, potential GDP is a constant $27 trillion regardless of the real interest rate. Given the $C + I + G$ line and the Y_{POT} line, we can determine the real interest rate.

The equilibrium real interest rate is 6 percent a year. At this real interest rate, the quantity of real GDP demanded equals potential GDP. Saving also equals investment. If the real interest rate were 8 percent a year, the quantity of real GDP demanded would be less than potential GDP and saving would exceed investment—a surplus of saving. The interest rate would fall. If the real interest rate were 4 percent a year, the quantity of real GDP demanded would exceed potential GDP and saving would be less than investment—a shortage of saving. The interest rate would rise.

This alternative way of viewing the equilibrium interest rate is most interesting when we use it to study an individual country and the forces that determine its net exports. This is our next task.

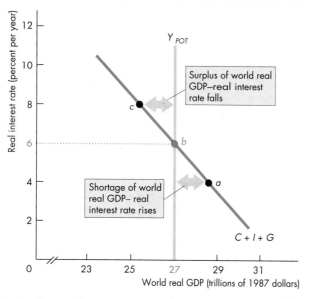

FIGURE 25.13

The Real Interest Rate

When the world economy is producing on its long-term trend, world real GDP equals potential GDP, which is shown by the Y_{POT} line. If the quantity of world real GDP demanded exceeds potential GDP, there is a shortage of world real GDP and the real interest rate rises. If the quantity of world real GDP demanded is less than potential GDP, there is a surplus supply of world real GDP and the real interest rate falls.

REVIEW

- At the equilibrium real interest rate, the world saving supply equals world investment demand and the demand for world GDP equals world potential GDP.

- The world oil price explosion of 1973–1974 increased oil exporters' incomes and increased saving supply. It also squeezed profit rates and decreased investment demand. The real interest rate fell to a low point.

- The 1980s expansion increased investment demand, but saving supply grew by less and the real interest rate rose.

- During the late 1980s, investment demand increased less than saving supply and the real interest rate fell.

We've now studied the decisions that determine investment, consumption expenditure, and saving, and we've seen how the real interest rate is determined. The real interest rate is determined by saving and investment in a global market. Our final task in this chapter is to return to the national economy and see how national investment, consumption, and saving decisions influence a country's net exports and its net lending to or borrowing from the rest of the world.

Net Exports and Equilibrium in the National Economy

IN THE NATIONAL ECONOMY, REAL GDP EQUALS consumption expenditure plus investment plus government purchases plus *net exports*. Each country determines its consumption expenditure, investment, and government purchases. We've seen that these consumption expenditure and investment decisions depend on the real interest rate. But we've also seen that the real interest rate is determined by *world* saving and investment. So what do *national* investment, consumption, and saving decisions determine?

The answer has two parts. First, each country contributes to world saving and investment and so helps to influence the world real interest rate. The larger the country, the greater is that influence. So, for example, the investment, consumption, and saving decisions of the United States, the European Union, and Japan have a significant impact on the world economy and influence the world real interest rate. Other countries individually have a less significant influence.

Second, for all countries regardless of their size, their investment, consumption, and saving decisions, along with the world real interest rate, determine their net exports. Net exports equals real GDP *minus* the total consumption expenditure, investment, and government purchases at the world interest rate. In the long run, when real GDP is equal to potential GDP net exports equal potential GDP minus the total of consumption expenditure, investment, and government purchases at the world interest rate.

Figure 25.14 illustrates the determination of U.S. net exports in the long run. Potential GDP in the United States is $5.3 trillion, as shown by the vertical line, Y_{POT}. The downward-sloping line is the $C + I + G$ line for the United States. This line tells us the quantity of real GDP demanded in the United States and it is derived just like the world $C + I + G$ line in Fig. 25.12. The world real interest rate is 6 percent a year. At this real interest rate, the quantity of $C + I + G$ demanded in the United States exceeds U.S. potential GDP by $0.2 trillion. This excess demand for goods and services spills over into the world economy and brings in imports that exceed exports. Net exports are negative and equal to –$0.2 trillion. The amount of net exports is shown by the arrow in the figure.

FIGURE 25.14

Net Exports and Equilibrium in the U.S. Economy

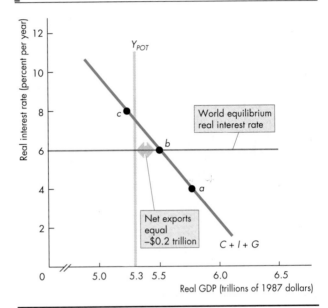

	Real interest rate (percent per year)	Consumption expenditure + Investment + Government purchases (C + I + G) (trillions of 1987 dollars)	Net exports (NX)	Potential GDP
a	4	5.8	–0.5	5.3
b	6	5.5	–0.2	5.3
c	8	5.2	+0.1	5.3

For three levels of the real interest rate, the table shows the levels of consumption expenditure plus investment plus government purchases (C + I + G), net exports (NX), and potential GDP. When the U.S. economy is producing on its long-term trend, real GDP equals potential GDP, which is shown by the Y_{POT} line at $5.3 trillion. World equilibrium determines the real interest rate (6 percent a year here). If the quantity of real GDP demanded exceeds potential GDP, as it does at points a and b, net exports are negative. At point b, net exports are –$0.2 trillion. If the quantity of real GDP demanded is less than potential GDP, as it is at point c, net exports are positive.

Net Exports and the Exchange Rate

What makes the U.S. net exports adjust in the long run to fill the gap between potential GDP and $C + I + G$? The answer is the exchange rate adjusts. Let's see why.

A country's export and import decisions depend on prices in that country compared with prices in the rest of the world. If you can buy an item from a Japanese producer at a lower price than you can buy it from a U.S. producer, the item will be imported by the United States and exported by Japan. The higher the prices of U.S.-produced goods and services relative to the prices of similar foreign-produced goods and services, the larger is the quantity of U.S. imports, other things remaining the same. For example, if the prices of Japanese-produced cars fall and the prices of U.S.-produced cars remain constant, U.S. car imports from Japan increase.

Similarly, if a person in Japan can buy an item from a U.S. producer at a lower price than he or she can buy it from a Japanese producer, that item will be exported by the United States and imported by

Japan. The lower the price of U.S.-made goods and services relative to the prices of similar goods and services made in other countries, the greater is the quantity of U.S. exports, other things remaining the same. For example, if the price of U.S.-produced cars falls while the prices of Japanese-produced cars remain constant, U.S. car exports to Japan increase.

The price comparisons we've just considered actually depend on three sets of prices:

1. Prices in the United States
2. Prices in Japan
3. The exchange rate between the U.S. dollar and the Japanese yen

Suppose the price of a U.S.-produced car is $20,000. A similar car produced in Japan might cost ¥2,000,000. To compare the price in the United States with the price in Japan, we need to convert the prices into common currency units. To make this conversion, we use the exchange rate between the U.S. dollar and the Japanese yen. If the exchange rate is $1 = ¥100, then a Japanese-produced car that costs ¥2,000,000 equivalently costs $20,000. Similarly, the

---

FIGURE 25.15

The Adjustment of Net Exports

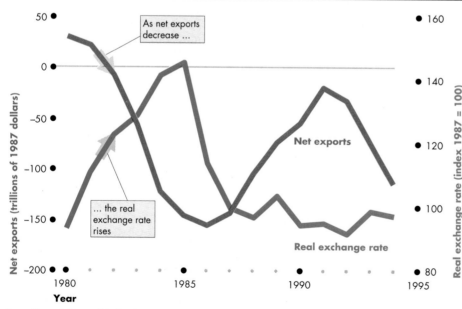

The real exchange rate adjusts to ensure that import and export decisions are compatible with consumption, investment, and government purchases decisions. A decrease in the real exchange rate increases net exports, and an increase in the real exchange rate decreases net exports, other things remaining the same. In the United States, the real exchange rate increased from 1980 through 1985 and net exports decreased. After 1985, the real exchange rate decreased and net exports increased.

Source: Economic Report of the President, 1995.

U.S.-produced car that costs $20,000 equivalently costs ¥2,000,000. If these two cars are very similar, most likely they will be neither exported nor imported by either country.

But suppose the exchange rate is $1 = ¥90. In this case, the Japanese-produced car that costs ¥2,000,000 now costs $22,222 and the U.S.-produced car that costs $20,000 now costs ¥1,800,000. If these two cars are very similar, most likely Japan will begin to import the U.S.-produced car.

On the other hand, suppose the exchange rate is $1 = ¥120. In this case, the Japanese-produced car that costs ¥2,000,000 now costs $16,667 and the U.S.-produced car that costs $20,000 now costs ¥2,400,000. At these prices, the United States will likely begin to import the Japanese-produced car.

The Real Exchange Rate   The three sets of prices that enable us to make international price comparisons can be summarized in a single *opportunity cost*. If the price of a U.S.-produced car is $20,000 and the price of a similar Japanese-produced car ¥2,000,000 and the exchange rate between the U.S. dollar and the Japanese yen is $1 = ¥100, then the opportunity cost of a Japanese-produced car is 1 U.S.-produced car. If the prices remain the same but the exchange rate changes to $1 = ¥90, then the opportunity cost of a Japanese-produced car is 1.11 U.S.-produced cars. If the prices remain the same but the exchange rate changes to $1 = ¥120, then the opportunity cost of a Japanese-produced car is 0.83 U.S.-produced cars.

To compare the prices of all goods and services, we use the concept of the real exchange rate. The **real exchange rate** is an index number that tells us the opportunity cost of foreign-produced goods and services in terms of U.S.-produced goods and services. Other things remaining the same, the lower the real exchange rate (the real value of the U.S. dollar in terms of other currencies), the greater is the demand by foreigners for U.S.-produced goods and services (for U.S. exports), and the smaller is the demand in the United States for foreign-produced goods and services (for U.S. imports). But exports minus imports are net exports so other things remaining the same, the higher the real exchange rate, the smaller is the value of U.S. net exports.

You can turn the last proposition around. The smaller is the value of U.S. net exports, the higher the real exchange rate (the higher is the real value of the U.S. dollar in terms of other currencies).

We can now connect the real exchange rate with the expenditure decisions. If consumption expenditure plus investment plus government purchases increase relative to potential GDP, then net exports decrease (and possibly become negative). In this case, the real exchange rate rises and net exports fall.

Does the real exchange rate actually change in the way we've just described? It does. Figure 25.15 shows the relationship between net exports and the real exchange rate for the United States. Net exports are shown as the red line graphed against the left scale. The real exchange rate is shown in blue and graphed against the right scale. This scale is inverted. The real exchange rate increases as you move down the scale. You can see that when the real exchange rate rises (the real value of the dollar rises), net exports fall and when the real exchange rate falls (the real value of the dollar falls), net exports rise.

R E V I E W

- Net exports adjust to fill the gap between potential GDP and $C + I + G$.
- The real exchange rate adjusts to make decisions about exports and imports compatible with decisions about consumption expenditure, saving, and investment.
- When consumption expenditure plus investment plus government purchases increases relative to potential GDP, the real exchange rate rises and net exports decrease.

◆ In this chapter, we've studied the factors that influence investment decisions and consumption and saving decisions. We've also studied the way these decisions interact in global markets to determine the real interest rate. Finally, we've studied the way the real interest rate determines consumption, investment, and the net exports in a national economy such as the United States.

We've now laid the foundation on which you can study both long-term economic growth and short-term fluctuations. In Chapter 26, you will learn how investment, consumption, and saving decisions influence the long-term growth of potential GDP. In Chapters 27 and 28, you will learn how these decisions influence our economy in the short run and create fluctuations around the long-term growth trend.

Interest Rates, Consumption, and Saving

The Wall Street Journal, December 6, 1994

Higher Costs for Variable-Rate Debt to Put Brakes on Consumer Spending

BY FRED R. BLEAKLEY

It's payback time on variable-rate loans.

As more and more variable-rate mortgages and credit cards are repriced in coming months, the long-awaited economic slowdown will gradually begin to take hold, economists say.

Call it "the reverse of the refi boom," says Susan Sterne of Economic Analysis Associates of Greenwich, Conn., referring to the billions of dollars freed up when consumers refinanced their mortgages at lower rates in 1992 and 1993. That extra cash in consumers' pockets triggered a spending spree and was a major force behind the economy's current strength. But as consumers spend more to service debt, there will be less money "left over for consumption and savings," Ms. Sterne says. ... with $900 billion of adjustable-rate home loans due to be reset at higher interest rates and $200 billion of credit-card debt tied to the prime rate—which has risen to 8.5% from 6% at the start of the year—economists say it's hard to imagine that the current pace of economic activity can continue. ...

Higher mortgage rates will curb home building and related home furnishing purchases, too. Besides making payments less affordable for first-time homebuyers, the higher rates are keeping existing home-owners where they are. St. Louis businessman Ed Stein last year refinanced a 10% fixed-rate mortgage on his home into one charging 6.875%. Now, instead of moving into a larger home, he'll build an addition and stay put. His current mortgage is "too good a deal," he says.

Credit-card holders are also in for a jolt, says Robert McKinley, president of Ram Research Corp. of Frederick, Md. Many didn't realize that the banks managing their card debt had switched to prime-based pricing, rather than the flat 19.8% rate that long had been standard, he says....

More than 70% of the $280 billion in outstanding card debt is repriced, mostly monthly, off the prime rate. ...

"If you know your monthly payments are going up next year, you may not buy a new car," says Maury Harris, chief economist of Paine Webber Inc. "It will definitely have an effect on people's spending." ...

Essence of THE STORY

■ $900 billion of home loans and $200 billion of credit-card debt have variable interest rates, and these interest rates increased during 1994.

■ The higher interest rates will decrease consumption expenditure and slow the growth of the economy.

■ During 1992 and 1993, interest rates on these same loans decreased and triggered spending that was a major force behind the recovery and expansion of the economy following the 1991 recession.

■ Higher home loan rates will decrease expenditure on new homes and home furnishings.

■ Uncertainty about future monthly payments will decrease spending on such items as new cars.

Economic

A N A L Y S I S

■ Figure 1 shows three interest rates: the rate on home mortgages, prime rate, and Moody's Aaa. Consumers pay higher rates than these, but consumer rates move in step with the rates shown here.

■ As reported in the news article, interest rates decreased from 1991 through 1993 and increased during 1994.

■ Consumption and saving plans depend on the *real interest rate*, not the nominal interest rate shown in Fig. 1.

■ Figure 2 shows the home mortgage rate again and two real interest rates. One is the real mortgage rate, which is the mortgage rate *minus* the inflation rate. The other is the real interest cost of home purchase. It is the home mortgage rate *minus* the inflation rate of house prices. The real interest cost of home purchase is more relevant to a homebuyer than the real mortgage interest rate is.

■ Figure 2 shows that the real home mortgage rate began to increase in mid-1993 and that it barely changed during 1994. It also shows that the real interest cost of home purchase decreased during the second half of 1994.

■ Figure 3 shows consumption expenditure and the real interest rate. You can see that the news article is correct when it says that a falling real interest rate brought a surge in consumption expenditure.

■ The rise in the real interest rate during 1993 brought a slight decrease in consumption expenditure—from 94 percent to 92.7 percent of disposable income—during 1994.

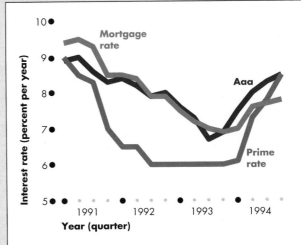

Figure 1   Interest rates

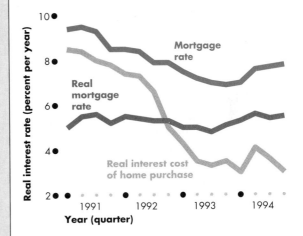

Figure 2   Real interest rates

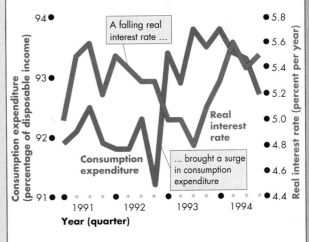

Figure 3   Consumption expenditure

S U M M A R Y

Capital and Interest

The capital stock increases by the amount of net investment, which fluctuates between $100 billion and $300 billion a year. Because net investment is usually positive, the capital stock grows steadily. Investment is business investment plus investment in new homes plus additions to inventories. Some government purchases are investment in social infrastructure capital.

The return on capital is the real interest rate—the interest rate on a loan minus the inflation rate. Real interest rates around the world move together. (pp. 595–597)

Investment Decisions

Gross investment is determined by two main factors: the real interest rate and expected profit rate.

The higher the expected profit rate on new capital, the greater is the amount of investment, other things remaining the same. The two main influences on the expected profit rate are the phase of the business cycle and advances in technology.

To decide whether to undertake an investment, a firm compares the expected profit rate with the opportunity cost of funds. This opportunity cost is the real interest rate. The lower the real interest rate, the greater is the amount of investment undertaken, other things remaining the same.

Investment demand is the relationship between the level of planned investment and the real interest rate, other things remaining the same. Investment demand changes when the expected profit rate changes. When firms expect a high profit rate, investment demand increases; when firms expect a low profit rate, investment demand decreases. (pp. 598–600)

Saving and Consumption Decisions

A household's consumption expenditure depends on its disposable income, the purchasing power of its net assets, and its expected future income. The higher a household's disposable income, purchasing power of its net assets, and expected future income, the greater is its consumption expenditure.

The relationship between consumption expenditure and the real interest rate is called consumption demand, and the relationship between saving and the real interest rate is called saving supply. As disposable income increases, other things remaining the same, both consumption demand and saving supply increase. An increase in the purchasing power of net assets or expected future income increases consumption demand and decreases saving supply. (pp. 601–607)

Long-Run Equilibrium in the Global Economy

Because capital is free to move internationally to seek the highest possible real rate of return, the real interest rate is determined in a global market. The equilibrium real interest rate makes global saving equal to global investment. Equivalently, the equilibrium real interest rate makes global consumption expenditure plus global investment plus global government purchases equal to global potential GDP. (pp. 608–612)

Net Exports and Equilibrium in the National Economy

In the national economy, foreign borrowing (the negative of net exports) fills the gap between domestic resources and investment. That is, net exports adjust to fill the gap between potential GDP and $C + I + G$, or, equivalently, they adjust to fill the gap between investment and national saving.

Changes in the real exchange rate make decisions about exports and imports compatible with decisions about investment, consumption, and saving. When investment exceeds national saving by a large amount, net exports become increasingly negative and the real exchange rate rises, making U.S.-produced goods expensive relative to foreign-produced goods. (pp. 613–615)

R E V I E W   Q U E S T I O N S

1. Which component of gross investment fluctuates the most, net investment or replacement investment?

2. Why does the capital stock grow smoothly when net investment fluctuates?

3. What is the real interest rate?

4. Describe how the real interest rate has changed since 1975.

5. What determines investment?

6. Why does a fall in the real interest rate increase investment?

7. List the main influences on consumption expenditure.

8. What is the consumption demand curve?

9. What is the saving supply curve?

10. What is the relationship between the saving supply curve and the consumption demand curve?

11. How do consumption demand and saving supply change when disposable income changes?

12. What are the marginal propensity to consume and the marginal propensity to save?

13. What happens to the consumption demand curve and the saving supply curve when expected future incomes or the purchasing power of assets increases?

14. Explain how the real interest rate is determined.

15. Describe the two approaches to determining the real interest rate and explain why they are equivalent.

16. How are U.S. net exports determined?

P R O B L E M S

◆ 1. A cellular phone assembly plant costs $10 million and has a life of one year. The firm will have to hire labor at a cost of $3 million and buy parts and fuel at a cost of a further $3 million. If the firm builds the plant, it will be able to produce cellular telephones that will sell for $17 million. Does it pay the firm to invest in this new production line at the following real interest rates:
   a.   5 percent a year?
   b.   10 percent a year?
   c.   15 percent a year?

2. Suppose the phone producer in problem 1 expects its total revenue to increase to $17.5 million with unchanged costs. What now is the highest real interest rate at which it will undertake the investment? How does the firm's investment demand curve change as a result of its expected profit rate increasing?

◆ 3. You are given the following information about the Batman family (Batman and Robin):

Consumption and Saving in 1994

Real interest rate (percent per year)	Consumption expenditure	Saving	Disposable income
	(thousands of dollars a year)		
4	80	20	100
6	75	25	100
8	60	40	100

Consumption and Saving in 1995

Real interest rate (percent per year)	Consumption expenditure	Saving	Disposable income
	(thousands of dollars a year)		
4	88.0	22.0	110
6	82.5	27.5	110
8	66.0	44.0	110

   a.   Draw a graph of the Batman family's consumption demand curve and saving supply curve for 1994 and 1995.
   b.   Calculate the Batman family's marginal propensity to consume.
   c.   Calculate their marginal propensity to save.

◆ 4. The economy of Alpha Centura, still isolated from all other planets, has the following consumption demand and investment demand schedules:

Real interest rate (percent per year)	Consumption expenditure	Investment
	(trillions of 3050 zips)	
4	28	7
5	24	6
6	20	5
7	16	4
8	12	3

Alpha Centura's government budget is balanced. Government purchases are 10 trillion zips. Potential GDP on Alpha Centura is 30 trillion zips.
   a.   What is the equilibrium real interest rate?
   b.   What is the equilibrium investment?
   c.   What is the equilibrium consumption expenditure?
   d.   Find the level of saving on Alpha Centura at each interest rate shown in the table.

◆ 5. Alpha Centura and Earth discover each other and begin to pursue intergalactic economic activity. The real interest rate on Earth is 6 percent a year. On Alpha Centura, it is the number you calculated for problem 6.
   a.   Which planet borrows from the other?
   b.   Do consumption and saving on Alpha Centura increase or decrease?
   c.   Do consumption and saving on Earth increase or decrease?

6. Study *Reading Between the Lines* on pp. 616–617 and then answer the following questions:
   a.   What happened to the real interest rate during 1994?
   b.   What happened to the real interest cost of buying a home during 1994?
   c.   Describe the relationship between the real interest rate and consumption expenditure during the 1990s expansion. Does the relationship agree with the theory of consumption demand and saving supply?

Chapter 26

Long-Term Economic Growth

After studying this chapter, you will be able to:

- Describe the long-term growth trends in the United States and other countries and regions

- Explain the main factors that influence the long-term growth rate of real GDP

- Explain the productivity growth slow-down in the United States during the 1970s

- Explain the rapid economic growth rates being achieved in East Asia

- Explain the theories of economic growth

- Describe the policies that might be used to speed up economic growth

Almost every year, we become more productive. Our economy expands, and our incomes grow. In the United States, real GDP per person almost doubled between 1960 and 1995. If you live in a dorm, chances are it was built during the 1960s and equipped with two electricity outlets, one for a desk lamp and one for a bedside lamp. Today, with the help of a power bar (or two), your room might bulge with a television and VCR, CD player, microwave, refrigerator,

Economic Miracles

coffee maker, toaster, and computer—the list goes on— that were not contemplated in the 1960s when the dorm you live in was built. What has brought about this growth in productivity and incomes? ◆ Although our economy expands, its growth is uneven. In some periods, such as the 1960s, growth is rapid. In other periods, such as the late 1970s and early 1980s, growth slows down. What makes our long-term growth rate vary? What can be done to prevent growth from slowing down? What can be done to speed up economic growth? ◆ We can see greater extremes of economic growth if we look at modern Asia. On the banks of the Li River in Southern China, Songman Yang breeds cormorants, amazing birds that he trains to fish and to deliver their catch to a basket on his simple bamboo raft. Songman's work, the capital equipment and technology he uses, and the income he earns are similar to those of his ancestors going back some 2,000 years. Yet all around Songman, in China's bustling villages, towns, and cities, people are participating in an economic miracle. They are creating businesses, investing in new technologies, developing both local and global markets, and experiencing income growth of more than 6 percent a year. Similar rapid economic growth is taking place in other economies in Asia such as Hong Kong, Korea, Singapore, and Taiwan. In all these countries, real GDP has doubled *three times*—an eightfold increase— between 1960 and 1995. Why have incomes in these Asian economies grown so rapidly? What makes an economic miracle?

◇ In this chapter we study long-term economic growth. We begin by looking more closely at the facts about long-term economic growth in the United States and other parts of the world. We then discover what makes real GDP grow, why some countries grow faster than others, and why the long-term growth rate some-times slows down. We'll also look at ways of achieving faster economic growth.

Long-Term Growth Trends

THE LONG-TERM GROWTH TRENDS THAT WE study in this chapter are the trends in *potential GDP*. Potential GDP growth has two components: population growth and growth in potential GDP per person. It is the growth of potential GDP per person that brings rising living standards. And it is changes in the growth of potential GDP per person that are the main causes for concern about economic growth. Let's look at the growth of real GDP per person in the United States.

Growth in the U.S. Economy

Figure 26.1 shows real GDP per person in the United States for the hundred years from 1895 to 1995. The average growth rate over this entire period is 1.7 percent a year. But the long-term growth rate has varied. For example, the growth rate slowed after 1973 to 1.4 percent a year, down from 2.5 percent a year dur-

ing the 1960s. This productivity growth slowdown was described in Chapter 22 (pp. 519–520).

You can see the present productivity growth slowdown in a longer perspective in Fig. 26.1 and can see that it is not unique. The the early years of the 1900s and the mid-1950s had even slower growth than we have today. The rapid growth of the 1960s was not unusual either. The 1920s was a period of similarly rapid growth.

In the middle of the graph are two extraordinary events: the Great Depression of the 1930s and World War II of the 1940s. The fall in real GDP during the depression and the bulge during the war obscure any changes in the long-term growth trend that might have occurred within these years. But between 1929 and 1953, averaging out the depression and the war, the long-term growth rate was 1.8 percent a year.

A major goal of this chapter is to explain why our economy grows and why the long-term growth rate varies. A related goal is to explain variations in the economic growth rate across countries. Let's look at some facts about these variations.

FIGURE 26.1

A Hundred Years of Economic Growth in the United States

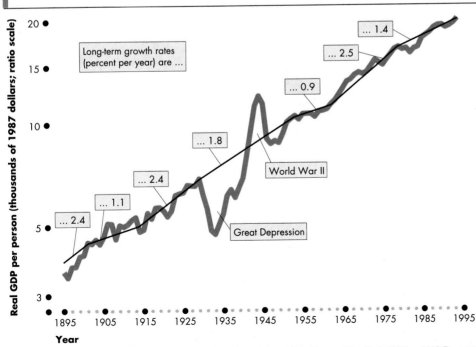

During the 100 years from 1895 to 1995, real GDP per person in the United States grew by 1.7 percent a year, on the average. The growth rate was above average during the 1920s and 1960s, and it was below average in 1901–1920, the 1950s, and 1974–1994.

Source: Angus Maddison, Oxford University Press, *Dynamic Forces in Capitalist Development*, (New York: 1991), and U.S. Department of Commerce, *National Income and Product Accounts of the United States*, (Washington D.C.: U.S. Government Printing Office).

Real GDP Growth in the World Economy

Figure 26.2 shows real GDP growth in the United States and in some other countries since 1960. The data shown in this figure are in 1985 dollars. Part (a) looks at the richest countries. The United States has the highest real GDP per person, and Canada has the second highest. But Canada has grown faster than the United States and so has been catching up.

Until 1984 the third richest countries were France, Germany, Italy, and the United Kingdom. They are shown in Fig. 26.2(a) as Europe Big 4. But in 1984 the fastest growing rich country, Japan, caught up with Europe Big 4. All the countries shown in Fig. 26.2(a) are catching up with the United States. Japan

has caught up most, Canada has got closest, and Europe Big 4 has caught up least.

Not all countries are growing faster than, and catching up with, the United States. Figure 26.2(b) looks at some of these. Africa and Central and South America were stagnating, not growing, during the 1980s. As a result, the gap between them and the United States widened. Western Europe other than the Big 4 countries and the former Communist countries of Central Europe grew during the 1970s and 1980s but at a rate that was roughly equal to that of the United States. So the gap remained constant.

The data used in Fig. 26.2 are not currently available beyond 1990. But other data (not shown in Fig. 26.2) suggest that after 1990, real GDP per person shrank in some of the countries of Central

---

FIGURE **26.2**

Economic Growth Around the World: Catch-Up or Not?

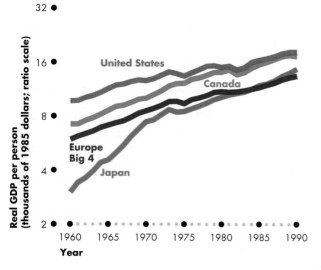

(a) Catch up?

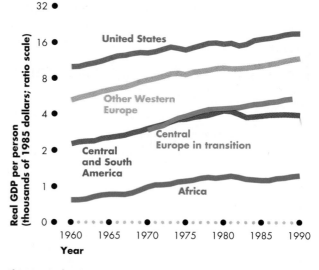

(b) No catch up?

Real GDP per person has grown throughout the world economy. Among the rich industrial countries (part a), real GDP growth has been faster in Canada, the big four Western European countries (France, Germany, Italy, and the United Kingdom), and Japan and they are catching up. The most spectacular growth was in Japan during the 1960s. The income level in Canada has also become closest to the U.S. income level.

Among a wider range of countries (part b), there is less sign of convergence. The gaps between the income levels of the United States, other Western European countries, Central Europe, Central and South America, and Africa have remained remarkably constant.

Source: Robert Summers and Alan Heston, New Computer Diskette (Mark 5.5), June 15, 1993, distributed by the National Bureau of Economic Research to update "The Penn World Table (Mark 5): An Expanded Set of International Comparisons, 1950–1988" *Quarterly Journal of Economics*, May 1991, 327–368.

Europe as they went through a process of traumatic political change.

Taking both parts of Fig. 26.2 together, we can see that the catch-up in real GDP per person that is visible in part (a) is not a global phenomenon. Some rich countries are catching up with the United States, but the gaps between the United States and many poor countries are not closing.

Another group of countries that in 1960 had low levels of real GDP per person are catching up with the United States in a dramatic way. These are Hong Kong, Korea, Singapore, and Taiwan. Figure 26.3

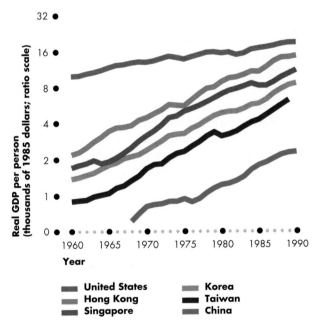

FIGURE   26.3
Catch-Up in Asia

The clearest examples of catch-up have occurred in five economies in Asia. Starting out in 1960 with incomes as little as one tenth of that in the United States, four Asian economies (Hong Kong, Korea, Singapore, and Taiwan) have substantially narrowed the gap on the United States. And from being a very poor developing country in 1960, China's income level now exceeds the income level that Hong Kong had in 1960. China is growing at a rate that is enabling it to continue to catch up with the United States.

Source: Robert Summers and Alan Heston, New Computer Diskette (Mark 5.5), June 15 1993, distributed by the National Bureau of Economic Research to update "The Penn World Table (Mark 5): An Expanded Set of International Comparisons, 1950–1988" Quarterly Journal of Economics, May 1991, 327–368.

shows how these countries are catching up with the United States. The figure also shows that China is catching up, but from a very long way behind. In 1968 (the earliest year for which we have data), China's real GDP per person was one twentieth that of the United States, but by 1990 it was one eighth.

The five Asian countries shown in Fig. 26.3 are like fast trains running on the same track at similar speeds and with a roughly constant gap between them. Hong Kong is the lead train and runs about 30 years in front of China, which is the last train. Real GDP per person in China in 1990 was similar to that in Hong Kong in 1960, thirty years earlier. Between 1960 and 1990, Hong Kong transformed itself from a poor developing country into one of the world's richest countries. It is possible that between 1990 and 2020, China will do the same. If this outcome does occur, it will be much more significant for the United States and the world economy than Hong Kong's growth because China is equivalent to more than 200 countries the size of Hong Kong. Whether China will continue on its current path of rapid growth is impossible to predict.

R E V I E W

■ Over the hundred years between 1895 and 1995, real GDP per person in the United States grew at an average rate of 1.7 percent a year. Slow growth occurred during the early 1900s, mid-1950s, and 1974–1994, and rapid growth occurred during the 1920s and 1960s.

■ Some rich countries are catching up with the United States, but the gaps between the United States and many poor countries are not closing.

■ Hong Kong, Korea, Singapore, Taiwan, and China are catching up fastest.

We've described some facts about economic growth in the United States and around the world. Our next task is to study the causes of economic growth. Economic growth is a complex process, and its causes are difficult to discover. We'll study the causes of economic growth in three stages. First, we'll describe the sources of growth. Second, we'll study growth accounting, which is an attempt to measure the quantitative importance of the sources of growth. Third, we'll study the theories of economic growth that explain how the sources of growth interact to determine the growth rate.

The Sources of Economic Growth

MOST HUMAN SOCIETIES HAVE LIVED FOR centuries and even thousands of years, like Songman Yang, with no economic growth. The key reason is that they have lacked some fundamental social institutions and arrangements that are essential preconditions for economic growth. Let's see what these preconditions are.

Preconditions for Economic Growth

The most basic precondition for economic growth is an appropriate *incentive* system. Three institutions are crucial to the creation of incentives. They are:

1. Markets
2. Property rights
3. Monetary exchange

You studied these institutions in Chapter 3 (pp. 57–58), so here we'll give you just a brief reminder of what you've already learned. Markets enable buyers and sellers to get information and to do business with each other, and market prices send signals to buyers and sellers that create incentives to increase or decrease the quantities demanded and supplied. Markets enable people to specialize and trade and to save and invest. But to work well, markets need property rights and monetary exchange.

Property rights are the social arrangements that govern the ownership, use, and disposal of factors of production and goods and services. They include the rights to physical property (land, buildings, and capital equipment), to financial property (claims by one person against another), and to intellectual property (such as inventions). Clearly established and enforced property rights give people an assurance that the income they earn and their savings will not be confiscated by a capricious government. Monetary exchange facilitates transactions of all kinds, including the orderly transfer of private property from one person to another. Property rights and monetary exchange create incentives for people to specialize and trade, to save and invest, and to discover new technologies.

No unique political system is necessary to deliver the preconditions for economic growth. Liberal democracy, founded on the fundamental principle of the rule of law, is the system that does the best job. It provides a solid base on which property rights can be established and enforced. But authoritarian political systems have sometimes provided an environment in which economic growth has occurred.

Early human societies, based on hunting and gathering, did not experience economic growth because they lacked the preconditions we've just described. Economic growth began when societies evolved these institutions. The presence of an incentive system and the institutions that create it does not guarantee that economic growth will occur. It permits economic growth but does not make that growth inevitable.

The simplest way in which growth happens when the appropriate incentive system exists is that people begin to specialize in the activities at which they have a comparative advantage and trade with each other. You saw in Chapter 3 how everyone can gain from such activity. By specializing and trading, everyone can acquire goods and services at the lowest possible cost. Equivalently, people can obtain a greater volume of goods and services from their labor.

As an economy moves from one with little specialization to one that is highly specialized, it grows. Real GDP per person increases and the standard of living rises. But once the economy is highly specialized, this source of economic growth runs its course.

For growth to continue, people must face incentives that encourage them to pursue three activities that generate ongoing economic growth. These activities are:

■ Saving and investment in new capital
■ Investment in human capital
■ Discovery of new technologies

These three sources of growth, which interact with each other, are the primary sources of the extraordinary growth in productivity during the past 200 years. Let's look at each in turn.

Saving and Investment in New Capital

Saving and investment in new capital increase the amount of capital per worker and increase human productivity. Human productivity took the most dramatic upturn when the amount of capital per worker increased during the Industrial Revolution. Production processes that use hand tools can create beautiful objects, but production methods that use large amounts of capital per worker, such as auto plant assembly lines, are much more productive. The accumulation of capital on farms, in textile factories, in iron foundries and steel mills, in coal mines, on building sites, in chemical plants, in auto plants, in banks and insurance companies, and in shopping malls has added incredibly to the productivity of our economy. The next time you see a Western movie, look carefully at the small amount of capital around. Try to imagine how productive you would be in such circumstances compared with your productivity today.

Investment in Human Capital

Human capital—the accumulated skill and knowledge of human beings—is the most fundamental source of economic growth. It is a source of both increased productivity and technological advance.

The development of one of the most basic human skills, writing, was the source of some of the earliest major gains in productivity. The ability to keep written records made it possible to extend the division of labor and to reap ever larger gains from specialization and exchange. Imagine how hard it would be to do any kind of business if all the accounts, invoices, and agreements existed only in people's memories.

Later, the development of mathematics laid the foundation for the eventual extension of knowledge about physical forces and chemical and biological processes. This base of scientific knowledge was the foundation for the technological advances of the Industrial Revolution 200 years ago and of today's Information Revolution.

But much human capital that is extremely productive is much more humble. It takes the form of millions of individuals learning and repetitively doing simple production tasks and becoming remarkably more productive in the tasks.

One carefully studied example illustrates the importance of this kind of human capital. Between 1941 and 1944 (during World War II), U.S. shipyards produced some 2,500 units of a cargo ship, called the Liberty Ship, to a standardized design. In 1941 it took 1.2 million person-hours to build a ship. By 1942 it took 600,000, and by 1943 it took only 500,000. Thousands of workers and managers learned from experience and accumulated human capital that more than doubled their productivity in two years.

Discovery of New Technologies

Saving and investment in new capital and the accumulation of human capital have made a large contribution to economic growth. But the contribution of technological change—of the discovery and the application of new technologies and new goods—has made an even greater contribution.

People are many times more productive today than they were a hundred years ago. We are not more productive because we have more steam engines per person and more horse drawn carriages per person. Rather, it is because we have the engines and transportation equipment that use technologies that were unknown a hundred years ago and that are more productive than the old technologies were. Technological change makes an enormous contribution to our increased productivity. It arises from formal research and development programs and from informal trial and error, and it involves discovering new ways of getting more out of our resources.

To reap the benefits of technological change, capital must increase. Some of the most powerful and far-reaching fundamental technologies are embodied in human capital—for example, language, writing, and mathematics. But most technologies are embodied in physical capital. For example, to reap the benefits of the internal combustion engine, millions of horse-drawn carriages and horses had to be replaced by automobiles; more recently, to reap the benefits of computerized word processing, millions of typewriters had to be replaced by PCs and printers.

REVIEW

- Economic growth cannot occur without institutional capital that creates incentives to specialize and exchange, save and invest, and develop new technologies.
- The most significant sources of economic growth are saving and investment in new capital, the growth of human capital, and the discovery of new technologies. These sources interact: Human capital creates new technologies, which are embodied in both human and physical capital.

We've described the sources of economic growth. Let's now see how we can begin to quantify their contributions by studying growth accounting.

Growth Accounting

REAL GDP GROWS BECAUSE THE QUANTITIES OF labor and capital grow and because technology advances. The purpose of **growth accounting** is to calculate how much real GDP growth has resulted from growth of labor and capital and how much is attributable to technological change.

The first task of growth accounting is to define productivity. **Productivity** is real GDP per hour of work. It is calculated by dividing real GDP by aggregate labor hours. (Chapter 23, pp. 551–555, explains how real GDP is measured and Chapter 24, pp. 575–576, explains how aggregate hours are measured.) We are interested in productivity because it determines how much income an hour of labor can earn. Figure 26.4 shows productivity for the period 1960–1994. You can see in this figure that productivity growth was most rapid during the 1960s and that it slowed down in 1973. You can also see that it speeded up again after 1983, but not to the pace of the 1960s.

The second (and main) task of growth accounting is to explain the fluctuations in productivity. Why was productivity growth fastest during the 1960s? Why did it slow down during the 1970s and then speed up again in the 1980s? Growth accounting answers these questions by dividing the growth in productivity into two components and then measuring the contribution of each. The components are:

1. Growth in capital per hour of labor
2. Technological change

The technological-change component contains everything that is not included in growth in capital per hour. In particular, it includes human capital. But as you've seen, human capital and technological change are intimately interrelated, so calling this catch-all component "technological change," while not exactly correct, is not seriously misleading.

The analytical engine of growth accounting is a relationship called the productivity function. Let's learn about this relationship and see how it is used.

The Productivity Function

The **productivity function** is a relationship that shows how real GDP per hour of labor changes as the amount of capital per hour of labor changes with no change in technology. Figure 26.5 illustrates the productivity function. Capital per hour of work is measured on the *x*-axis and real GDP per hour of work is

---

FIGURE 26.4

Real GDP per Hour of Work

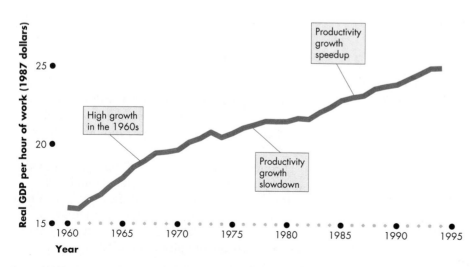

Real GDP divided by aggregate hours equals real GDP per hour of work, which is a broad measure of productivity. During the 1960s the productivity growth rate was high. It slowed during the 1970s and speeded up again during the 1980s.

Sources: U.S. Department of Commerce, *National Income and Product Accounts of the United States*, (Washington, D.C.: U.S. Government Printing Office); U.S. Department of Labor, Current Population Survey (Washington, D.C.: U.S. Government Printing Office).

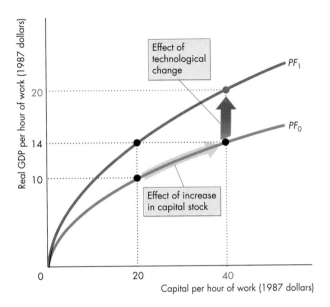

FIGURE 26.5

How Productivity Grows

Productivity can be measured by real GDP per hour of work, and it can grow for two reasons: (1) Capital per hour of work increases, and (2) technological advances occur. The productivity function, *PF*, shows the effects of an increase in capital per hour of work on productivity. Here, when capital per hour of work increases from \$20 to \$40, real GDP per hour of work increases from \$10 to \$14 along the productivity curve PF_0. Technological advance shifts the productivity function upward. Here, an advance in technology shifts the productivity function from PF_0 to PF_1. With this technological advance, real GDP per hour of work increases from \$14 to \$20 when there is \$40 of capital per hour of work.

measured on the *y*-axis. The figure shows two productivity functions as the curves labeled PF_0 and PF_1.

An increase in the amount of capital per hour of labor results in an increase in real GDP per hour of labor, which is shown by a movement along a productivity function. For example, on the curve labeled PF_0, when capital per hour of labor is \$20, real GDP per hour of labor is \$10. As capital per hour of labor increases to \$40, real GDP per hour of labor increases to \$14.

Technological change increases the amount of GDP per hour of labor that can be produced by a given amount of capital per hour of labor. It is shown

by an upward shift of the productivity function. For example, if capital per hour of work is \$20 and a technological change increases real GDP per hour of work from \$10 to \$14, the productivity function shifts upward from PF_0 to PF_1 in Fig. 26.5. Similarly, if capital per hour of work is \$40, the same technological change increases real GDP per hour of work from \$14 to \$20 and shifts the productivity function upward from PF_0 to PF_1.

To calculate the contributions of capital growth and technological change to productivity growth, we need to know the shape and slope of the productivity function. The shape of the productivity function reflects a fundamental economic law—the law of diminishing returns. The **law of diminishing returns** states that as the quantity of one input increases with the quantities of all other inputs remaining the same, output increases but by ever smaller increments. For example, in a factory that has a given amount of capital, as more labor is hired, production increases. But each *additional* hour of labor produces less *additional* output than the previous hour produced. Two typists working with one computer type fewer than twice as many pages per day as one typist working with one computer.

Applied to capital, the law of diminishing returns states that if a given number of hours of labor use more capital (with the same technology), the *additional* output that results from the *additional* capital gets smaller as the amount of capital increases. One typist working with two computers types fewer than twice as many pages per day as one typist working with one computer. More generally, one hour of labor working with \$40 of capital produces less than twice the output of one hour of labor working with \$20 of capital. But how much less? The answer is given by the *one third rule*.

The One Third Rule On the average, across all types of work, a one percent increase in capital per hour of labor, with no change in technology, brings a *one third of one percent* increase in output per hour of labor. In the aggregate a one percent increase in capital per hour of work, with no change in technology, brings a *one third of one percent* increase in real GDP per hour of work.

This one third rule, which was first discovered by Robert Solow of MIT, can be used to calculate the contributions of an increase in capital per hour of work and technological change to the growth of real GDP. Let's do such a calculation. Suppose that capital per hour of work grows by 3 percent a year and real GDP grows by 2.5 percent a year. The one third rule tells us that capital growth has contributed one third of 3 percent, which is 1 percent. The rest of the 2.5 percent growth of real GDP comes from technological change. That is, technological change has contributed 1.5 percent, which is the 2.5 percent growth of real GDP minus the estimated 1 percent contribution of capital growth.

Why the One Third Rule   Why is the one third rule used to separate contributions of capital growth and technological change to productivity growth? How do we know that one third is the correct proportion? The answer is that we don't know for sure, but there is one strong piece of evidence pointing to one third being the correct proportion. This evidence is the share of real GDP received by capital.

A fundamental principle of economics is that factors of production receive incomes in proportion to their contributions to production. On the average, capital receives one third of GDP and labor receives two thirds. (In 1994, for example, GDP was $6,738 billion and capital income was $2,180 billion, almost exactly one third of GDP). If the factors of production are rewarded in proportion to their contributions, then a one percent increase in capital brings a one third of one percent increase in real GDP. The one third rule is an average and not a hard and precise fixed number.

Accounting for the Productivity Growth Slowdown and Speedup

We can use the productivity function and the one third rule to study the reasons for the slowdown and subsequent speedup of productivity growth in the United States. Figure 26.6 shows you what has been happening.

1960 to 1973   The story begins in 1960, which is shown in Fig. 26.6(a), when capital per hour of work was $40 and real GDP per hour of work was $16. During the next 13 years, rapid technological change increased productivity and shifted the productivity function upward from PF_0 to PF_1. With no increase in capital per hour of work, real GDP per hour of work would have increased to $19.40. But capital per hour of work increased from $40 to $50. This increase in capital per hour of work increased real GDP per hour of work by a further $1.60 to $21.

You can see the one third rule at work here. The increase in capital per hour of work from $40 to $50 is a 25 percent increase. The increase in real GDP per hour of work from $19.40 to $21 is an 8.2 percent increase. The 8.2 percent increase in real GDP per hour of work equals one third of the 25 percent increase in capital per hour of work. The remaining increase in real GDP, 16.8 percent, is attributed to the advance in technology.

1973 to 1983   The story continues between 1973 and 1983 in Fig. 26.6(b). In 1973, capital per hour of work is $50 and real GDP per hour of work is $21, the place we ended up in Fig. 26.6(a). Capital per hour of work *decreased* in 1974 and even in 1975 was below its 1973 level. But by 1983, capital per hour of work had increased to $58, which is 16 percent higher than in 1973. Real GDP per hour of work increased by $1 dollar to $22, which is a 4.8 percent increase. This increase is slightly less than one third of 16 percent, so technological change made no contribution to real GDP growth during this period.

The reason for the productivity growth slowdown has now been isolated. It was not the result of slower growth in capital per hour of work. Rather it occurred because the contribution of technological change to real GDP growth dried up. Technological change itself did not stop. On the contrary, there was a lot of it. But the technological change that occurred did not increase productivity. Instead, it offset negative shocks to productivity. We'll look at those negative factors below.

1983 to 1994   The most recent episode in the story is shown in Fig. 26.6(c). It begins in 1983, when capital per hour of work was $58 and real GDP per hour of work was $22. Technological change shifted the productivity function upward from PF_1 to PF_2 and investment in new capital increased capital per hour of work from $58 to $64, a 10.3 percent increase. Real GDP per hour of work increased from $22 to $25, a 13.6 percent increase. Using the one third rule, the 10.3 percent increase in capital per hour of work increased real GDP per hour of work by 3.4 percent (3.4 is one third of 10.3). Technological change contributed the remaining 10.2 percent (13.6 percent minus 3.4 percent). Thus technological change resumed its contribution to productivity growth but at a slower pace than during the 1960s. Fluctuations in the pace of technological change are the key source of changes in the growth rate of productivity.

FIGURE 26.6
Growth Accounting and the Productivity Growth Slowdown

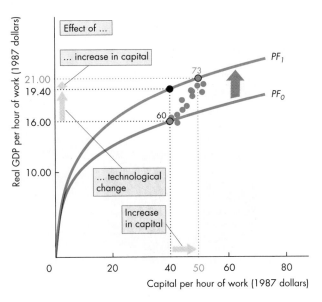

(a) 1960 to 1973

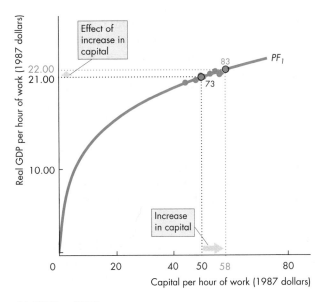

(b) 1973 to 1983

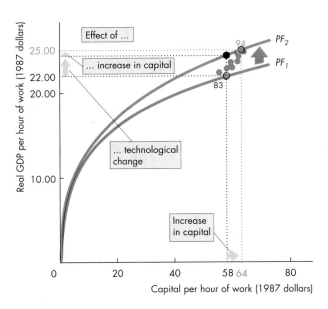

(c) 1983 to 1994

Between 1960 and 1973 (part a), which was a period of rapid productivity growth, capital per hour of work increased from $40 to $50, and technological progress shifted the productivity function upward from PF_0 to PF_1. Between 1973 and 1983 (part b), when potential GDP grew slowly, capital per hour of work increased from $50 to $58 but the productivity function did not shift. The technological change that occurred was offset by the negative effects of oil price shocks. Between 1983 and 1994 (part c), capital per hour of work increased from $58 to $64, and technological progress shifted the productivity function upward from PF_1 to PF_2. Although productivity growth was not as rapid as in the 1960s, the productivity growth rate did increase.

Sources: U.S. Department of Commerce, *National Income and Product Accounts of the United States* (Washington, D.C.: U.S. Government Printing Office); U.S. Department of Labor, *Current Population Survey* (Washington, D.C.: U.S. Government Printing Office); and the author's calculations.

Accounting for the Productivity Slowdown: A Summary

We can bring the elements we've been studying together and describe the productivity growth slowdown in term of those elements. Figure 26.7 summarizes them. Growth in aggregate hours slowed from 1.6 percent a year during the 1960s to 1.2 percent a year between 1973 and 1983. It then speeded up and grew at 1.7 percent a year after 1983. Growth in capital per hour contributed 0.55 percent per year to real GDP growth during the 1960s and increased to 0.6 percent a year between 1973 and 1983. But after 1983 its contribution fell to 0.3 percent a year. The major source of variation in productivity growth is the rate of technological change. This element slowed from 1.7 percent a year before 1973 to zero between 1973 and 1983 and then speeded up to 0.9 percent a year after 1983.

Technological Change During the Productivity Growth Slowdown

We've seen that during the productivity growth slowdown of the 1970s, the contribution of technological change dried up. But why? Three factors have been identified as being responsible. They are:

■ Energy price shocks
■ Environmental protection laws
■ Changes in the composition of output

Energy Price Shocks The price of oil quadrupled during 1973–1974 and quickly on the tail of this increase, the prices of coal and natural gas—substitutes for oil—also increased dramatically. Energy prices increased sharply again in 1979–1980.

The immediate effect of higher energy prices was an increase in the rate at which gas-guzzling automobiles, airplanes, and heating systems were scrapped. But this effect shows up in Fig. 26.6(b) as a leftward movement along the productivity function as capital per hour of labor decreased.

A longer drawn out effect was the development of new energy-saving technologies. Research and development efforts concentrated on developing new types of auto and airplane engines, heating furnaces, and industrial processes that used fuel more sparingly than their predecessors. As a result, despite a huge amount of technological change and investment in

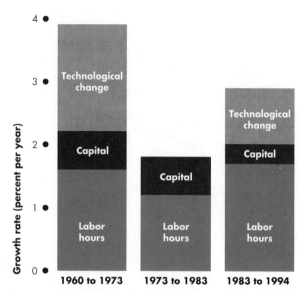

FIGURE 26.7

Real GDP Growth

Real GDP grows because aggregate hours grow, capital per hour grows, and technology advances. The growth in capital per hour of work contributed about 0.6 percent a year to the growth rate of real GDP from 1960 through 1983 but only 0.3 percent a year after 1983. The contribution of aggregate labor hours to growth fell slightly from 1.6 percent a year during the period 1960 through 1973 to 1.2 percent a year since 1973, but then increased to 1.7 percent a year after 1983. The contribution of technological change to real GDP growth has fluctuated much more than the contributions of capital per hour and aggregate hours and was zero during the decade from 1973 to 1983.

Sources: U.S. Department of Commerce, *National Income and Product Accounts of the United States* (Washington, D.C.: U.S. Government Printing Office); U.S. Department of Labor, *Current Population Survey* (Washington, D.C.: U.S. Government Printing Office); and the author's calculations.

new technologies, productivity did not increase. The new technologies produced a given amount of real GDP with a much smaller amount of fuel. That is, if we measured productivity in terms of GDP per barrel of oil (or its equivalent in other fuels), we would see big productivity gains during the 1970s and early 1980s. But to achieve these gains, we used a lot of labor and capital. So real GDP per hour of work did not grow quickly and the productivity function did not shift upward.

Environmental Protection Laws   During the 1970s, laws were introduced to protect the environment and improve the quality of the workplace. The benefits of these new laws were cleaner air and water and safer factories. But these benefits are not counted directly as production. So electric power utilities and other industries heavily affected by the new laws appeared to have a productivity problem, when actually they are contributing to the overall quality of life in ways that GDP fails to capture. If the value of these goods were added to real GDP per person, we would see that there was some productivity growth. That is, if the productivity function included the value that people place on a better environment as part of real GDP per hour of work, the productivity function would have shifted upward during the 1970s. So to some extent, the productivity slowdown was an illusion that resulted from mismeasurement of the value of production.

Changes in the Composition of Output   During the 1960s, a lot of our growth came from a movement of resources out of the farm sector into the small business sector. Farm productivity grows less quickly than small business productivity, so as resources move, average productivity grows quickly. During the 1970s and 1980s, the main movement of resources was out of manufacturing into services. Productivity growth in services is less than in manufacturing, so average productivity growth slowed. In the growth accounting exercise, this type of change shows up as a slowdown in aggregate productivity growth.

R E V I E W

■ Growth accounting separates out the contributions to economic growth of the growth of aggregate hours, capital per hour, and technological change.

■ The key to growth accounting is the *one third* rule—the rule that a 1 percent increase in capital per hour of work brings a one third of 1 percent increase in real GDP per hour of work.

■ Growth accounting isolates the reason for the productivity growth slowdown: Technological change made no contribution to real GDP growth between 1973 and 1983.

Growth Theory

WE'VE SEEN THAT REAL GDP GROWS WHEN aggregate hours of work grow, when the quantity of capital per hour of work grows, and when improvements in technology (including additions to human capital) bring increases in productivity. But what is the *cause* of economic growth and what is the *effect*? How do the influences on economic growth interact with each other to make some economies grow quickly and others grow slowly? And what are the deeper forces that make a country's long-term growth rate sometimes speed up and sometimes slow down?

The causes of economic growth are hard to unravel because so many factors interact with each other. Population growth might create pressures on land use that bring forth advances in plant biology that increase crop yields and advances in architecture and building technology that increase building heights. Here, population growth causes technological change, which in turns causes saving and investment, which in turn brings economic growth. Alternatively, a surplus of saving might lower interest rates and bring an increase in the pace of investment in human capital and physical capital that speed up the growth rate. Here, saving and investment have caused economic growth. A lucky break might bring an unlooked-for and unexpected technological advance that increases the productivity of labor and capital and brings forth a burst of saving and investment and rapid economic growth. Each of these possible sources of growth can operate.

But there are more complex interactions to consider. Rapid economic growth might set in motion a sequence of events that eventually bring that growth to an end. For example, other things remaining the same, growth in the labor force brings diminishing returns to labor and, again other things remaining the same, growth in the capital stock brings diminishing returns to capital. How do diminishing returns to labor and diminishing returns to capital influence the growth rate?

Let's look at the progress economists have made in finding the answers to these questions. There are three main theories of economic growth. They are:

■ Classical growth theory
■ Neoclassical growth theory
■ New growth theory

Classical Growth Theory

Classical growth theory is a theory of economic growth based on the view that population growth is determined by the level of income per person. This theory was suggested by Adam Smith, Thomas Robert Malthus, and David Ricardo, the leading economists of the late eighteenth century and early nineteenth century.

To understand classical growth theory, let's transport ourselves back to the world of 1776. Most of the 2.5 million people who live in the newly independent United States of America work on farms or on their own land and perform their tasks using simple tools

and animal power. They earn about 2 shillings (a little less than $12 dollars in today's money) for working a ten-hour day. Then advances in farming technology bring new types of ploughs and seeds that increase farm productivity. As farm productivity increases, farm production increases and some farm workers move from the land to the cities, where they get work producing and selling the expanding range of farm equipment. Incomes rise and the people seem to be prospering. But will the prosperity last? Classical growth theory says it will not.

Figure 26.8 illustrates classical growth theory and explains why it reaches a pessimistic conclusion. Before growth begins, the economy is in the situation

---

FIGURE **26.8**

Classical Growth Theory

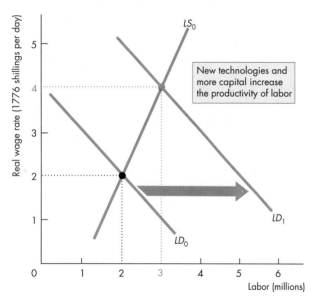

(a) Initial effect

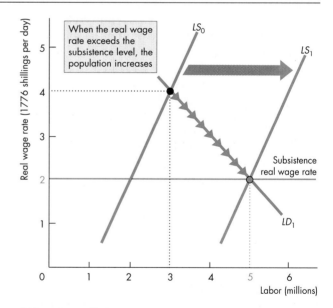

(b) Long-term effect

In classical growth theory, economic growth is temporary and the real wage rate keeps returning to the subsistence level. Initially, in part (a), the demand for labor is LD_0, and the supply of labor is LS_0. There are 2 million people employed, and they earn 2 shillings (1776 shillings) a day. An advance in technology and an increase in capital increase the productivity of labor, and the demand for labor increases to LD_1. The real wage rate rises to 4 shillings a day, and the quantity of labor supplied increases to 3 million.

The real wage rate is now above the subsistence real wage rate, which in this example is 2 shillings a day (part b). The population begins to increase. With an increase in population the supply of labor increases, and the labor supply curve shifts rightward to LS_1. As it does so, the real wage rate falls and the quantity of labor employed increases. The population stops growing when the real wage rate is back at the subsistence level.

shown in part (a). The labor demand curve is LD_0 and the labor supply curve is LS_0. There is equilibrium in the labor market: the quantity of labor demanded equals the quantity supplied at a real wage rate of 2 shillings a day and 2 million people are employed. (We will use constant 1776 prices in this example to keep it in its historical context.)

Advances in technology—in both agriculture and industry—lead to investment in new capital and labor becomes more productive. More and more businesses start up and try to hire the now more productive labor. So the demand for labor increases and the labor demand curve shifts rightward to LD_1. With this greater demand for labor, the real wage rate rises to 4 shillings a day and this higher wage rate brings an increase in the quantity of labor supplied (a movement along the labor supply curve). In the new situation, 3 million people are employed.

At this stage, economic growth has occurred and everyone has benefited from it. Real GDP has increased and real wages have also increased. But the classical economists believed that this new situation could not last and would be disturbed because it would induce an increase in the population.

Classical Theory of Population Growth   The classical theory of population growth is based on the idea of a subsistence real wage rate. The **subsistence real wage rate** is the minimum real wage rate needed to maintain life. By its definition, if the actual real wage rate is less than the subsistence real wage rate, some people cannot survive and the population decreases. But in classical theory, whenever the real wage rate exceeds the subsistence real wage rate, the population grows. This assumption, combined with diminishing returns to labor, has a very dismal implication—one that resulted in economics being called the *dismal science*. This implication is that no matter how much investment and technological change occurs, real wage rates are always pushed back toward the subsistence level.

Figure 26.8(b) shows this process. Here, the subsistence real wage rate is (by assumption) 2 shillings a day. The actual real wage rate, at the intersection of LS_0 and LD_1, is 2 shillings a day. Because the actual real wage rate exceeds the subsistence real wage rate, the population grows and the labor supply increases. The labor supply curve shifts rightward to LS_1. As it does so, the real wage rate falls and the quantity of labor demanded increases. Eventually, in the absence

of further technological change, the economy comes to rest at the subsistence real wage rate of 2 shillings a day, and 5 million people are employed.

The economy has grown, real GDP has increased, but a larger population is earning the subsistence real wage rate.

The Modern Theory of Population Growth
When the classical economists were developing their ideas about population growth, a population explosion was under way. In Britain and other Western European countries, advances in medicine and hygiene had lowered the death rate while the birth rate remained high. For several decades, population growth was extremely rapid. For example, after being relatively stable for several centuries, the population of Britain increased by 40 percent between 1750 and 1800 and by a further 50 percent between 1800 and 1830. At the same time, an estimated 1 million people (about 20 percent of the 1750 population) left Britain for America and Australia before 1800, and outward migration continued on a similar scale through the nineteenth century. Population growth on this scale alarmed Malthus and the other classical economists and was the empirical basis for their theory of population growth.

But eventually, the birth rate fell, and while the population continued to increase, its rate of increase was moderate. This slowdown in the population growth rate seemed to make the classical theory increasingly less relevant. It also eventually lead to the development of a modern economic theory of population growth.

The population growth rate is influenced by economic factors. Key among them is the opportunity cost of women's time. As women's wage rates have increased and their job opportunities have expanded, the opportunity cost of having children has increased. Faced with a higher opportunity cost, families have chosen to have a smaller number of children and the birth rate has fallen. Also the death rate has fallen as greater investment has been made in advances in medicine. But despite the influence of economic factors, to a good approximation, the rate of population growth is independent of the rate of economic growth. To the extent that there is a connection, as incomes increase, the population growth rate eventually decreases. This inverse relation between real income growth and population growth rate is contrary to the assumption of the classical economists and it invalidates their conclusions.

Neoclassical Growth Theory

Neoclassical growth theory is a theory of economic growth that explains how saving, investment, and economic growth respond to population growth and technological change. This theory was suggested during the 1950s by Robert Solow of MIT. In the neoclassical theory, the population growth rate influences the rate of economic growth. But economic growth does not influence population growth. Similarly, in neoclassical growth theory the rate of technological change influences the rate of economic growth, but economic growth does not influence the pace of technological change. Rather, technological change is determined by chance. When we get lucky, we have rapid technological change, and when bad luck strikes, the pace of technological advance slows down. But there is nothing we can do to influence its pace. When variables are determined outside a theory, they are called *exogenous* variables. Thus in the neoclassical growth theory population growth and technological change are exogenous.

At the heart of the neoclassical growth theory is the stock of capital and the *productivity function*—the relationship between capital per unit of labor and output per unit of labor. For simplicity, the theory assumes that people work a fixed number of hours and that everyone works. So it measures labor as the population. The faster the capital stock per person grows, the faster real GDP and income per person grows. But what determines the growth rate of the capital stock per person? The answer is the demand for and supply of capital per person.

The Demand for and Supply of Capital per Person Figure 26.9 illustrates the neoclassical growth theory by showing how the demand for and supply of capital determine the capital stock and its growth rate. In this figure, we measure the capital stock per person on the x-axis and the real interest rate on the y-axis. The demand for capital and the supply of capital are determined by investment and saving decisions, which are described in Chapter 25 (see pp. 597–607). Briefly, the lower the real interest rate, the larger is the number of capital projects that are profitable and the greater is the demand for capital. On the other hand, in the short run, the lower the interest rate, the less strong is the incentive to save rather than consume, and the smaller is the supply of capital.

In Fig. 26.9, the demand for capital is shown by the downward-sloping KD_0 curve in part (a). Along

this curve, as the real interest rate falls, other things remaining the same, the quantity of capital demanded increases. The supply of capital is shown by the upward-sloping KS_0 curve. Along this curve, as the real interest rate falls, other things remaining the same, the quantity of capital supplied decreases.

The real interest rate adjusts to achieve an equilibrium in which the quantity of capital demanded equals the quantity supplied. In Fig. 26.9, the economy is in equilibrium at a real interest rate of 4 percent a year and with a capital stock of $60,000 (part a). In the absence of technological change, capital per person converges to its equilibrium level. As a result, real GDP per person converges to a constant level and there is no economic growth.

But with technological change, real GDP per person grows. Figure 26.9 illustrates this growth process. A technological advance increases the productivity of capital and the demand for capital increases. The capital demand curve shifts rightward to KD_1. The greater demand for capital raises the real interest rate to 6 percent a year and the higher real interest rate brings forth an increase in saving (part a). The quantity of capital supplied increases to $70,000 per person.

The economy has experienced a period of economic growth. Because the capital stock per person has increased, output per person has increased. Also, labor has become more productive, and the demand for labor has increased, bringing an increase in real wages and employment. But economic growth continues beyond the point shown in Fig. 26.9(a). To understand why, we need to look at the neoclassical theory of saving.

Neoclassical Theory of Saving The neoclassical theory of saving is based on an idea called a constant rate of time preference. The **rate of time preference** is the target real interest rate that savers want to achieve. If the real interest rate exceeds the rate of time preference, saving is positive and the supply of capital increases. If the real interest rate is less than the rate of time preference, saving is negative and the supply of capital decreases. If the real interest rate equals the rate of time preference, people are happy with the amount of savings they have accumulated, so saving is zero.

Figure 26.9(b) illustrates the consequences of a constant rate of time preference. Here, the rate of time preference is 4 percent a year. So when the real interest rate rises to 6 percent a year, saving is positive and the supply of capital increases. The capital supply curve

FIGURE 26.9

Neoclassical Growth Theory

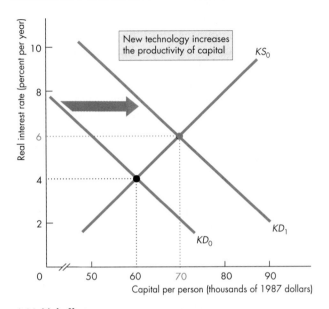

New technology increases the productivity of capital

(a) Initial effect

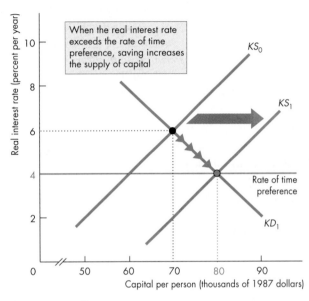

When the real interest rate exceeds the rate of time preference, saving increases the supply of capital

(b) Long-term effect

In neoclassical growth theory, economic growth results from technological change. Initially, in part (a), the demand for capital is KD_0 and the supply of capital is KS_0. The capital stock is $60,000 per person, and the real interest rate is 4 percent a year. An advance in technology increases the productivity of capital, and the demand for capital increases to KD_1. The real interest rate rises to 6 percent a year, and the quantity of capital supplied increases to $70,000.

The real interest rate is now above the rate of time preference, which in this example is 4 percent a year (part b). Saving is positive and the supply of capital increases to KS_1. The real interest rate falls and the quantity of capital per person increases. The quantity of capital per person stops growing when the real interest rate is again equal to the rate of time preference.

shifts rightward toward KS_1. As the supply of capital increases, the real interest rate falls and the quantity of capital demanded increases. Eventually, the economy reaches the point at which the real interest rate has fallen to equal the rate of time preference. At this point, saving is zero and the supply of capital is KS_1.

Throughout the process just described, real GDP per person has been increasing. The capital stock per person and real wage rates have also been increasing. The economy has experienced growth.

Ongoing exogenous advances in technology are constantly increasing the demand for capital and raising the real interest rate above the rate of time preference. The process that we've just examined repeats indefinitely to create an ongoing process of long-term economic growth.

Problems with Neoclassical Growth Theory

Neoclassical growth theory tells us how capital accumulation and saving interact to determine the economy's growth rate. But all economies have access to the same technologies, and capital is free to roam the globe seeking the highest available rate of return. So neoclassical growth theory predicts that growth rates and income levels per person around the globe will converge. While there is some sign of convergence among the rich countries (shown in Fig. 26.2a), convergence is slow and it does not appear to be imminent for all countries (as we saw in Fig. 26.2b).

New growth theory attempts to overcome this shortcoming of neoclassical growth theory. It also attempts to explain how the rate of technological change is determined.

New Growth Theory

New growth theory is a theory of economic growth based on the idea that technological change results from the choices that people make in the pursuit of ever greater profit. That is, technological change is *endogenous*. (New growth theory is sometimes called *endogenous growth theory* and sometimes also called *neo-Schumpeterian growth theory*—see *Economics in History*, p. 648–649).

New growth theory starts with four facts about market economies:

■ Discoveries result from choices and actions.
■ Discoveries bring profits.
■ Discoveries can be used by many people at the same time.
■ Physical activities can be replicated.

Discoveries and Choices   When people discover a new product or technique, they think of themselves as being lucky. They are right. But the pace at which new discoveries are made—the pace at which technology advances—is not determined by chance. It depends on how many people are looking for a new way of doing something and how intensively they are looking.

Discoveries and Profits   The spur to seeking new and better ways of producing is profit. The forces of competition are constantly squeezing profits, so to make a profit greater than the average, a person must constantly seek out either lower-cost methods of production or new and better products for which people are willing to pay a higher price. Inventors can maintain their above-average profits for several years by taking out a patent or copyright. But eventually, a new discovery is copied, and profits disappear. But in the meantime, above-average profit can be enjoyed, and when it disappears, another new innovation can possibly be found.

Discoveries Used by All   Once a profitable new discovery has been made, it is difficult to prevent other people from copying it. But also, unlike inputs such as labor and capital, the new discovery can be used by everyone who knows about it without reducing its availability to others. This fact means that as the benefits of a new discovery are dispersed through the economy, resources are made available to people who reap the benefit. These resources are free because these people didn't pay the price of making the discovery.

Replicating Activities   Replicas can be made of many (perhaps most) production activities. For example, there might be two, three, or fifty-three identical firms making fiber-optic cable using an identical assembly line and production technique. This fact means that the economy as a whole does not experience diminishing returns. (Each firm experiences diminishing returns, but the economy doesn't.)

These features of the economy can be summarized in the neat idea that knowledge—the stock of productive ideas that has been accumulated as a result of research and development efforts—is a special kind of capital that can be used by all and that is not subject to the law of diminishing returns. The implication of this simple and appealing idea is shown in Fig. 26.10, which illustrates new growth theory. In this figure, we measure the knowledge capital stock on the *x*-axis and the real interest rate on the *y*-axis.

The supply of knowledge capital is shown by the upward-sloping S_0 curve. Along this curve, as the real interest rate rises, other things remaining the same, the quantity of saving and of resources devoted to accumulating knowledge capital increases.

Because knowledge capital does not have diminishing returns, the demand for knowledge capital does not slope downward like the demand curve for other types of capital. If knowledge capital yields a higher return than the rate of time preference, the quantity of knowledge capital demanded is unlimited. And if knowledge capital yields a lower return than the rate of time preference, then the demand for knowledge capital is zero.

Initially, the rate of return on knowledge capital is 2 percent a year, shown by the line R_0 in Fig. 26.10(a). At this rate of return, and given the supply of knowledge capital curve, the equilibrium real interest rate is 2 percent a year and there is no knowledge capital. The economy is stuck at point *a*.

The invention of such basic tools as language and writing (the two most basic pieces of knowledge capital), and later the development of the scientific method and the establishment of communities of scientists and inventors and the research institutions that support them, brought an increase in the rate of return to knowledge capital. The rate of return line shifted upward to R_1. The initial effect of this increase in the return on knowledge capital was to increase the real interest rate to 6 percent a year and to bring forth an increase in the quantity of knowledge capital supplied (to $1 trillion in the figure). The economy moved to point *b*.

FIGURE 26.10

New Growth Theory

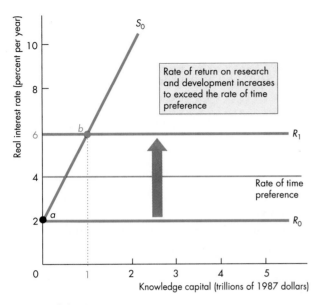

(a) Growth begins

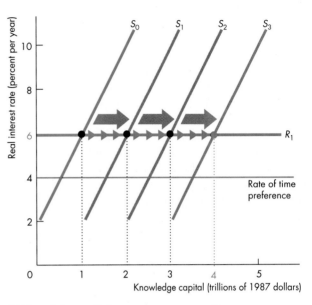

(b) Knowledge capital grows

In new growth theory, economic growth results from *endogenous* technological change. The returns to knowledge capital do not diminish, and growth proceeds indefinitely. Initially, in part (a), the rate of return on knowledge capital is R_0 and the supply of knowledge capital is S_0. The stock of knowledge capital is zero. The development of the scientific method and the creation of research and development organizations increases the rate of return on knowledge capital to R_1. The real interest rate rises to 6 percent a year, and the quantity of knowledge capital supplied increases to $1 trillion.

The real interest rate is now above the rate of time preference, which in this example is 4 percent a year (part b). Saving is positive, and the supply of knowledge capital increases. The knowledge capital supply curve shifts rightward successively to S_1, S_2, S_3, and so on. As it does so, the economy grows but the real interest rate does not fall because there are no diminishing returns to knowledge capital. Growth continues as long as the rate of return on knowledge capital exceeds the rate of time preference.

The economy has experienced a period of economic growth. Because the stock of knowledge capital has increased, real GDP has increased. But economic growth continues, and it continues indefinitely. The reason is that the real interest rate now exceeds the rate of time preference. So saving is positive, and the supply of capital (which includes knowledge capital) increases.

Figure 26.10(b) illustrates the process. The rate of time preference is 4 percent a year, and the rate of return on knowledge capital is 6 percent a year. With positive saving, the supply curve shifts rightward and continues to do so indefinitely. The speed with which the saving supply curve shifts rightward depends on

the extent to which the real interest rate exceeds the rate of time preference. The higher the rate of return on knowledge capital, the higher is the real interest rate and the faster the saving curve shifts rightward. So the faster the economy grows.

Unlike neoclassical theory, with its diminishing returns to capital, which eventually lowers the real interest rate to the rate of time preference, new growth theory has no such mechanism at work. Real GDP per person increases and does so indefinitely as long as people can undertake research and development that yields a higher return than the rate of time preference.

New growth theory sees the economy as a kind of perpetual motion mechanism. Economic growth is driven by our insatiable wants that lead us to pursue profit and innovate. The result of this process is new and better products. But new and better products result in new firms starting up and old firms going out of business. In this process, jobs are created and destroyed. The outcome is new and better jobs, more leisure, and more consumption. All this adds up to a higher standard of living. But our insatiable wants are still there, so the process continues, going round and round a circle of wants, profits, innovation, new products, and higher living standards.

The economy's growth rate depends on people's ability to innovate, the rate of return to innovation, and the rate of time preference, which influences the rate of saving. *Reading Between the Lines* on pp. 642–643 further explores the connection between saving and economic growth in the world economy.

R E V I E W

■ Economic growth arises from improvements in human capital, increases in the capital stock, and improvements in technology.
■ In classical growth theory, there is no long-term growth in the real wage rate because when the real wage rate exceeds its subsistence level, the population expands and diminishing returns lower the real wage rate to its subsistence level.
■ In neoclassical growth theory, growth results from technological advances that are themselves determined by chance.
■ In new growth theory, insatiable wants lead people to devote resources to innovation in the pursuit of above-average profit. The pace of innovation depends on the resources devoted to it. Profitable new discoveries are copied and replicated many times, so their benefits spread throughout the economy without diminishing returns.

You've now studied the theories of economic growth and have seen how ideas about economic growth have evolved. You can probe these ideas further and learn about the economists who have advanced growth theory in *Economics in History* on pp. 648–649. Your final task in this chapter is to see what can be done to speed up the growth rate.

Achieving Faster Growth

To ACHIEVE FASTER ECONOMIC GROWTH, WE MUST either increase the growth rate of capital per hour of work or increase the pace of technological advance. Let's begin to examine the polices that might speed up economic growth by looking at the miracle economies of Asia. How have they managed to grow so quickly?

The Miracle Economies

The full story of the miracle economies of the 1980s and 1990s has not yet been told. But the parts of the story that look relevant are:

■ High saving rate
■ High rate of investment in human capital
■ Learning-by-doing in high-technology industries

Singapore, Hong Kong, and China save a much larger fraction of income than we save in the United States. A high saving rate enables a country to accumulate physical capital and to invest in human capital at a rapid rate and thereby keep close to the frontier of new technologies. The miracle economies also concentrate on giving their labor forces experience with the latest technologies. Singapore has been the most aggressive in this respect. It has virtually replaced its entire capital stock and transformed its labor force every few years and now has one of the most adaptable and highly skilled labor forces in the world.

Policies for Faster Growth

The suggestions that come from growth theory to increase the economic growth rate all center on speeding up the pace of technological change and capital accumulation. The main suggestions are:

■ Stimulate saving
■ Subsidize research and development
■ Target high-technology industries
■ Encourage international trade

Stimulate Saving There is a direct link between economic growth and saving, so stimulating saving can also stimulate economic growth. It is not an accident that China, Hong Kong, Japan, Korea,

Singapore, and Taiwan have the highest growth rates. They also have the highest saving rates. It is also no accident that the countries of Africa have the lowest growth rates. They also have the lowest saving rates. The saving rates in the United States and the other rich countries are modest.

The most obvious way in which saving could be increased is by providing tax incentives. Some incentives already exist, but more effective measures are possible. For example, instead of taxing incomes (which means taxing both consumption and saving), we could tax only consumption. Such a tax would encourage additional saving and most likely increase the economy's growth rate.

Subsidize Research and Development Because everyone can use the fruits of research and development efforts, there is a tendency to allocate too few resources to these activities. It is true that inventions can be patented, but it is virtually impossible to prevent a near copy that does not violate a patent. For example, VisiCalc invented the spreadsheet, but it did not take long for Lotus Corporation to develop a similar product, the famous 1-2-3, and for Microsoft Corporation to bring out a Lotus 1-2-3 look-alike, Excel. Similarly, Intel developed the microprocessor that powers IBM and compatible PCs, but clones were soon developed that broke Intel's monopoly. Because inventions can be copied, the inventor's profit is limited, and the resources that a firm will allocate to making an invention or innovation are also limited.

This situation is one in which government subsidies might help. By using public funds to finance research and development that bring public benefits, it might be possible to encourage an efficient level of research. However, this solution is not foolproof. The main problem is that some mechanism must be designed for allocating the public funds. At present, universities and public research institutions such as NASA are the main channels through which public funds get used to finance research. It might be more productive to give public funds to private firms. But which firms?

Target High-Technology Industries One answer to the question "which firms?" is to direct the publicly funded research effort toward high-technology firms and industries. The argument is that by encouraging such industries, a country can become the first

to exploit a new technology and can earn above-average profits for a period while others are busy catching up. But to fully exploit the potential of a new technology, it must be marketed worldwide—hence the third element in the growth program.

Encourage International Trade Economists have always generally favored free international trade, and since the time of Adam Smith, they have appreciated the connection between trade and growth. But endogenous growth theory points to an advantage of international trade that had not previously been appreciated: *dynamic comparative advantage.* Dynamic comparative advantage is the ability to produce a good at a lower opportunity cost than that of any other supplier and results from being first in the field and getting the first crack at accumulating specialized human capital to exploit a new technology. Eventually, all countries can produce all goods at the same opportunity cost (to a reasonable approximation), but the first in a field can dominate that field for some time. However, there are many fields. Free international trade enables the firsts in the many fields to engage in mutually advantageous international trade.

As a technology ages and is copied, the dynamic comparative advantage disappears and a new field must be found. This is the story of Singapore over the past three decades as it has moved from textiles in the 1950s, through successively more complex electronic information technology products in the 1960s, 1970s, and 1980s, to the most advanced bio-technology products in the 1990s.

◆ In this chapter we've looked at long-term growth rates in the United States and around the world; we've studied the sources of economic growth; we've learned how we can measure the contributions of hours, capital, and technological change; and we've studied the theories of economic growth. Finally, we've seen some policy actions that might speed up growth rates.

Economic growth is the single most decisive factor in influencing a country's living standard, but it is not the only one. Another is the extent to which the country fully employs its scarce resources, especially its labor. In recent years, unemployment has become a severe problem for many countries. In Part 3 we study the fluctuations of real GDP and employment and unemployment around their long-term trends.

Saving and Growth

THE ECONOMIST, MAY 6, 1995

Rattling the Piggy Bank

When bond yields rose sharply last year many economists got into a tizzy about the possibility that the world would start to run short of capital. This triggered an avalanche of studies, of which the latest, from the IMF, finds some evidence for such fears. It is this savings shortfall, says the Fund, that is largely to blame for high real interest rates.

By saving rather than consuming current output, countries enjoy less jam today, but because these savings are invested they can look forward to higher income and consumption tomorrow. So if the total supply of savings (whether by individuals, firms, or governments) falls, global investment and hence growth will be constrained. ...

Countries that save more tend to grow faster. Over the past ten years, 14 of the 20 fastest-growing economies had savings rates of more than 25% of GDP. In contrast, 14 of the 20 slowest-growing economies had savings rates below 15%. But which way does the causality run?

Higher savings clearly boosts growth by spurring investment. But, intriguingly, the IMF argues that there is also evidence that faster growth itself causes savings rates to rise. Many East Asian economies, for example, enjoyed rapid growth before they began saving more. South Korea was one of the world's least thrifty countries in the early 1960s; now it is one of its biggest savers. This suggests that a virtuous circle connects growth and savings, with faster growth spurring higher savings and higher savings boosting growth. The reason this matters is that it implies that most of the savings needed to finance investment of fast-growing developing countries will be self-generated. ...

Essence of **THE STORY**

■ A study by the International Monetary Fund (IMF) says that interest rates increased during 1994 because saving decreased.

■ A low saving rate implies a low investment rate and a low growth rate of GDP.

■ Countries that save more tend to grow faster, but does a higher saving rate bring a higher growth rate or does a higher growth rate bring a higher saving rate?

■ The IMF says that faster growth causes the saving rate to rise.

■ If the IMF is correct, fast growth will produce the savings needed to sustain it.

Economic

A N A L Y S I S

■ For the world economy, a *closed economy*, saving (from all sources—individual, business, and government) equals investment.

■ Investment increases the capital stock, which brings higher productivity.

■ Figure 1 shows how the world saving rate (and investment rate) has fluctuated since 1960. It increased during the 1960s, peaked in 1974, and fluctuated around a slightly falling trend through the 1980s and into the 1990s.

■ Figure 2 shows the saving rates of the developing and industrial countries since 1970. The saving rate of the industrial countries has decreased, and that of the developing countries has increased.

■ The article is correct when it says that a decrease in world saving, other things remaining the same, brings an increase in the world average interest rate (see Chapter 25, pp. 609–610). But the article is not completely correct about the connection between a country's saving rate and its growth rate.

■ Figure 3 shows the relationship between the saving rate and the growth rate of more than 100 countries over the 30 years from 1960 to 1990. Some high savers are fast growers, but there are many exceptions, several of which are identified in the figure.

■ A high saving rate does not always bring fast growth (Venezuela and Gabon are counterexamples), and fast growth does not always bring a high saving rate (the Republic of Yemen, Malta, Lesotho, and Reunion are counterexamples.)

■ The reason why growth rates and saving rates are only loosely linked is that saving does not limit investment, and it is investment that brings growth. Capital is internationally mobile and people seek the highest available return on their savings. So capital flows into countries that offer the highest rate of return (for equal risk) and enables those countries to invest more than they save and grow faster.

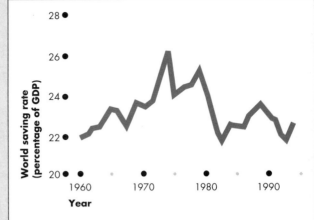

Figure 1   World saving rate

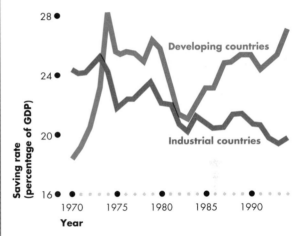

Figure 2   Saving rates

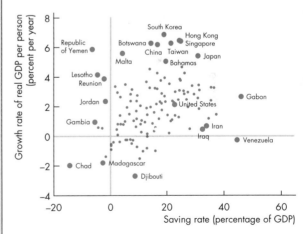

Figure 3   Saving and growth

Sources: Figures 1 and 2: International Monetary Fund and *The Economist* feature article. Figure 3: Robert Summers and Alan Heston, New Computer Diskette (Mark 5.5), June 15, 1993, distributed by the National Bureau of Economics Research to update "The Penn World Table (Mark 5): An Expanded Set of International Comparisons, 1950–1988" *Quarterly Journal of Economics*, May 1991, 327–368.

S U M M A R Y

Long-Term Growth Trends

Between 1895 to 1995, real GDP per person in the United States grew at an average rate of 1.7 percent a year. The early 1900s, mid-1950s, and 1974–1994 were the periods of slowest growth, and the 1920s and 1960s were periods of rapid growth.

Catch-up in real GDP per person occurs sometimes, but it is not a global phenomenon. Some rich countries are catching up with the United States, but the gaps between the United States and many poor countries are not closing. Canada, France, Germany, Italy, the United Kingdom, and Japan have grown faster than the United States and have been catching up. The gaps between the United States and Africa and between the United States and Central and South America have widened, and the gap between the United States and the former Communist countries of Central Europe has remained constant. Hong Kong, Korea, Singapore, and Taiwan and China are catching up fastest. (pp. 623–625)

The Sources of Economic Growth

Economic growth occurs when an *incentive* system, which is created by markets, property rights, and monetary exchange, encourages saving and investment in new capital, investment in human capital, and the discovery of new technologies. These factors are the main sources of economic growth. They interact to increase production and raise living standards. (pp. 626–627)

Growth Accounting

Growth accounting divides the sources of economic growth between the growth of aggregate hours and productivity growth, and it divides productivity growth between growth in capital per hour and technological change.

The analytical engine of growth accounting is the productivity function, which is the relationship between real GDP per hour of work and capital per hour of work, technology remaining the same. A change in capital per hour of work brings a movement along a productivity function, and technological change shifts the productivity function.

The contributions of capital growth and technological change to productivity growth are estimated by using the *one third rule*: a 1 percent increase in capital per hour of work brings a 1/3 percent increase in real GDP per hour of work.

Growth accounting isolates the reason for the productivity growth slowdown of the 1970s: Technological change made no contribution to real GDP growth. Four factors have been suggested as producing this situation: energy price shocks, changes in the composition of the labor force, environmental protection laws, and changes in the composition of output. (pp. 628–633)

Growth Theory

The three main theories of economic growth are classical theory, neoclassical theory, and new growth theory. In classical theory, the growth rate is determined by the population growth rate. The population grows whenever incomes rise above the *subsistence* level and declines whenever incomes fall below the subsistance level. This assumption combined with diminishing returns to labor implies that incomes will always be pushed back toward the subsistence level. In neoclassical growth theory, the growth rate is determined by the rate of technological change, which in turn is determined by chance. Ongoing technological change determines the long-term growth rate. In new growth theory, the growth rate depends on the costs and benefits of developing new technologies. (pp. 633–640)

Achieving Faster Growth

To achieve faster economic growth, we must increase the growth of capital per hour of work or increase the pace of technological advance.

The miracle economies grew quickly because they had a high saving rate and a high rate of investment in human capital, and they took advantage of learning-by-doing in high-technology industries. It might be possible to achieve faster growth by stimulating saving, subsidizing research and development, targeting (and possibly subsidizing) high-technology industries, and encouraging more international trade. (pp. 640–641)

Key Figures

Figure 26.1 A Hundred Years of Economic Growth in the United States, 623
Figure 26.5 How Productivity Grows, 629
Figure 26.6 Growth Accounting and the Productivity Growth Slowdown, 631
Figure 26.8 Classical Growth Theory, 634
Figure 26.9 Neoclassical Growth Theory, 637
Figure 26.10 New Growth Theory, 639

Key Terms

Classical growth theory, 634
Growth accounting, 628
Law of diminishing returns, 629
Neoclassical growth theory, 636
New growth theory, 638
Productivity, 628
Productivity function, 628
Rate of time preference, 636
Subsistence real wage rate, 635

R E V I E W   Q U E S T I O N S

1. What was the average growth rate of real GDP per person in the United States between 1895 and 1995?
2. Which countries have grown fastest and which have grown slowest?
3. Have levels of real GDP per person across countries caught up with each other?
4. What are the three necessary preconditions for economic growth to occur?
5. What three activities can create ongoing economic growth?
6. Explain how economic growth can occur even in the absence of investment and new technologies.
7. What is growth accounting?
8. What is the main concept used in growth accounting?
9. How are the effects of capital accumulation and technological change separated by growth accounting techniques?
10. What is the one third rule and how is it used?
11. Explain the main sources of economic growth in the United States.
12. What were the main sources of the productivity growth slowdown in the United States during the 1970s?
13. Why did technological advances not increase productivity during the 1970s?
14. What are the main theories of economic growth?
15. What are the key assumptions of classical growth theory?
16. What are the key assumptions of neoclassical growth theory?
17. What are the key assumptions of new growth theory?
18. Contrast neoclassical growth theory and new growth theory.
19. Describe the main reasons why the miracle economies of Asia have been so successful.
20. What are the main policy actions that governments might take to increase the growth rate?

P R O B L E M S

1. The following information has been discovered about the economy of Longland: The economy's productivity function is:

Capital per hour of work (1987 dollars per hour)	Real GDP per hour of work (1987 dollars per hour)
10	3.80
20	5.40
30	6.80
40	8.00
50	9.00
60	9.80
70	10.40
80	10.80

Does this economy conform to the one third rule? If so, explain why. If not, explain why not and also explain what rule, if any, it does conform to.

2. The figure illustrates the productivity function of Lotus Land in 1990 and 1995.

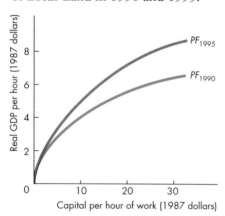

In 1990, capital per hour of work was $10 and in 1995 it was $25.

a. Does Lotus Land experience diminishing returns? Explain why or why not.

b. Use growth accounting to find the contribution of the change in capital between 1990 and 1995 to the growth of productivity in Lotus Land.

c. Use growth accounting to find the contribution of technological change between 1990 and 1995 to the growth of productivity in Lotus Land.

3. The figure illustrates the labor market in Desparado, a country that performs exactly as predicted by the Classical growth theory.

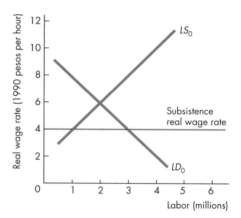

a. What is the real wage rate and level of employment in Desparado?

b. Is the population of Desparado growing, constant, or shrinking?

c. With no further change in technology and labor productivity, what is the eventual level of employment in Desparado and what is the eventual real wage rate?

4. The following information has been discovered about the economy of Cape Despair. The subsistence real wage rate is $7 an hour. Whenever the real wage rate rises above this level the population grows, and when the real wage rate falls below this level the population falls. With its current population, the demand and supply schedules for labor in Cape Despair are as follows:

Real wage rate (1987 dollars per hour)	Quantity of labor demanded (billions of hours per year)	Quantity of labor supplied (billions of hours per year)
3	8	4
5	7	5
7	6	6
9	5	7
11	4	8
13	3	9
15	2	10
17	1	11

Initially, the labor force of Cape Despair is constant, and the real wage is at its subsistence level. Then a technological advance increases the amount that firms are willing to pay for labor by $2 at each level of employment.

a. What is the initial level of employment and real wage rate in Cape Despair?

b. What happens to the real wage rate immediately following the technological advance?

c. What happens to the population growth rate following the technological advance?

d. What is the employment level when Cape Despair returns to a long-run equilibrium?

5. The figure illustrates the economy of Neoclassica, a country that behaves according to the predictions of the neoclassical growth model.

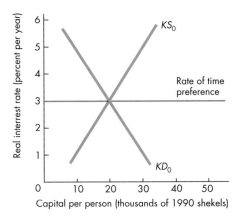

a. What is the real interest rate in Neoclassica?

b. What is the real amount of capital per person in Neoclassica?

   A technological advance increases the demand for capital by $10 thousand per person

c. What is the immediate effect of this change on the real interest rate and the amount of capital per person in Neoclassica?

d. With no further technological change, what is the eventual real interest rate and amount of capital per person in Neoclassica?

6. Martha's Island is an economy that behaves according to the neoclassical growth model. The rate of time preference is 3 percent a year. A technological advance increases the demand for capital and raises the interest rate to 5 percent a year. Describe what happens on Martha's Island.

7. The figure illustrates the economy of Romeria, a country that behaves according to the predictions of new growth theory. Initially, the rate of return on knowledge capital is 2 percent a year. It then rises to 6 percent a year.

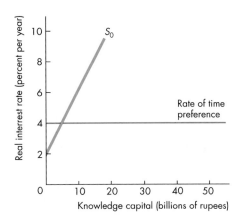

a. What initially is the real interest rate and quantity of knowledge capital in Romeria?

b. What is the immediate effect of the increase in the rate of return on knowledge capital to 6 percent a year on the real interest rate and the quantity of knowledge capital?

c. If the rate of return on knowledge capital remains at 6 percent a year, what happens in Romeria to the real interest rate, the quantity of knowledge capital, and real income per person?

8. What is the most effective way of speeding up the growth rate of the U.S. economy?

9. Set out your policy recommendations for speeding up the growth rate of the U.S. economy.

10. After studying *Reading Between the Lines* on pp. 642–643, answer the following questions:

a. For the world economy, why does an increase in the saving rate bring faster real GDP growth?

b. For an individual country, why does its saving not limit its investment?

c. Which countries have had the highest saving rates and the highest growth rates?

d. Which of the three economic growth theories—classical, neoclassical, and new—do you think best explains the facts about saving and growth rates in this news article?

"Economic progress, in capitalist society, means turmoil."

JOSEPH A. SCHUMPETER, *CAPITALISM, SOCIALISM AND DEMOCRACY.*

Economic Growth

THE ISSUES AND IDEAS

Technological change, capital accumulation, and population growth all interact to produce economic growth. But what is cause and what is effect, and can we expect productivity and income per person to keep on growing?

The classical economists of the eighteenth and nineteenth centuries believed that technological change and capital accumulation were the engines of growth. But they also believed that no matter how successful people were in inventing more productive technologies and investing in new capital, they were destined to live at the subsistence level. These economists based their conclusion on a belief that productivity growth causes population growth, which in turn causes productivity to fall. These classical economists believed that whenever economic growth raises income above the subsistence level, the population will increase. And, they went on to reason, the increase in population brings diminishing returns that lower productivity. As a result, incomes must always fall back to the subsistence level. Only when incomes are at the subsistence level is population growth held in check.

The new growth theories in the 1980s and 1990s stand the classical belief on its head. Today's theory of population growth is that rising income *slows* the population growth rate because it increases the opportunity cost of having children. Productivity and income grow because technology advances and the scope for further productivity growth, which is stimulated by the search for profit, is practically unlimited.

THEN...

IN 1830, a strong and experienced farm worker could harvest three acres of wheat in a day. The only capital employed was a scythe (to cut the wheat), which had been used since Roman times and a cradle (to lay the stalks on), which had been invented by Flemish farmers in the 15th century. With newly developed horse-drawn plows, harrows, and planters, farmers could plant more wheat then they could harvest. But despite big efforts, no one had been able to make a machine that could replicate the swing of a scythe. Then in 1831, 22-year-old Cyrus McCormick built a machine that worked. It scared the horse that pulled it, but it did in a matter of hours what three men could accomplish in a day. Technological change has increased productivity on farms and brought economic growth. Do the facts about productivity growth mean that the classical economists, who believed that diminishing returns would push us relentlessly back to a subsistence living standard, were wrong?

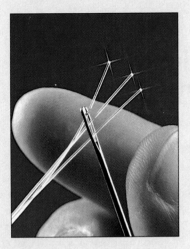

TODAY'S TECHNOLOGIES are expanding our horizons beyond the confines of our planet and are expanding our minds. Geosynchronous satellites bring us global television, voice and data communication, and more accurate weather forecasts, which incidentally increase agricultural productivity. In the foreseeable future, we may have superconductors that revolutionize the use of electric power, virtual reality theme parks and training facilities, pollution-free hydrogen cars, wristwatch telephones, and optical computers that we can talk to. Equipped with these new technologies, our ability to create yet more dazzling technologies will increase. Technological change begets technological change in an (apparently) unending process that makes us ever more productive and brings ever higher incomes.

Joseph Schumpeter

THE ECONOMISTS: JOSEPH SCHUMPETER, ROBERT SOLOW, AND PAUL ROMER

Joseph Schumpeter, who was born in Austria in 1883 and became a professor of economics at Harvard in the depths of the Great Depression in 1932, was the unwitting founder of modern growth theory. Schumpeter saw the development and diffusion of new technologies by profit-seeking entrepreneurs as the source of economic progress. But he saw economic progress as a process of *creative destruction*—the creation of new profit opportunities and the destruction of currently profitable businesses. When Schumpeter died, in 1950, he had achieved his self-expressed life ambition: He was the world's greatest economist.

Robert Solow, who was born in New York City in 1924 and is now a professor of economics at MIT, was one of Schumpeter's students. He gave modern growth theory its next push forward with the *neoclassical growth model,* for which he received the Nobel Prize for Economic Science.

But Paul Romer, who was born in Denver, Colorado, in 1955 and is now a professor of economics at the University of California, Berkeley, has transformed the way economists think about economic growth. Like Schumpeter, Romer believes that sustained economic growth arises from competition among firms. Firms try to increase their profits by devoting resources to creating new products and developing new ways of making existing products. One goal of Romer's research program is to understand why China and some other East Asian countries are growing quickly, while other countries are stagnating. Romer also wants to discover ways of designing economic incentives that foster faster growth.

Robert Solow

Paul Romer

part 6

Macroeconomic Fluctuations and Policies

Thomas J. Sargent, who teaches economics and econometrics at both Stanford University and the University of Chicago, was born in Pasadena, California, in 1943. He was an undergraduate at the University of California, Berkeley and a graduate student at Harvard University. Professor Sargent is well known for his theoretical work on rational expectations in macroeconomics, for his pioneering work on the problem of isolating the effects of policy changes so that truly effective macroeconomic stabilization might be achieved, and for work on learning and the relation between artificial intelligence and macroeconomics. Michael Parkin talked with Professor Sargent about his work.

TALKING WITH Thomas J. Sargent

Professor Sargent, a lot of your research resembles that of a natural scientist. Are you first and foremost a scientist or an economist?

Both scientists and economists use similar tools and methods to understand how things work: They observe, gather empirical data, build models, and try to predict the future. Economics involves measuring prices, quantities, and other aspects of economic activity and trying to understand them. Economists build models that help to predict and intervene to improve economic affairs. During this process, we also learn about our limits to predict and intervene.

I find that it is easy to communicate with other scientists because we speak the same statistical and mathematical language and are engaged in similar quests for understanding. I interact with physical and biological scientists on a regular basis at the Santa Fe Institute in New Mexico, which hosts scientific meetings for computer scientists, biologists, and economists. During the meetings, we exchange ideas about how to better understand the economy as a complex, evolving structure and how biological ideas about adaptation and evolution can be put to work in economics.

Economic systems, however, have some special features that physical and biological systems don't. An economic system is composed of individuals who are trying to figure out how the system works and to profit from this knowledge. By acting on our predictions of economic events, we alter events. For example, if people predict that IBM's profit is going to fall, they sell IBM stock and drive its price down.

You use a lot of high level mathematics in your work. How did you become proficient in the tools you need for your job? Did you take all the right courses when you were an undergraduate?
I confess that I suffered from math phobia in college and succeeded in avoiding math courses both in college and in graduate school. I ignored wise advice to study math that I received at the time from Dale Jorgenson, a professor, and Robert Hall, my classmate at Berkeley. But in America there are second chances. I started studying math seriously only after I was a professor at the University of Minnesota and was embarrassed because my students knew more math than I did. So I started studying math by auditing classes, one class at a time. After four or five years, I was less frightened of math. However, I still remain somewhat frightened.

When Robert Lucas first introduced rational expectations into macroeconomics in 1970, he touched off a revolution. Has that revolution spent its course? What have we learned that is lasting?
Robert Lucas certainly accelerated and shaped the revolution, but it would have happened without

The hyperinflations in five European countries after World War I... were all stabilized by drastic reductions in monetary growth rates and simultaneous reductions in government deficits.

him. The revolution was about building macroeconomics on the same foundation as microeconomics, a foundation grounded in the idea that people make rational choices and interact in markets that coordinate those choices. Viewed in this way, the revolution was inevitable.

The revolution has spent its course in the sense that rational expectations is no longer controversial. It is a standard tool among macroeconomists and microeconomists who study situations in which people's choices depend partly on their forecasts of the actions of others. For example, the decision to buy the stock of a corporation depends on forecasts of profits and dividends of the corporation.

You discovered, with Neil Wallace, that under some circumstances, policies designed to stabilize the economy can be ineffective. Did you then and do you now believe this policy irrelevance result is relevant to the real-world economy?
Neil and I showed that if unemployment is low when unanticipated inflation is high, the government can't lower unemployment

by increasing aggregate demand. It might do so once or even twice. But after a few repeated attempts to cut unemployment, the demand stimulation policy will become anticipated, and it will then influence the price level but not the level of unemployment. We really discovered an economic example of Abraham Lincoln's dictum that "you cannot fool all of the people all of the time."

The same idea implies that a well-executed anti-inflation policy can be highly effective. What is needed is a credible, widely anticipated, and drastic reduction in the money supply growth rate. The hyperinflations in five European countries after World War I—Germany, Austria, Poland, Hungary, and even Soviet Russia—were all stabilized by drastic reductions in monetary growth rates and simultaneous reductions in government deficits. Those countries experienced abrupt price level stabilizations and about as many real output increases as decreases. Somewhat more controversial, the stabilization in France in 1926 called the "Poincaré miracle" followed much the same lines, though the inflation that was going on in France was much smaller than the inflation that had recently occurred in Eastern Europe. Poincaré implemented a series of recommendations by a panel of experts, called the Sergeant Committee, which called for deficit reductions through tax increases and reductions in money supply growth. After the Poincaré miracle the French economy experienced a boom for several years.

The logic of the policy irrelevance result has nothing to say about the effects of government policies that work through avenues other than by inducing errors in people's forecasts. And there are many examples of such policies: investment and research and development effects on the growth rate, tax effects of the natural rate of unemployment, and so on.

...performing one's daily job is partly an investment in the acquisition of a form of capital. That is, a person's knowledge is a valuable commodity because its possession increases his or her future earnings potential.

You've spent a lot of time in recent years studying how people learn about the economic environment. What is learning? How do we study it? What have we learned about learning? How is it relevant to macroeconomic performance?

To make good economic choices, we must observe and discover patterns in the economy. Patterns, however, are difficult to distinguish because we observe an economy that is reacting both to fundamentals and to our beliefs about how the economy works. To understand the economy, we need to disentangle the influence of fundamentals from the influences of our changing beliefs. For example, suppose that inflation is caused by money supply growth, but nobody knows this fact. They believe, instead, that inflation is caused by El Niño, a warming of

the ocean surface off the western coast of South America that occurs every 4 to 12 years. When El Niño is present, inflation increases because everyone increases their prices. Nobody wants to get caught with too low a price. So, as El Niño comes and goes, the inflation rate rises and falls. Also, knowing about El Niño, the central bank creates enough money to prevent a liquidity crisis whenever El Niño hits. The learning problem is to figure out how the people in this economy gradually and eventually learn that they were wrong about El Niño and that inflation occurs only when the central bank increases the money supply.

In the last fifteen years, some economists have started studying how people learn about the eco-

nomic world. We are only just beginning to learn how models of learning influence macroeconomic performance. New work by Boyan Jovanovic and Yaw Nyarko at New York University is teaching us about statistical learning as a description of how people learn by doing. That is, people strengthen and improve their skills by repeatedly applying those skills over time. Kenneth Arrow of Stanford University formalized the idea that in situations in which you learn by doing—such as baseball, mathematics, and carpentry—performing one's daily job is partly an investment in the acquisition of a form of capital. That is, a person's knowledge is a valuable commodity because its possession increases his or her future earnings potential. This is a wonderful idea, but our implementations of it have been fairly vague until recently because we have been imprecise about what it is people learn through repeated performance. Jovanovic and Nyarko have been tightening that link by modeling repeated performance in terms of statistical sampling theory and studying how people's ideas can be expected to sharpen solely through their having been exposed to larger samples of experience.

William Brock and Black LeBaron at the University of Wisconsin are using sophisticated theories of learning from physics to explain some very puzzling observations from stock and commodities markets involving correlations between price change volatilities and trading volume. Jovanovic's and Mortensen's work on labor markets has taught us a lot about unemployment and job matching as information-gathering processes. For example, Jovanovic authored a model that explains why wages tend to rise with tenure on the job and why most quits and fires tend to occur early in tenure. Jovanovic explains these outcomes as responses to the ways firms and workers are learning about each others characteristics.

Rational expectations macroeconomics might tell us about economies that are in a settled and well-understood state. But what about the newly emerging market economies of Eastern Europe that have no history to guide us? How can we understand their performances?

Rational expectations theories study collections of people who interact in the context of well-understood rules and arrangements. They don't have much to

Economics is interesting because of the opportunities... it affords for unleashing one's natural curiosity about history, society, mathematics, and statistics.

say about situations in which the rules and social institutions are ill-formed and under discussion. Rational expectations theories impart to their users a prejudice in favor of well-specified and understood rules but little in the way of scientific machinery for studying what happens when the rules are up for grabs.

Rational expectations theories do have a lot to offer by way of describing which constellations of rules and arrangements would be desirable once they were implemented and understood. Andrew Atkeson and Patrick Kehoe of the University of Pennsylvania have constructed some theories of aspects of the transition in Eastern Europe that rest entirely on rational expectations and involve people adjusting to a clear understanding that laws, markets, trading relationships, and what to expect of others have been disrupted by the death of socialism. These theories remain controversial, partly because many economists see events in Eastern Europe in terms

of a situation in which the rules confronting people are unstable and unclear.

What is your advice to a student who is just setting out to become an economist? What are the things to study?

Economics is interesting because of the opportunities that it affords for unleashing one's natural curiosity about history, society, mathematics, and statistics. It is especially attractive to people with an interest in understanding what it takes to improve the governmental and business arrangements that we live with.

Aggregate Supply and Aggregate Demand

After studying
this chapter,
you will be
able to:

- Explain the purpose of the aggregate supply–aggregate demand model

- Explain what determines aggregate supply and aggregate demand

- Define macroeconomic equilibrium

- Explain the effects of changes in aggregate demand and aggregate supply on economic growth, inflation, and business cycles

- Explain the recent history of economic growth, inflation, and business cycles in the United States

Our economy is a bit like an ocean. Like the tide, the general direction or long-term trend of the economy is predictable and is governed by fundamental forces that are reasonably well understood. And like individual waves that ebb and flow, the economy rises and falls in a sequence of cycles that seem to repeat but are never quite like anything that went before and that are hard to predict.

Catching the Wave

World-class surfers know how to catch a wave and get a good ride. Like champion surfers, people who study the economy sometimes learn how to catch a wave and get a good economic ride. But the economic waves are hard to read. What makes the economy ebb and flow in waves around its long-term trend? ◆ Sometimes the economic waves rise high and then crash, as they did before the Great Depression in 1929. Sometimes they rise and roll on a high for a long period as they did during the mid-1980s. Sometimes the waves are inflationary as they were during the 1970s. And sometimes they hit a low and remain there for some time as they did during the Great Depression. What makes real GDP growth and inflation fluctuate in unpredictable ways? ◆ The U.S. economy is influenced by economic and political events in other parts of the world. For example, rapid economic and industrial expansion in Asia has increased competition in the markets for manufactured goods. The economy is also influenced by policy actions taken by the Administration, Congress, and the Federal Reserve. How do events in the rest of the world and domestic policy actions affect production and prices?

◈ To address questions like these, we need a model of macroeconomic fluctuations—of fluctuations around the long-term trends. Our main task in this chapter is to build such a model: the *aggregate supply–aggregate demand model*. Our second task is to use the aggregate supply–aggregate demand model to answer the questions we've just posed. You'll discover that the aggregate supply-aggregate demand model enables us to understand many economic events that have a major impact on our lives.

Aggregate Supply

THE PURPOSE OF THE AGGREGATE SUPPLY–
aggregate demand model is to understand and predict fluctuations of real GDP around potential GDP and fluctuations in the price level. The model uses an aggregate supply curve and an aggregate demand curve, each of which shows a relationship between real GDP and the price level. We begin by studying aggregate supply.

The *aggregate quantity of goods and services supplied* is the sum of the quantities of final goods and services produced by all firms in the economy, which is measured by real GDP. Aggregate supply is the relationship between the quantity of real GDP supplied and the price level (the GDP deflator), other things remaining the same. This relationship depends on the time frame we are considering and we distinguish two time frames for aggregate supply:

■ Long-run aggregate supply
■ Short-run aggregate supply

Long-Run Aggregate Supply

The economy is constantly bombarded by events that move real GDP away from potential GDP and, equivalently, that move the unemployment rate away from full employment. Following such an event, forces operate to take real GDP back toward potential GDP and restore full employment. The **macroeconomic long run** is a time frame that is sufficiently long for these forces to have done their work so that real GDP equals potential GDP and full employment prevails.

The **long-run aggregate supply curve** is the relationship between the quantity of real GDP supplied and the price level in the long run when real GDP equals potential GDP. Figure 27.1 illustrates long-run aggregate supply as the vertical line labeled *LAS*. Along the long-run aggregate supply curve, as the price level changes, real GDP remains at potential GDP, which in Fig. 27.1 is $6 trillion. The long-run aggregate supply curve is always vertical and located at potential GDP.

The long-run aggregate supply curve is vertical because potential GDP is independent of the price level. The reason for this independence is that a movement along the long-run aggregate supply curve is accompanied by changes in *two* sets of prices: the prices of goods and services (the price level) and the

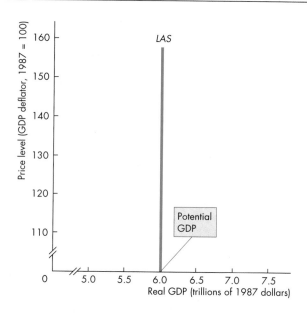

FIGURE 27.1

Long-Run Aggregate Supply

The long-run aggregate supply (*LAS*) curve shows the relationship between the quantity of real GDP supplied and the price level when real GDP equals potential GDP and there is full employment. This level of real GDP is independent of the price level so the *LAS* curve is vertical at potential GDP.

prices of factors of production. A 10 percent increase in the prices of goods and services is matched by a 10 percent increase in wage rates and in other factor prices. That is, the price level, wage rate, and other factor prices all change by the same percentage and *relative prices* and the *real wage rate* remain constant. When the price level changes but relative prices and the real wage rate remain constant, real GDP also remains constant.

Production at a Pepsi Plant   You can see why real GDP remains constant in these circumstances by thinking about production decisions at a Pepsi bottling plant. The plant has increased its production to the point at which it is making the largest available profit. It could increase production further but to do so it would have to incur additional costs that exceed the additional revenue from higher sales, so its profit would fall. In this situation, if the price of bottled Pepsi increased and wage rates and other bottling costs did not change, the firm would have an incentive to increase its production. The higher price for Pepsi would more than cover the extra cost of hiring more labor, and profit would rise. But if the price of bottled Pepsi increases and wage rates and other bottling costs also increase by the same percentage, the firm has no incentive to change its production. The extra revenue from the higher price just equals the extra cost of hiring more labor, so profit cannot be increased by increasing production. In this case, production remains constant.

What's true for Pepsi bottlers is also true for the producers of all goods and services. So aggregate production—real GDP—does not change when the price level and the prices of all factors of production change by the same percentage.

Short-Run Aggregate Supply

The **macroeconomic short-run** is a period during which real GDP has fallen below potential GDP (and unemployment has risen above the natural rate), or in which real GDP has risen above potential GDP (and unemployment has fallen below the natural rate). The short run is not a point in time and it is not a definite number of months or years that can be marked on a calendar. It is the normal state of the economy when real GDP is fluctuating around potential GDP.

The **short-run aggregate supply curve** is the relationship between the quantity of real GDP supplied and the price level in the short run when all other influences on production plans such as the money wage rate and raw materials prices remain constant. Figure 27.2 illustrates the short-run aggregate supply curve as the upward-sloping curve labeled *SAS*. This short-run aggregate supply curve is based on the aggregate supply schedule and each point on the aggregate supply curve corresponds to a row of the aggregate supply schedule. For example, point *a* on the short-run aggregate supply curve and row *a* of the schedule tell us that if the price level is 120, the quantity of real GDP supplied is $5 trillion.

At point *c* on the short-run aggregate supply curve and on row *c* of the schedule the price level is 130. At this price level, the quantity of real GDP supplied is $6 trillion, which equals potential GDP. If the price level is greater than 130, real GDP exceeds

FIGURE 27.2

Short-Run Aggregate Supply

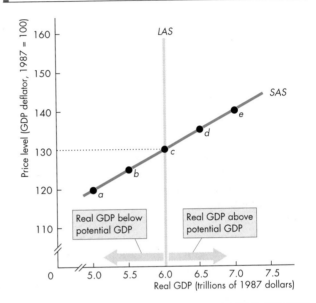

	Price Level (GDP deflator)	Real GDP (trillions of 1987 dollars)
a	120	5.0
b	125	5.5
c	130	6.0
d	135	6.5
e	140	7.0

The short-run aggregate supply (SAS) curve shows the relationship between the quantity of real GDP supplied and the price level when the money wage rate, other factor prices, and potential GDP are constant. The short-run aggregate supply curve SAS is based on the schedule in the table. The SAS curve is upward-sloping because firms' costs increase as the rate of output increases so a higher price is needed to bring forth an increase in the quantity produced.

potential GDP and if the price level is less than 130, real GDP is less than potential GDP. Equivalently, if the price level is greater than 130, unemployment is below the natural rate and if the price level is less than 130, unemployment is above the natural rate.

Back at the Pepsi Plant You can see why the short-run aggregate supply curve slopes upward by going back to the Pepsi bottling plant. Recall that the plant has increased its production to the point at which it is making the largest available profit. To increase production further, it must incur additional costs that exceed the additional revenue from higher sales, so its profit would fall. But if the price of bottled Pepsi rises and wage rates and other bottling costs don't change, the firm has an incentive to increase its production. The higher price for Pepsi more than covers the extra cost of hiring more labor, and its profit rises. So in this situation, the firm increases its production.

Again, what's true for Pepsi bottlers is also true for the producers of all goods and services. So when the price level rises and the money wage rate and other factor prices remain constant, the quantity of real GDP supplied increases.

Although Fig. 27.2 shows the short-run aggregate supply curve to be upward-sloping, which it normally is, for a very brief period the short-run aggregate supply curve is horizontal. The reason is that at the start of a short-run period, when spending, production, and sales begin to change, the price level does not change right away. Firms produce and sell the quantities demanded at the prices they have announced. So in this shortest of short runs, the *SAS* curve is horizontal: real GDP fluctuates but the price level is sticky. But this *sticky price* situation does not last for long. If sales increase, firms increase production and raise their prices. Similarly, if sales decrease, firms cut production and lower their prices. For the economy as a whole, if sales increase and with the money wage rate and other factor prices unchanged, the price level rises and the quantity of real GDP supplied increases. If sales decrease and the money wage rate and other factor prices remain unchanged, the price level falls and the quantity of real GDP supplied decreases.

Movements Along the *LAS* and *SAS* Curves

Figure 27.3 summarizes what you've just learned about the *LAS* and *SAS* curves. A *movement along* the *LAS* curve occurs when the price level changes but real GDP remains at potential GDP. The economy moves along the *LAS* curve only when the short-run adjustment process is complete and the price level, the money wage rate, and the prices of other factors

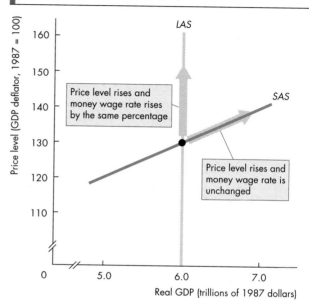

FIGURE 27.3
Movements Along the Aggregate Supply Curves

A rise in the price level with the money wage rate and other factor prices unchanged brings an increase in the quantity of real GDP supplied and a movement along the short-run aggregate supply curve. A rise in the price level with equal percentage rises in the money wage rate and other factor prices keeps the quantity of real GDP supplied constant and brings a movement along the long-run aggregate supply curve.

of production have all changed by the same percentage. Figure 27.3 illustrates a movement along the *LAS* curve when the price level, the money wage rate, and the prices of other factors of production all increase by the same percentage.

A *movement along* the *SAS* curve occurs when the price level changes but the money wage rate and other factor prices remain constant. Figure 27.3 illustrates a movement along the *SAS* curve when the price level *rises*. When the economy moves along the *SAS* curve, real GDP moves away from potential GDP.

You've now learned about the long-run and short-run aggregate supply curves and the factors that make the long-run aggregate supply curve vertical and the short-run aggregate supply curve slope upward. But what makes aggregate supply change? Let's find out.

Changes in Aggregate Supply

You've just seen that a change in the price level, other things remaining the same, brings a movement along the aggregate supply curves but it does not change aggregate supply. Aggregate supply changes when any other influence on production plans change. Let's study these influences beginning with those that affect long-run aggregate supply.

Changes in Long-Run Aggregate Supply Long-run aggregate supply changes when potential GDP changes and potential GDP changes for two reasons:

1. Growth of aggregate labor hours
2. Growth of productivity

Suppose there are two identical Pepsi bottling plants except that one employs 100 hours of labor and the other employs 10 hours of labor. The plant with more labor produces more bottles of Pepsi. The same is true for the economy as a whole. The larger the number of labor hours available, the greater is potential GDP, and the faster the growth rate of labor hours, the faster is the growth rate of potential GDP (other things remaining the same).

Growth in productivity means getting more output from given inputs (or the same output from fewer inputs). It is measured by the growth in real GDP per hour of labor. The growth in productivity is influenced by three main factors:

1. Growth of the capital stock
2. Growth of human capital
3. Technological change

Suppose one Pepsi plant has two production lines and the other has only one. The plant with two lines has more capital and produces more output than the other. For the economy as a whole, the larger the capital stock, the more productive is the labor force and the greater is the output that it can produce. Also, the faster the capital stock grows, the faster does real GDP grow. The capital-rich U.S. economy produces a vastly greater real GDP per hour of labor than nations that have a small amount of capital such as the developing countries. But the fast-growing capital stock of the Asian economies is bringing faster real GDP growth than the United States has achieved.

The manager of one Pepsi plant is an economics major with an MBA and its labor force has an average of 10 years experience. The manager of another identical plant has no business training and its labor force has just been hired and is new to bottling. The first plant has a higher stock of human capital than the second and its output is larger. For the economy as a whole, the larger the stock of *human capital*—the skills that people have acquired in school and through on-the-job training—the greater is real GDP, and the faster the stock of human capital grows, the faster real GDP grows (other things remaining the same).

One Pepsi plant has a production line that was designed in the 1970s before the computer age. Another uses the latest robot technology. Even with a smaller labor force, the second plant produces more bottles per day than the first plant. Technological change—inventing new and better ways of doing things—enables firms to produce more from any given amount of inputs. So even with a constant labor force and constant capital stock, improvements in technology increase production and increase aggregate supply. Technological advances are by far the most important source of increased production over the past two centuries. As a result of technological advances, in the United States today, one farmer can feed 100 people, and one autoworker can produce almost 14 cars and trucks in a year.

Changes in Short-Run Aggregate Supply All the factors that influence long-run aggregate supply also influence short-run aggregate supply. That is, if potential GDP increases, more real GDP is supplied in the long run but more real GDP is supplied at each price level in the short run. So if potential GDP increases, short-run aggregate supply increases.

The only influences on short-run aggregate supply that do not also change long-run aggregate supply are the money wage rate and the prices of other factors of production. Factor prices affect short-run aggregate supply through their influence on firms' costs. The higher the money wage rate and other factor prices, the higher are firms' costs and the smaller is the quantity that firms are willing to supply at each price level. Thus an increase in the money wage rate and other factor prices decreases short-run aggregate supply.

Why do factor prices affect short-run aggregate supply but not long-run aggregate supply? The answer lies in the definition of long-run aggregate supply. Along the long-run aggregate supply curve real GDP remains constant at potential GDP because when the money wage changes, the price level also changes by the same percentage.

FIGURE 27.4

Changes in Aggregate Supply

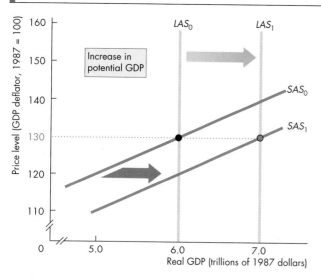

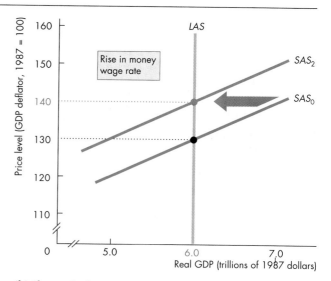

(a) Change in potential GDP shifts LAS and SAS

(b) Change in the money wage rate shifts SAS

In part (a), an increase in potential GDP increases both long-run aggregate supply and short-run aggregate supply and shifts both aggregate supply curves rightward from LAS_0 to LAS_1 and from SAS_0 to SAS_1. In part (b), a rise in the money wage rate

decreases short-run aggregate supply and shifts the short-run aggregate supply curve leftward from SAS_0 to SAS_2. A rise in the money wage rate does not change long-run aggregate supply so the LAS curve does not shift.

Shifts in LAS and SAS Figure 27.4 illustrates changes in long-run aggregate supply and short-run aggregate supply as shifts in the aggregate supply curves. Part (a) shows the effects of a change in potential GDP. Initially, the long-run aggregate supply curve is LAS_0 and short-run aggregate supply curve is SAS_0. An increase in labor hours or an increase in productivity increases potential GDP to $7 trillion. As a result, long-run aggregate supply increases and the long-run aggregate supply curve shifts rightward to LAS_1. Short-run aggregate supply also increases and the short-run aggregate supply curve shifts rightward to SAS_1.

Figure 27.4(b) shows the effects of an increase in the money wage rate (or other factor price) on aggregate supply. Initially, the short-run aggregate supply curve is SAS_0. A rise in the money wage rate *decreases* short-run aggregate supply and shifts the short-run aggregate supply curve leftward to SAS_2. Long-run aggregate supply does not change when the money wage rate changes, so the LAS curve remains at LAS.

REVIEW

- On the long-run aggregate supply curve, a change in the price level is accompanied by equal percentage changes in the money wage rate and other factor prices and the quantity of real GDP supplied is constant at potential GDP.

- On the short-run aggregate supply curve, a rise in the price level with no change in the money wage rate brings an increase in the quantity of real GDP supplied.

- An increase in labor hours and an increase in productivity increase potential GDP, which increases both long-run aggregate supply and short-run aggregate supply and shifts the LAS curve and the SAS curve rightward.

- An increase in the money wage rate (or other factor price) decreases short-run aggregate supply but leaves long-run aggregate supply unchanged. The SAS curve shifts leftward.

Aggregate Demand

THE AGGREGATE QUANTITY OF GOODS AND services produced is measured as real GDP—GDP valued in constant dollars. The average price of all these goods and services is measured by the GDP deflator. The purpose of the aggregate supply–aggregate demand model that you are studying in this chapter is to determine real GDP and the price level. We've learned about aggregate supply and we are now going to study aggregate demand.

The *aggregate quantity of goods and services demanded* is the sum of the consumption goods and services that households plan to buy, of investment goods that firms plan to buy, of goods and services that governments plan to buy, and of net exports that foreigners plan to buy. Thus the aggregate quantity of goods and services demanded depends on decisions made by households, firms, governments, and foreigners.

When we studied the demand for tapes in Chapter 4, we summarized the buying plans of households in a demand schedule and demand curve. Similarly, when we study the forces that influence aggregate buying plans, we summarize the decisions of households, firms, governments, and foreigners by using an aggregate demand schedule and aggregate demand curve. **Aggregate demand** is the entire relationship between the quantity of real GDP demanded and the price level (the GDP deflator).

Figure 27.5 illustrates aggregate demand as an aggregate demand schedule and as the downward-sloping curve labeled *AD*. This aggregate demand curve is based on the aggregate demand schedule and each point on the aggregate demand curve corresponds to a row of the aggregate demand schedule. For example, point *c'* on the aggregate demand curve and row *c'* of the aggregate demand schedule tells us that if the price level is 130, the quantity of real GDP demanded is $6 trillion.

In constructing the aggregate demand schedule and aggregate demand curve, we hold constant all the influences on the quantity of real GDP demanded other than the price level and the interest rate. As the price level changes, the interest rate also changes (for a reason that is explained below) and there is a movement along the aggregate demand curve. A change in any of the other influences on the quantity of real GDP demanded results in a new aggregate demand schedule and a shift in the aggregate demand curve.

FIGURE 27.5

Aggregate Demand

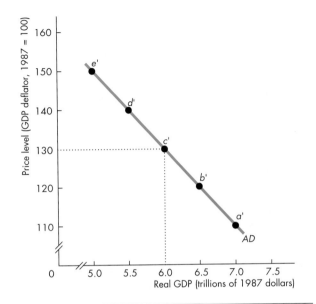

	Price Level (GDP deflator)	Real GDP (trillions of 1987 dollars)
a'	110	7.0
b'	120	6.5
c'	130	6.0
d'	140	5.5
e'	150	5.0

The aggregate demand curve (*AD*) shows the relationship between the quantity of real GDP demanded and the price level. The aggregate demand curve is based on the schedule in the table. Each point *a'* through *e'* on the curve corresponds to the row in the table identified by the same letter. Thus when the price level is 130, the quantity of real GDP demanded is $6.0 trillion, illustrated by point *c'* in the figure.

Let's look more closely at the effects of a change in the price level on the quantity of real GDP demanded. You can see from the numbers that describe the aggregate demand schedule that the higher the price level, the smaller is the quantity of real GDP demanded. The aggregate demand curve slopes downward. But why?

Why the Aggregate Demand Curve Slopes Downward

If the price of Pepsi rises, the quantity of Pepsi demanded decreases because some people can't afford to buy as much soda (an income effect) and because some people switch to drinking Coke and other sodas (a substitution effect). The demand curve for Pepsi slopes downward because of an income effect and a substitution effect.

The aggregate demand curve slopes downward for analogous reasons. Real GDP has three main substitutes: money, future real GDP, and foreign real GDP. These substitutes give rise to three influences of the price level on the quantity of real GDP demanded:

- Real money balances effect
- Intertemporal substitution effect
- International substitution effect

Real Money Balances Effect **Money** is currency and bank deposits—the things you use to buy goods and services and pay bills. **Real money** is the *purchasing power* of money or the quantity of goods and services that money will buy. It is measured by the quantity of money divided by the price level.

The **real money balances effect** is the change in the quantity of real GDP demanded that results from a change in the quantity of real money. The greater the quantity of real money (that is, the greater the purchasing power of money), the greater is the quantity of real GDP demanded. But the quantity of real money increases if the price level falls, so a fall in the price level brings an increase in the quantity of real GDP demanded and a movement along the aggregate demand curve.

To see how the real money balances effect works, think about your own spending plans. You have $5 to spend, and coffee costs $2.50 a cup. Your money can buy 2 cups of coffee. But if coffee cost $1 a cup, your $5 could buy 5 cups. The lower the price, the more you can buy with a given quantity of money so the greater is your purchasing power. And the greater your purchasing power, the more goods you plan to buy.

The real money balances effect is analogous to the income effect on the demand for individual goods and services. But income is a flow and money is a stock, which is part of wealth, so the two effects are not identical. The other two reasons for the downward-sloping aggregate demand curve are substitution effects.

Intertemporal Substitution Effect The **intertemporal substitution effect** is the change in the quantity of real GDP demanded resulting from a change in the *opportunity cost* of goods and services today in terms of goods and services in the future. The main influence on this opportunity cost is the *interest rate*. The higher the interest rate, the greater is the opportunity cost of buying today. By not buying today, but by saving instead, you can earn interest. The higher the interest rate, the greater is the amount you earn on your savings and the more you can buy in the future. So the higher the interest rate, the greater is the opportunity cost of buying today.

The interest rate is influenced by the price level. The higher the price level, other things remaining the same, the higher is the interest rate. The reason is connected to the *real money balances effect* that you've just learned about. With a higher price level, people have less purchasing power, so the amount they want to lend decreases and the amount they want to borrow increases (other things remaining the same). A decrease in the supply of loans and an increase in the demand for loans means that interest rates rise.

So as the price level rises, other things remaining the same, the interest rate also rises and the quantity of real GDP demanded decreases.

International Substitution Effect The **international substitution effect** is the change in the quantity of real GDP demanded resulting from a change in the *opportunity cost* of domestic goods (and services) in terms of foreign goods. An example is your decision to buy a Toyota car that was made in Japan instead of a GM car made in the United States. Another example is your decision to take a ski trip to the Canadian Rockies instead of to Colorado.

The higher the price level in the United States, other things remaining the same, the higher are the prices of U.S.-made goods and services relative to foreign-made goods and services and the fewer U.S.-made goods and services people buy. So the higher the price level, the smaller is the quantity of real GDP demanded.

For the three reasons just reviewed, the aggregate demand curve slopes downward. The higher the price level in the United States, the smaller is the quantity demanded of U.S.-made goods and services—U.S. real GDP. The lower the price level in the United States, the larger is the quantity demanded of U.S.-made goods and services—U.S. real GDP.

FIGURE 27.6
Changes in the Quantity of Real GDP Demanded

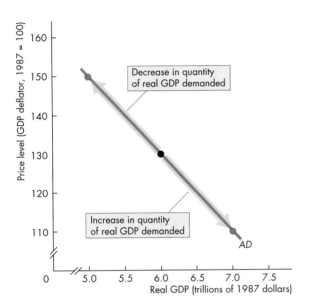

The quantity of real GDP demanded

Decreases if the price level *increases*   *Increases* if the price level *decreases*

because of the:

Real money balances effect

- An increase in the price level decreases the quantity of real money
- A decrease in the price level increases the quantity of real money

Intertemporal substitution effect

- An increase in the price level increases interest rates
- A decrease in the price level decreases interest rates

International substitution effect

- An increase in the price level increases the cost of domestic goods and services relative to foreign goods and services
- A decrease in the price level decreases the cost of domestic goods and services relative to foreign goods and services

Changes in the Quantity of Real GDP Demanded

When the price level changes (and the interest rate changes with it), other things remaining constant, there is a change in the quantity of real GDP demanded. Such a change is illustrated as a movement along the aggregate demand curve. Figure 27.6 illustrates changes in the quantity of real GDP demanded. It also summarizes the three reasons why the aggregate demand curve slopes downward.

We've now seen how the quantity of real GDP demanded changes when the price level (and interest rate) change. How do other influences on spending plans affect aggregate demand?

Changes in Aggregate Demand

The aggregate demand schedule and aggregate demand curve describe aggregate demand at a point in time. But aggregate demand frequently changes. As a consequence, the aggregate demand curve frequently shifts. The main influences on aggregate demand that shift the aggregate demand curve are:

- Expectations
- International factors
- Fiscal policy
- Monetary policy

Expectations

Expectations about all future economic conditions play a crucial role in determining people's decisions about spending on consumer goods and services and business decisions about spending on investment. Three expectations are very important: future incomes, future inflation, and future profits.

Expected Future Incomes   An increase in expected future income, other things remaining the same, increases the amount that households plan to spend today on consumption goods and consumer durables and increases aggregate demand. When households expect slow future income growth, or even a decline in income, they scale back their spending plans today, and aggregate demand decreases.

Expectations about future income growth were pessimistic during 1990, contributing to the decrease in spending that brought on the 1991 recession.

Expected Inflation   An increase in the expected inflation rate, other things remaining the same, leads to an increase in aggregate demand. The higher the expected inflation rate, the higher is the expected price of goods and services in the future and the lower is the expected real value of money and other financial assets in the future. As a consequence, when people expect a higher inflation rate, they plan to buy more goods and services today and hold smaller quantities of money and other financial assets. As a result, aggregate demand increases.

Inflation expectations increased during the 1970s and by 1980, people expected inflation to persist at close to 10 percent a year. This high expected inflation rate kept aggregate demand high through the late 1970s. But in 1982, a severe recession that resulted from tight monetary policy (see p. 665) lowered the inflation rate and inflation expectations also fell. This decrease in the expected inflation rate lowered aggregate demand (compared with what it would otherwise have been) through the rest of the 1980s and the early 1990s. But during 1994, with the economy expanding quickly, higher inflation became expected, which added to aggregate demand.

Expected Future Profits   A change in firms' expected future profit changes their demand for new capital equipment. For example, suppose that there has been a recent wave of technological change that has increased productivity. Firms might expect that large profit opportunities exist from using the latest technology. This expectation leads to an increase in demand for new plant and equipment and so to an increase in aggregate demand.

Profit expectations were pessimistic in 1991 and led to a decrease in aggregate demand. Expectations were optimistic through the mid-1990s and led to sustained increases in aggregate demand.

International Factors

There are two main international factors that influence aggregate demand. They are the foreign exchange rate and foreign income.

The Foreign Exchange Rate   A change in the U.S. price level, other things remaining constant, changes the prices of U.S.-produced goods and services *relative* to the prices of goods and services produced in other countries. Another influence on the price of U.S.-produced goods and services relative to those produced abroad is the *foreign exchange rate.* The foreign exchange rate is the amount of a foreign currency that you can buy with a U.S. dollar. For example, $1 might buy 100 Japanese yen.

The foreign exchange rate affects aggregate demand because it affects the prices that foreigners have to pay for U.S.-produced goods and services and the prices that we have to pay for foreign-produced goods and services. To see how, suppose that the dollar is worth 100 Japanese yen. You can buy a Fujitsu cellular telephone (made in Japan) that costs 12,500 yen for $125. What if for $110 you can buy a Motorola phone (made in the United States) that is just as good as the Fujitsu? In this case you will buy the Motorola phone.

But which phone will you buy if the value of the U.S. dollar rises to 125 yen and everything else remains the same? Let's work out the answer. At 125 yen per dollar you pay only $100 to buy the 12,500 yen needed to buy the Fujitsu phone. Since the Motorola phone costs $110, the Fujitsu is now cheaper, and you will substitute the Fujitsu for the Motorola. The demand for U.S.-made phones falls as the foreign exchange value of the dollar rises. So as the foreign exchange value of the dollar rises, everything else being held constant, aggregate demand decreases.

There have been huge swings in the foreign exchange value of the dollar through the 1990s, leading to large swings in aggregate demand.

Foreign Income   The income of foreigners affects the aggregate demand for U.S.-made goods and services. For example, an increase in income in Japan and Germany increases the demand by Japanese and German consumers and producers for U.S.-made consumption goods and capital goods and increases U.S. exports.

These sources of change in aggregate demand in the United States have been important ones since World War II. The rapid long-term economic growth of Japan and Western Europe and of some of the newly industrializing countries of the Pacific Rim, such as Hong Kong and Singapore, has led to a sustained increase in demand for U.S.-made goods and services. Also, fluctuations in income growth in the rest of the world have contributed to fluctuations in U.S. aggregate demand. For example, the slowdown in growth in Japan in the 1990s limited Japanese demand for U.S. imports and slowed the growth of aggregate demand in the United States.

Fiscal Policy

Decisions about government purchases of goods and services, taxes and transfer payments, and the government's deficit and debt are made by Congress in consultation with the administration and are brought together in the nation's annual budget. These decisions influence aggregate demand. The government's attempt to influence the economy by varying its purchases of goods and services, taxes and transfer payments, and its deficit and debt is called **fiscal policy**.

Government Purchases of Goods and Services
The scale of government purchases of goods and services has a direct effect on aggregate demand. If taxes are held constant, the more hospitals, highways, schools, and colleges the government funds, the larger are government purchases of goods and services and so the larger is aggregate demand. The most important changes in government purchases of goods and services arise from the state of international tension and conflict. In times of war, government purchases increase dramatically. In this century, government purchases increased sharply during World War II and then declined. They increased again during the Cold War era, expecially during the Vietnam War years of the late 1960s. They decreased when the Cold War ended in the early 1990s. These changes in spending exerted a large influence on aggregate demand. If the spending cuts in the "Contract with America" are implemented through the rest of the 1990s, aggregate demand will be decreased.

Taxes and Transfer Payments
A decrease in taxes increases aggregate demand. An increase in transfer payments—unemployment benefits, social security benefits, and welfare payments—also increases aggregate demand. Both of these influences operate by increasing households' *disposable* income. The higher the level of disposable income, the greater is the demand for goods and services. Because lower taxes and higher transfer payments increase disposable income, they also increase aggregate demand.

This source of changes in aggregate demand has been an important one in recent years. Through the late 1960s there was a large increase in government payments under various social programs, and these led to a large increase in aggregate demand. During the 1980s the Reagan tax cuts increased aggregate demand, and tax hikes in 1990 and 1993 decreased aggregate demand.

Monetary Policy

Decisions about the money supply and interest rates are made by the Federal Reserve Board (the Fed), a public agency that manages the nation's financial affairs. These decisions influence aggregate demand. The Fed's attempt to influence the economy by varying the money supply and interest rates is called **monetary policy**.

Money Supply
The money supply is determined by the Fed and the banks (in a process described in Chapters 30 and 31). The greater the *quantity of money*, the greater is the level of aggregate demand. An easy way to see why money affects aggregate demand is to imagine what would happen if the Fed borrowed the army's helicopters, loaded them with millions of dollars worth of new $10 bills, and sprinkled the bills like confetti across the nation. We would all stop whatever we were doing and rush out to pick up our share of the newly available money. But we wouldn't just put the money we picked up in the bank. We would spend some of it, so our demand for goods and services would increase. Although this story is pretty extreme, it does illustrate that an increase in the quantity of money increases aggregate demand.

In practice, changes in the quantity of money change interest rates and so have an additional influence on aggregate demand by changing investment and expenditure on consumer durables. When the Fed speeds up the rate at which it creates new money, banks have more funds to lend and interest rates fall. When the Fed slows down the pace at which it creates new money, banks have less funds to lend and interest rates rise. Thus a change in the quantity of money has a second effect on aggregate demand, operating through its effects on interest rates.

Interest Rates
If the Fed increases interest rates, households and firms change their borrowing, lending, and spending plans. They try to borrow less, lend more, and cut back their spending on durable goods—investment. The cut in spending on durable goods is a decrease in aggregate demand.

Fluctuations in the quantity of money and interest rates have been important sources of changes in aggregate demand. Rapid increases in the quantity of money through the 1970s made aggregate demand increase quickly and contributed to the inflation of those years; decreases in the growth rate of the quantity of money in 1980 and 1990 slowed aggregate

FIGURE 27.7

Changes in Aggregate Demand

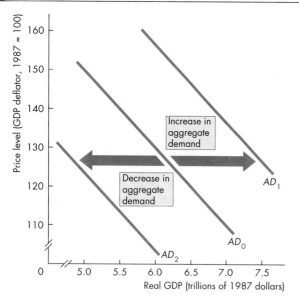

Aggregate demand

Decreases if

- Expected future income, inflation, or expected profits decrease

- The exchange rate increases or foreign income decreases

- Fiscal policy decreases government spending, increases taxes, or decreases transfer payments

- Monetary policy decreases the money supply and increases interest rates

Increases if

- Expected future income, inflation, or expected profits increase

- The exchange rate decreases or foreign income increases

- Fiscal policy increases government spending, decreases taxes, or increases transfer payments

- Monetary policy increases the money supply and decreases interest rates

Shifts of the Aggregate Demand Curve

We illustrate a change in aggregate demand as a shift in the aggregate demand curve. Figure 27.7 illustrates two changes in aggregate demand and summarizes the factors that bring about such changes. Aggregate demand is initially AD_0, which is the same as the aggregate demand curve in Fig. 27.5.

The aggregate demand curve shifts rightward, from AD_0 to AD_1, when expected future income increases, expected profit increases, the expected inflation rate increases, the foreign exchange rate falls, income in the rest of the world increases, government purchases of goods and services increase, taxes are cut, transfer payments increase, or the money supply increases and interest rates fall.

The aggregate demand curve shifts leftward, from AD_0 to AD_2, when expected future income decreases, expected future profit decreases, the expected inflation rate decreases, the foreign exchange rate rises, income in the rest of the world decreases, government purchases of goods and services decrease, taxes are increased, transfer payments decrease, or the money supply decreases and interest rates rise.

R E V I E W

- The aggregate demand curve shows the effect of a change in the price level on the quantity of real GDP demanded, other things remaining the same.

- An increase in the price level brings a decrease in the quantity of real GDP demanded because it decreases the quantity of real money balances, increases the price of goods in the present relative to goods in the future, and increases the price of domestic goods relative to foreign goods

- Other influences on aggregate spending plans (expectations, international factors, fiscal policy, and monetary policy) change aggregate demand and shift the aggregate demand curve.

You've seen how aggregate supply is determined in the long run and in the short run, and you've examined the main factors that change aggregate supply. You've also seen how aggregate demand is determined. Your next task is to see how aggregate supply and aggregate demand together determine real GDP and the price level.

demand growth and contributed to the recessions of those years. And more rapid money supply growth stimulated an expansion that began in 1992.

Let's now see how the influences on aggregate demand affect the aggregate demand curve.

Macroeconomic Equilibrium

THE PURPOSE OF THE AGGREGATE SUPPLY– aggregate demand model is to understand and predict changes in real GDP and the price level. To achieve this purpose, we combine aggregate supply and aggregate demand and determine macroeconomic equilibrium. There is a macroeconomic equilibrium for each of the time frames for aggregate supply: a long-run equilibrium and a short-run equilibrium. Long-run equilibrium is the state toward which the economy is heading. Short-run equilibrium describes the state of the economy at each point in time on its path toward long-run macroeconomic equilibrium. We'll begin our study of macroeconomic equilibrium by looking at the short run.

Determination of Real GDP and the Price Level

The aggregate demand curve tells us the quantity of real GDP demanded at each price level, and the short-run aggregate supply curve tells us the quantity of real GDP supplied at each price level. **Short-run macroeconomic equilibrium** occurs when the quantity of real GDP demanded equals the short-run quantity of real GDP supplied at the point of intersection of the *AD* curve and the *SAS* curve. Figure 27.8 illustrates such an equilibrium at a price level of 130 and real GDP of $6.0 trillion (points *c* and *c'*).

To see why this position is an equilibrium, let's work out what happens if the price level is something other than 130. Suppose, for example, that the price level is 140 and that real GDP is $7 trillion (at point *e*) on the *SAS* curve. The quantity of real GDP demanded is less than $7 trillion, so firms are unable to sell all their output. Unwanted inventories pile up, and firms cut both production and prices. Production and prices are cut until firms can sell all their output. This situation occurs only when real GDP is $6 trillion and the price level is 130.

Next consider what happens if the price level is 120 and real GDP is $5 trillion (at point *a*) on the *SAS* curve. The quantity of real GDP demanded exceeds $5 trillion, so firms are not able to meet demand. Inventories fall, and customers clamor for goods. So firms increase production and raise prices. Production and prices increase until firms can meet demand. This situation occurs only when real GDP is $6 trillion and the price level is 130.

FIGURE 27.8
Short-Run Equilibrium

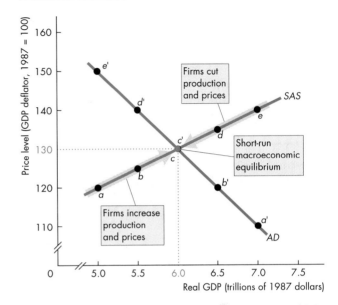

Short-run macroeconomic equilibrium occurs when real GDP demanded equals real GDP supplied at the intersection of the aggregate demand curve (AD) and the short-run aggregate supply curve (SAS). Here, such an equilibrium occurs at points *c* and *c'* where the price level is 130 and real GDP is $6.0 trillion. If the price level is 140 and real GDP is $7 trillion (point e), firms will not be able to sell all their output. They will decrease production and cut prices. If the price level is 120 and real GDP is $5 trillion (point a), people will not be able to buy all the goods they demanded. Firms will increase production and raise their prices. Only when the price level is 130 and real GDP is $6 trillion can firms sell all that they produce and people buy all that they demand. This is the short-run macroeconomic equilibrium.

Short-Run and Long-Run Macroeconomic Equilibrium

Long-run macroeconomic equilibrium occurs when real GDP equals potential GDP and there is full employment. Equivalently, long-run equilibrium occurs when the economy is on its *long-run* aggregate supply curve. Short-run macroeconomic equilibrium can occur at a real GDP that is less than, equal to, or greater than potential GDP. Figure 27.9 illustrates these three possible cases.

In part (a) there is a below full-employment equilibrium. A **below full-employment equilibrium** is a macroeconomic equilibrium in which potential GDP exceeds real GDP. The amount by which potential GDP exceeds real GDP is called a **recessionary gap**. This name reminds us that a gap has opened up between potential GDP and real GDP either because the economy has experienced a recession or because real GDP, while growing, has grown more slowly than potential GDP.

The below full-employment equilibrium illustrated in Fig. 27.9(a) occurs where aggregate demand

curve AD_0 intersects short-run aggregate supply curve SAS_0 at a real GDP of \$5 trillion and a price level of 130. The recessionary gap is \$1 trillion. The U.S. economy was in a situation similar to that shown in Fig. 27.9(a) in the early 1980s and again in the early 1990s. In those years, unemployment was high and real GDP was less than potential GDP.

Figure 27.9(b) is an example of long-run equilibrium or *full-employment equilibrium* in which real GDP equals potential GDP. In this example the equilibrium occurs where the aggregate demand curve AD_1 intersects the short-run aggregate supply curve

---

Three Cases of Macroeconomic Equilibrium

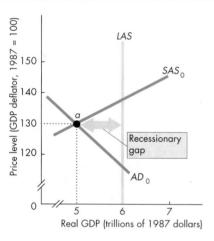

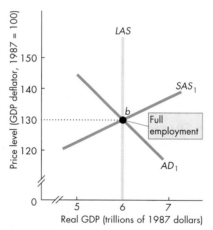

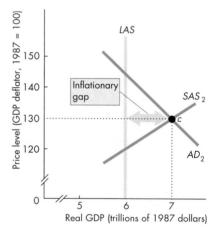

(a) Below full-employment equilibrium

(b) Long-run equilibrium

(c) Above full-employment equilibrium

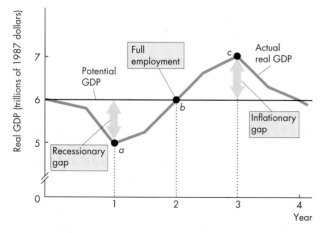

(d) Fluctuations in real GDP

Part (a) shows a below full-employment equilibrium in year 1; part (b) shows a long-run equilibrium in year 2; part (c) shows an above full-employment equilibrium in year 3. Part (d) shows how real GDP fluctuates around potential GDP in a business cycle. In year 1 there is a recessionary gap and the economy is at point *a* (in parts a and d). In year 2 there is full employment and the economy is at point *b* (in parts b and d). In year 3 there is an inflationary gap and the economy is at point *c* (in parts c and d).

SAS_1 at an actual and potential GDP of $6 trillion. The U.S. economy was in a situation such as that shown in Fig. 27.9(b) in mid-1994.

Figure 27.9(c) illustrates an above full-employment equilibrium. An **above full-employment equilibrium** is a macroeconomic equilibrium in which real GDP exceeds potential GDP. The amount by which real GDP exceeds potential GDP is called an **inflationary gap**. This name reminds us that a gap has opened up between real GDP and potential GDP that is creating inflationary pressure.

The above full-employment equilibrium illustrated in Fig. 27.9(c) occurs where the aggregate demand curve AD_2 intersects the short-run aggregate supply curve SAS_2 at a real GDP of $7 trillion and a price level of 130. There is an inflationary gap of $1 trillion. The U.S. economy was in a situation similar to that depicted in part (c) in 1988–1990.

The economy moves from one type of equilibrium to another as a result of fluctuations in aggregate demand and in short-run aggregate supply. These fluctuations produce fluctuations in real GDP and the price level. Figure 27.9(d) shows how real GDP fluctuates around potential GDP.

Long-Term Growth and Inflation

Long-term economic growth comes about because, over time, the long-run aggregate supply curve shifts rightward. The pace at which it shifts is determined by the growth rate of potential GDP.

Inflation comes about because, over time, the aggregate demand curve shifts rightward at a faster pace than the shift in the long-run aggregate supply curve. The pace at which the aggregate demand curve shifts is determined mainly by the growth rate of the quantity of money. At times when the quantity of money is increasing rapidly, aggregate demand is increasing quickly and the inflation rate is high. When the growth rate of the quantity of money slows down, other things remaining the same, the inflation rate eventually slows down.

But the economy does not experience steady real GDP growth and steady inflation. Instead, it fluctuates around its long-term growth path and its long-term inflation rate. When we study these fluctuations, we ignore the long-term trends. By doing so, we can see the short-term fluctuations more clearly.

Let's now look at some of the sources of fluctuations around the long-term trends.

Fluctuations in Aggregate Demand

Real GDP can fluctuate around its long-term trend either because of fluctuations in aggregate demand or fluctuations in aggregate supply. We'll study both sources of fluctuations. But first, let's work out the short-run and long-run effects on real GDP and the price level of a change in aggregate demand.

Let's suppose that the economy starts out at full employment and, as illustrated in Fig. 27.10(a), is producing $6 trillion worth of goods and services at a price level of 130. The economy is on the aggregate demand curve AD_0, the short-run aggregate supply curve SAS_0, and the long-run aggregate supply curve LAS.

Now suppose that the world economy grows more quickly and the demand for U.S.-made goods increases in Japan and Europe. The increase in U.S. exports increases aggregate demand and the aggregate demand curve shifts rightward. Suppose that the aggregate demand curve shifts from AD_0 to AD_1 in Fig. 27.10(a).

Faced with an increase in demand firms increase production and raise prices. For the economy as a whole, real GDP increases and the price level rises. Real GDP rises to $6.5 trillion and the price level rises to 135. In this short-run macroeconomic equilibrium, firms are producing the quantities they want to produce, given the price level and the money wage rate. But the economy is at an above full-employment equilibrium. Real GDP exceeds potential GDP, and there is an inflationary gap.

The increase in aggregate demand has increased the prices of all goods and services. Faced with higher prices, firms have increased their output rates. At this stage, prices of goods and services have increased but wage rates have not changed. (Recall that as we move along a short-run aggregate supply curve, wage rates are constant.)

The economy cannot produce in excess of potential GDP forever. Why not? What are the forces at work that bring real GDP back to potential GDP and restore full employment?

If the price level has increased and wage rates have remained constant, workers have experienced a fall in the purchasing power of their wages and firms' profits have increased. In these circumstances, workers demand higher wages, and firms, anxious to maintain their employment and output levels, meet those demands. If firms do not raise wage rates, they either lose workers or have to hire less productive ones.

FIGURE 27.10

An Increase in Aggregate Demand

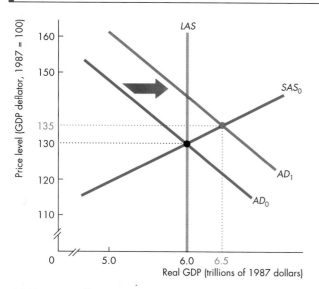

(a) Short-run effect

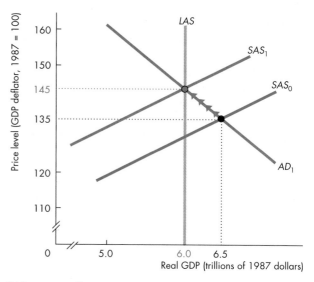

(b) Long-run effect

An increase in aggregate demand shifts the aggregate demand curve from AD_0 to AD_1. In the short-run equilibrium, real GDP is $6.5 trillion and the price level rises to 135. In this situation there is an inflationary gap. The money wage rate rises, and the short-run aggregate supply curve shifts leftward from SAS_0

to SAS_1 in part (b). As it shifts, it intersects the aggregate demand curve AD_1 at higher price levels and lower real GDP levels. Eventually, the price level rises to 145 and real GDP decreases to $6.0 trillion—potential GDP and full-employment.

As wage rates rise, the short-run aggregate supply curve begins to shift leftward. In Fig. 27.10(b) the short-run aggregate supply curve moves from SAS_0 toward SAS_1. The rise in wages and the shift in the *SAS* curve produce a sequence of new equilibrium positions. Along the adjustment path, real GDP falls and the price level rises, and the economy moves up along its aggregate demand curve as shown by the arrowheads in the figure. Eventually, wages will have risen by so much that the *SAS* curve is SAS_1. At this time, the aggregate demand curve AD_1 intersects SAS_1 at a full-employment equilibrium. The price level has risen to 145, and real GDP is back where it started, at potential GDP.

Throughout the adjustment process, higher wage rates raise firms' costs and, with rising costs, firms offer a smaller quantity of goods and services for sale at any given price level. By the time the adjustment is over, firms are producing the same amount as they initially produced but at higher prices and higher costs.

We've just worked out the effects of an increase in aggregate demand. A decrease in aggregate demand has effects that are similar but opposite to those that we've just studied. That is, a decrease in aggregate demand decreases real GDP to less than potential GDP and unemployment increases above its natural rate. A recessionary gap emerges. Firms cut prices. The lower price level increases the purchasing power of wages and increases firms' costs relative to their output prices because wages remain unchanged. Eventually, the slack economy leads to falling wage rates, and the short-run aggregate supply curve shifts rightward. Real GDP gradually returns to potential GDP, and full employment is restored. But the adjustment process will take a long time to complete because firms and workers will resist decreasing prices and wages.

You've seen how a change in aggregate demand changes real GDP and the price level. Let's now work out how real GDP and the price level change when aggregate supply changes.

Fluctuations in Aggregate Supply

Fluctuations in short-run aggregate supply can bring fluctuations in real GDP around potential GDP. We'll study a decrease in aggregate supply. Suppose that initially real GDP equals potential GDP. Then there is a large but temporary rise in the price of oil. (Such an increase occurred during the 1970s when OPEC used its market muscle). What happens to real GDP and the price level?

Figure 27.11 shows the effects of this rise in the price of oil. The aggregate demand curve is AD_0, the short-run aggregate supply curve is SAS_0, and the long-run aggregate supply curve is LAS. Equilibrium real GDP is $6 trillion, which equals potential GDP, and the price level is 130. Then the price of oil rises. Faced with a higher price of oil, firms' costs rise and they decrease production. Short-run aggregate supply

decreases, and the short-run aggregate supply curve shifts leftward to SAS_1.

As a result of this decrease in short-run aggregate supply, the economy moves to a new equilibrium where SAS_1 intersects the aggregate demand curve AD_0. The price level rises to 140, and real GDP decreases to $5.5 trillion. Because real GDP falls, the economy experiences recession. Because the price level increases, the economy experiences inflation. Such a combination of recession and inflation, called *stagflation*, actually occurred in the mid-1970s and early 1980s at the times of the OPEC oil price hikes.

Where the economy goes from this short-run equilibrium depends on whether aggregate demand changes. If aggregate demand does not change, the price of oil might eventually fall. Also, with real GDP below potential GDP and unemployment above the natural rate, the money wage rate might fall. But these adjustments are likely to take a very long time. More likely, aggregate demand will eventually be increased, in which case real GDP will increase and the price level will rise. As the price level increases, the relative price of oil falls. But if the oil producers keep on raising the price of oil and keep the relative price of oil high, potential GDP will fall and the economy will get stuck with a permanently smaller level of real GDP.

FIGURE 27.11
A Decrease in Aggregate Supply

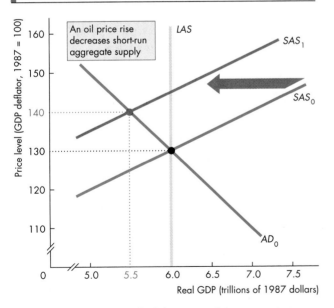

An increase in the price of oil decreases short-run aggregate supply and shifts the short-run aggregate supply curve from SAS_0 to SAS_1. Real GDP falls from $6.0 trillion to $5.5 trillion, and the price level increases from 130 to 140. The economy experiences both recession and inflation—stagflation.

REVIEW

■ Short-run macroeconomic equilibrium explains how real GDP and the price level change over time.

■ There are three types of short-run macroeconomic equilibrium: (1) below full-employment equilibrium (a situation in which potential GDP exceeds real GDP and there is a recessionary gap); (2) full-employment equilibrium (a situation in which real GDP equals potential GDP); and (3) above full-employment equilibrium (a situation in which real GDP exceeds potential GDP and there is an inflationary gap).

■ The price level fluctuates and real GDP fluctuates around potential GDP because of fluctuations in aggregate demand and short-run aggregate supply.

We've now seen how changes in aggregate supply and aggregate demand influence real GDP and the price level. Let's put our new knowledge to work and see how it helps us understand U.S. macroeconomic performance.

Long-Term Growth, Inflation, and Cycles in the U.S. Economy

THE ECONOMY IS CONTINUALLY CHANGING. If you imagine the economy as a video, then an aggregate supply–aggregate demand figure such as Fig. 27.11 is a freeze-frame. We're going to run the video—an instant replay—but keep our finger on the freeze-frame button, looking at some important parts of the previous action. Let's run the video from 1960.

Figure 27.12 shows the state of the economy in 1960 at the point of intersection of its aggregate demand curve AD_{60} and short-run aggregate supply curve SAS_{60}. Real GDP was $1.9 trillion, and the GDP deflator was 26 (less than one quarter of its 1994 level).

By 1994 the economy had reached the point marked by the intersection of aggregate demand curve AD_{94} and short-run aggregate supply curve SAS_{94}. Real GDP was $5.3 trillion, and the GDP deflator was 128.

There are three important features of the economy's path traced by the blue and red points:

- Long-term growth
- Inflation
- Cycles

Long-Term Growth

Over the years, real GDP grows—shown in Fig. 27.12 by the rightward movement of the points. The more rapid the growth rate of real GDP, the larger is the horizontal distance between successive dots in the figure. The force generating long-term growth is an increase in potential GDP, which increases long-run aggregate supply. Potential GDP increases because of labor force growth, the accumulation of capital (both physical plant and equipment and human capital), and technological change.

Inflation

The price level rises over the years—shown in Fig. 27.12 by the upward movement of the points. The larger the rise in the price level, the larger is the vertical distance between successive dots in the figure. The main force generating the persistent increase in the

FIGURE 27.12

Aggregate Supply and Aggregate Demand: 1960–1994

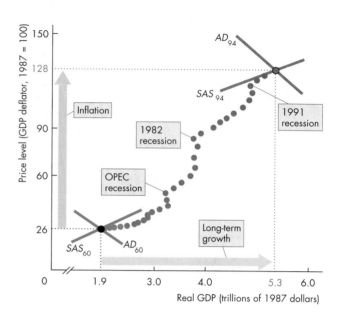

Each point indicates the value of the GDP deflator and real GDP in a given year. In 1960 these variables were determined by the intersection of the aggregate demand curve AD_{60} and the short-run aggregate supply curve SAS_{60}. Each point is generated by the gradual shifting of the AD and SAS curves. By 1994, the curves were AD_{94} and SAS_{94}. Real GDP grew, and the price level increased. But growth and inflation did not proceed smoothly. Real GDP grew quickly and inflation was moderate in the 1960s; real GDP growth sagged in 1974–1975 and again, more strongly, in 1982. Inflation was rapid during the 1970s but slowed after the 1982 recession. The period from 1982 to 1989 was one of strong, persistent recovery. A recession began in 1991, and a further expansion then followed.

price level is a tendency for aggregate demand to increase at a faster pace than the increase in long-run aggregate supply. All of the factors that increase aggregate demand and shift the aggregate demand curve influence the pace of inflation. But one factor—the growth of the quantity of money—is the most important source of *persistent* increases in aggregate demand and persistent inflation.

"Please stand by for a series of tones. The first indicates the official end of the recession, the second indicates prosperity, and the third the return of the recession."

Drawing by Mankoff; © 1991 The New Yorker Magazine, Inc.

Cycles

Over the years, the economy grows and shrinks in cycles—shown in Fig. 27.12 by the wavelike pattern made by the points, with the recessions highlighted. The cycles arise because both the expansion of short-run aggregate supply and the growth of aggregate demand do not proceed at a fixed, steady pace. Although the economy has cycles, recessions do not usually follow quickly on the heels of their predecessors; "double-dip" recessions like the one in the cartoon are rare.

The Evolving Economy: 1960–1994

During the 1960s, real GDP growth was rapid and inflation was low. This was a period of rapid increases in aggregate supply and of moderate increases in aggregate demand.

The mid-1970s were years of rapid inflation and recession—of stagflation. The major source of these developments was a series of massive oil price increases that shifted the short-run aggregate supply curve leftward and rapid increases in the quantity of money that shifted the aggregate demand curve rightward. Recession occurred because the aggregate supply curve shifted leftward at a faster pace than the aggregate demand curve shifted rightward.

The rest of the 1970s saw high inflation—the price level increased quickly—and only moderate growth in real GDP. This inflation was the product of

a battle between OPEC and the Fed. OPEC jacked up the price of oil, and stagflation ensued. The Fed was faced with a dilemma. Should it stimulate aggregate demand to restore full employment or should it keep the growth of aggregate demand in check?

The answer, delivered by Fed chairman Paul Volcker, was to keep aggregate demand growth in check. In Fig. 27.12 you can see the effects of Chairman Volcker's actions in 1979 to 1982. In this period, most people expected high inflation to persist, and wages grew at a rate consistent with those expectations. The short-run aggregate supply curve shifted leftward. Aggregate demand increased, but not fast enough to make inflation as high as most people expected. As a consequence, by 1982 the leftward shift of the short-run aggregate supply curve was so strong relative to the growth of aggregate demand that the economy went into a further deep recession.

During the years 1982 to 1990, capital accumulation and steady technological advance resulted in a sustained rightward shift of the long-run aggregate supply curve. Wage growth was moderate, and the short-run aggregate supply curve also shifted rightward. Aggregate demand growth kept pace with the growth of aggregate supply. Sustained but steady growth in aggregate supply and aggregate demand kept real GDP growing and inflation steady. The economy moved from a recession with real GDP less than potential GDP in 1981 to above full-employment in 1990. It was in this condition when a decrease in aggregate demand led to the 1991 recession. The economy again embarked on a path of expansion through 1994. The expansion from 1992 to 1994 and the emergence of an inflationary gap in 1994 created a dilemma for the Fed, which is explored further in *Reading Between the Lines* on pp. 674–675.

◆ The aggregate supply–aggregate demand model can be used to understand long-term growth, inflation, and business cycles. The model is a useful one because it enables us to keep our eye on the big picture—on the broad trends and cycles in inflation and real GDP. But the model lacks detail. It does not tell us as much as we need to know about the components of aggregate demand: consumption, investment, government purchases of goods and services, and exports and imports. It doesn't tell us what determines interest rates or wage rates or even, directly, what determines employment and unemployment. In the following chapters we're going to start to fill in that detail.

Aggregate Supply and Aggregate Demand in Action

THE AUSTRALIAN FINANCIAL REVIEW, DECEMBER 19, 1994

The Fed Likely to Delay Moving until New Year

REUTERS

The U.S. Federal Reserve meets today to consider raising interest rates for the seventh time this year, but most analysts are betting it will hold off from acting rather than spoil the Christmas cheer.

After boosting short-term rates sharply last month, the inflation-wary central bank is at a crossroads. It knows the economy is ending 1994 with a bang, but it expects growth to slow next year as the tighter credit begins to bite.

The result? A probable decision at today's meeting to delay a rate increase until after the start of the new year, when the Fed will have a better idea of how the economy performed during the crucial Christmas selling season. ...

But the delay is likely to be short-lived. Most analysts expect the central bank to resume raising interest rates next month. ...

Fed chairman, Dr Alan Greenspan, was as clear as he ever gets in signalling that higher rates are on the way in testimony to the US Congress earlier this month.

While insisting that he did not know whether the central bank would raise rates this week, Dr Greenspan painted a picture of an economy that was growing too fast for the Fed's liking and that was fuelling inflationary pressures in the process.

"We must remain alert to signs of inflationary pressures," he told Congress' Joint Economic Committee.

"If price increases are accommodated, they can become readily embedded in higher inflation expectations," Dr Greenspan said.

Reprinted with permission of Reuters.

■ The Fed met in mid-December 1994 to decide whether it should raise interest rates for the seventh time during the year.

■ The economy grew quickly in 1994, but because the Fed had already increased interest rates sharply, it expected growth to slow during 1995.

■ Most analysts expected the Fed to hold off an interest rate increase in December but to increase interest rates in January 1995.

■ Fed chairman Alan Greenspan said in testimony to Congress that the economy was growing too fast and that higher inflation might result.

Economic

A N A L Y S I S

■ Figure 1 shows that during 1994, real GDP grew quickly (at about 4 percent over the year) and surpassed the assumed level of potential GDP. It was expected to remain in excess of potential GDP throughout 1995.

■ Figure 2 shows that inflation decreased through mid-1994 but then began to increase.

■ Figure 3 interprets the events of 1994. In the fourth quarter of 1994, potential GDP was $5.4 trillion and the long-run aggregate supply curve was LAS_{94}. Real GDP exceeded potential GDP at $5.43 trillion, and the price level was 127.

■ Long-term economic growth was expected to increase long-run aggregate supply to about $5.5 trillion and to shift the LAS_{94} curve to LAS_{95} and the SAS curve to SAS_{95}.

■ Aggregate demand was growing more quickly than the long-term growth rate, and the aggregate demand curve was expected to be AD_{95}.

■ The forecast for 1995 was a real GDP increase to $5.6 trillion (about 3 percent) and a price level increase to 132 (inflation rate of about 4 percent). If these changes occurred, there would be an inflationary gap in 1995 of about $0.1 trillion, as shown in the figure.

■ The problem for the Fed was by how much to increase interest rates to slow the growth of aggregate demand.

■ But the Fed is always uncertain about the effects of its actions. Through 1994 it had increased interest rates from about 3 percent to almost 6 percent. Was this increase sufficient to restrain the growth of aggregate demand?

■ With the size of the inflationary gap shown in Fig. 3, not only would the price level rise by more than 4 percent during 1995, but the inflation rate would increase further in 1995 and beyond because of faster wage increases.

■ Alan Greenspan wanted to avoid the onset of such an inflation by limiting aggregate demand growth to eliminate the inflationary gap.

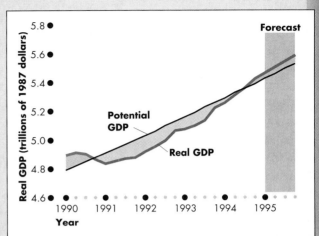

Figure 1 Real GDP and potential GDP

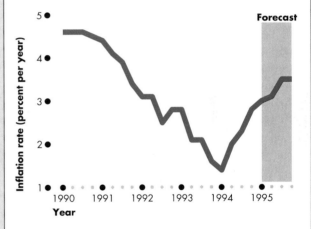

Figure 2 Inflation

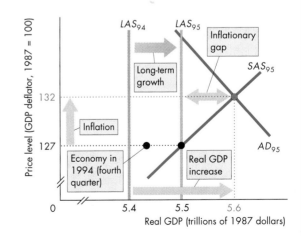

Figure 3 Aggregate supply and aggregate demand

S U M M A R Y

Aggregate Supply

In the long run, real GDP equals potential GDP and there is full employment. In the short run, real GDP deviates from potential GDP.

Long-run aggregate supply is the relationship between the quantity of real GDP supplied and the price level when real GDP equals potential GDP and there is full employment. The long-run aggregate supply curve is vertical—long-run aggregate supply is independent of the price level at potential GDP. Long-run aggregate supply changes only when potential GDP changes.

Short-run aggregate supply is the relationship between the quantity of real GDP supplied and the price level when wage rates and other factor prices are constant. The short-run aggregate supply curve is upward sloping—the higher the price level, the larger is the output that firms plan to supply. Short-run aggregate supply changes when factor prices change and when potential GDP changes. (pp. 656–660)

Aggregate Demand

Aggregate demand is the relationship between the quantity of real GDP demanded and the price level, all other influences remaining the same. The aggregate demand curve is downward sloping—the higher the price level, the smaller is the quantity of real GDP demanded. The aggregate demand curve slopes downward because the lower the price level, other things remaining the same, the greater is the quantity of *real* money, the lower is the cost of goods today compared with goods in the future, and the lower is the cost of domestic goods compared with foreign goods. So the lower the price level, the greater is the quantity of GDP demanded.

The main factors that change aggregate demand and shift the aggregate demand curve are expectations (especially expectations about future income, inflation, and profits), international factors (economic conditions in the rest of the world and the foreign exchange rate), fiscal policy (government purchases of goods and services, taxes, and transfer payments), and monetary policy (the money supply and interest rates). (pp. 661–666)

Macroeconomic Equilibrium

In a short-run macroeconomic equilibrium, real GDP and the price level are determined by aggregate demand and short-run aggregate supply. Short-run macroeconomic equilibrium tells us how real GDP and the price level evolve over time. In a long-run macroeconomic equilibrium, real GDP equals potential GDP. When equilibrium real GDP is less than potential GDP, there is a recessionary gap. When equilbrum real GDP exceeds potential GDP, there is an inflationary gap.

Long-term growth of real GDP occurs because potential GDP increases. Inflation occurs because aggregate demand grows more quickly than potential GDP. Fluctuations in real GDP and the price level occur because aggregate demand and short-run aggregate supply fluctuate. An increase in aggregate demand increases real GDP and the price level and creates an inflationary gap. The money wage rate rises, short-run aggregate supply decreases, the price level rises further, and real GDP eventually returns to potential GDP. An increase in factor prices decreases short-run aggregate supply, decreases real GDP and raises the price level—stagflation. (pp. 667–671)

Long-Term Growth, Inflation, and Cycles in the U.S. Economy

Long-term growth is the growth of potential GDP. Inflation persists in the U.S. economy because of steady increases in aggregate demand brought about by increases in the quantity of money. The U.S. economy experiences cycles because aggregate supply and aggregate demand change at an uneven pace.

During the 1960s, real GDP growth was rapid and inflation was low. Large oil price hikes in 1973 and 1974 resulted in stagflation. Restraint in aggregate demand growth in 1980 and 1981 resulted in a severe recession in 1982. Moderate increases in wage rates and steady technological advance and capital accumulation resulted in a sustained expansion from 1982 to 1989. A slowdown in aggregate demand growth brought recession in 1991, and an increase in aggregate demand growth brought an expansion through 1994. (pp. 672–673)

K E Y   E L E M E N T S

Key Figures

Key Terms

R E V I E W   Q U E S T I O N S

1. Name and distinguish between two macroeconomic time frames.

2. What is long-run aggregate supply?

3. What is short-run aggregate supply?

4. Distinguish between movements along the short-run and the long-run aggregate supply curves.

5. Consider the following events:
   a.   Potential GDP increases
   b.   The money wage rate rises
   c.   The price level rises
   d.   The money wage rate and the price level rise by the same percentages
   Say which of these events, if any, change (1) long-run aggregate supply but not short-run aggregate supply, (2) short-run aggregate supply but not long-run aggregate supply, (3) both short-run aggregate supply and long-run aggregate supply and which, if any, bring a movement along (4) the long-run aggregate supply curve, (5) the short-run aggregate supply curve, and (6) both the short-run and the long-run aggregate supply curves.

6. What is aggregate demand?

7. What is the difference between aggregate demand and the quantity of real GDP demanded?

8. List the main factors that affect aggregate demand.

9. Which of the following do not affect aggregate demand?
   a.   Quantity of money
   b.   Interest rates
   c.   Technological change
   d.   Human capital

10. Define short-run macroeconomic equilibrium.

11. Distinguish between a below full-employment equilibrium and full-employment equilibrium.

12. Work out the short-run and long-run effects of an increase in the quantity of money on the price level and real GDP.

13. Work out the short-run effect of an increase in the price of oil on the price level and real GDP.

14. What are the main factors generating growth, inflation, and cycles, in the U.S. economy?

P R O B L E M S

◆ 1. The following events occur that influence the economy of Toughtimes:
   - A deep recession hits the world economy
   - Oil prices rise sharply
   - Businesses expect huge losses in the near future.

   a. Explain the separate effects of each of these events on real GDP and the price level in Toughtimes, starting from a position of long-run equilibrium.

   b. Explain the combined effects of these events on real GDP and the price level in Toughtimes, starting from a position of long-run equilibrum.

   c. Explain what the Toughtimes government and Fed can do to overcome the problems faced by the economy.

◆ 2. The following events occur that influence the economy of Coolland:
   - A strong expansion in the world economy
   - Businesses expect huge profits in the near future
   - The Coolland government cuts its expenditure

   a. Explain the separate effects of each of these events on real GDP and the price level in Coolland, starting from a position of long-run equilibrium.

   b. Explain the combined effects of these events on real GDP and the price level in Coolland, starting from a position of long-run equilibrum.

   c. Explain why the Coolland government or Fed might want to take action to influence the Coolland economy.

◆ 3. The economy of Mainland has the following aggregate demand and supply schedules:

Price level	Real GDP demanded	Real GDP supplied in the short run
	(trillions of 1987 dollars)	
90	4.5	3.5
100	4.0	4.0
110	3.5	4.5
120	3.0	5.0
130	2.5	5.5
140	2.0	6.0

   a. Plot the aggregate demand curve and short-run aggregate supply curve in a figure.

   b. What are the values of real GDP and the price level in Mainland in a short-run macroeconomic equilibrium?

   c. Mainland's potential GDP is $5.0 trillion. Plot the long-run aggregate supply curve in the same figure in which you answered part (a).

   d. Is Mainland at, above, or below its natural rate of unemployment?

◆ 4. In problem 3, aggregate demand is increased by $1 trillion. What are the changes in real GDP and the price level in the short run?

◆ 5. In problem 3, aggregate supply decreases by $1 trillion. What is the new short-run macroeconomic equilibrium?

6. The following figure shows the aggregate supply and aggregate demand curves in an economy. Initially, short-run aggregate supply is SAS_0 and aggregate demand is AD_0. Then some events change aggregate demand and the aggregate demand curve shifts rightward to AD_1. Later, some further events change aggregate supply and the short-run aggregae supply curve shifts leftward to SAS_1.

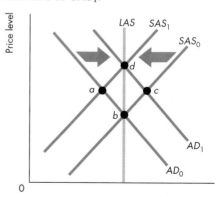

   a. What is the initial equilibrium point?

   b. What is the equilibrium point after the change in aggregate demand?

   c. What is the equilibrium point after the change in aggregate supply?

   d. What events could have changed aggregate demand from AD_0 to AD_1?

e. What events could have changed aggregate supply from SAS_0 to SAS_1?

f. After the increase in aggregate demand but before the increase in aggregate supply, is the real GDP greater than or less than potential GDP?

◆ 7. You are the President's economic advisor and you are trying to figure out where the U.S. economy is headed next year. You have the following forecasts:

Price level	Real GDP demanded	Short-run real GDP supplied	Potential GDP
		(trillions of 1987 dollars)	
115	6.5	3.5	5.2
120	6.0	4.5	5.2
125	5.5	5.5	5.2
130	5.0	6.5	5.2

This year, real GDP is $5.0 trillion, and the price level is 120. The President wants answers to the following questions:

a. What is your forecast of next year's real GDP?

b. What is your forecast of next year's price level?

c. What is your forecast of the inflation rate?

d. Will unemployment be above or below its natural rate?

e. Will there be a recessionary gap or an inflationary gap? By how much?

8. Carefully draw some figures similar to those in this chapter and use the information in problem 5 to explain:

a. What has to be done to aggregate demand to achieve full employment.

b. What the inflation rate is if aggregate demand is manipulated to achieve full employment.

9. After you have studied the account of the U.S. economic expansion during the 1990s in *Reading Between the Lines* on pp. 674–675:

a. Describe the main features of the economy in 1994 that worried Alan Greenspan.

b. In which periods was there a recessionary gap and in which was there an inflationary gap?

c. Draw a figure to illustrate the economy as shown in Fig. 1 in 1991 and 1994.

d. Draw a figure to illustrate the economy in 1995 if the Fed increased interest rates by too much and created a recession.

Expenditure Multipliers

After studying
this chapter,
you will be
able to:

- Explain how expenditure plans are determined when the price level is sticky

- Explain how real GDP is determined when the price level is sticky

- Explain the expenditure multiplier

- Explain how imports and taxes influence the multiplier

- Explain how recessions and expansions begin

- Explain the relationship between aggregate expenditure and aggregate demand

- Explain how the multiplier gets smaller as the price level changes

Economic Amplifier or Shock Absorber?

In the Red Rocks Amphitheater in Denver, Bonnie Raitt sings into a microphone in a barely audible whisper. Moving to a louder passage, she increases the volume of her voice and now, through the magic of electronic amplification, booms across the stadium, drowning out every other sound. ◆ Dennis Archer, the mayor of Detroit, and a secretary are being driven to a business meeting along one of the city's less well-repaired highways. (There are some pretty badly potholed highways in Detroit.) The car's wheels are bouncing and vibrating over some of the worst highways in the nation, but its passengers are completely undisturbed and the secretary's notes are written without a ripple, thanks to the car's efficient shock absorbers. ◆ Investment and exports fluctuate like the volume of Bonnie Raitt's voice and the uneven surface of a Detroit highway. How does the economy react to those fluctuations? Does it react like Dennis Archer's limousine, absorbing the shocks and providing a smooth ride for the economy's passengers? Or does it behave like Bonnie Raitt's amplifier, blowing up the fluctuations and spreading them out to affect the many millions of participants in an economic rock concert?

◈ You will explore these questions in this chapter. You learn how a recession or a recovery begins when a change in investment or exports triggers a larger change in *aggregate* expenditure and real GDP—like Bonnie Raitt's amplifier. You will also learn how, over the years, imports and income taxes have lowered the power of the amplifier. Finally, you will discover that in contrast to the initial amplification effect, the economy's imperfect shock absorbers, which are price and wage changes, pull real GDP back toward potential GDP. To achieve these objectives, we use a model called the *aggregate expenditure model*. This model explains changes in aggregate expenditure over a very short time frame during which prices do not change. We begin by describing the economy in this time frame.

Sticky Prices and Expenditure Plans

MOST FIRMS ARE LIKE YOUR LOCAL SUPERMARKET. They set their prices, advertise their products and services, and sell the quantities their customers are willing to buy. If they persistently sell a greater quantity that they plan to and are constantly running out of inventory, they eventually raise their prices. And if they persistently sell a smaller quantity than they plan to and have inventories piling up, they eventually cut their prices. But in the very short term their prices are sticky. They hold the prices they have set, and the quantities they sell depend on demand, not supply.

The Aggregate Implications of Sticky Prices

Sticky prices have two immediate implications for the economy as a whole:

1. Because each firm's price is sticky, the *price level* is sticky.
2. Because demand determines the quantities that each firm sells, *aggregate demand* determines the aggregate quantity of goods and services sold, which equals real GDP.

So to understand the fluctuations in real GDP when the price level is sticky, we must understand aggregate demand fluctuations. The aggregate expenditure model explains fluctuations in aggregate demand by identifying the forces that determine expenditure plans.

Expenditure Plans

The components of aggregate expenditure are:

- Consumption expenditure
- Investment
- Government purchases of goods and services
- Net exports (exports *minus* imports)

These four components of aggregate expenditure sum to real GDP (see Chapter 23, pp. 547–549). **Aggregate planned expenditure** is equal to *planned* consumption expenditure plus *planned* investment plus *planned* government purchases plus *planned* exports minus *planned* imports. Chapter 26 describes the influences on these expenditure plans and explains how in the long run, when real GDP equals potential GDP, expenditure plans determine the real interest rate. Chapter 27 combines aggregate demand, which is based on aggregate expenditure plans, with aggregate supply and explains how in the short run, real GDP deviates from potential GDP. Here, we look at expenditure plans on a much shorter-term horizon.

In the very short term, *planned* investment, *planned* government purchases, and *planned* exports are fixed. But *planned* consumption expenditure and *planned* imports are not fixed. They depend on the level of real GDP itself.

A Two-Way Link Between Aggregate Expenditure and GDP Because real GDP influences consumption expenditure and imports, and because consumption expenditure and imports are components of aggregate expenditure, there is a two-way link between aggregate expenditure and GDP. Other things remaining the same,

- An increase in real GDP increases aggregate planned expenditure, and
- An increase in aggregate expenditure increases real GDP.

You are going to learn how this two-way link between aggregate expenditure and real GDP determines real GDP when the price level is sticky. The starting point is to consider the first piece of the two-way link: the influence of real GDP on planned consumption expenditure and saving.

Consumption Function and Saving Function

Consumption and saving are influenced by several factors. The more important ones are:

- Real interest rate
- Disposable income
- Purchasing power of net assets
- Expected future income

The ways in which consumption and saving are influenced by these factors are explained in Chapter 25 (see pp. 601–602). In the short time frame we are considering, the real interest rate, the purchasing power of net assets, and expected future income are fixed. But disposable income is not fixed. It equals real GDP plus transfer payments minus taxes. So it depends on real GDP, which in turn depends on aggregate expenditure.

Consumption and Saving Plans   The table in Fig. 28.1 shows an example of the relationship among planned consumption expenditure, planned saving, and disposable income. It lists the consumption

expenditure and the saving that people plan to undertake at each level of disposable income. Notice that at each level of disposable income, consumption expenditure plus saving always equals disposable income. The reason is that households can only consume or save their disposable income. So planned consumption plus planned saving always equals disposable income.

FIGURE   28.1

Consumption Function and Saving Function

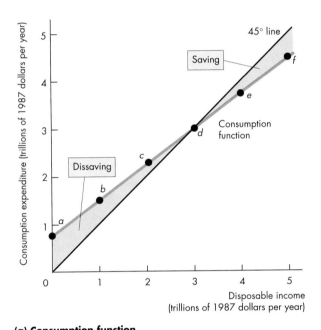

(a) Consumption function

	Disposable income	Planned consumption expenditure	Planned saving
		(trillions of 1987 dollars per year)	
a	0	0.75	−0.75
b	1	1.50	−0.50
c	2	2.25	−0.25
d	3	3.00	0
e	4	3.75	0.25
f	5	4.50	0.50

The table shows consumption expenditure and saving plans at various levels of disposable income. Part (a) of the figure shows the relationship between consumption expenditure and disposable income (the consumption function). Part (b) shows the relationship between saving and disposable income (the saving function). Points a through f on the consumption and saving functions correspond to the rows in the table.

The 45° line in part (a) is the line along which consumption expenditure equals disposable income. Consumption expenditure plus saving equals disposable income. When the consumption function is above the 45° line, saving is negative (dissaving occurs). When the consumption function is below the 45° line, saving is positive. At the point where the consumption function intersects the 45° line, all disposable income is consumed and saving is zero.

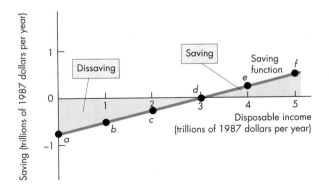

(b) Saving function

The relationship between consumption expenditure and disposable income, other things remaining the same, is called the **consumption function.** The relationship between saving and disposable income, other things remaining the same, is called the **saving function**. Let's study the consumption and saving functions, beginning with the consumption function.

Consumption Function   Figure 28.1(a) shows a consumption function. The y-axis measures consumption expenditure, and the x-axis measures disposable income. Along the consumption function the points labeled a through f correspond to the rows of the table. For example, point e shows that when disposable income is $4 trillion, consumption expenditure is $3.75 trillion. Along the consumption function, as disposable income increases, consumption expenditure also increases.

At point a on the consumption function, consumption expenditure is $0.75 trillion even though disposable income is zero. This consumption expenditure is called *autonomous consumption* and it is the amount of consumption expenditure that would take place in the short run, even if people had no current income. Consumption expenditure in excess of this amount is called *induced consumption*, which is expenditure that is induced by an increase in disposable income.

45° Line   Figure 28.1(a) also contains a line labeled "45° line." At each point on this line, consumption expenditure (on the y-axis) equals disposable income (on the x-axis). In the range over which the consumption function lies above the 45° line—between a and d—consumption expenditure exceeds disposable income; in the range over which the consumption function lies below the 45° line—between d and f—consumption expenditure is less than disposable income; and at a point at which the consumption function intersects the 45° line—at point d—consumption expenditure equals disposable income.

Saving Function   Figure 28.1(b) shows a saving function. The x-axis is exactly the same as that in part (a). The y-axis measures saving. Again, the points marked a through f correspond to the rows of the table. For example, point e shows that when disposable income is $4 trillion, saving is $0.25 trillion. Along the saving function, as disposable income increases, saving also increases. At disposable income

less than $3 trillion (point d), saving is negative. Negative saving is called *dissaving*. At disposable income greater than $3 trillion, saving is positive, and at $3 trillion, saving is zero.

Notice the connection between the two parts of Fig. 28.1. When consumption expenditure exceeds disposable income in part (a), saving is negative in part (b). When disposable income exceeds consumption expenditure in part (a), saving is positive in part (b). And when consumption expenditure equals disposable income in part (a), saving is zero in part (b).

When saving is negative (when consumption expenditure exceeds disposable income), past savings are used to pay for current consumption. Such a situation cannot last forever but it can occur if disposable income falls temporarily.

Marginal Propensities to Consume and Save

The extent to which consumption expenditure changes when disposable income changes depends on the marginal propensity to consume. The **marginal propensity to consume** (*MPC*) is the fraction of a *change* in disposable income that is consumed. It is calculated as the *change* in consumption expenditure (ΔC) divided by the *change* in disposable income (ΔYD) that brought it about. That is,

$$MPC = \frac{\Delta C}{\Delta YD}.$$

In the table in Fig. 28.1, when disposable income increases from $3 trillion to $4 trillion, consumption expenditure increases from $3 trillion to $3.75 trillion. The change in disposable income of $1 trillion brings about a change in consumption expenditure of $0.75 trillion. The *MPC* is $0.75 trillion divided by $1 trillion, which equals 0.75. In Fig. 28.1(a), the *MPC* is a constant 0.75. For example, an increase in disposable income from $2 trillion to $3 trillion increases consumption expenditure from $2.25 trillion to $3 trillion, so again, the *MPC* is 0.75.

The **marginal propensity to save** (*MPS*) is the fraction of a *change* in disposable income that is saved. It is calculated as the *change* in saving (ΔS) divided by the *change* in disposable income (ΔYD) that brought it about. That is,

$$MPS = \frac{\Delta S}{\Delta YD}.$$

Again, using the numbers in the table in Fig. 28.1, an increase in disposable income from $3 trillion to $4 trillion increases saving from zero to $0.25 trillion. The change in disposable income of $1 trillion brings about a change in saving of $0.25 trillion. The *MPS* is $0.25 trillion divided by $1 trillion, which equals 0.25. In Fig. 28.1(b), the *MPS* is a constant 0.25. For example, an increase in disposable income from $2 trillion to $3 trillion increases saving from −$0.25 trillion to zero, so again, the *MPS* is 0.25.

The marginal propensity to consume plus the marginal propensity to save always equals 1. They sum to 1 because consumption expenditure and saving exhaust disposable income. Part of each dollar increase in disposable income is consumed, and the remaining part is saved. You can see that these two marginal propensities sum to 1 by using the equation

$$\Delta C + \Delta S = \Delta YD.$$

Divide both sides of the equation by the change in disposable income to obtain

$$\frac{\Delta C}{\Delta YD} + \frac{\Delta S}{\Delta YD} = 1.$$

$\Delta C/\Delta YD$ is the *marginal propensity to consume* (*MPC*), and $\Delta S/\Delta YD$ is the *marginal propensity to save* (*MPS*), so

$$MPC + MPS = 1.$$

Marginal Propensities and Slopes   The marginal propensities to consume and save are shown by the slopes of the consumption function and the saving function. You can see the marginal propensity to consume as the slope of the consumption function in Fig. 28.2(a). A $1 trillion increase in disposable income from $3 trillion to $4 trillion is the base of the red triangle. The increase in consumption expenditure that results from this increase in income is $0.75 trillion and is the height of the triangle. The slope of the consumption function is given by the formula "slope equals rise over run" and is $0.75 trillion divided by $1 trillion, which equals 0.75—the *MPC*.

You can see the marginal propensity to save as the slope of the saving function in Fig. 28.2(b). A $1 trillion increase in disposable income from $3 trillion to $4 trillion (the base of the red triangle) increases saving by $0.25 trillion (the height of the triangle). The slope of the saving function is $0.25 trillion divided by $1 trillion, which equals 0.25—the *MPS*.

FIGURE   28.2

Marginal Propensities to Consume and Save

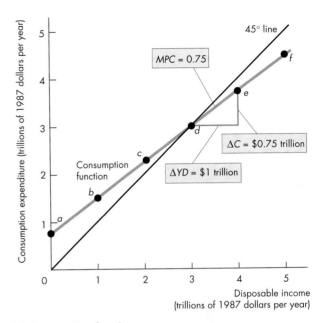

(a) Consumption function

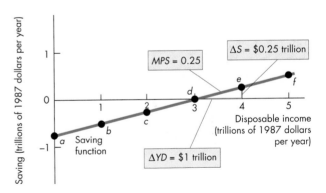

(b) Saving function

The marginal propensity to consume, *MPC*, is equal to the change in consumption expenditure divided by the change in disposable income, other things remaining the same. It is measured by the slope of the consumption function. In part (a) the *MPC* is 0.75. The marginal propensity to save, *MPS*, is equal to the change in saving divided by the change in disposable income, other things remaining the same. It is measured by the slope of the saving function. In part (b) the *MPS* is 0.25.

Other Influences on Consumption Expenditure and Saving

You've seen that a change in disposable income leads to changes in consumption expenditure and saving. A change in disposable income brings movements along the consumption function and saving function. A change in other influences on consumption expenditure and saving shifts both the consumption function and the saving function. These other factors include the real interest rate, expected future income, and the purchasing power net assets (see Chapter 25, pp. 601–602).

When the real interest rate falls or when the purchasing power of net assets or expected future income increases, consumption expenditure increases and saving decreases. Figure 28.3 shows the effects of these changes on the consumption function and the saving function. The consumption function shifts upward from CF_0 to CF_1, and the saving function shifts downward from SF_0 to SF_1. Such shifts commonly occur during the expansion phase of the business cycle because, at such times, expected future income increases.

When the real interest rate rises or when the purchasing power of net assets or expected future income decreases, consumption decreases and saving increases. Figure 28.3 also shows the effects of these changes on the consumption function and the saving function. The consumption function shifts downward from CF_0 to CF_2, and the saving function shifts upward from SF_0 to SF_2. Such shifts often occur when a recession begins because at such a time, expected future income decreases.

We've studied the theory of the consumption function. Let's now see how that theory applies to the U.S. economy.

The U.S. Consumption Function

Figure 28.4(a) shows the U.S. consumption function. Each point identified by a blue dot represents consumption expenditure and disposable income for a particular year. (The dots are for the years 1970–1994 and the even numbered years are identified in the figure.) The orange line shows the average relationship between consumption expenditure and disposable income and is an estimate of the U.S. consumption function.

FIGURE 28.3

Shifts in the Consumption and Saving Functions

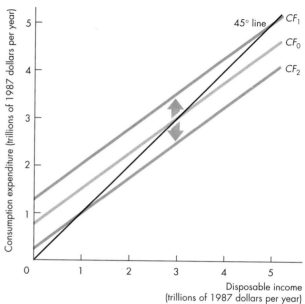

(a) Consumption function

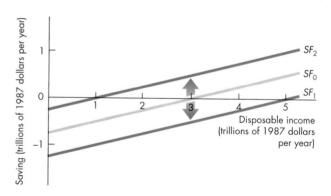

(b) Saving function

A fall in the real interest rate, an increase in the purchasing power of net assets, or an increase in expected future income increases consumption expenditure and decreases saving. It shifts the consumption function upward from CF_0 to CF_1 and shifts the saving function downward from SF_0 to SF_1. A rise in the real interest rate or a decrease in either the purchasing power of net assets or expected future income shifts the consumption function downward from CF_0 to CF_2 and shifts the saving function upward from SF_0 to SF_2.

The U.S. Consumption Function

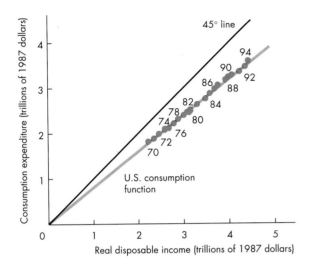

(a) Consumption as a function of disposable income

(b) Consumption as a function of real GDP

Real GDP	Disposable income	Consumption expenditure
(trillions of 1987 dollars per year)		
1.0	0.85	0.68
2.0	1.70	1.36
3.0	2.55	2.04
4.0	3.40	2.72

In part (a) each blue dot shows consumption expenditure and disposable income for a particular year. The orange line is an estimate of the U.S. consumption function. Its slope is the marginal propensity to consume, which is 0.8. Part (b) shows consumption expenditure as a function of real GDP. The slope of this function is 0.68. The table shows the connection between the two figures. Disposable income equals real GDP minus net taxes. The net tax rate is 15 percent, so disposable income (YD) is 85 percent of real GDP. With a marginal propensity to consume of 0.8, consumption expenditure is 0.8 × YD or 0.8 × 0.85 × real GDP, which is 0.68 × real GDP.

The slope of the U.S. consumption function in Fig. 28.4(a) is 0.8, which means that a $1 trillion increase in disposable income brings a $0.8 trillion increase in consumption expenditure. That is, on the average, over the period 1970–1994 the marginal propensity to consume in the United States was 0.8. Also, on the average, autonomous consumption is zero. That is, if disposable income were zero, consumption expenditure would also be zero.

The relationship between consumption expenditure and disposable income in any given year does not always fall exactly on the orange line. The reason is that the position of the consumption function in each year depends on other factors—such as the real interest rate, expected future income, and the purchasing power of net assets—that influence consumption expenditure and shift the consumption function.

Consumption as a Function of Real GDP

Because our goal is to determine real GDP when the price level is sticky, our next step is to link consumption expenditure with real GDP. Figure 28.4(b) shows this link in the United States. The blue dots illustrate the actual values of the two variables in each year, again for the period 1970–1994. The orange line shows the average relationship between consumption expenditure and real GDP.

Consumption expenditure is a function of real GDP because disposable income depends on real GDP. Disposable income is real GDP minus net taxes. *Net taxes* are equal to taxes paid to the government minus transfer payments (such as social security benefits) received from the government.

Net taxes increase as real GDP increases. Almost all the taxes that we pay—personal taxes, corporate taxes, and social security taxes—increase as our incomes increase. Transfer payments, such as social security and welfare benefits, decrease as our incomes increase. In 1995, net taxes were about 15 percent of real GDP. With net taxes equal to 15 percent of real GDP, disposable income is 85 percent of real GDP.

The table in Fig. 28.4 sets out the relationship between real GDP, disposable income, and consumption expenditure. For example, when real GDP is $4 trillion, disposable income is 85 percent of that amount, which is $3.4 trillion. And if the marginal propensity to consume is 0.8, as in Fig. 28.4(a), then consumption expenditure is 0.8 of $3.4 trillion, which is $2.72 trillion.

When consumption expenditure is plotted against real GDP, the slope of the curve tells us the amount by which consumption expenditure changes as real GDP changes. In Fig. 28.4 the slope is 0.68. When real GDP increases by $1 trillion, consumption expenditure increases by $0.68 trillion. This slope is equal to the marginal propensity to consume (0.8) multiplied by 1 minus the net tax rate (1 − 0.15 = 0.85).

Two components of aggregate planned expenditure are influenced by real GDP: consumption expenditure and imports. We've seen that consumption expenditure increases as real GDP increases. Let's now study the relationship between imports and real GDP.

Import Function

U. S. imports are determined by three main factors:

1. U.S. real GDP
2. Prices of foreign-made goods and services relative to the prices of similar U.S.-made goods and services
3. Foreign exchange rates

Other things being equal, the greater the U.S. real GDP, the larger is the quantity of U.S. imports.

For example, the growth in U.S. real GDP between 1983 and 1994 brought a huge increase in U.S. imports.

Other things again being equal, the lower the prices of foreign-made goods and services relative to the prices of similar U.S.-made goods and services, the larger is the quantity of U.S. imports. To compare prices of foreign-made and U.S.-made goods and services, we use foreign exchange rates. A **foreign exchange rate** is the value of one national money in terms of another, for example, the value of the U.S. dollar in terms of Japanese yen. The higher the value of the U.S. dollar against the yen, the more yen will one U.S. dollar buy and the cheaper are Japanese-made goods and services. That is, the higher the value of the U.S. dollar against other currencies, the larger are imports into the United States.

The response of imports to changes in prices and foreign exchange rates occurs slowly and is spread out over a long period. But real GDP influences imports quickly.

The relationship between imports and real GDP is called the **import function.** Figure 28.5(a) shows an import function. The x-axis measures real GDP, and the y-axis measures imports. The points labeled a through e in the figure correspond to the rows of the table. For example, point d indicates a real GDP of $4 trillion and imports of $1 trillion.

An increase in real GDP brings an increase in imports, and the magnitude of the increase in imports is determined by the marginal propensity to import. The **marginal propensity to import** is the fraction of an increase in real GDP that is spent on imports. It is calculated as the change in imports divided by the change in real GDP that brought it about, other things remaining the same. Along the import function in Fig. 28.5(a), the marginal propensity to import is a constant 0.25. That is, when real GDP increases by $1 trillion, imports increase by $0.25 trillion.

Figure 28.5(b) shows the U.S. import function. In 1970, the U.S. import function was IM_{70}. Along this import function, the marginal propensity to import is 0.07. A $1 trillion increase in U.S. real GDP increased imports by $0.07 trillion. Over the years, influences other than real GDP increased the marginal propensity to import and the U.S. import function has gradually become steeper. By 1994, it was IM_{94}. Along this import function, the marginal propensity to import is 0.15, more than twice the value in 1970.

FIGURE **28.5**

The Import Function

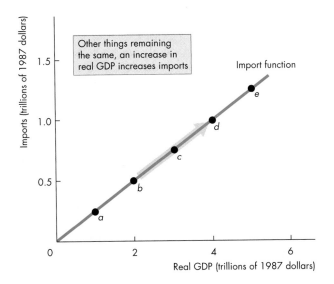

(a) An import function

	Real GDP	Imports
	(trillions of 1987 dollars per year)	
a	1	0.25
b	2	0.50
c	3	0.75
d	4	1.00
e	5	1.25

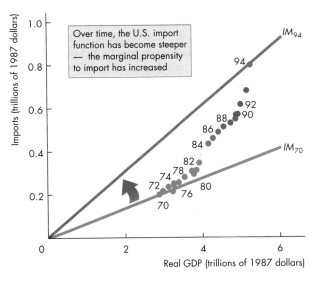

(b) The U.S. import function

Part (a) shows an import function, the relationship between imports and real GDP with all other influences on imports remaining constant. Here, the marginal propensity to import is 0.25. Part (b) shows the relationship between imports and real GDP in the United States. In 1970, the import function was IM_{70} and the marginal propensity to import was 0.07. By 1994, the marginal propensity to import had increased to 0.15 and the import function was IM_{94}.

R E V I E W

■ With a sticky price level, aggregate expenditure plans determine real GDP.

■ Two components of aggregate planned expenditure—consumption expenditure and imports—are influenced by real GDP.

■ The effects of real GDP on consumption expenditure and imports are determined by the marginal propensity to consume and the marginal propensity to import.

You've now completed your study of the first piece of the two-way link between aggregate expenditure and real GDP: the influence of real GDP on aggregate *planned* expenditure. You've seen how real GDP influences two components of aggregate planned expenditure, consumption expenditure and imports. Your next task is to study the second piece of the two-way link between aggregate expenditure and real GDP and see how the other components of aggregate planned expenditure—investment, government purchases, and exports—interact with consumption expenditure and imports to determine aggregate expenditure and real GDP when the price level is sticky.

Real GDP with a Sticky Price Level

YOU ARE NOW GOING TO DISCOVER HOW AGGREGATE expenditure plans interact to determine real GDP when the price level is sticky. First we will study the relationship between aggregate planned expenditure and real GDP. Second, we'll learn about the key distinction between *planned* expenditure and *actual* expenditure. And third, we'll study equilibrium expenditure, a situation in which aggregate planned expenditure and actual expenditure are equal.

The relationship between aggregate planned expenditure and real GDP can be described by either an aggregate expenditure schedule or an aggregate expenditure curve. The *aggregate expenditure schedule* lists aggregate planned expenditure generated at each level of real GDP. The *aggregate expenditure curve* is a graph of the aggregate expenditure schedule.

FIGURE 28.6
Aggregate Expenditure

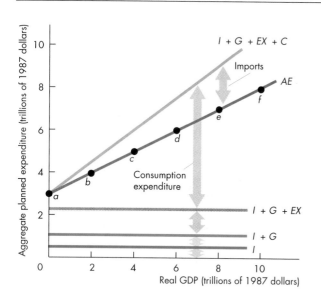

The aggregate expenditure schedule shows the relationship between aggregate planned expenditure and real GDP. Aggregate planned expenditure is the sum of planned consumption expenditure, investment, government purchases of goods and services, and exports minus imports. For example, in row *b* of the table, when real GDP is $2 trillion, planned consumption expenditure is $2.25 trillion, planned investment is $0.5 trillion, planned government purchases of goods and services are $0.55 trillion, planned exports are $1.2 trillion, and planned imports are $0.5 trillion. Thus when real GDP is $2 trillion, aggregate planned expenditure is $4 trillion ($2.25 + $0.5 + $0.55 + $1.2 − $0.5). The schedule shows that aggregate planned expenditure increases as real GDP increases. This relationship is graphed as the aggregate expenditure curve *AE*, the line *af*. The components of aggregate expenditure that increase with real GDP are consumption expenditure and imports. The other components—investment, government purchases, and exports—do not vary with real GDP.

	Real GDP (Y)	Consumption expenditure (C)	Investment (I)	Government purchases (G)	Exports (EX)	Imports (IM)	Aggregate planned expenditure (AE = C + I + G + EX − IM)
				(trillions of 1987 dollars)			
a	0	0.75	0.5	0.55	1.2	0.0	3
b	2	2.25	0.5	0.55	1.2	0.5	4
c	4	3.75	0.5	0.55	1.2	1.0	5
d	6	5.25	0.5	0.55	1.2	1.5	6
e	8	6.75	0.5	0.55	1.2	2.0	7
f	10	8.25	0.5	0.55	1.2	2.5	8

Aggregate Planned Expenditure and Real GDP

The table in Fig. 28.6 sets out an aggregate expenditure schedule together with the components of aggregate planned expenditure. To calculate aggregate planned expenditure at a given real GDP, we add the various components together. The first column of the table shows real GDP, and the second column shows the consumption expenditure generated by each level of real GDP. A $2 trillion increase in real GDP generates a $1.50 trillion increase in consumption expenditure—the *MPC* is 0.75.

The next two columns show investment and government purchases of goods and services. Investment depends on the real interest rate and the expected rate of profit (see Chapter 25, p. 598). At a given point in time these factors generate a level of investment that is independent of real GDP. Suppose this amount of investment is $0.5 trillion. Government purchases of goods and services are also independent of real GDP, and their value is $0.55 trillion.

The next two columns show exports and imports. Exports are influenced by events in the rest of the world, prices of foreign-made goods and services relative to the prices of similar U.S.-made goods and services, and foreign exchange rates. But they are not directly affected by real GDP in the United States. Exports are a constant $1.2 trillion. Imports increase as real GDP increases. A $2 trillion increase in real GDP generates a $0.5 trillion increase in imports—the marginal propensity to import is 0.25.

The final column shows aggregate planned expenditure—the sum of planned consumption expenditure, investment, government purchases of goods and services, and exports minus imports.

Figure 28.6 plots an aggregate expenditure curve. Real GDP is shown on the *x*-axis, and aggregate planned expenditure is shown on the *y*-axis. The aggregate expenditure curve is the red line *AE*. Points *a* through *f* on that curve correspond to the rows of the table. The *AE* curve is a graph of aggregate planned expenditure (the last column) plotted against real GDP (the first column).

Figure 28.6 also shows the components of aggregate expenditure. The constant components—investment (*I*), government purchases of goods and services (*G*), and exports (*EX*)—are shown by the horizontal lines in the figure. Consumption expenditure (*C*) is the vertical gap between the lines labeled *I + G + EX* and *I + G + EX + C*.

To construct the *AE* curve, subtract imports (*IM*) from the *I + G + EX + C* line. Aggregate expenditure is expenditure on U.S.-made goods and services. But the components of aggregate expenditure—*C*, *I*, and *G*—include expenditure on imported goods and services. For example, a student's purchase of a new motor bike is part of consumption expenditure, but if that motor bike is a Honda made in Japan, expenditure on it must be subtracted from consumption expenditure to find out how much is spent on goods and services produced in the United States—on U.S. real GDP. Money paid to Honda for motor bike imports from Japan does not add to aggregate expenditure in the United States.

Figure 28.6 shows that aggregate planned expenditure increases as real GDP increases. But as real GDP increases, only some of the components of aggregate planned expenditure increase. These components are consumption expenditure and imports. The sum of the components of aggregate expenditure that vary with real GDP is called **induced expenditure**. The sum of the components of aggregate expenditure that are not influenced by real GDP is called **autonomous expenditure**. The components of autonomous expenditure are investment, government purchases, exports, and autonomous consumption—that part of consumption expenditure that does not vary with real GDP. That is, autonomous expenditure is equal to the level of aggregate planned expenditure when real GDP is zero. In Fig. 28.6, autonomous expenditure is $3 trillion. And as real GDP increases from zero to $2 trillion, aggregate expenditure increases from $3 trillion to $4 trillion. Induced expenditure is $1 trillion—$4 trillion minus $3 trillion.

The aggregate expenditure curve summarizes the relationship between aggregate *planned* expenditure and real GDP. But what determines the point on the aggregate expenditure curve at which the economy operates? What determines *actual* aggregate expenditure?

Actual Expenditure, Planned Expenditure, and Real GDP

Actual aggregate expenditure is always equal to real GDP, as we saw in Chapter 23 (p. 555). But aggregate *planned* expenditure is not necessarily equal to actual aggregate expenditure and therefore is not necessarily equal to real GDP. How can actual expenditure and planned expenditure differ from each other?

Why don't expenditure plans get implemented? The main reason is that firms might end up with more inventories than planned or with less inventories than planned. People carry out their consumption expenditure plans, the government implements its planned purchases of goods and services, and net exports are as planned. Firms carry out their plans to purchase new buildings, plant, and equipment.

One component of investment, however, is the increase in firms' inventories of goods. When aggregate planned expenditure differs from real GDP, firms end up with more or less inventories than they had planned. If aggregate planned expenditure is less than real GDP, inventories increase; and if aggregate planned expenditure exceeds real GDP, inventories decrease.

FIGURE 28.7
Equilibrium Expenditure

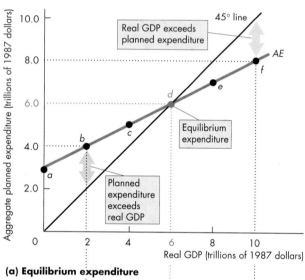

(a) Equilibrium expenditure

(b) Unplanned inventory changes

	Real GDP (Y)	**Aggregate planned expenditure** (AE)	**Unplanned inventory change** (Y − AE)
		(trillions of 1987 dollars)	
a	0	3	−3
b	2	4	−2
c	4	5	−1
d	6	6	0
e	8	7	1
f	10	8	2

The table shows expenditure plans at different levels of real GDP. When real GDP is $6 trillion, aggregate planned expenditure equals real GDP. Part (a) of the figure illustrates equilibrium expenditure, which occurs when aggregate planned expenditure equals real GDP at the intersection of the 45° line and the AE curve. Part (b) of the figure shows the forces that bring about equilibrium expenditure. When aggregate planned expenditure exceeds real GDP, inventories decrease—for example, point b in both parts of the figure. Firms increase production and real GDP increases. When aggregate planned expenditure is less than real GDP, inventories increase—for example, point f in both parts of the figure. Firms decrease production and real GDP decreases. When aggregate planned expenditure equals real GDP, there are no unplanned inventory changes and real GDP remains constant at equilibrium expenditure.

Equilibrium Expenditure

Equilibrium expenditure is the level of aggregate expenditure that occurs when aggregate *planned* expenditure equals real GDP. It is a level of aggregate expenditure and real GDP at which everyone's spending plans are fulfilled. When the price level is sticky, equilibrium expenditure determines real GDP. When aggregate planned expenditure and actual aggregate expenditure are unequal, a process of convergence toward equilibrium expenditure occurs. And throughout this convergence process, real GDP adjusts. Let's examine equilibrium expenditure and the process that brings it about.

Figure 28.7(a) illustrates equilibrium expenditure. The table sets out aggregate planned expenditure at various levels of real GDP. These values are plotted as points *a* through *f* along the *AE* curve. The 45° line shows all the points at which aggregate planned expenditure equals real GDP. Thus where the *AE* curve lies above the 45° line, aggregate planned expenditure exceeds real GDP; where the *AE* curve lies below the 45° line, aggregate planned expenditure is less than real GDP; and where the *AE* curve intersects the 45° line, aggregate planned expenditure equals real GDP. Point *d* illustrates equilibrium expenditure. At this point, real GDP is $6 trillion.

Convergence to Equilibrium

What are the forces that move aggregate expenditure toward its equilibrium level? To answer this question, we must look at a situation in which aggregate expenditure is away from its equilibrium level. Suppose that in Fig. 28.7, real GDP is $2 trillion. With real GDP at $2 trillion, actual aggregate expenditure is also $2 trillion. But aggregate *planned* expenditure is $4 trillion (point *b* in Fig. 28.7a). Aggregate planned expenditure exceeds *actual* expenditure. When people spend $4 trillion and firms produce goods and services worth $2 trillion, firms' inventories fall by $2 trillion (point *b* in Fig. 28.7b). Because the change in inventories is part of investment, *actual* investment is $2 trillion less than *planned* investment.

Real GDP doesn't remain at $2 trillion for very long. Firms have inventory targets based on their sales. When inventories fall below target, firms increase production to restore inventories to the target level. To increase inventories, firms hire additional labor and increase production. Suppose that they

increase production in the next period by $2 trillion. Real GDP increases by $2.0 trillion to $4.0 trillion. But again, aggregate planned expenditure exceeds real GDP. When real GDP is $4.0 trillion, aggregate planned expenditure is $5 trillion (point *c* in Fig. 28.7a). Again, inventories decrease, but this time by less than before. With real GDP of $4.0 trillion and aggregate planned expenditure of $5 trillion, inventories decrease by $1 trillion (point *c* in Fig. 28.7b). Again, firms hire additional labor, and production increases; real GDP increases yet further.

The process that we have just described—planned expenditure exceeds real GDP, inventories decrease, and production increases to restore the level of inventories—ends when real GDP has reached $6 trillion. At this real GDP there is an equilibrium. There are no unplanned inventory changes, and firms do not change their production.

You can do an experiment similar to the one we've just done but starting with a level of real GDP greater than equilibrium expenditure. In this case, planned expenditure is less than actual expenditure, inventories pile up, and firms cut production. As before, real GDP keeps on changing (decreasing this time) until it reaches its equilibrium level of $6.0 trillion.

REVIEW

- Equilibrium expenditure occurs when aggregate planned expenditure equals real GDP.
- Equilibrium expenditure results from an adjustment in real GDP.
- If real GDP and aggregate expenditure are less than their equilibrium levels, an unplanned fall in inventories leads firms to increase production, and real GDP increases.
- If real GDP and aggregate expenditure are greater than their equilibrium levels, an unplanned rise in inventories leads firms to decrease production, and real GDP decreases.

We've learned that when the price level is sticky, real GDP is determined by equilibrium expenditure. And we have seen how unplanned changes in inventories and the production response they generate brings a convergence toward equilibrium. We're now going to study *changes* in equilibrium and discover an economic amplifier called the multiplier.

The Multiplier

INVESTMENT AND EXPORTS CAN CHANGE FOR many reasons. A fall in the real interest rate might induce firms to increase their planned investment. A wave of innovation, such as occurred with the spread of multi-media computers in the 1990s, might increase expected future profits and lead firms to increase their planned investment. An economic boom in Western Europe and Japan might lead to a large increase in their expenditure on U.S.-produced goods and services—on U.S. exports. These are all examples of increases in autonomous expenditure.

When autonomous expenditure increases, aggregate expenditure increases, and so does equilibrium expenditure. The increase in equilibrium expenditure and real GDP is larger than the change in autonomous expenditure. The **multiplier** is the amount by which a change in autonomous expenditure is magnified or multiplied to determine the change in equilibrium expenditure and real GDP.

It is easiest to get the basic idea of the multiplier if we work with an example economy in which there are no income taxes and no imports. So we'll first assume that these factors are absent. Then, when you understand the basic idea, we'll bring these factors back into play and see what difference they make to the multiplier.

The Basic Idea of the Multiplier

Suppose that investment increases. The additional expenditure by businesses means that aggregate expenditure and real GDP increase. Disposable income also increases, and with no income taxes, real GDP and disposable income increase by the same amount. The increase in disposable income brings an increase in consumption expenditure. And the increased consumption expenditure adds even more to aggregate expenditure. Real GDP and disposable income increase further, and so does consumption expenditure. The initial increase in investment brings an even bigger increase in aggregate expenditure because it induces an increase in consumption expenditure. The magnitude of the increase in aggregate expenditure that results from an increase in autonomous expenditure is determined by the *multiplier*.

The table in Fig. 28.8 sets out aggregate planned expenditure. Initially, when real GDP is $5 trillion,

aggregate planned expenditure is $5.25 trillion. For each $1 trillion increase in real GDP, aggregate planned expenditure increases by $0.75 trillion. This aggregate expenditure schedule is shown in the figure as the aggregate expenditure curve AE_0. Initially, equilibrium expenditure is $6 trillion. You can see this equilibrium in row b of the table and in the figure where the curve AE_0 intersects the 45° line at the point marked b.

Now suppose that autonomous expenditure increases by $0.5 trillion. What happens to equilibrium expenditure? You can see the answer in Fig. 28.8. When this increase in autonomous expenditure is added to the original aggregate planned expenditure, aggregate planned expenditure increases by $0.5 trillion at each level of real GDP. The new aggregate expenditure curve is AE_1. The new equilibrium expenditure, highlighted in the table (row d'), occurs where AE_1 intersects the 45° line and is $8 trillion (point d'). At this real GDP, aggregate planned expenditure equals real GDP.

The Multiplier Effect

In Fig. 28.8, the increase in autonomous expenditure of $0.5 trillion increases equilibrium expenditure by $2 trillion. That is, the change in autonomous expenditure leads, like Bonnie Raitt's music-making equipment, to an amplified change in equilibrium expenditure. This amplified change is the *multiplier effect—* equilibrium expenditure increases by *more than* the increase in autonomous expenditure.

Initially, when autonomous expenditure increases, aggregate planned expenditure exceeds real GDP. As a result, inventories decrease. Firms respond by increasing production so as to restore their inventories to the target level. As production increases, so does real GDP. With a higher level of real GDP, *induced expenditure* increases. Thus equilibrium expenditure increases by the sum of the initial increase in autonomous expenditure and the increase in induced expenditure. In this example, induced expenditure increases by $1.5 trillion, so equilibrium expenditure increases by $2 trillion.

Although we have just analyzed the effects of an *increase* in autonomous expenditure, the same analysis applies to a decrease in autonomous expenditure. If initially the aggregate expenditure curve is AE_1, equilibrium expenditure and real GDP are $8 trillion. A decrease in autonomous expenditure of $0.5

FIGURE 28.8

The Multiplier

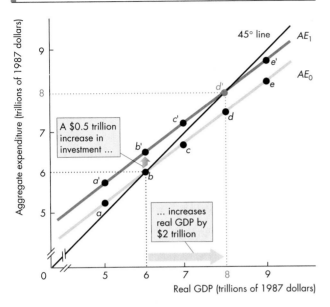

A $0.5 trillion increase in investment ...

... increases real GDP by $2 trillion

Real GDP (Y)	Aggregate planned expenditure			
	Original (AE₀)		New (AE₁)	
	(trillions of 1987 dollars)			
5	a	5.25	a'	5.75
6	b	6.00	b'	6.50
7	c	6.75	c'	7.25
8	d	7.50	d'	8.00
9	e	8.25	e'	8.75

A $0.5 trillion increase in autonomous expenditure shifts the AE curve upward by $0.5 trillion from AE_0 to AE_1. Equilibrium expenditure increases by $2 trillion from $6 trillion to $8 trillion. The increase in equilibrium expenditure is 4 times the increase in autonomous expenditure, so the multiplier is 4.

trillion shifts the aggregate expenditure curve downward by $0.5 trillion to AE_0. Equilibrium expenditure decreases from $8 trillion to $6 trillion. The decrease in equilibrium expenditure ($2 trillion) is larger than the decrease in autonomous expenditure that brought it about ($0.5 trillion).

Why Is the Multiplier Greater Than 1?

We've seen that equilibrium expenditure increases by more than the increase in autonomous expenditure. This makes the multiplier greater than 1. How come? Why does equilibrium expenditure increase by more than the increase in autonomous expenditure?

The multiplier is greater than 1 because of induced expenditure—an increase in autonomous expenditure *induces* further increases in expenditure. If General Motors spends $10 million on a new car assembly line, aggregate expenditure and real GDP immediately increase by $10 million. But that is not the end of the story. Engineers and construction workers now have more income, and they spend part of the extra income on cars, microwave ovens, vacations, and a host of other goods and services. Real GDP now rises by the initial $10 million plus the extra consumption expenditure induced by the $10 million increase in income. The producers of cars, microwave ovens, vacations, and other goods now have increased incomes, and they, in turn, spend part of the increase in their incomes on consumption goods and services. Additional income induces additional expenditure, which creates additional income.

We have seen that a change in autonomous expenditure has a multiplier effect on real GDP. But how big is the multiplier effect?

The Size of the Multiplier

Suppose that the economy is in a recession. Profit prospects start to look better, and firms are making plans for large increases in investment. The world economy is also heading toward expansion, and exports are increasing. The question on everyone's lips is: How strong will the expansion be? This is a hard question to answer. But an important ingredient in the answer is working out the size of the multiplier.

The *multiplier* is the amount by which a change in autonomous expenditure is multiplied to determine the change in equilibrium expenditure that it generates. To calculate the multiplier, we divide the change in equilibrium expenditure by the change in autonomous expenditure. Let's calculate the multiplier for the example in Fig. 28.8. Initially, equilibrium expenditure is $6 trillion. Then autonomous expenditure increases by $0.5 trillion, and equilibrium expenditure increases by $2 trillion to $8 trillion.

The multiplier is

$$\text{Multiplier} = \frac{\text{Change in equilibrium expenditure}}{\text{Change in autonomous expenditure}}$$
$$= \frac{\$2 \text{ trillion}}{\$0.5 \text{ trillion}}$$
$$= 4.$$

The Multiplier and the Marginal Propensity to Consume and Save

What determines the magnitude of the multiplier? The answer is the marginal propensity to consume. The larger is the marginal propensity to consume, the larger is the multiplier. To see why, let's do a calculation.

Aggregate expenditure and real GDP (Y) change because consumption expenditure (C) changes and investment (I) changes. The change in real GDP equals the change in consumption expenditure plus the change in investment. That is

Change in Y = Change in C + Change in I.

But the change in consumption expenditure is determined by the change in real GDP and the marginal propensity to consume. It is

Change in C = $MPC \times$ Change in Y.

Now combine these two facts to give

Change in Y = $MPC \times$ Change in Y + Change in I.

Now, solve for the change in Y as

$(1 - MPC) \times$ Change in Y = Change in I.

and rearranging,

$$\text{Change in } Y = \frac{\text{Change in } I}{(1 - MPC)}.$$

The multiplier that we want to calculate is

$$\text{Multiplier} = \frac{\text{Change in } Y}{\text{Change in } I},$$

so divide both sides of the previous equation by the change in I to give

$$\text{Multiplier} = \frac{\text{Change in } Y}{\text{Change in } I} = \frac{1}{(1 - MPC)}.$$

Using the numbers for Fig. 28.8, the MPC is 0.75 so the multiplier is

$$\text{Multiplier} = \frac{1}{(1 - 0.75)} = \frac{1}{0.25} = 4.$$

There is another formula for the multiplier. Because the marginal propensity to consume (MPC) plus the marginal propensity to save (MPS) sum to 1, the term $(1 - MPC)$ equals MPS. Therefore, another formula for the multiplier is

$$\text{Multiplier} = \frac{1}{MPS}.$$

Again using the numbers in Fig. 28.8, we have

$$\text{Multiplier} = \frac{1}{0.25} = 4.$$

Because the marginal propensity to save (MPS) is a fraction—a number between 0 and 1—the multiplier is greater than 1.

Figure 28.9 illustrates the multiplier process. In round 1, autonomous expenditure increases by $0.5 trillion (shown by the green bar). At this time, induced expenditure does not change, so aggregate expenditure and real GDP increase by $0.5 trillion. In round 2 the larger real GDP induces more consumption expenditure. Induced expenditure increases by 0.75 times the increase in real GDP, so the increase in real GDP of $0.5 trillion induces a further increase in expenditure of $0.375 trillion. This change in induced expenditure (the green bar in round 2), when added to the previous increase in expenditure (the blue bar in round 2), increases aggregate expenditure and real GDP by $0.875 trillion. The round 2 increase in real GDP induces a round 3 increase in expenditure. The process repeats through successive rounds. Each increase in real GDP is 0.75 times the previous increase. The cumulative increase in real GDP gradually approaches $2 trillion.

So far, we've ignored imports and income taxes. Let's now see how these two factors influence the multiplier.

Imports and Income Taxes

The multiplier is determined, in general, not only by the marginal propensity to consume but also by the marginal propensity to import and by the marginal tax rate. Imports make the multiplier smaller than it

FIGURE 28.9

The Multiplier Process

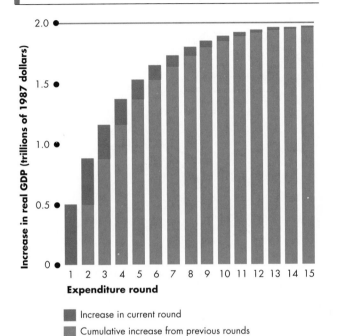

Autonomous expenditure increases in round 1 by $0.5 trillion. As a result, real GDP increases by the same amount. With a marginal propensity to consume of 0.75, each additional dollar of real GDP induces an additional 0.75 of a dollar of aggregate expenditure. The round 1 increase in real GDP induces an increase in consumption expenditure of $0.375 trillion in round 2. At the end of round 2, real GDP has increased by $0.875 trillion. The extra $0.375 trillion of real GDP in round 2 induces a further increase in consumption expenditure of $0.281 trillion in round 3. Real GDP increases yet further to $1.156 trillion. This process continues with real GDP increasing by ever smaller amounts. When the process comes to an end, real GDP has increased by a total of $2 trillion.

otherwise would be. To see why, think about what happens following an increase in investment. An increase in investment increases real GDP, which in turn increases consumption expenditure. But part of investment and part of the consumption expenditure are expenditure on imported goods and services, not U.S.-produced goods and services. It is the expenditure on only U.S.-produced goods and services that increases real GDP in the United States.

Income taxes also make the multiplier smaller than it otherwise would be. Again, think about what happens following an increase in investment. An increase in investment increases real GDP. Because income taxes increase with income, the increase in real GDP increases income taxes. And the increase in income taxes decreases disposable income. Consumption expenditure depends on disposable income, so the greater the increase in income taxes, the smaller is the increase in consumption expenditure, other things remaining the same. It is only the increase in *disposable* income that induces an increase in consumption expenditure.

The marginal propensity to import and the marginal tax rate together with the marginal propensity to consume determine the slope of the *AE* curve and the multiplier. The multiplier is equal to 1 divided by (1 − slope of the *AE* curve). Figure 28.10 compares two situations. In Fig. 28.10(a), there are no imports and no taxes. The slope of the *AE* curve equals the marginal propensity to consume, which is 0.75 and the multiplier is 4. In Fig. 28.10(b), imports and income taxes decrease the slope of the *AE* curve to 0.5. In this case, the multiplier is 2.

Over time, the value of the multiplier changes as tax rates change and as the marginal propensity to consume and the marginal propensity to import change. These ongoing changes make the multiplier hard to predict. But they do not change the fundamental fact that an initial change in autonomous expenditure leads to a magnified change in aggregate expenditure and real GDP.

Now that we've studied the multiplier and the factors that influence its magnitude, let's use what we've learned to gain some insights into business cycle turning points.

Business Cycle Turning Points

At business cycle turning points, the economy moves from expansion to recession or from recession to expansion. Economists understand these turning points like seismologists understand earthquakes. They know quite a lot about the forces and mechanisms that produce them but they can't predict them. The forces that bring business cycle turning points are the swings in autonomous expenditure such as investment and exports. The mechanism that gives momentum to the economy's new direction is the multiplier. Let's use what we've now learned to examine these turning points.

FIGURE 28.10

The Multiplier and the Slope of the *AE* Curve

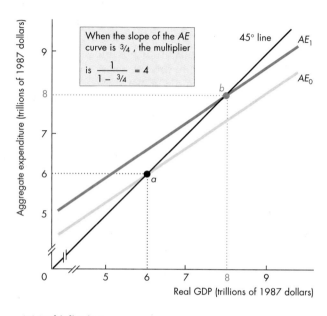

(a) Multiplier is 4

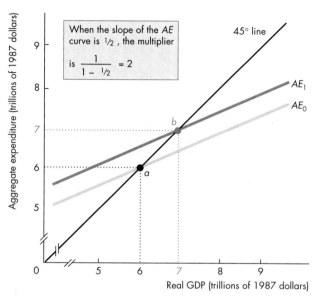

(a) Multiplier is 2

Imports and income taxes make the *AE* curve less steep and reduce the value of the multiplier. In part (a) with no imports and income taxes, the slope of the *AE* curve is 0.75 (the marginal propensity to consume) and the multiplier is 4. But with

imports and income taxes, the slope of the *AE* curve is less than the marginal propensity to consume. In part (b) the slope of the *AE* curve is 0.5. In this case the multiplier is 2.

An Expansion Begins An expansion is triggered by an increase in autonomous expenditure that increases aggregate planned expenditure. At the moment the economy turns the corner into expansion, aggregate planned expenditure exceeds real GDP. In this situation, firms see their inventories taking an unplanned dive. The expansion now begins. To meet their inventory targets, firms increase production, and real GDP begins to increase. This initial increase in real GDP brings higher incomes that stimulate consumption expenditure. The multiplier process kicks in, and the expansion picks up speed.

A Recession Begins The process we've just described works in reverse at a business cycle peak. A recession is triggered by a decrease in autonomous expenditure that decreases aggregate planned expenditure. At the moment the economy turns the corner

into recession, real GDP exceeds aggregate planned expenditure. In this situation, firms see unplanned inventories piling up. The recession now begins. To lower their inventories, firms cut production, and real GDP begins to decrease. This initial decrease in real GDP brings lower incomes that cut consumption expenditure. The multiplier process reinforces the initial cut in autonomous expenditure, and the recession takes hold.

The Next U.S. Recession? During 1994, inventories increased rapidly in the United States. Were these inventory changes planned or unplanned? If they were planned, they would *not* trigger a change in production. But if they were unplanned, firms would cut production and real GDP would begin to fall. A new recession would be on us. The crucial issue of the timing of the next U.S. recession is explored in *Reading Between the Lines* on pp. 704–705.

R E V I E W

- A change in autonomous expenditure changes real GDP by an amount determined by the multiplier.
- The multiplier is larger, the greater the marginal propensity to consume, the smaller the marginal propensity to import, and the smaller the marginal tax rate.
- Fluctuations in autonomous expenditure bring business cycle turning points.

We've seen that the economy does not operate like the shock absorbers on Dennis Archer's car. The economy's potholes are changes in investment and exports. And while the price level is sticky, these economic potholes are not smoothed out. Instead, they are amplified. But we've considered only the adjustments in spending that occur in the very short term when the price level is sticky. What happens when the price level changes? And what happens in the long run? Let's answer these questions.

The Multiplier, Real GDP, and the Price Level

WHEN FIRMS ARE HAVING TROUBLE KEEPING UP with sales and their inventories fall below target, they increase production, but at some point they raise their prices. Similarly, when firms find unwanted inventories piling up, they decrease production, but eventually they cut their prices. So far, we've studied the macroeconomic consequences of firms changing their production levels when their sales change, but we haven't looked at the effects of price changes. When individual firms change their prices, the economy's price level changes.

To study the simultaneous determination of real GDP and the price level, we use the *aggregate supply–aggregate demand model*, which is explained in Chapter 27. We also need to work out the connection between the aggregate supply–aggregate demand model and the equilibrium expenditure model that we've used in this chapter. The key to the relationship between these two models is the distinction between the aggregate *expenditure* curve and the aggregate *demand* curve.

Aggregate Expenditure and Aggregate Demand

The aggregate expenditure curve is the relationship between the aggregate planned expenditure and real GDP, all other influences on aggregate planned expenditure remaining the same. The aggregate demand curve is the relationship between the aggregate quantity of goods and services demanded and the price level, all other influences on aggregate demand remaining the same. Let's explore the links between these two relationships.

Aggregate Expenditure and the Price Level

At a given price level, there is a given level of aggregate planned expenditure. But if the price level changes, so does aggregate planned expenditure. Why? There are three main reasons:[1]

1. Real money balances effect
2. Intertemporal substitution effect
3. International substitution effect

Real money is the purchasing power of money, which is measured by the quantity of money divided by the price level. A rise in the price level, other things remaining the same, decreases the quantity of real money and a smaller quantity of real money decreases aggregate planned expenditure—*the real money balances effect*. A rise in the price level, other things remaining the same, makes current goods and services more costly relative to future goods and services and results in a delay in purchases—*the intertemporal substitution effect*. A rise in the price level, other things remaining the same, makes U.S.-produced goods more expensive relative to foreign-produced goods and services and increases imports and decreases exports—*the international substitution effect*.

When the price level rises, each of these effects reduces aggregate planned expenditure at each level of real GDP. As a result, when the price level rises, the aggregate expenditure curve shifts downward. A fall in the price level has the opposite effect. When the price level falls, the aggregate expenditure curve shifts upward.

---

[1]These reasons are explained more fully in Chapter 27, pp. 662–663.

Figure 28.11(a) illustrates these effects. When the price level is 130, the aggregate expenditure curve is AE_0, which intersects the 45° line at point b. Equilibrium expenditure is $6 trillion. If the price level increases to 170, the aggregate expenditure curve shifts downward to AE_1, which intersects the 45° line at point a. Equilibrium expenditure is $4 trillion. If the price level decreases to 90, the aggregate expenditure curve shifts upward to AE_2, which intersects the 45° line at point c. Equilibrium expenditure is $8 trillion.

We've just seen that when the price level changes, other things remaining the same, the aggregate expenditure curve shifts and the equilibrium expenditure changes. And when the price level changes, other things remaining the same, there is a movement along the aggregate demand curve. Figure 28.11(b) illustrates these movements. At a price level of 130 the aggregate quantity of goods and services demanded is $6 trillion—point b on the aggregate demand curve AD. If the price level increases to 170, the aggregate quantity of goods and services demanded decreases to $4 trillion. There is a movement along the aggregate demand curve to point a. If the price level decreases to 90, the aggregate quantity of goods and services demanded increases to $8 trillion. There is a movement along the aggregate demand curve to point c.

Each point on the aggregate demand curve corresponds to a point of equilibrium expenditure. The equilibrium expenditure points a, b, and c in Fig. 28.11(a) correspond to the points a, b, and c on the aggregate demand curve in Fig. 28.11(b).

When the price level changes, other things remaining the same, the aggregate expenditure curve shifts and there is a movement along the aggregate demand curve. When any other influence on aggregate planned expenditure changes, both the aggregate expenditure curve and the aggregate demand curve shift. For example, an increase in investment or in exports increases both aggregate planned expenditure and aggregate demand and shifts both the AE curve and the AD curve. Figure 28.12 illustrates the effect of such an increase.

Initially, the aggregate expenditure curve is AE_0 in part (a) and the aggregate demand curve is AD_0 in part (b). The price level is 130, real GDP is $6 trillion, and the economy is at point a in both parts of the figure. Now suppose that investment increases by $1 trillion. At a constant price level of 130, the aggregate expenditure curve shifts upward to AE_1. This curve intersects the 45° line at an equilibrium expenditure of $8 trillion (point b). This equilibrium expenditure

FIGURE 28.11

Aggregate Demand

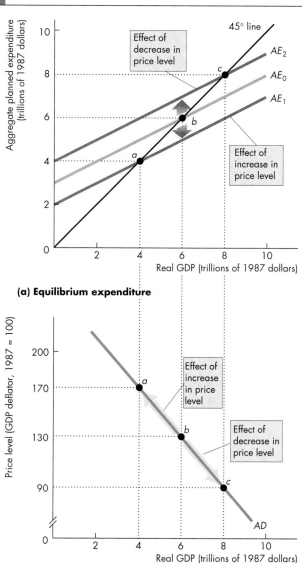

(a) Equilibrium expenditure

(b) Aggregate demand

A change in the price level shifts the AE curve and results in a *movement along* the AD curve. When the price level is 130, the AE curve is AE_0, and equilibrium expenditure is $6 trillion at point b. When the price level rises to 170, the AE curve is AE_1, and equilibrium expenditure is $4 trillion at point a. When the price level falls to 90, the AE curve is AE_2, and equilibrium expenditure is $8 trillion at point c. Points a, b, and c on the AD curve in part (b) correspond to the equilibrium expenditure points a, b, and c in part (a).

A Change in Aggregate Demand

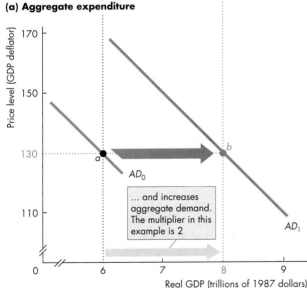

(a) Aggregate expenditure

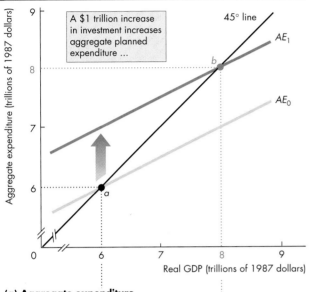

(b) Aggregate demand

The price level is 130. When the aggregate expenditure curve is AE_0 (part a), the aggregate demand curve is AD_0 (part b). An increase in autonomous expenditure shifts the AE curve upward to AE_1. In the new equilibrium real GDP is $8 trillion (at b). Because the quantity of real GDP demanded at a price level of 130 increases to $8 trillion, the AD curve shifts rightward to AD_1.

of $8 trillion is the aggregate quantity of goods and services demanded at a price level of 130, as shown by point b in part (b). Point b lies on a new aggregate demand curve. The aggregate demand curve has shifted rightward to AD_1.

But how do we know by how much the AD curve shifts? The answer is determined by the multiplier. The larger the multiplier, the larger is the shift in the aggregate demand curve that results from a given change in autonomous expenditure. In this example the multiplier is 2. A $1 trillion increase in investment produces a $2 trillion increase in the aggregate quantity of goods and services demanded at each price level. That is, a $1 trillion increase in autonomous expenditure shifts the aggregate demand curve rightward by $2 trillion.

A decrease in autonomous expenditure shifts the aggregate expenditure curve downward and shifts the aggregate demand curve leftward. You can see these effects by reversing the change that we've just studied. Suppose that the economy is initially at point b on the aggregate expenditure curve AE_1 and the aggregate demand curve AD_1. A decrease in autonomous expenditure shifts the aggregate planned expenditure curve downward to AE_0. The aggregate quantity of goods and services demanded falls from $8 trillion to $6 trillion, and the aggregate demand curve shifts leftward to AD_0.

We can summarize what we have just discovered in the following way: An increase in autonomous expenditure arising from some source other than a change in the price level shifts the AE curve upward and the AD curve rightward. The magnitude of the shift of the AD curve is determined by the change in autonomous expenditure and the multiplier.

Equilibrium GDP and the Price Level

In Chapter 27, we learned that aggregate demand and short-run aggregate supply determine equilibrium real GDP and the price level. We've now put aggregate demand under a more powerful microscope and have discovered that a change in investment (or in any component of autonomous expenditure) changes aggregate demand and shifts the aggregate demand curve. The magnitude of the shift depends on the multiplier. But whether a change in autonomous expenditure results ultimately in a change in real GDP, a change in the price level, or some combination of the two depends on aggregate supply. There are two time frames to consider:

1. The short run
2. The long run

First we'll see what happens in the short run. Then we'll look at the long run.

An Increase in Aggregate Demand in the Short Run

Figure 28.13 describes the economy. In part (a), the aggregate expenditure curve is AE_0, and equilibrium expenditure is $6 trillion—point a. In part (b), aggregate demand is AD_0, and the short-run aggregate supply curve is SAS. (Look at Chapter 10 if you need to refresh your understanding of this curve.) Equilibrium is at point a, where the aggregate demand and short-run aggregate supply curves intersect. The price level is 130, and real GDP is $6 trillion.

Now suppose that investment increases by $1 trillion. With the price level sticky at 130, the aggregate expenditure curve shifts upward to AE_1. Equilibrium expenditure increases to $8 trillion—point b in part (a). In part (b) the aggregate demand curve shifts rightward by $2 trillion, from AD_0 to AD_1. How far the aggregate demand curve shifts is determined by the multiplier when the price level is sticky. But with this new aggregate demand curve, the price level does not remain fixed. The price level rises and as it does so, the aggregate expenditure curve shifts downward. The short-run equilibrium occurs when the aggregate expenditure curve has shifted downward to AE_2 and the new aggregate demand curve, AD_1, intersects the short-run aggregate supply curve. Real GDP is $7.6 trillion and the price level is 136 (at point c).

When price level effects are taken into account, the increase in investment still has a multiplier effect on real GDP, but the effect is smaller than it would be if the price level were sticky. The steeper the slope of the short-run aggregate supply curve, the larger is the increase in the price level and the smaller is the multiplier effect on real GDP.

An Increase in Aggregate Demand in the Long Run

Figure 28.14 illustrates the long-run effect of an increase in aggregate demand. In the long run, real GDP equals potential GDP and there is full employment. Potential GDP is $6 trillion and the long-run aggregate supply curve is LAS. Initially, the economy is at point a (parts a and b).

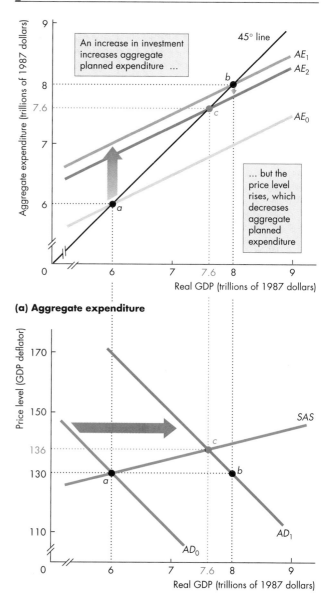

FIGURE 28.13

The Short-Run Multiplier

(a) Aggregate expenditure

(b) Aggregate demand

An increase in investment shifts the AE curve from AE_0 to AE_1 (part a) and shifts the AD curve from AD_0 to AD_1 (part b). At the price level 130 there is a shortage. The price level rises, and the higher price level shifts the AE curve downward to AE_2. The economy moves to point c in both parts. With flexible prices, the multiplier is smaller than when prices are sticky.

FIGURE 28.14
The Long-Run Multiplier

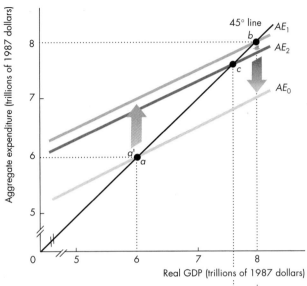

(a) Aggregate expenditure

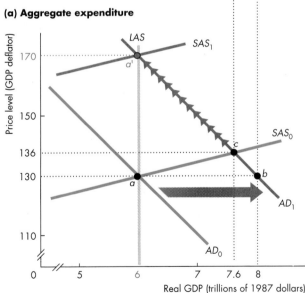

(b) Aggregate demand

Starting from point *a*, an increase in investment shifts the *AE* curve to AE_1 and shifts the *AD* curve to AD_1. In the short run, the economy moves to point *c*. In the long run, the money wage rate rises, the *SAS* curve shifts to SAS_1, the *AE* curve shifts back to AE_0, the price level rises, and real GDP falls. The economy moves to point *a'* and the long-run multiplier is zero.

Investment increases by $1 trillion. The aggregate expenditure curve shifts to AE_1 and the aggregate demand curve shifts to AD_1. With no change in the price level, the economy would move to point *b*. But the price level rises to 136 and real GDP increases to $7.6 trillion. With the higher price level, the *AE* curve shifts to AE_2. The economy is now in a short-run equilibrium at point *c*. With real GDP above potential GDP and the labor force more than fully employed, there are shortages of labor and the money wage rate rises. The higher money wage rate increases costs, which decreases short-run aggregate supply and shifts the *SAS* curve leftward to SAS_1. As a result, the price level rises and real GDP decreases. There is a movement along AD_1 and the *AE* curve shifts downward toward AE_0. When the money wage rate and the price level have increased by the same percentage, real GDP is again equal to potential GDP and the economy is at point *a'*. The long-run multiplier is zero.

R E V I E W

■ A change in the price level shifts the *AE* curve and brings a movement along the *AD* curve.

■ A change in autonomous expenditure that is not caused by a change in the price level shifts both the *AE* curve and the *AD* curve, and the multiplier determines the magnitude of the shift in the *AD* curve.

■ The increase in real GDP that results from an increase in autonomous expenditure is smaller than the increase in aggregate demand.

■ An increase in aggregate demand at full employment leaves real GDP unchanged but increases the price level. The long-run multiplier is zero.

◆ We've now seen how real GDP deviates from its long-term growth path when aggregate demand fluctuates, and we've studied the multiplier effect that amplifies the disturbances to aggregate demand.

In the next three chapters we're going to see how macroeconomic policy can be used to smooth economic fluctuations. In Chapter 29 we study fiscal policy and discover what the government can do (and can't do) with taxes and its own spending to smooth economic fluctuations and stimulate production. In Chapters 30 and 31 we study money and the actions the Fed can take to smooth fluctuations and to keep inflation in check.

From Expansion to Recession: But When?

NATIONAL ECONOMIC TRENDS, APRIL, 1994

Inventory Changes and the Business Cycle

BY DONALD S. ALLEN

The robust growth of Gross Domestic Product (GDP) in 1994 was due in large part to a buildup of business inventory. The 1994 increase in business inventory was $47.8 billion in 1987 dollars, contributing 1 percentage point of the 4.1 percent increase in GDP, and following a $15.3 billion increase in 1993. Most post-war recessions have been preceded by a rise in inventory levels. Does the 1994 buildup of inventory portend another downturn? Not necessarily.

The impact of inventory increases on the business cycle depends on whether they are planned or unplanned. *Unplanned* increases in inventory are undesirable and are usually followed by scaled-back production or purchases until inventory levels return to normal. Such decreases in production can trigger layoffs and sluggish demand throughout the economy. Planned increases in inventory, on the other hand, contribute positively to economic expansions and do not lead to corrections. ...

Fundamental changes in inventory management methods may also have permanently changed the relationship between inventory and recessions. ... The manufacturing sector has adopted more efficient inventory management techniques and contributed heavily to the decline in the aggregate inventory-to-sales ratio. Innovations like just-in-time delivery allow production to respond faster to changes in demand, minimizing unplanned inventory accumulation. Some analysts believe this will reduce the severity of business cycles over the long run.

The Federal Reserve Bank of St. Louis

Essence of THE STORY

■ Investment in business inventories in 1994 was $47.8 billion (1987 dollars), up from $15.3 billion in 1993.

■ Most recessions are preceded by an increase in inventory levels, but not all increases in inventories bring recession.

■ The impact of inventory increases on the business cycle depends on whether they are planned or unplanned. Only *unplanned* increases in inventories are followed by recession.

■ Innovations such as just-in-time delivery allow production to respond faster to changes in demand and to minimize unplanned inventory investment and might have changed the relationship between inventory and recessions.

Economic

A N A L Y S I S

■ Figure 1 shows the quarterly changes in inventories, and Fig. 2 shows the quarterly ratio of inventories to sales from 1990 through 1994.

■ When the last recession began, in the second quarter of 1990, the change in inventories increased, and so did the ratio of inventories to sales. These increases were *unplanned*.

■ Through the 1990–1991 recession, inventories fell. When the expansion began, the change in inventories began to rise.

■ Throughout the expansion, which began in mid-1991, the change in inventories increased (Fig. 1), but through 1993, the ratio of inventories to sales decreased (Fig. 2).

■ In 1994 the change in inventories increased quickly, and the ratio of inventories to sales also increased.

■ It is not possible to say whether the 1994 increase in inventories was planned or unplanned. If it was planned, the expansion will continue at least through 1995 and into 1996, perhaps for longer. If it was unplanned, a recession will probably be triggered when the change in

inventories falls to restore inventories to their planned level.

■ The steady fall in the ratio of inventories to sales during the 1990s is part of a longer process described in the article and shown in Fig. 3. At its peak in 1974 the ratio of inventories to sales was 4.1 percent. This level of inventory is equivalent to 15 days' sales. At its trough in the first quarter of 1994 the ratio was 2.25 percent, which is equivalent to 8 days' sales.

■ The article says that some analysts believe that the lower inventory-to-sales ratio will lessen the severity of the business cycle. There is no sign of such a development. The ratio of inventories to sales has been falling since the mid-1970s, and the business cycle has been even more severe during this period than it was when the ratio was much higher during the 1960s.

■ If inventories act as a cushion against fluctuations in demand, smaller inventories can bring bigger rather than smaller fluctuations in production. Economists are still trying to work out exactly how inventories and the business cycle interact.

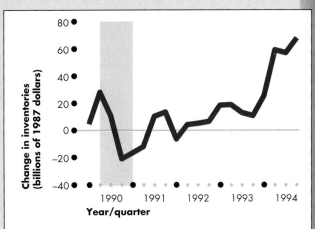

Figure 1 Change in inventories

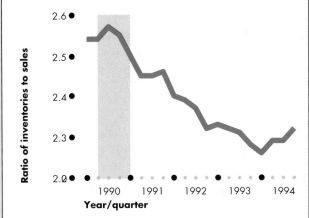

Figure 2 Inventories to sales ratio

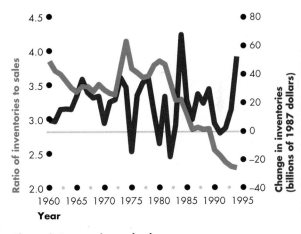

Figure 3 Inventories and sales

■ For now, we can tell when we are in a recession or an expansion, but we can't predict when the next turning point will occur.

SUMMARY

Sticky Prices and Expenditure Plans

When the price level is sticky, expenditure plans determine real GDP. There is a two-way relationship between aggregate expenditure and real GDP. An increase in real GDP brings an increase in aggregate *planned* expenditure, and an increase in aggregate expenditure brings an increase in real GDP.

Planned consumption expenditure is described by the consumption function—the relationship between consumption expenditure and disposable income. *Planned* saving is described by the saving function—the relationship between saving and disposable income. The influence of disposable income on consumption expenditure is determined by the marginal propensity to consume (*MPC*), which is equal to the slope of the consumption function. Similarly, the influence of disposable income on saving is determined by the marginal propensity to save (*MPS*), which is equal to the slope of the saving function.

The influence of real GDP on imports is described by the import function. An increase in real GDP brings an increase in imports, and the magnitude of the increase in imports is determined by the marginal propensity to import. (pp. 682–689)

Real GDP with a Sticky Price Level

The aggregate expenditure curve shows the relationship between aggregate *planned* expenditure and real GDP. *Actual* aggregate expenditure is always equal to real GDP. But aggregate *planned* expenditure is not necessarily equal to actual aggregate expenditure and real GDP.

Equilibrium expenditure occurs when aggregate planned expenditure equals actual expenditure and real GDP. When aggregate planned expenditure and real GDP are unequal, a process of convergence toward equilibrium expenditure occurs. When real GDP is below its equilibrium level, an unplanned fall in inventories stimulates production, which increases real GDP. When real GDP is above its equilibrium level, an unplanned rise in inventories brings a decrease in production, which decreases real GDP. (pp. 690–693)

The Multiplier

The multiplier is the magnified effect of a change in autonomous expenditure on real GDP. The basic idea of the multiplier is that an increase in investment (or any other component of autonomous expenditure) increases real GDP and disposable income, which in turn increases consumption expenditure and adds more to real GDP than did the initial increase in investment.

The multiplier is equal to 1 divided by the marginal propensity to save. The larger the marginal propensity to consume, the smaller the marginal propensity to save and so the larger is the multiplier. The multiplier is also influenced by the marginal propensity to import and by the marginal income tax rate. For a given marginal propensity to consume, the larger the marginal propensity to import and the higher the marginal tax rate, the smaller is the multiplier. (pp. 694–699)

The Multiplier, Real GDP, and the Price Level

The aggregate demand curve is the relationship between the quantity of real GDP demanded and the price level, other things remaining the same. The aggregate expenditure curve is the relationship between aggregate planned expenditure and real GDP, other things remaining the same. At a given price level, there is a given aggregate expenditure curve. A change in the price level changes aggregate planned expenditure and shifts the aggregate expenditure curve. A change in the price level also creates a movement along the aggregate demand curve. Thus a movement along the aggregate demand curve is associated with a shift in the aggregate expenditure curve.

A change in autonomous expenditure that is not caused by a change in the price level shifts the aggregate expenditure curve and also shifts the aggregate demand curve. The magnitude of the shift in the aggregate demand curve depends on the size of the multiplier and the change in autonomous expenditure.

Because real GDP and the price level are determined by both aggregate demand and aggregate supply, the short-run multiplier is smaller than when the price level is sticky. The long-run multiplier in zero. (pp. 699–703)

K E Y   E L E M E N T S

Key Figures

Key Terms

R E V I E W   Q U E S T I O N S

1. What are the main implications of sticky prices for the economy as a whole?
2. Explain the two-way relationship between real GDP and aggregate expenditure.
3. What is the main influence on consumption expenditure and saving in the short term?
4. What are the consumption function and the saving function? What is the relationship between them?
5. What is the marginal propensity to consume? Why is it less than 1?
6. Explain the relationship between the marginal propensities to consume and to save.
7. What determines the slope of the consumption function?
8. Explain the relationship between consumption expenditure and GDP.
9. What are the import function and the marginal propensity to import?
10. What are the aggregate expenditure schedule and the aggregate expenditure curve?
11. Distinguish between induced expenditure and autonomous expenditure.
12. How is equilibrium expenditure determined?
13. Explain how a recovery gets going when aggregate planned expenditure exceeds real GDP.
14. Explain why an increase in autonomous expenditure shifts the aggregate expenditure curve.
15. What is the multiplier?
16. Explain the multiplier process.
17. What determines the size of the multiplier?
18. Explain the influences of the marginal propensity to consume, imports, and taxes on the size of the multiplier.
19. Describe the relationship between the aggregate expenditure curve and the aggregate demand curve.
20. Explain why the aggregate expenditure curve shifts downward when the price level increases.
21. What happens to the aggregate expenditure curve and the aggregate demand curve when the price level changes and everything else is constant?
22. Explain why an increase in autonomous expenditure increases aggregate demand.
23. Explain why the multiplier is larger when the price level is sticky than when it changes.
24. Explain why the multiplier is zero in the long run.

PROBLEMS

1. You are given the following information about the economy of Heron Island:

Disposable income (millions of dollars per year)	Consumption expenditure (millions of dollars per year)
0	5
10	10
20	15
30	20
40	25

Calculate Heron Island's
   a. Marginal propensity to consume.
   b. Saving at each level of disposable income.
   c. Marginal propensity to save.

2. Turtle Island is a closed economy, the people of Turtle Island pay no incomes taxes, and the price level is sticky. The figure illustrates the components of aggregate planned expenditure on Turtle Island.

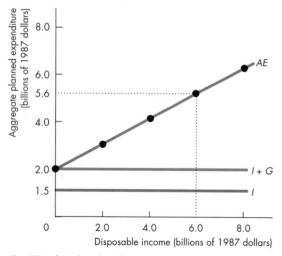

On Turtle Island, what is
   a. Autonomous expenditure?
   b. The marginal propensity to consume?
   c. Aggregate planned expenditure when real GDP is $6 billion?
   d. If real GDP is $4 billion, what is happening to inventories?
   e. If real GDP is $6 billion, what is happening to inventories?
   f. What is the multiplier?

3. You are given the following information about the economy of Zeeland: Autonomous consumption expenditure is $100 billion, and the marginal propensity to consume is 0.9. Investment is $460 billion, government purchases of goods and services are $400 billion, and net taxes are a constant $400 billion—they do not vary with income.
   a. What is the consumption function?
   b. What is the equation that describes the aggregate expenditure curve?
   c. Calculate equilibrium expenditure.
   d. If investment falls to $360 billion, what is the change in equilibrium expenditure and what is the size of the multiplier?

4. Suppose that in problem 3, the price level is 100 and real GDP equals potential GDP.
   a. If investment increases by $100 billion, what happens to the quantity of real GDP demanded?
   b. In the short run, does equilibrium real GDP increase by more than, less than, or the same amount as the increase in the quantity of real GDP demanded?
   c. In the long run, does equilibrium real GDP increase by more than, less than, or the same amount as the increase in the quantity of real GDP demanded?
   d. In the short run, does the price level in Zeeland rise, fall, or remain unchanged?
   e. In the long run, does the price level in Zeeland rise, fall, or remain unchanged?

5. Study *Reading Between the Lines* on pp. 704–705, and then answer the following questions:
   a. If the 1994 investment in inventories was *unplanned*, what is the implication for real GDP and aggregate expenditure and inventory investment during 1995? Use a figure like Fig. 28.7 to answer this question.
   b. If the 1994 investment in inventories was *planned*, what is the implication for real GDP and aggregate expenditure and inventory investment during 1995? Use figures like Figs. 28.7 and 28.8 in your answer.
   c. Critically appraise the view that a low inventories-to-sales ratio will decrease the severity of the business cycle.

The Federal Budget and Fiscal Policy

After studying this chapter, you will be able to:

- Describe the federal budget process

- Describe the recent history of federal expenditures, tax revenues, and the budget deficit

- Distinguish between automatic and discretionary fiscal policy

- Define and explain the fiscal policy multipliers

- Explain the effects of fiscal policy in both the short run and the long run

- Distinguish between and explain the demand-side and the supply-side effects of fiscal policy

Balancing Acts on Capitol Hill

In 1995 the federal government planned to spend $1,609 billion, or 23 cents of every dollar that Americans earn. What are the effects of government spending on the economy? Does it create jobs? Or does it destroy them? And does a dollar spent by the government on goods and services have the same effect as a dollar spent by someone else? ◆ Although the federal government planned to *spend* 23 cents of every dollar earned, it did not plan to tax us by that amount. Its plans were for tax revenues of $1,436 billion or 21 cents of every dollar earned. What are the effects of taxes on the economy? Do taxes harm employment and economic growth? ◆ The plan to have tax revenues fall short of expenditures is not new on Capitol Hill. The last time the federal government budget was in surplus was 1969. In the 26 years since then, the federal government's debt has increased from $278 billion to $3,640 billion—a *thirteenfold increase*. If these numbers are too big to mean anything, divide them by the U.S. population to find *your* share. Government debt per person has grown from $1,400 in 1969 to $14,000 in 1995. Does it matter if the government doesn't balance its books? What are the effects of an ongoing government deficit and accumulating debt? Does it slow economic growth? Does it impose a burden on future generations—on you and your children? What must be done to balance the budget? Can it be done by cutting spending? Or must taxes be increased? Or can spending be cut so severely that taxes can also be cut?

◆ These are the questions that you will explore in this chapter. We'll begin by describing the federal budget and the process of creating it. We'll also look at the recent history of the budget. We'll then use the multiplier analysis of Chapter 28 and the aggregate supply-aggregate demand model of Chapter 27 to study the effects of the budget on the economy.

The Federal Budget

THE ANNUAL STATEMENT OF THE EXPENDITURES and tax revenues of the government of the United States together with the laws and regulations that approve and support those expenditures and taxes make up the **federal budget**.

1. To finance the activities of the federal government
2. To stabilize the economy

The first purpose of the federal budget—and its original purpose—is to ensure that funds are available to finance the business of the government. Until the Great Depression years of the 1930s the federal budget had no other purpose. The second purpose is to pursue the government's fiscal policy. **Fiscal policy** is the use of the federal budget to achieve macroeconomic objectives such as full employment, sustained long-term economic growth, and price level stability. It is on this second purpose that we focus in this chapter.

The Institutions and Laws

Fiscal policy is made by the President and Congress on an annual time line that is shown in Figure 29.1.

The Roles of the President and Congress In February of each year, the President *proposes* a budget to Congress, and in September, after Congress has passed the budget acts, he either signs those acts into law or vetoes them. In approving or vetoing the budget acts, the President is in a "take it or leave it" situation. He does not have a *line-item veto,* a veto power to eliminate specific items in the budget and approve others. Many state governors do have a line-item veto, but the President of the United States does not. Although the President proposes and ultimately approves the budget, it is Congress that makes the budget decisions.

Congress begins its work on the budget with the President's proposal. The House of Representatives and the Senate develop their own budget ideas in their respective House and Senate Budget Committees. Formal conferences between the two houses eventually resolve differences of view, and a series of spending acts and an overall budget act are usually passed by both houses before the start of the fiscal year. A *fiscal year* is a year that runs from October 1 to September

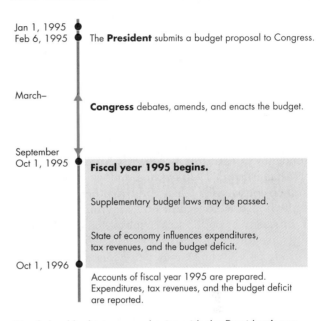

FIGURE 29.1

The Federal Budget Time Line in 1995–96

Jan 1, 1995
Feb 6, 1995 — The **President** submits a budget proposal to Congress.

March– — **Congress** debates, amends, and enacts the budget.

September
Oct 1, 1995 — **Fiscal year 1995 begins.**

Supplementary budget laws may be passed.

State of economy influences expenditures, tax revenues, and the budget deficit.

Oct 1, 1996 — Accounts of fiscal year 1995 are prepared. Expenditures, tax revenues, and the budget deficit are reported.

The federal budget process begins with the President's proposals in February. Congress debates and amends these proposals and enacts a budget before the start of the fiscal year on October 1. The President either signs into law or vetoes the budget acts. As events evolve through the fiscal year, Congress might pass supplementary budget laws. The budget outcome is calculated after the end of the fiscal year.

30 in the next calendar year. *Fiscal 1995* is the fiscal year that *begins* on October 1, 1995.

During a fiscal year, Congress often passes supplementary budget laws, and the budget outcome is influenced by the evolving state of the economy. For example, if a recession begins, tax revenues fall and welfare payments increase.

The Employment Act of 1946 Fiscal policy operates within the framework of the landmark **Employment Act of 1946** in which Congress declared that

> …it is the continuing policy and responsibility of the Federal Government to use all practicable means … to coordinate and utilize all its plans, functions, and resources … to promote maximum employment, production, and purchasing power.

This act recognized a role for government actions to reduce unemployment, keep the economy expanding, and keep inflation in check. The *Full Employment and Balanced Growth Act of 1978*, more commonly known as the *Humphrey-Hawkins Act*, went further than the 1946 employment act and set a specific target of 4 percent for the unemployment rate. The President is responsible for achieving the goals of these acts and, under the 1946 act, must describe the current economic situation and the policies he believes are needed in an annual *Economic Report of the President*. The President is assisted in this task by the Council of Economic Advisers.

The Council of Economic Advisers   The President's **Council of Economic Advisers** (CEA) was established in 1946 by the Employment Act. The Council consists of a Chair and two other members, all of whom are economists on leave from their regular university or public service jobs. Members typically serve for two to three years. In 1995, the Chair of President Clinton's Council of Economic Advisers was Joseph E. Stiglitz of Stanford University and the two members were Martin Neil Baily of the

University of Maryland and Alicia H. Munnell. The main work of the Council is to monitor the economy and to keep the President and the public well informed about the current state of the economy and the best available forecasts of where it is heading. This economic intelligence activity is one source of data that informs the budget-making process.

We've described the purposes of the federal budget and the process of its creation. Let's now look at the content of the federal budget.

Highlights of the 1995 Budget

Table 29.1 shows the main items in the federal budget proposed by President Clinton in 1995. The numbers are projected amounts for the fiscal year beginning on October 1, 1995—fiscal 1995. Notice first the three main parts of the table: *tax revenues* are the government's receipts, *expenditures* are the government's outlays, and the *deficit* is the amount by which the government's expenditures exceed its tax revenues.

Tax Revenues   Tax revenues were projected to be $1,436 billion in fiscal 1995. These revenues come from four sources:

1. Personal income taxes
2. Social insurance taxes
3. Corporate income taxes
4. Indirect taxes

The largest source of revenue is *personal income taxes*, which in 1995 were expected to be $599 billion. These are the taxes paid by individuals on their incomes. The second largest source is *social insurance taxes*. These are the taxes paid by workers and their employers to finance the government's social insurance programs such as Social Security. Third in size are *corporate income taxes*. These are the taxes paid by companies on their profits. Finally, the smallest source of federal revenues are *indirect taxes*. These are taxes on the sale of gasoline, alcoholic drinks, and a few other items.

Expenditures   Expenditures are classified in three categories:

1. Transfer payments
2. Purchases of goods and services
3. Debt interest

TABLE   29.1

Federal Budget in Fiscal 1995

Item	Projections (billions of dollars)
Tax Revenues	**1,436**
Personal income taxes	599
Social insurance taxes	573
Corporate income taxes	171
Indirect taxes	94
Expenditures	**1,609**
Transfer payments	954
Purchases of goods and services	438
Debt interest	217
Deficit	**173**

Source: *Economic Report of the President*, 1995, Table B-82.

The largest item of expenditure, *transfer payments*, are payments to individuals, businesses, other levels of government, and the rest of the world. In 1995, this item was expected to be $954 billion. It includes Social Security benefits, Medicare and Medicaid, unemployment checks, welfare payments, farm subsidies, grants to state and local governments, aid to developing countries, and dues to international organizations such as the United Nations.

Purchases of goods and services are expenditures on final goods and services, and in 1995 they were expected to total $438 billion. These expenditures include those on national defense, the NASA space program, research on cures for AIDS, computers for the Internal Revenue Service, government cars and trucks, federal highways, and dams. This component of the federal budget is *government purchases of goods and services* that appears in the circular flow of expenditure and income and in the national income and product accounts (see Chapter 23, pp. 548–552).

Debt interest is the interest on the government debt minus interest received by the government on its own investments. In 1995 this item was expected to be $217 billion—more than half the expenditure on goods and services. This interest payment is large because the government has a large debt—over $3 trillion ($3,000 billion). This large debt has arisen from large and persistent deficits.

Deficit The government's budget balance is equal to its tax revenues minus its expenditures. That is,

Budget balance = Tax revenues – Expenditures.

If tax revenues exceed expenditures, the government has a **budget surplus**. If expenditures exceed tax revenues, the government has a **budget deficit**. If tax revenues equal expenditures, the government has a **balanced budget**. In 1995, with projected expenditures of $1,609 billion and tax revenues of $1,436 billion, the government projected a budget deficit of $173 billion.

Big numbers like these are hard to visualize. To get a better sense of their magnitudes we often express them as percentages of GDP. Expressing them in this way lets us see how large government is relative to the size of the economy and also helps us to study *changes* in the scale of government over time.

How typical is the federal budget of 1995? Let's look at its recent history.

The Budget in Historical Perspective

Figure 29.2 shows the government's tax revenues, expenditures, and budget deficit since 1978. Throughout this period there was a budget deficit.

FIGURE 29.2

The Budget Deficit

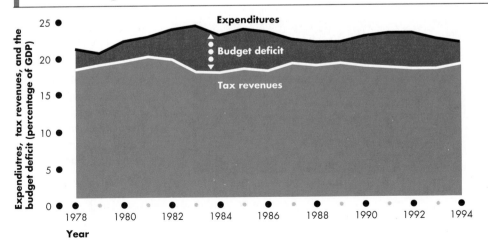

The figure records the federal government's expenditures, tax revenues, and budget deficit from 1978 to 1995. In the late 1970s the deficit was small and decreasing, but during the 1980s it became large and persisted. The budget deficit arose from the combination of a decrease in tax revenues and an increase in expenditures.

Source: *Economic Report of the President*, 1995.

The deficit was small and decreasing between 1978 and 1979, but it then increased and reached a peak in 1983 of 5.3 percent of GDP. It declined from 1983 through 1989 but averaged more than 3 percent of GDP through the entire decade of the 1980s. The deficit climbed again during the 1990–1991 recession and then decreased during the 1990s expansion.

Why did the government deficit grow in the early 1980s and remain high? The immediate answer is that expenditures increased and tax revenues decreased. But which components of expenditures increased and which sources of tax revenues decreased? Let's look at tax revenues and expenditures in a bit more detail.

Tax Revenues   Figure 29.3(a) shows the components of tax revenues as percentages of GDP between 1978 and 1994. Total tax revenues increased between 1978 and 1981 and then declined through 1986. Most of the decline was in corporate and personal

FIGURE 29.3

Federal Government Tax Revenues and Expenditures

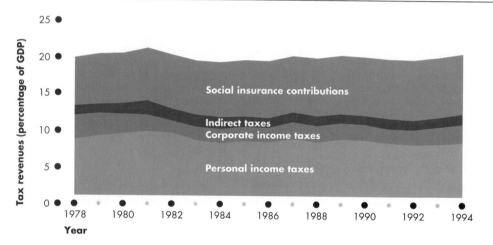

(a) Tax revenues

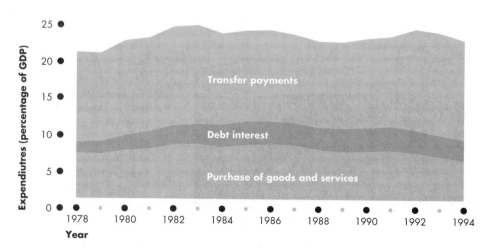

(b) Expenditures

Part (a) shows the four components of government tax revenues: personal income taxes, corporate income taxes, indirect taxes, and social insurance contributions. Revenues from personal and corporate income taxes declined during the early 1980s. The other two components of tax revenues remained steady.

Part (b) shows three components of government expenditures: purchases of goods and services, debt interest, and transfer payments. Purchases of goods and services fluctuated but did not increase. Transfer payments fluctuated most and did increase, especially during the early 1980s. Debt interest increased steadily during the 1980s as the budget deficit fed on itself.

Source: Economic Report of the President, 1995.

income taxes, and the decline resulted from tax cuts passed in the Economic Recovery Tax Act of 1981. From 1986 through 1991, tax revenues did not change much as a percentage of GDP. But they increase slightly after 1992.

Expenditures   Figure 29.3(b) shows the components of government expenditures as percentages of GDP, between 1978 and 1994. Total expenditures decreased between 1978 and 1979 and then increased sharply between 1979 and 1983. Expenditures then declined slightly through 1989 before increasing again to 1992. After 1992, total expenditures decreased. Both purchases of goods and services and transfer payments fluctuated. The item that increased most persistently was debt interest. To understand why, we need to see the connection between the deficit and government debt.

Deficit and Debt   Government debt is the total amount of borrowing by the government. It is the sum of past deficits minus the sum of past surpluses. If the government has a deficit, its debt increases; if it has a surplus, its debt decreases. Once a persistent deficit emerged during the 1980s, the deficit began to feed on itself. The deficit led to increased borrowing; increased borrowing led to larger interest payments; and larger interest payments led to a larger deficit. That is the story of the increasing deficit of the 1980s.

   Figure 29.4 shows the history of government debt since 1945. At the end of World War II, debt (as a percentage of GDP) was at an all-time high of 114 percent. Huge wartime deficits had increased debt to the point that it exceeded real GDP. Postwar budget surpluses lowered the debt to GDP ratio through 1974, by which time it stood at 24 percent, its lowest point since World War II. Small deficits increased the debt to GDP ratio slightly through the 1970s, and large deficits increased it dramatically between 1981 and 1986. During the late 1980s the ratio continued to increase but at a more moderate rate. It grew quickly again during the 1990–1991 recession, but its growth rate slowed when the economy recovered during 1993 and 1994.

Debt and Capital   When individuals and businesses incur debts, they usually do so to buy capital—assets that yield a return. In fact, the main point of debt is to enable people to buy assets that will earn a return that exceeds the interest paid on

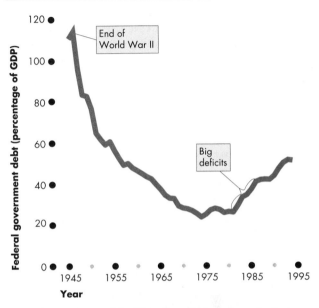

FIGURE 29.4

The Federal Government Debt

Federal government debt (the accumulation of past budget deficits less past budget surpluses) was more than 100 percent of GDP at the end of World War II. Debt as a percentage of GDP fell through 1974 but then started to increase. After a further brief decline during the late 1970s, it exploded during the 1980s and continued to increase through the 1990s.

Source: Economic Report of the President, 1995.

the debt. The government is similar to individuals and businesses in this regard. Much government expenditure is on public assets that yield a return. Highways, major irrigation schemes, public schools and universities, public libraries, and the stock of national defense capital all yield a social rate of return that probably far exceeds the interest rate the government pays on its debt.

   But total government debt, which is around $3 trillion, is more than twice the value of the public capital stock, which in 1993 was about $1.3 trillion. So some government debt has been incurred to finance public consumption expenditure. It is this aspect of government debt that is a potential concern.

   How does the U. S. government deficit compare with deficits in other countries?

The Budget Deficit in Global Perspective

Is the United States unusual in running a budget deficit? Do other countries have budget deficits or do they have budget surpluses? Figure 29.5 answers these questions. Almost all countries have budget deficits in today's world. To make the deficits comparable across countries, we measure the deficits as percentages of GDP. The biggest deficits relative to GDP are found in the Middle East and in the countries of Central Europe that are making a transition from a

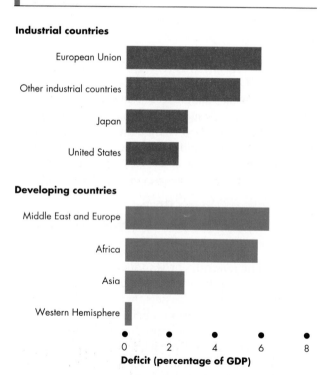

FIGURE 29.5

Government Deficits Around the World

Industrial countries

European Union

Other industrial countries

Japan

United States

Developing countries

Middle East and Europe

Africa

Asia

Western Hemisphere

0   2   4   6   8
Deficit (percentage of GDP)

Governments in most countries have budget deficits. The largest ones are in the Middle East and Europe, and the smallest are in the developing countries in the Western Hemisphere—Central and South America. The U.S. federal government deficit is at the low end of the scale.

Source: World Economic Outlook, October 1994, International Monetary Fund, Washington, D.C., Tables A14 and A19.

heavily regulated economy to a market economy (see Chapter 37, pp. 944–945). The smallest deficits relative to GDP are found in the developing countries of the Western Hemisphere. The U.S. budget deficit is *smaller* than that of most countries. It is even smaller than Japan's and the average of the rich industrial countries in Europe.

Budget Reform and Deficit Reduction

Many attempts have been made by both the major political parties to limit government expenditures and bring the federal deficit under control. But so far, all such attempts have failed. Everyone agrees with the *general idea* of either cutting spending or increasing taxes, but getting general agreement on *which programs* to cut or *which taxes* to raise is hard. Few people want *their own* programs cut or taxes increased. So when Congress gets down to the details, the practical issue of votes weighs more heavily than the idea of cutting the deficit.

The most recent deficit-cutting plan, which is part of the 1995 Republican Congress's "Contract with America," is ongoing, and we will not know until the late 1990s whether is has succeeded. But the task is as heavy as the cartoon suggests.

Contract with America   In 1995 the Senate and House Budget Committees proposed two alternative plans for balancing the federal budget by 2002. Under the Senate plan, expenditures would be cut by $961 billion through the seven years 1996–2002. Slowing the growth of Medicare and Medicaid would account for $432 billion of this cut. But expenditures in all areas of government except Social Security and defense would be cut, and some government departments, including the Department of Commerce, would disappear. Over this same seven-year period, the House plan is to cut expenditures by a larger amount—$1.4 trillion—and also to cut tax revenues by $350 billion. To achieve these objectives, Medicare and Medicaid would be cut more deeply, the Departments of Energy and Education would be abolished, and farm subsidies and other federal subsidies such as that to public television would be phased out.

These deficit reduction projections are not concrete, irrevocable plans, and like previous attempts, they might not succeed. Let's look at one of these previous attempts to eliminate the deficit.

*The Economist, May 13–19, 1995;
reprinted by permission of Oliphant.*

Omnibus Budget Reconciliation Act of 1990   In the Omnibus Budget Reconciliation Act of 1990, Congress attempted to impose budget discipline on itself and to lower the federal budget deficit by more than $0.5 trillion by 1995. The Act contained spending caps and rules to prevent new programs from increasing total federal spending. Any spending increases in one program were to be offset by spending decreases in other programs. And if this requirement was violated, across-the-board spending cuts were to be made to remain within the spending cap.

To see what happened through the four years following the passage of this Act, glance back at Fig. 29.2 (p. 713). In 1990 the deficit was 4 percent of GDP. During 1991 and 1992 the deficit *increased* to almost 5 percent of GDP. It then decreased to 4 percent in 1993 and 3 percent in 1994. But the dollar magnitude of the deficit was larger in 1994 than it had been in 1990.

Despite these facts, we can't conclude that this earlier attempt at deficit reduction was a failure. In the absence of the 1990 Act, the budget deficit would probably have increased even more than it did. Also, the Omnibus Budget Reconciliation Act permitted expenditures to rise during a recession, and 1991 was a recession year. But this earlier attempt was a failure in the sense that it did not reduce the deficit.

Balanced Budget Amendment   Some people want to go further than a congressional self-imposed balanced budget strategy such as the 1990 legislation or the 1995 plan to balance the budget by 2002. They want to amend the Constitution of the United States to include a formula for requiring the federal government to balance its budget. Many economists, including Nobel laureates Milton Friedman and

James Buchanan, advocate a balanced budget amendment to the Constitution.

Those who favor a balanced budget amendment argue two things. First, the process of debating and achieving the amendment would itself increase the level of awareness of the importance of financial discipline on the government. Second, once such an amendment were in place, Congress would have a cast-iron excuse for not satisfying all the many claims and demands imposed upon it and would, in effect, be able to take refuge behind the balanced budget law.

Most economists believe that a cyclically unbalanced budget, with a deficit when real GDP is below potential GDP and a surplus when real GDP exceeds potential GDP, brings greater macroeconomic stability than a budget that is balanced every year. What we need, they argue, is a budget that is balanced in the long run. But it would be very difficult to frame an effective balanced budget law when the time frame over which the budget must balance is longer than one year and possibly even longer than the life of one Congress (two years).

Line-Item Veto   Another suggested change in the budget process is to give the President a line-item veto. Some people believe that giving the President this power would bring a sharper and more precise scalpel to bear on the spending-cutting process. But it has to be borne in mind that the budget itself emerges as a result of compromise and is the best attempt of the Congress to balance competing claims on public resources. If the President had such a veto power, the lobbying effort on the executive branch itself would likely increase, and there would be no guarantee that the President would be tougher on spending than Congress is.

Tax Reform   Few people want to balance the budget by increasing taxes. As you've just seen, the House plan for the seven years through 2002 is to *cut* tax revenues. But politicians and economists are constantly striving to design tax arrangements that are more efficient and that bring in higher tax revenues. One suggestion that was being actively discussed in 1995 is for a flat tax. A **flat tax** is a tax that is levied at the same rate on all income. Supporters of such a tax say that although it would not redistribute incomes as much as our current taxes do, it would bring in more tax revenues because it would strengthen incentives for high income earners to work more and save more. A flat tax would also remove some of the distortions created by the current tax system, such as the over consumption of housing services by the wealthy. Opponents of a flat tax worry about its effects on the distribution of income and question its effects on incentives.

State and Local Budgets

The *total government* sector of the United States includes state and local governments as well as the federal government. In 1994, when federal government expenditures were $1,538 billion, state and local expenditures were $719 billion. Most of these expenditures were on public schools, colleges, and universities ($350 billion); local police and fire services; and roads.

It is the total government sector that influences the aggregate economy. But state and local budgets are not designed, as the federal budget is, with the specific goal of stabilizing the aggregate economy. On the contrary, sometimes, when the aggregate economy needs an injection of additional expenditures, state and local governments cut their expenditures and deficits. Such changes in expenditures occurred during the 1990–1991 recession when many states both cut their expenditures and increased taxes.

R E V I E W

- Fiscal policy is created by Congress and the President, and is a key tool designed to influence employment and economic activity.
- Each year, the budget is proposed by the President in February and amended and enacted by Congress. The fiscal year begins on October 1.
- For many years, the federal government has run a budget deficit and federal debt has grown.

We have now described the federal budget. Next we study the effects of fiscal policy. We'll begin by learning about its effects on expenditure plans when the price level is sticky. You will see that fiscal policy has multiplier effects like the expenditure multipliers explained in Chapter 28. Then we'll study the influences of fiscal policy on both aggregate demand and aggregate supply and look at its short-run and long-run effects on real GDP and the price level.

Fiscal Policy Multipliers

FISCAL POLICY ACTIONS CAN EITHER BE AUTOMATIC or discretionary. **Automatic fiscal policy** is a change in fiscal policy that is triggered by the state of the economy. For example, an increase in unemployment triggers an *automatic* increase in payments to the unemployed. A fall in incomes triggers an *automatic* decrease in tax receipts. That is, this type of fiscal policy adjusts automatically. **Discretionary fiscal policy** is a policy action that is initiated by an act of Congress. It requires a change in tax laws or in some spending program. For example, an increase in the income tax rate and an increase in defense spending are discretionary fiscal policy actions. That is, discretionary fiscal policy is a deliberate policy action.

We begin by studying the effects of *discretionary* changes in government spending and taxes. To focus on the essentials, we'll initially study a model economy that is simpler than the one in which we live. In our model economy there is no international trade and the taxes are all lump sum. **Lump-sum taxes** are taxes that do not vary with real GDP. They are fixed by the government, and they change only when the government changes them. Lump-sum taxes are rare in reality, and they are generally considered to be unfair because the rich and the poor pay the same amount of tax. (Margaret Thatcher, a former Prime Minister of Britain, lost her job because of a lump-sum tax called the "poll tax," which was a fixed tax per person to pay for local government services.) We use lump-sum taxes in our model economy only because they make the principles we are studying easier to understand. Once we've grasped the principles, we'll explore our real economy with its international trade and income taxes—taxes that *do* vary with real GDP.

Like our real economy, the model economy we study is constantly bombarded by shocks. Exports fluctuate because incomes fluctuate in the rest of the world. And business investment fluctuates because of swings in profit expectations and interest rates. These fluctuations set up multiplier effects that begin a recession or an expansion. If a recession takes hold, unemployment increases and incomes fall. If an expansion becomes too strong, inflationary pressures build up. To minimize the effects of these swings in spending, the government might change either its purchases of goods and services or taxes. By changing either of these items, the government can influence aggregate expenditure and real GDP. But it also changes its budget deficit or surplus. An alternative fiscal policy action is to change purchases and taxes together so that the budget balance does not change. We are going to study the initial effects of these discretionary fiscal policy actions in the very short run when the price level is sticky. Each of these actions creates a multiplier effect on real GDP. These multipliers are:

- The government purchases multiplier
- The lump-sum tax multiplier
- The balanced budget multiplier

The Government Purchases Multiplier

The **government purchases multiplier** is the amount by which a change in government purchases of goods and services is multiplied to determine the change in equilibrium expenditure that it generates.

Government purchases are a component of aggregate expenditure. So when government purchases change, aggregate expenditure changes and so does real GDP. The change in real GDP induces a change in consumption expenditure, which brings an additional change in aggregate expenditure. A multiplier process ensues. This multiplier process is like the one described in Chapter 28 (pp. 694–697). Let's look at an example.

Cape Canaveral Multiplier   Before the National Aeronautics and Space Administration (NASA) built a major space launching facility at Cape Canaveral in Florida in the 1960s, the Cape was a quiet place. The injection of government purchases to build the space launching and research facility created jobs in the region. Because construction workers and NASA workers spent most of their incomes locally, consumption expenditure increased. Retail stores and hotels and motels opened and hired yet more people and, in the process, created yet bigger incomes. These incomes were also spent in the area, so spending and incomes rose still further. Today, the government purchases that kicked the process off have dried to a trickle.

The Size of the Multiplier   Table 29.2 illustrates the government purchases multiplier with a numerical example. The first column lists various possible levels of real GDP. Our task is to find equilibrium expenditure and the change in real GDP when government purchases change. The second column shows taxes. They are fixed at $0.5 trillion, regardless of the level of real GDP. (This is an assumption that keeps your attention on the key idea and makes the calculations easier to do.) The third column calculates disposable income. Because taxes are a lump sum, disposable income equals real GDP minus the $0.5 trillion of taxes. For example, in row *b*, real GDP is $6 trillion and disposable income is $5.5 trillion. The next column shows consumption expenditure. In this example the *marginal propensity to consume* is 0.75 or 3/4. That is, a $1 increase in disposable income brings a 75 cent increase in consumption expenditure. Check this fact by calculating

---

TABLE 29.2

The Government Purchases Multiplier

	Real GDP (Y)	Taxes (T)	Disposable income (Y – T)	Consumption expenditure (C)	Investment (I)	Initial government purchases (G)	Initial aggregate planned expenditure (AE = C + I + G)	New government purchases (G')	New aggregate planned expenditure (AE' = C + I + G')
					(trillions of dollars)				
a	5.0	0.5	4.5	3.75	1.0	0.5	5.25	1.0	5.75
b	6.0	0.5	5.5	4.50	1.0	0.5	6.00	1.0	6.50
c	7.0	0.5	6.5	5.25	1.0	0.5	6.75	1.0	7.25
d	8.0	0.5	7.5	6.00	1.0	0.5	7.50	1.0	8.00
e	9.0	0.5	8.5	6.75	1.0	0.5	8.25	1.0	8.75

the increase in consumption expenditure when disposable income increases by $1 trillion from row *b* to row *c*. Consumption expenditure increases by $0.75 trillion. The next column shows investment, which is a constant of $1 trillion. The next column shows the initial level of government purchases, which is $0.5 trillion. Aggregate planned expenditure is the sum of consumption expenditure, investment, and government purchases.

Equilibrium expenditure and real GDP occur when aggregate planned expenditure equals real GDP. In this example, equilibrium expenditure is $6 trillion (highlighted in row *b* of the table.)

The final two columns of the table show what happens when government purchases increase by $0.5 trillion to $1 trillion. Aggregate planned expenditure increases by $0.5 trillion at each level of real GDP. At the initial real GDP of $6 trillion (row *b*), aggregate planned expenditure increases to $6.5 trillion.

Because aggregate planned expenditure now exceeds real GDP, inventories decrease and firms increase production. Output, incomes, and expenditure increase. Increased incomes induce a further increase in expenditure. But the induced increase in aggregate planned expenditure is less than the increase in income, and eventually a new equilibrium is reached. The new equilibrium is at a real GDP of $8 trillion (highlighted in row *d*).

A $0.5 trillion increase in government purchases has increased equilibrium expenditure and real GDP by $2 trillion. Therefore the government purchases multiplier is 4. The size of the multiplier depends on the marginal propensity to consume, which in this example is 3/4. The following formula shows the connection between the government purchases multiplier and the marginal propensity to consume (*MPC*):

$$\text{Government purchases multiplier} = \frac{1}{(1 - MPC)}.$$

Let's check this formula by using the numbers in the above example. The marginal propensity to consume is 3/4, so the government purchases multiplier is 4.

Figure 29.6 illustrates the government purchases multiplier. Initially, aggregate planned expenditure is shown by the curve labeled AE_0. The points on this curve, labeled *a* through *e*, correspond with the rows of Table 29.2. This aggregate expenditure curve intersects the 45° line at the equilibrium level of real GDP, which is $6 trillion.

FIGURE 29.6

The Government Purchases Multiplier

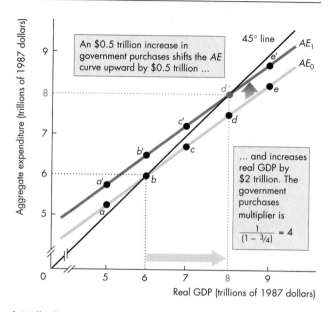

Initially, the aggregate expenditure curve is AE_0, and real GDP is $6 trillion (at point *b*). An increase in government purchases of $0.5 trillion increases aggregate planned expenditure at each level of real GDP by $0.5 trillion. The aggregate expenditure curve shifts upward from AE_0 to AE_1—a parallel shift. At the initial real GDP of $6 trillion, aggregate planned expenditure is now $6.5 trillion. Because aggregate planned expenditure is greater than real GDP, real GDP increases. The new equilibrium is reached when real GDP is $8 trillion—the point at which the AE_1 curve intersects the 45° line (at *d'*). In this example the government purchases multiplier is 4.

When government purchases increase by $0.5 trillion, the aggregate expenditure curve shifts upward by that amount to AE_1. With this new aggregate expenditure curve, equilibrium real GDP increases to $8 trillion. The increase in real GDP is 4 times the increase in government purchases. The government purchases multiplier is 4.

You've seen that in the very short term, when the price level is sticky, an increase in government purchases increases real GDP. But to produce more output, more people must be employed, so in the short term an increase in government purchases can create jobs.

Increasing its purchases of goods and services is one way in which the government can try to stimulate the economy. A second way in which the government might act to increase real GDP in the very short run is by decreasing lump-sum taxes. Let's see how this action works.

The Lump-Sum Tax Multiplier

The **lump-sum tax multiplier** is the amount by which a change in lump-sum taxes is multiplied to determine the change in equilibrium expenditure that it generates. An *increase* in taxes leads to a *decrease* in disposable income and a *decrease* in aggregate expenditure. The amount by which aggregate expenditure initially changes is determined by the marginal propensity to consume. In our example the marginal propensity to consume is 3/4, so a $1 tax cut increases disposable income by $1 and increases aggregate expenditure initially by 75 cents.

This initial change in aggregate expenditure has a multiplier just like the government purchases multiplier. We've seen that the government purchases multiplier is $1/(1 - MPC)$. Because a tax *increase* leads to a *decrease* in expenditure, the lump-sum tax multiplier is *negative*. And because a change in lump sum taxes changes aggregate expenditure initially by only MPC multiplied by the tax change, the lump-sum tax multiplier is equal to

$$\text{Lump-sum tax multiplier} = \frac{-MPC}{(1 - MPC)}.$$

In our example the marginal propensity to consume is 3/4, so the lump-sum tax multiplier is

$$\text{Lump-sum tax multiplier} = \frac{-\dfrac{3}{4}}{(1 - \dfrac{3}{4})} = -3.$$

Figure 29.7 illustrates the lump-sum tax multiplier. Initially, the aggregate expenditure curve is AE_0, and equilibrium expenditure is $8 trillion. Taxes increase by $1 trillion, and disposable income falls by that amount. With a marginal propensity to consume of 3/4, aggregate expenditure decreases initially by $0.75 trillion and the aggregate expenditure curve shifts downward by that amount to AE_1. Equilibrium expenditure and real GDP fall by $3 trillion to $5 trillion. The lump-sum tax multiplier is –3.

FIGURE 29.7

The Lump-Sum Tax Multiplier

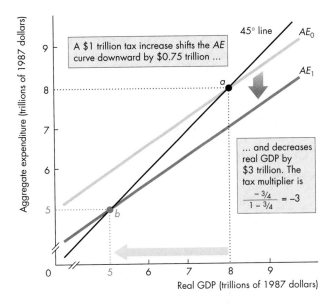

Initially, the aggregate expenditure curve is AE_0, and equilibrium expenditure is $8 trillion. The marginal propensity to consume is 0.75. Lump-sum taxes increase by $1 trillion, so disposable income falls by $1 trillion. The decrease in aggregate expenditure is found by multiplying this change in disposable income by the marginal propensity to consume and is $1 trillion x 0.75 = $0.75 trillion. The aggregate expenditure curve shifts *downward* by this amount to AE_1. Equilibrium expenditure decreases by $3 trillion, from $8 trillion to $5 trillion. The lump-sum tax multiplier is –3.

Lump-Sum Transfer Payments   The lump-sum tax multiplier also tells us the effects of a change in lump-sum transfer payments. Transfer payments are like negative taxes, so an increase in transfer payments works like a decrease in taxes. Because the tax multiplier is negative, a decrease in taxes increases expenditure. An increase in transfer payments also increases expenditure. So the lump-sum transfer payments multiplier is positive. It is

$$\frac{\text{Lump-sum transfer}}{\text{payments multiplier}} = \frac{MPC}{(1 - MPC)}.$$

The Balanced Budget Multiplier

A balanced budget fiscal policy action is one that changes *both* government purchases and taxes by the same amount so that the government's budget deficit or surplus remains *unchanged*. The **balanced budget multiplier** is the amount by which a simultaneous and equal change in government purchases and taxes is multiplied to determine the change in equilibrium expenditure. What is the multiplier effect of this fiscal policy action?

To find out, we must combine the government purchases multiplier and the lump-sum tax multiplier. These two multipliers are

$$\text{Government purchases multiplier} = \frac{1}{(1 - MPC)}.$$

$$\text{Lump-sum tax multiplier} = \frac{-MPC}{(1 - MPC)}.$$

Adding these two multipliers gives the balanced budget multiplier, which is

$$\text{Balanced budget multiplier} = \frac{(1 - MPC)}{(1 - MPC)}.$$

$$= 1.$$

The balanced budget multiplier is smaller than the other multipliers, but it is not zero. This fact means that, in principle, if a recession is expected, fiscal policy can be used to increase aggregate planned expenditure without increasing the government deficit.

Induced Taxes and Entitlement Spending

In the examples we've studied so far, taxes are lump-sum taxes. But in reality, net taxes (taxes minus transfer payments) vary with the state of the economy.

On the tax revenues side of the budget, the government passes tax laws that define the tax *rates* to be paid, not the tax *dollars* to be paid. As a consequence, tax *revenues* depend on real GDP. We call those taxes that vary as real GDP varies **induced taxes.** If the economy is in an expansion phase of the business cycle, induced taxes increase because real GDP increases. If the economy is in a recession phase of the business cycle, induced taxes decrease because real GDP decreases.

On the government expenditures side of the budget, the government creates programs that entitle suitably qualified individuals and businesses to receive benefits. The spending on such programs is called **entitlement spending,** and it results in transfer payments that depend on the economic state of individual citizens and businesses. For example, when the economy is in a recession, unemployment is high, the number of people experiencing economic hardship from poverty increases, and a larger number of firms and farms experience hard times. Government transfer payments increase in response to the increased economic hardship. When the economy experiences boom conditions, expenditure on programs to compensate for economic hardship declines.

The existence of induced taxes and entitlement payments decreases the government purchases and lump-sum tax multipliers because they loosen the link between real GDP and disposable income and so dampen the effect of a change in real GDP on consumption expenditure. When real GDP increases, induced taxes increase and entitlement payments decrease, so disposable income does not increase by as much as the increase in real GDP. As a result, consumption expenditure does not increase by as much as it otherwise would have done and the multiplier effect is reduced.

The extent to which induced taxes and entitlement payments decrease the multiplier depends on the *marginal tax rate*. The marginal tax rate is the proportion of an additional dollar of real GDP that flows to the government in net taxes (taxes minus transfer payments). The higher the marginal tax rate, the larger is the proportion of an additional dollar of real GDP that is paid to the government and the smaller is the induced change in consumption expenditure. The smaller the change in consumption expenditure induced by a change in real GDP, the smaller is the multiplier effect of a change in government purchases or lump-sum taxes.

International Trade and Fiscal Policy Multipliers

Not all expenditure on final goods and services in the United States is on U.S.-produced goods and services. Some of it is on imports—foreign-produced goods and services. The extent to which an additional dollar of real GDP is spent on imports is determined by the *marginal propensity to import*. Expenditure on imports does not generate U.S. real GDP and does not lead to an increase in U.S. consumption expenditure. The larger the marginal propensity to import, the smaller is the increase in consumption expenditure induced by an increase in real GDP and the smaller are the government purchases and lump-sum tax multipliers. (Imports affect the fiscal policy multipliers in exactly the same way that they influence the investment multiplier, as explained in Chapter 28, see pp. 696–697.)

In today's increasingly global economy in which the marginal propensity to import is much greater than it was 20 years ago, the fiscal policy multipliers are smaller than they used to be.

So far, we've studied *discretionary* fiscal policy. Let's now look at *automatic* stabilizers.

Automatic Stabilizers

Automatic stabilizers are mechanisms that operate without the need for explicit action by the government. Their very name is borrowed from engineering and conjures images of shock absorbers, thermostats, and sophisticated devices that keep airplanes and ships steady in turbulent air and seas. Automatic fiscal stabilizers arise from the fact that income taxes and transfer payments fluctuate with real GDP. If real GDP begins to fall, tax revenues also fall and transfer payments rise. These changes in taxes and transfers affect the economy and the balance of the government's budget—its surplus or deficit. Let's study the budget deficit over the business cycle.

Fiscal Policy over the Business Cycle Figure 29.8 shows the business cycle and fluctuations in the budget deficit since 1975. Part (a) shows the fluctuations of real GDP around potential GDP. Part (b) shows the federal budget deficit. Both parts highlight recessions by shading those periods. By comparing the two parts of the figure, you can see the relationship between the business cycle and the budget deficit. As a rule, when the economy is in the expansion phase of a business cycle, the budget deficit declines. (In the figure, a declining deficit means a deficit that is getting closer to zero.) As the expansion slows before the recession begins, the budget deficit increases. It continues to increase during the recession and for a further period after the recession is over. Then, when the expansion is well under way, the budget deficit declines again.

FIGURE 29.8

The Business Cycle and the Budget Deficit

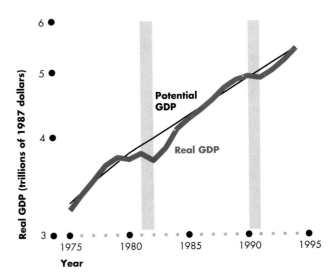

(a) Growth and recessions

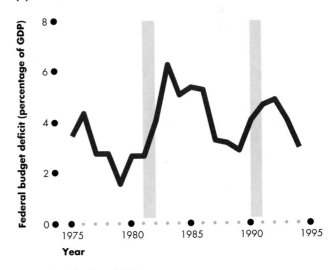

(b) Federal budget deficit

As real GDP fluctuates around potential GDP (part a), the budget deficit fluctuates (part b). During a recession (shaded years), tax revenues decrease, transfer payments increase, and the budget deficit increases. The deficit also increases *before* a recession as real GDP growth slows and *after* a recession before real GDP growth speeds up.

Source: Economic Report of the President, 1995, and the author's calculations.

The budget deficit fluctuates with the business cycle because both tax revenues and expenditures fluctuate with real GDP. As real GDP increases during an expansion, tax revenues increase and transfer payments decrease, so the budget deficit automatically decreases. As real GDP decreases during a recession, tax revenues decrease and transfer payments increase, so the budget deficit automatically increases.

As investment or exports fluctuate, real GDP fluctuates. And as real GDP fluctuates, tax revenues fluctuate and so the budget deficit fluctuates. For example, when a large increase in investment causes the economy to boom, real GDP increases by a multiple of the increase in investment. But the multiplier effect of the increase in investment is reduced by the automatic increase in tax revenues and decrease in the budget deficit (or increase in a budget surplus). The higher tax revenues act as an automatic stabilizer. They decrease disposable income and induce a decrease in consumption expenditure. This decrease in consumption expenditure dampens the effects of the initial increase in investment on aggregate expenditure and moderates the increase in equilibrium expenditure and real GDP. The expansion slows.

Conversely, when a large decrease in investment is pushing the economy into recession, tax revenues decrease and the budget deficit increases (or the budget surplus decreases). Again, tax revenues—this time lower revenues—act as an automatic stabilizer. They limit the fall in disposable income and moderate the extent of the decline in aggregate expenditure and real GDP. The recession slows.

Because the budget deficit increases when the economy is in recession and decreases when the economy is in an expansion, economists have developed a modified deficit concept called the cyclically adjusted deficit. The **cyclically adjusted deficit** is the budget deficit that would occur if the economy were at full employment.

The Cyclically Adjusted Deficit   The cyclically adjusted deficit is a measure for judging whether the budget deficit is cyclical or structural. The budget deficit is cyclical only if it is present because real GDP is less than potential GDP. In this state, taxes are temporarily low and transfer payments are temporarily high. The budget deficit is structural—there is a **structural deficit**—if expenditures exceed tax revenues when real GDP equals potential GDP. The two terms "cyclically adjusted deficit" and "structural deficit" are equivalent.

Figure 29.9 illustrates the deficit and the concept of the structural deficit. The blue curve shows expenditures. The expenditures curve slopes downward because the higher the level of real GDP, the lower is the level of transfer payments so the lower is the level of government expenditures. The green curve shows tax revenues. The tax revenues curve slopes upward because most components of tax revenues increase as incomes and real GDP increase.

In Fig. 29.9, if real GDP is $7 trillion, the government has a *balanced budget*. Expenditures and tax

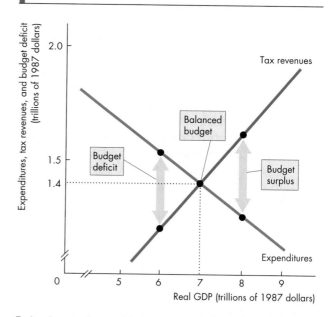

FIGURE 29.9

Cyclical and Structural Deficits

Federal expenditures (blue line) decrease as real GDP increases because transfer payments decrease. Tax revenues (green line) increase as real GDP increases because most taxes are linked to income and expenditures. If real GDP is $7 trillion, the government has a *balanced budget*. If real GDP is less than $7 trillion, expenditures exceed tax revenues and the government has a budget deficit. If real GDP exceeds $7 trillion, expenditures are less than tax revenues and the government has a budget surplus. If potential GDP is $7 trillion, there is no structural deficit—the budget deficits and surpluses are cyclical. But if potential GDP is less than $7 trillion, there is a structural deficit.

revenues each equal $1.4 trillion. If real GDP is less than $7 trillion, expenditures exceed tax revenues and there is a budget deficit. And if real GDP is greater than $7 trillion, expenditures are less than tax revenues and there is a budget surplus.

To determine whether there is a structural deficit, we need to know potential GDP. First, suppose that potential GDP is $7 trillion. In this case, the structural deficit is zero. As real GDP fluctuates over the business cycle, the budget fluctuates around zero and alternates between a surplus and a deficit.

Second, suppose that potential GDP is $6 trillion. In this case, the budget is in deficit at full employment: There is a structural deficit. In a recession the deficit increases, and in an expansion the deficit decreases. But even at the peak of a business cycle, the budget might still be in deficit. The deficit cycles with the business cycle but it rarely and perhaps never gets into surplus. The deficit in this example behaves like the U.S. deficit shown in Fig. 29.8.

Finally, suppose that potential GDP is $8 trillion. In this case, the budget is in surplus at full employment: There is a structural surplus. In a recession the surplus decreases, and in an expansion the surplus increases. Even at the trough of a business cycle, there might still be a surplus. The government budget balance cycles with the business cycle but the budget rarely and perhaps never goes into deficit.

REVIEW

- In the very short run when the price level is sticky, a change in government purchases or lump-sum taxes has a multiplier effect on real GDP.
- The multiplier effect of a change in government purchases is greater than that of a change in lump-sum taxes because a dollar of taxes initially changes aggregate expenditure by less than a dollar.
- The presence of income taxes and international trade reduces the fiscal policy multipliers.
- Income taxes and entitlement programs work as automatic stabilizers to dampen the business cycle.

We have now seen the immediate effects of fiscal policy when the price level is sticky. The next task is to see how, with the passage of more time and with some price level adjustments, these multiplier effects are modified.

Fiscal Policy in the Short Run and the Long Run

WE'VE SEEN HOW REAL GDP RESPONDS TO changes in fiscal policy when the price level is sticky and all the adjustments that take place are in spending, income, and production. The time frame over which this response occurs is very short. Once production starts to change, regardless of whether it increases or decreases, prices also start to change. The price level and real GDP change together and the economy moves to a new short-run equilibrium.

To study the simultaneous changes in real GDP and the price level that result from fiscal policy, we use the aggregate supply–aggregate demand model of Chapter 27. In the long run, both the price level and the money wage rate respond to fiscal policy. As these further changes take place, the economy gradually moves toward a new long-run equilibrium. We also use the aggregate supply–aggregate demand model to study these questions.

We are going to investigate the response of real GDP and the price level to fiscal policy in the short run and in the long run. To do so, we must study the effects of fiscal policy on both aggregate demand and aggregate supply. We begin by looking at its effects on aggregate demand.

Fiscal Policy and Aggregate Demand

You learned about the relationship between aggregate demand, aggregate expenditure, and equilibrium expenditure in Chapter 28. You are now going to use what you learned there to work out what happens to aggregate demand, the price level, real GDP, and jobs when fiscal policy changes. We'll start by looking at the effects of a change in fiscal policy on aggregate demand.

Fiscal Policy and Aggregate Demand Figure 29.10 shows the effects of an increase in government purchases on aggregate demand. Initially, the aggregate expenditure curve is AE_0 in part (a), and the aggregate demand curve is AD_0 in part (b). The price level is 130, real GDP is $6 trillion, and the economy is at point a in both parts of the figure. Now suppose that government purchases increase by $0.5 trillion.

At a constant price level of 130, the aggregate expenditure curve shifts upward to AE_1. This curve intersects the 45° line at an equilibrium expenditure of $8 trillion at point b. This amount is the aggregate quantity of goods and services demanded at a price level of 130, as shown by point b in part (b). Point b lies on a new aggregate demand curve. The aggregate demand curve has shifted rightward to AD_1.

The distance by which the aggregate demand curve shifts rightward is determined by the government purchases multiplier. The larger the multiplier, the larger is the shift in the aggregate demand curve resulting from a given change in government purchases. In this example a $0.5 trillion increase in government purchases produces a $2 trillion increase in the aggregate quantity of goods and services demanded at each price level. The multiplier is 4. So the $0.5 trillion increase in government purchases shifts the aggregate demand curve rightward by $2 trillion.

Figure 29.10 shows the effects of an increase in government purchases. But a similar effect occurs for *any* expansionary fiscal policy. An **expansionary fiscal policy** is an increase in government expenditures or a decrease in tax revenues.

Figure 29.10 can also be used to illustrate the effects of a contractionary fiscal policy. A **contractionary fiscal policy** is a decrease in government expenditures or an increase in tax revenues. In this case, start at point b in each part of the figure and decrease government expenditure or increase taxes. Aggregate demand decreases from AD_1 to AD_0.

Equilibrium GDP and the Price Level in the Short Run We've seen how an increase in government purchases increases aggregate demand. Let's now see how it changes real GDP and the price level. Figure 29.11(a) describes the economy. Aggregate demand is AD_0, and the short-run aggregate supply curve is *SAS*. (Check back to Chapter 10 if you need to refresh your understanding of the *SAS* curve.) Equilibrium is at point a, where the aggregate demand and short-run aggregate supply curves intersect. The price level is 130, and real GDP is $6 trillion.

An increase in government purchases of $0.5 trillion shifts the aggregate demand curve rightward from AD_0 to AD_1. While the price level is sticky at 130, the economy moves toward point b and real GDP increases toward $8 trillion. But during the adjustment process, the price level does not remain constant. It gradually rises and the economy moves along the short-run aggregate supply curve to the

FIGURE 29.10

Government Purchases and Aggregate Demand

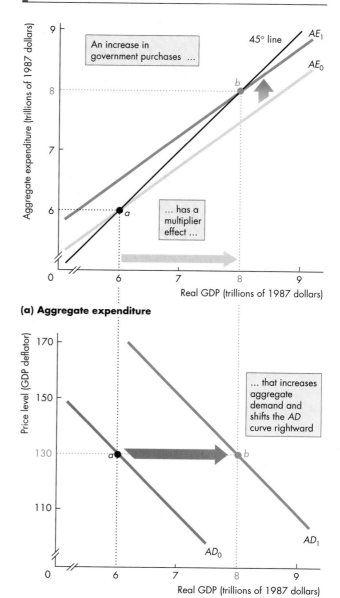

(a) Aggregate expenditure

(b) Aggregate demand

The price level is 130, aggregate planned expenditure is AE_0 (part a), and aggregate demand is AD_0 (part b). An increase in government purchases shifts the AE curve to AE_1 and equilibrium real GDP to $8 trillion. The aggregate demand curve shifts rightward to AD_1.

FIGURE 29.11

Fiscal Policy, Real GDP, and the Price Level

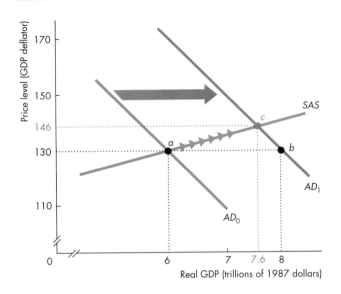

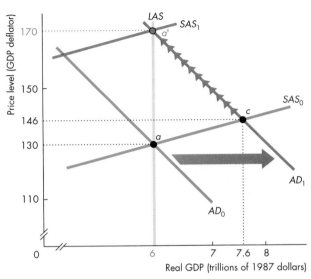

(a) Short-run effect

An increase in government purchases shifts the AD curve from AD_0 to AD_1. With a sticky price level, the economy would have moved to point *b*. But the price level rises and the economy moves to point *c*. The price level increases to 146, and real GDP increases to $7.6 trillion.

(b) Long-run effect

At point *c*, real GDP exceeds potential GDP and unemployment is below the natural rate. The wage rate rises and short-run aggregate supply decreases. The SAS curve shifts leftward to SAS_1 and the economy moves to point *a'*. The price level rises to 170, and real GDP returns to $6 trillion.

point of intersection of the short-run aggregate supply curve and the new aggregate demand curve—point *c*. The price level rises to 146 and real GDP increases to $7.6 trillion.

When we take the price level effect into account, the increase in government purchases still has a multiplier effect on real GDP, but the effect is smaller than it would be if the price level remained constant. Also, the steeper the slope of the short-run aggregate supply curve, the larger is the increase in the price level, the smaller is the increase in real GDP, and the smaller is the government purchases multiplier. But the multiplier is not zero.

In the long run, real GDP equals potential GDP—the economy is at full-employment equilibrium. When real GDP equals potential GDP, an increase in aggregate demand has the same short-run effect as we've just worked out, but its long-run effect is different.

Fiscal Expansion at Potential GDP

Suppose that real GDP is equal to potential GDP, which means that unemployment is equal to the natural rate of unemployment. Suppose also that the unemployment rate and the natural rate are high. The natural rate of unemployment fluctuates for the reasons explained in Chapter 24 (see pp. 579–580). But suppose that the government mistakenly thinks that unemployment is above the natural rate and tries to lower unemployment by increasing its own purchases.

Figure 29.11(b) shows the effect of an expansionary fiscal policy when real GDP equals potential GDP. In this example, potential GDP is $6 trillion. Aggregate demand increases and the aggregate demand curve shifts rightward from AD_0 to AD_1. The short-run equilibrium, point *c*, is an above full-employment equilibrium. The labor force is more than fully employed, and there are shortages of labor. Wage rates begin to increase. Higher wage rates increase costs, and short-run aggregate supply decreases. The SAS curve begins to shift leftward from SAS_0 to SAS_1. The economy moves up the aggregate demand curve AD_1 toward point a'.

Eventually, when all adjustment to wage rates and the price level have been made, the price level is 170 and real GDP is again at potential GDP of $6 trillion. The multiplier in the long run is zero. There has been a temporary decrease in the unemployment rate during the process you've just looked at, but not a permanent decrease.

Limitations of Fiscal Policy

Because the short-run fiscal policy multipliers are not zero, expansionary fiscal policy can be used to increase real GDP and decrease the unemployment rate in a recession. Contractionary fiscal policy can also be used if the economy is overheating to decrease real GDP and help to keep inflation in check. But the use of fiscal policy is limited by two factors.

First, the legislative process is slow, which means that it is difficult to take fiscal policy actions in a timely way. The economy might be able to benefit from fiscal stimulation right now, but it will take Congress many months, and perhaps more than a year, to act. By the time the action is taken, the economy might need an entirely different fiscal medicine.

Second, it is not always easy to tell whether real GDP is below (or above) potential GDP. A change in aggregate demand can move real GDP away from potential GDP or a change in aggregate supply can change real GDP and change potential GDP. This difficulty is a serious one because, as you've seen, fiscal stimulation at full employment leads to a rise in the price level and has no long-run effect on real GDP.

Fiscal Policy and Aggregate Supply

So far we've considered only the demand-side effects of fiscal policy. But fiscal policy also has supply-side effects. On the expenditures side, the government buys capital goods, which increases the quantity of real GDP supplied. On the tax revenues side, taxes on labor income act as a disincentive to work and decrease the quantity of labor employed and the quantity of real GDP supplied. With fewer people employed, the jobless rate is higher.

Similarly, taxes on interest income weaken the incentive to save and invest and so decrease the quantity of capital and decrease the quantity of real GDP supplied. This effect is an ongoing one that affects not only the current *level* of real GDP but the growth rate of potential GDP.

The influences of fiscal policy on the quantity of real GDP supplied mean that to assess the impact of an expansionary fiscal policy, especially a tax cut, we must take into account changes in both aggregate demand and aggregate supply.

Figure 29.12(a) shows the most likely supply-side effects of a tax cut. The tax cut increases aggregate demand and shifts the AD curve rightward, just as before. But a tax cut that increases the incentive to work also increases aggregate supply. It shifts the long-run and short-run aggregate supply curves rightward. Here we focus on the short-run and show the effect on the SAS curve, which shifts rightward to SAS_1. In this example, the tax cut has a large effect on aggregate demand and a small effect on aggregate supply. The aggregate demand curve shifts rightward by a larger amount than the rightward shift in the short-run aggregate supply curve. The outcome is a rise in the price level and an increase in real GDP. But notice that the price level rises by *less* and real GDP increases by *more* than would occur if there were no supply-side effects.

During the 1980s, when Ronald Reagan was President, a group of economists knows as *supply-siders* became prominent. Supply-siders believed that tax cuts would strengthen incentives and have a large effect on aggregate supply. Figure 29.12(b) shows the effects that supply-siders believe might occur. A tax cut still has a large effect on aggregate demand, but it has a similarly large effect on aggregate supply. The aggregate demand curve and the short-run aggregate supply curve shift rightward by similar amounts. In this particular case the price level remains constant and real GDP increases. A slightly larger increase in aggregate supply would have brought a fall in the price level, a possibility that some supply-siders believe could occur.

The general point that everyone agrees with is that an expansionary fiscal policy that strengthens incentives to produce increases real GDP by more and is less inflationary than one that does not change or that weakens incentives to produce.

We've studied the long-run effects of government expenditures and tax revenues, but we haven't studied the long-run effects of the budget deficit. What are those effects?

FIGURE **29.12**

Supply-Side Effects of Fiscal Policy

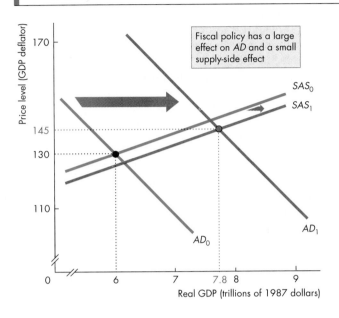

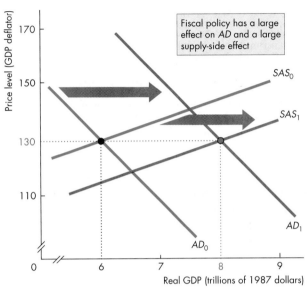

(a) The traditional view

A tax cut increases aggregate demand and shifts the AD curve rightward from AD_0 to AD_1 (both parts). Such a policy change also has a supply-side effect. If the supply-side effect is small, the SAS curve shifts rightward from SAS_0 to SAS_1 in part (a). The demand-side effect dominates the supply-side effect, real GDP increases, and the price level rises.

(b) The supply-side view

If the supply-side effect of a tax cut is large, the SAS curve shifts to SAS_1 in part (b). In this case the supply-side effect is as large as the demand-side effect. Real GDP increases, and the price level remains constant. But if the supply-side effect were larger than the demand-side effect, the price level would actually fall.

A Burden of Future Generations?

A common and popular view is that the budget deficit places a burden on future generations. The idea behind this view is that the current generation is enjoying the benefits of government expenditures but is not paying for all those benefits. The budget deficit is financed by selling bonds, and future generations will pay either in the form of ongoing interest payments or in repayment of the debt now being incurred.

But wait. Doesn't the interest paid each year get financed with tax revenues collected each year? So how can the deficit be a burden to *future* generations? It might be a burden to those members of the future generation who pay taxes, but it must be a benefit to those who receive the interest payments. In the aggregate the burden and the benefit cancel out.

Although in the aggregate the interest paid equals the tax revenues collected, there might still be undesirable redistribution effects. For example, one feature of our present budget deficit is that some government debt is being bought not by Americans but by foreign investors. So part of the future burden of the current deficit is that future U.S. taxpayers will have to pay sufficient tax revenues so that the interest can be paid to foreign holders of U.S. government debt. In this case the burden on future U.S. taxpayers, like yourself and your children, will exceed the interest received by American holders of U.S. government debt.

There's another way in which today's budget deficit can make people poorer tomorrow: By slowing investment today, the rate of growth of real GDP will slow and the stock of productive capital equipment available for future generations will be smaller. This phenomenon is called "crowding out."

Crowding Out

Crowding out is the tendency for an increase in government purchases of goods and services to bring a decrease in investment. If crowding out does occur, there will be a larger stock of government debt and a smaller stock of capital in the future. Unproductive government debt replaces productive capital.

Crowding out does *not* occur if:

■ Real GDP is less than potential GDP.
■ The budget deficit arises from the government's purchases of capital on which the return equals (or exceeds) that on privately purchased capital.

Crowding out *does* occur if:

■ Real GDP equals or exceeds potential GDP.
■ The government purchases consumption goods and services or capital on which the return is less than that on privately purchased capital.

Real GDP and Potential GDP   If real GDP equals (or exceeds) potential GDP, an increase in government purchases of goods and services (and an increase in the budget deficit) must result in a decrease in consumption or investment expenditure. But if real GDP is below potential GDP, it is possible that an increase in government purchases (and an increase in the budget deficit) could result in an increase in real GDP (and a decrease in the unemployment rate). In such a case, the budget deficit does not completely crowd out other expenditure.

Productive Government Purchases   Much of what the government purchases is productive capital. Building highways, dams, airports, schools, and universities are some obvious examples. But there are some not-so-obvious examples of productive government purchases that have an investment element. Expenditure on teachers' and health care workers'

FIGURE 29.13

The Deficit, Borrowing, and Crowding Out

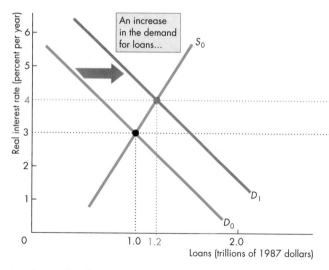

(a) The market for loans

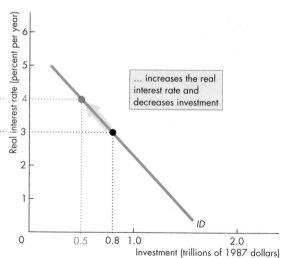

(b) Investment

Part (a) shows the market for loans. The demand for loans is D_0, and the supply of loans is S_0. The equilibrium quantity of loans is $1 trillion and the real interest rate is 3 perent a year. In part (b), the investment demand curve is *ID* and at an interest rate of 3 percent a year, investment is $0.8 trillion. The government runs a deficit, which it finances by borrowing. The

government's increased demand for loans increases the market demand and shifts the demand curve rightward to D_1. The real interest rate rises to 4 percent a year and in part (b), investment decreases to $0.5 trillion. The deficit crowds out investment in productive capital.

wages are investments in productive human capital. Defense expenditure protects our resources and is also productive capital expenditure. To the extent that the deficit results from our acquisition of such assets, it does not crowd out productive capital. On the contrary, it contributes to it.

But government purchases can crowd out the accumulation of productive private capital.

How Crowding Out Occurs   Crowding out occurs if the government's deficit increases the real interest rate and decreases investment. Figure 29.13 shows how this outcome arises. Part (a) shows the demand and supply curves for loans. Initially, the demand for loans is D_0 and the supply of loans is S_0. The real interest rate is 3 percent a year and the quantity of loans made is $1 trillion a year. Part (b) shows investment. The investment demand curve ID shows how investment depends on the opportunity cost of funds, the real interest rate. At a real interest rate of 3 percent, investment is $0.8 trillion. Now suppose that the government begins to run a deficit and it borrows to finance the deficit. The government's demand for loans is added to the original demand and the demand curve is part (a) shifts rightward to D_1. There is no change in the supply of loans so the real interest rate rises to 4 percent. At this interest rate, investment decreases to $0.5 trillion in part (b). Because investment has decreased, the capital stock is lower than it would have been. The government deficit has crowded out investment, and government debt has crowded out productive capital.

Ricardian Equivalence

Some economists do not believe that budget deficits crowd out investment. On the contrary, they argue, debt financing and paying for government spending with tax revenues are equivalent. The level of purchases of goods and services matters. Government purachases can crowd out investment and increase the real interest rate. But the way in which government purchases are financed is irrelevant.

The first economist to advance this idea (known as *Ricardian equivalence*) was the great English economist David Ricardo. Ricardo's idea has been given a forceful restatement by Robert Barro of Harvard University. Barro argues as follows: If the government decreases its tax revenues and increases its deficit, people are smart enough to recognize that the government

must increase taxes in the future to pay the increased interest charges on the debt being issued today and, eventually, to repay the debt. In recognition of having to pay higher taxes in the future, people will cut their consumption now and save more. They'll increase their saving so that when the higher taxes are finally levied, they will have accumulated sufficient wealth to meet those tax liabilities without a further cut in consumption. The increased saving matches the decreased taxes and national saving is unchanged.

Whether Ricardian equivalence is relevant to the U.S. economy is controversial and unsettled. Most economists believe that Ricardian equivalence has no practical relevance for the U.S. economy. Deficits have the potential to redistribute resources across generations and if Ricardian equivalence really works, people's consumption and saving choices must prevent any such redistribution. But for such an outcome to occur, people must be as concerned about the consumption of future generations as they are about their own consumption. Most economists believe that while people do care about future generations, they don't care enough to make Ricardian equivalence relevant.

But Ricardian equivalence has many defenders and the empirical evidence against it is not decisive.

R E V I E W

■ In the short run, changes in government purchases and taxes change the price level. The multiplier effect on real GDP is smaller than when the price level is sticky.

■ In the long run, fiscal policy actions influence wage rates, the price level, interest rates, and the level and growth rate of aggregate supply.

■ The long-run effects of a budget deficit are possibly slower economic growth and less capital and lower incomes in the future, but whether these consequences do arise is controversial.

◆ You have now completed your study of the effects of fiscal policy. You've seen how fiscal policy influences the way real GDP fluctuates around its trend and how it influences the long-term growth rate of real GDP. Your next task is to study the other main arm of macroeconomic policy: monetary policy. We begin in the next chapter by describing the monetary system of a modern economy.

Fiscal Policy in Action

THE ECONOMIST, MAY 20, 1995

Battle Stations

The fun is over; now the revolution begins. If, that is, there is to be a revolution. The approval by Republican-dominated budget committees in both the House and the Senate of their deficit-reduction plans—which are really government-reduction plans—opens the way for the big brawl that the "Contract with America" merely hinted at.

The House and Senate agree on the destination: balancing the budget in 2002 by squeezing spending dramatically. But they use different paths to get there. The House scores for audacity. It eliminates more agencies than the Senate (including three cabinet departments), cuts a bit deeper into programmes such as farm subsidies and health care, and generally would cause a little more mayhem. Having done all that, it throws a $350 billion tax cut back to the voters, and raises defence spending a touch too.

The Senate scores points for integrity. Unlike the House, it eschews gimmicky assumptions about inflation and interest rates. It also achieves its deficit reductions faster and without givebacks. ...

Still, the similarities are large. Both plans would freeze "discretionary" government spending (most of what government does apart from writing entitlement cheques to people) for seven years: an ambitious operation. Both count on taking large bites out of the spiralling health programmes—which, nonetheless, would still grow swiftly. ...

The pitfalls for Republicans are many, and the anti-deficit plans still only plans. "Remember," says Robert Reischauer, a former Congressional Budget Office director, "we haven't begun to shoot real bullets yet." The work of actually turning the budgetary schemes into law will occupy Congress right through the autumn; and, once irate lobbies and reluctant congressmen and the hostile president (with his veto) are placated, the result may yet be much more modest than this week's bold beginning.

Essence of THE STORY

■ During 1995, Congress began to implement the fiscal policy content in the Republicans' "Contract with America."

■ The House and Senate each proposed to balance the budget by 2002.

■ The House assumed lower interest rates than the Senate, cut farm subsidies and health care by more, gave a $350 billion tax cut (which the Senate did not), and achieved its deficit reduction later.

■ Both plans froze "discretionary" government spending for seven years, and both cut health programs, but health spending would still grow.

■ The deficit reduction laws that are eventually passed might turn out to be more modest than the deficit reduction projections.

Economic

A N A L Y S I S

■ Figure 1 shows four alternative federal budget projections through 2002. The CBO baseline projection is a prediction by the Congressional Budget Office of the deficit path that would occur with unchanged policies. The other three are the President's proposal and the House and Senate projections.

■ Consistent with the news article, the Senate and the House have the same 2002 target but plan to get there at different speeds.

■ The Senate plan is for an approximately equal annual fall in the deficit.

■ The House plan sees no fall in the deficit until 1998 and even by 2000 has a deficit of more than $100 billion.

■ What are the likely effects of the proposed cuts in government expenditures and deficit if they do actually occur? The likely effects are different for the House and Senate plans.

■ Figure 2 shows the possible effects of the House plan. The expenditure cuts will decrease aggregate demand from AD_0 to AD_1.

■ Because the expenditure cuts are bunched at the end of the period, interest rates will not fall by much, investment will not increase, and aggregate supply will be unaffected. Real GDP might fall below potential GDP when the spending cuts occur.

■ Figure 3 shows the possible effects of the Senate plan. The expenditure cuts will decrease aggregate demand from AD_0 to AD_1.

■ Because the plan cuts expenditures every year by similar amounts, it will probably lower interest rates, boost investment, and increase aggregate supply.

■ In Fig. 3, potential GDP is assumed to increase to $6.8 trillion and the short-run aggregate supply curve shifts to SAS_1. The real GDP growth rate increases, and the inflation rate slows

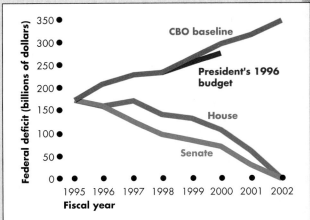

Figure 1 Federal budget projections

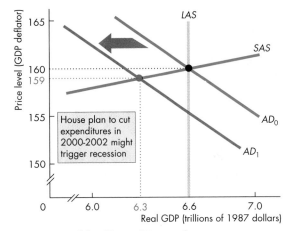

Figure 2 Possible effects of House plan

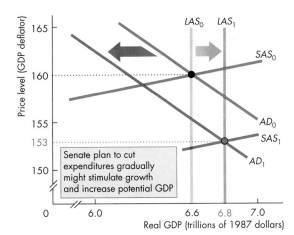

Figure 3 Possible effects of Senate plan

S U M M A R Y

The Federal Budget

The federal budget finances the activities of the government and is used to achieve full employment, sustained long-term economic growth, and price level stability. The budget is proposed by the President, amended and enacted by Congress, and signed into law by the President.

Federal tax revenues come from personal income taxes, social insurance taxes, corporate income taxes, and indirect taxes. Federal expenditures include transfer payments, purchases of goods and services, and debt interest. The budget balance is equal to tax revenues minus expenditures.

If government expenditures exceed tax revenues, the government has a budget deficit; if government expenditures are less than tax revenues, the government has a budget surplus; and if government expenditures equal tax revenues, the government has a balanced budget.

The government budget deficit increased during the early 1980s and has remained high since then. The reasons for the increased deficit of the 1980s is a decrease in corporate and personal income taxes and a persistent increase in debt interest payments. With an ongoing deficit, government debt has increased. At the end of World War II, debt (as a percentage of GDP) was at an all-time high. It declined through 1974 but has increased since then. Almost all countries have budget deficits in today's world, and the U.S. budget deficit relative to GDP is *smaller* than that of most countries. Attempts to decrease the budget deficit have so far had only limited success.

The total government sector of the United States includes the federal, state, and local governments. (pp. 711–718)

Fiscal Policy Multipliers

Fiscal policy actions are either automatic and triggered by the state of the economy or discretionary and initiated by an act of Congress. The government purchases multiplier equals $1/(1 - MPC)$. The lump-sum tax multiplier equals $-MPC/(1 - MPC)$. The transfer payments multiplier is equal in magnitude to the lump-sum tax multiplier but is positive. The balanced budget multiplier equals 1.

Income taxes, entitlement payments, and imports make each of the multipliers smaller than it otherwise would be. Income taxes and entitlement payments also bring fluctuations in tax revenues and transfer payments over the business cycle and help the shock-absorbing capacities of the economy. (pp. 718–725)

Fiscal Policy in the Short Run and the Long Run

An expansionary fiscal policy (an increase in government purchases or a decrease in taxes) increases aggregate demand and shifts the aggregate demand curve rightward. It increases real GDP and raises the price level. A contractionary fiscal policy (a decrease in government purchases or an increase in taxes) decreases aggregate demand and shifts the aggregate demand curve leftward. It decreases real GDP and lowers the price level. In the short run, the fiscal policy multipliers are smaller than when the price level is sticky.

In the long run, when real GDP equals potential GDP, an expansionary fiscal policy increases the price level but leaves real GDP unchanged. The fiscal policy multipliers are zero.

Fiscal policy has supply-side effects because the government buys capital goods that increase aggregate supply and because increases in taxes weaken the incentives to work, save, and invest. These supply-side influences mean that an expansionary fiscal policy increases real GDP and if the supply-side effect is stronger than the demand-side effect, an expansionary fiscal policy might lower the price level.

A deficit can place a long-run burden on future generations for two reasons. First, it might result in increased international debt. In this case, part of the income of future generations will be paid to foreigners instead of being used for consumption or investment. Second, it might result in a smaller future stock of productive capital, which means that future production will be lower than it otherwise could have been. This outcome results from "crowding out," which is the tendency for public expenditure to displace private expenditure. The controversial Ricardian equivalence view is that a deficit is equivalent to a tax. Government expenditure crowds out private expenditure but the way the expenditure is financed is irrelevant. (pp. 725–731)

KEY ELEMENTS

REVIEW QUESTIONS

1. Describe the main purposes of the federal budget.
2. Describe the process that creates a federal budget.
3. List the four main sources of federal tax revenues and the three main components of federal expenditures.
4. List the main changes in taxes and government spending that are associated with the increase in the federal government deficit during the 1980s.
5. Compare the U.S. federal deficit with deficits in other regions and countries.
6. Describe the main attempts at budget reform designed to decrease the deficit.
7. Distinguish between automatic and discretionary fiscal policy.
8. Explain why an increase in government purchases has a multiplier effect on real GDP when the price level is sticky.

9. Explain why the lump-sum tax multiplier is smaller than the government purchases multiplier.
10. Explain why there is an increase in real GDP when both taxes and expenditures increase by the same amount.
11. Explain how induced taxes and entitlement spending influence the fiscal policy multipliers.
12. Explain how international trade influences the fiscal policy multipliers.
13. Explain how the deficit fluctuates over the business cycle and define the structural deficit.
14. Explain how the multiplier effect is modified in the short run when the price level begins to change.
15. Explain what happens following an increase in government purchases if real GDP equals potential GDP.
16. Explain why the deficit can be a burden on future generations.

P R O B L E M S

◆ 1. In the economy of Zapland, the marginal propensity to consume is 0.9. Investment is $50 billion, government purchases of goods and services are $40 billion, and lump-sum taxes are $40 billion. Zapland has no exports and no imports.
   a. The government cuts its purchases of goods and services to $30 billion. What is the change in equilibrium expenditure?
   b. What is the value of the government purchases multiplier?
   c. The government continues to purchase $40 billion worth of goods and services and cuts lump-sum taxes to $30 billion. What is the change in equilibrium expenditure?
   d. What is the value of the tax multiplier?
   e. The government simultaneously cuts both its purchases of goods and services and taxes to $30 billion. What is the change in equilibrium expenditure?
   f. What is the value of the balanced budget multiplier?

◆ 2. Suppose that the price level in the economy of Zapland as described in problem 1 is 100. The economy is also at full employment.
   a. If the government of Zapland increases its purchases of goods and services by $10 billion, what happens to the quantity of real GDP demanded?
   b. How does Zapland's aggregate demand curve change? Draw a two-part diagram that is similar to Fig. 29.10 to illustrate the change in both the AE curve and the AD curve.
   c. In the short run, does equilibrium real GDP increase by more than, less than, or the same amount as the increase in the quantity of real GDP demanded?
   d. In the long run, does equilibrium real GDP increase by more than, less than, or the same amount as the increase in the quantity of real GDP demanded?
   e. In the short run, does the price level in Zapland rise, fall, or remain unchanged?
   f. In the long run, does the price level in Zapland rise, fall, or remain unchanged?

◆ 3. In the figure, aggregate demand is initially AD_0 and short-run aggregate supply is initially SAS_0. A tax cut increases aggregate demand to AD_1. This same tax cut influences incentives and increases aggregate supply. At first, there is no supply-side effect. Then short-run aggregate supply increases to SAS_1. Eventually, short-run aggregate supply increases to SAS_2.

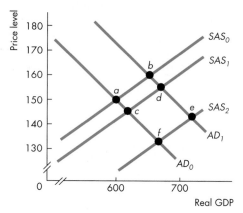

Use the letters in the figure and the values on the axes to trace the path of the economy and to answer the following questions.
   a. What is the initial equilibrium point and the initial equilibrium values of real GDP and the price level before the tax cut occurs?
   b. What is the immediate effect of the tax cut before its supply-side effects begin to occur?
   c. How do real GDP and the price level change when short-run aggregate supply increases to SAS_1?
   d. How do real GDP and the price level change when short-run aggregate supply increases to SAS_2?

4. Study *Reading Between the Lines* on pp. 732–733 and then answer the following questions:
   a. What are the main differences in the deficit reduction plans of the House of Representatives and the Senate?
   b. Which plan, the House plan or the Senate plan, will have the bigger supply-side effects and why?
   c. Which plan, the House plan or the Senate plan, will have the bigger negative effects on real GDP and employment and why?

Money

After studying this chapter, you will be able to:

- Define money and describe its functions

- Explain the economic functions of banks and other financial institutions

- Describe the financial innovations of the 1980s

- Explain how banks create money

- Explain why the quantity of money is an important economic magnitude

- Explain the quantity theory of money

Money, like fire and the wheel, has been around for a very long time. An incredible array of items have served as money. Wampum (beads made from shells) was used by North American Indians, whale's teeth were used by Fijians, and tobacco was used by early American colonists. Cakes of salt served as money in Ethiopia and Tibet. Today, when we want to buy something, we use coins or bills, write a check, or present a credit card.

Money Makes the World Go Around

Tomorrow, we'll use a "smart card" that keeps track of spending and that our pocket computer can read. Are all these things money? ◆ When we deposit some coins or notes into a bank, is that still money? And what happens when the bank lends the money in our deposit to someone else? How can we get our money back if it's been lent out? Does lending by banks create money—out of thin air? ◆ In the 1970s you had either a savings deposit that earned interest or a checking deposit that didn't. Today, there's a wide variety of accounts that provide the convenience of a checking deposit and the income of a savings deposit. Why were these new kinds of bank deposits introduced? ◆ During the 1970s the quantity of money in existence in the United States increased quickly, but in the 1980s it increased at a slower pace. In Russia and in some Latin American countries the quantity of money is increasing at an extremely rapid pace. In Switzerland and Germany the quantity of money has increased at a slower pace. Does the rate of increase in the quantity of money matter? What are the effects of an increasing quantity of money on our economy?

◈ In this chapter we'll study that useful invention: money. We'll look at its functions, its different forms, and the way it is defined and measured in the United States today. We'll also study banks and other financial institutions and explain how they create money. Finally, we'll examine the effects of money on the economy.

What Is Money?

WHAT DO WAMPUM, TOBACCO, AND NICKELS AND dimes have in common? Why are they all examples of money? To answer these questions, we need a definition of money. **Money** is any commodity or token that is generally acceptable as the means of payment. A **means of payment** is a method of settling a debt. When a payment has been made, there is no remaining obligation between the parties to a transaction. So what wampum, tobacco, and nickels and dimes have in common is that they have served (or still do serve) as the means of payment. But money has three other functions:

- Medium of exchange
- Unit of account
- Store of value

Medium of Exchange

A *medium of exchange* is an object that is generally accepted in exchange for goods and services. Money acts as such a medium. Without money it would be necessary to exchange goods and services directly for other goods and services—an exchange called **barter**. For example, if you want to buy a hamburger, you offer the paperback novel you've just finished reading in exchange for it. Barter requires a *double coincidence of wants*, a situation that occurs when Erika wants to buy what Kazia wants to sell and Kazia wants to buy what Erika wants to sell. To get your hamburger, you must find someone who's selling hamburgers and who wants your paperback novel. Money guarantees that there is a double coincidence of wants because people with something to sell will always accept money in exchange for it. Money acts as a lubricant that smoothes the mechanism of exchange.

Unit of Account

A *unit of account* is an agreed measure for stating the prices of goods and services. To get the most out of your budget, you have to figure out, among other things, whether seeing one more movie is worth the price you have to pay, not in dollars and cents, but in terms of the number of ice-cream cones, sodas, and cups of coffee that you have to give up. It's easy to do such calculations when all these goods have prices in terms of dollars and cents (see Table 30.1). If a movie costs $6 and a six-pack of soda costs $3, you know right away that seeing one more movie costs you 2 six-packs of soda. If jelly beans are 50¢ a pack, one more movie costs 12 packs of jelly beans. You need only one calculation to figure out the opportunity cost of any pair of goods and services.

But imagine how troublesome it would be if your local movie theater posted its price as 2 six-packs of soda, and if the convenience store posted the price of a six-pack of soda as 2 ice-cream cones, and if the ice-cream shop posted the price of a cone as 3 packs of

---

TABLE 30.1

The Unit of Account Function of Money Simplifies Price Comparisons

Good	Price in money units	Price in units of another good
Movie	$6.00 each	2 six-packs of soda
Soda	$3.00 per six-pack	2 ice-cream cones
Ice cream	$1.50 per cone	3 packs of jelly beans
Jelly beans	$0.50 per pack	2 cups of coffee
Coffee	$0.25 per cup	1 local phone call

Money as a unit of account: One movie costs $6 and one cup of coffee costs 25¢, so one movie costs 24 cups of coffee ($6.00 ÷ 25¢ = 24).

No unit of account: You go to a movie theater and learn that the price of a movie is 2 six-packs of soda. You go to a candy store and learn that a pack of jelly beans costs 2 cups of coffee. But how many cups of coffee does seeing a movie cost you? To answer that question, you go to the convenience store and find that a six-pack of soda costs 2 ice-cream cones. Now you head for the ice-cream shop, where an ice-cream cone costs 3 packs of jelly beans. Now you get out your pocket calculator: 1 movie costs 2 six-packs of soda, or 4 ice-cream cones, or 12 packs of jelly beans, or 24 cups of coffee!

jelly beans, and if the candy store priced a pack of jelly beans as 2 cups of coffee! Now how much running around and calculating do you have to do to figure out how much that movie is going to cost you in terms of the soda, ice cream, jelly beans, or coffee that you must give up to see it? You get the answer for soda right away from the sign posted on the movie theater, but for all the other goods you're going to have to visit many different stores to establish the price of each commodity in terms of another and then calculate prices in units that are relevant for your own decision. Cover up the column labeled "price in money units" in Table 30.1 and see how hard it is to figure out the number of local phone calls it costs to see one movie. It's enough to make a person swear off movies! How much simpler it is for everyone to express their prices in terms of dollars and cents.

Store of Value

Any commodity or token that can be held and exchanged later for goods and services is called a *store of value*. Money acts as a store of value. If it did not, it would not be acceptable in exchange for goods and services. The more stable the value of a commodity or token, the better it can act as a store of value, and the more useful it is as money. There are no stores of value that are completely safe. The value of a physical object, such as a house, a car, or a work of art, fluctuates over time. The value of commodities and tokens used as money also fluctuate, and when there is inflation, they persistently fall in value.

The objects used as money have evolved over many centuries. We can identify four main forms of money:

- Commodity money
- Convertible paper money
- Fiat money
- Deposit money

Commodity Money

A physical commodity that is valued in its own right and is also used as a means of payment is **commodity money**. An amazing array of items have served as commodity money at different times and places,

four of which were described in the chapter opener. But the most common commodity monies have been coins made from metals such as gold, silver, and copper. The first known coins were made in Lydia, a Greek city-state, at the beginning of the seventh century B.C.

There are two problems with commodity money. First, there is a constant temptation to cheat on the value of the money. Two methods of cheating have been commonly used: clipping and debasement. *Clipping* is reducing the size of coins by an imperceptible amount, thereby lowering their metallic content. *Debasement* is the creation of a coin that has a lower silver or gold content (the balance being made up of some cheaper metal).

The temptation to lower the value of commodity money led to a phenomenon known as Gresham's Law, after the sixteenth century English financial expert Sir Thomas Gresham. **Gresham's Law** is the tendency for bad (debased) money to drive good (not debased) money out of circulation. To see why Gresham's Law works, suppose you are paid with two coins, one debased and the other not. Each coin has the same value if you use it to buy goods. But the good coin is more valuable as a commodity than it is as money. You will not, therefore, use the good coin as money. You will always pay with a debased coin (if you have one). In this way, bad money drives good money out of circulation.

The second problem with commodity money is its opportunity cost. Gold and silver used as money could be used to make jewelry or ornaments instead. This opportunity cost creates incentives to find alternatives to the commodity itself for use in the exchange process. One such alternative is a paper claim to commodity money.

Convertible Paper Money

When a paper claim to a commodity circulates as a means of payment, that claim is called **convertible paper money**. The first known example of paper money occurred in China during the Ming dynasty (A.D. 1368–1399). This form of money was also used extensively throughout Europe in the Middle Ages.

The inventiveness of goldsmiths and their clients led to the widespread use of convertible paper money. Because gold was valuable, goldsmiths had well-guarded safes in which to keep their own gold. They also rented space to artisans and others who wanted to put their gold in safekeeping and issued a receipt entitling them to reclaim their "deposits" on demand. (These receipts were similar to the coat check token that you get at a theater or museum.) Because the gold receipts entitled the holder of the receipt to reclaim gold, they were "as good as gold" and circulated as money. When Isabella bought some land from Henry, she simply gave him a gold receipt for the appropriate value. The gold receipt was convertible paper money. It was *backed* by the gold held by a goldsmith and was *convertible* into commodity money—gold.

Fractional Backing—The Origin of Banking

Once a convertible paper money system is operating and people are using paper claims to gold rather than gold itself as the means of payment, goldsmiths notice that their vaults are storing a lot of gold that is never withdrawn. This gives them a brilliant idea. Why not lend people gold receipts? The goldsmith can charge interest on the loan, and the loan is created just by writing on a piece of paper. As long as the number of such receipts created is not too large in relation to the stock of gold in the goldsmith's safe, the goldsmith is in no danger of not being able to honor his promise to convert receipts into gold on demand. The gold in the goldsmith's safe is a *fraction* of the gold receipts in circulation. By this device, *fractionally backed* convertible paper money was invented.

Between 1879 and 1933 the United States was on a **gold standard**, a monetary system with fractionally backed convertible paper in which a dollar could be converted into gold at a guaranteed value on demand. From 1933 until 1971 it was illegal for U.S. citizens to hold gold coins or ingots, but the U.S. Treasury stood ready to convert dollars into gold at $35 per ounce of gold for foreign central banks and foreign governments. In 1971, with the market price of gold far greater than $35 an ounce, the convertibility of the U.S. dollar into gold was finally abandoned.

Even with fractionally backed paper money, valuable commodities that could be used for other productive activities are tied up in the exchange process. There remains an incentive to find a yet more efficient way of facilitating exchange and of freeing up the commodities used to back the paper money. This alternative is fiat money.

Fiat Money

The term *fiat* means "let it be done" or "by order of the authority." **Fiat money** is an intrinsically worthless (or almost worthless) commodity that serves the functions of money. Some of the earliest fiat monies were the continental currency issued during the American Revolution and the "greenbacks" issued during the Civil War, which circulated until 1879. These early experiments with fiat money failed because prices increased rapidly and money lost its value. But despite this poor start, fiat money has become the main type of money used today.

The bills and coins that we use in the United States today—collectively known as **currency**—are examples of fiat money. They are money because the government declares them to be so with the words "This note is legal tender for all debts, public and private," which you can find printed on every dollar bill. Because of the creation of fiat money, people are willing to accept a piece of paper with a special watermark, printed in green ink, and worth not more than a few cents as a commodity, in exchange for $100 worth of goods and services. The small metal alloy disk that we call a quarter is worth almost nothing as a piece of metal, but it pays for a local phone call and many other small commodities. The replacement of commodity money by fiat money enables the commodities themselves to be used productively.

Deposit Money

In the modern world there is a fourth type of money: deposit money. **Deposit money** consists of deposits at banks and other financial institutions such as S&Ls. This type of money is an accounting entry in an electronic database in the banks' and other financial institutions' computers. It is money because it is used to settle debts. In fact, it is the main means of settling debts in modern societies. The owner of a deposit transfers ownership to another person simply by writing a check—an instruction to a bank—that tells the bank to change its database, debiting the account of one depositor and crediting the account of another.

We'll have more to say about deposit money shortly. But before doing so, let's look at the different forms of money and their relative magnitudes in the United States today.

Money in the United States Today

In the United States today, money consists of *currency* and *deposits* at banks and other financial institutions. There are different types of deposits and, as a result, different measures of money. The two main measures of money are known as **M1** and **M2**. M1 consists of currency and traveler's checks plus checking deposits owned by individuals and businesses. M1 does *not* include currency held by banks, and it does not include currency and checking deposits owned by the U.S. government. M2 consists of M1 plus saving deposits and time deposits. Time deposits are deposits that have a fixed term to maturity. (There is a third official definition of money, M3, which consists of M2 plus large-scale time deposits and term deposits.) Table 30.2 gives the definitions of M1 and M2.

Are M1 and M2 Really Money?   Money is the means of payment. So the test of whether an asset is money is whether it serves as a means of payment. Currency passes the test. But what about deposits? Checking deposits are money because they can be transferred from one person to another by writing a check. Such a transfer of ownership is equivalent to handing over currency. Because M1 consists of currency plus checking deposits and each of these is a means of payment, *M1 is money*.

But what about M2? Some of the savings deposits in M2 are just as much a means of payment as the checking deposits in M1. You can use the ATM at the grocery store checkout or gas station and transfer funds directly from your saving account to pay for your purchase. But other saving deposits are not means of payment. These deposits are known as *liquid assets*. **Liquidity** is the property of being instantly convertible into a means of payment with little loss in value. Because most of the deposits in M2 are quickly and easily converted into currency or checking deposits, they are operationally similar to M1, but technically they are not money.

Deposits Are Money but Checks Are Not

In defining money, we included, along with currency, deposits at banks and other financial institutions. But we did not count the checks that people write as money. Why are deposits money and checks not?

To see why deposits are money but checks are not, think about what happens when Colleen buys some roller blades for $200 from Rocky's Rollers.

TABLE 30.2

Two Measures of Money

M1	▪ Currency held outside banks
	▪ Traveler's checks
	▪ Checking deposits at commercial banks
	▪ Checking deposits at S&Ls, savings banks, and credit unions
M2	▪ M1
	▪ Savings deposits
	▪ Small time deposits
	▪ Money market mutual funds and other deposits

M1 consists of currency (pennies, nickels, dimes, and quarters and Federal Reserve bank notes, that is, dollar bills of various denominations) and checking deposits owned by individuals and businesses. The currency component of M1 is only that held outside the banks. Currency held by banks and checking accounts owned by the U.S. government are not part of M1. M2 is M1 plus savings deposits, time deposits, and money market mutual funds.

When Colleen goes to Rocky's shop, she has $500 in her deposit account at the Laser Bank. Rocky has $1,000 in his deposit account—at the same bank, as it happens. The total deposits of these two people is $1,500. On June 11, Colleen writes a check for $200. Rocky takes the check to Laser Bank right away and deposits it. Rocky's bank balance rises from $1,000 to $1,200. But when the bank credits Rocky's account with $200, it also debits Colleen's account $200, so her balance falls from $500 to $300. The total deposits of Colleen and Rocky are still the same as before: $1,500. Rocky now has $200 more and Colleen has $200 less than before. These transactions are summarized in Table 30.3.

This transaction has transferred money from Colleen to Rocky. The check itself was never money. There wasn't an extra $200 worth of money while the check was in circulation. The check was an instruction to the bank to transfer money from Colleen to Rocky.

In the example, Colleen and Rocky use the same bank. The same story, but with additional steps,

TABLE 30.3

Paying by Check

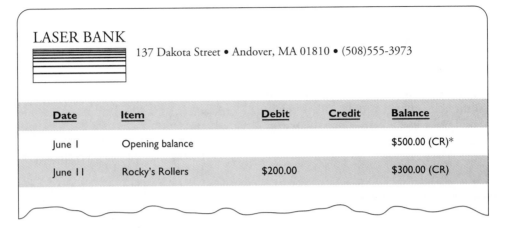

Colleen's checking deposit account

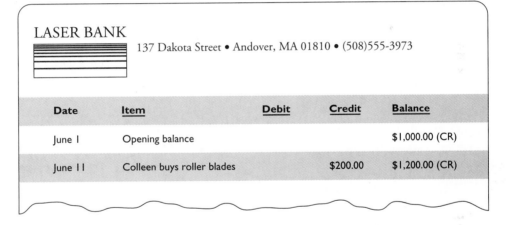

Rocky's Rollers' checking deposit account

CR means "credit": The bank owes the depositor.

describes what happens if Colleen and Rocky use different banks. Rocky's bank credits the check to Rocky's account and then takes the check to a check-clearing center. The check is then sent to Colleen's bank, which pays Rocky's bank $200 and then debits Colleen's account $200. This process can take a few days, but the principles are the same as when two people use the same bank.

Credit Cards Are Not Money So checks are not money. But what about credit cards? Isn't having a credit card in your wallet and presenting the card to pay for your roller blades the same thing as using money? Why aren't credit cards somehow valued and counted as part of the quantity of money?

When you pay by check, you are frequently asked to prove your identity by showing your driver's license. It would never occur to you to think of your driver's license as money. It's just an ID card. A credit card is also an ID card but one that lets you take a loan at the instant you buy something. When you sign a credit card sales slip, you are saying: "I agree to pay for these goods when the credit card company bills me." Once you get your statement from the credit card company, you must make the minimum payment due (or clear your balance). To make that payment you need money—you need to have currency or a checking deposit to pay the credit card company. So although you use a credit card when you buy something, the credit card is not the *means of payment*, and it is not money.

Figure 30.1 summarizes the components of money in the United States today. You can see that currency is a small part of our money. It accounts for 31 percent of M1 and 10 percent of M2. Checking deposits total more than currency and account for 69 percent of M1 and 22 percent of M2. Currency and checking deposits together, M1, is only 32 percent of M2.

REVIEW

- Money is the means of payment and has three functions: medium of exchange, unit of account, and store of value.
- A commodity can serve as money, but modern societies use fiat money and deposit money.
- The main component of money in the United States today is deposits at banks and other financial institutions.
- Neither checks nor credit cards are money.

We've seen that the main component of money in the United States is deposits at banks and other financial institutions. Let's take a closer look at these institutions.

FIGURE 30.1
Two Measures of Money

	$ billions
M2	**$3,600**
Money market mutual funds and other deposits	$375
Time deposits	$818
Savings deposits	$1,259
M1	**$1,148**
Checking deposits	$794
Currency and traveler's checks	$354

The M1 measure of money consists of all the assets that are a means of payment: currency, traveler's checks, and checking deposits that are used by individuals and businesses at commercial banks and other financial institutions. M1 makes up 31 percent of the M2 measure of money. M2 consists of M1 plus savings deposits, time deposits, and money market mutual funds.

Source: Economic Report of the President, 1994.

Financial Intermediaries

WE ARE GOING TO STUDY THE BANKING AND financial system by first describing the variety of financial intermediaries that operate in the United States today. Then we'll examine the operations of banks and of other financial intermediaries. After describing the main features of financial intermediaries, we'll examine their economic functions, describing what they produce and how they make a profit.

A **financial intermediary** is a firm that takes deposits from households and firms and makes loans to other households and firms. There are five types of financial intermediaries whose deposits are components of the nation's money:

- Commercial banks
- Savings and loan associations
- Savings banks and credit unions
- Money market mutual funds

Let's begin by looking at the commercial banks.

Commercial Banks

A **commercial bank** is a private firm, licensed either by the Comptroller of the Currency (in the U.S. Treasury) or by a state agency to receive deposits and make loans. There are close to 13,000 commercial banks in the United States today. To describe the operations of commercial banks, it is useful to study their balance sheets.

The *balance sheet* of a bank (or of any other business) is a list of assets, liabilities, and net worth. *Assets* are what the bank *owns*, *liabilities* are what the bank *owes*, and *net worth*, which is equal to assets minus liabilities, is the value of the bank to its stockholders—its owners. A bank's balance sheet can be described by the equation

$$\text{Liabilities} + \text{Net worth} = \text{Assets.}$$

Among a bank's liabilities are the deposits that are part of the nation's money. Your deposit at the bank is a liability to your bank (and an asset to you) because the bank must repay your deposit (and sometimes the interest on it too) whenever you decide to take your money out of the bank.

Profit and Prudence: A Balancing Act   The aim of a bank is to maximize its net worth—its value to its stockholders. To achieve this objective, a bank lends the money deposited with it at interest rates that are higher than the rates it pays for deposits. But a bank must perform a delicate balancing act. Lending is risky, and the more a bank ties up its deposits in high-risk, high-interest rate loans, the bigger its chance of not being able to repay its depositors. And if depositors perceive a high risk of not being repaid, they withdraw their funds and create a crisis for the bank. So a bank must be prudent in the way it uses its deposits, balancing security for the depositors against profit for its stockholders.

Reserves and Loans   To achieve security for its depositors, a bank divides its funds into two parts: reserves and loans. **Reserves** are cash in a bank's vault plus its deposits at Federal Reserve banks. (We'll study the Federal Reserve banks in Chapter 31.) The cash in a bank's vaults is a reserve to meet the demands that its customers place on it—it keeps that automatic teller replenished every time you and your friends have raided it for money for a midnight pizza. A commercial bank's deposit at the Federal Reserve is similar to your deposit at your own bank. Commercial banks use these deposits in the same way that you use your bank account. A commercial bank deposits cash into or draws cash out of its account at the Federal Reserve and writes checks on that account to settle debts with other banks.

If a bank kept all its assets as cash in its vault or as deposits at the Federal Reserve, it wouldn't make any profit. In fact, it keeps only a small fraction of its funds in reserves and lends the rest. A bank has three types of loans or assets. They are:

1. *Liquid assets* are U.S. government Treasury bills and commercial bills. These assets are the banks' first line of defense if they need cash. They can be sold and instantly converted into cash with virtually no risk of loss. Because liquid assets are virtually risk free, they have a low interest rate.

2. *Investment securities* are longer-term U.S. government bonds and other bonds. These assets can be sold quickly and converted into cash but at prices that fluctuate. Because their prices fluctuate, these assets are riskier than liquid assets, but they also have a higher interest rate.

3. *Loans* are commitments of fixed amounts of money for agreed-upon periods of time. Most banks' loans are made to corporations to finance the purchase of capital equipment and inventories and to households—personal loans—to finance consumer durable goods, such as cars or boats. The outstanding balances on credit card accounts are also bank loans. Loans are the riskiest assets of a bank because they cannot be converted into cash until they are due to be repaid. And some borrowers default and never repay. Because they are the riskiest of a bank's assets, they also carry the highest interest rate.

Commercial bank deposits are one component of the nation's money. But other financial intermediaries also take deposits that form part—an increasing part—of the nation's money. The largest of these other financial intermediaries are the S&Ls.

Savings and Loan Associations

A **savings and loan association** (S&L) is a financial intermediary that traditionally obtained its funds from savings deposits (called shares) and that made long-term mortgage loans to home buyers. Before 1980, S&Ls were prevented by regulation from offering checking deposits and were restricted to making mostly mortgage loans. Furthermore, the interest rate on these loans was fixed. Many mortgage loans had a term of 30 years, so a large number of mortgages still outstanding in the late 1970s had been written in the early 1950s, when the S&Ls were able to borrow at 3 percent a year and lend at 6 percent a year. But in the late 1970s, interest rates were much higher than they had been during the 1950s and 1960s, and the S&Ls had to pay more for deposits than they were making on their older mortgages.

Because of the plight of the S&Ls, Congress loosened the restrictions on them in 1980, permitting them to offer checking deposits and make high-interest consumer and commercial loans. Two years later, the Garn-St. Germain Depository Institutions Act loosened the restrictions on the S&Ls yet further, enabling them to invest a larger part of their funds in high-risk commercial real estate ventures. The way in which they used their greater freedom led the S&Ls to a crisis in the late 1980s. The majority of the S&Ls survived the crisis but many became bankrupt.

Savings Banks and Credit Unions

A **savings bank** is a financial intermediary owned by its depositors that accepts savings deposits and makes mostly mortgage loans. These institutions perform functions similar to those of S&Ls. The key difference is that savings banks, also called *mutual* savings banks, are owned by their depositors.

A **credit union** is a financial intermediary owned by its depositors that accepts savings deposits and makes mostly consumer loans. The key difference between a savings bank and a credit union is that a credit union is owned by a social or economic group such as a firm's employees.

Money Market Mutual Funds

A **money market mutual fund** is a financial institution that obtains funds by selling shares and uses these funds to buy highly liquid assets such as U.S. Treasury bills. Money market mutual fund shares act like the deposits at commercial banks and other financial intermediaries. Shareholders can write checks on their money market mutual fund accounts. But there are restrictions on most of these accounts. For example, the minimum deposit accepted might be $2,500, and the smallest check a depositor is permitted to write might be $500.

The Economic Functions of Financial Intermediaries

All financial intermediaries make a profit from the spread between the interest rate they pay on deposits and the interest rate at which they lend. Why can financial intermediaries borrow at a low interest rate and lend at a higher one? What services do they perform that makes their depositors willing to put up with a low interest rate and their borrowers willing to pay a higher one?

Financial intermediaries provide four main services that people are willing to pay for:

- Creating liquidity
- Minimizing the cost of obtaining funds
- Minimizing the cost of monitoring borrowers
- Pooling risk

Creating Liquidity   Financial intermediaries create liquidity. *Liquid* assets are those that are easily and with certainty convertible into money. Some of the liabilities of financial intermediaries are themselves money; others are highly liquid assets that are easily converted into money.

Financial intermediaries create liquidity by borrowing short and lending long. Borrowing short means taking deposits but standing ready to repay them on short notice (and on even no notice in the case of checking deposits). Lending long means making loan commitments for a prearranged, and often quite long, period of time. For example, when a person makes a deposit with a savings and loan association, that deposit can be withdrawn at any time. But the S&L makes a lending commitment for perhaps more than 20 years to a homebuyer.

Minimizing the Cost of Obtaining Funds
Finding someone from whom to borrow can be a costly business. Imagine how troublesome it would be if there were no financial intermediaries. A firm that was looking for $1 million to buy a new production plant would probably have to hunt around for several dozen people from whom to borrow in order to acquire enough funds for its capital project. Financial intermediaries lower those costs. The firm needing $1 million can go to a single financial intermediary to obtain those funds. The financial intermediary has to borrow from a large number of people, but it's not doing that just for this one firm and the million dollars it wants to borrow. The financial

intermediary can establish an organization that is capable of raising funds from a large number of depositors and can spread the cost of this activity over a large number of borrowers.

Minimizing the Cost of Monitoring Borrowers

Lending money is a risky business. There's always a danger that the borrower may not repay. Most of the money lent gets used by firms to invest in projects that they hope will return a profit. But sometimes those hopes are not fulfilled. Checking up on the activities of a borrower and ensuring that the best possible decisions are being made for making a profit and avoiding a loss are costly and specialized activities. Imagine how costly it would be if each and every household that lent money to a firm had to incur the costs of monitoring that firm directly. By depositing funds with a financial intermediary, households avoid those costs. The financial intermediary performs the monitoring activity by using specialized resources that have a much lower cost than what each household would incur if it had to undertake the activity individually.

Pooling Risk   As we noted above, lending money is risky. There is always a chance of not being repaid—of default. The risk of default can be reduced by lending to a large number of different individuals. In such a situation, if one person defaults on a loan, it is a nuisance but not a disaster. In contrast, if only one person borrows and that person defaults on the loan, the entire loan is a write-off. Financial intermediaries enable people to pool risk in an efficient way. Thousands of people lend money to any one financial intermediary, and, in turn, the financial intermediary re-lends the money to hundreds, perhaps thousands, of individual firms. If any one firm defaults on its loan, that default is spread across all the depositors with the intermediary, and no individual depositor is left exposed to a high degree of risk.

R E V I E W

- Most of the nation's money is made up of deposits in financial intermediaries: commercial banks, savings and loan associations, savings banks, credit unions, and money market mutual funds.
- The main economic functions of financial intermediaries are to create liquidity, to minimize the cost of obtaining funds and of monitoring borrowers, and to pool risk.

Financial Regulation, Deregulation, and Innovation

FINANCIAL INTERMEDIARIES ARE HIGHLY REGULATED institutions. But regulation is not static, and in the 1980s, some important changes in their regulation as well as deregulation took place. Also, the institutions are not static. In their pursuit of profit, they constantly seek lower-cost ways of obtaining funds, monitoring borrowers, pooling risk, and creating liquidity. They also are inventive in seeking ways to avoid the costs imposed on them by financial regulation. Let's take a look at regulation, deregulation, and innovation in the financial sector in recent years.

Financial Regulation

Financial intermediaries face two types of regulation:

- Deposit insurance
- Balance sheet rules

Deposit Insurance   The deposits of most financial intermediaries are insured by the Federal Deposit Insurance Corporation (FDIC). The FDIC is a federal agency that receives its income from compulsory insurance premiums paid by commercial banks and other financial intermediaries. The FDIC operates two separate insurance funds: the Bank Insurance Fund (BIF), which insures deposits in commercial banks, and the Saving Association Insurance Fund (SAIF), which insures the deposits of S&Ls, savings banks, and credit unions. Each of these funds insures deposits of up to $100,000.

The existence of deposit insurance provides protection for depositors in the event that a financial intermediary fails. But it also limits the incentive for the owner of a financial intermediary to make safe investments and loans. Some economists believe that deposit insurance played an important role in worsening the problems faced by S&Ls in the 1980s. Depositors did not worry about risk because their deposits were insured. The S&L owners making high-risk loans knew they were making a one-way bet. If their loans paid off, they made a high rate of return. If they failed and could not meet their obligations to the depositors, the insurance fund would step in. Bad loans were good business!

Because of this type of problem, all financial intermediaries face regulation of their balance sheets.

Balance Sheet Rules   The most important balance sheet regulations are:

- Capital requirements
- Reserve requirements
- Deposit rules
- Lending rules

Capital requirements are the minimum amount of an owner's own financial resources that must be put into an intermediary. This amount must be sufficiently large to discourage owners from making loans that are too risky. *Reserve requirements* are rules setting out the minimum percentages of deposits that must be held in currency or other safe, liquid assets. These minimum percentages vary across the different types of intermediaries and deposits; they are largest for checking deposits and smallest for long-term savings deposits. *Deposit rules* are restrictions on the different types of deposits that an intermediary may take. These are the rules that historically have created the sharpest distinctions between the various institutions. For example, commercial banks offered checking accounts while other institutions offered only savings accounts. *Lending rules* are restrictions on the proportions of different types of loans that an intermediary may make. Like deposit rules, these rules also helped to create sharp distinctions between the various institutions. Before 1980, commercial banks were the only intermediaries that were permitted to make commercial loans, and S&Ls and savings banks were restricted to making mostly mortgage loans to home buyers.

To enable S&Ls and savings banks to compete with commercial banks for funds, a ceiling was imposed on the interest rates that banks could pay on deposits. This interest ceiling regulation was known as *Regulation Q*. Also, commercial banks were not permitted to pay interest on checking deposits.

Deregulation in the 1980s

In 1980, Congress passed the Depository Institutions' Deregulation and Monetary Control Act (DIDMCA). The DIDMCA removed many of the distinctions between commercial banks and other financial intermediaries. It permitted nonbank financial intermediaries to compete with commercial banks in a wider range of lending business. At the same time it permitted the payment of interest on checking deposits so that NOW accounts and ATS accounts could be offered by all deposit-taking institutions—banks and non-banks.[1] It also extended the powers of the Federal Reserve to place reserve requirements on all depository institutions. Despite the general direction of deregulation, this move brought a greater measure of central control over the financial system that had previously existed and represented a strengthening of the Fed's control.

The ability of S&Ls and savings banks to compete for lending business with commercial banks was further strengthened in 1982 with the passage of the Garn-St. Germain Depository Institutions Act. This legislation further eased restrictions on the scale of commercial lending that S&Ls and savings banks could undertake.

Another important regulatory change occurred in 1986: the abolition of Regulation Q. With the abolition of Regulation Q, a fiercely competitive environment was created. In this environment there was rapid innovation in the types of deposits offered, and also rapid growth in money market mutual funds.

Financial Innovation

The development of new financial products—of new ways of borrowing and lending—is called **financial innovation**. The aim of financial innovation is to lower the cost of borrowing or to increase the return from lending or, more simply, to increase the profit from financial intermediation. There are three main influences on financial innovation:

- Economic environment
- Technology
- Regulation

The pace of financial innovation was remarkable during the 1980s and 1990s, and all three of these forces played a role.

---

[1] A NOW account is a Negotiable Order of Withdrawal account; "negotiable order of withdrawal" is another name for a check. An ATS account is an Automatic-Transfer Savings account—a savings account that is linked to a checking account. Funds are automatically tranferred between the two accounts.

Economic Environment   Some of the innovation was a response to high inflation and high interest rates. An important example is the development of variable interest rate mortgages. Traditionally, house purchases have been financed by mortgage loans at a guaranteed interest rate. Rising interest rates brought rising borrowing costs for S&Ls, and because they were committed to fixed interest rates on their mortgages, the industry incurred severe losses. The creation of variable interest rate mortgages has taken some of the risk out of long-term lending for house purchases.

Technology   Other financial innovations resulted from technological change, most notably that associated with the decreased cost of computing and long-distance communication. The spread in the use of credit cards and the development of international financial markets—for example, the increased importance of Eurodollars—are consequences of technological change.[2]

Regulation   A good deal of financial innovation takes place to avoid regulation. For example, Regulation Q, which prevented banks from paying interest on checking deposits, gave the impetus to devising new types of deposits on which checks could be written and interest paid, thereby getting around the regulation.

Deregulation, Innovation, and Money

Deregulation and financial innovation that have led to the development of new types of deposit accounts have brought important changes in the composition of the nation's money. In 1960, M1 consisted of only currency and checking deposits at commercial banks. In the 1990s, other new types of checking deposits have expanded while traditional checking deposits have declined. Similar changes have taken place in the composition of M2. Savings deposits have declined, while time deposits and money market mutual funds have expanded.

R E V I E W

■ Financial intermediaries are required to insure their deposits, and their lending is regulated.

■ The 1980s saw a wave of financial deregulation that blurred the distinction between commercial banks and other financial institutions.

■ Financial intermediaries constantly seek new ways of making a profit and react to the changing economic environment, new technologies, and regulations.

■ Deregulation and innovation have brought new types of deposits that changed the composition of the nation's money.

How Banks Create Money

BANKS CREATE MONEY.[3] BUT THIS DOESN'T MEAN that they have smoke-filled back rooms in which counterfeiters are busily working. Remember, most money is deposits, not currency. What banks create is deposits, and they do so by making loans. But the amount of deposits they can create is limited by their reserves.

Reserves: Actual and Required

We've seen that banks don't have $100 in bills for every $100 that people have deposited with them. In fact, a typical bank today has $1.25 in currency and another $1.15 on deposit at a Federal Reserve bank, a total reserve of $2.40, for every $100 deposited in it. No need for panic. Banks have learned, from experience, that these reserve levels are adequate for ordinary business needs.

The fraction of a bank's total deposits that are held in reserves is called the **reserve ratio**. The value of the reserve ratio is influenced by the actions of a bank's depositors. If a depositor withdraws currency from a bank, the reserve ratio decreases. If a depositor puts currency into a bank, the reserve ratio increases.

The **required reserve ratio** is the ratio of reserves to deposits that banks are required, by regulation, to hold. A bank's *required reserves* are equal to its deposits multiplied by the required reserve ratio. Actual reserves minus required reserves are **excess reserves**. Whenever banks have excess reserves, they are able to create money.

To see how banks create money, we'll look at two model banking systems. In the first, there is only one bank; in the second, there are many banks.

Creating Deposits by Making Loans in a One-Bank Economy

In the model banking system that we'll study, there is only one bank, and its required reserve ratio is 25 percent. That is, for each dollar deposited, the bank keeps 25¢ in reserves and lends the rest. The balance sheet of One-and-Only Bank is shown in Fig. 30.2(a). On January 1, its deposits are $400 million, and its reserves are 25 percent of this amount—$100 million. Its loans are equal to deposits minus reserves and are $300 million.

The story begins with Al Capone, who has decided to end his career of crime. He has been holding all his money in currency and has a nest egg of $1 million. On January 2, Al decides to put his $1 million on deposit at the One-and-Only bank. On the day that Al makes his deposit, the One-and-Only bank's balance sheet changes. The new situation is shown in Fig. 30.2(b). The bank now has $101 million in reserves and $401 million in deposits. It still has loans of $300 million.

The bank now has *excess reserves*. With reserves of $101 million, the bank would like to have deposits of $404 million and loans of $303 million. Because it is the One-and-Only bank, the manager knows that the reserves will remain at $101 million. That is, she knows that when she makes a loan, the amount lent remains on deposit at the One-and-Only bank. She knows, for example, that all the suppliers of Sky's-the-Limit Construction are also depositors of One-and-Only. So she knows that if she makes the loan that Sky's-the-Limit has just requested, the deposit she lends will never leave One-and-Only. When Sky's-the-Limit uses part of its new loan to pay $100,000 to I-Dig-It Excavating Company for some excavations, the One-and-Only bank simply moves the funds from Sky's-the-Limit's checking account to I-Dig-It's checking account.

So on January 3, the manager of One-and-Only calls Sky's-the-Limit's accountant and offers to lend the maximum that she can. How much does she lend? She lends $3 million. By lending $3 million, One-and-Only's balance sheet changes to the one shown in Fig. 30.2(c). Loans increase by $3 million to $303 million. The loan shows up in Sky's-the-Limit's deposit initially, and total deposits increase to $404 million—$400 million plus Al Capone's deposit of $1 million plus the newly created deposit of $3 million. The bank now has no excess reserves and has reached the limit of its ability to create money.

FIGURE 30.2

Creating Money at the One-and-Only Bank

(a) Balance sheet on January 1

Assets (millions of dollars)		Liabilities (millions of dollars)	
Reserves	$100	Deposits	$400
Loans	$300		
Total	$400	Total	$400

(b) Balance sheet on January 2

Assets (millions of dollars)		Liabilities (millions of dollars)	
Reserves	$101	Deposits	$401
Loans	$300		
Total	$401	Total	$401

(c) Balance sheet on January 3

Assets (millions of dollars)		Liabilities (millions of dollars)	
Reserves	$101	Deposits	$404
Loans	$303		
Total	$404	Total	$404

In part (a) the One-and-Only Bank has deposits of $400 million, loans of $300 million, and reserves of $100 million. The bank's required reserve ratio is 25 percent. When the bank receives a deposit of $1 million (part b), it has excess reserves. It lends $3 million and creates a further $3 million of deposits. Deposits increase by $3 million, and loans increase by $3 million (in part c).

The Deposit Multiplier

The **deposit multiplier** is the amount by which an increase in bank reserves is multiplied to calculate the increase in bank deposits. That is,

$$\text{Deposit multiplier} = \frac{\text{Change in deposits}}{\text{Change in reserves}}.$$

In the example we've just worked through, the deposit multiplier is 4. The $1 million increase in reserves created a $4 million increase in deposits. The deposit multiplier is linked to the required reserve ratio by the following equation

$$\text{Deposit multiplier} = \frac{1}{\text{Required reserve ratio}}.$$

In the example the required reserve ratio is 25 percent, or 0.25. That is,

$$\text{Deposit multiplier} = \frac{1}{0.25}$$
$$= 4.$$

Creating Deposits by Making Loans with Many Banks

If you told the loans officer at your own bank that she creates money, she wouldn't believe you. Bankers see themselves as lending the money they receive from others, not creating money. But in fact, even though each bank lends only what it receives, the banking *system* creates money. To see how, let's look at another example.

Figure 30.3 is going to keep track of what is happening in the process of money creation by a banking system in which each bank has a required reserve ratio of 25 percent. The process begins when Art decides to decrease his currency holding and put $100,000 on deposit. Now Art's bank has $100,000 of new deposits and $100,000 of additional reserves. With a required reserve ratio of 25 percent, the bank keeps $25,000 on reserve and lends $75,000 to Amy. Amy writes a check for $75,000 to buy a copy-shop franchise from Barb. At this point, Art's bank has a new deposit of $100,000, new loans of $75,000, and new reserves of $25,000. You can see this situation in Fig. 30.3 as the first row of the "running tally."

For Art's bank, that is the end of the story. But it's not the end of the story for the entire banking system. Barb deposits her check for $75,000 in another bank, which has an increase in deposits and reserves of $75,000. This bank puts 25 percent of its increase in deposits ($18,750) into reserve and lends $56,250 to Bob. And Bob writes a check to Carl to pay off a business loan. The current state of play is seen in Fig. 30.3. Now total bank reserves have increased by $43,750 ($25,000 plus $18,750), total loans have increased by $131,250 ($75,000 plus $56,250), and total deposits have increased by $175,000 ($100,000 plus $75,000).

When Carl takes his check to his bank, its deposits and reserves increase by $56,250, $14,063 of which it keeps in reserve and $42,187 of which it lends. This process continues until there are no excess reserves in the banking system. But the process takes a lot of further steps. One additional step is shown in Fig. 30.3. The figure also shows the final tallies—reserves increase by $100,000, loans increase by $300,000, and deposits increase by $400,000.

The sequence in Fig. 30.3 is the first four stages of the entire process. To figure out the entire process, look closely at the numbers in the figure. At each stage, the loan is 75 percent (0.75) of the previous loan and the deposit is 0.75 of the previous deposit. Call that proportion L, ($L = 0.75$). The complete sequence is

$$1 + L + L^2 + L^3 + \ldots .$$

Remember, L is a fraction, so at each stage in this sequence the amount of new loans gets smaller. The total number of loans made at the end of the process is the above sum, which is[4]

$$\frac{1}{(1 - L)}.$$

---

[4]Both here and in the expenditure multiplier process in Chapter 28, the sequence of values is called a convergent geometric series.

To find the sum of a series such as this, begin by calling the sum S. Then write out the sum as
$$S = 1 + L + L^2 + L^3 + \ldots.$$
Multiply by L to get,
$$LS = L + L^2 + L^3 + \ldots$$
and then subtract the second equation from the first to get.
$$S(1 - L) = 1$$
or
$$S = \frac{1}{(1 - L)}.$$

FIGURE 30.3

The Multiple Creation of Bank Deposits

The sequence

Deposit $100,000		
Reserve $25,000	Loan $75,000	
	Deposit $75,000	
	Reserve $18,750	Loan $56,250
		Deposit $56,250
	Reserve $14,063	Loan $42,187
		Deposit $42,187
	Reserve $10,547	Loan $31,640

and so on ...

The running tally

Reserves	Loans	Deposits
$25,000	$75,000	$100,000
$43,750	$131,250	$175,000
$57,813	$173,437	$231,250
$68,360	$205,077	$273,437
•	•	•
•	•	•
▼	▼	▼
$100,000	$300,000	$400,000

When a bank receives deposits, it keeps 25 percent in reserves and lends 75 percent. The amount lent becomes a new deposit at another bank. The next bank in the sequence keeps 25 percent and lends 75 percent, and the process continues until the banking system has created enough deposits to eliminate its excess reserves. The running tally tells us the amounts of deposits and loans created at each stage. At the end of the process, an additional $100,000 of reserves creates an additional $400,000 of deposits.

If we use the numbers from the example, the total increase in deposits is

$$\$100,000 + 75,000 + 56,250 + 42,190 + \ldots$$
$$= \$100,000 \, (1 + 0.75 + 0.5625 + 0.4219 + \ldots)$$
$$= \$100,000 \, (1 + 0.75 + 0.75^2 + 0.75^3 + \ldots)$$
$$= \$100,000 \, \frac{1}{(1 - 0.75)}$$
$$= \$100,000 \, \frac{1}{(0.25)}$$
$$= \$100,000 \, (4)$$
$$= \$400,000.$$

By using the same method, you can check that the totals for reserves and loans are the ones shown in Fig. 30.3.

So even though each bank lends only the money it receives, the banking system as a whole does create money by making loans. The amount created is exactly the same in a multibank system as in a one-bank system.

The Deposit Multiplier in the United States

The deposit multiplier in the United States works in the same way as the deposit multiplier we've just worked out for a model economy. But the deposit multiplier in the United States differs from the one we've just calculated for three reasons. First, the required reserve ratio of U.S. banks is smaller than the 25 percent we used here. Second, U.S. banks sometimes choose to hold excess reserves. Third, not all the loans made by banks return to them in the form of reserves. Some of the loans remain outside the banks and are held as currency. The smaller required reserve ratio makes the U.S. multiplier larger than the multiplier in the above example. But the other two factors make the U.S. multiplier smaller.

R E V I E W

▪ Banks create deposits by making loans, and the amount they can lend is determined by their reserves and the required reserve ratio.

▪ Each time a bank makes a loan, both deposits at other banks and required reserves increase.

▪ When deposits are at a level that makes required reserves equal to actual reserves, the banks have reached the limit of their ability to create money.

▪ A change in reserves brings about a multiple change in deposits, and the deposit multiplier equals 1 divided by the required reserve ratio.

We've now seen what money is and how banks create it. The amount of money created by the banks has a powerful influence on the economy. Our next task is to examine that influence.

Money, Real GDP, and the Price Level

YOU NOW KNOW THAT IN A MODERN ECONOMY such as that of the United States today, most of the money is bank deposits. You've seen that banks actually create money by making loans. Does the quantity of money created by the banking and financial system matter? What effect does money have? Does it matter whether the quantity of money increases quickly or slowly? In particular, how does the quantity of money influence real GDP, the price level, and the inflation rate?

We're going to answer these questions first by using the aggregate supply–aggregate demand model, which explains how money affects real GDP and the price level in the short run. Then we're going to study a theory called the quantity theory of money, which explains how money growth influences inflation in the long run. We'll also look at some historical and international evidence on the relationship between money growth and inflation.

The Short-Run Effects of a Change in the Quantity of Money

Figure 30.4 illustrates the *AS-AD* model that explains how real GDP and the price level are determined in the short run. (For a full explanation of the *AS-AD* model, see Chapter 27, pp. 656–668.) We are going to use this model to study the short-run effects of a change in the quantity of money on real GDP and the price level. Potential GDP is $6 trillion, and the long-run aggregate supply curve is *LAS*. The short-run aggregate supply curve is *SAS*. Initially, the aggregate demand curve is AD_0. Equilibrium real GDP is $5.5 trillion, and the price level is 125 at the intersection of the *AD* curve and the *SAS* curve.

FIGURE 30.4

Short-Run Effects of Change in Quantity of Money

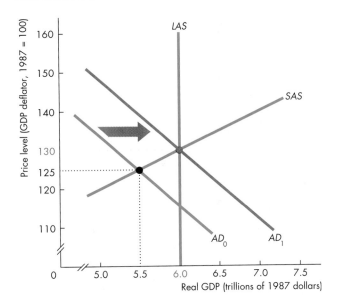

Real GDP is less than potential GDP. An increase in the quantity of money increases aggregate demand and shifts the aggregate demand curve rightward from AD_0 to AD_1. The price level rises to 130, and real GDP expands to $6 trillion. The increase in the quantity of money increases real GDP to potential GDP.

Banks, flush with excess reserves, make loans, and the loans create money. This increase results from the process of money creation we've just studied. With more money in their bank accounts and more loans, people plan to increase their consumption expenditure and businesses plan to increase their investment. Aggregate demand increases, and the aggregate demand curve shifts rightward to AD_1. A new equilibrium emerges at the intersection point of AD_1 and SAS. Real GDP expands to $6 trillion, and the price level rises to 130. Real GDP now equals potential GDP, and there is full employment. This increase in the quantity of money has increased both real GDP and the price level.

Now imagine the reverse situation. Real GDP is initially $6 trillion, and the price level is 130 at the intersection point of AD_1 and SAS. The quantity of money *decreases*. With *less* money in their bank accounts, people and businesses plan to decrease their expenditures. Aggregate demand decreases, and the aggregate demand curve shifts leftward to AD_0. A recession occurs as real GDP shrinks to $5.5 trillion and the price level falls to 125.

These influences of the quantity of money on real GDP and the price level are *short-run* effects. In the long run, a change in the quantity of money, perhaps surprisingly, has no effect on real GDP. All its effects are on the price level. Let's see why this outcome occurs.

The Long-Run Effects of a Change in the Quantity of Money

Figure 30.5 explains how real GDP and the price level are determined in both the short run and the long run. Again, potential GDP is $6 trillion and the long-run aggregate supply curve is *LAS*. The short-run aggregate supply curve is SAS_1. Initially, the aggregate demand curve is AD_1. Equilibrium real GDP is $6 trillion, and the price level is 130. So real GDP equals potential GDP, and there is full employment.

Now suppose the quantity of money increases. Aggregate demand increases, and the aggregate demand curve shifts rightward to AD_2. The new short-run equilibrium is at the intersection point of AD_2 and SAS_1. The price level rises to 134, and real GDP expands to $6.5 trillion. This short-run adjustment has put real GDP above potential GDP and has

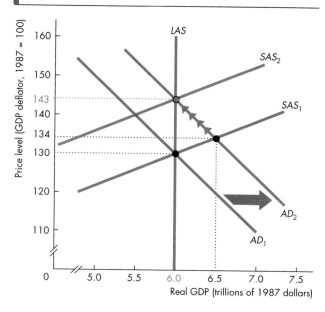

FIGURE 30.5

Long-Run Effects of Change in Quantity of Money

Real GDP equals potential GDP. An increase in the quantity of money shifts the aggregate demand curve from AD_1 to AD_2. The price level rises to 134, and real GDP increases to $6.5 trillion. Real GDP exceeds potential GDP, and the money wage rate rises. Short-run aggregate supply decreases, and the *SAS* curve shifts leftward from SAS_1 to SAS_2. Real GDP returns to potential GDP, and the price level rises to 143. In the long run, the increase in the quantity of money increases the price level and has no effect on real GDP.

decreased unemployment below the natural rate. A shortage of labor makes the money wage rate rise. As the money wage rate rises, short-run aggregate supply decreases and the *SAS* curve shifts leftward toward SAS_2. As short-run aggregate supply decreases, the price level rises to 143 and real GDP decreases back to potential GDP at $6 trillion.

Thus from one full-employment equilibrium to another, an increase in the quantity of money increases the price level and has no effect on real GDP. This relationship between the quantity of money and the price level at full employment is made more precise by the quantity theory of money, which tells us about the quantitative link between money growth and inflation.

The Quantity Theory of Money

The **quantity theory of money** is the proposition that in the long run, an increase in the quantity of money brings an equal percentage increase in the price level. The original basis of the quantity theory of money is a concept known as *the velocity of circulation* and an equation called *the equation of exchange*.

The **velocity of circulation** is the average number of times a dollar of money is used annually to buy the goods and services that make up GDP. GDP is equal to the price level (P) multiplied by real GDP (Y); that is,

$$GDP = PY.$$

Call the quantity of money M. The velocity of circulation, V, is determined by the equation

$$V = PY/M.$$

For example, if GDP is $6.0 trillion and the quantity of money is $3 trillion, the velocity of circulation is 2.

On the average, each dollar of money circulates twice in its use to purchase the final goods and services that make up GDP; that is, each dollar of money is used twice in a year to buy GDP.

Figure 30.6 shows the history of the velocity of circulation of both M1 and M2, the two main official definitions of money. You can see that the velocity of circulation of M1 increased between 1945 and 1980 and fluctuated through the 1980s and 1990s. In contrast, the velocity of circulation of M2 has been remarkably stable. The reason why the velocity of M1 has increased is that deregulation and financial innovation have created new types of deposits and payments technologies that are substitutes for M1. As a result, the quantity of M1 per dollar of GDP has decreased, and equivalently, the velocity of circulation of M1 has increased. The reason why the velocity of M2 has been almost constant is that the new types of deposits that have replaced M1 are part of M2. So the ratio of M2 to GDP and the velocity of circulation of M2 have been much more stable.

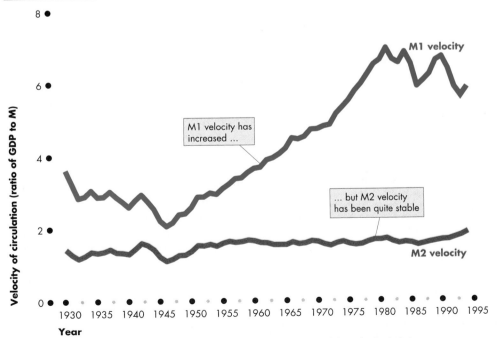

FIGURE 30.6

The Velocity of Circulation in the United States: 1930-1994

M1 velocity

M1 velocity has increased ...

... but M2 velocity has been quite stable

M2 velocity

Velocity of circulation (ratio of GDP to M)

Year

The velocity of circulation of M1 has increased over the years because financial innovation has developed M1 substitutes. The velocity of circulation of M2 has been relatively stable because the M1 substitutes that have resulted from financial innovation are new types of deposits that are part of M2.

Sources: *Historical Statistics of the United States*, *Economic Report of the President*, 1995, and the author's calculations.

The **equation of exchange** states that the quantity of money (M) multiplied by the velocity of circulation (V) equals GDP, or

$$MV = PY.$$

Given the definition of the velocity of circulation, this equation is always true—it is true by definition. With M equal to $3 trillion and V equal to 2, MV is equal to $6.0 trillion, the value of GDP.

The equation of exchange becomes the quantity theory of money by making two assumptions:

1. The velocity of circulation is not influenced by the quantity of money.
2. Potential GDP is not influenced by the quantity of money.

If these two assumptions are true, the equation of exchange tells us that in the long run, a given percentage change in the quantity of money brings about an equal percentage change in the price level. You can see why by solving the equation of exchange for the price level. Dividing both sides of the equation by real GDP (Y) gives

$$P = (V/Y)M.$$

In the long run, real GDP, Y, equals potential GDP, so if potential GDP and velocity are not influenced by the quantity of money, the relationship between the change in the price level (ΔP) and the change in the quantity of money (ΔM) is

$$\Delta P = (V/Y) \Delta M.$$

Divide this equation by the previous one ($P = (V/Y)M$) to get

$$\Delta P/P = \Delta M/M.$$

($\Delta P/P$) is the percentage increase in the price level and ($\Delta M/M$) is the percentage increase in the quantity of money. So this equation is the quantity theory of money: In the long run, the percentage increase in the price level equals the percentage increase in the quantity of money.

The Quantity Theory and the *AS-AD* Model

The quantity theory of money can be interpreted in terms of the *AS-AD* model. The aggregate demand curve is a relationship between the quantity of real GDP demanded (Y) and the price level (P), other things remaining constant. We can obtain such a relationship from the equation of exchange,

$$MV = PY.$$

Dividing both sides of this equation by real GDP (Y) gives

$$P = MV/Y.$$

This equation may be interpreted as describing an aggregate demand curve. In Chapter 27 (pp. 661–663) you saw that the aggregate demand curve slopes downward: as the price level increases, the quantity of real GDP demanded decreases. The above equation also shows such a relationship between the price level and the quantity of real GDP demanded. For a given quantity of money (M) and a given velocity of circulation (V) the higher the price level (P), the smaller is the quantity of real GDP demanded (Y).

In general, when the quantity of money changes, the velocity of circulation might also change. But the quantity theory asserts that velocity is not influenced by the quantity of money. If this assumption is correct, an increase in the quantity of money increases aggregate demand and shifts the aggregate demand curve upward by the same amount as the percentage change in the quantity of money.

The quantity theory of money also asserts that real GDP, which in the long run equals potential GDP, is not influenced by the quantity of money. This assertion is true in the *AS-AD* model in the long run when the economy is on its long-run aggregate supply curve. Figure 30.5 shows the quantity theory result in the *AS-AD* model. Initially, the economy is on the long-run aggregate supply curve *LAS* and at the intersection of the aggregate demand curve AD_1 and the short-run aggregate supply curve SAS_1. A 10 percent increase in the quantity of money shifts the aggregate demand curve from AD_1 to AD_2. This shift, measured by the vertical distance between the two demand curves, is 10 percent. In the long run, wages rise (also by 10 percent) and shift the *SAS* curve leftward to SAS_2. A new long-run equilibrium occurs at the intersection of AD_2 and SAS_2. Real GDP remains at potential GDP of $6 trillion, and the price level rises to 143. The new price level is 10 percent higher than the initial one (143 – 130 = 13, which is 10 percent of 130).

So the *AS-AD* model predicts the same outcome as the quantity theory of money. The *AS-AD* model also predicts a less precise relationship between the quantity of money and the price level in the short run than in the long run. For example, Fig. 30.4 shows that if we start out at a below-full employment equilibrium, an increase in the quantity of money increases real GDP. In this case a 10 percent increase in the money supply increases the price level from 125 to 130—a 4 percent increase. That is, the price level increases by a smaller percentage than the percentage increase in the quantity of money.

How good a theory is the quantity theory of money? Let's answer this question by looking at the relationship between money and the price level, both historically and internationally.

Historical Evidence on the Quantity Theory of Money

The percentage increase in the price level is the inflation rate, and the percentage increase in the quantity of money is the money supply growth rate. So the quantity theory predictions can be cast in terms of money growth and inflation. The quantity theory predicts that at a given level of potential GDP and in the long run, the inflation rate will equal the money growth rate. But over time, potential GDP expands. Taking this expansion into account, the quantity theory predicts that in the long run, the inflation rate will equal the money growth rate minus the growth rate of potential GDP.

We can test the quantity theory of money by looking at the historical relationship between money growth and inflation in the United States. Figure 30.7 shows two views of this relationship for the years between 1930 and 1994. In both parts of the figure, the inflation rate is the percentage change in the GDP deflator and the two alternative money growth rates are based on M1 and M2. Part (a) shows year-to-year changes in money and the price level. These changes show the short-run relationship between money growth and inflation. Part (b) shows decade average changes. These changes average out the year-to-year fluctuations and enable us to see the long-run relationship between the variables. If the quantity theory is a reasonable guide to reality, there should be a strong correlation between inflation and money growth in the decade average data and a weak correlation in the year-to-year data.

The data are broadly consistent with the quantity theory. The money growth rate and the inflation rate are correlated, but the relationship is not precise. During World War II, money growth increased sharply, while inflation remained low. After the war, inflation exploded, while money growth remained

steady. Between 1950 and 1994 the inflation rate fluctuated less than the fluctuations in the money growth rate. The year-to-year fluctuations in money growth and inflation, which contain short-run influences (in part a) show a weak correlation, and the decade average fluctuations in money growth and inflation (in part b) show a stronger correlation.

International Evidence on the Quantity Theory of Money

Another way to test the quantity theory of money is to look at the cross-country relationship between money growth and inflation. Figure 30.8 shows this relationship for 60 countries during the 1980s. By looking at a decade average, we again are smoothing out the short-run effects of money growth and focusing on the long-run effects. There is in these data an unmistakable tendency for high money growth to be associated with high inflation. Some further evidence from the experience of Brazil during the 1980s can be seen in *Reading Between the Lines* on pp. 760–761.

Correlation, Causation, and Other Influences

Both the historical evidence for the United States and the international data tell us that in the long run, money growth and inflation are correlated. But the correlation between money growth and inflation does not tell us that money growth causes inflation. Money growth might cause inflation; inflation might cause money growth; or some third variable might simultaneously cause inflation and money growth.

According to the quantity theory and according to the *AS-AD* model, causation runs from money growth to inflation. But neither theory denies the possibility that at different times and places, causation might run in the other direction or that some third factor might be the root cause of both rapid money growth and inflation. One possible third factor is a large and persistent government budget deficit that gets financed by newly created money.

But some occasions give us an opportunity to test our assumptions about causation. One of these is World War II and the years immediately following it. Rapid money growth during the war years accompanied by price controls almost certainly caused the postwar inflation. The inflationary consequences of

FIGURE 30.7

Money Growth and Inflation in the United States

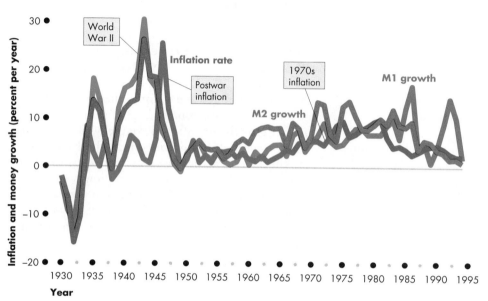

(a) Year-to-year change in money supply and the price level

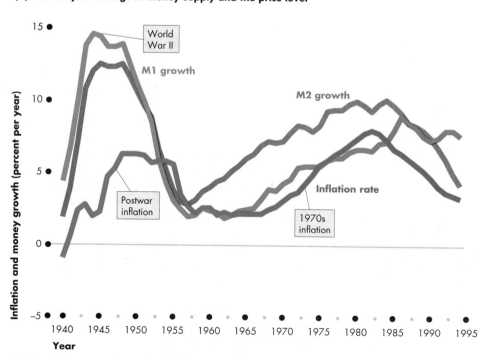

(b) Decade average change in money supply and the price level

Year-to-year fluctuations in money growth and inflation (part a) are loosely correlated, but decade average fluctuations in money growth and inflation (part b) are closely correlated. The burst of postwar inflation was caused by rapid money growth during World War II, and the rise in inflation during the 1970s was caused by more rapid money growth during the 1960s.

Sources: Historical Statistics of the United States, Economic Report of the President, 1995, and the author's calculations.

FIGURE 30.8

FIGURE 30.8
Money Growth and Inflation in the World Economy

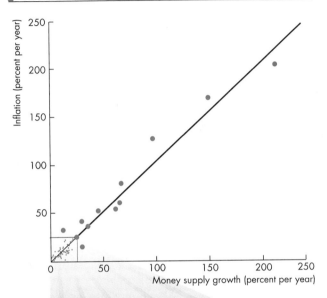

(a) All countries

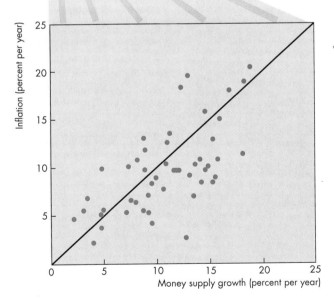

(b) Low-inflation countries

Inflation and money growth in 60 countries (in part a) and low-inflation countries (in part b) show a clear positive relationship between money growth and inflation.

Source: Federal Reserve Bank of St. Louis, *Review,* May/June 1988, p. 15.

the money growth was delayed by the controls but not removed. It is inconceivable that this was an example of reverse causation—of postwar inflation causing wartime money growth. Another is the late 1960s and 1970s. Rapid money growth that began during the 1960s almost certainly caused the high and persistent inflation of the 1970s.

The combination of historical and international correlations between money growth and inflation and independent evidence about the direction of causation lead to the conclusion that the quantity theory is correct in the long run. It explains the long-term fundamental source of inflation. But the quantity theory is not correct in the short run. To understand the short-term fluctuations in inflation, the joint effects of a change in the quantity of money on real GDP, the velocity of circulation, and the price level must be explained. The *AS-AD* model provides this explanation. It also points to the possibility of other factors that influence both aggregate supply and aggregate demand influencing the inflation rate independently of the money growth rate in the short run.

REVIEW

■ The quantity of money influences the price level and real GDP.

■ In the short run, an increase in the quantity of money increases aggregate demand and increases both the price level and real GDP.

■ In the long run, when real GDP equals potential GDP, an increase in the quantity of money brings an equal percentage increase in the price level (the quantity theory of money).

■ The long-run historical and international evidence on the relationship between money growth and inflation supports the quantity theory.

◆ In the next chapter we're going to study the Fed and monetary policy. We'll see how the Fed's actions can change the quantity of money. We'll also learn how the Fed is able to influence interest rates, which in turn influence aggregate demand. It is through its effects on the quantity of money and interest rates and their wider ramifications that the Fed is able to help steer the course of the economy. Then, in Chapter 32, we'll return to the problem of inflation and explore more deeply its causes, consequences, and ways of keeping it under control.

Unstable Money

THE NEW YORK TIMES, JULY 25, 1993

In Brazil, Wild Ways to Counter Wild Inflation

By JAMES BROOKE

RIO DE JANEIRO, July 20—At a fashion industry fair, a clothing manufacturer and boutique owner haggled recently over payment for blouses to be delivered in October. Mistrusting Government-manipulated dollar exchange rates and inflation indexes, buyer and seller finally agreed on a neutral pricing unit: bars of margarine.

Pricing blouses according to the margarine standard is but one of many ways Brazilians have developed to survive, and sometimes thrive, amid high inflation.

Since 1980, Brazil has had 4 currencies, 5 wage-and-price freezes, 9 economic stabilization programs, 11 inflation indexes, 12 finance ministers, and an accumulated inflation rate of 146 billion percent. Without the currency changes, a cup of coffee that sold in 1980 for 15 cruzeiros would sell today for 22 billion cruzeiros.

The cardinal rule is to keep no cash, or to spend it as quickly as possible.

"My currency is the electronic cash card," Carlos Decotelli, an economist for the Brazilian Institute for Capital Markets, said recently. "I left my house this morning without any cruzeiros in my pocket. I told the taxi driver to stop at a money machine. They are on every corner now."

Others use checks to pay for taxis, pizzas, and even newspapers. Most bank accounts bear interest daily. The 30 percent monthly rates, which sound fabulous elsewhere, merely keep account holders abreast of inflation. ...

Another inflation dodge is to use credit cards. By timing a purchase carefully, a shopper can get a free 30-day float, by which time the real cost of his purchase will have dropped by 30 percent. ...

Essence of **THE STORY**

■ Since 1980, Brazil has had an accumulated inflation rate of 146 billion percent.

■ To cope with the unstable value of money, some people use bars of margarine as a unit of account.

■ To avoid losses, people hold as little cash as possible and use electronic cash card and checks as much as possible.

■ Bank deposits pay interest at a rate of 30 percent a month, which just keeps up with inflation.

■ By timing credit card purchases, it is possible to get a 30-day loan that gets paid off with money that is worth 30 percent less than when the goods were bought.

Economic

A N A L Y S I S

■ The last time the inflation rate in Brazil dipped below 100 percent a year was 1982. Through the 1980s, Brazil's inflation increased, and by 1989 it exceeded 1,000 percent a year. The rate peaked in July 1994, when it briefly hit 5,600 percent a year.

■ Figure 1 shows the record of Brazil's inflation. It also shows the money growth rate in Brazil over this same period.

■ When inflation is as high and variable as it has been in Brazil, money ceases to work well as a medium of exchange, a unit of account, or a store of value.

■ You can see in the news article that people use ingenious ways of getting around these problems, but not without incurring costs. It takes time to haggle about the price of a blouse and decide to use a margarine standard. And it takes time to stop the taxi at the cash machine to pay the fare (especially if there is a line at the cash machine).

■ Brazil's experience is so extreme that it enables us to test the quantity theory of money in a much sharper way than we can on the much more limited inflation experience of the United States.

■ The quantity theory predicts that there will be a correlation between money growth and inflation, and Figure 1 shows that there is such a correlation in Brazil. But look closely at the graph.

■ In 1990, when the inflation rate leapt to 3,000 percent a year, the money growth rate also increased, but only to around 2,000 percent a year.

■ Why did inflation jump by so much more than money growth? The answer is that the velocity of circulation increased.

■ To account for experiences like those in Brazil, a more sophisticated version of the quantity theory is used that recognizes that when the inflation rate increases, the velocity of circulation sometimes also increases.

■ The reason for this response to high inflation is that people try to hold as little money as possible—as described in the news article—to avoid incurring losses from holding an asset whose value is falling rapidly.

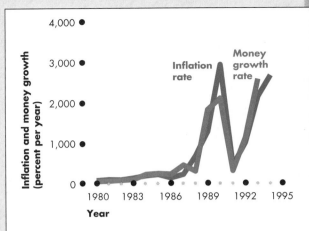

Figure 1 Money growth and inflation

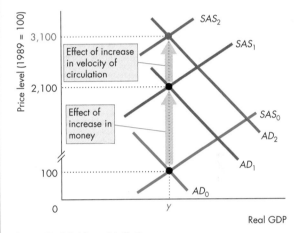

Figure 2 *AS-AD* and inflation

■ If interest is paid on bank deposits at a rate equal to the inflation rate, this increase in velocity does not occur. But in 1990 the inflation rate outstripped the interest rate on deposits. As a result, an increase in the money stock and increase in velocity both increased aggregate demand.

■ Figure 2 illustrates these *two* effects in 1990. In 1989 the aggregate demand curve was AD_0, and the short-run aggregate supply curve was SAS_0. The increase in

money increased aggregate demand to AD_1, and the anticipation of inflation increased wages and decreased aggregate supply to SAS_1. On its own, this factor would have taken the inflation rate to around 2,000 percent.

■ The increase in velocity increased aggregate demand further to AD_2, and the anticipation of this additional inflation increased wages and decreased aggregate supply to SAS_2. This additional factor took the inflation rate up to 3,000 percent.

761

"Inflation is always and everywhere a monetary phenomenon."

MILTON FRIEDMAN, *THE COUNTER-REVOLUTION IN MONETARY THEORY.*

Money and Inflation

THE ISSUES AND IDEAS

The combination of history and economics has taught us a lot about the causes of inflation. Severe inflation—hyperinflation—arises from a breakdown of the normal fiscal policy processes at times of war or political upheaval. Tax revenues fall short of government spending, and the gap between them is filled by printing money. As inflation increases, the quantity of money that is needed to make payments increases, and there can even be a *shortage* of money. So the rate of money growth is increased yet further, and prices rise yet faster. Eventually, the monetary system collapses. Such was the experience of Germany in the 1920s and Brazil in the 1990s.

In earlier times, when commodities were used as money, inflation resulted from the discovery of new sources of money. The most recent occurrence of this type of inflation was at the end of the nineteenth century when gold, then used as money, was discovered in Australia, the Klondike, and South Africa.

In modern times, inflation has resulted from increases in the money supply that has accommodated increases in costs. The most dramatic of such inflations occurred during the 1970s when oil price increases were accommodated by the Fed and other central banks around the world.

To avoid inflation, money supply growth must be held in check. But at times of severe cost-push pressure, central banks feel a strong tug in the direction of avoiding recession and accommodating the cost-push.

Yet some countries have avoided inflation more effectively than others. A key source of success is central bank independence. In low-inflation countries, such as Germany and Japan, the central bank decides how much money to create and at what level to set interest rates and does not take instructions from the government. In high-inflation countries, such as the United Kingdom and Italy, the central bank takes direct orders from the government about interest rates and money supply growth. This connection between central bank independence and inflation has been noticed by the architects of a new monetary system for the European Union, who are modeling the European Central Bank on Germany's Bundesbank.

THEN...

WHEN INFLATION is especially rapid, as it was in Germany in 1923, money becomes almost worthless. In Germany at that time, bank notes were more valuable as fire kindling than as money, and the sight of people burning Reichmarks was a common one. To avoid having to hold money for too long, wages were paid and spent twice a day. Banks took deposits and made loans, but at interest rates that compensated depositors and the bank for the falling value of money, interest rates that could exceed 100 percent a month. The price of a dinner would increase during the course of an evening, making lingering over coffee a very expensive pastime.

In 1994, Brazil had a computer-age hyperinfla-tion, an inflation rate that was close to 50 percent a month. Banks installed ATMs on almost every street corner and refilled them several times an hour. Brazilians tried to avoid holding currency. As soon as they were paid, they went shopping and bought enough food to get them through to the next payday. Some shoppers filled as many as six carts on a single monthly trip to the supermarket. Also, instead of using currency, Brazilians used credit cards whenever possible. But they paid their card balances off quickly because the interest rate on unpaid balances was 50 percent a month. Only at such a high interest rate was it worthwhile for banks to lend to cardholders, because banks themselves were paying interest rates of 40 percent a month to induce depositors to keep their money in the bank.

David Hume

THE ECONOMISTS: DAVID HUME AND MILTON FRIEDMAN

Born in Edinburgh, Scotland, in 1711, and a close friend of Adam Smith, David Hume was a philosopher, histor-ian, and economist of extraordinary breadth. His first book, by his own description, "fell dead-born from the press." But his essays, on topics ranging from love and marriage, and the immortality of the soul, to money, interest, and the balance of payments, were widely read and earned him a considerable fortune. Hume gave the first clear account of the way in which an increase in the quantity of money causes an increase in prices. He even anticipated the discovery, some 220 years later, of the Phillips curve and the Keynesian theory of aggregate demand.

Milton Friedman, now a Senior Fellow at the Hoover Institution at Stanford University, was from 1946 to

1983 one of the leading members of the "Chicago School," an approach to economics developed at the University of Chicago and based on the views that free markets allocate resources efficiently and that stable and low money supply growth delivers macroeconomic stabilty. Friedman was awarded the Nobel Prize for Economic Science for his work on money and other macroeconomic problems.

By reasoning from basic economic principles, Friedman predicted that persistent demand stimulation would *not* increase output but *would* cause inflation. When output growth slowed and inflation broke out in the 1970s, Friedman seemed like a prophet, and for a time, his policy prescription, known as "monetarism," was embraced around the world.

Milton Friedman

SUMMARY

What Is Money?

Money is the means of payment, and it has three functions. It is a medium of exchange, a unit of account, and a store of value. The earliest forms of money were commodities. In the modern world we use a fiat money system. The biggest component of money is deposit money.

The two main measures of money in the United States today are M1 and M2. M1 consists of currency held outside banks, traveler's checks, and checking deposits. M2 includes M1 plus savings deposits, time deposits, and money market mutual funds. M1 is the means of payment, but the additional items in M2 are easily converted into M1 and are highly liquid. Checking deposits are money, but checks and credit cards are not money. (pp. 739–744)

Financial Intermediaries

The main financial intermediaries whose liabilities are money are commercial banks, savings and loan associations, savings banks, credit unions, and money market mutual funds. These institutions take in deposits, hold cash reserves to ensure that they can meet their depositors' demands for currency, and use the rest of their financial resources either to buy securities or to make loans. Financial intermediaries make a profit by borrowing at a lower interest rate than that at which they lend. All financial intermediaries provide four main economic services: They create liquidity, minimize the cost of obtaining funds, minimize the cost of monitoring borrowers, and pool risks. (pp. 744–747)

Financial Regulation, Deregulation, and Innovation

Financial intermediaries are regulated to protect depositors. Deposits are insured by the FDIC, owners of intermediaries are required to put a certain minimum amount of their own financial resources into the institution, minimum cash and liquid assets reserves are specified, and lending rules are imposed.

Before 1980, S&Ls and savings banks were permitted to make only mortgage loans to home buyers and were excluded from making commercial loans. Interest rates on savings deposits were controlled by Regulation Q, and commercial banks were not permitted to pay interest on checking deposits.

Deregulation in the 1980s removed restrictions on nonbank financial intermediaries and thereby enabled them to compete with commercial banks for lending business and permitted interest to be paid on checking deposits. Regulation Q was abolished in 1986.

The continual search for profitable financial opportunities leads to financial innovation—to the creation of new financial products such as new types of deposits and loans. NOW accounts and ATS accounts are examples of some of the new financial products of the 1980s. Deregulation and financial innovation have brought important changes in the composition of the nation's money. (pp. 747–749)

How Banks Create Money

Banks create money by making loans. When a loan is made to one person and the amount lent is spent, much of it ends up as someone else's deposit. The total quantity of deposits that can be supported by a given amount of reserves (the deposit multiplier) is equal to 1 divided by the required reserve ratio. (pp. 749–753)

Money, Real GDP, and the Price Level

The quantity of money affects aggregate demand. An increase in the quantity of money increases aggregate demand and, in the short run, increases both the price level and real GDP. Over the long run, real GDP grows and fluctuates around its full-employment level, and increases in the quantity of money bring increases in the price level. The quantity theory of money predicts that an increase in the quantity of money increases the price level by the same percentage as the quantity of money increased and leaves real GDP unchanged. Both historical and international evidence suggests that the quantity theory of money is correct on the average. The quantity of money exerts a powerful influence on the price level. But in the short run, it also influences real GDP. (pp. 753–759)

K E Y   E L E M E N T S

R E V I E W   Q U E S T I O N S

1. What is money? What are its functions?

2. What are the different forms of money?

3. What are the two main measures of money in the United States today?

4. Are checks and credit cards money? Explain your answer.

5. What are financial intermediaries? What are the types of financial intermediaries in the United States? What are the main deposit-taking institutions other than commercial banks?

6. What are the economic functions of financial intermediaries?

7. How do banks make a profit and how do they create money?

8. Describe the main types of financial regulation that financial intermediaries face.

9. Describe the deregulation of financial intermediaries that took place in the 1980s.

10. What is financial innovation? Explain the financial innovation that took place in the 1980s.

11. Define the deposit multiplier. Explain why it equals 1 divided by the required reserve ratio.

12. What does the aggregate supply–aggregate demand model predict about the effects of a change in the quantity of money on the price level and real GDP when the economy is initially
    a. In a recession?
    b. At full employment?

13. What is the equation of exchange and the velocity of circulation? What assumptions are necessary to make the equation of exchange the quantity theory of money?

14. What is the U.S. and international evidence on the quantity theory of money?

PROBLEMS

1. In the United States today, money includes which of the following items?
   a. Federal Reserve banknotes in the Bank of America's cash machines
   b. Your Visa card
   c. The quarters inside public phones
   d. Federal Reserve banknotes in your wallet
   e. The check you have just written to pay for your rent
   f. The loan you took out last August to pay for your school fees

2. Which of the following items are fiat money? Which are deposit money?
   a. Checking deposits at Citicorp
   b. IBM shares held by individuals
   c. The Susan B. Anthony dollar coin
   d. U.S. government securities
   e. NOW accounts

3. As the cruzeiro loses its ability to function as money, which of these commodities is most likely to take its place in the Brazilian economy?
   a. Tractor parts
   b. Packs of cigarettes
   c. Loaves of bread
   d. Impressionist paintings
   e. Economists trading cards
   Explain your answer by referring to the three basic functions of money.

4. Sara withdraws $1,000 from her savings account at the Lucky S&L, keeps $50 in cash, and deposits the balance in her checking account at the Bank of America. What is the immediate change in M1 and M2?

5. The commercial banks in Desertland have:

Reserves	$250 million
Loans	$1,000 million
Deposits	$2,000 million
Total assets	$2,500 million

   a. Construct the commercial banks' balance sheet. If you are missing any assets, call them "other assets"; if you are missing any liabilities, call them "other liabilities."
   b. Calculate the banks' reserve ratio.
   c. If banks hold no excess reserves, calculate the deposit multiplier.

6. An immigrant arrives in New Transylvania with $1,200. The $1,200 is put into a bank deposit. All the banks in New Transylvania have a required reserve ratio of 10 percent.
   a. What is the initial increase in the quantity of money of New Transylvania?
   b. What is the initial increase in the quantity of bank deposits when the immigrant arrives?
   c. How much does the immigrant's bank lend out?
   d. Set out the transactions that take place and calculate the amount lent and the amount of deposits created, assuming that all the funds lent are returned to the banking system in the form of deposits.
   e. By how much has the quantity of money increased after the banks have made 20 loans?
   f. What is the total increase in the quantity of money, in bank loans, and in bank deposits?

7. Quantecon is a country in which the quantity theory of money operates. The country has a constant population, capital stock, and technology. In year 1, real GDP was $400 million, the price level was 200, and the velocity of circulation of money was 20. In year 2, the quantity of money was 20 percent higher than in year 1.
   a. What was the quantity of money in year 1?
   b. What was the quantity of money in year 2?
   c. What was the price level in year 2?
   d. What was the level of real GDP in year 2?
   e. What was the velocity of circulation in year 2?

8. Study *Reading Between the Lines* on pp. 760–761 and then answer the following questions:
   a. How has Brazil coped with the problem of finding a stable unit of account?
   b. What has happened to the velocity of circulation of money in Brazil?
   c. How do people protect themselves from a falling value of money in Brazil?
   d. Why has Brazil's inflation rate been higher than its money supply growth rate in some years? Does this fact contradict the quantity theory of money?

Chapter 31

The Federal Reserve and Monetary Policy

After studying
this chapter,
you will be
able to:

- Describe the structure of the Federal Reserve System (the Fed)

- Describe the tools used by the Fed to conduct its monetary policy

- Explain what an open market operation is and how it works

- Explain how an open market operation changes the money supply

- Explain what determines the demand for money

- Explain how the Fed influences interest rates

- Explain how interest rates influence the economy

In 1987, William Greider's *Secrets of the Temple: How the Federal Reserve Runs the Country* made the *New York Times* best seller list. This book was popular partly because it was (and is) a good read and partly because it let its reader in on some secrets—the secrets of a mysterious Fed. What exactly is the Fed? What tools does it possess? And how does it use them? ◆ One thing the Fed

Temple of Secrets

does is to manage the nation's money. The amount of money in existence is surprisingly large. Enough currency—coins and Federal Reserve bills—circulates in the United States today for every person to have a wallet stuffed with $1,360. In addition, enough money is deposited in banks and other financial institutions for every person to have a deposit of more than $12,500. What determines the amount of currency and bank deposits in existence? How does the Fed change the amount of money floating around the economy? And why do individuals and businesses hold so much money? ◆ At the end of 1993, short-term interest rates—interest rates on short-term loans—were at a 30-year low. Then, through 1994 and early 1995, these interest rates increased. Almost every month, the newspapers ran stories about the rising interest rates under headlines such as "The Fed pushes interest rates higher to check inflation." How does the Fed change interest rates? How do interest rates influence the economy? And how do higher interest rates keep inflation in check?

◆ In this chapter you will learn about the Fed and monetary policy. You will learn how the Fed influences interest rates and how interest rates influence the economy. You'll discover that interest rates depend, in part, on the amount of money in existence. You will also discover how the Fed influences the quantity of money to influence interest rates as it attempts to smooth the business cycle and keep inflation in check.

The Federal Reserve System

THE CENTRAL BANK OF THE UNITED STATES IS the **Federal Reserve System**. A **central bank** is a bank's bank and a public authority charged with regulating and controlling a nation's monetary and financial institutions and markets. As the banks' bank, the Fed provides banking services to commercial banks such as Chase Manhattan and the Bank of America. But a central bank is not a citizens' bank. That is, the Fed does not provide general banking services for businesses and individual citizens.

The Fed conducts the nation's **monetary policy**, which means that it adjusts the quantity of money in circulation. The Fed's goals in its conduct of monetary policy are to keep inflation in check, maintain full employment, moderate the business cycle, and maintain adequate long-term growth. Complete success in the pursuit of these goals is impossible, and the Fed's more modest goal is to improve the performance of the economy and to get closer to the goals than a "hands off" approach would achieve. Whether the Fed succeeds in improving economic performance is a matter on which there is a variety of opinion.

Our goal in this chapter is to learn about the tools available to the Fed in its conduct of monetary policy and the effects of the Fed's actions on the economy. Our starting point is to examine the origins and describe the structure of the Fed.

The Origins of the Federal Reserve System

The Fed was created by the Federal Reserve Act of 1913. Previous attempts to establish a central bank had been made but central banking and a deep hostility to central power—visible in the checks and balances built into the Constitution—just did not seem to mix. Each time it was proposed that a central bank be established, the proposal hit roadblocks. During this period, there was a series of severe national bank panics. In 1907, bank failures and depositors' losses were so severe that the critics of central banking became a minority. The serious financial turmoil of 1907 led to the emergence of a consensus on the need for a central bank, and this consensus finally found expression in the Federal Reserve Act of 1913.

By the time the Fed was created, most other countries already had a central bank. The first such banks were established in Sweden and England in the seventeenth century. But their origins were very different from that of the Fed. They were set up as private banks designed to solve the financial problems of monarchs. These banks gradually evolved into modern central banks, eventually becoming publicly owned corporations. Central banks, as their name suggests, concentrate the power to control and influence the banking system in a single center. In setting up the Federal Reserve System, care was taken to design a central bank that diffused and decentralized, as far as possible, responsibility for monetary policy. The result was a central bank with a unique structure, unlike all other central banks. Let's examine that structure.

The Structure of the Federal Reserve System

There are three key elements in the structure of the Federal Reserve System:

- The Board of Governors
- The Regional Federal Reserve Banks
- The Federal Open Market Committee

The Board of Governors   The Board of Governors of the Federal Reserve System consists of seven members appointed by the President of the United States and confirmed by the Senate. The board is located in Washington, D.C. Each member is appointed for a 14-year term, and the terms are staggered so that one place on the board becomes vacant every two years. One of the members of the board is its chairman for a renewable term of four years.

The Federal Reserve Banks   There are 12 Federal Reserve banks, one for each of 12 Federal Reserve districts shown in Fig. 31.1. Each Federal Reserve bank has nine directors, three of whom are appointed by the Board of Governors and six of whom are elected by the commercial banks in the Federal Reserve district. The directors of the regional Federal Reserve banks appoint the bank's president, and this appointment is approved by the Board of Governors.

The Federal Reserve Bank of New York (or the New York Fed, as it is usually called) occupies a special place in the Federal Reserve System. It is the New York Fed that implements some of the Fed's most important policy decisions.

FIGURE 31.1

The Federal Reserve System

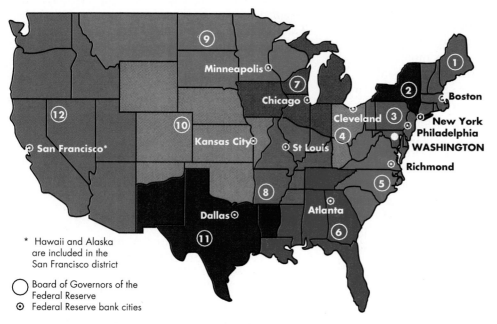

The nation is divided into 12 Federal Reserve districts, each having a Federal Reserve bank. (Some of the larger districts also have branch banks.) The Board of Governors of the Federal Reserve System is located in Washington, D.C.

* Hawaii and Alaska are included in the San Francisco district

○ Board of Governors of the Federal Reserve
⊙ Federal Reserve bank cities

Source: *Federal Reserve Bulletin*, published monthly.

The Federal Open Market Committee   The **Federal Open Market Committee** (FOMC) is the main policy-making organ of the Federal Reserve System. The FOMC consists of the following voting members:

- The chairman of the Board of Governors
- The other six members of the Board of Governors
- The president of the Federal Reserve Bank of New York
- The presidents of the other regional Federal Reserve banks (of whom, on a yearly rotating basis, only four vote)

The FOMC meets every six weeks to review the state of the economy and to formulate detailed policy actions to be carried out by the New York Fed.

The Fed's Power Center

A description of the formal structure of the Fed gives the impression that power in the Fed resides with the Board of Governors. In practice, it is the chairman of the Board of Governors who has the largest influence on the Fed's monetary policy actions, and this position has been held by some remarkable individuals. One of these is Paul Volcker, who was appointed in 1979 by President Carter and reappointed in 1983 by President Reagan. Volcker eradicated inflation but helped to create one of the most severe post-war recessions. Another is Alan Greenspan, who was appointed by President Reagan in 1987 and reappointed by President Bush in 1992. Greenspan must be replaced or reappointed as Fed chairman before March 1996.

The chairman's power and influence stem from three sources. First, it is the chairman who controls the agenda and who dominates the meetings of the FOMC. Second, day-to-day contact with a large staff of economists and other technical experts provides the chairman with detailed background briefings on monetary policy issues. Third, the chairman is the spokesperson for the Fed and the main point of contact of the Fed with the President and government and with foreign central banks and governments.

The Fed's Policy Tools

The Federal Reserve System has many responsibilities, but we'll examine its single most important one: regulating the amount of money floating around in the United States. How does the Fed control the money supply? It does so by adjusting the reserves of the banking system. It is also by adjusting the reserves of the banking system and by standing ready to make loans to banks that the Fed is able to prevent banking panics and bank failures. The Fed uses three main policy tools to achieve its objectives:

- Required reserve ratios
- Discount rate
- Open market operations

Required Reserve Ratios   All depository institutions in the United States are required to hold a minimum percentage of deposits as reserves. This minimum percentage is known as a *required reserve ratio*. The Fed determines a required reserve ratio for each type of deposit. Table 31.1 shows the ratios in force at the end of 1994.

By increasing required reserve ratios, the Fed can create a shortage of reserves for the banking system and decrease bank lending. A decrease in lending decreases the money supply by a process similar to that described in Chapter 30 (see pp. 749–752). We'll look at this process later in this chapter.

Although changes in required reserve ratios can be used to influence the money supply, the Fed only rarely uses this policy tool. That is, the Fed does not often *change* required reserve ratios as an active tool to *change* the money supply.

TABLE 31.1

Required Reserve Ratios

Type of deposit	Minimum required reserves (percentage of deposits)
Checking and saving deposits: $0–$54 million	3
Checking and saving deposits: more than $54 million	10
Time deposits	0

Source: Federal Reserve Bulletin (May 1995).

Discount Rate   The **discount rate** is the interest rate at which the Fed stands ready to lend reserves to commercial banks. A change in the discount rate is proposed to the FOMC by the Board of Directors of at least one of the 12 Federal Reserve banks and is approved by the Board of Governors. A rise in the discount rate makes it more costly for banks to borrow reserves from the Fed and encourages them to cut back their lending, which reduces the money supply. A fall in the discount rate makes it less costly for banks to borrow reserves from the Fed and stimulates bank lending, which increases the money supply.

The discount rate is most effective when the banking system has a shortage of reserves and the commercial banks are borrowing from the Fed. If the banks have a surplus of reserves and are not borrowing from the Fed, the level of the discount rate has no immediate impact on bank profits so a change in the discount rate has a limited effect on bank lending and the quantity of money. But the Fed can determine whether or not the banking system has a shortage or surplus of reserves. It does so by using its third monetary policy tool, open market operations.

Open Market Operations   An **open market operation** is the purchase or sale of government securities—U.S. Treasury bills and bonds—by the Federal Reserve System in the open market. The term "open market" refers to commercial banks and the general public but not the federal government. Thus when the Fed conducts an open market operation, it makes a transaction with a bank or some other business but it does not transact with the federal government.

Open market operations influence the money supply. We'll study the details of this influence in the next section. Briefly, when the Fed sells government securities, it receives payment with bank deposits and bank reserves, which creates tighter monetary and credit conditions. With lower reserves, the banks cut their lending, and the money supply decreases. When the Fed buys government securities, it pays for them with bank deposits and bank reserves, which creates looser monetary and credit conditions. With extra reserves, the banks increase their lending, and the money supply increases.

The structure and policy tools of the Federal Reserve System are summarized in Fig. 31.2. The most actively used of the Fed's policy tools is the open market operation. To understand how open market operations work, we need to know about the Fed's balance sheet.

FIGURE 31.2

FIGURE 31.2
The Structure of the Fed

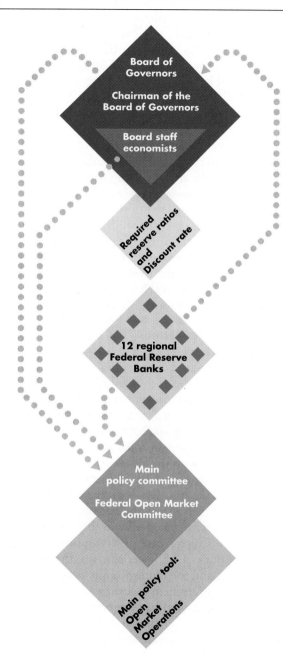

The Board of Governors sets required reserve ratios and, on the proposal of the 12 Federal Reserve banks, sets the discount rate. The Board of Governors and presidents of the regional Federal Reserve banks sit on the FOMC to determine open market operations.

The Fed's Balance Sheet

The balance sheet of the Federal Reserve System for December 1994 is set out in Table 31.2. The assets on the left side are what the Fed owns, and the liabilities on the right side are what it owes. The Fed's four main assets are:

1. Gold and foreign exchange
2. U.S. government securities
3. Loans to banks
4. Other assets

The Fed's holdings of gold and foreign exchange are its international reserves. Most of the Fed's foreign exchange consists of deposits by the Fed at other central banks. The Fed's holdings of U.S. government securities are the backing for the money that the Fed creates. Loans to banks are loans of reserves on which the Fed charges the banks the discount rate.

The Fed's two main liabilities are:

1. Federal Reserve notes in circulation
2. Banks' deposits

The Federal Reserve notes in circulation are the bank notes that we use in our daily transactions. Some of these notes are in circulation with the public; others are in the tills and vaults of banks and other financial institutions. Banks' deposits are the deposits of commercial banks, which are part of the reserves of those banks.

You might be wondering why Federal Reserve notes are considered a liability of the Fed. When

TABLE 31.2
The Fed's Balance Sheet, December 1994

Assets (billions of dollars)		Liabilities (billions of dollars)	
Gold and foreign exchange	19.3	Federal Reserve notes in circulation	381.5
U.S. government securities	374.1		
Loans to banks	0.2	Banks' deposits	30.8
Other assets (net)	18.7		
Total assets	412.3	Monetary base	412.3

Source: *Federal Reserve Bulletin* (May 1995).

notes were invented, they gave their owner a claim on the gold reserves of the issuing bank. Such notes were *convertible paper money*. The holder of such a note could convert the note on demand into gold (or some other commodity such as silver) at a guaranteed price. Thus when a bank issued a note, it was holding itself liable to convert that note into gold or silver. Modern bank notes are nonconvertible. A *nonconvertible note* is a bank note that is not convertible into any commodity and that obtains its value by government fiat—hence the term fiat money. Such bank notes are considered the legal liability of the bank that issues them, but they are backed not by commodity reserves but by holdings of securities and loans. Federal Reserve notes are backed by the Fed's holdings of U.S. government securities.

The Fed's liabilities, together with coins in circulation (coins are issued by the Treasury and are not liabilities of the Fed), make up the monetary base. That is, the **monetary base** is the sum of Federal Reserve notes, coins, and banks' deposits at the Fed. The monetary base is so called because it acts like a base that supports the nation's money supply. The larger the monetary base, the greater is the quantity of money.

R E V I E W

- The Federal Reserve System is the central bank of the United States.
- A central bank conducts a nation's monetary policy and supervises the financial system.
- The Fed's policy tools are required reserve ratios, the discount rate, and open market operations.
- Required reserve ratios are set by the Board of Governors.
- The discount rate is set by the Board of Governors on the recommendation of the regional federal reserve banks.
- Open market operations are determined by the Federal Open Market Committee (FOMC).

Next, we're going to study the connection between the monetary base and the quantity of money. We'll first see how the Fed changes the monetary base, and then we'll see how the monetary base influences the quantity of money.

Controlling the Money Supply

THE FED CONSTANTLY MONITORS AND ADJUSTS the quantity of money in the economy. To change the quantity of money, the Fed can use any of its three tools: required reserve ratios, discount rate, and open market operations. Required reserve ratios are changed infrequently. The discount rate and open market operations are used more frequently. Let's see how these tools work.

How Required Reserve Ratios Work

When the Fed *increases* the required reserve ratio, the banks must hold more reserves. To increase their reserves, the banks must *decrease* their lending, and the quantity of money *decreases*. When the Fed *decreases* the required reserve ratio, the banks may hold less reserves. To decrease their reserves, the banks *increase* their lending, and the quantity of money *increases*.

How the Discount Rate Works

When the Fed *increases* the discount rate, the banks must pay a higher price for any reserves that they borrow from the Fed. Faced with higher cost of reserves, the banks try to get by with smaller reserves. But with a given required reserve ratio, the banks must also *decrease* their lending to decrease their reserves. So the quantity of money *decreases*. When the Fed *decreases* the discount rate, the banks pay a lower price for any reserves that they borrow from the Fed. Faced with lower cost of reserves, the banks are willing to borrow more reserves and *increase* their lending. So the quantity of money *increases*.

How an Open Market Operation Works

When the Fed *buys* securities in an open market operation, the monetary base *increases*, banks *increase* their lending, and the quantity of money *increases*. When the Fed *sells* securities in an open market operation, the monetary base *decreases*, banks *decrease* their lending, and the quantity of money *decreases*. Open market operations are used more frequently than the other two tools and are the most complex in their operation. So we'll study this tool in greater detail than the other two.

When the Fed conducts an open market operation, the reserves of the banking system (a component of the monetary base) change. To see why this outcome occurs, we'll trace the effects of an open market operation both when the Fed *buys* securities and when it *sells* securities.

The Fed Buys Securities   Suppose the Fed buys $100 million of U.S. government securities in the open market. There are two cases to consider: when the Fed buys from a commercial bank and when it buys from the public (a person or business that is not a commercial bank). The outcome is essentially the same in either case, but you need to be convinced of this fact, so we'll study the two cases, starting with the simplest case, in which the Fed buys from a commercial bank.

Buy from Commercial Bank   When the Fed buys $100 million of securities from the Manhattan Commercial Bank, two things happen:

1. The Manhattan Commercial Bank has $100 million less securities, and the Fed has $100 million more securities.

2. The Fed pays for the securities by crediting the Manhattan Commercial Bank's deposit account at the Fed with $100 million.

Figure 31.3(a) shows the effects of these actions on the balance sheets of the Fed and the Manhattan Commercial Bank. Ownership of the securities passes from the commercial bank to the Fed, so the bank's assets decrease by $100 million and the Fed's assets increase by $100 million, as shown by the blue arrow running from the Manhattan Commercial Bank to the Fed. The Fed pays for the securities by crediting the Manhattan Commercial Bank's deposit account— its reserves—at the Fed with $100 million, as shown by the green arrow running from the Fed to the Manhattan Commercial Bank. This action increases the monetary base and increases the reserves of the banking system.

The Fed's assets increase by $100 million, and its liabilities also increase by $100 million. The commercial bank's total assets remain constant, but their composition changes. Its holdings of government securities decrease by $100 million, and its deposits at the Fed increase by $100 million. So the bank has additional reserves, which it can use to make loans.

FIGURE   31.3

The Fed Buys Securities in the Open Market

(a) The Fed buys securities from a commercial bank

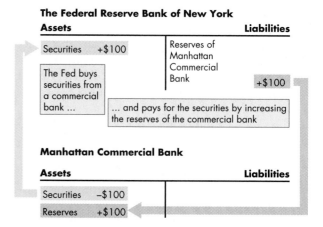

(b) The Fed buys securities from the public

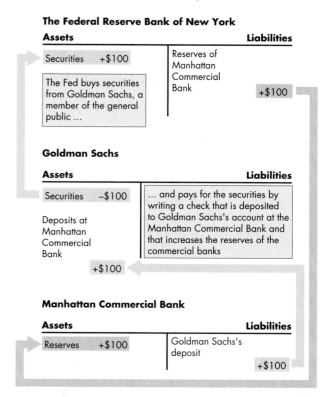

We've just seen that when the Fed buys government securities from a bank, the bank's reserves increase. But what happens if the Fed buys government securities from the public—say from Goldman Sachs, a financial services company?

Buy from Public When the Fed buys $100 million of securities from Goldman Sachs, three things happen:

1. Goldman Sachs has $100 million less securities, and the Fed has $100 million more securities.
2. The Fed pays for the securities with a check for $100 million drawn on itself, which Goldman Sachs deposits in its account at the Manhattan Commercial Bank.
3. The Manhattan Commercial Bank collects payment of this check from the Fed, and $100 million is deposited in Manhattan's deposit account at the Fed.

Figure 31.3(b) shows the effects of these actions on the balance sheets of the Fed, Goldman Sachs, and the Manhattan Commercial Bank. Ownership of the securities passes from Goldman Sachs to the Fed, so Goldman Sachs's assets decrease by $100 million and the Fed's assets increase by $100 million, as shown by the blue arrow running from Goldman Sachs to the Fed. The Fed pays for the securities with a check payable to Goldman Sachs, which it deposits in the Manhattan Commercial Bank. This payment increases Goldman Sachs's deposit at the Manhattan Commercial Bank by $100 million, as shown by the green arrow running from the Fed to Manhattan Commercial Bank. It also increases Manhattan's reserves by $100 million, as shown by the red arrow running from the Manhattan Commercial Bank to Goldman Sachs. Just as when the Fed buys from a bank, this action increases the monetary base and increases the reserves of the banking system.

Again, the Fed's assets increase by $100 million, and its liabilities also increase by $100 million. Goldman Sachs has the same total assets as before, but their composition has changed. It now has more money and fewer securities. The Manhattan Commercial Bank's total assets increase, and so do its liabilities. Its deposits at the Fed—its reserves—increase by $100 million, and its deposit liability to Goldman Sachs increases by $100 million. Because its reserves have increased by the same amount as its deposits, the bank has excess reserves, which it can use to make loans.

We've now studied what happens when the Fed buys government securities from either a bank or the public. Let's reinforce what we've learned by examining the reverse case, in which the Fed *sells* securities.

The Fed Sells Securities Suppose the Fed sells $100 million of U.S. government securities in the open market. Again, there are two cases to consider: when the Fed sells to a commercial bank and when it sells to the public.

Sell to Commercial Bank When the Fed sells $100 million of securities to the Manhattan Commercial Bank, two things happen:

1. The Manhattan Commercial Bank has $100 million more securities, and the Fed has $100 million less securities.
2. The Manhattan Commercial Bank pays for the securities by using its deposit account at the Fed.

Figure 31.4(a) shows the effects of these actions on the balance sheets of the Fed and the Manhattan Commercial Bank. Ownership of the securities passes from the Fed to the commercial bank, so the bank's assets increase by $100 million and the Fed's assets decrease by $100 million—as shown by the blue arrow running from the Fed to the Manhattan Commercial Bank. The Manhattan Commercial Bank pays for the securities by using its deposit account—its reserves—at the Fed. These reserves fall by $100 million, as shown by the green arrow running from the Manhattan Commercial Bank to the Fed. This action decreases the monetary base and decreases the reserves of the banking system.

The Fed's assets decrease by $100 million and its liabilities also decrease by $100 million. The commercial bank's total assets remain constant, but their composition changes. Its deposits at the Fed decrease by $100 million, and its holdings of government securities increase by $100 million. So the bank has fewer reserves and cuts back on the amount of loans.

Sell to Public When the Fed sells $100 million of securities to Goldman Sachs, three things happen:

1. Goldman Sachs has $100 million more securities, and the Fed has $100 million fewer securities.
2. Goldman Sachs pays for the securities with a check for $100 million drawn on its account at the Manhattan Commercial Bank.
3. The Manhattan Commercial Bank pays this check from its reserves at the Fed.

FIGURE 31.4

The Fed Sells Securities in the Open Market

(a) The Fed sells securities to a commercial bank

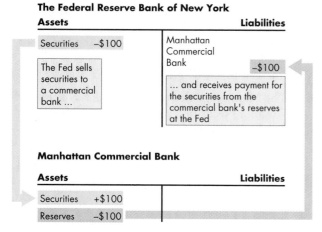

(b) The Fed sells securities to the public

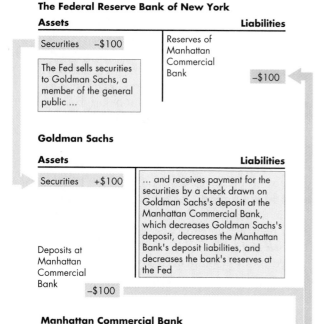

Figure 31.4(b) shows the effects of these actions on the balance sheets of the Fed, Goldman Sachs, and the Manhattan Commercial Bank. Ownership of the securities passes from the Fed to Goldman Sachs, so Goldman Sachs's assets increase by $100 million and the Fed's assets decrease by $100 million, as shown by the blue arrow running from the Fed to Goldman Sachs. Goldman Sachs pays for the securities with a check drawn on its account at the Manhattan Commercial Bank. This payment decreases Goldman Sachs's deposit at the Manhattan Commercial Bank by $100 million, as shown by the red arrow running from Goldman Sachs to the Manhattan Commercial Bank. It also decreases Manhattan's reserves by $100 million, as shown by the green arrow running from the Manhattan Commercial Bank to the Fed. Just as when the Fed sells to a bank, this action decreases the monetary base and decreases the reserves of the banking system.

Again, the Fed's assets decrease by $100 million, and its liabilities also decrease by $100 million. Goldman Sachs has the same total assets as before, but their composition has changed. It now has a smaller deposit and more securities. The Manhattan Commercial bank's total assets decrease, and so do its liabilities. Its deposits at the Fed—its reserves—decrease by $100 million, and its deposit liability to Goldman Sachs decreases by $100 million. Because its reserves have decreased by the same amount as its deposits, the bank has a shortage of reserves, and it must decrease its loans.

The effects of an open market operation on the balance sheets of the Fed and the banks that we've just described are not the end of the story—they are just the beginning. With an increase in their reserves, the banks are able to make more loans, which increases the quantity of money. With a decrease in reserves, the banks must cut back on their loans, which decreases the quantity of money.

A change in the quantity of money that results from an open market operation has ripple effects through the economy. First, it has a multiplier effect on the quantity of money. Second, it changes interest rates. Third, it changes aggregate expenditure and real GDP. We are going to study these ripple effects in the rest of this chapter. We begin by studying the multiplier effect of an open market operation on the quantity of money. To do so, we build on the link between bank reserves and bank deposits that you studied in Chapter 30. But here we examine a related broader link between the monetary base and the quantity of money.

Monetary Base and Bank Reserves

We've defined the *monetary base* as the sum of Federal Reserve notes, coins, and banks' deposits at the Fed. The monetary base is held either by banks as *reserves* or outside the banks as currency in circulation. When the monetary base increases, both bank reserves and currency in circulation increase. But only the increase in bank reserves can be used by banks to make loans and create additional money. An increase in currency held outside the banks is called a **currency drain**. A currency drain reduces the amount of additional money that can be created from a given increase in the monetary base.

The **money multiplier** is the amount by which a change in the monetary base is multiplied to determine the resulting change in the quantity of money. It is related to, but differs from, the deposits multiplier that we studied in Chapter 30. The *deposits multiplier* is the amount by which a change in bank reserves is multiplied to determine the change in the bank deposits.

Let's now look at the money multiplier.

The Multiplier Effect of an Open Market Operation

Let's work out the multiplier effect of an open market operation in which the Fed buys securities from the banks. In this case, although the open market operation increases the banks' reserves, it has no immediate effect on the quantity of money. The banks are holding more reserves and fewer securities, and they have excess reserves. When the banks have excess reserves, the sequence of events shown in Fig. 31.5 takes place.

FIGURE 31.5

A Round in the Multiplier Process Following an Open Market Operation

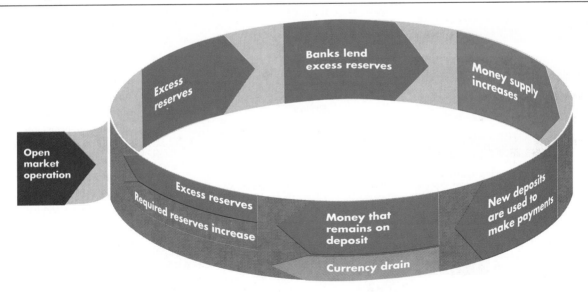

An open market operation increases bank reserves and creates excess reserves. Banks lend the excess reserves, and new loans are used to make payments. Households and firms receiving payments keep some of the receipts in the form of currency—a currency drain—and place the rest on deposit in banks. The increase in bank deposits increases banks' reserves but also increases banks' required reserves. Required reserves increase by less than actual reserves, so the banks still have some excess reserves, though less than before. The process repeats until excess reserves have been eliminated.

These events are as follows:

- Banks lend excess reserves.
- Money supply increases.
- New deposits are used to make payments.
- Some of the new money remains on deposit in banks.
- Some of new money is held as currency—a *currency drain*.
- Banks' required reserves increase.
- Excess reserves decrease, but remain positive.

The sequence repeats in a series of rounds, but each round begins with a smaller quantity of excess reserves than did the previous one. The process continues until excess reserves have finally been eliminated.

Figure 31.6 keeps track of the magnitudes of the increases in reserves, loans, deposits, currency, and money that results from an open market operation of $100,000. In this figure, the *currency drain* is 33.33 percent and the *required reserve ratio* is 10 percent. These numbers are assumed to keep the arithmetic simple.

The Fed buys $100,000 of securities from the banks. The banks' reserves increase by this amount, but deposits do not change. The banks have excess reserves of $100,000, and they lend those reserves. When the banks lend $100,000 of excess reserves, $66,667 remains in the banks as deposits and $33,333 drains off and is held outside the banks as currency. The quantity of money has now increased by $100,000—the increase in deposits plus the increase in currency holdings.

The increased bank deposits of $66,667 generates an increase in required reserves of 10 percent of that amount, which is $6,667. Actual reserves have

---

FIGURE 31.6

The Multiplier Effect of an Open Market Operation

The Sequence

Open Market Operation $100,000

Loan $100,000

Currency $33,333 | Deposit $66,667

Reserve $6,667 | Loan $60,000

Currency $20,000 | Deposit $40,000

Reserve $4,000 | Loan $36,000

Currency $12,000 | Deposit $24,000

and so on ...

The Running Tally

	Reserves	Deposits	Currency	Money
		$66,667	$33,333	$100,000
	$6,667	$106,667	$53,333	$160,000
	$10,667	$130,667	$65,333	$196,000
	•	•	•	•
	•	•	•	•
	▼	▼	▼	▼
	$16,667	$166,667	$83,333	$250,000

When the Fed provides the banks with $100,000 of additional reserves in an open market operation, the banks lend those reserves. Of the amount lent, $33,333 (33.33 percent) leaves the banks in a currency drain and $66,667 remains on deposit. With additional deposits, required reserves increase by $6,667 (10 percent required reserve ratio) and the banks lend $60,000. Of this amount, $20,000 leaves the banks in a currency drain and $40,000 remains on deposit. The process repeats until the banks have created enough deposits to eliminate their excess reserves. An additional $100,000 of reserves creates $250,000 of money.

FIGURE 31.7

The Cumulative Effects of an Open Market Operation

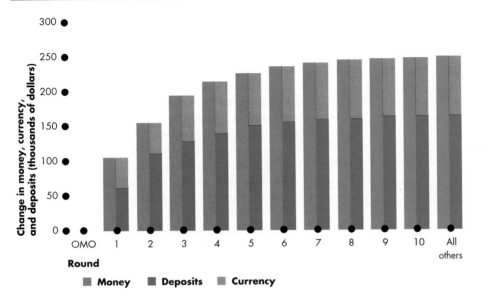

A $100,000 open market operation (OMO) creates excess reserves. When loans are made with these reserves, bank deposits and currency holdings increase. Each time new loans are made, part of the loan drains out from the banks and is held as currency, and part of the loan stays in the banking system in the form of additional deposits and additional reserves. Banks continue to increase their lending until excess reserves have been eliminated. The magnitude of the ultimate increase in the money supply is determined by the money multiplier.

increased by the same amount as the increase in deposits—$66,667. So the banks now have excess reserves of $60,000. At this stage we have gone around the circle shown in Fig. 31.5 once. The process we've just described repeats but begins with excess reserves of $60,000. Figure 31.6 shows the next two rounds. At the end of the process, the quantity of money has increased by $250,000.

Figure 31.7 illustrates the accumulated increase in the quantity of money and in its components—bank deposits and currency. When the open market operation takes place (labeled OMO in the figure), there is no initial change in either the quantity of money or its components. Then, after the first round of bank lending, the quantity of money increases by $100,000—the size of the open market operation. In successive rounds, the quantity of money and its components continue to increase but by successively smaller amounts until, after 10 rounds, the quantities of currency and deposits and their sum, the quantity of money, have almost reached the values to which they are ultimately heading.

You've seen how an open market purchase increases the quantity of money. An open market *sale* works similarly but it *decreases* the quantity of money.

R E V I E W

- When the Fed buys securities in the open market, the monetary base and bank reserves increase and an expansion of bank lending increases the quantity of money.
- When the Fed sells securities in the open market, the monetary base and bank reserves decrease and a contraction of bank lending decreases the quantity of money.

The Fed's objective in taking actions that influence the quantity of money is not simply to affect the money supply for its own sake. It is to influence the course of the economy. But the Fed's influence on aggregate demand is indirect. The Fed's immediate objective is to move interest rates up or down. And the Fed achieves this objective by changing the quantity of money. To work out the effects of the Fed's actions on interest rates, we need to work out how and why interest rates change when the quantity of money changes. We'll discover the answer to these questions by first studying the demand for money.

The Demand for Money

THE AMOUNT OF MONEY WE RECEIVE EACH WEEK in payment for our labor is income—a flow. The amount of money that we hold in our wallet or in a deposit account at the bank is an inventory—a stock. There is no limit to how much income—or flow— we would like to receive each week. But there is a limit to how big an inventory of money each of us would like to hold, on the average.

The Influences on Money Holding

The quantity of money that people choose to hold depends on four main factors:

- The price level
- The interest rate
- Real GDP
- Financial innovation

Let's look at each of them.

The Price Level   The quantity of money measured in current dollars is called the quantity of *nominal money*. The quantity of nominal money demanded is proportional to the price level, other things remaining the same. That is, if the price level (GDP deflator) increases by 10 percent, people will want to hold 10 percent more nominal money than before, other things being equal. What matters is not the number of dollars that you hold but their buying power. If you hold $20 to buy your weekly movies and soda, you will increase your money holding to $22 dollars if the prices of movies and soda—and your wage rate—increase by 10 percent.

The quantity of money measured in constant dollars (for example, in 1987 dollars) is called *real money*. Real money is equal to nominal money divided by the price level. The quantity of real money demanded is independent of the price level. In the above example you held $20, on the average, at the original price level. When the price level increased by 10 percent, you increased your average cash holding by 10 percent, keeping your *real* cash holding constant. Your $22 dollars at the new price level is the same quantity of *real money* as your $20 dollars at the original price level.

The Interest Rate   A fundamental principle of economics is that as the opportunity cost of something increases, people try to find substitutes for it. Money is no exception. The higher the opportunity cost of holding money, other things being equal, the lower is the quantity of real money demanded. But what is the opportunity cost of holding money? It is the interest rate. To see why, recall that the opportunity cost of any activity is the value of the best alternative forgone. The alternative to holding money is holding an interest-earning financial asset such as a savings bond or Treasury bill. By holding money instead, you forgo the interest that you otherwise would have received. This forgone interest is the opportunity cost of holding money.

Money loses value because of inflation. Why isn't the inflation rate part of the cost of holding money? It is: Other things being equal, the higher the expected inflation rate, the higher are interest rates and the higher, therefore, is the opportunity cost of holding money. (The forces that make interest rates change to reflect changes in the expected inflation rate are described in Chapter 32 on pp. 814–816.)

Real GDP   The quantity of money that households and firms plan to hold depends on the amount they are spending, and the quantity of money demanded in the economy as a whole depends on aggregate expenditure—real GDP.

Again, suppose that you hold an average of $20 to finance your weekly purchases of movies and soda. Now imagine that the prices of these goods and of all other goods remain constant but that your income increases. As a consequence you now spend more, and you also keep a larger amount of money on hand to finance your higher volume of expenditure.

Financial Innovation   Several innovations by financial institutions have changed the quantity of money held. The major ones are the widespread use of:

1. Daily interest checking deposits
2. Automatic transfers between checking and savings deposits
3. Automatic teller machines
4. Credit cards

These innovations have occurred because of the development of low-cost computing power. Without computers it would be too costly to calculate the interest owing on daily balances, to switch funds from one account to another automatically, to get cash at midnight on a street corner, or to shuffle sales slips and keep credit card records.

The Demand for Money Curve

The *demand for money* is the relationship between the quantity of real money demanded and the interest rate, when all other influences on the amount of money that people wish to hold remain the same. Figure 31.8 shows a demand for money curve, *MD*. When the interest rate rises, everything else remaining the same, the opportunity cost of holding money rises and the quantity of money demanded decreases—there is a movement along the demand for money curve. Similarly, when the interest rate falls, the opportunity cost of holding money falls and the quantity of money demanded increases—there is a downward movement along the demand for money curve.

Shifts in the Demand Curve for Real Money

A change in real GDP or financial innovation changes the demand for money and shifts the demand curve for real money. Figure 31.9 illustrates the change in the demand for money. A decrease in real GDP decreases the demand for money and shifts the demand curve leftward from MD_0 to MD_1. An increase in real GDP has the opposite effect. It increases the demand for money and shifts the demand curve rightward from MD_0 to MD_2.

The influence of financial innovation on the demand for money curve is more complicated. It might increase the demand for some types of deposits, decrease the demand for others, and decrease the demand for currency. We'll look at the effects of financial innovation by studying the demand for money in the United States.

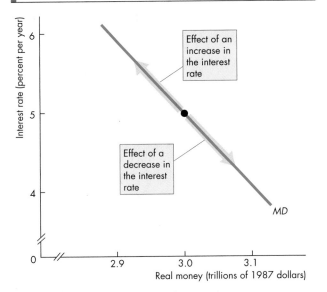

FIGURE 31.8
The Demand for Money

The demand for money curve, *MD*, shows the relationship between the quantity of money that people plan to hold and the interest rate, other things remaining the same. The interest rate is the opportunity cost of holding money. A change in the interest rate brings a movement along the demand curve.

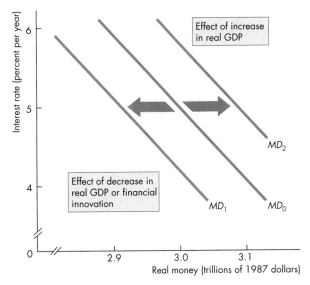

FIGURE 31.9
Changes in the Demand for Money

A decrease in real GDP decreases the demand for money and shifts the demand curve leftward from MD_0 to MD_1. An increase in real GDP increases the demand for money and shifts the demand curve rightward from MD_0 to MD_2. Financial innovation generally decreases the demand for money.

The Demand for Money in the United States

Figure 31.10 shows the relationship between the interest rate and the quantity of real money demanded in the United States between 1970 and 1994. Each dot shows the interest rate and the amount of real money held in a given year. In 1970, the demand for M1 (shown in part a) was MD_{70}. During the early 1970s, the evolution of new financial products decreased the demand for M1 (currency and checking deposits) and this financial innovation shifted the demand for M1 curve leftward to MD_{76}. But over the years, real GDP growth increases the demand for M1

and by 1994 the demand for M1 curve had shifted rightward to MD_{94}.

In 1970, the demand for M2 (shown in part b) was MD_{70}. The financial innovation that decreased the demand for M1 during the period did not decrease demand for M2. The reason is that most of the new financial products were M2 deposits. So from 1970 through 1989, the demand for M2 increased and the demand for M2 curve shifted rightward to MD_{89}. But in the period after 1989, the main innovations were in financial products that compete with deposits of all kinds. So the demand for M2 decreased and the demand for M2 curve shifted leftward to MD_{94}.

FIGURE 31.10

The Demand for Money in United States

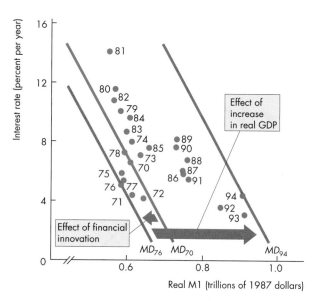

(a) M1 demand

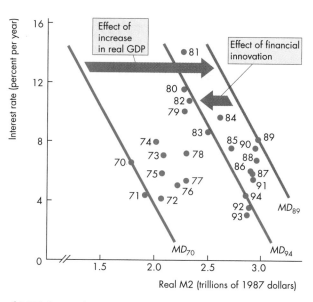

(b) M2 demand

The dots show the quantity of real money and the interest rate in each year between 1970 and 1994. In 1970, the demand for M1 was MD_{70} in part (a). The demand for M1 decreased during the early 1970s because of financial innovation and the demand curve shifted leftward to MD_{76}. But the demand for M1 has increased because of real GDP growth and by 1994, the

demand curve had shifted rightward to MD_{94}. In 1970, the demand for M2 curve was MD_{70} in part (b). The growth of real GDP increased the demand for M2 and by 1989 the demand curve had shifted rightward to MD_{89}. During the 1990s, new substitutes for M2 decreased the demand for M2 and the demand curve shifted leftward to MD_{94}.

Source: Economic Report of the President, 1994, and the author's calculations and assumptions.

REVIEW

- The demand for money curve shows the relationship between the quantity of real money demanded and the interest rate with all other influences on money holding unchanged.
- An increase in the interest rate decreases the quantity of money demanded and brings a movement along the demand curve for real money.
- Other influences on the quantity of real money demanded are real GDP and financial innovation.
- An increase in real GDP increases the demand for money and shifts the demand curve rightward.
- Financial innovations have decreased the demand for M1. These innovations initially increased the demand for M2, but later the demand for M2 also decreased.

We now know what determines the demand for money. And we've seen that a key factor is the interest rate—the opportunity cost of holding money. But what determines the interest rate? Let's find out.

Interest Rate Determination

AN INTEREST RATE IS THE PERCENTAGE YIELD ON a financial security such as a *bond* or a *stock*. The higher the price of a financial asset, other things remaining the same, the lower is the interest rate. An example will make this relationship clear. Suppose the Federal government sells a bond that promises to pay $10 a year. If the price of the bond is $100, the interest rate is 10 percent per year—$10 is 10 percent of $100. If the price of the bond is $50, the interest rate is 20 percent—$10 is 20 percent of $50. And if the price of the bond is $200, the interest rate is 5 percent—$10 is 5 percent of $200.

You've just seen the link between the price of a bond and the interest rate. People divide their wealth between bonds (and other interest-bearing financial assets) and money, and the amount they hold as money depends on the interest rate. We can study the forces that determine the interest rate either in the market for bonds or the market for money. Because the Fed can influence the *supply* of money, we focus on the market for money.

Money Market Equilibrium

The interest rate is determined by the supply of and the demand for money. The quantity of money supplied is determined by the actions of the banking system and the Fed. On any given day, the supply of money is a fixed quantity. The *real* quantity of money supplied is equal to the nominal quantity supplied divided by the price level. At a given moment in time, there is a particular price level, and so the quantity of real money supplied is also a fixed amount. The supply curve of real money is shown in Fig. 31.11 as the vertical line labeled *MS*. The quantity of real money supplied is $3.0 trillion.

The demand for money depends on the price level, real GDP, and the interest rate. On any given day, the price level and real GDP are fixed and

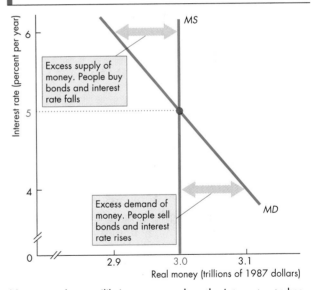

FIGURE 31.11
Money Market Equilibrium

Money market equilibrium occurs when the interest rate has adjusted to make the quantity of money demanded equal to the quantity supplied. Here, equilibrium occurs at an interest rate of 5 percent. At interest rates above 5 percent, the quantity of money demanded is less than the quantity supplied, so people buy bonds and the interest rate falls. At interest rates below 5 percent, the quantity of real money demanded exceeds the quantity supplied, so people sell bonds and the interest rate rises. Only at 5 percent is the quantity of real money in existence willingly held.

changes in the quantity of money demanded depend only on the interest rate. Figure 31.11 shows a demand for money curve, *MD*, for a given real GDP and price level.

Equilibrium   When the quantity of money supplied equals the quantity of money demanded, the money market is in equilibrium. Figure 31.11 illustrates equilibrium in the money market. Equilibrium is achieved by changes in the interest rate. If the interest rate is too high, people demand a smaller quantity of money than the quantity supplied. They are holding too much money. In this situation they try to get rid of money by buying bonds. As they do so, the price of a bond rises and the interest rate falls. Conversely, if the interest rate is too low, people demand a larger quantity of money than the quantity supplied. They are holding too little money. In this situation they try to get more money by selling bonds. As they do so, the price of a bond falls and the interest rate rises. Only when the interest rate is at the level at which people are holding the quantity of money supplied do they willingly hold the money and take no actions that change the interest rate.

Changing the Interest Rate

Suppose that the economy is overheating and the Fed fears inflation. It decides to take action to decrease aggregate demand and spending. To do so, it wants to raise interest rates and discourage borrowing and expenditure on goods and services. What does the Fed do?

The Fed sells securities in the open market. As it does so, it mops up bank reserves and induces the banks to cut their lending. The banks make a smaller quantity of new loans each day until the stock of loans outstanding has fallen to a level that is consistent with the new lower level of reserves. The money supply decreases.

Suppose that the Fed undertakes open market operations on a sufficiently large scale to decrease the money supply from $3.0 trillion to $2.9 trillion. As a consequence, the supply curve of real money shifts leftward, as shown in Figure 31.12, from *MS*₀ to *MS*₁.

The demand for money is shown by *MD*. With an interest rate of 5 percent, and with $2.9 trillion of money in the economy, firms and households are now holding less money than they wish to hold. They attempt to increase their money holding by selling financial assets. As they do so, the prices of bonds

FIGURE   31.12

Interest Rate Changes

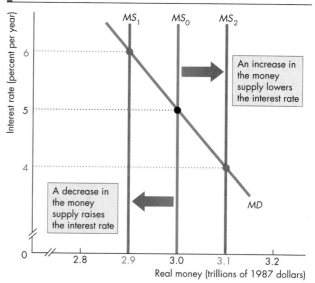

An open market sale of securities shifts the money supply curve leftward to *MS*₁ and the interest rate rises to 6 percent. An open market purchase of securities shifts the money supply curve rightward to *MS*₂ and the interest rate falls to 4 percent.

and stocks fall and the interest rate rises. When the interest rate has increased to 6 percent, people are willing to hold the smaller $2.9 trillion stock of money that the Fed and the banks have created.

Conversely, suppose that the Fed fears recession and decides to stimulate spending by increasing the money supply. If the Fed increases the real money supply to $3.1 trillion, the supply of money curve shifts rightward from *MS*₀ to *MS*₂. Equilibrium occurs when the interest rate has fallen to 4 percent.

R E V I E W

■ Short-term interest rates are determined by the demand for and supply of money. When the quantity of money demanded equals the quantity supplied, the interest rate is at its equilibrium level.

■ To increase the interest rate, the Fed sells securities and decreases the money supply. To decrease the interest rate, the Fed buys securities and increases the money supply.

Monetary Policy

YOU HAVE NOW LEARNED A GREAT DEAL ABOUT the Fed, the monetary policy actions it can take, and the effects of those actions on short-term interest rates. Most of the "secrets of the temple" have been revealed. But you are possibly thinking: All this sounds nice in theory, but does it really happen? Does the Fed actually do the things we've learned about in this chapter? Indeed, it does happen, sometimes with dramatic effect.

To see the Fed in action, we'll do two things. First, we'll look at the fluctuations in short-term interest rates in the United States since 1970 and see how the Fed has influenced those fluctuations. Second, we'll focus on two episodes in the life of the Fed, one from the turbulent years of the early 1980s when the Fed was struggling to eradicate a stubborn inflation and the other from the period since the stock market crash of 1987 through which the Fed as tried to keep inflation in check without killing economic growth.

The Fed in Action

You've seen that the immediate effect of the Fed's actions is a change in the short-term interest rate. Figure 31.13 shows the course of four short-term interest rates since 1970:

1. The 3-month Treasury bill rate, which is the interest rate paid by the federal government on 3-month loans

2. The 6-month commercial bill rate, which is the interest rate paid by large corporations on 6-month loans

3. The discount rate, which is the interest rate charged to banks by the Fed when the banks borrow reserves

4. The federal funds rate, which is the interest rate that the banks charge each other on overnight loans of reserves

Notice how closely these four interest rates move together. The interest rate that the Fed directly controls is the discount rate, and the rate that it closely

---

FIGURE 31.13

Short-Term Interest Rates

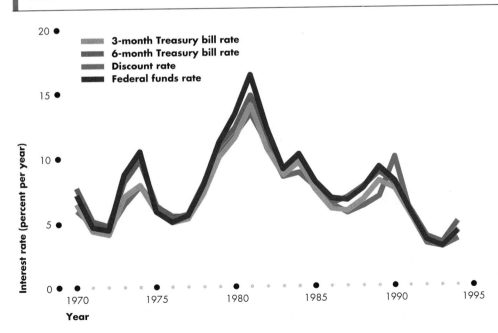

The Fed directly determines the discount rate (the rate at which the Fed lends reserves to banks) and closely monitors the federal funds rate (the rate at which banks lend reserves to each other). All short-term interest rates move up and down together, so the Fed influences all short-term rates such as the 3-month Treasury bill rate (the rate at which the federal government borrows in the short-term) and the 6-month commercial bill rate (the rate at which big corporations borrow in the short-term).

Source: *Economic Report of the President, 1995*, Table B72.

monitors is the federal funds rate, but because the short-term rates all move up and down together, the Fed is effectively able to influence all these rates.

Do short-term interest rates rise and fall in response to changes in the quantity of money, as the theory we've just studied predicts? Mostly they do, but not quite always. Figure 31.14 illustrates this connection. It shows the federal funds rate and a measure of the quantity of money. This measure of money is M2 expressed as a percentage of GDP. The reason for looking at M2 is that it is this measure of money that the Fed has placed greatest emphasis on. The reason for expressing M2 as a percentage of GDP is that we can see both the supply side and demand side effects on interest rates in a single measure. Interest rates rise if the quantity of money decreases. Interest rates also rise if the demand for money increases. But the demand for money increases if GDP increases. So the ratio of M2 to GDP rises either if the supply of money increases (M2 increases) or the demand for money decreases (GDP decreases).

You can see by studying Fig. 31.14 that between 1970 and 1990, the rises and falls in the interest rate are exactly matched by decreases and increases in the ratio of M2 to GDP. An increase in the supply of money relative to the demand for money brought a fall in the interest rate (1970–1972, 1974–1977, 1981–1986). A decrease in the supply of money relative to the demand for money brought a rise in the interest rate (1972–1974, 1977–1981, and 1986–1989).

You can also see in Fig. 31.14 that after 1990, the relationship between money and interest rates broke down. When the interest rate fell through 1993, the M2 to GDP ratio did not increase. The reason is that the demand for M2 fell because of the availability of some new substitute ways of holding wealth—bond and equity mutual funds. These funds were growing through the 1980s, but they grew more quickly during the 1990s, and their growth disturbed the traditional relationship between M2 and short-term interest rates. After 1990, the Fed began to pay less attention to M2—see *Reading Between the Lines* on pp. 790–791.

FIGURE 31.14

Money and Interest Rates

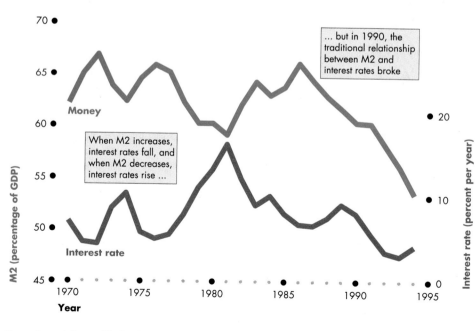

When the ratio of M2 to GDP (measured on the left scale) rises, either the supply of money increases or the demand for money decreases. The result, before 1990, is a fall in the federal funds rate (measured on the right scale). Similarly, when the ratio of M2 to GDP falls, either the supply of money has decreased or the demand for money has increased and (again before 1990) the federal funds rate rises. After 1990, the relationship between M2 and interest rates broke down because new substitutes for M2 decreased the demand for M2.

Source: *Economic Report of the President*, 1995, Tables B1, B68, and B72, and the author's calculations.

You've now seen that we can explain short-term interest rate fluctuations as arising from fluctuations in the supply of money relative to the demand for money. But this relationship doesn't tell us whether actions by the Fed or fluctuations in GDP brought the fluctuations in the M2 to GDP ratio. Do the Fed's own actions move interest rates around? Let's answer this question by looking at two episodes in the life of the Fed.

Paul Volcker's Fed At the start of Paul Volcker's term of office as chairman of the Fed, which began in August 1979, the United States was locked in the grips of double-digit inflation. Volcker ended that inflation. He did so by forcing interest rates sharply upward from 1979 through 1981. This increase in interest rates resulted from the Fed using open market operations and increases in the discount rate to keep the banks short of reserves, which in turn held back the growth in the supply of loans and of money relative to the growth in their demand.

As we saw in Fig. 31.12, to increase interest rates, the Fed has to cut the real money supply. In practice, because the economy is growing and because prices are rising, a *slowdown* in nominal money supply growth is enough to increase interest rates. It is not necessary to actually *cut* the nominal money supply.

When Volcker became chairman of the Fed, the money supply was growing at more than 8 percent a year. Volcker slowed down that money supply growth to 6.5 percent in 1981. As a result, interest rates increased. The Treasury bill rate—the rate at which the government borrows—increased from 10 percent to 14 percent. The rate at which big corporations borrow increased from 9 percent to 14 percent. Mortgage rates—the rates at which home buyers borrow—increased from 11 percent to 15 percent. The economy went into recession. The money supply growth slowdown and interest rate hike cut back the growth rate of aggregate demand. Real GDP fell, and the inflation rate slowed down.

Alan Greenspan's Fed Alan Greenspan became chairman of the Fed in August 1987. In the two preceding years, the money supply had grown at a rapid pace, interest rates had tumbled, and the stock market had boomed. Then, suddenly and with no warning, stock prices fell, bringing fears of economic calamity and recession. This was Alan Greenspan's first test as Fed chairman.

The Fed's immediate reaction to the new situation was to emphasize the flexibility and sensitivity of the financial system and to make reserves plentiful to avoid any fear of a banking crisis. But as the months passed, it became increasingly clear that the economy was not heading for any kind of a recession. Unemployment continued to fall, income growth continued to be strong, and the fears that emerged were of inflation, not recession.

Seeking to avoid a serious upturn in inflation, the Fed slowed money growth and, just as Paul Volcker had done eight years earlier, forced interest rates sharply upward. Open market operations were targeted toward creating a shortage of reserves in the banking system to slow down the growth rate of the money supply. As a consequence, during the year from May 1988 to May 1989, the M1 measure of the money supply was virtually constant and the M2 measure grew by only 2.4 percent, both down from growth rates of around 5 percent a year earlier and down from around 10 percent a year before the stock market crash. The slowdown in money supply growth had the effect implied by the model that you have been studying in this chapter. Interest rates increased throughout 1988. The interest rate on U.S. government 3-month Treasury bills increased from less than 6 percent a year at the start of 1988 to almost 9 percent a year by early 1989.

As 1989 advanced, concern about inflation remained, but renewed fears of recession returned as an increasing number of signs of a slowing economy emerged. Interest rates were gradually lowered, and the money supply was permitted to grow more quickly. By 1990, recession had become a reality. At first, the Fed's reaction was to adopt a neutral position, waiting for signs of recovery from an increase in investment and consumption expenditure. But as the months passed and recovery seemed elusive, the Fed eventually began to act vigorously to stimulate spending with a series of interest rate cuts. During 1991, interest rates declined by three percentage points as the Fed tried to encourage an increase in borrowing and spending.

By mid-1991, the recovery had begun, and real GDP expanded. By 1994, the expansion was brisk and the ever recurring fear of renewed inflation returned. Through that year, the Fed gradually tightened the anti-inflation screw. It increased interest rates almost every month of 1994. Its goal was to slow the expansion but without provoking a new recession.

Profiting by Predicting the Fed

Every day the Fed influences interest rates by its open market operations. By buying securities and increasing the money supply, the Fed can lower interest rates; by selling securities and lowering the money supply, the Fed can increase interest rates. Sometimes such actions are taken to offset other influences and keep interest rates steady. At other times the Fed moves interest rates up or down. The higher the interest rate, the lower is the price of a bond; the lower the interest rate, the higher is the price of a bond. Thus predicting interest rates is the same as predicting bond prices. Predicting that interest rates are going to fall is the same as predicting that bond prices are going to rise—a good time to buy bonds. Predicting that interest rates are going to rise is the same as predicting that bond prices are going to fall—a good time to sell bonds.

Because the Fed is the major player whose actions influence interest rates and bond prices, predicting the Fed is profitable and a good deal of effort goes into that activity. But people who anticipate that the Fed is about to increase the money supply buy bonds right away, pushing their prices upward and pushing interest rates downward *before* the Fed acts. Similarly, people who anticipate that the Fed is about to decrease the money supply sell bonds right away, pushing their prices downward and pushing interest rates upward before the Fed acts. In other words, bond prices and interest rates change as soon as the Fed's actions are foreseen. By the time the Fed actually takes its actions, if those actions are correctly foreseen, they have no effect. The effects occur in anticipation of the Fed's actions. Only changes in the money supply that are not foreseen change the interest rate at the time that those changes occur.

The Ripple Effects of Monetary Policy

You've now seen that the Fed's actions do indeed change interest rates and that the Fed tries to influence the course of the economy. These monetary policy measures work by changing aggregate demand. When the Fed slows money growth and pushes interest rates up, it decreases aggregate demand, which in turn slows both real GDP growth and inflation. When the Fed speeds money growth and lowers interest rates, it increases aggregate

demand, which in turn speeds real GDP growth and inflation. The mechanism through which aggregate demand changes involves several channels. Higher interest rates bring a decrease in consumption expenditure and investment. Tighter bank credit brings fewer loans and reinforces the effects of higher interest rates on consumption expenditure and investment.

Higher interest rates bring an increase in the exchange rate that makes U.S. exports more expensive and makes imports less costly. So net exports decrease. The decreases in consumption, investment, and net exports all combine to decrease aggregate demand, which in turn slows the gorwth rate of real GDP and the inflation rate. Schematically, the effects of the Fed's actions ripple through the economy in the following way:

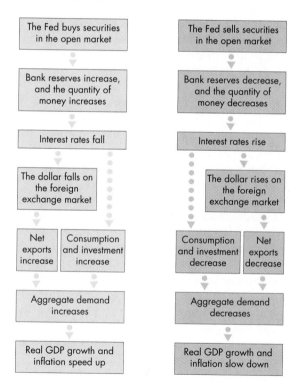

Interest Rates and the Business Cycle

You've seen the connection between the Fed's actions and interest rates in Fig. 31.14. What about the ripple effects that we've just described? Do they really occur? Do changes in interest rates ultimately influence the real GDP growth rate? Yes they do. You can see these effects in Fig. 31.15. The blue line in this

---

FIGURE 31.15

Interest Rates and Real GDP Growth

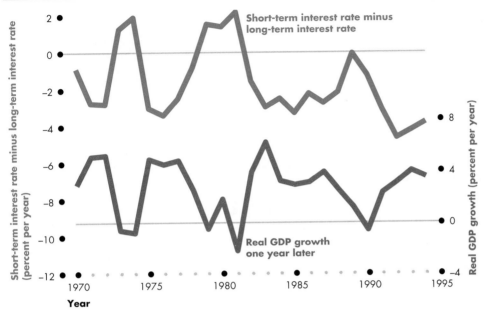

When the Fed increases short-term interest rates, the short-term rate rises above the long-term rate and, later, real GDP growth slows down. Similarly, when the Fed decreases short-term interest rates, the short-term rate falls below the long-term rate and, later, real GDP growth speeds up.

Source: *Economic Report of the President,* 1995, Tables B1 and B72, and the author's calculations.

---

figure shows the short-term interest rate minus the long-term interest rate. The short-term interest rate is influenced by the Fed in the way that you studied earlier in this chapter. The long-term interest rate is determined by saving and investment plans (see Chapter 25, pp. 608–609) and by long-term inflation expectations (see Chapter 32, pp. 814–816). The red line in Fig. 31.15 is the real GDP growth rate *one year later.* You can see that when short-term interest rates rise or long-term interest rates fall, the real GDP growth rate slows down in the following year. Long-term interest rates fluctuate less than short-term rates, so when short-term rates rise above long-term rates, it is because the Fed has pushed short-term rates upward. And when short-term rates fall below long-term rates, it is because the Fed has pushed short-term rates downward. So when the Fed stimulates aggregate demand (pushes short-term rates downward), the GDP growth rate speeds up, and when the Fed lowers aggregate demand (pushes short-term rates upward), the real GDP growth rate slows down. The inflation rate also increases and decreases in sympathy with these fluctuations in real GDP growth.

REVIEW

- The Fed directly controls the discount rate, closely monitors the federal funds rate, and influences all short-term interest rates.
- Fluctuations in short-term interest rates mirror fluctuations in the ratio of M2 to GDP.
- When the money supply change is *un*anticipated, interest rates change at the same time as the change in the money supply. When a money supply change is *anticipated,* interest rates change ahead of the change in the money supply.
- When the Fed lowers (raises) interest rates, aggregate demand increases (decreases) and real GDP growth and inflation speed up (slow down).

◆ In this chapter we've studied the determination of interest rates and seen how the Fed can influence interest rates. We've also seen how interest rates influence aggregate demand. In the next chapter we're going to explore the influence of money and other factors on inflation.

The Fed in Action

THE NEW YORK TIMES, NOVEMBER 16, 1994

Federal Reserve Increases Interest Rates by 3/4 Point; Jump Is Largest Since 1981

By KEITH BRADSHER

WASHINGTON, Nov 15—Determined to prevent strong economic growth from feeding inflation, the Federal Reserve raised short-term interest rates today by the largest amount since 1981 and left open the possibility of further increases. Banks followed by raising the rates they charge for loans.

The increases are likely to show up immediately in the rates charged millions of Americans on everything from home equity loans to credit cards to small-business loans. Already, interest rates on 30-year mortgages that were available at slightly more than 7 percent at the start of the year have risen to 9.05 percent.

While rising rates are intended to slow economic growth, the Federal Reserve's five previous increases, which began in February, have had mixed results. Some industries, like auto making, that depend on customers who need loans have had robust sales, while others, like home building, have begun to slow. Critics of the Federal Reserve say that interest rate changes take up to 18 months to show results and that the previous increases may yet do so. ...

Essence of THE STORY

■ In November 1994 the Fed increased short-term interest rates by three quarters of a percentage point, the sixth increase in 1994 and the largest increase since 1981.

■ The interest rates paid by millions of Americans on home loans, credit cards, and small-business loans increased immediately.

■ The Fed's intent was to slow economic growth and contain inflation.

■ The Fed's five previous rate increases in 1994 had mixed results. Auto sales remained firm, but home building slowed.

■ The Fed's critics say that interest rate changes take up to 18 months to work, so the effects of the previous increases had not yet been felt at the end of 1994.

Economic

A N A L Y S I S

■ Throughout 1994 and in early 1995 the Fed raised the discount rate and the federal funds rate (Figure 1) to slow the growth of real GDP and inflation.

■ The discount rate is set directly by the Fed. It is the rate at which the Fed is willing to lend reserves to the banks.

■ To change the federal funds rate, the Fed must change bank reserves. Figure 2 shows you how bank reserves decreased during 1994 and the first quarter of 1995.

■ To decrease bank reserves, the Fed undertakes open market operations. It sells government securities, and as these securities are paid for, bank reserves decrease.

■ Figure 3 shows how the demand for and supply of bank reserves determine the federal funds rate.

■ The banks' demand for reserves during 1994 and early 1995 is RD. This demand curve is just like the demand for money curve for the economy as a whole. The lower the federal funds rate, the greater is the quantity of reserves demanded by the banks.

■ In February 1994, after the Fed's first interest rate increase, the supply of bank reserves was RS_0. With this supply, the equilibrium interest rate was 3.25 percent a year.

■ By August 1994 the Fed had decreased the supply of reserves to RS_1 and pushed the federal funds rate up to 4.5 percent a year.

■ In November 1994 (the event described in the news article) the Fed decreased the supply of reserves to RS2 and pushed the federal funds rate up to 5.25 percent a year.

■ Because the Fed's actions increased the federal funds rate, the banks immediately increased the interest rates at which they were willing to lend.

■ Faced with higher interest rates, businesses and individuals gradually decreased their borrowing and spending. But decisions to cut borrowing and spending are spread out over many months—perhaps as long as 18 months as the news article says.

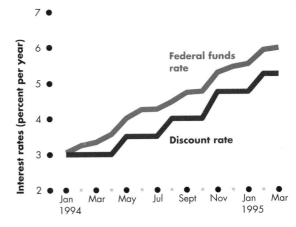

Figure 1 Interest rates

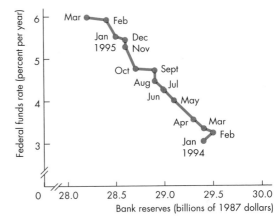

Figure 2 Bank reserves

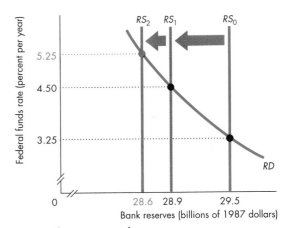

Figure 3 The money market

■ Actions taken by the Fed to increase interest rates during 1994 and early 1995 will slow down spending through 1995 and 1996.

S U M M A R Y

The Federal Reserve System

The Federal Reserve System is the central bank of the United States. The Fed consists of the Board of Governors and 12 regional Federal Reserve banks. The main policy-making committee is the Federal Open Market Committee. The Fed influences the economy by setting the required reserve ratio for banks and other deposit-taking institutions, by setting the discount rate—the interest rate at which it is willing to lend reserves to the banking system—and by open market operations. (pp. 769–773)

Controlling the Money Supply

By buying government securities in the market (an open market purchase), the Fed is able to increase the monetary base and the reserves available to banks. As a result, there is an expansion of bank lending and the quantity of money increases. By selling government securities, the Fed is able to decrease the monetary base and the reserves of banks and other financial institutions, thereby curtailing loans and decreasing the quantity of money. The overall effect of a change in the monetary base on the money supply is determined by the money multiplier. (pp. 773–779)

The Demand for Money

The quantity of money demanded is the amount of money that people plan to hold on the average. The quantity of nominal money demanded is proportional to the price level, and the quantity of real money demanded depends on the interest rate and real GDP. A higher interest rate induces a smaller quantity of real money demanded—a movement along the demand curve for real money. A higher level of real GDP induces a larger demand for money—a shift in the demand curve for real money. Technological changes in the financial sector also change the demand for money and shift the demand curve for real money. (pp. 780–783)

Interest Rate Determination

Changes in interest rates achieve equilibrium in the markets for money and financial assets. There is an inverse relationship between the interest rate and the price of a financial asset. The higher the interest rate, the lower is the price of a financial asset. Money market equilibrium achieves an interest rate (and an asset price) that makes the quantity of real money available willingly held. If the quantity of real money is increased by the actions of the Fed, the interest rate falls and the prices of financial assets rise. (pp. 783–784)

Monetary Policy

The Fed directly controls the discount rate and it closely targets the federal funds rate but all short-term rates fluctuate together and the Fed influences all short-term interest rates. The fluctuations in short-term interest rates are closely mirrored by fluctuations in the ratio of M2 to GDP. This ratio increases when the supply of money (M2) increases and when the demand for money (determined by GDP) decreases. Before 1990, rises and falls in the interest rate are matched by decreases and increases, respectively, in the ratio of M2 to GDP. After 1990, the relationship between M2 and interest rates broke down because of the growth of bond and equity mutual funds, which are substitutes for M2 and decreased the demand for M2.

People attempt to profit by predicting the actions of the Fed. To the extent that they can predict the Fed, interest rates and the price of financial assets move in anticipation of the Fed's actions rather than in response to them. As a consequence, interest rates change when the Fed changes the money supply only if the Fed catches people by surprise. Anticipated changes in the money supply produce interest rate changes by themselves.

When the Fed lowers interest rates, it increases aggregate demand, which speeds real GDP growth and inflation. And when the Fed raises interest rates, it decreases aggregate demand, which slows real GDP growth and inflation. (pp. 785–789)

KEY ELEMENTS

REVIEW QUESTIONS

1. What are the three main elements in the structure of the Federal Reserve System?

2. What are the three policy tools of the Fed? Which of these is the Fed's most frequently used tool?

3. If the Fed wants to decrease the quantity of money, does it buy or sell U.S. government securities in the open market?

4. Describe the events that take place when banks have excess reserves.

5. What is the money multiplier?

6. Distinguish between nominal money and real money.

7. What is the opportunity cost of holding money?

8. What do we mean by the demand for money?

9. What determines the demand for money?

10. What happens to the interest rate on a bond if the price of the bond increases?

11. How does equilibrium come about in the money market?

12. What happens to the interest rate if the money supply increases?

13. Explain the ripple effects of the Fed's actions when it increases the interest rate.

14. Explain why it pays people to try to predict the Fed's actions.

P R O B L E M S

1. You are given the following information about the economy of Nocoin: The banks have deposits of $300 billion. Their reserves are $15 billion, two thirds of which is in deposits with the central bank. There are $30 billion notes outside the banks. There are no coins in Nocoin!
   a. Calculate the monetary base.
   b. Calculate the currency drain.
   c. Calculate the money supply.
   d. Calculate the money multiplier.

2. Suppose that the Bank of Nocoin, the central bank, undertakes an open market purchase of securities of $0.5 million. What happens to the money supply? Explain why the change in the money supply is not equal to the change in the monetary base.

3. You are given the following information about the economy of Miniland: For each $1 increase in real GDP, the demand for money increases by one quarter of a dollar, other things remaining the same. Also, if the interest rate increases by 1 percentage point (for example, from 4 percent to 5 percent), the quantity of real money demanded falls by $50. If real GDP is $4,000 and the price level is 1,
   a. At what interest rate is no money held?
   b. How much real money is held at an interest rate of 10 percent a year?
   c. Draw a graph of the demand for money.

4. Given the demand for money in Miniland, if the price level is 1, real GDP is $4,000, and the real money supply is $750,
   a. What is the equilibrium interest rate?
   b. What is the equilibrium quantity of real money held?

5. Suppose that the Bank of Miniland, the central bank, wants to lower the interest rate by 1 percentage point. By how much would it have to change the real money supply to achieve that objective?

6. The figure shows the demand for real money in Miniland.

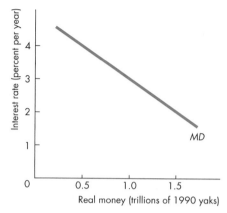

   a. In the figure, draw the supply of money curve if the interest rate in Miniland is 3 percent a year.
   b. Suppose that the Bank of Miniland (the central bank) wants to lower the interest rate by 1 percentage point. By how much must it change the real money supply to achieve that objective? Draw the new supply of money curve.
   c. Suppose that to change the quantity of money in b), the Bank of Miniland uses open market operations. Does the Bank of Miniland make an open market purchase or an open market sale of securities?

7. Study *Reading Between the Lines* on pp. 790–791 and then answer the following questions:
   a. Why did the Fed increase interest rates during 1994?
   b. Which tools did the Fed use to increase interest rates? Explain how those tools work.
   c. What have been the effects of the Fed's actions on the economy during 1994 and 1995?
   d. What are the problems with the Fed's actions?

Inflation

After studying this chapter, you will be able to:

- Distinguish between inflation and a one-time rise in the price level

- Explain the different ways in which inflation can be generated

- Describe how people try to forecast inflation

- Explain the short-run and long-run relationships between inflation and unemployment

- Explain the short-run and long-run relationships between inflation and interest rates

- Describe the political origins of inflation

From Rome to Russia

At the end of the third century A.D., Roman Emperor Diocletian struggled to contain an inflation that raised prices by more than 300 percent a year. At the end of the twentieth century, Russian President Boris Yeltsin struggled to contain a severe inflation that raised prices at a rate of close to 1,000 percent a year. But the most rapid recent inflations have been in Brazil, where the inflation rate hit 40 percent *per month* in 1994, and in Zaire, which had an inflation rate of 75 percent *per month*. What causes rapid inflation? ◆ In comparison with the cases just described, the United States has had remarkable price stability. Nevertheless, during the 1970s the U.S. price level more than doubled—an inflation of more than 100 percent over the decade. Today, along with the other rich industrial countries, the United States has a low inflation rate at about 2.5 percent a year. Why do some countries have a low inflation rate? And why did a more serious inflation break out in the United States during the 1970s? ◆ Most of life's big economic decisions— whether to buy or rent a home, whether to save more for retirement—turn on what is going to happen to inflation. Will inflation increase so our savings buy less? Will inflation decrease so our debts are harder to repay? To make good decisions, we need good forecasts of inflation, and not for just next year but for many years into the future. How do people try to forecast inflation? And how do expectations of inflation influence the economy? ◆ As the inflation rate rises and falls, the unemployment rate and interest rates also fluctuate. What are the links between inflation and the economy that make unemployment and interest rates fluctuate when inflation fluctuates?

◇ In this chapter you will learn about the forces that generate inflation, the effects of inflation, and the way in which people try to forecast inflation. You will pull together several of the threads you have been following through your study of macroeconomics. In particular, you will use the *AS-AD* model of Chapter 27 and the analysis of the money market of Chapter 31 and put them to work in understanding the process of inflation. But first, let's recall what inflation is and how its rate is measured.

Inflation and the Price Level

WE DON'T HAVE MUCH INFLATION TODAY, BUT during the 1970s it was a major problem. **Inflation** is a process in which the *price level is rising* and *money is losing value.* Two features of this definition of inflation must be emphasized. First, inflation is a *monetary* phenomenon. It is the price *level* and therefore the *value of money* that is changing, not the price of some particular commodity. For example, if the price of oil rises but prices of computers fall such that the price level (an average of prices) is constant, there is no inflation. Second, inflation is an ongoing *process,* not a one-time affair. Figure 32.1 illustrates this distinction. In part (a) the price level rises continuously. In part (b) the price level rises at the beginning of 1993, a one-time rise, but is constant at other times. The economy in part (a) experiences inflation, but the economy in part (b) does not. It has a one-time rise in its price level.

To measure the inflation *rate,* we calculate the annual percentage change in the price level.

For example, if this year's price level is 126 and last year's price level was 120, the inflation rate is 5 percent per year. That is,

$$\text{Inflation rate} = \frac{126 - 120}{120} \times 100$$

$$= 5 \text{ percent per year.}$$

This equation shows the connection between the *inflation rate* and the *price level.* For a given price level last year, the higher the price level in the current year, the higher is the inflation rate. If the price level is *rising,* the inflation rate is *positive.* If the price level rises at a *faster* rate, the inflation rate *increases.* Also, the higher the price level, the lower is the value of money, and the higher the inflation rate.

Inflation can result from either an increase in aggregate demand or a decrease in aggregate supply. These two sources of impulses that can get an inflation started are called:

- Demand pull
- Cost push

We'll first study a demand-pull inflation.

FIGURE 32.1

Inflation Versus a One-Time Rise in the Price Level

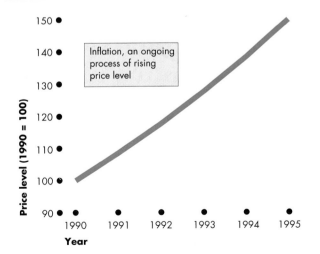

(a) Inflation

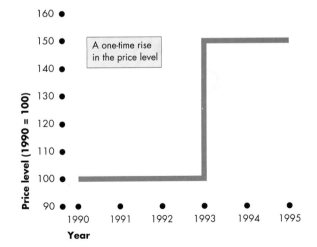

(b) One-time rise in price level

An economy experiences inflation when the price level rises persistently, as shown in part (a). An economy experiences a one-time rise in the price level if some disturbance increases the price level but does not set off an ongoing process of a rising price level, as shown in part (b).

Demand-Pull Inflation

AN INFLATION THAT RESULTS FROM AN INITIAL increase in aggregate demand is called **demand-pull inflation**. Such an inflation may arise from any individual factor that increases aggregate demand such as an:

- Increase in the money supply
- Increase in government purchases
- Increase in exports

Inflation Effect of an Increase in Aggregate Demand

Suppose that last year the price level was 130 and real GDP was $6 trillion. Potential GDP was also $6 trillion. Figure 32.2(a) illustrates this situation. The aggregate demand curve is AD_0, the short-run aggregate supply curve is SAS_0, and the long-run aggregate supply curve is LAS.

In the current year, aggregate demand increases to AD_1. Such a situation arises if, for example, the Fed loosens its grip on the money supply, or the government increases its purchases of goods and services, or exports increase. With no change in potential GDP, and with no change in the money wage rate, the long-run aggregate supply curve and the short-run aggregate supply curve remain at LAS and SAS_0. The economy moves to the point where the aggregate demand curve AD_1 intersects the short-run aggregate supply curve. The price level rises to 135, and real GDP increases above potential GDP to $6.5 trillion. The economy experiences a 3.8 percent rise in the price level (a price level of 135 compared with 130 in the previous year) and a rapid expansion of real GDP. Unemployment falls below the natural rate. The next step in the unfolding story is a rise in wages.

FIGURE 32.2

A Demand-Pull Rise in the Price Level

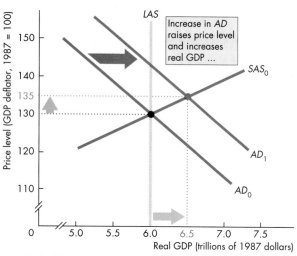

(a) Initial effect

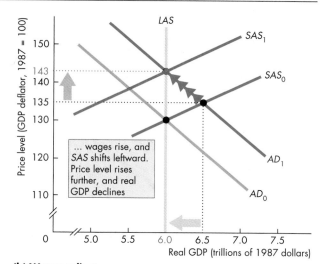

(b) Wages adjust

In part (a) the aggregate demand curve is AD_0, the short-run aggregate supply curve is SAS_0, and the long-run aggregate supply curve is LAS. The price level is 130, and real GDP is $6 trillion, its long-run level. Aggregate demand increases to AD_1 (because, for example, the Fed increases the money supply or the government increases its purchases of goods and services or exports increase). The new equilibrium occurs where AD_1 intersects SAS_0. The price level rises to 135, and real GDP increases to $6.5 trillion. In part (b), starting from above full employment, wages begin to rise and the short-run aggregate supply curve shifts leftward toward SAS_1. The price level rises further, and real GDP returns to its long-run level.

Wage Response

Real GDP cannot remain above potential GDP forever. With unemployment below its natural rate, there is a shortage of labor. In this situation, wages begin to rise. As they do so, short-run aggregate supply decreases and the SAS curve starts to shift leftward. The price level rises further, and real GDP begins to decrease.

With no further change in aggregate demand—the aggregate demand curve remains at AD_1—this process comes to an end when the short-run aggregate supply curve has shifted to SAS_1 in Fig. 32.2(b). At this time, the price level has increased to 143 and real GDP has returned to potential GDP of $6 trillion, the level from which it started.

A Demand-Pull Inflation Process

The process we've just studied eventually comes to an end when, for a given increase in aggregate demand, wages have adjusted enough to restore the real wage rate to its full-employment level. We've studied a one-time rise in the price level like that described in Fig. 32.1(b). For inflation to proceed, aggregate demand must persistently increase.

The only way in which aggregate demand can persistently increase is if the quantity of money persistently increases. Suppose the government has a large budget deficit that it finances by creating more and more money each year. In this situation, aggregate demand increases year after year. The aggregate demand curve keeps shifting rightward. This persistent increase in aggregate demand puts continual upward pressure on the price level. The economy now experiences demand-pull inflation.

Figure 32.3 illustrates the process of demand-pull inflation. The starting point is the same as that shown in Fig. 32.2. The aggregate demand curve is AD_0, the short-run aggregate supply curve is SAS_0, and the long-run aggregate supply curve is LAS. Real GDP is $6 trillion, and the price level is 130. Aggregate demand increases, shifting the aggregate demand curve to AD_1. Real GDP increases to $6.5 trillion, and the price level rises to 135. The economy is at an above full-employment equilibrium. There is a shortage of labor and the wage rate rises, shifting the short-run aggregate supply curve to SAS_1. The price level rises to 143, and real GDP returns to potential GDP.

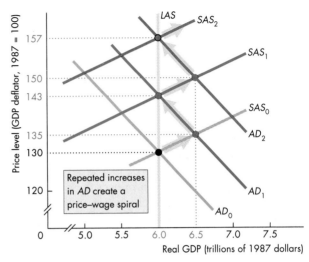

FIGURE 32.3

A Demand-Pull Inflation Spiral

Each time the money supply increases, aggregate demand increases, and the aggregate demand curve shifts rightward from AD_0 to AD_1 to AD_2, and so on. Each time real GDP goes above potential GDP and unemployment goes below the natural rate, the money wage rate rises and the short-run aggregate supply curve shifts leftward from SAS_0 to SAS_1 to SAS_2, and so on. As aggregate demand continues to increase, the price level rises from 130 through 135, 143, 150, to 157, and so on. There is a perpetual demand-pull inflation. Real GDP fluctuates between $6 trillion and $6.5 trillion.

But the money supply increases again, and aggregate demand continues to increase. The aggregate demand curve shifts rightward to AD_2. The price level rises further to 150, and real GDP again exceeds potential GDP at $6.5 trillion. Yet again, the wage rate rises and decreases short-run aggregate supply. The SAS curve shifts to SAS_2, and the price level rises further to 157. As the money supply continues to grow, aggregate demand increases and the price level rises in an ongoing demand-pull inflation process.

The process you have just studied generates inflation—an ongoing process of a rising price level.

Demand-Pull Inflation in Kalamazoo You may better understand the inflation process that we've just described by considering what is going on in an individual part of the economy, such as a Kalamazoo soda-bottling plant. Initially, when aggregate demand increases, the demand for soda increases and the price of soda rises. Faced with a higher price, the soda plant works overtime and increases production. Conditions are good for workers in Kalamazoo, and the soda factory finds it hard to hang onto its best people. To do so, it has to offer higher wages. As wages increase, so do the soda factory's costs.

What happens next depends on what happens to aggregate demand. If aggregate demand remains constant (as in Fig. 32.2b), the firm's costs are increasing but the price of soda is not increasing as quickly as its costs. Production is scaled back. Eventually, wages and costs increase by the same percentage as the price of soda. In real terms, the soda factory is in the same situation as initially—before the increase in aggregate demand. The bottling plant produces the same amount of soda and employs the same amount of labor as before the increase in demand.

But if aggregate demand continues to increase, so does the demand for soda, and the price of soda rises at the same rate as wages. The soda factory continues to operate above full employment, and there is a persistent shortage of labor. Prices and wages chase each other upward in an unending spiral.

Demand-Pull Inflation in the United States   A demand-pull inflation like the one you've just studied occurred in the United States during the 1960s. In 1960, inflation was a moderate 2 percent a year, but its rate increased slowly to 3 percent by 1966. Then, in 1967, a large increase in government purchases on the Vietnam War and an increase in spending on social programs, together with an increase in the growth rate of the money supply, increased aggregate demand more quickly. As a consequence, the rightward shift of the aggregate demand curve speeded up and the price level increased more quickly. Real GDP moved above potential GDP and the unemployment rate fell below the natural rate.

With unemployment below the natural rate, the money wage rate started to rise more quickly and the short-run aggregate supply curve shifted leftward. The Fed responded with a further increase in the money supply growth rate and a demand-pull inflation spiral unfolded. By 1970, the inflation rate had reached 5 percent a year.

For the next few years, aggregate demand grew even more quickly and the inflation rate kept rising. By 1975, its rate had almost reached 10 percent a year.

R E V I E W

■ Demand-pull inflation begins when an increase in aggregate demand increases real GDP and increases the price level.
■ At above-full employment the wage rate rises, short-run aggregate supply decreases, real GDP decreases, and the price level rises further.
■ If aggregate demand keeps increasing, wages chase prices in an unending inflation spiral.

Next, let's see how shocks to aggregate supply can create a cost-push inflation.

Cost-Push Inflation

AN INFLATION THAT RESULTS FROM AN INITIAL increase in costs is called **cost-push inflation**. The two main sources of increases in costs are:

1. An increase in money wage rates
2. An increase in the money prices of raw materials

At a given price level, the higher the cost of production, the smaller is the amount that firms are willing to produce. So if money wage rates rise or if the prices of raw materials (for example, oil) rise, firms decrease their supply of goods and services. Aggregate supply decreases, and the short-run aggregate supply curve shifts leftward.[1] Let's trace the effects of such a decrease in short-run aggregate supply on the price level and real GDP.

Initial Effect of a Decrease in Aggregate Supply

Suppose that last year the price level was 130 and real GDP was $6 trillion. Potential real GDP was also $6 trillion. Figure 32.4 illustrates this situation. The aggregate demand curve was AD_0, the short-run aggregate supply curve was SAS_0, and the long-run aggregate supply curve was LAS. In the current year,

---

[1] Some cost-push forces, such as an increase in the price of oil accompanied by a decrease in the availability of oil, can also decrease long-run aggregate supply. We'll ignore such effects here and examine cost-push factors that change only short-run aggregate supply.

FIGURE 32.4

A Cost-Push Rise in the Price Level

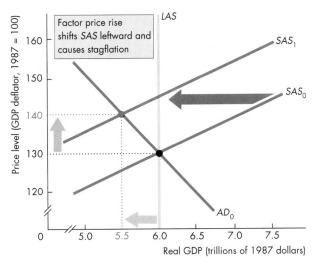

Initially, the aggregate demand curve is AD_0, the short-run aggregate supply curve is SAS_0, and the long-run aggregate supply curve is LAS. A decrease in aggregate supply (for example, resulting from an increase in the world price of oil) shifts the short-run aggregate supply curve to SAS_1. The economy moves to the point where the short-run aggregate supply curve SAS_1 intersects the aggregate demand curve AD_0. The price level rises to 140, and real GDP decreases to $5.5 trillion. The economy experiences inflation and a contraction of real GDP—*stagflation*.

a sharp increase in world oil prices decreases short-run aggregate supply. The short-run aggregate supply curve shifts leftward to SAS_1. The price level rises to 140, and real GDP decreases to $5.5 trillion. The combination of a rise in the price level and a fall in real GDP is called **stagflation**.

An event like the one you've just studied brings about a one-time rise in the price level like that in Fig. 32.1(b). It does not cause inflation. In fact, a supply shock on its own cannot cause inflation. Something more must happen to enable a one-time supply shock, which causes a one-time rise in the price level, to be converted into a process of money supply growth and ongoing inflation. The money supply must persistently increase. And it often does increase, as you will now see.

Aggregate Demand Response

When real GDP falls, the unemployment rate rises above the natural rate. In such a situation there is usually an outcry of concern and a call for action to restore full employment. Suppose that the Fed increases the money supply. Aggregate demand increases. In Fig. 32.5 the aggregate demand curve shifts rightward to AD_1. The increase in aggregate demand has restored full employment. But the price level rises to 143, a 10 percent increase over the original price level.

A Cost-Push Inflation Process

Suppose now that the oil producers, who see the prices of everything that they buy with the dollars they receive increase by 10 percent, decide to increase the price of oil again. Figure 32.6 continues the story.

FIGURE 32.5

Aggregate Demand Response to Cost Push

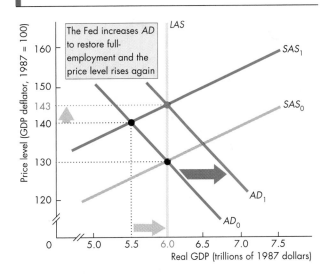

Following a cost-push increase in the price level, real GDP is below potential GDP and unemployment is above the natural rate. If the Fed responds by increasing aggregate demand to restore full employment, the aggregate demand curve shifts rightward to AD_1. The economy returns to full employment, but at the expense of more inflation. The price level rises to 143.

The short-run aggregate supply curve now shifts to SAS_2, and another bout of stagflation ensues. The price level rises further to 154, and real GDP falls to $5.5 trillion. Unemployment increases above its natural rate. If the Fed responds yet again with an increase in the money supply, aggregate demand increases and the aggregate demand curve shifts to AD_2. The price level rises even higher—to 157—and full employment is again restored. A cost-push inflation spiral results. But if the Fed does not respond, the economy remains below full employment.

You can see that the Fed has a dilemma. If it increases the money supply to restore full employment, it invites another oil price hike that will call forth yet a further increase in the money supply.

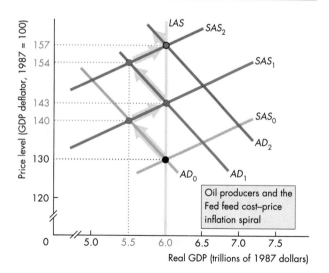

FIGURE 32.6

A Cost-Push Inflation Spiral

When a cost increase (for example, an increase in the world oil price) decreases short-run aggregate supply from SAS_0 to SAS_1, the price level rises to 140 and real GDP decreases to $5.5 trillion. The Fed responds with an increase in the money supply that shifts the aggregate demand curve from AD_0 to AD_1. The price level rises again to 143, and real GDP returns to $6 trillion. A further cost increase occurs, which shifts the short-run aggregate supply curve again, this time to SAS_2. Stagflation is repeated, and the price level now rises to 154. The Fed responds again, and the cost-price inflation spiral continues.

Inflation will rage along at a rate decided by the oil-exporting nations. If the Fed keeps the lid on money supply growth, the economy operates with a high level of unemployment.

Cost-Push Inflation in Kalamazoo What is going on in the Kalamazoo soda-bottling plant when the economy is experiencing cost-push inflation? When the oil price increases, so do the costs of bottling soda. These higher costs decrease the supply of soda, increasing its price and decreasing the quantity produced. The soda plant lays off some workers. This situation will persist until either the Fed increases aggregate demand or the price of oil falls. If the Fed increases aggregate demand, as it did in the mid-1970s, the demand for soda increases and so does its price. The higher price of soda brings higher profits, and the bottling plant increases its production. The soda factory rehires the laid-off workers.

Cost-Push Inflation in the United States A cost-push inflation like the one you've just studied occurred in the United States during the 1970s. It began in 1974 when the Organization for Petroleum Exporting Countries (OPEC) raised the price of oil fourfold. The higher oil price decreased aggregate supply, which caused the price level to rise more quickly and real GDP to shrink. The Fed then faced a dilemma. Would it increase the quantity of money and accommodate the cost-push forces or would it keep aggregate demand growth in check by limiting money growth? In 1975, 1976, and 1977 the Fed repeatedly allowed the money supply to grow quickly, and inflation proceeded at a rapid rate. In 1979 and 1980, OPEC was again able to push oil prices higher. On that occasion the Fed decided not to respond to the oil price hike with an increase in the money supply. The result was a recession but also, eventually, a fall in inflation.

R E V I E W

- Cost-push inflation starts with an increase in the money wage rate or in the money price of a raw material that decreases aggregate supply.

- Real GDP decreases and the price level rises—*stagflation* occurs.

- If the Fed increases aggregate demand to restore full employment, a freewheeling cost-push inflation ensues.

Anticipating Inflation

REGARDLESS OF WHETHER INFLATION IS DEMAND-pull or cost-push, the failure to correctly *anticipate* it results in unintended consequences. These unintended consequences impose costs on firms and workers in the labor market and on borrowers and lenders in the capital market. Let's examine these costs.

Unanticipated Inflation in the Labor Market

Unanticipated inflation has two main consequences for the operation of the labor market:

- Redistribution of income
- Departure from full employment

Redistribution of Income Unanticipated inflation redistributes income between employers and workers. Sometimes employers gain at the expense of workers, and sometimes they lose. If an unexpected increase in aggregate demand increases the inflation rate, then wages will not have been set high enough. Profits will be higher than expected, and wages will buy fewer goods than expected. In this case, employers gain at the expense of workers. But if aggregate demand is expected to increase at a rapid rate and it fails to do so, workers gain at the expense of employers. With a high inflation rate anticipated, wages are set too high and profits are squeezed. Redistributions between employers and workers create an incentive for both firms and workers to try to forecast inflation correctly.

Departures from Full Employment Redistribution brings gains to some and losses to others. But departures from full employment impose costs on everyone. To see why, let's return to the soda-bottling plant in Kalamazoo.

If the bottling plant and its workers do not anticipate inflation, but inflation occurs, the money wage rate does not rise to keep up with inflation. The real wage rate falls, and the firm tries to hire more labor and increase production. But because the real wage rate has fallen, the firm has a hard time attracting the labor it wants to employ. It pays overtime rates to its existing work force, and because it runs its plant at a faster pace, it incurs higher plant maintenance and parts replacement costs. But also, because the real wage rate has fallen, workers begin to quit the bottling plant to find jobs that pay a real wage rate that is closer to one prevailing before the outbreak of inflation. This labor turnover imposes additional costs on the firm. So even though its production increases, the firm incurs additional costs, and its profits do not increase as much as they otherwise would. The workers incur additional costs of job search, and those who remain at the bottling plant wind up feeling cheated. They've worked overtime to produce the extra output, and when they come to spend their wages, they discover that prices have increased, so their wages buy a smaller quantity of goods and services than expected.

If the bottling plant and its workers anticipate a high inflation rate that does not occur, they increase the money wage rate by too much, and the real wage rate rises. At the higher real wage rate, the firm lays off some workers and the unemployment rate increases. Those workers who keep their jobs gain, but those who become unemployed lose. Also, the bottling plant loses because its output and profits fall.

Unanticipated Inflation in the Capital Market

Unanticipated inflation has two consequences for the operation of the capital market. They are:

- Redistribution of income
- Too much or too little lending and borrowing

Redistribution of Income Unanticipated inflation redistributes income between borrowers and lenders. Sometimes borrowers gain at the expense of lenders and sometimes they lose. When inflation is unexpected, interest rates are not set high enough to compensate lenders for the falling value of money. In this case, borrowers gain at the expense of lenders. But if inflation is expected and then fails to occur, interest rates are set too high. In this case, lenders gain at the expense of borrowers. Redistributions of income between borrowers and lenders create an incentive for both groups to try to forecast inflation correctly.

Too Much or Too Little Lending and Borrowing If the inflation rate turns out to be either higher or lower than expected, the interest rate does not incorporate a correct allowance for the falling value of money and the real interest rate is either lower or higher than it otherwise would be. When the real interest rate turns out to be too low, which occurs when inflation is *higher* than expected, borrowers wish they had borrowed more and lenders wish they had lent less. Both groups would have made different lending and borrowing decisions with greater foresight about the inflation rate. When the real interest rate turns out to be too high, which occurs when inflation is *lower* than expected, borrowers wish they had borrowed less and lenders wish they had lent more. Again, both groups would have made different lending and borrowing decisions with greater foresight about the inflation rate.

So unanticipated inflation imposes costs regardless of whether the inflation turns out to be higher or lower than anticipated. The presence of these costs gives everyone an incentive to forecast inflation correctly. Let's see how people go about this task.

How People Forecast Inflation

People devote considerable resources to forecasting inflation. Some people specialize in economic forecasting and make a living from it. Other people buy the services of these specialists. The specialist forecasters are economists who work for public and private macroeconomic forecasting agencies and for banks, insurance companies, labor unions, and large corporations. The returns these specialists make depend on the quality of their forecasts, so they have a strong incentive to forecast as accurately as possible. The most accurate forecast possible is one that is correct on the average and that has the minimum possible range of error.

Specialist forecasters use statistical models of the economy that are based on (but more detailed than) the aggregate supply–aggregate demand model that you are studying in this book.

Predicting People's Forecasts

Economics tries to predict the choices that people make. Because people's choices depend on their forecasts, we must predict their forecasts to predict their choices. How can we predict people's forecasts?

We assume that people are rational in their use of information. In particular, we assume that they use all relevant information available to them. If some information is available that can lead to a better forecast, it will be used. We call a forecast based on all available relevant information a **rational expectation**.

A rational expectation has two features:

1. It is correct on the average.
2. The range of the forecast error is as small as possible.

A forecast that is correct *on the average* is not always correct. Suppose you forecast the outcome of tossing a coin 10 times. You predict that there will be 5 heads and 5 tails. On the average (repeating the experiment of coin tossing many times) you are correct. But often you will get 6 heads and 4 tails.

The assumption that people use all the relevant information when they make forecasts does not tell us what information they actually use. So we make one further assumption. They use the *information that economic theory predicts is relevant.* For example, to predict people's expectations of the price of orange juice, we use the economic model of demand and supply, together with all the available information about the positions of the demand and supply curves for orange juice. To make a prediction about people's expectations of the price level and inflation, we use the economic model of aggregate supply and aggregate demand.

Let's see how we can use the model of aggregate supply and aggregate demand to work out the rational expectation of the price level.

Rational Expectation of the Price Level

We use the aggregate supply–aggregate demand model to forecast the price level in much the same way that a meteorologist uses a model of the atmosphere to forecast the weather. But there is a difference between the meteorologist's model of the atmosphere and the economist's model of the economy. In the meteorologist's model, tomorrow's weather does not depend on people's forecast of it. In the economist's model, next year's price level *does* depend on people's forecast of it. To work out the rational expectation of the price level, we must take account of this dependence of the actual price level on the forecasted price level.

We're going to work out the rational expectation of the price level, using Fig. 32.7 to guide our analysis. The aggregate supply–aggregate demand model predicts that the price level is at the point of intersection of the aggregate demand and short-run aggregate supply curves. To forecast the price level, therefore, we have to forecast the positions of these curves.

FIGURE 32.7

Rational Expectation of the Price Level

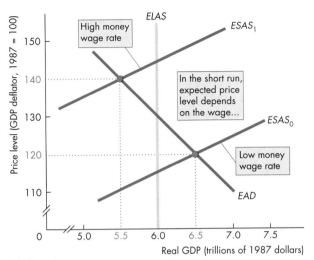

(a) The short run

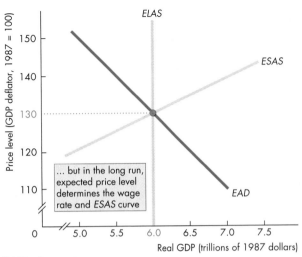

(b) The long run

In the short run, part (a), wages are fixed and the rational expectation of the price level occurs at the point of intersection of curves *ESAS* and *EAD*. With a low money wage rate, the expected short-run aggregate supply curve is *ESAS₀* and the rational expectation of the price level is 120. With a high money wage rate, the expected short-run aggregate supply

curve is *ESAS₁* and the rational expectation of the price level is 140. In the long run, part (b), wages are flexible and the rational expectation of the price level occurs at the intersection of *ELAS* and *EAD*. The money wage rate is expected to adjust to place the expected short-run aggregate supply curve, *ESAS*, through the intersection of *ELAS* and *EAD*.

To forecast the position of the aggregate demand curve, we must forecast all the variables that influence aggregate demand. Suppose that we have done this and that our forecast is given by the curve *EAD*, the *expected* aggregate demand curve.

Our next task is to forecast the position of the short-run aggregate supply curve. The variables that determine short-run aggregate supply are summarized by just two things:

1. Potential GDP
2. The money wage rate

Suppose that we have made the best forecast we can of potential GDP and that we expect it to be $6 trillion. Potential GDP determines long-run aggregate supply, so the *expected* long-run aggregate supply curve is *ELAS* in Fig. 32.7.

The short-run aggregate supply curve intersects the long-run aggregate supply curve but its position depends on the money wage rate. To forecast the

money wage rate, we must deal with two cases:

- The short run
- The long run

Rational Expectations in the Short Run   In the short run, the money wage rate is set, so forecasting it is easy. The forecast is the current actual wage rate. Given that fixed wage rate and the expected long-run aggregate supply curve, *ELAS*, there is an expected short-run aggregate supply curve. In Fig. 32.7(a), if the money wage rate is low, then the expected short-run aggregate supply curve is *ESAS₀*.

The rational expectation of the price level is the point of intersection of *EAD* and *ESAS₀*, a price level of 120. The rational expectation of inflation is calculated as the percentage amount by which the forecasted future price level exceeds the current price level. For example, if the current price level is 110 and next year's forecasted price level is 120, the expected inflation rate over the year is 9 percent.

There is also a rational expectation of real GDP. Given the wage rate and the expected short-run aggregate supply curve $ESAS_0$, the rational expectation is that real GDP will be $6.5 trillion and unemployment will be less than the natural rate.

Figure 32.7(a) shows another case—one in which the money wage rate is high. With this higher money wage rate, the expected short-run aggregate supply curve is $ESAS_1$. Here, the rational expectation of the price level is determined at the point of intersection of EAD and $ESAS_1$, an expected price level of 140. If the current price level is 110, the expected inflation rate over the year is 27 percent. The economy is expected to have an equilibrium real GDP of $5.5 trillion and to have unemployment exceeding the natural rate.

Rational Expectations in the Long Run   In the long run, the expected price level is determined by expected aggregate demand, EAD, and expected long-run aggregate supply, $ELAS$. The money wage rate is flexible and adjusts to achieve full employment. That is, the money wage rate adjusts so that the expected short-run aggregate supply curve, $ESAS$, passes through the intersection point of the EAD and $ELAS$ curves.

Figure 32.7(b) illustrates the long-run rational expectation of the price level. The forecasted price level, 130, is determined at the intersection point of the EAD and $ELAS$ curves. Here we forecast the position of the short-run aggregate supply curve and the price level at the same time.

You've now seen how we try to predict the inflation forecasts that people make when those forecasts are rational expectations. Suppose people make accurate forecasts of inflation. Does the forecast of inflation influence the inflation process itself? To answer this question, we must study anticipated inflation.

Anticipated Inflation

In the demand-pull and cost-push inflations that we studied earlier in this chapter, money wages are sticky. When aggregate demand increases, either to set off a demand-pull inflation or to accommodate a cost-push inflation, the money wage does not change immediately. But if people correctly anticipate increases in aggregate demand, they will adjust money wage rates so as to keep up with anticipated inflation.

In this case, inflation proceeds with real GDP equal to potential GDP and unemployment equal to

the natural rate. Figure 32.8 explains why. Suppose that last year the price level was 130 and real GDP was $6 trillion, which is also potential GDP. The aggregate demand curve was AD_0, the aggregate supply curve was SAS_0, and the long-run aggregate supply curve was LAS. Because real GDP equals potential GDP, the actual price level equals the expected price level.

Suppose that potential GDP does not change and is not expected to change, so the actual and expected long-run aggregate supply curves do not change. Also suppose that aggregate demand is expected to increase and that the expected aggregate demand curve for this year is AD_1. We can now calculate the rational expectation of the price level for this year. It is a price level of 143, the price level at which the new expected aggregate demand curve intersects the expected long-run aggregate supply curve. The expected inflation rate is 10 percent, the percentage change in the price level from 130 to 143.

In anticipation of this inflation, money wage rates rise and the short-run aggregate supply curve shifts leftward. In particular, given that expected inflation is 10 percent, the short-run aggregate supply curve for next year (SAS_1) passes through the long-run aggregate supply curve (LAS) at the expected price level.

If aggregate demand turns out to be the same as expected, the actual aggregate demand curve is AD_1. The intersection point of AD_1 and SAS_1 determines the actual price level—where the price level is 143. Between last year and this year, the price level increased from 130 to 143 and the economy experienced an inflation rate of 10 percent, the same as the inflation rate that was anticipated. If this anticipated inflation is ongoing, in the following year aggregate demand increases (as anticipated) and the aggregate demand curve shifts to AD_2. The money wage rate rises to reflect the anticipated inflation and the short-run aggregate supply curve shifts to SAS_2. The price level rises by a further 10 percent to 157.

What has caused this inflation? The immediate answer is that because people expected inflation, wages were increased and prices increased. But the expectation was correct. Aggregate demand was expected to increase, and it did increase. Because aggregate demand was *expected* to increase from AD_0 to AD_1, the short-run aggregate supply curve shifted up from SAS_0 to SAS_1. Because aggregate demand actually did increase by the amount that was expected, the actual aggregate demand curve shifted from AD_0 to AD_1. The combination of the anticipated and actual shifts

Unanticipated Inflation

When aggregate demand increases by *more* than expected, there is some unanticipated inflation that looks just like the demand-pull inflation that you studied earlier. Some inflation is expected, and the money wage rate is set to reflect that expectation. The *SAS* curve intersects the *LAS* curve at the expected price level. Aggregate demand then increases, but by more than expected. So the *AD* curve intersects the *SAS* curve at a level of real GDP that exceeds potential GDP. With real GDP above potential GDP and unemployment below the natural rate, the money wage rate rises. So the price level rises further. If aggregate demand increases again, a demand-pull inflation spiral unwinds.

When aggregate demand increases by *less* than expected, there is some unanticipated inflation that looks like the cost-push inflation that you studied earlier. Again, some inflation is expected, and the money wage rate is set to reflect that expectation. The *SAS* curve intersects the *LAS* curve at the expected price level. Aggregate demand then increases, but by less than expected. So the *AD* curve intersects the *SAS* curve at a level of real GDP below potential GDP. Aggregate demand increases to restore full employment. But if aggregate demand is expected to increase by more than it actually does, wages again rise, short-run aggregate supply again decreases, and a cost-push spiral unwinds.

We've seen that only when inflation is unanticipated does real GDP depart from potential GDP. When inflation is anticipated, real GDP remains at potential GDP. Does this mean that an anticipated inflation has no costs?

The Costs of Anticipated Inflation

The cost of an anticipated inflation depends on its rate. At a moderate rate of 2 or 3 percent a year, the cost is probably small. But as the anticipated inflation rate rises, so does its cost and an anticipated inflation at a rapid rate can be extremely expensive. The costs of anticipated inflation can be summarized under four broad headings:

■ "Bootleather costs"
■ Other transactions costs
■ Decrease in potential GDP
■ Fall in long-term growth rate

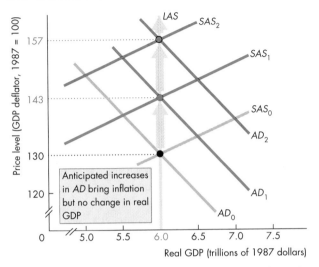

FIGURE 32.8
Anticipated Inflation

Potential real GDP is $6 trillion. Last year, aggregate demand was AD_0, and the short-run aggregate supply curve was SAS_0. The actual price level was the same as the expected price level—130. This year, aggregate demand is expected to increase to AD_1. The rational expectation of the price level changes from 130 to 143. As a result, wages rise and the short-run aggregate supply curve shifts up to SAS_1. If aggregate demand actually increases as expected, the actual aggregate demand curve AD_1 is the same as the expected aggregate demand curve. Equilibrium occurs at a real GDP of $6 trillion and an actual price level of 143. The inflation is correctly anticipated. Next year the process continues with aggregate demand increasing as expected to AD_2 and wages rising to shift the short-run aggregate supply curve to SAS_2. Again, real GDP remains at $6 trillion and the price level rises, as anticipated, to 157.

of the aggregate demand curve rightward produced an increase in the price level that was anticipated.

Only if aggregate demand growth is correctly forecasted does the economy follow the course described in Fig. 32.8. If the expected growth rate of aggregate demand is different from its actual growth rate, the expected aggregate demand curve shifts by an amount that is different from the actual aggregate demand curve. The inflation rate departs from its expected level, and to some extent, there is unanticipated inflation.

"Bootleather Costs" The "bootleather costs" of inflation are costs that arise from an increase in the velocity of circulation of money and an increase in the amount of running around that people do to try to avoid incurring losses from the falling value of money.

When money loses value at a rapid anticipated rate, it does not function well as a store of value and people try to avoid holding money. They spend their incomes as soon as they receive them, and firms pay out incomes—wages and dividends—as soon as they receive revenue from their sales. The velocity of circulation increases. During the 1920s when inflation in Germany reached *hyperinflation* levels (rates in excess of 50 percent a month), wages were paid and spent twice in a single day!

The bootleather costs have been estimated to be between 1 percent and 2 percent of GDP for a 10 percent inflation. For a rapid inflation they are much more.

Other Transactions Costs The bootleather costs of inflation are transactions costs—costs of making transactions. But other transactions costs are influenced by the inflation rate as well. At high anticipated inflation rates, people seek alternatives to money as a means of payment and use tokens and commodities or even barter, all of which are less efficient than money as a means of payment. For example, in Israel during the 1980s, when inflation reached 1,000 percent a year, the U.S. dollar started to replace the increasingly worthless shekel. As a result, people had to keep track of the exchange rate between the shekel and the dollar hour by hour and had to engage in many additional and costly transactions in the foreign exchange market.

Decrease in Potential GDP Because anticipated inflation increases transactions costs, it diverts resources from producing goods and services and it decreases potential GDP. The faster the anticipated inflation rate, the greater is the decrease in potential GDP and the further leftward does the *LAS* curve shift.

Fall in Long-Term Growth Rate The most serious cost of an anticipated inflation is a fall in the long-term growth rate of GDP. This cost has three sources. The first comes from the way in which inflation interacts with the tax system. Anticipated inflation swells the dollar returns on investments. But dollar returns are taxed, so the effective tax rate rises.

This effect becomes serious at even modest inflation rates. Let's consider an example.

Suppose the real interest rate is 4 percent a year and the tax rate is 50 percent. With no inflation, the nominal interest rate is also 4 percent a year and 50 percent of this rate is taxable. The real *after-tax* interest rate is 2 percent a year (50 percent of 4 percent). Now suppose the inflation rate is 4 percent a year so the nominal interest rate is 8 percent a year. The *after-tax* nominal rate is 4 percent a year (50 percent of 8 percent). Now subtract the 4 percent inflation rate from this amount and you see that the *after-tax real interest rate* is zero! The true tax rate on interest income is 100 percent. If the inflation rate was greater than 4 percent in this example, the true tax rate would exceed 100 percent and the after-tax real interest rate would be negative.

With a low or possibly even negative after-tax real interest rate, the incentive to save is weakened and the saving rate falls. With a fall in saving, the pace of capital accumulation slows and so does the long-term growth rate of real GDP.

The second source of a fall in the economic growth rate arises because when the inflation rate is high, there is increased uncertainty about the long-term inflation rate. Will inflation remain high for a long time or will price stability be restored? This increased uncertainty makes long-term planning difficult and gives people a shorter term focus. Investment falls and so the growth rate slows.

The third source of a fall in the economic growth rate arises because instead of concentrating on the activities at which they have a comparative advantage, people find it more profitable to search for ways of avoiding the losses that inflation inflicts. As a result, inventive talent that might otherwise work on productive innovations works on finding ways of profiting from the inflation instead.

The economic growth costs of inflation are estimated to be much higher than the bootleather and other transactions costs and range between 5 percent and 7 percent of GDP for a 10 percent inflation. The U.S. productivity growth slowdown of the 1970s can be partly attributed to the inflation outburst that occurred during those years.

There are many examples of rapid anticipated inflations around the world, especially in Argentina, Bolivia and Brazil; in Russia and other Eastern European countries; and in some of the African countries where the cost of anticipated inflation are much greater than the numbers given here.

REVIEW

- Wrong inflation forecasts are costly, and to minimize forecasting errors, people use all the available information and make a *rational expectation*.
- Anticipated changes in aggregate demand and aggregate supply result in anticipated inflation.
- A rapid anticipated inflation diverts resources from producing goods and services and decreases potential GDP.

You've seen that an increase in aggregate demand that is not fully anticipated increases both the price level and real GDP. It also decreases unemployment. Similarly, a decrease in aggregate demand that is not fully anticipated decreases the price level and real GDP. It also increases unemployment. Do these relationships mean that there is a tradeoff between inflation and unemployment? That is, does low unemployment always bring inflation and does low inflation bring high unemployment? We explore these questions next.

Inflation and Unemployment: The Phillips Curve

THE AGGREGATE SUPPLY–AGGREGATE DEMAND model focuses on the price level and real GDP. Knowing how these two variables change, we can work out what happens to the inflation rate and the unemployment rate. But the model does not place inflation and unemployment at the center of the stage.

A more direct way of studying inflation and unemployment uses a relationship called the Phillips curve. The Phillips curve approach uses the same basic ideas as the *AS-AD* model, but it focuses directly on inflation and unemployment. The Phillips curve is so named because it was popularized by New Zealand economist A.W. Phillips. A **Phillips curve** is a curve that shows a relationship between inflation and unemployment. There are two time frames for Phillips curves:

- The short-run Phillips curve
- The long-run Phillips curve

The Short-Run Phillips Curve

The **short-run Phillips curve** is a curve that shows the relationship between inflation and unemployment, holding constant:

1. The expected inflation rate
2. The natural unemployment rate

You've just seen what determines the expected inflation rate. The natural rate of unemployment and the factors that influence it are explained in Chapter 24 on pp. 579–580.

Figure 32.9 shows a short-run Phillips curve, *SRPC*. Suppose that the expected inflation rate is 10 percent a year and the natural unemployment rate is

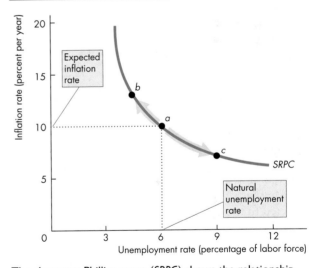

FIGURE 32.9

A Short-Run Phillips Curve

The short-run Phillips curve (*SRPC*) shows the relationship between inflation and unemployment at a given expected inflation rate and given natural unemployment rate. With an expected inflation rate of 10 percent a year and a natural unemployment rate of 6 percent, the short-run Phillips curve passes through point *a*. An unanticipated increase in aggregate demand lowers unemployment and increases inflation—a movement up the short-run Phillips curve. An unanticipated decrease in aggregate demand increases unemployment and lowers inflation—a movement down the short-run Phillips curve.

6 percent, point *a* in the figure. A short-run Phillips curve passes through this point. If inflation rises above its expected rate, unemployment falls below its natural rate. This joint movement in the inflation rate and the unemployment rate is illustrated as a movement up the short-run Phillips curve from point *a* to point *b* in the figure. Similarly, if inflation falls below its expected rate, unemployment rises above the natural rate. In this case there is movement down the short-run Phillips curve from point *a* to point *c*.

This negative relationship between inflation and unemployment along the short-run Phillips curve is explained by the aggregate supply–aggregate demand model. Figure 32.10 shows the connection between the two approaches. Initially, the aggregate demand curve is AD_0, the short-run aggregate supply curve is SAS_0, and the long-run aggregate supply curve is *LAS*. Real GDP is $6 trillion and the price level is 100. Aggregate demand is expected to increase and the aggregate demand curve is expected to shift rightward to AD_1. Anticipating this increase in aggregate demand, the money wage rate rises, which shifts the short-run aggregate supply curve to SAS_1. What happens to actual inflation and real GDP depends on the *actual* change in aggregate demand.

First, suppose that aggregate demand actually increases by the amount expected so the aggregate demand curve shifts to AD_1. The price level rises from 100 to 110 and the inflation rate is an anticipated 10 percent a year. Real GDP remains at potential GDP and unemployment remains at the natural rate. The economy moves to point *a* in Fig. 32.10 and it can equivalently be described as being at point *a* on the short-run Phillips curve in Fig. 32.9.

Alternatively, suppose that aggregate demand is expected to increase to AD_1 but actually increases by more than expected to AD_2. The price level now rises to 113, a 13 percent inflation rate. Real GDP increases above potential GDP and unemployment falls below the natural rate. We can now describe the economy as moving to point *b* in Fig. 32.10 or at point *b* on the short-run Phillips curve in Fig. 32.9.

Finally, suppose that aggregate demand is expected to increase to AD_1 but actually remains at AD_0. The price level now rises to 107, a 7 percent inflation rate. Real GDP falls below potential GDP and unemployment rises above the natural rate. We can now describe the economy as moving to point *c* in Fig. 32.10 or at point *c* on the short-run Phillips curve in Fig. 32.9.

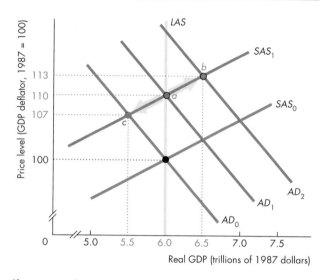

FIGURE 32.10

AS-AD and the Short-Run Phillips Curve

If aggregate demand is expected to increase and shift the aggregate demand curve from AD_0 to AD_1, then the money wage rate rises by an amount that shifts the short-run aggregate supply curve from SAS_0 to SAS_1. The price level rises to 110, a 10 percent rise, and the economy is at point *a* in this figure and at point *a* on the short-run Phillips curve in Fig. 32.9. If, with the same expectations, aggregate demand increases and shifts the aggregate demand curve from AD_0 to AD_2, the price level rises to 113, a 13 percent rise, and the economy is at point *b* in this figure and at point *b* on the short-run Phillips curve in Fig. 32.9. If, with the same expectations, aggregate demand does not change, the price level rises to 107, an 7 percent rise, and the economy is at point *c* in this figure and at point *c* on the short-run Phillips curve in Fig. 32.9.

The short-run Phillips curve is like the short-run aggregate supply curve. A movement along the *SAS* curve that brings a higher price level and an increase in real GDP is equivalent to a movement along the short-run Phillips curve that brings an increase in the inflation rate and a decrease in the unemployment rate. (Similarly, a movement along the *SAS* curve that brings a lower price level and a decrease in real GDP is equivalent to a movement along the short-run Phillips curve that brings a decrease in the inflation rate and an increase in the unemployment rate.)

The Long-Run Phillips Curve

The **long-run Phillips curve** is a curve that shows the relationship between inflation and unemployment when the actual inflation rate equals the expected inflation rate. The long-run Phillips curve is vertical at the natural unemployment rate. It is shown in Fig. 32.11 as the vertical line *LRPC*. The long-run Phillips curve tells us that any anticipated inflation rate is possible at the natural unemployment rate. This proposition is the same as the one you discovered in the *AS-AD* model. When inflation is anticipated, real GDP equals potential GDP. And with real GDP equal to potential GDP, unemployment is at the natural rate.

FIGURE 32.11

Short-Run and Long-Run Phillips Curves

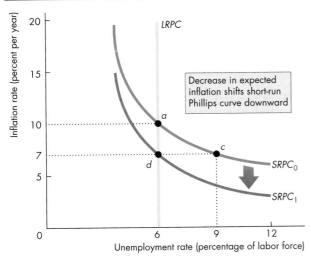

The long-run Phillips curve is *LRPC*, a vertical line at the natural unemployment rate. A fall in expected inflation shifts the short-run Phillips curve downward by the amount of the fall in the expected inflation rate. For example, when the expected inflation rate falls from 10 percent a year to 7 percent a year, the short-run Phillips curve shifts downward from $SRPC_0$ and $SRPC_1$. The new short-run Phillips curve intersects the long-run Phillips curve at the new expected inflation rate—point *d*. With the original expected inflation rate (of 10 percent), an actual inflation rate of 7 percent a year would occur at an unemployment rate of 9 percent, at point *c*.

When the expected inflation rate changes, the short-run Phillips curve shifts. If the expected inflation rate is 10 percent a year, the short-run Phillips curve is $SRPC_0$. If the expected inflation rate falls to 7 percent a year, the short-run Phillips curve shifts downward to $SRPC_1$. The distance by which the short-run Phillips curve shifts downward when the expected inflation rate falls is equal to the change in the expected inflation rate.

To see why the short-run Phillips curve shifts when the expected inflation rate changes, let's do an experiment. The economy is at full employment, and a fully anticipated inflation is raging at 10 percent a year. The Fed now begins a permanent attack on inflation by slowing money supply growth. Aggregate demand growth slows down, and the inflation rate falls to 7 percent a year. At first, this decrease in inflation is unanticipated, so wages continue to rise at their original rate, shifting the short-run aggregate supply curve leftward at the same pace as before. Real GDP falls, and unemployment increases. In Fig. 32.11 the economy moves from point *a* to point *c* on the short-run Phillips curve $SRPC_0$.

If the actual inflation rate remains steady at 7 percent a year, eventually this rate will come to be expected. As this happens, wage growth slows down and the short-run aggregate supply curve shifts leftward less quickly. Eventually, it shifts leftward at the same pace at which the aggregate demand curve is shifting rightward. The actual inflation rate equals the expected inflation rate, and full employment is restored. Unemployment is back at its natural rate. In Fig. 32.11 the short-run Phillips curve has shifted from $SRPC_0$ to $SRPC_1$ and the economy is at point *d*.

An increase in the expected inflation rate has the opposite effect to that shown in Fig. 32.11. Starting at point *d* with an expected inflation rate of 7 percent a year, suppose the actual inflation rate rises to 10 percent a year. The unemployment rate falls as the economy moves along $SRPC_1$. If the actual inflation rate remains at 10 percent a year, this rate will eventually become the expected inflation rate. As this happens, the short-run Phillips curve shifts upward from $SRPC_1$ to $SRPC_0$ and the economy moves to point *a*.

Shifts in the short-run Phillips curve like the ones we've just studied have occurred in the United States during the past 35 years. We'll look at these real-world examples below. But first we'll examine another important source of shifts in the Phillips curve: changes in the natural rate of unemployment.

Changes in the Natural Unemployment Rate

The natural unemployment rate changes for many reasons that are explained in Chapter 24 (pp. 579–580). A change in the natural unemployment rate shifts both the short-run and long-run Phillips curves. Figure 32.12 illustrates such shifts. If the natural unemployment rate increases from 6 percent to 9 percent, the long-run Phillips curve shifts from $LRPC_0$ to $LRPC_1$, and if expected inflation is constant at 10 percent a year, the short-run Phillips curve shifts from $SRPC_0$ to $SRPC_1$. Because the expected inflation rate is constant, the short-run Phillips curve $SRPC_1$ intersects the long-run curve $LRPC_1$ (point e) at the same inflation rate at which the short-run Phillips curve $SRPC_0$ intersects the long-run curve $LRPC_0$ (point a).

FIGURE 32.12

A Change in the Natural Unemployment Rate

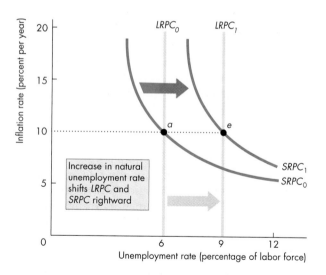

A change in the natural unemployment rate shifts both the short-run and long-run Phillips curves. Here the natural unemployment rate increases from 6 percent to 9 percent, and the two Phillips curves shift right to $SRPC_1$ and $LRPC_1$. The new long-run Phillips curve intersects the new short-run Phillips curve at the expected inflation rate—point e.

The Phillips Curve in the United States

Figure 32.13 shows the relationship between inflation and unemployment in the United States. Begin by looking at part (a), a scatter diagram of inflation and unemployment since 1960. Each dot in the figure represents the combination of inflation and unemployment for a particular year. As you can see, there does not appear to be any clear relationship between inflation and unemployment. We certainly cannot see a Phillips curve similar to that shown in Fig. 32.9.

But we can interpret the data with a short-run Phillips curve that shifts. Figure 32.13(b) shows this interpretation. In the 1960s, the natural rate of unemployment was 5 percent and the expected inflation rate was 2 percent a year (point a) and the short-run Phillips curve for this period is shown as $SRPC_0$. In the early 1970s, the natural rate of unemployment was still 5 percent but the expected inflation rate increased to 6 percent a year (point b) and the short-run Phillips curve shifted upward to $SRPC_1$.

In 1974, a large increase in oil prices disrupted the economy and had profound effects on both the natural unemployment rate, which increased to 8 percent, and the expected inflation rate, which increased briefly to 9 percent a year (point c). The short-run Phillips curve in 1975 shifted upward and rightward to $SRPC_3$. Through the rest of the 1970s, the natural unemployment rate remained at 8 percent but the expected inflation rate fell to 6 percent a year (point d) and the short-run Phillips curve was $SRPC_2$. In 1981, the expected inflation rate increased again to 9 percent a year and the short-run Phillips curve returned to $SRPC_3$.

Through the 1980s, both the expected inflation rate and the natural unemployment rate fell. By 1990, the natural unemployment rate was 6 percent and the expected inflation rate was 3 percent (point e) and the short-run Phillips curve was back at $SRPC_1$. Although in the 1990s the economy is on the same short-run Phillips curve as in the early 1970s ($SRPC_1$), the two periods are different. In the early 1970s, the natural unemployment rate was 5 percent and the expected inflation rate was 6 percent a year, while in the 1990s, the natural unemployment rate is 6 percent and the expected inflation rate is 3 percent a year. Thus although the short-run Phillips curves for these two periods are similar, a different combination of expected inflation and natural unemployment rates underlies the two curves.

FIGURE 32.13

Phillips Curves in the United States

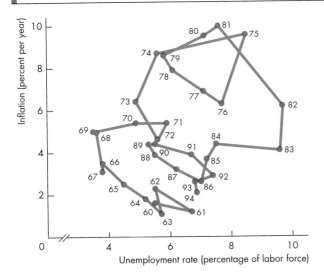

(a) Time sequence

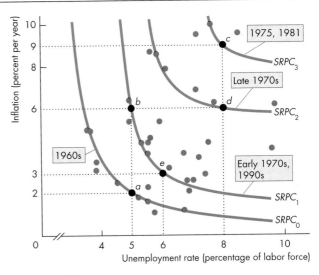

(b) Four Phillips curves

In part (a) each dot represents the combination of inflation and unemployment for a particular year in the United States. There is no clear relationship between the two variables. Part (b) interprets the data with a shifting short-run Phillips curve. In the 1960s, the natural unemployment rate was 5 percent and the expected inflation rate was 2 percent a year (point *a*) and the short-run Phillips curve was $SRPC_0$. In the early 1970s, the natural unemployment rate was 5 percent and the expected inflation rate was 6 percent a year (point *b*) and the short-run Phillips curve was $SRPC_1$. By 1975, the natural unemployment rate had increased to 8 percent and the expected

inflation rate was 9 percent a year (point *c*) and the short-run Phillips curve was $SRPC_3$. During the rest of the 1970s, the natural unemployment rate remained at 8 percent but the expected inflation rate fell to 6 percent a year (point *d*) and the short-run Phillips curve was $SRPC_2$. In 1981, the short-run Phillips curve briefly returned to $SRPC_3$. Then, through the 1980s, the natural unemployment rate and the expected inflation rate fell. By 1990 the natural unemployment rate was 6 percent and the expected inflation rate was 3 percent (point *e*) and the economy was back on $SRPC_1$.

Source: Economic Report of the President, 1995, and the author's assumptions and calculations.

- Unanticipated changes in the inflation rate bring movements along the short-run Phillips curve.
- An unanticipated increase in the inflation rate lowers the unemployment rate, and an unanticipated decrease in the inflation rate raises the unemployment rate.
- A change in the expected inflation rate shifts the short-run Phillips curve (upward for an increase in inflation and downward for a decrease in inflation) by an amount equal to the change in the expected inflation rate.

- A change in the natural unemployment rate shifts both the short-run and long-run Phillips curves (rightward for an increase in the natural rate and leftward for a decrease).
- The relationship between inflation and unemployment in the United States can be interpreted by a short-run Phillips curve that shifts.

So far, we've studied the effects of inflation on real GDP, real wages, employment, and unemployment. But inflation lowers the value of money and changes the real value of the amounts borrowed and repaid. As a result, interest rates are influenced by inflation. Let's see how.

Interest Rates and Inflation

IN THE EARLY 1990S, CORPORATIONS COULD borrow at interest rates of less than 5 percent a year. But in the early 1980s, interest rates were around 16 percent a year. Why do interest rates fluctuate so much and why were they so high in the early 1980s? Part of the answer is explained in Chapter 25 where the forces that determine the real interest rate are explained. The **real interest rate** is the *nominal* interest rate minus the inflation rate. Fluctuations in the real interest rate are caused by fluctuations in saving supply and investment demand. But another part of the answer, and a major part, is that the inflation rate was low during the 1990s and high during the early 1980s. With changes in the inflation rate, nominal interest rates change to make borrowers pay the amount that compensates lenders for the fall in the value of money. Let's see how inflation affects borrowers and lenders.

The Effects of Inflation on Borrowers and Lenders

The *nominal* interest rate is the price paid by a borrower to compensate a lender for two things: the amount loaned and the fall in the value of money that results from inflation. The *real* interest rate is the price paid by a borrower to compensate a lender only for the amount loaned. It is the real cost of a loan to the borrower and the real return on a loan to the lender. The forces of demand and supply determine an equilibrium real interest rate that does not depend on the inflation rate. These same forces also determine an equilibrium nominal interest rate that does depend on the inflation rate and that equals the equilibrium real interest rate plus the expected inflation rate.

To see why these outcomes occur, imagine that there is no inflation and that the nominal interest rate is 4 percent a year. The real interest rate is also 4 percent a year. The amount that businesses and people want to borrow equals the amount that businesses and people want to lend at this real interest rate. Walt Disney Corporation is willing to pay an interest rate of 4 percent a year to get the funds it needs to pay for its global investment in new theme parks. Sue and thousands of people like her are willing to lend

Disney the amount it needs for its theme parks if they can get a *real* return of 4 percent a year. (Sue wants to buy a new car, and she plans to save enough to do so.)

Now suppose inflation breaks out at a steady 6 percent a year. All dollar prices and values, including theme park profits and car prices rise by 6 percent a year. If Disney was willing to pay a 4 percent interest rate when there was no inflation, it is now willing to pay 10 percent interest. The reason is that its profits are rising by 6 percent a year, so it is *really* paying only 4 percent. Similarly, if Sue was willing to lend at a 4 percent interest rate when there was no inflation, she is now willing to lend only if she gets 10 percent interest. The price of the car Sue is planning on buying is rising by 6 percent a year, so she is *really* getting only a 4 percent interest rate.

Because borrowers are willing to pay the higher rate and lenders are willing to lend only if they receive the higher rate, when inflation is anticipated, the *nominal interest rate* increases by an amount equal to the expected inflation rate. The *real interest rate* remains constant. The real interest rate might change because the supply of saving or investment demand has changed for some other reason. But a change in the expected inflation rate alone does not change the real interest rate.

We've seen why the behavior of borrowers and lenders makes the nominal interest rate change when the expected inflation rate changes. Let's look at the mechanism in the money market that brings this change about. We'll first see what happens when the price level changes but the change is *not* anticipated. Then we'll see what happens when the price level keeps on rising and the inflation is anticipated.

Interest Rates and Unanticipated Inflation

We'll work out the effects of inflation on interest rates by using Fig. 32.14, which is similar to Fig. 31.12 (p. 784). Initially, the economy is at full employment, and there is no inflation and none is expected. The *real* quantity of money is $5 trillion, and the money supply curve is MS_0. The demand for money curve is MD, and the interest rate is 4 percent a year. This interest rate is both the *nominal* interest rate and the *real* interest rate. To see why, recall that

$$\text{Real interest rate} = \text{Nominal interest rate} - \text{Inflation rate}.$$

FIGURE **32.14**

Money Growth, Inflation, and the Interest Rate

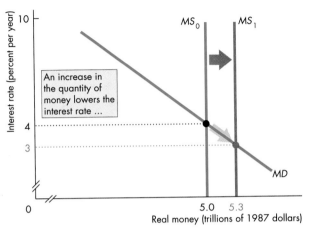

(a) Unanticipated increase in money

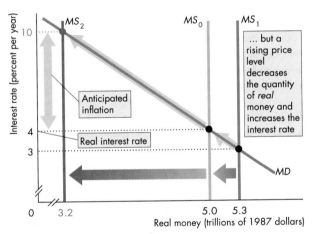

(b) Anticipated money growth

Initially, there is no inflation and none is expected. The demand for money curve is *MD*, the supply of money curve is MS_0, and the interest rate (*nominal* and *real*) is 4 percent a year. The quantity of money increases and the money supply curve shifts to MS_1. In part (a), the nominal interest rate falls to 4 percent a year. In part (b), as the price level rises, the quantity of real money decreases and the interest rate rises. If the quantity of money keeps increasing and if people anticipate higher inflation, the price level rises and the quantity of real money falls until the interest rate has increased by an amount equal to the anticipated inflation rate.

Because the inflation rate is zero, the real and nominal interest rates are the same.

Now suppose that the Fed increases the quantity of money to $5.3 trillion—a 6 percent increase. The money supply curve shifts rightward to MS_1. The nominal interest rate falls to 3 percent a year.

The lower interest rate now begins to have a ripple effect through the economy. With a lower interest rate, aggregate demand increases and the price level begins to rise. The higher price level *decreases* the quantity of *real* money and the money supply curve shifts leftward. When the price level has increased to 6 percent, the same as the percentage increase in the quantity of money, the quantity of real money is back at its original level of $5 trillion and the interest rate is back at 4 percent.

Interest Rates and Anticipated Inflation

Now suppose that the Fed increases the quantity of money by 6 percent a year every year. Aggregate demand is increasing and inflation is running at 6 percent a year. At first, the inflation is not anticipated. So the amount of money and other assets that people plan to hold, and the amount they plan to spend, are based on a nominal interest rate of 4 percent a year, an expectation of no inflation, and a real interest rate of 4 percent a year.

But when people begin to anticipate inflation, their plans change. With an interest rate of 4 percent and some inflation expected, people believe that the real interest rate has fallen. In this situation they decide to hold a smaller quantity of money because its real value is expected to fall. They decide to hold a smaller quantity of other financial assets because the real interest rate they expect to earn has fallen. And, anticipating higher future prices, people increase their demand for goods and services.

The increase in demand for goods and services increases aggregate demand. So aggregate demand is now increasing for two reasons: the quantity of money is increasing and people are demanding more goods in anticipation of them costing even more in the future. These two sources of increase in aggregate demand increase the inflation rate to a level that, for a while, exceeds the rate at which the quantity of money is increasing. As a result the quantity of *real* money decreases. The money supply curve shifts leftward and the interest rate rises.

In Fig. 32.14(b), by the time the quantity of real money has fallen to $3.2 trillion and the supply of money curve is MS_2, the nominal interest rate has increased to 10 percent a year. The real interest rate is back at its original level of 4 percent a year. In this situation, people's spending plans return to their original levels. Aggregate demand now increases only because of the increasing quantity of money. The inflation rate and the growth rate of the money supply are equal, the real money supply is constant, and the economy is in a long-run equilibrium.

We've seen that an unanticipated inflation leads to a decrease in the nominal interest rate and that an anticipated inflation leads to an increase in the nominal interest rate and no change in the real interest rate. Therefore the higher the anticipated inflation rate, the higher is the nominal interest rate. To the extent that inflation is in fact anticipated, interest rates and the inflation rate will move up and down together. Let's see whether they do.

Inflation and Interest Rates in the United States

Figure 32.15 shows the relationship between inflation and nominal interest rates in the United States between 1960 and 1994. Each point represents a year. The interest rate is that paid by large corporations on 6-month loans. The blue line shows the relationship between the nominal interest rate and the inflation rate if the real interest rate is constant at 2.1 percent a year, which is its actual average value in this period. When the red dot lies above the blue line, the real interest rate exceeds 2.1 percent a year and when the red dot lies below the blue line, the real interest rate is less than 2.1 percent a year.

You can see that there is a positive relationship between the inflation rate and the interest rate, but the real interest rate has not been constant. During the 1960s, inflation and nominal interest rates were low. In the early 1970s inflation began to increase, but it was not expected to increase much and certainly not to persist. As a result, nominal interest rates did not rise very much at that time. During the late 1970s and early 1980s, inflation of close to 10 percent a year came to be expected as an ongoing and highly persistent phenomenon. As a result, nominal interest rates increased to around 15 percent a year. Then in 1984 and 1985 the inflation rate fell—at first unexpectedly. Interest rates began to fall but not nearly as quickly as

FIGURE 32.15

Inflation and the Interest Rate

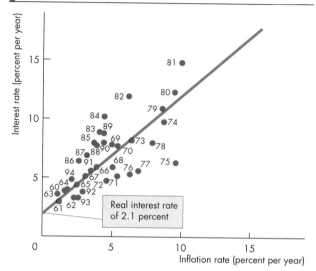

Other things remaining the same, the higher the expected inflation rate, the higher is the nominal interest rate. A graph showing the relationship between nominal interest rates and the actual inflation rate reveals that the influence of inflation on nominal interest rates is a powerful one.

Source: Economic Report of the President, 1995.

the inflation rate. Short-term interest rates fell more quickly than long-term interest rates because, at that time, it was expected that inflation would be lower in the short term but not as low in the longer term.

By the 1990s, inflation and the nominal interest rate had returned to their 1960s levels and with inflation near to its expected rate, the real interest rate was close to its long-term average of 2.1 percent a year.

The relationship between inflation and interest rates is even more dramatically illustrated by international experience. For example, in recent years, Chile has experienced an inflation rate of around 30 percent with nominal interest rates of about 40 percent. Brazil has experienced inflation rates and nominal interest rates of 40 percent a *month*. At the other extreme, countries such as Japan and Belgium have low inflation and low nominal interest rates.

■ The nominal interest rate is the rate that is actually paid and received in the marketplace.

■ The real interest rate is the rate that is *really* paid and received when the effects of inflation are taken into account.

■ The real interest rate is equal to the nominal interest rate minus the inflation rate.

■ There is a strong correlation between the inflation rate and the nominal interest rate—other things remaining the same, an anticipated increase in the inflation rate brings an equal increase in the nominal interest rate.

The Politics of Inflation

WE NOTED AT THE BEGINNING OF THIS CHAPTER that inflation has plagued nations over many centuries, from the Roman empire to modern Russia. (There are examples of inflation from even earlier times going back to the earliest civilizations.) What are the deeper sources of inflation that are common to all these vastly different societies? The answer lies in the political situation. There are two main political sources of inflation. They are:

■ Inflation tax
■ Errors in forecasting the natural unemployment rate

Inflation Tax

Inflation is not a tax in the usual sense. Governments don't pass inflation tax laws like income tax and sales tax laws. But inflation works just like a tax. One way in which a government can finance its expenditure is by selling bonds. These bonds are sold on the bond market. Whenever the Fed buys some federal government's bonds, it pays for them with new money—with an increase in the monetary base. When government expenditure is financed in this way, the quantity of money increases. So the government gets revenue from inflation just as if it had increased taxes. And the holders of money pay this tax to the government. They do so because the real value of their money holdings decreases at a rate equal to the inflation rate.

Inflation is not a major revenue source for the U.S. federal government; its average is less than 2 percent of total revenue. But in some countries it is the main revenue source. The closing years of the Roman empire and the transition years to a market economy in Russia and Eastern Europe are examples. In the case of the Roman empire, the empire had grown beyond its capacity to administer the collection of taxes on a scale sufficient to cover the expenditures of the government. In the case of Russia, the traditional source of government revenue was from state-owned enterprises. In the transition to a market economy, government revenue from these enterprises dried up but expenditure commitments did not decline in line with this loss of revenue. In both cases, the government financed its expenditures by creating money and the resulting increase in the quantity of money caused inflation.

Errors in Forecasting the Natural Unemployment Rate

The Fed sometimes speeds up money growth in an attempt to lower the unemployment rate. But if unemployment has increased because the natural unemployment rate has increased, such a monetary policy ends up increasing the inflation rate. In deciding the appropriate monetary policy, the Fed must make a judgment about potential GDP and the natural unemployment rate. In 1994, the Fed believed that unemployment was falling below the natural rate and decided to slow the pace of money growth to prevent inflation from breaking out. This episode is explored further in *Reading Between the Lines* on pp. 818–819.

■ Inflation is a source of government revenue—inflation is a tax—and when conventional revenue sources are inadequate, an inflation tax is used.

■ Inflation might also arise from unforeseen changes in the natural unemployment rate.

◆ You have now completed your study of inflation. This material, together with that on economic growth (Chapter 27), gives a good overview of the long-term problems that confront a modern economy such as that of the United States. Our task in the following chapter is to focus more sharply on the problems of the business cycle and unemployment.

Anticipating Inflation

THE CHICAGO TRIBUNE, MAY 9, 1994

Will Inflation Reappear, or Is It Different Now?

BY JOHN N. MACLEAN

When the United Steelworkers of America came to the negotiating table with Inland Steel Industries Inc. last year, the No. 1 issue on the workers' agenda could be summed up in two words: job security.

Gone were the days when the steelworkers, the autoworkers, the truckers, and other unionized workers went into negotiations with the No. 1 issue that also took two words: more money.

That episode should give pause to those who think a strong employment report, such as the one on Friday, will bring another round of inflation, with wages and prices chasing each other. Wall Street reacted that way Friday, sending the Dow Jones industrial average down more than 50 points at one point on fears of renewed inflation.

The case for inflation stands or falls on the traditional wage-price spiral. Floods in the Midwest may wash out a corn crop and temporarily raise prices, but events such as that cannot by themselves cause the sort of sustained, devastating inflation that afflicted the U.S. economy in the late 1970s and early 1980s.

The only commodity capable of such damage is oil. The industrialized world amounts to a petroleum culture. When the oil lifeline was threatened twice in the 1970s, inflation roared and caused deep harm. [But] right now, the world is awash with oil. ...

So, can inflation rise again?

A tug of war exists between financial analysts who say things are different this time and inflation can't easily reappear and financial markets that say things are not different this time and inflation looms on the horizon.

It's fun to make the case for things being different. American business has shown extraordinary resilience in reinventing itself, raising productivity and producing quality. ...

It's no fun to write about the jobs side of restructuring and less fun to be its victim. But it's an important element, too. ...

Where, then, could a wage-price spiral start?

At the moment only the faintest of indicators gives any sign of such activity. The markets themselves are the main indicator.

Months before the Fed began raising interest rates in February, long-term bond prices began falling, sending yields upward. ...

That's the market's way of saying, "Watch out, inflation lies ahead." ...

Essence of THE STORY

■ In 1993, months before the Fed started to raise interest rates, bond prices fell and bond yields increased. These changes were read as signs that bond holders expected renewed inflation.

■ But inflation can resume only if a traditional wage-price (cost-push) spiral breaks out, and there was little sign of pressures that could create such a spiral.

■ Increases in productivity and restructuring had brought a slack labor market and in 1994, labor union negotiators were more concerned about job security than pay increases, so there was no sign of wages causing renewed inflation.

■ A rise in the price of oil (such as occurred twice in the 1970s) could trigger an inflation, but there was no sign of a shortage of oil.

■ Nonetheless, the bond market says, "Watch out, inflation lies ahead."

Economic

A N A L Y S I S

■ Interest rates on bonds began to increase in 1993, several months before the Fed started to push interest rates upward.

■ Figure 1 shows three government bond interest rates—*nominal* interest rates—month by month through 1993 and 1994. They are the interest rates on 30-year, 10-year, and 3-year bonds.

■ The figure shows that all three interest rates began to rise in November 1993, three months before the Fed started to put upward pressure on interest rates in February 1994.

■ But the magnitude of the rise in rates was small. Between October 1993 and February 1994, nominal interest rates increased by an average of 0.6 percentage point.

■ The nominal interest rate equals the real interest rate plus the expected inflation rate. So if the real interest rate did not change during this period, the expected inflation rate increased by 0.6 percentage point. For example, if the expected inflation rate in October was 2.8 percent a year, the actual inflation rate at that time, then a 3.4 percent a year inflation was being anticipated by February.

■ The bond market then says, "Watch out for a tiny upturn in the inflation rate."

■ Figure 2 interprets these bond market developments and the Fed's actions by using expectations about aggregate supply and aggregate demand.

■ In the winter of 1993–1994, bond holders and the Fed were trying to forecast the economy in 1995. Potential GDP was expected to grow to about $6.9 trillion, so the expected long-run aggregate supply curve was $ELAS_{95}$.

■ Before October 1993, aggregate demand was expected to increase and to be EAD_0 in 1995. The price level was expected to rise from 126 in 1994 to 129 in 1995, an inflation rate of around 2.4 percent.

■ Wage agreements for 1995 incorporated this expectation, so the short-run aggregate supply curve was $ESAS_{95}$.

■ After October 1993, bond holders expected the aggregate demand curve to shift to EAD_1. The inflation rate was expected to increase to about 3 percent, and real GDP was expected to rise above potential GDP.

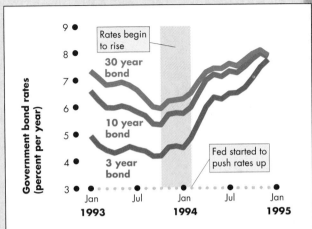

Figure 1 Government bond rates

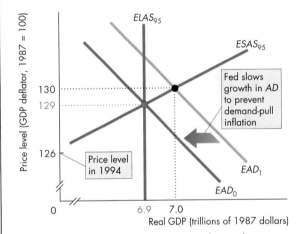

Figure 2 Aggregate supply–aggregate demand

■ By February 1994 the Fed agreed with the bond market and took action to slow the growth of aggregate demand. Its aim was to ensure that aggregate demand grew by the amount previously expected.

■ The news article is a bit misleading in the way it identifies the origins of inflation with wage and price rises. A wage increase or a rise in prices, even key prices like that of oil, does not cause inflation. It can cause a one-time rise in the price level. But only the Fed can cause inflation—an ongoing process of a rising price level.

SUMMARY

Inflation and the Price Level

Inflation is a process of persistently rising prices and falling value of money. The price level rises when the inflation rate is positive and falls when the inflation rate is negative. The price level rises *faster* when the inflation rate *increases* and *slower* when the inflation rate *decreases*. (p. 797)

Demand-Pull Inflation

Demand-pull inflation arises from increasing aggregate demand. Its main sources are increases in the money supply or in government puchases. When aggregate demand increases, real GDP and the price level rise. Wages then begin to rise and short-run aggregate supply decreases, which raises the price level still further. If aggregate demand keeps increasing, the price level keeps on rising. Wages respond, aggregate demand increases again, and a price-wage inflation spiral ensues. (pp. 798–800)

Cost-Push Inflation

Cost-push inflation can result from any factor that decreases aggregate supply, and the main factors are increasing wage rates and increasing prices of key raw materials. These sources of a decreasing aggregate supply bring increasing costs that lower real GDP and increase the price level. An increase in the money supply to restore full employment increases aggregate demand, which results in a yet higher price level and higher real GDP. If the original source of cost-push inflation repeats, costs rise again and the short-run aggregate supply curve shifts leftward again. If the money supply increases again, the price level rises even higher. Inflation proceeds at a rate determined by the cost-push forces. (pp. 800–802)

Anticipating Inflation

Forecasts of inflation are rational expectations if they are based on the aggregate supply–aggregate demand model and use all the available information on the positions of the aggregate demand and aggregate supply curves. A moderate anticipated inflation has a small cost. But a rapid anticipated inflation is costly and decreases potential GDP. (pp. 803–809)

Inflation and Unemployment: The Phillips Curve

The short-run Phillips curve, which slopes downward, shows the relationship between inflation and unemployment when the expected inflation rate and the natural unemployment rate are constant. The long-run Phillips curve, which is vertical, shows that when the actual inflation rate equals the expected inflation rate, the unemployment rate equals the natural unemployment rate. Unexpected changes in the inflation rate bring movements along the short-run Phillips curve. Changes in expected inflation shift the short-run Phillips curve. Changes in the natural unemployment rate shift both the short-run and long-run Phillips curves. There is no clear relationship between inflation and unemployment in the United States, but the joint movements in those variables can be interpreted in terms of a shifting short-run Phillips curve. (pp. 809–813)

Interest Rates and Inflation

The higher the expected inflation rate, the higher is the nominal interest rate. As the anticipated inflation rate rises, borrowers willingly pay a higher interest rate and lenders successfully demand a higher interest rate. So the nominal interest rate equals the real interest rate plus the expected inflation rate. (pp. 814–817)

The Politics of Inflation

Inflation is a source government revenue—a tax—and its rate increases when the government's financial needs exceed the income tax and other tax revenues. Inflation can also increase if the Fed speeds up money growth when the natural unemployment rate rises. (p. 817)

K E Y   E L E M E N T S

Key Figures

Key Terms

R E V I E W   Q U E S T I O N S

1. Distinguish between a one-time change in the price level and inflation.

2. Distinguish between the price level and the inflation rate.

3. Distinguish between demand-pull inflation and cost-push inflation.

4. Explain how a demand-pull inflation spiral occurs.

5. Explain how a cost-push inflation spiral occurs.

6. Why is unanticipated inflation costly? Suggest some of the losses that an individual would suffer in labor markets as well as in asset markets.

7. Explain why unanticipated inflation does more than redistribute income.

8. What is a rational expectation? Explain the two features of a rational expectation.

9. What is the rational expectation of the price level in
   a. The short run?
   b. The long run?

10. Explain how anticipated inflation arises.

11. Why is anticipated inflation costly?

12. What does the short-run Phillips curve show?

13. What does the long-run Phillips curve show?

14. What have been the main shifts in the U.S. short-run Phillips curve during the 1970s, 1980s, and 1990s?

15. What is the connection between expected inflation and nominal interest rates?

PROBLEMS

1. Work out the effects on the price level of the following unexpected events:
   a. An increase in the money supply
   b. An increase in government purchases of goods and services
   c. An increase in income taxes
   d. An increase in investment demand
   e. An increase in the wage rate
   f. An increase in labor productivity

2. Work out the effects on the price level of the events listed in problem 1 when they are correctly anticipated.

◆ 3. The figure shows an economy's long-run aggregate supply curve, *LAS*, aggregate demand curve AD_0, and short-run aggregate supply curve SAS_0. Wages are flexible and aggregate demand is *expected* to be AD_1.

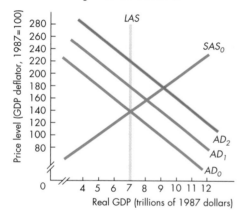

   a. What is the expected price level?
   b. What is expected inflation rate?
   c. If aggregate demand actually increases to AD_1, what is the actual inflation rate and real GDP?
   d. If aggregate demand actually increases to AD_1, is the unemployment rate less than, greater than, or equal to the natural rate of unemployment?
   e. If aggregate demand actually increases to AD_2, what is the actual inflation rate and real GDP?
   f. If aggregate demand actually increases to AD_2, is the unemployment rate less than, greater than, or equal to the natural rate of unemployment?

   g. If aggregate demand remains constant at AD_0, what is the actual inflation rate and real GDP?
   h. If aggregate demand remains constant at AD_0, is the unemployment rate less than, greater than, or equal to the natural rate of unemployment?

◆ 4. In the economy of problem 3, aggregate demand is expected to increase to AD_2.
   a. What is the new *SAS* curve if the money wage rate is fixed?
   b. What is the new *SAS* curve if the money wage rate is flexible?
   c. In (a) and (b) is real GDP expected to be at, above, or below potential GDP?

◆ 5. In the economy in problem 4, aggregate demand actually increases to AD_1.
   a. What is the actual price level in the short run?
   b. What is actual real GDP in the short run?
   c. What is the actual price level in the long run?
   d. What is actual real GDP in the long run?

◆ 6. In 1995 the expected aggregate demand schedule for 1996 is as follows:

Price level (GDP deflator)	Expected real GDP demanded (trillions of 1987 dollars)
120	4.0
121	3.9
122	3.8
123	3.7
124	3.6

In 1995 the potential real GDP is $3.8 trillion and the real GDP expected for 1996 is $3.9 trillion. Calculate the 1995 rational expectation of the price level for 1996 if wages are
   a. Fixed until 1996.
   b. Going to be renegotiated before 1996.

7. An economy has a natural unemployment rate of 4 percent when its expected inflation is 6 percent. Its inflation and unemployment history is as follows:

Inflation rate (percent per year)	Unemployment rate (percent)
10	2
8	3
6	4
4	5
2	6

a. Draw a diagram of this economy's short-run and long-run Phillips curves.

b. If the actual inflation rate rises from 6 percent a year to 8 percent a year, what is the change in the unemployment rate? Explain why it occurs.

c. If the natural unemployment rate rises to 5 percent, what is the change in the unemployment rate? Explain why it occurs.

d. Go back to (b). If the expected inflation rate falls to 4 percent a year, what is the change in the unemployment rate? Explain why it occurs.

8. Study *Reading Between the Lines* on pp. 818–819 and then answer the following questions:

a. What does the news article say about the likelihood of inflation returning in the next year or two?

b. What do the financial markets say about expectations of renewed inflation?

c. What steps has the Fed taken to avoid renewed inflation?

d. Draw on what you have learned in this chapter about the causes of inflation, and write a critique of the theory of inflation that implicitly lies behind this news article.

The Business Cycle

After studying
this chapter,
you will be
able to:

- Distinguish among the different theories of the business cycle

- Explain the Keynesian and monetarist theories of the business cycle

- Explain the new classical and new Keynesian theories of the business cycle

- Explain real business cycle theory

- Describe the origins of and the mechanisms at work during two recent recessions

- Describe the origins of and the mechanisms at work during the Great Depression

Must What Goes Up Always Come Down?

The 1920s were years of unprecedented prosperity for Americans. After the horrors of World War I (1914–1918), the economic machine was back at work, producing such technological marvels as cars and airplanes, telephones and vacuum cleaners. Houses and apartments were being built at a frantic pace. Then, almost without warning, in October 1929, came a devastating stock market crash. Overnight, the values of stocks and shares trading on Wall Street fell by 30 percent. During the four succeeding years, there followed the most severe economic contraction in recorded history. By 1933, real GDP had fallen by 30 percent; unemployment had increased to 25 percent of the labor force; and employment was down 20 percent. What caused the Great Depression? ◆ By the standard of the Great Depression, recent recessions have been mild. But recessions have not gone away. Our economy has experienced 15 recessions since 1920 and 10 since the end of World War II in 1945. Over the 16 months from November 1973 through March 1975, real GDP fell by 5 percent. It fell by 2.5 percent over a period of 6 months in 1980. It fell again in a back-to-back recession by 3 percent over a period of 16 months in 1981–1982. Most recently, it decreased by 1.4 percent over a period of 8 months in 1990–1991. Between these recessions, expansions took real GDP and income per person to new heights. Since the 1990–1991 recession, real GDP has soared. By the end of 1994, it stood some 12 percent higher than it had in the 1990–1991 recession and 10 percent higher than its peak before that recession. What causes a repeating sequence of recessions and expansions in our economy? Must what goes up always come down? Will we have another recession? When? Before 2000?

◈ We are going to explore the business cycle in this chapter. You will see how all the strands of macroeconomics that you've been following come together and weave a complete picture of the forces and mechanisms that generate economic growth and fluctuations in production, employment and unemployment, and inflation.

Cycle Patterns, Impulses, and Mechanisms

YOU'VE LOOKED AT THE BUSINESS CYCLE AT several points in your study of macroeconomics. You met it first in Chapter 22, which defines the phases of the cycle and describes its history. You saw how unemployment fluctuates over the business cycle in Chapter 24. In Chapter 27 you learned about a framework for studying the business cycle—the aggregate supply–aggregate demand model. In Chapter 28 you focused on business cycle turning points and the inventory changes and expenditure multiplier effects that operate as the economy swings from expansion to recession and recession to expansion. In Chapter 29 you studied the ways in which fiscal policy influences and is influenced by the business cycle. Finally, you saw in Chapters 30 through 32 how money influences economic fluctuations and how inflation and the business cycle intertwine.

You've also looked at another type of economic fluctuation, the productivity growth slowdown of the 1970s. This slowdown is not classified as a business cycle event, but it has some similarities. It is part of an overall process of economic growth, the pace of which fluctuates. The processes of growth and of the business cycle are intimately connected. In fact, according to one view, they are all manifestations of the same phenomenon.

This chapter brings all these strands in your previous study of macroeconomics together and gives you an opportunity both to review what you have learned and to put it to work in a focused way in interpreting and making sense of particular episodes in our economic history.

We'll get moving by first returning to the facts about the business cycle and looking at the complex patterns it makes.

Business Cycle Patterns

The *business cycle* is an irregular and nonrepeating up-and-down movement of business activity that takes place around a generally rising trend and that shows great diversity. Each recession, expansion, and turning point has been dated by the National Bureau of Economic Research (NBER). The NBER has identified 15 recessions and expansions since 1920. On the average, recessions have lasted for just over a

year and real GDP has fallen from peak to trough by more than 6 percent. Expansions have lasted for almost 4 years on the average, and real GDP has increased from trough to peak by an average of 22 percent. But these averages hide huge variations from one cycle to another.

Figure 33.1 shows the range of variation across the different recessions and expansions. You can see that the Great Depression was much more severe than anything that followed it. According to the NBER, the contraction of real GDP that created the Great Depression began in August 1929 and ended in March 1933 and over this 43-month period, real GDP shrank by 33 percent. The second most severe recession was also in the 1930s. Another relatively severe recession occurred at the end of World War II in 1945. The only other recession that comes close to these is the OPEC recession of 1974–1975, which lasted for 16 months during which real GDP fell by 5 percent. The other recessions since 1950, including the most recent 1990–1991 recession, have been much milder than those of the 1930s. The biggest expansion occurred during World War II. But the other two big expansions were in the 1960s and 1980s. There is no correlation between the length of an expansion and the length of the preceding recession.

With this enormous diversity of experience, there is no simple explanation for the business cycle. Also, there is no (currently available) way of forecasting when the next turning point will come. But there is a body of theory about the business cycle that helps us to understand its causes. A good place to begin studying this theory is to distinguish the possible ways in which cycles can be created.

Cycle Impulses and Mechanisms

Cycles are a widespread physical phenomenon. In a tennis match, the ball cycles from one side of the court to the other and back again. Every day, the earth cycles from day to night and back to day. A child on a rocking horse creates a cycle as the horse swings to and fro.

The tennis ball cycle is the simplest. It is caused by the actions of the players. Each time the ball changes direction (at each turning point), the racket (an outside force) is applied. The day-night-day cycle is the most subtle. This cycle is caused by the rotation of the earth. No new force is applied each day to make the sun rise and set. It happens because of the

---

FIGURE 33.1
Some Business Cycle Patterns

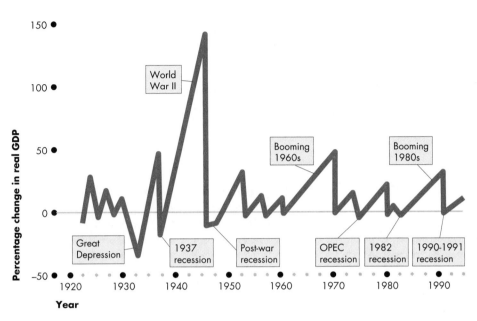

Recessions have lasted from 43 months during the Great Depression, when real GDP fell by 33 percent, to 6 months in 1980, when real GDP fell by 2.5 percent. The mildest recession lasted through most of 1970, when real GDP fell by 1 percent. Recessions have been less severe in the post World War II period. Expansions have lasted from 6 months in 1980 to more than 100 months during the 1960s. Expansions have become longer and stronger during the post World War II period.

Source: National Bureau of Economic Research and the author's calculations.

---

design of the objects that interact to create the cycle. Nothing happens at a turning point (sunrise and sunset) that is any different from what is happening at other points except that the sun comes into or goes out of view. The child's rocking horse cycle is a combination of these two cases. To start the horse rocking, some outside force must be exerted (as in the tennis ball cycle). But once the horse is rocking, the to-and-fro cycle continues for some time with no further force being applied (as in the day-night-day cycle). The rocking horse cycle eventually dies out unless the horse is pushed again, and each time the horse is pushed, the cycle temporarily becomes more severe.

The economy is a bit like all three of these examples. It can be hit by shocks (like a tennis ball) that send it in one direction or another, it can cycle indefinitely (like the turning of day into night), and it can cycle in swings that get milder until another shock sets off a new burst of bigger swings (like a rocking horse). While none of these analogies is perfect, they all contain some insights into the business cycle.

Different theories of the cycle emphasize different outside forces (different tennis rackets) and different cycle mechanisms (different solar system and rocking horse designs).

Although there are several different theories of the business cycle, they all agree about one aspect of the cycle: the central role played by investment and the accumulation of capital.

The Central Role of Investment and Capital

Whatever the shocks are that hit the economy, they hit one crucial variable: investment. Recessions begin when investment in new capital slows down, and they turn into expansions when investment speeds up. Investment and capital interact like the spinning earth and the sun to create an ongoing cycle.

In an expansion, investment proceeds at a rapid rate and the capital stock grows quickly. But rapid capital growth means that the amount of capital per hour of labor is growing. Equipped with more capital, labor becomes more productive. But the *law of diminishing returns* begins to operate. (Recall that the law of diminishing returns states that as the quantity of capital increases, with the quantity of labor remaining the same, the gain in productivity from the additional units of capital eventually diminishes—see Chapter 26, p. 629). Diminishing returns to capital bring a fall in the profit rate and with a lower profit rate, the incentive to invest weakens. As a result, investment eventually falls. When it falls by a large amount, recession begins.

In a recession, investment is low and the capital stock grows slowly. In a deep recession, the capital stock might actually fall. Slow capital growth (or even a falling capital stock) means that the amount of capital per hour of labor is falling. With a low amount of capital per hour of labor, businesses begin to see opportunities for profitable investment and the pace of investment eventually picks up. As it does so, recession turns into expansion.

The AS-AD Model

Investment and capital are a crucial part of the business cycle mechanism but they are just one part. To study the broader business cycle mechanism, we need a broader framework. That framework is the *AS-AD* model of Chapter 27. All the theories of the business cycle can be described in terms of the *AS-AD* model. Theories differ both in what they identify as the impulse and in the cycle mechanism. But all theories can be thought of as making assumptions about the factors that make either aggregate supply or aggregate demand fluctuate and assumptions about how they interact with each other to create a business cycle. Business cycle impulses can affect either the supply side or the demand side of the economy or both. But there are no pure supply-side theories. We will classify all theories of the business cycle as either:

- Aggregate demand theories
- Real business cycle theory

We'll study the aggregate demand theories first. Then we'll study real business cycle theory, which is a more recent approach that isolates a shock that has both aggregate supply and aggregate demand effects.

Aggregate Demand Theories of the Business Cycle

THREE TYPES OF AGGREGATE DEMAND THEORY OF the business cycle have been proposed. They are:

- Keynesian theory
- Monetarist theory
- Rational expectations theories

Keynesian Theory

The **Keynesian theory of the business cycle** regards volatile expectations as the main source of economic fluctuations. This theory is distilled from Keynes' *General Theory of Employment, Interest, and Money*. We'll explore the Keynesian theory by looking at its main impulse and the mechanism that converts that impulse into a real GDP cycle.

Keynesian Impulse   The *impulse* in the Keynesian theory of the business cycle is *expected future sales and profits*. A change in expected future sales and profits changes the demand for new capital and changes the level of investment.

Keynes had a sophisticated theory about *how* expected sales and profits are determined. He reasoned that these expectations would be volatile because most of the events that shape the future are unknown and impossible to forecast. So, he reasoned, news or even rumors about future tax rate changes, interest rate changes, advances in technology, global economic and political events, or any other of the thousands of relevant factors that influence sales and profits change expectations in ways that can't be quantified but that have large effects.

To emphasize the volatility and diversity of sources of changes in expected sales and profits, Keynes described these expectations as *animal spirits*. In using this term, Keynes was not saying that expectations are irrational. Rather, he meant that because future sales and profits are impossible to forecast, it might be rational to take a view about them based on rumors, guesses, intuition, and instinct. Further, it might be rational to *change* one's view of the future, perhaps radically, in the light of scraps of new information.

Keynesian Cycle Mechanism   In the Keynesian theory, once a change in animal spirits has changed investment, a cycle mechanism begins to operate that has two key elements. First, the initial change in investment has a multiplier effect. The change in investment changes *aggregate* expenditure, real GDP, and disposable income. The change in disposable income changes consumption expenditure, and aggregate demand changes by a multiple of the initial change in investment. (This mechanism is described in detail in Chapter 28, pp. 694–695.) The aggregate demand curve shifts rightward in an expansion and leftward in a recession.

The second element of the Keynesian cycle mechanism is the response of real GDP to a change in aggregate demand. The short-run aggregate supply curve is horizontal (or nearly so). With a horizontal *SAS* curve, swings in aggregate demand translate into swings in real GDP with no changes in the price level. But the short-run aggregate supply curve depends on the money wage rate. If the money wage rate is fixed (sticky), the *SAS* curve does not move. And if the money wage rate changes, the *SAS* curve shifts. In the Keynesian theory the response of the money wage rate to changes in aggregate demand are *asymmetric*.

On the downside, when aggregate demand decreases and unemployment rises, the money wage rate does not change. It is completely rigid in the down direction. With a decrease in aggregate demand and no change in the money wage rate, the economy gets stuck in an unemployment equilibrium. There are no natural forces operating to restore full employment. The economy remains in that situation until animal spirits are lifted and investment increases again.

On the upside, when aggregate demand increases and unemployment falls below the natural rate, the money wage rate rises quickly. It is flexible in the up direction. At above full employment, the horizontal *SAS* curve plays no role and only the vertical *LAS* curve is relevant. With an increase in aggregate demand and an accompanying rise in the money wage rate, the price level rises quickly to eliminate the shortages and bring the economy back to full employment. The economy remains in that situation until animal spirits fall and investment and aggregate demand decrease.

Figures 33.2 and 33.3 illustrate the Keynesian theory of the business cycle by using the aggregate supply–aggregate demand model. In Fig. 33.2 the economy is initially at full employment (point *a*) on

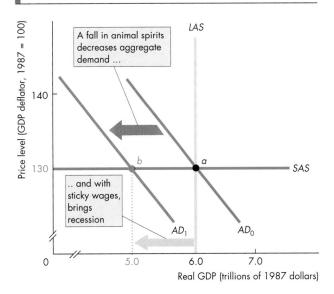

A Keynesian Recession

The economy is operating at point *a* at the intersection of the long-run aggregate supply curve, *LAS*; the short-run aggregate supply curve, *SAS*; and the aggregate demand curve, *AD*₀. A Keynesian recession begins when a fall in animal spirits causes investment demand to decrease. Aggregate demand decreases and the *AD* curve shifts leftward to *AD*₁. With sticky money wages, real GDP decreases to $5 trillion and the price level does not change. The economy moves to point *b*.

the long-run aggregate supply curve, *LAS*; the aggregate demand curve, *AD*₀; and the short-run aggregate supply curve, *SAS*. A fall in animal spirits decreases investment, and a multiplier process decreases aggregate demand. The aggregate demand curve shifts leftward to *AD*₁. With a fixed money wage rate, real GDP falls to $5 trillion and the economy moves to point *b*. Unemployment has increased and there is a surplus of labor, but the money wage rate does not fall, and the economy remains at point *b* until some force moves it away.

That force is shown in Fig. 33.3. Here, starting out at point *b*, a rise in animal spirits increases investment. The multiplier process kicks in, and aggregate demand increases. The *AD* curve shifts to *AD*₂ and real GDP begins to increase. An expansion is underway. As long as real GDP remains below potential

FIGURE 33.3

A Keynesian Expansion

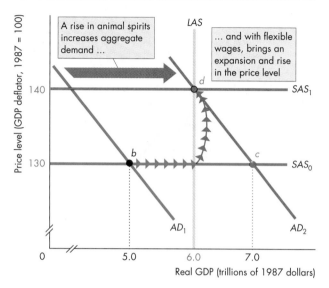

Starting at point *b*, a Keynesian expansion begins when a rise in animal spirits causes investment demand to increase. Aggregate demand increases and the *AD* curve shifts rightward to *AD*$_2$. With sticky money wages, real GDP increases to $6 trillion. But the economy does not go all the way to point *c*. When full employment is reached, the money wage rate rises and the *SAS* curve shifts upward toward *SAS*$_1$. The price level rises as the economy heads toward point *d*.

GDP ($6 trillion in this example), the money wage rate and the price level remain constant. But real GDP never increases to point *c*, the point of intersection of *SAS*$_0$ and *AD*$_2$. The reason is that once real GDP exceeds potential GDP and unemployment falls below the natural rate, the money wage rate begins to rise and the *SAS* curve starts to shift upward toward *SAS*$_1$. As the money wage rate rises, the price level also rises and real GDP growth slows down. The economy follows a path like the one shown by the arrows connecting point *b*, the initial equilibrium, with point *d*, the final equilibrium.

The Keynesian business cycle is mainly like a tennis match. It is caused by outside forces—animal spirits—that change direction and set off a process that ends at an equilibrium that must be hit again by the outside forces to disturb it.

Monetarist Theory

The **monetarist theory of the business cycle** regards fluctuations in the money stock as the main source of economic fluctuations. This theory is distilled from the writings of Milton Friedman and several other economists. We'll explore the monetarist theory as we did the Keynesian theory, by looking first at its main impulse and second at the mechanism that creates a cycle in real GDP.

Monetarist Impulse   The *impulse* in the monetarist theory of the business cycle is the *growth rate of the quantity of money*. A speedup in money growth brings expansion, and a slowdown in money growth brings recession. The source of the change in the growth rate of the quantity of money is the monetary policy actions of the Fed.

Monetarist Cycle Mechanism   In the monetarist theory, once the Fed has changed the money growth rate, a cycle mechanism begins to operate that, like the Keynesian mechanism, first affects aggregate demand. When the money growth rate increases, the quantity of real money in the economy increases. Interest rates fall, and real money balances increase. The foreign exchange rate also falls—the dollar loses value on the foreign exchange market. These initial financial market effects begin to spill over into other markets. Investment demand and exports increase, and consumers spend more on durable goods. These initial changes in expenditure have a multiplier effect, just as investment has in the Keynesian theory. Through these mechanisms a speedup in money growth shifts the aggregate demand curve rightward and brings an expansion. Similarly, a slowdown in money growth shifts the aggregate demand curve leftward and brings a recession.

The second element of the monetarist cycle mechanism is the response of aggregate supply to a change in aggregate demand. The short-run aggregate supply curve is upward-sloping. With an upward-sloping *SAS* curve, swings in aggregate demand translate into swings in both real GDP and the price level. But monetarists believe that real GDP deviations from full-employment are temporary in both directions.

In monetarist theory, the money wage rate is only *temporarily sticky*. When aggregate demand decreases and unemployment rises, the money wage rate eventually begins to fall. As the money wage rate falls, so does the price level and after a period of adjustment, full employment is restored. When aggregate demand increases and unemployment falls below the natural rate, the money wage rate begins to rise. As the money wage rate rises, so does the price level and through a period of adjustment, real GDP returns to potential GDP and the unemployment rate returns to the natural rate.

Figure 33.4 illustrates the monetarist theory. In part (a) the economy is initially at full employment (point *a*) on the long-run aggregate supply curve, *LAS*; the aggregate demand curve, AD_0; and the short-run aggregate supply curve, SAS_0. A slowdown in the money growth rate decreases aggregate demand, and the aggregate demand curve shifts leftward to AD_1.

Real GDP decreases to \$5.5 trillion, and the economy goes into recession (point *b*). Unemployment increases and there is a surplus of labor. The money wage rate begins to fall. As the money wage falls, the short-run aggregate supply curve starts to shift rightward toward SAS_1. The price level falls, and real GDP begins to expand as the economy moves to point *c,* its new full-employment equilibrium.

Figure 33.4(b) shows the effects of the opposite initial money shock—a speedup in money growth. Here, starting out at point *c*, a rise in the money growth rate increases aggregate demand and shifts the *AD* curve to AD_2. Both real GDP and the price level increase as the economy moves to point *d*, the point

---

FIGURE 33.4

A Monetarist Business Cycle

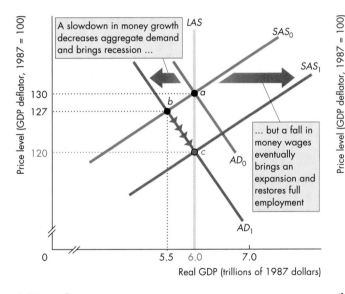

(a) Recession

(b) Expansion

A monetarist recession begins when a slowdown in money growth decreases aggregate demand. The *AD* curve shifts leftward from AD_0 to AD_1 (in part a). With sticky money wages, real GDP decreases to \$5.5 trillion and the price level falls to 127 as the economy moves from point *a* to point *b*. With a surplus of labor, the money wage rate falls and the *SAS* curve shifts rightward to SAS_1. The price level falls further, and real GDP returns to potential GDP at point *c*.

Starting at point *c* (part b), a monetarist expansion begins when an increase in money growth increases aggregate demand and shifts the *AD* curve rightward to AD_2. With sticky money wages, real GDP rises to \$6.5 trillion, the price level rises to 123, and the economy moves to point *d*. With a shortage of labor, the money wage rate rises and the *SAS* curve shifts toward SAS_2. The price level rises and real GDP decreases to potential GDP as the economy heads toward point *e*.

of intersection of SAS_1 and AD_2. With real GDP above potential GDP and unemployment below the natural rate, the money wage rate begins to rise and the SAS curve starts to shift leftward toward SAS_2. As the money wage rate rises, the price level also rises and real GDP decreases. The economy moves from point d to point e, its new full-employment equilibrium.

The monetarist business cycle is like a rocking horse. It needs an outside force to get it going, but once going, it rocks to and fro (but just once). It doesn't matter what the outside force is. If it is a money growth slowdown, the economy cycles with a recession followed by expansion. If it is a money growth speedup, the economy cycles with an expansion followed by recession.

Rational Expectations Theories

A **rational expectation** is a forecast that is based on all the available relevant information (see Chapter 32, p. 804). Rational expectations theories of the business cycle are theories based on the view that money wages are determined by a rational expectation of the price level. Two distinctly different rational expectations theories of the cycle have been proposed. A **new classical theory of the business cycle** regards *unanticipated* fluctuations in aggregate demand as the main source of economic fluctuations. This theory is based on the work of Robert E. Lucas, Jr., (see *Economics in History* on pp. 854–855) and several other economists, including Thomas J. Sargent (see Talking with Thomas Sargent on pp. 650–653). A different **new Keynesian theory of the business cycle** regards *both anticipated and unanticipated* fluctuations in aggregate demand as sources of economic fluctuations. We'll explore these theories as we did the Keynesian and monetarist theories, by looking first at the main impulse and second at the cycle mechanism.

Rational Expectations Impulse   The *impulse* that distinguishes the rational expectations theories from the other aggregate demand theories of the business cycle is the *unanticipated change in aggregate demand*. A larger than anticipated increase in aggregate demand brings an expansion and a smaller than anticipated increase in aggregate demand brings a recession. Any factor that influences aggregate demand—for example, fiscal policy, monetary policy, or developments in

the world economy that influence exports—whose change is not anticipated, can bring a change in real GDP.

Rational Expectations Cycle Mechanisms   To describe the rational expectations cycle mechanisms, we'll deal first with the new classical version. When aggregate demand decreases, if the money wage rate doesn't change, real GDP and the price level both decrease. The fall in the price level increases the *real* wage rate, and employment decreases and unemployment rises. In the new classical theory, these events occur only if the decrease in aggregate demand is not anticipated. If the decrease in aggregate demand *is* anticipated, the price level is expected to fall and both firms and workers will agree to a lower money wage rate. By doing so, they can prevent the real wage from rising and avoid a rise in the unemployment rate.

Similarly, if firms and workers anticipate an increase in aggregate demand, they expect the price level to rise and will agree to a higher money wage rate. By doing so, they can prevent the real wage rate from falling and avoid a fall in the unemployment rate below the natural rate.

Only fluctuations in aggregate demand that are unanticipated and not taken into account in wage agreements bring changes in real GDP. *Anticipated* changes in aggregate demand change the price level but they leave real GDP and unemployment unchanged and do not create a business cycle.

New Keynesian economists, like new classical economists, believe that money wages are influenced by rational expectations of the price level. But new Keynesians emphasize the long-term nature of most wage contracts. They say that *today's* money wages are influenced by *yesterday's* rational expectations. These expectations, which were formed in the past, are based on old information that might now be known to be incorrect. After they have made a long-term wage agreement, both firms and workers might anticipate a change in aggregate demand, which they expect will change the price level. But because they are locked into their agreement, they are unable to change money wages. So money wages are sticky in the new Keynesian theory and with sticky money wages, even an *anticipated* change in aggregate demand changes real GDP.

New classical economists believe that long-term contracts are renegotiated when conditions change to make them outdated. So they do not regard long-term contracts as an obstacle to money wage flexibility, provided both parties to an agreement recognize the changed conditions. If both firms and workers expect the price level to change, they will change the agreed money wage rate to reflect that shared expectation. In this situation, anticipated changes in aggregate demand change the money wage rate and the price level and leave real GDP unchanged.

The distinctive feature of both versions of the rational expectations theory of the business cycle is the role of unanticipated changes in aggregate demand and Fig. 33.5 illustrates its effect on real GDP and the price level.

Potential GDP is $6 trillion and the long-run aggregate supply curve is *LAS*. Aggregate demand is expected to be *EAD*. Given potential GDP and *EAD*, the money wage rate is set at the level that is expected to bring full employment. At this money wage rate, the short-run aggregate supply curve is *SAS*. Imagine that initially aggregate demand equals expected aggregate demand, so there is full employment. Real GDP is $6 trillion and the price level is 130. Then, unexpectedly, aggregate demand turns out to be less than expected and the aggregate demand curve shifts leftward to AD_0 (in Fig. 33.5a). Many different aggregate demand shocks, such as a slowdown in the money

---

FIGURE 33.5

A Rational Expectations Business Cycle

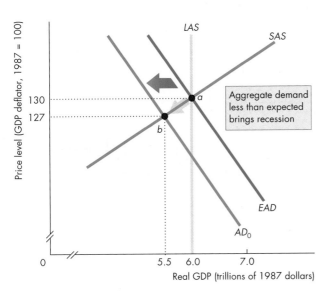

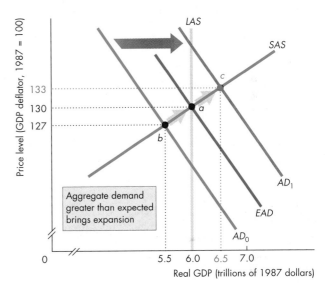

(a) Recession

The economy is expected to be at point *a* at the intersection of the long-run aggregate supply curve, *LAS*, the short-run aggregate supply curve *SAS*, and the *expected* aggregate demand curve, *EAD*. A rational expectations recession begins when an unanticipated fall in aggregate demand shifts the *AD* curve leftward to AD_0. With money wage rates based on the expectation that aggregate demand will be *EAD*, real GDP falls to $5.5 trillion and the price level falls to 127 as the economy moves to point *b*. As long as aggregate demand is *expected* to be *EAD*, there is no change in the money wage rate.

(b) Expansion

A rational expectations expansion begins when an unanticipated rise in aggregate demand shifts the *AD* curve rightward from AD_0 to AD_1. With money wage rates based on the expectation that aggregate demand will be *EAD*, real GDP increases to $6.5 trillion and the price level rises to 133 as the economy moves to point *c*. Again, as long as aggregate demand is *expected* to be *EAD*, there is no change in the money wage rate.

growth rate or a collapse of exports, could have caused this shift. A recession begins. Real GDP falls to $5.5 trillion and the price level falls to 127. The economy moves to point *b*. Unemployment increases and there is a surplus of labor. But aggregate demand is expected to be at *EAD* so the money wage rate doesn't change and the short-run aggregate supply curve remains at *SAS*.

The recession ends when aggregate demand increases again to its expected level. And a larger shock that takes aggregate demand to a level that exceeds *EAD* brings an expansion. In Fig. 33.5(b), the aggregate demand curve shifts rightward to AD_1. Such an increase in aggregate demand might be caused by a speedup in the money growth rate or an export boom. Real GDP now increases to $6.5 trillion and the price level rises to 133. The economy moves to point *c*. Unemployment is now below the natural rate. But aggregate demand is expected to be at *EAD* so the money wage rate doesn't change and the short-run aggregate supply curve remains at *SAS*.

Fluctuations in aggregate demand between AD_0 and AD_1 around expected aggregate demand *EAD* bring fluctuations in real GDP and the price level between points *b* and *c*.

The two versions of the rational expectations theory differ in their predictions about the effects of a change in expected aggregate demand. The new classical theory predicts that as soon as expected aggregate demand changes, the money wage rate also changes so the *SAS* curve shifts. The new Keynesian theory predicts that the money wage rate changes only gradually when new contracts are made so that the *SAS* curve moves only slowly. This difference between the two theories is crucial for policy. According to the new classical theory, anticipated policy actions change the price level only and have no effect on real GDP and unemployment. The reason is that when policy is expected to change, the money wage rate changes so the *SAS* curve shifts and offsets the effects of the policy action on real GDP. In contrast, in the new Keynesian theory, because money wages change only when new contracts are made, even anticipated policy actions change real GDP and can be used in an attempt to stabilize the cycle.

Like the monetarist business cycle, these rational expectations cycles are similar to rocking horses. They need an outside force to get going, but once going the economy rocks around its full employment point. The new classical horse rocks faster and comes to rest more quickly than the new Keynesian horse.

AS-AD General Theory

All the theories of the business cycle that we've considered can be viewed as particular cases of the more general *AS-AD* theory. In this more general theory the impulses of both the Keynesian and monetarist theories can change aggregate demand. A multiplier effect makes aggregate demand change by more than any initial change in one of its components. The money wage rate can be viewed as responding to changes in the expected price level. Even if the money wage is flexible, it will change only to the extent that price level expectations change. As a result, the money wage rate will adjust gradually.

Although in all three types of business cycle theory that we've considered, the cycle is caused by fluctuations in aggregate demand, the possibility that an occasional aggregate supply shock might occur is not ruled out. A recession could occur because aggregate supply falls. For example, a widespread drought that cuts agricultural production could cause a recession in an economy that has a large agricultural sector. But these aggregate demand theories of the cycle regard aggregate supply shocks as rare rather than normal events. Aggregate demand fluctuations are the normal ongoing sources of fluctuations.

R E V I E W

■ Keynesian theory says that the business cycle is caused by volatile expectations about future sales and profits—*animal spirits*—a multiplier effect, and sticky money wages.

■ Monetarist theory says that the business cycle is caused by the Fed speeding up and slowing down the growth rate of money, which changes spending plans.

■ New classical and new Keynesian theories (rational expectations theories) say that the business cycle is caused by unanticipated fluctuations in aggregate demand. In the new classical theory the money wage rate responds to price level expectations, and in the new Keynesian theory the money wage rate is set by long-term contracts.

A new theory of the business cycle challenges this mainstream and traditional aggregate demand theories that you've just studied. It is called the real business cycle theory. Let's take a look at this new cycle theory.

Real Business Cycle Theory

THE NEWEST FURY OF THE BUSINESS CYCLE, known as **real business cycle theory** (or RBC theory), regards random fluctuations in productivity as the main source of economic fluctuations. These productivity fluctuations are assumed to result mainly from fluctuations in the pace of technological change, but they might also have other sources such as international disturbances, climate fluctuations, or natural disasters. The origins of real business cycle theory can be traced to the rational expectations revolution set off by Robert E. Lucas, Jr., but the first demonstration of the power of this theory was given by Edward Prescott and Finn Kydland, and by John Long and Charles Plosser. Today, real business cycle theory is part of a broad research agenda called *dynamic general equilibrium analysis*, and hundreds of young macroeconomists do research on this topic.

Like our study of the aggregate demand theories, we'll explore RBC theory by looking first at its impulse and second at the mechanism that converts that impulse into a cycle in real GDP.

The RBC Impulse

The *impulse* in RBC theory is the *growth rate of productivity that results from technological change.* RBC theorists believe this impulse to be generated mainly by the process of research and development that leads to the creation and use of new technologies. Sometimes technological progress is rapid and productivity grows quickly; at other times, progress is slow and productivity grows moderately. Occasionally, technological change is so far-reaching that it makes a large amount of existing capital, especially human capital, obsolete. It also, initially, destroys jobs and shuts down businesses. These initial effects of far-reaching technological change *decrease* productivity and can trigger a recession. Ultimately, such technological change creates both jobs and businesses and brings massive gains in productivity. Other shocks such as the world oil embargo of the mid-1970s, can temporarily decrease productivity.

To isolate the RBC theory impulse—the growth rate of productivity that results from technological change—economists use the tool of growth accounting, which is explained in Chapter 26, on pp. 628–630.

FIGURE 33.6

The Real Business Cycle Impulse

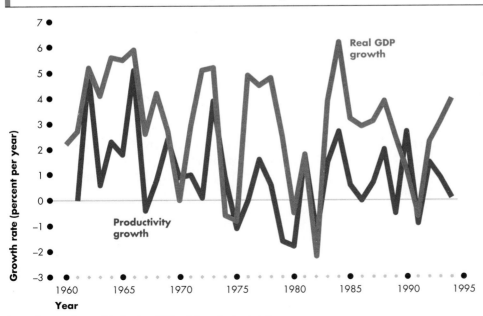

The real business cycle is caused by changes in technology that bring fluctuations in the growth rate of productivity. The fluctuations in productivity growth shown here are calculated by using growth accounting (the one third rule) to remove the contribution of capital accumulation to productivity growth. Productivity fluctuations are correlated with real GDP fluctuations. Economists are not sure what the productivity variable actually measures or what causes it to fluctuate.

Source: *Economic Report of the President*, 1995, and the author's calculations.

Figure 33.6 shows the RBC impulse for the United States from 1960 to 1994. The figure also shows that fluctuations in productivity growth are correlated with real GDP fluctuations.

The RBC Mechanism

The mechanism that creates the business cycle according to RBC theory is more complex and intricate than the aggregate demand theory mechanisms. Two immediate effects follow from a change in productivity that get an expansion or a contraction going:

1. Investment demand changes.
2. The demand for labor changes.

We'll study these effects and their consequences during a recession. In an expansion they work in the direction opposite to what is described here.

A wave of technological changes makes some existing capital obsolete and temporarily lowers productivity. Firms expect the future profits to fall and see their labor productivity falling. With lower profit expectations they cut back their purchases of new capital, and with lower labor productivity they plan to lay off some workers. So the initial effect of a temporary fall in productivity is a decrease in investment demand and a decrease in the demand for labor.

Figure 33.7 illustrates these two initial effects of a decrease in productivity. Part (a) shows investment demand, ID, and saving supply, SS (both of which are explained in Chapter 25, pp. 598–599 and 602–603). Initially, investment demand is ID_0, and the equilibrium investment and saving are $1 trillion at a real interest rate of 6 percent a year. A decrease in productivity decreases investment demand and the ID curve shifts leftward to ID_1. The real interest rate falls to 4 percent, and investment and saving decrease to $0.7 trillion.

Part (b) shows the demand for labor, LD, and the supply of labor, LS (which are explained in Chapter 24, p. 582). Initially, the demand for labor is LD_0, and equilibrium employment is 200 billion hours a year at a real wage rate of $15 an hour. The decrease in productivity decreases the demand for labor, and the LD curve shifts leftward to LD_1.

Before we can determine the new level of employment and real wage rate, we need to take a ripple effect into account—the key ripple effect in RBC theory.

The Key Decision: When to Work? According to RBC theory, people decide *when* to work by doing a cost-benefit calculation. They compare the return from working in the current period with the *expected* return from working in a later period. You make such a comparison every day in school. Suppose your goal in this course is to get an A. To achieve this goal, you work pretty hard most of the time. But during the few days before the midterm and final exams, you work especially hard. Why? Because you believe that the return from studying close to the exam is greater than the return from studying when the exam is a long time away. So during the term, you take time off for the movies and other leisure pursuits, but at exam time, you work every evening and weekend.

Real business cycle theory says that workers behave like you. They work fewer hours, sometimes zero hours, when the real wage rate is temporarily low, and they work more hours when the real wage rate is temporarily high. But to properly compare the current wage rate with the expected future wage rate, workers must use the real interest rate. If the real interest rate is 6 percent a year, a real wage of $1 an hour earned this week will become $1.06 a year from now. If the real wage rate is expected to be $1.05 an hour next year, today's real wage of $1 looks good. By working longer hours now and shorter hours a year from now, a person can get a 1 percent higher real wage. But suppose the real interest rate is 4 percent a year. In this case, $1 earned now is worth $1.04 next year. Working fewer hours now and more next year is the way to get a 1 percent higher real wage.

So the when-to-work decision depends on the real interest rate. The lower the real interest rate, other things remaining the same, the smaller is the supply of labor. Many economists believe this *intertemporal substitution* effect to be of negligible size. RBC theorists believe that the effect is large, and it is the key element in the RBC mechanism.

You've seen in Fig. 33.7(a) that the decrease in investment demand lowers the real interest rate. This fall in the real interest rate lowers the return to current work and decreases the supply of labor. In Fig. 33.7(b) the labor supply curve shifts leftward to LS_1. The effect of a productivity shock on the demand for labor is larger than the effect of the fall in the real interest rate on the supply of labor. That is, the LD curve shifts farther leftward than does the LS curve. As a result, the real wage rate falls to $14.50 an hour and the level of employment falls to 195 billion hours. A recession has begun and is intensifying.

FIGURE 33.7

Factor Markets in a Real Business Cycle

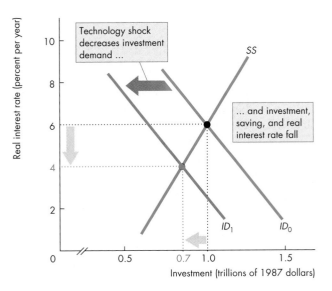

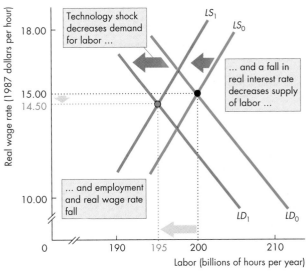

(a) Investment, saving, and interest rate

(b) Labor and wage rate

Saving supply is *SS* (part a), and initially, investment demand is ID_0. The real interest rate is 6 percent, and saving and investment are \$1 trillion. In the labor market (part b) the demand for labor is LD_0 and the supply of labor is LS_0. The real wage rate is \$15 an hour, and employment is 200 billion hours. A technological change temporarily decreases productivity, and both investment demand and the demand for labor decrease.

The two demand curves shift leftward to ID_1 and LD_1. In part (a) the real interest rate falls to 4 percent a year and investment and saving decrease. In part (b) the fall in the real interest rate decreases the supply of labor (the when-to-work decision) and the supply curve shifts leftward to LS_1. Employment falls to 195 billion hours, and the real wage rate falls to \$14.50 an hour. A recession is underway.

Real GDP and the Price Level   The next part of the RBC story traces the consequences of the changes you've just seen for real GDP and the price level. With a decrease in employment, aggregate supply decreases, and with a decrease in investment demand, aggregate demand decreases. Figure 33.8 illustrates these effects, using the *AS-AD* framework. Initially, the long-run aggregate supply curve is LAS_0, and the aggregate demand curve is AD_0. The price level is 130, and real GDP is \$6 trillion. There is no short-run aggregate supply curve in this figure because in RBC theory, the *SAS* curve has no meaning. The labor market moves relentlessly toward its equilibrium, and the money wage rate adjusts freely (either upward or downward) to ensure that the real wage rate keeps the quantity of labor demanded equal to the quantity supplied. In RBC theory, unemployment

is always at the natural rate, and the natural rate fluctuates over the business cycle because the amount of job search fluctuates.

The decrease in employment decreases total production, and aggregate supply decreases. The *LAS* curve shifts leftward to LAS_1. The decrease in investment demand decreases aggregate demand, and the *AD* curve shifts leftward to AD_1. The price level falls to 127, and real GDP decreases to \$5.8 trillion. The economy has gone through a recession.

What Happened to Money?   The name *real* business cycle theory is no accident. It reflects the central prediction of the theory. The business cycle is caused by real things, not by nominal or monetary things. If the quantity of money changes, aggregate demand changes. But if there is no real change—with no

FIGURE 33.8

AS-AD in a Real Business Cycle

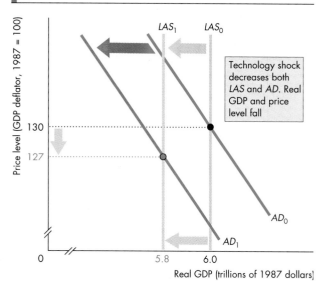

Initially, the long-run aggregate supply curve is *LAS₀*, and the aggregate demand curve is *AD₀*. Real GDP is $6 trillion (which equals potential GDP), and the price level is 130. There is no *SAS* curve in the real business cycle theory because the money wage rate is flexible. The technological change described in Fig. 33.7 temporarily decreases potential GDP, and the *LAS* curve shifts leftward to *LAS₁*. The fall in investment demand decreases aggregate demand, and the *AD* curve shifts leftward to *AD₁*. Real GDP falls to $5.8 trillion, and the price level falls to 127. The economy goes into recession.

change in the use of the factors of production and no change in potential GDP—the change in money changes only the price level. In real business cycle theory, this outcome occurs because the aggregate supply curve is the *LAS* curve, which pins real GDP down at potential GDP, so that when *AD* changes only the price level changes.

Cycles and Growth   The shock that drives the business cycle of RBC theory is the same as the force that generates economic growth: technological change. On the average, as technology advances, productivity grows. But it grows at an uneven pace. You saw this fact when you studied growth accounting in

Chapter 26. There, we focused on slow-changing trends in productivity growth. Real business cycle theory uses the same idea but says that there are frequent shocks to productivity that are mostly positive but that are occasionally negative.

Criticisms of Real Business Cycle Theory

RBC theory is controversial, and when economists discuss it, they often generate more heat than light. Its detractors claim that its basic assumptions are just too incredible. Money wages *are* sticky, they claim, so to assume otherwise is at odds with a clear fact. Intertemporal substitution is too weak, they say, to account for large fluctuations in labor supply and employment with small real wage changes.

But what really kills the RBC story, say most economists, is an implausible impulse. Technology shocks are not capable of creating the swings in productivity that growth accounting reveals. These swings in productivity are caused by something, they concede, but they are as likely to be caused by *changes in aggregate demand* as by technology. If the fluctuations in productivity are caused by aggregate demand fluctuations, then the traditional demand theories are needed to explain them. Fluctuations in productivity do not cause the cycle but are caused by it!

Building on this theme, the critics point out that the so-called productivity fluctuations that growth accounting measures are correlated with changes in the growth rate of money and other indicators of changes in aggregate demand.

Defense of Real Business Cycle Theory

The defenders of RBC theory claim that the theory works. It explains the macroeconomic facts about the business cycle and is consistent with the facts about economic growth. In effect, a single theory explains *both growth and cycles*. The growth accounting exercise that explains slowly changing trends also explains the more frequent business cycle swings. Its defenders also claim that RBC theory is consistent with a wide range of *micro*economic evidence about labor supply decisions, labor demand and investment demand decisions, and information on the distribution of income between labor and capital.

RBC theorists acknowledge that money and the business cycle are correlated. That is, rapid money growth and expansion go together, and slow money growth and recession go together. But, they argue, causation does not run from money to real GDP as the traditional aggregate demand theories state. Instead, they view causation as running from real GDP to money—so-called reverse causation. In a recession, the initial fall in investment demand that lowers the interest rate decreases the demand for bank loans and lowers the profitability of banking. So banks increase their reserves and decrease their loans. The quantity of bank deposits and hence the quantity of money decreases. This reverse causation is responsible for the correlation between money growth and real GDP according to real business cycle theory.

Its defenders also argue that the RBC view is significant because it at least raises the possibility that the business cycle is efficient. The business cycle does not signal an economy that is misbehaving; it is business as usual. If this view is correct, it means that policy designed to smooth the cycle is misguided. Smoothing the troughs can be done only by taking out the peaks. But peaks are bursts of investment to take advantage of new technologies in a timely way. So smoothing the cycle means delaying the benefits of new technologies.

R E V I E W

- Real business cycle (RBC) theory says that economic fluctuations are caused by technological change that makes productivity growth fluctuate.
- A fall in productivity decreases both investment demand and the demand for labor and lowers the real interest rate. The lower real interest rate decreases the supply of labor and employment, and the real wage rate falls.
- A fall in productivity decreases both long-run aggregate supply and aggregate demand and decreases both real GDP and the price level.

You've now reviewed the main theories of the business cycle. Your next task is to examine some actual business cycles. In pursuing this task, we will focus on the recession phase of the cycle. We'll do this mainly because it is the recessions that cause the most trouble. We begin by looking at two recent recessions.

Two Recent Recessions

IN THE THEORIES OF THE BUSINESS CYCLE THAT you've studied, recessions can be triggered by a variety of forces, some on the aggregate demand side and some on the aggregate supply side. Let's identify the shocks that triggered two recent recessions: the OPEC recession of 1974–1975 and the 1990–1991 recession.

The OPEC Recession

During the early 1970s the U.S. economy was progressing unremarkably. Real GDP was on trend and growing at a rate similar to its long-run average growth rate. Unemployment ranged between 5 and 6 percent, and inflation ranged between 3 and 6 percent a year. More and more people were enjoying and sharing in the benefits of sustained economic expansion.

Then, toward the end of 1973, the U.S. and world economies were dealt a devastating blow. The Organization of Petroleum Exporting Countries (OPEC), which controlled 68 percent of world oil production (outside the Communist countries), imposed an oil embargo and increased the price of a barrel of oil from $2.60 to $11.65—a 348 percent increase. The price hike had dramatic macroeconomic effects. For the next two years, the U.S. economy went into a severe recession.

Figure 33.9 shows the severity of the OPEC recession and illustrates the forces that caused the recession by using the mainstream AS-AD framework. Before the oil price hike, the aggregate demand and short-run aggregate supply curves were AD_{73} and SAS_{73}, respectively. Real GDP was $3.3 trillion, and the GDP deflator was 41. Through the subsequent two years, aggregate demand continued to increase and the aggregate demand curve shifted rightward to AD_{75}. When OPEC increased the price of crude oil, the prices of other fuels as well as the prices of many other raw materials also increased. The index of all commodity prices excluding fuel increased by 63 percent in 1973 and 24 percent in 1974. Labor costs also started to increase more quickly. As a result of these factor price increases, the short-run aggregate supply curve shifted leftward to SAS_{75}. This shift in the short-run aggregate supply curve, triggered by the oil price increase, was the single most significant

FIGURE 33.9

The OPEC Recession

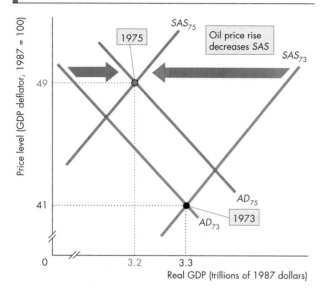

In 1973 the economy was on its aggregate demand curve, AD_{73}, and its short-run aggregate supply curve, SAS_{73}, with real GDP at \$3.3 trillion and a GDP deflator of 41. Between 1973 and 1975, aggregate demand continued to increase at a moderate pace and the aggregate demand curve shifted to AD_{75}. In 1974, OPEC increased the price of oil by 348 percent. Other input prices and wages increased and the short-run aggregate supply curve shifted to SAS_{75}. The large shift of the SAS curve combined with the moderate shift of the AD curve led to stagflation—a decrease in real GDP and an acceleration of inflation.

event producing the OPEC recession. Real GDP fell to \$3.2 trillion, and the GDP deflator increased to 49—an almost 20 percent increase in the price level over the two years of recession. Thus during the OPEC recession, real GDP decreased and the inflation rate increased. This combination of events gave rise to a new word, *stagflation*, a combination of falling real GDP and rising inflation.

The 1990–1991 Recession

At the beginning of 1990 the economy was at full employment. The unemployment rate was just above 5 percent, and inflation was steady at 4 percent a year. But the events of 1990 disturbed this situation

and brought an end to the longest peacetime expansion in U.S. history.

The dominant events of 1990 were the Persian Gulf crisis and the ensuing Gulf War triggered by Saddam Hussein's invasion of Kuwait. The Gulf crisis brought shocks to both aggregate demand and aggregate supply. The aggregate demand shocks went in both directions. First, fiscal policy became less restrained as government purchases increased to cope with the military consequences of the crisis. The Gulf situation also increased uncertainty about expected sales and profits, which brought a fall in investment. With a fall in investment, aggregate demand decreased. Although fiscal policy was working in the direction opposite to this change in investment, it was not strong enough to prevent aggregate demand from decreasing.

FIGURE 33.10

The 1990–1991 Recession

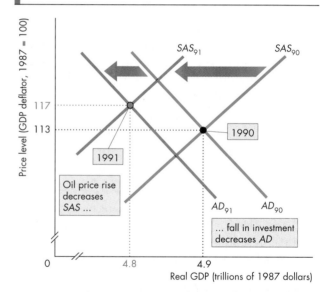

In 1990 the economy was on its aggregate demand curve, AD_{90}, and its short-run aggregate supply curve, SAS_{90}, with real GDP at \$4.9 trillion and a GDP deflator of 113. A large increase in oil prices decreased aggregate supply and shifted the short-run aggregate supply curve to SAS_{91}. Uncertainty surrounding the world economy lowered profit expectations, leading to a fall in investment and a decrease in aggregate demand. The aggregate demand curve shifted to AD_{91}. The combination of a decrease in both aggregate supply and aggregate demand puts the economy into recession.

On the supply side, the Gulf crisis put the world energy markets into turmoil yet again. Between April 1990 and October 1990 the price of crude oil more than doubled. This oil price increase operated in a way similar to that of the 1970s. It decreased short-run aggregate supply.

Figure 33.10 shows how the combined effects of these forces started the 1990–1991 recession. In mid-1990 the economy was on aggregate demand curve AD_{90} and short-run aggregate supply curve SAS_{90} with real GDP at \$4.9 trillion and the GDP deflator at 113. By mid-1991 the short-run aggregate supply curve had shifted to SAS_{91}, and investment uncertainty had shifted the aggregate demand curve to AD_{91}. Real GDP had decreased to \$4.8 trillion. The GDP deflator increased to 117, which slowed the inflation rate slightly to 3.5 percent over the year.

You've seen how aggregate demand and aggregate supply changed in two recent recessions. What happened in the labor market during these recessions?

The Labor Market in the OPEC Recession

During the OPEC recession the real wage rate fell from \$12.55 an hour in 1973 to \$12.43 an hour in 1975.[1] Aggregate hours decreased from 157 billion in 1973 to 155 billion in 1975. What caused this decrease in both employment and the real wage rate? We've seen that there are two views about the labor market. The traditional view is that the money wage rate is sticky and changes only gradually. The real business cycle view is that the money wage rate is flexible and adjusts to keep the labor market in equilibrium. Let's see how these two views explain the changes in the real wage rate and employment during the OPEC recession.

Sticky Wage Theory   Figure 33.11 illustrates the labor market in 1973 and 1975 according to the sticky wage view. In 1973 the demand for labor was LD_{73} and the supply of labor was LS_{73}. The real wage rate, \$12.55 an hour, and the level of employment, 157 billion hours, are determined at the intersection of these two curves. The unemployment rate in 1973

---

[1] The measure of real wage rates used here is aggregate wages, salaries, and benefits divided by aggregate hours—see Figure 24.5, p. 576.

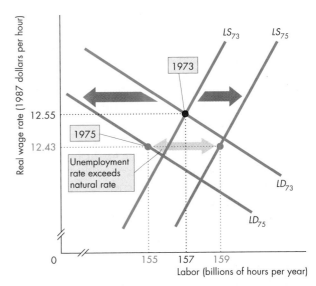

FIGURE 33.11
The Sticky Wage View

In 1973, the demand for labor was LD_{73} and the supply of labor was LS_{73}. If the quantity of labor demanded equaled the quantity supplied in 1973, the real wage rate of \$12.55 and employment of 157 billion hours are at the point of intersection of LD_{73} and LS_{73}. The OPEC oil price hike lowered the productivity of labor, so the demand for labor decreased and the demand for labor curve shifted leftward to LD_{75}. An increase in the population increased the supply of labor and shifted the supply curve rightward to LS_{75}. The real wage rate fell, but not by enough to bring about equality between the quantities of labor supplied and demanded. The quantity demanded was 155 billion hours, but the quantity supplied was 159 billion hours. Unemployment increased.

was 4.9 percent, which we will assume was equal to the natural rate, so there was full employment. (This is an assumption, not a fact.)

The OPEC oil price hike lowered labor productivity, which in turn decreased the demand for labor. The labor demand curve shifted leftward to LD_{75}. There were four main reasons for this decrease in labor productivity. First, OPEC restricted the supply of crude oil, which meant that some firms experienced temporary shortages of fuel and so had to slow down production. Second, faced with higher energy prices, firms economized on the use of energy. For example, transportation companies lowered truck speeds and airlines pruned schedules to get better payloads. Again, production per hour of labor fell. Third, labor resources that were previously used in production were redirected to designing and building more fuel-efficient equipment. For example, automakers designed smaller, more fuel-efficient cars. Yet again, production per work-hour fell. Fourth, gas-guzzling planes and road vehicles and energy-hungry furnaces and industrial equipment were scrapped at a more rapid than normal pace, a process that decreased the capital stock and so further cut labor productivity.

In the sticky wage view, the real wage rate is determined in the short run by the gradually changing money wage rate and the price level. Between 1973 and 1975 the money wage rate increased by 18 percent. But the price level increased by 19 percent, so the real wage rate fell by 1 percent to $12.43. At this real wage rate, and with the new demand for labor curve, employment decreased to 155 billion hours in 1975.

Through 1974 and 1975 the population increased, and as a result, the supply of labor increased. If there were no other influences on the supply of labor, the supply curve shifted rightward from LS_{73} to LS_{75}. At the real wage rate of $12.43, the quantity of labor supplied was 159 billion hours. Unemployment increased above the natural rate. The unemployment rate increased from 4.9 percent in 1973 to 8.5 percent in 1975.

What were the forces preventing the real wage rate from falling in 1975? Given that both the money wage rate and the price level had increased by almost 20 percent, it seems hard to believe that the money wage was sticky. The flexible wage theory has an answer.

Flexible Wage Theory The flexible wage theory is that the money wage rate adjusts to maintain equality between the quantity of labor demanded and the quantity supplied. Fluctuations in unemployment are fluctuations in the natural rate of unemployment. Let's examine the OPEC recession again and see how we can interpret it in terms of this alternative theory.

Figure 33.12 illustrates the flexible wage view of the OPEC recession. The 1973 demand and supply curves, LD_{73} and LS_{73}, are identical to those in Fig. 33.11, and they determine the 1973 (assumed) full-employment equilibrium. Following the oil price hike, the demand for labor fell and the demand curve shifted leftward to LD_{75}, just as it did in Fig. 33.11.

So far, the flexible wage and sticky wage stories have been the same. The difference arises on the supply side of the labor market. An increase in the population increased the supply of labor. But a fall in the real interest rate—the when-to-work decision—decreased the supply of labor. The real interest rate, which had been around 1 percent a year in 1973, fell to almost *minus* 1 percent a year in 1975. With a low (negative) real interest rate, 1975 was for many people a good year in which to borrow and look for a better job rather than work. This factor was so strong, according to the flexible wage view, that it more than counteracted the increase in the population. So the supply of labor decreased. The labor supply curve shifted leftward to LS_{75} in Fig. 33.12.

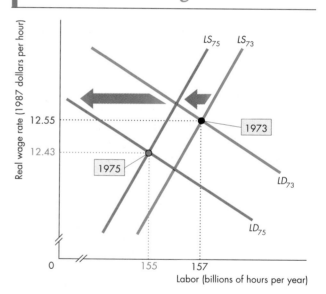

FIGURE 33.12

The Flexible Wage View

During the OPEC recession the real wage rate fell from $12.55 an hour to $12.43 an hour, and employment fell from 157 billion hours to 155 billion hours. These movements of the real wage rate and employment are consistent with the flexible wage theory. A fall in the real interest rate made 1975 a bad year for working and a good year for searching for a better job, so the supply of labor decreased. The supply of labor curve shifted leftward to LS_{75} and the 1975 equilibrium is at the intersection of LD_{75} and LS_{75}. According to the flexible wage theory, the increase in unemployment that occurred between 1973 and 1975 is interpreted as a temporary increase in the natural rate of unemployment.

The new supply of labor curve intersected the new demand for labor curve at a real wage rate of $12.43 an hour and an employment level of 155 billion hours. You can't see it in Fig. 33.12, but the natural rate of unemployment increased through 1975, according to the flexible wage view. In deciding not to work, more people searched for new and better jobs, so job search and unemployment increased. People who had previously worked in energy-using jobs looked for higher-paid energy-saving jobs.

We've interpreted the labor market in the OPEC recession in two ways. Can we also interpret the 1990–1991 recession in these same two ways?

The Labor Market in the 1990–1991 Recession

During the 1990–1991 recession the real wage rate *increased* from $14.31 an hour in 1990 to $14.44 an hour in 1991, and aggregate hours decreased from 203 billion in 1990 to 201 billion in 1992. Why did the real wage rate increase when hours decreased and the economy was in recession?

Sticky Wage Theory   A sticky wage story can be told about money wages in the 1990–1991 recession that is based on the rational expectations theories of the business cycle. According to this view, the money wage rate in 1991 was determined by decisions made in 1990 based on the price level then expected for 1991. Prices had increased during 1990 by about 4.5 percent a year. Assuming this rate would continue through 1991 and allowing for a small expected rise in labor productivity, employers and workers agreed to increase the money wage rate by almost 5 percent.

In reality, the inflation rate slowed in 1991 to less than 4 percent. As a result, the real wage rate increased by 1 percent. With an increase in the real wage rate, the quantity of labor demanded decreased and employment fell.

Can the flexible wage theory interpret the 1990–1991 change in employment and the real wage rate?

Flexible Wage Theory   The flexible wage theory has a difficult time accounting for the events we've just described. For the real wage rate to rise and employment to fall, the supply of labor must have decreased and by more than the decrease in the demand for labor. But the influences on the supply of labor worked in the wrong direction in 1991. The working-age population increased that year by almost 1 percent. More significant, though, the real interest rate *increased*. So the when-to-work decision and the population change both increased the supply of labor.

The failure of a simple flexible wage theory to explain the rise in the real wage rate and the fall in employment does not mean that the entire approach is invalid. Many economists believe that a more detailed microeconomic story about labor reallocation across sectors and changes in wage rates for individual jobs can explain even the 1990–1991 recession in terms of flexible wages.

Determining which of the two wage theories is correct is not just an academic curiosity. It is crucial for the design of anti-recessionary policy. If the flexible wage theory is correct, there is only one aggregate supply curve—the vertical long-run aggregate supply curve. This fact means that any attempt to bring the economy out of recession by increasing aggregate demand—for example, by lowering interest rates and increasing the money supply or by fiscal policy measures—is doomed to failure and can result only in a higher price level (more inflation). Conversely, if the sticky wage theory is correct, then the short-run aggregate supply curve slopes upward. An increase in aggregate demand, although increasing the price level somewhat, increases real GDP and will bring the economy out of a recession.

R E V I E W

- The OPEC recession was triggered by a supply shock—an increase in the price of oil.
- The 1990–1991 recession was triggered by a supply shock—the Gulf crisis, which increased the price of oil—and a demand shock—increased uncertainty, which lowered investment demand.
- The labor market can be interpreted by using either the sticky wage theory or the flexible wage theory during the OPEC recession but by using only the sticky wage theory during the 1990–1991 recession.

You've now seen how business cycle theory can be used to interpret two recent recessions. But can we use business cycle theory to explain the greatest of recessions—the Great Depression? Let's find out.

The Great Depression

THE LATE 1920S WERE YEARS OF ECONOMIC boom. New houses and apartments were built on an unprecedented scale, new firms were created, and the capital stock of the nation expanded. At the beginning of 1929, U.S. real GDP exceeded potential GDP and the unemployment rate was a low 3.2 percent. But as that eventful year unfolded, increasing signs of economic weakness began to appear. The most dramatic events occurred in October when the stock market collapsed, losing more than one third of its value in two weeks. The four years that followed were years of monstrous economic depression.

Figure 33.13 shows the dimensions of the Great Depression. On the eve of the Great Depression in 1929, the economy was on aggregate demand curve AD_{29} and short-run aggregate supply curve SAS_{29}. Real GDP was $822 billion (1987 dollars), and the GDP deflator was 12.5.

In 1930 there was a widespread expectation that the price level would fall, and the money wage rate fell. With a lower money wage rate, the short-run aggregate supply curve shifted from SAS_{29} to SAS_{30}. But increased pessimism and uncertainty decreased investment, and the demand for consumer durables and aggregate demand decreased to AD_{30}. In 1930, real GDP decreased to $749 billion (a 9 percent decrease) and the price level fell to 12.1 (a 3 percent fall).

In a normal recession the economy might have remained below full employment for a year or so and then started to expand. But the recession of 1930 was not a normal one. In 1930 and the next two years, the economy was further bombarded with huge negative demand shocks (the sources of which we'll look at in a moment). The aggregate demand curve shifted leftward all the way to AD_{33}. With a depressed economy the price level was expected to fall, and wages fell in line with those expectations. The money wage fell from 55¢ an hour in 1930 to 44¢ an hour by 1933. As a result of lower wages, the aggregate supply curve shifted from SAS_{30} to SAS_{33}. But the size of the shift of the short-run aggregate supply curve was much less than the decrease in aggregate demand. As a result, the aggregate demand curve and the short-run aggregate supply curve intersected in 1933 at a real GDP of $587 billion (a decrease of 29 percent from 1929) and a GDP deflator of 9.5 (a decrease of 24 percent from 1929).

FIGURE 33.13
The Great Depression

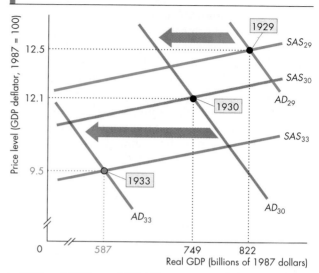

In 1929 real GDP was $822 billion and the GDP deflator was 12.5—at the intersection of AD_{29} and SAS_{29}. Increased pessimism and uncertainty resulted in a decrease in investment, and aggregate demand decreased to AD_{30}. The capital stock increased and wages decreased, so the short-run aggregate supply curve shifted to SAS_{30}. Real GDP and the price level fell. In the next three years, decreases in the money supply and investment lowered aggregate demand, shifting the aggregate demand curve to AD_{33}. Again, to some degree, the decrease in aggregate demand was anticipated, so wages fell and the short-run aggregate supply curve shifted to SAS_{33}. By 1933, real GDP had fallen to $587 billion (71 percent of its 1929 level) and the GDP deflator had fallen to 9.5 (76 percent of its 1929 level).

Although the Great Depression brought enormous hardship, the distribution of that hardship was uneven. Twenty-five percent of the work force had no jobs at all. Also at that time, there were virtually no organized social security and unemployment programs in place. So for many families there was virtually no income. But the pocketbooks of those who kept their jobs barely noticed the Great Depression. It is true that wages fell from 57¢ an hour in 1929 to 44¢ an hour in 1933. But at the same time, the price level fell by a larger percentage, so real wages actually increased. Thus people who had jobs became better off during the Great Depression.

You can begin to appreciate the magnitude of the Great Depression if you compare it with the two recessions that we studied earlier in this chapter. Between 1973 and 1975, real GDP fell by 1.8 percent. From mid-1990 to mid-1991 it fell by 1.6 percent. A hypothetical 1999 Great Depression would lower real GDP by 30 percent, to less than its 1979 level.

Why the Great Depression Happened

The late 1920s were years of economic boom, but they were also years of increasing uncertainty. The main source of increased uncertainty was international. The world economy was going through tumultuous times. The patterns of world trade were changing as Britain, the traditional economic powerhouse of the world, began its period of relative economic decline and new economic powers such as Japan began to emerge. International currency fluctuations and the introduction of restrictive trade policies by many countries (see Chapter 35) further increased the uncertainty faced by firms. There was also domestic uncertainty arising from the fact that there had been such a strong boom in recent years, especially in the capital goods sector and housing. No one believed that this boom could continue, but there was great uncertainty as to when it would end and how the pattern of demand would change.

This environment of uncertainty led to a slowdown in consumer spending, especially on new homes and household appliances. By the fall of 1929, the uncertainty had reached a critical level and contributed to the stock market crash. The stock market crash, in turn, heightened people's fears about economic prospects in the foreseeable future. Fear fed fear. Investment collapsed. The building industry almost disappeared. An industry that had been operating flat out just two years earlier was now building virtually no new houses and apartments. It was this drop in investment and a drop in consumer spending on durables that led to the initial leftward shift of the aggregate demand curve from AD_{29} to AD_{30} in Fig. 33.13.

At this stage, what became the Great Depression was no worse than many previous recessions had been. What distinguishes the Great Depression from previous recessions are the events that followed between 1930 and 1933. But economists, even to this day, have not come to agreement on how to interpret those events. One view, argued by Peter Temin,[2] is that spending continued to fall for a wide variety of reasons—including a continuation of increasing pessimism and uncertainty. According to Temin's view, the continued contraction resulted from a collapse of expenditure that was independent of the decrease in the quantity of money. The investment demand curve shifted leftward. Milton Friedman and Anna J. Schwartz have argued that the continuation of the contraction was almost exclusively the result of the subsequent worsening of financial and monetary conditions.[3] According to Friedman and Schwartz, it was a severe cut in the money supply that lowered aggregate demand, prolonging the contraction and deepening the depression.

Although there is disagreement about the causes of the contraction phase of the Great Depression, the disagreement is not about the elements at work but about the degree of importance attached to each. Everyone agrees that increased pessimism and uncertainty lowered investment demand, and everyone agrees that there was a massive contraction of the real money supply. Temin and his supporters assign primary importance to the fall in autonomous expenditure and secondary importance to the fall in the money supply. Friedman and Schwartz and their supporters assign primary responsibility to the money supply and regard the other factors as being of limited importance.

Let's look at the contraction of aggregate demand a bit more closely. Between 1930 and 1933 the nominal money supply decreased by 20 percent. This decrease in the money supply was not directly induced by the Fed's actions. The *monetary base* (currency in circulation and bank reserves) hardly fell at all. But the bank deposits component of the money supply suffered an enormous collapse. It did so primarily because a large number of banks failed. Before the Great Depression, fueled by increasing stock prices and booming business conditions, bank loans expanded. But after the stock market crash and the downturn, many borrowers found themselves in hard economic times. They could not pay the interest on their loans, and they could not meet the agreed

---

[2] Peter Temin, *Did Monetary Forces Cause the Great Depression?* (New York; W. W. Norton, 1976).

[3] This explanation was developed by Milton Friedman and Anna J. Schwartz in *A Monetary History of the United States 1867–1960.* (Princeton: Princeton University Press, 1963), Chapter 7.

repayment schedules. Banks had deposits that exceeded the realistic value of the loans that they had made. When depositors withdrew funds from the banks, the banks lost reserves. Many of them simply couldn't meet their depositors' demands to be repaid.

Bank failures feed on themselves and create additional failures. Seeing banks fail, people become anxious to protect themselves and so take their money out of the banks. Such were the events of 1930. The quantity of notes and coins in circulation increased, and the volume of bank deposits declined. But the very action of taking money out of the bank to protect one's wealth accentuated the process of banking failure. Banks were increasingly short of cash and unable to meet their obligations.

What role did the stock market crash of 1929 play in producing the Great Depression? It certainly created an atmosphere of fear and panic and probably also contributed to the overall air of uncertainty that dampened investment spending. It also reduced the wealth of stockholders, encouraging them to cut back on their consumption spending. But the direct effect of the stock market crash on consumption, although a contributory factor to the Great Depression, was not the major source of the drop in aggregate demand. It was the collapse in investment arising from increased uncertainty that brought the 1930 decline in aggregate demand.

The stock market crash was a predictor of severe recession. It reflected the expectations of stockholders concerning future profit prospects. As those expectations became pessimistic, people sold their stocks. There were more sellers than buyers and the prices of stocks were bid lower and lower. That is, the behavior of the stock market was a consequence of expectations about future profitability, and those expectations were lowered as a result of increased uncertainty.

Can It Happen Again?

Because we have an incomplete understanding of the causes of the Great Depression, we cannot be sure whether such an event will happen again. The economic turmoil of the 1920s that preceded the depression certainly can happen again. But there are some significant differences between the economy of the 1990s and that of the 1930s that make a severe depression much less likely today than it was 60 years ago. The most significant features of the economy that make severe depression less likely today are:

- Bank deposit insurance
- The Fed's role as lender of last resort
- Taxes and government spending
- Multi-income families

Let's examine these in turn.

Bank Deposit Insurance   As a result of the Great Depression, the federal government established, in the 1930s, the Federal Deposit Insurance Corporation (FDIC). The FDIC insures bank deposits for up to $100,000 per deposit, so most depositors need no longer fear bank failure. If a bank fails, the FDIC pays the deposit holders. With federally insured bank deposits, the key event that turned a fairly ordinary recession into the Great Depression is most unlikely to occur. It was the fear of bank failure that caused people to withdraw their deposits from banks. The aggregate consequence of these individually rational acts was to cause the very bank failures that were feared. With deposit insurance, most depositors have nothing to lose if a bank fails and so have no incentive to take actions that are likely to give rise to that failure.

Some recent events reinforce this conclusion. With massive failures of S&Ls in the 1980s and with bank failures in New England in 1990 and 1991, there was no tendency for depositors to panic and withdraw their funds in a self-reinforcing run on similar institutions.

Lender of Last Resort   The Fed is the lender of last resort in the U.S. economy. If a single bank is short of reserves, it can borrow reserves from other banks. If the entire banking system is short of reserves, banks can borrow from the Fed. By making reserves available (at a suitable interest rate), the Fed is able to make the quantity of reserves in the banking system respond flexibly to the demand for those reserves. Bank failure can be prevented, or at least contained to cases in which bad management practices are the source of the problem. Widespread failures of the type that occurred in the Great Depression can be prevented.

It is now generally agreed that the Fed made a serious mistake in its handling of monetary policy during the Great Depression. With one eye on the international situation, the Fed *increased* the discount rate sharply from 1.5 percent to 3.5 percent just when the banks needed to borrow more. It was only long after the event, when Friedman and Schwartz examined the contraction years of the Great Depression, that economists came to realize that the Fed would have had to *decrease* the discount rate and *increase* the monetary base to have prevented the intensification of the contraction. Now that this lesson has been learned and there is such widespread agreement about the matter, there is at least some chance that the mistake will not be repeated.

The last time the Fed was confronted by a similar problem, although on a much smaller scale, was in October 1987. At that time, a severe stock market crash triggered fears of a new Great Depression. The Fed Chairman, Alan Greenspan, told the U.S. banking and financial community that the Fed had both the ability and the intent to maintain calm financial conditions and to supply sufficient reserves to ensure that the banking system did not begin to contract.

Taxes and Government Spending The government sector was a much smaller part of the economy in 1929 than it has become today. On the eve of that earlier recession, government purchases of goods and services were less than 9 percent of GDP. Today, government purchases exceed 20 percent of GDP. Government transfer payments were less than 6 percent of GDP in 1929. Today, they exceed 15 percent of GDP.

A larger level of government purchases of goods and services means that when recession hits, a large component of aggregate demand does not decline. But government transfer payments are the most sensitive economic stabilizer. When the economy goes into recession and depression, more people qualify for unemployment compensation and social security. As a consequence, although disposable income decreases, the extent of the decrease is moderated by the existence of such programs. Consumption expenditure, in turn, does not decline by as much as it would in the absence of such government programs. The limited decline in consumption spending further limits the overall decrease in aggregate expenditure, thereby limiting the magnitude of an economic downturn.

Multi-Income Families At the time of the Great Depression, families with more than one wage earner were much less common than they are today. The labor force participation rate in 1929 was around 55 percent. Today, it is 67 percent. Thus even if the unemployment rate increased to around 25 percent today, close to 50 percent of the adult population

would actually have jobs. During the Great Depression, less than 40 percent of the adult population had work. Multi-income families have greater security than single-income families. The chance of both (or all) income earners in a family losing their jobs simultaneously is much lower than the chance of a single earner losing work. With greater family income security, family consumption is likely to be less sensitive to fluctuations in family income that are seen as temporary. Thus when aggregate income falls, it does not induce a cut in consumption. For example, during the OPEC recession, as real GDP fell, personal consumption expenditure actually increased. In 1990–1991, when real GDP fell by $30 billion, consumption expenditure fell by only $13 billion.

For the four reasons we have just reviewed, it appears that the economy has better shock-absorbing characteristics today than it had in the 1920s and 1930s. Even if there is a collapse of confidence, leading to a fall in investment, today's shock absorbers will not translate that initial shock into the large and prolonged fall in real GDP and rise in unemployment that occurred more than 60 years ago.

Because the economy is now more immune to severe recession than it was in the 1930s, even a stock market crash of the magnitude that occurred in 1987 had barely noticeable effects on spending. A crash of a similar magnitude in 1929 resulted in the near collapse of housing investment and consumer durable purchases. In the period following the 1987 stock market crash, investment and spending on durable goods hardly changed.

None of this is to say that there might not be a deep recession or even a Great Depression in the last half of the 1990s (or beyond). But it would take a very severe shock to trigger one.

◆ We have now completed our study of the business cycle. During an expansion, analysts use the theories you have studied to try to forecast the next recession. You can see an example of this activity in *Reading Between the Lines* on pp. 848–849.

We have also completed our study of the science of macroeconomics and learned about the influences on long-term economic growth and inflation as well as the business cycle. We have discovered that these issues pose huge policy challenges. How can we speed up the rate of economic growth while at the same time keeping inflation low and avoiding big swings of the business cycle? Our task in the next chapter is to study these macroeconomic policy challenges.

Anticipating Recession

FORTUNE, JULY 10, 1995

The Recession Watch Is On

BY LOUIS S. RICHMAN

There's no doubt about it: The U.S. economy took a big dive this spring. ....

Any time growth sinks to within hailing distance of zero, it's time to search the sky for warning signs that the economy is heading into a recession. ... But despite the suddenly gloomier outlook, few forecasters are ready to predict a recession just yet. Most are interpreting the latest indicators of a sharper-than-expected slide as evidence that manufacturers are acting decisively to reduce their overbuilt inventories. ...

Most forecasters are counting on several still solid fundamentals to bring growth back up to speed once the inventory correction has run its course by midsummer. The first is that there are good reasons to believe consumers will keep spending. While personal incomes increased by a bare 0.4% in April, and after-tax disposable income dropped a consumption-crimping 0.7%, shoppers haven't deserted the malls entirely. Retail sales have edged up slightly, and even sales of cars and light trucks rebounded in May. ...

The second reason not to panic is that business investment is hanging tough. Capital spending has been the mainstay of the expansion and should remain robust well into 1996. New orders for capital goods excluding aircraft soared at a 28% annual rate during the first quarter, and most forecasters expect orders to continue to grow at double-digit rates through the end of the year. ...

The final reason for optimism is that exports are gaining strength. True, the collapse of the Mexican peso this year took the salsa out of exports to America's third-largest trading partner. And the escalation of trade tensions with Japan—our No. 2 trading partner despite the fuss about the bilateral deficit—could cause U.S. exports there to contract. But the effects of the dollar's decline that began earlier this year are only just beginning to show up in new export orders. ...

Those are all good reasons to hope for the best. Another is that the economy remains apparently free of the kinds of excesses that produce recessions, such as high inflation or steeply rising interest rates. In the end, though, the mood of American consumers, as much as anything else, will determine the outcome. Inventory cycles turn into recessions when people become anxious about their jobs and begin reducing their spending. That in turn prompts companies to further curtail output and hiring, creating more waves of consumer anxiety. Should demand stay below forecasts and inventories remain high for several more months, then profits will erode, capital spending plans will be put on hold, and down we will assuredly go.

Essence of THE STORY

■ U.S. economic growth slowed in the first quarter of 1995 and prompted forecasters to revisit their predictions for the rest of 1995 and 1996.

■ But in mid-year, forecasters saw three sources of strength that led them to expect no recession in 1995: consumption expenditure, business investment, and exports were all holding up.

■ The absence of high inflation or steeply rising interest rates was also seen as a promising sign.

■ Recession begins, says the news article, when people become anxious about their jobs and reduce their spending. That prompts companies to cut output and hiring, which feeds consumer anxiety.

■ If demand stays below forecast and inventories remain high for several more months, investment will fall and a recession will begin.

Economic

ANALYSIS

■ Because a recession can be triggered by many factors and economists do not completely understand the business cycle mechanism, it is impossible to forecast when an expansion will end.

■ In looking for signs of recession, people use their own preferred theory of the business cycle.

■ The theory used in this news article—a consumer sentiment theory—is not a standard economic theory, but it is often seen in the media.

■ The article says that the cycle impulses are consumer confidence (anxiety about jobs), inflation, and steeply rising interest rates.

■ If consumers become anxious about jobs, they cut spending. Lower spending keeps inventories high, slows production, and produces job conditions that validate the anxiety that started the problem. Investment falls, and recession begins.

■ This description of recession does not agree with the data. Consumption expenditure usually turns down *after* the recession begins.

■ Figure 1 shows how the components of aggregate expenditure changed during the 1990–1991 recession. Real GDP began to shrink in the third quarter of 1990. But consumption expenditure did not fall until the fourth quarter of 1990. In contrast, investment had begun to fall in the second quarter of 1990. Investment, not consumption expenditure, is usually the first component of expenditure to fall during a recession.

■ Figure 1 also shows that exports held up right through the 1990–1991 recession. This fact makes exports a poor indicator of recession. Exports are strong because the world is getting smaller as transportation and communication costs fall.

■ Figure 2 shows that unemployment is also not an early indicator of recession. In most recessions, unemployment lags. During the 1990–1991 recession the unemployment rate did not increase sharply until the fourth quarter of 1990, which was the second quarter of the recession.

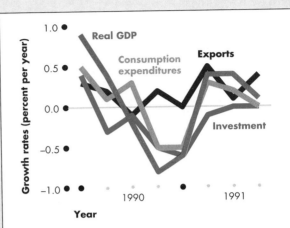

Figure 1 Components of aggregate expenditure

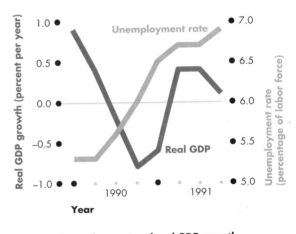

Figure 2 Unemployment and real GDP growth

■ Two things that made a 1995–1996 recession look possible in 1995 were a slowdown of money growth and a rise in real interest rates through 1994 and early 1995.

■ The real interest rate on long-term bonds paid by large firms increased from 5 percent at the beginning of 1994 to 7.5 percent at the beginning of 1995. Such a large rise in the real interest rate could trigger a slowdown in investment and eventually bring recession.

SUMMARY

Cycle Patterns, Impulses, and Mechanisms

Since 1920, there have been fifteen recessions and expansions. The Great Depression was the most severe contraction of real GDP and the postwar recessions have been milder than the prewar recessions. The economy can be hit (like a tennis ball), cycle indefinitely (like the turning of day into night), and cycle in swings that get milder until another shock hits (like a rocking horse). (pp. 826–828)

Aggregate Demand Theories of the Business Cycle

Aggregate demand theories of the cycle are based on the aggregate supply–aggregate demand model. Keynesian theory is based on volatile expectations about future sales and profits. Monetarist theory regards fluctuations in the money stock as the main source of economic fluctuations. Rational expectations theories identify unanticipated fluctuations in aggregate demand as the main source of economic fluctuations. (pp. 828–834)

Real Business Cycle Theory

In real business cycle (RBC) theory, economic fluctuations are caused by fluctuations in the influence of technological change on productivity growth. A temporary slowdown in the pace of technological change decreases investment demand and both the demand for labor and supply of labor.

The name *real* business cycle theory reflects the central prediction of the theory that the business cycle is caused by real things and not by money. (pp. 835–839)

Two Recent Recessions

The OPEC recession was triggered by an increase in the price of oil and an oil embargo. These events decreased aggregate supply. Aggregate demand also decreased but not by as much as aggregate supply. As a consequence, real GDP decreased and the price level increased at an accelerating pace. The

phenomenon gave rise to a new economic term: stagflation.

The 1990–1991 recession resulted from the Gulf crisis, which increased the price of oil—a decrease in aggregate supply—and increased uncertainty and decreased investment—a decrease in aggregate demand. The result was a fall in real GDP with little change in the inflation rate.

The labor market during the OPEC recession can be interpreted by using either the sticky wage theory or the flexible wage theory. But the labor market during the 1990–1991 recession cannot be interpreted by a simple flexible wage theory because the real interest rate *increased* in 1991. (pp. 839–843)

The Great Depression

The Great Depression that began in 1929 lasted longer and was more severe than any depression before it or since. The Great Depression started with increased uncertainty and pessimism, which brought a fall in investment (especially in housing) and spending on consumer durables. Increased uncertainty and pessimism also brought on the stock market crash. The crash added to the pessimistic outlook, and further spending cuts occurred. There then followed a near total collapse of the financial system. Banks failed and the money supply fell, resulting in a continued fall in aggregate demand. Expectations of falling prices led to falling wages, but the fall in aggregate demand continued to exceed expectations and real GDP continued to decline.

The Great Depression itself produced a series of reforms that make a repeat of such a depression much less likely. The most significant of these were the Fed's willingness to act as lender of last resort and the introduction of federal bank deposit insurance, both of which reduced the risk of bank failure and financial collapse. Higher taxes and government spending have given the economy greater resistance against depression, and an increased labor force participation rate provides a greater measure of security, especially for families with more than one wage earner. For these reasons an initial change in either aggregate demand or aggregate supply is much less likely to translate into depression than it did in the early 1930s. (pp. 844–847)

R E V I E W   Q U E S T I O N S

1. Describe an average recession and expansion.
2. Have recessions been getting more severe or less severe?
3. Distinguish between a cycle impulse and a cycle mechanism, and identify the impulse and mechanism in three analogies given in this chapter.
4. What is the Keynesian theory of the business cycle? Carefully distinguish between its impulse and its mechanism.
5. What is the monetarist theory of the business cycle? Carefully distinguish between its impulse and its mechanism.
6. What are the rational expectations theories of the business cycle? Carefully distinguish between their impulses and their mechanisms.
7. What is the key difference between new classical theory and new Keynesian theory of the business cycle?
8. What is the impulse that causes economic fluctuations according to real business cycle theory?
9. In real business cycle theory what happens to investment demand and the demand for labor if a technological change brings a large increase in productivity?
10. How is the labor supply decision influenced by the real interest rate?
11. Why is there no short-run aggregate supply curve in real business cycle theory?

12. List the main arguments against and in favor of real business cycle theory.
13. When did the Great Depression and the OPEC recession occur?
14. What triggered the OPEC recession and the 1990–1991 recession?
15. Which one of the OPEC recession and the 1990–1991 recession was a period of stagflation?
16. Describe the changes in employment and real wages in the OPEC recession. What is the sticky wage theory of these changes? What is the flexible wage theory of these changes?
17. Describe the changes in employment and real wages in the 1990–1991 recession. What is the sticky wage theory of these changes? What is the flexible wage theory of these changes?
18. Describe the changes in real GDP, employment and unemployment, and the price level that occurred during the Great Depression years of 1929–1933.
19. What were the main causes of the onset of the Great Depression in 1929?
20. What events in 1931 and 1932 led to the continuation and increasing severity of the fall in real GDP and the rise in unemployment?
21. What four features of today's economy make it less likely now than in 1929 that a Great Depression will occur? Why is it less likely?

P R O B L E M S

1. Here is a news report about the past year in Gloomland:

   "Business confidence is low. Firms have cut back on investment and laid off tens of thousands of workers. Productivity has collapsed. Real GDP has decreased, and the price level, the real wage rate, the real interest rate, and the money supply have all fallen."

   Try to explain these events by using the alternative theories of the business cycle. Are the facts as reported inconsistent with any of the theories? Use diagrams to illustrate your reasoning.

2. Here is a news report about the past year in Coolland:

   "Business confidence is high. Business investment is booming. Jobs are easy to find and firms have a hard time hiring. Productivity growing rapidly. Real GDP has increased and the price level is stable."

   Try to explain these events by using the alternative theories of the business cycle. Are the facts as reported inconsistent with any of the theories? Use diagrams to illustrate your reasoning.

3. Use carefully drawn figures to illustrate the evolution of the economy during the recession of 1981–1982 and the expansion through the 1980s according to:
   a. Keynesian theory (like Figs. 33.2 and 33.3);
   b. Monetarist theory (like Fig. 33.4);
   c. Rational expectations theories (like Fig. 33.5);
   d. Real business cycle theory (like Figs. 33.7 and 33.8).

4. The figure illustrates the economy of Virtualreality. When the economy is in a long-run equilibrium, it is at points *b*, *e*, and *h*. When a recession occurs in Virtualreality, the economy moves away from these points to one of the two oher points identified in each of the three parts of the figure.
   a. If the Keynesian theory is the correct explanation for the recession, to which points does the economy move?
   b. If the monetarist theory is the correct explanation for the recession, to which points does the economy move?

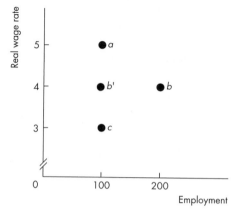

(a) Labor market

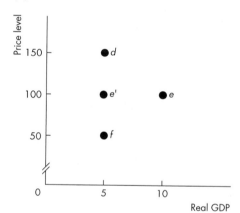

(b) AS-AD

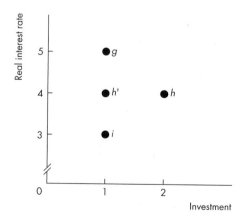

(c) Investment

c. If the new classical rational expectations theory is the correct explanation for the recession, to which points does the economy move?

d. If the new Keynesian rational expectations theory is the correct explanation for the recession, to which points does the economy move?

e. If real business cycle theory is the correct explanation for the recession, to which points does the economy move?

5. Suppose that when the recession occurs in Virtualreality, as shown in the figure accompanying problem 4, the economy moves to *a*, *f*, and *i*. Which, if any, theory of the businesss cycle explains this outcome?

6. Suppose that when the recession occurs in Virtualreality, as shown in the figure accompanying problem 4, the economy moves to *c*, *f*, and *i*. Which, if any, theory of the business cycle explains this outcome?

7. Suppose that when the recession occurs in Virtualreality, as shown in the figure accompanying problem 4, the economy moves to *a*, *d*, and *i*. Which, if any, theory of the business cycle explains this outcome?

8. Suppose that when the recession occurs in Virtualreality, as shown in the figure accompanying problem 4, the economy moves to c, *d*, and *i*. Which, if any, theory of the business cycle explains this outcome?

9. Suppose that when the recession occurs in Virtualreality, as shown in the figure accompanying problem 4, the economy moves to *a*, *f*, and *g*. Which, if any, theory of the business cycle explains this outcome?

10. There are two economies, Flexiland and Fixland. These economies are identical in every way except that in Flexiland, real wages are flexible and maintain equality between the quantities of labor demanded and supplied. In Fixland, wages are sticky but the money wage rate is set so that, *on the average*, the quantity of labor demanded equals the quantity supplied.

a. Explain which economy has the higher average unemployment rate.

b. Explain which economy has the larger fluctuations in unemployment.

11. During the OPEC recession, real wages fell from $12.55 an hour to $12.43 an hour. Employment fell from 157 billion hours to 155 billion hours. How can these changes be explained by the sticky wage and flexible wage theories?

12. During the 1990–1991 recession, real wages increased from $14.31 in 1990 to $14.44 in 1991, and employment decreased from 203 billion hours in 1990 to 201 billion hours in 1991. How can these changes be explained by the sticky and flexible wage theories?

13. Compare and contrast the recessions of 1974–1975 and 1990–1991. In what ways are they similar, and in what ways do they differ?

14. List all of the features of the U.S. economy in 1995 that you can think of that are consistent with a pessimistic outlook for 1996–1997.

15. List all of the features of the U.S. economy in 1995 that you can think of that are consistent with an optimistic outlook for 1996–1997.

16. How do you think the U.S. economy is going to evolve over the next year or two? Explain your predictions, drawing on the pessimistic and optimistic factors that you have listed in the previous two questions and on your knowledge of macroeconomic theory.

17. Study *Reading Between the Lines* on pp. 848–849 and then answer the following questions:

a. What are the main signs that forecasters look for to signal that a recession is not far in the future?

b. How do consumption expenditure and inventories change at the onset of a recession?

c. What were the main developments in the U.S. economy in 1995 that led to anxieties about a new recession?

d. What were the main developments in the U.S. economy in 1995 that made a near-future recession look unlikely?

e. Compare the theory of recession in the news article with the aggregate demand theories and real business cycle theory that are explained in this chapter.

> *"We don't want to manage the U.S. economy. And we don't think anybody else should take the job either."*
>
> ROBERT E. LUCAS, JR., PERSONAL INTERVIEW

Business Cycles

THE ISSUES AND IDEAS

Economic activity has fluctuated between boom and bust for as long as we've kept records. The range of fluctuations was especially pronounced during the nineteenth and early twentieth centuries.

Understanding the sources of economic fluctuations has turned out to be difficult. One reason is that there are no simple patterns. Every new episode of the business cycle is different from its predecessor in some way. Some cycles are long and some are short, some are mild and some are severe, some begin in the United States and some begin abroad. We never know with any certainty when the next turning point (down or up) is coming or what will cause it. A second reason is that the apparent waste of resources during a recession or depression seems to contradict the very foundation of economics: Resources are limited and people have unlimited wants—there is scarcity. A satisfactory theory of the business cycle must explain why scarce resources don't *always* get fully employed.

One theory is that recessions result from insufficient aggregate demand. The solution is to increase government spending, cut taxes, and cut interest rates. But demand stimulation must not be overdone. Countries that stimulate aggregate demand too much, such as Brazil, find their economic growth rates sagging, unemployment rising, and inflation accelerating.

Today's new theory, real business cycle theory, predicts that fluctuations in aggregate demand have *no* effect on output and employment and change only the price level and inflation rate. But this theory ignores the *real* effects of financial collapse of the type that occurred in the 1930s. If banks fail on a large scale and people lose their wealth, other firms also begin to fail and jobs are destroyed. Unemployed people cut their spending, and output falls yet further. Demand stimulation may not be called for, but action to ensure that sound banks survive certainly is.

While economists are trying to understand the sources of the business cycle, the government and the Fed are doing the best they can to moderate the cycle. In the years since World War II, there appears to have been some success. Although the business cycle has not disappeared, it has become much less severe.

THEN...

WHAT HAPPENS to the economy when people lose confidence in banks? They withdraw their funds. These withdrawals feed on themselves, creating a snowball of withdrawals and, eventually, panic. Short of funds with which to repay depositors, banks call in loans and previously sound businesses are faced with financial distress. They close down and lay off workers. Recession deepens and turns into depression. Bank failures and the resulting decline in the nation's supply of money and credit were a significant factor in deepening and prolonging the Great Depression. But they taught us the importance of stable financial institutions and gave rise to the establishment of federal deposit insurance to prevent future financial collapse.

How can a building that was designed to be a shop have no better use than to be boarded up and left empty? Not enough aggregate demand, say the Keynesians. Not so, say the real business cycle theorists. Technological change has reduced the building's current productivity as a shop to zero. But its expected future productivity is sufficiently high that it is not efficient to refit the building for some other purpose.

All unemployment, whether of buildings or of people, can be explained in a similar way. For example, how can it be that during a recession, a person who has been trained as a shop clerk is without work? Not enough aggregate demand is one answer. Another is that the current productivity of shop clerks is low but their expected future productivity is sufficiently high that it does not pay an unemployed clerk to retrain for a job that is currently available.

Robert E. Lucas, Jr.

The Economist: Robert E. Lucas, Jr.

Many economists, past and present, have advanced our understanding of business cycles. But one contemporary economist stands out. He is Robert E. Lucas, Jr., of the University of Chicago, who was the 1995 recipient of the Nobel Prize for Economic Science. In 1970, Lucas, then a 32-year-old professor at Carnegie-Mellon University, challenged the Keynesian theories of economic fluctuations and launched a new macroeconomic revolution that was based on two principles: People and businesses make rational decisions based on rational expectations, and markets reconcile individual decisions by balancing supply and demand, even in a recession. Like all scientific revolutions, the one touched off by Lucas was controversial. Twenty years later, the concept of rational expectations (whether right or wrong) is accepted by most economists. But the idea that in a recession when unemployment is high, supply equals demand remains controversial and is even distasteful to some economists. Along with his teacher Milton Friedman, Lucas believes that governments cannot smooth out business cycles and that their attempts to do so are misguided and sometimes do more harm than good.

Macroeconomic Policy Challenges

After studying this chapter, you will be able to:

- Describe the goals of macroeconomic policy

- Describe the main features of fiscal policy and monetary policy since 1960

- Explain how fiscal policy and monetary policy influence long-term economic growth

- Distinguish between and evaluate fixed-rule and feedback-rule policies to stabilize the business cycle

- Explain how fiscal policy influences the natural unemployment rate

- Evaluate fixed-rule and feedback-rule policies to contain inflation and explain why lowering inflation usually brings recession

What Can Policy Do?

The U.S. economy had an outstanding year in 1994. Real GDP expanded by 4 percent, unemployment fell to 5.4 percent, and inflation remained low with only a 2.7 percent rise in the Consumer Price Index. The United States was not alone in achieving a strong macroeconomic performance in 1994. Real GDP expanded in Canada by more than 4 percent and in the developing countries of Asia by 8 percent. But not all countries and regions shared in this solid growth. Japan's real GDP expanded by a lackluster 0.9 percent, and in Russia, real GDP shrank for the fourth successive year to less than two thirds its 1990 level. ◆ There were clouds, even in the U.S. economic sky. Interest rates increased through the year, and the federal budget deficit stubbornly held up at more than 3 percent of GDP. Also, no one believed that U.S. real GDP growth of 4 percent a year could be maintained. The longer-term trend in potential GDP growth has been a little more than 2 percent a year, so as actual real GDP overtook potential GDP, the fear of renewed inflation was awakened, to be followed, most likely, by another recession. ◆ The wide variety of macroeconomic performance raises questions about macroeconomic policy. What can policy do to improve macroeconomic performance? Can the federal government use its fiscal policy to speed up long-term growth, keep inflation in check, and maintain a low unemployment rate? Can the Fed use its monetary policy to achieve any of these ends? Are some policy goals better achieved by fiscal policy and some by monetary policy? What specific policy actions do the best job? Are some ways of conducting policy better than others?

◆ In this chapter we're going to study the challenges of using policy to influence the U.S. economy and achieve the highest sustainable long-term growth rate and low unemployment while avoiding high inflation. At the end of the chapter you will have a clearer and deeper understanding of the macroeconomic policy problems facing the United States today and of the debates that surround us concerning those problems.

Policy Goals

MACROECONOMIC POLICY GOALS FALL INTO TWO big categories: domestic and international. We study international macroeconomic policy issues in Chapters 35 and 36. Here, we focus on domestic policy. The four main domestic macroeconomic policy goals are to:

- Achieve the highest sustainable rate of potential GDP growth
- Smooth out avoidable business cycle fluctuations
- Maintain low unemployment
- Maintain low inflation

Potential GDP Growth

Rapid sustained real GDP growth can make a profound contribution to economic well being. With a growth rate of 2 percent a year, it takes more than 30 years for production to double. With a growth rate of 5 percent a year, production more than doubles in just 15 years. And with a growth rate of 10 percent a year like some Asian countries are achieving, production doubles in just 7 years. The limits to *sustainable* growth are determined by the availability of natural resources, by environmental considerations, and by the willingness of people to save and invest in new capital and new technologies rather than consume everything they produce.

How fast can the economy grow over the long term? Between 1988 and 1994, through one complete business cycle, potential GDP grew at a rate of 2.1 percent a year. Because the U.S. population grows at about 1 percent a year, a real GDP growth rate of 2.1 percent a year translates to a growth rate of real GDP per person of 1.1 percent a year, which means that output per person doubles every 64 years. Most economists believe that the U.S. economy can do better than it did over the past few years and maintain a long-term growth rate of potential GDP of 2.5 percent a year. This growth rate would double output per person every 48 years. But a few economists believe that with the right policies, sustainable growth of 5 percent a year is possible. This growth rate would double output per person every 18 years, increase it more than sixfold over 48 years, and increase it more than twelvefold in 64 years. So increasing the long-term growth rate is of critical importance.

The Business Cycle

Potential GDP probably does not grow at a constant rate. Fluctuations in the pace of technological advance and in the pace of investment in new capital bring fluctuations in potential GDP. So some fluctuations in real GDP represent fluctuations in potential GDP. But when real GDP grows less quickly than potential GDP, output is lost, and when real GDP grows more quickly than potential GDP, bottlenecks arise. Keeping real GDP growth steady and equal to potential GDP growth avoids these problems.

It is not known how smooth real GDP growth can be made. Real business cycle theory regards all the fluctuations in real GDP as fluctuations in potential GDP. The aggregate demand theories regard most of the fluctuations in real GDP as being avoidable deviations from potential GDP.

Unemployment

When real GDP growth slows, unemployment increases and rises above the natural rate of unemployment. The higher the unemployment rate, the longer is the time taken by unemployed people to find jobs. Productive labor is wasted, and there is a slowdown in the accumulation of human capital. If high unemployment persists, serious psychological and social problems arise for the unemployed workers and their families.

When real GDP growth speeds up, unemployment decreases and falls below the natural rate of unemployment. The lower the unemployment rate, the harder it becomes for expanding industries to get the labor they need to keep growing. If extremely low unemployment persists, serious bottlenecks and production dislocations occur.

Keeping unemployment at the natural rate avoids both of these problems. But just what is the natural rate of unemployment? Assessments vary. The actual average unemployment rate over the most recent business cycle—1988 to 1994—was 6.2 percent. Most economists would put the natural rate at about 6 percent. A few economists believe that the natural rate is lower than this, perhaps as low as 5 percent. At the other extreme, real business cycle theorists believe the natural rate fluctuates and equals the actual unemployment rate.

If the natural rate of unemployment becomes high, then a goal of policy becomes lowering the natural rate itself. This goal is independent of smoothing the business cycle.

Inflation

When inflation fluctuates unpredictably, money becomes less useful as a measuring rod for conducting transactions. In extreme cases it becomes useless and is abandoned as the means of payment. Borrowers and lenders and employers and workers must take on extra risks. Keeping the inflation rate steady and predictable avoids these problems.

What is the most desirable inflation rate? Some economists say that the *rate* of inflation doesn't matter much as long as the rate is *predictable*. But most economists believe that price stability, which they translate as an inflation rate of between 0 and 3 percent, is desirable. The reason why zero is not the target is that some price increases are due to quality improvements—a measurement bias in the price index—so a positive average *measured* inflation rate is equivalent to price stability.

FIGURE 34.1

Macroeconomic Performance: Real GDP and Inflation

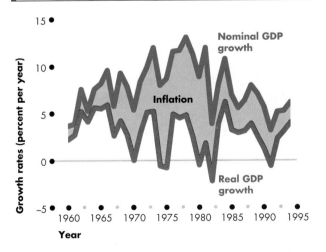

Real GDP growth and inflation fluctuate a great deal and during the 1970s, inflation mushroomed (the green shaded area) and real GDP growth slowed. This macroeconomic performance falls far short of the goals of a high and stable real GDP growth rate and low and predictable inflation.

Source: The Economic Report of the President, 1995.

The Two Core Policy Indicators: Real GDP Growth and Inflation

Although macroeconomic policy pursues the four goals we've just considered, the goals are not independent ones. Three of these goals—increasing the real GDP growth rate, smoothing the business cycle, and maintaining low unemployment—are linked together. Real GDP growth tells us directly about the long-term goal of high sustainable growth and the business cycle. It also has a strong link to unemployment. If growth becomes too rapid, unemployment falls below the natural rate and if growth becomes too slow, unemployment rises above the natural rate. So keeping real GDP growing steadily at its maximum sustainable rate is equivalent to avoiding business fluctuations and keeping unemployment at the natural rate.

There are some connections between real GDP growth and inflation, but over the long run, these two variables are largely independent. So two variables, real GDP growth and inflation, define the core policy targets.

Policy performance, judged by the two core policy targets—real GDP growth and inflation—is shown in Fig. 34.1. Here the red line shows real GDP growth. Real GDP growth averaged 4 percent a year during the 1960s, but after 1970, the growth rate fell to less than 2.5 percent a year. Real GDP growth has fluctuated between a high of 6.2 percent in 1984 and a low of –2.2 percent in 1982. The green shaded area shows inflation. The inflation rate was low during the 1960s, exploded during the 1970s, and then fell through the 1980s. During the 1990s, inflation returned to its 1960s level.

R E V I E W

- The goals of domestic macroeconomic policy are the highest sustainable rate of potential GDP growth, small business cycle fluctuations, low unemployment and low inflation.
- Keeping real GDP growing steadily at its highest sustainable rate is equivalent to avoiding business cycle fluctuations and keeping unemployment at the natural rate.

We've examined the policy goals. Let's now look at the policy tools and the way they have been used.

Policy Tools and Performance

THE TOOLS THAT ARE USED TO TRY TO ACHIEVE macroeconomic performance objectives are fiscal policy and monetary policy. **Fiscal policy**, which is described in Chapter 29, is the use of the federal budget to achieve macroeconomic objectives. The detailed fiscal policy tools are tax rates, benefit rates, and government purchases of goods and services. These tools work by influencing aggregate supply and aggregate demand in the ways explained in Chapter 29. **Monetary policy**, which is described in Chapter 31, is the adjustment of the quantity of money in circulation and interest rates by the Federal Reserve (the Fed) to achieve macroeconomic objectives. These tools work by changing aggregate demand. How have the tools actually been used in the United States? Let's answer this question by summarizing the main directions of fiscal and monetary policy over the years since 1960.

Fiscal Policy Since 1960

Figure 34.2 gives a broad summary of fiscal policy since 1960. It shows the levels of government revenues and expenditures and the budget balance (each as a percentage of GDP). So that you can see the political context of fiscal policy, the figure also shows the terms of administrations and the names of the incumbent presidents.

Fiscal policy was mildly expansionary during the Kennedy years and strongly expansionary during the later Johnson years when the Vietnam War buildup occurred. During Nixon's presidency, spending growth was kept moderate. But under the pressure of the first OPEC oil shock, spending soared during Ford's presidency. The Carter years began with spending cuts but then spending climbed to a new high. During the first Reagan term, spending continued to increase at first but it was later held in check and then during the second Reagan term, spending was cut. The Bush administration worked hard to keep spending in check and was initially committed to "no new taxes," but in mid-term, taxes increased as

---

FIGURE 34.2

The Fiscal Policy Record: A Summary

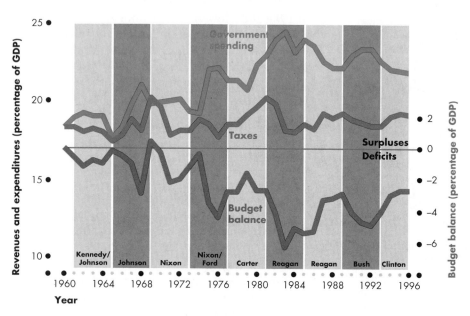

Fiscal policy is summarized here by the performance of government spending, taxes, and the budget balance. Spending has been on an upward trend and because spending has increased more than taxes, a deficit has emerged. Cycles in spending and taxes have resulted in cycles in the deficit that often have been expansionary in the year before an election and contractionary in the year following an election.

Source: *The Economic Report of the President,* 1995, and the author's calculations.

a percentage of GDP. As the 1991 recession intensified and the 1992 election drew closer, tax cuts became the rage, especially in Congress, and revenues decreased. Revenues increased and spending decreased during the Clinton presidency.

The budget balance tells an interesting story. During the terms of Johnson, Nixon, and Ford and the first Reagan term, the budget deficit decreased in the immediate post-election year and increased as the next election approached.

Let's now look at monetary policy.

Monetary Policy Since 1960

Figure 34.3 shows three broad measures of monetary policy. They are the growth rate of M2, the federal funds rate, and the real federal funds rate. The M2 growth rate tells us how monetary policy was influencing an important determinant of aggregate demand. The federal funds rate tells us how the Fed was acting to change money growth. And the real federal funds rate tells us how the Fed was acting on

the opportunity cost of short-term funds that influences spending plans.

Figure 34.3 also identifies the election years, the presidents, and the Fed chairs. The Fed has had five chairs during this period. Notice that the term of a Fed chair does not coincide with the term of a president. William McChesney Martin was a long-serving chair, whose term began in 1951. He retired in 1969 and was replaced by Arthur Burns, who served until 1977. William Miller had the shortest term and was replaced by Paul Volcker in 1979. The next chair, Alan Greenspan, was appointed by President Reagan in 1987 and served under three presidents.

First, let's look at some of the monetary policy trends. During the 1960s the M2 growth rate averaged 7 percent a year and ranged between a low of 4 percent in 1969 and a high of 9 percent in 1967. It then increased to average 10 percent a year between 1970 and 1983 and hit a peak of 14 percent in 1976. M2 growth then fell sharply from 12 percent in 1983 down to less than 1 percent in 1994. The federal funds rate also has some trends. It trended upward from 1960 through 1981 and then trended downward.

FIGURE   34.3

The Monetary Policy Record: A Summary

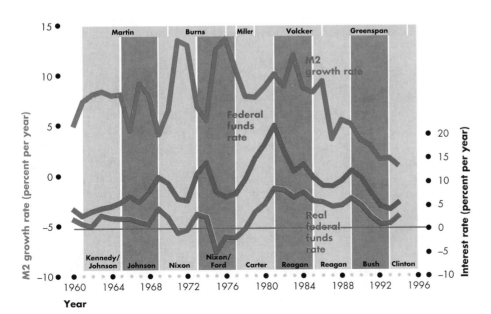

The monetary policy record is summarized here by the growth rate of M2 and the federal funds rate. Fluctuations in M2 growth have coincided with elections, the growth rate usually increasing in the year before an election. Important exceptions are 1979–1980 and 1991–1992, when monetary policy did not become expansionary and the incumbent President lost the election.

Source: *The Economic Report of the President,* 1995.

The real federal funds rate fell through 1975 and then increased and remained high through most of the 1980s. It fell during the early 1990s but then began to rise again through 1994.

The general upward trend in M2 growth brought the 1970s inflation, which brought rising *nominal* interest rates but, at first, falling real interest rates. The subsequent sharp downward trend in M2 growth brought falling inflation and falling nominal interest rates, but was accompanied by high real interest rates.

Next, look at the cycles. The peaks and troughs in M2 growth more or less coincide with the opposite turning points in the federal funds rate. When the Fed cuts the federal funds rate, M2 growth speeds up; when the Fed increases the federal funds rate, M2 growth slows down. But notice also a remarkable fact about the monetary policy cycles. There is a distinct tendency for the federal funds rate to rise and the M2 growth rate to decrease immediately following an election and for the federal funds rate to fall and the M2 growth rate to increase as the next election approaches. Usually, the incumbent president or his party's successor has won the election. There are two breaks in the M2 growth pattern, one during the term of Jimmy Carter and the other during the term of George Bush. In 1980 and in 1992, M2 growth did not rise sharply. Carter and Bush both lost their re-election bids. A coincidence? Perhaps, but the pattern is quite strong, and presidents certainly take a keen interest in what the Fed is up to.

R E V I E W

■ The macroeconomic policy tools are fiscal policy and monetary policy.

■ Fiscal policy was expansionary during the Kennedy, Johnson (Vietnam War), Ford (first OPEC oil shock), and Reagan years; moderate during the Nixon and Bush years; and contractionary during the Carter and Clinton years.

■ Money supply growth increased at the end of the 1960s and remained high through the 1970s. It slowed through the 1980s and 1990s.

You've now studied the goals of policy and seen the broad trends and cycles in fiscal and monetary policy. Let's now study the ways in which policy might be used better to achieve its goals. We'll begin by looking at long-term growth policy.

Long-Term Growth Policy

THE SOURCES OF THE LONG-TERM GROWTH OF potential GDP, which are explained in Chapter 27 (p. 659), are the accumulation of physical and human capital and the advance of technology. Chapter 27 briefly examines the range of policies that might achieve faster growth. Here, we probe more deeply into the problem of boosting the long-term growth rate.

The factors that determine long term growth result from millions of individual decisions; the role of government in influencing growth is limited. Nevertheless, policy can influence the private decisions on which long term growth depends in three areas. Such a policy would increase:

■ National saving
■ Investment in human capital
■ Investment in new technologies

National Saving

National saving equals private saving plus government saving. Figure 34.4 shows national saving and its private and government components since 1960. From 1960 through 1982, national saving (green line) fluctuated around an average of 17 percent of GDP. There then began a steady slide that saw national saving sink to 12 percent of GDP in 1992. Private saving (blue line) actually increased as a percentage of GDP between 1960 and 1984, when it peaked at 20 percent of GDP. Government saving (the vertical gap between the blue line and the green line) fluctuated around zero before 1975 and became increasingly negative (government dissaving) during the 1980s.

The data you have just examined are for *gross* saving. Each year, national wealth grows by the amount of *net* saving, which equals gross saving minus the value of capital that is scrapped during the year. Figure 34.4 shows U.S. net saving as a percentage of GDP. You can see that net saving (red line) has followed a falling trend since the mid-1970s. It has fallen faster than gross saving. The reason is that capital has depreciated more quickly. During the 1960s, depreciation ranged between 8 percent and 9 percent of GDP. This percentage edged upward and was around

11 percent by the mid-1990s. In the 1982 recession, it reached 13 percent of GDP. As a result of the fall in gross saving and the increase in the depreciation rate, net saving in the United States sank to an all-time low of 1.1 percent of GDP in 1992.

U.S. investment, one of the engines of growth, is not limited by U.S. saving. The reason is that foreign saving can be harnessed to finance U.S. investment. But boosting the U.S. saving rate can help to bring faster real GDP growth for two reasons. First, the U.S. economy is a significant proportion of the world economy, so an increase in U.S. saving would increase world saving and bring lower real interest rates around the world. With lower real interest rates, investment would be boosted everywhere. The U.S. economy and the world economy could grow faster. Second, with more domestic saving, there might be an increase in domestic investment in high-risk–high-return new technologies that could boost U.S. growth.

How can national saving be increased? The two points of attack are:

- Increasing government saving
- Increasing private saving

Increasing Government Saving Government saving has been negative since 1975, and its average during the 1990s has been –3.4 percent of GDP. Increasing government saving means reducing or eliminating the federal deficit. Chapter 29 (pp. 716–718) describes the measures that are being pursued to eliminate the federal deficit by 2002. But as is explained in Chapter 29, achieving a substantial cut in the deficit will be hard work and will be achieved only by cuts in such sensitive areas as Social Security, Medicaid, and Medicare.

Increasing Private Saving Private saving has fallen from its peak of the mid-1980s, but even in the low years of 1992 and 1993, private saving was the same percentage of GDP it had been in 1960. The main way in which government actions can boost private saving is by increasing the after-tax rate of return on saving. This is what government policy has sought to do, but on only one type of asset: individual retirement accounts (IRAs). By putting their savings into IRAs, people can avoid income tax on their interest income. But they cannot use their IRAs (without tax penalties) until they reach the age of 59. Also, there are limits to the amount that can be accumulated tax-free in an IRA. The Clinton administration has proposed expanding IRAs.

Private saving probably could be stimulated more effectively by cutting taxes on interest income across the board and replacing the lost government revenue from such a tax cut with a national consumption tax or a national sales tax. Whether such restructuring of taxes is politically feasible or desirable is a question that goes beyond the scope of macroeconomics.

Private Saving and Inflation Inflation erodes the value of money and other financial assets such as bonds, and uncertainty about future inflation discourages saving. One further policy, therefore, that increases the saving rate is a monetary policy that preserves stable prices and minimizes uncertainty about the future value of money. Chapter 32 (pp. 807–808) spells out the broader connection between inflation and real GDP and explains why low inflation brings greater output and faster growth.

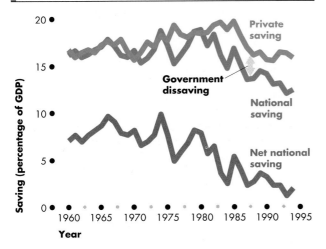

FIGURE   34.4

Saving Rates in the United States: 1960–1994

The U.S. national saving (green line) peaked in 1979 and has fallen since that year. Both government saving and private saving have contributed to the fall. U.S. net saving (red line) has fallen even faster than national saving and has been on a downward trend since the mid-1970s. It hit an all-time low of 1.1 percent of GDP in 1992.

Source: The Economic Report of the President, 1995.

Investment in Human Capital

The accumulation of human capital plays a crucial role in economic growth, and two areas are relevant: schooling and on-the-job experience. Economic research shows that both schooling and on-the-job training pay. That is, on the average, the greater the number of years a person remains in school and the greater the number of years of work experience, the higher are that person's earnings. Furthermore, schooling and on-the-job experience don't simply pay; they yield a high rate of return.

If education and on-the-job training yield higher earnings, why does the government need a policy toward investment in human capital? Why can't people simply be left to get on with making their own decisions about how much human capital to acquire? The answer is that the *social* returns to human capital probably exceed the *private* returns. The extra productivity that comes from the *interactions* of well-educated and experienced people exceeds what each individual could achieve alone. So, left to ourselves, we would probably accumulate too little human capital. Let's look at some aspects of education and training policies.

Education and Training Policies   The main way in which governments attempt to increase the amount of human capital is by providing subsidized or, more often, free schooling. They also help to set the standards of achievement for the school system.

The United States has achieved a high standard on some dimensions of schooling but not on all dimensions. For example, in 1992, 62 percent of high school graduates enrolled in post-secondary education (one of the highest percentages in the world) but 13 percent of high school students dropped out and did not graduate.

The Goals 2000: Educate America Act of 1994 is an attempt to improve the quality of schooling, especially for those who benefit least at present. The Act pays special attention to improving each child's state of preparation for school and performance in school, especially in mathematics and science, two areas in which U.S. schoolchildren are not leading the world. A further feature of Goals 2000 is to improve college access, especially for adults who can benefit from retraining.

The scope for government involvement in these areas is limited, but the government can set an example as an employer and it can encourage best-practice training programs for workers.

Investment in New Technologies

Investment in new technologies is the third area in which policy can influence economic growth. As Chapter 26 explains, investment in new technologies is special for two reasons. First, it appears not to run into the problem of diminishing returns that plague the other types of capital and the other factors of production. Second, the benefits of new technologies spill over to influence all parts of the economy, not just the firms undertaking the investment. For these reasons, increasing the rate of investment in new technologies appears to be a particularly promising way of boosting long-term growth. But how can government policy influence the pace of technological change?

Government can fund and provide tax incentives for research and development activities. Through the National Science Foundation, the public universities, and various research establishments, governments fund a large amount of basic research. Also, the federal government encourages business research with a Research and Experiment Tax Credit (R&E credit). This credit is available to firms that spend more on research and development than some threshold amount. The idea is to stimulate more expenditure on these activities than would occur otherwise. The effectiveness of the R&E credit is not certain but some research says it is a cost effective way of boosting research.

R E V I E W

- Long-term growth policies focus on increasing saving and increasing investment in human capital and new technologies.
- The U.S. net saving rate has been on a negative trend since the mid-1970s. To increase the saving rate, government saving and the after-tax return on private saving must be increased and inflation must be kept in check.
- Human capital investment might be increased with improved education and on-the-job training programs.
- Investment in new technologies can be encouraged by government funding and tax incentives.

We've seen how government might use its fiscal and monetary policies to influence long-term growth. How can it influence the business cycle and unemployment? Let's now address this question.

Business Cycle and Unemployment Policy

MANY DIFFERENT FISCAL AND MONETARY POLICIES can be pursued to stabilize the business cycle and cyclical unemployment. But all these polices fall into three broad categories:

- Fixed-rule policies
- Feedback-rule policies
- Discretionary policies

Fixed-Rule Policies

A **fixed-rule policy** specifies an action to be pursued independently of the state of the economy. An everyday life example of a fixed rule is a stop sign. It says, "Stop regardless of the state of the road ahead—even if no other vehicle is trying to use the road." One fixed-rule policy, proposed by Milton Friedman, is to keep the quantity of money growing at a constant rate year in and year out, regardless of the state of the economy to make the *average* inflation rate zero. Another fixed-rule policy is to balance the federal budget. Fixed rules are rarely followed in practice, but they have some merits in principle, and later in this chapter, we will study how they would work if they were pursued.

Feedback-Rule Policies

A **feedback-rule policy** specifies how policy actions respond to changes in the state of the economy. A yield sign is an everyday feedback rule. It says, "Stop if another vehicle is attempting to use the road ahead, but otherwise, proceed." A macroeconomic feedback-rule policy is one that changes the money supply, interest rates, or even tax rates in response to the state of the economy. Some feedback-rules guide the actions of policy makers. For example, the Fed's Federal Open Market Committee used a feedback rule when it kept pushing interest rates ever higher through 1994 in response to persistently falling unemployment and strong real GDP growth. Other feedback-rule policies are automatic. Examples are the automatic increase in tax revenues and decrease in transfer payments during an expansion and the automatic decrease in tax revenues and increase in transfer payments during a recession.

Discretionary Policies

A **discretionary policy** responds to the state of the economy in a possibly unique way that uses all the information available, including perceived lessons from past "mistakes." An everyday discretionary policy occurs at an unmarked intersection. Each driver uses discretion in deciding whether to stop and how slowly to approach the intersection. Most macroeconomic policy actions have an element of discretion because every situation is to some degree unique. For example, through 1994 the Fed increased interest rates several times but by small increments. It might have delayed increasing rates until it was more sure that higher rates were needed and then increased them in a larger increment. The Fed used discretion based on lessons it had learned from earlier expansions. But despite the fact that all policy actions have an element of discretion, they can be regarded as modifications of a basic feedback-rule policy.

We'll study the effects of business cycle policy by comparing the performance of real GDP and the price level under a fixed rule and a feedback rule. Because the business cycle can result from demand shocks or supply shocks, we need to consider these two cases. We'll begin by studying demand shocks.

Stabilizing Aggregate Demand Shocks

We'll study an economy that starts out at full employment and has no inflation. Figure 34.5 illustrates this situation. The economy is on aggregate demand curve AD_0 and short-run aggregate supply curve SAS. These curves intersect at a point on the long-run aggregate supply curve, LAS. The GDP deflator is 130, and real GDP is $6 trillion. Now suppose that there is an unexpected and temporary decrease in aggregate demand. Let's see what happens.

Perhaps investment decreases because of a wave of pessimism about the future, or perhaps exports decrease because of a recession in the rest of the world. Regardless of the origin of the decrease in aggregate demand, the aggregate demand curve shifts leftward, to AD_1 in Fig. 34.5. Aggregate demand curve AD_1 intersects the short-run aggregate supply curve, SAS, at a GDP deflator of 125 and a real GDP of $5.5 trillion. The economy is in a recession. Real GDP is less than potential GDP, and unemployment is above its natural rate.

FIGURE 34.5

A Decrease in Aggregate Demand

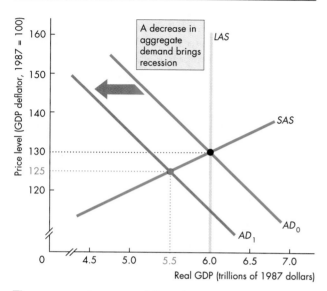

The economy starts out at full employment on aggregate demand curve AD_0 and short-run aggregate supply curve SAS, the two curves intersecting on the long-run aggregate supply curve, LAS. Real GDP is $6 trillion, and the GDP deflator is 130. A fall in aggregate demand (due to pessimism about future profits, for example) unexpectedly shifts the aggregate demand curve to AD_1. Real GDP falls to $5.5 trillion, and the GDP deflator falls to 125. The economy is in a recession.

Assume that the decrease in aggregate demand from AD_0 to AD_1 is temporary. As confidence in the future improves, firms' investment picks up, or as economic expansion proceeds in the rest of the world, exports gradually increase. As a result, the aggregate demand curve gradually returns to AD_0, but it takes some time to do so.

We are going to work out how the economy responds under two alternative policies during the period in which aggregate demand gradually increases to its original level: a fixed rule and a feedback rule.

Fixed Rule: Monetarism   The fixed rule that we'll study here is one in which government purchases of goods and services, taxes, and the deficit remain constant and the money supply remains constant. Neither fiscal policy nor monetary policy responds to the depressed economy. This is the rule advocated by

monetarists. A **monetarist** is an economist who believes that fluctuations in the money stock are the main source of economic fluctuations—the monetarist theory of the business cycle (see Chapter 33, p. 830).

Figure 34.6(a) illustrates the response of the economy under a fixed rule when the decrease in aggregate demand to AD_1 is *temporary*. Gradually, aggregate demand returns to its original level and the aggregate demand curve shifts rightward to AD_0. As it does so, real GDP and the GDP deflator gradually increase. The GDP deflator gradually returns to 130 and real GDP to $6 trillion, as shown in Fig. 34.6(a). Throughout this process, the economy experiences more rapid growth than usual but beginning from a state in which real GDP is less than potential GDP. Also throughout the adjustment, unemployment remains above the natural rate.

Figure 34.6(b) illustrates the response of the economy under a fixed rule when the decrease in aggregate demand to AD_1 is *permanent*. Gradually, with unemployment above the natural rate, the money wage rate falls and the short-run aggregate supply curve shifts rightward to SAS_1. As it does so, real GDP gradually increases and the GDP deflator falls. Real GDP gradually returns to potential GDP of $6 trillion and the GDP deflator gradually falls to 115, as shown in Fig. 34.6(b). Again, throughout the adjustment, real GDP is less than potential GDP and unemployment exceeds the natural rate.

Let's contrast the adjustment under a fixed rule with that under a feedback-rule policy.

Feedback Rule: Keynesian Activism   The feedback rule that we'll study is one in which government purchases of goods and services increase, taxes decrease, the deficit increases, and the money supply increases when real GDP falls below potential GDP. In other words, both fiscal policy and monetary policy become expansionary when real GDP is less than potential GDP. When real GDP exceeds potential GDP, both policies operate in reverse, becoming contractionary. This rule is advocated by Keynesian activists. A **Keynesian activist** is an economist who believes that fluctuations in aggregate demand combined with sticky wages (and/or sticky prices) are the main source of economic fluctuations—the Keynesian and new Keynesian theories of the business cycle (see Chapter 33, pp. 828–834).

Figure 34.6(c) illustrates the response of the economy under this feedback rule policy. When aggregate demand decreases to AD_1, the expansionary fiscal and

FIGURE 34.6

Two Stabilization Policies: Aggregate Demand Shock

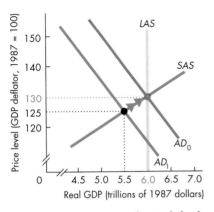

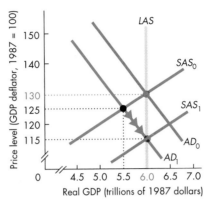

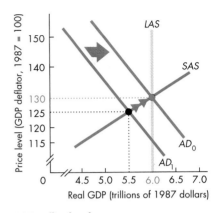

(a) Fixed rule: temporary demand shock   **(b) Fixed rule: permanent demand shock**   **(c) Feedback rule**

Aggregate demand has fallen from AD_0 to AD_1 and the economy is in a recession. Real GDP has fallen to $5.5 trillion and the GDP deflator has fallen to 125. A fixed-rule stabilization policy (parts a and b) leaves aggregate demand at AD_1, so real GDP remains at $5.5 trillion and the GDP deflator remains at 125. If the aggregate demand shock is temporary (part a), aggregate demand subsequently returns to its original level and the aggregate demand curve shifts back to AD_0. As it does, real GDP increases back to $6 trillion and the GDP deflator increases to 130. If the demand shock is permanent (part b),

aggregate demand remains at AD_1. Eventually, because unemployment is above the natural rate, the money wage rate falls and the SAS curve shfits to SAS_1. The price level falls further (to a GDP deflator of 115) and real GDP returns to $6 trillion. Part (c) shows a feedback rule. With the economy in recession, expansionary fiscal and monetary policies increase aggregate demand and shift the aggregate demand curve from AD_1 to AD_0. Real GDP returns to $6 trillion and the GDP deflator returns 130.

monetary policies increase aggregate demand, shifting the aggregate demand curve immediately to AD_0. As other influences begin to increase aggregate demand, fiscal and monetary policies become contractionary and hold the aggregate demand curve steady at AD_0. Real GDP is held steady at $6 trillion, and the GDP deflator remains at 130.

The Two Rules Compared   Under a fixed-rule policy the economy goes into a recession and stays there for as long as it takes for aggregate demand to increase again under its own steam. Only gradually does the aggregate demand curve return to its original position and the recession come to an end.

Under a feedback-rule policy, the economy is pulled out of its recession by the policy action. Once back at potential GDP, real GDP is held there by a gradual, policy-induced decrease in aggregate demand that exactly offsets the increase in aggregate demand coming from private spending decisions.

The price level and real GDP decrease and increase by exactly the same amounts under the two policies, but real GDP stays below potential GDP for longer with a fixed rule than it does with a feedback rule.

The Fed's Feedback Rule: 1992–1994   The Fed tried to operate a feedback rule like the one you've just studied between 1992 and 1995. At the end of 1992, real GDP was below potential GDP and unemployment was above the natural rate. Through 1992 the Fed gradually lowered interest rates and speeded up money growth. The economy expanded. By 1994, real GDP was almost back at potential GDP and was growing faster than potential GDP. To prevent an outbreak of inflation, the Fed gradually increased interest rates and slowed money growth. Its aim was to engineer what has been called a "soft landing," in which real GDP growth slows and real GDP converges on potential GDP without overshooting or turning downward into recession.

So Feedback Rules Are Better? Isn't it obvious that a feedback rule is better than a fixed rule? Can't the government and the Fed use feedback rules to keep the economy close to full employment with a stable price level? Of course, unforecasted events—such as a collapse in business confidence—will hit the economy from time to time. But by responding with a change in tax rates, spending, interest rates, and money supply, can't the government and the Fed minimize the damage from such a shock? It appears to be so from our analysis, and the Fed seems to have done a pretty good job during 1992–1994.

Despite the apparent superiority of a feedback rule, many economists remain convinced that a fixed rule stabilizes aggregate demand more effectively than a feedback rule does. These economists assert that fixed rules are better than feedback rules because:

- Potential GDP is not known.
- Policy lags are longer than the forecast horizon.
- Feedback-rule policies are less predictable than fixed-rule policies.

Let's look at these assertions.

Knowledge of Potential GDP To decide whether a feedback policy needs to stimulate or retard aggregate demand, it is necessary to determine whether real GDP is currently above or below potential GDP. But potential GDP is not known with certainty. It depends on a large number of factors, one of which is the level of employment when unemployment is at its natural rate. But uncertainty and disagreement exist about how the labor market works, so we can only estimate the natural rate of unemployment. As a result, there is uncertainty about the *direction* in which a feedback policy should be pushing the level of aggregate demand.

Policy Lags and the Forecast Horizon The effects of policy actions taken today are spread out over the following two years or even more. But no one is able to forecast accurately that far ahead. The forecast horizon of the policy makers is less than 1 year. Further, it is not possible to predict the precise timing and magnitude of the effects of policy actions. Thus feedback policies that react to today's economy may be inappropriate for the state of the economy at that uncertain future date when the policy's effects are felt.

For example, suppose that today the economy is in recession. The Fed reacts with an increase in the money supply growth rate. When the Fed puts on the monetary accelerator, the first reaction is a fall in interest rates. Some time later, lower interest rates produce an increase in investment and the purchases of consumer durable goods. Some time still later, this increase in expenditure increases income; higher income in turn induces higher consumption expenditure. Later yet, the higher expenditure increases the demand for labor, and eventually, wages and prices rise. The sectors in which the spending increases occur vary, and so does the impact on employment. It can take anywhere from 9 months to 2 years for an initial action by the Fed to cause a change in real GDP, employment, and the inflation rate.

By the time the Fed's actions are having their maximum effect, the economy has moved on to a new situation. Perhaps a world economic slowdown has added a new negative effect on aggregate demand that is offsetting the Fed's expansionary actions. Or perhaps a boost in business confidence has increased aggregate demand yet further, adding to the Fed's own expansionary policy. Whatever the situation, the Fed can take the appropriate actions today only if it can forecast those future shocks to aggregate demand.

Thus to smooth the fluctuations in aggregate demand, the Fed needs to take actions today, based on a forecast of what will be happening over a period stretching 2 or more years into the future. It is no use taking actions a year from today to influence the situation that then prevails. By then it will be too late.

If the Fed is good at economic forecasting and bases its policy actions on its forecasts, then the Fed can deliver the type of aggregate-demand-smoothing performance that we assumed in the model economy that we studied earlier in this chapter. But if the Fed takes policy actions that are based on today's economy rather than on the forecasted economy a year into the future, then those actions will often be inappropriate ones.

When unemployment is high and the Fed puts its foot on the accelerator, it speeds the economy back to full employment. But the Fed cannot see far enough ahead to know when to ease off the accelerator and gently tap the brake, holding the economy at its full-employment point. Usually, the Fed keeps its foot on the accelerator for too long, and after the Fed has taken its foot off the accelerator pedal, the economy races through the full-employment point and starts to experience shortages and inflationary pressures. Eventually, when inflation increases and unemployment falls below its natural rate, the Fed steps on the brake, pushing the economy back below full employment.

The Fed's own reactions to the current state of the economy has become one of the major sources of fluctuations in aggregate demand and the major factor that people have to forecast to make their own economic choices.

During 1994 the Fed tried hard to avoid the problems just described. It increased interest rates early in the expansion and by small increments. In 1995, after real GDP growth slowed down but before any serious signs of recession were on the horizon, it began to cut interest rates. Whether the Fed now knows enough to avoid some of the mistakes of the past is too early to tell. But its actions during 1992–1995 were gentler and better timed than in previous cycles.

The problems for fiscal policy feedback rules are similar to those for monetary policy but are more severe because of the lags in the implementation of fiscal policy. The Fed can take actions relatively quickly. But before a fiscal policy action can be taken, the entire legislative process must be completed. Thus even before a fiscal policy action is implemented, the economy may have moved on to a new situation that calls for a different feedback policy from the one that is in the legislative pipeline.

Predictability of Policies   To make decisions about long-term contracts for employment (wage contracts) and for borrowing and lending, people have to anticipate the future course of prices—the future inflation rate. To forecast the inflation rate, it is necessary to forecast aggregate demand. And to forecast aggregate demand, it is necessary to forecast the policy actions of the government and the Fed.

If the government and the Fed stick to rock-steady, fixed rules for tax rates, spending programs, and money supply growth, then policy itself cannot be a contributor to unexpected fluctuations in aggregate demand.

In contrast, when a feedback rule is being pursued, there is more scope for the policy actions to be unpredictable. The main reason is that feedback rules are not written down for all to see. Rather, they have to be inferred from the behavior of the government and the Fed.

Thus with a feedback policy it is necessary to predict the variables to which the government and Fed react and the extent to which they react. Consequently, a feedback rule for fiscal and monetary policies can create more unpredictable fluctuations in aggregate demand than a fixed rule can.

Economists disagree about whether those bigger fluctuations offset the potential stabilizing influence of the predictable changes the Fed makes. No agreed measurements have been made to settle this dispute. Nevertheless, the unpredictability of the Fed in its pursuit of feedback policies is an important fact of economic life. And the Fed does not always go out of its way to make its reactions clear. Even in Congressional testimony, Federal Reserve Board chairmen are reluctant to make the Fed's actions and intentions entirely plain. (It has been suggested that two former chairmen of the Federal Reserve Board, the pipe-puffing Arthur Burns and the cigar-puffing Paul Volcker, carried their own smokescreens around with them, as if to exemplify the Fed's mysteriousness and unpredictability. The nonsmoking Alan Greenspan seems to be running a more open and predictable Fed.)

It is not surprising that the Fed seeks to keep *some* of its actions behind a smokescreen. First, the Fed wants to maintain as much freedom of action as possible and so does not want to state with too great a precision the feedback rules that it will follow in any given circumstances. Second, the Fed is part of a political process and, although legally independent of the federal government, is not immune to subtle influence. For at least these two reasons, the Fed does not specify feedback rules as precisely as the one we've analyzed in this chapter. As a result, the Fed cannot deliver an economic performance that has the stability that we generated in the model economy.

To the extent that the Fed's actions are discretionary and unpredictable, they lead to unpredictable fluctuations in aggregate demand. These fluctuations, in turn, produce fluctuations in real GDP, employment, and unemployment.

If it is difficult for the Fed to pursue a predictable feedback stabilization policy, it is probably impossible for Congress to do so. The stabilization policy of Congress is formulated in terms of spending programs and tax laws. Because these programs and laws are the outcome of a political process that is constrained only by the Constitution, there can be no effective way in which a predictable feedback fiscal policy can be adhered to.

We reviewed three reasons why feedback-rule policies might not be more effective than fixed-rule policies in controlling aggregate demand. But there is a fourth reason why some economists prefer fixed rules: Not all shocks to the economy are on the demand side. Most advocates of feedback rules believe that most fluctuations do come from aggregate demand. Some advocates of fixed rules believe that aggregate supply fluctuations are the dominant ones. Let's now see how aggregate supply fluctuations affect the economy under a fixed rule and a feedback rule. We will also see why those economists who believe that aggregate-supply fluctuations are the dominant ones also favor a fixed rule rather than a feedback rule.

Stabilizing Aggregate Supply Shocks

Real business cycle theorists believe that fluctuations in real GDP (and in employment and unemployment) are caused not by fluctuations in aggregate demand but by fluctuations in productivity growth. According to real business cycle theory, there is no useful distinction between long-run aggregate supply and short-run aggregate supply. Because wages are flexible, the labor market is always in equilibrium and unemployment is always at its natural rate. The vertical long-run aggregate supply curve is also the short-run aggregate supply curve. Fluctuations occur because of shifts in the long-run aggregate supply curve. Normally, the long-run aggregate supply curve shifts to the right—the economy expands. But the pace at which the long-run aggregate supply curve shifts to the right varies. Also, on occasion, the long-run aggregate supply curve shifts leftward, bringing a decrease in aggregate supply and a fall in real GDP.

If the real business cycle theory is correct, economic policy that influences the aggregate demand curve has no effect on real GDP. But it does affect the price level. If a feedback-rule policy is used to increase aggregate demand every time real GDP decreases, and if the real business cycle theory is correct, the feedback-rule policy will make price level fluctuations more severe than they otherwise would be. To see why, consider Fig. 34.7.

Imagine that the economy starts out on aggregate demand curve AD_0 and long-run aggregate supply curve LAS_0 at a GDP deflator of 130 and with real GDP equal to $6 trillion. Now suppose that the long-run aggregate supply curve shifts to LAS_1. An actual decrease in long-run aggregate supply can occur as a result of a severe drought or other natural catastrophe or perhaps as the result of a disruption of international trade such as the OPEC embargo of the 1970s.

FIGURE 34.7

Responding to a Productivity Growth Slowdown

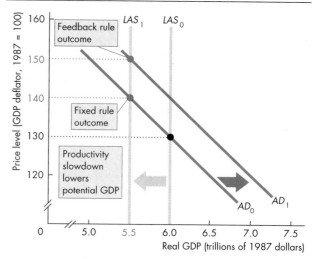

A productivity growth slowdown shifts the long-run aggregate supply curve from LAS_0 to LAS_1. Real GDP decreases to $5.5 trillion, and the GDP deflator rises to 140. With a fixed rule, there is no change in the money supply, taxes, or government spending; aggregate demand stays at AD_0; and that is the end of the matter. With a feedback rule, the Fed increases the money supply and the Congress cuts taxes or increases spending, intending to increase real GDP. Aggregate demand shifts to AD_1, but the result is an increase in the price level—the GDP deflator rises to 150—with no change in real GDP.

Fixed Rule With a fixed rule, the fall in the long-run aggregate supply has no effect on the policies of the Fed or the government and no effect on aggregate demand. The aggregate demand curve remains AD_0. Real GDP falls to $5.5 trillion, and the GDP deflator increases to 140.

Feedback Rule Now suppose that the Fed and the government use feedback rules. In particular, suppose that when real GDP decreases, the Fed increases the money supply and Congress enacts a tax cut to increase aggregate demand. In this example the money supply and tax cut shift the aggregate demand curve to AD_1. The policy goal is to bring real GDP back to $6 trillion. But the long-run aggregate supply curve has shifted, and so potential GDP has decreased to $5.5 trillion. The increase in aggregate demand cannot bring forth an increase in output if the economy does not have the capacity to produce that output. So real GDP stays at $5.5 trillion but the price level rises still further—the GDP deflator goes to 150. You can see that in this case the attempt to stabilize real GDP using a feedback-rule policy has no effect on real GDP but generates a substantial price level increase.

We've now seen some of the shortcomings of using feedback rules for stabilization policy. Some economists believe that these shortcomings are serious and want to constrain Congress and the Fed so that they use fixed rules. Others, regarding the potential advantages of feedback rules as greater than their costs, advocate the continued use of such policies but with an important modification that we'll now look at.

Nominal GDP Targeting

Nominal GDP targeting is an attempt to keep the growth rate of nominal GDP steady. This policy target was first proposed by a leading Keynesian activist, James Tobin of Yale University. It is a policy that recognizes the strengths of a fixed rule but that regards the monetarist fixed rule as inappropriate. Instead, nominal GDP targeting uses feedback rules for fiscal and monetary policy to hit a fixed nominal GDP growth target.

Because nominal GDP growth equals the real GDP growth rate plus the inflation rate, keeping nominal GDP growth steady does not directly target either real GDP growth or inflation. But nominal GDP usually grows quickly because the inflation rate is high. And nominal GDP usually grows slowly because real GDP growth is negative—the economy is in recession. So the idea is that, by keeping nominal GDP growth steady, both excessive inflation and severe recession might be avoided.

Nominal GDP targeting uses feedback rules. Expansionary fiscal and/or monetary actions increase aggregate demand when nominal GDP is below target and contractionary fiscal and/or monetary actions decrease aggregate demand when nominal GDP is above target. The main problem with nominal GDP targeting is that there are long and variable time lags between the identification of a need to change aggregate demand and the effects of the policy actions that are taken.

Natural Rate Policies

The business cycle and unemployment policies we've considered have been directed at smoothing the business cycle and minimizing *cyclical unemployment*. It is also possible to pursue policies directed toward lowering the natural rate of unemployment. But there are no simple and costless ways of lowering the natural rate of unemployment. Let's look at two possible ways.

The main policy tools that influence the natural rate of unemployment are unemployment compensation and the minimum wage. But to use these tools, the government faces tough trade-offs. To lower the natural rate of unemployment, the government could lower the unemployment compensation rate, or shorten the period for which compensation is paid, or restrict compensation to people who undertake training programs that increase the likelihood of their finding jobs. These possible policy actions might create hardship and have a cost that exceeds the cost of a high natural rate of unemployment.

Alternatively, the government might lower the minimum real wage rate either by holding the minimum money wage rate constant and letting inflation cut the minimum real wage rate or by cutting the minimum money wage rate. Either way, the government faces the trade-off between real wages and the natural rate of unemployment.

R E V I E W

- Fixed-rule policies keep fiscal and monetary policy set steady and independent of the state of the economy.
- Feedback policies cut taxes, increase spending, and speed up money supply growth when the economy is in recession and reverse these measures when the economy is overheating.
- The successful use of feedback rules requires knowledge of whether the economy has been hit by an aggregate demand or an aggregate supply shock, an ability to forecast as far ahead as the policy actions have effects, and clarity about the feedback rules being used.

We've studied growth policy and business cycle and unemployment policy. Let's now study inflation policy.

Inflation Policy

THERE ARE TWO INFLATION POLICY PROBLEMS. In times of price level stability the problem is to prevent inflation from breaking out. In times of inflation the problem is to reduce its rate and restore price stability. Preventing inflation from breaking out means avoiding both demand-pull and cost-push forces. Avoiding demand-pull inflation is the flip side of avoiding demand-driven recession and is achieved by stabilizing aggregate demand. So the business cycle and unemployment policy we've just studied is also an anti-inflation policy. But avoiding cost-push inflation raises some special issues that we need to consider. So we will look at two issues for inflation policy:

■ Avoiding cost-push inflation
■ Slowing inflation

Avoiding Cost-Push Inflation

Cost-push inflation is inflation that has its origins in cost increases. In 1973–1974 and again in 1980, the world oil price exploded. Cost shocks such as these become inflationary if they are accommodated by an increase in the quantity of money. Such an increase in the quantity of money can occur if a monetary policy feedback rule is used. A fixed-rule policy for the money stock makes cost-push inflation impossible. Let's see why.

Figure 34.8 shows the economy at full employment. Aggregate demand is AD_0, short-run aggregate supply is SAS_0, and long-run aggregate supply is LAS. Real GDP is $6 trillion, and the GDP deflator is 130. Now suppose that OPEC tries to gain a temporary advantage by increasing the price of oil. The short-run aggregate supply curve shifts leftward from SAS_0 to SAS_1.

FIGURE   34.8

Responding to an OPEC Oil Price Increase

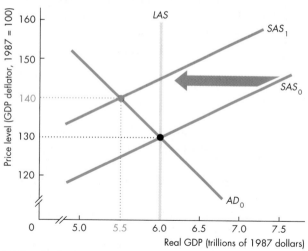

(a) Fixed rule

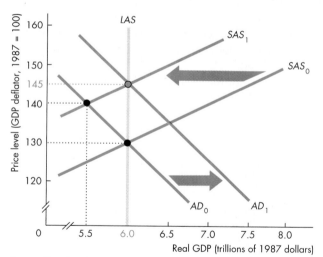

(b) Feedback rule

The economy starts out on AD_0 and SAS_0, with a GDP deflator of 130 and real GDP of $6 trillion. OPEC forces up the price of oil, and the short-run aggregate supply curve shifts to SAS_1. Real GDP decreases to $5.5 trillion, and the GDP deflator increases to 140. With a fixed-rule policy (part a), the Fed makes no change to aggregate demand. The economy stays in

a recession until the price of oil falls again and the economy returns to its original position. With a feedback-rule policy (part b), the Fed injects additional money and the aggregate demand curve shifts to AD_1. Real GDP returns to $6 trillion (potential GDP), but the GDP deflator increases to 145. The economy is set for another round of cost-push inflation.

Monetarist Fixed Rule Figure 34.8(a) shows what happens if the Fed follows a fixed rule for monetary policy and the government follows a fixed rule for fiscal policy. Suppose that the fixed rule is for zero money growth and no change in taxes or government purchases of goods and services. With these fixed rules, the Fed and the government pay no attention to the fact that there has been an increase in the price of oil. No policy actions are taken. The short-run aggregate supply curve has shifted to SAS_1, but the aggregate demand curve remains at AD_0. The GDP deflator rises to 140, and real GDP falls to $5.5 trillion. The economy has experienced *stagflation*. With unemployment above the natural rate, the money wage rate will eventually fall. The low level of real GDP and low sales will probably also bring a fall in the price of oil. These events shift the short-run aggregate supply curve back to SAS_0. The GDP deflator will fall to 130 and real GDP will increase to $6 trillion. But this adjustment might take a long time.

Keynesian Feedback Rule Figure 34.8(b) shows what happens if the Fed and government operate a feedback rule. The starting point is the same as before—the economy is on SAS_0 and AD_0 with a GDP deflator of 130 and real GDP of $6 trillion. OPEC raises the price of oil, and the short-run aggregate supply curve shifts to SAS_1. Real GDP decreases to $5.5 trillion, and the price level rises to 140.

A feedback rule is followed. With potential GDP perceived to be $6 trillion and with actual real GDP at $5.5 trillion, the Fed pumps money into the economy and the government increases its spending and lowers taxes. Aggregate demand increases and the aggregate demand curve shifts rightward to AD_1. The price level rises to 145 and real GDP returns to $6 trillion. The economy moves back to full employment but at a higher price level. The Fed responded in the way we've just described to the first wave of OPEC price increases in the mid-1970s.

OPEC now sees the same advantage in forcing up the price of oil again. A new rise in the price of oil decreases aggregate supply, and the short-run aggregate supply curve shifts leftward once more. The Fed chases it with an increase in aggregate demand, and the economy is in a freewheeling inflation. Realizing this danger, the Fed did *not* respond to the second wave of OPEC price increases in the early 1980s as it had done before. Instead, the Fed held firm and even slowed down the growth of aggregate demand to further dampen the inflation consequences of OPEC's actions.

Incentives to Push Up Costs You can see that there are no checks on the incentives to push up costs if the Fed accommodates price hikes. If some group sees a temporary gain from pushing up the price at which they are selling their resources and if the Fed always accommodates to prevent unemployment and slack business conditions from emerging, then cost-push elements will have a free rein. But when the Fed pursues a fixed-rule policy, the incentive to attempt to steal a temporary advantage from a price increase is severely weakened. The cost of higher unemployment and lower output is a consequence that each group will have to face and recognize.

Thus a fixed rule can deliver steady inflation, while a feedback rule, in the face of cost-push pressures, leaves inflation free to rise and fall at the whim of whichever group believes a temporary advantage to be available from pushing up its price.

Slowing Inflation

So far, we've concentrated on *avoiding* inflation. But often the problem is not to avoid inflation but to tame it. The United States was in such a situation during the late 1970s and early 1980s. How can inflation, once it has set in, be cured? We'll look at two cases:

- A surprise inflation reduction
- A credible announced inflation reduction

A Surprise Inflation Reduction We'll use two equivalent approaches to study the problem of lowering inflation: the aggregate supply–aggregate demand model and the Phillips curve. The *AS-AD* model tells us about real GDP and the price level, while the Phillips curve, which is explained in Chapter 32 (pp. 809–813), lets us keep track of inflation and unemployment.

Figure 34.9 illustrates the economy at full employment with inflation raging at 10 percent a year. In part (a) the economy is on aggregate demand curve AD_0 and short-run aggregate supply curve SAS_0. Real GDP is $6 trillion, and the GDP deflator is 130. With real GDP equal to potential GDP on the *LAS* curve, the economy is at full employment. Equivalently, in part (b), the economy is on its long-run Phillips curve, *LRPC*, and short-run Phillips curve, $SRPC_0$. The inflation rate of 10 percent a year is anticipated, so unemployment is at its natural rate, 6 percent of the labor force.

FIGURE 34.9

Lowering Inflation

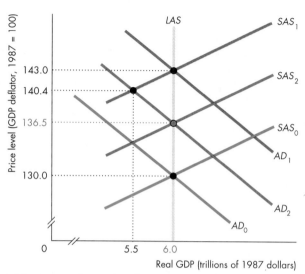

(a) Aggregate demand and aggregate supply

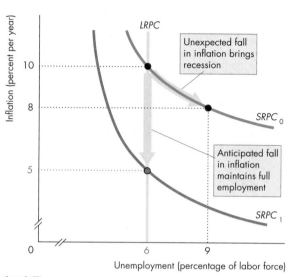

(b) Phillips curves

In part (a), aggregate demand is AD_0, short-run aggregate supply is SAS_0, and real GDP and potential GDP are $6 trillion on the long-run aggregate supply curve LAS. The aggregate demand curve is expected to shift and actually shifts to AD_1. The short-run aggregate supply curve shifts to SAS_1. The GDP deflator rises to 143 but real GDP remains at $6 trillion. Inflation is proceeding at a 10 percent a year and this inflation rate is anticipated. In part (b), which shows this same situation, the economy on the short-run Phillips curve $SRPC_0$ and on the long-run Phillips curve $LRPC$. Unemployment is at the natural rate of 6 percent and inflation is 10 percent a year.

An unexpected slowdown in aggregate demand growth means that the aggregate demand curve shifts from AD_0 to AD_2, real GDP falls to $5.5 trillion, and inflation slows to 8 percent (GDP deflator is 140.4). Unemployment rises to 9 percent as the economy slides down $SRPC_0$. An anticipated, credible, announced slowdown in aggregate demand growth means that when the aggregate demand curve shifts from AD_0 to AD_2, the short-run aggregate supply curve shifts from SAS_0, to SAS_2. The short-run Phillips curve shifts to $SRPC_1$. Inflation slows to 5 percent, real GDP remains at $6 trillion, and unemployment remains at its natural rate of 6 percent.

Next year, aggregate demand is *expected* to increase and the aggregate demand curve in Fig. 34.9(a) is expected to shift rightward from AD_0 to AD_1. In expectation of this increase in aggregate demand, wages increase to shift the short-run aggregate supply curve from SAS_0 to SAS_1. If expectations are fulfilled, the GDP deflator rises to 143—a 10 percent inflation—and real GDP remains at potential GDP. In part (b) the economy remains at its original position—unemployment is at the natural rate, and the inflation rate is 10 percent a year.

Suppose that when no one is expecting the Fed to change its policy, the Fed actually tries to slow inflation. It increases interest rates and slows money

growth. Aggregate demand growth slows, and the actual aggregate demand curve (in part a) shifts from AD_0 to AD_2. With no change in the expected inflation rate, wage rates rise by the same amount as before and the short-run aggregate supply curve shifts leftward from SAS_0 to SAS_1. Real GDP decreases to $5.5 trillion, and the GDP deflator rises to 140.4—an inflation rate of 8 percent a year. In Fig. 34.9(b) the economy moves along the short-run Phillips curve $SRPC_0$ as unemployment rises to 9 percent and inflation falls to 8 percent a year. The Fed's policy has succeeded in slowing inflation, but at the cost of recession. Real GDP is below potential GDP, and unemployment is above its natural rate.

A Credible Announced Inflation Reduction

Suppose that instead of simply slowing down the growth of aggregate demand, the Fed announces its intention ahead of its action and in a credible and convincing way so that its announcement is believed. That is, the Fed's policy is anticipated. Because the lower level of aggregate demand is expected, wages increase at a pace consistent with the lower level of aggregate demand. The short-run aggregate supply curve (in Fig. 34.9a) shifts leftward from SAS_0 but only to SAS_2. Aggregate demand increases by the amount expected, and the aggregate demand curve shifts from AD_0 to AD_2. The GDP deflator rises to 136.5—an inflation rate of 5 percent a year—and real GDP remains at potential GDP.

In Fig. 34.9(b) the lower expected inflation rate shifts the short-run Phillips curve downward to $SRPC_1$, and inflation falls to 5 percent a year, while unemployment remains at its natural rate of 6 percent.

Inflation Reduction in Practice

When the Fed in fact slowed down inflation in 1981, we all paid a very high price. The Fed's monetary policy action was unpredicted. As a result, it occurred in the face of wages that had been set at too high a level to be consistent with the growth of aggregate demand that the Fed subsequently allowed. The consequence was recession—a decrease in real GDP and a rise in unemployment. Couldn't the Fed have lowered inflation without causing recession by telling people far enough ahead of time that it did indeed plan to slow down the growth rate of aggregate demand?

The answer appears to be no. The main reason is that people form their expectations of the Fed's action (as they form expectations about anyone's actions) on the basis of actual behavior, not on the basis of stated intentions. How many times have you told yourself that it is your firm intention to take off 10 unwanted pounds or to keep within the budget and put a few dollars away for a rainy day, only to discover that, despite your very best intentions, your old habits win out in the end?

To form expectations of the Fed's actions, people look at the Fed's past *actions*, not its stated intentions. On the basis of such observations—called Fed-watching—they try to work out what the Fed's policy is, to forecast its future actions, and to forecast the effects of those actions on aggregate demand and

inflation. The Greenspan Fed, like the Volcker Fed that preceded it, has built a reputation for being anti-inflationary. That reputation is valuable because it helps the Fed to contain inflation and lowers the cost of eliminating inflation if it temporarily returns. The reason is that with a low expected inflation rate, the short-run Phillips curve is in a favorable position (like $SRPC_1$ in Fig. 34.9b). The situation faced by the Fed in 1995 is explored more fully in *Reading Between the Lines* on pp. 876–877.

A Truly Independent Fed

A radical suggestion for strengthening the Fed's reputation as the guardian of price stability is to make the Fed more independent of government and to charge it with the single responsibility of achieving and maintaining price level stability. Some central banks are more independent than the Fed. The German and Swiss central banks are the best examples. Another example is the New Zealand central bank. All these central banks have the responsibility of stabilizing prices but not real GDP and of pursuing their objective without interference from the government. Recent research on central bank performance has strengthened the view that a more independent central bank can deliver a lower average inflation rate without creating either a higher unemployment rate or a lower real GDP growth rate.

R E V I E W

- A fixed rule gives more effective protection against a cost-push inflation than a feedback rule does.
- When inflation is tamed, a recession usually results because people form policy expectations based on past policy actions.
- A more independent Fed pursuing only price stability could possibly achieve price stability with greater credibility and at lower cost in terms of unemployment and lost production.

◆ You have now completed your study of macroeconomics and of the problems and challenges of improving macroeconomic performance. In this study, your main focus has been the U.S. economy. In the remaining chapters we shift our focus and study some vital international issues.

Stabilization Policy Dilemma

The Wall Street Journal, January 24, 1995

Business and Academia Clash Over a Concept: 'Natural' Jobless Rate

by Amanda Bennett

Are too many Americans at work for the economy's own good?

Absolutely, says Martin Feldstein, a Harvard University professor ... By Mr. Feldstein's calculations, unemployment already has fallen way below the level he believes is sure to trigger steadily rising inflation—even if the economy begins slowing soon on its own. "We are ... into the danger zone," he says.

Nonsense, retorts Dana Mead, chairman of Tenneco Inc. in Houston. Economists who talk that way, he maintains, just don't understand how American companies have tied wage increases to productivity gains, shifted work overseas and learned to produce more with fewer people. ...

As the economy continues heating up, so too does the battle between the ivied halls and the factory floor. On one side, the weapon is economic theory. On the other, day-to-day experience. Much hangs in the balance: If theory bears out, the Federal Reserve Board courts inflation if it keeps interest rates too low; if many businesses' observations are correct, the Fed risks choking off the economic expansion by raising rates too high. ...

To understand the roots of the debate, it helps to look at an arcane economic concept developed back in the late 1960s by Edmund Phelps, now a professor of economics at Columbia University, and by Milton Friedman, the Nobel Prize-winning economist. It is called ... the "natural" rate of unemployment. ... [I]f unemployment falls below the natural rate, inflation won't stop rising until the jobless rate retreats. "If the labor market stays overtight, each year there will be another point added to the inflation rate," says Prof. Phelps. "It will go on rising, up and up and up higher and higher."...

Many economists ... say that the natural rate has changed in the past, going from about 5.4% in the 1960s, to just above 7% in the 1970s, and declining to about 6.4% in the 1980s....

Prof. Phelps says he has lowered his own estimate of the natural rate...to 6% from 6.5%....

Essence of THE STORY

■ Martin Feldstein believes that by January 1995, unemployment had fallen into the danger zone that would trigger rising inflation.

■ Dana Mead believes that the 1994 expansion could continue without increasing inflation because companies have increased productivity, tied wages to productivity, and are willing to expand overseas to avoid rising labor costs.

■ In Feldstein's view, the Fed risks inflation if it keeps interest rates too low. In Mead's view, the Fed risks choking off the expansion by raising rates too high.

■ The debate turns on the concept of the natural rate of unemployment. If unemployment falls below the natural rate, the inflation rate increases.

■ Economists believe that the natural rate increased from about 5.4 percent in the 1960s to above 7 percent in the 1970s and then declined to about 6.4 percent in the 1980s.

Economic

A N A L Y S I S

■ The Fed faces a constant stabilization policy dilemma: whether to tighten or loosen its grip on money growth by raising or lowering short-term interest rates.

■ In early 1995 there was no doubt that the economy had been expanding rapidly and the unemployment rate had fallen sharply through the previous year.

■ There was also no doubt that the Fed had already tightened its grip on money growth by raising short-term interest rates on 10 occasions through 1994.

■ But had the Fed done enough to slow the growth of aggregate demand and prevent inflation from returning? Or had it done too much and created the danger of choking off the expansion?

■ The theory of inflation predicts that the inflation rate rises if aggregate demand grows more quickly than long-run aggregate supply and takes real GDP above potential GDP. Equivalently, the inflation rate rises if the unemployment rate falls below the natural rate.

■ The three figures show how the change in the inflation rate and the unemployment rate have been related since 1960.

■ In the 1960s the natural rate of unemployment was about 5.4 percent (Fig. 1). In the 1970s it was about 7.5 percent (Fig. 2), and in the late 1980s and 1990s it fell to about 6 percent (Fig. 3).

■ When the unemployment rate goes into the "danger zone" below the natural rate, the inflation rate usually increases (there was only one exception, in 1967). When the unemployment rate exceeds the natural rate, the inflation rate usually falls.

■ By studying the shifting relationship between the change in the inflation rate and the unemployment rate, the Fed tries to estimate the natural rate and decide whether to tighten or loosen its monetary policy.

■ There is no evidence in the data shown in the figures to believe that the optimistic business view about the possibility of continued inflation-free expansion was possible in 1995. The Feldstein view looked solid.

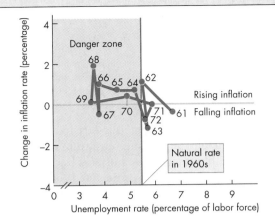

Figure 1 The 1960s

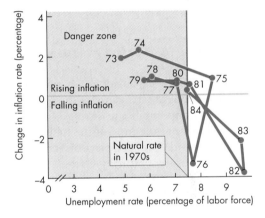

Figure 2 The 1970s and early 1980s

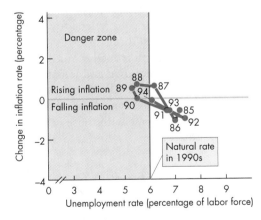

Figure 3 The late 1980s and early 1990s

■ But Friedman's belief that no one knows the natural rate is correct. The natural rate keeps changing, and although we can see what it has been, we cannot know its current and future level.

■ The fact that the natural rate cannot be known with certainty is one of the reasons that Friedman urges a fixed-rule policy that does not try to revive a flagging economy or hold back a buoyant one.

S U M M A R Y

Policy Goals

The goals of macroeconomic policy are to achieve the highest sustainable rate of long-term real GDP growth, smooth out avoidable business fluctuations, maintain low unemployment, and avoid inflation.

These four goals boil down to two: real GDP growth and inflation. Keeping real GDP growing steadily at its maximum sustainable rate is equivalent to avoiding business fluctuations and keeping unemployment at the natural rate. (pp. 858–859.)

Policy Tools and Performance

Fiscal policy was mildly expansionary during the Kennedy years, strongly expansionary during the Vietnam War buildup, moderate during Nixon's presidency, expansionary at the time of the first OPEC oil shock during Ford's presidency, contractionary at first but then expansionary during Carter's presidency, expansionary during the Reagan years, moderate during the Bush presidency, and contractionary during the Clinton presidency.

The M2 growth rate increased during the 1970s, peaked in 1976, and then began to fall. In 1994, M2 grew by less than 1 percent. The federal funds rate trended upward from 1960 through 1981 and then trended downward. The real federal funds rate fell through 1975 and then increased and remained high through most of the 1980s. It fell during the early 1990s but then began to rise again through 1994. The cycles in M2 growth coincide with those in the federal funds rate. (pp. 860–862)

Long-Term Growth Policy

The sources of the long-term growth of potential GDP are the accumulation of physical and human capital and the advance of technology. Policies to increase the long-term growth rate focus on increasing saving and investment in human capital and new technologies.

To increase the saving rate, government saving, which has been negative since 1975, must be increased or incentives for private saving must be strengthened by increasing the after-tax rate of return.

Human capital investment might be increased with improved education (the Goals 2000: Educate America Act of 1994 is an attempt to do this) and by improving on-the-job training programs.

Investment in new technologies can be encouraged by tax incentives such as those in the federal government's Research and Experiment Tax Credit (R&E credit). (pp. 862–864)

Business Cycle and Unemployment Policy

In the face of an aggregate demand shock, a fixed-rule policy takes no action to counter the shock. As a result, there are fluctuations in real GDP and the price level. A feedback-rule policy adjusts tax rates, government purchases, or the money supply to offset the effects of other influences on aggregate demand. An ideal feedback rule keeps the economy at full employment, with stable prices.

Some economists argue that feedback rules make the economy less stable because they require greater knowledge of the state of the economy than we have, operate with time lags that extend beyond the forecast horizon, and introduce unpredictability about policy reactions.

In the face of a productivity growth slowdown, a fixed rule results in smaller output (and more unemployment) and a higher price level. A feedback rule that increases the money supply or cuts tax rates to stimulate aggregate demand results in an even higher price level and higher inflation. Output (and unemployment) follows the same course as with a fixed rule.

By using feedback policies to target nominal GDP growth, it might be possible to avoid the extremes of inflation and recession. (pp. 865–871)

Inflation Policy

A fixed rule minimizes the threat of cost-push inflation. A feedback rule validates cost-push inflation and leaves the price level and inflation rate free to move to wherever they are pushed.

Inflation can be tamed, at little or no cost in terms of lost output or excessive unemployment, by slowing the growth of aggregate demand in a credible and predictable way. But usually, when inflation is slowed down, a recession occurs. (pp. 872–875)

KEY ELEMENTS

Key Figures

Key Terms

REVIEW QUESTIONS

1. What are the goals of macroeconomic policy?
2. Describe the main features of fiscal policy since 1960.
3. Describe the main features of monetary policy since 1960.
4. Explain the main ways in which policy can try to speed up potential GDP growth.
5. Explain the distinction between a fixed-rule policy and a feedback-rule policy.
6. Analyze the effects of a temporary decrease in aggregate demand if the Fed adopts a fixed-rule policy.
7. Analyze the behavior of real GDP and the price level in the face of a permanent decrease in aggregate demand when the Fed adopts

   a. A fixed-rule monetary policy
   b. A feedback-rule policy.

8. Explain the main problems in using fiscal policy for stabilizing the economy.
9. Why do economists disagree with each other on the appropriateness of fixed-rule and feedback-rule policies?
10. Analyze the effects of a rise in the price of oil on real GDP and the price level if the Fed employs
    a. A fixed-rule policy.
    b. A feedback-rule policy.
11. Explain nominal GDP targeting and why it reduces real GDP fluctuations and inflation.
12. Explain why the Fed's credibility affects the cost of lowering inflation.

PROBLEMS

1. A productivity growth slowdown has occurred. Explain its possible origins and describe a policy package that is designed to speed up growth again.

2. The economy is experiencing 10 percent inflation and 7 percent unemployment. Set out policies for the Fed and Congress to pursue that will lower both inflation and unemployment. Explain how and why your proposed policies will work.

3. The economy shown in the figure is initially on aggregate demand curve AD_0 and short-run aggregate supply curve SAS_0. Then aggregate demand decreases and the aggregate demand curve shifts leftward to AD_1.

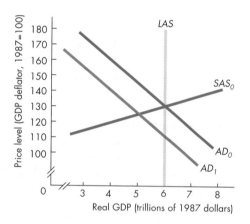

a. What is the initial equilibrium real GDP and price level?
b. If the decrease in aggregate demand is temporary and the government follows a fixed-rule fiscal policy, what happens to real GDP and the price level? Trace the immediate effects and the adjustment as aggregate demand returns to its original level.
c. If the decrease in aggregate demand is temporary and the government follows a feedback-rule fiscal policy, what happens to real GDP and the price level? Trace the imme-

diate effects and the adjustment as aggregate demand returns to its original level.
d. If the decrease in aggregate demand is permanent and the government follows a fixed-rule fiscal policy, what happens to real GDP and the price level?

4. The economy is booming, and inflation is beginning to rise, but it is widely agreed that a massive recession is just around the corner. Weigh the advantages and disadvantages of the Congress pursuing a fixed-rule policy and a feedback-rule policy.

5. The economy is in a recession, and inflation is falling. It is widely agreed that a strong recovery is just around the corner. Weigh the advantages and disadvantages of the Fed pursuing a fixed-rule and a feedback-rule policy.

6. The President has hired you to draw up an economic plan that will maximize the chance of the President being re-elected.
a. What are the macroeconomic stabilization policy elements in that plan?
b. What do you have to make the economy do in an election year?
c. What policy actions would help the President achieve re-election?
(In dealing with this problem, be careful to take into account the effects of your proposed policy on expectations and the effects of those expectations on actual economic performance.)

7. Study *Reading Between the Lines* on pp. 876–877 and then answer the following questions:
a. What do Martin Feldstein and Dana Mead disagree about and why does it matter?
b. Use the theory of the Phillips curve to explain why Martin Feldstein believes the U.S. economy entered the "danger zone" in 1995?
c. What are the policy options for the Fed and the federal government in a situation like that described in this news article?

TALKING WITH Jacob A. Frenkel

Jacob A. Frenkel, who is Governor of the Bank of Israel, was born in Tel Aviv, in 1943. He was an undergraduate at the Hebrew University at Jerusalem and a graduate student at the University of Chicago, where he earned his Ph.D. in 1970 and then taught for 17 years, becoming the David Rockefeller Professor of International Economics. He left Chicago to become the Economic Counselor and Director of Research at the International Monetary Fund from 1987–1991.

Dr. Frenkel is an influential international economist who has made many contributions to improving our understanding of the forces that influence exchange rates, interest rates, and the balance of international payments. Michael Parkin talked with Jacob Frenkel about his work and about the challenges facing the world economy in the 1990s.

Dr. Frenkel, what drew you into economics?
The choice was rather accidental. When I started my undergraduate studies, I was working polishing diamonds and attended evening classes. I had only four courses to choose from: economics, political science, statistics, and sociology. I chose to study economics and political science and quickly became intrigued by economics, particularly by macroeconomics. As a graduate student at the University of Chicago I was fortunate to have courses in monetary economics and international economics from the giants of the time, including Milton Friedman, Lloyd Metzler, Harry Johnson, and Bob Mundell.

The International Monetary Fund (IMF), where you made an outstanding contribution to research on international economic questions, was established to help manage a world of fixed exchange rates. What was your role in the IMF?
My own entry into the IMF was in the context of participating in the G7 discussions on the interdependent world economy. My initial task was to provide a global perspective on the debate and design of economic policies. During this period, the research department developed a variety of analytical and empirical perspectives on these issues including economic indicators, the role of

the international reserves, and the evolving world.

We recognized that we were gravitating at that time toward a world in which there was no single reserve currency, greater unification within Europe, and with the emergence of a new economic center in the Pacific. In this period, the exchange system was evolving. Small developing countries with no well-developed capital markets—and later transitional economies—had to make choices of the appropriate exchange rate regimes.

What is the IMF's role in today's world of floating exchange rates?
Today, the IMF has three major roles. The first is its traditional role: It assists developing countries to design stabilization policies, accompanied by structural measures, that enhance the flexibility of the economy. The IMF monitors their economic development and acts as a catalyst for financial assistance.

The second is to provide advice to countries even when they do not borrow from the IMF. This function will increase in importance because in the longer run, private capital markets will provide financial assistance.

The third ties these things together: The IMF interacts with countries within a multilateral setting where the global perspective is taken.

What does the Governor of the Bank of Israel do?
The Governor of the Bank of Israel wears two hats. First, he is in charge of monetary policy and the traditional tasks of the central bank including bank supervision. The central bank in Israel is highly independent. Monetary policy decisions that concern interest rates are made exclusively by the Bank of Israel without any

involvement of the government. The Bank of Israel is also responsible for the day-to-day operation of the exchange market.

Second, the governor is the chief economic advisor to the government, which is unique to Israel. In this capacity, he participates in

cabinet meetings that involve economic matters and is involved in the broad range of economic issues that go beyond the narrow scope of monetary policy.

How does your involvement in the broader political arena influence the independence of the Bank?
It requires a very delicate balance between the economic advisor role that calls for proximity to government and the independence necessary for the conduct of monetary policy that calls for distance. I think that each governor finds his own balance. As far as I'm concerned, I have no doubt that monetary policy in Israel is conducted with complete independence and with a focus that is entirely set on proper professional economic consideration.

Israel has had extraordinary economic growth in the past year. To what do you attribute this economic success story?
In 1994, real GDP growth was 6 $\frac{1}{2}$ percent. This was healthy growth, with the business sector growing at 7 $\frac{1}{2}$ percent. Each year

since 1990, growth has ranged around 6 percent.

A major impetus to economic performance during the first part of this decade has been the influx of immigrants primarily from the former Soviet Union. They have proven to be a major engine of

[Governments] do not have the discipline of profit and loss and the guidance and discipline of shareholders.

growth. As in all countries, absorbing new immigrants into society and into the workforce is not an easy task. However, I think that we have been successful.

Our strategy relies heavily on the private sector to absorb immigrants. Since the beginning of the decade our population has increased by about one fifth, yet our unemployment rate is now significantly lower than what it was before the start of the mass immigration. This means that our economy is capable of generating more new jobs than new entrants to the labor market. A large percentage of immigrants have gained employment.

I think that our rapid growth is the result of consistent economic policy, coupled with good immigration policies. Every year our exports have increased at a double-digit rate, which is much faster than the growth of GDP. This has happened despite our markets abroad being in recession at the beginning of the decade. In the last two years, we've penetrated into completely new markets, especially in Asia, China, and India.

Can you say more about the content of your economic policy?

First, budget deficit reduction. We have a budget-deficit reduction law, which requires continuous reduction in the budget deficit: Each year the budget deficit must be a smaller percentage of GDP than it was in the preceding year. We are now in the fourth year, and we are on track. I project the budget deficit in 1994 will be about 2 percent of GDP. At the beginning of the decade, it was more than 6 percent.

Second, trade liberalization. We have a free trade agreement with the United States and also a special agreement with the European Union. Vis-à-vis third-world countries, four years ago, we adopted a unilateral multi-year tariff-reduction scheme. Each year we cut our tariffs unilaterally. As we have opened up our economy to international competition, competition at home has increased significantly. The government has committed itself to a trajectory of multi-year tariff reductions. So far, so good.

Third, inflation target. Since the beginning of 1992, we have adopted an inflation target and it has served us very well. Also since 1992, we have adopted an exchange rate regime, which we call a "crawling band." We set the slope of the band to be consistent with our inflation target. At the beginning of the year, we set an inflation target. Then we subtract from it the average inflation rate in our trading partners, and this is the slope of the "crawling band." That is, we set the trajectory for the nominal magnitude of the economy. We are forward looking. We do not change the slope of our "crawling band" according to past inflation but rather according to targeted inflation. All the nominal magnitudes of the economy converge to be consistent with that target.

To summarize, our economic policy is cast in the medium term: multi-year budget deficit reduction, multi-year trade liberalization, and a forward-looking exchange rate regime that is consistent with our long-term inflation target.

But your inflation rate is still high.

While inflation is high—and higher than our trading partners—we are now on a downward trend. Interest rate policies and monetary policy had to be very austere during 1994. This austerity meant that monetary policy could not be popular, which provided a real test for the independence of the Bank of Israel.

Could you tell me about your inflation?

Up to 1985, we've had hyperinflation. In 1985, there was a massive stabilization program and inflation got stuck. Inflation averaged 18 percent a year from 1986 to 1991, then fell in 1992–1993 to around 10 to 12 percent. In 1994, it climbed to about 14 percent. I think in 1995 inflation will be in the 8 to 11 percent range.

One of the things that we have learned is that if a sector of the economy is rigid and out of line with the rest of the economy, a microeconomic issue can be transformed into a macroeconomic difficulty. In our case, it has been housing. The flow of immigrants into Israel has increased the demand for housing. Indeed, housing prices increased between two and three times as much as the price level. So the relative price of housing increased very significantly, and this increase has been a major component of the inflationary pressure.

Why do you think central banks have such a hard time controlling inflation?

I would attribute it to at least three things. First, our economy has lived in an inflationary environment for many, many years. A lot of effort was put into the creation of institutions, like indexation, that helped us to live with inflation. But these institutions may have reduced the incentive to fight inflation with the illusion that you protect yourself with indexation. I think that experience suggests that this is indeed illusory and there is no mechanism whatsoever that can be full protection against inflation. Rather than learning to live with inflation, one should fight it.

If you are disinflating and you are doing so within a setting that has not yet dismantled many of the things that are allegedly protecting you from inflation, you create an inertia and you create some rigidities that prove to be difficult on the down side.

Second, in most societies, there are still quite a few people that were born with a Phillips Curve in their heads; that is, with the notion that there is a permanent tradeoff between inflation and unemployment. It takes bitter experience to remove that obstacle and get into the mindset that all of these alleged tradeoffs and the gains from them are really illusory in the medium term. But when it comes to solidifying the anti-inflation culture, you really need to overcome the notion of a trade-off that is still in the heads of quite a few.

Third, our science has not yet found an easy way to reduce inflation in a steady way without having a period in which real interest rates are relatively high for a relatively long time. I think that societies and policy makers must understand that this is a necessary price to pay, which is worthwhile paying sooner rather than later. Typically, most countries must go through such a period.

As far as Israel is concerned, I am pleased to say that the Israeli society and policy makers have gone through all three. Real interest rates are high and people understand why they are high. Policy makers recognize that it is a necessary price to pay. That's why I'm optimistic that we are going to see a significant decline in the inflation rate.

If we think of the world economy as an economic laboratory in which experiments are being conducted, what, for you, are the clearest lessons for economic policy that come from the experiments currently being undertaken?
Lesson No. 1: To control inflation, a country must have an independent central bank. If you divide countries into those with low inflation and high inflation, or rising and falling inflation, I think that you can see the degree of the independence of the central banks. The degree of independence reflects the reality of the political system, which typically has a shorter time horizon than the economic system requires. Therefore, society must protect itelf from that reality by having an independent central bank.

Lesson No. 2: A country can't have sustainable growth without engaging in the world trading system. The interaction of trade policies, structural policies that ensure flexibility and nondistortion, and economic stability is becoming more important and apparent. If you look at the real cost of reform in Eastern Europe and transformation in Central Europe, you realize that a very large fraction of that cost comes from the collapse of their trading systems. Put the other way around, I think it is suggestive of the cure. For me, the GATT agreement is much more than just the dismantling of tariffs;

rather it's an extraordinary victory of philosophy that in the new world, no country can afford to be a small island at the side of the larger economic world. A small country's only chance is to become an integral part of that world, and

the only way to survive as an integral part of that world is to have a competitive, efficient economic system.

Lesson No. 3: The private sector stands no chance in competing against government. Governments are guided by different considerations. They do not have the discipline of profit and loss and the guidance and discipline of shareholders. Therefore, in the long term large governments lose and in the short term the private sector loses. It is in the best interest of the economy to get the size of the public sector as small as you can.

Lesson No. 4: The future is much closer to the present than many politicians think. Which

means that if a country is running large budget deficits that are not sustainable, the marketplace will not be patient. The market extrapolates the consequences into the future and translates them immediately into the present.

… in the new world, no country can afford to be a small island at the side of the larger economic world…. [it must] have a competitive, efficient economic system.

Suppose a student wants to pursue a career in economics with an international policy orientation. What is the best combination of undergraduate courses to pursue?
Courses that build analytical skills are useful. In addition to economics, take a range of courses including philosophy, math, history, and political science. Seek out professors and peers who will challenge and inspire you to excel. It's also important to remain attentive to the economic and political changes in the world by reading, traveling, and exposing yourself to diverse cultures. Know who the policy makers are and what impact their decisions have on the world.

Trading with the World

After studying
this chapter,
you will be
able to:

- Describe the trends and patterns in international trade

- Explain comparative advantage and explain why all countries can gain from international trade

- Explain how economies of scale and diversity of taste lead to gains from trade

- Explain why trade restrictions reduce the volume of imports and exports and reduce our consumption possibilities

- Explain the arguments used to justify trade restrictions and show how they are flawed

- Explain why we have trade restrictions

Silk Routes and Sucking Sounds

Since ancient times, people have expanded their trading as far as technology allowed. Marco Polo opened up the silk route between Europe and China in the thirteenth century. Today, container ships laden with cars and machines and Boeing 747s stuffed with farm-fresh foods ply sea and air routes, carrying billions of dollars worth of goods. Why do people go to such great lengths to trade with those in other nations? ◆ Low-wage Mexico has entered into a free trade agreement with high-wage Canada and the United States—the North American Free Trade Agreement, or NAFTA. According to Texas billionaire Ross Perot, this agreement will cause a "giant sucking sound" as jobs are transferred from Michigan to Mexico. Is Ross Perot right? How can we compete with a country that pays its workers a fraction of U.S. wages? Are there any industries, besides perhaps the Hollywood movie industry, in which we have an advantage? ◆ In 1930, Congress passed the Smoot-Hawley Act, which imposed a 45 percent tariff (rising to 60 percent by 1933) on one third of U.S. imports. This move provoked widespread retaliation and a tariff war among the world's major trading countries. After World War II, a process of trade liberalization brought about a gradual reduction of tariffs. What are the effects of tariffs on international trade? Why don't we have completely unrestricted international trade?

◈ In this chapter, we're going to learn about international trade. We'll discover how *all* nations can gain by specializing in producing the goods and services in which they have a comparative advantage and trading with other countries. We'll discover that all countries can compete, no matter how high their wages. We'll also explain why, despite the fact that international trade brings benefits to all, countries restrict trade.

Patterns and Trends in International Trade

THE GOODS AND SERVICES THAT WE BUY FROM people in other countries are called **imports**. The goods and services that we sell to people in other countries are called **exports**. What are the most important things that we import and export? Most people would probably guess that a rich nation such as the United States imports raw materials and exports manufactured goods. Although that is one feature of U.S. international trade, it is not its most important feature. The vast bulk of our exports *and* imports is manufactured goods. We sell foreigners earth-moving equipment, airplanes, supercomputers, and scientific equipment, and we buy televisions, VCRs, blue jeans, and T-shirts from them. Also, we are a major exporter of agricultural products and raw materials. We also import and export a huge volume of services. Let's look at the international trade of the United States in a recent year.

U.S. International Trade

Table 35.1 classifies U.S. international trade in four major categories: agricultural products, industrial supplies and materials, manufactured goods, and services. The second column gives the value of U.S. exports, and the third column gives the value of U.S. imports. The fourth column tells us the balance of trade in the various categories. The **balance of trade** is the value of exports minus the value of imports. If the balance is positive, then the value of exports exceeds the value of imports and the United States is a **net exporter**. But if the balance is negative, the value of imports exceeds the value of exports and the United States is a **net importer**.

Trade in Goods About 80 percent of U.S. international trade is trade in goods, and 20 percent is trade in services. Of the categories of goods traded, by far the most important is manufactured goods. The total value of exports of manufactured goods is less than that of imports—the United States is a net importer of manufactured goods. The United States is also a net importer of industrial supplies. It is a net exporter of agricultural products and services.

Figure 35.1 highlights some of the major items of U.S. imports and exports of goods. The largest

TABLE 35.1
U.S. Exports and Imports in 1994

Category	Exports	Imports	Balance of trade
	(billions of dollars)		
Agricultural products	47	31	16
Industrial supplies and materials (excluding agricultural)	121	165	−44
Manufactured goods	335	473	−138
Services	195	135	60
Total	698	804	−106

Source: *Survey of Current Business* (March 1995), vol. 75.

items of both imports and exports are capital goods (other than automotive vehicles and parts which are shown in a separate category). Our imports of consumer goods and automotive vehicles and parts (shown by the red bars) are twice the value of exports of those items (shown by the blue bars).

Trade in Services One fifth of U.S. international trade is not of goods but of services. You may be wondering how a country can "export" and "import" services. Let's look at some examples.

Suppose that you decided to vacation in France, traveling there on an Air France flight from New York. What you buy from Air France is not a good, but a transportation service. Although the concept may seem odd at first, in economic terms you are importing that service from France. The money you spend in France on hotel bills and restaurant meals is also classified as the import of services. Similarly, the vacation taken by a French student in the United States counts as an export of services to France.

When we import TV sets from South Korea, the owner of the ship that carries those TV sets might be Greek and the company that insures the cargo might be British. The payments that we make for the transportation and insurance to the Greek and British companies are also payments for the import of ser-

FIGURE 35.1
U.S. Exports and Imports: 1994

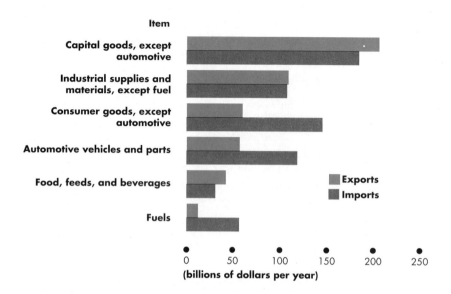

We export large quantities of capital goods such as machinery, aircraft and other transportation equipment. We also export large quantities of industrial supplies and this trade is balanced. We export consumer goods and automotive vehicles and parts, but we import even larger quantities of some of these items. We also import large quantities of fuel.

Source: *Survey of Current Business* (March 1995), vol. 75.

vices. Similarly, when an American shipping company transports California wine to Tokyo, the transportation cost is an export of a service to Japan.

The importance of the various components of trade in services is set out in Table 35.2. As you can see, travel and transportation are the largest items, accounting for more than 50 percent of exports and 60 percent of imports. We also do a large amount of international trade in intellectual property (royalties and license fees).

Geographical Patterns

The United States has trading links with almost every part of the world. Figure 35.2 shows the scale of these links and the way they have changed since 1960. In 1960 (part a), our trade was primarily with Europe, Canada, and Latin American countries. Japan and Asia were small trading partners. In 1994 (part b), our trade with Asia dominated that with our traditional trading partners. Our *imports* from Japan and Asian countries such as China, Hong Kong, Singapore, South Korea, and Taiwan were 45 percent of total imports. Also, our international trade deficit was almost exclusively with the Asian countries.

TABLE 35.2
U.S. Trade in Services in 1994

	Exports	Imports	Balance of trade
		(billions of dollars)	
Travel and transportation	102	81	21
Royalties and license fees	23	6	17
Education	8	1	7
Financial services and insurance	8	10	−2
Telecommunications	3	7	−4
Military services	11	11	0
Other services	40	19	21
Total	195	135	60

Source: *Survey of Current Business* (March 1995), vol. 75.

Trends in Trade

International trade has become an increasingly important part of our economic life. In 1960, we exported less than 5 percent of total output and imported only 4 1/2 percent of the goods and services that we consumed ourselves. Over the years since then, these percentages have steadily increased, and today they are more than double their levels of 1960.

On the export side, all the major commodity categories have shared in the increased volume of international trade. Machinery, food, and raw materials have remained the largest components of exports and have roughly maintained their share in total exports.

But there have been dramatic changes in the composition of imports. Food and raw material imports have declined steadily. Imports of fuel increased dramatically in the 1970s but declined in the 1980s. Imports of machinery of all kinds, after being a fairly stable percentage of total imports until the middle 1980s, now approach 50 percent of total imports.

Figure 35.3 shows the United States' overall *balance of trade* (of goods and services) since 1960. As you can see, there was a surplus (a positive balance) during the early 1960s. The balance then fluctuated around zero until the mid-1970s. But in the years since the mid-1970s, the balance of U.S. international trade has been on a downward trend, and throughout the 1980s and 1990s, the excess of imports over exports (negative balance of trade) has been large.

Balance of Trade and International Borrowing

When people buy more than they sell, they have to finance the difference by borrowing or by selling their assets. When they sell more than they buy, they can use the surplus to make loans to others and to buy assets. This simple principle that governs the income and expenditure and borrowing and lending of individuals and firms is also a feature of our balance of trade. If we import more than we export, we have to finance the difference by borrowing from foreigners or by selling our assets to them. When we export more than we import, we make loans to foreigners or buy their assets to enable them to buy goods in excess of the value of the goods they have sold to us.

This chapter does *not* cover the factors that determine the balance of trade and the scale of

---

FIGURE 35.2

The Geographical Pattern of U.S. International Trade

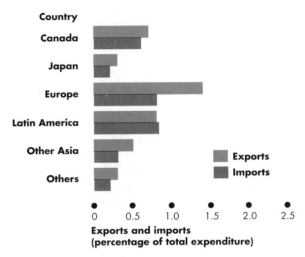

(a) 1960

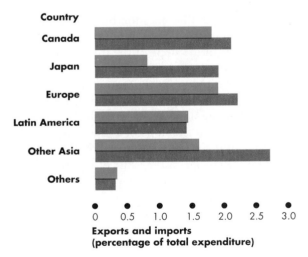

(b) 1994

In 1960, the United States' largest trading partners were Europe, Canada, and the countries of Latin America. By 1994, trade with Japan and other Asian countries had expanded to overtake that with our traditional trading partners. Also, the percentage of expenditure accounted for by international trade had expanded.

Source: Survey of Current Business, (March 1995), vol. 75.

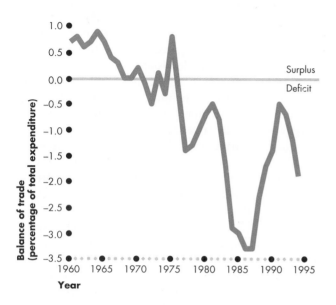

FIGURE 35.3

The U.S. Balance of Trade

The balance of trade was positive (a surplus) in most years between 1960 and 1975. Since 1976, the balance has been negative (a deficit).

Source: Economic Report of the President, 1995.

international borrowing, lending, and asset transactions that finance that balance. It is concerned with understanding the volume, pattern, and directions of international trade rather than its balance. So that we can keep our focus on these topics, we'll build a model in which there is no international borrowing and lending—just international trade in goods and services. Because there is no international borrowing or lending, the trade balance must be zero. We'll find that we are able to understand what determines the volume, pattern, and direction of international trade and also establish its benefits and the costs of trade restrictions within this framework. This model can be expanded to include international borrowing and lending, but this extension does not change the conclusions that we'll reach here about the factors that determine the volume, pattern, directions, and benefits of international trade.

Let's now begin to study those factors.

Opportunity Cost and Comparative Advantage

LET'S APPLY THE LESSONS THAT WE LEARNED IN Chapter 3 about the gains from trade between Mark and Marjorie to the trade between nations. We'll begin by recalling how we can use the production possibility frontier to measure opportunity cost.

Opportunity Cost in Farmland

Farmland (a fictitious country) can produce grain and cars at any point inside or along its production possibility frontier (PPF) shown in Fig. 35.4. (We're holding constant the output of all the other goods that Farmland produces.) The Farmers (the people of Farmland) are consuming all the grain and cars that they produce, and they are operating at point *a* in the figure. That is, Farmland is producing and consuming 15 billion bushels of grain and 8 million cars each year. What is the opportunity cost of a car in Farmland?

We can answer that question by calculating the slope of the production possibility frontier at point *a*. The magnitude of the slope of the frontier measures the opportunity cost of one good in terms of the other. To measure the slope of the frontier at point *a*, place a straight line tangential to the frontier at point *a* and calculate the slope of that straight line. Recall that the formula for the slope of a line is the change in the value of the variable measured on the *y*-axis divided by the change in the value of the variable measured on the *x*-axis as we move along the line. Here, the variable measured on the *y*-axis is billions of bushels of grain, and the variable measured on the *x*-axis is millions of cars. So the slope is the change in the number of bushels of grain divided by the change in the number of cars.

As you can see from the red triangle at point *a* in the figure, if the number of cars produced increases by 2 million, grain production decreases by 18 billion bushels. Therefore the magnitude of the slope is 18 billion divided by 2 million, which equals 9,000. To get one more car, the people of Farmland must give up 9,000 bushels of grain. Thus the opportunity cost of 1 car is 9,000 bushels of grain. Equivalently, 9,000 bushels of grain cost 1 car. For the people of Farmland, these opportunity costs are the prices they

FIGURE 35.4

Opportunity Cost in Farmland

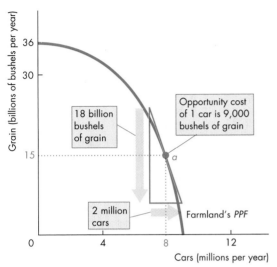

Farmland produces and consumes 15 billion bushels of grain and 8 million cars a year. That is, it produces and consumes at point *a* on its production possibility frontier. Opportunity cost is equal to the magnitude of the slope of the production possibility frontier. The red triangle tells us that at point *a*, 18 billion bushels of grain must be forgone to get 2 million cars. That is, at point *a*, 2 million cars cost 18 billion bushels of grain. Equivalently, 1 car costs 9,000 bushels of grain or 9,000 bushels cost 1 car.

---

face. The price of a car is 9,000 bushels of grain, and the price of 9,000 bushels of grain is 1 car.

Opportunity Cost in Mobilia

Figure 35.5 shows Mobilia's production possibility frontier. Like the Farmers, the Movers (the people in Mobilia) consume all the grain and cars that they produce. Mobilia consumes 18 billion bushels of grain a year and 4 million cars, at point *a'*.

Let's calculate the opportunity costs in Mobilia. At point *a'*, the opportunity cost of a car is equal to the magnitude of the slope of the red line tangential to the production possibility frontier *(PPF)*. You can see from the red triangle that the magnitude of the

FIGURE 35.5

Opportunity Cost in Mobilia

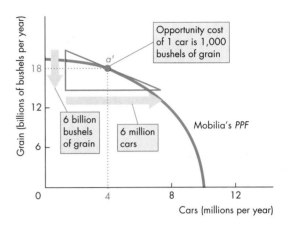

Mobilia produces and consumes 18 billion bushels of grain and 4 million cars a year. That is, it produces and consumes at point *a'* on its production possibility frontier. Opportunity cost is equal to the magnitude of the slope of the production possibility frontier. The red triangle tells us that at point *a'*, 6 billion bushels of grain must be forgone to get 6 million cars. That is, at point *a'*, 6 million cars cost 6 billion bushels of grain. Equivalently, 1 car costs 1,000 bushels of grain or 1,000 bushels cost 1 car.

---

slope of Mobilia's production possibility frontier is 6 billion bushels of grain divided by 6 million cars, which equals 1,000 bushels of grain per car. To get one more car, the people of Mobilia must give up 1,000 bushels of grain. Thus the opportunity cost of 1 car is 1,000 bushels of grain, or, equivalently, the opportunity cost of 1,000 bushels of grain is 1 car. These are the prices faced in Mobilia.

Comparative Advantage

Cars are cheaper in Mobilia than in Farmland. One car costs 9,000 bushels of grain in Farmland but only 1,000 bushels of grain in Mobilia. But grain is cheaper in Farmland than in Mobilia—9,000 bushels of grain costs only 1 car in Farmland, while that same amount of grain costs 9 cars in Mobilia.

Mobilia has a comparative advantage in car production. Farmland has a comparative advantage in grain production. A country has a **comparative advantage** in producing a good if it can produce that good at a lower opportunity cost than any other country.

Let's see how opportunity cost differences and comparative advantage generate gains from international trade.

Gains from Trade

IF MOBILIA BOUGHT GRAIN FOR WHAT IT COSTS Farmland to produce it, then Mobilia could buy 9,000 bushels of grain for 1 car. That is much lower than the cost of growing grain in Mobilia, for there it costs 9 cars to produce 9,000 bushels of grain. If the Movers can buy grain at the low Farmland price, they will reap some gains.

If the Farmers can buy cars for what it costs Mobilia to produce them, they will be able to obtain a car for 1,000 bushels of grain. Because it costs 9,000 bushels of grain to produce a car in Farmland, the Farmers would gain from such an opportunity.

In this situation, it makes sense for Movers to buy their grain from Farmers and for Farmers to buy their cars from Movers. Let's see how such profitable international trade comes about.

Reaping the Gains from Trade

We've seen that the Farmers would like to buy their cars from the Movers and that the Movers would like to buy their grain from the Farmers. Let's see how the two groups do business with each other, concentrating attention on the international market for cars.

Figure 35.6 illustrates such a market. The quantity of cars *traded internationally* is measured on the *x*-axis. On the *y*-axis, we measure the price of a car. This price is expressed as the number of bushels of grain that a car costs—the opportunity cost of a car. If no international trade takes place, the price of a car in Farmland is 9,000 bushels of grain, indicated by point *a* in the figure. Again, if no trade takes place, the price of a car in Mobilia is 1,000 bushels of grain, indicated by point *a'* in the figure. The no-trade points *a* and *a'* in Fig. 35.6 correspond to the points

FIGURE 35.6

International Trade in Cars

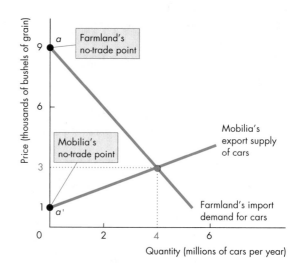

As the price of a car decreases, the quantity of imports demanded by Farmland increases—Farmland's import demand curve for cars is downward-sloping. As the price of a car increases, the quantity of cars supplied by Mobilia for export increases—Mobilia's export supply curve of cars is upward-sloping. Without international trade, the price of a car is 9,000 bushels of grain in Farmland (point *a*) and 1,000 bushels of grain in Mobilia (point *a'*).

With free international trade, the price of a car is determined where the export supply curve intersects the import demand curve—a price of 3,000 bushels of grain. At that price, 4 million cars a year are imported by Farmland and exported by Mobilia. The value of grain exported by Farmland and imported by Mobilia is 12 billion bushels a year, the quantity required to pay for the cars imported.

identified by those same letters in Figs. 35.4 and 35.5. The lower the price of a car (in terms of grain), the greater is the quantity of cars that the Farmers are willing to import from the Movers. This fact is illustrated by the downward-sloping curve, which shows Farmland's import demand for cars.

The Movers respond in the opposite direction. The higher the price of cars (in terms of bushels of grain), the greater is the quantity of cars that Movers are willing to export to Farmers. This fact is reflected in Mobilia's export supply of cars—the upward-sloping line in Fig. 35.6.

The international market in cars determines the equilibrium price and quantity traded. This equilibrium occurs where the import demand curve intersects the export supply curve. In this case, the equilibrium price of a car is 3,000 bushels of grain. Four million cars a year are exported by Mobilia and imported by Farmland. Notice that the price at which cars are traded is lower than the initial price in Farmland but higher than the initial price in Mobilia.

Balanced Trade

The number of cars exported by Mobilia—4 million a year—is exactly equal to the number of cars imported by Farmland. How does Farmland pay for its cars? By exporting grain. How much grain does Farmland export? You can find the answer by noticing that for 1 car, Farmland has to pay 3,000 bushels of grain. Hence, for 4 million cars, they have to pay 12 billion bushels of grain. Thus Farmland's exports of grain are 12 billion bushels a year. Mobilia imports this same quantity of grain.

Mobilia is exchanging 4 million cars for 12 billion bushels of grain each year, and Farmland is doing the opposite, exchanging 12 billion bushels of grain for 4 million cars. Trade is balanced between these two countries. The value received from exports equals the value paid out for imports.

Changes in Production and Consumption

We've seen that international trade makes it possible for Farmers to buy cars at a lower price than that at which they can produce them for themselves. Equivalently, Farmers can sell their grain for a higher price. International trade also enables Movers to sell their cars for a higher price. Equivalently, Movers can buy grain for a lower price. Thus everybody gains. How is it possible for *everyone* to gain? What are the changes in production and consumption that accompany these gains?

An economy that does not trade with other economies has identical production and consumption possibilities. Without trade, the economy can consume only what it produces. But with international

trade, an economy can consume different quantities of goods from those that it produces. The production possibility frontier describes the limit of what a country can produce, but it does not describe the limits to what it can consume. Figure 35.7 will help you to see the distinction between production possibilities and consumption possibilities when a country trades with other countries.

First of all, notice that the figure has two parts, part (a) for Farmland and part (b) for Mobilia. The production possibility frontiers that you saw in Figs. 35.4 and 35.5 are reproduced here. The slopes of the two black lines in the figure represent the opportunity costs in the two countries when there is no international trade. Farmland produces and consumes at point *a*, and Mobilia produces and consumes at *a'*. Cars cost 9,000 bushels of grain in Farmland and 1,000 bushels of grain in Mobilia.

Consumption Possibilities The red line in each part of Fig. 35.7 shows the country's consumption possibilities with international trade. These two red lines have the same slope, and the magnitude of that slope is the opportunity cost of a car in terms of grain on the world market—3,000 bushels per car. The *slope* of the consumption possibilities line is common to both countries because its magnitude equals the *world* price. But the position of a country's consumption possibilities line depends on the country's production possibilities. A country cannot produce outside its production possibility curve, so its consumption possibility curve touches its production possibility curve. Thus Farmland could choose to consume at point *b* with no international trade or, with international trade, at any point on its red consumption possibilities line.

Free Trade Equilibrium With international trade, the producers of cars in Mobilia can get a higher price for their output. As a result, they increase the quantity of car production. At the same time, grain producers in Mobilia get a lower price for their grain, and so they reduce production. Producers in Mobilia adjust their output by moving along their production possibility frontier until the opportunity cost in Mobilia equals the world price (the opportunity cost in the world market). This situation arises when Mobilia is producing at point *b'* in Fig. 35.7(b).

But the Movers do not consume at point *b'*. That is, they do not increase their consumption of cars and

FIGURE 35.7

Expanding Consumption Possibilities

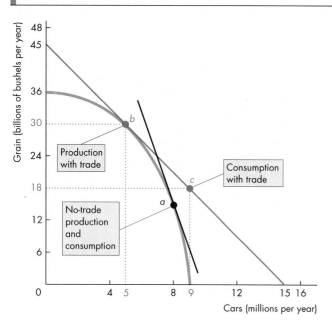

(a) Farmland

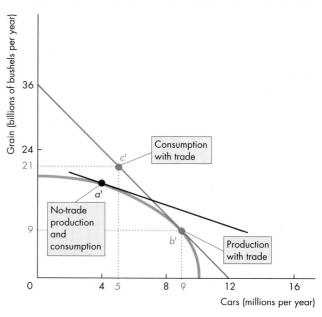

(b) Mobilia

With no international trade, the Farmers produce and consume at point *a* and the opportunity cost of a car is 9,000 bushels of grain (the slope of the black line in part a). Also, with no international trade, the Movers produce and consume at point *a'* and the opportunity cost of 1,000 bushels of grain is 1 car (the slope of the black line in part b).

Goods can be exchanged internationally at a price of 3,000 bushels of grain for 1 car along the red line in each part of the figure. In part (a), Farmland decreases its production of cars and increases its production of grain, moving from *a* to *b*.

It exports grain and imports cars, and it consumes at point *c*. The Farmers have more of both cars and grain than they would if they produced all their own consumption goods—at point *a*.

In part (b), Mobilia increases car production and decreases grain production, moving from *a'* to *b'*. Mobilia exports cars and imports grain, and it consumes at point *c'*. The Movers have more of both cars and grain than they would if they produced all their own consumption goods—at point *a'*.

decrease their consumption of grain. Instead, they sell some of their car production to Farmland in exchange for some of Farmland's grain. They trade internationally. But to see how that works out, we first need to check in with Farmland to see what's happening there.

In Farmland, producers of cars now get a lower price and producers of grain get a higher price. As a consequence, producers in Farmland decrease car production and increase grain production. They adjust their outputs by moving along the production

possibility frontier until the opportunity cost of a car in terms of grain equals the world price (the opportunity cost on the world market). They move to point *b* in part (a). But the Farmers do not consume at point *b*. Instead, they trade some of their additional grain production for the now cheaper cars from Mobilia.

The figure shows us the quantities consumed in the two countries. We saw in Fig. 35.6 that Mobilia exports 4 million cars a year and Farmland imports those cars. We also saw that Farmland exports 12 billion bushels of grain a year and Mobilia imports that grain. Thus Farmland's consumption of grain is 12 billion bushels a year less than it produces, and its consumption of cars is 4 million a year more than it produces. Farmland consumes at point *c* in Fig. 35.7(a).

Similarly, we know that Mobilia consumes 12 billion bushels of grain more than it produces and 4 million cars fewer than it produces. Thus Mobilia consumes at *c'* in Fig. 35.7(b).

Calculating the Gains from Trade

You can now literally see the gains from trade in Fig. 35.7. Without trade, Farmers produce and consume at *a* (part a)—a point on Farmland's production possibility frontier. With international trade, Farmers consume at point *c* in part (a)—a point *outside* the production possibility frontier. At point *c*, Farmers are consuming 3 billion bushels of grain a year and 1 million cars a year more than before. These increases in consumption of both cars and grain, beyond the limits of the production possibility frontier, are the gains from international trade.

Movers also gain. Without trade, they consume at point *a'* in part (b)—a point on Mobilia's production possibility frontier. With international trade, they consume at point *c'*—a point outside the production possibility frontier. With international trade, Mobilia consumes 3 billion bushels of grain a year and 1 million cars a year more than without trade. These are the gains from international trade for Mobilia.

Gains for All

In popular discussions about international trade, we hear about the need for a "level playing field" and other measures to protect people from foreign competition. International trade seems like a type of contest in which there are winners and losers. But the trade between the Farmers and the Movers that you've just studied does not create winners and losers. Everyone wins. Sellers add the net demand of foreigners to their domestic demand, and so their market expands. Buyers are faced with domestic supply plus net foreign supply and so have a larger total supply available to them. As you know, prices increase when there is an increase in demand and decrease when there is an increase in supply. Thus the

increased demand (from foreigners) for exports increases their price, and the increased supply (from foreigners) of imports decreases their price. Gains in one country do not bring losses in another. Everyone, in this example, gains from international trade.

Absolute Advantage

Suppose that in Mobilia, fewer workers are needed to produce any given output of either grain or cars than in Farmland—productivity is higher in Mobilia than in Farmland. In this situation, Mobilia has an absolute advantage over Farmland. A country has an **absolute advantage** if it has greater productivity than another country in the production of all goods. With an absolute advantage, can't Mobilia outsell Farmland in the markets for both cars and grain? Why, if Mobilia has greater productivity than Farmland, does it pay Mobilia to buy *anything* from Farmland?

The answer is that the cost of production in terms of the factors of production employed is irrelevant for determining the gains from trade. It does not matter how many resources are required to produce 1,000 bushels of grain or a car. What matters is how many cars must be given up to produce an additional bushel of grain or how much grain must be given up to produce an additional car. That is, what matters is the opportunity cost of one good in terms of the other good. (For a further explanation of why absolute advantage does not influence the gains from trade, see Chapter 3, pp. 55–56.)

Mobilia might have an absolute advantage in the production of all goods, but it cannot have a comparative advantage in the production of all goods. The statement that the opportunity cost of a car in Mobilia is lower than that in Farmland is identical to the statement that the opportunity cost of grain is higher in Mobilia than in Farmland. Thus *whenever opportunity costs diverge, everyone has a comparative advantage in something.* All countries can potentially gain from international trade.

This lesson has powerful implications for the world economy today. It means that countries like the United States that have high productivity can gain from trade with countries that have low productivity like Mexico.

The story of the discovery of the logic of the gains from international trade is presented in *Economics in History* on pp. 914–915.

R E V I E W

■ When countries have divergent opportunity costs, they can gain from international trade.

■ Each country can buy some goods and services from another country at a lower opportunity cost than that at which it can produce them for itself.

■ Gains arise when each country increases its production of those goods and services in which it has a comparative advantage (goods and services that it can produce at an opportunity cost that is lower than that of other countries) and trades some of its production for that of other countries.

■ All countries gain from international trade. Everyone has a comparative advantage at something.

Gains from Trade in Reality

THE GAINS FROM TRADE THAT WE HAVE JUST studied between Farmland and Mobilia in grain and cars occur in a model economy—in a world economy that we have imagined. But these same phenomena occur every day in the real global economy.

Comparative Advantage in the Global Economy

We buy cars made in Japan, and American producers of grain and lumber sell large parts of their output to Japanese households and firms. We buy cars and machinery from European producers and sell airplanes and computers to Europeans in return. We buy shirts and fashion goods from the people of Hong Kong and sell them machinery in return. We buy TV sets and VCRs from South Korea and Taiwan and sell them financial and other services as well as manufactured goods in return. We make some kinds of machines, and the Europeans and Japanese make other kinds, and we exchange one type of manufactured good for another.

These are all examples of international trade generated by comparative advantage, just like the international trade between Farmland and Mobilia in our model economy. All international trade arises from comparative advantage, even when trade is in similar goods such as tools and machines. At first thought, it seems puzzling that countries exchange manufactured goods. Why doesn't each developed country produce all the manufactured goods its citizens want to buy? Let's look a bit more closely at this question.

Trade in Similar Goods

Why does it make sense for the United States to produce automobiles for export and at the same time to import large quantities of them from Canada, Japan, Korea, and Western Europe? Wouldn't it make more sense to produce all the cars that we buy here in the United States? After all, we have access to the best technology available for producing cars. Auto workers in the United States are surely as productive as their fellow workers in Canada, Western Europe, and the Pacific countries. Capital equipment, production lines, robots, and the like used in the manufacture of cars are as available to U.S. car producers as they are to any others. This line of reasoning leaves a puzzle concerning the sources of international trade of similar goods produced by similar people using similar equipment. Why does it happen? Why does the United States have a comparative advantage in some types of cars and Japan and Europe in others?

Diversity of Taste The first part of the answer to the puzzle is that people have a tremendous diversity of taste. Let's stick with the example of cars. Some people prefer a sports car, some prefer a limousine, some prefer a regular, full-size car, and some prefer a minivan. In addition to size and type of car, there are many other dimensions in which cars vary. Some have low fuel consumption, some have high performance, some are spacious and comfortable, some have a large trunk, some have four-wheel drive, some have front-wheel drive, some have manual transmission, some have automatic transmission, some are durable, some are flashy, some have a radiator grill that looks like a Greek temple, others look like a wedge. People's preferences across these many dimensions vary.

The tremendous diversity in tastes for cars means that people would be dissatisfied if they were forced to consume from a limited range of standardized cars. People value variety and are willing to pay for it in the marketplace.

Economies of Scale   The second part of the answer to the puzzle is economies of scale. *Economies of scale* are the tendency, present in many production processes, for the average cost of production to be lower, the larger the scale of production. In such situations, larger and larger production runs lead to ever lower average production costs. Many manufactured goods, including cars, experience economies of scale. For example, if a car producer makes only a few hundred (or perhaps a few thousand) cars of a particular type and design, the producer must use production techniques that are much more labor-intensive and much less automated than those employed to make hundreds of thousands of cars in a particular model. With short production runs and labor-intensive production techniques, costs are high. With very large production runs and automated assembly lines, production costs are much lower. But to obtain lower costs, the automated assembly lines have to produce a large number of cars.

It is the combination of diversity of taste and economies of scale that determines opportunity cost, produces comparative advantages, and generates such a large amount of international trade in similar commodities. If every car bought in the United States today were made in the United States—if no cars were imported—and if the present range of diversity and variety were available, production runs would be remarkably short. Car producers would not be able to reap economies of scale.

But with international trade, each car manufacturer has the whole world market to serve. Each producer can specialize in a limited range of products and then sell its output to the entire world market. This arrangement enables large production runs on the most popular cars and feasible production runs even on the most customized cars demanded by only a handful of people in each country.

The situation in the market for cars is also present in many other industries, especially those producing specialized equipment and parts. For example, the United States exports computer central processor chips but imports memory chips, exports mainframe computers but imports PCs, exports specialized video equipment but imports VCRs. Thus international exchange of similar but slightly differentiated manufactured products is a highly profitable activity.

This type of trade can be understood with exactly the same model of international trade that we studied earlier. Although we normally think of cars as a single commodity, we have to think of sports cars, sedans, and so on as different goods. Different countries, by specializing in a few of these "goods," are able to enjoy economies of scale and therefore a comparative advantage in their production.

You can see that comparative advantage and international trade bring gains regardless of the goods being traded. When the rich countries of the European Union, Japan, and the United States import raw materials from the Third World and from Australia and Canada, the rich importing countries gain, and so do the exporting countries. When we buy cheap TV sets, VCRs, shirts, and other goods from low-wage countries, both we and the exporters gain from the trade. It's true that if we increase our imports of cars and produce fewer cars ourselves, jobs in our car industry disappear. But jobs in other industries, industries in which we have a comparative advantage, expand. After the adjustment is completed, people whose jobs have been lost find employment in the expanding industries and buy goods produced in other countries at even lower prices than those at which they were available before. The gains from international trade are not necessarily gains for some at the expense of losses for others.

But changes in comparative advantage that lead to changes in international trade patterns can take a long time to adjust to. For example, the increase in automobile imports and the corresponding relative decline in domestic car production have not brought increased wealth for displaced auto workers. Good new jobs take time to find, and often people spend a period of prolonged search putting up with inferior jobs and lower wages than they had before. Thus only in the long run does everyone potentially gain from international specialization and trade. Short-run adjustment costs that can be large and relatively prolonged are borne by the people who have lost their comparative advantage. Some of the people who lose their jobs may be too old for it to be worth their while to make the move to another region of the country or industry, and so they never share in the gains.

Partly because of the costs of adjustment to changing international trade patterns, but partly also for other reasons, governments intervene in international trade, restricting its volume. Let's examine what happens when governments restrict international trade. We'll contrast restricted trade with free trade. We'll see that free trade brings the greatest possible benefits. We'll also see why, in spite of the benefits of free trade, governments sometimes restrict trade.

Trade Restrictions

GOVERNMENTS RESTRICT INTERNATIONAL TRADE to protect domestic industries from foreign competition. The restriction of international trade is called **protectionism**. There are two main protectionist methods employed by governments:

1. Tariffs
2. Nontariff barriers

A **tariff** is a tax that is imposed by the importing country when an imported good crosses its international boundary. A **nontariff barrier** is any action other than a tariff that restricts international trade. Examples of nontariff barriers are quantitative restrictions and licensing regulations limiting imports. We'll consider nontariff barriers in more detail below. First, let's look at tariffs.

The History of Tariffs

U.S. tariffs today are modest compared with their historical levels. Figure 35.8 shows the average tariff rate—total tariffs as a percentage of total imports. You can see in this figure that this average reached a peak of 20 percent in 1933. In that year, three years after the passage of the Smoot-Hawley Act, one third of imports was subject to a tariff and on those imports, the tariff rate was 60 percent. (The average tariff in Fig. 35.8 for 1933 is 60 percent multiplied by 0.33, which equals 20 percent). Today, the average tariff rate is only 4 percent. Two thirds of U.S. imports is now subject to a tariff, but on those imports, the tariff rate is only 6 percent. (The average tariff in Fig. 35.8 for 1994 is 6 percent multiplied by 0.67, which equals 4 percent.)

The reduction in tariffs since World War II followed the establishment of the General Agreement on Tariffs and Trade (GATT). The **General Agreement on Tariffs and Trade** is an international agreement designed to limit government intervention to restrict international trade. It was negotiated immediately following World War II and was signed in October 1947. Its goal is to liberalize trading activity and to provide an organization to administer more liberal trading arrangements. GATT has a small bureaucracy located in Geneva, Switzerland.

Since the formation of GATT, several rounds of negotiations have taken place that have resulted in general tariff reductions. One of these, the Kennedy Round that began in the early 1960s, resulted in large tariff cuts starting in 1967. Another, the Tokyo Round, resulted in further tariff cuts in 1979.

The most recent, the Uruguay Round, which started in 1986 and was completed in 1994, was the most ambitious and comprehensive of the rounds. It was an agreement among 115 countries to lower tariffs and to prevent protection through subsidies or favorable treatment from government purchases. The agreement has been described as the biggest tax cut in the history of the world, and the gains from greater specialization and exchange are predicted to boost world output by 1 percent a year.

The most significant parts of the Uruguay Round agreement are the phasing out of many agricultural subsidies, the strengthening of intellectual property rights (copyrights and patents), and the creation of a new World Trade Organization (WTO). Membership of the WTO brings greater obligations on countries to observe the GATT rules and makes subsidies much harder to use as an alternative to tariffs and other forms of protection. President Clinton signed the Uruguay Round agreements and Congress ratified them in 1994.

In addition to the agreements under the GATT and the WTO, the United States is a party to the North American Free Trade Agreement (NAFTA), which became effective on January 1, 1994. Under this agreement, barriers to international trade between the United States, Canada, and Mexico will be virtually eliminated after a 15-year phasing-in period (10 years for Canada-U.S. trade under an earlier Canada–United States Free Trade Agreement that became effective on January 1, 1989). NAFTA appears to be boosting both exports and imports among the three members. *Reading Between the Lines* on pp. 908–909 takes a closer look at U.S.-Mexico trade during the first three months of NAFTA. As this agreement becomes more effective, other countries of Central and South America can be expected to make efforts to join.

In other parts of the world, trade barriers have virtually been eliminated among the member countries of the European Union, which has created the largest unified tariff-free market in the world. In 1994, discussions among the Asia-Pacific Economic group (APEC) led to an agreement in principle to work toward a free-trade area that embraces China, all the economies of East Asia and the South Pacific, and the United States and Canada. These countries

FIGURE 35.8
U.S. Tariffs: 1930–1994

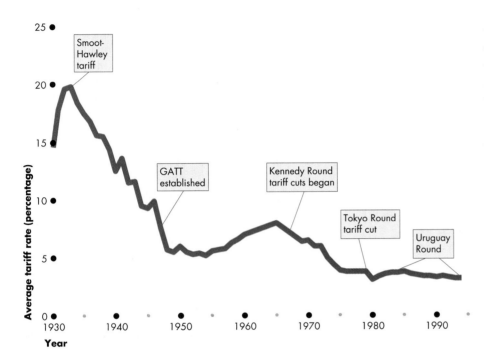

The Smoot-Hawley Act, which was passed in 1930, took U.S. tariffs to a peak average rate of 20 percent in 1933. (One third of imports was subject to a tariff rate of 60 percent.) Since the establishment of GATT in 1947, tariffs have steadily declined in a series of negotiating rounds, the most significant of which are identified in the figure. Tariffs are now as low as they have ever been.

Sources: U.S. Bureau of the Census, *Historical Statistics of the United States, Colonial Times to 1970*, Bicentennial Edition, Part 1 (Washington, D.C., 1975); Series U-212: *Statistical Abstract of the United States: 1986*, 106th edition (Washington, D.C., 1985); and *Statistical Abstract of the United States: 1994*, 114th edition (Washington, D.C., 1994).

include the fastest-growing economies and hold the promise of heralding a global free-trade area.

The effort to achieve freer trade underlines the fact that trade in some goods is still subject to extremely high tariffs. The highest tariffs faced by U.S. buyers are those on textiles and footwear. A tariff of more than 10 percent (on the average) is imposed on almost all our imports of textiles and footwear. For example, when you buy a pair of blue jeans for $20, you pay about $5 more than you would if there were no tariffs on textiles. Other goods protected by tariffs are agricultural products, energy and chemicals, minerals, and metals. The meat, cheese, and sugar that you consume cost significantly more because of protection than they would with free international trade.

The temptation on governments to impose tariffs is a strong one. First, tariffs provide revenue to the government. Second, they enable the government to satisfy special interest groups in import-competing industries. But, as we'll see, free international trade

brings enormous benefits that are reduced when tariffs are imposed. Let's see how.

How Tariffs Work

To analyze how tariffs work, let's return to the example of trade between Farmland and Mobilia. Figure 35.9 shows the international market for cars in which these two countries are the only traders. The volume of trade and the price of a car are determined at the point of intersection of Mobilia's export supply curve of cars and Farmland's import demand curve for cars.

In Fig. 35.9, these two countries are trading cars and grain in exactly the same way that we analyzed in Fig. 35.6. Mobilia exports cars, and Farmland exports grain. The volume of car imports into Farmland is 4 million a year, and the world market price of a car is 3,000 bushels of grain. To make the example more concrete and real, Fig. 35.9 expresses prices in dollars rather than in units of grain and is based on a money

FIGURE 35.9

The Effects of a Tariff

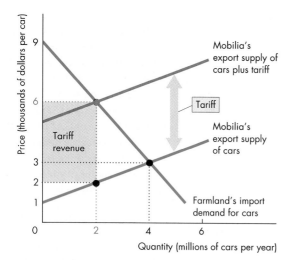

Farmland imposes a tariff on car imports from Mobilia. The tariff increases the price that Farmers have to pay for cars. It shifts the supply curve of cars in Farmland leftward. The vertical distance between the original supply curve and the new one is the amount of the tariff, $4,000 per car. The price of cars in Farmland increases, and the quantity of cars imported decreases. The government of Farmland collects a tariff revenue of $4,000 per car—a total of $8 billion on the 2 million cars imported. Farmland's exports of grain decrease because Mobilia now has a lower income from its exports of cars.

price of grain of $1 a bushel. With grain costing $1 a bushel, the money price of a car is $3,000.

Now suppose that the government of Farmland, perhaps under pressure from car producers, decides to impose a tariff on imported cars. In particular, suppose that a tariff of $4,000 per car is imposed. (This is a huge tariff, but the car producers of Farmland are pretty fed up with competition from Mobilia.) What happens?

The first part of the answer is obtained by studying the effects on the supply of cars in Farmland. Cars are no longer going to be available at the Mobilia export supply price. The tariff of $4,000 must be added to that price—the amount paid to the government of Farmland on each car imported. As a consequence, the supply curve in Farmland shifts upward by the amount of the tariff as shown in Fig.

35.9. The new supply curve becomes that labeled "Mobilia's export supply of cars plus tariff." The vertical distance between Mobilia's export supply curve and the new supply curve is the tariff imposed by the government of Farmland—$4,000 a car.

The next part of the answer is found by determining the new equilibrium. Imposing a tariff has no effect on the demand for cars in Farmland and so has no effect on Farmland's import demand for cars. Thus Farmland's import demand curve is unchanged. The new equilibrium occurs where the new supply curve intersects Farmland's import demand curve for cars. That equilibrium is at a price of $6,000 a car and with 2 million cars a year being imported. Imports fall from 4 million to 2 million cars a year. At the higher price of $6,000 a car, domestic car producers increase their production. Domestic grain production decreases as resources are moved into the expanding car industry.

The total expenditure on imported cars by the Farmers is $6,000 a car multiplied by the 2 million cars imported ($12 billion). But not all of that money goes to the Movers. They receive $2,000 a car, or $4 billion for the 2 million cars. The difference—$4,000 a car, or a total of $8 billion for the 2 million cars—is collected by the government of Farmland as tariff revenue.

Obviously, the government of Farmland is happy with this situation. It is now collecting $8 billion that it didn't have before. But what about the Farmers? How do they view the new situation? The demand curve tells us the maximum price that a buyer is willing to pay for one more unit of a good. As you can see from Farmland's import demand curve for cars, if one more car could be imported, someone would be willing to pay almost $6,000 for it. Mobilia's export supply curve of cars tells us the minimum price at which additional cars are available. As you can see, one additional car would be supplied by Mobilia for a price only slightly more than $2,000. Thus because someone is willing to pay almost $6,000 for a car and someone else is willing to supply one for little more than $2,000, there is obviously a gain to be had from trading an extra car. In fact, there are gains to be had—willingness to pay exceeds the minimum supply price—all the way up to 4 million cars a year. Only when 4 million cars are being traded is the maximum price that a Farmer is willing to pay equal to the minimum price that is acceptable to a Mover. Thus restricting international trade reduces the gains from international trade.

It is easy to see that the tariff has lowered the total amount Farmland pays for imports. With free trade, Farmland was paying $3,000 a car and buying 4 million cars a year from Mobilia. Thus the total amount paid to Mobilia for imports was $12 billion a year. With a tariff, Farmland's imports have been cut to 2 million cars a year and the price paid to Mobilia has also been cut to only $2,000 a car. Thus the total amount paid to Mobilia for imports has been cut to $4 billion a year. Doesn't this fact mean that Farmland is now importing less than it is exporting and has a balance of trade surplus?

To answer that question, we need to figure out what's happening in Mobilia. We've just seen that the price that Mobilia receives for cars has fallen from $3,000 to $2,000 a car. Thus the price of cars in Mobilia has fallen. But the price of grain remains at $1 a bushel. So the relative price of cars has fallen, and the relative price of grain has increased. With free trade, the Movers could buy 3,000 bushels of grain for one car. Now they can buy only 2,000 bushels for a car. With a higher relative price of grain, the quantity demanded by the Movers decreases. As a result, Mobilia imports less grain. But because Mobilia imports less grain, Farmland exports less grain. In fact, Farmland's grain industry suffers from two sources. First, there is a decrease in the quantity of grain sold to Mobilia. Second, there is increased competition for inputs from the now expanded car industry. Thus the tariff leads to a contraction in the scale of the grain industry in Farmland.

It seems paradoxical at first that a country imposing a tariff on cars would hurt its own export industry, lowering its exports of grain. It may help to think of it this way: Movers buy grain with the money they make from exporting cars to Farmland. If they export fewer cars, they cannot afford to buy as much grain. In fact, in the absence of any international borrowing and lending, Mobilia has to cut its imports of grain by exactly the same amount as the loss in revenue from its export of cars. Grain imports into Mobilia will be cut back to a value of $4 billion, the amount that can be paid for by the new lower revenue from Mobilia's car exports. Thus trade is still balanced in this post-tariff situation. Although the tariff has cut imports, it has also cut exports, and the cut in the value of exports is exactly equal to the cut in the value of imports. The tariff therefore has no effect on the balance of trade—it reduces the volume of trade.

The result that we have just derived is perhaps one of the most misunderstood aspects of interna-

tional economics. On countless occasions, politicians and others have called for tariffs to remove a balance of trade deficit or have argued that lowering tariffs would produce a balance of trade deficit. They reach this conclusion by failing to work out all the implications of a tariff. Because a tariff raises the price of imports and cuts imports, the easy conclusion is that the tariff reduces the balance of trade deficit. But there is a second round effect: the tariff changes the *volume* of exports as well. The equilibrium effects of a tariff are to reduce the volume of trade in both directions and the value of imports and exports by the same amount. The balance of trade itself is left unaffected.

Learning the Hard Way   Although the analysis that we have just worked through leads to the clear conclusion that tariffs cut both imports and exports and make both countries worse off, we have not found that conclusion easy to accept. Time and again in our history, we have imposed high tariff barriers on international trade (as Fig. 35.8 illustrates). Whenever tariff barriers are increased, trade collapses. The most vivid historical example of this interaction of tariffs and trade occurred during the Great Depression years of the early 1930s when, in the wake of the Smoot-Hawley tariff increases and the retaliatory tariff changes that other countries introduced as a consequence, world trade almost dried up.

Let's now turn our attention to the other range of protectionist weapons—nontariff barriers.

Nontariff Barriers

There are two important forms of nontariff barriers:

1. Quotas
2. Voluntary export restraints

A **quota** is a quantitative restriction on the import of a particular good. It specifies the maximum amount of the good that may be imported in a given period of time. A **voluntary export restraint** is an agreement between two governments in which the government of the exporting country agrees to restrain the volume of its own exports. Voluntary export restraints are often called VERs.

Nontariff barriers have become important features of international trading arrangements in the period since World War II, and there is general agreement that nontariff barriers are now a more severe impediment to international trade than tariffs.

Quotas are especially important in the textile industries, where there exists an international agreement called the Multifiber Arrangement, which establishes quotas on a wide range of textile products. Agriculture is also subject to extensive quotas. Voluntary export restraints are particularly important in regulating the international trade in cars between Japan and the United States.

It is difficult to quantify the effects of nontariff barriers in a way that makes them easy to compare with tariffs, but some studies have attempted to do just that. Such studies attempt to assess the tariff rate that would restrict trade by the same amount as the nontariff barriers do. With such calculations, nontariff barriers and tariffs can be added together to assess the total amount of protection. When we add nontariff barriers to tariffs for the United States, the overall amount of protection increases more than threefold—equivalent to about an 18 percent tariff. Even so, the United States is one of the least protectionist countries in the world. Total protection in the European Union is higher, and that in other developed countries and Japan is higher still. The less developed countries and some of the newly industrializing countries have the highest protection rates of all.

How Quotas and VERs Work

To understand how nontariff barriers affect international trade, let's return to the example of trade between Farmland and Mobilia. Suppose that Farmland imposes a quota on car imports. Specifically, suppose that the quota restricts imports to not more than 2 million cars a year. What are the effects of this action?

The answer is found in Fig. 35.10. The quota is shown by the vertical red line at 2 million cars a year. Because it is illegal to import more than that number of cars, car importers buy only that quantity from Mobilia producers. They pay $2,000 a car to the Mobilia producers. But what do the car importers sell their cars for? The answer is $6,000 each. Because the import supply of cars is restricted to 2 million cars a year, people with cars for sale will be able to get $6,000 each for them. The quantity of cars imported equals the quantity determined by the quota.

Importing cars is now obviously a profitable business. An importer gets $6,000 for an item that costs

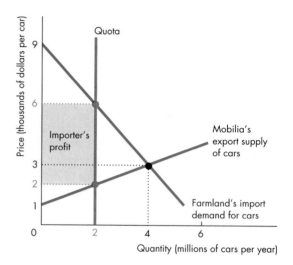

.FIGURE 35.10

The Effects of a Quota

Farmland imposes a quota of 2 million cars a year on car imports from Mobilia. That quantity appears as the vertical line labeled "Quota." Because the quantity of cars supplied by Mobilia is restricted to 2 million, the price at which those cars will be traded increases to $6,000. Importing cars is profitable because Mobilia is willing to supply cars at $2,000 each. There is competition for import quotas—rent seeking.

only $2,000. Thus there is severe competition among car importers for the available quotas. The pursuit of the profits from quotas is called "rent seeking."

The value of imports—the amount paid to Mobilia—declines to $4 billion, exactly the same as in the case of the tariff. Thus with lower incomes from car exports and with a higher relative price of grain, Movers cut back on their imports of grain in exactly the same way that they did under a tariff.

The key difference between a quota and a tariff lies in who gets the profit represented by the difference between the import supply price and the domestic selling price. In the case of a tariff, that difference goes to the government of the importing country. In the case of a quota, that difference goes to the person who has the right to import under the import quota regulations.

A voluntary export restraint is like a quota arrangement in which quotas are allocated to each exporting country. The effects of voluntary export restraints are similar to those of quotas but differ from them in that the gap between the domestic price and the export price is captured not by domestic importers but by the foreign exporter. The government of the exporting country has to establish procedures for allocating the restricted volume of exports among its producers.

"Invisible" Nontarriff Barriers

In addition to quotas and VERs, there are thousands of nontariff barriers that are virtually impossible to detect—that are almost invisible. They arise from domestic laws that are not (necessarily) aimed at restricting foreign competition but they have that effect. For example, in a few countries (most notably Britain, Japan, Australia, and New Zealand) highway traffic drives on the left. This apparently harmless law effectively restricts competition from foreign car makers. Of course a car produced in the United States can be fitted out with its steering wheel and controls on the right but only at an additional cost. And the cost depends on the volume of sales.

R E V I E W

- When a country opens itself up to international trade and trades freely at world market prices, it expands its consumption possibilities.
- When trade is restricted, some of the gains from trade are lost.
- A country might be better off with restricted trade than with no trade but not as well off as it could be if it engaged in free trade.
- A tariff reduces the volume of imports, but it also reduces the volume of exports.
- Under both free trade and restricted trade (and without international borrowing and lending), the value of imports equals the value of exports. With restricted trade, both the total value of exports and the total value of imports are lower than under free trade, but trade is still balanced.

We've now learned about the gains from international trade and we've studied the effects of different ways in which trade can be restricted. Let's now look at the arguments about restricting international trade.

The Case Against Protection

FOR AS LONG AS NATIONS AND INTERNATIONAL trade have existed, people have debated whether a country is better off with free international trade or with protection from foreign competition. The debate continues, but for most economists, a verdict has been delivered and is the one you have just explored. Free trade is the arrangement most conducive to prosperity, and protection creates more problems than it solves. We've seen the most powerful case for free trade in the example of how Farmland and Mobilia both benefit from their comparative advantage. But there is a broader range of issues in the free-trade versus protection debate. Let's review these issues.

A country might restrict international trade and impose tariffs or quotas in an attempt to achieve three goals. They are:

- Achieving national security
- Stimulating the growth of new industries
- Encouraging competition and restraining monopoly

Let's see how protection might be used to try to achieve these goals.

National Security

The national security argument for protection is that a country is better off if it protects its strategic industries—industries that produce defense equipment and armaments and the industries on which the defense industries rely for their raw materials and other intermediate inputs. This argument for protection runs into three overwhelming counter-arguments.

First, it is an argument for the protection of *every* industry. In a time of war, there is no industry that does not contribute to national defense. Agriculture, ore and coal mining, oil and natural gas extraction, the manufacture of steel and other metals, vehicles, aircraft, ships, machinery of all kinds, and services such as banking and insurance are all vital to a nation's defense. To protect every industry would require a tariff or quota on the import of all goods and services that can be traded.

Second, the cost of lower output must be weighed against the benefit of greater national security. There is no clear and objective way of making this cost-benefit calculation. In practice, it is made in the political arena, and once a national security argument is given respectability, it is exploited by anyone who can lay remote claim to its being relevant. Makers of paper clips and nail scissors will lobby as vigorously as weapons designers and shipbuilders.

Third, even if the case is made for maintaining or increasing the output of a strategic industry, there is always a more efficient way of doing so than by protecting the industry from international competition. A direct subsidy to the firms in a strategic industry that is financed out of taxes on all sectors of the economy keeps the industry operating at the scale judged appropriate, and the presence of unfettered international competition prevents the prices faced by consumers from rising.

New Industries

The second argument that is used to justify protection is the **infant-industry argument**—the proposition that protection is necessary to enable an infant industry to grow into a mature industry that can compete in world markets. The argument is based on the idea of *dynamic comparative advantage*, which can arise from *learning-by-doing* (see Chapter 3).

There is no doubt that learning-by-doing is a powerful engine of productivity growth and that comparative advantage evolves and changes because of on-the-job experience. But these facts do not justify protection.

First, the infant-industry argument is valid only if the benefits of learning-by-doing *not only* accrue to the owners and workers of the firms in the infant industry but also *spill over* to other industries and parts of the economy. For example, there are huge productivity gains from learning-by-doing in the manufacture of aircraft. But almost all of these gains benefit the stockholders and workers of Boeing, McDonnell Douglas, and other aircraft producers. Because the people making the decisions, bearing the risk, and doing the work are the ones who benefit, they take the dynamic gains into account when they decide on the scale of their activities. In this case, almost no benefits spill over to other parts of the economy, so there is no need for government assistance to achieve an efficient outcome.

Second, even if the case is made for protecting an infant industry, it is more efficient to do so by a subsidy to the firms in the infant industry, with the subsidy financed out of taxes. Such a subsidy would keep the industry operating at the scale judged appropriate, and free international trade would keep the prices faced by consumers at their world market levels.

Restraining Monopoly

The third argument used to justify protection is the dumping argument. **Dumping** occurs when a foreign firm sells its exports at a lower price than its cost of production. Dumping might be used by a firm that wants to gain a global monopoly. In this case, the foreign firm sells its output at a price below its cost to drive domestic firms out of business. When the domestic firms have gone, the foreign firm takes advantage of its monopoly position and charges a higher price for its product. Dumping is usually regarded as a justification for temporary countervailing tariffs.

But there are powerful reasons to resist the dumping argument for protection. First, it is virtually impossible to detect dumping because it is hard to determine a firm's costs. As a result, the test for dumping is whether a firm's export price is below its domestic price. But this test is a weak one because it can be rational for a firm to charge a low price in markets in which the quantity demanded is highly sensitive to price and a higher price in a market in which demand is less price-sensitive.

Second, there are virtually no goods that are natural global monopolies. So even if all the domestic firms did get driven out of business in some industry, it would always be possible to find several and usually many alternative foreign sources of supply and to buy at prices determined in competitive markets.

Third, if a good or service were a truly global natural monopoly, the best way of dealing with it would be by regulation—just as in the case of domestic monopolies. Such regulation would require international cooperation.

The three arguments for protection that we've just examined have an element of credibility. The counter-arguments are in general stronger, so these arguments do not make the case for protection. But they are not the only arguments that you might encounter. The many other arguments that are commonly heard are quite simply wrong. They are fatally flawed. The most common of them are that protection:

- Saves jobs
- Allows us to compete with cheap foreign labor
- Brings diversity and stability
- Penalizes lax environmental standards
- Prevents rich countries from exploiting developing countries

Saves Jobs

The argument is: When we buy shoes from Brazil or shirts from Taiwan, U.S. workers lose their jobs. With no earnings and poor prospects, these workers become a drain on welfare and spend less, causing a ripple effect of further job losses. The proposed solution to this problem is to ban imports of cheap foreign goods and protect U.S. jobs. The proposal is flawed for the following reasons.

First, free trade does cost some jobs, but it also creates other jobs. It brings about a global rationalization of labor and allocates labor resources to their highest-value activities. Because of international trade in textiles, tens of thousands of workers in the United States have lost jobs because textile mills and other factories have closed. But tens of thousands of workers in other countries have gotten jobs because textile mills have opened there. And tens of thousands of U.S. workers have gotten better-paying jobs than textile workers because other export industries have expanded and created more jobs than have been destroyed.

Second, imports create jobs. They create jobs for retailers that sell imported goods and firms that service those goods. They also create jobs by creating incomes in the rest of the world, some of which are spent on imports of U.S.-made goods and services.

Although protection does save jobs, it does so at inordinate cost. For example, textile jobs are protected in the United States by quotas imposed under an international agreement called the Multifiber Arrangement. It has been estimated by the U.S. International Trade Commission (ITC) that because of quotas, 72,000 jobs exist in textiles that would otherwise disappear and annual clothing expenditure in the United States is $15.9 billion or $700 per family higher than it would be with free trade. Equivalently, the ITC estimates that each textile job saved costs $221,000 a year.

Allows Us to Compete with Cheap Foreign Labor

With the removal of protective tariffs in U.S. trade with Mexico, Ross Perot said we would hear a "giant sucking sound" of jobs rushing to Mexico (one of which is shown in the cartoon). Let's see what's wrong with this view.

The labor cost of a unit of output equals the wage rate divided by labor productivity. For example, if a U.S. auto worker earns $30 an hour and produces 15 units of output an hour, the average labor cost of a unit of output is $2. If a Mexican auto assembly worker earns $3 an hour and produces 1 unit of output an hour, the average labor cost of a unit of output is $3. Other things remaining the same, the higher a worker's productivity, the higher is the worker's wage rate. High-wage workers have high productivity. Low-wage workers have low productivity.

Although high-wage U.S. workers are more productive, on the average, than low-wage Mexican workers, there are differences across industries. U.S. labor is relatively more productive in some activities than in others. For example, the productivity of U.S. workers in producing movies, financial services, and customized computer chips is relatively higher than in the production of metals and some standardized

"I don't know what the hell happened—one minute I'm at work in Flint, Michigan, then there's a giant sucking sound and suddenly here I am in Mexico."

Drawing by M. Stevens; © 1993
The New Yorker Magazine, Inc.

machine parts. The activities in which U.S. workers are relatively more productive than their Mexican counterparts are those in which the United States has a *comparative advantage*. By engaging in free trade, increasing our production and exports of the goods and services in which we have a comparative advantage and decreasing our production and increasing our imports of the goods and services in which our trading partners have a comparative advantage, we can make ourselves and the citizens of other countries better off.

Brings Diversity and Stability

A diversified investment portfolio is less risky than one that has all the eggs in one basket. The same is true for an economy's production. A diversified economy fluctuates less than an economy that produces only one or two goods.

But big, rich, diversified economies like those of the United States, Japan, and Europe do not have this type of stability problem. Even a country like Saudi Arabia that produces almost only one good (oil) can benefit from specializing in the activity at which it has a comparative advantage and then investing in a wide range of other countries to bring greater stability to its income and consumption.

Penalizes Lax Environmental Standards

A new argument for protection that was used extensively in the Uruguay Round of GATT and in the NAFTA negotiations is that many poorer countries, such as Mexico, do not have the same environment policies that we have and, because they are willing to pollute and we are not, we cannot compete with them without tariffs. So if they want free trade with the richer and "greener" countries, they must clean up their environments to our standards.

The environment argument for trade restrictions is weak. First, it is not true that all poorer countries have significantly lower environmental protection standards than the United States has. Many poor countries and the former communist countries of Eastern Europe do have bad records on the environment. But some countries, one of which is Mexico, have strict laws, and they enforce them. Second, a poor country cannot afford to be as concerned about its environment as a rich country can. The best hope for a better environment in Mexico and in other developing countries is rapid income growth through free trade. As their incomes grow, developing countries such as Mexico will have the *means* to match their desires to improve their environment.

Prevents Rich Countries from Exploiting Developing Countries

Another new argument for protection is that international trade must be restricted to prevent the people of the rich industrial world from exploiting the poorer people of the developing countries, forcing them to work for slave wages.

Wage rates in some developing countries are indeed very low. But by trading with developing countries, we increase the demand for the goods that these countries produce, and, more significantly, we increase the demand for their labor. When the demand for labor in developing countries increases, the wage rate also increases. So, far from exploiting people in developing countries, trade improves their opportunities and increases their incomes.

We have reviewed the arguments that are commonly heard in favor of protection and the counter-arguments against them. There is one counter-argument to protection that is general and quite overwhelming. Protection invites retaliation and can trigger a trade war. The best example of a trade war occurred during the Great Depression of the 1930s when the Smoot-Hawley Tariff was introduced. Country after country retaliated with its own tariff, and in a short period, world trade had almost disappeared. The costs to all countries were large and led to a renewed international resolve to avoid such self-defeating moves in the future. They also led to the creation of GATT and are the impetus behind NAFTA, APEC, and the European Union.

Why Is Trade Restricted?

Why, despite all the arguments against protection, is trade restricted? The key reason is that consumption possibilities increase *on the average* but not everyone shares in the gain and some people even lose. Free trade brings benefits to some and costs to others, with total benefits exceeding total costs. It is the uneven distribution of costs and benefits that is the principal source of impediment to achieving more liberal international trade.

Returning to our example of trade in cars and grain between Farmland and Mobilia, the benefits from free trade accrue to all the producers of grain and those producers of cars who would not have to bear the costs of adjusting to a smaller car industry. These costs are transition costs, not permanent costs. The costs of moving to free trade are borne by those car producers and their employees who have to become grain producers. The number of people who gain will, in general, be enormous compared with the number who lose. The gain per person will therefore be rather small. The loss per person to those who bear the loss will be large. Because the loss that falls on those who bear it is large, it will pay those people to incur considerable expense to lobby against free trade. On the other hand, it will not pay those who gain to organize to achieve free trade. The gain from trade for any one individual is too small for that individual to spend much time or money on a political organization to achieve free trade. The loss from free trade will be seen as being so great by those bearing that loss that they *will* find it profitable to join a political organization to prevent free trade. Each group is optimizing—weighing benefits against costs and choosing the best action for themselves. The anti-free-trade group will, however, undertake a larger quantity of political lobbying than the pro-free-trade group.

Compensating Losers

If, in total, the gains from free international trade exceed the losses, why don't those who gain compensate those who lose so that everyone is in favor of free trade? To some degree, such compensation does take place. When Congress approved the NAFTA deal with Canada and Mexico, it set up a $56 million fund to support and retrain workers who lost their jobs because of the new trade agreement. During the first six months of the operation of NAFTA, only 5,000 workers applied for benefits under this scheme.

The losers from freer international trade are also compensated indirectly through the normal unemployment compensation arrangements. But only limited attempts are made to compensate those who lose from free international trade. The main reason why full compensation is not attempted is that the costs of identifying all the losers and estimating the value of their losses would be enormous. Also, it would never be clear whether a person who has fallen on hard times is suffering because of free trade or for other

reasons, perhaps reasons that are largely under the control of the individual. Furthermore, some people who look like losers at one point in time may, in fact, wind up gaining. The young auto worker who loses his job in Michigan and becomes a computer assembly worker in Minneapolis resents the loss of work and the need to move. But a year or two later, looking back on events, he counts himself fortunate. He has made a move that has increased his income and given him greater job security.

It is because we do not, in general, compensate the losers from free international trade that protectionism is such a popular and permanent feature of our national economic and political life.

REVIEW

- Trade restrictions aimed at national security goals, stimulating the growth of new industries, and restraining foreign monopoly have little merit.
- Trade restrictions to save jobs, compensate for low foreign wages, make the economy more diversified, compensate for costly environmental policies, and protect developing countries from being exploited are misguided.
- The main arguments against trade restrictions are that subsidies and antitrust policies can achieve domestic goals more efficiently than protection and that protection can trigger a trade war in which all countries lose.

◆ You've now seen how free international trade enables all nations to gain from specialization and trade. By producing goods in which we have a comparative advantage and trading some of our production for that of others, we expand our consumption possibilities. Placing impediments on that trade restricts the extent to which we can gain from specialization and trade. By opening our country up to free international trade, the market for the things that we sell expands and the relative price rises. The market for the things that we buy also expands and the relative price falls.

In the next chapter, we're going to study how international trade is financed and also learn why unbalanced international trade arises. We'll discover the forces that determine the U.S. balance of payments and the value, in terms of foreign currency, of our dollar.

Free Trade in Action

LOS ANGELES TIMES, MAY 20, 1994

U.S. Exports to Mexico Flourish under NAFTA

BY CHRIS KRAUL

Record growth in U.S. exports to Mexico during the first quarter of 1994 was a bright light in the U.S. Commerce Department's trade report issued Thursday—and evidence that the North American Free Trade Agreement is living up to its billing.

The easing of tariffs that began when NAFTA took effect Jan. 1 helped boost U.S. exports to Mexico to $11.8 billion in the three months ended March 31— 16% higher than the first quarter of 1993. It was the highest quarterly level of exports to Mexico ever recorded, the department said.

"This is very positive," Lehman Bros. economist Lawrence Krohn said. "The whole purpose of NAFTA was to pro-mote trade and exploitation of comparative advantage, and it looks like it's happening."

Sales of U.S.-made electrical machinery, paper, trucks and cereals led the increases. They were among the trade categories on which tariffs were either reduced or eliminated.

Under NAFTA, tariffs on most goods produced and traded within the U.S.-Mexico-Canada trade zone are being phased out over 15 years. But Assistant Secretary of Commerce Charles Meissner said NAFTA is already paying dividends, accounting for "over half of U.S. export growth and one-third of U.S. import growth so far in 1994. ..."

First-quarter imports of Mexican goods and services grew to $11.3 billion, up 22% from the same period in 1993, bolstering proponents' view that NAFTA is a good policy for Mexico as well.

Reprinted by permission.

Essence of THE STORY

■ The North American Free Trade Agreement (NAFTA) took effect on January 1, 1994. Under NAFTA, tariffs on most goods produced and traded among the United States, Mexico, and Canada will be phased out over 15 years.

■ During the first quarter of 1994, U.S. exports to Mexico grew by 16 percent to a record level of $11.8 billion, and U.S. imports from Mexico grew by 22 percent to $11.3 billion.

■ The biggest export increases were of U.S.-made electrical machinery, paper, trucks, and cereals—all items on which tariffs were cut.

■ Lehman Bros. economist Lawrence Krohn said that NAFTA was achieving its purpose, which is to stimulate trade and increase the benefits of comparative advantage.

Economic

A N A L Y S I S

■ On January 1, 1994, the United States, Mexico, and Canada began a process of tariff reduction that by 2009 will have eliminated most restrictions on trade among the three countries.

■ Some tariffs were cut on signing of the agreement, and the effects were quick to appear in the volume of trade between the United States and Mexico.

■ The figure shows why U.S. exports to Mexico increased. Mexico's demand for trucks is shown by the curve D_M, and the supply curve for trucks produced in Mexico is S_M.

■ The opportunity cost of producing trucks in the United States is P_1. International competition in the market for trucks forces the United States to offer trucks at their opportunity cost, so the supply curve of trucks from the United States to Mexico is S_{US}.

■ Before NAFTA came into effect, Mexico imposed a tariff on U.S.-made trucks. To determine the price at which U.S. trucks sold in Mexico, we must add the tariff to the U.S. supply price P_1. The supply curve facing Mexicans was the blue line S_{US} + tariff.

■ The price of trucks in Mexico was P_0, and at this price, the quantity of trucks produced in Mexico was Q_0. The quantity demanded was C_0, and imports made up the difference.

■ The light blue rectangle shows the total amount paid by Mexico for trucks imported from the United States.

■ When NAFTA cut tariffs on trucks, the supply curve of trucks faced by Mexicans shifted to the red curve S_{US}. The price of trucks in Mexico fell to P_1, and at this price, the quantity of trucks produced in Mexico decreased to Q_1. The quantity demanded increased to C_1, and imports increased to make up the difference.

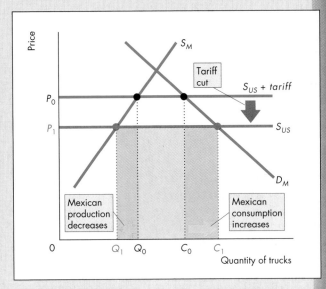

■ The value of imports increased by the amounts shown as the dark blue rectangles in the figure.

■ U.S. imports from Mexico increased for reasons similar to those you've just studied. The tariff cut lowered the price of U.S. imports from Mexico.

■ With a lower price of imports from Mexico, U.S. production decreased and the quantity demanded increased. Imports increased to fill the gap between the decrease in production and the increase in the quantity demanded.

■ In 1993, Mexico exported about 14 percent of its output. The United States exported 10 percent of its output, and Canada exported 29 percent.

■ As the economies of these countries continue to grow and to specialize in the activities in which each has a comparative advantage, trade among them will expand further.

■ Mexico, with a population more than three times that of Canada, will possibly one day account for a larger share of U.S. trade than Canada does today.

SUMMARY

Patterns and Trends in International Trade

Large flows of trade take place between countries. Resource-rich countries exchange natural resources for maufactured goods, and resource-poor countries import resources in exchange for their own manufactured goods. But most international trade is in manufactured goods exchanged among rich industrialized countries. The volume of trade has grown; trade with Asia has grown most. (pp. 887–890)

Opportunity Cost and Comparative Advantage

When opportunity costs differ between countries, the country with the lowest opportunity cost of producing a good is said to have a comparative advantage in that good. Comparative advantage is the source of the gains from international trade. (pp. 890–492)

Gains from Trade

Countries can gain from trade if their opportunity costs differ. Through trade, each country can obtain goods at a lower opportunity cost than it could if it produced all goods at home. Trading allows consumption to exceed production. By specializing in producing the good in which it has a comparative advantage and then trading some of that good for imports, a country can consume at points outside its production possibility frontier.

In the absence of international borrowing and lending, trade is balanced as prices adjust to reflect the international supply of and demand for goods. The world price balances the production and consumption plans of the trading parties. At the equilibrium price, trade is balanced. For imported goods, consumption equals domestic production plus imports. For exported goods, consumption equals domestic production minus exports.

A country can have an absolute advantage, but not a comparative advantage, in the production of all goods. Whenever opportunity costs diverge, every country has a comparative advantage in something (pp. 892–896)

Gains from Trade in Reality

Comparative advantage explains the enormous volume and diversity of international trade that takes place in the world. But much trade takes the form of exchanging similar goods for each other—one type of car for another. Such trade arises because of economies of scale in the face of diversified tastes. By specializing in producing a few goods, having long production runs, and then trading those goods internationally, consumers in all countries can enjoy greater diversity of products at lower prices. (pp. 896–897)

Trade Restrictions

A country can restrict international trade by imposing tariffs or nontariff barriers such as quotas and voluntary export restraints. All trade restrictions raise the domestic price of imported goods, lower the volume of imports, and reduce the total value of imports. They also reduce the total value of exports by the same amount as the reduction in the value of imports. (pp. 898–903)

The Case Against Protection

The arguments that protection is necessary for national security, infant industries, and to prevent dumping, are weak. Every industry contributes to national defense; in an infant industry, the benefits of learning-by-doing accrue to the owners and workers; it is unlikely that a foreign firm will sell below cost to gain a global monopoly because there are virtually no goods that are global natural monopolies.

The arguments that protection saves jobs, allows us to compete with cheap foreign labor, makes the economy diversified and stable, and is needed to offset the costs of environmental policies are fatally flawed.

Trade is restricted despite the fact that it is beneficial because protection brings a small loss to a large number of people and a large gain per person to a small number of people. Those who gain from protection undertake more political lobbying than those who lose from it. (pp. 903–907)

K E Y   E L E M E N T S

Key Figures

Key Terms

R E V I E W   Q U E S T I O N S

1. What are the main exports and imports of the United States?
2. How does the United States trade services internationally?
3. Which items of international trade have been growing the most quickly in recent years?
4. What is the balance of trade? In what circumstances would the United States be a net exporter?
5. With which countries does the United States do most of its international trade?
6. In 1994, to which country did the United States export the largest amounts of goods and services?
7. In 1994, from which country did the United States import the largest amount of goods and services?
8. Describe how the U.S. balance of trade has changed since 1960.
9. What is comparative advantage? Why does it lead to gains from international trade?
10. Explain what the gains from trade are.
11. Explain why international trade brings gains to all countries.
12. Distinguish between comparative advantage and absolute advantage.
13. Explain why all countries have a comparative advantage in something.
14. Explain why, when a country begins to trade, the price received for the good exported rises and the price paid for the good imported falls.
15. Explain why we import and export such large quantities of certain similar goods—such as cars.
16. What are the main ways in which we restrict international trade?
17. What are the GATT and the WTO? When was each established and what is its role?
18. What is NAFTA? When did it begin, and what have its effects to date been?
19. What are the effects of a tariff?
20. What are the effects of a quota?
21. What are the effects of a voluntary export restraint?
22 What is dumping? Explain why it occurs.
23. Describe the main trends in tariffs and nontariff barriers.
24. What are the main arguments for trade restrictions? Explain the flaw in each argument.
25. Why do countries restrict international trade?

P R O B L E M S

◆ 1. Figures 35.4 and 35.5 illustrate Farmland's and Mobilia's production possibilities.
   a. Calculate Farmland's opportunity cost of a car when it produces 2 million cars a year.
   b. Calculate Mobilia's opportunity cost of a car when it produces 8 million cars a year.
   c. With no trade, Farmland produces 2 million cars and Mobilia produces 8 million cars. Which country has a comparative advantage in the production of cars?
   d. If there is no trade between Farmland and Mobilia, how much grain is consumed and how many cars are bought in each country?

◆ 2. Suppose that the two countries in problem 1 trade freely.
   a. Which country exports grain?
   b. What adjustments will be made to the amount of each good produced by each country?
   c. What adjustment will be made to the amount of each good consumed by each country?
   d. What can you say about the price of a car under free trade?

◆ 3. Compare the total production of each good produced in problems 1 and 2.

4. Compare the situation in problems 1 and 2 with that analyzed in this chapter (pp. 890–891). Why does Mobilia export cars in the chapter but import them in problem 2?

◆ 5. The following figure depicts the international market for soybeans.

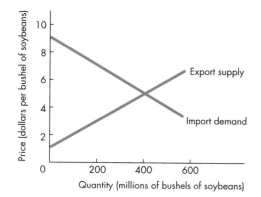

   a. If the two countries did not engage in international trade, what would be the prices of soybeans in the two countries?
   b. What is the world price of soybeans if there is free trade between these countries?
   c. What quantities of soybeans are exported and imported?
   d. What is the balance of trade?

6. If the country in problem 5 that imports soybeans imposes a tariff of $2 per bushel, what is the world price of soybeans and what quantity of soybeans gets traded internationally? What is the price of soybeans in the importing country? Calculate the tariff revenue.

◆ 7. The importing country in problem 5(b) imposes a quota of 300 million bushels on imports of soybeans.
   a. What is the price of soybeans in the importing country?
   b. What is the revenue from the quota?
   c. Who gets this revenue?

◆ 8. The exporting country in problem 5(b) imposes a VER of 300 million bushels on its exports of soybeans.
   a. What is the world price of soybeans now?
   b. What is the revenue of soybean growers in the exporting country?
   c. Which country gains from the VER?

9. Suppose that the exporting country in problem 5(b) subsidizes production by paying its farmers $1 a bushel for soybeans harvested.
   a. What is the price of soybeans in the importing country?
   b. What action might soybean growers in the importing country take? Why?

10. Countries Atlantis and Magic Kingdom produce only food and balloon rides and have the following production possibility frontiers:
   a. If Atlantis produces at point *a*, what is its opportunity cost of a balloon ride?
   b. What are the consumption possibilities of Atlantis?
   c. If Magic Kingdom produces at point *a'*, what is its opportunity cost of a balloon ride?

d. What are the consumption possibilites of Magic Kingdom?

e. Which country has a comparative advantage in producing food?

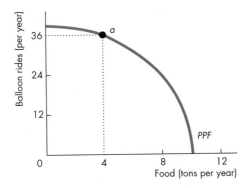

(a) Atlantis

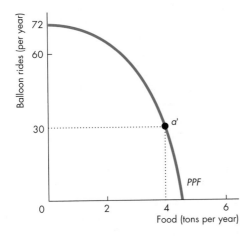

(b) Magic Kingdom

11. If Atlantis and Magic Kingdom in problem 10 enter into a free trade agreement:

a. How does the price of balloon rides in each country change?

b. How does the price of food in each country change?

c. Which country exports balloon rides?

d. Which country exports food?

e. What are the gains from trade for each country?

f. Are there any losers as a result of the free trade agreement?

12. Study *Reading Between the Lines* on pp. 908–909, and then answer the following questions.

a. What happened to international trade between the United States and Mexico during the first three months of NAFTA?

b. How did NAFTA contribute to the change in U.S. exports to Mexico during the first three months of NAFTA?

c. How did NAFTA contribute to the change in U.S. imports from Mexico during the first three months of NAFTA?

d. Who gained from NAFTA—the United States, Mexico, or both?

e. What do you predict will happen to trade between the United States and Canada and between Mexico and Canada as a result of NAFTA?

f. Find the data for international trade between Mexico and the United States for the most recent three months. Did exports and imports between the two countries continue to change in the same direction as they did in the first three months of NAFTA? Use what you have learned about the causes of international trade to interpret the most recent changes. (You can find the data in the *Survey of Current Business,* which is published by the U.S. Department of Commerce, in the March, June, September, and December issues each year. Look in the Table of Contents under "U.S. International Transactions, ..." and then turn to Table 2.)

> *"*Free trade, one of the greatest blessings which a government can confer on a people, is in almost every country unpopular.*"*
>
> LORD MACAULAY (1800–1859); *ESSAY ON MITFORD'S HISTORY OF GREECE*

Understanding the Gains from International Trade

THE ISSUES AND IDEAS

Until the mid-eighteenth century, it was generally believed that the purpose of international trade was to keep exports greater than imports and pile up gold. If gold was accumulated, it was believed, the nation would prosper; and if gold was lost through an international deficit, the nation would be drained of money and impoverished. These beliefs are called *mercantilism*, and the *mercantilists* were pamphleteers who advocated with missionary fervor the pursuit of an international surplus. If exports did not exceed imports, the mercantilists wanted imports restricted.

In the 1740s, David Hume explained that as the quantity of money (gold) changes, so also does the price level, and the nation's *real* wealth is unaffected. In the 1770s, Adam Smith argued that import restrictions would reduce the gains from specialization and make a nation poorer, and 30 years later, David Ricardo proved the law of comparative advantage and demonstrated the superiority of free trade. Mercantilism was intellectually bankrupt but remained politically powerful.

Gradually, through the nineteenth century, the mercantilist influence waned, and North America and Western Europe prospered in an environment of increasingly free international trade. But despite remarkable advances in economic understanding, mercantilism never quite died. It had a brief and devastating revival in the 1920s and 1930s when tariff hikes brought about the collapse of international trade and accentuated the Great Depression. It subsided again after World War II with the establishment of the General Agreement on Tariffs and Trade (GATT).

But mercantilism lingers on. The Japan–United States 'trade war' of 1995 and fears that NAFTA will bring economic ruin to the United States are modern manifestations of mercantilism. It would be interesting to have David Hume, Adam Smith, and David Ricardo commenting on these views. But we know what they would say—the same things that they said to the eighteenth-century mercantilists. And they would still be right today.

THEN...

In the eighteenth century, when mercantilists and economists were debating the pros and cons of free international exchange, the available transportation technology severely limited the gains from international trade. Sailing ships with tiny cargo holds took close to a month to cross the Atlantic Ocean. But the potential gains were large, and so was the incentive to cut shipping costs. By the 1850s, the clipper ship had been developed, cutting the journey from Boston to Liverpool to only 12 1/4 days. Half a century later, 10,000-ton steamships were sailing between America and England in just 4 days. As sailing times and costs declined, the gains from international trade increased and the volume of trade expanded.

THE CONTAINER ship has revolutionized international trade and contributed to its continued expansion. Today, most goods cross the oceans in "containers"—metal boxes—packed into and piled on top of ships like this one. Container technology has cut the cost of ocean shipping by economizing on handling and by making cargoes harder to steal, lowering insurance costs. It is unlikely that there would be much international trade in goods such as television sets and VCRs without this technology. High-value and perishable cargoes such as flowers and fresh foods, as well as urgent courier packages, travel by air. Every day, dozens of cargo-laden 747s fly between every major U.S. city and destinations across the Atlantic and Pacific oceans.

David Ricardo

THE ECONOMISTS: FROM SMITH AND RICARDO TO GATT

David Ricardo (1772–1823) was a highly successful 27-year-old stockbroker when he stumbled on a copy of Adam Smith's *Wealth of Nations* (see p. 65) on a weekend visit to the country. He was immediately hooked and went on to become the most celebrated economist of his age and one of the all-time great economists. One of his many contributions was to develop the principle of comparative advantage, the foundation on which the modern theory of international trade is built. The example that he used to illustrate this principle was the trade between England and Portugal in cloth and wine.

The General Agreement on Tariffs and Trade (GATT) was established as a reaction against the devastation wrought by the beggar-my-neighbor tariffs imposed during the 1930s. But it is also a triumph for the logic first worked out by Smith and Ricardo.

The Balance of Payments and the Dollar

After studying this chapter, you will be able to:

- Explain how international trade is financed

- Describe a country's balance of payments accounts

- Explain what determines the amount of international borrowing and lending

- Explain why the United States changed from being a lender to being a borrower in the mid-1980s

- Explain how the foreign exchange value of the dollar is determined

- Explain why the foreign exchange value of the dollar fluctuates

A Climbing Debt and a Tumbling Dollar

In 1988 the United States owned $1.9 trillion in assets abroad and foreigners owned $1.9 trillion of assets in the United States. Before 1988, U.S. residents' ownership of foreign assets exceeded foreigners' ownership of assets in the United States, and since 1988 the balance has tipped increasingly the other way. During these years, foreign entrepreneurs like Australian-born Rupert Murdoch and Sony's Akio Mori roamed the United States with giant shopping carts and loaded them up with such items as Twentieth Century Fox, the Rockefeller Center, and MGM. Why have foreigners been buying more U.S. real estate and businesses than Americans have been buying abroad?

◆ In 1971, one U.S. dollar was enough to buy 360 Japanese yen. In mid-1995, that same dollar bought only 84 yen. But the slide from 360 to 84 yen was not a smooth one. At some times, the dollar held its own or even rose in value against the Japanese currency, as it did, for example, in 1982. But at other times, the dollar's slide was precipitous, as in the period between 1985 and 1988 and again in 1995. The dollar has fallen in value not only against the Japanese currency. During the first six months of 1995 it fell against the German mark, the French franc, the Swiss franc, and the British pound. But the dollar gained in value against the Italian lira and held steady against the Canadian dollar. What makes our dollar fluctuate in value against other currencies? Why were the fluctuations particularly extreme during the 1980s? Is there anything we can do to stabilize the value of the dollar?

◻ The issues of international economics have become important matters for all Americans, and we're going to study these issues in this chapter. We're going to discover why the U.S. economy has become so attractive for foreign investors, why the dollar fluctuates against the values of other currencies, and why interest rates vary from country to country.

Financing International Trade

WHEN 47TH STREET PHOTO IN NEW YORK CITY imports Sony CD players, it does not pay for them with U.S. dollars—it uses Japanese yen. And when a French construction company buys an earth mover from Caterpillar, Inc., it uses U.S. dollars. Whenever we buy things from another country, we use the currency of that country to make the transaction. It doesn't make any difference what the item being traded is; it might be a consumption good or a capital good, a building, or even a firm.

We're going to study the markets in which money—different types of currency—is bought and sold. But first we're going to look at the scale of international trading and borrowing and lending and at the way in which we keep our records of these transactions. Such records are called the balance of payments accounts.

Balance of Payments Accounts

A country's **balance of payments accounts** records its international trading, borrowing, and lending. There are in fact three balance of payments accounts:

1. Current account
2. Capital account
3. Official settlements account

The **current account** records payments for imports of goods and services from abroad, receipts from exports of goods and services sold abroad, net interest paid abroad, and net transfers (such as foreign aid payments). The *current account balance* equals exports minus imports, net interest, and net transfers. The **capital account** records foreign investment in the United States minus U.S. investment abroad. The **official settlements account** records the change in official U.S. reserves. **Official U.S. reserves** are the government's holdings of foreign currency. If U.S. official reserves increase, the *official settlements account balance* is negative. The reason is that holding foreign money is like investing abroad. U.S. investment abroad is a minus item in the capital account and in the official settlements account. (By the same reasoning, if official reserves decrease, the *official settlements account balance* is positive.)

The sum of the balances on the three accounts always equals zero. That is, to pay for our current account deficit, either we must borrow more from abroad than we lend abroad, or our official reserves must decrease to cover the shortfall.

Table 36.1 shows the U.S. balance of payments accounts in 1994. Items in the current account and capital account that provide foreign currency to the United States have a plus sign; items that cost the United States foreign currency have a minus sign. The table shows that in 1994, U.S. imports exceeded U.S. exports and the current account had a deficit of $155.7 billion. How do we pay for imports that exceed the value of our exports? That is, how do we pay for our current account deficit? We pay by borrowing from the rest of the world. The capital account tells us by how much. We borrowed $314.6 billion but made loans of $131.0 billion. Thus our identified net foreign borrowing was $183.6 billion. There is also a statistical discrepancy of $33.2 billion in the capital account. Actually, this discrepancy represents a

TABLE 36.1

U.S. Balance of Payments Accounts in 1994

Current account	(billions of dollars)
Imports of goods and services	−804.4
Exports of goods and services	+698.0
Net interest income	−15.2
Net transfers	−34.1
Current account balance	−155.7
Capital account	
Foreign investment in the United States	+314.6
U.S. investment abroad	−131.0
Statistical discrepancy	−33.2
Capital account balance	+150.4
Official settlements account	
Decrease in official U.S. reserves	5.3

Source: Survey of Current Business (March 1995), vol. 75.

combination of capital and current account transactions such as unidentified borrowing from the rest of the world, illegal international trade—for example, the import of illegal drugs—and transactions that are not reported in order to illegally evade tariffs or other international trade protection measures.

Our net borrowing from abroad minus our current account deficit is the change in official U.S. reserves. In 1994 those reserves decreased by $5.3 billion (net borrowing from foreigners was $150.4 billion, the current account deficit was $155.7 billion, and the difference, $5.3 billion, was the decrease in official reserves).

The numbers in Table 36.1 give a snapshot of the balance of payments accounts in 1994. Figure 36.1 puts that snapshot into perspective by showing the balance of payments between 1975 and 1994. Because the economy grows and the price level rises, changes in the dollar value of the balance of payments do not convey much information. To remove the influences of growth and inflation, Fig. 36.1 shows the balance of payments as a percentage of nominal GDP.

As you can see, the capital account balance is almost a mirror image of the current account balance. The official settlements balance is very small in comparison with the balances on these other two accounts. A large current account deficit (and capital account surplus) emerged during the 1980s but declined from 1987 to 1991. Since then it has increased again.

You will perhaps obtain a better understanding of the balance of payments accounts and the way in which they are linked together if you consider the income and expenditure, borrowing and lending, and bank account of an individual.

Individual Analogy   An individual's current account records the income from supplying the services of factors of production and the expenditure on goods and services. Consider, for example, Joanne. She worked in 1995 and earned an income of $25,000. Joanne has $10,000 worth of investments that earned her an interest income of $1,000. Joanne's current account shows an income $26,000. Joanne spent $18,000 buying goods and services for consumption. She also bought a new house, which

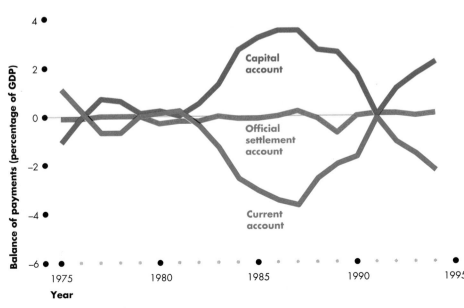

FIGURE   36.1

The Balance of Payments: 1975–1994

During the 1970s, fluctuations in the balance of payments were small, but during the 1980s a large current account deficit arose. That deficit decreased in the late 1980s but increased again after 1991. The capital account balance mirrors the current account balance. When the current account balance is negative, the capital account balance is positive—we borrow from the rest of the world. Fluctuations in the official settlements balance are small in comparison with fluctuations in the current account balance and the capital account balance.

Source: Economic Report of the President, 1995.

cost her $60,000. So Joanne's total expenditure was $78,000. The difference between her expenditure and income is $52,000 ($78,000 minus $26,000). This amount is Joanne's current account deficit.

To pay for expenditure of $52,000 in excess of her income, Joanne has to use the money that she has in the bank or has to take out a loan. In fact, Joanne took a mortgage of $50,000 to help buy her house. This mortgage was the only borrowing that Joanne did, so her capital account surplus was $50,000. With a current account deficit of $52,000 and a capital account surplus of $50,000, Joanne is still $2,000 short. She got that $2,000 from her own bank account. Her cash holdings decreased by $2,000.

Joanne's income from her work is analogous to a country's income from its exports. Her income from her investments is analogous to a country's interest income from foreigners. Her purchases of goods and services, including her purchase of a house, are analogous to a country's imports. Joanne's mortgage—borrowing from someone else—is analogous to a country's borrowing from the rest of the world. The change in her own bank account is analogous to the change in the country's official reserves.

Borrowers and Lenders, Debtors and Creditors

A country that is borrowing more from the rest of the world than it is lending to it is called a **net borrower**. Similarly, a **net lender** is a country that is lending more to the rest of the world than it is borrowing from it. A net borrower might be going deeper into debt or might simply be reducing its net assets held in the rest of the world. The total stock of foreign investment determines whether a country is a debtor or creditor. A **debtor nation** is a country that during its entire history has borrowed more from the rest of the world than it has lent to it. It has a stock of outstanding debt to the rest of the world that exceeds the stock of its own claims on the rest of the world. The United States became a debtor nation in 1989. A **creditor nation** is a country that has invested more in the rest of the world than other countries have invested in it. The largest creditor nation today is Japan.

At the heart of the distinction between a net borrower/net lender and a debtor/creditor nation is the distinction between flows and stocks, which you have encountered many times in your study of macroeconomics. Borrowing and lending are flows—amounts borrowed or lent per unit of time. Debts are stocks—amounts owed at a point in time. The flow of borrowing and lending changes the stock of debt. But the outstanding stock of debt depends mainly on past flows of borrowing and lending, not on the current period's flows. The current period's flows determine the *change* in the stock of debt outstanding.

The United States is a newcomer to the ranks of net borrower nations. Throughout the 1960s and most of the 1970s the United States had a surplus on its current account and a deficit on its capital account. Thus the country was a net lender to the rest of the world. It was not until 1983 that the United States became a significant net borrower from the rest of the world. Between 1983 and 1987, its borrowing increased each year. It then decreased and was briefly zero in 1991, after when it started to increase again. The average foreign borrowing by the United States between 1983 and 1994 was $106 billion a year.

Most countries are net borrowers like the United States. But a small number of countries, including Japan and oil-rich Saudi Arabia and Venezuela, are huge net lenders.

The United States is not only a net borrower nation. It is also a debtor nation. That is, its total stock of borrowing from the rest of the world exceeds its lending to the rest of the world. The largest debtor nations are the capital-hungry developing countries. The international debt of these countries grew from less than a third to more than a half of their gross domestic product during the 1980s and created what was called the "Third World debt crisis."

Should the United States be concerned about the switch from being a net lender to being a net borrower? The answer to this question depends mainly on what the net borrower is doing with the borrowed money. If borrowing is financing investment that in turn is generating economic growth and higher income, borrowing is not a problem. If the borrowed money is being used to finance consumption, then higher interest payments are being incurred, and as a consequence, consumption will eventually have to be reduced. In this case the more the borrowing and the longer it goes on, the greater is the reduction in consumption that will eventually be necessary. We'll see below whether the United States is borrowing for investment or for consumption.

Current Account Balance

What determines a country's current account balance and net foreign borrowing? You've seen that exports and imports are the main items in the current account. Exports minus imports are called net exports (NX). We can define the current account balance (CAB) as:

$$CAB = NX + \text{Net interest income} + \text{Net transfers}.$$

Fluctuations in net exports are the main source of fluctuations in the current account balance. The other two items are small and have trends but do not fluctuate much. So we can study the current account balance by looking at what determines net exports.

We need to begin by recalling and using some of the things that we learned about the national income accounts in Chapter 23. Table 36.2 will refresh your memory and summarize the necessary calculations for you. Part (a) lists the national income variables that are needed, with their symbols.

Part (b) tells us about the injections into and the leakages from the circular flow of income and expenditure. Equation (1) reminds us that the injections are investment (I), government purchases of goods and services (G), and exports (EX). Equation (2) reminds us that the leakages are saving (S), net taxes (NT), and imports (IM). In Chapter 23, we learned that injections equal leakages. Subtracting equation (2) from equation (1) in the table gives equation (3). We write the equality of leakages and injections this way to highlight the sector surpluses and deficits.

The **government sector surplus or deficit** is equal to net taxes minus government purchases of goods and services. If that number is positive, the government sector has a surplus; if the number is negative, it has a deficit. The government sector deficit is different from the federal government deficit: It is the sum of the deficits of the federal, state, and local governments.

The **private sector surplus or deficit** is the difference between saving and investment. If saving exceeds investment, the private sector has a surplus to lend to other sectors. If investment exceeds saving, the private sector has a deficit that has to be financed by borrowing from other sectors.

Part (c) calculates the values of these deficits and surpluses for the United States in 1994. As you can see, net exports were –$102 billion, a deficit of $102 billion. The government sector's revenue from net taxes was $1,041 billion and it purchased $1,174 billion worth of goods and services. The government sector deficit was $133 billion. The private sector

saved $1,069 billion and invested $1,038 billion, so it had a surplus of $31 billion.

As you can see from these calculations, the net exports deficit is equal to the sum of the government sector deficit and the private sector surplus. In the United States in 1994 the private sector had a surplus of $31 billion and the government sector had a deficit of $133 billion. The government sector deficit minus the private sector surplus equaled the net exports deficit of $102 billion.

Part (d) of Table 36.2 shows you how investment is financed. To increase investment, either private saving, the government sector surplus or borrowing from the rest of the world (net exports deficit) must increase.

The calculations that we've just performed are really nothing more than bookkeeping. We've manipulated the national income accounts and discovered that net exports equals the sum of the government sector deficit and the private sector surplus. But these calculations do reveal a fundamental fact: Our net exports and our current account deficit can change only if either our government sector deficit changes or our private sector surplus changes.

We've seen that our net exports are equal to the sum of the government sectors deficit and the private sector surplus. Why is the private sector surplus equal to the government's budget deficit so that net exports are zero? Does an increase in the government sector deficit necessarily bring a decrease in net exports and an increase in the current account deficit?

You can see the answer to this question by looking at Fig. 36.2. In that figure, the government sector (federal, state, and local governments) budget balance is plotted alongside the current account balance. To remove the effects of growth and inflation, each balance is measured as a percentage of nominal GDP. Between 1977 and 1989 (shaded in Fig. 36.2) the current account and the government sector deficits moved in similar ways. Before 1977 and after 1989 the two deficits moved in opposite directions. When the paths of the government sector deficit and the current account deficit diverge, their divergence is accommodated by a change in the private sector surplus.

To understand the history of the current account balance and the government sector budget balance shown in Fig. 36.2, we need to consider two extreme possible relationships among the three sector balances:

■ The Ricardian case
■ The twin deficits case

TABLE 36.2

Net Exports, Net Foreign Borrowing, and the Financing of Investment

	Symbols and equations	United States in 1994 (billions of dollars)
(a) Variables		
Investment	I	1,038
Government purchases of goods and services	G	1,174
Exports of goods and services	EX	716
Imports of goods and services	IM	818
Saving	S	1,069
Net taxes	NT	1,041
(b) Injections and leakages		
Injections	(1) $I + G + EX$	
Leakages	(2) $S + NT + IM$	
Difference between (1) and (2)	(3) $0 = (I - S) + (G - NT) + (EX - IM)$	
(c) Surpluses and deficits		
Net exports	(4) $EX - IM$	$716 - 818 = -102$
Government sector	(5) $NT - G$	$1,041 - 1,174 = -133$
Private sector	(6) $S - I$	$1,069 - 1,038 = 31$
(d) Financing investment		
Investment is financed by the sum of:		
private saving,	S	1,069
net government saving, and	$NT - G$	-133
borrowing from the rest of the world	$IM - EX$	102
That is,	(7) $I = S + (NT - G) + (IM - EX)$	$1,038 = 1,069 - 133 + 102$

Source: Economic Report of the President, 1995.

FIGURE 36.2

The Twin Deficits

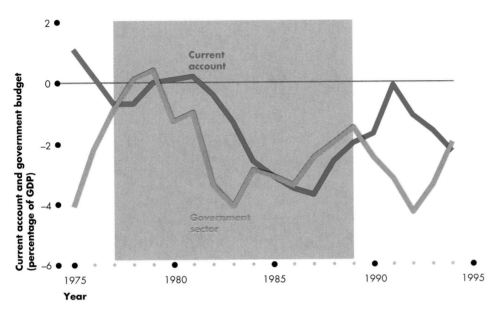

Between 1977 and 1989 (shaded) the current account deficit and the government budget deficit moved in sympathy with each other. These similar movements lead to the concept of the *twin deficits*. Before 1977 and after 1989 the two deficits moved in opposite directions. The relationship between the twin deficits is broken by fluctuations in saving minus investment.

Source: Economic Report of the President, 1995.

The Ricardian Case

Changes in the government sector deficit can also influence private sector saving and investment and so change the private sector surplus. The Ricardian case is one in which a change in the government sector deficit induces an equal offsetting change in the private sector surplus and leaves the current account balance unchanged. The name "Ricardian" is used because this case arises from the *Ricardian equivalence*, which is explained in Chapter 29 (p. 731).

Suppose the government cuts taxes and increases the deficit. People will recognize that the lower taxes and larger deficit mean that taxes must *rise* later to pay the higher interest on the growing debt. *Ricardian equivalence* is the view that people will regard future taxes as *equivalent* to the current tax cut and will not feel any better off. Because people feel no better off with the tax cut, they do not increase their consumption. Instead, they increase their saving by an amount equal to the decrease in the tax bill. The private surplus increases to exactly offset the increase in the government deficit, and the current account balance is unchanged.

The Twin Deficits Case

The tendency for the current account deficit and the government deficit to move together during the late 1970s and 1980s created the idea that there was a mechanism that made them **twin deficits**.

The twin deficits can arise when two conditions prevail: Real GDP is at potential GDP and capital is perfectly mobile among countries. In this situation, suppose the government increases its purchases and increases the government deficit.

With the economy at full employment, the increase in aggregate demand that comes from the additional government purchases increases imports and/or decreases exports, and the current account deficit increases. Saving does not change because there is no change in either disposable income or the interest rate, the two factors that determine saving. Investment does not change because there is no change in the interest rate. Foreign capital flows in to finance the increased government deficit. So the private sector surplus is unchanged, and the current account changes to offset the change in the government deficit.

This extreme case does not occur away from full employment. If the increase in government purchases increases real GDP and increases disposable income, saving increases and the private sector surplus also increases. The extreme case does not occur if capital is not completely mobile. In this case the change in government purchases increases the interest rate, investment decreases, and the private sector surplus increases. So if an increase in the government deficit increases real GDP or induces higher interest rates, it increases the private sector surplus.

The combination of these possible cases creates the variety of responses of the current account balance to changes in the government deficit.

Is U.S. Borrowing for Consumption or Investment?

You've seen that in 1994, private saving exceeded private investment by $31 billion and government purchases exceeded net taxes by $133 billion. Net exports were a negative $102 billion and this amount was borrowed from abroad. So our international borrowing (along with our private sector surplus) is being used to finance a government deficit.

Whether U.S. borrowing is for consumption or investment depends on the division of government purchases between consumption goods and capital goods. The government accounts reveal that in 1994, $121 billion was spent on structures such as improved highways and dams. This expenditure is government investment. It adds to the nation's stock of capital and increases productivity. A further $108 billion was spent on durable goods. The rest, $945 billion, was spent on nondurable goods and services. But we cannot conclude that all of this expenditure is government consumption. Much of it was on education and health care services. Are these expenditures consumption or investment? To a degree, they are consumption. But they have an investment component because they add to the stock of *human capital*. The human capital that comes from a better educated and healthier labor force increases productivity in just the same way that an improved highway increases productivity.

It is clear that public investment expenditure exceeds the government deficit. So it is equally clear that our international borrowing is not being used to finance consumption but to finance public investment in physical and human capital.

REVIEW

- When we buy goods from or invest in the rest of the world, we use foreign currency; and when foreigners buy goods from or invest in the United States, they use U.S. currency.
- We record international transactions in the balance of payments accounts—current account (exports and imports of goods and services), capital account (net foreign borrowing or lending), and official settlements account (change in holdings of a foreign currencies).
- The current account deficit is equal to the sum of the government sector deficit and the private sector surplus.
- Changes in the government sector deficit can change both the private sector surplus and the current account deficit.

Foreign Exchange and the Dollar

WHEN WE BUY FOREIGN GOODS OR INVEST IN another country, we have to obtain some of that country's currency to make the transaction. When foreigners buy U.S.-produced goods or invest in the United States, they have to obtain some U.S. dollars. We get foreign currency, and foreigners get U.S. dollars in the foreign exchange market. The **foreign exchange market** is the market in which the currency of one country is exchanged for the currency of another. The foreign exchange market is not a place like a downtown flea market or produce market. The market is made up of thousands of people—importers and exporters, banks, and specialists in the buying and selling of foreign exchange, called foreign exchange brokers. The foreign exchange market opens on Monday morning in Hong Kong, which is still Sunday evening in New York. As the day advances, markets open in Singapore, Tokyo, Bahrain, Frankfurt, London, New York, Chicago, and San Francisco. As the West Coast markets close, Hong Kong is only an hour away from opening for the next day of business. As Fig. 36.3 shows, the sun barely sets on the foreign exchange market and on any given day, billions of dollars change hands.

FIGURE 36.3

The Global Foreign Exchange Market

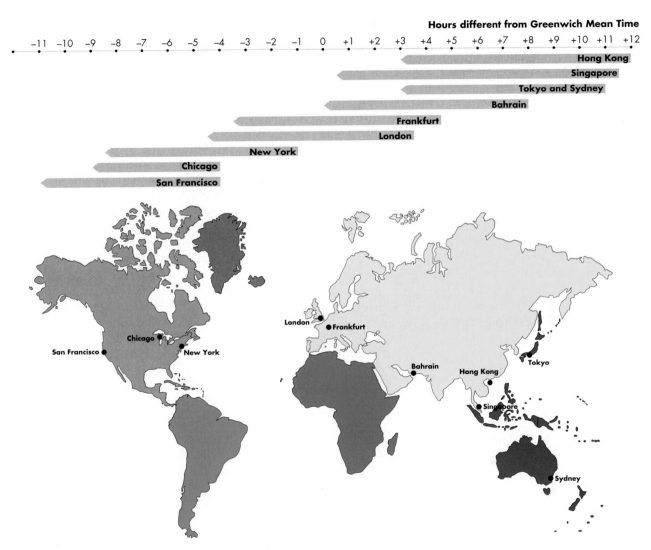

The foreign exchange market barely closes. The day begins in Hong Kong, and as the globe spins, markets open up in Singapore, Tokyo, Sydney, Bahrain, Frankfurt, London, New York, Chicago, and San Francisco. By the time the West Coast markets close, Hong Kong is almost ready to begin another day.

Source: Based on a similar map in Steven Husted and Michael Melvin, *International Economics,* Harper & Row Publishers Inc., 1989, and data from *Euromoney,* April 1979, p. 14.

The price at which one currency exchanges for another is called a **foreign exchange rate**. For example, in June 1995, one U.S. dollar bought 84 Japanese yen. The exchange rate was 84 yen per dollar. We've just expressed the exchange rate between the yen and the dollar as a number of yen per dollar. Equivalently, we could express the exchange rate in terms of dollars per yen. That exchange rate in June 1995 was $0.012 per yen, or 1.2 cents per yen. (A yen was worth a bit more than a penny.)

The actions of the foreign exchange brokers make the foreign exchange market highly efficient. Exchange rates are almost identical around the world. If U.S. dollars were cheap in London and expensive in Tokyo, people would buy in London and sell in Tokyo. The London price would rise and the Tokyo price would fall until the prices were equal.

Foreign Exchange Systems

Foreign exchange rates are of critical importance for millions of people. They affect the costs of our foreign vacations and our imported cars. They affect the number of dollars that we end up getting for the oranges and beef that we sell to Japan and the cars and trucks that we sell to Mexico. Because of its importance, governments pay a great deal of attention to what is happening in foreign exchange markets and, more than that, take actions that are designed to achieve what they regard as desirable movements in exchange rates. In deciding how to act in the foreign exchange market, a government must choose among three alternative strategies that give rise to three foreign exchange systems. They are:

1. Fixed exchange rate
2. Flexible exchange rate
3. Managed exchange rate

A **fixed exchange rate** is a system in which the value of a country's currency is pegged by the country's central bank. If the United States adopted a fixed exchange rate, the government would declare the U.S. dollar to be worth a certain number of units of some other currency and would instruct the Fed to take actions on the foreign exchange market to maintain the dollar's declared value. We'll study what those foreign exchange market actions would be below.

A **flexible exchange rate** is a system in which the value of a country's currency is determined by market forces in the absence of central bank intervention. If the United States adopted a flexible exchange rate, the Fed would take no actions on the foreign exchange market.

A **managed exchange rate** is a system in which the value of a country's currency is not fixed at some preannounced level but is influenced by central bank intervention in the foreign exchange market. Most currencies, including the U.S. dollar, have been on a managed exchange rate system in recent years.

Before we learn how the foreign exchange market operates in these three systems, let's look at the recent history of the foreign exchange market.

Recent Exchange Rate History

At the end of World War II the major countries of the world set up the International Monetary Fund (IMF). The **International Monetary Fund** is an international organization that monitors balance of payments and exchange rate activities. The IMF is located in Washington, D.C. It was created during World War II. In July 1944, at Bretton Woods, New Hampshire, 44 countries signed the Articles of Agreement of the IMF. The agreement established a worldwide system of fixed exchange rates between currencies. The anchor for this fixed exchange rate system was gold. One ounce of gold was defined to be worth 35 U.S. dollars. All other currencies were pegged to the U.S. dollar at a fixed exchange rate. For example, the Japanese yen was set at 360 yen per dollar; the British pound was set to be worth $4.80. Although the fixed exchange rate system established in 1944 served the world well during the 1950s and early 1960s, it came under increasing strain in the late 1960s, and by 1971 the system had almost collapsed. In the period since 1971 the world has operated with different nations adopting a variety of flexible and managed exchange rate arrangements as well as fixed exchange rates. Some currencies have increased in value, and others have declined. The U.S. dollar is among the currencies that have declined. The Japanese yen is the currency that has had the most spectacular increase in value.

Figure 36.4 shows what happened to the exchange rate of the U.S. dollar between 1975 and 1995. The orange line shows the value of the dollar against the Japanese yen. The value of the dollar has fallen against the yen—the dollar has depreciated. **Currency depreciation** is the fall in the value of one currency in terms of another currency. For example, in 1975 the dollar was worth 297 yen, and in 1995 it was worth 84 yen. So the dollar has depreciated by 213 yen or almost 72 percent of its 1975 value.

Although the dollar has depreciated in terms of the Japanese yen, it has not depreciated, on the average, in terms of all other currencies. To study the average value of the U.S. dollar against other currencies we use the trade-weighted index. The **trade-weighted index** is the value of a basket of currencies

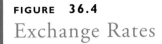

FIGURE 36.4

Exchange Rates

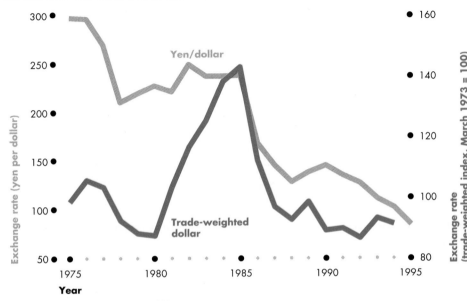

The exchange rate is the price at which two currencies can be traded. The yen-dollar exchange rate, expressed as yen per dollar, shows that the dollar has fallen in value—depreciated—against the yen. An index of the value of the U.S. dollar against all currencies shows that the U.S. dollar depreciated between 1976 and 1980, appreciated through 1985, depreciated sharply through 1988, and then fluctuated around a slightly falling trend during the 1990s.

Source: Economic Report of the President, 1995.

in which the weight placed on each currency is related to its importance in U.S. international trade. Table 36.3 gives an example of the calculation of the trade-weighted index. In this example we suppose that the United States trades with only three countries: Canada, Japan, and Great Britain. Fifty percent of the trade is with Canada, 30 percent with Japan, and 20 percent with Great Britain. In year 1, the U.S. dollar is worth 1.25 Canadian dollars, 100 Japanese yen, and 0.50 British pounds. Imagine putting these three currencies into a "basket" worth 100 U.S. dollars, where 50 percent of the value of the basket is in Canadian dollars, 30 percent is in Japanese yen, and 20 percent is in British pounds. In year 1, the index number for the basket is 100.

Suppose that in year 2, the exchange rates change as shown in the table. The U.S. dollar remains constant against the Canadian dollar, goes down in value against the Japanese yen, so one U.S. dollar buys only 90 Japanese yen, and goes up in value against the British pound, so one U.S. dollar buys 0.55 British pound. What is the change in the value of the basket? The percentage changes in the value of the U.S. dollar against each currency are

calculated in the table. The dollar goes down against the Japanese yen by 10 percent and up against the British pound by 10 percent. Applying the trade weights to these percentage changes, we can calculate the weighted average change in the value of the U.S. dollar. Because the weight on the Japanese yen is 0.3 and that on the British pound is 0.2, the yen is more important than the pound. That is, a larger fraction of the basket's value consists of yen than of pounds. The weighted average value of the basket falls by 1 percent. The trade-weighted index declines by 1 percent and is 99. In this example the U.S. dollar has depreciated, on the average, against the other three currencies.

The calculation that we have just worked through used hypothetical numbers. Figure 36.4 shows how the U.S. dollar has actually fluctuated against other currencies on the average in the period 1975 to 1994. The trade-weighted dollar appreciated in 1976 but then depreciated through 1980. Between 1980 and 1985 it appreciated strongly; then, through 1988 it depreciated almost equally strongly. After 1988, the trade-weighted dollar fluctuated around a slightly downward path.

TABLE 36.3

Trade-Weighted Index Calculation

Currency	Trade weight	Exchange rate (Units of foreign currency per U.S. dollar)		Percentage change	
		Year 1	Year 2	Unweighted	Weighted
Canadian dollar	0.5	1.25	1.25	0	0
Japanese yen	0.3	100	90	−10	−3
British pound	0.2	0.50	0.55	+10	+2
Total	1.0				−1

Trade-weighted index: Year 1 = 100

Year 2 = 99

You can see that the view we get about the exchange rate of the dollar depends a great deal on which measure of the exchange rate we use. Has the dollar increased or decreased in value since 1990? The dollar has fallen in value against the yen (and against the D-mark). But against a trade-weighted basket of currencies, the dollar has increased in value.

REVIEW

■ There are three possible foreign exchange market systems: fixed, flexible, and managed.

■ Between the end of World War II and 1971 the world economy had a fixed exchange rate system. Since 1971 it has had a mixture of flexible and managed systems.

■ The U.S. dollar has fluctuated against the currencies of its trading partners and has depreciated against the yen.

Why has the U.S. dollar depreciated so steeply against the yen? Why did it climb in value against the currencies of most countries during the early 1980s and then collapse after 1985? To answer questions like these, we need to know what determines the exchange rate.

Exchange Rate Determination

THE EXCHANGE RATE IS THE PRICE OF THE DOLLAR in terms of other currencies. Just like any other price, the exchange rate is determined by demand and supply—by the demand for and supply of dollars. But what exactly do we mean by the demand for and supply of dollars? And what is the quantity of dollars?

The quantity of dollars demanded in the foreign exchange market is the amount that people would buy on a given day at a particular exchange rate (price) if they found a willing seller. The quantity of dollars supplied in the foreign exchange market is the amount that people would sell on a given day at a particular exchange rate (price) if they found a willing buyer. What determines the quantities of dollars demanded and supplied?

To answer this question, we need to think about the alternative to demanding and supplying dollars. For a demander of dollars the alternative is to hang onto foreign currency. For a supplier of dollars the alternative is to hang onto dollars. The decision to buy dollars is also the decision to hold dollars; The decision to sell dollars is also the decision to hold foreign currency.

To understand the forces that determine demand and supply in the foreign exchange market, we need to study people's decisions about the quantities of dollars and foreign currencies to hold. Let's see what we mean by the quantity of dollars held.

The Quantity of U.S. Dollars

The **quantity of U.S. dollar assets** (which we'll call the **quantity of dollars**) is the *net stock* of financial assets denominated in U.S. dollars held outside the Fed and the government. Three things about the quantity of dollars need to be emphasized.

First, the quantity of dollars is a *stock*, not a *flow*. People make decisions about the quantity of dollars to hold (a stock) and about the quantities to buy and sell (flows) in the foreign exchange market. But it is the decision about how many dollars to hold (the stock) that determines whether people plan to buy or sell dollars (the flow).

Second, the quantity of dollars is a stock *denominated in U.S. dollars.* The denomination of an asset defines the units in which a debt must be repaid. It is possible to make a loan using any currency of denomination. The U.S. government could borrow Japanese yen. If it did borrow in yen, it would issue a bond denominated in yen. Such a bond would be a promise to pay an agreed number of yen on an agreed date. It would not be a dollar debt and, even though issued by the U.S. government, would not be part of the supply of dollars. Many governments actually do issue bonds in currencies other than their own. The Canadian government, for example, issues bonds denominated in U.S. dollars.

Third, the supply of dollars is a *net* supply—the quantity of assets *minus* the quantity of liabilities. This fact means that the quantity of dollars supplied does not include dollar assets created by private households, firms, financial institutions, or foreigners. The reason is that when a private debt is created, there is both an asset (for the holder) and a liability (for the issuer), so the *net* financial asset is zero. For example, if Pat loans Matt $1,000, then Pat's asset of $1,000 cancels Matt's $1,000 liability. The quantity of dollars includes only the dollar liabilities of the federal government *plus* those of the Fed. This quantity is equal to the government debt held outside the Fed plus the dollar liabilities of the Fed—the monetary base. That is,

$$\text{Quantity of dollars} = \text{Government debt held outside the Fed} + \text{Monetary base}.$$

We've now seen what dollar assets are. Let's now study the demand for and the supply of these assets and also see what makes the demand and supply change.

The Demand for Dollars

The law of demand applies to dollars just as it does to anything else that people value. The quantity of dollars demanded increases when the price of a dollar in terms of foreign currency falls and decreases when the price of a dollar in terms of foreign currency rises. Suppose, for example, that the dollar is trading at 85 yen per dollar. If the price of a dollar rises to 90 yen per dollar, with everything else the same, the quantity of dollars demanded decreases; if the price of a dollar falls to 80 yen per dollar, with everything else the same, the quantity of dollars demanded increases. There are two separate reasons why the law of demand applies to dollars:

- Transactions effect
- Expected capital gains effect

Transactions Effect A transactions cost is incurred whenever a foreign currency is converted into dollars. This transactions cost can be avoided by holding an inventory of dollars. With such an inventory it is not necessary to convert foreign currency into dollars on the foreign exchange market each time a dollar payment must be made. The larger the value of dollar payments, the larger is the inventory of dollars that people hold. But the value of dollar payments depends on the exchange rate. The lower the value of the dollar, with everything else the same, the cheaper are U.S.-produced goods and services. Both U.S. residents and foreigners will plan to buy more U.S.-produced goods and services and less foreign-produced goods and services. The demand for U.S. exports increases and U.S. demand for imports decreases. Foreigners demand more dollars to pay for U.S. exports, and we demand fewer units of foreign currency and more dollars as we switch from importing foreign goods and services to buying U.S.-produced goods and services. Hence the lower the value of the dollar, the larger is the value of dollar payments and the greater is the quantity of dollars demanded.

FIGURE 36.5

The Demand for Dollar Assets

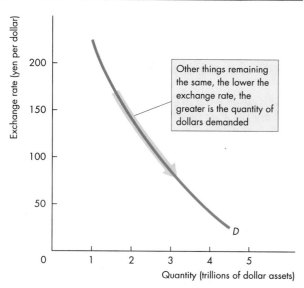

Other things remaining the same, the lower the exchange rate, the greater is the quantity of dollars demanded

The quantity of dollar assets that people demand, other things remaining the same, depends on the exchange rate. The lower the exchange rate (the smaller the number of yen per dollar), the larger is the quantity of dollar assets demanded. The increased quantity demanded arises from an increase in the volume of dollar trade (the Japanese buy more U.S.-produced goods and services, and we buy fewer Japanese-produced goods and services) and an increase in the expected appreciation (or decrease in the expected depreciation) of dollar assets.

Expected Capital Gains Effect Suppose you think the dollar will be worth 85 yen by the end of the month. If the dollar is trading today at 90 yen per dollar and if your prediction about the future value of the dollar is correct, you can make yourself a quick capital gain. Suppose you sell $1,000 and buy yen today. You get 90,000 yen for your $1,000. If the exchange rate at the end of the month is 85 yen per dollar, as you predict it will be, you can sell your 90,000 yen for $1,059 (90,000 divided by 85 approximately equals 1,059) You've made a profit of $59 on these transactions. If you are pretty confident about your prediction, you will not hold dollars during the current month. You will hold yen instead.

If the dollar is trading today not at 90 but at 80 yen per dollar and if your prediction about the future value of the dollar—85 yen—is correct, you will incur a capital loss if you undertake the transactions we've just looked at. If you sell $1,000 and buy yen today, you now get only 80,000 yen for your $1,000. If the exchange rate at the end of the month is 85 yen per dollar, as you predict it will be, you will sell your 80,000 yen for $941 (80,000 divided by 85 approximately equals 941). You've incurred a loss of $59 on these transactions. If you are confident about your prediction, you will hang onto your dollars during the current month. You will *not* hold yen.

For a given expected future value of the dollar, the lower the current value of the dollar, the greater is the expected capital gain from holding dollars and the greater is the quantity of dollars demanded.

Figure 36.5 shows the relationship between the exchange rate (the price of the U.S. dollar in terms of yen) and the quantity of dollar assets demanded—the demand curve for dollar assets. When the exchange rate changes, other things remaining the same, there is a movement along the demand curve.

Changes in the Demand for Dollars

Any other influence on the quantity of dollar assets that people want to hold results in a shift in the demand curve. Demand either increases or decreases. These other influences are:

■ U.S. GDP
■ The expected future value of the dollar
■ The U.S. interest rate differential

U.S. GDP You've seen that transactions costs can be avoided by holding an inventory of dollars and that the larger the value of dollar payments, the larger is the inventory of dollars that people hold. A major influence on the value of dollar payments is U.S. GDP. An increase in U.S. GDP brings an increase in the value of dollar payments, which increases the demand for dollars. When the demand for dollars increases, the demand curve for dollars shifts rightward.

The Expected Future Value of the Dollar You've seen that for a given expected future value of the dollar, the lower the current value of the dollar, the greater is the expected capital gain from holding dollars and the greater is the quantity of dollars demanded. But what happens if the expected future value of the dollar changes while the current exchange rate is unchanged?

You can answer this question by returning to the capital gain example. Suppose the dollar is trading at 85 yen per dollar and you think that the value of the dollar is going to fall to 80 yen per dollar by the end of the month. You are confident in your view, and you buy 85,000 yen with your $1,000. At the end of the month, the dollar falls to 80 yen as you predicted it would. You now sell your 85,000 yen and buy dollars. At 80 yen per dollar, you collect $1062.50. You have made a capital gain. In this circumstance you hold yen rather than dollars during this month. But suppose the dollar is trading at 85 yen per dollar and you think that the value of the dollar is going to rise to 90 yen per dollar by the end of the month. If in this situation you make the transactions we've just considered, you will incur a capital loss. Your $1,000 still buys 85,000, but when you sell these yen at the end of the month for 90 yen per dollar, you collect only $944.44. In this circumstance you would hold dollars rather than yen during this month.

The lower the expected future value of the dollar, other things remaining the same, the smaller is the demand for dollars (and the greater is the demand for other currencies). Similarly, the higher the expected future value of the dollar, other things remaining the same, the greater is the demand for dollars (and the smaller is the demand for other currencies).

The U.S. Interest Rate Differential People and businesses buy financial assets to make a return that has two components: a capital gain and an interest rate. You've just seen how the expected capital gain is determined by the current exchange rate and the expected future exchange rate. Let's now look at the interest component of the return on financial assets.

People can hold dollar assets or foreign currency assets. To choose the currency in which to hold their wealth, people look at the interest rate on dollar assets and compare it with the interest rate on a foreign currency asset. The interest rate on a dollar asset minus the interest rate on a foreign currency asset is called the **U.S. interest rate differential**. If the interest rate on U.S. dollar assets increases and the interest rate on a foreign currency asset remains constant, the U.S. interest rate differential increases. The larger the U.S. interest rate differential, the greater is the demand for dollar assets.

TABLE 36.4
The Demand for Dollar Assets

THE LAW OF DEMAND

The quantity of dollar assets demanded

Increases if:	*Decreases if:*
■ The foreign exchange rate falls	■ The foreign exchange rate rises

CHANGES IN DEMAND

The demand for dollar assets

Increases if:	*Decreases if:*
■ U.S. GDP increases	■ U.S. GDP decreases
■ The expected future value of the dollar rises	■ The expected future value of the dollar falls
■ The U.S. interest rate differential increases	■ The U.S. interest rate differential decreases

Table 36.4 summarizes the above discussion of the influences on the demand for dollars.

The Supply of Dollars

Remember that the *flows* of dollars and other currencies through the foreign exchange market are determined by decisions about *stocks*. A decrease in the demand for dollars brings a flow of dollars onto the foreign exchange market. But this flow of dollars onto the market is *not* what we mean when we talk about the *supply of dollars*. The supply of dollars is the quantity of dollar assets available for people to hold.

The quantity of dollars supplied is determined by the actions of the government and the Fed. We've seen that the quantity of dollars is equal to government debt plus the monetary base. Of these two items the monetary base is by far the smaller. But it plays a crucial role in determining the supply of dollars. The behavior of the monetary base depends crucially on the foreign exchange rate system.

In a fixed exchange rate system the supply curve of dollar assets is horizontal at the chosen exchange rate. The Fed stands ready to supply whatever quantity of dollar assets is demanded in exchange for foreign currency assets at the fixed exchange rate. In a managed exchange rate system the Fed wants to smooth fluctuations in the exchange rate, and the supply curve of dollar assets is upward-sloping. The higher the exchange rate, the larger is the quantity of dollar assets supplied by the Fed in exchange for foreign currency assets. In a flexible exchange rate system a fixed quantity of dollar assets is supplied, regardless of the exchange rate. As a consequence, in a flexible exchange rate system the supply curve of dollar assets is vertical.

Changes in the Supply of Dollars

There are two ways in which the quantity of dollars supplied can change:

1. The federal government has a budget deficit or surplus
2. The Fed buys or sells foreign currency assets

The Federal government influences the quantity of dollar assets supplied through its budget. If the federal government has a budget deficit, it borrows by issuing bonds, which are denominated in U.S. dollars. The sale of new federal government bonds to finance a deficit increases the supply of dollar assets. Similarly, if the federal government has a budget surplus, it buys back previously issued bonds and the supply of dollar assets decreases.

The Fed influences the quantity of dollars supplied through its transactions in the foreign exchange market. If the Fed buys foreign currency, it increases the quantity of dollar assets supplied. If the Fed sells foreign currency, it decreases the quantity of dollar assets supplied.

An open-market operation in which the Fed buys or sells government securities changes the monetary base but does not change the quantity of dollar assets supplied. It changes the composition of dollar assets supplied. For example, if the Fed buys government bonds, the quantity of dollar bonds decreases and the monetary base increases. But the increase in the monetary base equals the decrease in dollar bonds, so the total quantity of dollar assets remains unchanged.

Table 36.5 summarizes the above discussion of the influences on the supply of dollar assets.

TABLE 36.5

The Supply of Dollar Assets

SUPPLY

Fixed exchange rate system
The supply curve of dollar assets is horizontal at the fixed exchange rate.

Managed exchange rate
To smooth fluctuations in the exchange rate, the quantity of dollar assets supplied by the Fed increases if the foreign currency price of the dollar rises and decreases if the foreign currency price of the dollar falls. The supply curve of dollar assets is upward-sloping.

Flexible exchange rate
The supply curve of dollar assets is vertical.

CHANGES IN SUPPLY

The supply of dollar assets

Increases if:	*Decreases if:*
■ The U.S. government has a deficit	■ The U.S. government has a surplus
■ The Fed buys foreign currency	■ The Fed sells foreign currency

The Market for Dollars

Let's now bring the demand and supply sides of the market for dollar assets together and determine the exchange rate. Figure 36.6 shows how the exchange rate is determined in the three systems: fixed, flexible, and managed exchange rates. The demand side of the market is the same in the three cases, but the supply side differs. First, let's look at a fixed exchange rate system such as that from the end of World War II to 1971.

Fixed Exchange Rate   Figure 36.6(a) illustrates this case. The supply curve of dollars, S, is horizontal at the fixed exchange rate of 100 yen per dollar. If the demand curve is D_0, the quantity of dollar assets is Q_0. An increase in demand to D_1 results in an increase in the quantity of dollar assets from Q_0 to Q_1 but no change in the exchange rate.

FIGURE 36.6

Three Exchange Rate Systems

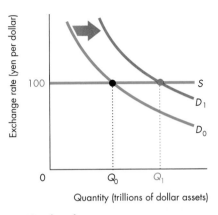

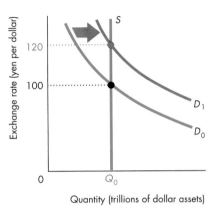

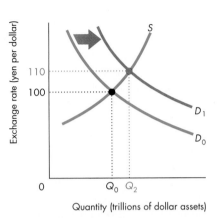

(a) Fixed exchange rate   **(b) Flexible exchange rate**   **(c) Managed exchange rate**

In a fixed exchange rate system (part a) the Fed stands ready to supply dollar assets or to take dollar assets off the market (supplying foreign currency in exchange) at a fixed exchange rate. The supply curve for dollar assets, S, is horizontal. Fluctuations in demand lead to fluctuations in the quantity of dollar assets outstanding and to fluctuations in the nation's official holdings of foreign exchange. If demand increases from D_0 to D_1, the quantity of dollar assets increases from Q_0 to Q_1 and the exchange rate does not change. In a flexible exchange rate system (part b) the quantity of dollar assets is fixed, so the supply curve is vertical. An increase in the demand for dol-

lar assets from D_0 to D_1 results only in an increase in the value of the dollar—the exchange rate rises from 100 to 120 yen per dollar. The quantity of dollar assets remains constant at Q_0. In a managed exchange rate system (part c) the Fed has an upward-sloping supply curve of dollar assets. If demand increases from D_0 to D_1, the dollar appreciates but the quantity of dollar assets supplied also increases—from Q_0 to Q_2. The increase in the quantity of dollar assets supplied moderates the rise in the value of the dollar but does not completely prevent it as in the case of fixed exchange rates.

Flexible Exchange Rate   Next look at Fig. 36.6(b), which shows what happens in a flexible exchange rate system. In this case the quantity of dollar assets supplied is fixed at Q_0, so the supply curve of dollar assets is vertical. If the demand curve for dollars is D_0, the exchange rate is 100 yen per dollar. If the demand for dollars increases from D_0 to D_1, the exchange rate increases to 120 yen per dollar.

Managed Exchange Rate   Finally, consider a managed exchange rate system, which appears in Fig. 36.6(c). Here, the supply curve is upward-sloping. When the demand curve is D_0, the exchange rate is 100 yen per dollar. If demand increases to D_1, the exchange rate rises but only to 110 yen per dollar. Compared with the flexible exchange rate case, the same increase in demand results in a smaller increase

in the exchange rate when it is managed. The reason is that the quantity supplied increases in the managed exchange rate case but not in the flexible exchange rate case.

Exchange Rate System and Official Settlements Balance   The behavior of the official settlements balance depends on the foreign exchange rate system. The official settlements account of the balance of payments records the change in the country's official holdings (by the government and the Fed) of foreign currency. In a fixed exchange rate system (as shown in Fig. 36.6a), every time the demand for dollar assets changes, the Fed must change the quantity of dollar assets supplied to match it. When the Fed has to increase the quantity of dollar assets supplied, it does so by offering dollar assets in exchange for foreign currency assets. In this case the official holdings of foreign exchange increase and the official settlements balance is positive. If the demand for dollar assets decreases, the Fed must decrease the quantity of dollar assets supplied. To decrease the quantity of dollars supplied, the Fed buys dollars and pays for them with its foreign exchange reserves. In this case official U.S. foreign exchange reserves decrease and the official settlements balance is negative. Thus with a fixed exchange rate, fluctuations in the demand for dollar assets result in fluctuations in official reserves and an official settlements balance that is not zero.

In a flexible exchange rate system there is no Fed intervention in the foreign exchange market. Regardless of what happens to the demand for dollars, no action is taken to change the quantity of dollars supplied. Therefore there is no change in the country's official reserves. In this case the official settlements balance is zero.

With a managed exchange rate, official holdings of foreign exchange are adjusted to meet fluctuations in demand but in a less extreme manner than in a fixed exchange rate system. As a consequence, fluctuations in the official settlements balance are smaller in a managed exchange rate system than in a fixed exchange rate system.

Why Is the Exchange Rate So Volatile?

We've seen times, especially recently, when the dollar-yen exchange rate has moved dramatically. On most of these occasions the dollar has depreciated spectacularly, but on some occasions it has appreciated strongly.

The main reason why the exchange rate fluctuates so remarkably is that fluctuations in supply and demand are not always independent of each other. Sometimes a change in supply will trigger a change in demand that reinforces the effect of the change in supply. Let's see how these effects work by looking at two episodes: one in which the dollar appreciated and one in which it depreciated.

An Appreciating Dollar: 1981–1982

Between 1981 and 1982 the dollar appreciated against the yen, rising from 220 to 250 yen per dollar. Figure 36.7(a) explains why this happened. In 1981 the demand and supply curves were those labeled D_{81} and S_{81}. The foreign exchange value of the dollar was 220 yen—where the supply and demand curves intersect. The period between 1981 and 1982 was one of severe recession in the United States. This recession was brought about in part by the Fed pur-

suing a very restrictive monetary policy. The Fed permitted interest rates to rise sharply, cutting back on the supply of dollar assets. The direct effect was a shift in the supply curve from S_{81} to S_{82}—a decrease in the supply of dollars. But higher U.S. interest rates induced an increase in demand for dollars to take advantage of the higher interest rates. As a result, the demand curve shifted from D_{81} to D_{82}. These two shifts reinforced each other, increasing the exchange rate to 250 yen per dollar.

A Depreciating Dollar: 1995

There was a spectacular depreciation of the dollar in terms of yen from 100 yen per dollar in December 1994 to 84 yen per dollar in mid-1995. This fall came about in the following way. First, in December 1994 the demand and supply curves were those labeled D_{94} and S_{94} in Fig. 36.7(b). The yen price of the dollar—the price at which these two curves intersect—was 100 yen per dollar. Through 1994 the U.S. economy expanded quickly. But the federal budget deficit remained large. With a large federal budget deficit the supply of dollar assets increased and the supply of dollars curve shifted rightward from S_{94} to S_{95}. With no other influences on the exchange rate, the dollar would have depreciated somewhat. In Fig. 36.7(b) the fall in the exchange rate would have been to 96 yen per dollar (just an example of the fall that might have occurred). But as the exchange rate began to fall, further falls became widely expected. Because the expected future value of the dollar fell, the demand for dollar assets decreased from D_{94} to D_{95}. The result of this combined increase in supply and decrease in demand was a dramatic fall in the value of the dollar to 84 yen in mid-1995.

Forecasting the Future Value of the Dollar

Can we use the theory of the exchange rate to get rich by forecasting future changes in the exchange rate so we can buy at a low price and sell at a high one? The answer, unfortunately, is no. The reason is that if some information becomes available that tells us that the exchange rate is going to rise, a large volume of buying takes place. So the exchange rate rises immediately to reflect the new information. Similarly, if some new information tells us that the exchange rate is going to fall, a large volume of selling makes the exchange rate fall immediately. The foreign exchange rate always reflects the currently available information about its likely future value and no model exists for reliably forecasting *future* exchange rate changes.

FIGURE 36.7
Why the Exchange Rate Is So Volatile

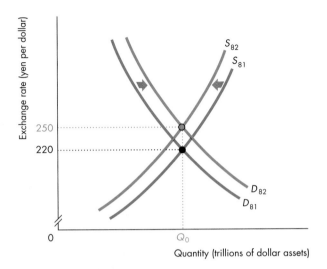

(a) 1981 to 1982

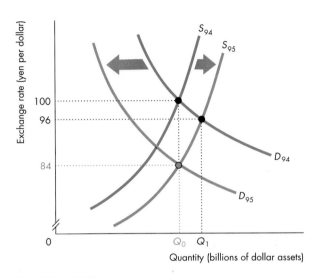

(b) 1994 to 1995

The exchange rate is volatile because shifts in the demand and supply curves for dollar assets are not independent of each other. Between 1981 and 1982 (part a) the dollar appreciated from 220 to 250 yen per dollar. This appreciation arose because the supply curve of dollar assets shifted leftward and higher interest rates induced an increase in demand for dollar assets, shifting the demand curve rightward. The result was a large increase in the foreign exchange value of the dollar.

Between December 1994 and mid-1995 (in part b) the quantity of dollar assets increased and the supply curve of dollars shifted rightward. The exchange rate fell—for example, to 96 yen. As the dollar fell in value, further falls were expected, so the demand for dollars decreased and the demand curve shifted leftward. The result was a steep fall in the exchange rate, from 100 yen in December 1994 to 84 yen per dollar in mid-1995.

R E V I E W

- The exchange rate is determined by the demand for and supply of dollars.

- In a fixed exchange rate system a change in the demand for dollars is matched by a change in the quantity of dollars supplied by the Fed, and the exchange rate does not change.

- In a flexible exchange rate system, fluctuations in the exchange rate can be large because the quantity of dollar assets remains constant as the demand for dollars fluctuates.

- In a managed exchange rate system the Fed tries to smooth fluctuations in the exchange rate by

changing the quantity of dollars supplied when the demand for dollars changes but by less than in a fixed exchange rate system.

◆ You've now discovered what determines a country's current account balance and the value of its currency. You've seen that the main influences on current account balance are the government budget deficit and private saving and investment. You've also seen that a major influence on the exchange rate is the quantity of dollar assets that the government and the Fed permit to be created.

In the final chapter we're going to look at some further global economic issues by examining the problems faced by newly emerging market economies in Asia and Central Europe.

Foreign Exchange Markets in Action

THE ECONOMIST, MARCH 11, 1995

Dial C for Chaos

In the end, on March 8th, he finally said it. The dollar's weakness, confessed Alan Greenspan in testimony on Capitol Hill, was "unwelcome and troublesome." But the confession from the Fed's chairman came after many days during which the United States had appeared as cool as a cucumber about the panic in the world's currency markets, even though the dollar had fallen to new post-1945 lows against both the yen and the D-mark. ...

It is easy to find explanations for the tumble. The dollar has been unsettled by America's contribution to a $50 billion international aid package for Mexico. Investors have switched from dollars to D-marks in the belief that American interest rates have peaked, whereas those in Germany are likely to rise this year. And the dollar has been sliding for a more fundamental reason: both American and international investors are diversifying their portfolios. On this view, the dollar, like sterling during its crises of the 1960s and 1970s, could become a victim of its reserve-currency status, as investors start to reduce disproportionate holdings.

Many explanations; and, in contrast to the dollar turbulence of the 1980s, oddly little concerted action from central banks to prop the dollar up. Indeed, both the Fed and the Clinton administration had until this week given the impression that they were far happier to tolerate a weaker dollar than to squeeze the domestic economy yet again by raising interest rates. Why?

One cause of the calmness of American policy-makers is that the dollar's overall trade-weighted exchange rate has remained pretty stable in spite of the greenback's plunge against the other big currencies. This is because Canada and Mexico account for almost 30% of America's trade, and the dollar has risen against the sickly currencies of these two trade partners. Germany and Japan, with their lusty currencies, account for less than a fifth of American trade. ...

Essence of THE STORY

■ In 1995, the dollar fell to new post-1945 lows against both the yen and the Deutsche mark (D-mark) because:

(1) a U.S. contribution to an international aid package for Mexico unsettled the market;

(2) investors believed that U.S. interest rates had peaked but German rates were likely to rise, so they switched into D-marks; and

(3) investors were diversifying their portfolios and holding fewer U.S. dollar assets.

■ U.S. policy makers were calm about the dollar because its trade-weighted exchange rate had remained fairly stable.

■ Canada and Mexico account for almost 30 percent of U.S. international trade, while Germany and Japan account for less than 20 percent.

■ The U.S. dollar had risen against the Canadian dollar and the Mexican peso.

Economic

A N A L Y S I S

■ At the beginning of March 1995, when this news article was written, the dollar had fallen against the Japanese yen and the German D-mark (Fig. 1) but it had risen against the Canadian dollar and Mexican peso (Fig. 2) and had been more steady on a trade-weighted basis (Fig. 3).

■ But in the few following months, a much bigger slide set in. The dollar continued to fall against the yen and the D-mark, it began to fall against the Canadian dollar, and the trade-weighted dollar also fell. Only against the peso did the dollar keep on climbing.

■ Over a period as short as these few months, the supply of dollar assets did not increase by much. So the decrease in the value of the dollar was caused by a decrease in the demand for dollar assets.

■ As well as the three influences on the demand for dollars are identified in the news article, other factors have operated.

■ As the economies of Japan and Germany have become stronger, their assets and their currencies have become more attractive to international investors.

■ So the value of dollar financed trade has fallen, and as a result, the demand for dollars has also fallen. This too has contributed to the decrease in the demand for dollars and to the fall in the value of the dollar.

■ The U.S. dollar has risen against the peso because Mexico has created peso assets at a faster rate than the demand for those assets has grown.

■ The U.S. dollar rose against the Canadian dollar because Canada has created Canadian dollar assets at a faster pace than the demand for those assets has grown.

■ The trade-weighted dollar is influenced most by the Canadian dollar and second by the peso. It began to fall when the Canadian dollar started to rise against the U.S. dollar.

■ Canada and Mexico account for almost 30 percent of U.S. international trade, while Germany and Japan account for less than 20 percent.

■ The U.S. dollar had risen against the Canadian dollar and the Mexican peso.

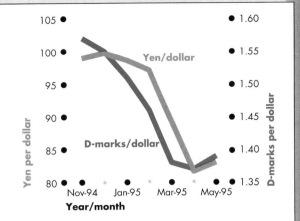

Figure 1 The dollar, yen, and D-mark

Figure 2 The dollar, Canadian dollar, and Peso

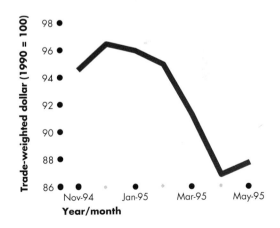

Figure 3 The trade-weighted dollar

SUMMARY

Financing International Trade

International trade, borrowing, and lending are financed by using foreign currency. A country's international transactions are recorded in its balance of payments accounts. The current account records receipts and expenditures connected with the sale and purchase of goods and services, as well as interest income received from and paid to the rest of the world and transfers to and from the rest of the world. The capital account records international borrowing and lending transactions. The official settlements account shows the increase or decrease in the country's official holdings of foreign reserves.

Historically, the United States has been a net lender to the rest of the world, but in 1989 that situation changed and the United States became a net borrower and a net debtor.

The net exports deficit is equal to the government sector deficit plus the private sector surplus. Changes in the government sector deficit change both the private sector surplus and the current account deficit, but during the late 1970s and 1980s the government sector deficit and the current deficit account were twin deficits. (pp. 918–924)

Foreign Exchange and the Dollar

Foreign currency is obtained in exchange for domestic currency in the foreign exchange market. The exchange rate can be fixed, flexible, or managed. A fixed exchange rate is one that is pegged by a central bank. A flexible exchange rate is one that adjusts freely with no central bank intervention in the foreign exchange market. A managed exchange rate is one in which the central bank smoothes out fluctuations but does not peg the rate at a fixed value. (pp. 924–928)

Exchange Rate Determination

The exchange rate is determined by the demand for and supply of dollar assets. The lower the exchange rate, the greater is the quantity of dollars demanded. A change in the exchange rate brings a movement along the demand curve for dollars. Changes in U.S. GDP, the expected future exchange rate, and the U.S. interest differential change the demand for dollar assets and shifts the demand curve.

The supply of dollar assets depends on the exchange rate system. In a fixed exchange rate system the supply curve is horizontal; in a flexible exchange rate system the supply curve is vertical; in a managed exchange rate system the supply curve is upward-sloping. The position of the supply curve depends on the government's budget and the Fed's monetary policy. The larger the budget deficit or the greater the purchases of foreign currency by the Fed, the greater is the supply of dollar assets.

Fluctuations in the exchange rate occur because of fluctuations in the demand for and supply of dollar assets and sometimes these fluctuations are large. Large fluctuations arise from interlinked changes in demand and supply. A change in supply often induces a change in demand that reinforces the effect on the exchange rate. (pp. 928–935)

KEY ELEMENTS

REVIEW QUESTIONS

1   What are the transactions that are recorded in a country's current account, capital account, and official settlements account?

2. What is the relationship between the balance on the current account, the capital account, and the official settlements account?

3. Distinguish between a country that is a net borrower and one that is a creditor. Are net borrowers always creditors? Are creditors always net borrowers?

4. What is the connection between a country's net exports and the government sector deficit and the private sector surplus?

5. Why do fluctuations in the government sector balance lead to fluctuations in the current account balance?

6. Distinguish among the three exchange rate systems: fixed, flexible, and managed.

7. Review the main influences on the quantity of dollar assets that people demand.

8. Review the influences on the supply of dollar assets.

9. How does the supply curve of dollars differ in the three exchange rate systems?

10. Why does the foreign exchange value of the dollar fluctuate so much?

PROBLEMS

1. The citizens of Silecon, whose currency is the grain, conduct the following transactions in 1995:

Item	Billions of grains
Imports of goods and services	350
Exports of goods and services	500
Borrowing from the rest of the world	60
Lending to the rest of the world	200
Increase in official holdings of foreign currency	10

a. Set out the three balance of payments accounts for Silecon.
b. Does Silecon have a flexible exchange rate?

2. You are told the following about Ecflex, a country with a flexible exchange rate whose currency is the band:

Item	Billion bands
GDP	100
Consumption expenditure	60
Government purchases of goods and services	24
Investment	22
Exports of goods and services	20
Government budget deficit	4

Calculate the following for Ecflex:
a. Imports of goods and services
b. Current account balance
c. Capital account balance
d. Net taxes
e. Private sector surplus

3. A country's currency appreciates, and its official holdings of foreign currency increase. What can you say about:
a. The exchange rate system being pursued by the country?
b. The country's current account balance?
c. The country's official settlements account?

4. The foreign exchange market is shown in the figure. The demand for dollars decreases from D_0 to D_1.

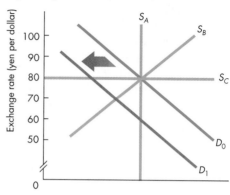

a. Explain the influences on the market that might have caused this fall in the demand for dollars.
b. Which curve is the supply of dollars if the exchange rate is fixed? Explain what happens to the exchange rate and the official settlements account balance in this case when the demand for dollars decreases from D_0 to D_1.
c. Which curve is the supply of dollars if the exchange rate is flexible? Explain what happens to the exchange rate and the official settlements account balance in this case when the demand for dollars decreases from D_0 to D_1.
d. Which curve is the supply of dollars if the exchange rate is managed? Explain what happens to the exchange rate and the official settlements account balance in this case when the demand for dollars decreases from D_0 to D_1.

5. The figure at the top of p. 941 illustrates the flows of income and expenditure in Dream Land in 1994. The amounts are in millions of dollars.

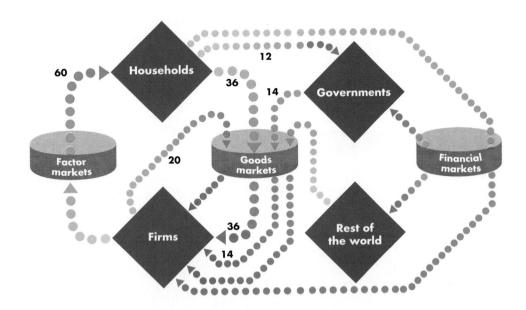

GDP in Dream Land in 1994 was $60 million.
a. Calculate Dream Land's net exports.
b. Calculate saving in Dream Land.
c. How is Dream Land's investment financed?

6. The figure shows the trade-weighted indexes of the U.S. dollar, the pound, the French franc, the Deutsche mark and the yen.

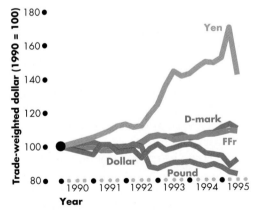

Source: International Financial Statistics

a. Describe how each of these currencies has appreciated and depreciated on the average against other currencies.
b. Compare the yen, the pound, and the U.S. dollar. Which currency has appreciated on the average against the U.S. dollar and which has depreciated?
c. Compare the Deutsche mark and the French franc. What do you think has happened to the exchange rate between the French franc and the Deutsche mark?

7. Study *Reading Between the Lines* on pp. 936–937 and then answer the following questions.
a. What events in the foreign exchange market does the news article describe?
b. What are the main explanations given by the article for the fluctuations in the foreign exchange rate?
c. Which of the explanations is the most plausible?
d. How can the Fed and the administration influence the dollar?

37

Emerging Economies

After studying this chapter, you will be able to:

- Describe how income is distributed and is changing in the world economy of the 1990s

- Explain the fundamental economic problem that confronts all nations and the alternative systems that have been used to cope with it

- Describe the process of transition in the emerging economies of Russia and other Central European countries

- Describe the process of economic growth in China

The Berlin Wall has fallen, and Germany is reunited. East Germany's centrally planned economy has been replaced by a market economy. Russia, Ukraine, Poland, Hungary, and the Czech and Slovak Republics have abandoned central economic planning and are making a painful transition toward a market economy. Why are these countries abandoning central planning and jumping on the

Dramatic Economic Change

market bandwagon? ◆ Dramatic change is also taking place in Asia. In 1946, as World War II ended, China was a desperately poor country. It went through a revolution in 1949, when it was taken over by a communist regime that did little to help its people prosper. But by the mid-1970s, China began to transform its economy. Over the years since then, more than a billion people, scattered across the countryside and crowded into some of the world's largest cities, have begun to experience income growth that is simply extraordinary. How has China managed to unshackle itself from poverty? What steps has China taken to unleash the forces of economic expansion?

◇ This chapter brings you full circle and returns to the fundamental economic problem of scarcity and the alternative ways in which people try to cope with it. You've studied the way the economy of the United States operates. You are now going to look at the bigger picture and examine economies that are emerging from either relative economic underdevelopment or an alternative economic system, that of socialist central planning. You are going to look at the process of revolutionary change that is taking place in the world economy during the 1990s. But to set the scene, we're first going to look at a snapshot of the world economy in the mid-1990s.

A Snapshot of the World Economy

THE WORLD ECONOMY CONSISTS OF MORE THAN 5 billion people, who live in 181 countries. In 1990, the most recent year for which comparable data are available for a large number of countries, world average annual income per person was $4,500. Which countries earn more than this average and which earn less? How is world income distributed around the average? And how quickly is the situation changing because of economic growth? We are going to answer these questions in this snapshot of the world economy. But to do so, and to study the anatomy of the world economy, we need a scheme for classifying countries.

Classification of Countries

Many different country classification schemes exist, and none are perfect. But a commonly used scheme is one devised by the International Monetary Fund (IMF). It has three major groups of countries:

- Industrial countries
- Developing countries
- Countries in transition

Industrial Countries   The IMF's first group is made up of 23 countries. They are the Group of Seven, or G-7 (Canada, France, Germany, Italy, Japan, United Kingdom, and United States), the other 14 Western European countries, plus Australia and New Zealand. Figure 37.1 shows these countries in blue.

Developing Countries   The IMF's second group has 130 countries, which cover the Western Hemisphere other than the United States and Canada, Asia other than Japan, the Middle East, and Africa. Figure 37.1 shows these countries in red (Western Hemisphere), orange (Asia and the Middle East), and green (Africa). Four Asian countries in this group, Hong Kong, South Korea, Singapore, and Taiwan, are more similar to the members of the industrial group than to the other developing countries. They are sometimes called Newly Industrializing Countries, or NICs, and are identified separately in yellow in Fig. 37.1.

Countries in Transition   The countries in transition are the 28 countries that have emerged from the former Soviet Union together with the countries of Central Europe that were closely allied and linked with the former Soviet Union. Figure 37.1 shows these countries in gray.

Let's now see how these three country groups differ in terms of incomes per person and income growth rates.

Incomes Per Person

Income per person ranges from $18,400 a year in the United States to $365 a year—a dollar a day—in the African nation of Chad. Figure 37.1 shows some of the details of the distribution across the major countries and regions of the world. In the Western Hemisphere outside Canada and the United States, the average annual income of $3,900 contains a range from $8,500 in the Caribbean islands of Trinidad and Tobago to $1,200 in Guyana. In Western Europe, the average annual income of $12,900 contains a range from $17,700 in Switzerland to $6,500 in Portugal. In Africa, the average annual income of $1,300 contains a range from $5,700 in the Indian Ocean island of Mauritius and $3,200 in South Africa to $365 in Chad. Average incomes for the countries in transition (gray on the map) are not known with sufficient accuracy and detail for international comparisons to be made. But data for a few of these countries show their average annual incomes to be around $5,000.

Income Distribution

Figure 37.2 summarizes the world distribution in the form of a Lorenz curve. A **Lorenz curve** plots the cumulative percentage of income against the cumulative percentage of population. If income is equally distributed, the Lorenz curve is a straight diagonal line running from the origin. With an equal distribution of income, each 1 percent of the population receives 1 percent of the income. The degree of inequality is indicated by the extent to which the Lorenz curve departs from the line of equality. The blue Lorenz curve in Fig. 37.2 shows the degree of inequality in the world economy. The poorest 20 percent of the world's population lives in countries that earn only 4.5 percent of world income. The richest

FIGURE 37.1

World Income per Person in 1990

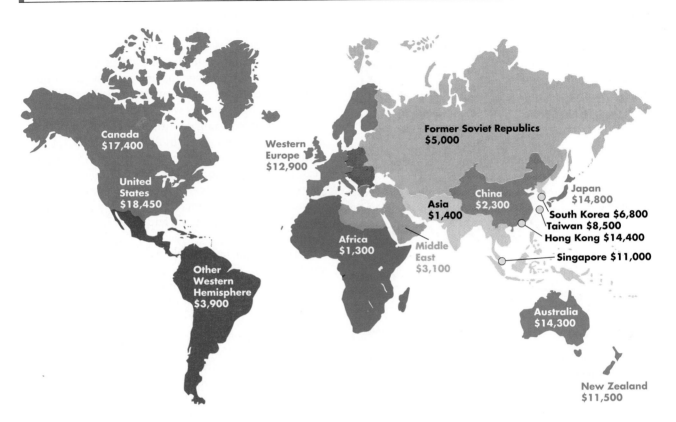

Canada
$17,400

United
States
$18,450

Western
Europe
$12,900

Former Soviet Republics
$5,000

Japan
$14,800

China
$2,300

South Korea $6,800
Taiwan $8,500
Hong Kong $14,400

Asia
$1,400

Africa
$1,300

Middle
East
$3,100

Singapore $11,000

Other
Western
Hemisphere
$3,900

Australia
$14,300

New Zealand
$11,500

The industrial countries (blue) have the highest incomes per person. The developing countries of Africa (green) and Asia (light orange) have the lowest incomes per person, followed by China (dark orange), the Middle East (orange), and the Western Hemisphere countries other than Canada and the United States (red). Four developing countries in Asia (yellow) have rapidly growing incomes and are closing the gap on the industrial countries. The European countries in transition are those of Central Europe (gray) and the former Soviet Union (light gray).

Source: Robert Summers and Alan Heston, "The Penn World Table (Mark 5): An Expanded Set of International Comparisons, 1950–1988," *Quarterly Journal of Economics,* May 1991: 327–368 [updated to 1990 on New Computer Diskette Supplement (Mark 5.5), June 15, 1993].

20 percent of the world's population lives in countries that earn 63 percent of world income.

Figure 37.2 also shows a Lorenz curve for the United States.[1] This curve shows the degree of inequality of income in the United States. The figure also reveals that the distribution of world income across countries is more unequal than the distribution of U.S. income across families. The poorest 20 percent of U.S. families earn 5 percent of total U.S. income—similar to the poorest 20 percent of the world's population. But the richest 20 percent of U.S. families earn 44 percent of total U.S. income—much less than the 63 percent of total world income earned by the 20 percent of the world's population who live in the richest countries.

The picture of the world economy contained in Figs. 37.1 and 37.2 is static. It shows the world at a point in time. But the world is changing. Many poor

---

[1] The world data are country incomes, while the United States data are family incomes.

FIGURE 37.2

The World Lorenz Curve: 1990

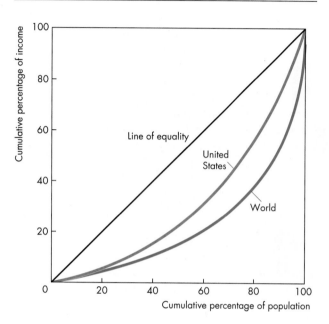

The Lorenz curve plots the cumulative percentage of income against the cumulative percentage of population. If income were distributed equally across the population, the Lorenz curve would be a straight diagonal line—the line of equality.

Sources: Robert Summers and Alan Heston, "The Penn World Table (Mark 5): An Expanded Set of International Comparisons, 1950–1988," *Quarterly Journal of Economics,* May 1991: 327–368 [updated to 1990 on New Computer Diskette Supplement (Mark 5.5), June 15, 1993]; and *Current Population Reports, Consumer Income,* Series P-60, Nos. 167 and 168 (Washington, D.C.: U.S. Department of Commerce, Bureau of the Census, 1990).

people live in countries in which rapid economic growth is taking place. As a result of economic growth and development, millions of people now enjoy living standards that were undreamed of by their parents and inconceivable to their grandparents. In the countries in transition, change is taking place, and although it holds hope for the future, its present effects are putting the lives of millions of people under severe strain. Let's end our snapshot of the world economy by looking at some of the changes in incomes that have taken place in the past several years.

Economic Growth and Decline

World income per person has grown at an average rate of 2.6 percent a year during the ten years 1986–1995. But the rate has varied across countries. Figure 37.3(a) shows that aggregate income in the industrial countries (the green line) has grown at a slower pace than that in the developing countries (the orange line). The average income growth rate of the industrial countries was 2.2 percent a year, and that of the developing countries was 5.1 percent a year. Within the developing countries, income per person grew at 7.5 percent a year in Asia but at only 1.1 percent a year in Africa. At a growth rate of 7.5 percent a year, the *level* of income per person doubles in 10 years. At a growth rate of 1.1 percent a year, the level of income per person increases by only a little more than 10 percent in 10 years and takes 70 years to double.

Most countries have shared in economic growth, even if the pace has varied. But a few countries have experienced declining incomes. These are the countries in transition—the former Soviet Union and other Central European countries. Figure 37.3(b) shows the rate of change in income in these countries (the blue line). Incomes have *fallen* at an average rate of 3.4 percent a year during the years shown in the figure. In the year of greatest decline, 1992, incomes fell by almost 16 percent. To place this period of economic transition in perspective, Fig. 37.3(c) shows the growth rate in the countries in transition (the blue line) alongside the growth rate of income in the United States 60 years earlier during the Great Depression (the red line). During the 10 years from 1926 to 1935, incomes in the United States fell at an average rate of 0.5 percent a year. Viewed in this perspective, it is clear that the transition taking place in Central Europe and Russia is a very costly process.

Why are the countries of East Asia expanding so quickly? Why are Russia and the other countries in transition having such a painful time? Part of the answer to both of these questions lies in the economic system employed and to changes in that system. The economies of East Asia rely on a *decentralized market mechanism.* In contrast, until recently, the economies in transition relied on a *centralized command mechanism* that they are dismantling and replacing with a market system. Let's look at these different economic systems and see how they differ in the way they try to cope with the economic problem.

FIGURE 37.3

World Economic Growth

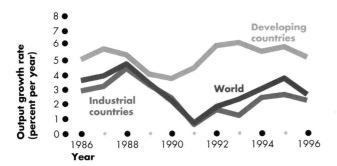

(a) Developing and industrial countries

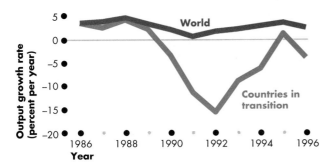

(b) Countries in transition

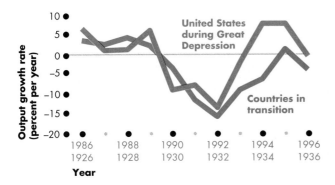

(c) Another Great Depression

The developing countries are experiencing faster economic growth than the industrial countries (part a). The countries in transition have experienced declining incomes (part b), and the scale of their income decline has exceeded the decline in income in the United States during the Great Depression, 60 years earlier (part c). (The data for 1995 and 1996 are projections.)

Source: World Economic Outlook, October 1994, International Monetary Fund, Washington D.C.

Alternative Economic Systems

THE ECONOMIC PROBLEM ARISES FROM THE universal fact of scarcity—we want to consume more goods and services than the available resources make possible. Figure 37.4 illustrates the economic problem. People have preferences about what goods and services to consume and how to make use of the factors of production that they own or control. Techniques of production—technologies—are available to transform factors of production into goods and services. The economic problem is to choose the quantities of goods and services to produce—*what*—the ways to produce them—*how*—the timing of production—*when*—the location of production—*where*—and the distribution of goods and services to each individual—*who.*

What, how, when, and *where* goods and services are produced and *who* gets them depend on how the economy is organized. Different systems deliver different outcomes. Let's examine the different economic systems.

The economic systems of the world's 180 countries vary in many different ways. But two characteristics of an economic system are crucial. They are:

■ Property rights
■ Incentives

Property Rights

Property rights are the social arrangements that govern the ownership, use, and disposal of factors of production and goods and services. Economic systems differ in the way they assign property rights to capital and land. These property rights may be granted to individuals, the state, or a mixture of the two. The private ownership of capital and land enables people to create and operate their own firms. It also enables them to buy and sell capital, land, and firms freely at the going market prices. State ownership of capital and land enables bureaucrats and managers to control the use of these resources in state-owned firms, but it does not permit this control to be passed to others in a market transaction.

In practice, no economy has pure private ownership or pure and exclusive state ownership. For example, in an economy with widespread private owner-

FIGURE 37.4

The Fundamental Economic Problem

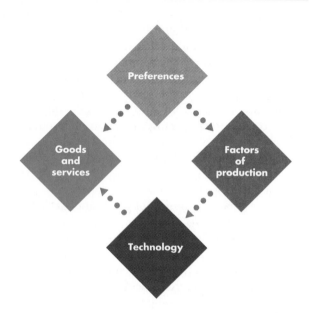

People have preferences about goods and services and the use of factors of production. Technologies are available for transforming factors of production into goods and services. People want to consume more goods and services than can be produced with the available factors of production and technology. The fundamental economic problem is to choose *what* goods and services to produce, *how, when,* and *where* to produce them, and *who* gets them. Different economic systems deliver different solutions to this problem.

ship, the freedom to buy and sell firms is modified by antitrust laws. Also, national defense or the public interest might be invoked to limit private ownership and to justify public ownership. Such limitations operate to restrict private ownership and promote public ownership of beaches and areas of natural scenic beauty.

In an economy that has predominantly state ownership, people sometimes own small plots of land and their homes. Also, in many economies, private ownership and state ownership exist side by side. In such cases, the state acts like a private firm and can buy capital, land, or even a production enterprise from its existing owner.

Incentives

Incentives are inducements to take certain actions. They can be rewards (carrots) for taking actions that bring benefits or penalties (sticks) for taking actions that impose costs. There are two sources of the rewards and penalties that create incentives:

- Market prices
- Laws and regulations

Market Prices An incentive system based on market prices is one in which people respond to the price signals they receive and the price signals themselves respond to people's actions. For example, suppose a severe frost in Florida wipes out the orange crop one year. The supply of orange juice falls. As a result, the price of orange juice rises. Faced with the higher price, people have an *incentive* to economize on orange juice and they decrease the quantity demanded. At the same time, the higher price of orange juice induces an increase in the demand for apple juice, a substitute for orange juice. As a result, the prices of apples and apple juice also rise. With higher prices for orange juice and apple juice, orange and apple growers in other countries have an *incentive* to increase the quantity supplied.

Laws and Regulations An incentive system based on laws and regulations is one in which people are rewarded or punished in a variety of nonmonetary ways to induce them to take particular actions. For example, a manager might reward a salesperson for achieving a sales goal with more rapid promotion or a bigger office. Alternatively, a salesperson might be punished for failing to achieve a sales goal by being moved to a less desirable sales district. When an entire economy is operated on administrative incentives, everyone, from the highest political authority to the lowest-ranked worker, faces nonmonetary rewards and punishments from their immediate superiors.

When the incentive system is based on laws and regulations, prices are determined by the law, not by the forces of demand and supply. For example, a government might want everyone to have access to low-cost bread. As a result, bread might be priced at a few cents a loaf. At this price, people have an *incentive* to buy lots of bread. Poor children might even use stale loaves as footballs! This use of bread apparently did actually occur in the former Soviet Union.

Types of Economic Systems

Economic systems differ in how they combine property rights and incentives. Figure 37.5 illustrates the range of possibilities. There are two extreme types and many hybrid types of economic systems. The extreme types are capitalism and socialism. **Capitalism** is a system with private ownership of capital and land and incentives based on market prices. **Socialism** is a system with state ownership of capital and land and incentives based on laws and regulations.

No country uses an economic system that precisely corresponds to one of these extreme types, but the United States, Japan, and Hong Kong come closest to being capitalist economies, and the former Soviet Union, China before the 1980s, Cuba, and North Korea come closest to being socialist economies.

The many hybrid economic systems combine private ownership with state ownership and incentives based on market prices with incentives based on laws and regulations. **Market socialism** (also called **decentralized planning**) is an economic system that combines state ownership of capital and land with incentives based on a mixture of market prices

and laws and regulations. Hungary and Poland have used market socialism. In such economies, administrators set the prices at which firms and shops buy their inputs and sell their outputs and then leave those organizations free to choose the quantities of inputs and outputs. But the prices set by the administrators respond to the forces of demand and supply. That is, the laws of demand and supply hold.

Another combination is welfare state capitalism. **Welfare state capitalism** combines the private ownership of capital and land with state intervention in markets that modifies the price signals to which people respond. Sweden, the United Kingdom, and other Western European countries are examples of such economies.

Capitalism has evolved over thousands of years and is not the invention of a single philosopher. But Adam Smith was the first economist to probe the workings of capitalism and explain how the invisible hand of the price mechanism guides resources to their highest-value uses. In contrast, socialism was invented. It was first imagined by Karl Marx and Friedrich Engels during the nineteenth century, and then refined and put into practice in the Soviet Union during the 1930s by Joseph Stalin and in China during the 1950s by Mao Zedong.

FIGURE 37.5

Alternative Economic Systems

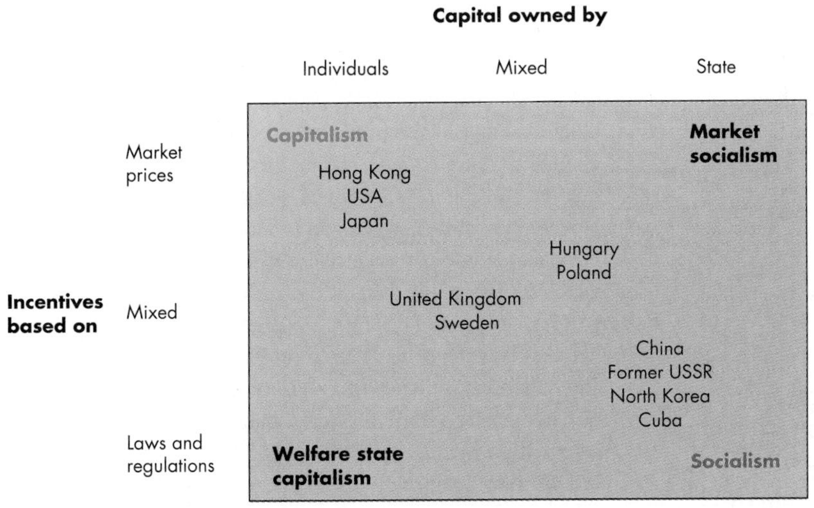

Capital owned by

	Individuals	Mixed	State
Market prices	Capitalism Hong Kong USA Japan		**Market socialism**
Incentives based on — Mixed		United Kingdom Sweden	Hungary Poland China Former USSR North Korea Cuba
Laws and regulations	**Welfare state capitalism**		Socialism

Under capitalism, individuals own capital—farms, factories, plant, and equipment—and incentives are created by market prices. Under socialism, the state owns capital and land, and incentives are created by a planning and command system. Market socialism combines state ownership of capital with market price incentives and laws and regulations. Welfare state capitalism combines private capital ownership with a high degree of state intervention in markets that changes incentives.

Alternative Systems Compared

Because all economic systems are a combination of the two extreme cases—capitalism and socialism—we can study the essence of any system by studying the two extreme types. Let's see how capitalism and socialism cope with scarcity.

How Capitalism Copes with Scarcity

Figure 37.6 shows how capitalism copes with scarcity. Households own the factors of production and are free to use those factors and the incomes they receive from the sale of their services in any way they choose. These choices are governed by their preferences. The preferences of households are all-powerful in a capitalist economy.

Households choose the quantity of each factor of production to supply, and firms choose the quantity of each factor of production to demand. Firms choose the quantity of each good or service to supply, and households choose the quantity of each to demand. These choices respond to prices in factor markets and goods markets. An increase in a factor price gives households an incentive to increase the quantity supplied of that factor and gives firms an incentive to decrease the quantity demanded. An increase in the price of a good gives firms an incentive to increase the quantity supplied of that good and gives households an incentive to decrease the quantity demanded. Factor prices adjust to bring the quantities demanded of the factors into equality with the quantities supplied, and goods prices adjust to bring the quantities demanded of the goods into equality with the quantities supplied.

In Fig. 37.6, factors of production flow from households through factor markets to firms, and goods and services flow through goods markets from firms to households. *What* is produced, *how, when,* and *where* it is produced, and *who* gets what is produced are determined by the preferences of the households, the resources that they own, and the technologies available to the firms.

No one *plans* a capitalist economy. Doctors perform nearly miraculous life-saving surgery by using sophisticated computer-controlled equipment. The equipment is designed by medical and electronic engineers, programmed by mathematicians, financed by insurance companies and banks, and bought and

FIGURE 37.6

Capitalism's Solution to the Economic Problem

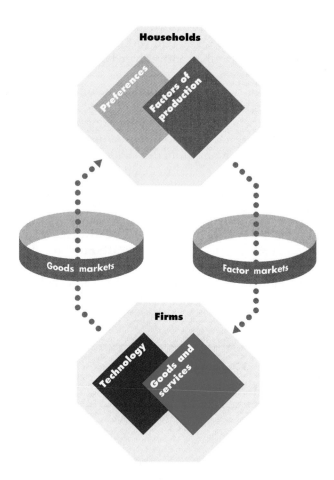

Under capitalism, the preferences of households dictate the choices that are made. Households own the factors of production and sell the services of those factors in factor markets. Households decide which goods and services to consume and buy them in goods markets. Firms decide what to produce and which factors of production to employ, selling their output in goods markets and buying their inputs in factor markets. The markets find the prices that bring the quantities demanded and quantities supplied into equality for each factor of production and each good or service. Capitalism economizes on information because households and firms need to know only the prices of various goods and factors that they buy and sell.

installed by hospital administrators. Each individual household and firm involved in this process allocates the resources that it controls in the way that seems best for it. Each firm tries to maximize its profit, and each household tries to maximize its utility. These plans are coordinated in the markets for health-care equipment, computers, engineers, computer programmers, insurance, hospital services, nurses, doctors, and hundreds of other markets for items that range from anesthetic chemicals to paper gowns.

When a surgeon performs an operation, an incredible amount of information is used. Yet no one person or firm possesses all this information. It is not centralized in one place. The capitalist economic system economizes on information. Each household or firm needs to know very little about the other households and firms with which it does business. The reason is that *prices convey most of the information it needs.* By comparing the prices of factors of production, each household chooses the quantity of each factor to supply. And by comparing the prices of goods and services, it chooses the quantity of each to buy. Similarly, by comparing the prices of factors of production, each firm chooses the quantity of each factor to use, and by comparing the prices of goods and services, it chooses the quantity of each to supply.

How Socialism Copes with Scarcity

Figure 37.7 shows how socialism copes with scarcity. In this case, the preferences of a group of administrators called *planners* carry the most weight. Those preferences dictate the activities of the production enterprises. The planners control capital and natural resources, directing them to the uses that satisfy their priorities. The planners also decide what types of jobs will be available, and the state plays a large role in the allocation of the only factor of production owned by households—labor.

The decisions of the planners are formalized in a central plan. A **central plan** is a detailed economic blueprint that sets out *what* will be produced, *how, when,* and *where* it will be produced, and *who* will get what is produced, and that establishes a set of sanctions and rewards designed to ensure that the plan is fulfilled as fully as possible.

The central plan is communicated to state-owned enterprises, which use the factors of produc-

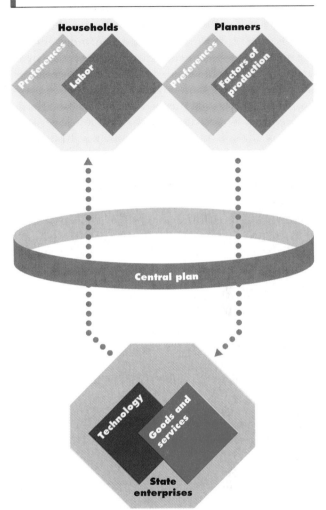

FIGURE 37.7

Socialism's Solution to the Economic Problem

Under socialism, the planners' preferences dictate the choices that are made. The planners control all the capital and natural resources owned by the state. Planners draw up plans and issue orders that determine how these resources will be used in the production of goods and services. Households decide which goods and services to consume and buy. State enterprises produce the goods and services and employ the factors of production required by the central plan. The output of state enterprises is shipped to other enterprises in accordance with the plan. Prices are set by the planners to achieve social objectives and bear no relation to the quantities demanded and quantities supplied.

tion and the available technologies to produce goods and services. These goods and services are supplied to households in accordance with the central plan. Each individual household's purchases are determined by its preferences, but the total amount available is determined by the central plan.

A centrally planned economy has prices, but they do not adjust to make the quantity demanded and the quantity supplied equal. Instead, they are set by the planners to achieve social objectives. For example, the prices of staple food products are usually set at low levels so that even the poorest families can afford an adequate diet. Setting such prices at low levels results in chronic shortages and long lines. In such a situation, prices do not provide the main incentives and people respond to the penalties and rewards that superiors impose on and give to their subordinates.

R E V I E W

- Capitalism copes with scarcity by permitting households and firms to decide how to use the factors of production that they own and coordinates these decisions through markets.
- Socialism copes with scarcity by central planning and state ownership—planners decide what to produce and communicate their plans to state-owned enterprises.

Let's now look at some of the formerly socialist economies that are in transition.

Economic Transition in Russia and Central Europe

WE'LL BEGIN OUR LOOK AT ECONOMIES IN transition with the republics that once made up the Soviet Union, the place where socialist central planning was developed and from which it spread to other countries in central Europe.

History of the Soviet Union

The Soviet Union, or the Union of Soviet Socialist Republics (USSR), was founded in 1917 following the Bolshevik Revolution led by Vladimir Ilyich Lenin. After more than 70 turbulent years, the Soviet Union collapsed in 1991 and was replaced by 16 independent republics, the largest of which are Russia and Ukraine. The 16 republics are resource-rich and diverse. Their land area is almost three times that of the United States; their population is 290 million, 20 percent larger than that of the United States; they have vast reserves of coal, oil, iron ore, natural gas, timber, and almost every other mineral resource. They are republics of enormous ethnic diversity with Russians making up 50 percent of the population and many European, Asian, and Arabic ethnic groups making up the other 50 percent. A compact economic history of the Soviet Union appears in Table 37.1.

Although the Soviet Union was founded in 1917, its economic management system was not put in place until 1928. The architect of this system was Joseph Stalin. The financial, manufacturing, and transportation sectors of the economy had been placed under state ownership and control by Lenin. Stalin added the farms to this list. He replaced the market mechanism with a command planning mechanism, initiating a series of five-year plans that placed their major emphasis on setting and attaining goals for the production of capital goods. The production of consumer goods was given a secondary place, and personal economic conditions were harsh. With emphasis on the production of capital goods, the Soviet economy grew quickly.

By the 1950s, after Stalin's death, steady economic growth continued, but the emphasis in economic planning gradually shifted away from capital goods toward consumer goods production. But there was also a large emphasis on both military equipment and space exploration. In the 1960s, the growth rate began to sag, and by the 1970s and early 1980s, the Soviet economy was running into serious problems. Productivity was actually declining, especially in agriculture but also in industry. Growth slowed, and by some estimates, income per person began to fall.

It was in this situation that Mikhail Gorbachev came to power with plans to restructure the Soviet economy. His plan was based on the idea of increased individual accountability and rewards based on performance. But Gorbachev remained fully committed to the socialist idea of state ownership and central planning. He pursued reform within the system rather than reform of the system. Because his reform plans were gradual and evolutionary, they had little

TABLE 37.1	

Key Periods in the Economic History of the Soviet Union

Period	Main economic events/characteristics
1917–1921 (Lenin)	■ Bolshevik Revolution ■ Nationalization of banking, industry, and transportation ■ Forced requisitioning of agricultural output
1921–1924 (Lenin)	■ New Economic Policy, 1921 ■ Market allocation of most resources
1928–1953 (Stalin)	■ Abolition of market ■ Introduction of command planning and five-year plans ■ Collectivization of farms ■ Emphasis on capital goods and economic growth ■ Harsh conditions
1953–1970 (Khrushchev to Brezhnev)	■ Steady growth ■ Increased emphasis on consumer goods
1970–1985 (Brezhnev to Chernenko)	■ Deteriorating productivity in agriculture and industry ■ Slowdown in growth
1985–1991 (Gorbachev)	■ *Perestroika*—reforms based on increased accountability
1991	■ Breakup of the Soviet Union

As a unified political entity, the Soviet Union effectively disintegrated following an unsuccessful coup to topple Mikhail Gorbachev in August 1991. What emerged from that coup was a loose federation of independent republics. Political freedoms began to be enjoyed in the late 1980s under President Gorbachev's programs of *perestroika* (restructuring) and *glasnost* (openness). These freedoms released nationalist and ethnic feelings that had been held in check for 50 years and created a virtual explosion of political activity. At the same time, the economies of the new republics underwent tumultuous change.

We are going to look at that change. But to understand it, we need to see how the Soviet Union operated before abandoning its central planning system.

Soviet-Style Central Planning

Soviet-style central planning was a method of economic planning and control that had four key elements:

■ Administrative hierarchy

■ Iterative planning process

■ Legally binding commands

■ Taut and inflexible plans

Administrative Hierarchy   A large and complex hierarchy implemented and controlled the central economic plan that determined almost every aspect of economic activity. At the top of the hierarchy was the state's *political* authority, and at the bottom were factories and farms that produced the goods and services. In between were layer upon layer of superiors and subordinates, with superiors wielding absolute and arbitrary power over their subordinates.

Iterative Planning Process   An iterative process is a repetitive series of calculations that get closer and closer to a solution. Central planning is an iterative process. A plan is proposed and adjustments are repeatedly made until all the elements of the plan are consistent with each other. But a plan is not arrived at as the result of a set of neat calculations performed on a computer. Rather, the process involves a repeated sequence of communications of proposals and reactions down and up the administrative hierarchy.

In the Soviet Union the process began with a big picture set of objectives or directives by the highest

effect, either for good or ill. But the fact that they did not speed up the economy's growth rate and improve the conditions in which ordinary citizens lived put the Soviet Union under severe political strain that was soon to bring about truly revolutionary change.

political authority. These directives were translated into targets by the planning ministry and retranslated into ever more detailed targets as they were passed down the hierarchy. Tens of millions of raw materials and intermediate goods featured in the detailed plans of the Soviet Union, which filled 70 volumes, or 12,000 pages, each year.

When the targets were specified as production plans for individual products, the factories reacted with their own assessments of what was feasible. Reactions as to feasibility were passed back up the hierarchy, and the central planning ministry made the targets and reports of feasibility consistent. A good deal of bargaining took place in this process: superiors demanded the impossible and subordinates claimed the requests to be infeasible.

Legally Binding Commands   Once the planning ministry had a consistent (even if infeasible) plan, the plan was given the force of law in a set of binding commands from the political authority. The commands were translated into increasing detail as they passed down the chain of command and were implemented by the production units in a way that most nearly satisfied the superiors of each level.

Taut and Inflexible Plans   In the Soviet Union, the targets set by superiors for their subordinates were infeasible. The idea was that in the attempt to do the impossible, more would be achieved than if an easily attained goal were set. The outcome of this planning process was a set of taut and inflexible plans. A taut plan is one that has no slack built into it. If one unit fails to meet its planned targets, all the other units that rely on the output of the first unit will fail to meet their targets also. An inflexible plan is one that has no capacity for reactions to changing circumstances.

Faced with impossible targets, factories produced a combination of products that enabled their superiors to report plan fulfillment, but the individual items produced did not meet the needs of the other parts of the economy. Imbalances in the central plan rippled through the entire economy and disrupted production. No factory received exactly the quantity and types of inputs needed, and the economy was unable to respond to changes in circumstances. In practice, the plan for the current year was the outcome of the previous year plus a wished-for but unattainable increment.

Living Standards in the 1980s

Figure 37.8 puts the problems of the Soviet economy in sharp focus. This figure compares the mid-1980s productivity and consumption levels of the Soviet Union with those of the United States, Western Europe (Germany, France, and Italy), Japan, and Portugal. As you can see, average worker productivity in the Soviet Union, measured by output per worker, was less than 40 percent of the output per worker in the United States and lagged considerably behind those of the other Western European countries and Japan.

A similar picture is painted by comparing consumption per worker and consumption per person. The capitalist country whose levels of productivity and consumption were most similar to those of the Soviet Union is Portugal, a relatively poor Western European country.

FIGURE   37.8

Productivity in the Soviet Union and Other Countries

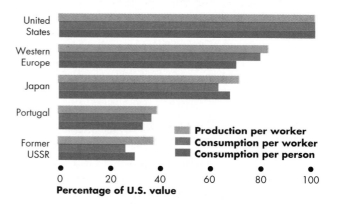

Productivity per worker in the Soviet Union in the mid-1980s was less than 40 percent of its level in the United States and similar to the level in Portugal. Consumption per worker and consumption per person were even lower, at less than 30 percent of the U.S. level. The Soviet Union lagged considerably behind Western Europe and Japan in both productivity and consumption.

Source: Abram Bergson, "The USSR Before the Fall: How Poor and Why," *Journal of Economic Perspectives*, Vol. 5, No. 4, (Fall 1991): 29–44.

Market Economy Reforms

By 1990, there was widespread dissatisfaction throughout the Soviet Union with the economic planning system. Incomes were falling, and the old political order was under severe strain. It was in this climate that a process of transition toward a market economy began. This process had three main elements:

- Relaxing central plan enforcement
- Deregulating prices
- Permitting limited private ownership of firms

Relaxing Central Plan Enforcement The transition in all three areas was one of gradual change. But the relaxation of central plan enforcement was the fastest and the most far-reaching element of the transition. The idea was that by relaxing central control over the annual plan and permitting the managers of state enterprises greater freedom to act like the managers of private firms, enterprises would be able to respond to changing circumstances without having to wait for orders from the central planners.

Deregulating Prices Price deregulation was gradual and covered a limited range of products. The idea of removing price controls was to allow the price mechanism to allocate scarce resources to their highest-value uses. Shortages would disappear and be replaced by available but in some cases expensive goods and services. Higher prices would strengthen the incentive for producers to increase output and increase the quantities supplied.

Permitting Limited Private Ownership of Firms
The move toward the private ownership of firms was extremely gradual. It was recognized that there were shortages of many goods and services. Faced with this problem it was hoped that by permitting private ownership of firms, enterprising individuals would pursue profit opportunities, increase production, and eliminate the shortages. At the same time, suspicion of private enterprise was deep-seated so moves in this direction were slow.

The transition process faced severe problems. One of these problems was that of unlearning the old methods of the centrally planned economy. But deeper transition problems arose from the nature of the system being replaced. Let's now study the major transition problems Russia faces.

Transition Problems

Three major problems confront Russia and the other republics of the former Soviet Union that complicate their transition to the capitalist market economic system. They are:

- Value and legal systems that are alien to capitalism
- Collapse of traditional trade flows
- Fiscal crisis

Value and Legal Systems Seventy years of socialist dictatorship and a feudal society that preceded it have left a legacy of values and memories that are alien to the rapid and successful establishment of a capitalist, market economy. The political leaders and people of the former Soviet Union have no personal experience of free political institutions and markets. And they have been educated, both formally and informally, to believe in a political creed in which traders and speculators are not just shady characters, but criminals. Unlearning these values will be a slow and perhaps painful process.

The legal system is also unsuited to the needs of a market economy in two ways. First, there are no well-established property rights and methods of protecting those rights. Second, and more important, there is no tradition for the government to behave like individuals and firms before the rule of law. In the Soviet system, the government *was* the law. Its economic plan and the arbitrary decisions made by the superiors at each level in the hierarchy were the only law that counted. Rational, self-promoting actions taken outside the plan were illegal.

Collapse of Traditional Trade Flows When a centrally administered empire collapses, the ensuing political reorganization can have devastating economic consequences. The most serious of these is the collapse of traditional trade flows. The Soviet Union was a highly interdependent grouping of republics organized on a wheel-hub basis with Moscow at its center. The most heavily dependent republic, Belarus, delivered 70 percent of its output to other republics and received a similar value of goods from them. Even the least dependent republic, Kazakhstan, traded 30 percent of its output with the other republics. The vast amount of interrepublic trade, managed by the central planners and channeled through the Moscow hub, meant that individual enterprise managers had little knowledge of where their products ended up or of where their inputs originated.

With the collapse of the central plan, managers must search for supplies and for markets. Because they have not yet built new networks of information, shortages of raw materials and other material inputs are common, and the lack of markets stunts production. This problem can be solved by the activities of specialist traders and speculators, but the emergence of intermediaries is proving to be slow because of political attitudes toward this type of activity.

Fiscal Crisis   Under its central planning system, the central government of the Soviet Union collected taxes in an arbitrary way. One source of revenue was a tax on consumer goods, the rate of which was increased to eliminate shortages. With prices now being free to adjust to eliminate shortages, this source of government revenue has dried up. Another source (the major source) of revenue was the profits of the state enterprises. Because the state owned these enterprises, it also received the profits. With the collapse of central planning and the decentralization of control and privatization of state enterprises, this source of revenue has also declined.

Money played virtually no role in the Soviet Union's system of central planning. Workers received their wages in currency and used it to purchase consumer goods and services. But for the state enterprises and the government, money was just a unit for keeping records. With the collapse of central planning, money became more important, especially for the government. And with the loss of its traditional sources of revenue but no cut in its spending, a government budget deficit emerged. The government was forced to cover this deficit by printing money, and the result was inflation. By 1992 inflation had reached 1,300 percent, where it remained through 1993. With substantial international help, inflation was lowered to around 200 percent a year in 1994 and was in prospect of being lowered less than 20 percent a year by 1996—see *Reading Between the Lines* on pp. 962–963.

Economic Transition in Central Europe

East Germany, the Czech and Slovak republics, Hungary, and Poland—formerly planned economies of Central Europe—are also making transitions to market economies. Let's take a look at the transition process in these countries.

East Germany

On October 3, 1990, the 16 million people of East Germany became citizens of a new united Germany, a country with a combined population of 80 million. Even before the formal reunification of Germany, East Germany had begun to dismantle its Soviet-style planning system and replace it with a market economy.

The former East Germany adopted the monetary system of West Germany, deregulated its prices, and opened itself up to free trade with its western partner. State enterprises were permitted to fail in competition with private western firms, private firms were permitted to open up in the former East Germany, and a massive sell-off of state enterprises took place.

The process of selling state enterprises began by the creation of a state corporation called Treuhandanstalt (which roughly translates as "Trust Corporation") that took over the assets of the almost 11,000 state enterprises of East Germany. The idea was then to sell off these enterprises in an orderly way over a period of a few years. In its first year of operation, Treuhandanstalt disposed of more than 4,000 firms. Most of these firms were sold to the private sector, but about 900 firms were closed down or merged with other firms. By the mid-1990s, the process of privatization was far advanced.

The loss of jobs resulting from this rapid shake-out of state enterprises was large. Even by July 1990, before the two Germanies were reunited, unemployment in East Germany had reached one third of the labor force. It has remained high and will do so for some years. But the safety net of the West German social security system is cushioning the blow to individual workers and their families.

East Germany has no fiscal policy crisis and no inflation problem. It has adopted the West German taxation and monetary systems and has assured financial stability. But the transition for East Germany will last for several more years, even though it will be the most rapid transition imaginable.

Czech Republic and Slovak Republic

Czechoslovakia removed its communist government in what was called the "Velvet Revolution" in November 1989 and almost immediately embarked on a program of economic reforms aimed at replacing its centrally planned economy with a market system.

The first step was the freeing of wages, prices, and interest rates. This step was accomplished quickly, but the emergence of well-functioning markets did not immediately follow. Financial markets were especially nervous, and a shortage of liquidity created a financial crisis.

The second step was privatization. Czechoslovakia pursued a so-called two-track policy of "little privatization" and "big privatization." "Little privatization" is the sale or, where possible, the return to their former owners, of small businesses and shops. "Big privatization" is the sale of shares in the large industrial enterprises. One feature of this privatization process is the issue of vouchers to citizens that can be used to buy shares in former state enterprises.

Czechoslovakia's transition was slowed down by the decision of its people to divide into two parts, the Czech Republic and the Slovak Republic. Production in Czechoslovakia fell by 16 percent in 1991 and by a further 8.5 percent in 1992. But in 1993, the two new countries turned the corner. Production was roughly constant in the Czech Republic and increased by 1 percent in the Slovak Republic. Both economies expanded in 1994.

These republics not only had a relatively rapid transition to an expanding market economy, but also avoided the worst excesses of inflation. Inflation peaked at 59 percent a year in 1991. By 1994, inflation had slowed to 18 percent in the Slovak Republic and to 9 percent in the Czech Republic. Unemployment rates were also low in these countries—climbing to a peak of 16 percent in the Slovak Republic and to only 4 percent in the Czech Republic.

Hungary

Hungary has been in a long transition toward a capitalist, market economy. The process began in the 1960s when central planning was replaced by decentralized planning based on a price system. Hungary has also established a taxation system similar to that in the market economies. But the privatization of large-scale industry began only in the 1990s and has proceeded slowly.

Because of its gradualism, Hungary's transition has been less disruptive than that in Russia and the other countries of the former Soviet Union. But Hungary has felt the repercussions of economic restructuring of the other Eastern European countries with which it has traditionally had the strongest trade

links, so it has suffered some modest economic decline in its transition. Production fell by 10 percent in 1991, Hungary's worst year, and began to grow again only in 1994.

Like the Czech and Slovak Republics, Hungary has avoided rampant inflation (consumer prices have increased at a steady 20 to 30 percent a year throughout the 1990s) and has had relatively modest unemployment (climbing to a peak of 12 percent).

Poland

Severe shortages, black markets, and inflation were the jumping off point for Poland's journey toward a market economy, a journey that began in September 1989 when a noncommunist government that included members of the trade union Solidarity took office. The new government has deregulated prices, and black markets have disappeared. Poland has also pursued a policy of extreme financial restraint, bringing the state budget and inflation under control.

Privatization has also been on a fast track in Poland. Under the "Mass Privatization Scheme," the shares of 400 state enterprises have been transferred through a "Privatization Fund" to the entire adult population. This method of privatization creates a giant insurance company that owns most of the production enterprises and that is in turn owned by private shareholders.

Poland's economy has responded well to these measures. Production fell in 1989 and 1990 by a total of 20 percent, but by 1992 it was growing again. The growth rate increased in both 1993 and 1994. At the same time, Poland brought a severe inflation under control. It cut the rate at which consumer prices were rising from 600 percent a year in 1993 to only 30 percent a year in 1994. The transition brought more unemployment in Poland than it did in the other countries we've just looked at. Its unemployment rate climbed each year through 1994, by which time it had reached 17 percent.

We've seen that economic decline accompanied the economic transition of the countries of the former Soviet Union and Central Europe. Production has fallen in every country and by an extremely large amount in Russia. But the rate of output loss varies and in some cases is modest.

The economic change that is taking place in China is as profound as that in the transition economies that we've just studied. But there, the process is accompanied by rapid and unprecedented expansion. Let's now turn our attention to China.

China's Emerging Market Economy

CHINA IS THE WORLD'S LARGEST NATION. IN 1994, its population exceeded 1.2 billion—almost a quarter of the world's population. Chinese civilization is ancient and has a splendid history, but the modern nation—the People's Republic of China—dates only from 1949. Table 37.2 gives a compact summary of key periods in the economic history of the People's Republic.

Modern China began when a revolutionary communist movement, led by Mao Zedong, captured control of the country and forced its previous leader, Chiang Kai-shek (Jiang Jie-shi), onto the island of Formosa—now Taiwan.

During the early years of the People's Republic, urban manufacturing industries were taken over and operated by the state and the farms were collectivized. Also, primary emphasis was placed on the production of capital equipment.

The Great Leap Forward

In 1958, Mao Zedong set the Chinese economy on what he called a **Great Leap Forward**—an economic plan based on small-scale, labor-intensive production. The Great Leap Forward paid little or no attention to linking individual pay to individual effort. Instead, a revolutionary commitment to the success of collective plans was relied upon. The Great Leap Forward was an economic failure. Productivity increased, but so slowly that living standards hardly changed. In the agricultural sector, massive injections of modern, high-yield seeds, improved irrigation, and chemical fertilizers were insufficient to enable China to feed its population. The country became the world's largest importer of grains, edible vegetable oils, and even raw cotton.

The popular explanation within China for poor performance, especially in agriculture, was that the country had reached the limits of its arable land and

TABLE 37.2

Key Periods in the Economic History of the People's Republic of China

Period	Main economic events/characteristics
1949	■ People's Republic of China established under Mao Zedong
1949–1952	■ Economy centralized under a new communist government
	■ Emphasis on heavy industry and "socialist transformation"
1952–1957	■ First five-year plan
1958–1960	■ The Great Leap Forward: an economic reform plan based on labor-intensive production methods
	■ Massive failure
1966	■ Cultural Revolution: revolutionary zealots
1976	■ Death of Mao Zedong
1978	■ Deng Xiaoping's reforms: liberalization of agriculture and introduction of individual incentives
	■ Growth rates accelerated
1989	■ Democracy movement; government crackdown
1990s	■ Continued rapid economic growth

that its population explosion was so enormous that agriculture was being forced to use substandard areas for farming. But it is much more likely that the key problem was the adoption of inefficient techniques. A further problem was that the revolutionary and ideological motivation for the Great Leap Forward degenerated into what came to be called the Cultural Revolution. Revolutionary zealots denounced productive managers, engineers, scientists, and scholars and banished them to the life of the peasant. Schools and universities were closed, and the accumulation of human capital was severely disrupted.

Deng Xiaoping's Reforms

By 1978, two years after Mao Zedong's death, the new Chinese leader, Deng Xiaoping, proclaimed major economic reforms. Collectivized agriculture was abolished. Agricultural land was distributed among households on long-term leases. In exchange for a lease, a household agreed to pay a fixed tax and contracted to sell part of its output to the state. But the household made its own decisions on cropping patterns and the quantity and types of fertilizers and other inputs to use, and it hired its own workers. Markets for farm produce were liberalized, and farmers received higher prices for their output. Also, the state increased the prices it paid to farmers, especially for cotton and other nongrain crops.

The results of Deng Xiaoping's reforms have been astounding. Annual growth rates of output of cotton and oil-bearing crops increased a staggering 14-fold. Soybean production, which had been declining at an annual rate of 1 percent between 1957 and 1978, now started to grow at 4 percent a year. Growth rates of yields per acre also increased dramatically. By 1984, a country that six years earlier had been the world's largest importer of agricultural products became a food exporter!

China has gone even further and is encouraging foreign investment and joint ventures. In addition, China has created capital markets, including a stock market.

Motivated partly by political considerations, China proclaims the virtues of what it calls the "one country, two systems" approach to economic management. One political source of this movement is the existence of two capitalist enclaves in which China has a close interest: Taiwan and Hong Kong. China claims sovereignty over Taiwan. Therefore it wants to create an atmosphere in which it will become possible for China to be "reunified" at some future date. But capitalist "islands" are also emerging in other cities such as Hong Kong's close neighbor Guangzhou, the capital of the most dynamic province, Guangdong, and Shanghai.

The results of this move toward capitalism in China are summarized in the country's dramatic growth statistics. Between 1978 and 1994, output per person grew at an average rate of 7.5 percent a year—a 3.2-fold increase in outcome per person over the 16-year period. Between 1982 and 1988, output per person grew at 7.8 percent a year, and between 1991 and 1994, it grew at 9.5 percent a year.

FIGURE 37.9

Economic Growth in China

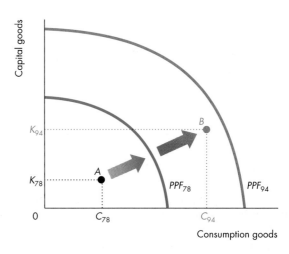

When China began its reforms in 1978, it was operating *inside* its production possibility frontier, PPF_{78}, at a point such as A, where it produced C_{78} consumption goods and K_{78} capital goods. Capital accumulation and technological change shifted the PPF outward to PPF_{94}. China's income growth has resulted partly from moving closer to its PPF and partly from a shifting PPF. By 1994, the economy was producing at a point such as B, where it produced C_{94} consumption goods and K_{94} capital goods.

No one knows how long China can keep growing at rates like these. Part of the problem of forecasting its future growth is the fact that past growth is the combined effect of becoming more efficient and expanding production possibilities. Figure 37.9 illustrates the distinction between these two sources of growth. In 1978, China's production possibility frontier was PPF_{78}. But because it was using an inefficient system of central economic planning, China was wasting resources and producing at a point such as A, *inside* its production possibility frontier. The economic reforms of 1978 helped China's economy to become more efficient and to move closer to its PPF. At the same time, the reforms increased the incentives to save and invest and also increased the flow of foreign capital and enterprise into China. As a result, over the years, the country's production possibilities have expanded. By 1994, the production possibility frontier had shifted outward to PPF_{94}. Production expanded, and in 1994, it was at point B and closer to its PPF than it had been in 1978, before the reforms. The production of consumption goods increased almost threefold from C_{78} to C_{94}, and the production of capital goods increased more than threefold from K_{78} to K_{94}.

Once China's economy becomes efficient and operates on its PPF, the growth rate will probably slow somewhat. Whether it will slow to the rates of Hong Kong and Singapore—a growth of income per person of around 5 percent a year—or to the rate of the United States—a growth rate of around 2 percent a year—is impossible to tell. But on its 1990s growth path, China is closing the gap with the United States and is set to become the world's largest economy before the year 2000.[2]

China is not only experiencing rapid growth of real income per person but also increasing its international competitiveness. Its exports have grown during the 1980s and 1990s at a much faster rate than its output. In 1994, China's exports were 19 percent of what it produced.

How has China achieved this dramatic success?

China's Success

China's success in achieving a high rate of economic growth has resulted from four features of its reforms.[3] They are:

■ Massive rate of entry of new nonstate firms
■ Large increases in the productivity and profitability of state firms
■ An efficient taxation system
■ Gradual price deregulation

Entry of Nonstate Firms   The most rapidly growing sector of the Chinese economy is industrial firms located in rural areas. In recent years, this sector has grown at an annual rate of 17.5 percent. In 1978, it

produced 22 percent of the nation's industrial output, and by 1993, it was producing close to 50 percent of total industrial output. By contrast, the state-owned firms—the firms organized by the state under its national plan—shrank (relatively) from producing 78 percent of total output in 1978 to about 50 percent in the mid-1990s.

The entry of new firms created a dramatic increase in competition both among the new firms and between the new firms and the state firms. This competition spurred both nonstate and state firms into greater efficiency and productivity.

Increases in Productivity and Profitability of State Firms   China has not privatized its economy by selling state firms. Instead, privatization has come from the entry of new firms. State firms have continued to operate, and the government has a strong incentive to ensure that these firms are profitable. If state firms make no profit, the government collects no taxes from them.

To achieve the greatest possible profit and tax revenue, the Chinese economic planners have changed the incentives faced by the managers of state enterprises to resemble those of the market incentives faced by nonstate firms. Managers of state-owned firms are paid according to the firm's performance—similar to managers in private firms.

The Chinese system gives incentives for managers of state enterprises to be extremely enterprising and productive. As a result of this new system, the Chinese government is now able to auction off top management jobs. Potential managers bid for the right to be manager. The manager who offers the best promise of performance, backed by a commitment of personal wealth, is the one who gets the job.

Efficient Taxation System   Firms (both private and state firms) are taxed, but the tax system is unusual and different from that in our own economy. Firms are required to pay a fixed amount of profit to the government. Once that fixed amount of tax has been paid, the firm keeps any additional profit. In contrast, the tax system in the United States requires firms to pay a fixed percentage of their profits in tax. Thus in the United States, more profit means higher taxes, while in China, taxes are set independently of a firm's profit level. The Chinese system creates much stronger incentives than does our own system for firms to seek out and pursue profitable ventures.

---

[2] Because the population of China is 4.5 times that of the United States, when income per person in China exceeds 22 percent of that in the United States, China's output will exceed that of the United States. In 1994, according to the most generous estimates, output per person in China was about 17 percent of that in the United States. If China and the United States maintain their current growth rates, output in China will exceed that in the United States by about 1998.

[3] This section is based on John McMillan and Barry Naughton, "How to Reform a Planned Economy: Lessons from China," Graduate School of International Relations and Pacific Studies, University of California, San Diego, 1991.

Gradual Price Reform   China has not abandoned planning its prices. The socialist planning system keeps the prices of manufactured goods fairly high and keeps domestic prices higher than world prices. This pricing arrangement makes private enterprise production in China extremely profitable. In 1978, when the nonstate sector was small, the profit rate in that sector was almost 40 percent. With such a high profit rate, there was a tremendous incentive for enterprising people to find niches and engage in creative and productive activity. The forces of competition have gradually lowered prices. By 1990, rates of return had fallen to 10 percent. The price movements were gradual. There was no big bang adjustment of prices—no abandonment of the planning mechanism and introduction of a rip-roaring free market system.

Growing Out of the Plan   As a result of the reforms adopted in the 1970s and pursued vigorously since that time, the Chinese economy has gradually become a much more market-oriented economy and is, in effect, growing out of its central plan.[4] The proportion of the economy accounted for by private enterprise and market-determined prices has gradually increased, and the proportion accounted for by state enterprises and planned and regulated prices has gradually decreased.

To sustain this process, changes in fiscal policy and monetary policy have been necessary. The reform of the economy has entailed the redesigning of the tax system. In a centrally planned economy, the government's tax revenues come directly through its pricing policy. Also, the government, as the controller of all financial institutions, receives all of the nation's saving. When the central planning system is replaced by the market system, the government must establish a tax collection agency similar to the Internal Revenue Service of the United States. Also, it must develop financial markets so that households' savings can be channeled into the growing private firms to finance their investment in new buildings, plant, and equipment.

Despite the reform of its tax system, the government of China spends more than it receives in tax revenue and covers its deficit by the creation of money. The result is inflation. But inflation in China is

not out of control, because the rapid growth of economic activity absorbs a great deal of the new money.

Whether China has found a way of making the transition from socialism to capitalism relatively painless is controversial. The violent suppression of the democracy movement in Tiananmen Square in the summer of 1989 suggests that China might have bought economic gains at the expense of political freedoms. But the experiment in comparative *economic* systems that is currently going on in China is one of the most exciting that the world has seen. Economists of all political shades of opinion will closely watch its outcome, and its lessons will be of enormous value for future generations—whatever those lessons turn out to be.

R E V I E W

■ China embarked on a process of economic reform in 1978 that created a dynamic market economy alongside its socialist economy.

■ Since 1978, China's rate of economic expansion has been rapid and income per person has increased more than threefold.

■ China's success has resulted from unleashing market incentives.

◆ Rapid income growth in Asia and other parts of the world is increasing the number of people who live in rich industrial countries. The transition to a market economy is changing Central Europe. But the world has seen change of historical proportions before. The transformation of the economies of formerly war-torn Germany and Japan into the economic powerhouses of today is one example. Throughout all this change—past, present, and future—our knowledge and understanding of the economic forces that produce the change and are unleashed by it have been getting gradually better. There remains a great deal that we do not understand. But we have made some progress. The economic principles presented in this book summarize this progress and the current state of knowledge. As the world continues to change, you will need a compass to guide you into unknown terrain. The principles of economics are that compass!

[4]Barry Naughton, "Growing Out of the Plan: Chinese Economic Reform, 1978–90," Graduate School of International Relations and Pacific Studies, University of California, San Diego, 1992.

Russia's Macroeconomic Performance

The Wall Street Journal, November 28, 1994

Russia's Economic News: It's Not All Bad

by Steve Leisman

MOSCOW—Russia's stormy transition to a market economy is a story of fired ministers, a plunging ruble, soaring inflation, and even violence. The cabinet has been reshuffled six times, most recently last month, and a parliament has been dissolved by military force.

Yet despite the fears about hyperinflation and an end to economic liberalization that were expressed after each government shakeup, the reforms have shown surprising resilience. Indeed, the economy—albeit still precarious—has been having its best year since reforms began in 1992, when Russia broke with its socialist past by freeing prices.

After three years of decline following the collapse of the Soviet Union, Russia's potentially vast economy started growing again in October. Prices are expected to rise a relatively modest 150% this year, compared with 840% in 1993. Outside investment has begun to filter in, with estimates that foreigners this year pumped [in] $2.5 billion to $3 billion. ...

President Boris Yeltsin gathered hundreds of legislative, regional, and industrial leaders in the Kremlin to drum up enthusiasm for the economy and continued reforms. "Until now, the Russian economy has remained in crisis. Now, we are close to overcoming that stage," Mr. Yeltsin said. "In 1995, we'll start an offensive. We will complete financial stabilization and move on to creating conditions for economic revival and growth." ...

The country still lacks coherent tax and civil codes. The government keeps promising tax reform ...but it hasn't delivered. ...

The government's hope these days is that if it tames inflation, other reforms will fall into line. The 1995 budget proposal, now before Parliament, aims to lower inflation to between 1% and 1.5% monthly. It was 11.8% in October. ...

If a [budget] proposal similar to the current one passes, lending institutions such as the World Bank and International Monetary Fund are ready to inject as much as $13 billion into Russia, covering half the projected budget deficit of 7.8% of gross domestic product. ... An additional $6 billion could come from the IMF to support the ruble in a plan to peg it to the dollar. ...

Essence of THE STORY

■ Russia's transition to a market economy has been accompanied by falling real GDP, a falling ruble, and high inflation.

■ But after three years of decline, Russia's economy started growing again in October 1994. Inflation in 1994 was expected to be 150 percent a year, down from 840 percent a year in 1993.

■ Foreign investment in 1994 was expected to be $2.5 billion to $3 billion.

■ The core of the government's plan is to lower inflation from its October 1994 rate of 11.8 percent a month to between 1 percent and 1.5 percent a month.

■ Loans of $13 billion from the World Bank and International Monetary Fund would be used to cover half the projected government budget deficit of 7.8 percent of GDP.

■ An additional $6 billion from the IMF might be used to peg the ruble to the U.S. dollar.

Economic

A N A L Y S I S

■ Figure 1 shows the International Monetary Fund's (IMF) estimates of Russia's real GDP growth rate between 1991 and 1994 and its projections for 1995 and 1996.*

■ Although the news article says that real GDP grew in October 1994, the IMF estimate of the growth rate for 1994 and its projected growth rate for 1995 are negative—they show a *fall* in real GDP.

■ The IMF expects real GDP to start growing again in 1996.

■ Figure 2 shows the IMF's estimates of Russia's inflation between 1991 and 1994 and its projections for 1995 and 1996.

■ You can see that inflation peaked at 1,350 percent in 1992 and was, as reported in the article, more than 800 percent in 1993. The IMF projects an inflation rate of 143 percent for 1995 and 12.3 percent for 1996.

■ The news article reports a target inflation rate of 1 percent to 1.5 percent a month.

*Figure 1 and Figure 2 are based on data from *World Economic Outlook*, May 1995, International Monetary Fund, Washington, D.C.

■ These monthly inflation rates translate to a range of 13 percent to 20 percent a year, which are lower than the IMF projection for 1995, but similar to the IMF projection for 1996.

■ Even if Russia does not lower its inflation rate further, but maintains its current rate, it will have avoided *hyperinflation*.

■ Russia's problem of eliminating inflation arises from its government budget deficit. With no tax reform, Russia has a government budget deficit of $26 billion, which is 7.8 percent of GDP.

■ Even if the World Bank and IMF lend Russia $13 billion to finance half of its budget deficit, Russia must find the other $13 billion.

■ Without a well-functioning capital market, Russia will print new money (additional rubles) to finance the other half of its deficit.

■ It is unlikely that Russia can sell bonds to foreigners.

■ The news article states that foreign lending to Russia was $2.5 billion to $3 billion in 1994.

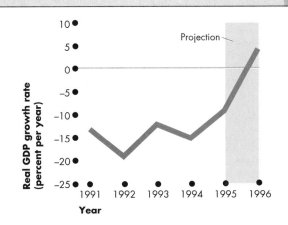

Figure 1 Real GDP growth

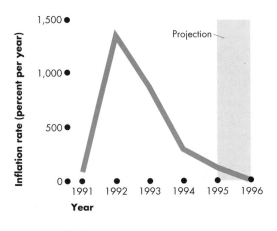

Figure 2 Inflation rate

■ This amount is small in comparison to the government's deficit and it is commercial lending that is seeking a profit, not money, for the Russian government.

■ So even if the IMF and World Bank finance half of Russia's government deficit, this financing will likely only be sufficient to lower the inflation rate to around half its present level.

■ Even if Russia could lower its inflation rate to between 13 percent and 20 percent a year, talk of pegging the ruble to the dollar is misplaced.

■ The ruble will depreciate against the dollar at a rate that reflects the gap between the Russian and U.S. inflation rates.

■ In 1995 the U.S. inflation rate was about 3 percent a year, so a good deal of ruble depreciation remains likely, no matter how much the IMF lends Russia.

S U M M A R Y

A Snapshot of the World Economy

More than 5 billion people live in 181 countries, 23 of which are industrial, 130 developing, and 28 economies in transition. In 1990, average income per person was $4,500 a year. The poorest 20 percent of the world's population live in countries that earn only 4.5 percent of world income while the richest 20 percent live in countries that earn 63 percent of world income. World average income per person grew at an average rate of 2.6 percent a year during the ten years 1986 to 1995. Income growth was slower in industrial countries than in developing countries and income growth was faster in Asia than in Africa. In the former Soviet Union and other Central European countries in transition, incomes fell, and in the most extreme cases by more than they fell in the United States 60 years earlier during the Great Depression. (pp. 944–947)

Alternative Economic Systems

The economic problem is the universal fact of scarcity. Different economic systems deliver different solutions to the economic problem determining *what, how, when,* and *where* goods and services are produced and *who* gets them. Alternative economic systems vary along two dimensions: property rights (ownership of capital and land) and the incentives people face. Capital and land may be owned by individuals, the state, or a mixture of the two. Incentives may be based on market prices, laws and regulations, or a mixture of the two.

Economic systems differ in the ways in which they combine property rights and incentives. Capitalism is based on the private ownership of capital and land and on market price incentives. Socialism is based on state ownership of capital and land and on incentives based on laws and regulations. Market socialism combines state ownership of capital and land with incentives based on a mixture of market prices and laws and regulations. Welfare state capitalism combines the private ownership of capital and land with state intervention in markets that changes the price signals to which people respond. (pp. 947–952)

Economic Transition in Russia and Central Europe

Between 1917 and 1990, the Soviet Union had a planned, socialist economy. It began a process of transition toward the market economy in the late 1980s. It relaxed its central plan, deregulated prices, and introduced limited private ownership of firms. The transition was gradual but it ran into severe problems. The most important were: value and legal systems alien to capitalism, the collapse of traditional trade flows, and the emergence of a large state budget deficit and inflation.

The formerly planned economies of East Germany, Czechoslovakia, Hungary, and Poland are also making transitions to market economies. East Germany's transition has been the most dramatic and the most complete. The Czech Republic and the Slovak Republic have deregulated wages, prices, and interest rates and are privatizing their industries. Hungary began to move toward a market economy during the 1960s when central planning was replaced by decentralized planning. Poland has deregulated prices, pursued a policy of financial restraint that has brought inflation under control, and put privatization on a fast track. (pp. 952–958)

China's Emerging Market Economy

Since the foundation of the People's Republic of China in 1949, economic management has been through turbulent changes. At first, the state took over manufacturing and farms were collectivized. It then introduced the Great Leap Forward, which in turn degenerated into the Cultural Revolution. China at first grew quickly with heavy reliance on state planning and the production of capital equipment, but growth slowed, and at times, income per person actually fell. In 1978, China revolutionized its economic management, placing greater emphasis on private incentives and markets. Productivity grew at a rapid rate and income per person increased.

China's high rate of economic growth has resulted from competition between private and state firms, productivity increases in state firms, an efficient taxation system, and price deregulation. (pp. 958–961)

R E V I E W   Q U E S T I O N S

1. What are the average incomes per person in the main regions and types of countries?

2. Compare the distribution of income among families in the United States with the distribution of income among countries in the world. Which distribution is more unequal?

3. What is the fundamental economic problem that any economic system must cope with?

4. What are the main economic systems? Set out the key features of each.

5. Give examples of countries that are capitalist, socialist, market socialist, and welfare state capitalist. (Name some countries other than those in Fig. 37.5.)

6. How does capitalism cope with the economic problem? What determines how much of each good to produce?

7. How does socialism cope with the economic problem? What determines how much of each good to produce?

8. How does market socialism determine the price of each good and quantity of it that is produced?

9. List the main economic events in the history of the Soviet Union before its collapse in 1991.

10. Describe the main elements in the Soviet Union's central planning system.

11. Compare the standard of living and productivity in the Soviet Union before its collapse with that in the United States and other countries.

12. Why did the Soviet economy begin to fail in the 1980s?

13. What are the main features of the transition program in the former Soviet Union?

14. What are the main problems faced by the republics of the former Soviet Union?

15. What are the problems that the Central European countries face as they make the transition to a market economy?

16. What are the main episodes in China's economic management since 1949?

17. Explain why China has grown so quickly.

18. Describe the economic experiment that is going on in China.

P R O B L E M S

1. A poor country has 10 percent of the income of a rich country. The poor country achieves a growth rate of 10 percent per year, and the rich country achieves a growth rate of 5 percent per year. How many years will it take income in the poor country to catch up with that of the rich country?

2. Three countries are identified in the figure by A, B, and C.

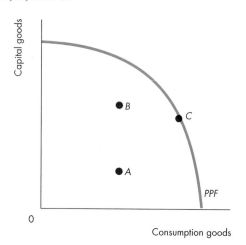

a. Which country or countries most likely use a market mechanism and which a central planning mechanism?

b. Which country most likely has the fastest rate of economic growth and which the slowest?

c. Which country has the greatest scope for increasing incomes by becoming more efficient in the use of its resources?

d. Which country most resembles China today?

e. Which country most resembles Russia today?

3. Compare and contrast the methods being used in the former Soviet Union with those of China and explain why the economy of China is growing more rapidly than that of the former Soviet Union.

4. Compare and contrast the methods being used in the former Soviet Union with those of the other countries in transition in Central Europe.

5. Study *Reading Between the Lines* on pp. 962–963 and then answer the following questions:

a. What are the main problems that have accompanied Russia's transition to a market economy?

b. What inflation target is Russia aiming to achieve in 1996?

c. How is Russia planning on achieving its inflation target?

d. How are the World Bank and the International Monetary Fund helping Russia achieve its goals?

e. Why is it premature to talk of pegging the ruble to the dollar?

Glossary

Above full-employment equilibrium A situation in which macroeconomic equilibrium occurs at a level of real GDP above long-run real GDP.

Absolute advantage A person has an absolute advantage in the production of two goods if by using the same quantities of inputs, that person can produce more of both goods than another person; a country has an absolute advantage if its output per unit of inputs of all goods is larger than that of another country.

Adverse selection The tendency for people to enter into agreements in which they can use their private information to their own advantage and to the disadvantage of the less-informed party.

Aggregate demand The relationship between the aggregate quantity of goods and services demanded (real GDP demanded) and the price level (the GDP deflator) everything else held constant.

Aggregate hours The total number of hours worked by all the people employed, both full time and part time, during a year.

Aggregate planned expenditure The expenditure that economic agents (households, firms, governments, and foreigners) plan to undertake in given circumstances.

Allocative efficiency A situation that occurs when no resources are wasted—when no one can be made better off without someone else being made worse off. Allocative efficiency is also called *Pareto efficiency.*

Antitrust law A law that regulates and prohibits certain kinds of market behavior, such as monopoly and monopolistic practices.

Automatic fiscal policy A change in fiscal policy that is triggered by the state of the economy.

Automatic stabilizer A mechanism that decreases the fluctuations in aggregate expenditure resulting from fluctuations in a component of aggregate expenditure.

Autonomous expenditure The sum of those components of aggregate planned expenditure that are not influenced by real GDP.

Average cost pricing rule A rule that sets price equal to average total cost.

Average fixed cost Total fixed cost per unit of output—total fixed cost divided by output.

Average product The average productivity of a factor of production—total product divided by the quantity of the factor employed;

Average revenue The revenue per unit of output sold—total revenue divided by the quantity sold. Average revenue also equals price.

Average total cost Total cost per unit of output.

Average variable cost Total variable cost per unit of output.

Balanced budget A government budget in which tax revenues and expenditures are equal.

Balanced budget multiplier The amount by which simultaneous and equal changes in government purchases and taxes are multiplied to determine the change in equilibrium expenditure.

Balance of payments accounts A country's record of international trading, borrowing, and lending.

Balance of trade The value of exports minus the value of imports.

Barriers to entry Legal or natural impediments protecting a firm from competition from potential new entrants.

Barter The direct exchange of one good or service for other goods and services.

Below full-employment equilibrium A macroeconomic equilibrium in which potential GDP exceeds real GDP.

Big trade-off The conflict between equity and efficiency.

Bilateral monopoly A situation in which there is a single seller (a monopoly) and a single buyer (a monopsony).

Black market An illegal trading arrangement in which buyers and sellers do business at a price higher than the legally imposed price ceiling.

Bond A legally enforceable debt obligation to pay specified amounts of money at specified future dates.

Bond market A market in which the bonds of corporations and governments are traded.

Budget deficit A government's budget balance that is negative—expenditures exceed tax revenues.

Budget line The limits to a household's consumption choices.

Budget surplus A government's budget balance that is positive—tax revenues exceed expenditures.

Bureaucrat A hired official who works in a government department at either the federal, state, or local level and who produces public goods and services.

Business cycle The periodic but irregular up-and-down movement in economic activity, measured by fluctuations in real GDP and other macroeconomic variables.

Capital The equipment, buildings, tools, and manufactured goods that are used in the production of goods and services.

Capital account A record of a country's international borrowing and lending transactions.

Capital accumulation The growth of capital resources.

Capital gain The income received by selling a stock, bond, or asset for a higher price than the price paid for it.

Capital stock The stock of plant, equipment, buildings (including residential housing), and inventories.

Capitalism An economic system with private ownership of capital and land and incentives based on market prices.

Capture theory A theory of regulation that states that the regulations are supplied to satisfy the demand of producers to maximize producer surplus—to maximize economic profit.

Cartel A group of firms that has entered into a collusive agreement to restrict output so as to increase prices and profits.

Central bank A public authority charged with regulating and controlling a country's monetary policy and financial institutions and markets.

Central plan A detailed economic blueprint that sets out what will be produced, how, when, and where it will be produced, and who will get what is produced, and that establishes a set of sanctions and rewards designed to ensure that the plan is fulfilled as fully as possible.

Ceteris paribus   Other things being equal—all other relevant things remaining the same.

Change in demand   A change in buyers' plans that occurs when some influence on those plans   other than the price of the good changes. It is illustrated by a shift of the demand curve.

Change in supply   A change in sellers' plans that occurs when some influence on those plans other than the price of the good changes. It is illustrated by a shift of the supply curve.

Change in the quantity demanded   A change in buyers' plans that occurs when the price of a good changes but all other influences on buyers' plans remains unchanged. It is illustrated by a movement along the demand curve.

Change in the quantity supplied   A change in sellers' plans that occurs when the price of a good changes but all other influences on sellers' plans remain unchanged. It is illustrated by a movement along the supply curve.

Choke price   The price at which the quantity demanded of a natural resource is zero.

Classical growth theory   A theory of economic growth based on the view that population growth is determined by the level of income per person.

Coase theorem   The proposition that if property rights exist and transactions costs are low, private transactions are efficient—equivalently, there are no externalities.

Collective bargaining   A process of negotiation between representatives of employers and unions.

Collusive agreement   An agreement between two (or more) producers to restrict output so as to increase prices and profits.

Commercial bank   A private firm, licensed either by the Comptroller of the Currency (in the U.S. Treasury) or by a state agency to receive deposits and make loans.

Commodity money   A physical commodity that is valued in its own right and also used as a means of payment.

Comparative advantage   A person or country has a comparative advantage in an activity if that person or country can perform the activity at a lower opportunity cost than anyone else or any other country.

Complement   A good that is used in conjunction with another good.

Constant returns to scale Technological conditions under which a given percentage increase in all the firm's inputs results in the firm's output increasing by the same percentage.

Consumer efficiency   A situation that occurs when consumers cannot make themselves better off by reallocating their budget.

Consumer equilibrium   A situation in which a consumer has allocated his or her income in the way that maximizes his or her utility.

Consumer Price Index (CPI)   An index that measures the average level of prices of the goods and services typically consumed by an urban American family.

Consumer surplus   The value that the consumer places on a good minus the price paid for it.

Consumption demand   The relationship between consumption expenditure and the real interest rate, other things remaining the same.

Consumption expenditure   The total payment made by households on consumption goods and services.

Consumption function   The relationship between consumption expenditure and disposable income, other things held constant.

Contestable market   A market structure in which there is one firm (or a small number of firms) and because of freedom of entry and exit, the firm (or firms) faces competition from potential entrants and so operates like a perfectly competitive firm.

Cooperative equilibrium   The outcome of a collusive agreement between players when each player responds rationally to a credible threat from another player to inflict heavy damage if an agreement is broken.

Contractionary fiscal policy   A decrease in government expenditures or an increase in tax revenues.

Convertible paper money   A paper claim to a commodity (such as gold) that circulates as a means of payment.

Copyright   A government-sanctioned exclusive right granted to the inventor of a good, service, or productive process to produce, use, and sell the invention for a given number of years.

Cost-push inflation   Inflation that results from an initial increase in costs.

Council of Economic Advisers (CEA)   A President's council whose main work is to monitor the economy and keep the President and the public well informed about the current state of the economy and the best available forecasts of where it is heading.

Craft union   A group of workers who have a similar range of skills but work for many different firms in many different industries and regions.

Credit union   A financial intermediary owned by its depositors, who are a social or economic group, that accepts savings deposits and makes consumer loans.

Creditor nation   A country that has invested more in the rest of the world than other countries have invested in it.

Cross elasticity of demand   The responsiveness of the demand for a good to the price of a substitute or complement, other things remaining the same. It is calculated as the percentage change in the quantity demanded of the good divided by the percentage change in the price of the substitute or complement.

Cross-section graph   A graph that shows the values of an economic variable for different groups in a population at a point in time.

Crowding out   The tendency for an increase in government purchases of goods and services to bring a decrease in investment.

Currency   The bills and coins that we use today.

Currency depreciation   The fall in the value of one currency in terms of another currency.

Currency drain   An increase in currency held outside banks.

Current account   A record of receipts from the sale of goods and services to foreigners, the payments for goods and services bought from foreigners, the interest income received from and paid to foreigners, and gifts and other transfers (such as foreign aid payments) received from and paid to foreigners.

Cyclical unemployment The unemployment arising from the slowdown in the pace of economic expansion.

Cyclically adjusted deficit The budget deficit that would occur if the economy were at full employment.

Deadweight loss A measure of allocative inefficiency. It is equal to the loss in total surplus (consumer surplus plus producer surplus) that results from producing less than the efficient level of output.

Debtor nation A country that during its entire history has borrowed more from the rest of the world than it has lent to it. It has a stock of outstanding debt to the rest of the world that exceeds the stock of its own claims on the rest of the world.

Decentralized planning An economic system that combines state ownership of capital and land with incentives based on a mixture of market prices and laws and regulations.

Decreasing returns to scale Technological conditions under which a given percentage increase in all the firm's inputs results in the firm's output increasing by a smaller percentage.

Demand The relationship between the quantity of a good that consumers plan to buy and the price of the good, with all other influences on buyers' plans remaining the same. It is described by a demand schedule and illustrated by a demand curve.

Demand curve A curve that shows the relationship between the quantity demanded of a good and its price, all other influences on consumers' planned purchases remaining the same.

Demand-pull inflation Inflation that results from an initial increase in aggregate demand.

Deposit money Deposits at banks and other financial institutions; an accounting entry in an electronic database in the banks' and other financial institutions' computers.

Deposit multiplier The amount by which an increase in bank reserves is multiplied to calculate the increase in bank deposits.

Depreciation The decrease in the value of capital stock or the value of a durable input that results from wear and tear and the passage of time.

Derived demand Demand for an item not for its own sake but for use in the production of goods and services.

Diminishing marginal rate of substitution The general tendency for the marginal rate of substitution of one good for another to diminish as a consumer increases consumption of the first good.

Diminishing marginal returns The tendency for the marginal product of a variable factor eventually to diminish as additional units of the variable factor are employed.

Diminishing marginal utility The marginal utility that a consumer gets from a good decreases as more of the good is consumed.

Direct relationship A relationship between two variables that move in the same direction.

Discounting The conversion of a future amount of money to its present value.

Discount rate The interest rate at which the Fed stands ready to lend reserves to commercial banks.

Discouraged workers People who do not have jobs and would like to work but have stopped seeking work.

Discretionary fiscal policy A policy action that is initiated by an act of Congress.

Discretionary policy A policy that responds to the state of the economy in a possibly unique way that uses all the information available, including perceived lessons from past "mistakes."

Diseconomies of scale Technological conditions under which long-run average cost increases as output increases.

Dominant strategy equilibrium The outcome of a game in which there is a single best strategy (a dominant strategy) for each player, regardless of the strategy of the other players.

Dumping The sale of a good in a foreign market for a lower price than in the domestic market or for a lower price than its cost of production.

Duopoly A market structure in which two producers of a good or service compete.

Dynamic comparative advantage A comparative advantage that a person or country possesses as a result of having specialized in a particular activity and then, as a result of learning-by-doing, becoming the producer with the lowest opportunity cost.

Economic depreciation The decrease in the market price of a piece of capital over a given period.

Economic efficiency A situation that occurs when the cost of producing a given output is as low as possible.

Economic growth The expansion of production possibilities that results from capital accumulation and technological change.

Economic information Data on prices, quantities, and qualities of goods and services and factors of production.

Economic model A description of some aspect of the economic world that includes only those features of the world that are needed for the purpose at hand.

Economic profit A firm's total revenue minus its opportunity cost.

Economic rent The income received by the owner of a factor of production in excess of the amount required to induce that owner to offer the factor for use.

Economic stability The absence of wide fluctuations in the economic growth rate, the level of employment, and average prices.

Economic theory A generalization that summarizes what we think we understand about the economic choices that people make and the performance of industries and entire economies.

Economics The study of the choices people make to cope with scarcity.

Economies of scale Technological conditions under which long-run average cost decreases as output increases.

Economies of scope Decreases in average total cost made possible by increasing the range of goods produced.

Economy A mechanism that allocates scarce resources among competing uses.

Efficiency wage The wage rate that maximizes profit.

Efficient market A market in which the actual price embodies all currently available relevant information.

Elastic demand   Demand with a price elasticity greater than 1; other things remaining the same, the percentage change in the quantity demanded exceeds the percentage change in price.

Elasticity of supply   The responsiveness of the quantity supplied of a good to a change in its price, other things remaining the same.

Employment Act of 1946   A landmark Congressional act that recognized a role for government actions to reduce unemployment, keep the economy expanding, and keep inflation check.

Employment-to-population ratio   The percentage of people of working age who have jobs.

Entitlement spending   Spending on government programs that entitle suitably qualified individuals and businesses to receive benefits and that result in transfer payments that depend on the economic state of individual citizens and businesses.

Entrants   People who enter the labor force.

Entrepreneurial ability   A special type of human resource that organizes the other three factors of production—labor, land, and capital—and makes business decisions, innovates, and bears business risk.

Equation of exchange   An equation that states that the quantity of money multiplied by the velocity of circulation equals GDP.

Equilibrium expenditure   The level of aggregate planned expenditure that equals real GDP.

Equilibrium price   The price at which the quantity demanded equals the quantity supplied.

Equilibrium quantity   The quantity bought and sold at the equilibrium price.

Equity   In economics, equity has two meanings: economic justice or fairness and the owner's stake in a business.

Excess reserves   A bank's actual reserves minus its required reserves.

Exchange efficiency   A situation in which a good or service is exchanged at a price that equals both the marginal social benefit and the marginal social cost of the good or service.

Excise tax   A tax on the sale of a good or service. The tax is paid when the good or service is bought.

Excludable good   A good is excludable if its benefits can be restricted to the person who has paid for the good.

Exhaustible natural resources   Natural resources that can be used only once and that cannot be replaced once they have been used.

Expansion   A business cycle phase in which there is a speedup in the pace of economic activity.

Expansionary fiscal policy   An increase in government expenditure or a decrease in tax revenues.

Expected utility   The average utility arising from all possible outcomes.

Exports   The goods and services that we sell to people in other countries.

External benefits   Benefits that accrue to members of the society other than the buyer of the good.

External costs   Costs that are borne by members of society other than the producer of the good.

External economies   Factors beyond the control of a firm that lower the firm's costs as the industry produces a larger output.

Externality   A cost or a benefit arising from an economic activity that affects people other than those who decide the scale of the activity.

Factors of production   The economy's productive resources—land, labor, capital, and entrepreneurial ability.

Federal budget   A statement of the federal government's financial plan, itemizing programs and their costs, tax revenues, and the proposed deficit or surplus.

Federal Open Market Committee   The main policy-making organ of the Federal Reserve System.

Federal Reserve System   The central bank of the United States.

Feedback-rule policy   A rule that specifies how policy actions respond to changes in the state of the economy.

Fiat money   An intrinsically worthless (or almost worthless) commodity that serves the functions of money.

Financial innovation   The development of new financial products—new ways of borrowing and lending.

Financial intermediary   An institution that receives deposits and makes loans.

Firm   An institution that hires factors of production and that organizes those factors to produce and sell goods and services.

Fiscal policy   The government's attempt to influence the economy by varying its purchases of goods and services and taxes to smooth the fluctuations in aggregate expenditure; use of the federal budget to achieve macroeconomic objectives such as full employment, sustained long-term economic growth, and price level stability.

Fixed cost   The cost of a fixed input; a cost that is independent of the output level.

Fixed exchange rate   A system in which the value of a country's currency is pegged by the country's central bank.

Fixed-rule policy   A rule that specifies an action to be pursued independently of the state of the economy.

Flat tax   A tax that is levied at the same rate on all income.

Flexible exchange rate   A system in which the value of a country's currency is determined by market forces in the absence of central bank intervention.

Flow   A quantity per unit of time.

Foreign exchange market   The market in which the currency of one country is exchanged for the currency of another.

Foreign exchange rate   The price at which one currency exchanges for another.

Four-firm concentration ratio   A measure of market power that is calculated as the sales of the four largest firms in an industry as a percentage of total industry sales.

Free rider   A person who consumes a good without paying for it.

Frictional unemployment   Unemployment arising from normal labor turnover—new entrants are constantly coming into the labor market, and firms are constantly laying off workers and hiring new workers.

Full employment   A situation in which the number of people looking for a job equals the number of job vacancies.

Game theory   A method of analyzing strategic behavior.

GDP deflator   A price index that measures the average level of the prices of all goods and services that make up GDP.

General Agreement on Tariffs and Trade (GATT)   An international agreement designed to limit government intervention to restrict international trade.

Gold standard   A monetary system with fractionally backed convertible paper in which a dollar could be converted into gold at a guaranteed value on demand.

Government debt   The total amount of borrowing that the government has undertaken and the total amount that it owes to households, firms, and foreigners.

Government purchases   Goods and services bought by the government.

Government purchases multiplier   The amount by which a change in government purchases of goods and services is multiplied to determine the change in equilibrium expenditure that it generates.

Government sector surplus or deficit   An amount equal to net taxes minus government purchases of goods and services.

Great Depression   A decade (1929–1939) of high unemployment and stagnant production throughout the world economy.

Great Leap Forward   An economic plan for post revolutionary China based on small-scale, labor-intensive production.

Gresham's Law   The tendency for bad (debased) money to drive good (not debased) money out of circulation.

Gross domestic product (GDP)   The value of all final goods and services produced in the economy in a year.

Gross investment   The amount spent on replacing depreciated capital and on net additions to the capital stock.

Gross investment   The purchase of new capital goods during a given time period.

Growth accounting   A method of calculating how much real GDP growth has resulted from growth of labor and capital and how much is attributable to technological change.

Herfindahl-Hirschman Index   A measure of market power, that is cal-

culated as the sum of the square of the market share (as a percentage) of each of the largest 50 firms (or all firms if there are fewer than 50) in a market.

Hotelling Principle   The proposition that the market for the stock of a natural resource is in equilibrium when the price of the resource is expected to rise at a rate equal to the interest rate on similarly risky assets.

Human capital   The skill and knowledge of people, arising from their education and on-the-job training.

Hysteresis   The idea that the natural rate of unemployment depends on the path of the actual unemployment rate; where the unemployment rate ends up depends on where it has been.

Implicit rental rate   The rent that a firm pays to itself for the use of the assets that it owns.

Import function   The relationship between imports and real GDP.

Imports   The goods and services that we buy from people in other countries.

Incentive   An inducement to take a particular action.

Incentive regulation scheme   A regulation that gives a firm an incentive to operate efficiently and keep costs under control.

Income effect   The change in consumption that results from a change in the consumer's income, other things remaining the same.

Income elasticity of demand   The responsiveness of demand to a change in income, other things remaining the same. It is calculated as the percentage change in the quantity demanded divided by the percentage change in income.

Increasing marginal returns   The tendency for the marginal product of a variable factor initially to increase as additional units of the variable factor are employed.

Increasing returns to scale   Technological conditions under which a given percentage increase in all the firm's inputs results in the firm's output increasing by a larger percentage

Indifference curve   A line that shows combinations of goods among which a consumer is indifferent.

Induced expenditure   The part of aggregate planned expenditure on

U.S.-produced goods and services that varies as real GDP varies.

Induced taxes   Taxes that vary as real GDP varies.

Industrial union   A group of workers who have a variety of skills and job types but who work for the same firm or industry.

Inelastic demand   A demand with a price elasticity between 0 and 1; the percentage change in the quantity demanded is less than the percentage change in price.

Infant-industry argument   The argument that protection is necessary to enable an infant industry to grow into a mature industry that can compete in world markets.

Inferior good   A good for which demand decreases as income increases.

Inflation   An upward movement in the average level of prices; a process in which the price level is rising and money is losing value.

Inflationary gap   Actual real GDP minus long-run real GDP when actual real GDP is above long-run real GDP.

Information cost   The cost of acquiring information on prices, quantities, and qualities of goods and services and factors of production—the opportunity cost of economic information.

Insider-outsider theory   A theory of job rationing that says that to be productive, new workers—outsiders—must receive on-the-job training from existing workers—insiders.

Intellectual property rights   Property rights for discoveries owned by the creators of knowledge.

Interest rate   The amount received by a lender and paid by a borrower expressed as a percentage of the amount of the loan.

Intermediate goods and services   Goods and services that are used as inputs into the production process of another good or service.

International Monetary Fund (IMF)   An international organization that monitors balance of payments and exchange rate activities.

International substitution effect   The substitution of domestic goods and services for foreign goods and services or of foreign goods and services for domestic goods and services.

Intertemporal substitution effect The substitution of goods and services now for goods and services later or of goods and services later for goods and services now.

Inverse relationship A relationship between variables that move in opposite directions.

Investment The purchase of new plant, equipment, and buildings and additions to inventories.

Investment demand The relationship between the level of planned investment and real interest rate, all other influences on investment held constant.

Isocost line A line that shows all the combinations of capital and labor that can be bought for a given total cost.

Isocost map A series of isocost lines, each one for a different total cost.

Isoquant A curve that shows the different combinations of labor and capital that are required to produce a given quantity of output.

Isoquant map A series of isoquant lines, each for a different quantity of output.

Job leavers People who voluntarily quit their jobs.

Job losers People who are laid off, either permanently or temporarily, from their jobs.

Job rationing The practice of paying employed people a wage that creates an excess supply of labor, a shortage of jobs, and increases the natural rate of unemployment.

Job search The activity of people looking for acceptable vacant jobs.

Keynesian activist An economist who believes that fluctuations in aggregate demand combined with sticky wages (and/or sticky prices) are the main source of economic fluctuations.

Keynesian theory of the business cycle A theory that regards volatile expectations as the main source of economic fluctuations.

Labor The time and effort that people allocate to producing goods and services.

Labor demand curve A curve that shows the quantity of labor that firms

plan to hire at each possible real wage rate.

Labor force The total number of employed and unemployed workers.

Labor force participation rate The proportion of the working age population that is either employed or unemployed (but seeking employment).

Labor supply curve A curve that shows the quantity of labor that households plan to supply at each possible real wage rate.

Labor union An organized group of workers whose purpose is to increase their wages and to influence their other job conditions.

Land All the natural resources used to produce goods and services.

Law of diminishing marginal rate of substitution As a firm increases the amount of labor and at the same time decreases the amount of capital so as to produce the same output, the marginal rate of substitution of labor for capital diminishes.

Law of diminishing returns A law stating that as the quantity of one input increases with the quantities of all other inputs remaining the same, output increases but by ever smaller increments.

Law of diminishing returns As a firm increases the quantity of a variable factor, given the quantities of other factors (fixed factors), the marginal product of the variable factor eventually diminishes.

Learning-by-doing People become more productive in an activity (learn) just by repeatedly producing a particular good or service (doing).

Least-cost technique The combination of inputs that minimizes the total cost of producing a given output.

Legal monopoly A market structure in which there is one firm and entry is restricted by the granting of a public franchise, license, patent or copyright or the firm has acquired ownership of a significant portion of a key resource.

Limit pricing The practice of charging a price below the monopoly profit-maximizing price and producing a quantity greater than that at which marginal revenue equals marginal cost so as to deter entry.

Linear relationship A relationship between two variables that is illustrated by a straight line.

Liquidity The property of being instantly convertible into a means of payment with little loss in value.

Loan market A market in which households and firms make and receive loans.

Long run A period of time in which a firm can vary the quantities of all its inputs.

Long-run aggregate supply curve A curve showing the quantity of real GDP supplied and the price level when there is full employment.

Long-run cost The cost of production when a firm uses the economically efficient plant size.

Long-run industry supply curve A curve that shows how the quantity supplied by an industry varies as the market price varies, after all the possible changes in plant size and the number of firms in the industry have been made.

Long-run macroeconomic equilibrium A situation that occurs when real GDP equals potential GDP and there is full employment.

Long-run Phillips curve A curve that shows the relationship between inflation and unemployment when the actual inflation rate equals the expected inflation rate.

Lorenz curve A curve that graphs the cumulative percentage of income or wealth against the cumulative percentage of families or population.

Lump-sum tax multiplier The amount by which a change in lump-sum taxes is multiplied to determine the change in equilibrium expenditure that it generates.

Lump-sum taxes Taxes that are fixed by the government and do not vary with real GDP.

M1 A measure of money that consists of currency and traveler's checks plus checking deposits owned by individuals and businesses.

M2 A measure of money that consists of M1 plus savings deposits and time deposits.

Macroeconomic long run A period that is sufficiently long for the prices of all the factors of production to have adjusted to any disturbance.

Macroeconomic short run A period during which the prices of goods and services change in response to changes in demand and supply but the prices of factors of production do not change.

Macroeconomics   The study of the national economy and the global economy, the way that economic aggregates grow and fluctuate, and the effects of government actions on them.

Managed exchange rate   A system in which the value of a country's currency is not fixed at some preannounced level but is influenced by central bank intervention in the foreign exchange market.

Marginal benefit   The extra benefit received from a small increase in the consumption of a good or service. It is calculated as the increase in total benefit divided by the increase in consumption.

Marginal cost   The change in total cost that results from a unit increase in output. It is calculated as the increase in total cost divided by the increase in output.

Marginal cost pricing rule   A rule that sets the price of a good or service equal to the marginal cost of producing it.

Marginal product   The extra output produced as a result of a small increase in the variable factor. It is calculated as the increase in total product divided by the increase in the variable factor employed, when the quantities of all other factors are constant.

Marginal propensity to consume   The fraction of the last dollar of disposable income that is spent on consumption goods and services.

Marginal propensity to import   The fraction of the last dollar of real GDP spent on imports.

Marginal propensity to save   The fraction of the last dollar of disposable income that is saved.

Marginal rate of substitution   The rate at which a person will give up one good in order to get more of another good and at the same time remain indifferent.

Marginal rate of substitution of labor for capital   The decrease in the quantity of capital per unit increase in the quantity of labor so that the output produced remains constant.

Marginal revenue   The extra total revenue received from selling one additional unit of the good or service. It is calculated as the change in total revenue divided by the change in quantity sold.

Marginal revenue product   The extra total revenue received from employing one more unit of a factor of production while the quantity of all other factors remains the same. It is calculated as the increase in total revenue divided by the increase in the quantity of the factor.

Marginal social benefit   The marginal benefit received by the producer of a good (marginal private benefit) plus the marginal benefit received by other members of society (external benefit).

Marginal social cost   The marginal cost incurred by the producer of a good (marginal private cost) plus the marginal cost imposed on other members of society (external cost).

Marginal utility   The change in total utility resulting from a one-unit increase in the quantity of a good consumed.

Marginal utility per dollar spent   The marginal utility obtained from the last unit of a good consumed divided by the price of the good.

Market   Any arrangement that enables buyers and sellers to get information and to do business with each other.

Market activity   People undertake market activity when they buy goods and services in goods markets or sell the services of the factors of production that they own in factor markets.

Market demand   The total demand of a good or service by everyone in the population. It is illustrated by the market demand curve.

Market failure   The failure of an unregulated market to achieve an efficient allocation of resources.

Market socialism   An economic system that combines state ownership of capital and land with incentives based on a mixture of market prices and laws and regulations.

Means of payment   A method of settling a debt.

Median voter theorem   The proposition that political parties will pursue policies that appeal most to the median voter.

Merger   The combining of the assets of two firms to form a single, new firm.

Microeconomics   The study of the decisions of people and businesses, the interactions of those decisions in markets, and the effects of government regulation and taxes on the prices and quantities of goods and services.

Minimum wage law   A regulation that prohibits labor services being paid at less than a specified wage rate.

Monetarist   An economist who believes that fluctuations in the money stock are the main source of economic fluctuations.

Monetarist theory of the business cycle   A theory that regards fluctuations in the money stock as the main source of economic fluctuations.

Monetary base   The sum of the Federal Reserve notes, coins, and banks' deposits at the Fed.

Monetary exchange   A system in which some commodity or token serves as the medium of exchange.

Monetary policy   The Federal Reserve's attempt to achieve macroeconomic objectives by adjusting the quantity of money in circulation and interest rates.

Money   Any commodity or token that is generally acceptable as a means of payment for goods and services.

Money market mutual fund   A financial institution that obtains funds by selling shares and that uses these funds to buy highly liquid assets such as U.S. Treasury bills.

Money multiplier   The amount by which a change in the monetary base is multiplied to determine the resulting change in the quantity of money.

Monopolistic competition   A market structure in which a large number of firms compete with each other by making similar but slightly different products.

Monopoly   An industry that produces a good or service for which no close substitute exists and in which there is one supplier that is protected from competition by a barrier preventing the entry of new firms.

Monopsony   A market structure in which there is just a single buyer.

Moral hazard   A situation in which one of the parties to an agreement has an incentive, after the agreement is made, to act in a manner that brings additional benefits to himself or herself at the expense of the other party.

Multiplier   The change in equilibrium real GDP divided by the change in autonomous expenditure.

Nash equilibrium   The outcome of a game that occurs when player A takes the best possible action given the action of player B, and player B takes the best possible action given the action of player A.

National saving   Private saving plus government saving. Also equals GDP minus consumption expenditure minus government purchases.

Natural monopoly   A monopoly that occurs when one firm can supply the entire market at a lower price than two or more firms can.

Natural rate of unemployment   The unemployment rate when the economy is at full employment.

Natural resources   The nonproduced factors of production, which can be exhaustible or nonexhaustible.

Negative income tax   A redistribution scheme that gives every family a *guaranteed annual income* and decreases the family's benefit at a specified *benefit-loss rate* as its market income increases.

Negative relationship   A relationship between variables that move in opposite directions.

Neoclassical growth theory   A theory of economic growth that explains how saving, investment, and economic growth respond to population growth and technological change.

Net borrower   A country that is borrowing more from the rest of the world than it is lending to it.

Net exporter   A country whose value of exports exceeds its value of imports—its balance of trade is positive.

Net exports   The expenditure by foreigners on U.S.-produced goods minus the expenditure by U.S. residents on foreign-produced goods—exports minus imports.

Net importer   A country whose value of imports exceeds its value of exports—its balance of trade is negative.

Net investment   The change in the capital stock in a given period of time. It is calculated as gross investment minus depreciation.

Net lender   A country that is lending more to the rest of the world than it is borrowing from it.

Net present value   The present value of the future flow of marginal revenue product generated by capital minus the cost of the capital.

Net taxes   Taxes paid to governments minus transfer payments received from governments.

New classical theory of the business cycle   A rational expectations theory of the business cycle that regards unanticipated fluctuations in aggregate demand as the main source of economic fluctuations.

New growth theory   A theory of economic growth based on the idea that technological change results from the choices that people make in the pursuit of every greater profit.

New Keynesian theory of the business cycle   A rational expectations theory of the business cycle that regards unanticipated fluctuations in aggregate demand as the main source of economic fluctuations.

Nominal GDP   The output of final goods and services valued at current prices.

Nominal GDP targeting   An attempt to keep the growth rate of nominal GDP steady.

Nominal interest rate   The interest rate actually paid and received in the marketplace.

Nonexcludable good   A good that it is impossible, or extremely costly, to prevent someone from benefiting from.

Nonexhaustible natural resources   Natural resources that can be used repeatedly without depleting what is available for future use.

Nonmarket activity   Leisure and nonmarket production activities, including education and training, shopping, cooking, and other activities in the home.

Nonrival good   A good that has the characteristic that one person's consumption of it does not decrease the quantity available for another person to consume.

Nontariff barrier   Any action other than a tariff that restricts international trade.

Normal good   A good for which demand increases as income increases.

Normal profit   The expected return for supplying entrepreneurial ability.

Official settlements account   An account showing the net increase or decrease in a country's holdings of foreign currency.

Official U.S. reserves   The government's holdings of foreign currency.

Oligopoly   A market structure in which a small number of producers compete with each other.

Open market operation   The purchase or sale of government securities by the Federal Reserve System designed to influence the money supply.

Opportunity cost   The opportunity cost of an action is the best forgone alternative.

Patent   A government-sanctioned exclusive right granted to the inventor of a good, service, or productive process to produce, use, and sell the invention for a given number of years.

Payoff matrix   A table that shows the payoffs for every possible action by each player for every possible action by each other player.

Perfect competition   A market structure in which there are many firms; each firm sells an identical product; there are many buyers; there are no restrictions on entry into the industry; firms in the industry have no advantage over potential new entrants; and firms and buyers are completely informed about the price of each firm's product.

Perfectly elastic demand   Demand with an infinite price elasticity; the quantity demanded is infinitely responsive to a change in price.

Perfectly inelastic demand   Demand with a price elasticity of zero; the quantity demanded remains constant when the price changes.

Phillips curve   A curve that shows a relationship between inflation and unemployment.

Political equilibrium   A situation in which the choices of voters, politicians, and bureaucrats are all compatible and in which no one group can improve its position by making a different choice.

Positive relationship   A relationship between two variables that move in the same direction.

Potential GDP   A situation in which all the economy's labor, capital, land, and entrepreneurial ability are fully employed.

Poverty   A state in which a family's income is too low to be able to buy the quantities of food, shelter, and clothing that are deemed necessary.

Present value   The amount of money that, if invested today, will grow to be as large as a given future amount when the interest that it will earn is taken into account.

Price ceiling   A regulation that makes it illegal to charge a price higher than a specified level.

Price level   The average level of prices as measured by a price index.

Price discrimination   The practice of charging some customers a lower price than others for an identical good or of charging an individual customer a lower price per unit on a large purchase than on a small one, even though the cost of servicing all customers is the same.

Price effect   The change in consumption that results from a change in the price of a good or service, other things remaining the same.

Price elasticity of demand   The responsiveness of the quantity demanded of a good to a change in its price, other things remaining the same.

Price taker   A firm that cannot influence the price of the good or service it produces.

Principal-agent problem   The problem of devising compensation rules that induce an agent to act in the best interest of a principal.

Principle of minimum differentiation   As competitors attempt to appeal to the maximum number of clients or voters, they tend to make themselves identical.

Principle of substitution   When the opportunity cost of an activity increases, people substitute other activities that have lower opportunity costs.

Private information   Information that is available to one person but is too costly for anyone else to obtain.

Private sector surplus or deficit   The difference between saving and investment.

Producer efficiency   A situation in which the economy is producing at a point on its production possibilities frontier.

Producer surplus   The price a producer gets for a good or service minus the opportunity cost of producing it.

Product differentiation   Making a good or service slightly different from that of a competing firm.

Production efficiency   A situation in which it is not possible to produce more of one good without producing less of some other good.

Production function   The relationship that shows how the maximum output attainable varies as quantities of all inputs vary.

Production possibility frontier   The boundary between those combinations of goods and services that can be produced and those that cannot.

Productivity   The amount of output produced per unit of inputs used to produce it.

Productivity function   A relationship that shows how real GDP per hour of labor changes as the amount of capital per hour of labor changes with no change in technology.

Productivity growth slowdown   A slowdown in the growth rate of output per person.

Progressive income tax   A tax on income at a marginal rate that increases with the level of income.

Property rights   Social arrangements that govern the ownership, use, and disposal of factors of production and goods and services.

Proportional income tax   A tax on income that remains at a constant rate, regardless of the level of income.

Protectionism   The restriction of international trade.

Public good   A good or service that can be consumed simultaneously by everyone and from which no one can be excluded.

Public interest theory   A theory of regulation that states that regulations are supplied to satisfy the demand of consumers and producers to maximize total surplus—that is, to attain allocative efficiency.

Quantity demanded   The amount of a good or service that consumers plan to buy during a given time period at a particular price.

Quantity of U.S. dollar assets   The net stock of financial assets denominated in U.S. dollars held outside the Fed and the government.

Quantity supplied   The amount of a good or service that producers plan to sell during a given time period at a particular price.

Quantity theory of money   The proposition that in the long run, an increase in the quantity of money brings an equal percentage increase in the price level.

Quota   A quantitative restriction on the import of a particular good.

Rate of return regulation   A regulation that determines a regulated price by setting the price at a level that enables the regulated firm to earn a specified target percent return on its capital.

Rate of time preference   The target real interest rate that savers want to achieve.

Rational expectation   A forecast based on all available relevant information.

Rational ignorance   The decision not to acquire information because the cost of doing so exceeds the expected benefit.

Real business cycle theory   A theory that regards random fluctuations in productivity that result from technological change as the main source of economic fluctuations.

Real exchange rate   An index number that gives the opportunity cost of foreign-produced goods and services in terms of U.S.-produced goods and services.

Real Gross Domestic Product (GDP)   The output of final goods and services valued at prices prevailing in the base period.

Real income   The quantity of a good that a consumer's income will buy. It is the consumer's income expressed in units of a good and is calculated as income divided by the price of the good.

Real interest rate   The interest rate paid by a borrower and received by a lender after taking into account the change in the value of money resulting from inflation; the nominal interest rate minus the inflation rate.

Real money   A measure of money based on the quantity of goods and services it will buy.

Real money balances effect   The influence of a change in the quantity of real money on the quantity of real GDP demanded.

Real wage rate The wage rate per hour expressed in constant dollars.

Recession A downturn in the level of economic activity in which real GDP falls in two successive quarters.

Recessionary gap Long-run real GDP minus actual real GDP when actual real GDP is below long-run real GDP.

Reentrants People who reenter the labor force.

Regressive income tax A tax on income at a marginal rate that decreases with the level of income.

Relative price The ratio of the price of one good or service to the price of another good or service. A relative price is an opportunity cost.

Rent ceiling A regulation that makes it illegal to charge a rent higher than a specified level.

Rent seeking The activity of searching out or creating a monopoly from which an economic profit can be made.

Required reserve ratio The ratio of reserves to deposits that banks are required, by regulation, to hold.

Reservation price The highest price that a buyer is willing to pay for a good.

Reservation wage The lowest wage rate for which a person will supply labor to the market. Below that wage, the person will not supply labor.

Reserve ratio The fraction of a bank's total deposits that are held in reserves.

Reserves Cash in a bank's vault plus the bank's deposits at Federal Reserve banks.

Returns to scale The increase in output that results when a firm increases all its inputs by the same percentage.

Risk A situation in which more than one outcome might occur and the probability of each possible outcome can be estimated.

Rival good A good that has the characteristic that one person's consumption of it decreases the consumption available to someone else.

Saving Income minus consumption. Saving is measured in the national income accounts as disposable income (income less taxes) minus consumption expenditure.

Saving function The relationship between saving and disposable income, other things held constant.

Savings and loan association (S&L) A financial intermediary that traditionally obtained its funds from savings deposits (called shares) and that made long-term mortgage loans to home buyers.

Savings bank A financial intermediary owned by its depositors that accepts savings deposits and makes mortgage loans.

Saving supply The relationship between saving and the real interest rate, other things remaining the same.

Scarcity The universal state in which wants exceed resources.

Scatter diagram A diagram that plots the value of one economic variable against the value of another.

Search activity The time spent in looking for someone with whom to do business.

Short run The short run in microeconomics has two meanings. For the firm, it is the period of time in which the quantity of at least one of its inputs is fixed and the quantities of the other inputs can be varied. The fixed input is usually capital—that is, the firm has a given plant size. For the industry, the short run is the period of time in which each firm has a given plant size and the number of firms in the industry is fixed.

Short-run aggregate supply curve A curve showing the relationship between the quantity of real GDP supplied and the price level, everything else held constant.

Short-run industry supply curve A curve that shows how the quantity supplied by the industry varies as the market price varies when the plant size of each firm and the number of firms in the industry remain the same.

Short-run macroeconomic equilibrium A situation that occurs when the quantity of real GDP demanded equals the short-run quantity of real GDP supplied at the point of intersection of the AD curve and the SAS curve.

Short-run Phillips curve A curve showing the relationship between inflation and unemployment, the expected inflation rate and the natural unemployment rate held constant.

Shutdown point The price and output level at which the firm just covers its total variable cost. In the short run, the firm is indifferent between producing the profit-maximizing output and shutting down temporarily. If it produces, it makes a loss equal to its total fixed cost.

Signal An action taken outside a market that conveys information that can be used by that market.

Slope The change in the value of the variable measured on the y-axis divided by the change in the value of the variable measured on the x-axis.

Socialism An economic system with state ownership of capital and land and on incentives based on laws and regulations.

Stagflation The combination of a rise in the price level and a fall in real GDP.

Stock A quantity that exists at a point in time.

Stock market A market in which the stocks of corporations are traded.

Strategies All the possible actions of each player in a game.

Structural deficit A budget that is in deficit even though real GDP equals potential GDP; expenditures are high relative to tax revenues over the entire business cycle.

Structural unemployment The unemployment that arises when there is a decline in the number of jobs available in a particular region or industry.

Subsidy A payment made by the government to producers that depends the level of output.

Subsistence real wage rate The minimum real wage rate needed to maintain life.

Substitute A good that can be used in place of another good.

Substitution effect The effect of a change in price of one good or service on a consumer's consumption of goods and services when the consumer remains indifferent between the original and the new consumption bundles—that is, the consumer remains on the same indifference curve.

Sunk cost The past economic depreciation of a firm's capital (buildings, plant, and equipment).

Supply The relationship between the quantity of a good that producers plan to sell and the price of the good, with all other influences on sellers' plans remaining the same. It is described by a supply schedule and illustrated by a supply curve.

Supply curve A curve that shows the relationship between the quantity supplied and the price of a good, all other influences on producers' planned sales remaining the same.

Takeover The purchase of the stock of one firm by another firm.

Tariff A tax on an import by the government of the importing country.

Technological efficiency A situation that occurs when it is not possible to increase output without increasing inputs.

Technological progress The development of new and better ways of producing goods and services and the development of new goods.

Time-series graph A graph that measures time (for example, months or years) on the x-axis and the variable or variables in which we are interested on the y-axis.

Total cost The sum of the costs of all the inputs a firm uses in production.

Total fixed cost The total cost of the fixed inputs.

Total product The total output produced by a firm in a given period of time.

Total revenue The value of a firm's sales. It is calculated as the price of the good multiplied by the quantity sold.

Total revenue test A method of estimating the price elasticity of demand by observing the change in total revenue that results from a change in the price, when all other influences on the quantity sold remain the same.

Total surplus The sum of consumer surplus and producer surplus.

Total utility The total benefit or satisfaction that a person gets from the consumption of goods and services.

Total variable cost The total cost of the variable inputs.

Trade-off A constraint that entails giving up one thing to get something else.

Trade-weighted index The value of a basket of currencies in which the weight placed on each currency is related to its importance in U.S. international trade.

Transactions costs The costs incurred in searching for someone with whom to do business, in reaching an agreement about the price and other aspects of the exchange, and in ensuring that the terms of the agreement are fulfilled.

Transfer earnings The income that an owner of a factor of production requires to induce the owner to supply the factor.

Trend A general direction (rising or falling) in which a variable is moving over the long term.

Twin deficits The tendency for the current account deficit and the government deficit to move together.

Uncertainty A situation in which more than one event might occur but it is not known which will occur.

Unemployed A person who does not have a job but is available for work, willing to work, and has made some effort to find work within the previous four weeks.

Unemployment rate The number of people unemployed expressed as a percentage of the labor force.

Unit elastic demand Demand with a price elasticity of 1; the percentage change in the quantity demanded equals the percentage change in price.

U.S. interest rate differential The interest rate on a dollar asset minus the interest rate on a foreign currency asset.

Utility The benefit or satisfaction that a person gets from the consumption of a good or service.

Utility of wealth The amount of utility that a person attaches to a given amount of wealth.

Value The maximum amount that a person is willing to pay for a good.

Value added The value of a firm's output minus the value of the intermediate goods bought from other firms.

Variable cost A cost that varies with the output level. It is the cost of a variable input.

Velocity of circulation The average number of times a dollar of money is used annually to buy the goods and services that make up GDP.

Voluntary export restraint An agreement between two countries in which the government of the exporting country agrees to reduce the volume of its own exports to the other country.

Voluntary export restraint A self-imposed restriction by an exporting country on the volume of its exports of a particular good. Voluntary export restraints are often called VERs.

Wants Unlimited desires or wishes that people have for goods and services.

Wealth The current market value of what a household owns. It is equal to the current market value of the household's past saving plus any inheritances it has received.

Wealth The value of all the things that people own.

Welfare state capitalism An economic system that combines the private ownership of capital and land with state intervention in markets that modify the price signals to which people respond.

Working-age population The total number of people aged 16 years and over who are not in jail, hospital, or some other form of institutional care.

Index

Key concepts and pages where they are defined appear in **boldface type**. Page numbers followed by n indicate footnotes.

Credits

(continuation from p. ii)

Part 1: Douglass North (pp. 1–4), © Bill Stover.

Chapter 3: Pin factory (p. 64), Culver Pictures. Woman holding silicon wafer (p. 65), Tony Stone Images. Adam Smith (p. 65), The Bettmann Archive.

Chapter 4: Scene along the railroad route (p. 94), The Bettmann Archive. Newark Airport (p. 95), Steve Proehl/The Image Bank. Antoine-Augustin Cournot (p. 95), Stock Montage. Alfred Marshall (p. 95), Stock Montage.

Part 2: Ernst Berndt (pp. 142–144), © Susan Van Etten.

Chapter 8: Women in cannery (p. 188), California Museum of Photography, University of California, Riverside. All rights reserved. Modern business woman and man (p. 189), Richard Wood/The Picture Cube. William Stanley Jevons (p. 189), Macmillan Press. Jeremy Bentham (p. 189), The Bettmann Archive.

Chapter 9: Reebok stock certificate (p. 197), Adapted courtesy of Reebok International Ltd. Kinpo Electronics stock certificate (p. 198), Adapted courtesy of Kinpo Electronics, Inc. Reprinted with permission.

Chapter 10: 1920s Ford assembly line (p. 242), The Bettmann Archive. Michael Dell (p. 243), Will Van Overbeek. Ronald Coase (p. 243), David Joel/David

Joel Photography, Inc. Jacob Viner (p. 243), Archives of the University, Department of Rare Books and Special Collections, Princeton University Libraries.

Part 3: James Heckman (pp. 327–329), © Bruce Powell.

Chapter 14: Chicago traffic jam, 1892 (p. 354), The Bettmann Archive. Cartoon of stacked cars (p. 355), *The Economist,* 9/14/91; reprinted by permission of Robert Hunt. Thomas Robert Malthus (p. 355), The Bettmann Archive. Harold Hotelling (p. 355), Harold Hotelling, Jr.

Part 4: Glenn Loury (pp. 419–422), © Susan Van Etten.

Chapter 21: Water pollution (p. 508), © Jim Baron/The Image Finders. Boat on Lake Erie (p. 509), Pat Mullen. James Buchanan (p. 509), George Mason University, photo by Carl Zitzman. Arthur Cecil Pigou (p. 509), By courtesy of the National Portrait Gallery, London.

Part 5: Christina Romer (pp. 513–516), © Jane Scherr.

Chapter 22: Workers destroying spinning jenny in England (p. 542), The Bettmann Archive. AT&T Network Center (p. 543), © AT&T. Jean-Baptiste Say (p. 543), The Library of Congress. John Maynard Keynes (p. 543), Stock Montage.

Chapter 26: McCormick's first reaping machine, ca. 1834 (p. 648), The Granger Collection. Fiber optics (p. 649), © The Stock Market/Jon Feingersh. Joseph Schumpeter (p. 649), The Bettmann Archive. Robert Solow (p. 649), © L. Barry Hetherington. Paul Romer (p. 649), © Christopher Irion.

Part 6: Thomas J. Sargent (pp. 650–653), © Bruce Powell.

Chapter 30: German housewife burning Reichmarks in 1923 (p. 762), UPI/Bettmann. Brazilians stocking up on food before price increase (p. 763), © Carlos Humberto TDC/Contact Press Images. David Hume (p. 763), The Bettmann Archive. Milton Friedman (p. 763), Marshall Henrichs/Addison-Wesley.

Chapter 33: Depositors outside door of closed bank (p. 854), The Bettmann Archive. Boarded-up shop (p. 855), © Susan van Etten. Robert E. Lucas, Jr. (p. 855), Marshall Henrichs/Addison-Wesley.

Part 7: Jacob A. Frenkel (pp. 881–884), © Photo Galia.

Chapter 35: Poster advertising ships sailing for California (p. 914), The Bettmann Archive. Container ship (p. 915), M. Fife/SuperStock. David Ricardo (p. 915), The Bettman Archive.

Macroeconomic data for the United States: 1959–1994

Year	Gross domestic product (Y)	Personal consumption expenditures (C)	Gross private domestic investment (I)	Government purchases of goods and services (G)	Net exports (NX)	Unemployment rate (percentage of all workers)	GDP deflator (1987 = 100)	M1	M2
	(billions of 1987 dollars)							(billions of dollars)	
1959	1,928.8	1,178.9	296.4	475.3	−21.8	5.5	25.6	140.0	297.8
1960	1,970.8	1,210.8	290.8	476.9	−7.6	5.5	26.0	140.7	312.3
1961	2,023.8	1,238.4	289.4	501.5	−5.5	6.7	26.3	145.2	335.5
1962	2,128.1	1,293.3	321.2	524.2	−10.5	5.5	26.9	147.8	362.7
1963	2,215.6	1,341.9	343.3	536.6	5.8	5.7	27.2	153.3	393.2
1964	2,340.6	1,417.2	371.8	549.1	2.5	5.2	27.7	160.3	424.8
1965	2,470.5	1,497.0	413.0	566.9	−6.4	4.5	28.4	167.9	459.3
1966	2,616.2	1,573.8	438.0	622.4	−18.0	3.8	29.4	172.0	480.0
1967	2,685.2	1,622.4	418.6	667.9	−23.7	3.8	30.3	183.3	524.3
1968	2,796.9	1,707.5	440.1	686.8	−37.5	3.6	31.8	197.4	566.3
1969	2,873.0	1,771.2	461.3	682.0	−41.5	3.5	33.4	203.9	589.5
1970	2,873.9	1,813.5	429.7	665.8	−35.2	4.9	35.2	214.4	628.1
1971	2,955.9	1,873.7	481.5	652.4	−45.9	5.9	37.1	228.3	712.7
1972	3,107.1	1,978.4	532.2	653.0	−56.5	5.6	38.8	249.2	805.2
1973	3,268.6	2,066.7	591.7	644.2	−34.1	4.9	41.3	262.8	861.0
1974	3,248.1	2,053.8	543.0	655.4	−4.1	5.6	44.9	274.3	908.5
1975	3,221.7	2,097.5	437.6	663.5	23.1	8.5	49.2	287.5	1,023.2
1976	3,380.8	2,207.3	520.6	659.2	−6.4	7.7	52.3	306.3	1,163.6
1977	3,533.3	2,296.6	600.4	664.1	−27.8	7.1	55.9	331.3	1,286.5
1978	3,703.5	2,391.8	664.6	677.0	−29.9	6.1	60.3	358.2	1,388.6
1979	3,796.8	2,448.4	669.7	689.3	−10.6	5.8	65.5	382.5	1,497.0
1980	3,776.3	2,447.1	594.4	704.2	30.7	7.1	71.7	408.5	1,629.3
1981	3,843.1	2,476.9	631.1	713.2	22.0	7.6	78.9	436.3	1,793.3
1982	3,760.3	2,503.7	540.5	723.6	−7.4	9.7	83.8	474.3	1,953.2
1983	3,906.6	2,619.4	599.5	743.8	−56.1	9.6	87.2	521.0	2,187.6
1984	4,148.5	2,746.1	757.5	766.9	−122.0	7.5	91.0	552.1	2,377.9
1985	4,279.8	2,865.8	745.9	813.4	−145.3	7.2	94.4	619.9	2,575.0
1986	4,404.5	2,969.1	735.1	855.4	−155.1	7.0	96.9	724.5	2,818.2
1987	4,539.5	3,052.2	749.3	881.5	−143.1	6.2	100.0	750.1	2,920.1
1988	4,718.6	3,162.4	773.4	886.8	−104.0	5.5	103.9	787.4	3,081.4
1989	4,838.0	3,223.3	784.0	904.4	−73.7	5.3	108.5	794.7	3,239.8
1990	4,897.3	3,272.6	746.8	932.6	−54.7	5.5	113.3	826.4	3,353.0
1991	4,867.6	3,259.4	683.8	944.0	−19.5	6.7	117.6	897.7	3,455.2
1992	4,979.3	3,349.5	725.3	936.9	−32.3	7.4	120.9	1,024.8	3,509.0
1993	5,134.5	3,458.7	819.9	929.8	−73.9	6.8	123.5	1,128.4	3,567.9
1994	5,342.3	3,578.5	955.5	922.5	−114.2	6.1	126.1	1,147.6	3,600.0

Sources: GDP: 1959–1994, *Economic Report of the President*, 1995, Table B-2; unemployment: 1959–1994, *Economic Report of the President*, 1995, Table B-40; GDP deflator: 1959–1994, *Economic Report of the President*, 1995, Table B-3; money supply, *Economic Report of the President*, 1995, Table B-68.

	Federal, state, and local government receipts and expenditures			Bond yields and interest rates	
	Receipts	Expenditures	Surplus or deficit (–)	U.S. Treasury bills	Corporate bonds
Year	(billions of dollars)			(percent per year)	
1959	128.8	131.9	–3.1	3.4	4.4
1960	138.8	135.2	3.6	2.9	4.4
1961	144.1	147.1	–3.0	2.4	4.4
1962	155.8	158.7	–2.9	2.8	4.3
1963	167.5	165.9	1.6	3.2	4.3
1964	172.9	174.5	–1.6	3.5	4.4
1965	187.0	185.8	1.2	4.0	4.5
1966	210.7	211.6	–1.0	4.9	5.1
1967	226.4	240.2	–13.7	4.3	5.5
1968	260.9	265.5	–4.6	5.3	6.2
1969	294.0	284.0	10.0	6.7	7.0
1970	299.8	311.2	–11.5	6.5	8.0
1971	318.9	338.1	–19.2	4.3	7.4
1972	364.2	368.1	–3.9	4.1	7.2
1973	408.5	401.6	6.9	7.0	7.4
1974	450.7	455.2	–4.5	7.9	8.6
1975	465.8	530.6	–64.8	5.8	8.8
1976	532.6	570.9	–38.3	5.0	8.4
1977	598.4	615.2	–16.8	5.3	8.0
1978	673.2	670.3	2.9	7.2	8.7
1979	754.7	745.3	9.4	10.0	9.6
1980	825.7	861.0	–35.3	11.5	11.9
1981	941.9	972.3	–30.3	14.0	14.2
1982	960.5	1,069.1	–108.6	10.7	13.8
1983	1,016.4	1,156.2	–139.8	8.6	12.0
1984	1,123.6	1,232.4	–108.8	9.6	12.7
1985	1,217.0	1,342.2	–125.3	7.5	11.4
1986	1,290.8	1,437.5	–146.8	6.0	9.0
1987	1,405.2	1,516.9	–111.7	5.8	9.4
1988	1,492.4	1,590.7	–98.3	6.7	9.7
1989	1,622.6	1,700.1	–77.5	8.1	9.3
1990	1,709.1	1,847.5	–138.4	7.5	9.3
1991	1,759.0	1,944.9	–185.9	5.4	8.8
1992	1,849.1	2,106.9	–257.8	3.5	8.1
1993	1,970.6	2,185.6	–215.0	3.0	7.2
1994	—	2,257.1	—	4.3	8.0

Sources: Receipts, expenditures, and deficit: *Economic Report of the President,* 1995, Table B-83; Treasury bill and corporate bond rates: *Economic Report of the President,* 1995, Table B-72.